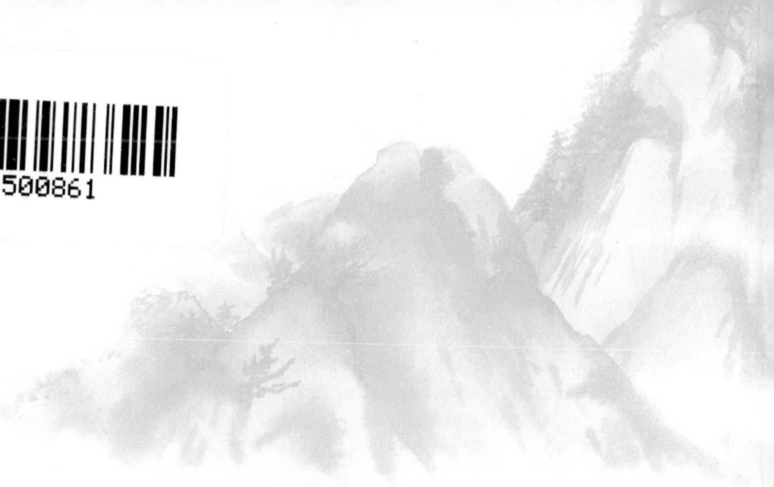

FUSHIGI YÛGI

STORY & ART BY

YUU WATASE

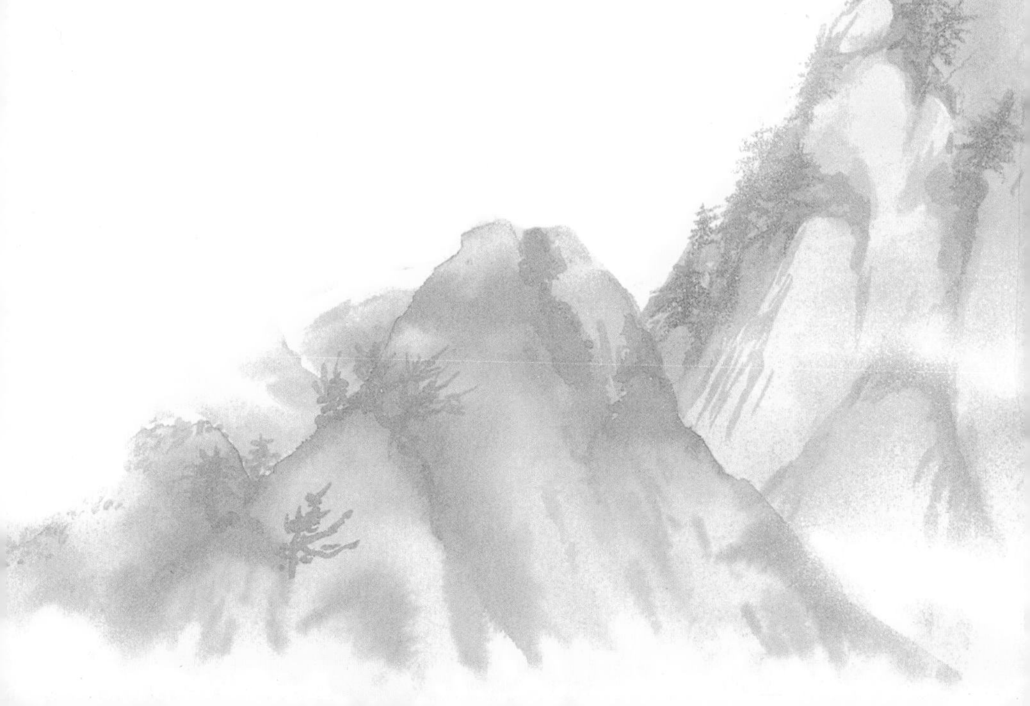

FUSHIGI YÛGI
Volume 4
VIZBIG Edition

Story and Art by **Yuu Watase**

English Adaptation **Yuji Oniki** & **William Flanagan**
Translation Assist **Kaori Kawakubo Inoue**
Touch-up Art & Lettering **Bill Spicer**
VIZBIG Edition Touch-up Art & Lettering **Freeman Wong**
VIZBIG Edition Design **Hidemi Sahara**
First Edition Editor **William Flanagan**
Shôjo Edition Editor **Elizabeth Kawasaki** & **Frances E. Wall**
VIZBIG Edition Editor **Nancy Thistlethwaite**

Original Japanese edition "FUSHIGI YÛGI"
published by SHOGAKUKAN Inc.

Printed in China

Published by VIZ Media, LLC
P.O. Box 77010
San Francisco, CA 94107

10 9 8 7 6 5 4 3 2
First printing, December 2009
Second printing, April 2015

VIZBIG EDITION

VIZ media
www.viz.com

RATED T+ FOR OLDER TEEN
PARENTAL ADVISORY
FUSHIGI YÛGI is rated T+ for
Older Teen and is recommended
for ages 16 and up.
ratings.viz.com

FUSHIGI YÛGI

THE MYSTERIOUS PLAY

VOLUME 10
ENEMY

VOLUME 11
VETERAN

VOLUME 12
GIRLFRIEND

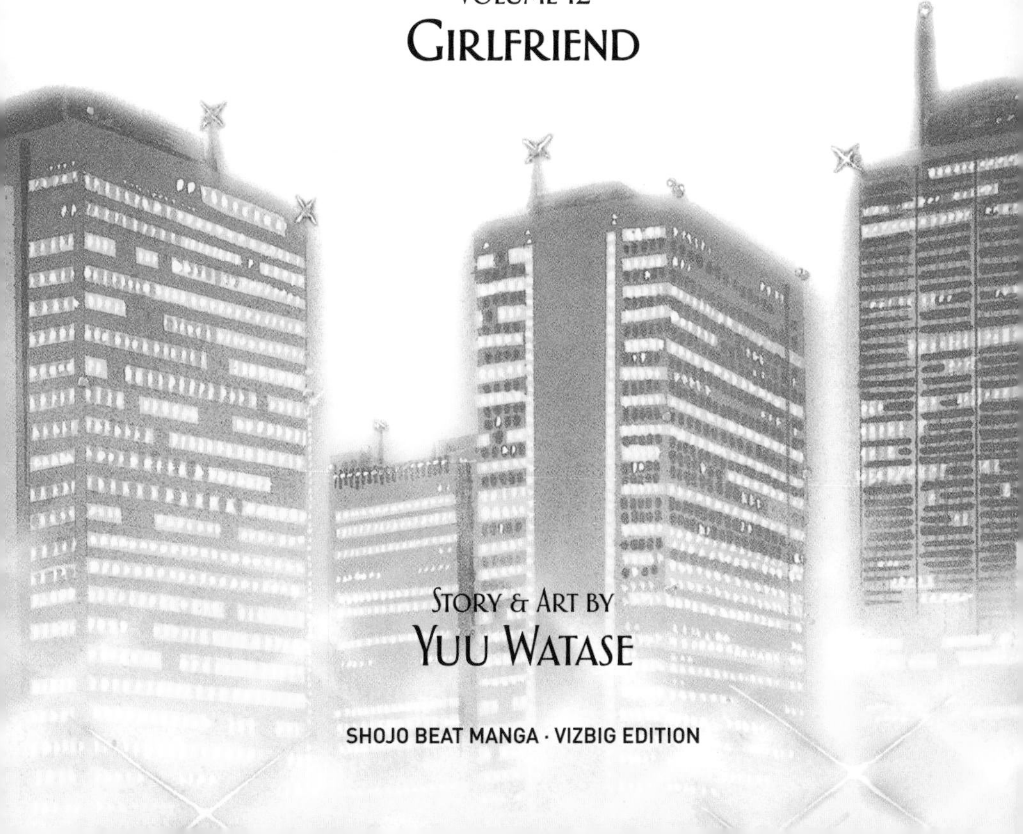

STORY & ART BY
YUU WATASE

SHOJO BEAT MANGA · VIZBIG EDITION

Contents

Volume 12: Girlfriend

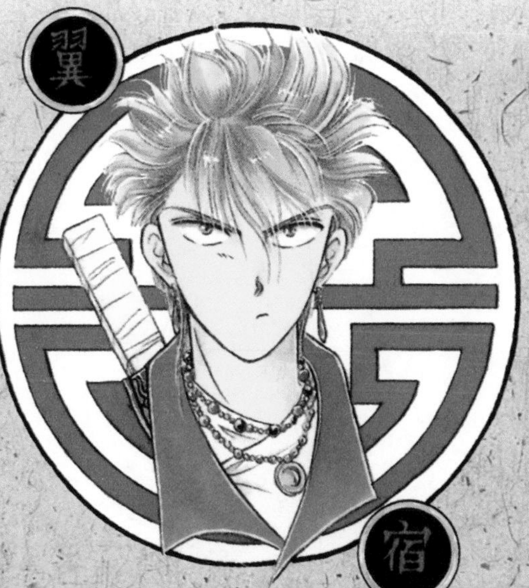

翼
宿

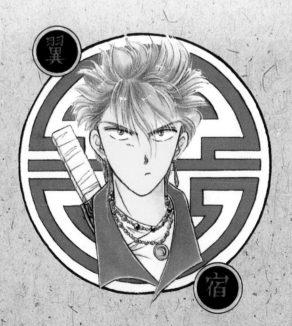

CAST OF CHARACTERS
ANCIENT CHINA
SUZAKU CELESTIAL WARRIORS

Tamahome
Tamahome is obsessed with money, but he loves Miaka deeply.

Nuriko
Nuriko is besotted with the emperor and has superhuman strength.

Hotohori
Hotohori is the emperor of Hong-Nan.

Chichiri
Chichiri can appear and disappear at will.

Mitsukake
Mitsukake is a former recluse who practices medicine.

Tasuki
Tasuki is the leader of a gang of mountain bandits.

Chiriko
Chiriko is a 13-year-old boy who is studying to become a government minister.

SEIRYU CELESTIAL WARRIORS

Nakago
Nakago is a strong warrior from Qu-Dong who commands the other Seiryu Celestial Warriors.

Suboshi
Suboshi is the twin brother of Amiboshi. He cares for Yui.

Amiboshi
Amiboshi pretended to be a Suzaku Celestial Warrior.

Miboshi
Miboshi is the abbot of an ancient monastery.

Soi
Soi can attack using lightning.

Tomo
Tomo has the power to enshroud his enemies in illusions.

Ashitare
Ashitare is a wolf-like beast.

PRESENT-DAY JAPAN

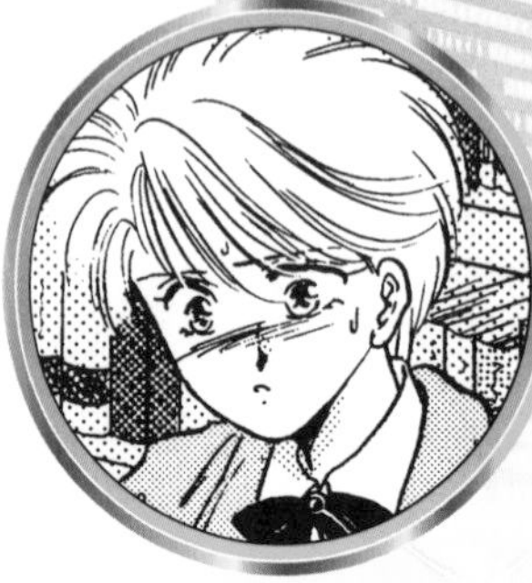

Yui

Yui is Miaka's best friend. She gets better grades than Miaka.

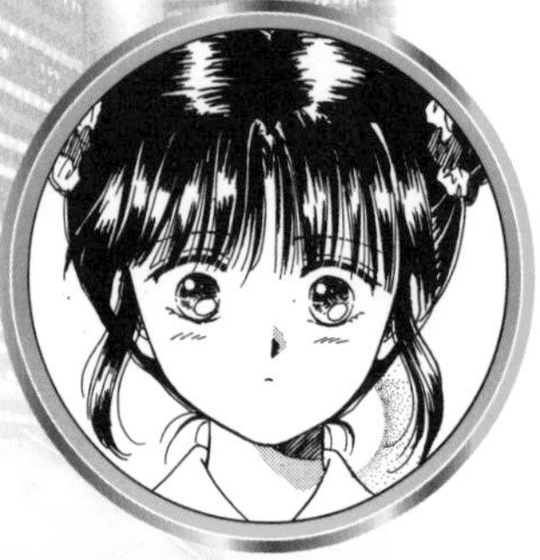

Miaka

Miaka is a chipper junior high student who is studying for high school entrance exams. She loves food.

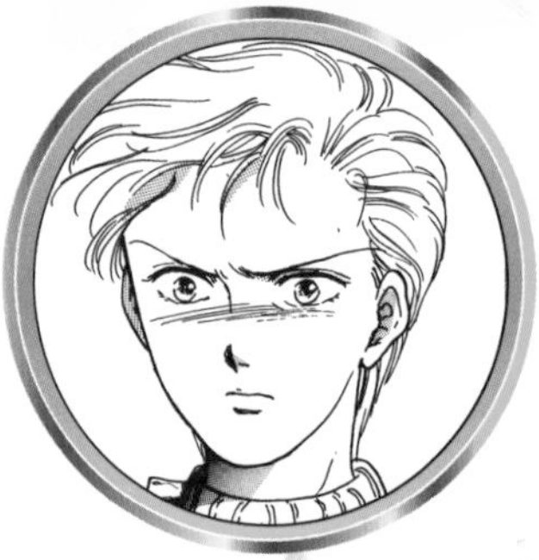

Miaka's Mom

She's a divorced single mom who wants Miaka to get into Jonan, a prestigious high school.

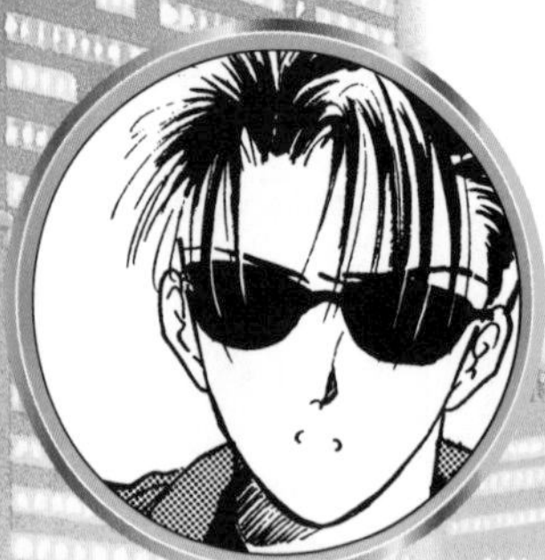

Tetsuya

Tetsuya is a friend of Keisuke's who is helping him research *The Universe of the Four Gods.*

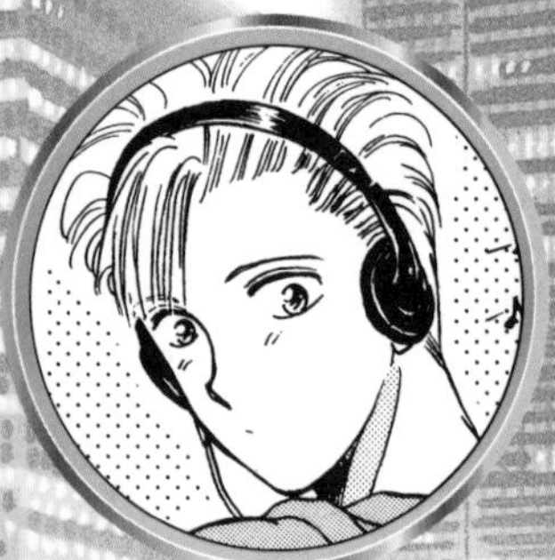

Keisuke

Keisuke is Miaka's brother. He knows Miaka is under a lot of pressure from their mother.

Fushigi Yûgi

Volume 10: Enemy

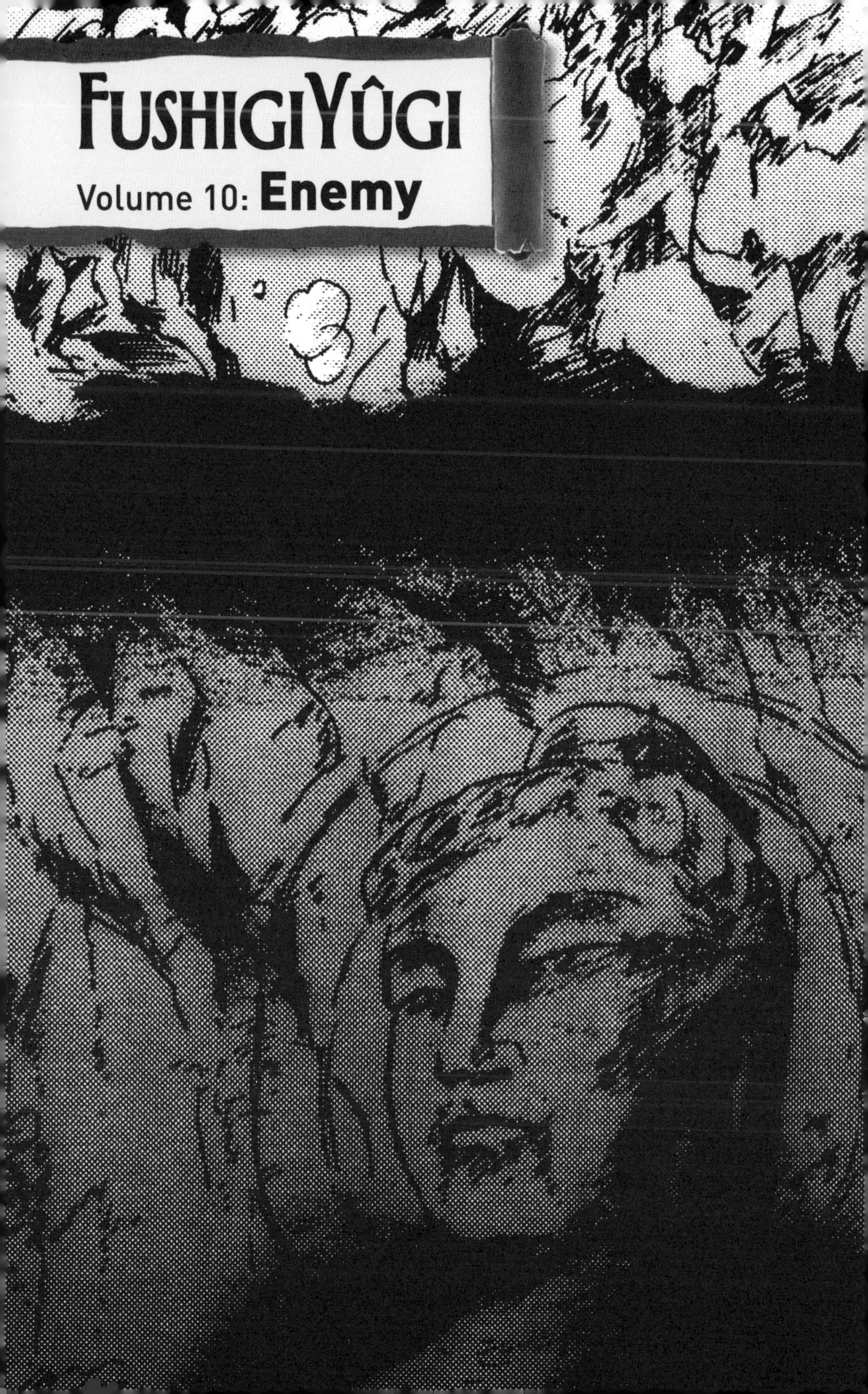

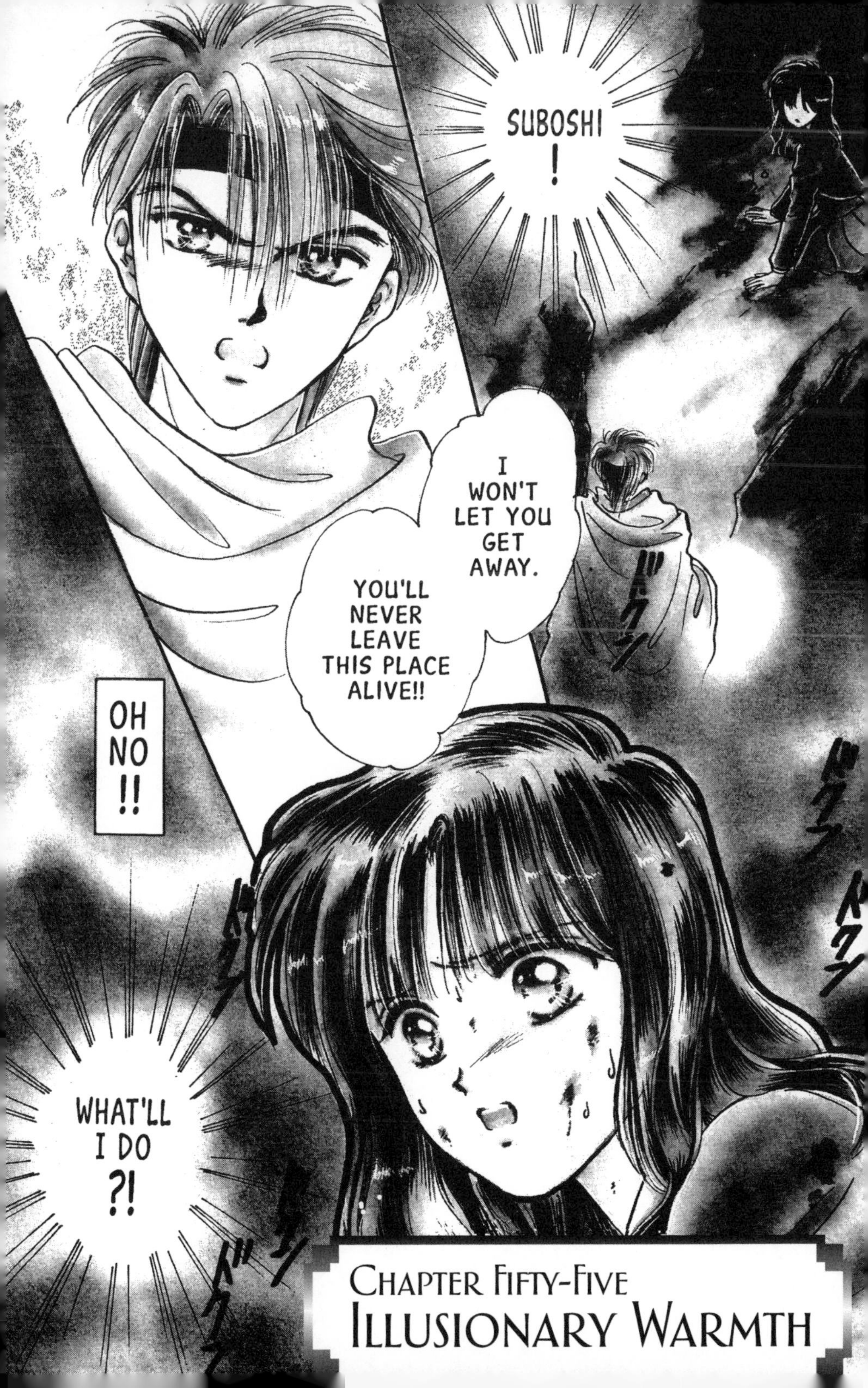
SUBOSHI !
I WON'T LET YOU GET AWAY.
YOU'LL NEVER LEAVE THIS PLACE ALIVE!!
OH NO !!
WHAT'LL I DO ?!
CHAPTER FIFTY-FIVE
ILLUSIONARY WARMTH

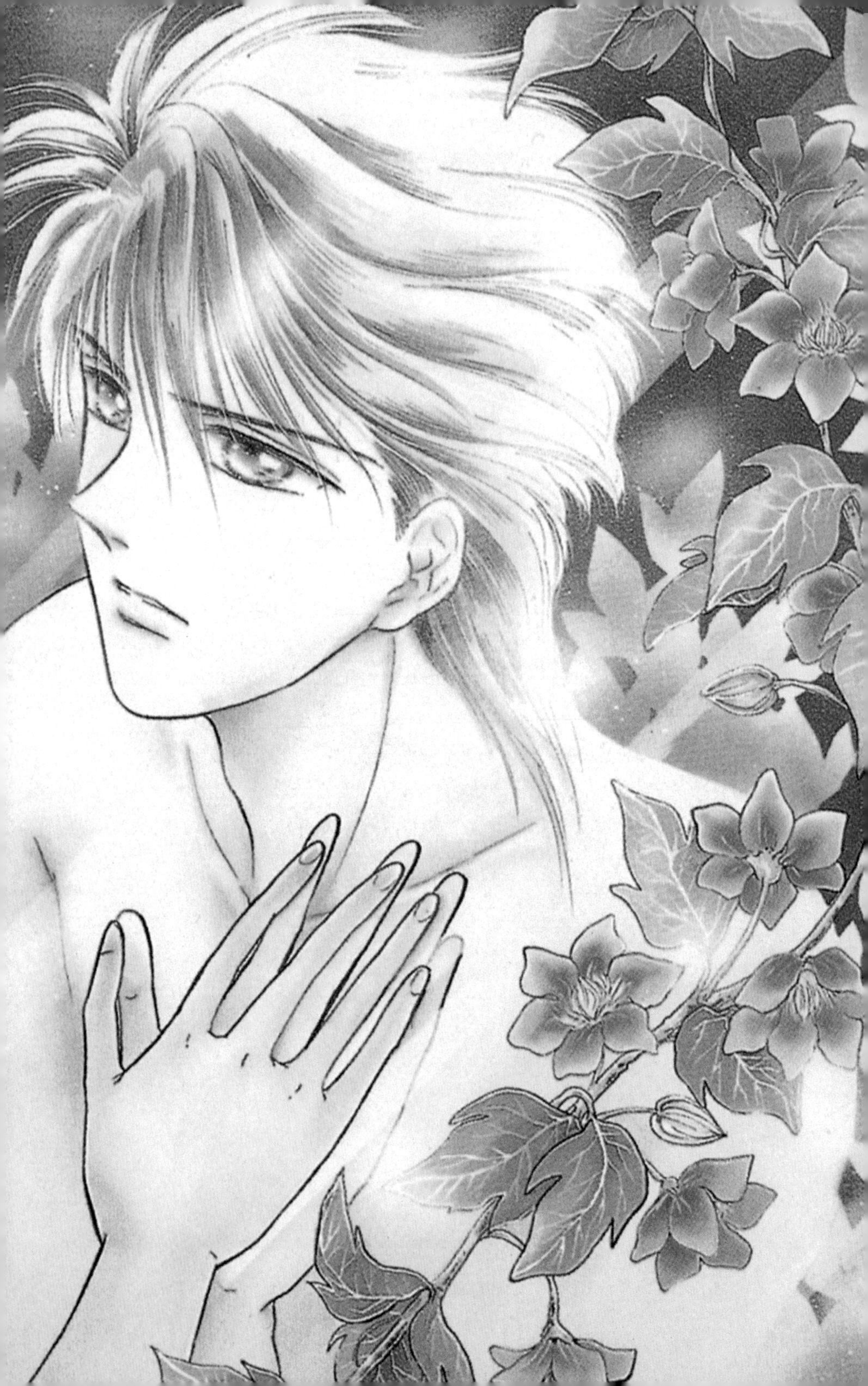

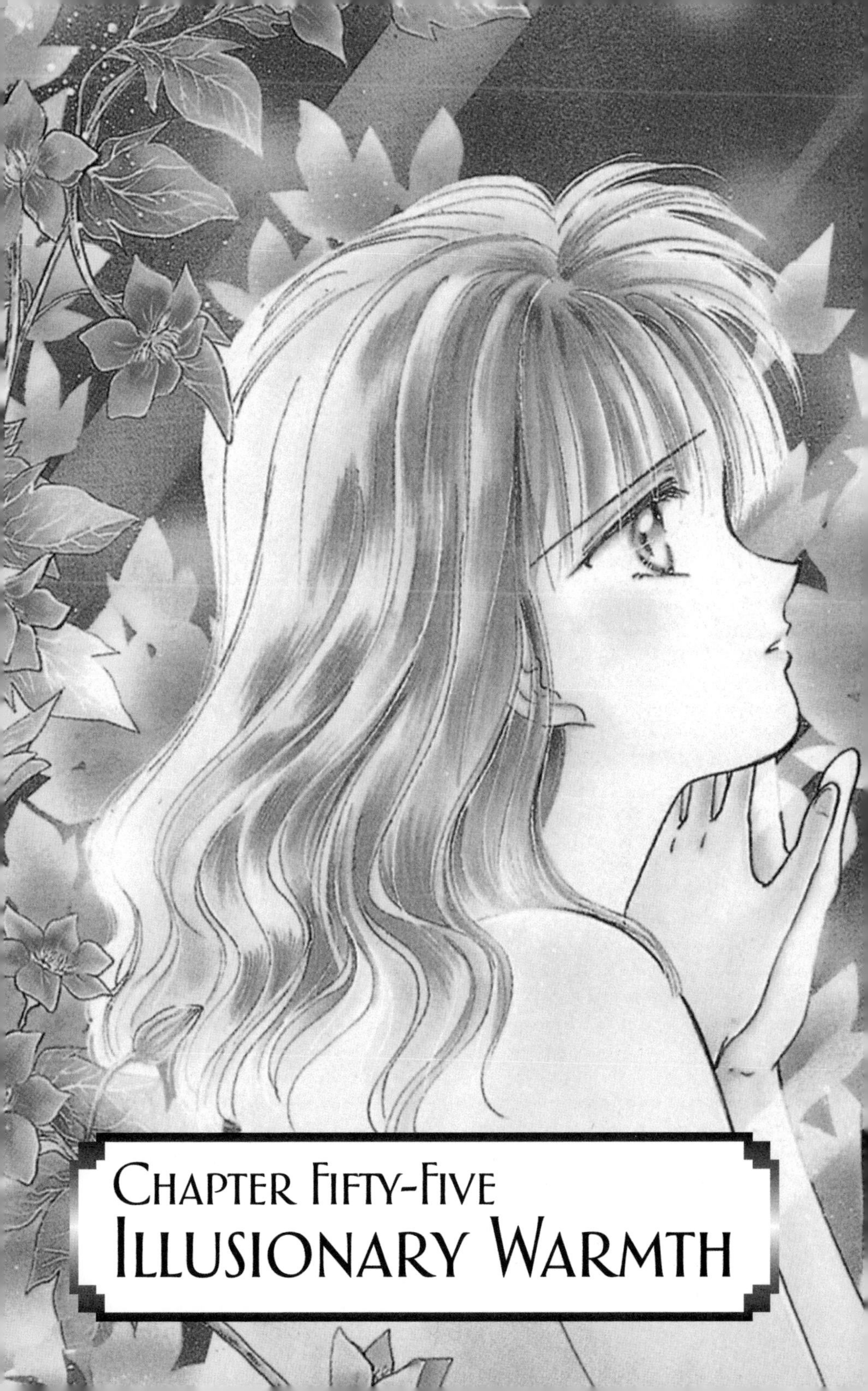

Chapter Fifty-Five
Illusionary Warmth

? **本 郷 唯**
HON GŌ YUI

N A K A G O
Y U I

- He comes from an immigrant tribe of the far west.
- Commander of 2/3 of Qu-Dong's armed forces.
- No living family or friends.
- 25 years old.
- Height: 6' 4" (193 cm)
- Ability: Chi attack techniques.
- Hobbies: Making Tamahome miserable (ha ha!).
- Personality: Beyond cold, he's Arctic ice! His name is a misnomer (a dwelling for the heart); his plans and actions show a complete lack of mercy. He allows for no emotional distraction nor wasted action. Once someone's usefulness is exhausted, the person is eliminated. On the other hand, he has an undeniable charisma that allows him to skillfully manipulate people. But what goes on in his mind remains a mystery.

- Birth Place: Tokyo. Miaka's classmate, 15 years old.
- An only child. Latchkey kid--both parents work.
- Height: 5' 3" (162 cm)
- Weight: 108 lbs. (49 kg)
- Vision: Right 20/18, Left 20/15
- Blood type: AB
- Hobbies: Reading (mysteries), music.
- Personality: In keeping with her looks, she is more mature than an average 15-year-old. Bold and confident in everything she does. Tends to see the world in black and white. Passionate, but passion turns to fury with betrayal. On the outside, she's supremely self-confident, but underneath, she longs for someone to take care of her.

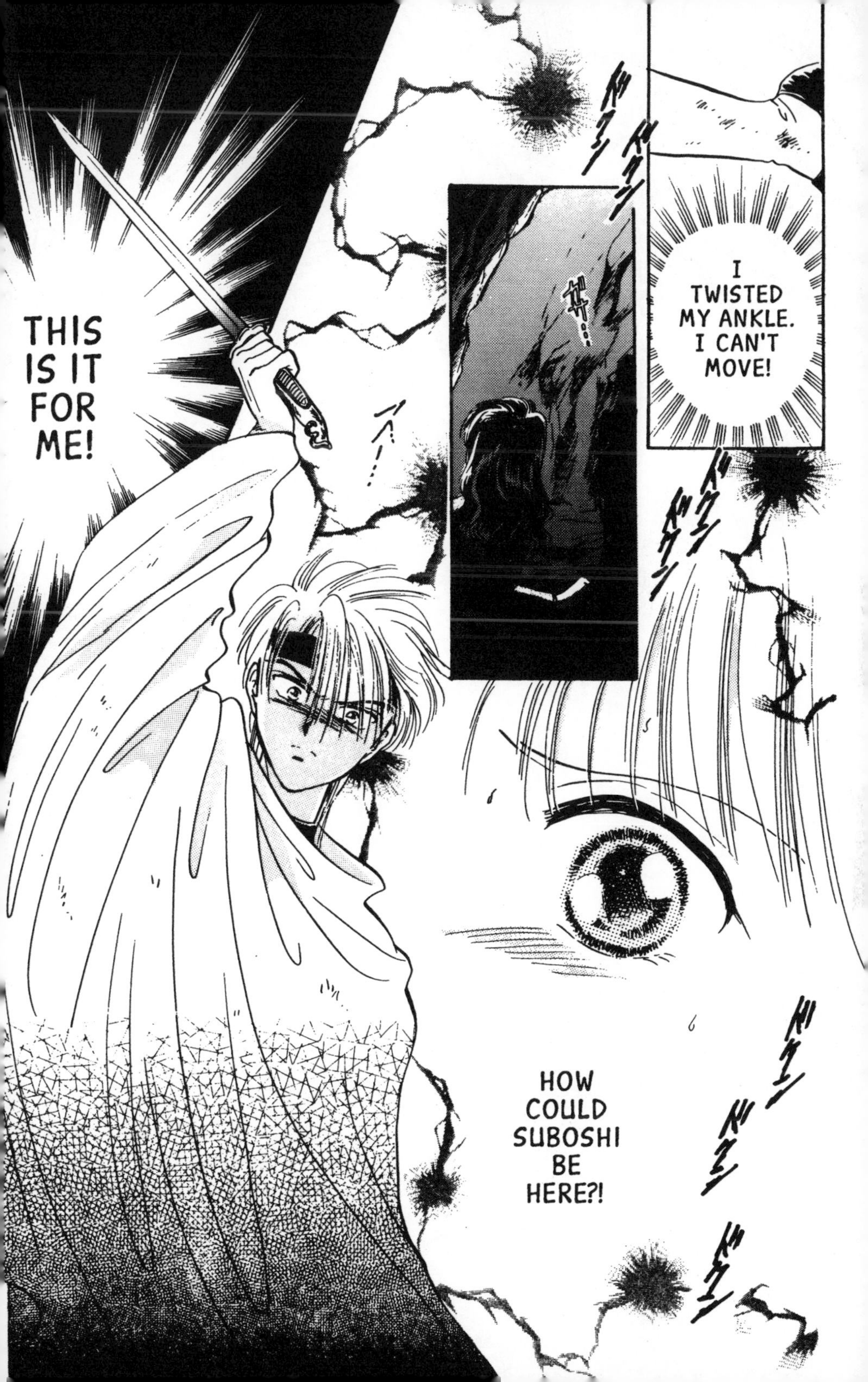
I TWISTED MY ANKLE. I CAN'T MOVE!
THIS IS IT FOR ME!
HOW COULD SUBOSHI BE HERE?!

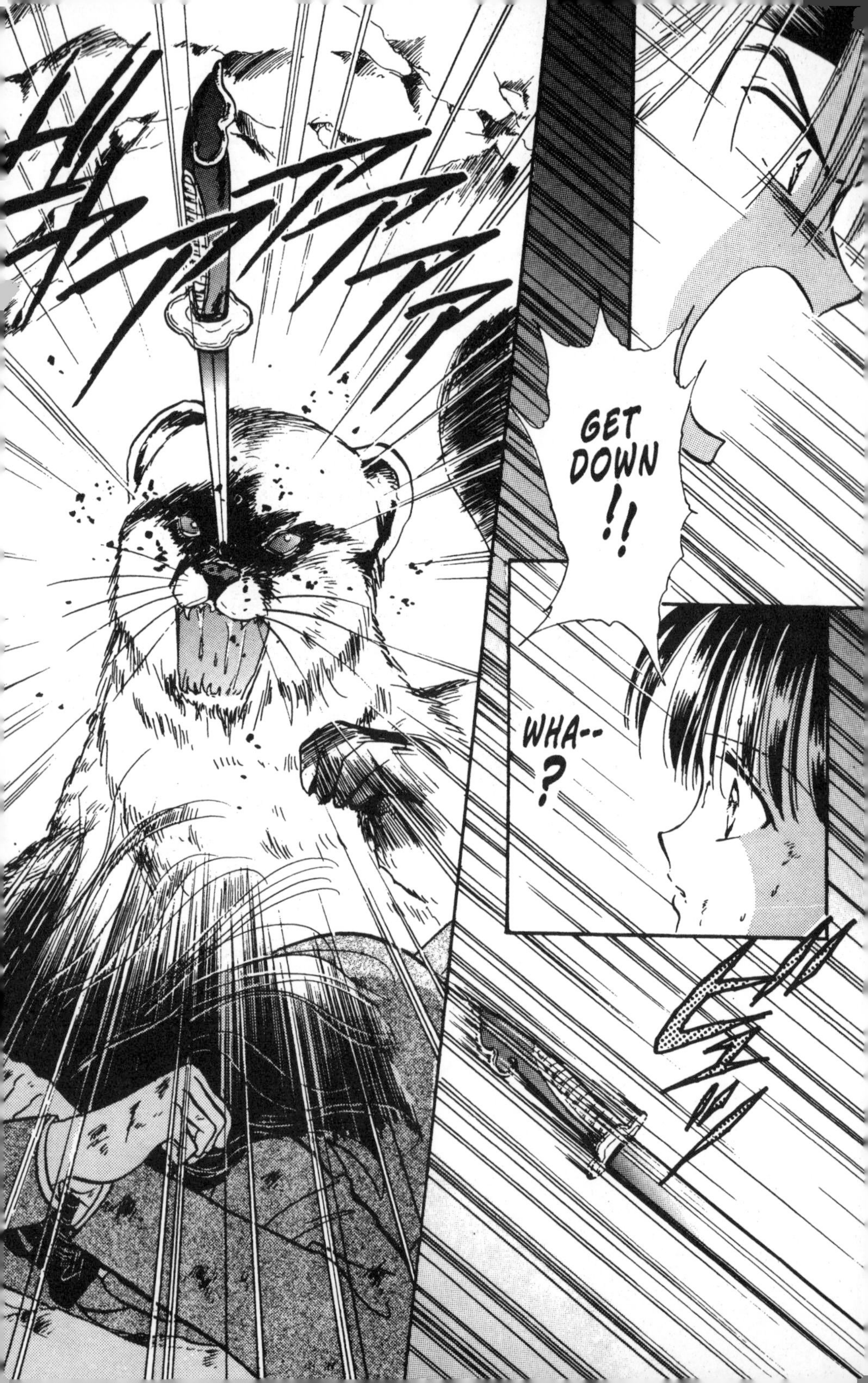
GET DOWN!!
WHA--?

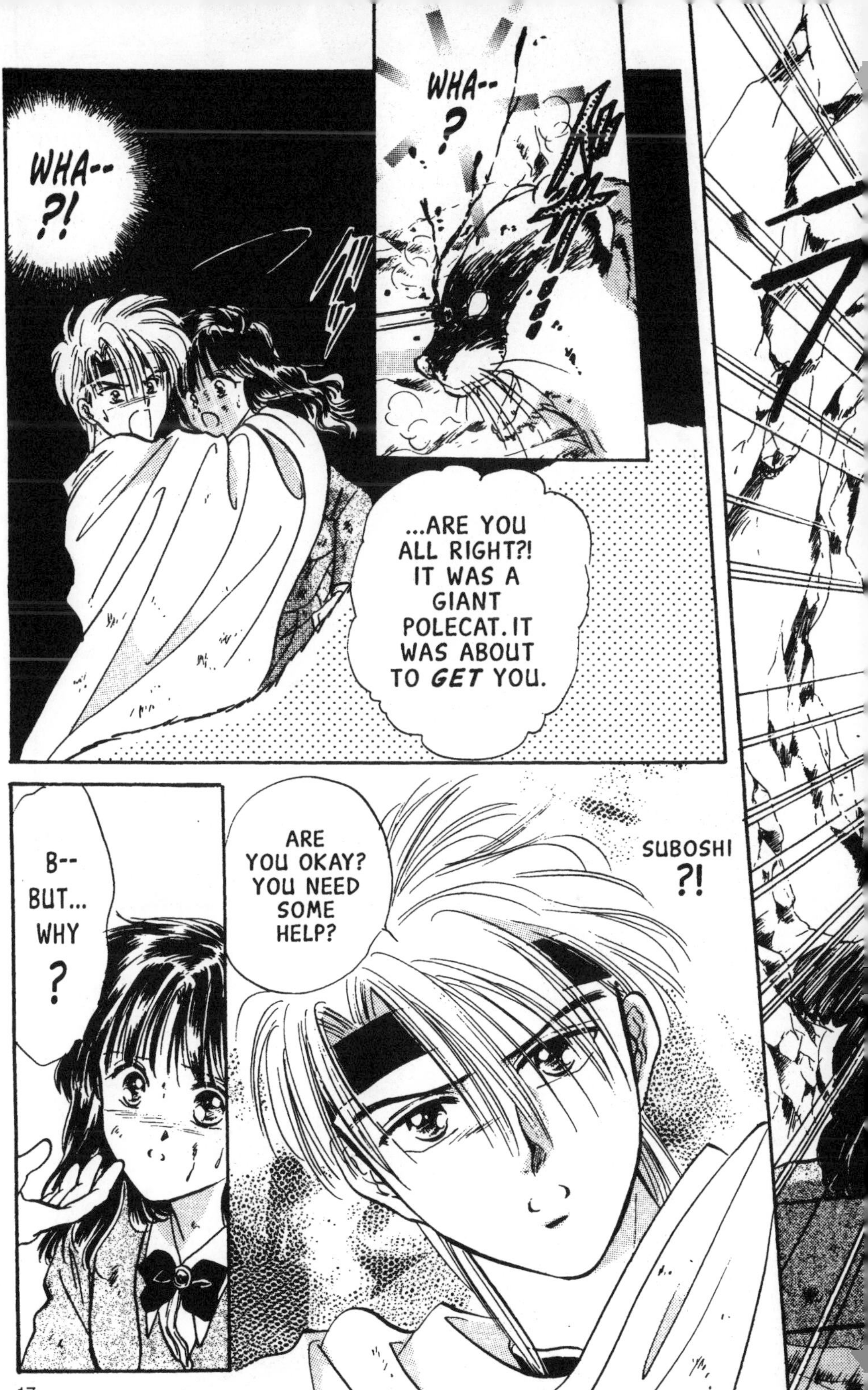
WHA-- ?
WHA-- ?!
...ARE YOU ALL RIGHT?! IT WAS A GIANT POLECAT. IT WAS ABOUT TO *GET* YOU.
SUBOSHI ?!
ARE YOU OKAY? YOU NEED SOME HELP?
B-- BUT... WHY ?

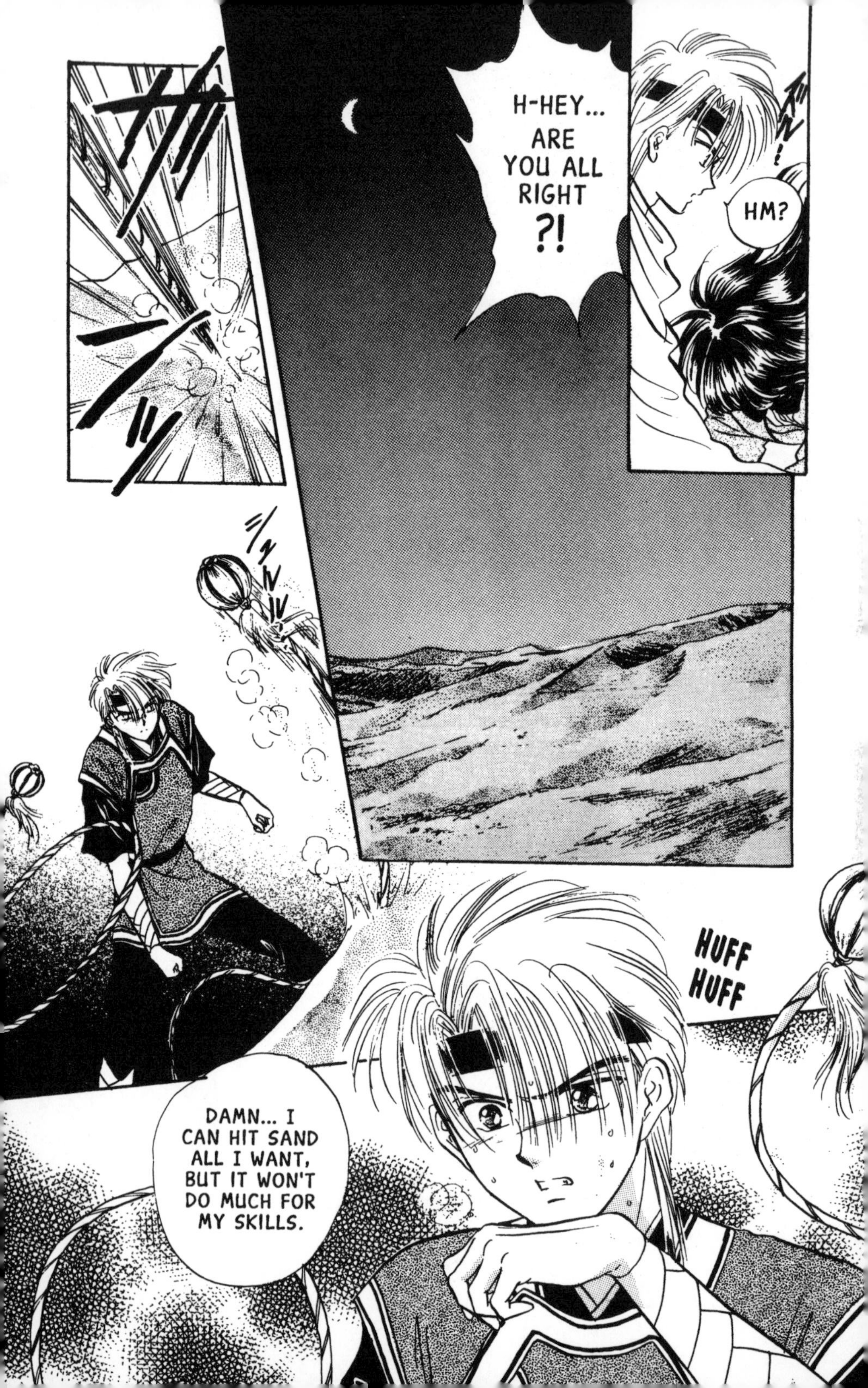
H-HEY... ARE YOU ALL RIGHT ?!
HM?
HUFF HUFF
DAMN... I CAN HIT SAND ALL I WANT, BUT IT WON'T DO MUCH FOR MY SKILLS.

Hello, it's me, Watase. I just pulled my first all-nighter in quite a while, so I'm totally zoning out... ZZZZ... Hey, wake up! No sleep for me!

I don't really have a theme for this column (how much of a theme can you have in a 1/3-page column like this?)... so I'll just write down whatever comes to my numb mind.

In this story, there's a concept called the 28 constellations. For those who haven't read FY serialized in *Shojo Comic*, it had an issue with a supplementary chart of astrological fortunes based on the 28 constellations. Apparently, that was the first time a chart like that has ever appeared in Japan! I tried it, and it was really fun! According to the editor who wrote the text, it was from an Indian 27-constellation astrology system that made its way as far as China! The characters (y'know, my characters) like Chichiri and Tamahome had their own personalities and attributes which ended up corresponding to the historical charts! It really surprised me.

I think my star sign was one of the constellations in Byakko. I forgot which one. I read the astrologer's notes and it was so similar to my story. That was another surprise!

"Eastern Seiryu" was the sea god representing the waters from which life springs. "Northern Genbu" is the cycle of death and rebirth as represented by the turtle and snake. (As far as death goes, there's Nuriko and Hikitsu. And rebirth means you're reincarnated. Of course, that was just a coincidence.) "Western Byakko" represents worship of holy mountains. Western China is surrounded by mountains. And the sea is in the east. See?

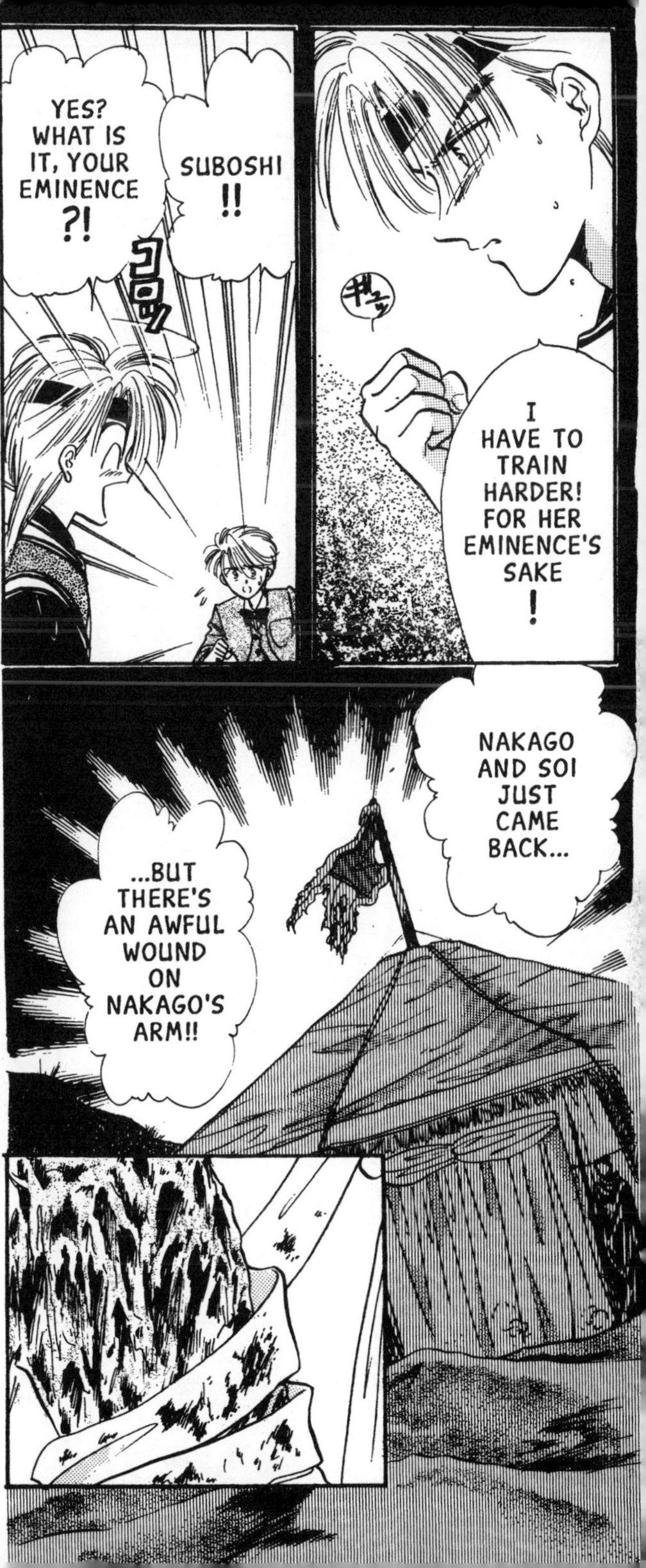
I HAVE TO TRAIN HARDER! FOR HER EMINENCE'S SAKE!
SUBOSHI!!
YES? WHAT IS IT, YOUR EMINENCE?!
NAKAGO AND SOI JUST CAME BACK...
...BUT THERE'S AN AWFUL WOUND ON NAKAGO'S ARM!!

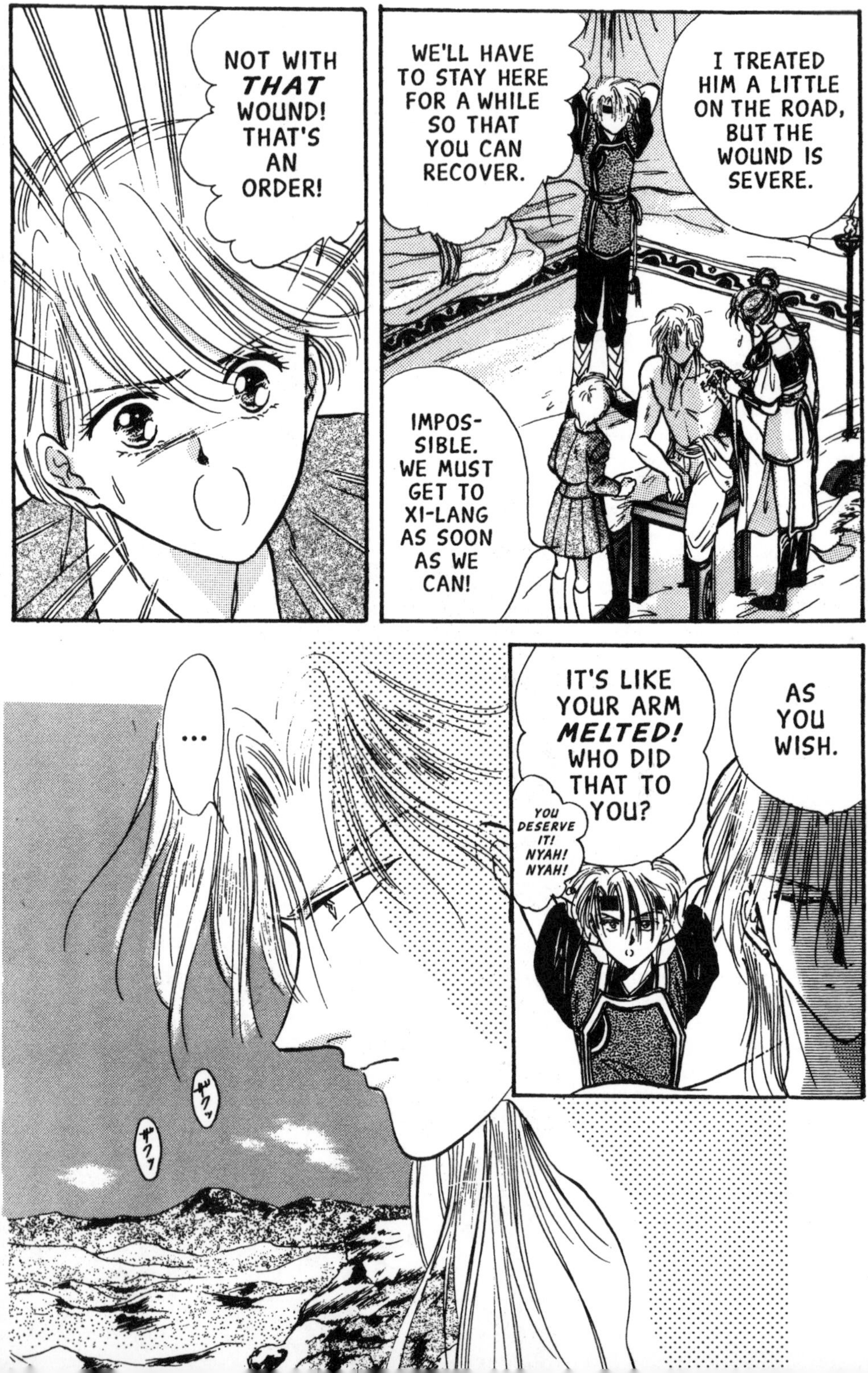
I TREATED HIM A LITTLE ON THE ROAD, BUT THE WOUND IS SEVERE.
WE'LL HAVE TO STAY HERE FOR A WHILE SO THAT YOU CAN RECOVER.
IMPOSSIBLE. WE MUST GET TO XI-LANG AS SOON AS WE CAN!
NOT WITH *THAT* WOUND! THAT'S AN ORDER!
AS YOU WISH.
IT'S LIKE YOUR ARM *MELTED!* WHO DID THAT TO YOU?
YOU DESERVE IT! NYAH! NYAH!
...
ザクッ
ザクッ

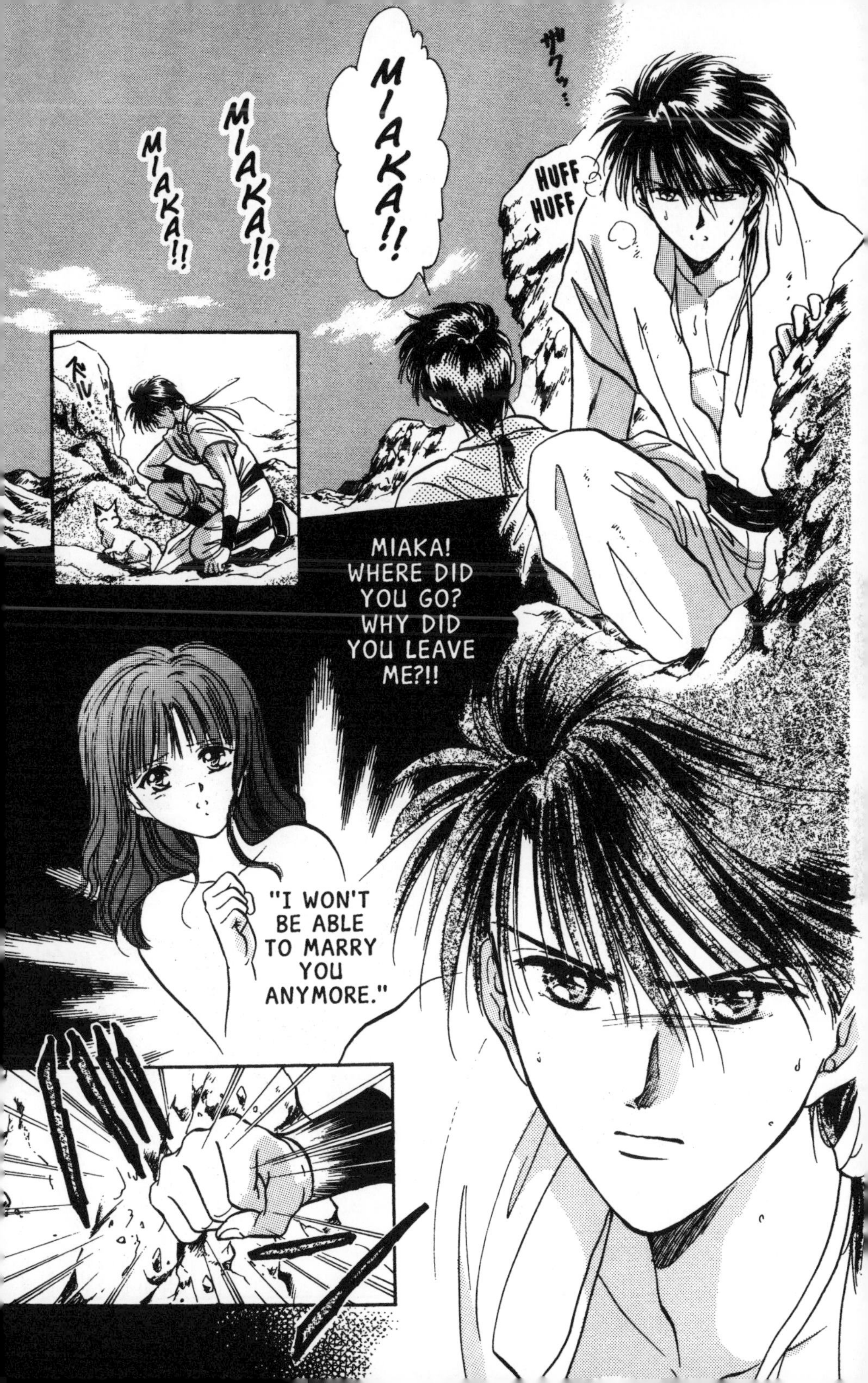
HUFF HUFF
MIAKA!!
MIAKA!!
MIAKA!!
MIAKA! WHERE DID YOU GO? WHY DID YOU LEAVE ME?!!
"I WON'T BE ABLE TO MARRY YOU ANYMORE."

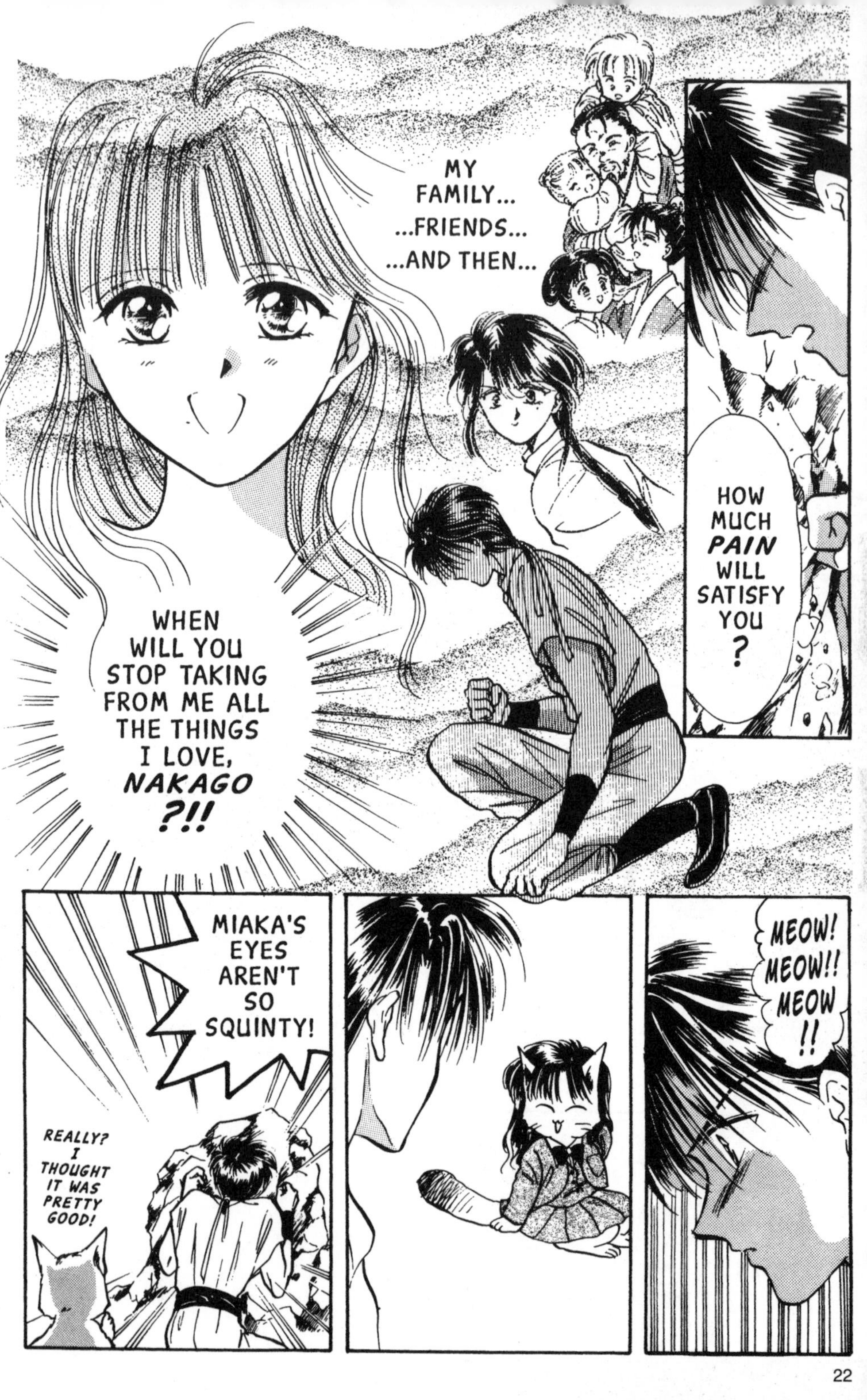
HOW MUCH PAIN WILL SATISFY YOU?
MY FAMILY...
...FRIENDS...
...AND THEN...
WHEN WILL YOU STOP TAKING FROM ME ALL THE THINGS I LOVE, NAKAGO?!!
MEOW! MEOW!! MEOW!!
MIAKA'S EYES AREN'T SO SQUINTY!
REALLY? I THOUGHT IT WAS PRETTY GOOD!

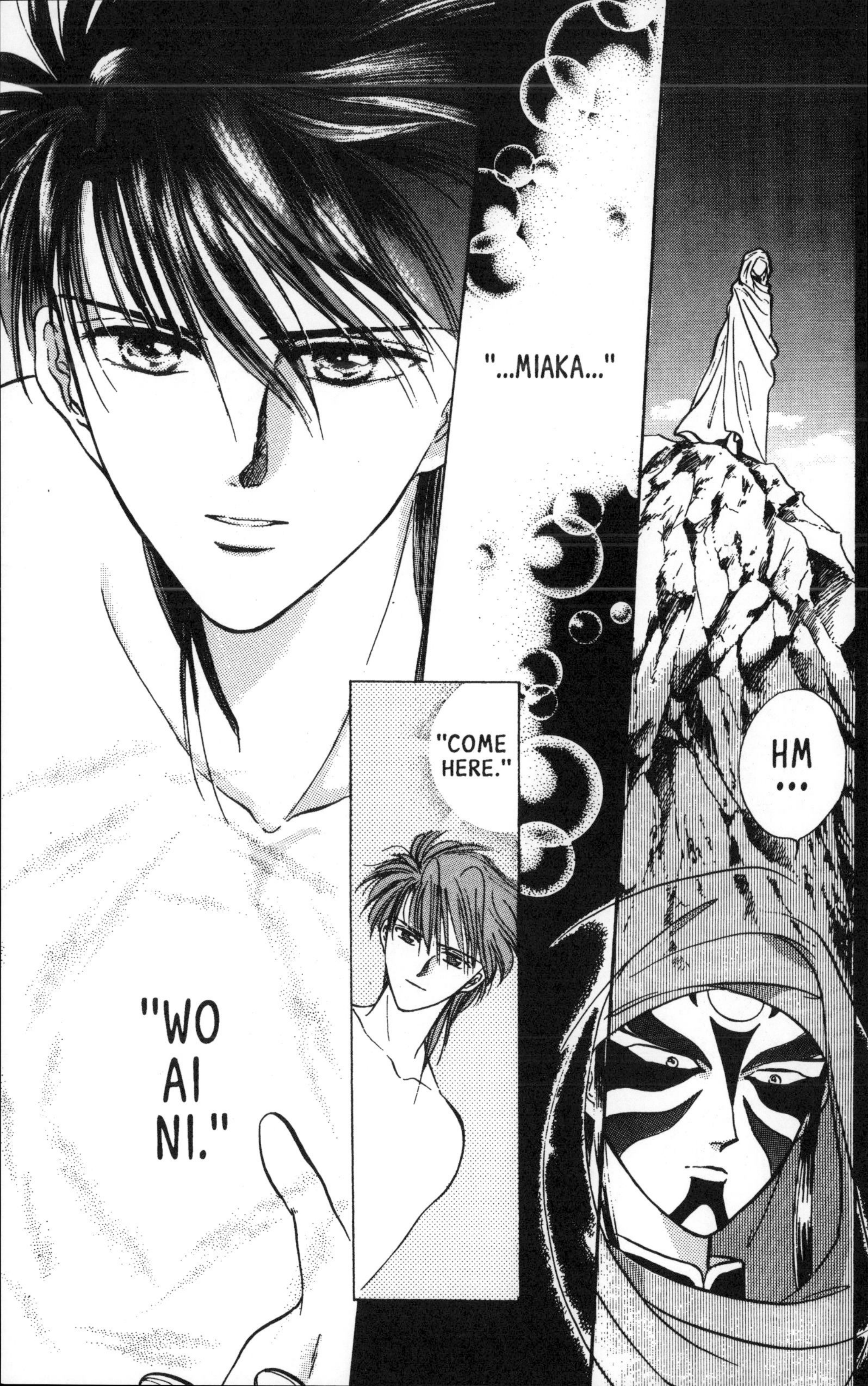
HM...
"...MIAKA..."
"COME HERE."
"WO AI NI."

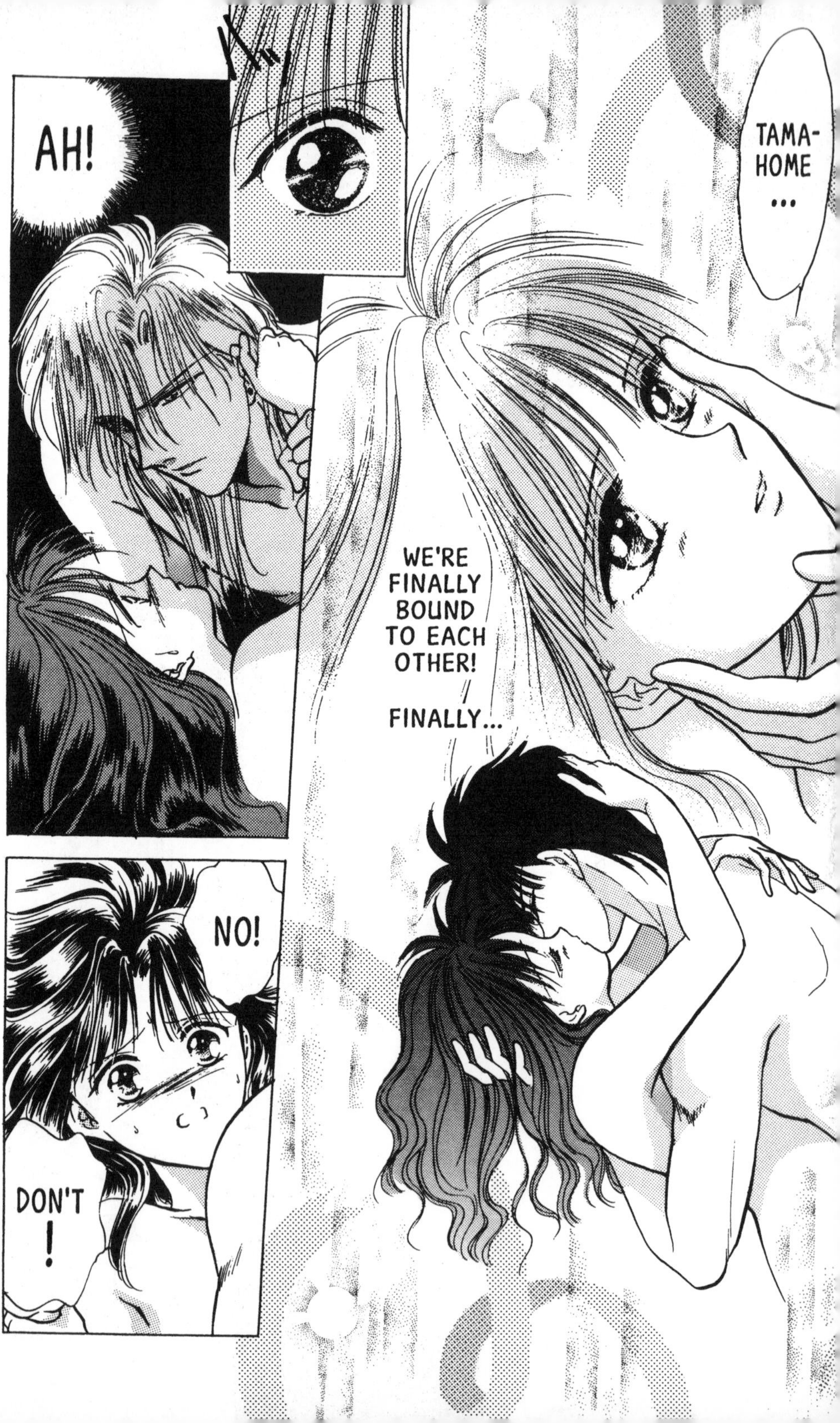
TAMA-HOME ...
WE'RE FINALLY BOUND TO EACH OTHER!
FINALLY...
AH!
NO!
DON'T !

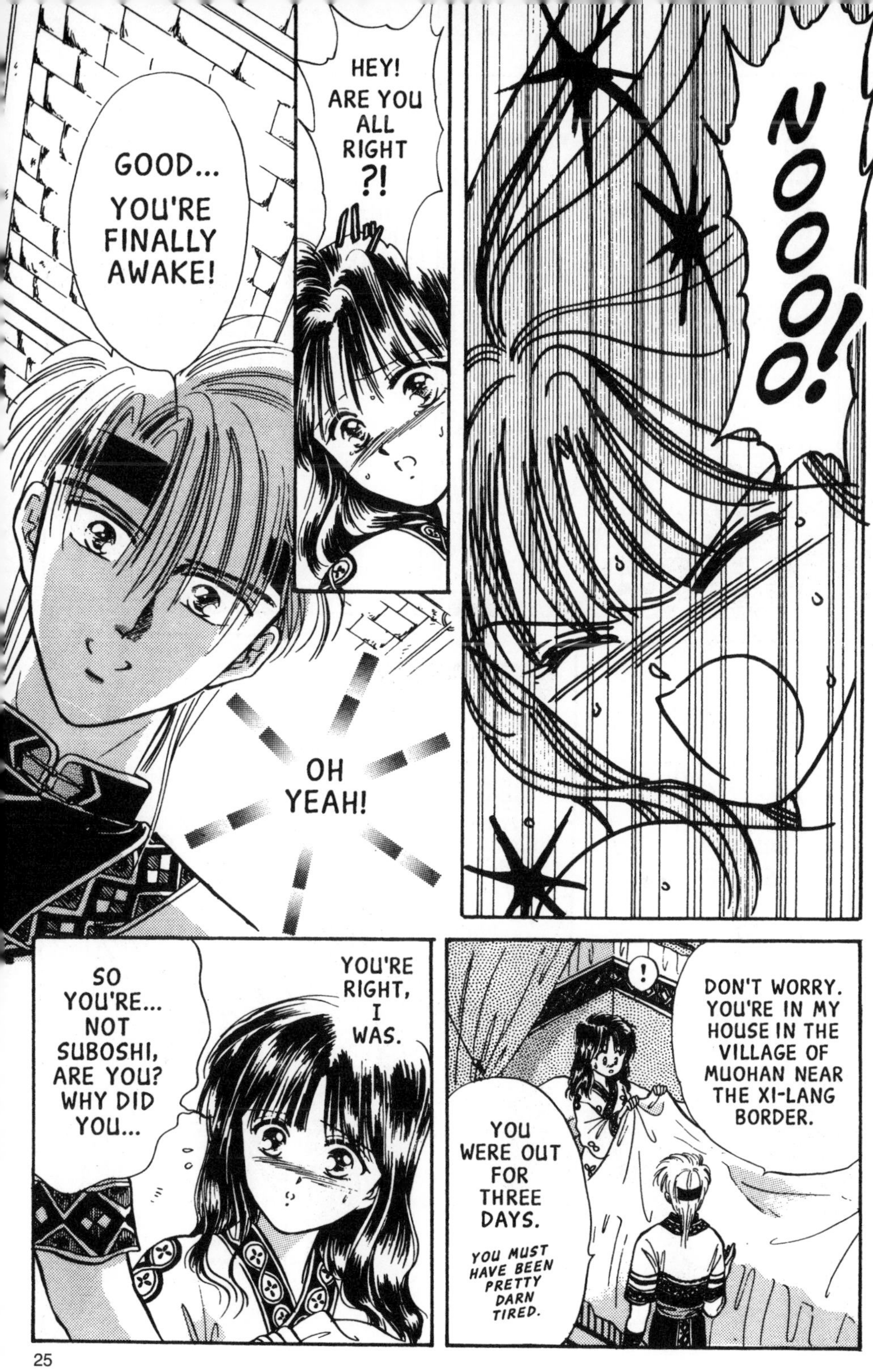
NOOOOO!
HEY! ARE YOU ALL RIGHT ?!
GOOD... YOU'RE FINALLY AWAKE!
OH YEAH!
!
DON'T WORRY. YOU'RE IN MY HOUSE IN THE VILLAGE OF MUOHAN NEAR THE XI-LANG BORDER.
YOU WERE OUT FOR THREE DAYS.
YOU MUST HAVE BEEN PRETTY DARN TIRED.
YOU'RE RIGHT, I WAS.
SO YOU'RE... NOT SUBOSHI, ARE YOU? WHY DID YOU...

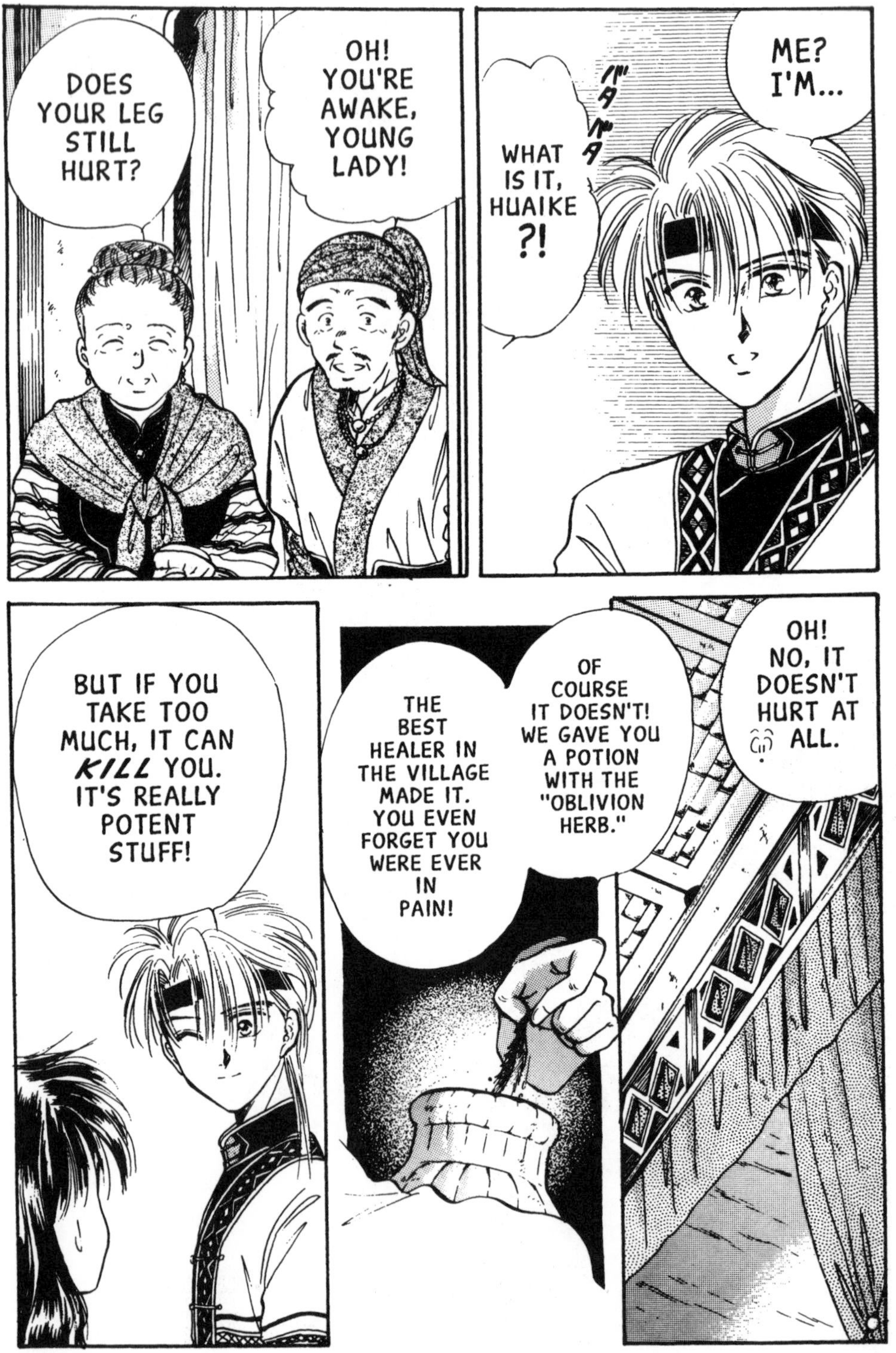
ME? I'M...
バタバタ
WHAT IS IT, HUAIKE?!
OH! YOU'RE AWAKE, YOUNG LADY!
DOES YOUR LEG STILL HURT?
OH! NO, IT DOESN'T HURT AT ALL.
OF COURSE IT DOESN'T! WE GAVE YOU A POTION WITH THE "OBLIVION HERB."
THE BEST HEALER IN THE VILLAGE MADE IT. YOU EVEN FORGET YOU WERE EVER IN PAIN!
BUT IF YOU TAKE TOO MUCH, IT CAN *KILL* YOU. IT'S REALLY POTENT STUFF!

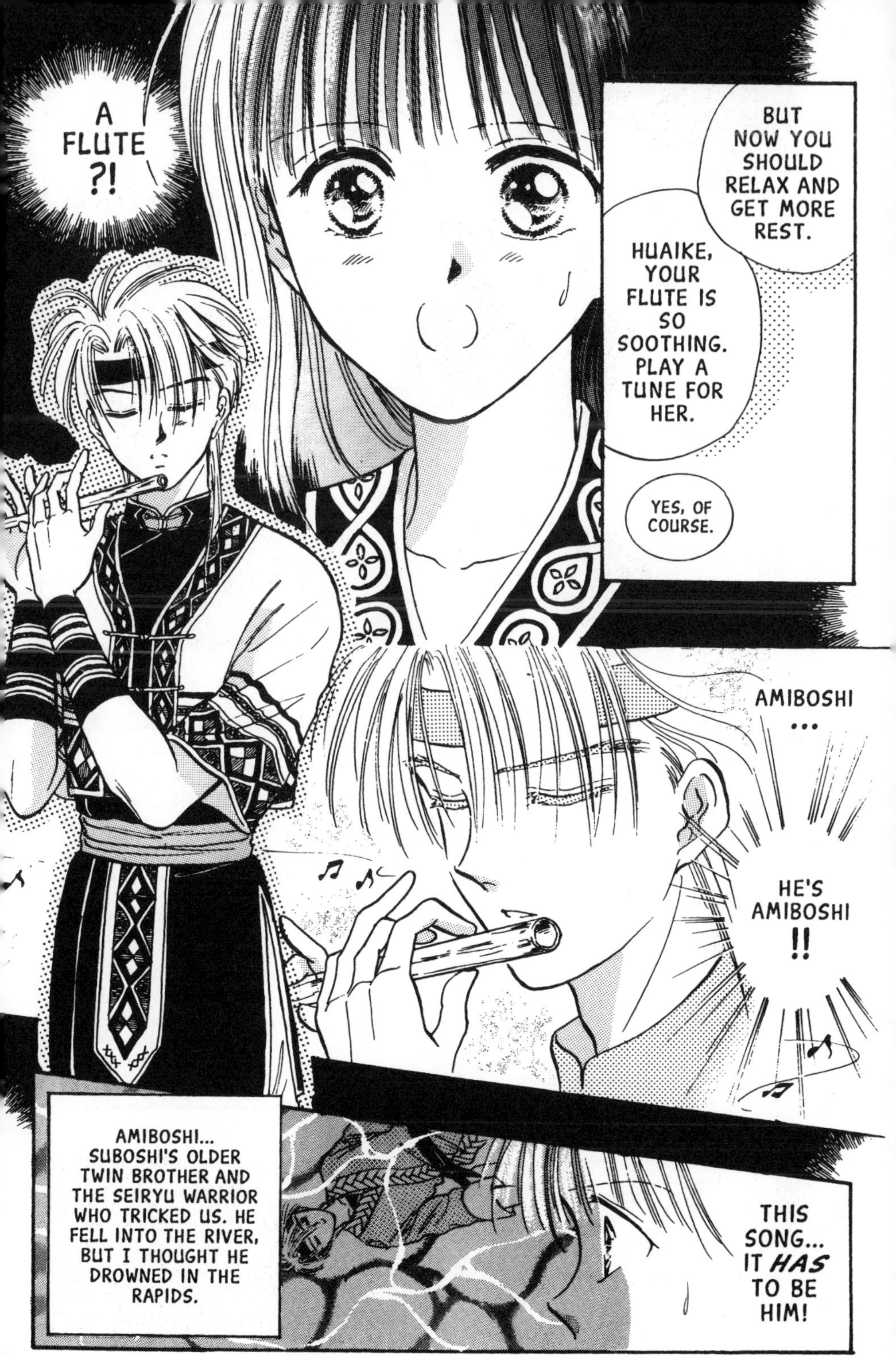
BUT NOW YOU SHOULD RELAX AND GET MORE REST.
HUAIKE, YOUR FLUTE IS SO SOOTHING. PLAY A TUNE FOR HER.
YES, OF COURSE.
A FLUTE ?!
AMIBOSHI ...
HE'S AMIBOSHI !!
THIS SONG... IT *HAS* TO BE HIM!
AMIBOSHI... SUBOSHI'S OLDER TWIN BROTHER AND THE SEIRYU WARRIOR WHO TRICKED US. HE FELL INTO THE RIVER, BUT I THOUGHT HE DROWNED IN THE RAPIDS.

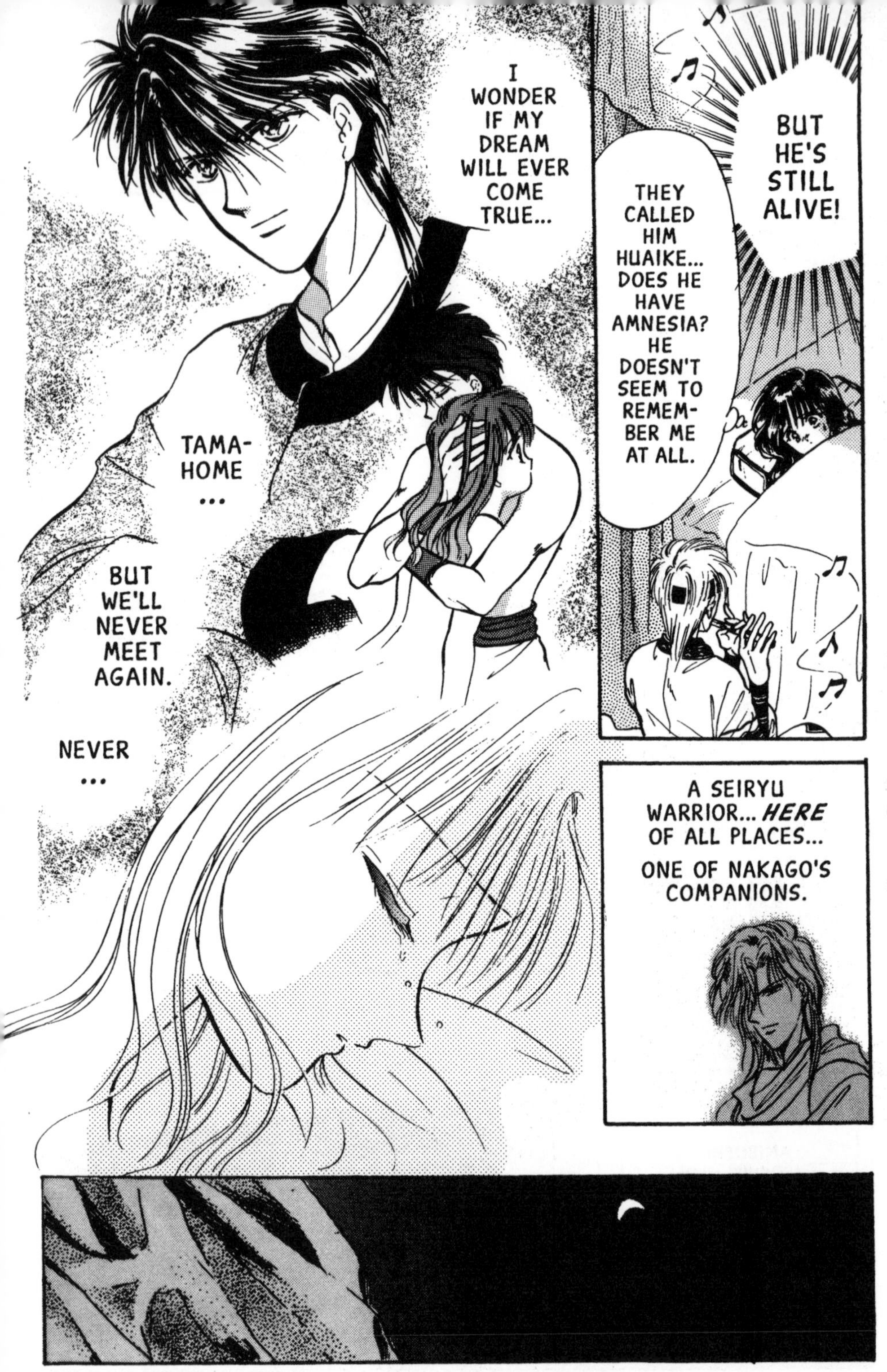
BUT HE'S STILL ALIVE!
THEY CALLED HIM HUAIKE... DOES HE HAVE AMNESIA? HE DOESN'T SEEM TO REMEMBER ME AT ALL.
A SEIRYU WARRIOR... *HERE* OF ALL PLACES...
ONE OF NAKAGO'S COMPANIONS.
I WONDER IF MY DREAM WILL EVER COME TRUE...
TAMA-HOME...
BUT WE'LL NEVER MEET AGAIN.
NEVER...

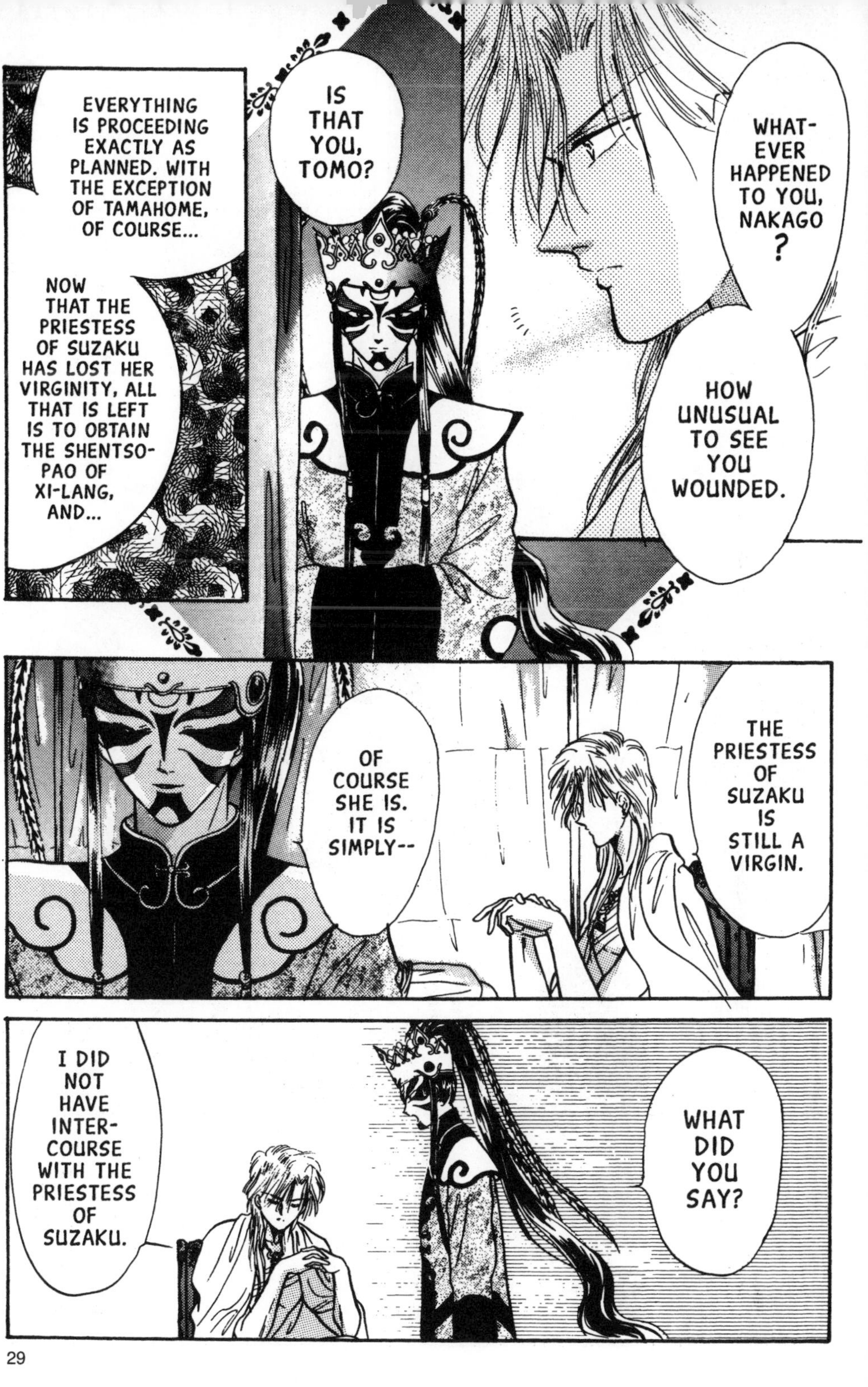
WHAT-EVER HAPPENED TO YOU, NAKAGO?
HOW UNUSUAL TO SEE YOU WOUNDED.
IS THAT YOU, TOMO?
EVERYTHING IS PROCEEDING EXACTLY AS PLANNED. WITH THE EXCEPTION OF TAMAHOME, OF COURSE...
NOW THAT THE PRIESTESS OF SUZAKU HAS LOST HER VIRGINITY, ALL THAT IS LEFT IS TO OBTAIN THE SHENTSO-PAO OF XI-LANG, AND...
THE PRIESTESS OF SUZAKU IS STILL A VIRGIN.
OF COURSE SHE IS. IT IS SIMPLY--
WHAT DID YOU SAY?
I DID NOT HAVE INTER-COURSE WITH THE PRIESTESS OF SUZAKU.

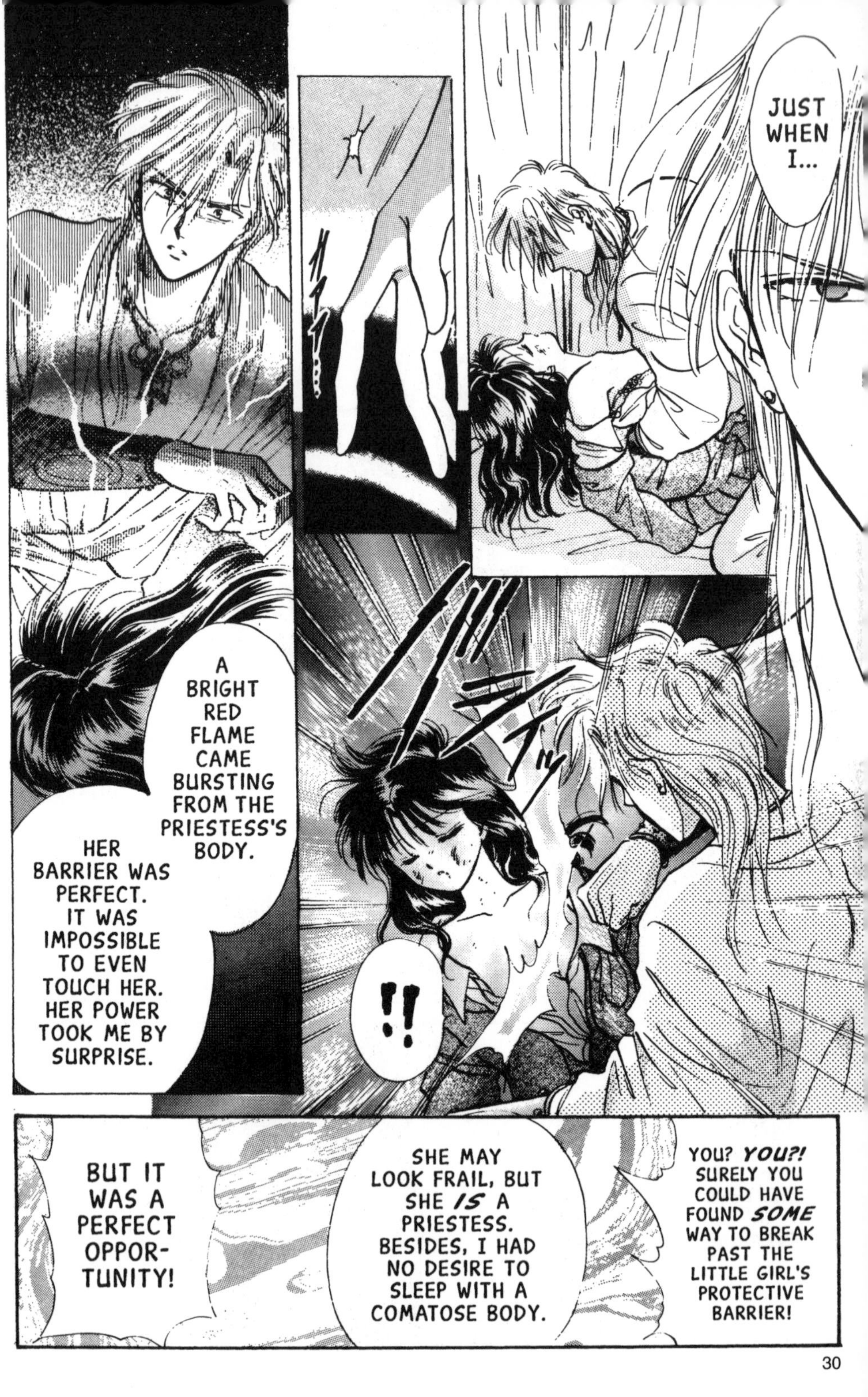
JUST WHEN I...
!!
A BRIGHT RED FLAME CAME BURSTING FROM THE PRIESTESS'S BODY.
HER BARRIER WAS PERFECT. IT WAS IMPOSSIBLE TO EVEN TOUCH HER. HER POWER TOOK ME BY SURPRISE.
YOU? *YOU?!* SURELY YOU COULD HAVE FOUND *SOME* WAY TO BREAK PAST THE LITTLE GIRL'S PROTECTIVE BARRIER!
SHE MAY LOOK FRAIL, BUT SHE *IS* A PRIESTESS. BESIDES, I HAD NO DESIRE TO SLEEP WITH A COMATOSE BODY.
BUT IT WAS A PERFECT OPPORTUNITY!

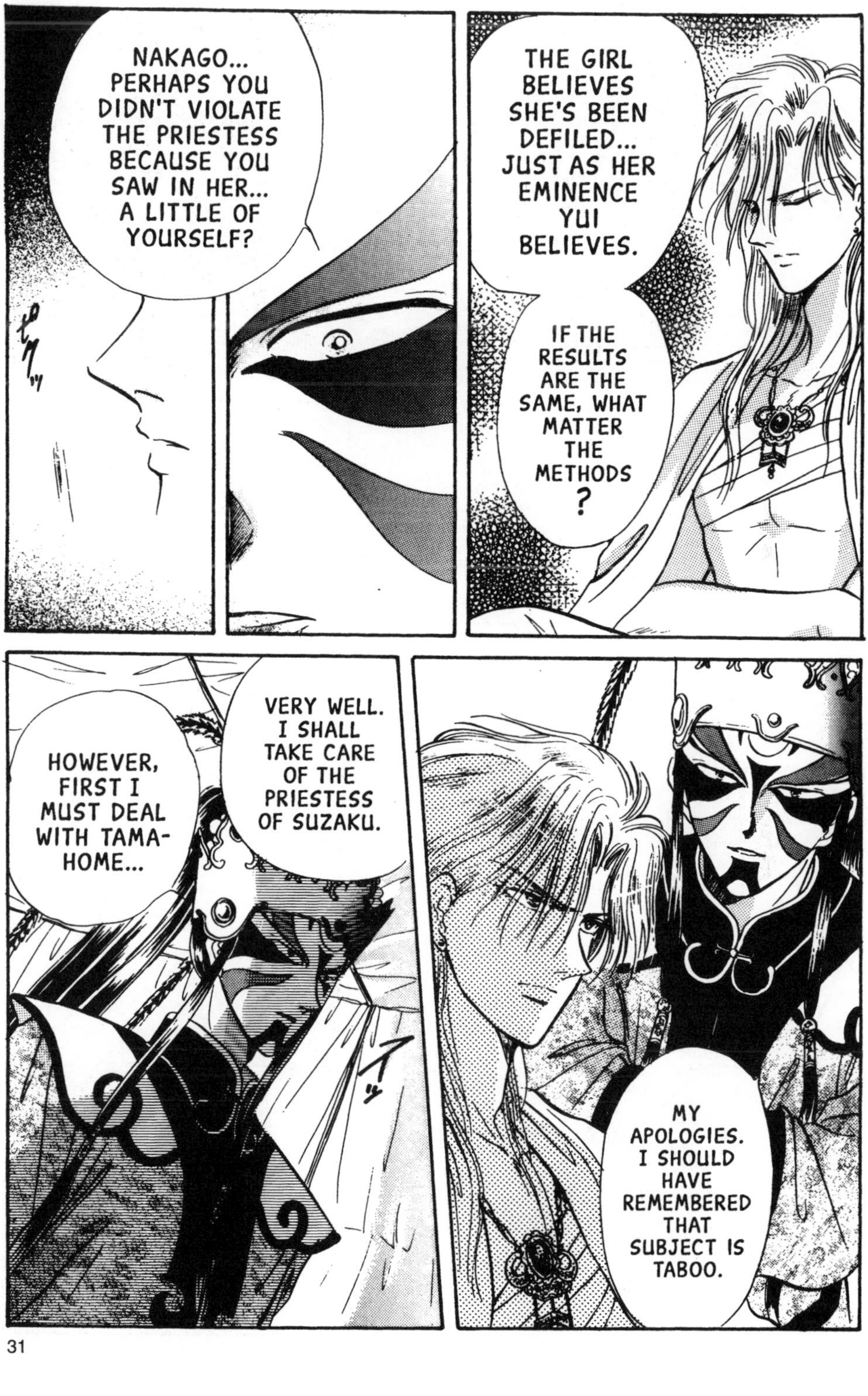
THE GIRL BELIEVES SHE'S BEEN DEFILED... JUST AS HER EMINENCE YUI BELIEVES.
IF THE RESULTS ARE THE SAME, WHAT MATTER THE METHODS?
NAKAGO... PERHAPS YOU DIDN'T VIOLATE THE PRIESTESS BECAUSE YOU SAW IN HER... A LITTLE OF YOURSELF?
MY APOLOGIES. I SHOULD HAVE REMEMBERED THAT SUBJECT IS TABOO.
VERY WELL. I SHALL TAKE CARE OF THE PRIESTESS OF SUZAKU.
HOWEVER, FIRST I MUST DEAL WITH TAMA-HOME...

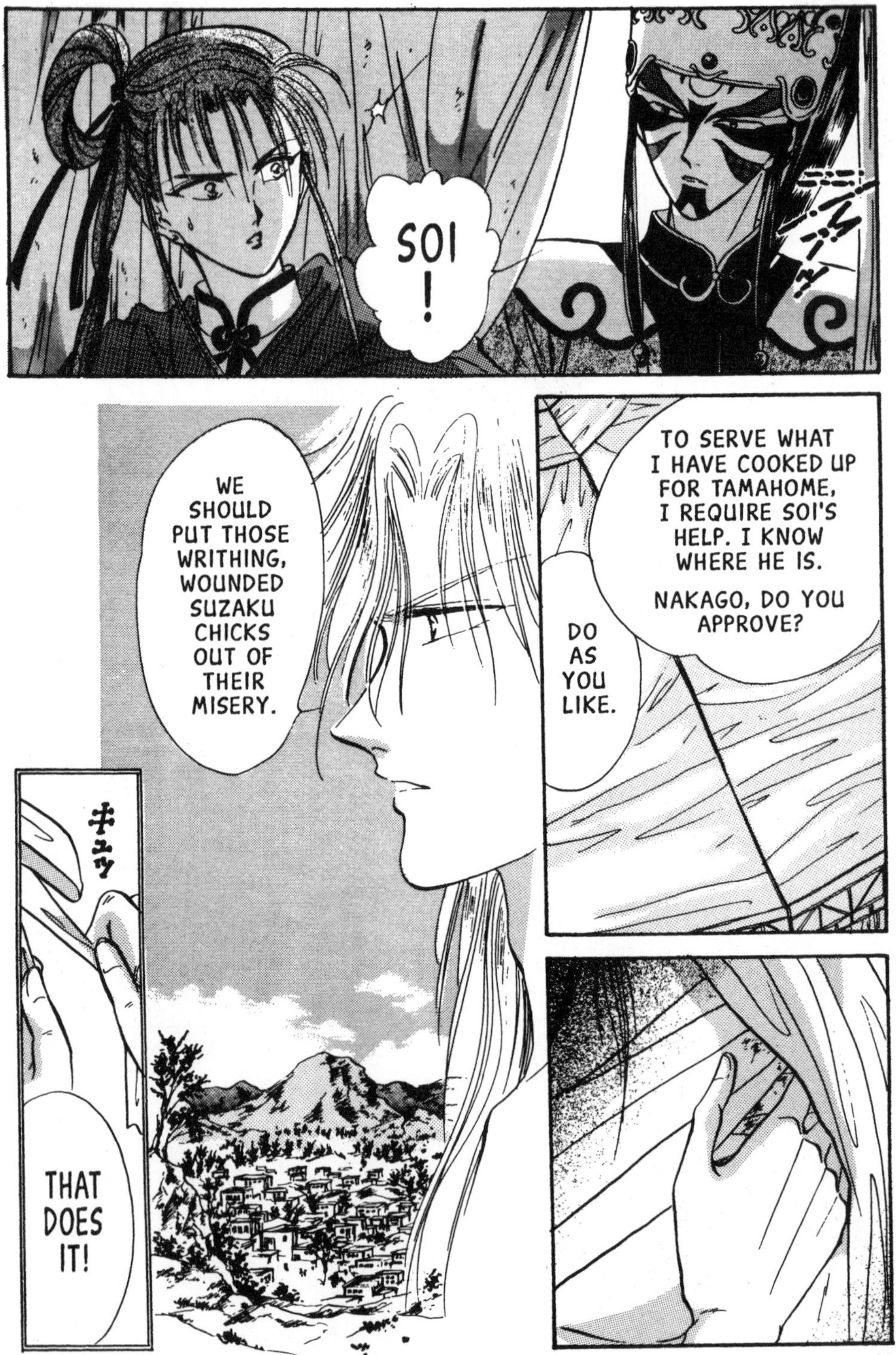
SOI!
TO SERVE WHAT I HAVE COOKED UP FOR TAMAHOME, I REQUIRE SOI'S HELP. I KNOW WHERE HE IS.
NAKAGO, DO YOU APPROVE?
DO AS YOU LIKE.
WE SHOULD PUT THOSE WRITHING, WOUNDED SUZAKU CHICKS OUT OF THEIR MISERY.
キュッ
THAT DOES IT!

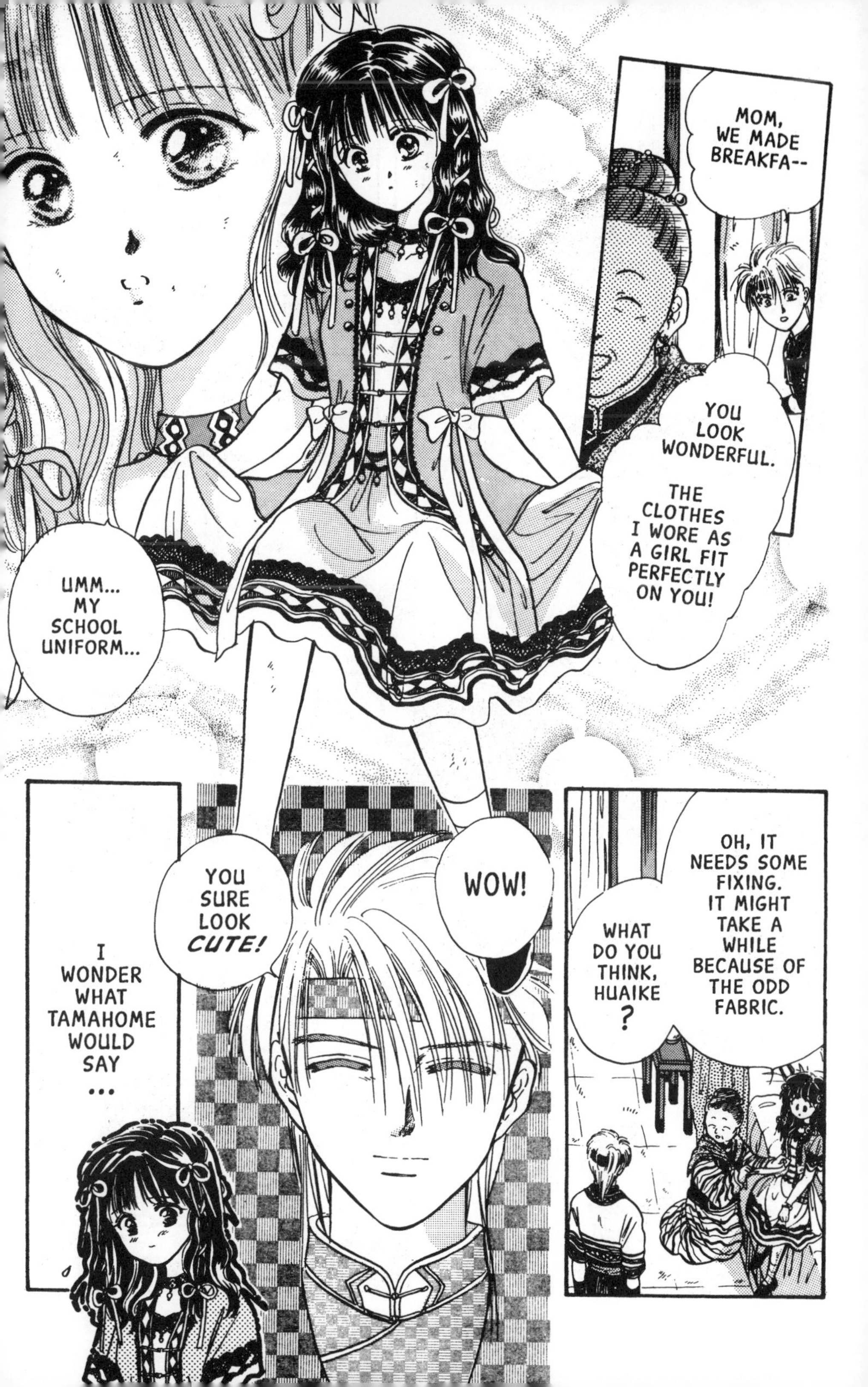
MOM, WE MADE BREAKFA--
YOU LOOK WONDERFUL.
THE CLOTHES I WORE AS A GIRL FIT PERFECTLY ON YOU!
UMM... MY SCHOOL UNIFORM...
OH, IT NEEDS SOME FIXING. IT MIGHT TAKE A WHILE BECAUSE OF THE ODD FABRIC.
WHAT DO YOU THINK, HUAIKE?
WOW!
YOU SURE LOOK *CUTE!*
I WONDER WHAT TAMAHOME WOULD SAY ...

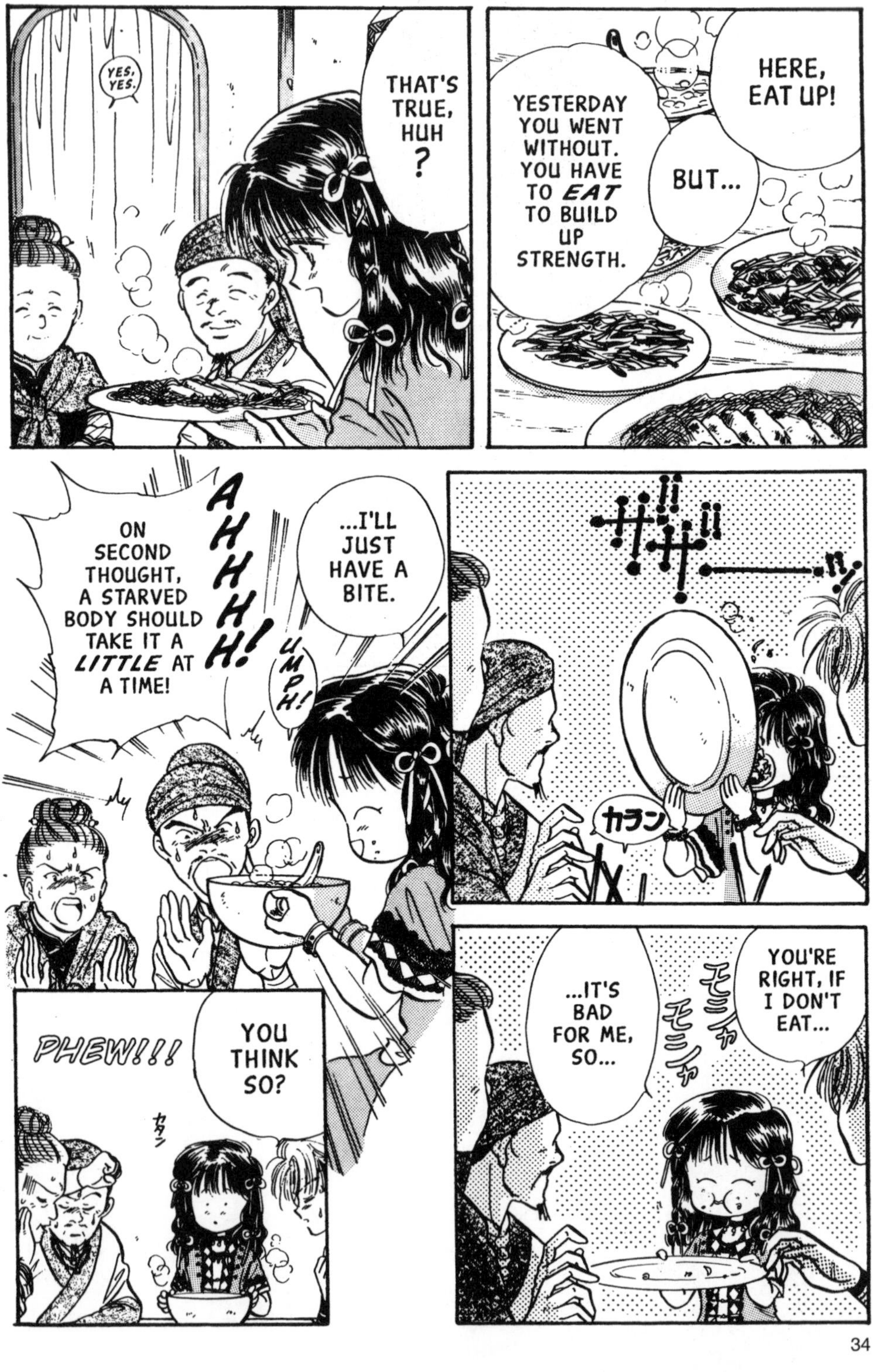
HERE, EAT UP!
BUT...
YESTERDAY YOU WENT WITHOUT. YOU HAVE TO *EAT* TO BUILD UP STRENGTH.
THAT'S TRUE, HUH?
YES, YES.
サササ
カラン
YOU'RE RIGHT, IF I DON'T EAT...
モシャ モシャ
...IT'S BAD FOR ME, SO...
...I'LL JUST HAVE A BITE.
UMPH!
AHHHHH!
ON SECOND THOUGHT, A STARVED BODY SHOULD TAKE IT A *LITTLE* AT A TIME!
YOU THINK SO?
PHEW!!!
カタン

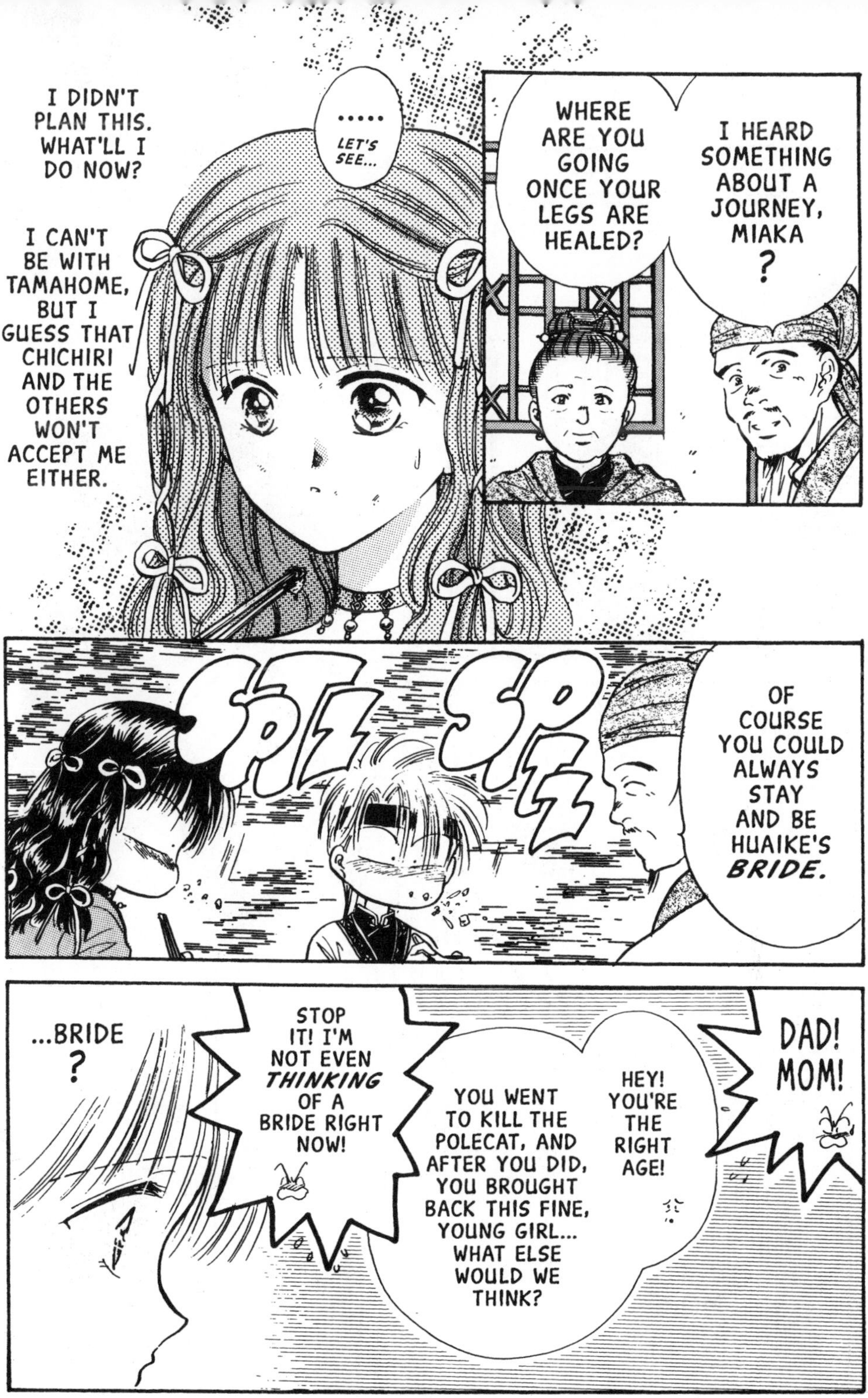
I HEARD SOMETHING ABOUT A JOURNEY, MIAKA ?
WHERE ARE YOU GOING ONCE YOUR LEGS ARE HEALED?
.....
LET'S SEE...
I DIDN'T PLAN THIS. WHAT'LL I DO NOW?
I CAN'T BE WITH TAMAHOME, BUT I GUESS THAT CHICHIRI AND THE OTHERS WON'T ACCEPT ME EITHER.
OF COURSE YOU COULD ALWAYS STAY AND BE HUAIKE'S *BRIDE.*
SPIZ
SPIZ
DAD! MOM!
HEY! YOU'RE THE RIGHT AGE!
YOU WENT TO KILL THE POLECAT, AND AFTER YOU DID, YOU BROUGHT BACK THIS FINE, YOUNG GIRL... WHAT ELSE WOULD WE THINK?
STOP IT! I'M NOT EVEN *THINKING* OF A BRIDE RIGHT NOW!
...BRIDE ?

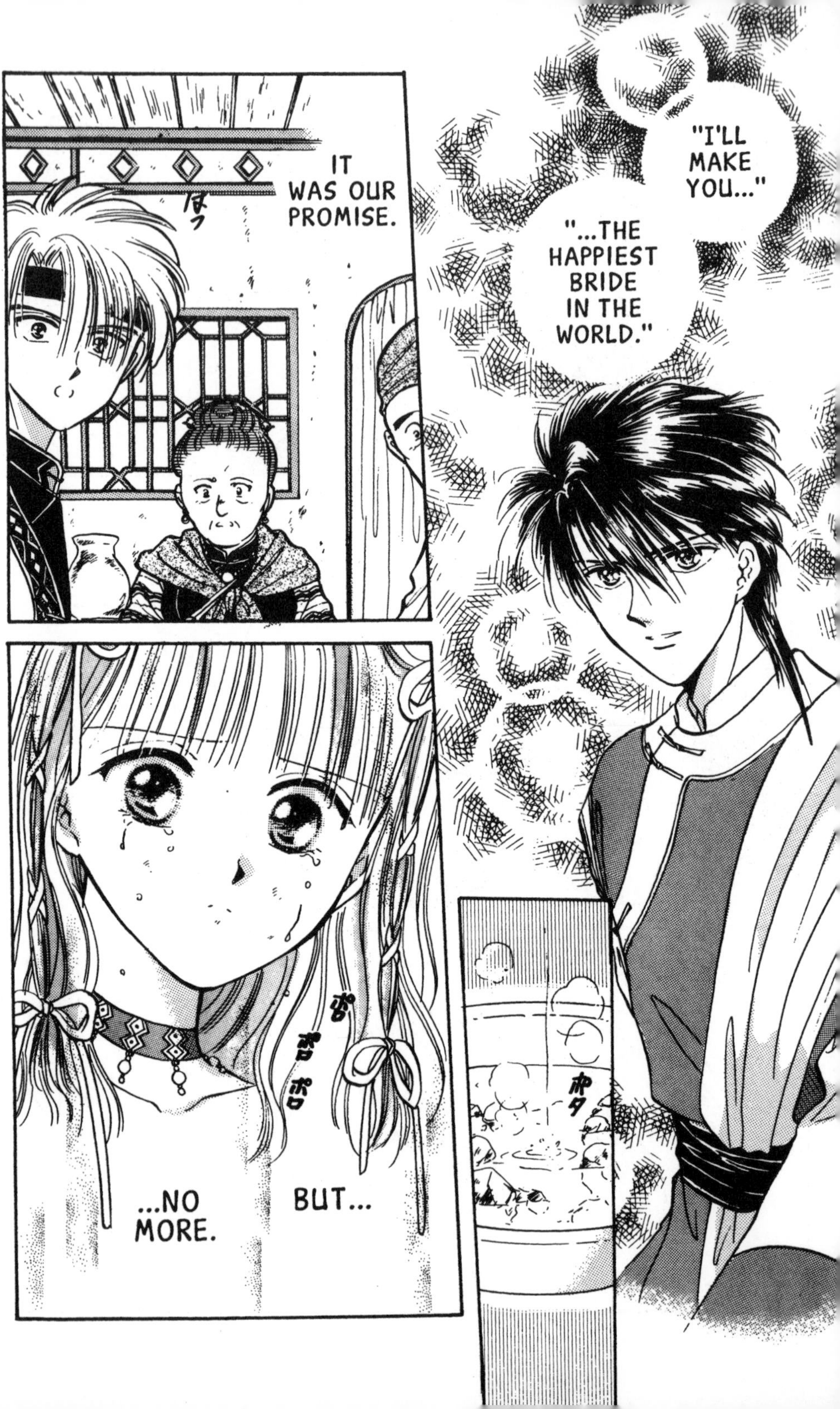
"I'LL MAKE YOU..."
"...THE HAPPIEST BRIDE IN THE WORLD."
はっ
IT WAS OUR PROMISE.
ポロ
ポロ ポロ
BUT...
...NO MORE.
ホタ

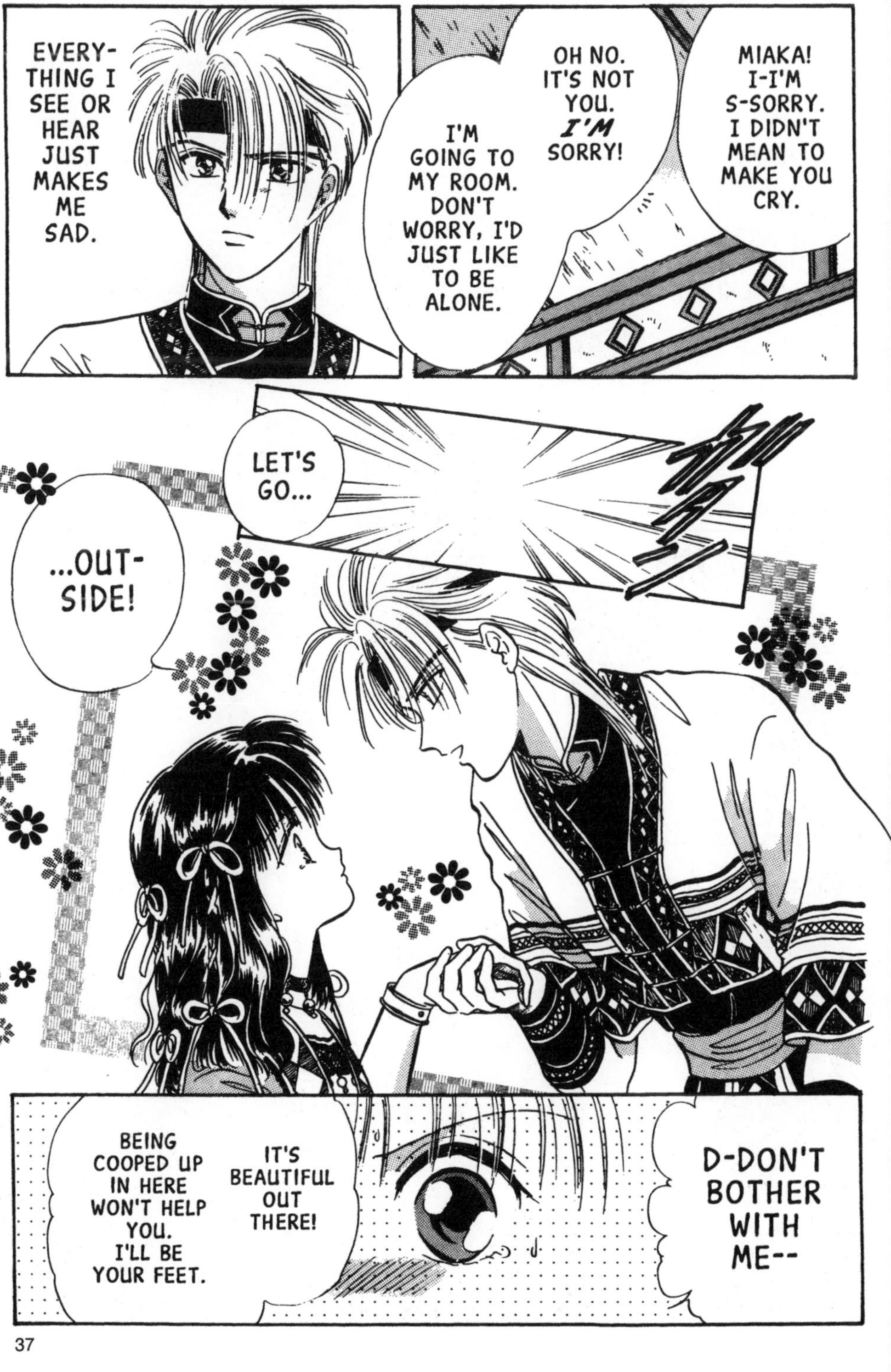
MIAKA! I-I'M S-SORRY. I DIDN'T MEAN TO MAKE YOU CRY.
OH NO. IT'S NOT YOU. *I'M* SORRY!
I'M GOING TO MY ROOM. DON'T WORRY, I'D JUST LIKE TO BE ALONE.
EVERY-THING I SEE OR HEAR JUST MAKES ME SAD.
LET'S GO...
...OUT-SIDE!
D-DON'T BOTHER WITH ME--
IT'S BEAUTIFUL OUT THERE!
BEING COOPED UP IN HERE WON'T HELP YOU. I'LL BE YOUR FEET.

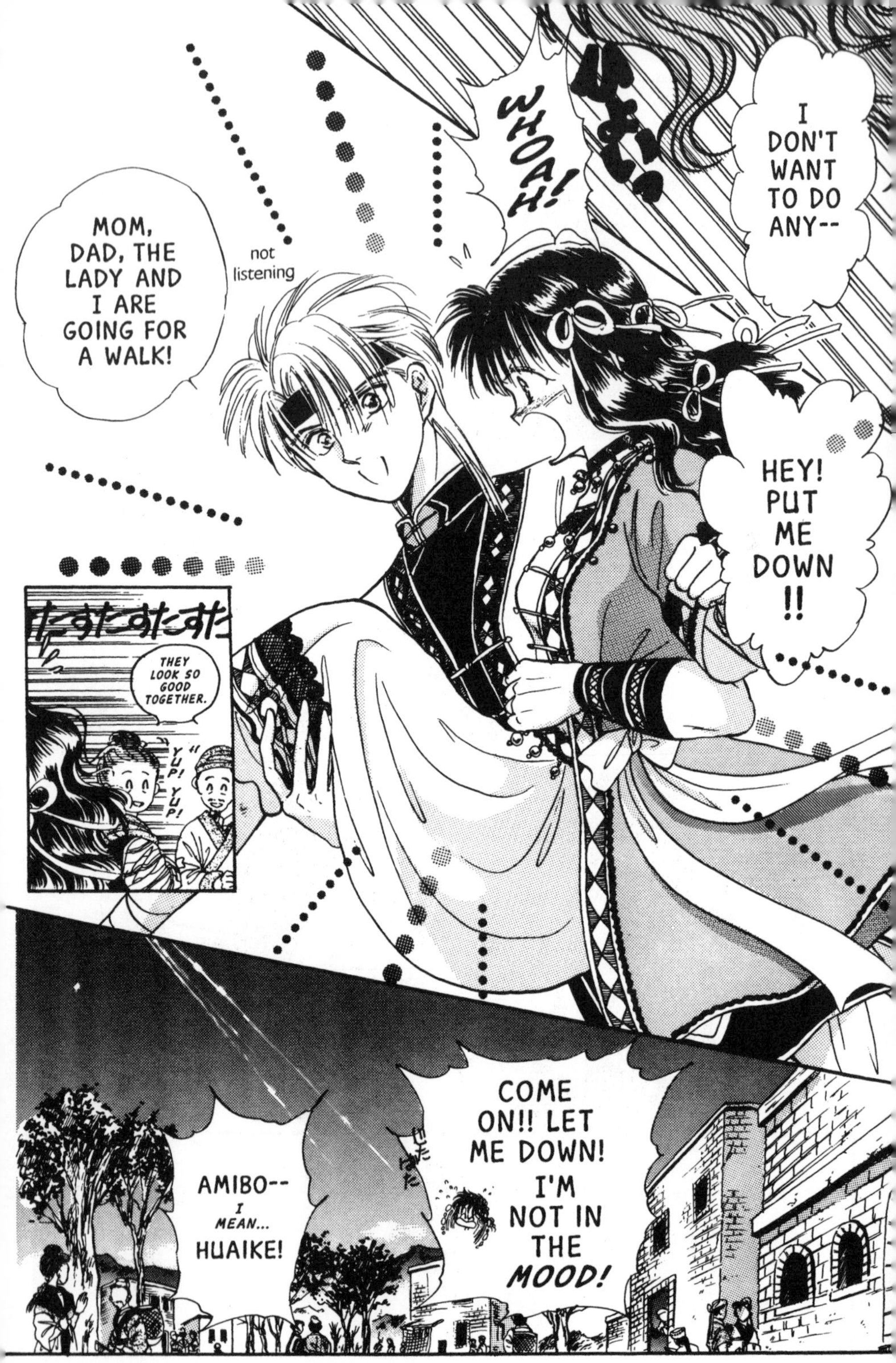
I DON'T WANT TO DO ANY--
WHOAH!
MOM, DAD, THE LADY AND I ARE GOING FOR A WALK!
not listening
HEY! PUT ME DOWN!!
THEY LOOK SO GOOD TOGETHER.
YUP! YUP!
COME ON!! LET ME DOWN!
I'M NOT IN THE *MOOD*!
AMIBO-- I MEAN... HUAIKE!

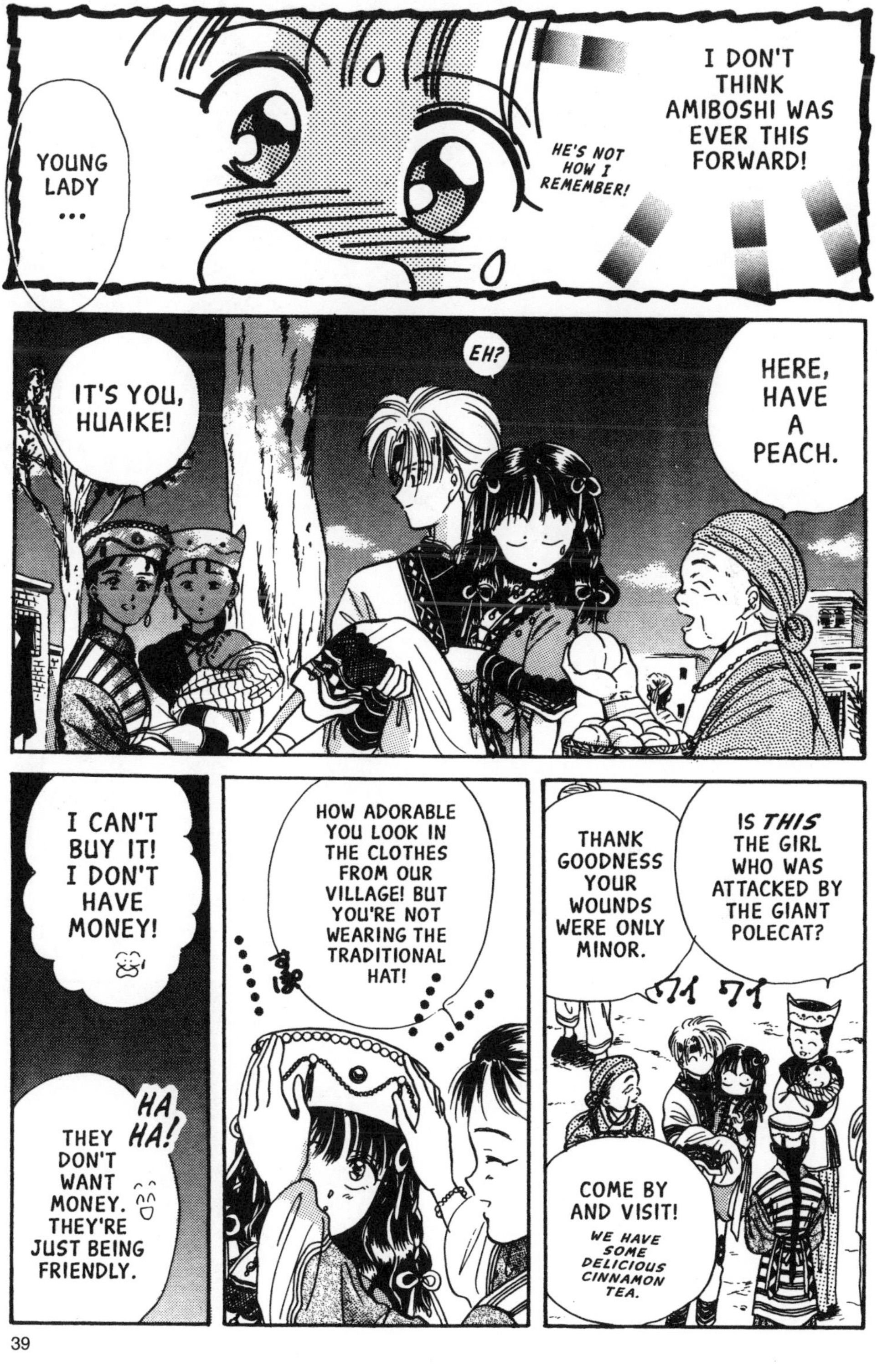
I DON'T THINK AMIBOSHI WAS EVER THIS FORWARD!
HE'S NOT HOW I REMEMBER!
YOUNG LADY...
HERE, HAVE A PEACH.
EH?
IT'S YOU, HUAIKE!
IS *THIS* THE GIRL WHO WAS ATTACKED BY THE GIANT POLECAT?
THANK GOODNESS YOUR WOUNDS WERE ONLY MINOR.
ワイ ワイ
COME BY AND VISIT!
WE HAVE SOME DELICIOUS CINNAMON TEA.
HOW ADORABLE YOU LOOK IN THE CLOTHES FROM OUR VILLAGE! BUT YOU'RE NOT WEARING THE TRADITIONAL HAT!
I CAN'T BUY IT! I DON'T HAVE MONEY!
HA HA!
THEY DON'T WANT MONEY. THEY'RE JUST BEING FRIENDLY.

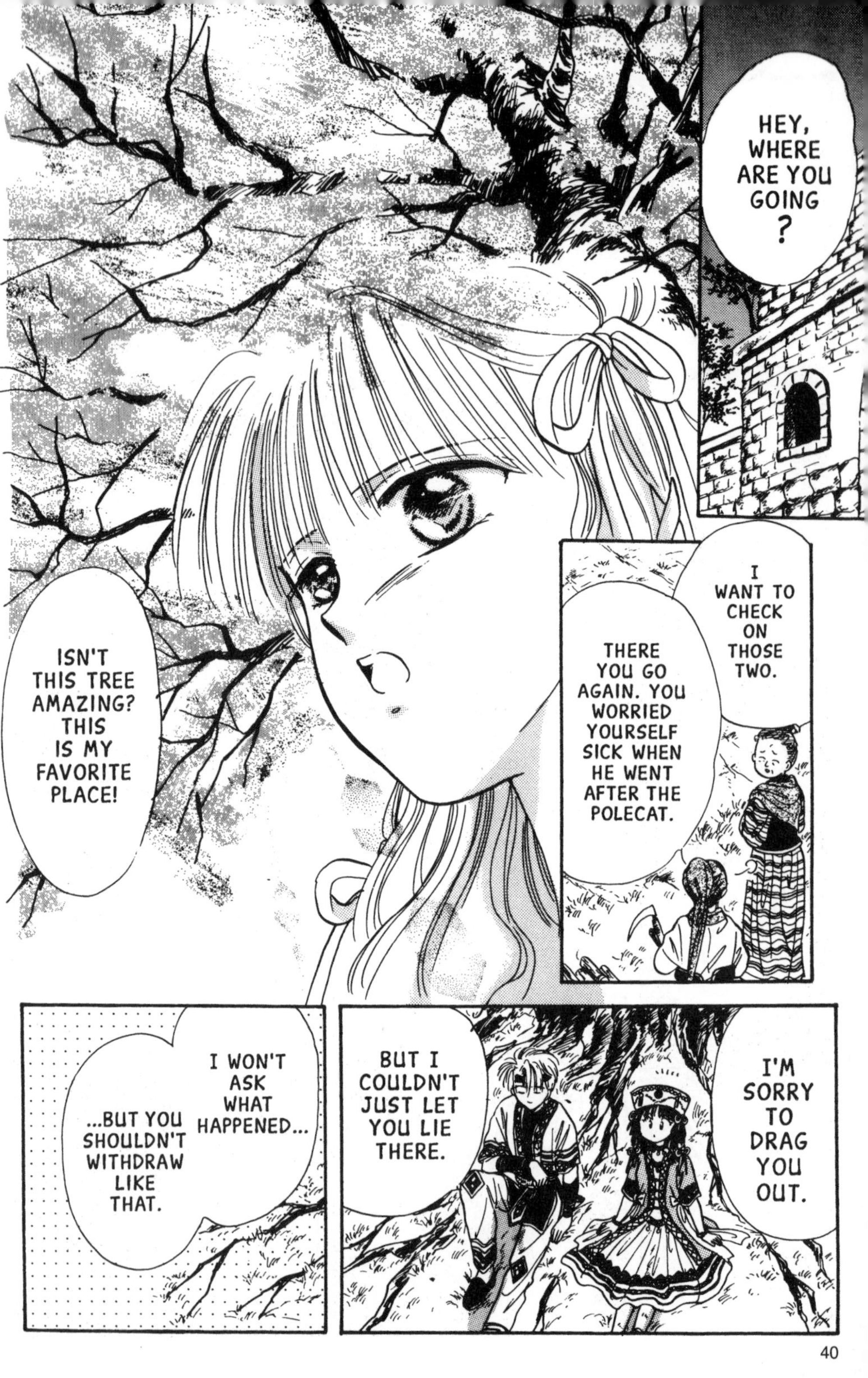
HEY, WHERE ARE YOU GOING?
I WANT TO CHECK ON THOSE TWO.
THERE YOU GO AGAIN. YOU WORRIED YOURSELF SICK WHEN HE WENT AFTER THE POLECAT.
ISN'T THIS TREE AMAZING? THIS IS MY FAVORITE PLACE!
I'M SORRY TO DRAG YOU OUT.
BUT I COULDN'T JUST LET YOU LIE THERE.
I WON'T ASK WHAT HAPPENED...
...BUT YOU SHOULDN'T WITHDRAW LIKE THAT.

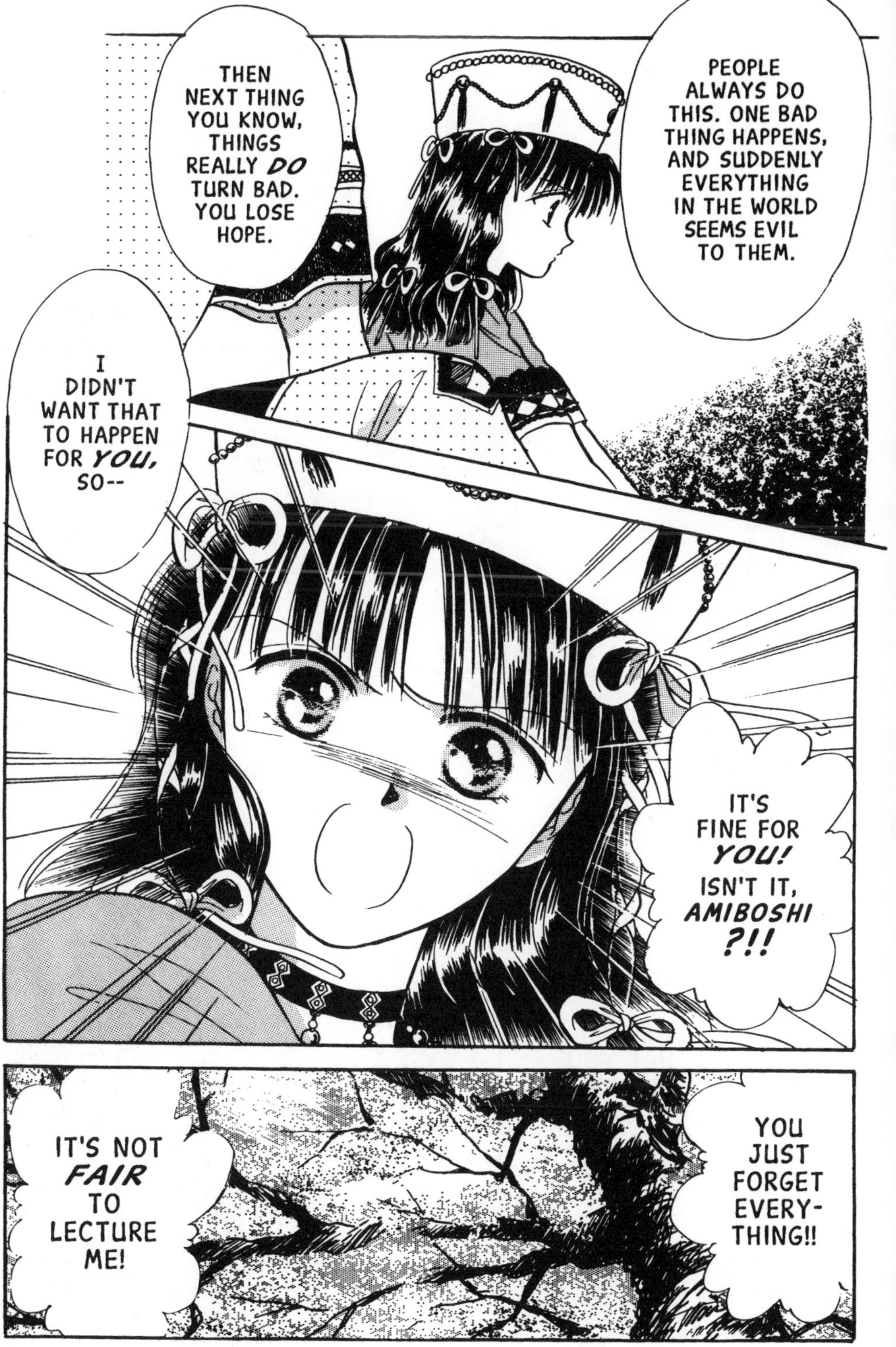
PEOPLE ALWAYS DO THIS. ONE BAD THING HAPPENS, AND SUDDENLY EVERYTHING IN THE WORLD SEEMS EVIL TO THEM.
THEN NEXT THING YOU KNOW, THINGS REALLY *DO* TURN BAD. YOU LOSE HOPE.
I DIDN'T WANT THAT TO HAPPEN FOR *YOU,* SO--
IT'S FINE FOR *YOU!* ISN'T IT, *AMIBOSHI ?!!*
YOU JUST FORGET EVERY-THING!!
IT'S NOT *FAIR* TO LECTURE ME!

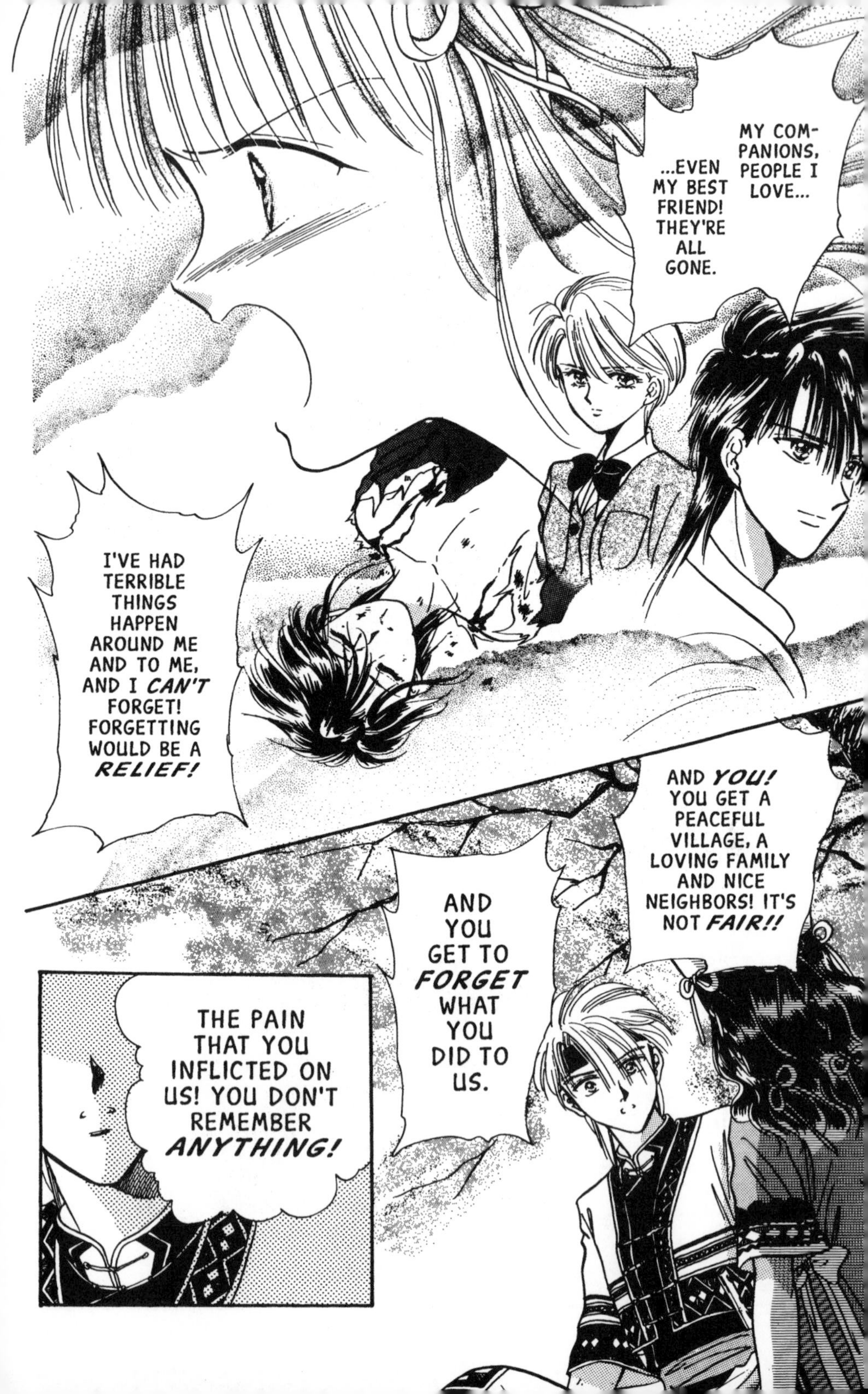
MY COMPANIONS, PEOPLE I LOVE...
...EVEN MY BEST FRIEND! THEY'RE ALL GONE.
I'VE HAD TERRIBLE THINGS HAPPEN AROUND ME AND TO ME, AND I CAN'T FORGET! FORGETTING WOULD BE A RELIEF!
AND YOU! YOU GET A PEACEFUL VILLAGE, A LOVING FAMILY AND NICE NEIGHBORS! IT'S NOT FAIR!!
AND YOU GET TO FORGET WHAT YOU DID TO US.
THE PAIN THAT YOU INFLICTED ON US! YOU DON'T REMEMBER ANYTHING!

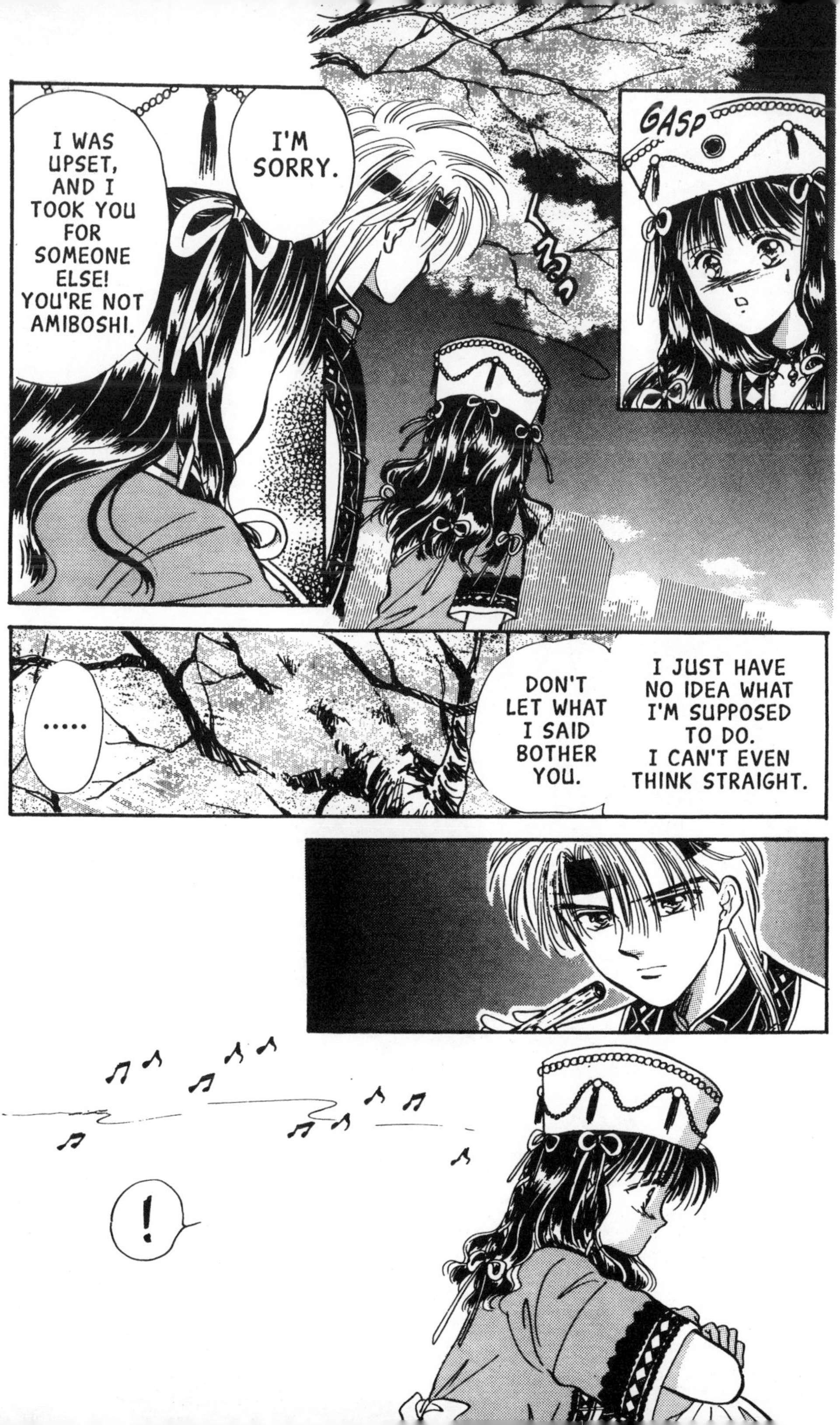
GASP
I'M SORRY.
I WAS UPSET, AND I TOOK YOU FOR SOMEONE ELSE! YOU'RE NOT AMIBOSHI.
I JUST HAVE NO IDEA WHAT I'M SUPPOSED TO DO. I CAN'T EVEN THINK STRAIGHT.
DON'T LET WHAT I SAID BOTHER YOU.
.....
!

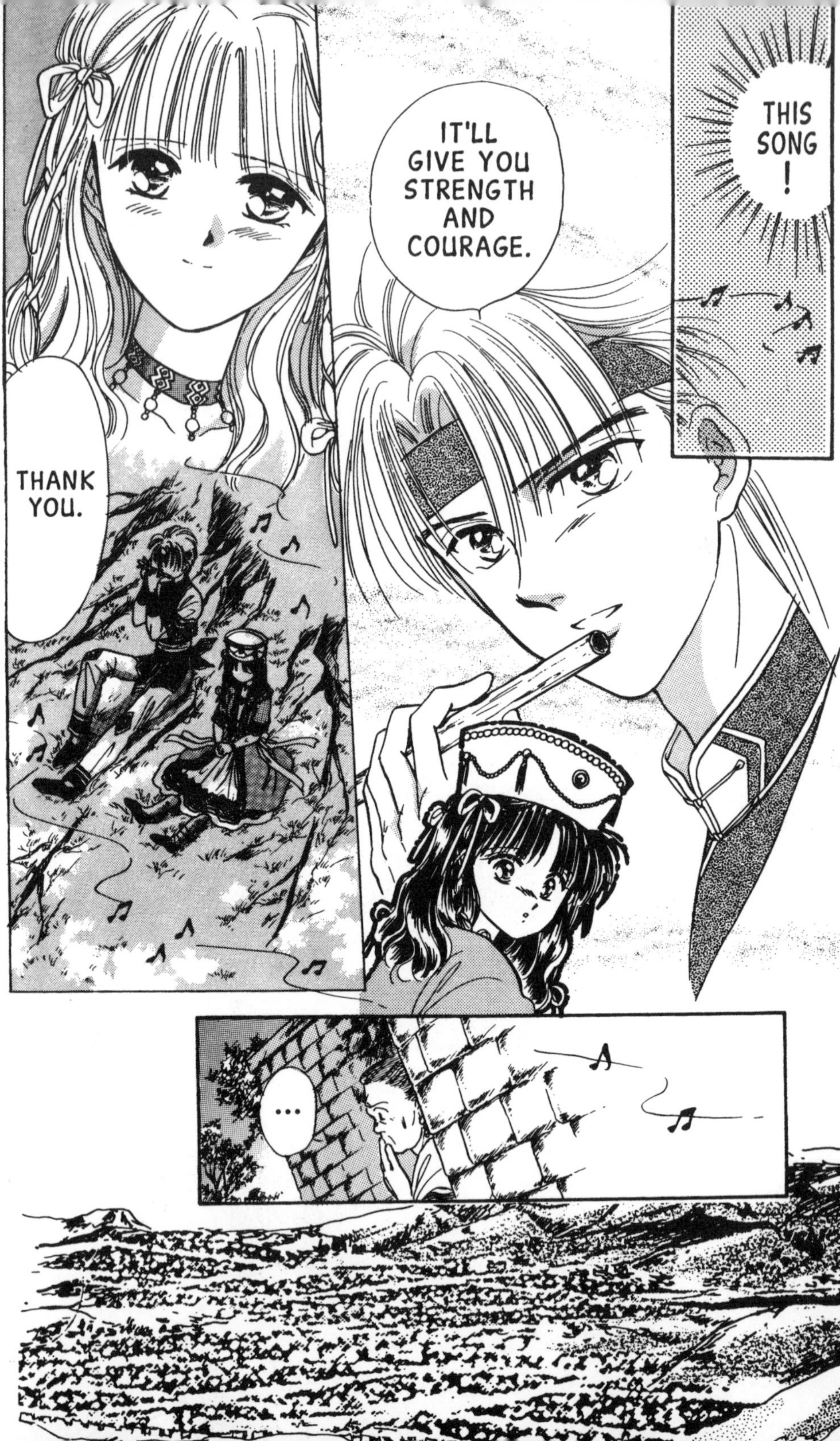
THIS SONG !
IT'LL GIVE YOU STRENGTH AND COURAGE.
THANK YOU.
...

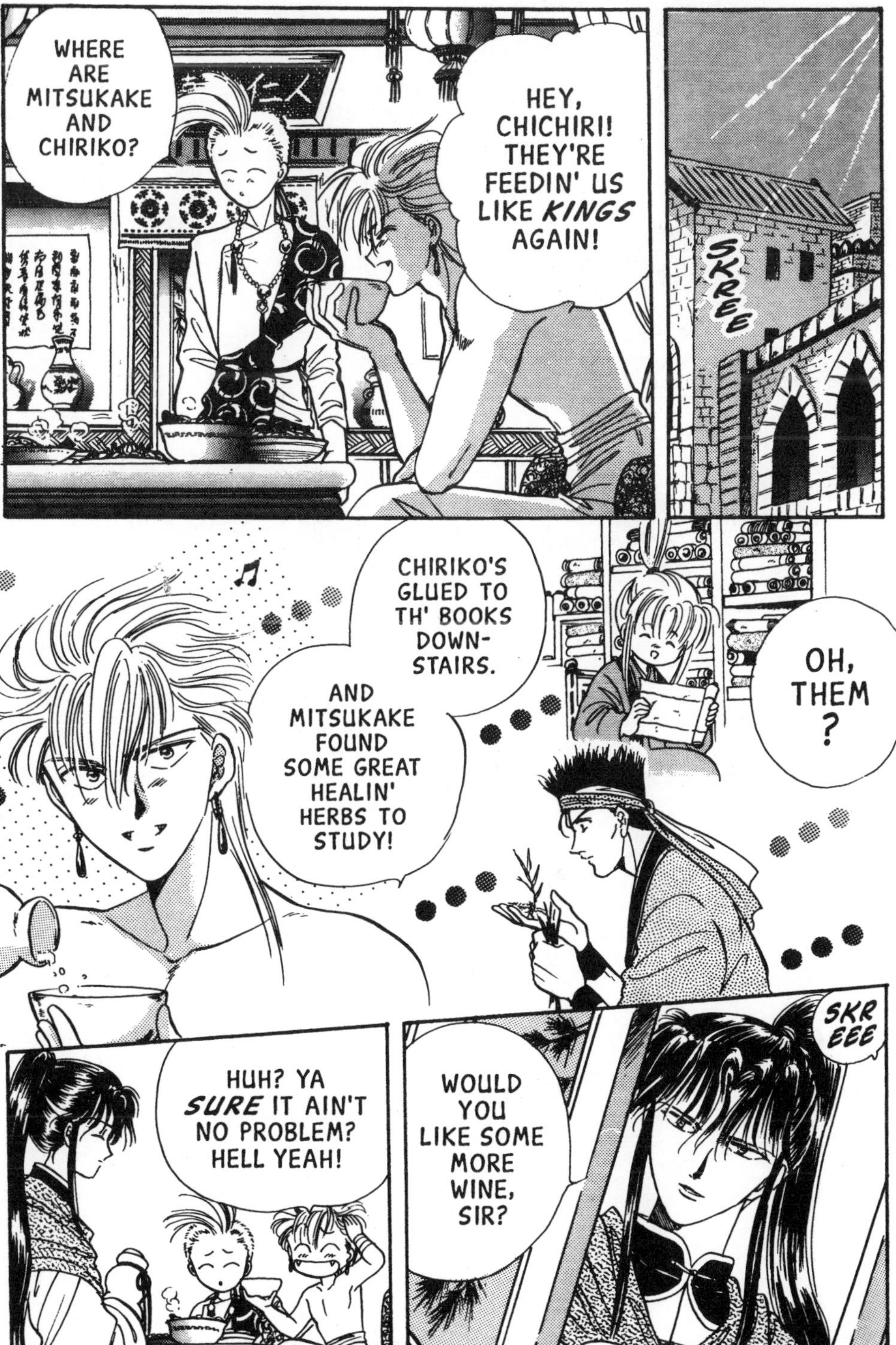
SKREE
HEY, CHICHIRI! THEY'RE FEEDIN' US LIKE *KINGS* AGAIN!
WHERE ARE MITSUKAKE AND CHIRIKO?
OH, THEM?
CHIRIKO'S GLUED TO TH' BOOKS DOWN-STAIRS.
AND MITSUKAKE FOUND SOME GREAT HEALIN' HERBS TO STUDY!
SKR EEE
WOULD YOU LIKE SOME MORE WINE, SIR?
HUH? YA *SURE* IT AIN'T NO PROBLEM? HELL YEAH!

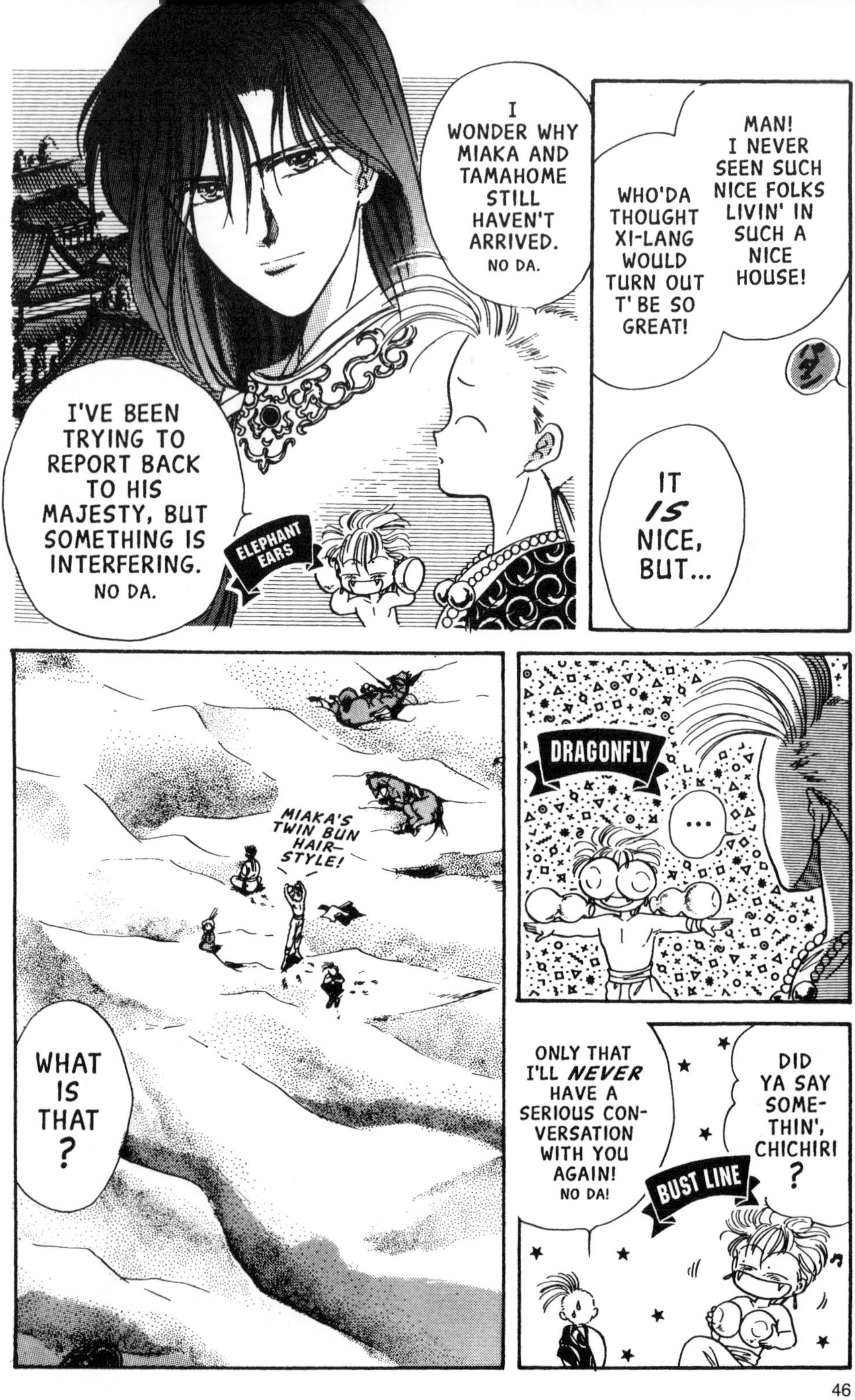
MAN! I NEVER SEEN SUCH NICE FOLKS LIVIN' IN SUCH A NICE HOUSE!
WHO'DA THOUGHT XI-LANG WOULD TURN OUT T' BE SO GREAT!
IT IS NICE, BUT...
I WONDER WHY MIAKA AND TAMAHOME STILL HAVEN'T ARRIVED. NO DA.
I'VE BEEN TRYING TO REPORT BACK TO HIS MAJESTY, BUT SOMETHING IS INTERFERING. NO DA.
ELEPHANT EARS
DRAGONFLY
...
DID YA SAY SOMETHIN', CHICHIRI?
ONLY THAT I'LL NEVER HAVE A SERIOUS CONVERSATION WITH YOU AGAIN! NO DA!
BUST LINE
MIAKA'S TWIN BUN HAIR-STYLE!
WHAT IS THAT?

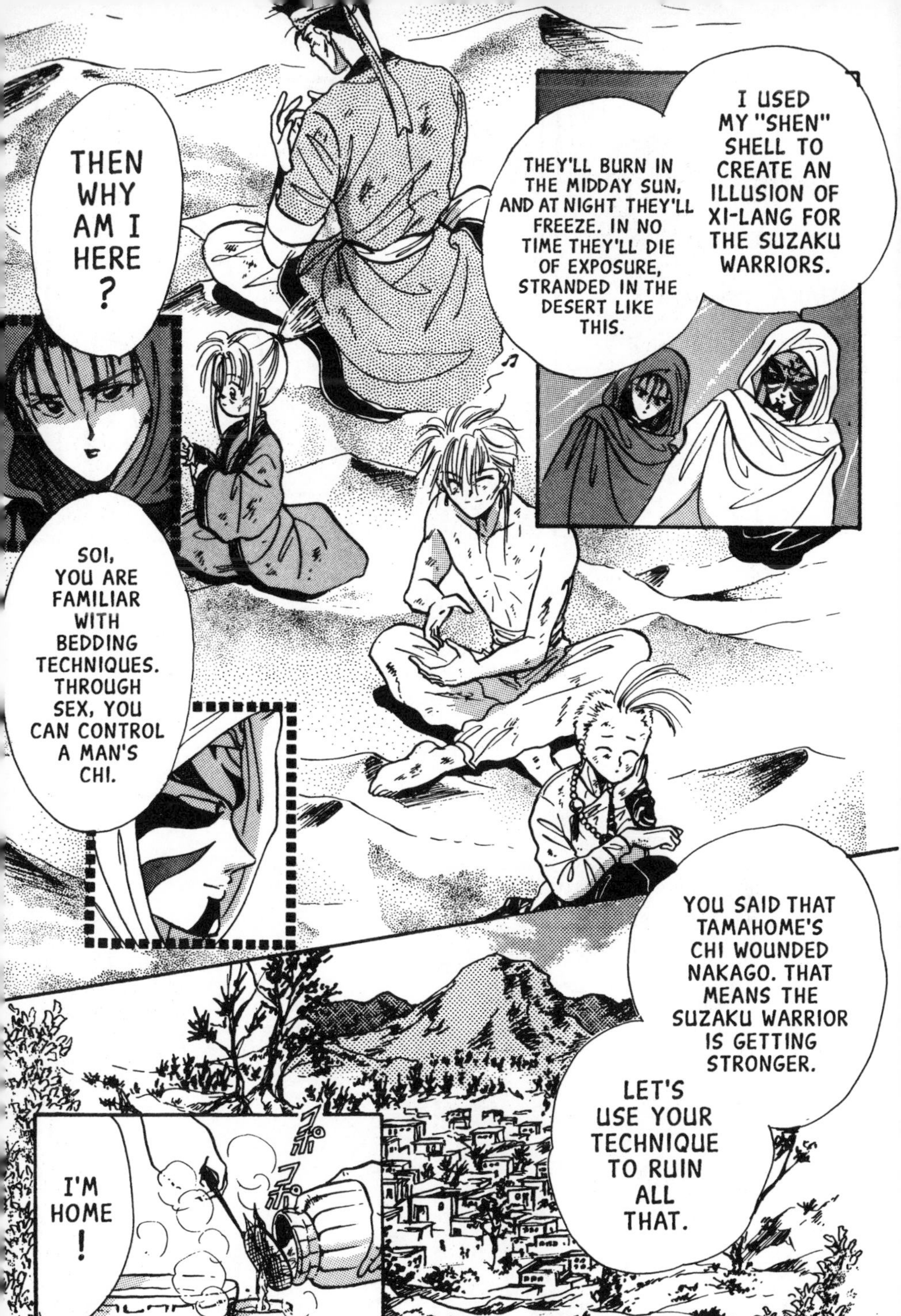
I USED MY "SHEN" SHELL TO CREATE AN ILLUSION OF XI-LANG FOR THE SUZAKU WARRIORS.
THEY'LL BURN IN THE MIDDAY SUN, AND AT NIGHT THEY'LL FREEZE. IN NO TIME THEY'LL DIE OF EXPOSURE, STRANDED IN THE DESERT LIKE THIS.
THEN WHY AM I HERE?
SOI, YOU ARE FAMILIAR WITH BEDDING TECHNIQUES. THROUGH SEX, YOU CAN CONTROL A MAN'S CHI.
YOU SAID THAT TAMAHOME'S CHI WOUNDED NAKAGO. THAT MEANS THE SUZAKU WARRIOR IS GETTING STRONGER.
LET'S USE YOUR TECHNIQUE TO RUIN ALL THAT.
I'M HOME!

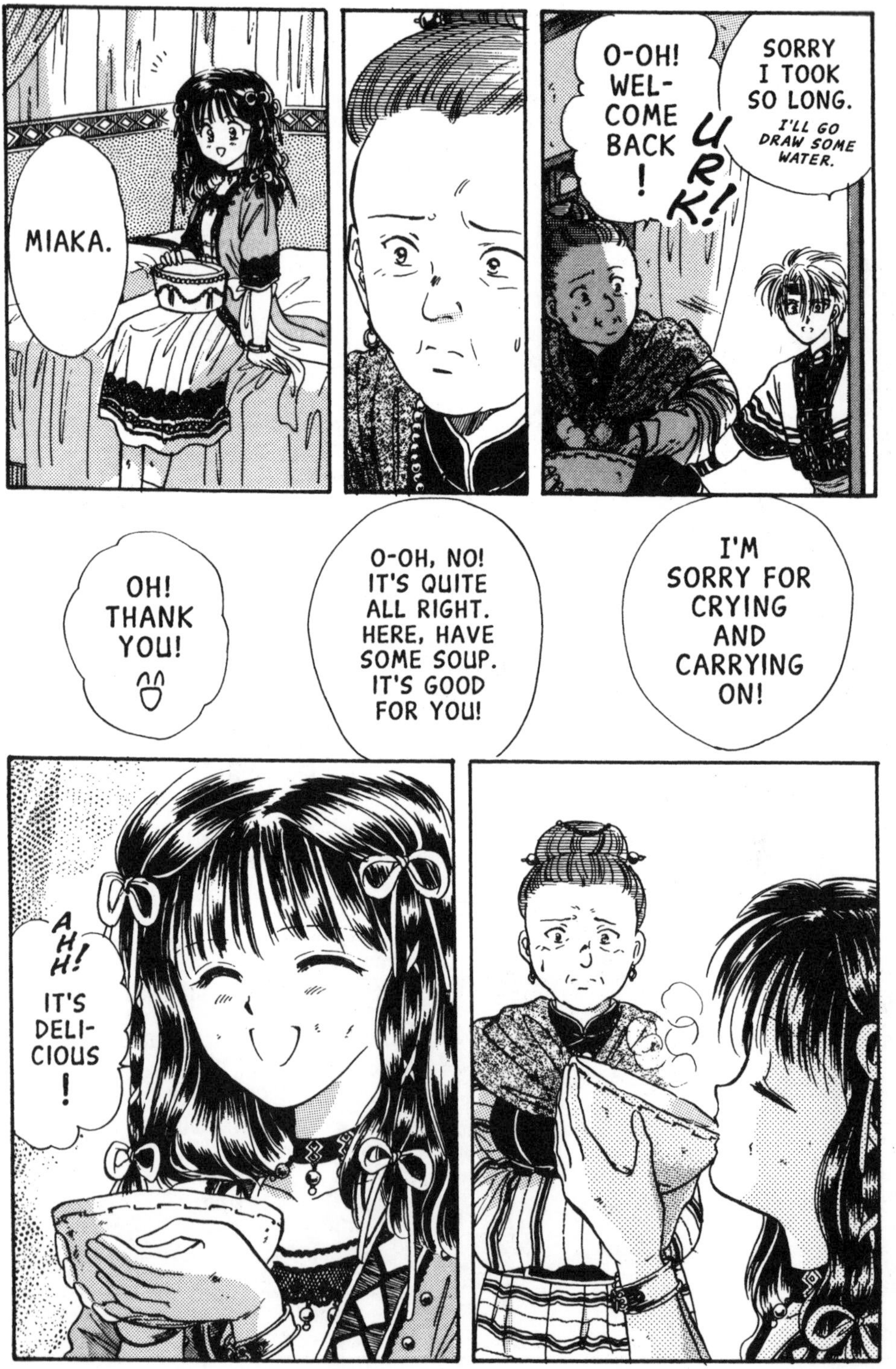
SORRY I TOOK SO LONG.
I'LL GO DRAW SOME WATER.
URK!
O-OH! WEL-COME BACK!
MIAKA.
I'M SORRY FOR CRYING AND CARRYING ON!
O-OH, NO! IT'S QUITE ALL RIGHT. HERE, HAVE SOME SOUP. IT'S GOOD FOR YOU!
OH! THANK YOU!
AHH!
IT'S DELI-CIOUS!

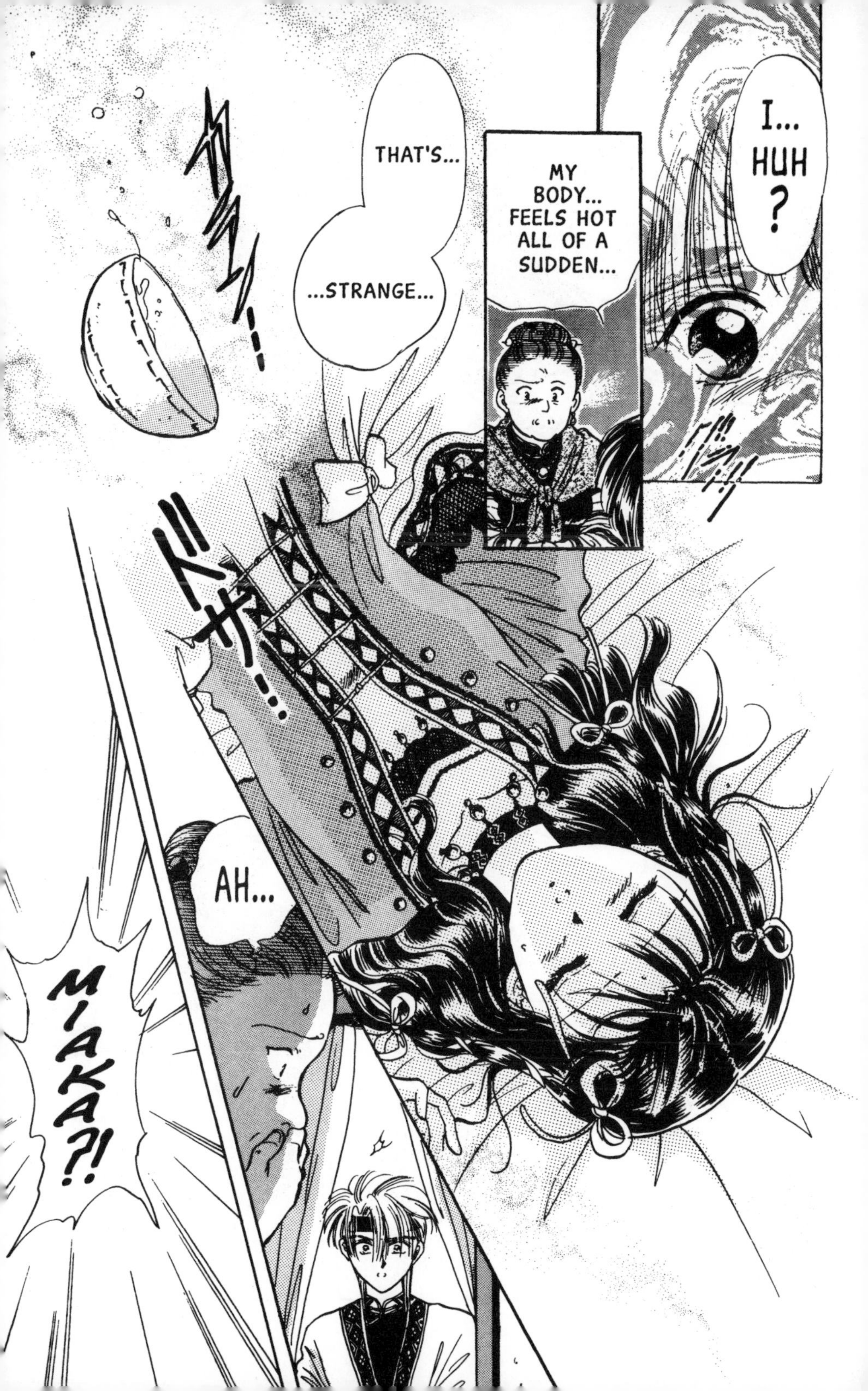
I... HUH?
MY BODY... FEELS HOT ALL OF A SUDDEN...
THAT'S...
...STRANGE...
AH...
MIAKA?!

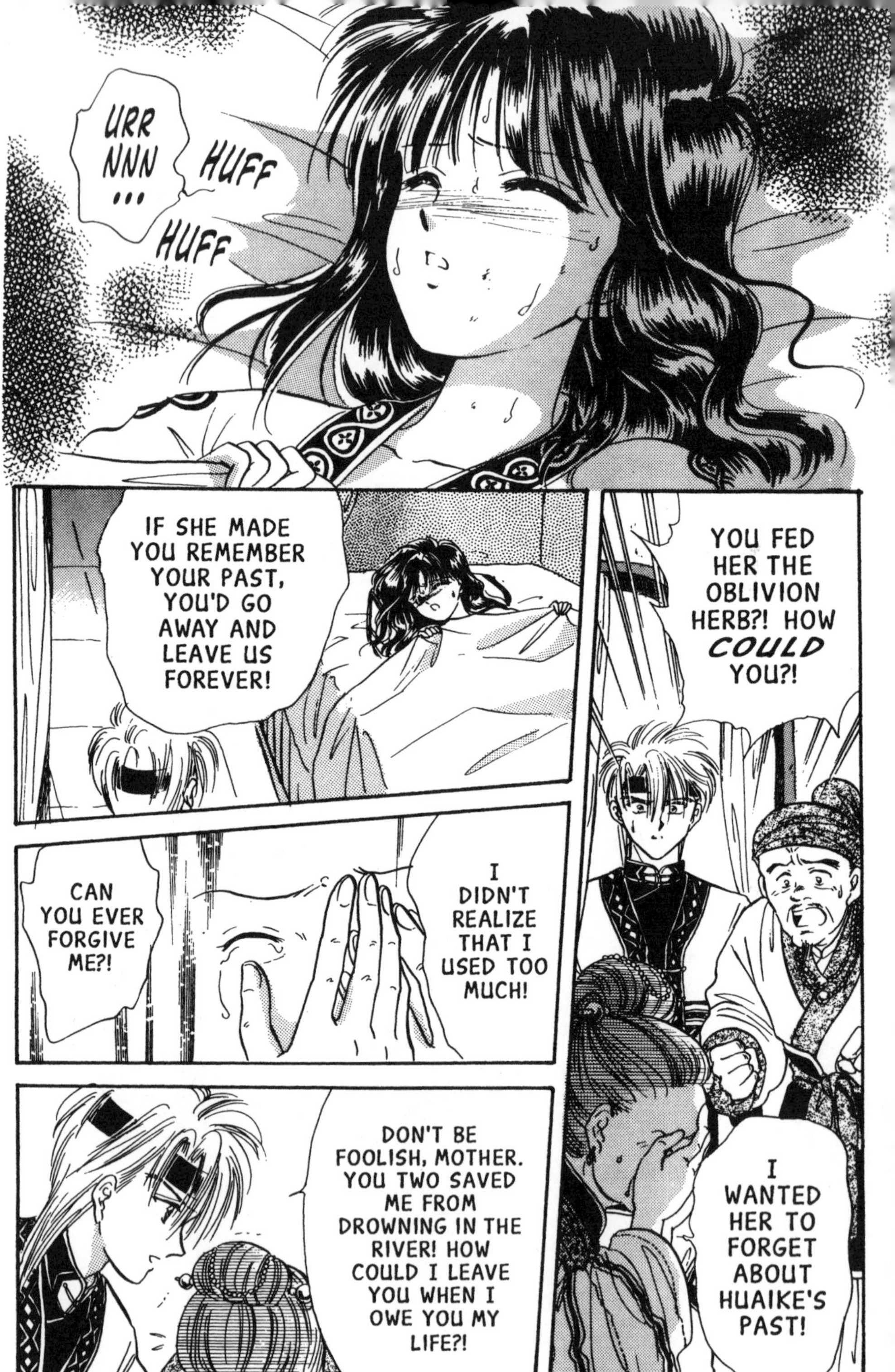
URR NNN...
HUFF
HUFF
YOU FED HER THE OBLIVION HERB?! HOW COULD YOU?!
I WANTED HER TO FORGET ABOUT HUAIKE'S PAST!
IF SHE MADE YOU REMEMBER YOUR PAST, YOU'D GO AWAY AND LEAVE US FOREVER!
I DIDN'T REALIZE THAT I USED TOO MUCH!
CAN YOU EVER FORGIVE ME?!
DON'T BE FOOLISH, MOTHER. YOU TWO SAVED ME FROM DROWNING IN THE RIVER! HOW COULD I LEAVE YOU WHEN I OWE YOU MY LIFE?!

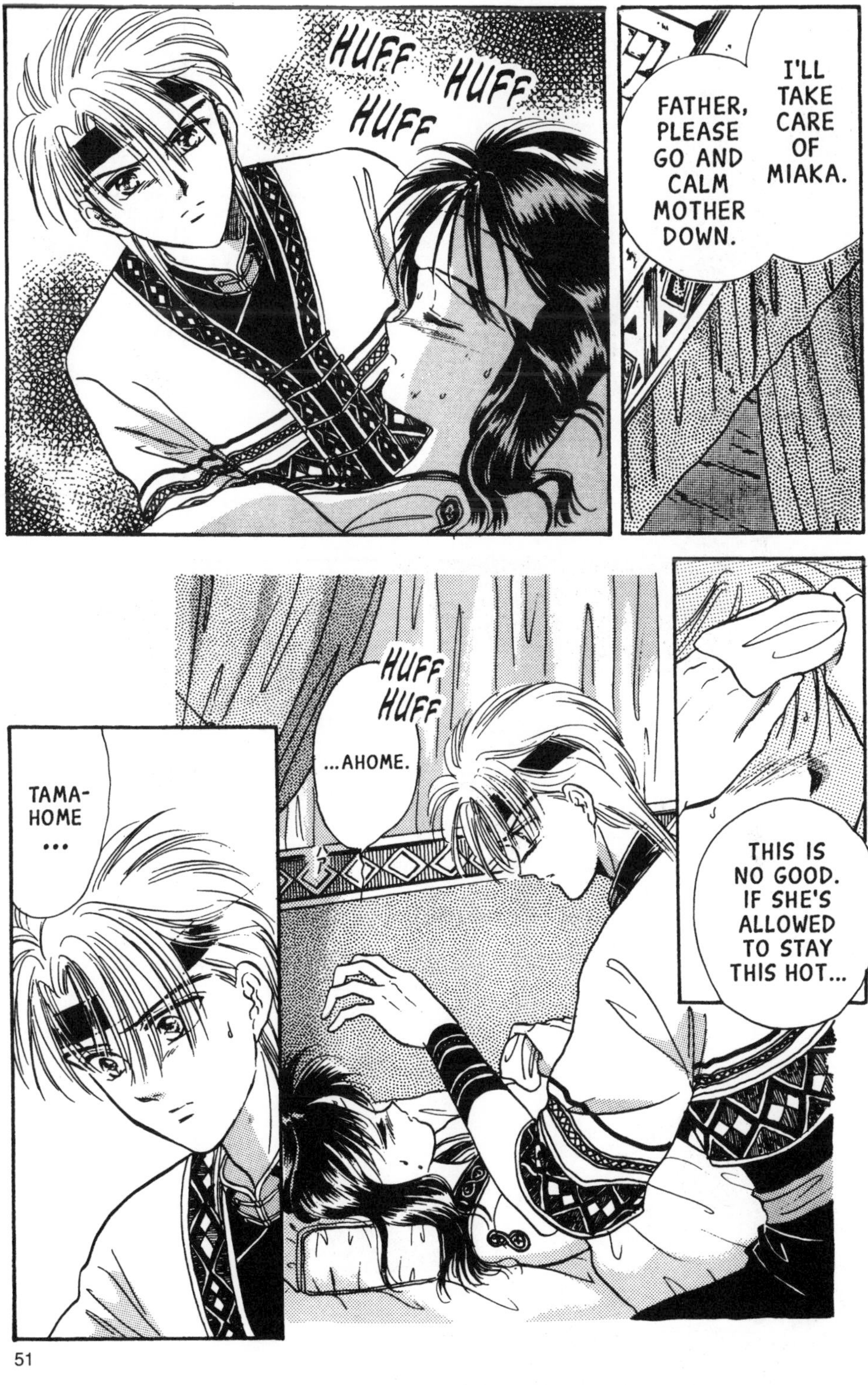
I'LL TAKE CARE OF MIAKA.
FATHER, PLEASE GO AND CALM MOTHER DOWN.
HUFF HUFF HUFF
THIS IS NO GOOD. IF SHE'S ALLOWED TO STAY THIS HOT...
HUFF HUFF
...AHOME.
TAMA-HOME ...

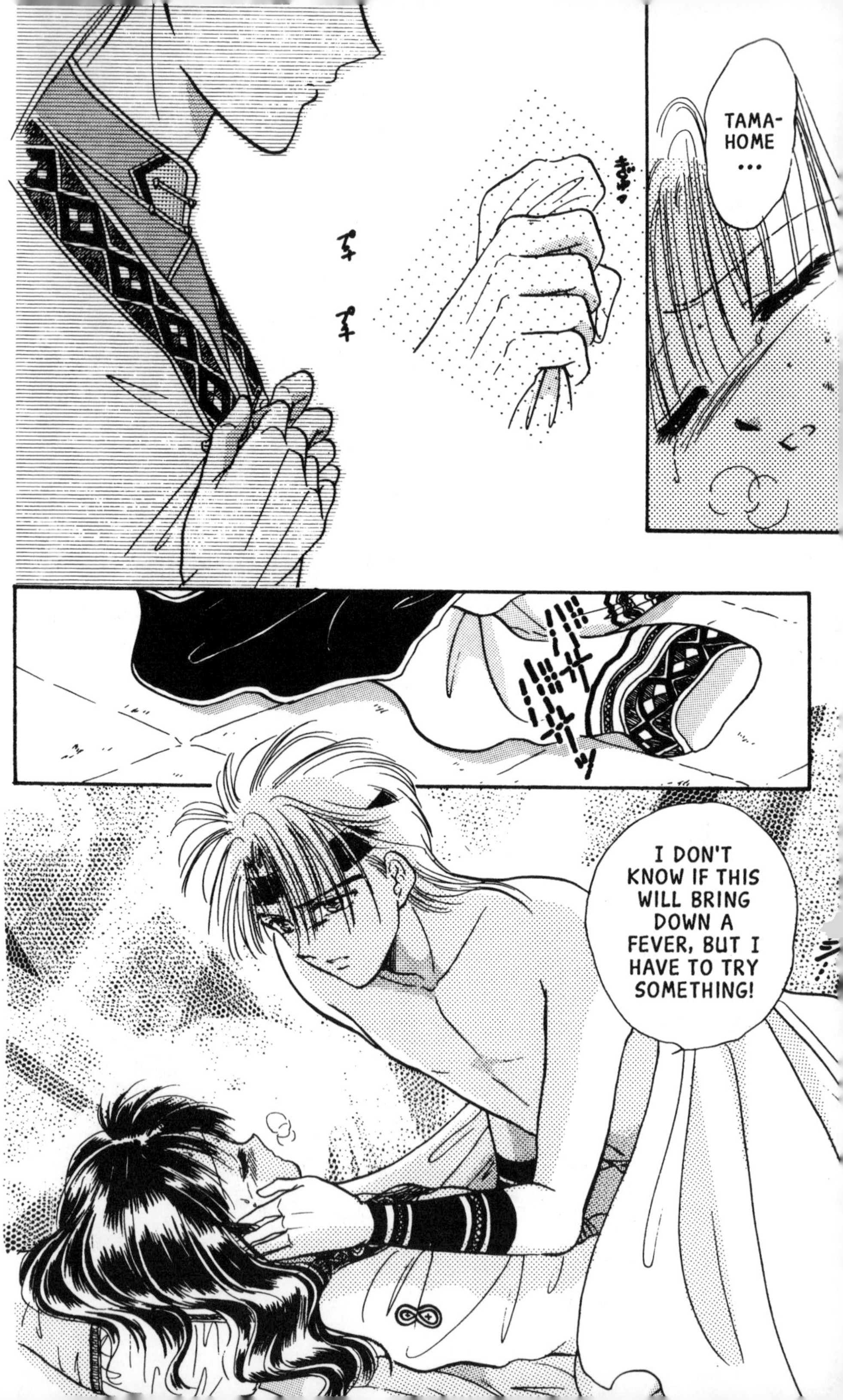
TAMA-HOME ...
I DON'T KNOW IF THIS WILL BRING DOWN A FEVER, BUT I HAVE TO TRY SOMETHING!

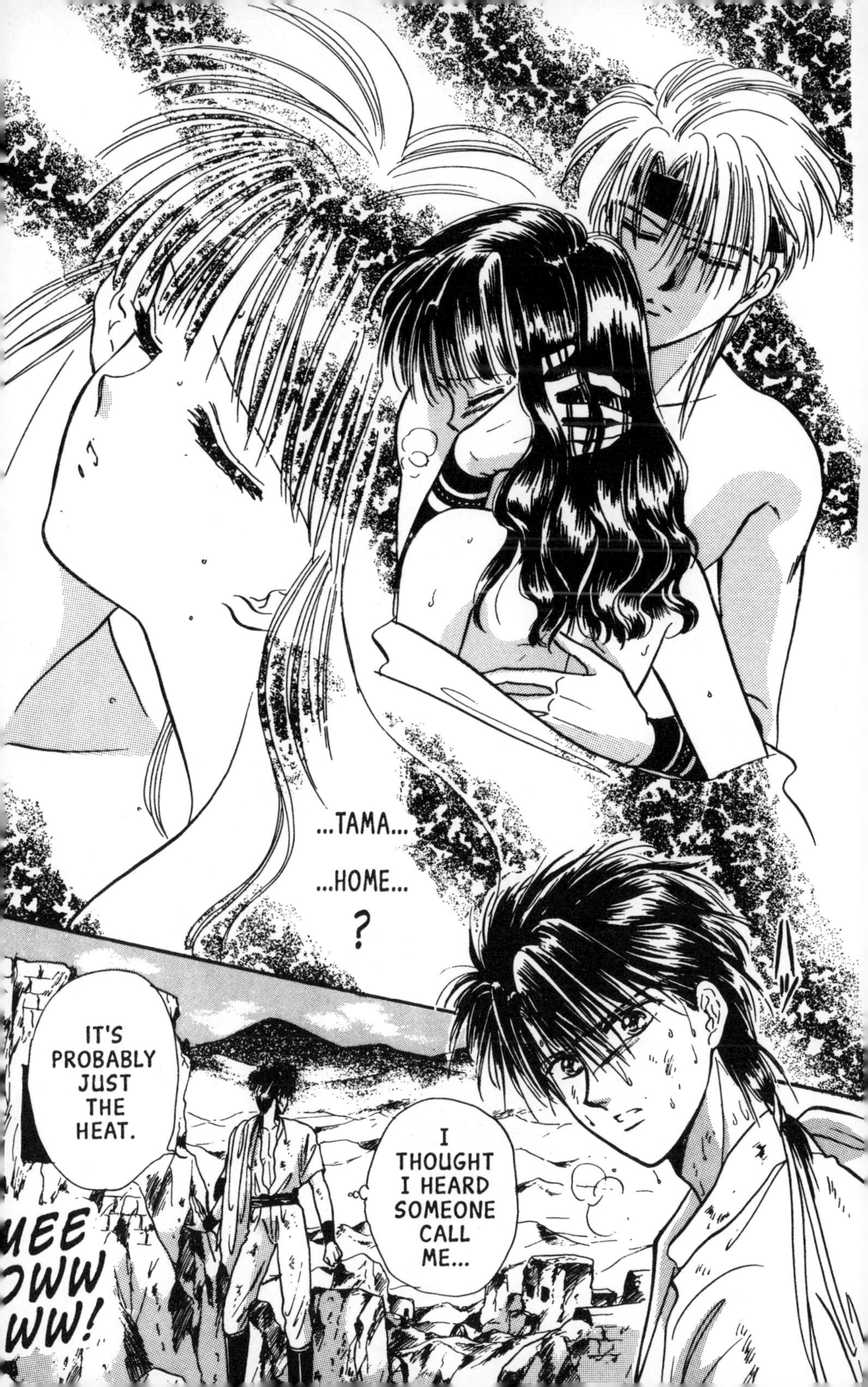
...TAMA...
...HOME...
?
I THOUGHT I HEARD SOMEONE CALL ME...
IT'S PROBABLY JUST THE HEAT.
UEE OWW WW!

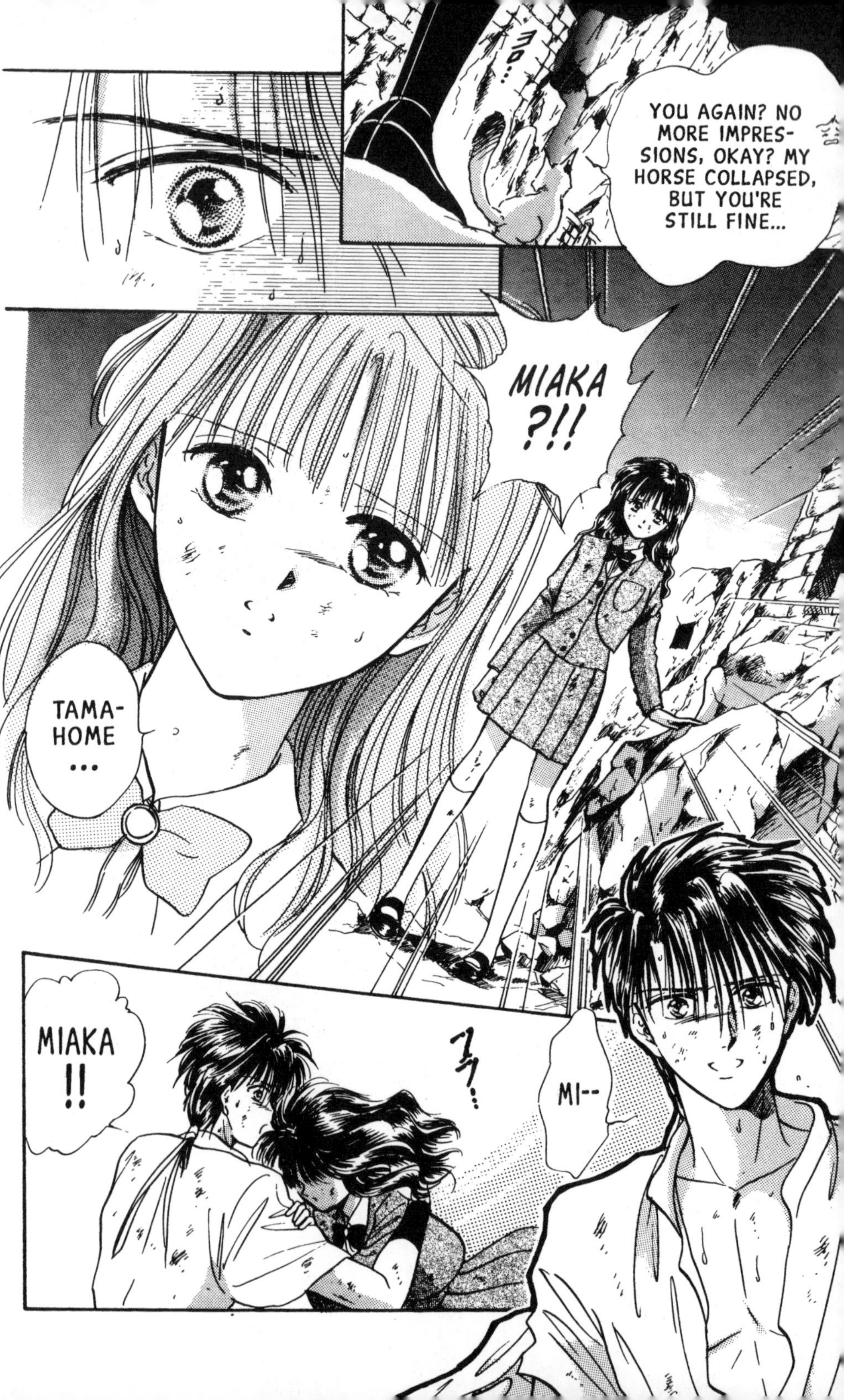
YOU AGAIN? NO MORE IMPRESSIONS, OKAY? MY HORSE COLLAPSED, BUT YOU'RE STILL FINE...
MIAKA ?!!
TAMA-HOME ...
MI--
MIAKA !!

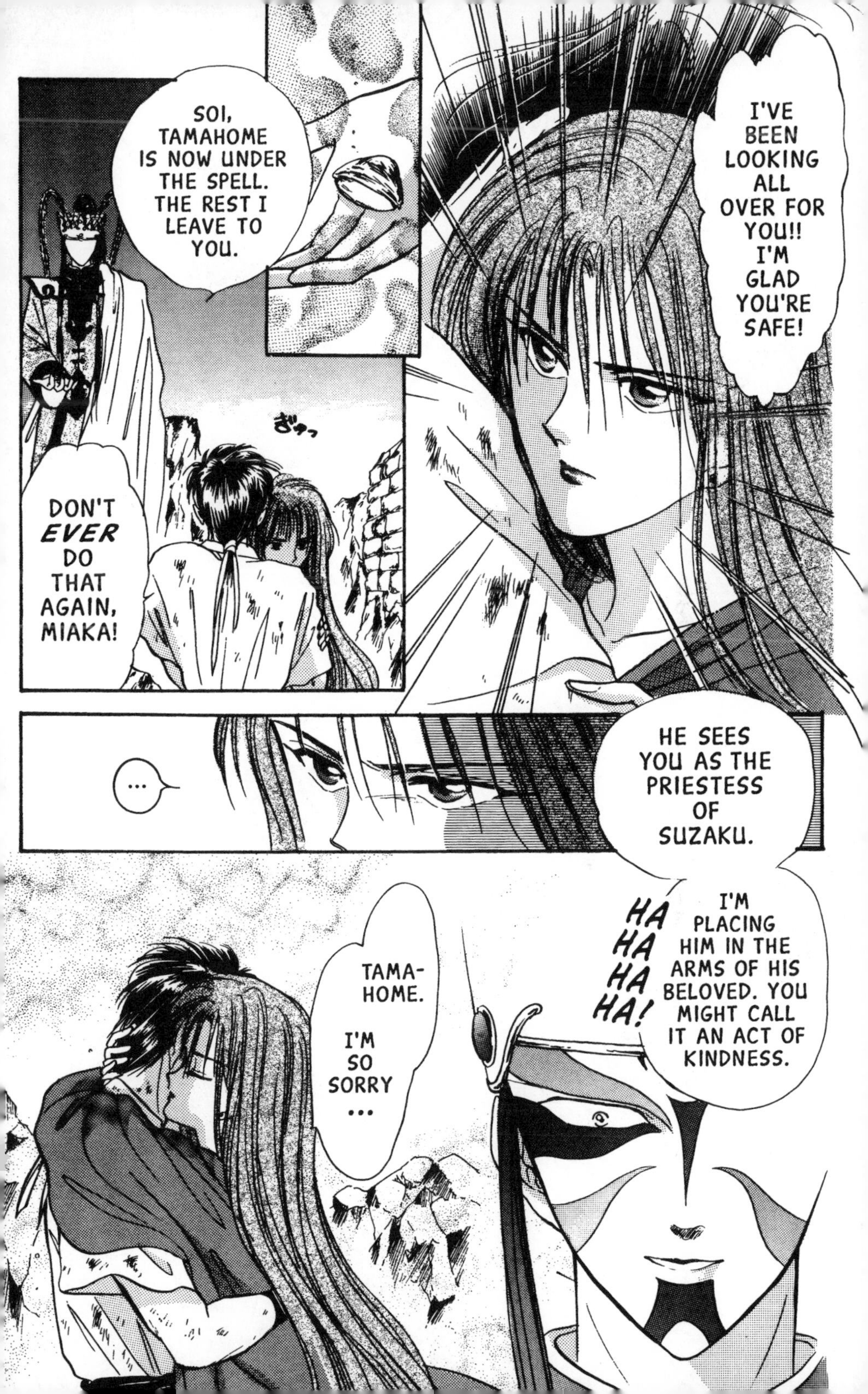
I'VE BEEN LOOKING ALL OVER FOR YOU!! I'M GLAD YOU'RE SAFE!
SOI, TAMAHOME IS NOW UNDER THE SPELL. THE REST I LEAVE TO YOU.
ぎゅっ
DON'T *EVER* DO THAT AGAIN, MIAKA!
HE SEES YOU AS THE PRIESTESS OF SUZAKU.
...
HA HA HA HA!
I'M PLACING HIM IN THE ARMS OF HIS BELOVED. YOU MIGHT CALL IT AN ACT OF KINDNESS.
TAMA-HOME.
I'M SO SORRY ...

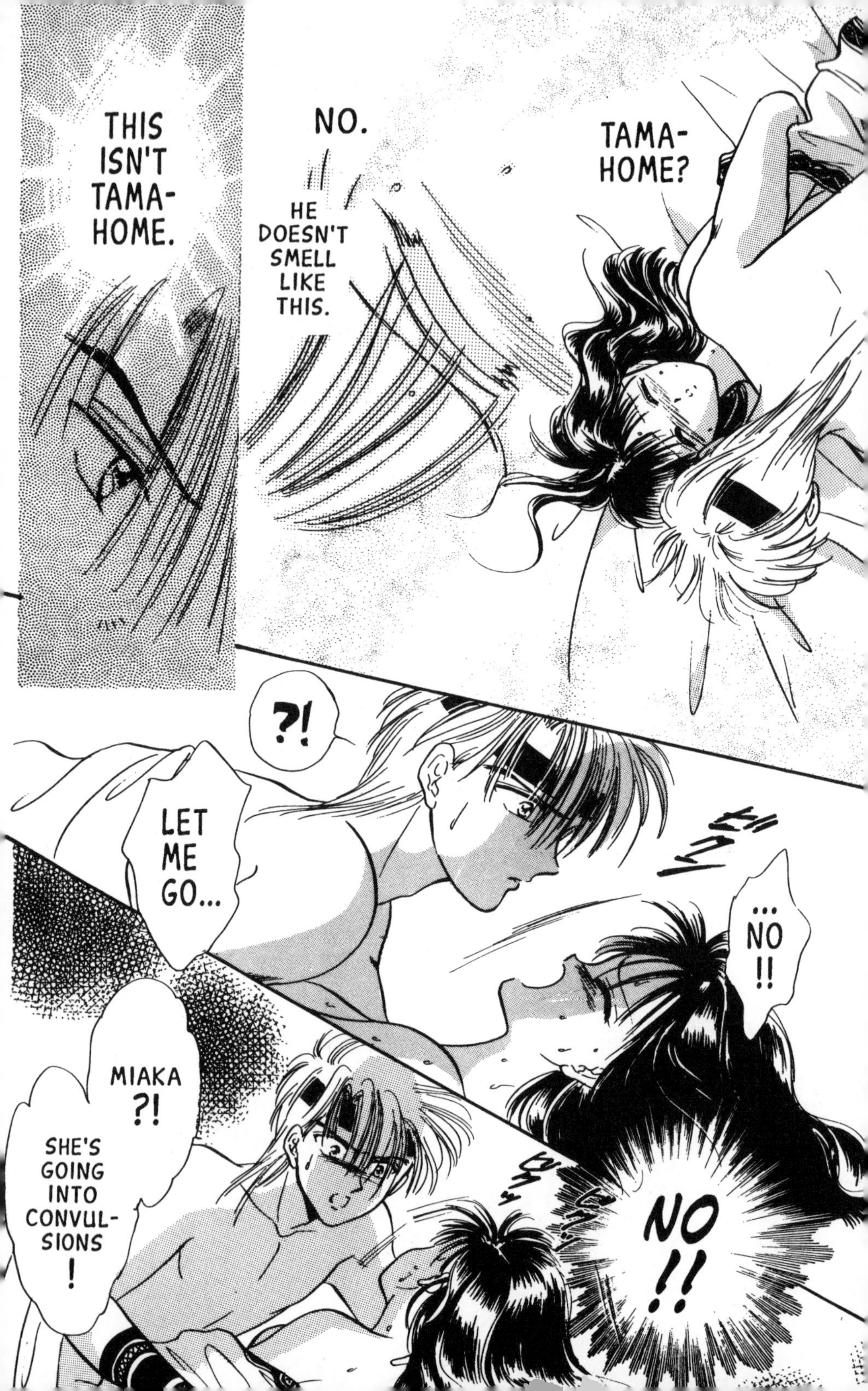
TAMA-HOME?
NO.
HE DOESN'T SMELL LIKE THIS.
THIS ISN'T TAMA-HOME.
?!
LET ME GO...
...NO!!
NO!!
MIAKA?!
SHE'S GOING INTO CONVULSIONS!

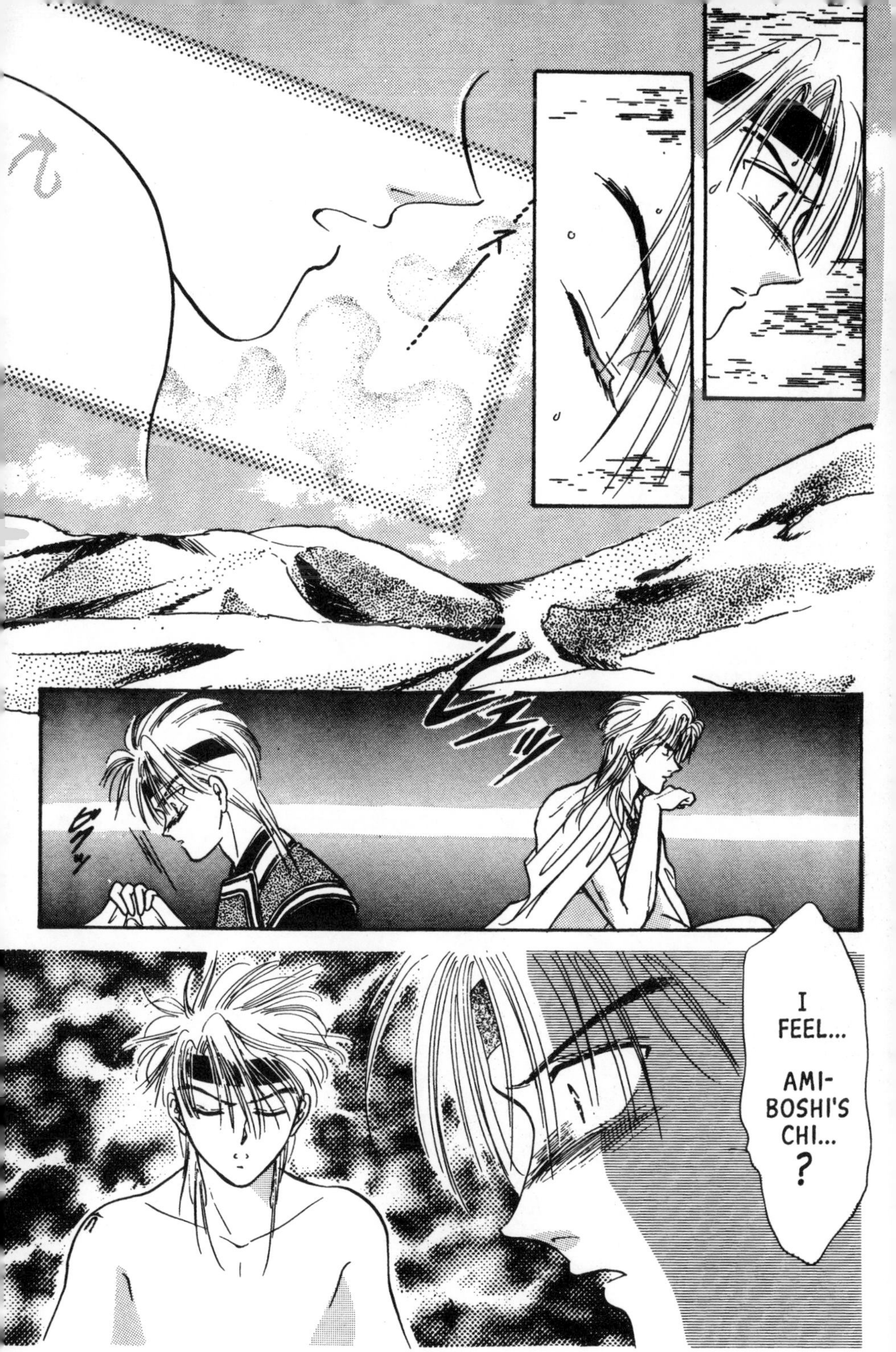
I FEEL... AMI-BOSHI'S CHI...?

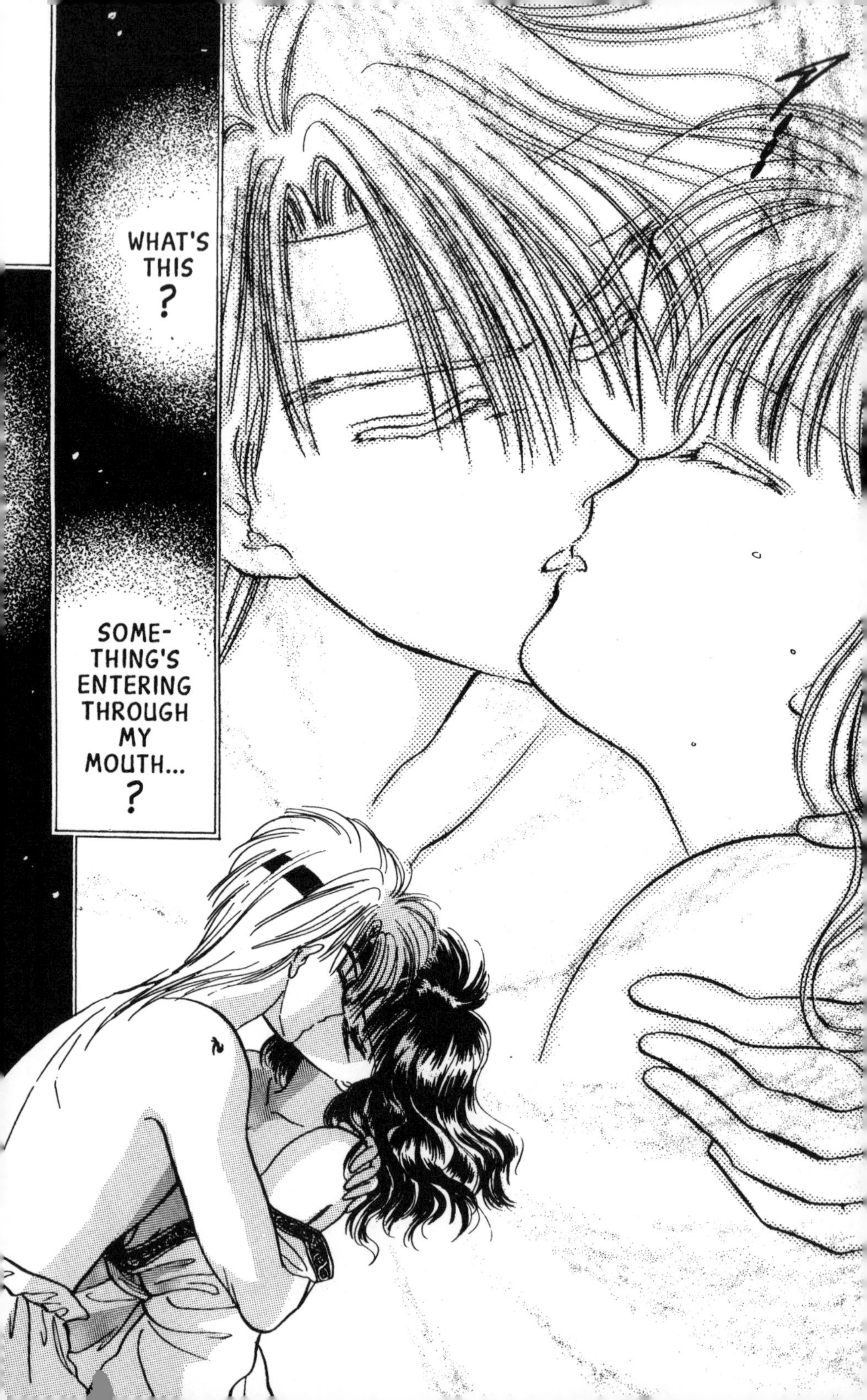
WHAT'S THIS ?
SOME-THING'S ENTERING THROUGH MY MOUTH... ?

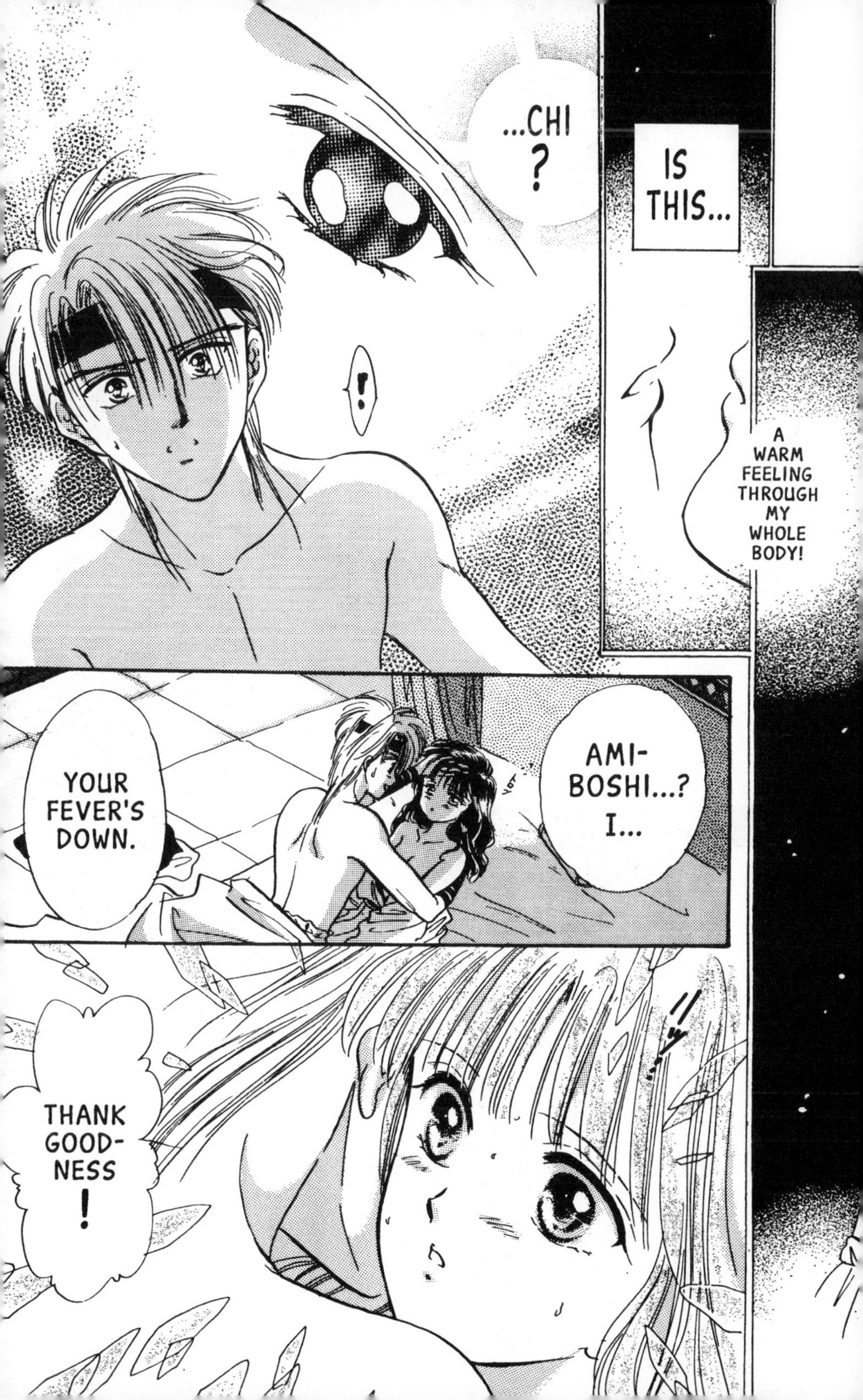
IS THIS...
A WARM FEELING THROUGH MY WHOLE BODY!
...CHI ?
!
AMI-BOSHI...? I...
YOUR FEVER'S DOWN.
THANK GOOD-NESS !

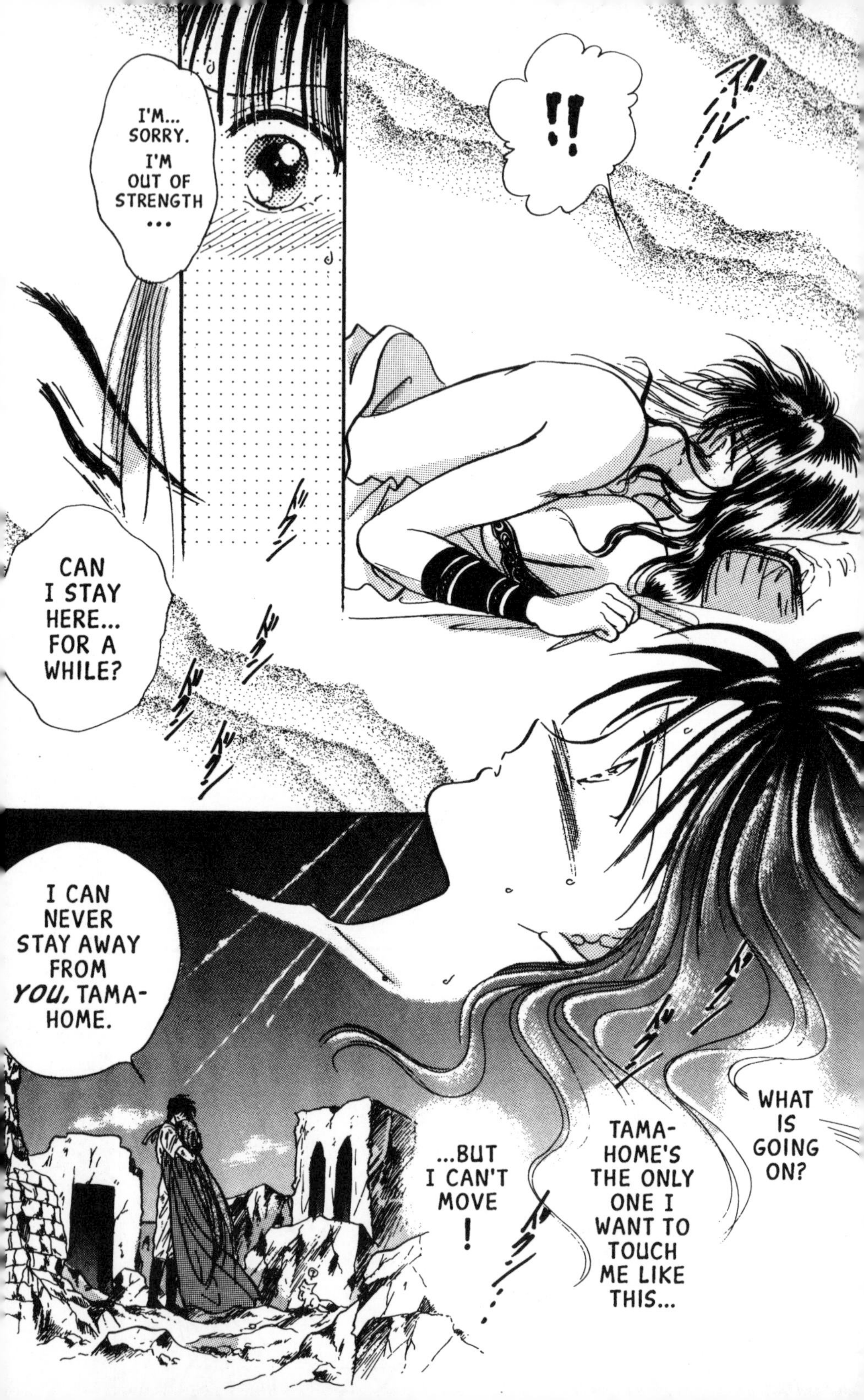
!!
I'M... SORRY. I'M OUT OF STRENGTH...
CAN I STAY HERE... FOR A WHILE?
WHAT IS GOING ON?
TAMA-HOME'S THE ONLY ONE I WANT TO TOUCH ME LIKE THIS...
...BUT I CAN'T MOVE!
I CAN NEVER STAY AWAY FROM *YOU,* TAMA-HOME.

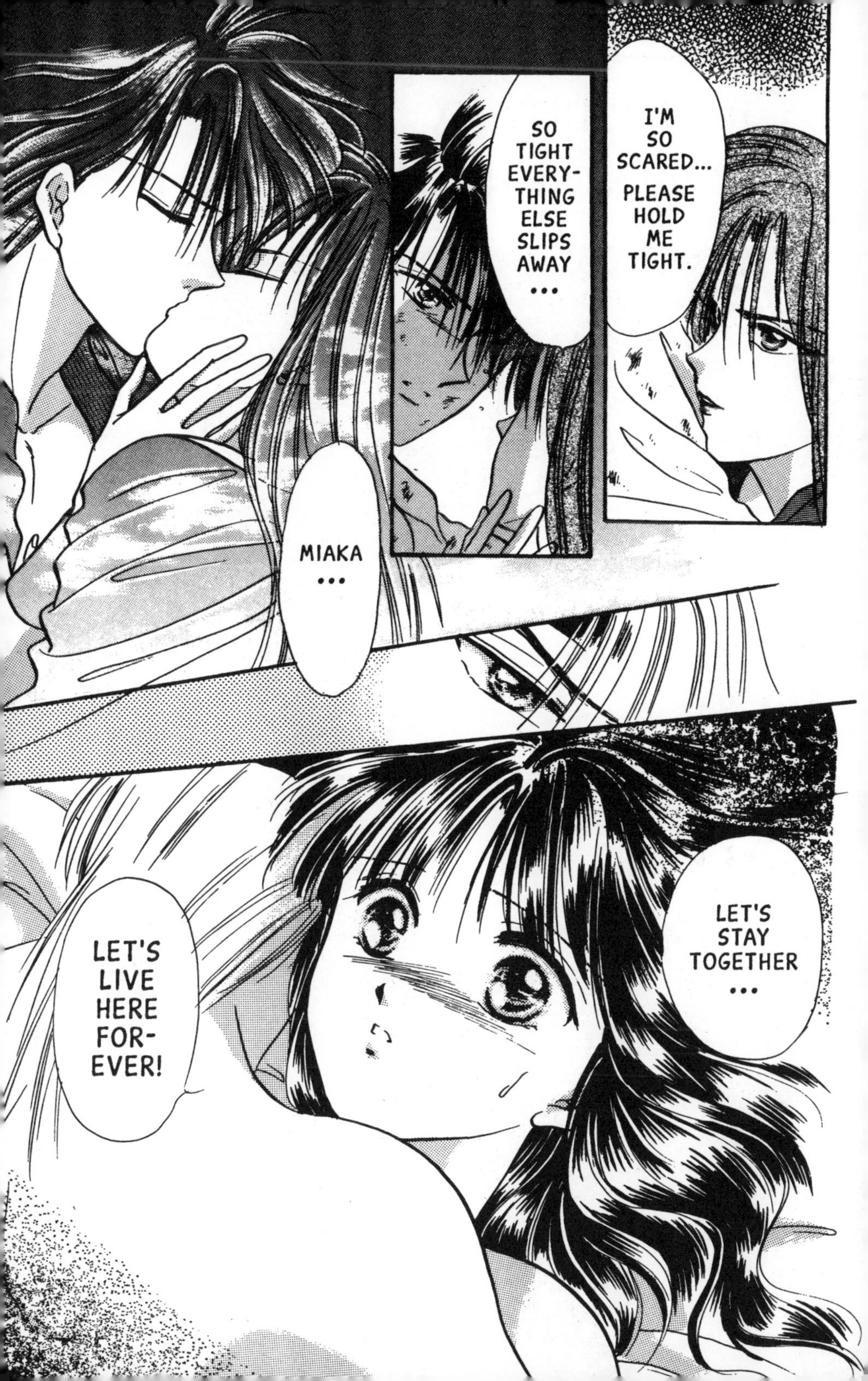
I'M SO SCARED...
PLEASE HOLD ME TIGHT.
SO TIGHT EVERY-THING ELSE SLIPS AWAY...
MIAKA...
LET'S STAY TOGETHER...
LET'S LIVE HERE FOR-EVER!

Chapter Fifty-Six
Dawn for the Heart

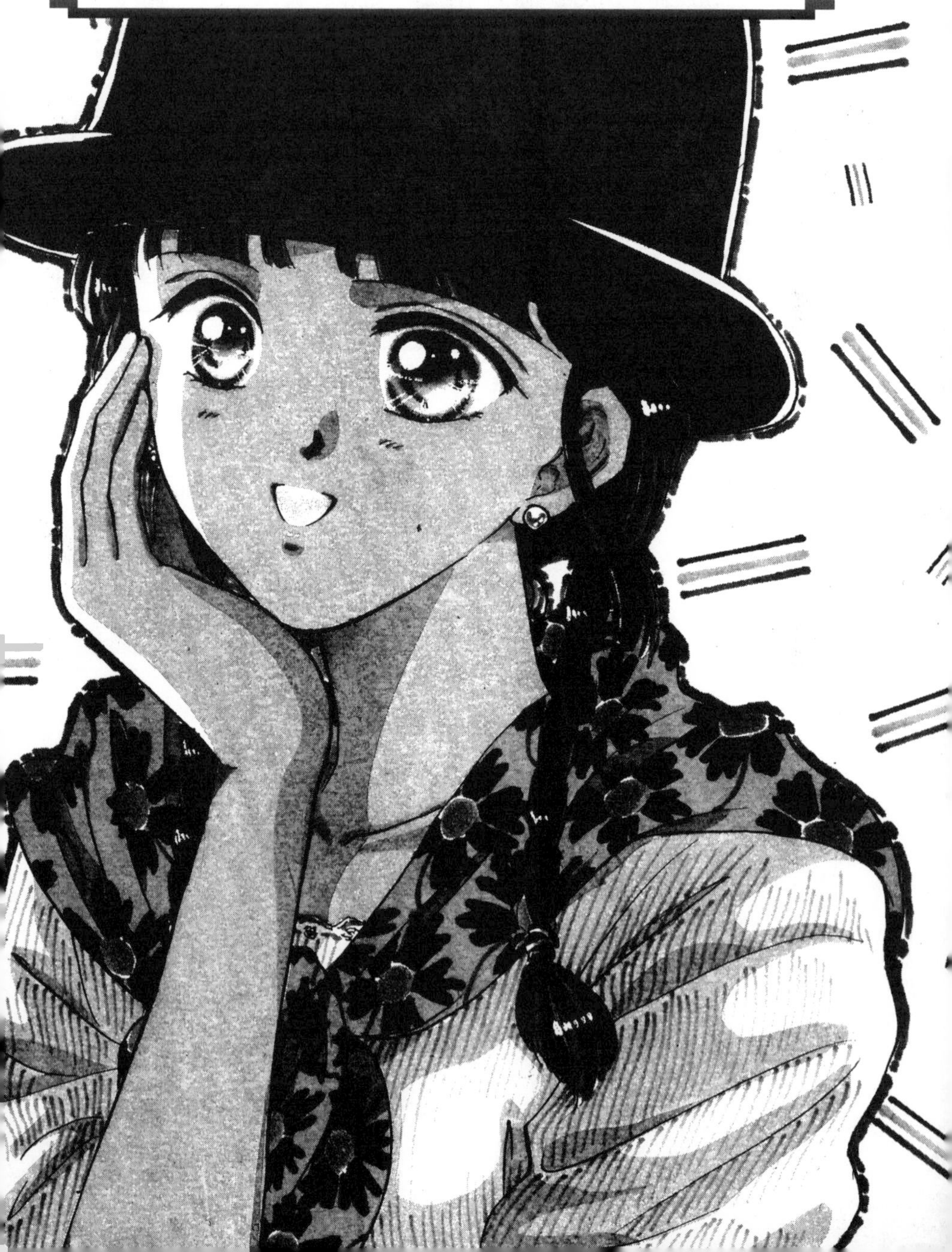

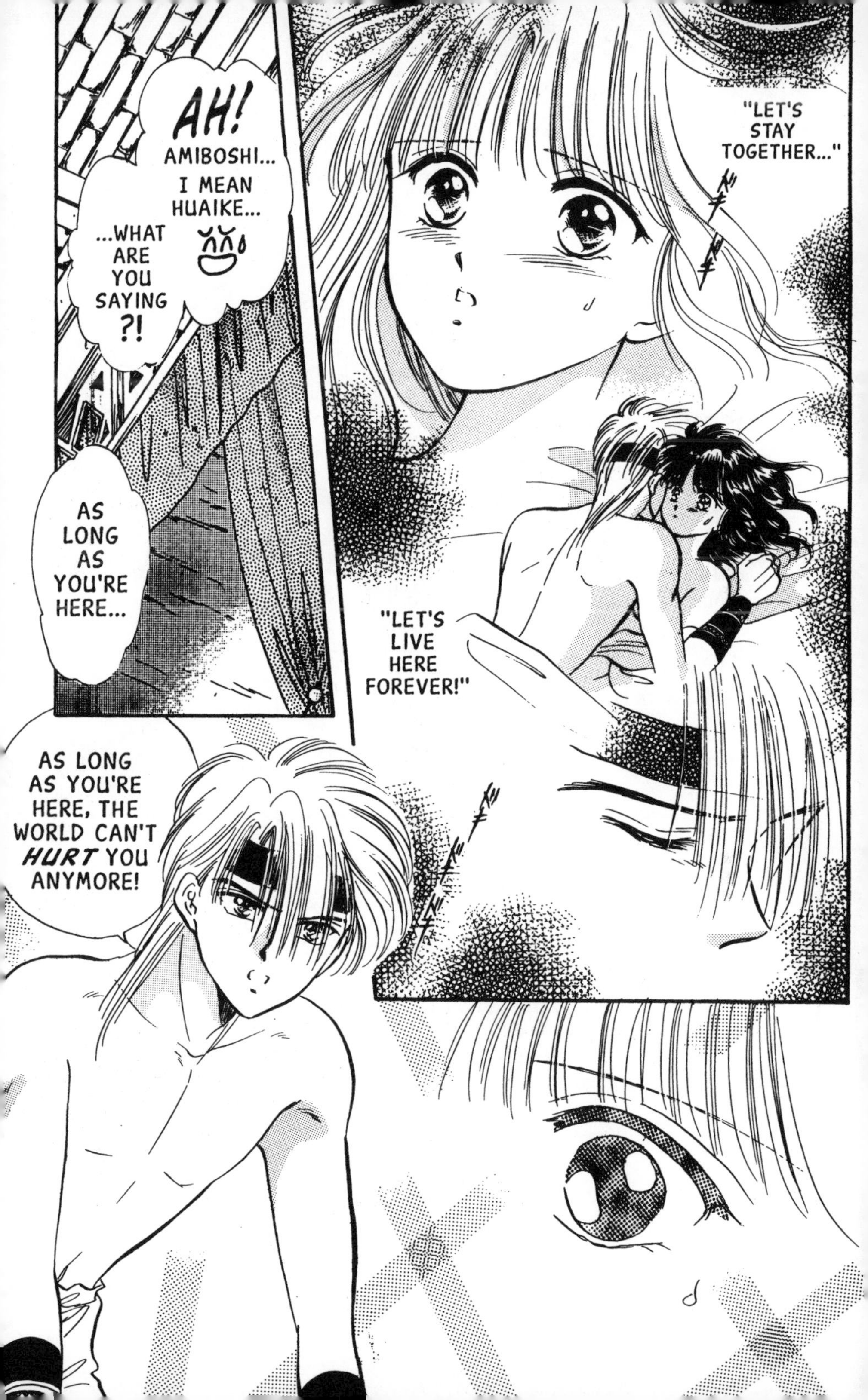
"LET'S STAY TOGETHER..."
"LET'S LIVE HERE FOREVER!"
AH! AMIBOSHI... I MEAN HUAIKE...
...WHAT ARE YOU SAYING ?!
AS LONG AS YOU'RE HERE...
AS LONG AS YOU'RE HERE, THE WORLD CAN'T *HURT* YOU ANYMORE!

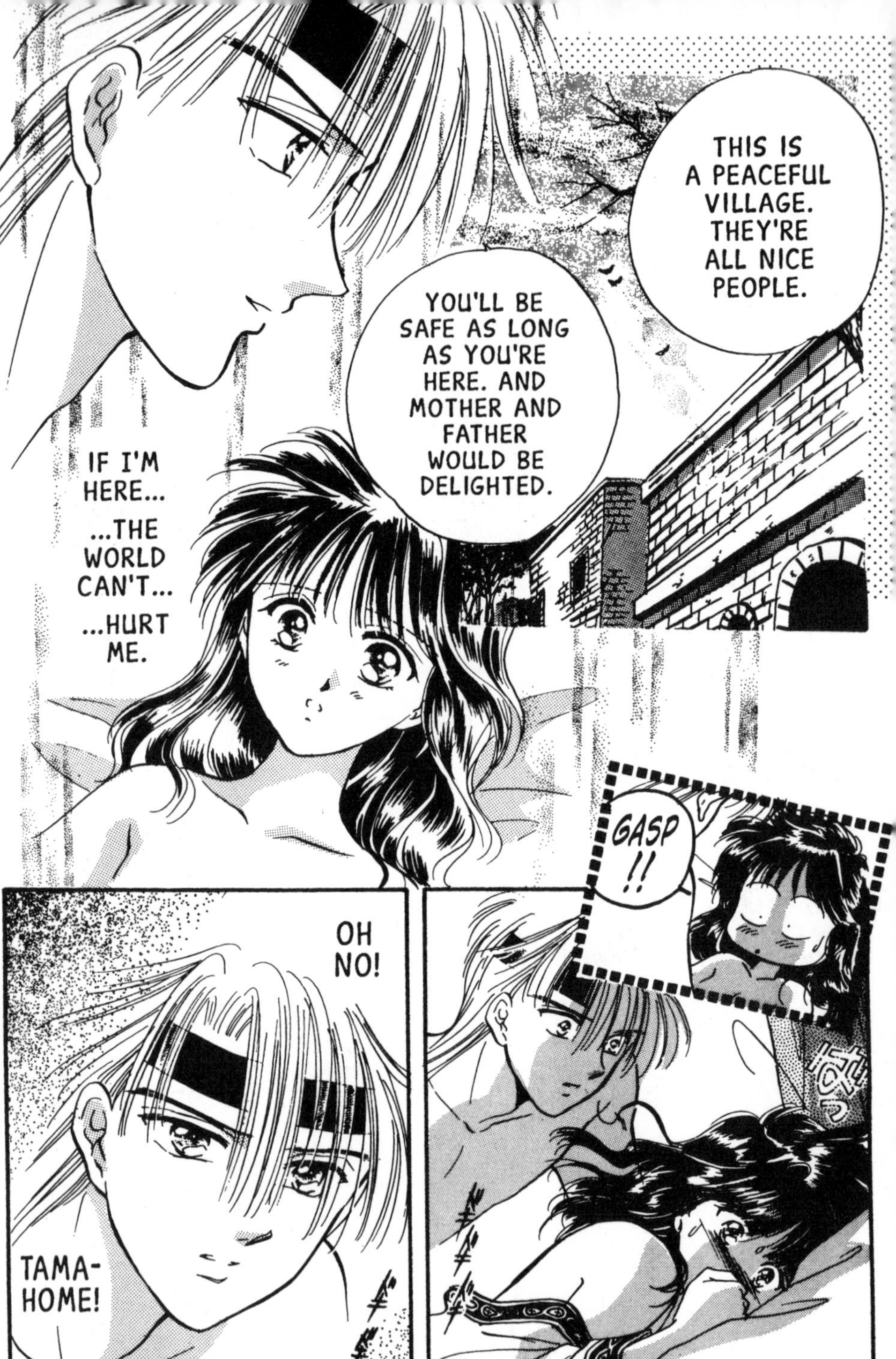
THIS IS A PEACEFUL VILLAGE. THEY'RE ALL NICE PEOPLE.
YOU'LL BE SAFE AS LONG AS YOU'RE HERE. AND MOTHER AND FATHER WOULD BE DELIGHTED.
IF I'M HERE...
...THE WORLD CAN'T...
...HURT ME.
GASP !!
OH NO!
TAMA-HOME!

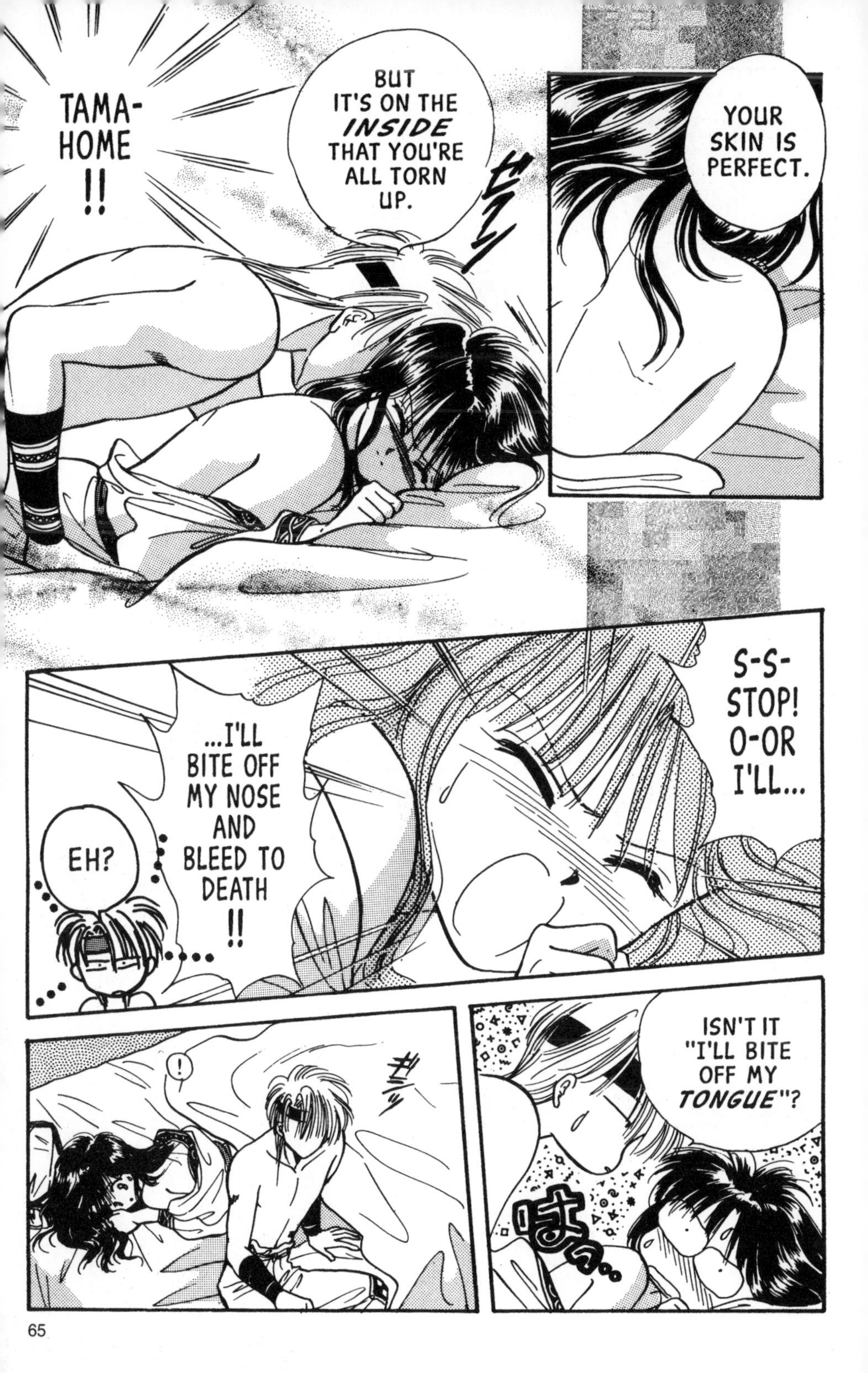
YOUR SKIN IS PERFECT.
BUT IT'S ON THE *INSIDE* THAT YOU'RE ALL TORN UP.
TAMA-HOME!!
S-S-STOP! O-OR I'LL...
...I'LL BITE OFF MY NOSE AND BLEED TO DEATH!!
EH?
ISN'T IT "I'LL BITE OFF MY *TONGUE*"?
はっ
!

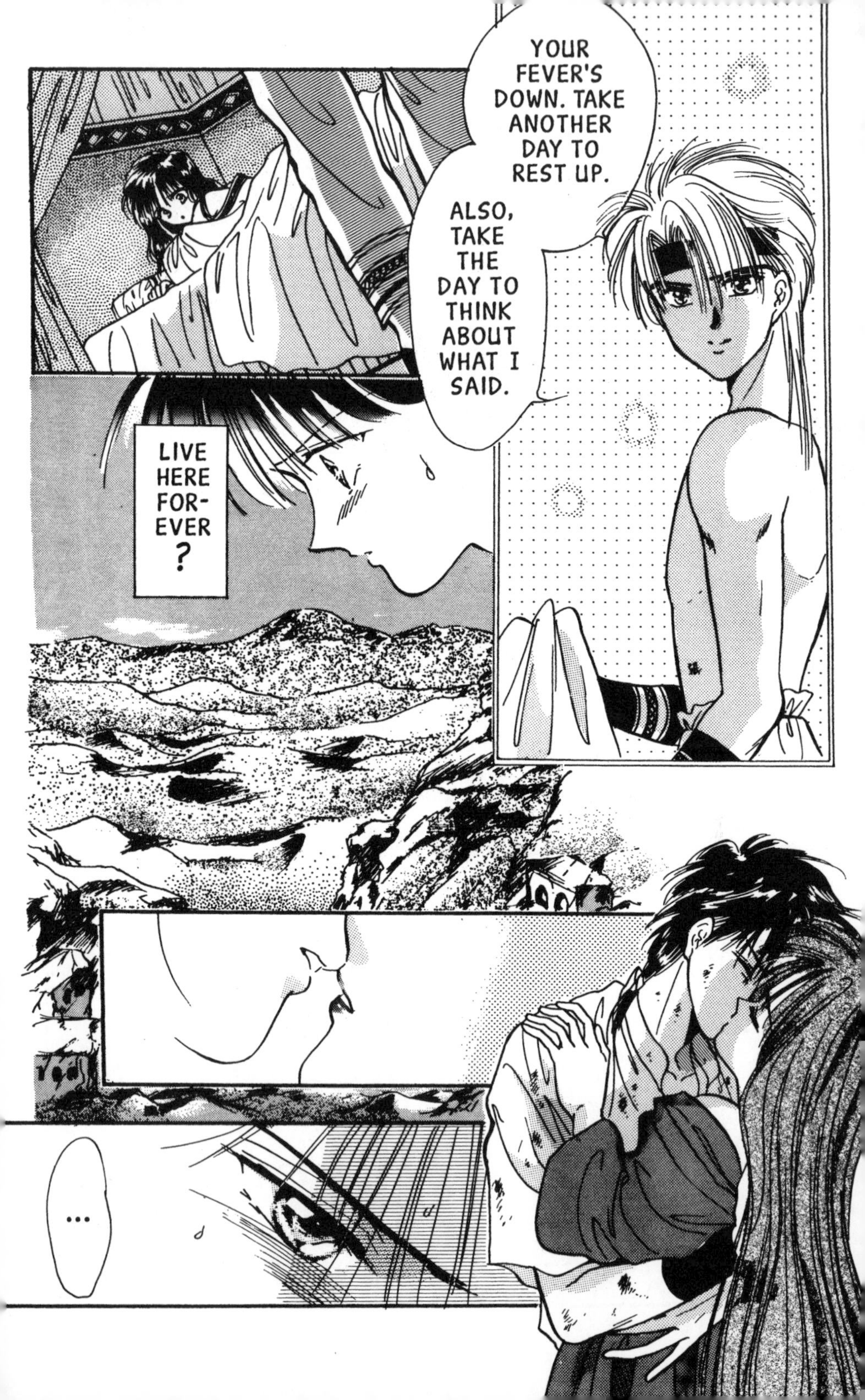
YOUR FEVER'S DOWN. TAKE ANOTHER DAY TO REST UP.
ALSO, TAKE THE DAY TO THINK ABOUT WHAT I SAID.
LIVE HERE FOR-EVER?
...

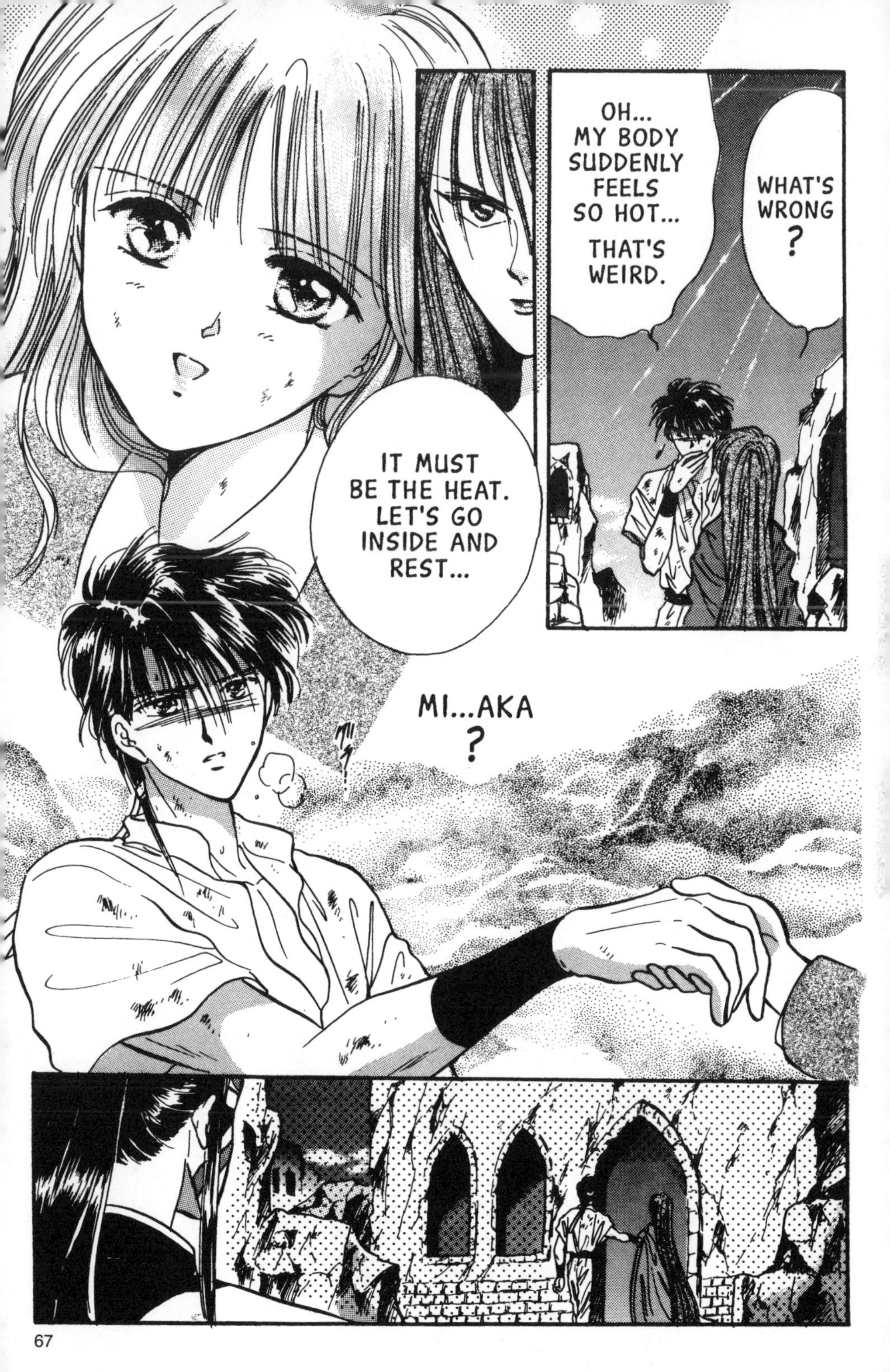
WHAT'S WRONG?
OH... MY BODY SUDDENLY FEELS SO HOT... THAT'S WEIRD.
IT MUST BE THE HEAT. LET'S GO INSIDE AND REST...
MI...AKA?

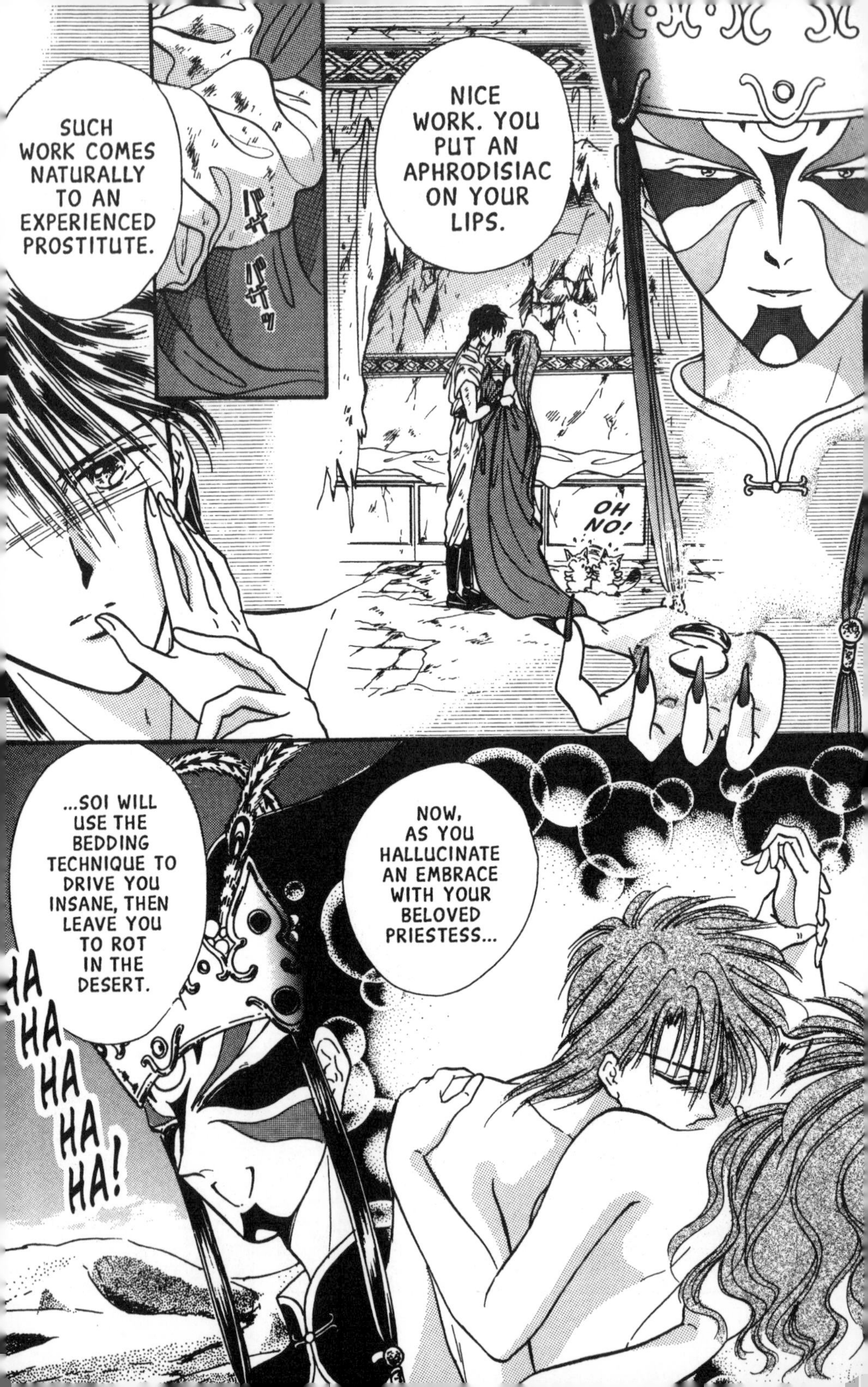
NICE WORK. YOU PUT AN APHRODISIAC ON YOUR LIPS.
OH NO!
SUCH WORK COMES NATURALLY TO AN EXPERIENCED PROSTITUTE.
NOW, AS YOU HALLUCINATE AN EMBRACE WITH YOUR BELOVED PRIESTESS...
...SOI WILL USE THE BEDDING TECHNIQUE TO DRIVE YOU INSANE, THEN LEAVE YOU TO ROT IN THE DESERT.
HAHAHAHAHA!

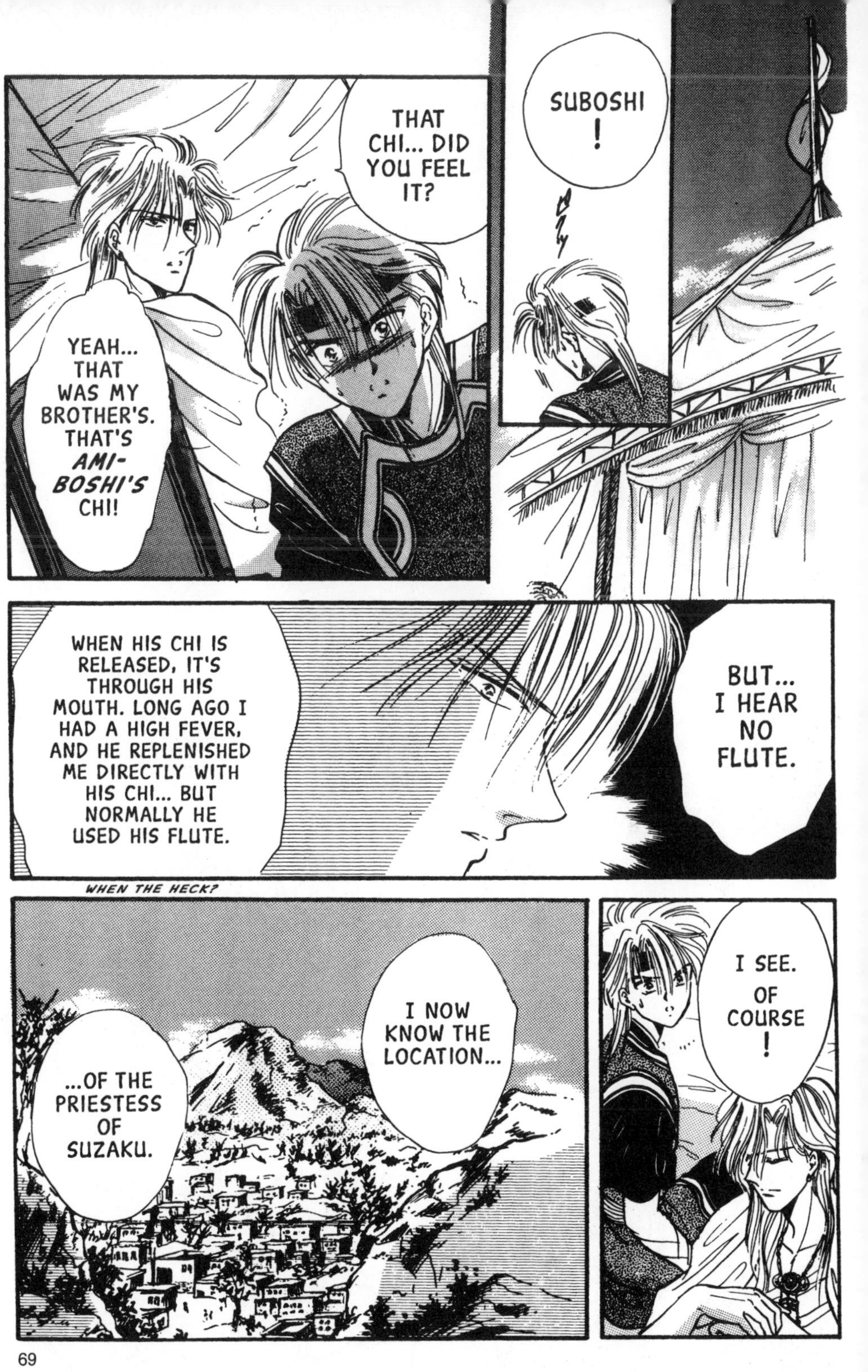
SUBOSHI!
THAT CHI... DID YOU FEEL IT?
YEAH... THAT WAS MY BROTHER'S. THAT'S *AMIBOSHI'S* CHI!
BUT... I HEAR NO FLUTE.
WHEN HIS CHI IS RELEASED, IT'S THROUGH HIS MOUTH. LONG AGO I HAD A HIGH FEVER, AND HE REPLENISHED ME DIRECTLY WITH HIS CHI... BUT NORMALLY HE USED HIS FLUTE.
WHEN THE HECK?
I SEE. OF COURSE!
I NOW KNOW THE LOCATION...
...OF THE PRIESTESS OF SUZAKU.

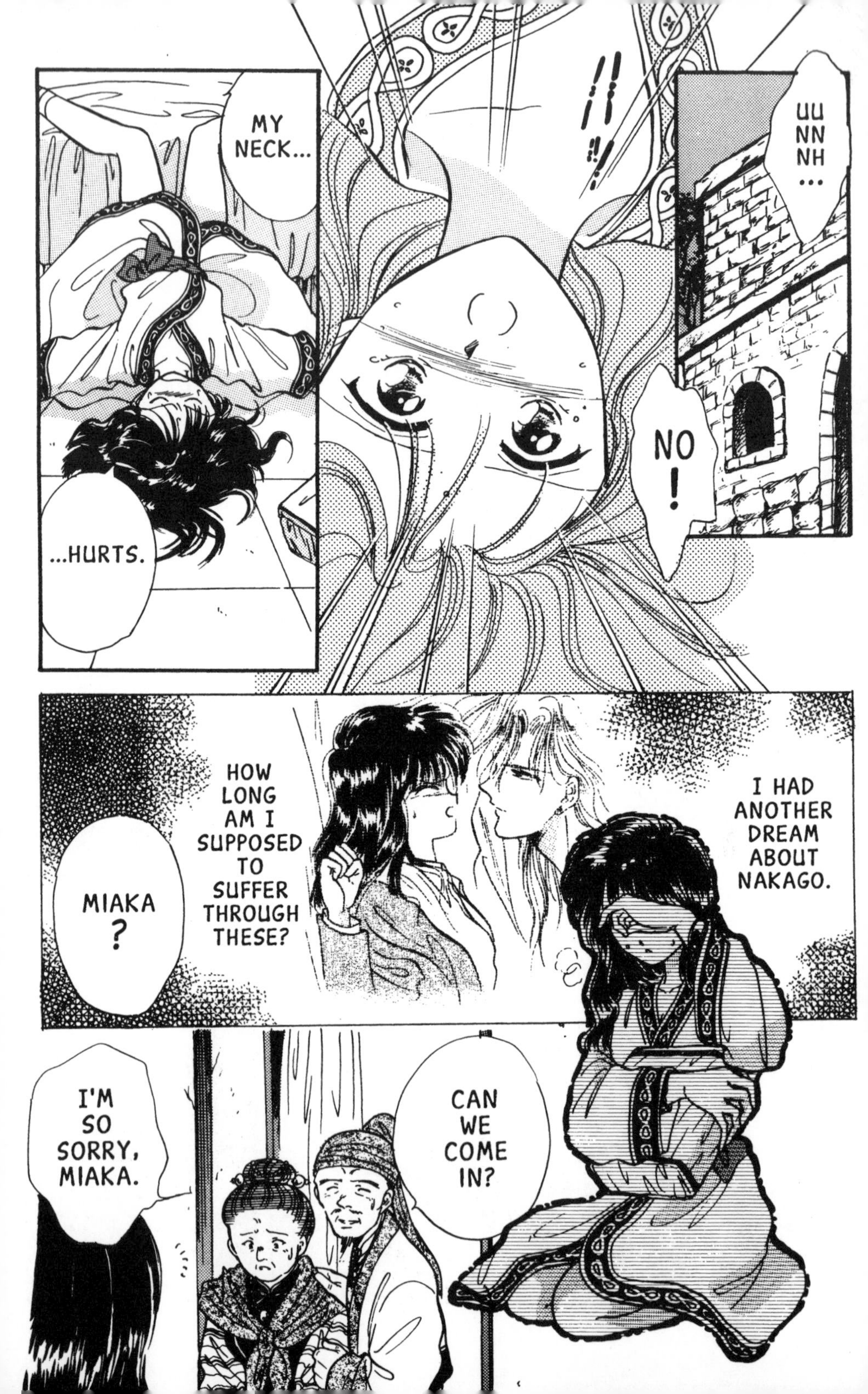
UUNNNH...
NO!
MY NECK...
...HURTS.
I HAD ANOTHER DREAM ABOUT NAKAGO.
HOW LONG AM I SUPPOSED TO SUFFER THROUGH THESE?
MIAKA?
CAN WE COME IN?
I'M SO SORRY, MIAKA.

(Continued)...

Now to continue with the southern Suzaku constellations.
The South had a symbolic meaning for the ancient Chinese emperor. While the Heavenly Ruler (Tai Yi-Jun) took care of the heavens, the earthly emperor was to rule the world from his throne in the south. *H-how lucky can Hotohori get?*
The symbol for the South, the character for "Su" in Suzaku, represented the holy power of eternal life. In other words, the bird of eternal life (the Hōō, firebird or Phoenix). Amazingly, it was thought that once Suzaku was summoned, eternal peace would reign over the land!! Is that true, China?! That's the plot of *Fushigi Yūgi*! I was shocked!
Later this "North Star 28 Constellation Astrology" was applied, not only to the national interests, but to individuals as well. Suzaku guides the fates of love (with the name Hōō, the "Hō" part is male, and the "ō" part is female). So the Chinese people used to pray for love to the Suzaku constellations in the south. *Best of luck!*
By the way, I had no idea this kind of astrology even existed in Ancient China. It shocked the heck out of me!
Or maybe it was no coincidence that I chose the Suzaku for Miaka! L-Love? Well, I suppose.
Also, when I began this story, I came up with the characters and assigned each of them to constellations. But much to my surprise, when I casually looked up their meanings, I discovered (this really bowls me over!) that many of the stars corresponded to the characters' personalities!

To be continued...

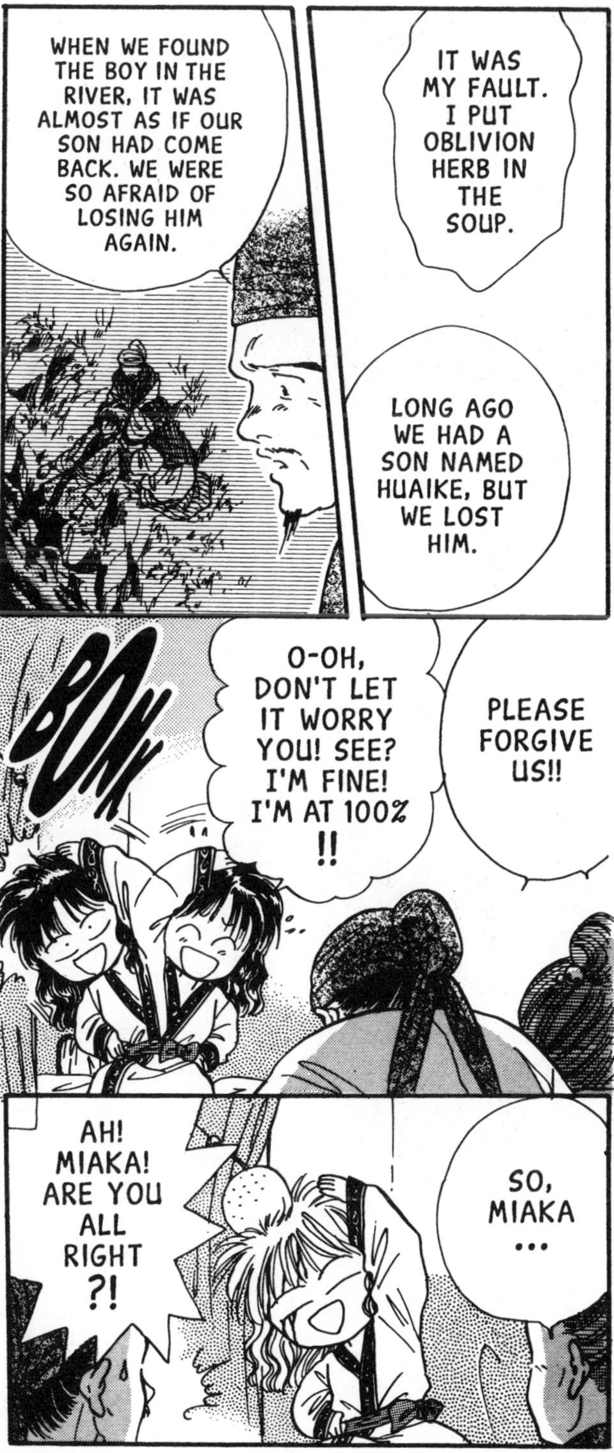
IT WAS MY FAULT. I PUT OBLIVION HERB IN THE SOUP.
LONG AGO WE HAD A SON NAMED HUAIKE, BUT WE LOST HIM.
WHEN WE FOUND THE BOY IN THE RIVER, IT WAS ALMOST AS IF OUR SON HAD COME BACK. WE WERE SO AFRAID OF LOSING HIM AGAIN.
PLEASE FORGIVE US!!
O-OH, DON'T LET IT WORRY YOU! SEE? I'M FINE! I'M AT 100% !!
BONK
SO, MIAKA...
AH! MIAKA! ARE YOU ALL RIGHT ?!

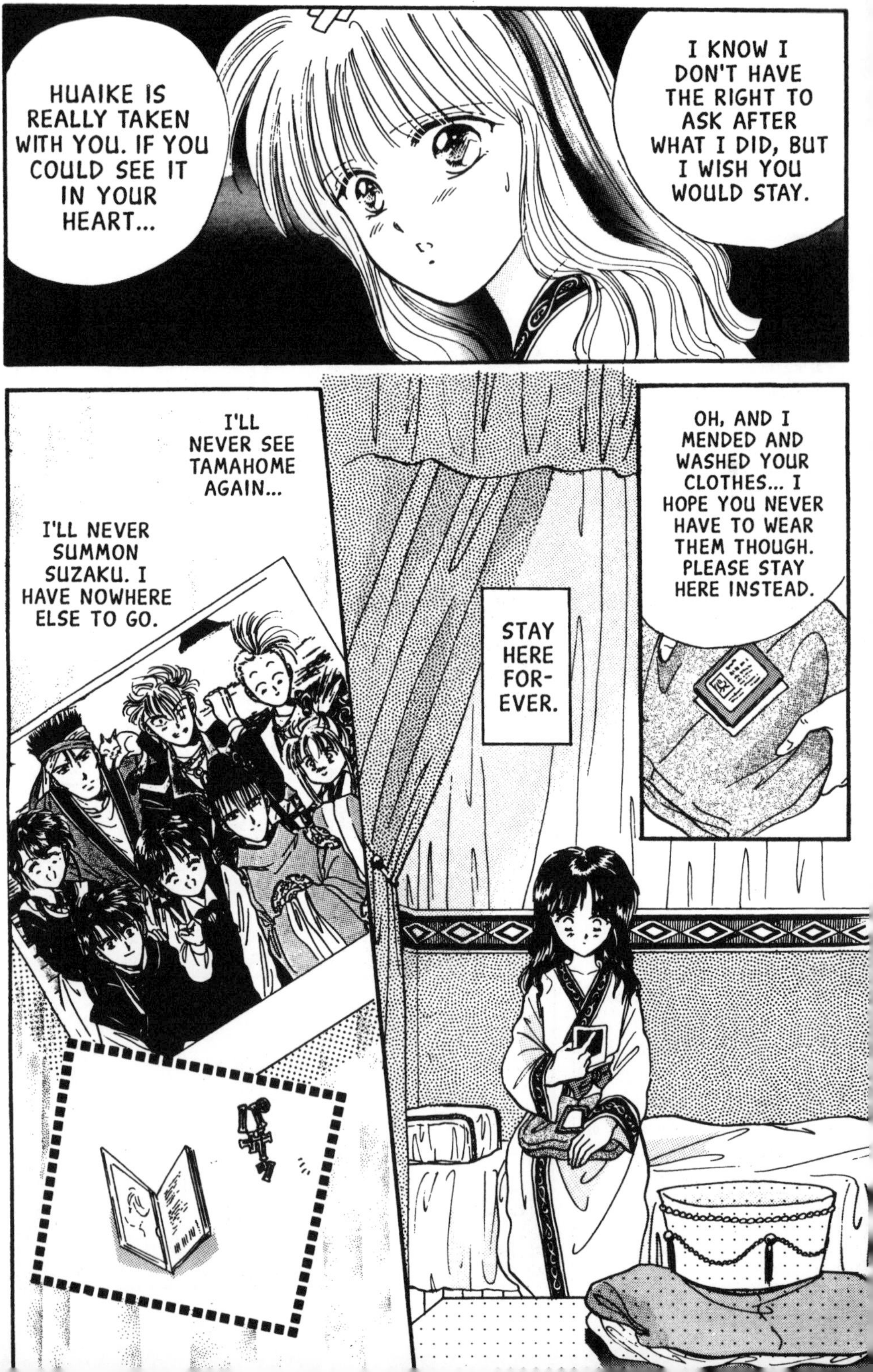
I KNOW I DON'T HAVE THE RIGHT TO ASK AFTER WHAT I DID, BUT I WISH YOU WOULD STAY.
HUAIKE IS REALLY TAKEN WITH YOU. IF YOU COULD SEE IT IN YOUR HEART...
OH, AND I MENDED AND WASHED YOUR CLOTHES... I HOPE YOU NEVER HAVE TO WEAR THEM THOUGH. PLEASE STAY HERE INSTEAD.
STAY HERE FOR-EVER.
I'LL NEVER SEE TAMAHOME AGAIN...
I'LL NEVER SUMMON SUZAKU. I HAVE NOWHERE ELSE TO GO.

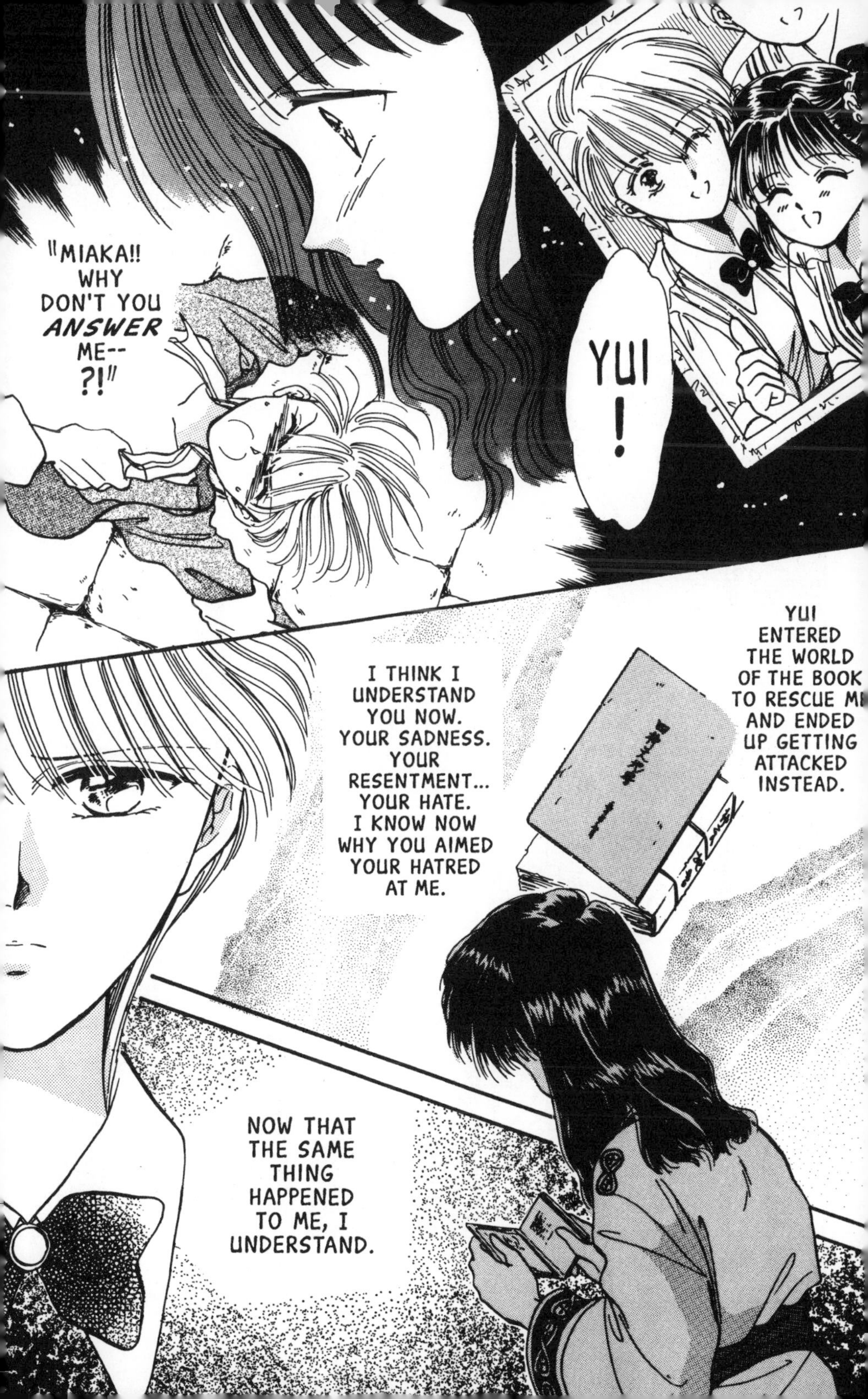
YUI!
"MIAKA!! WHY DON'T YOU *ANSWER* ME--?!"
YUI ENTERED THE WORLD OF THE BOOK TO RESCUE M AND ENDED UP GETTING ATTACKED INSTEAD.
I THINK I UNDERSTAND YOU NOW. YOUR SADNESS. YOUR RESENTMENT... YOUR HATE. I KNOW NOW WHY YOU AIMED YOUR HATRED AT ME.
NOW THAT THE SAME THING HAPPENED TO ME, I UNDERSTAND.

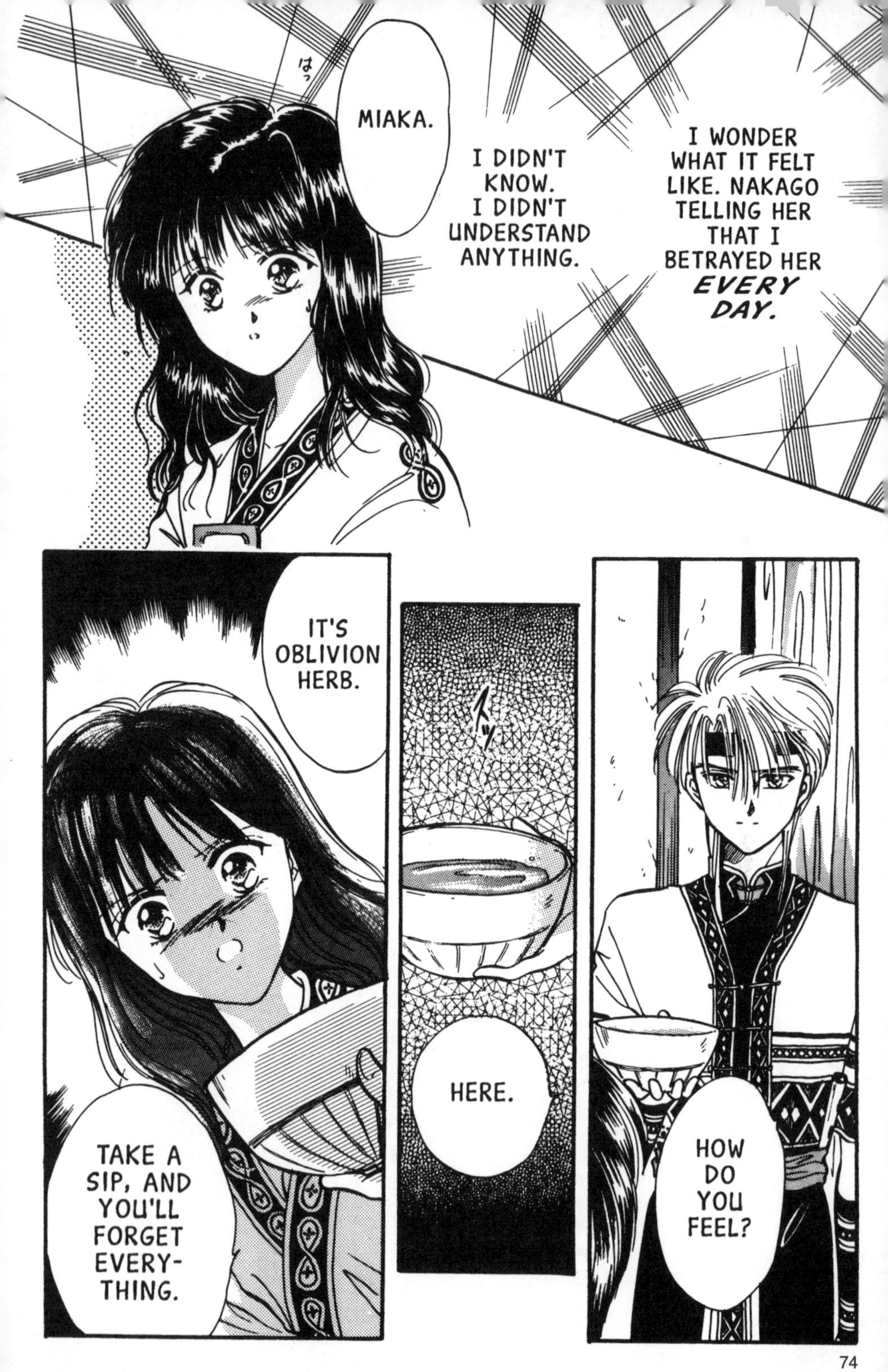
I WONDER WHAT IT FELT LIKE. NAKAGO TELLING HER THAT I BETRAYED HER *EVERY DAY.*
I DIDN'T KNOW. I DIDN'T UNDERSTAND ANYTHING.
MIAKA.
はっ
HOW DO YOU FEEL?
スッ
HERE.
IT'S OBLIVION HERB.
TAKE A SIP, AND YOU'LL FORGET EVERY-THING.

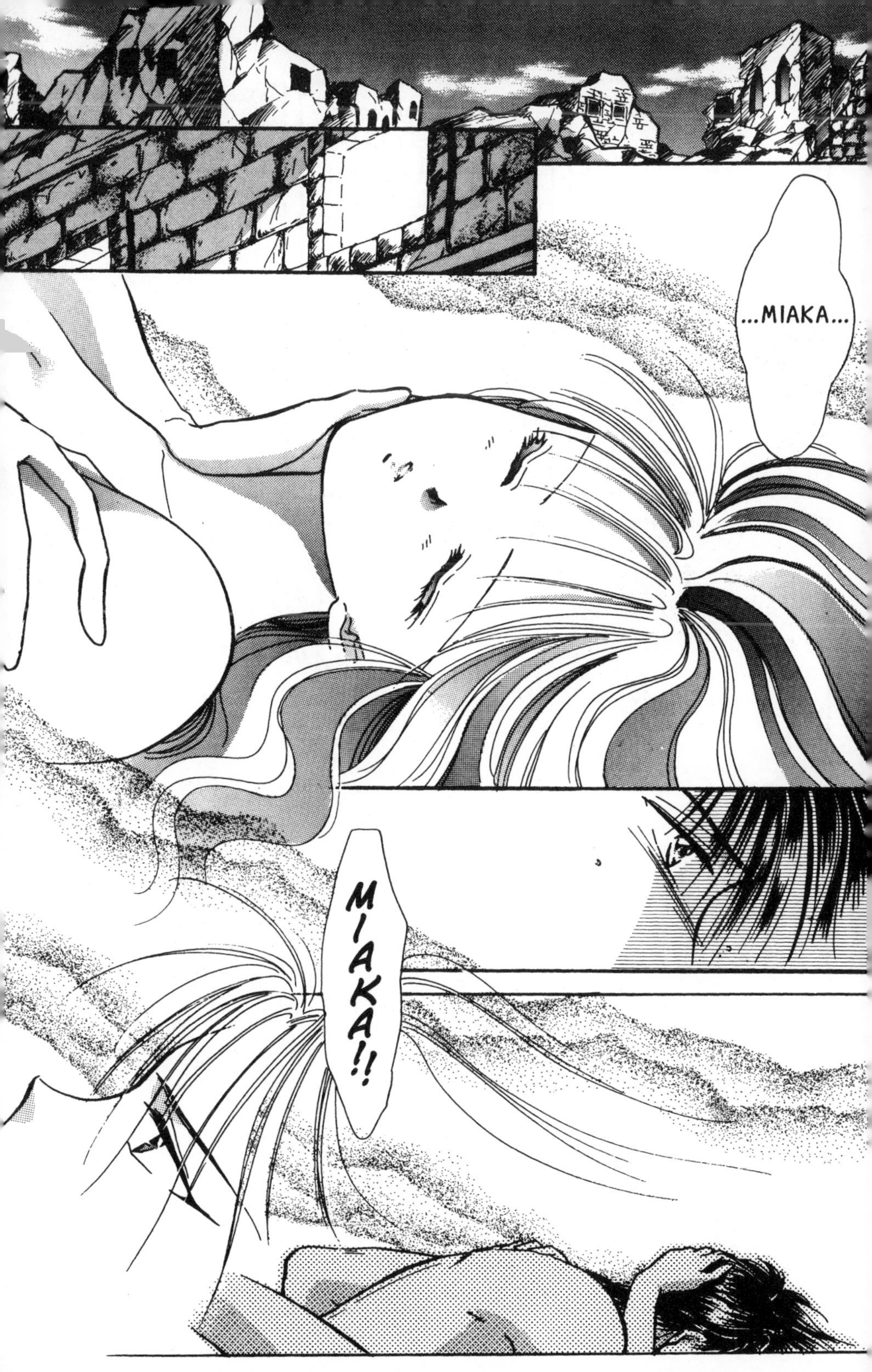
...MIAKA...
MIAKA!!

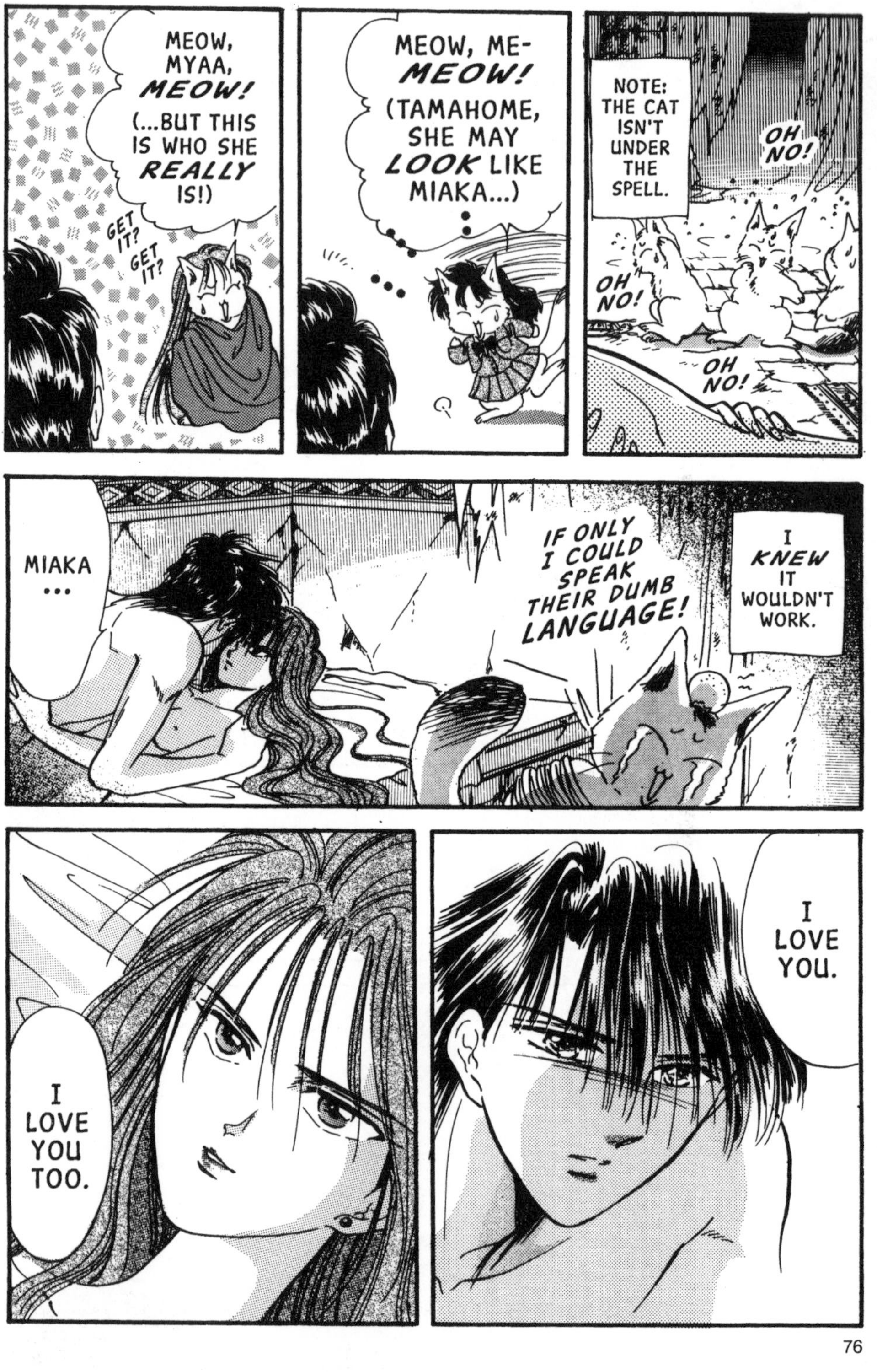
NOTE: THE CAT ISN'T UNDER THE SPELL.
OH NO!
OH NO!
OH NO!
MEOW, ME-MEOW! (TAMAHOME, SHE MAY LOOK LIKE MIAKA...)
...
MEOW, MYAA, MEOW! (...BUT THIS IS WHO SHE REALLY IS!)
GET IT? GET IT?
I KNEW IT WOULDN'T WORK.
IF ONLY I COULD SPEAK THEIR DUMB LANGUAGE!
MIAKA...
I LOVE YOU.
I LOVE YOU TOO.

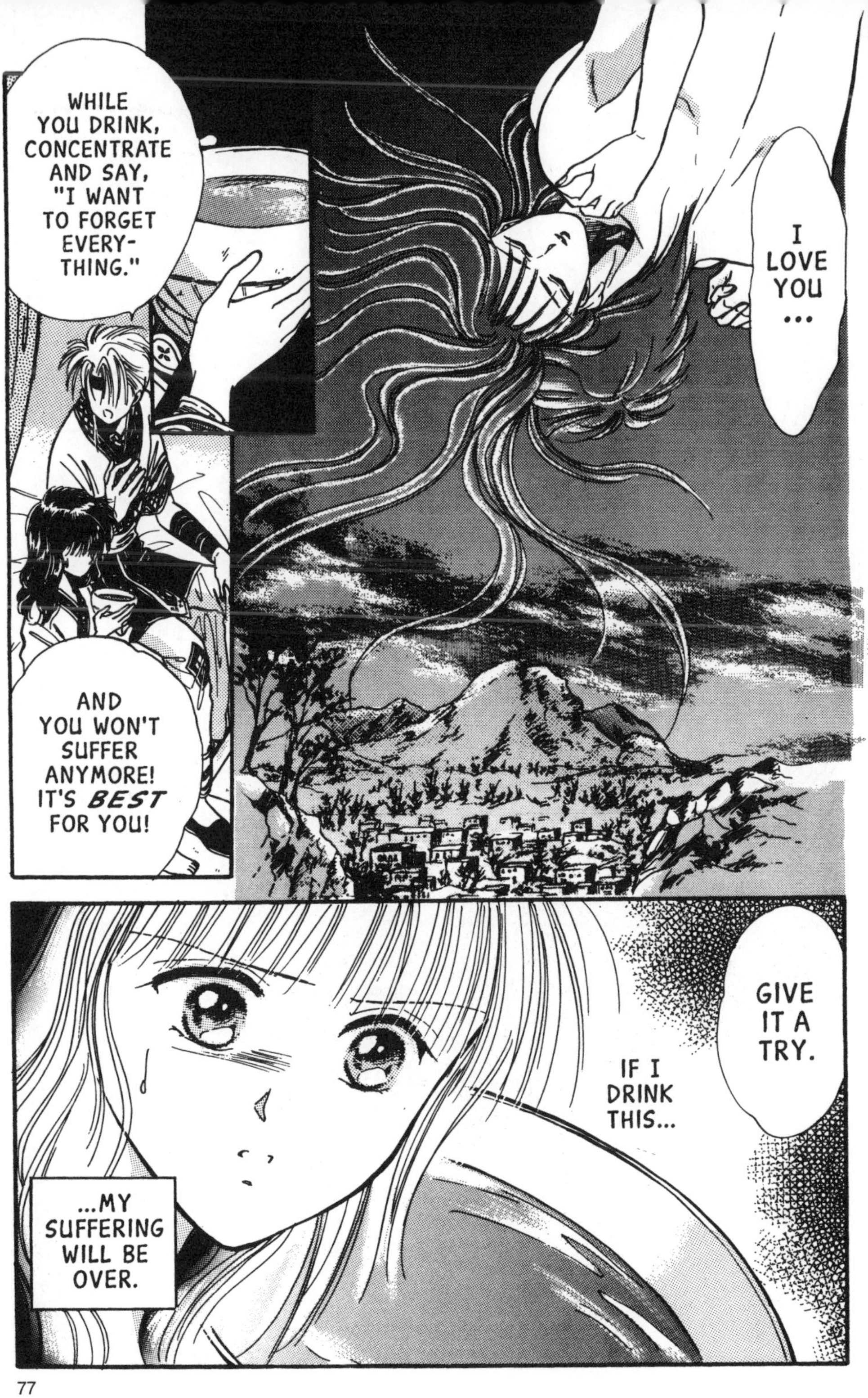
I LOVE YOU ...
WHILE YOU DRINK, CONCENTRATE AND SAY, "I WANT TO FORGET EVERY-THING."
AND YOU WON'T SUFFER ANYMORE! IT'S *BEST* FOR YOU!
GIVE IT A TRY.
IF I DRINK THIS...
...MY SUFFERING WILL BE OVER.

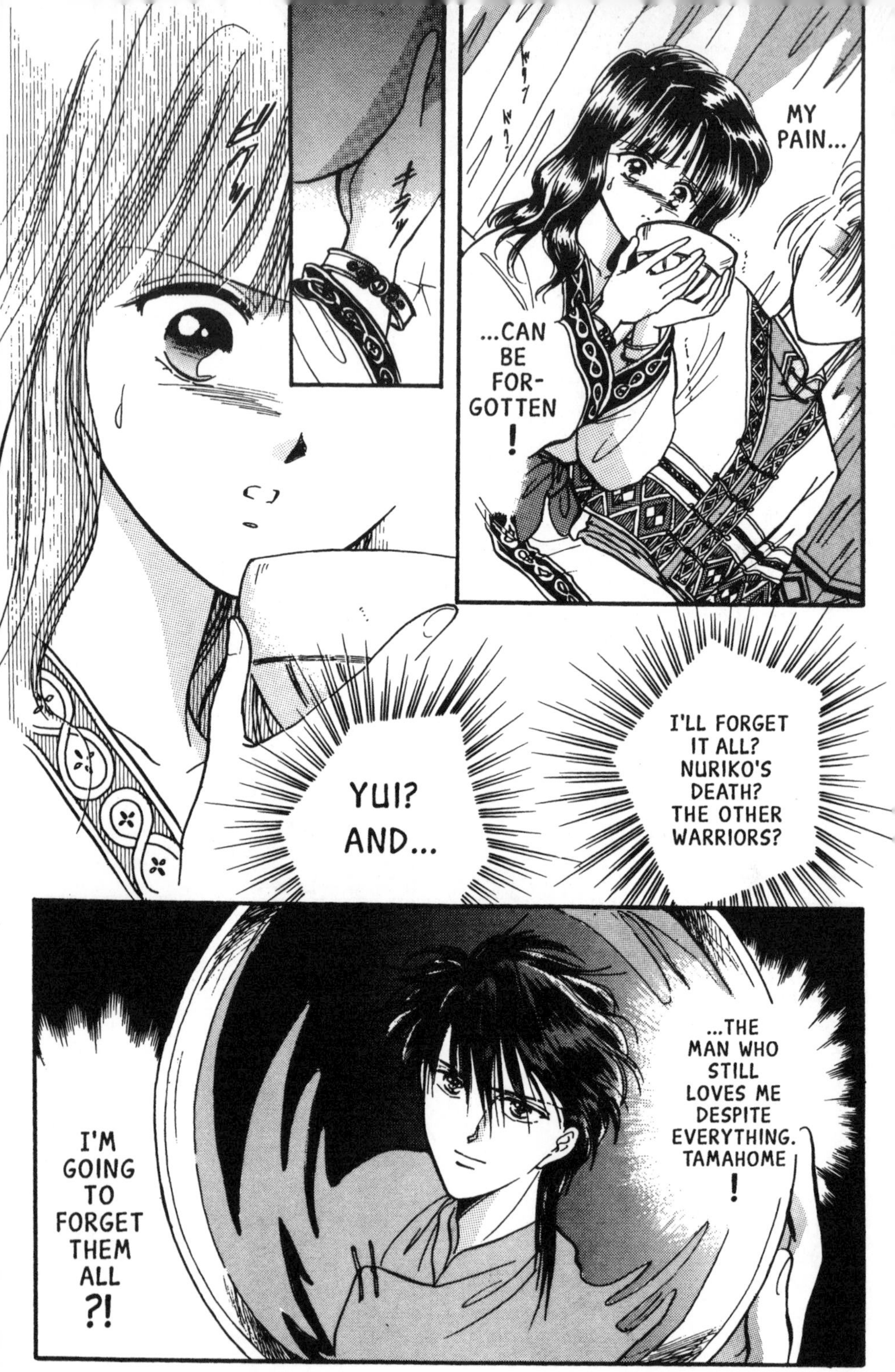
MY PAIN...
...CAN BE FORGOTTEN!
I'LL FORGET IT ALL? NURIKO'S DEATH? THE OTHER WARRIORS?
YUI? AND...
...THE MAN WHO STILL LOVES ME DESPITE EVERYTHING. TAMAHOME!
I'M GOING TO FORGET THEM ALL?!

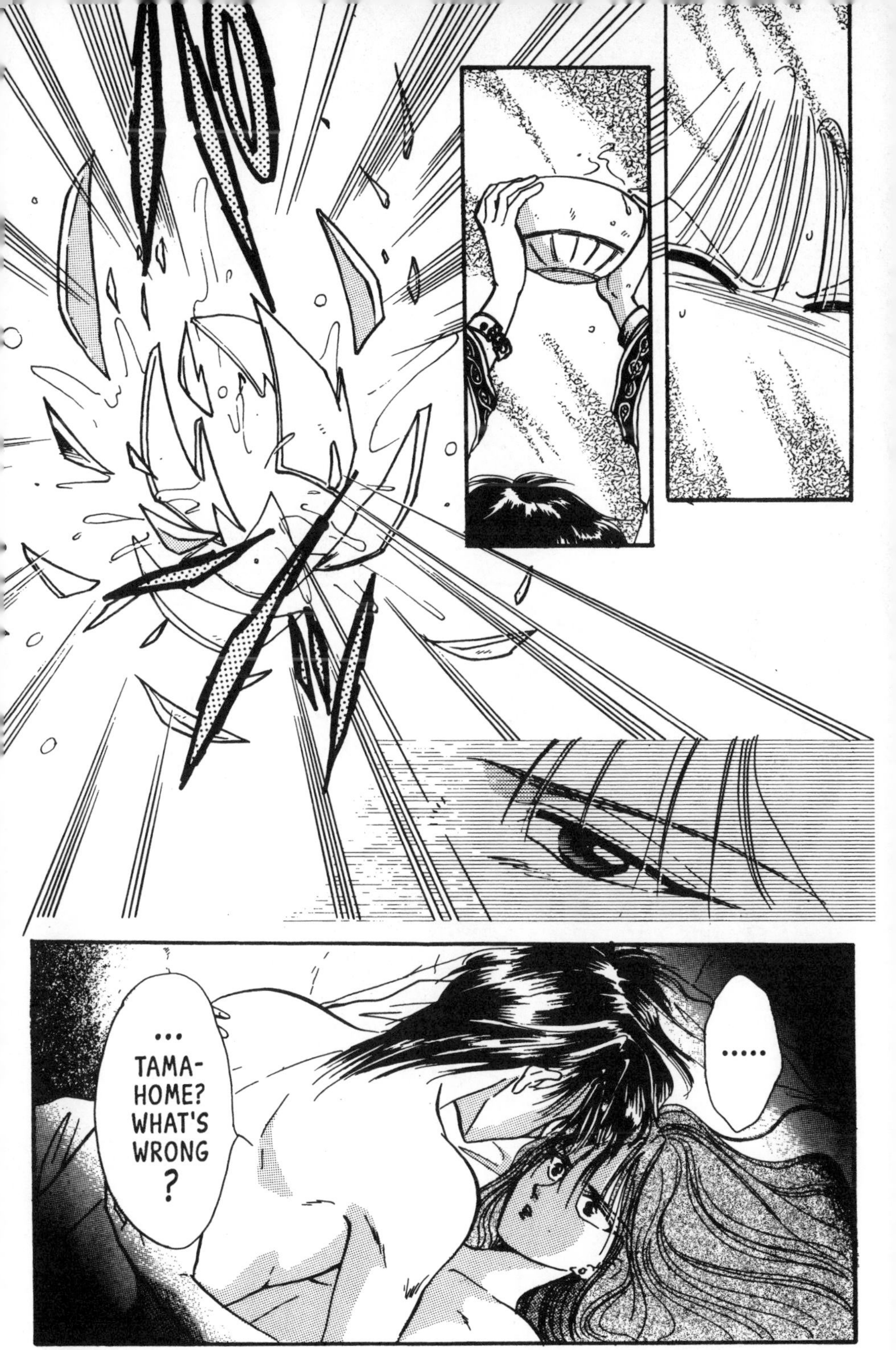
.....
... TAMA-HOME? WHAT'S WRONG ?

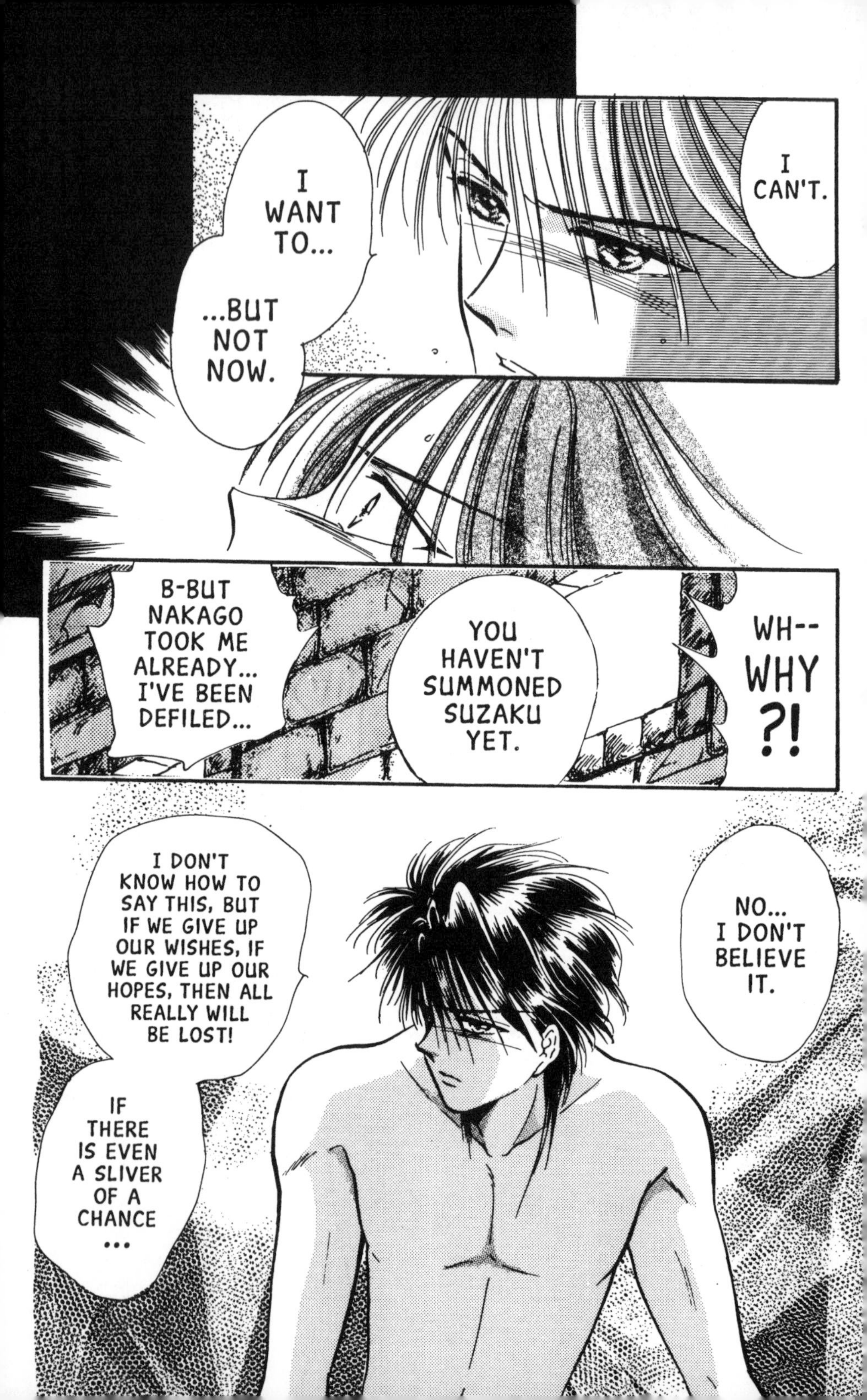
I CAN'T.
I WANT TO...
...BUT NOT NOW.
WH-- WHY?!
YOU HAVEN'T SUMMONED SUZAKU YET.
B-BUT NAKAGO TOOK ME ALREADY... I'VE BEEN DEFILED...
NO... I DON'T BELIEVE IT.
I DON'T KNOW HOW TO SAY THIS, BUT IF WE GIVE UP OUR WISHES, IF WE GIVE UP OUR HOPES, THEN ALL REALLY WILL BE LOST!
IF THERE IS EVEN A SLIVER OF A CHANCE...

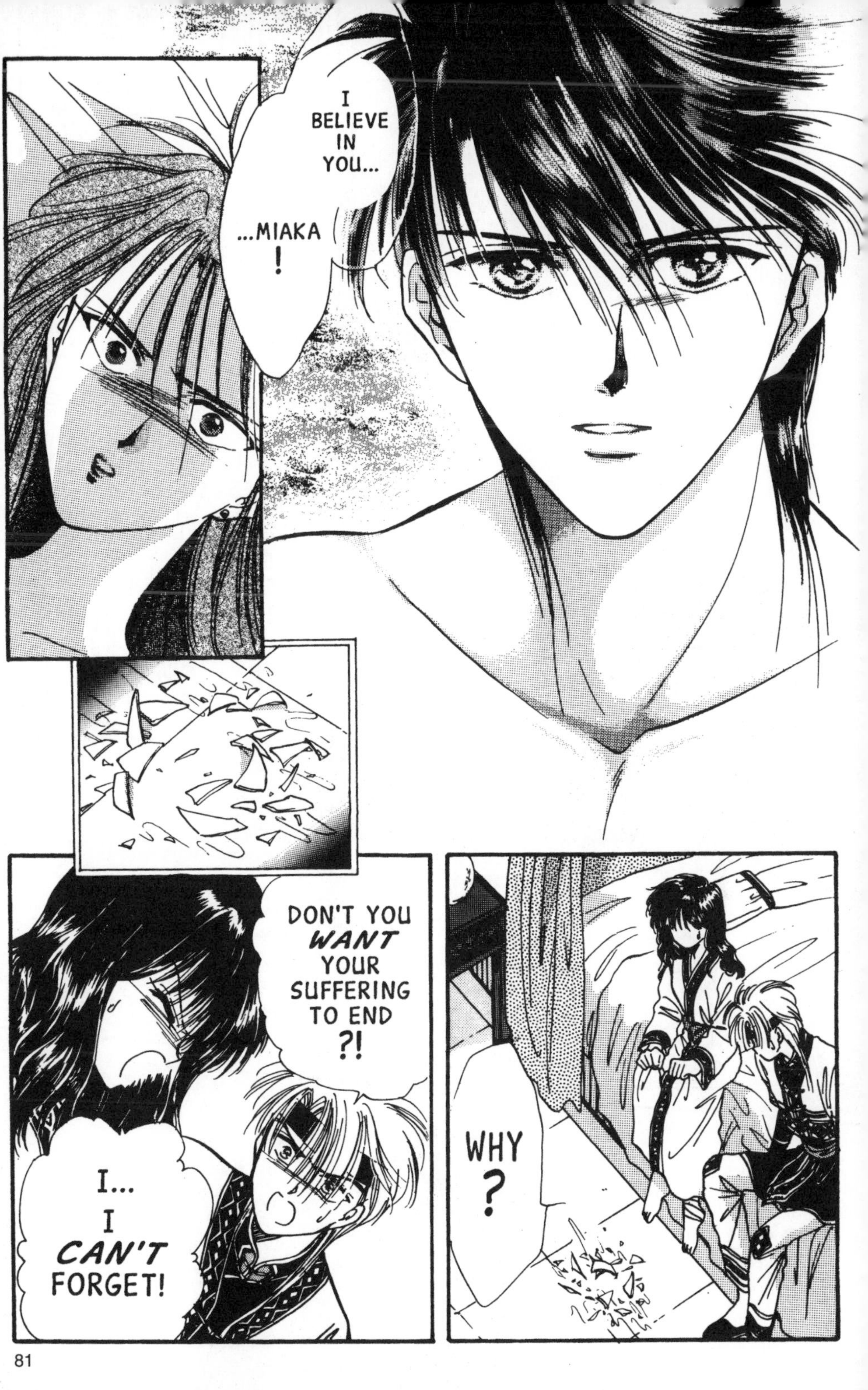
I BELIEVE IN YOU...
...MIAKA!
WHY?
DON'T YOU *WANT* YOUR SUFFERING TO END?!
I... I *CAN'T* FORGET!

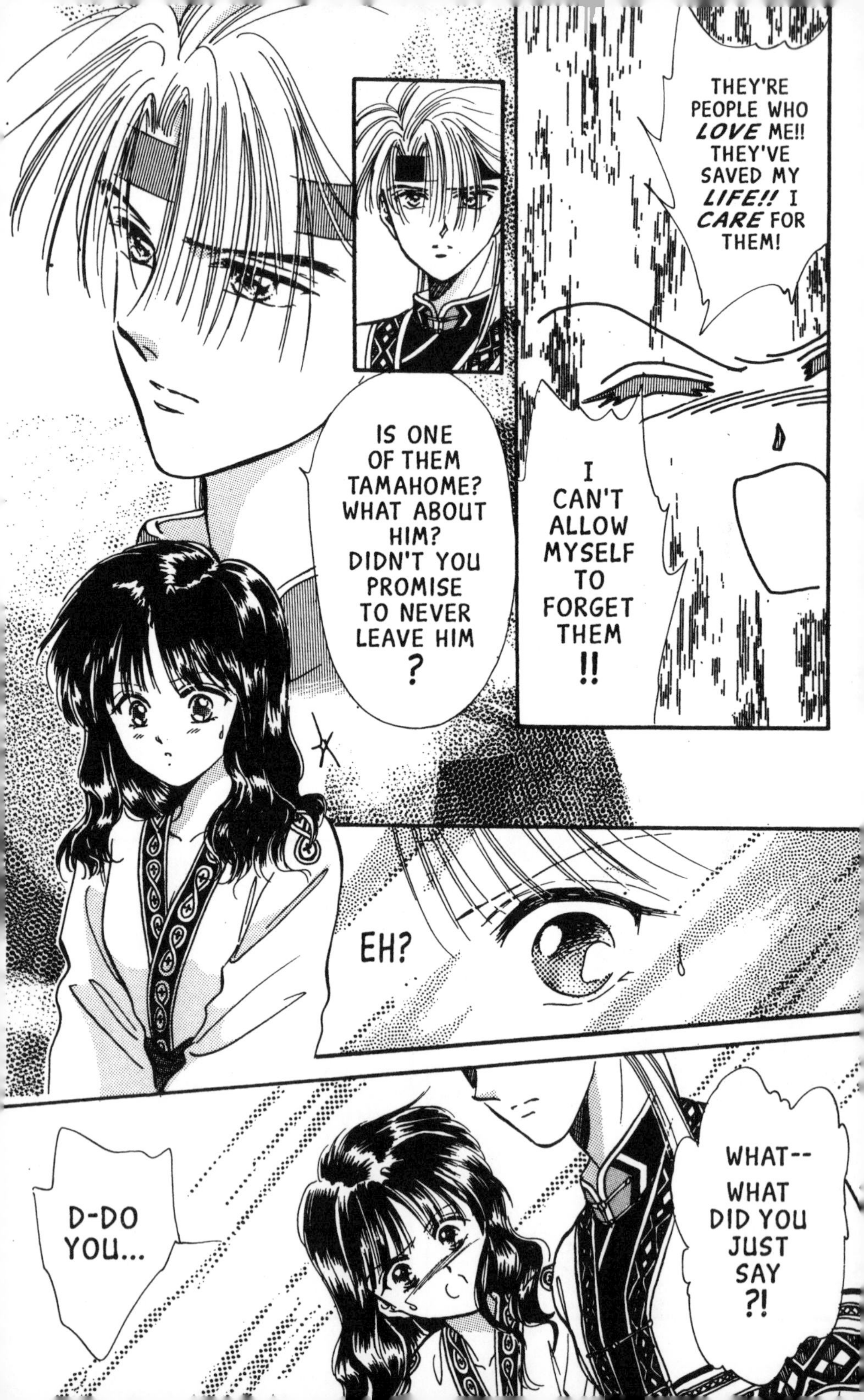
THEY'RE PEOPLE WHO *LOVE* ME!! THEY'VE SAVED MY *LIFE!!* I *CARE* FOR THEM!
I CAN'T ALLOW MYSELF TO FORGET THEM!!
IS ONE OF THEM TAMAHOME? WHAT ABOUT HIM? DIDN'T YOU PROMISE TO NEVER LEAVE HIM?
EH?
WHAT-- WHAT DID YOU JUST SAY?!
D-DO YOU...

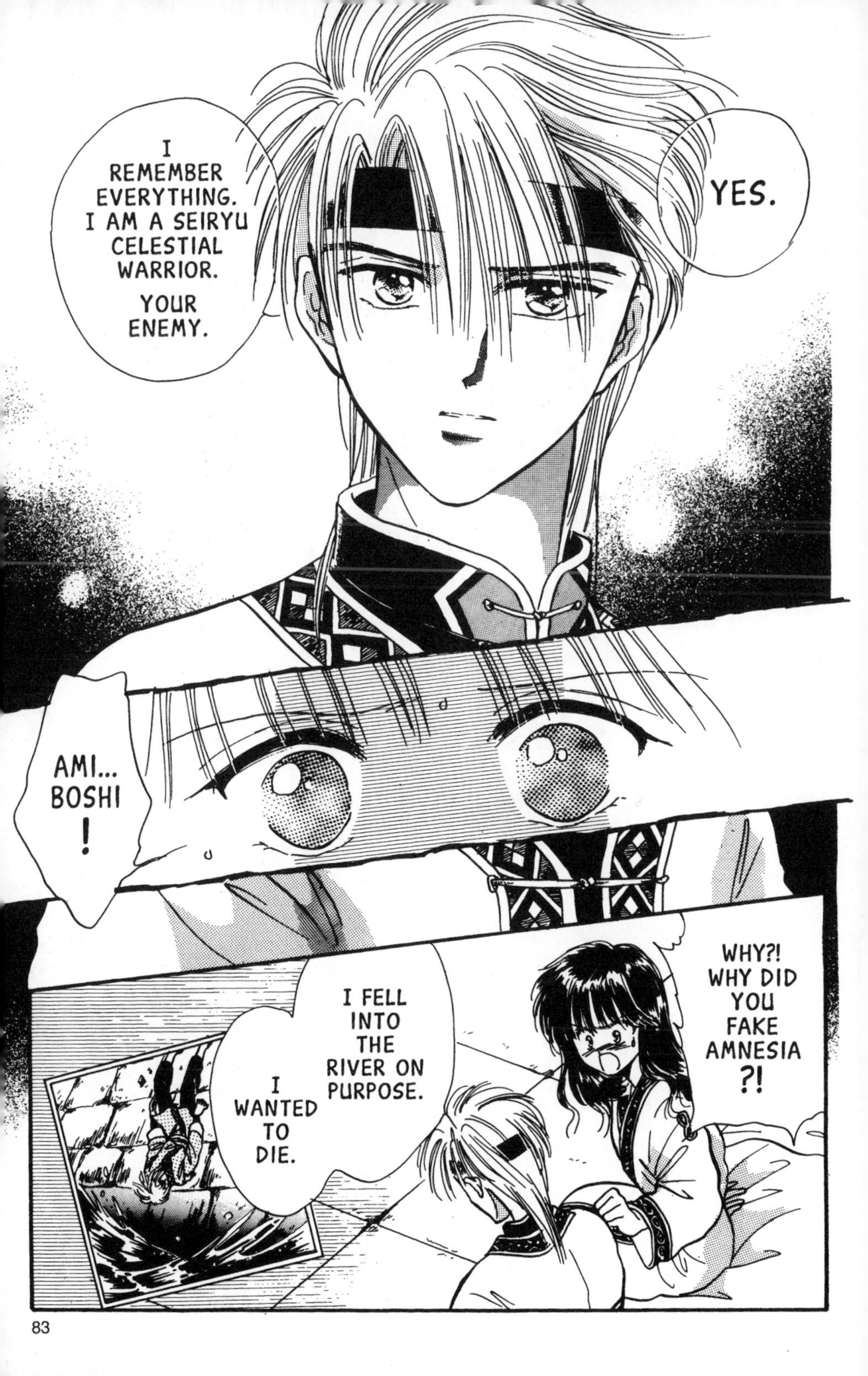
YES.
I REMEMBER EVERYTHING. I AM A SEIRYU CELESTIAL WARRIOR.
YOUR ENEMY.
AMI... BOSHI!
WHY?! WHY DID YOU FAKE AMNESIA?!
I FELL INTO THE RIVER ON PURPOSE.
I WANTED TO DIE.

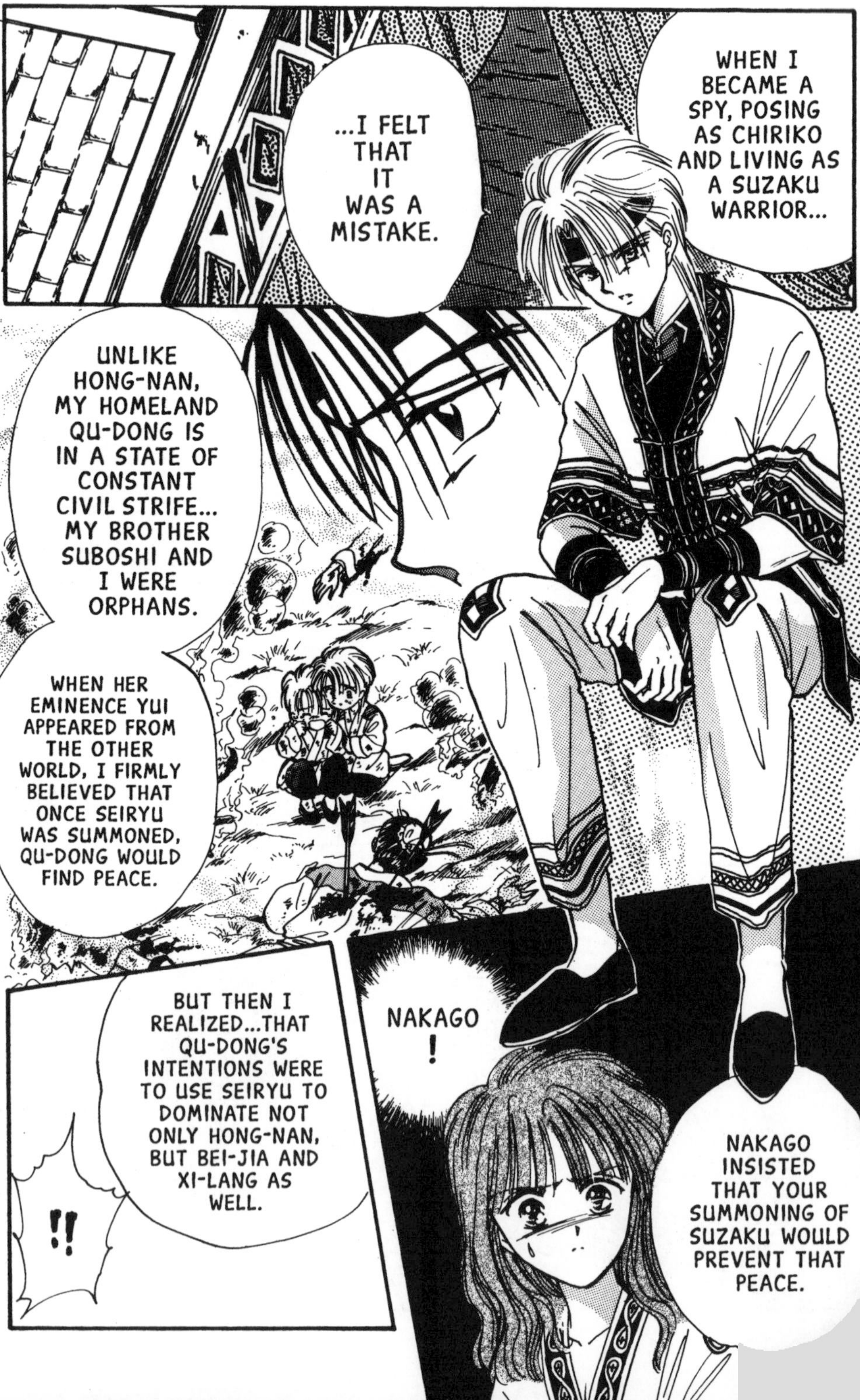
WHEN I BECAME A SPY, POSING AS CHIRIKO AND LIVING AS A SUZAKU WARRIOR...
...I FELT THAT IT WAS A MISTAKE.
UNLIKE HONG-NAN, MY HOMELAND QU-DONG IS IN A STATE OF CONSTANT CIVIL STRIFE... MY BROTHER SUBOSHI AND I WERE ORPHANS.
WHEN HER EMINENCE YUI APPEARED FROM THE OTHER WORLD, I FIRMLY BELIEVED THAT ONCE SEIRYU WAS SUMMONED, QU-DONG WOULD FIND PEACE.
NAKAGO INSISTED THAT YOUR SUMMONING OF SUZAKU WOULD PREVENT THAT PEACE.
NAKAGO !
BUT THEN I REALIZED...THAT QU-DONG'S INTENTIONS WERE TO USE SEIRYU TO DOMINATE NOT ONLY HONG-NAN, BUT BEI-JIA AND XI-LANG AS WELL.
!!

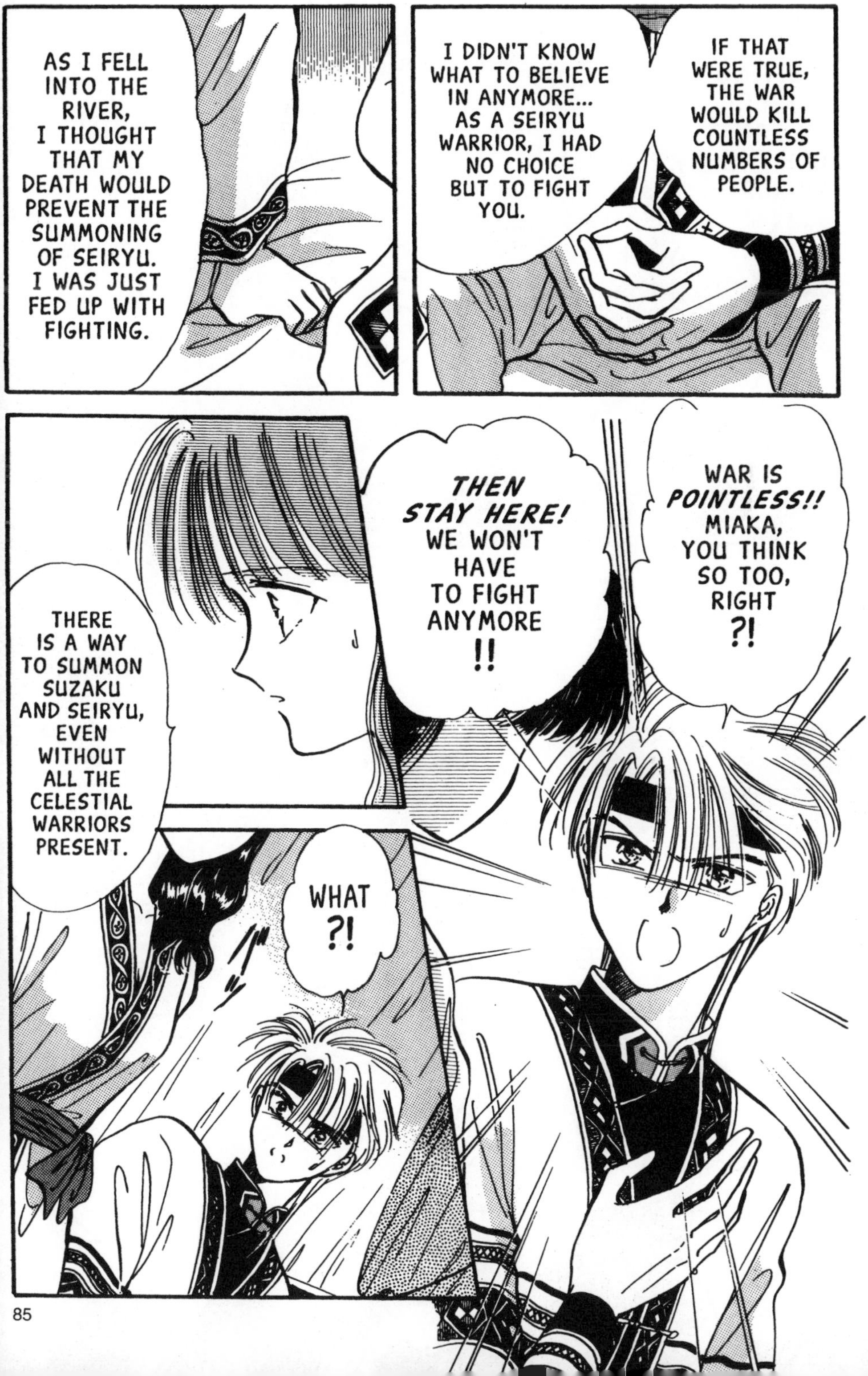
IF THAT WERE TRUE, THE WAR WOULD KILL COUNTLESS NUMBERS OF PEOPLE.
I DIDN'T KNOW WHAT TO BELIEVE IN ANYMORE... AS A SEIRYU WARRIOR, I HAD NO CHOICE BUT TO FIGHT YOU.
AS I FELL INTO THE RIVER, I THOUGHT THAT MY DEATH WOULD PREVENT THE SUMMONING OF SEIRYU. I WAS JUST FED UP WITH FIGHTING.
WAR IS *POINTLESS!!* MIAKA, YOU THINK SO TOO, RIGHT ?!
THEN STAY HERE! WE WON'T HAVE TO FIGHT ANYMORE !!
THERE IS A WAY TO SUMMON SUZAKU AND SEIRYU, EVEN WITHOUT ALL THE CELESTIAL WARRIORS PRESENT.
WHAT ?!

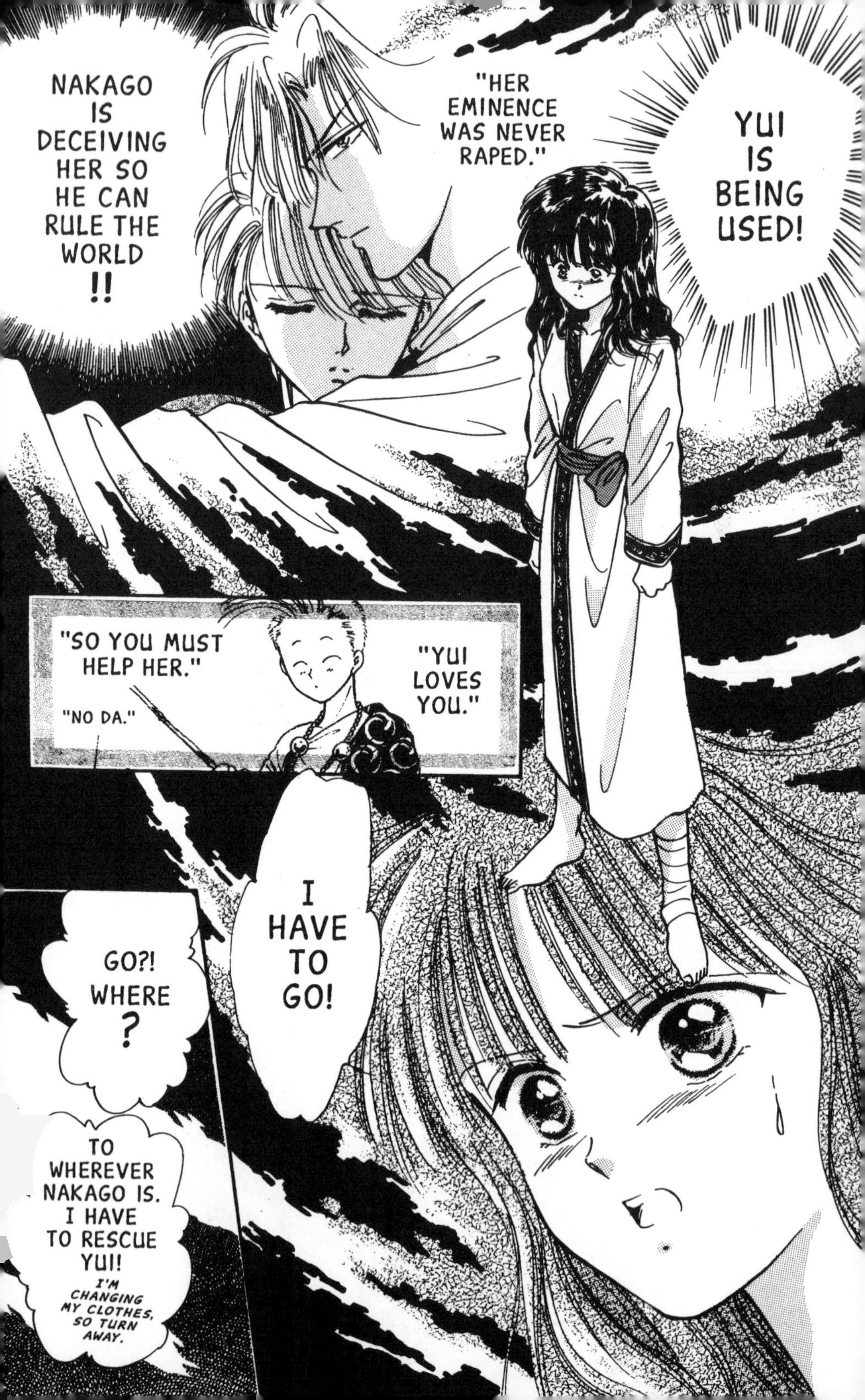

"HER EMINENCE WAS NEVER RAPED."
YUI IS BEING USED!
NAKAGO IS DECEIVING HER SO HE CAN RULE THE WORLD!!
"YUI LOVES YOU."
"SO YOU MUST HELP HER."
"NO DA."
I HAVE TO GO!
GO?! WHERE?
TO WHEREVER NAKAGO IS. I HAVE TO RESCUE YUI!
I'M CHANGING MY CLOTHES, SO TURN AWAY.

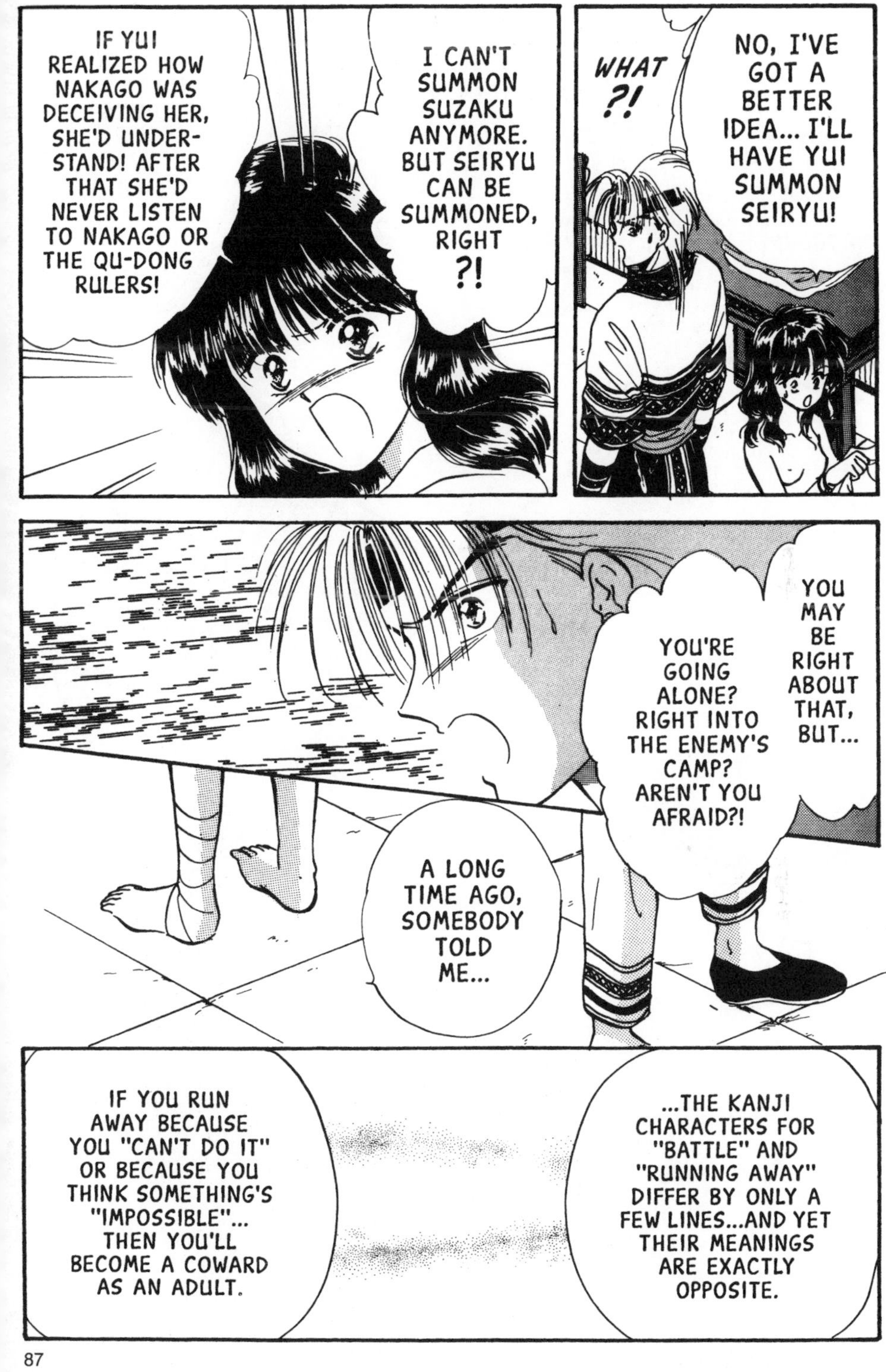
NO, I'VE GOT A BETTER IDEA... I'LL HAVE YUI SUMMON SEIRYU!
WHAT ?!
I CAN'T SUMMON SUZAKU ANYMORE. BUT SEIRYU CAN BE SUMMONED, RIGHT ?!
IF YUI REALIZED HOW NAKAGO WAS DECEIVING HER, SHE'D UNDER-STAND! AFTER THAT SHE'D NEVER LISTEN TO NAKAGO OR THE QU-DONG RULERS!
YOU MAY BE RIGHT ABOUT THAT, BUT...
YOU'RE GOING ALONE? RIGHT INTO THE ENEMY'S CAMP? AREN'T YOU AFRAID?!
A LONG TIME AGO, SOMEBODY TOLD ME...
...THE KANJI CHARACTERS FOR "BATTLE" AND "RUNNING AWAY" DIFFER BY ONLY A FEW LINES...AND YET THEIR MEANINGS ARE EXACTLY OPPOSITE.
IF YOU RUN AWAY BECAUSE YOU "CAN'T DO IT" OR BECAUSE YOU THINK SOMETHING'S "IMPOSSIBLE"... THEN YOU'LL BECOME A COWARD AS AN ADULT.

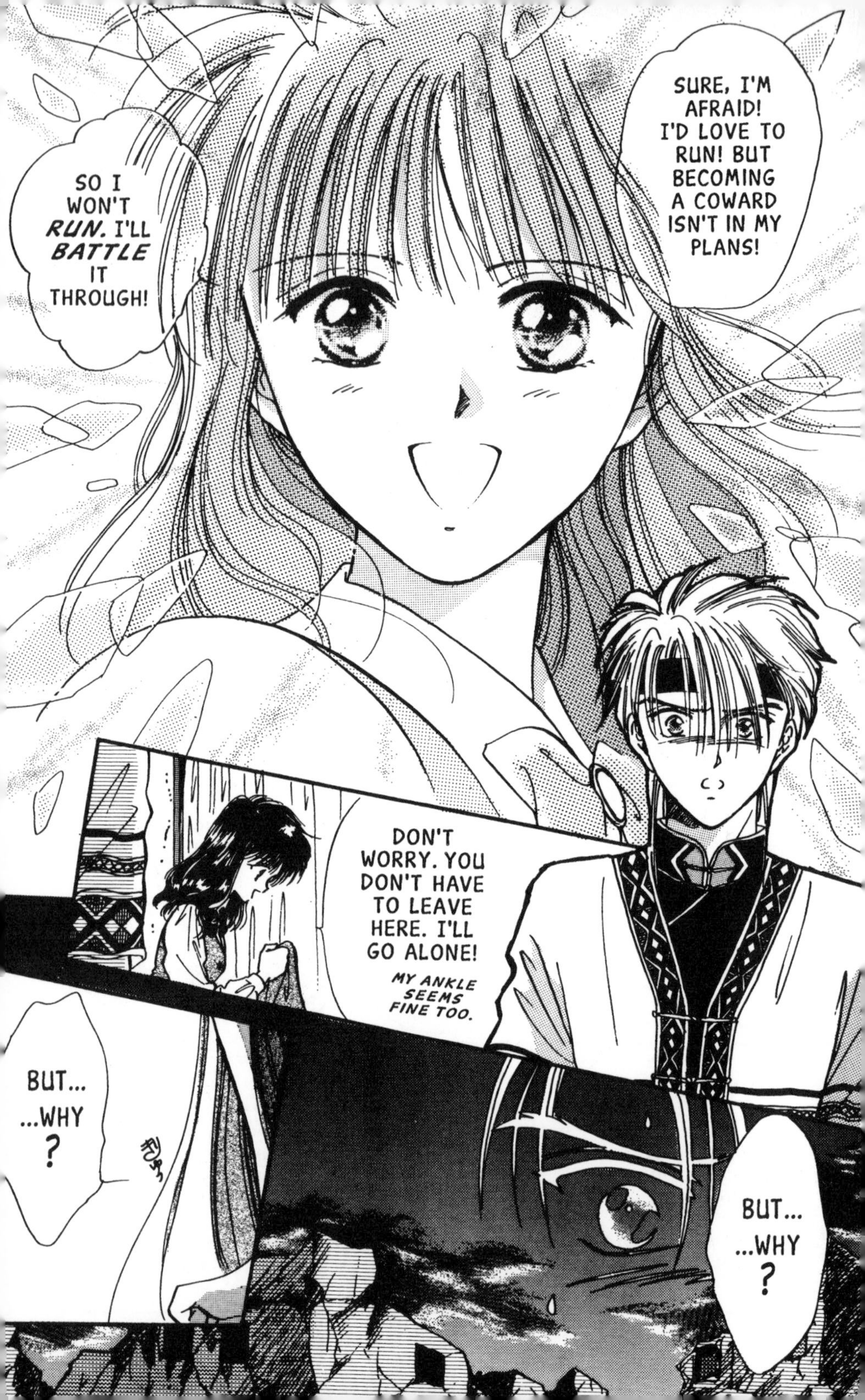
SURE, I'M AFRAID! I'D LOVE TO RUN! BUT BECOMING A COWARD ISN'T IN MY PLANS!
SO I WON'T *RUN.* I'LL *BATTLE* IT THROUGH!
DON'T WORRY. YOU DON'T HAVE TO LEAVE HERE. I'LL GO ALONE!
MY ANKLE SEEMS FINE TOO.
BUT... ...WHY ?
BUT... ...WHY ?

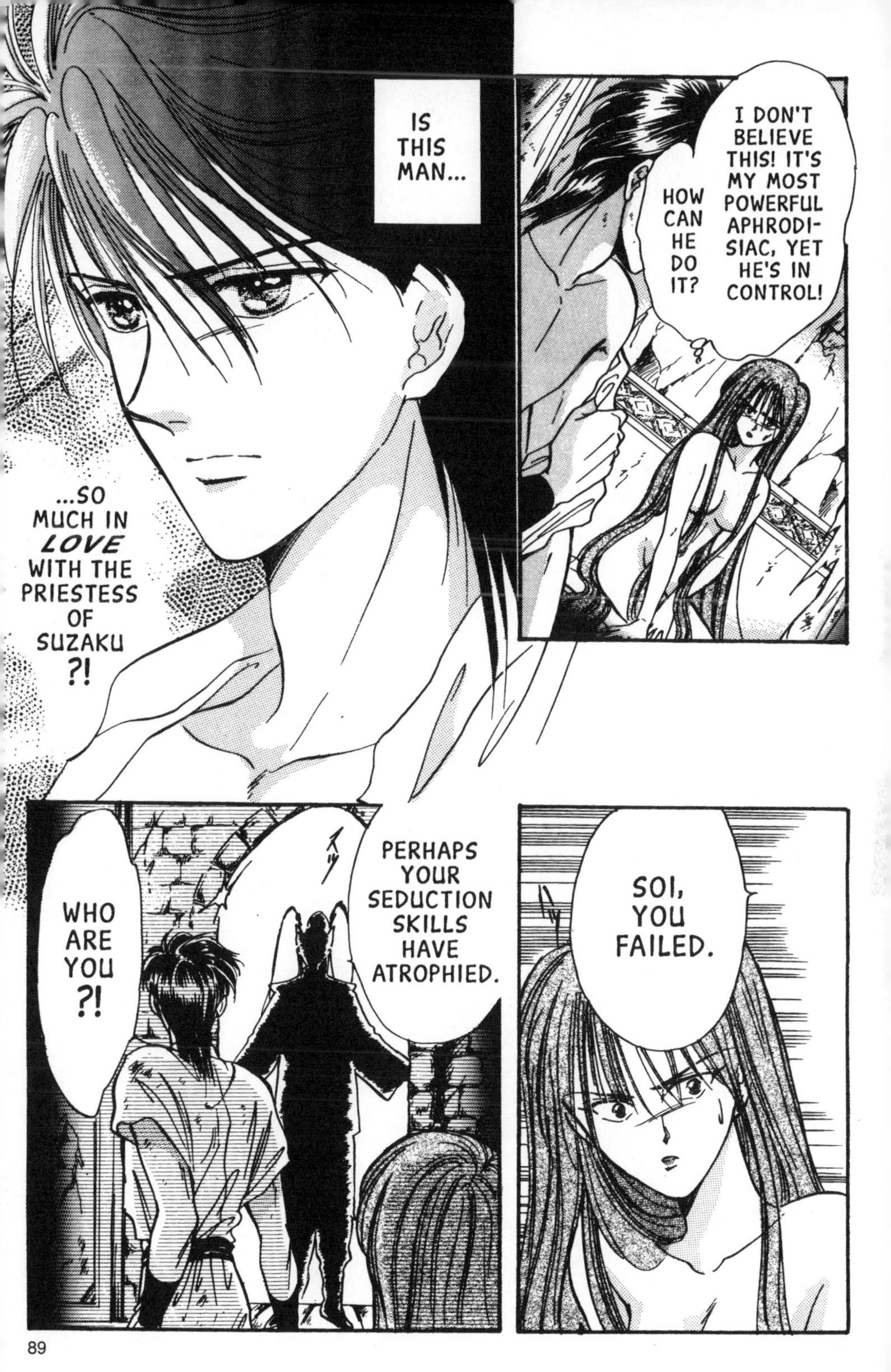
I DON'T BELIEVE THIS! IT'S MY MOST POWERFUL APHRODISIAC, YET HE'S IN CONTROL!
HOW CAN HE DO IT?
IS THIS MAN...
...SO MUCH IN *LOVE* WITH THE PRIESTESS OF SUZAKU ?!
SOI, YOU FAILED.
PERHAPS YOUR SEDUCTION SKILLS HAVE ATROPHIED.
WHO ARE YOU ?!

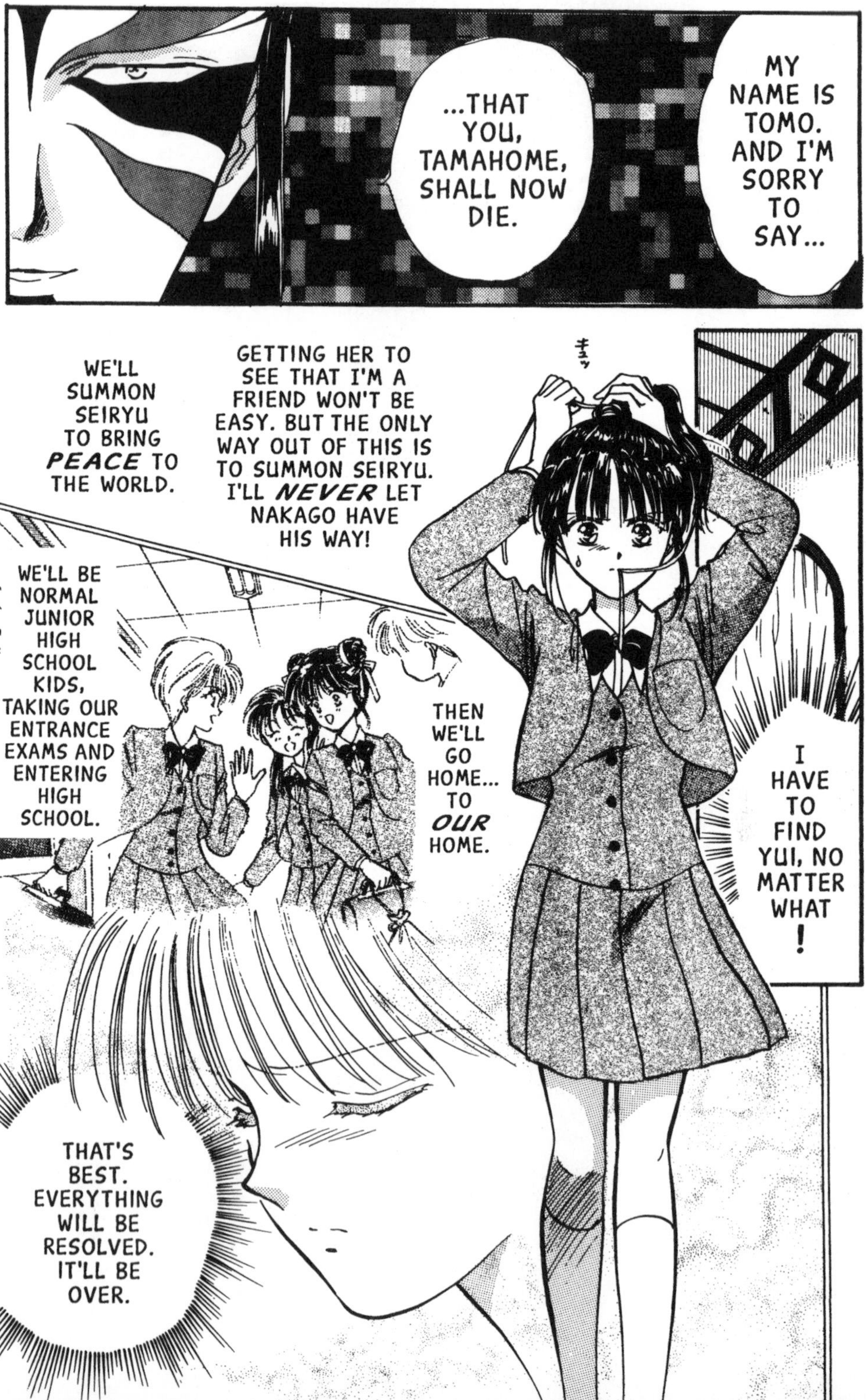
MY NAME IS TOMO. AND I'M SORRY TO SAY...
...THAT YOU, TAMAHOME, SHALL NOW DIE.
キュッ
I HAVE TO FIND YUI, NO MATTER WHAT!
GETTING HER TO SEE THAT I'M A FRIEND WON'T BE EASY. BUT THE ONLY WAY OUT OF THIS IS TO SUMMON SEIRYU. I'LL *NEVER* LET NAKAGO HAVE HIS WAY!
WE'LL SUMMON SEIRYU TO BRING *PEACE* TO THE WORLD.
THEN WE'LL GO HOME... TO *OUR* HOME.
WE'LL BE NORMAL JUNIOR HIGH SCHOOL KIDS, TAKING OUR ENTRANCE EXAMS AND ENTERING HIGH SCHOOL.
THAT'S BEST. EVERYTHING WILL BE RESOLVED. IT'LL BE OVER.

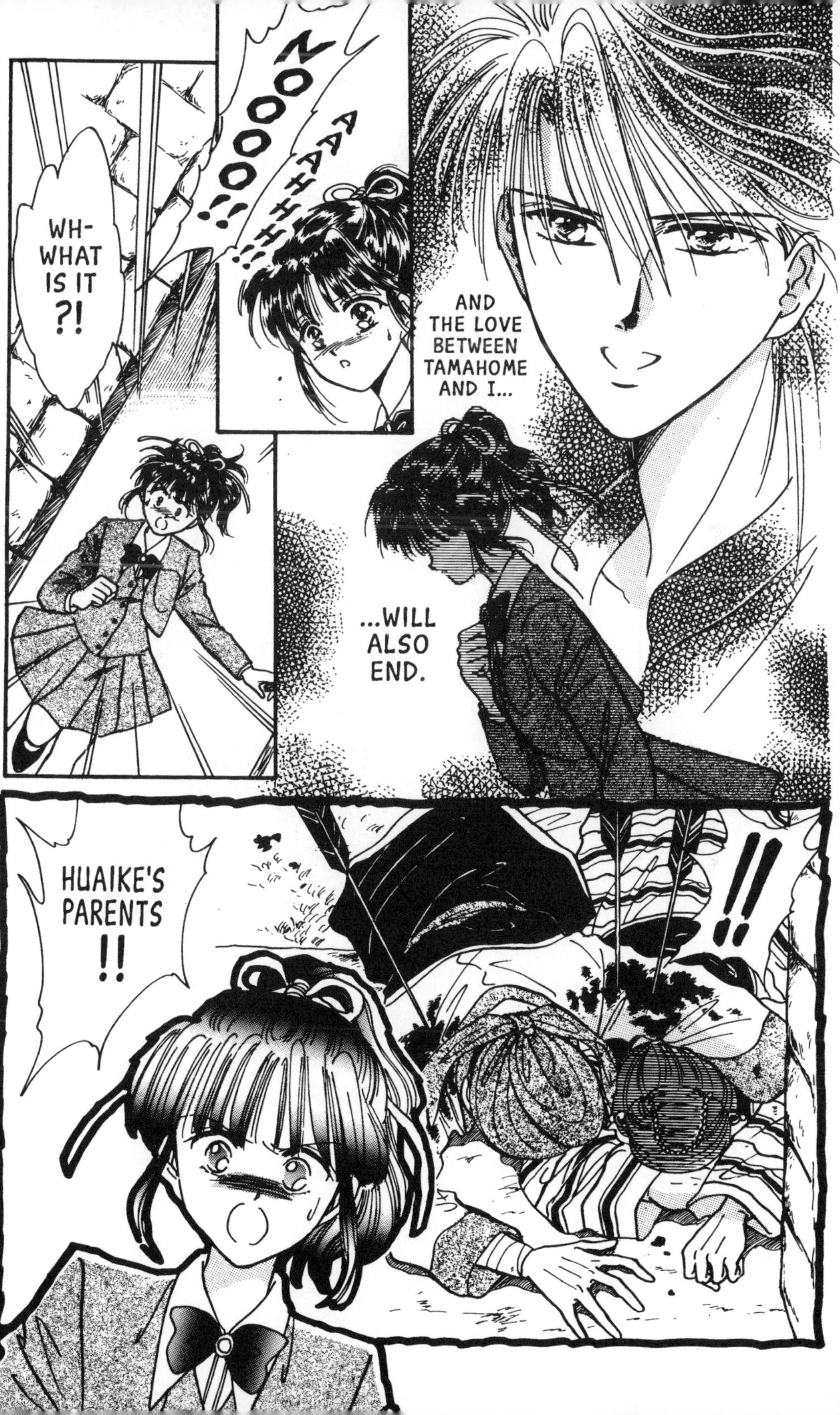
AND THE LOVE BETWEEN TAMAHOME AND I...
...WILL ALSO END.
NOOOOO!!
AAAHHHH!!
WH-WHAT IS IT ?!
!!
HUAIKE'S PARENTS !!

ふしぎ悪戯

FUSHIGI AKUGI
THE MALICIOUS PLAY

From volume 7 (Ah, the memories!)

Long Overdue: Fushigi Akugi The Malicious Play (8)

I'LL HOLD YOU UNTIL YOU'RE FINISHED ...

URGH.

Thank you for sending me all those dōjinshi and tapes, Ms. Haruta (great parody!). It was all really interesting! The Tasuki novel and the notebook with all your friends' drawings! I also received a Ranma 1/2 video and cute illustrations from someone who is now an animator. I'd like to have all the fan art and character portraits from you readers displayed somewhere. Can I?

The idea came from several readers ... I-I still don't know your names! Sorry! ♡

.....

Why am I always in these dōjinshi?!

It never ends! They call me Akago, Inago, Mukago, Chicago ...

Are you that jealous, Nakago? Then why don't you cuddle up with Tamahome ... (krak)

SUBOSHI ...

I WANNA DO THAT!

BGM: Final Fantasy IV (3 CD set)

The names of each celestial warrior were written on each of these handmade chocolates!

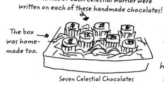

The box was homemade too.

Seven Celestial Chocolates

I had quite a few that were homemade. Here are two samples.

I ran out of space to write it in volume 9, but I wanted to thank you for all the Valentine's Day chocolates! (Come on, that was so long ago!) Thank you so much!

There were so many others I received. Even ones that had love letters (?) to Fushigi characters. Everyone was so thrilled! There was one that was called "Nuriko in Heaven." A note to the fan who sent a gift to Mitsukake, in the CD Book II, he talks a lot more than he does in the manga. In fact he even laughs.

Tamahome Love

12 cm diameter

2-3 cm thick (Who'd take the trouble to measure this?)

This was awesome!

All kinds of topping on the strawberry chocolate.

MNCH MNCH

Wow, there's almond inside!

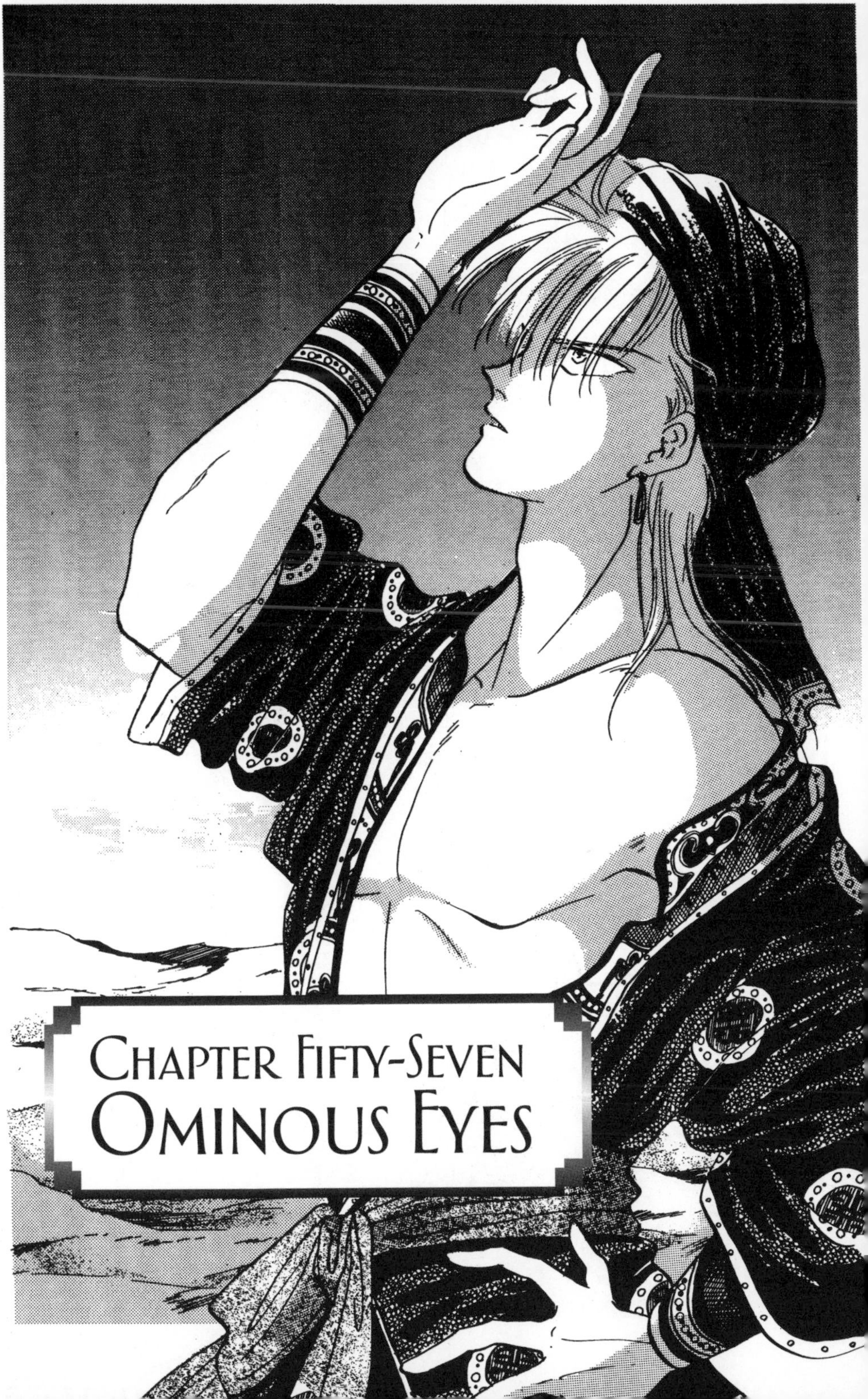
Chapter Fifty-Seven
Ominous Eyes

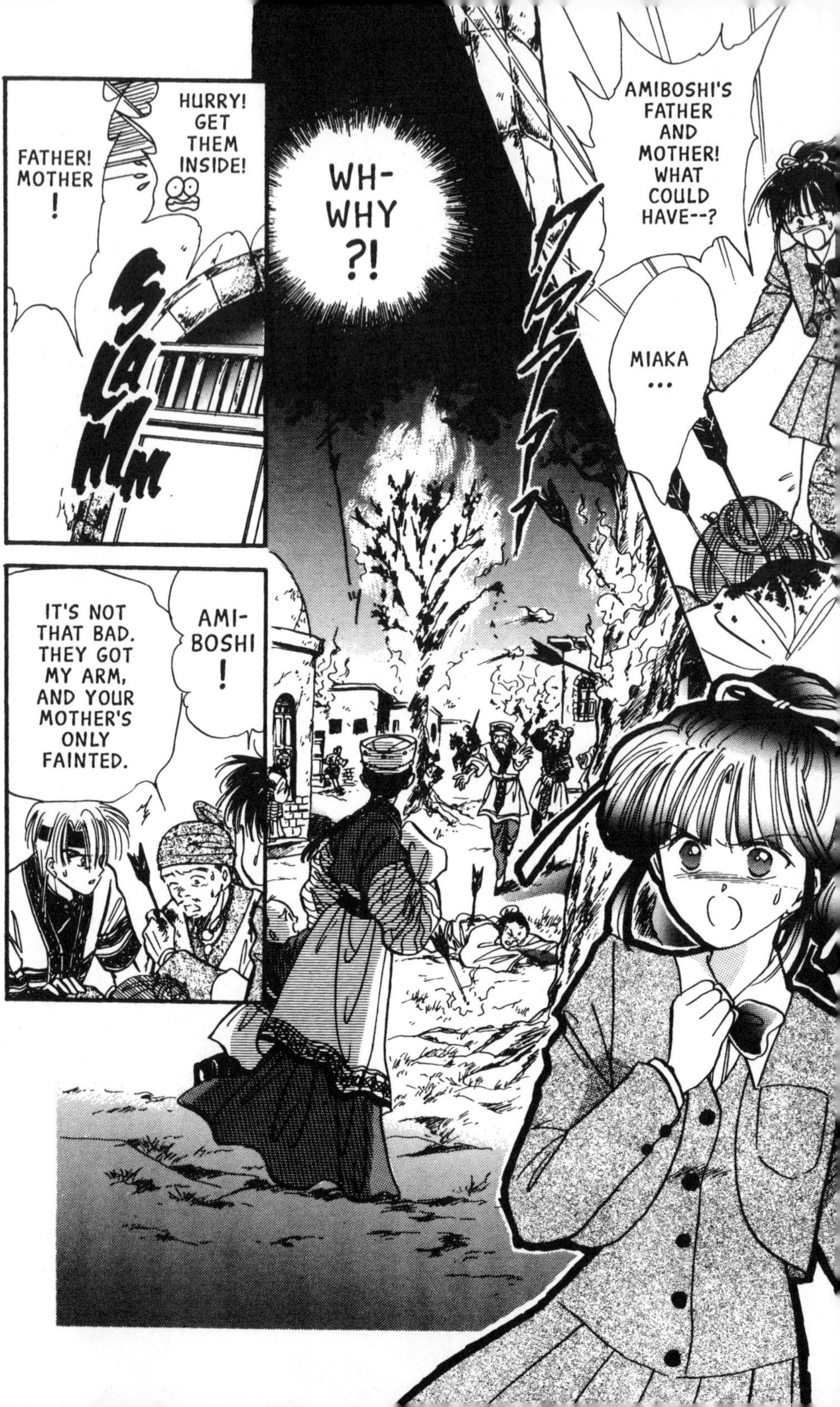
AMIBOSHI'S FATHER AND MOTHER! WHAT COULD HAVE--?
MIAKA...
WH-WHY?!
HURRY! GET THEM INSIDE!
FATHER! MOTHER!
SLAMM
AMIBOSHI!
IT'S NOT THAT BAD. THEY GOT MY ARM, AND YOUR MOTHER'S ONLY FAINTED.

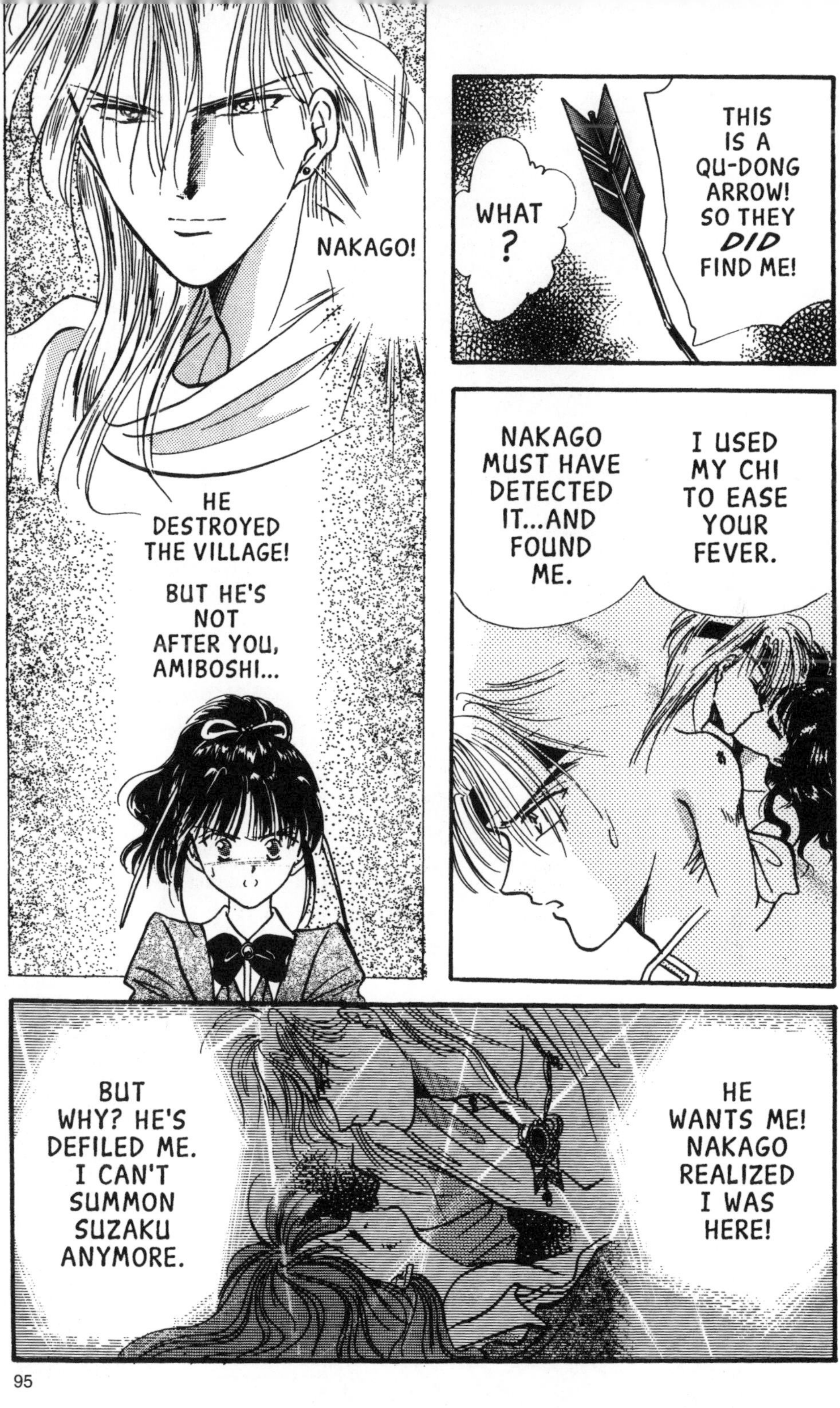
THIS IS A QU-DONG ARROW! SO THEY *DID* FIND ME!
WHAT ?
I USED MY CHI TO EASE YOUR FEVER.
NAKAGO MUST HAVE DETECTED IT...AND FOUND ME.
NAKAGO!
HE DESTROYED THE VILLAGE!
BUT HE'S NOT AFTER YOU, AMIBOSHI...
HE WANTS ME! NAKAGO REALIZED I WAS HERE!
BUT WHY? HE'S DEFILED ME. I CAN'T SUMMON SUZAKU ANYMORE.

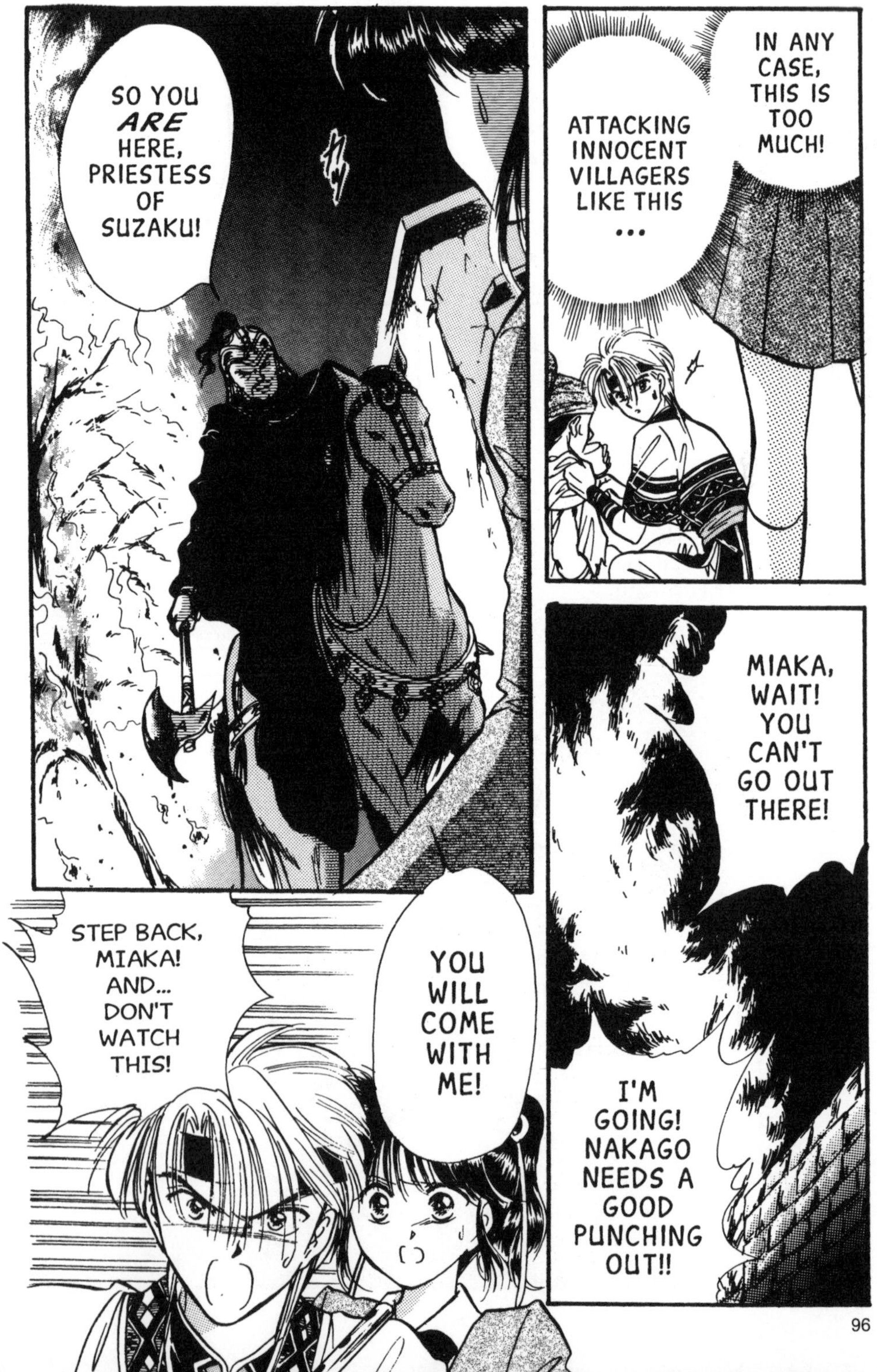
IN ANY CASE, THIS IS TOO MUCH!
ATTACKING INNOCENT VILLAGERS LIKE THIS ...
MIAKA, WAIT! YOU CAN'T GO OUT THERE!
I'M GOING! NAKAGO NEEDS A GOOD PUNCHING OUT!!
SO YOU *ARE* HERE, PRIESTESS OF SUZAKU!
YOU WILL COME WITH ME!
STEP BACK, MIAKA! AND... DON'T WATCH THIS!

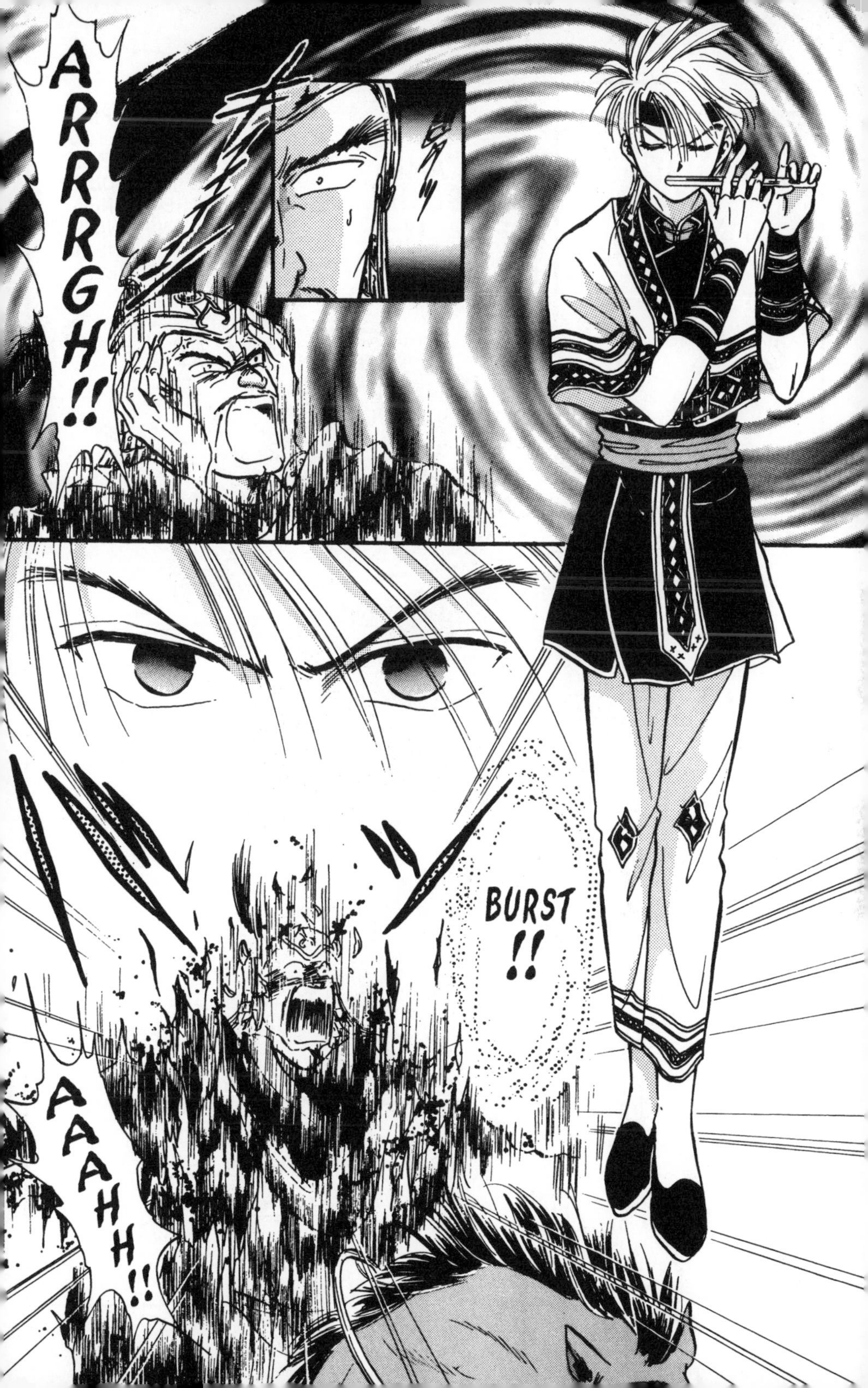
ARRRGH!!
BURST !!
AAAHH!!

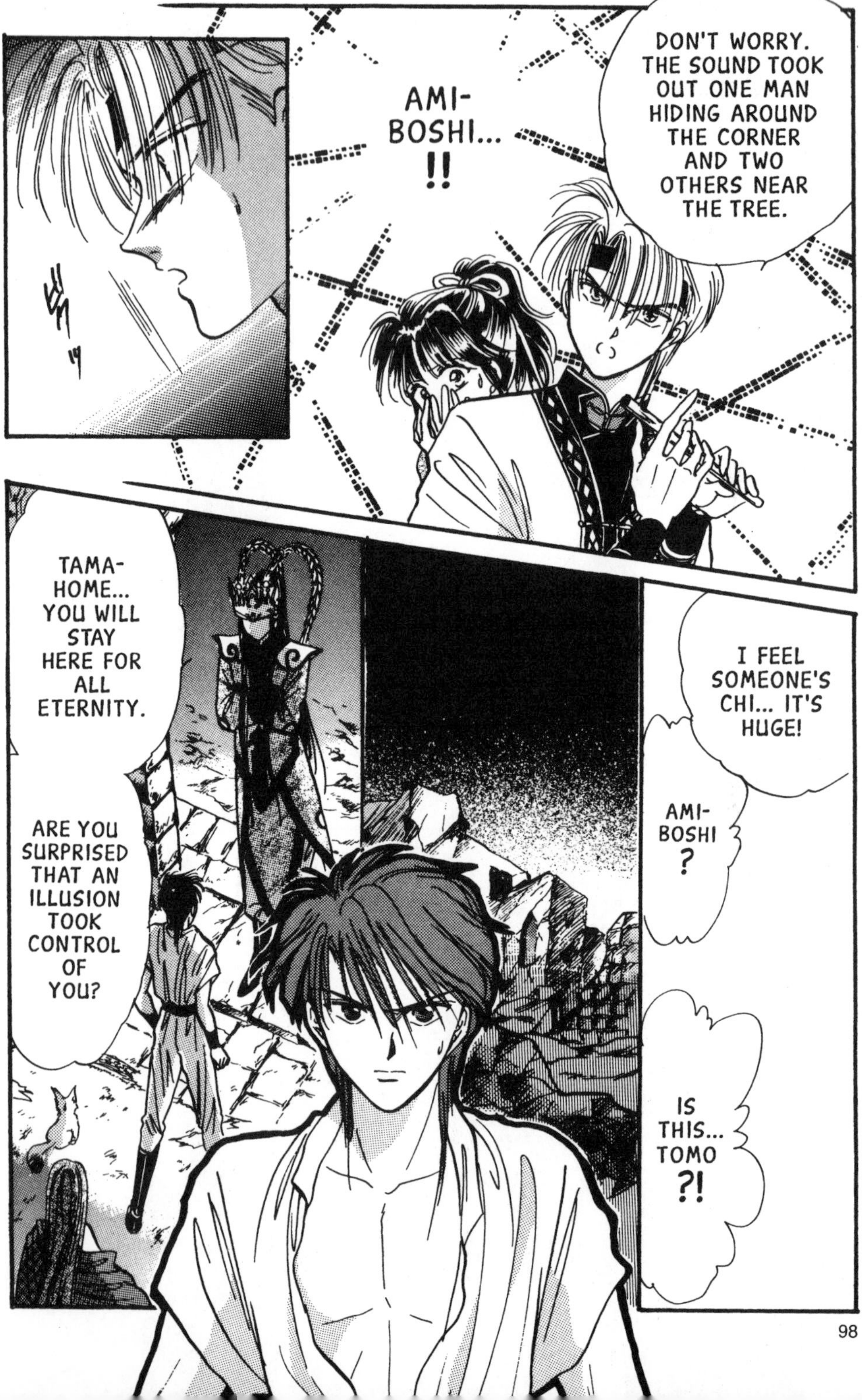
DON'T WORRY. THE SOUND TOOK OUT ONE MAN HIDING AROUND THE CORNER AND TWO OTHERS NEAR THE TREE.
AMI-BOSHI...!!
I FEEL SOMEONE'S CHI... IT'S HUGE!
AMI-BOSHI?
IS THIS... TOMO?!
TAMA-HOME... YOU WILL STAY HERE FOR ALL ETERNITY.
ARE YOU SURPRISED THAT AN ILLUSION TOOK CONTROL OF YOU?

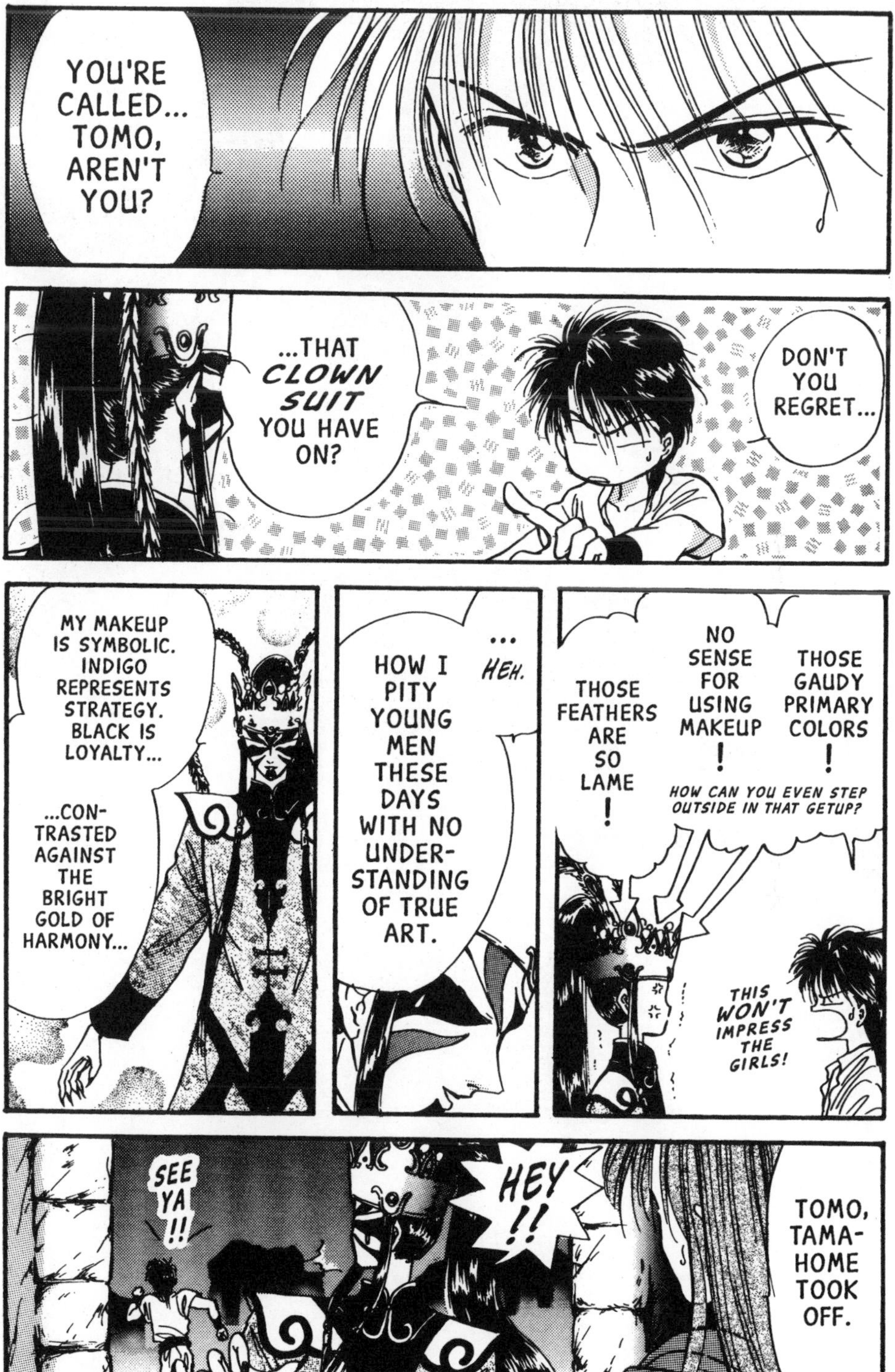
YOU'RE CALLED... TOMO, AREN'T YOU?
DON'T YOU REGRET...
...THAT CLOWN SUIT YOU HAVE ON?
THOSE GAUDY PRIMARY COLORS!
NO SENSE FOR USING MAKEUP!
THOSE FEATHERS ARE SO LAME!
HOW CAN YOU EVEN STEP OUTSIDE IN THAT GETUP?
THIS WON'T IMPRESS THE GIRLS!
...HEH.
HOW I PITY YOUNG MEN THESE DAYS WITH NO UNDERSTANDING OF TRUE ART.
MY MAKEUP IS SYMBOLIC. INDIGO REPRESENTS STRATEGY. BLACK IS LOYALTY...
...CONTRASTED AGAINST THE BRIGHT GOLD OF HARMONY...
TOMO, TAMAHOME TOOK OFF.
HEY!!
SEE YA!!

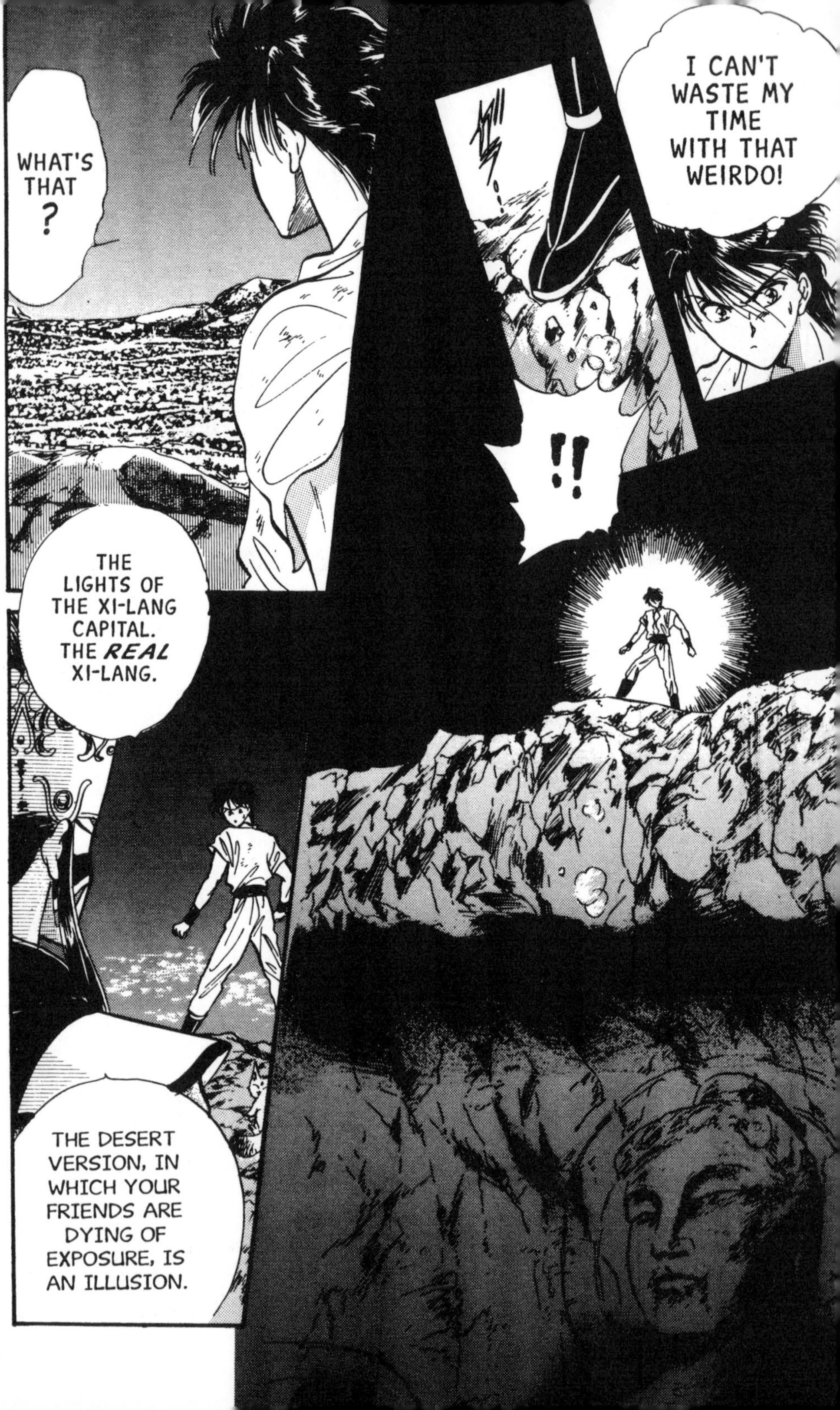
I CAN'T WASTE MY TIME WITH THAT WEIRDO!
!!
WHAT'S THAT?
THE LIGHTS OF THE XI-LANG CAPITAL. THE *REAL* XI-LANG.
THE DESERT VERSION, IN WHICH YOUR FRIENDS ARE DYING OF EXPOSURE, IS AN ILLUSION.

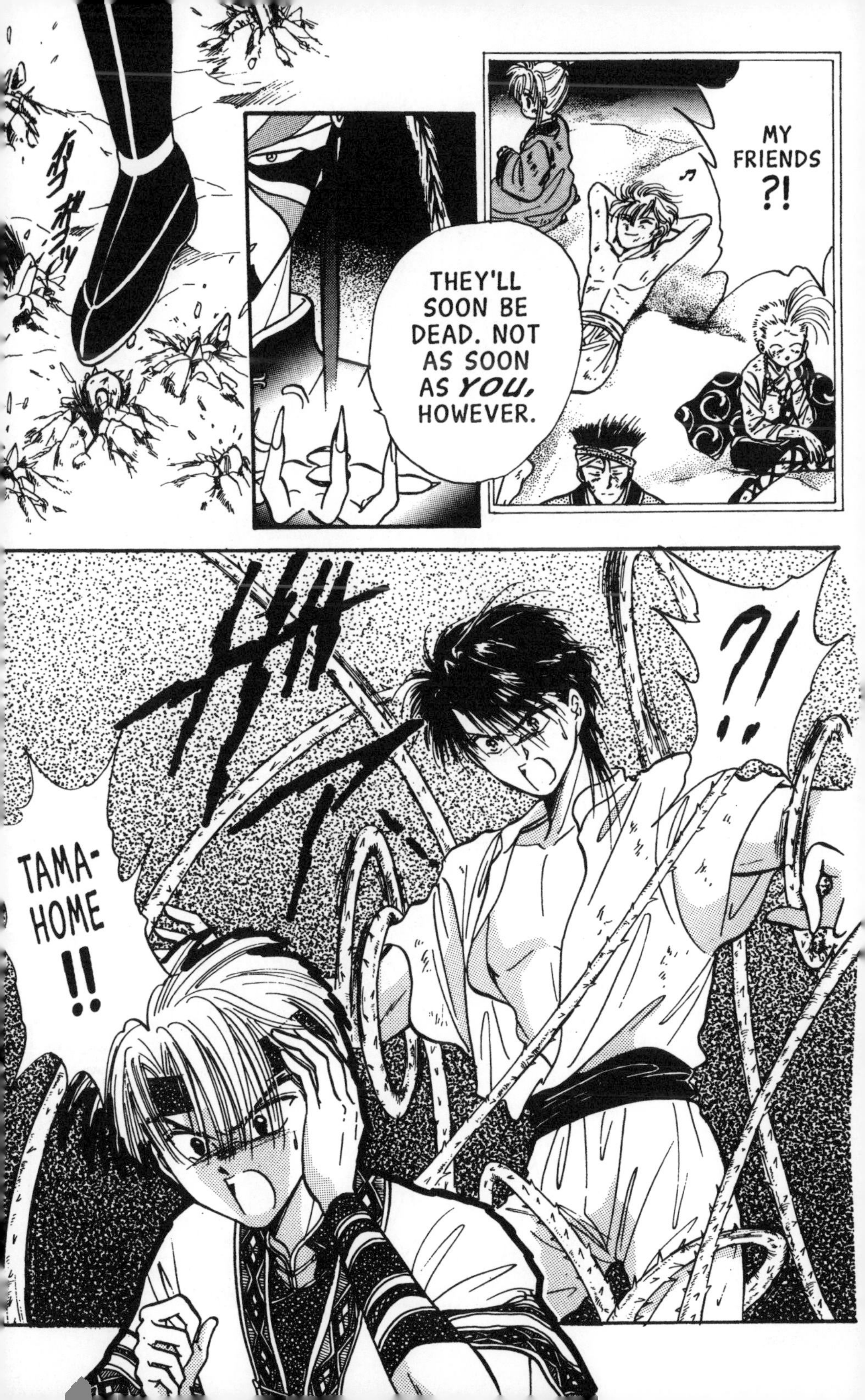
MY FRIENDS ?!
THEY'LL SOON BE DEAD. NOT AS SOON AS *YOU,* HOWEVER.
?!
TAMA-HOME !!

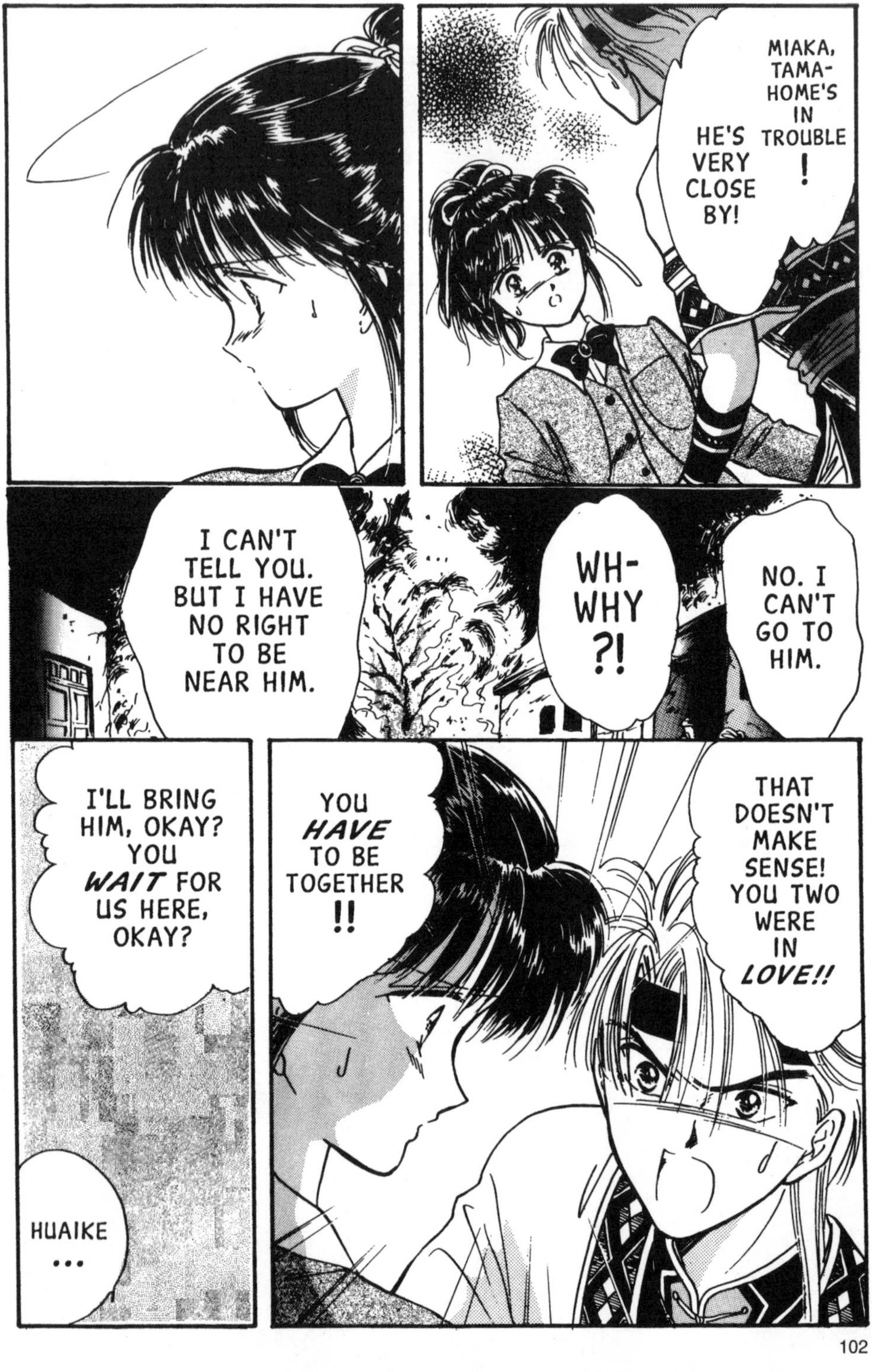
MIAKA, TAMA-HOME'S IN TROUBLE!
HE'S VERY CLOSE BY!
NO. I CAN'T GO TO HIM.
WH-WHY?!
I CAN'T TELL YOU. BUT I HAVE NO RIGHT TO BE NEAR HIM.
THAT DOESN'T MAKE SENSE! YOU TWO WERE IN *LOVE!!*
YOU *HAVE* TO BE TOGETHER!!
I'LL BRING HIM, OKAY? YOU *WAIT* FOR US HERE, OKAY?
HUAIKE...

Here are the details. First, Tamahome. When I found out the meaning for his kanji was "man with courage," I stopped short! I started looking up the other characters and burst out laughing.

"Nuriko" = graceful beauty
"Hotohori" = a highly ranked person
"Tasuki" = help, assistance, protection

Then, "Chichiri" means hometown. "Chiriko" means to widen and spread. "Mitsukake" means to suffer. As for the Seiryu warriors—*Are you even interested?*—I hadn't checked them before, so I'll look them up now! *Watase pulls out her kanji character dictionary.*

"Su" of "Suboshi" = to compete, fight. *Wow!*
"Ami" of "Amiboshi" = go far, cut off
"Soi" = to draw near, to be wed
"Tomo" = despicable... Ha ha!
"Ashitare" = back, the end
"Mi" of "Miboshi" = trash collecting, and...

What the--? Now this is a shock for me!! "...sitting cross-legged"?! Those who've been reading FY serialized in the magazine must know how Miboshi has always remained in that sitting position the whole time!! Geez!!

"Nakago" = prudence (strategy, maybe?), center, considerate... hmm. There are a lot of other meanings, but I highlighted the ones that match him.

Oh yeah, my assistant did a reading of Tamahome's name and found that it signified "poverty, looks after others, loses family, gentle in appearance but strong inside" (wait, isn't it the other way around?) That really took me by surprise.

You might think I'm lying, but this was all a coincidence. Really! I find it a little frightening myself.

The world can work in mysterious ways...!!

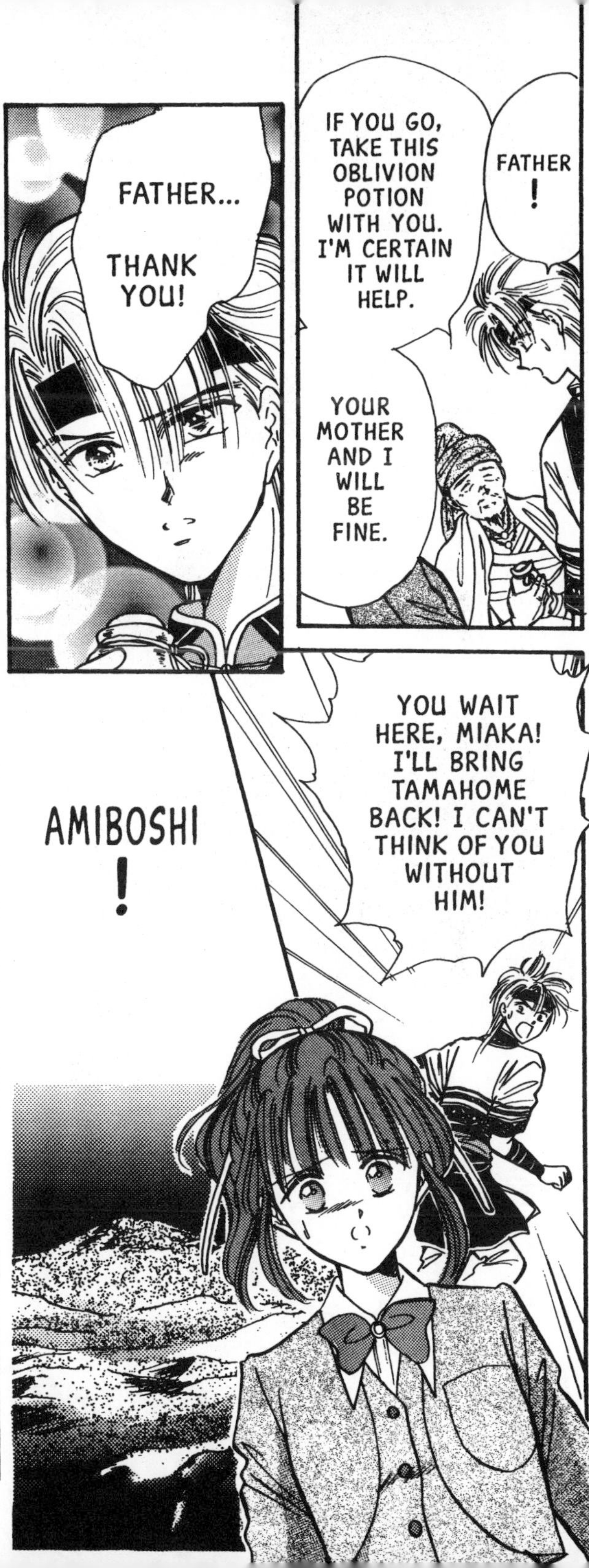
FATHER!
IF YOU GO, TAKE THIS OBLIVION POTION WITH YOU. I'M CERTAIN IT WILL HELP.
YOUR MOTHER AND I WILL BE FINE.
FATHER... THANK YOU!
YOU WAIT HERE, MIAKA! I'LL BRING TAMAHOME BACK! I CAN'T THINK OF YOU WITHOUT HIM!
AMIBOSHI!

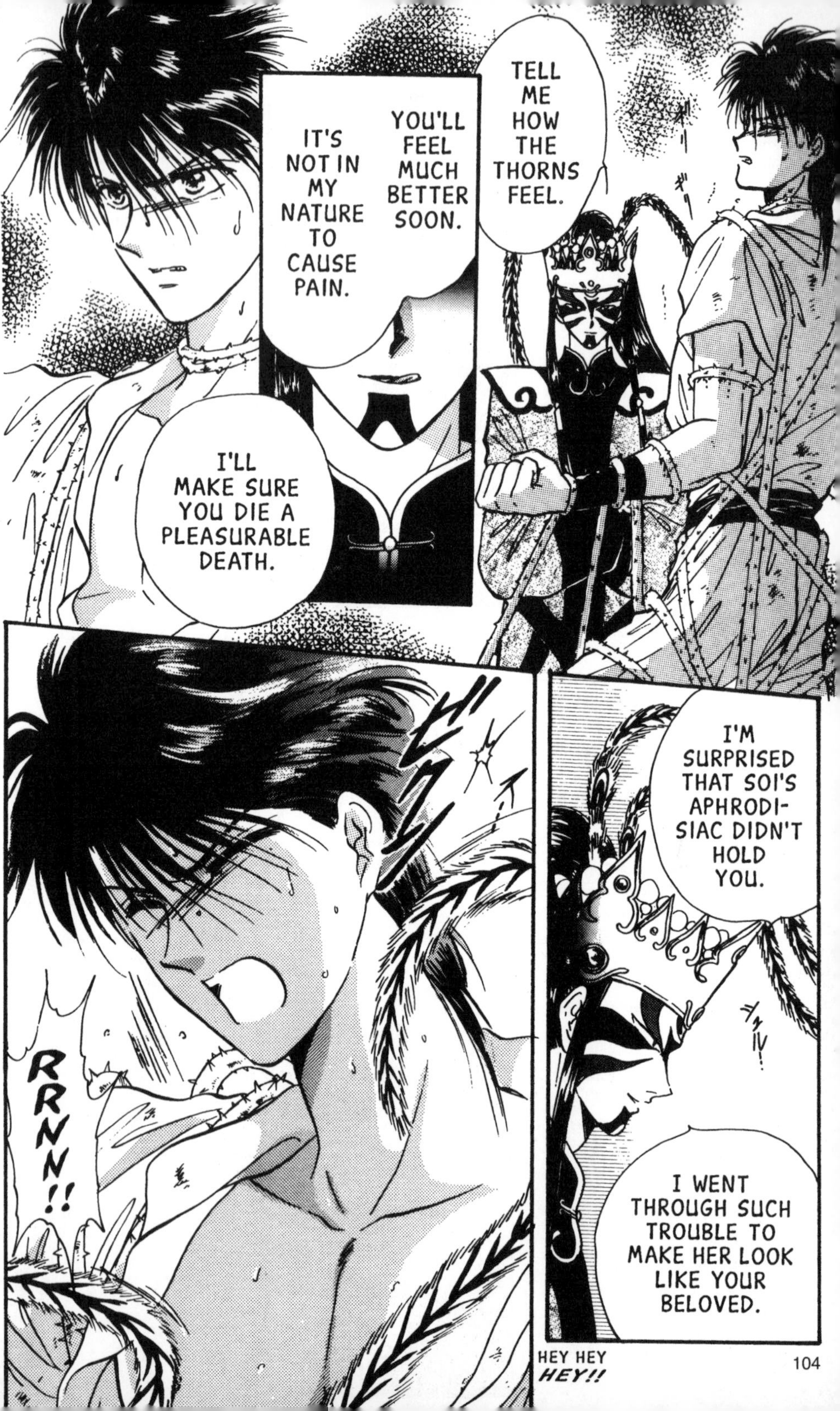
TELL ME HOW THE THORNS FEEL.
YOU'LL FEEL MUCH BETTER SOON.
IT'S NOT IN MY NATURE TO CAUSE PAIN.
I'LL MAKE SURE YOU DIE A PLEASURABLE DEATH.
I'M SURPRISED THAT SOI'S APHRODISIAC DIDN'T HOLD YOU.
I WENT THROUGH SUCH TROUBLE TO MAKE HER LOOK LIKE YOUR BELOVED.
RRNN!!
HEY HEY HEY!!

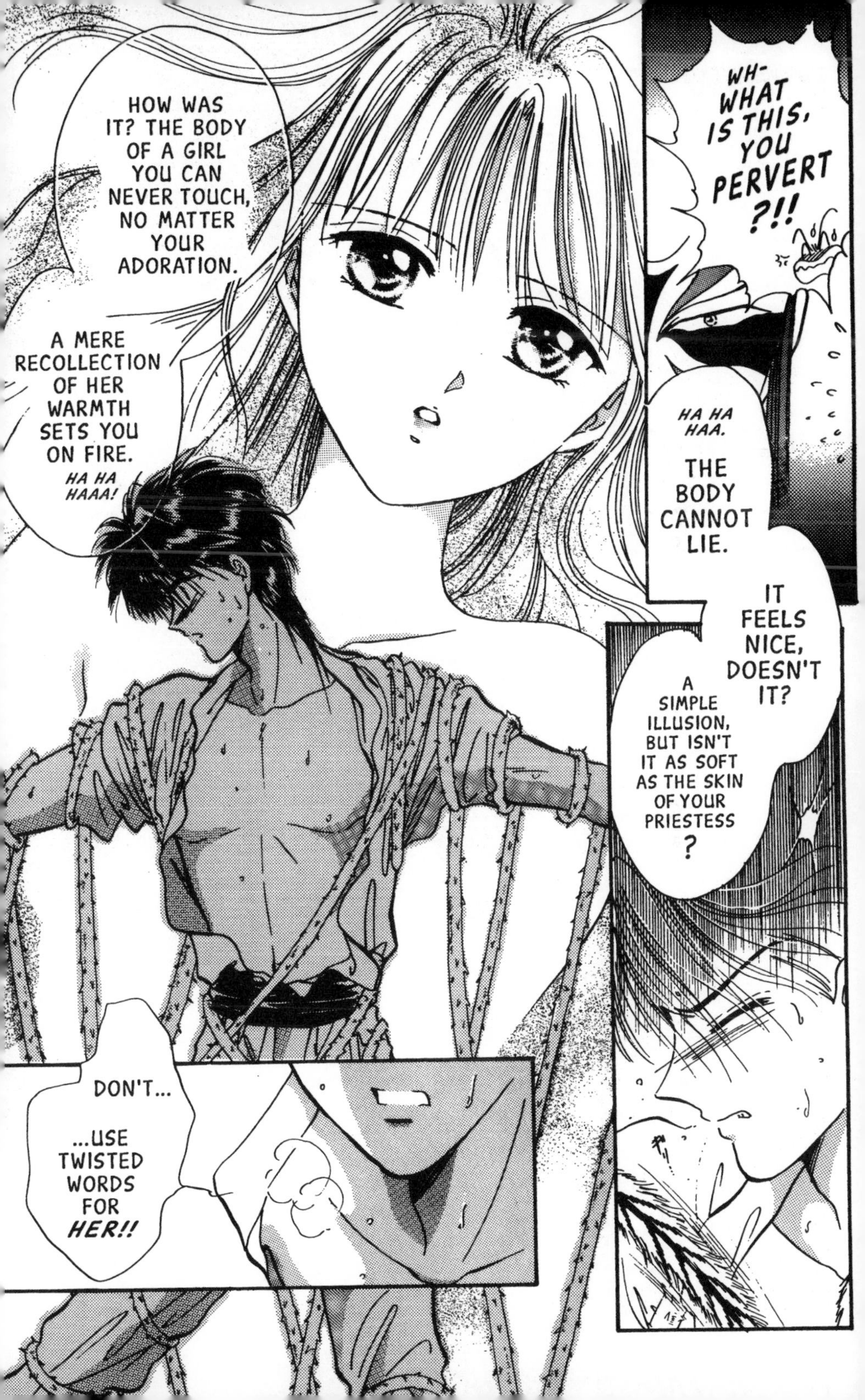
WH-WHAT IS THIS, YOU PERVERT?!!
HA HA HAA.
THE BODY CANNOT LIE.
IT FEELS NICE, DOESN'T IT?
A SIMPLE ILLUSION, BUT ISN'T IT AS SOFT AS THE SKIN OF YOUR PRIESTESS?
HOW WAS IT? THE BODY OF A GIRL YOU CAN NEVER TOUCH, NO MATTER YOUR ADORATION.
A MERE RECOLLECTION OF HER WARMTH SETS YOU ON FIRE.
HA HA HAAA!
DON'T...
...USE TWISTED WORDS FOR HER!!

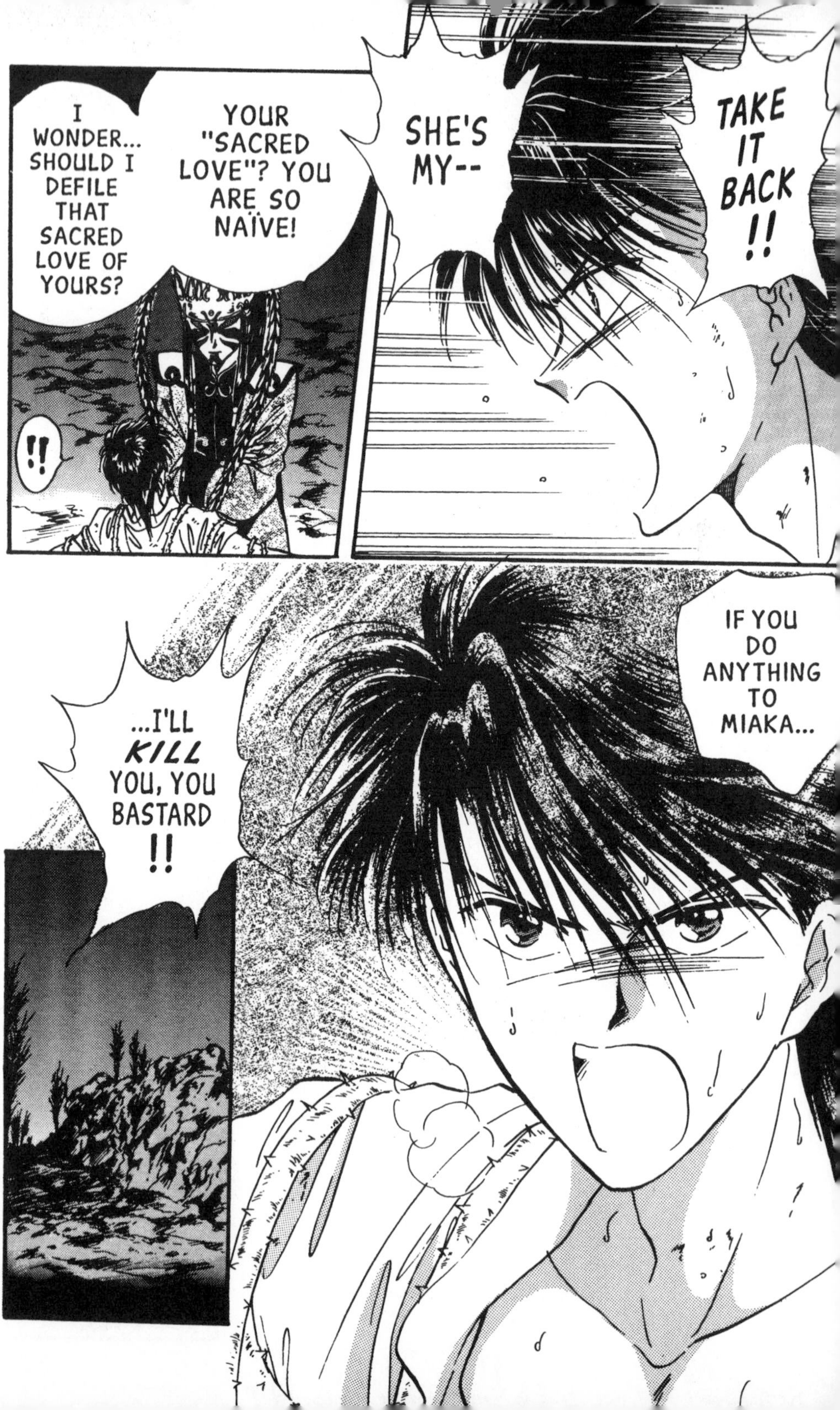
TAKE IT BACK!!
SHE'S MY--
YOUR "SACRED LOVE"? YOU ARE SO NAÏVE!
I WONDER... SHOULD I DEFILE THAT SACRED LOVE OF YOURS?
!!
IF YOU DO ANYTHING TO MIAKA...
...I'LL *KILL* YOU, YOU BASTARD!!

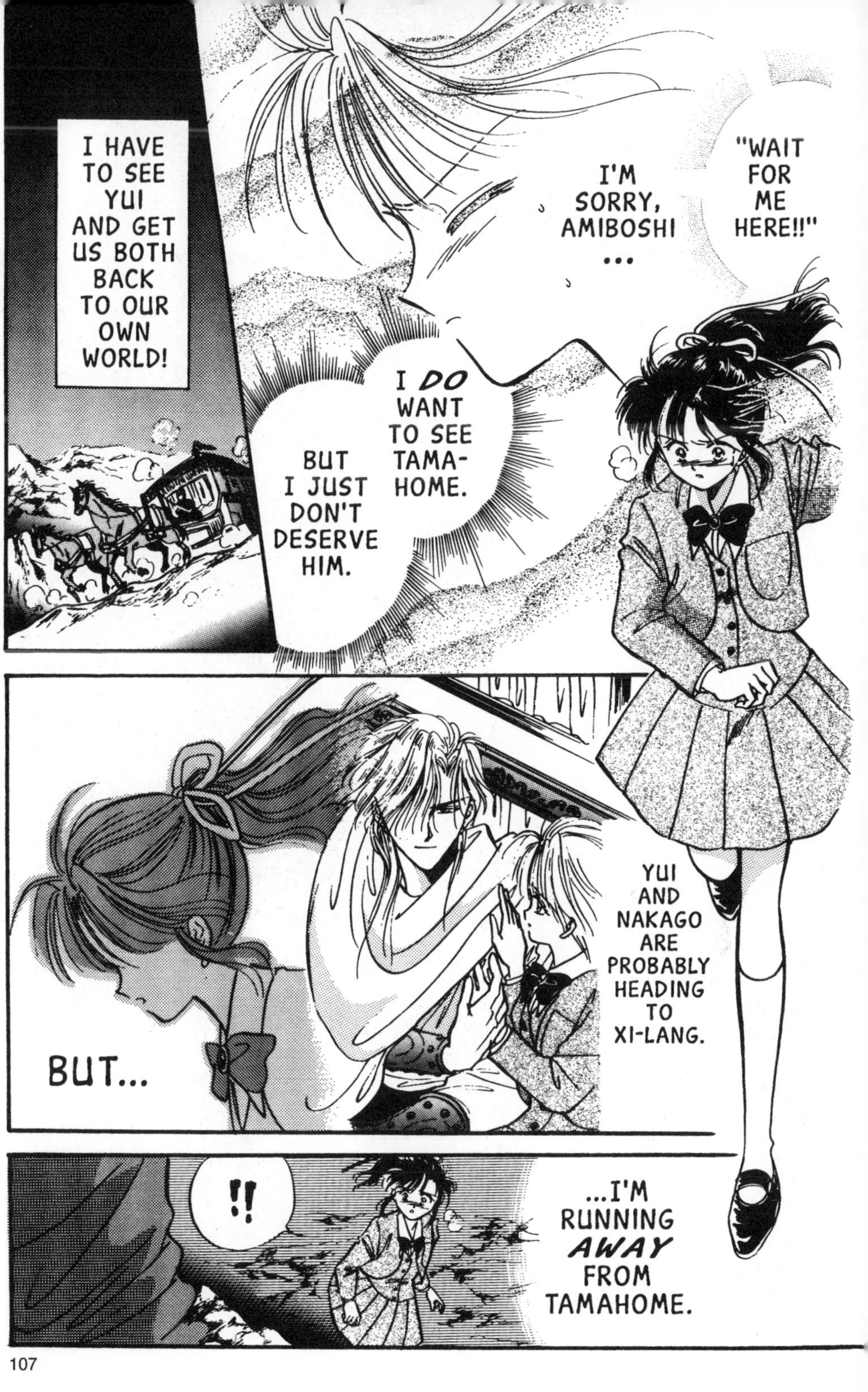
"WAIT FOR ME HERE!!"
I'M SORRY, AMIBOSHI...
I *DO* WANT TO SEE TAMAHOME.
BUT I JUST DON'T DESERVE HIM.
I HAVE TO SEE YUI AND GET US BOTH BACK TO OUR OWN WORLD!
YUI AND NAKAGO ARE PROBABLY HEADING TO XI-LANG.
BUT...
...I'M RUNNING *AWAY* FROM TAMAHOME.
!!

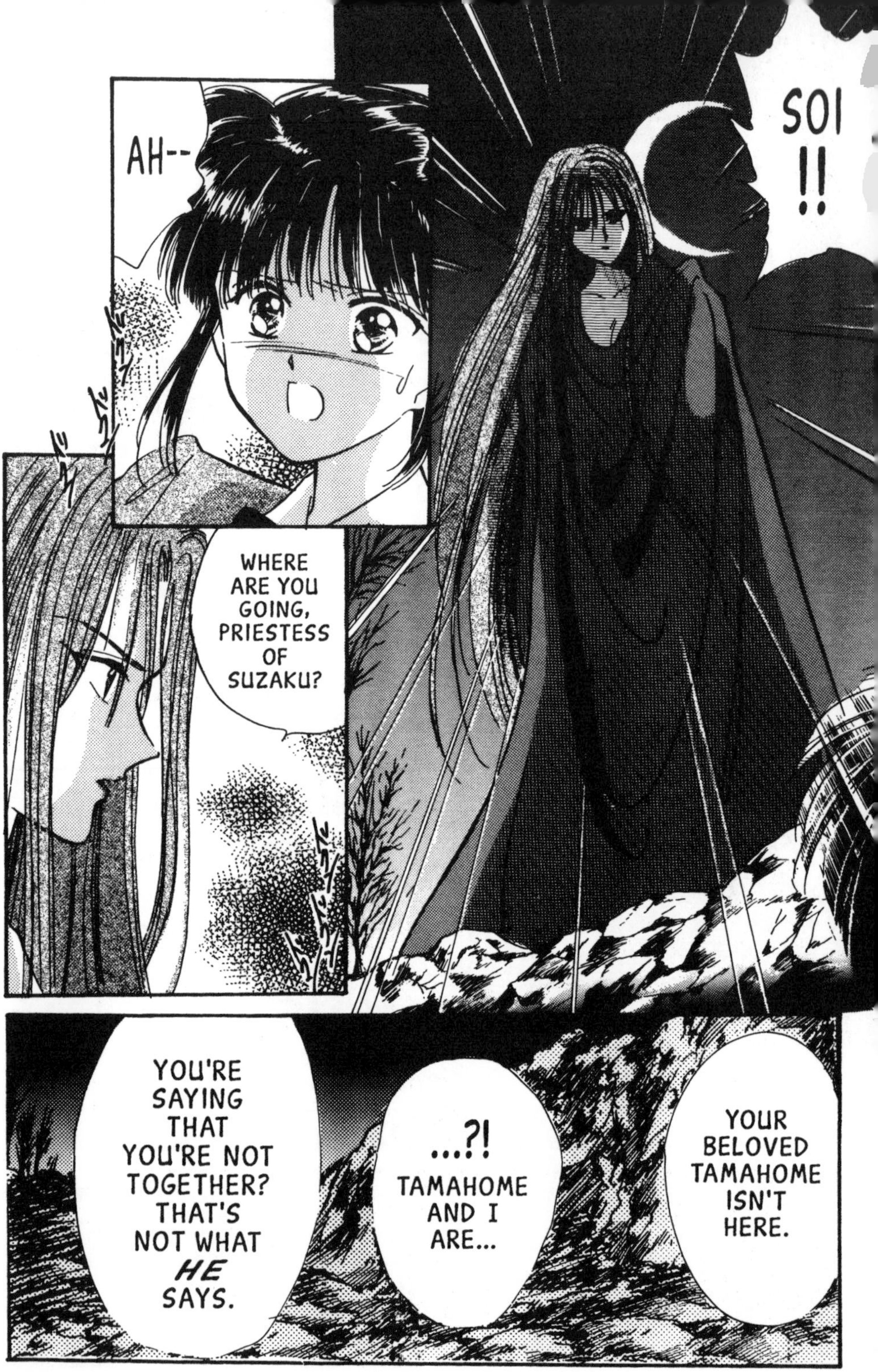
SOI!!
AH--
WHERE ARE YOU GOING, PRIESTESS OF SUZAKU?
YOUR BELOVED TAMAHOME ISN'T HERE.
...?! TAMAHOME AND I ARE...
YOU'RE SAYING THAT YOU'RE NOT TOGETHER? THAT'S NOT WHAT *HE* SAYS.

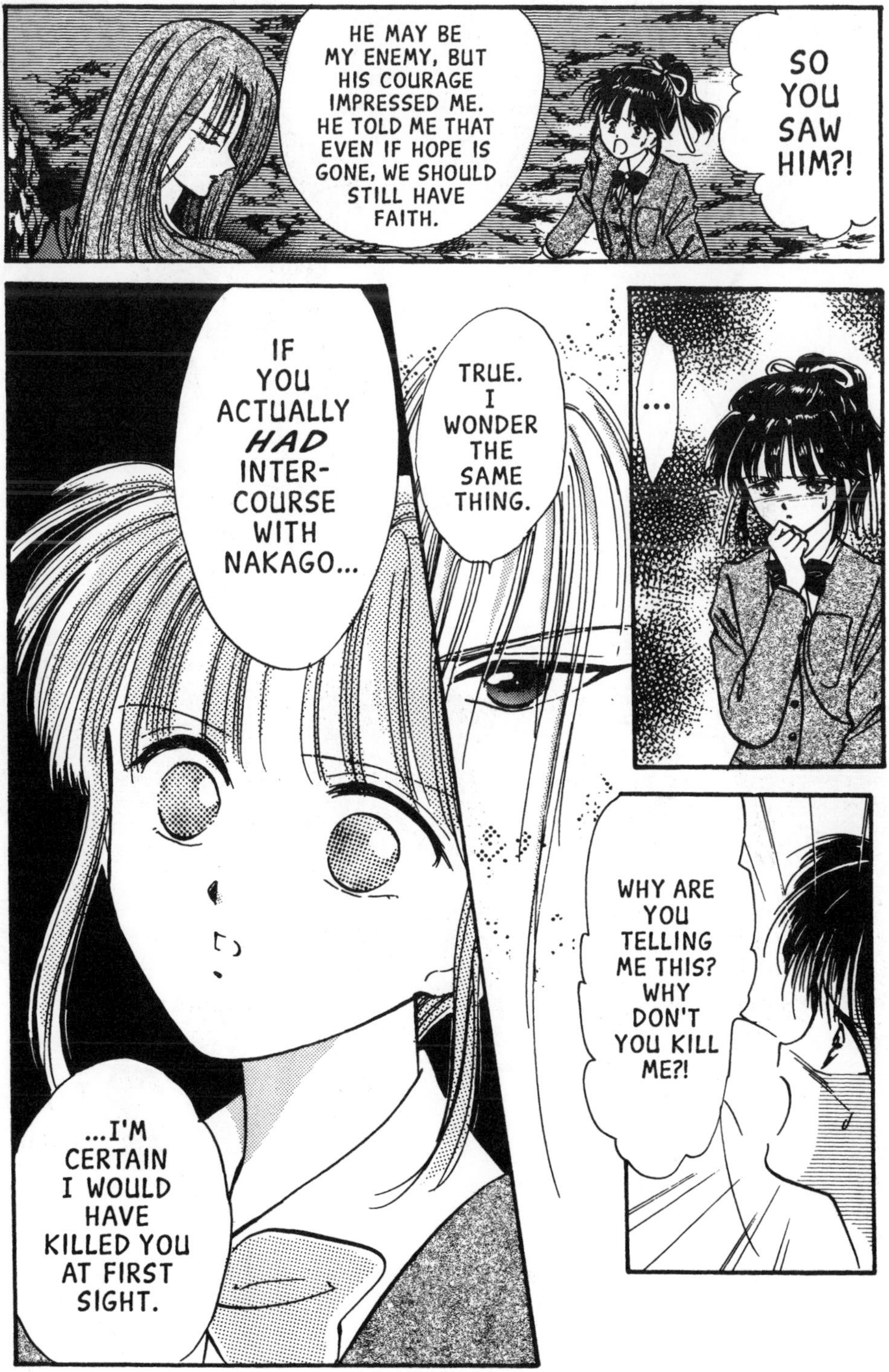
SO YOU SAW HIM?!
HE MAY BE MY ENEMY, BUT HIS COURAGE IMPRESSED ME. HE TOLD ME THAT EVEN IF HOPE IS GONE, WE SHOULD STILL HAVE FAITH.
...
WHY ARE YOU TELLING ME THIS? WHY DON'T YOU KILL ME?!
TRUE. I WONDER THE SAME THING.
IF YOU ACTUALLY *HAD* INTER-COURSE WITH NAKAGO...
...I'M CERTAIN I WOULD HAVE KILLED YOU AT FIRST SIGHT.

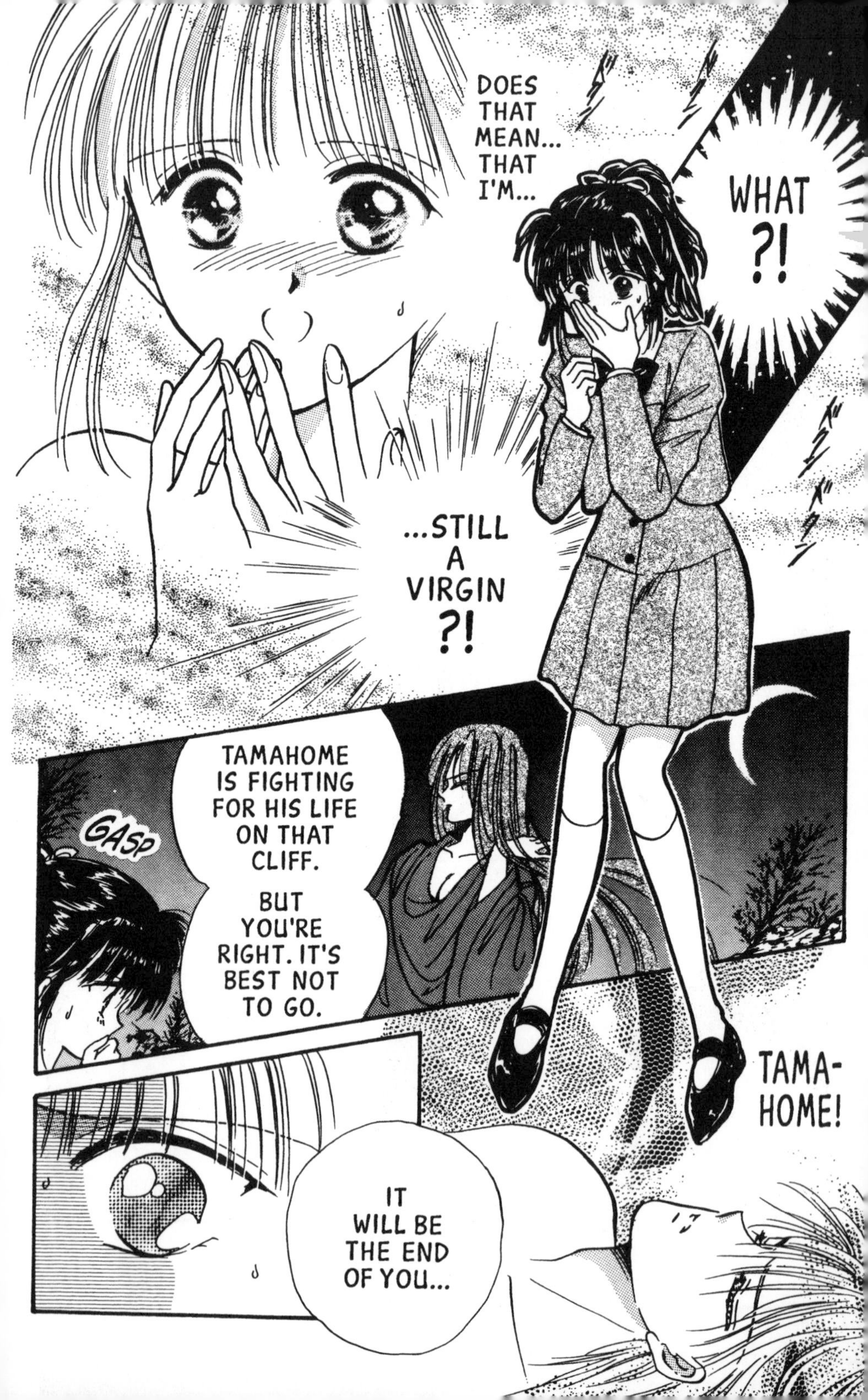
WHAT ?!
DOES THAT MEAN... THAT I'M...
...STILL A VIRGIN ?!
TAMAHOME IS FIGHTING FOR HIS LIFE ON THAT CLIFF.
BUT YOU'RE RIGHT. IT'S BEST NOT TO GO.
GASP
TAMA-HOME!
IT WILL BE THE END OF YOU...

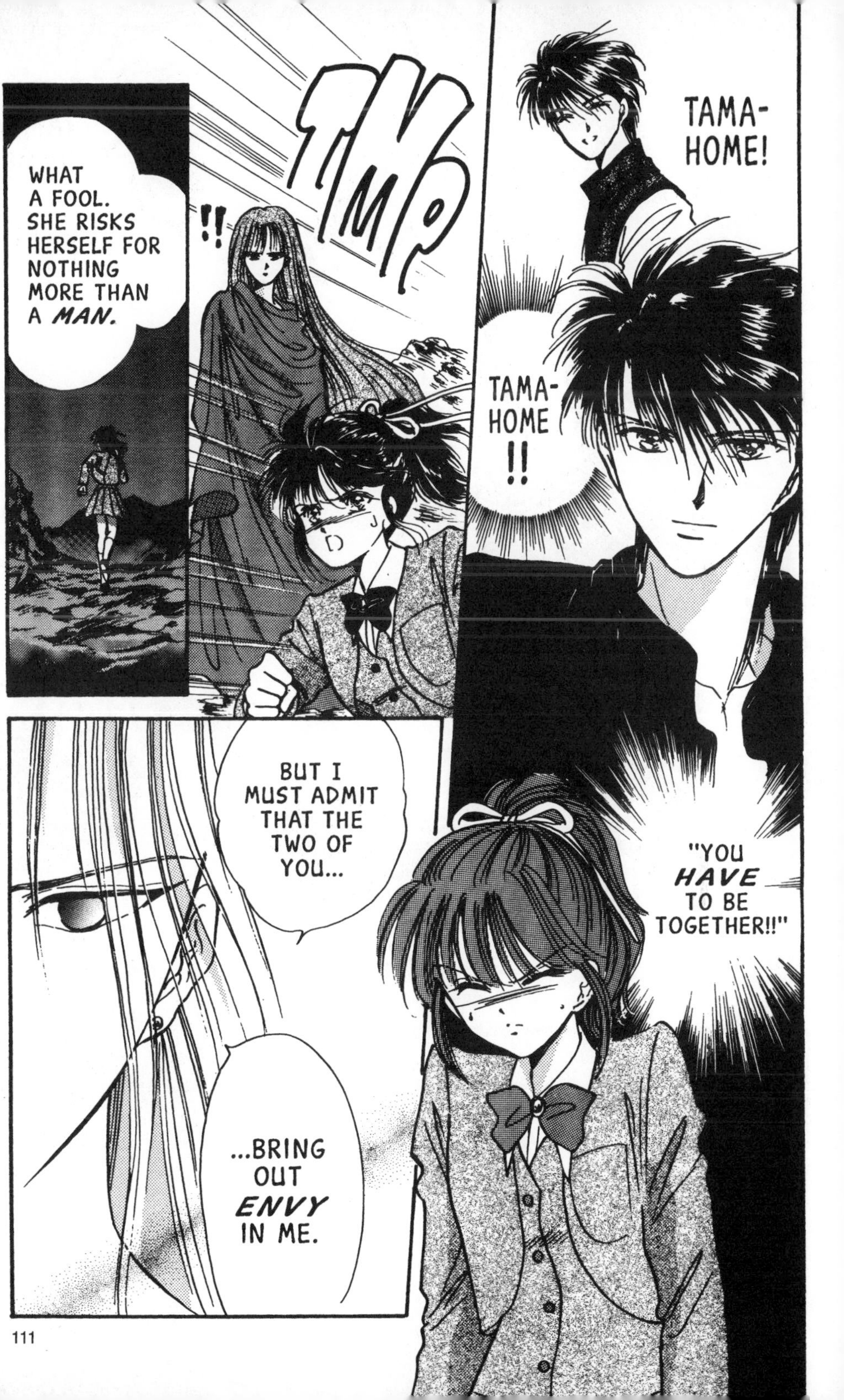
TAMA-HOME!
TAMA-HOME!!
TMP
!!
WHAT A FOOL. SHE RISKS HERSELF FOR NOTHING MORE THAN A *MAN.*
"YOU *HAVE* TO BE TOGETHER!!"
BUT I MUST ADMIT THAT THE TWO OF YOU...
...BRING OUT *ENVY* IN ME.

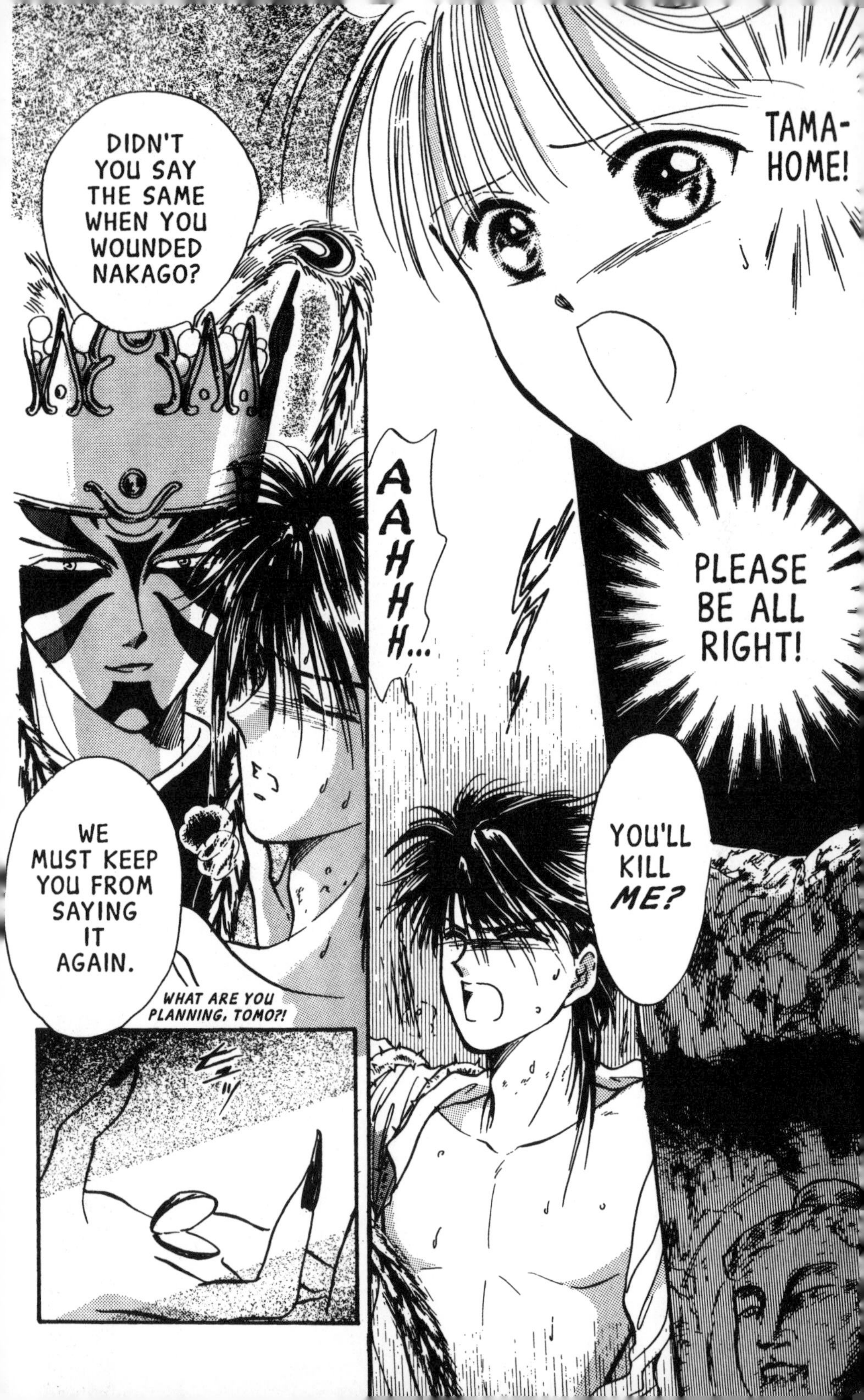
TAMA-HOME!
PLEASE BE ALL RIGHT!
AAHHHH...
YOU'LL KILL *ME?*
DIDN'T YOU SAY THE SAME WHEN YOU WOUNDED NAKAGO?
WE MUST KEEP YOU FROM SAYING IT AGAIN.
WHAT ARE YOU PLANNING, TOMO?!

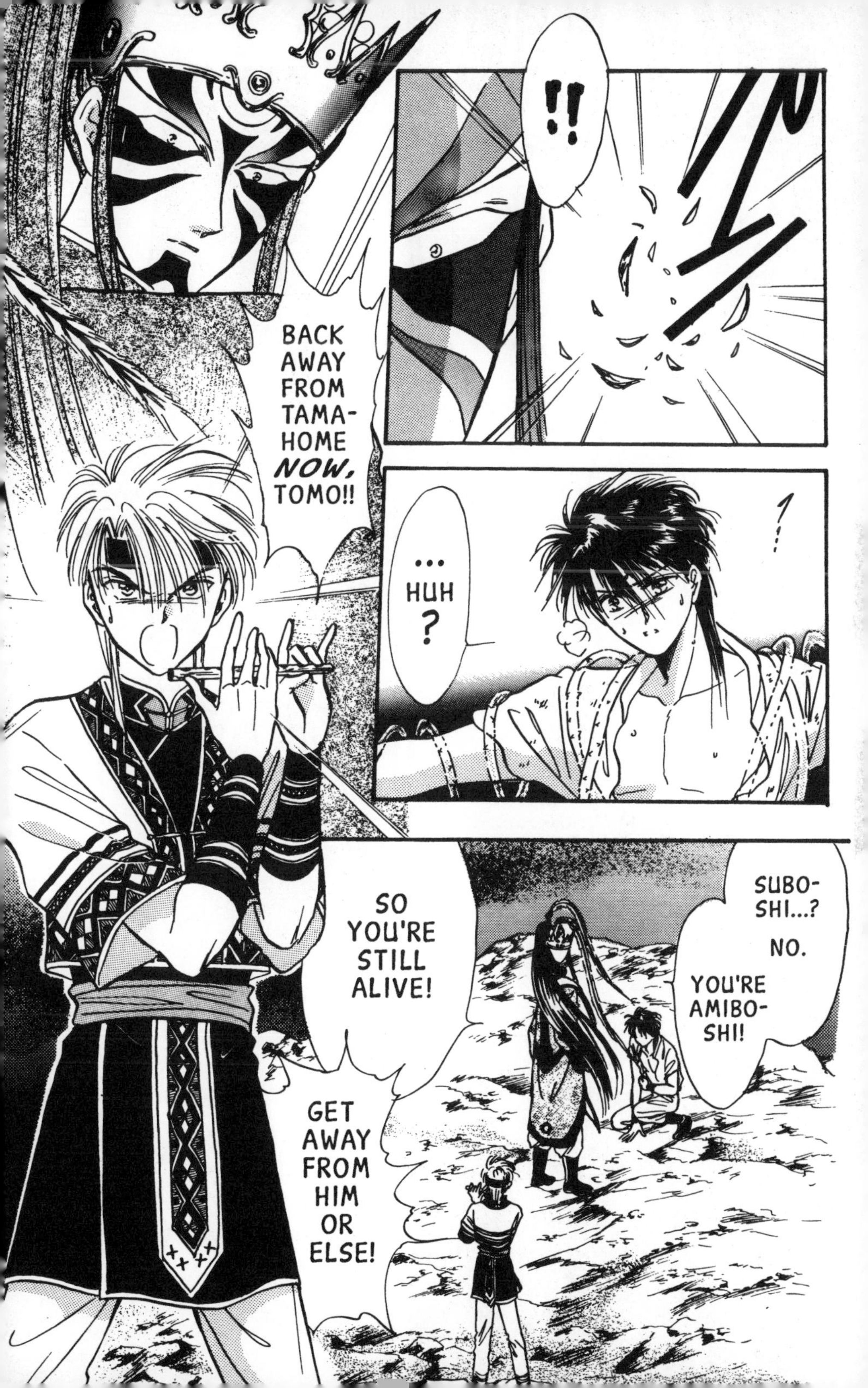
BACK AWAY FROM TAMAHOME *NOW,* TOMO!!
!!
...HUH?
SUBO-SHI...? NO. YOU'RE AMIBO-SHI!
SO YOU'RE STILL ALIVE!
GET AWAY FROM HIM OR ELSE!

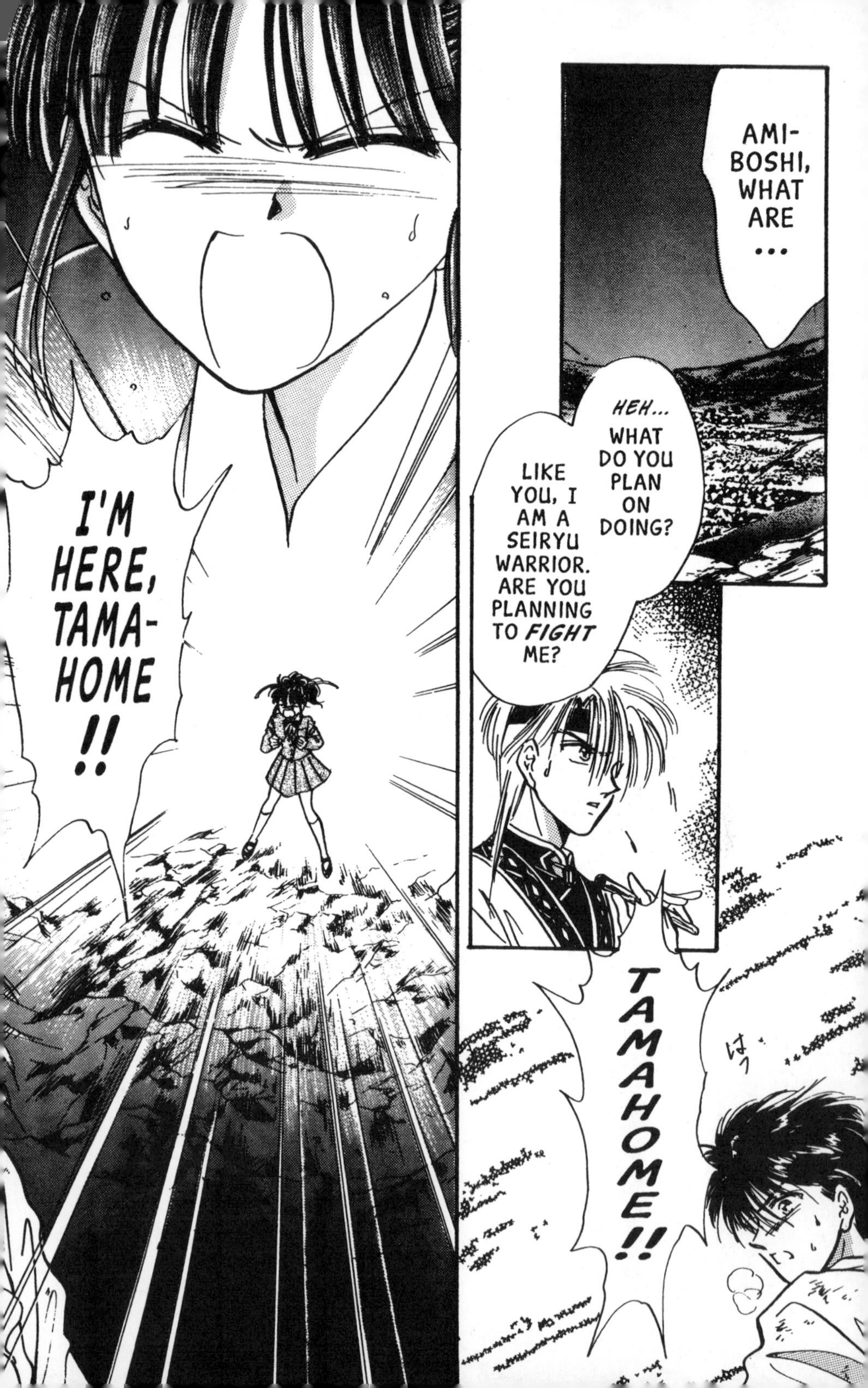
AMI-BOSHI, WHAT ARE...
HEH... WHAT DO YOU PLAN ON DOING?
LIKE YOU, I AM A SEIRYU WARRIOR. ARE YOU PLANNING TO FIGHT ME?
TAMAHOME!!
はっ
I'M HERE, TAMA-HOME!!

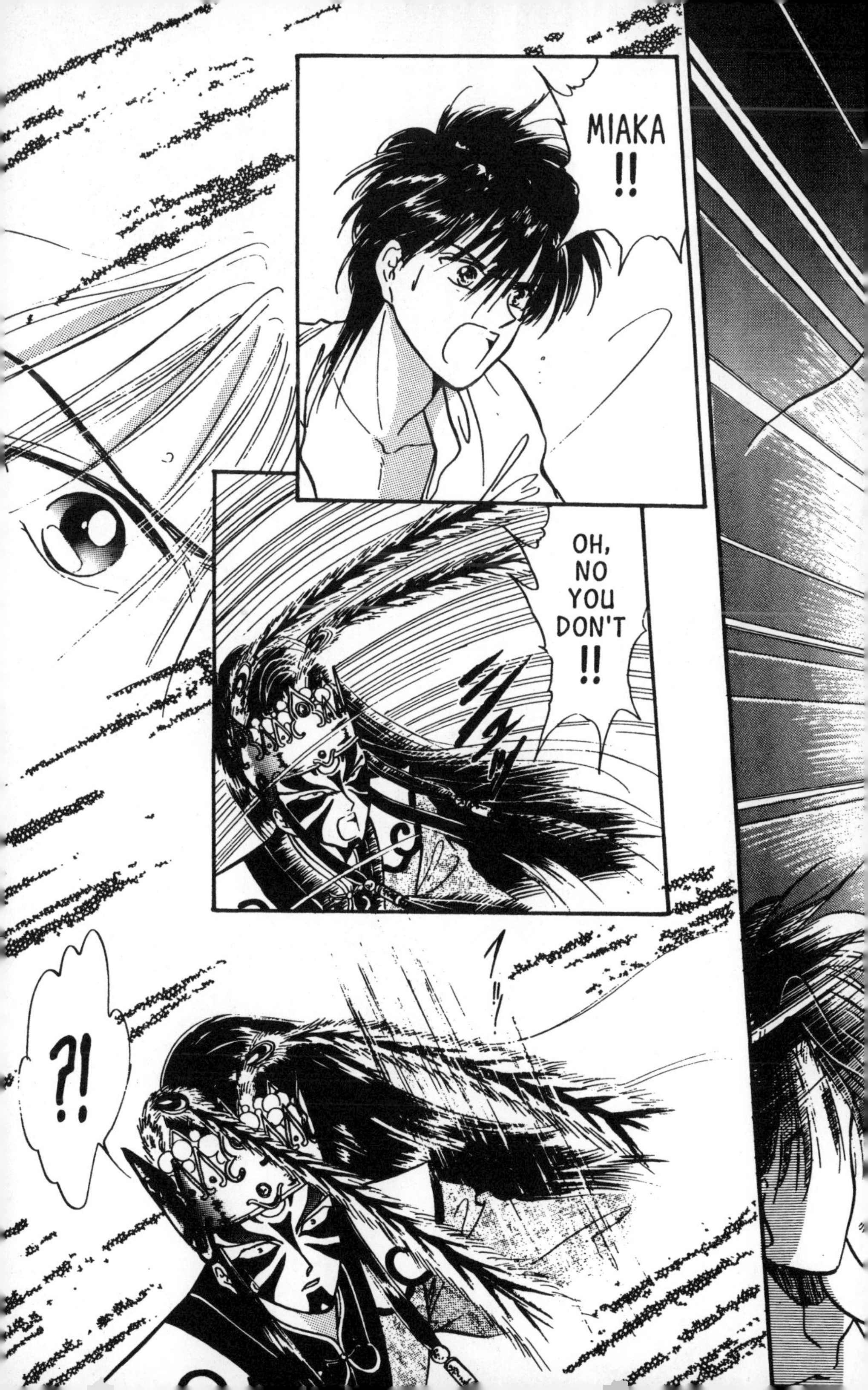
MIAKA !!
OH, NO YOU DON'T !!
?!

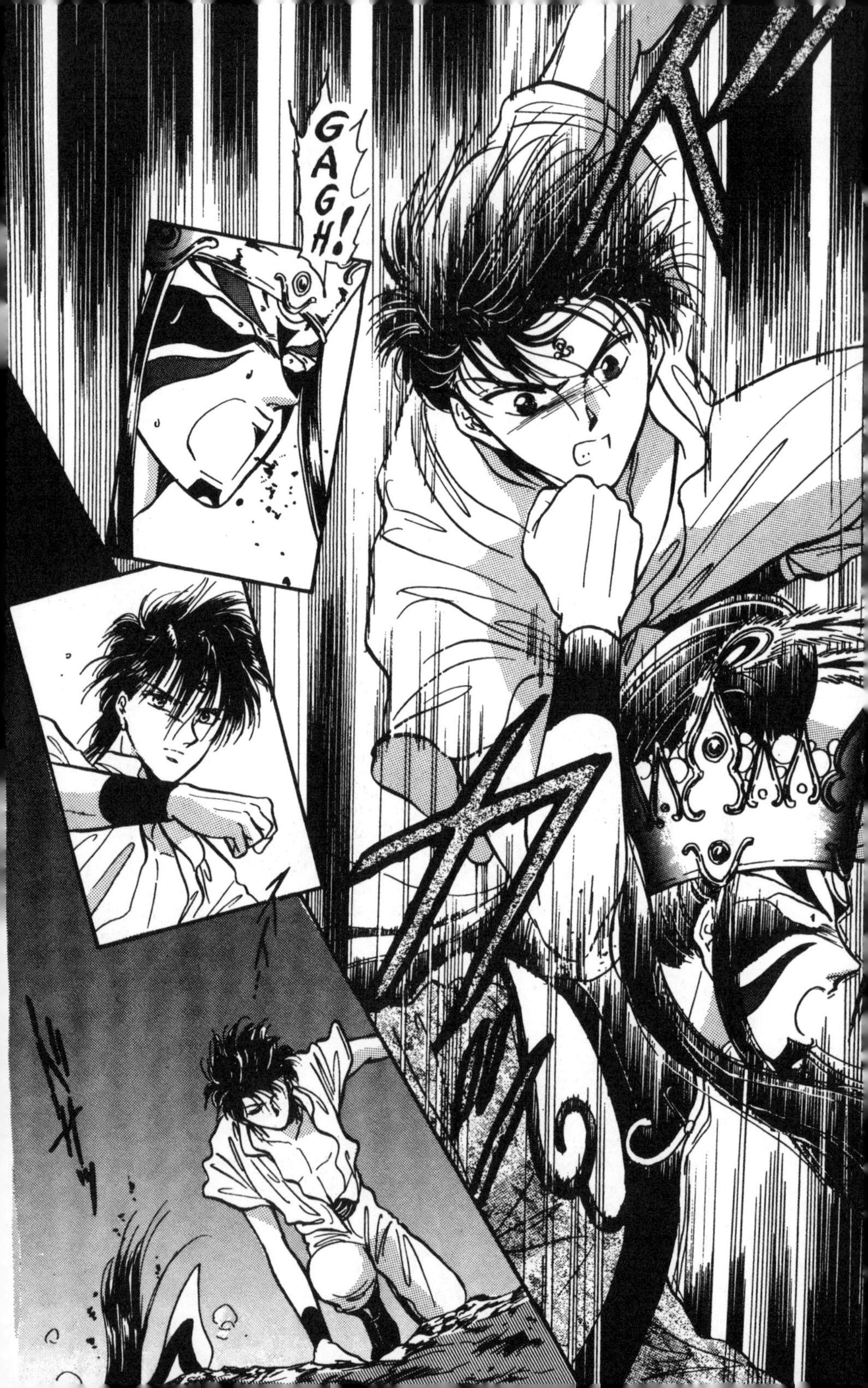
GAGH!

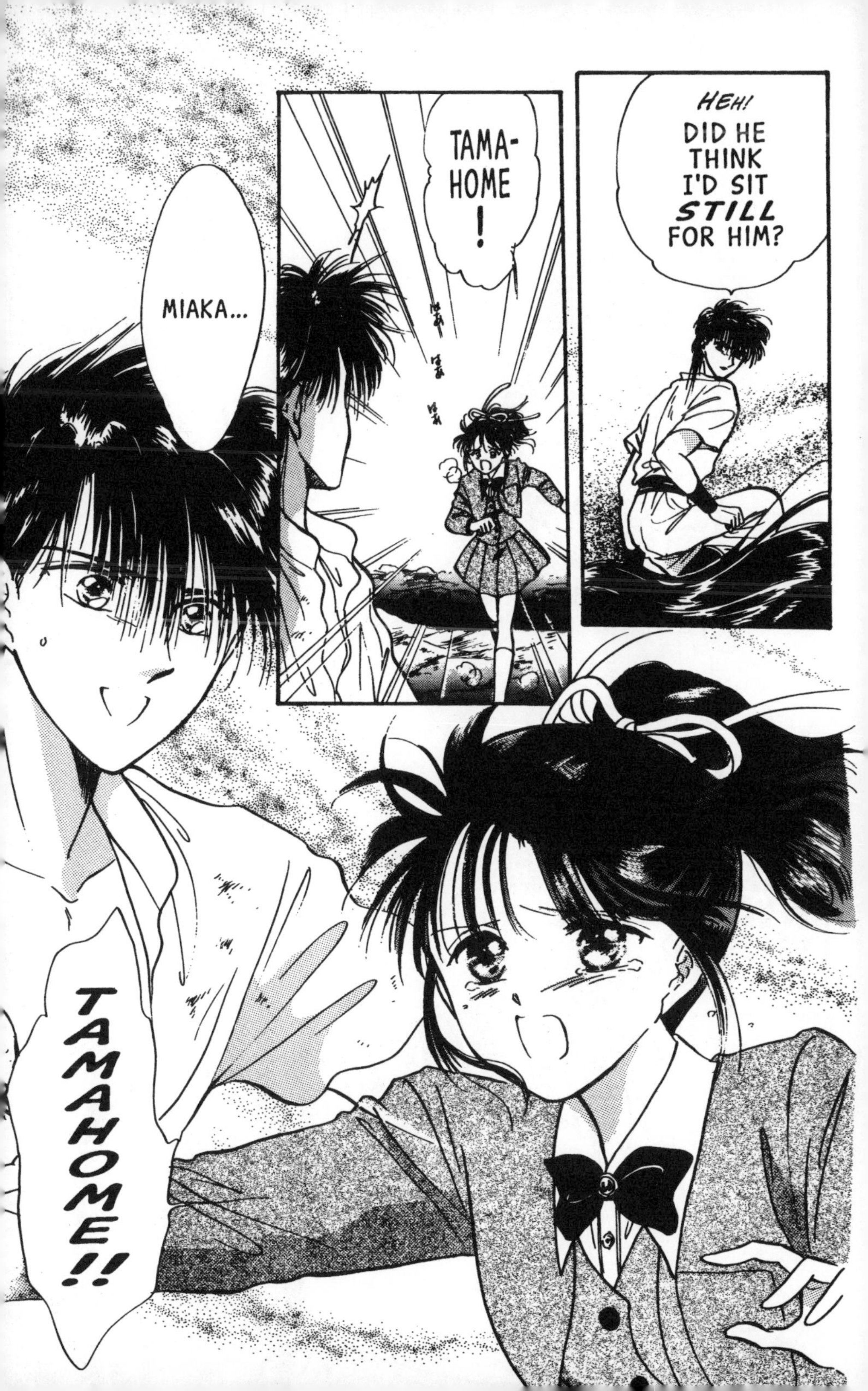
HEH! DID HE THINK I'D SIT STILL FOR HIM?
TAMA-HOME!
MIAKA...
TAMAHOME!!

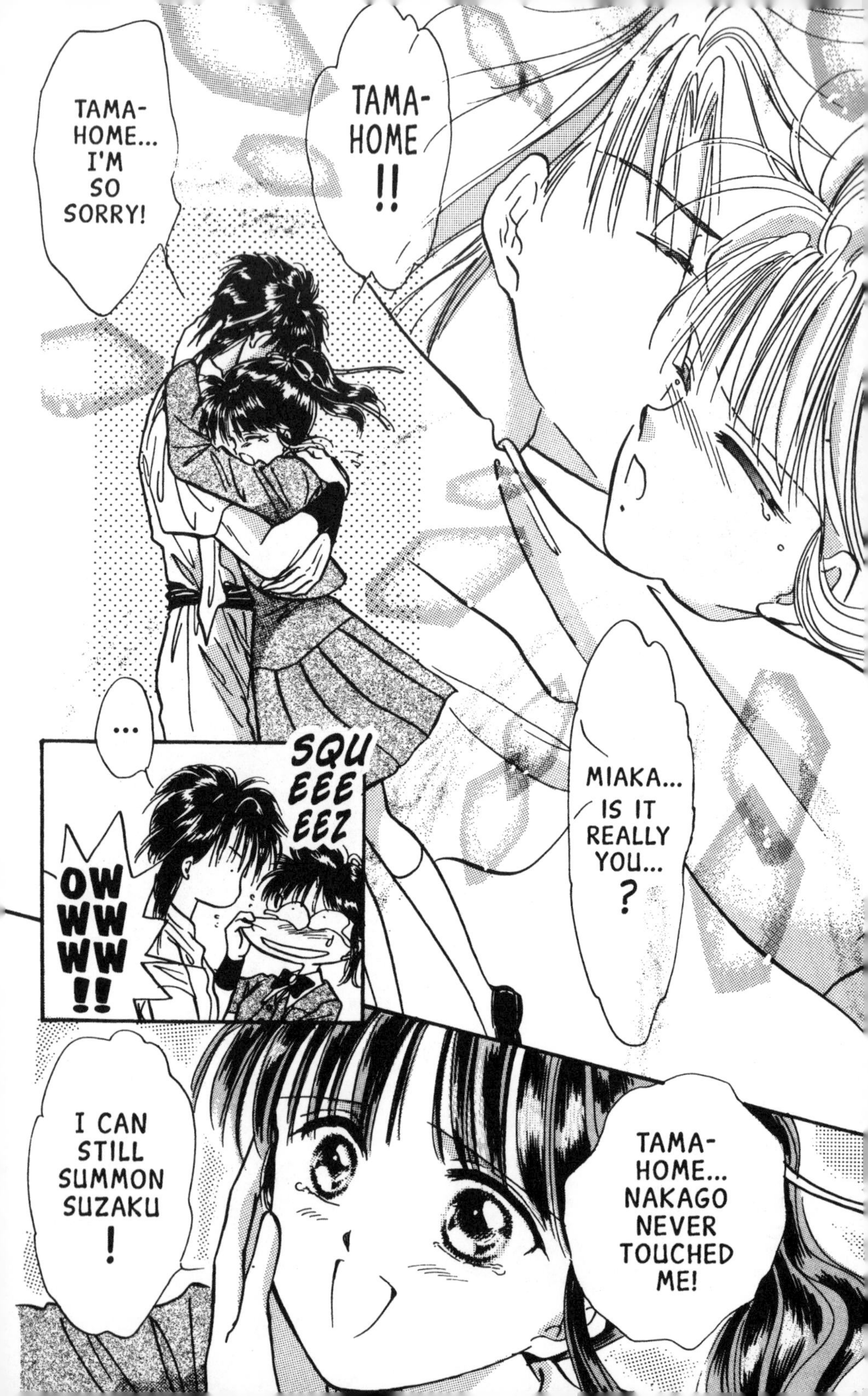
TAMA-HOME!!
TAMA-HOME... I'M SO SORRY!
MIAKA... IS IT REALLY YOU...?
...
SQUEEEEEZ
OWWWWWW!!
TAMA-HOME... NAKAGO NEVER TOUCHED ME!
I CAN STILL SUMMON SUZAKU!

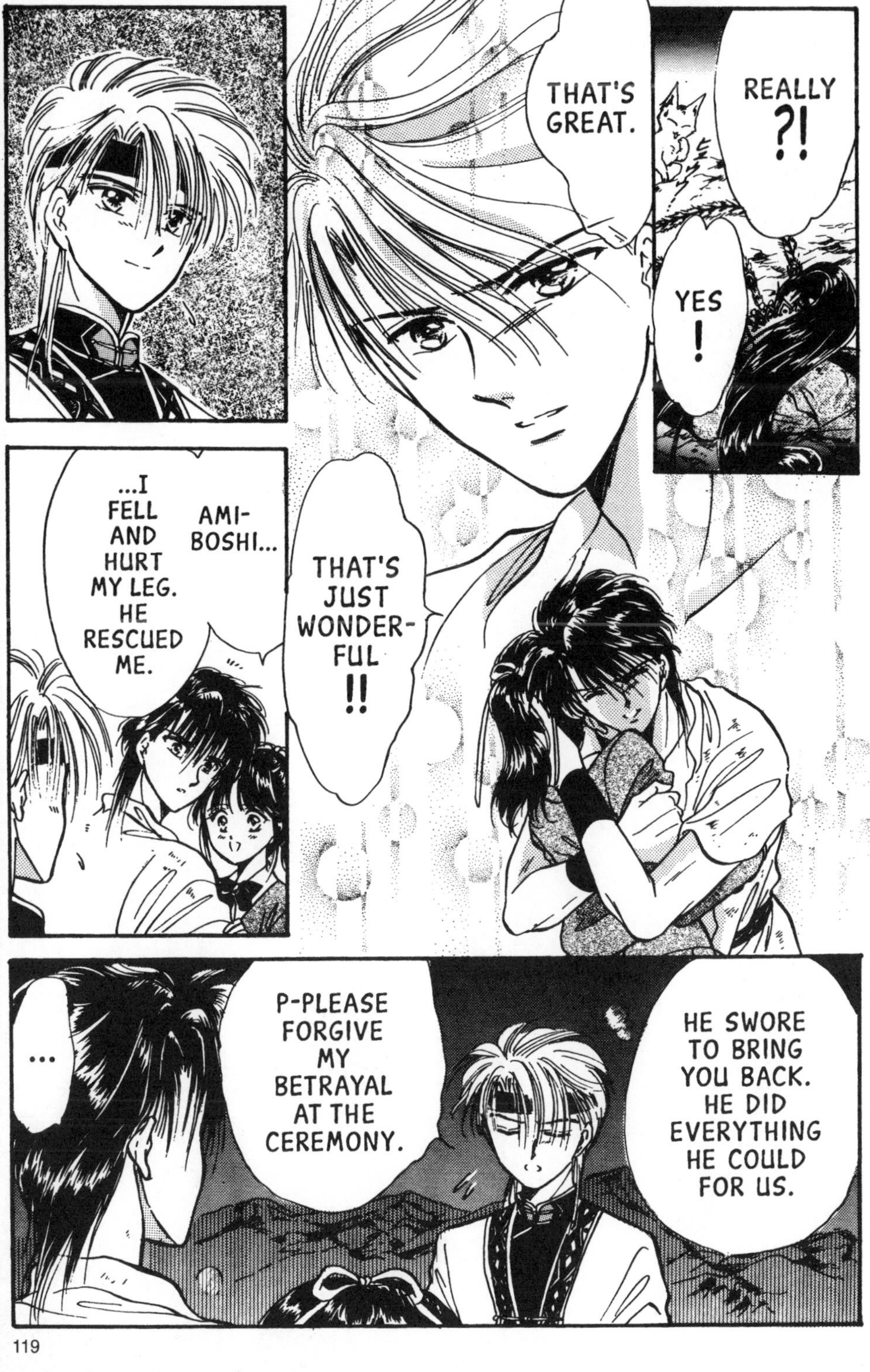

REALLY ?!
YES !
THAT'S GREAT.
THAT'S JUST WONDERFUL !!
AMI-BOSHI...
...I FELL AND HURT MY LEG. HE RESCUED ME.
HE SWORE TO BRING YOU BACK. HE DID EVERYTHING HE COULD FOR US.
P-PLEASE FORGIVE MY BETRAYAL AT THE CEREMONY.
...

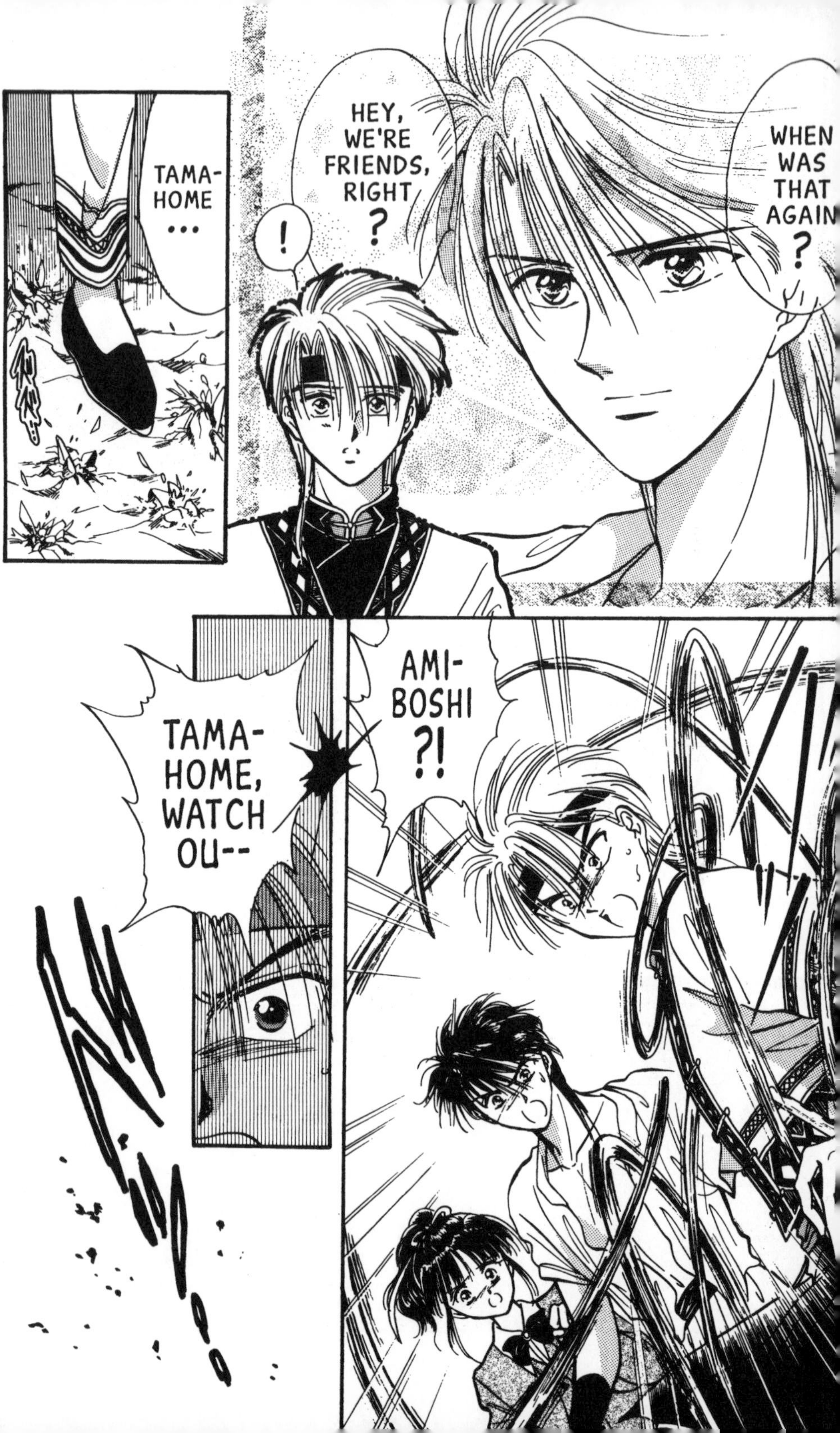
WHEN WAS THAT AGAIN?
HEY, WE'RE FRIENDS, RIGHT?
!
TAMA-HOME...
AMI-BOSHI?!
TAMA-HOME, WATCH OU--

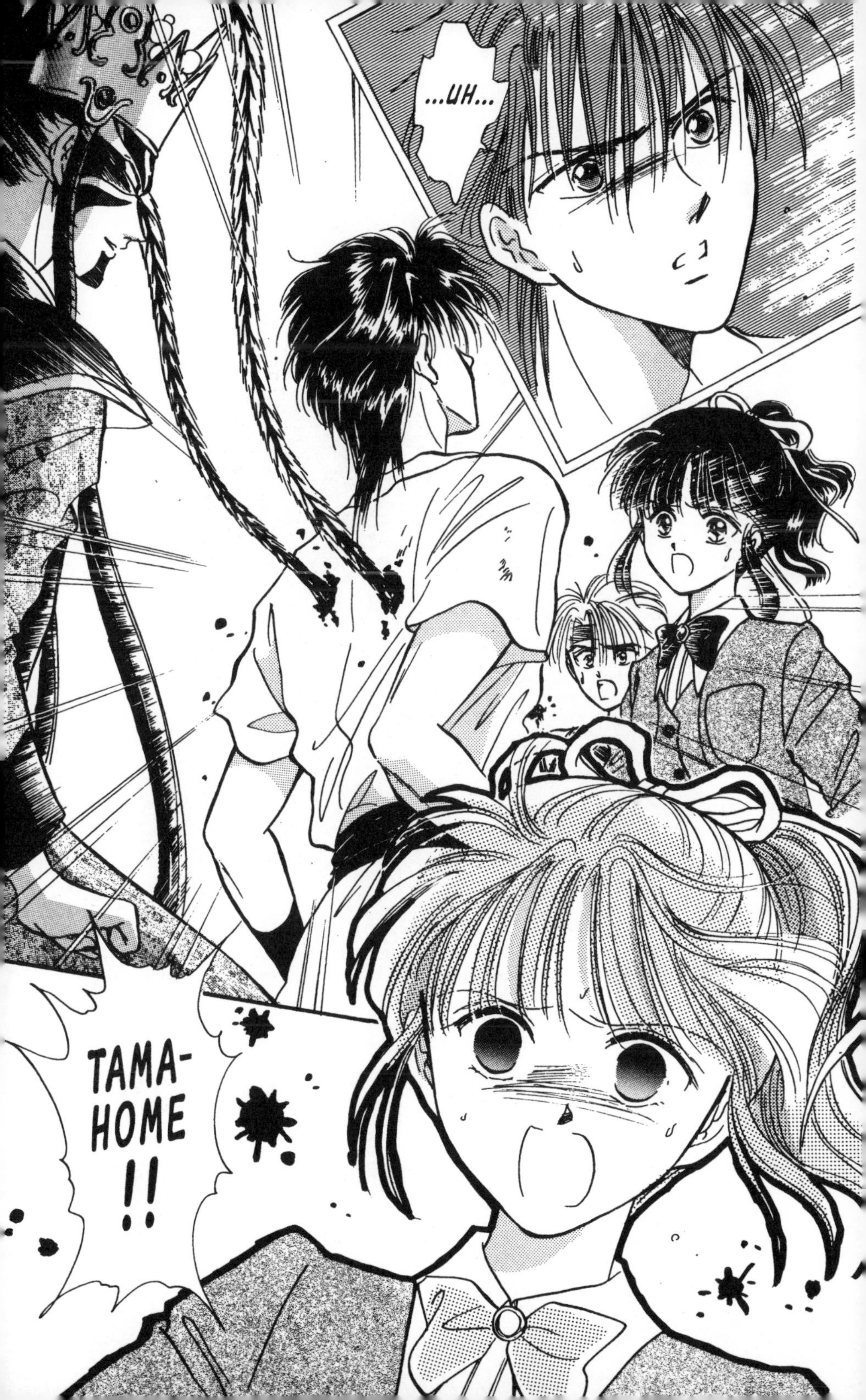
...UH...
TAMA-HOME !!

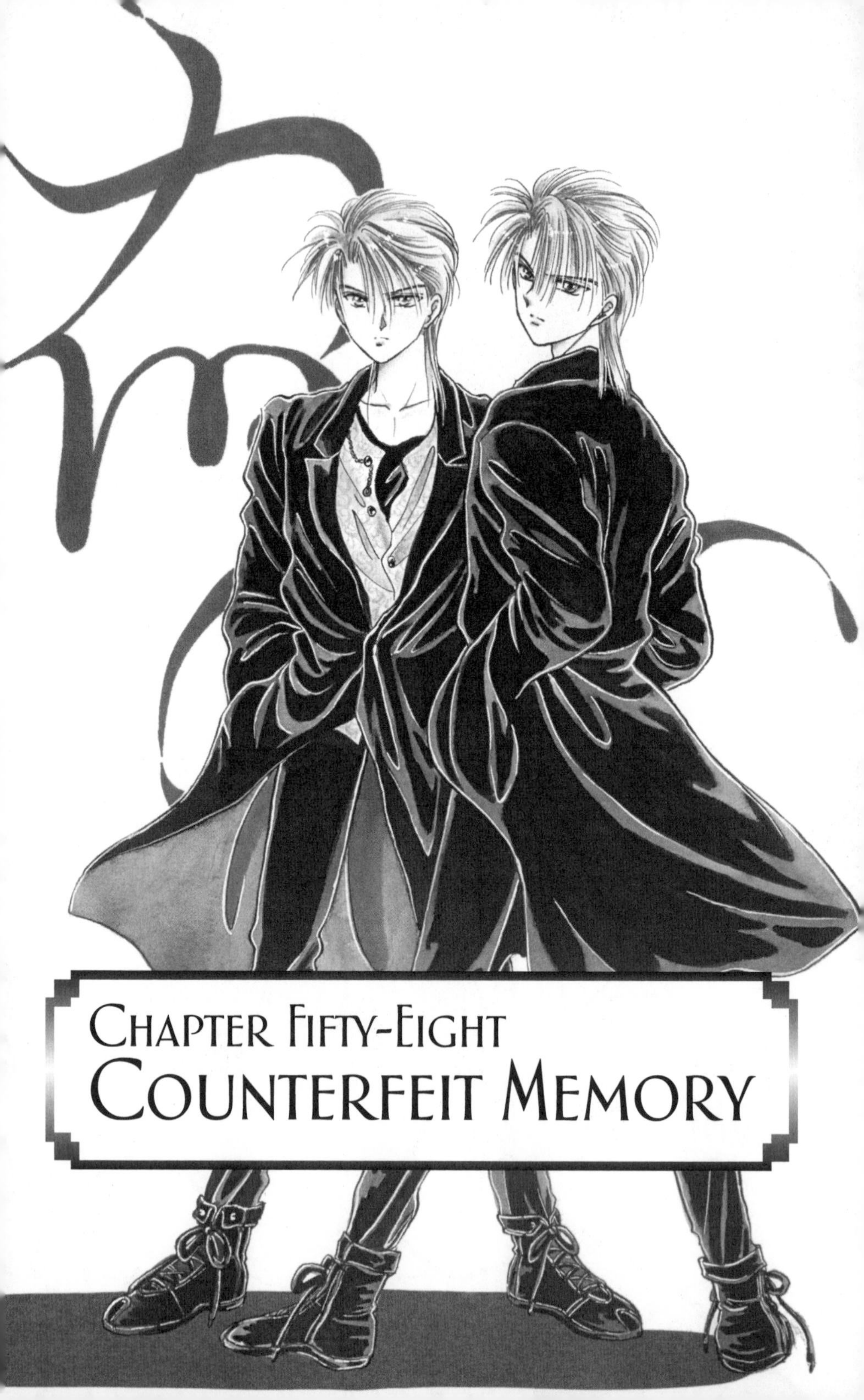
Chapter Fifty-Eight
Counterfeit Memory

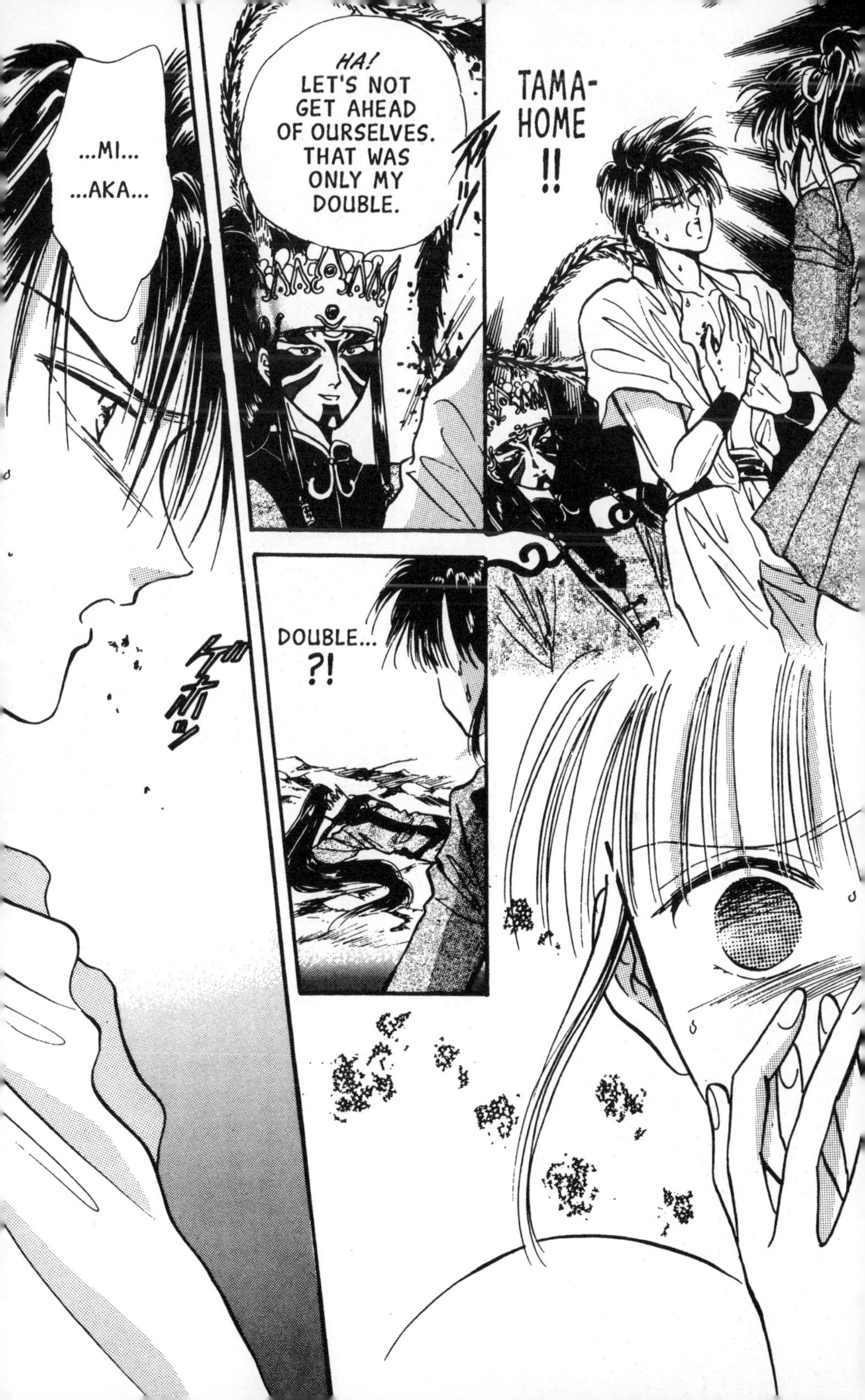
TAMA-HOME !!
HA! LET'S NOT GET AHEAD OF OURSELVES. THAT WAS ONLY MY DOUBLE.
DOUBLE... ?!
...MI... ...AKA...

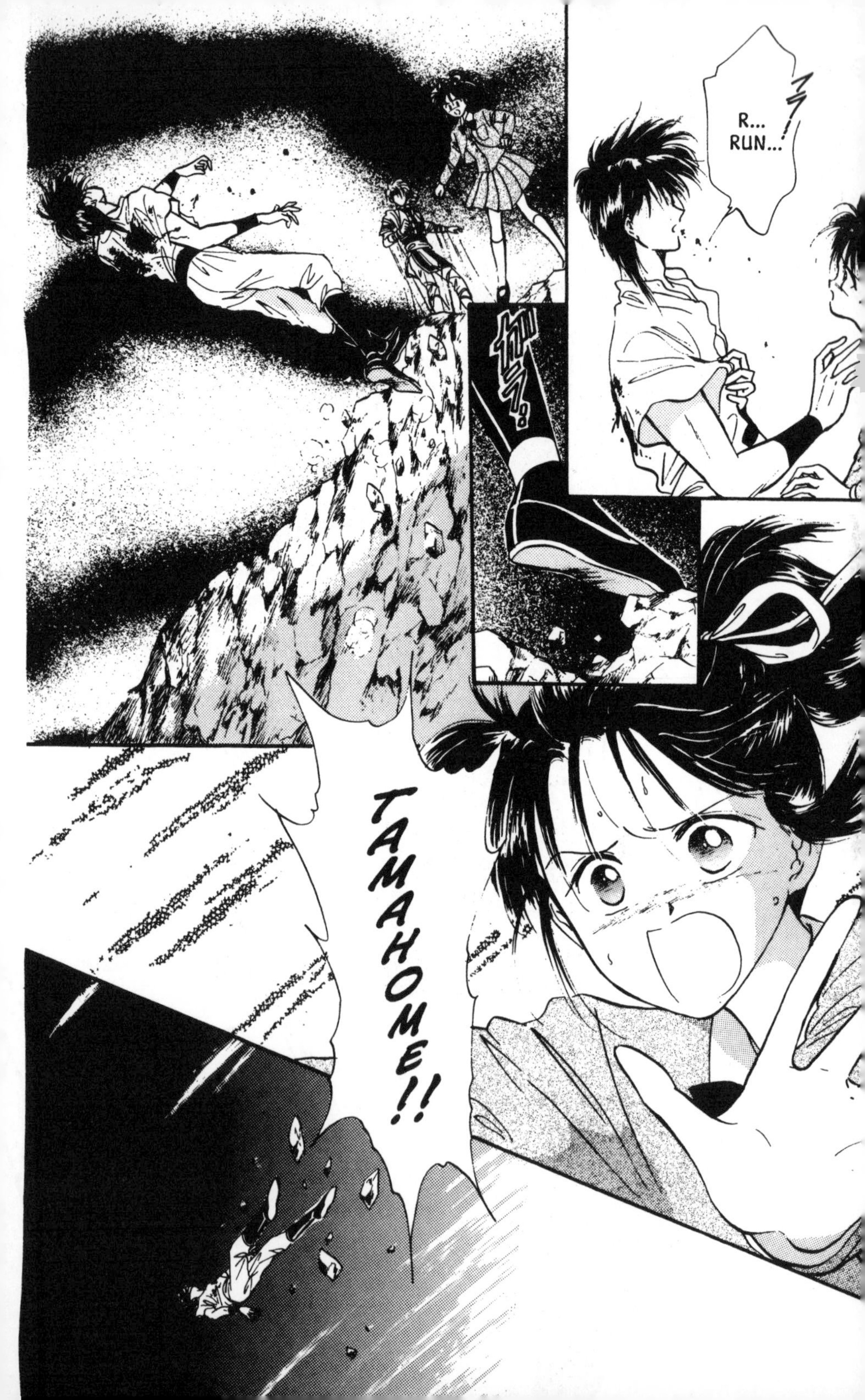
R... RUN...!
TAMAHOME!!

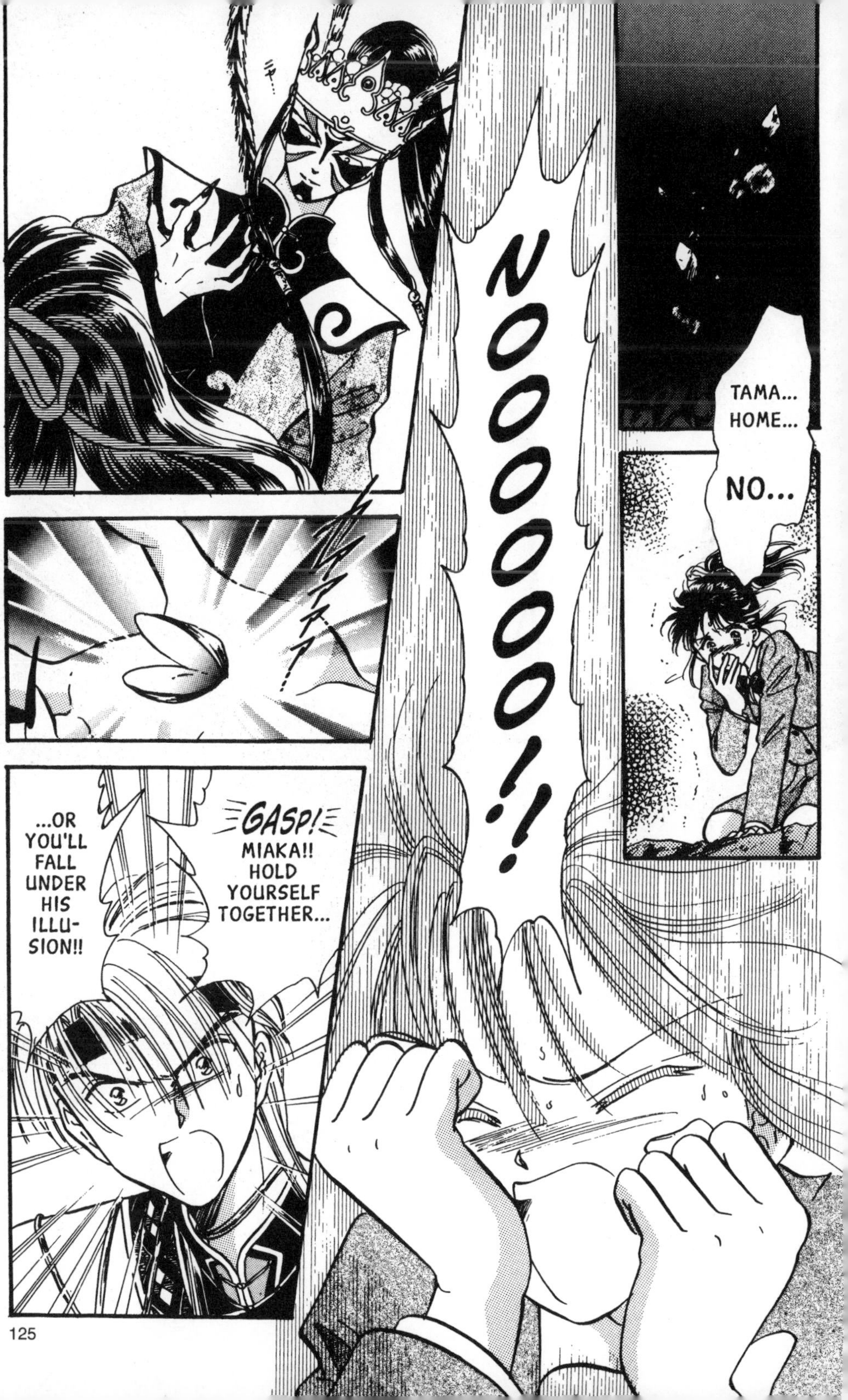
TAMA... HOME...
NO...
NOOOOOO!!
ニヤ…
GASP!
MIAKA!! HOLD YOURSELF TOGETHER...
...OR YOU'LL FALL UNDER HIS ILLUSION!!

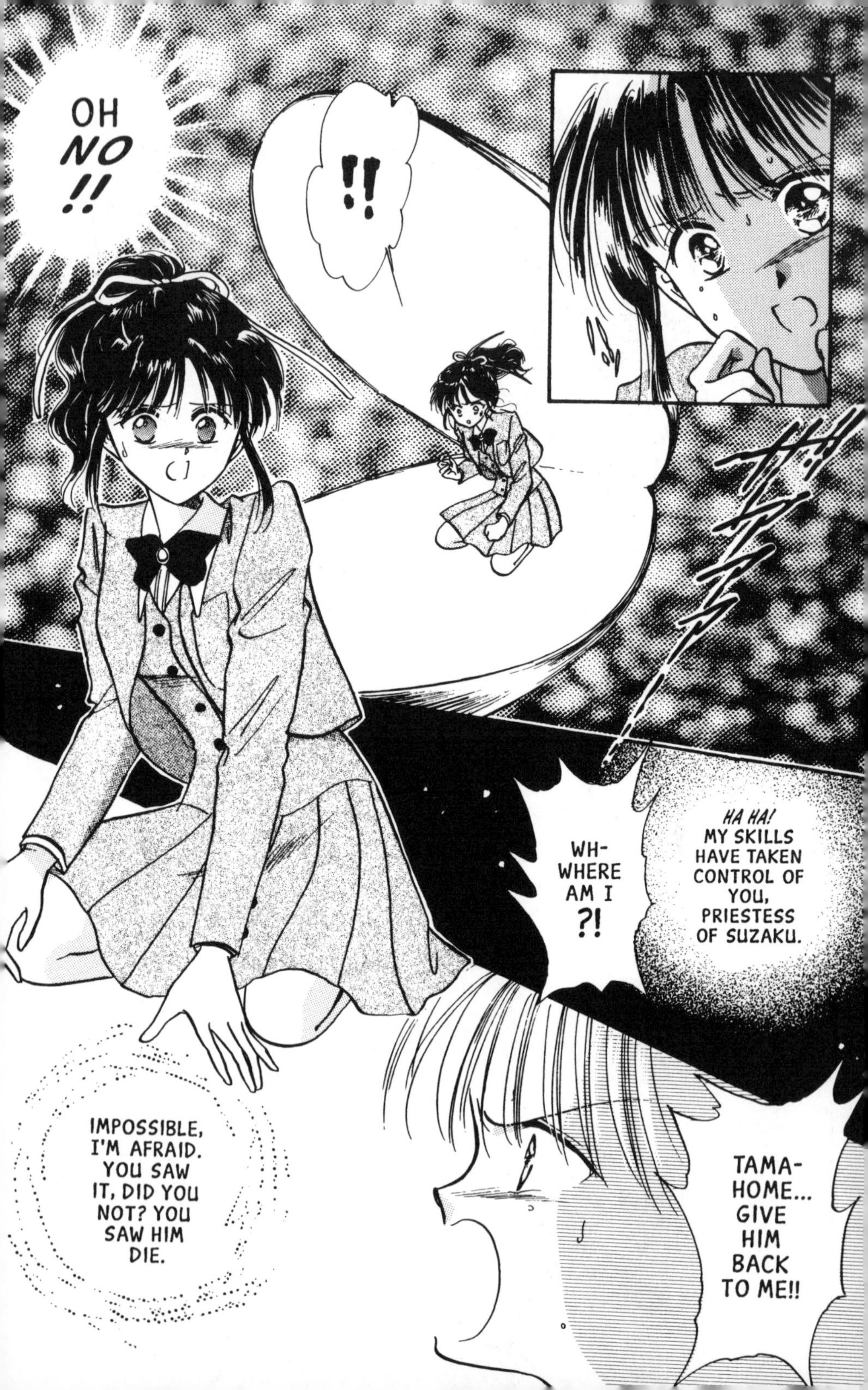
!!
OH NO!!
HA HA! MY SKILLS HAVE TAKEN CONTROL OF YOU, PRIESTESS OF SUZAKU.
WH-WHERE AM I ?!
TAMA-HOME... GIVE HIM BACK TO ME!!
IMPOSSIBLE, I'M AFRAID. YOU SAW IT, DID YOU NOT? YOU SAW HIM DIE.

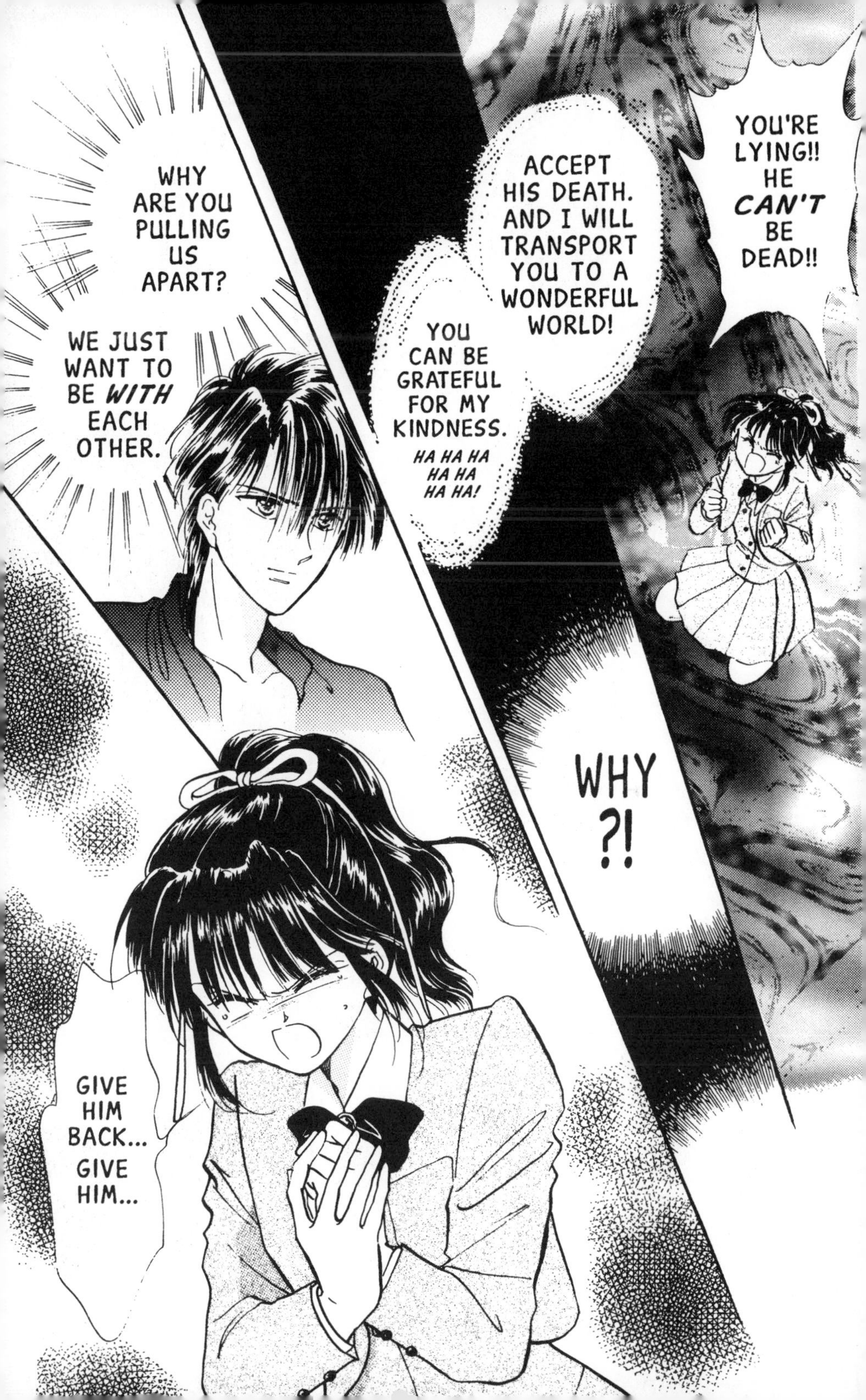
YOU'RE LYING!! HE *CAN'T* BE DEAD!!
ACCEPT HIS DEATH. AND I WILL TRANSPORT YOU TO A WONDERFUL WORLD!
YOU CAN BE GRATEFUL FOR MY KINDNESS.
HA HA HA HA HA HA HA!
WHY ARE YOU PULLING US APART?
WE JUST WANT TO BE *WITH* EACH OTHER.
WHY ?!
GIVE HIM BACK... GIVE HIM...

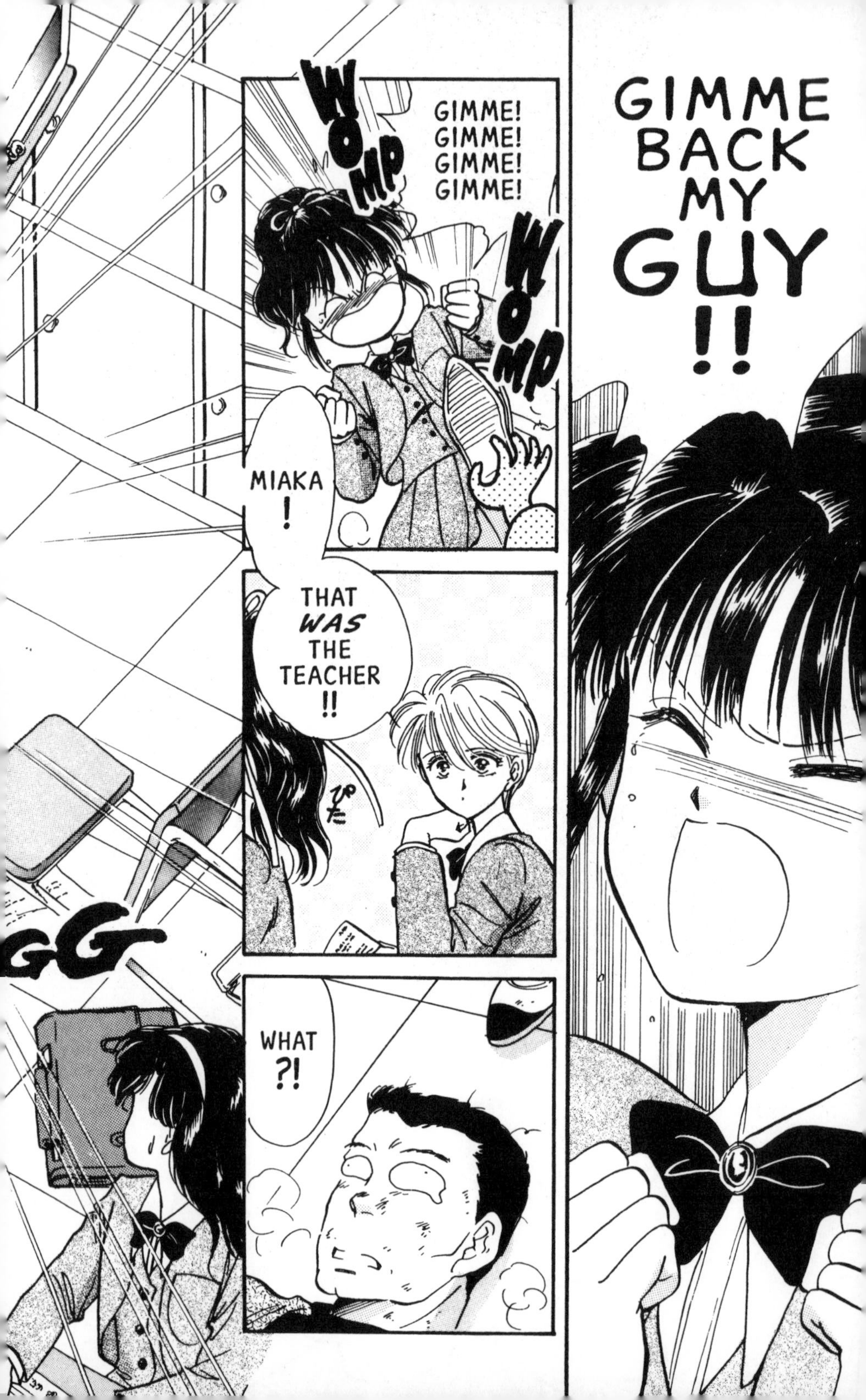
GIMME BACK MY GUY!!
WOMP
WOMP
GIMME! GIMME! GIMME! GIMME!
MIAKA!
THAT *WAS* THE TEACHER!!
WHAT?!
GG

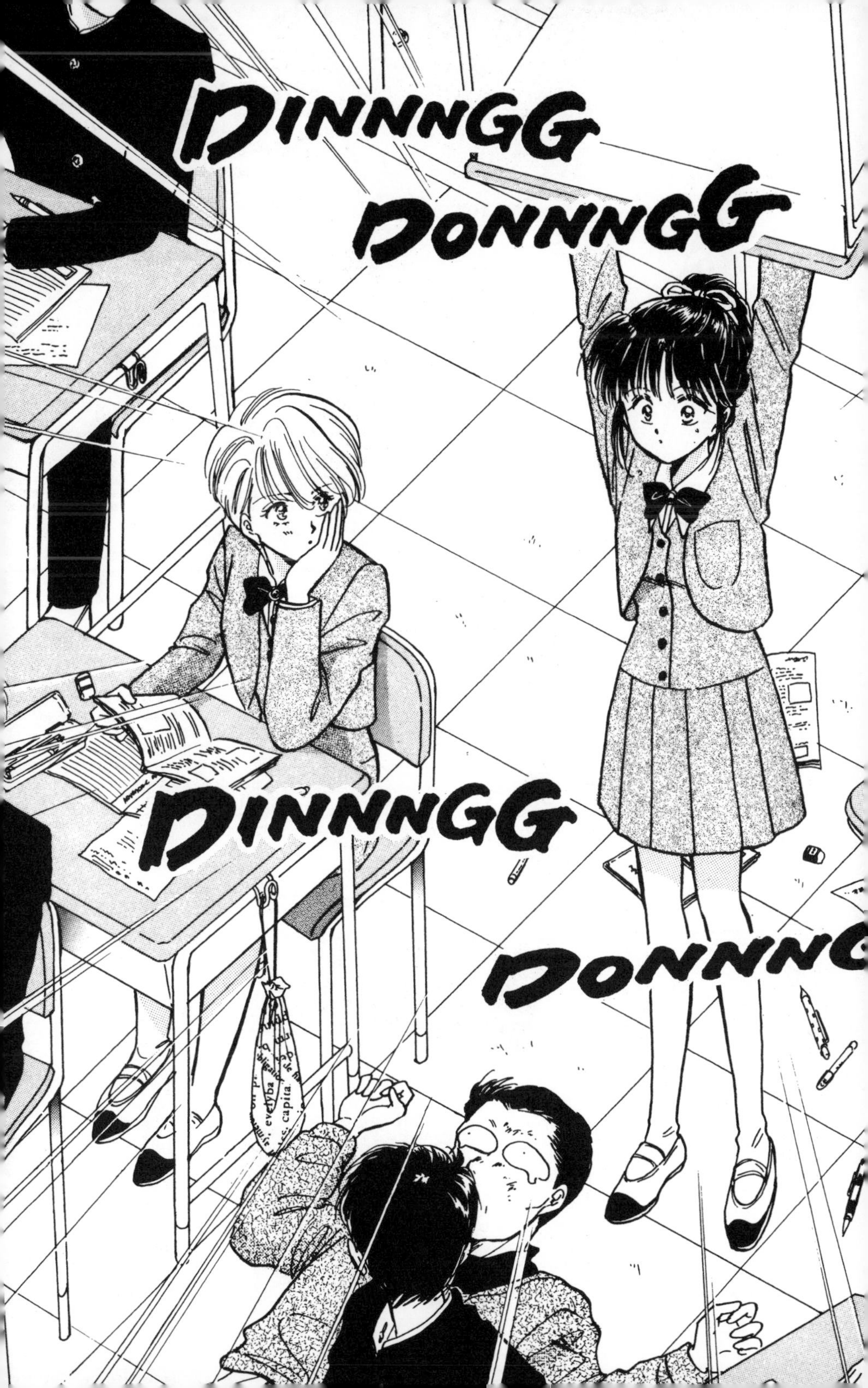
DINNNGG
DONNNGG
DINNNGG
DONNN

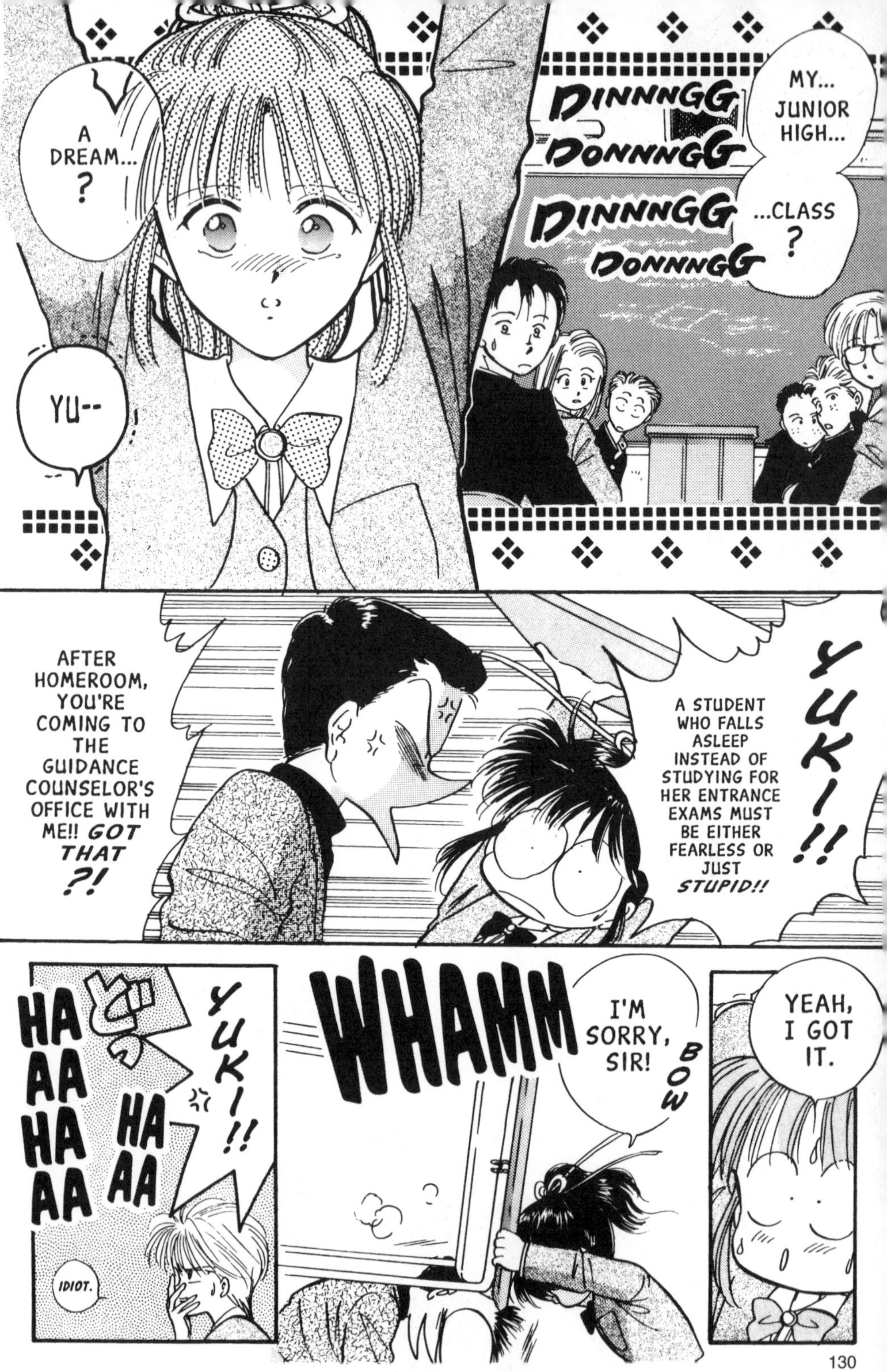
DINNNGG DONNNGG
DINNNGG DONNNGG
MY... JUNIOR HIGH...
...CLASS ?
A DREAM... ?
YU--
YUKI!!
A STUDENT WHO FALLS ASLEEP INSTEAD OF STUDYING FOR HER ENTRANCE EXAMS MUST BE EITHER FEARLESS OR JUST *STUPID!!*
AFTER HOMEROOM, YOU'RE COMING TO THE GUIDANCE COUNSELOR'S OFFICE WITH ME!! *GOT THAT ?!*
YEAH, I GOT IT.
I'M SORRY, SIR!
BOW
WHAMM
YUKI!!
どっ
HA HA HA HA HA HA
HA HA AA AA
IDIOT.

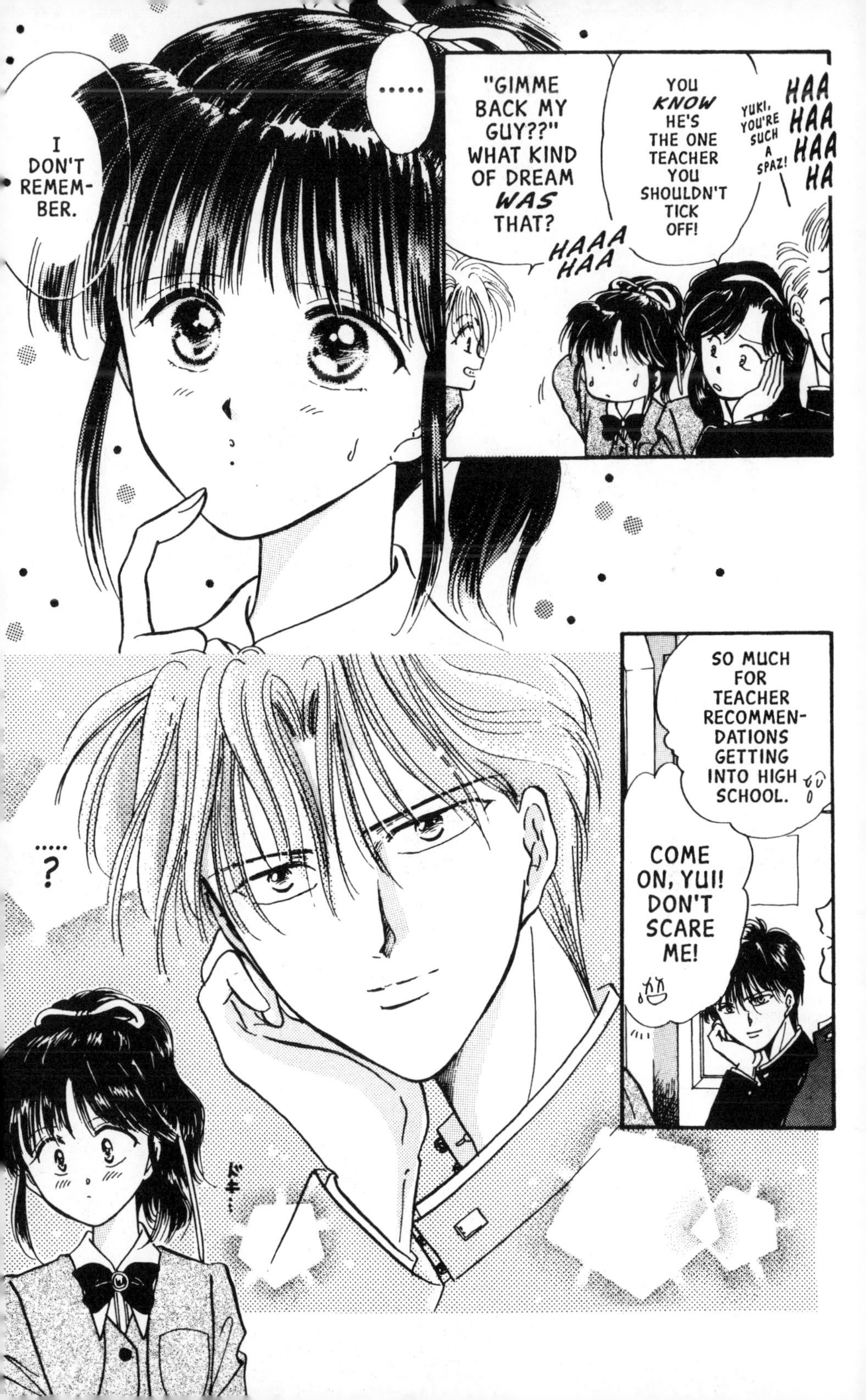
HAA HAA HAA HA
YUKI, YOU'RE SUCH A SPAZ!
YOU KNOW HE'S THE ONE TEACHER YOU SHOULDN'T TICK OFF!
"GIMME BACK MY GUY??" WHAT KIND OF DREAM WAS THAT?
HAAA HAA
.....
I DON'T REMEMBER.
SO MUCH FOR TEACHER RECOMMENDATIONS GETTING INTO HIGH SCHOOL.
COME ON, YUI! DON'T SCARE ME!
..... ?

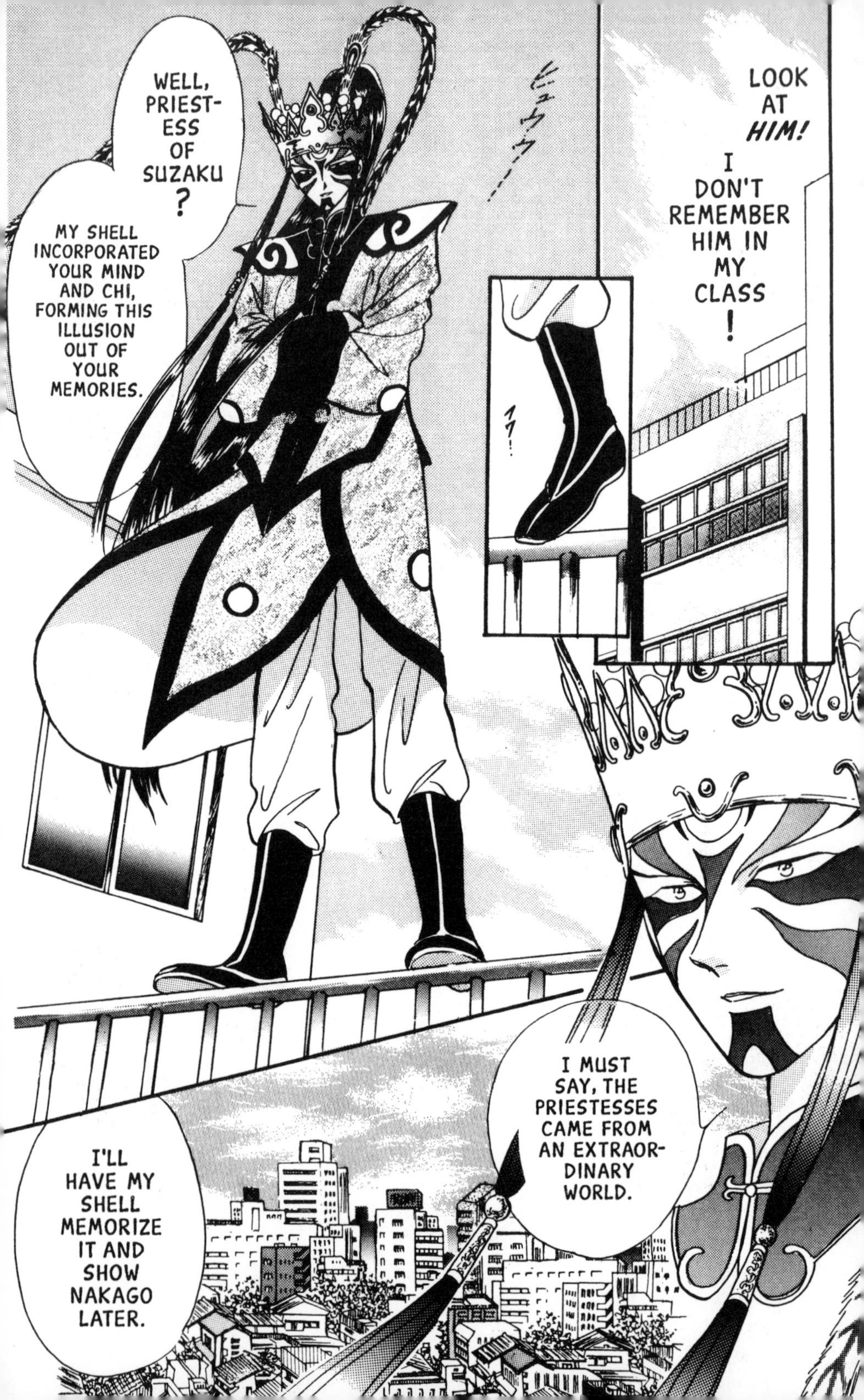
LOOK AT *HIM!*
I DON'T REMEMBER HIM IN MY CLASS!
WELL, PRIESTESS OF SUZAKU?
MY SHELL INCORPORATED YOUR MIND AND CHI, FORMING THIS ILLUSION OUT OF YOUR MEMORIES.
I MUST SAY, THE PRIESTESSES CAME FROM AN EXTRAORDINARY WORLD.
I'LL HAVE MY SHELL MEMORIZE IT AND SHOW NAKAGO LATER.

Now to change the subject. Here, something I read in your recent fan mail. It says that *Fushigi Yūgi* graphic novels and merchandise showed up on TV in Hanakin Dataland. I didn't know about it at all and didn't watch the series. My editors didn't know about it either! Meanwhile, my '94 calendar showed up all the time in the TV drama *Tanin no Fukō wa Mitsu no Aji* (The Delicious Woes of Others) which made me happy! It was a while ago. By the way, the second CD book will be released on August 3. This time, it is amazing, if I do say so myself. First of all, there are so many voice actors. 14 actors. 14!! There are the leads Noriko Hidaka (Miaka), Toshihiko Seki (Tamahome), Wakana Yamazaki (Yui), Yasunori Matsumoto (Hotohori), Minami Takayama (Nuriko), Rin Mizuhara (Tai Yi-Jun)!! Then on top of that, Kazuki Yao (Tasuki), Kappei Yamaguchi (Chichiri), Megumi Origasa (Chiriko), Jurota Osugi (Mitsukake), Tetsuya Iwanaga (Amiboshi), and Ryutaro Okiayu (Nakago) were in it. Eiji Yanagisawa and Toru Furusawa gave a fierce (so fierce it terrified me) performance as the men attacking Yui. I was so impressed I had to write them all down!! My right hand's trembling. What a terrific cast!! Tremble, tremble! They're all on the same recording! What a great deal. I actually visited a recording session at the studio... but given my origins as an anime fan, I completely lost control, went haywire, lost my mind, went nuts, etc.

OH BOY! OH BOY! OH BOY! OH BOY!

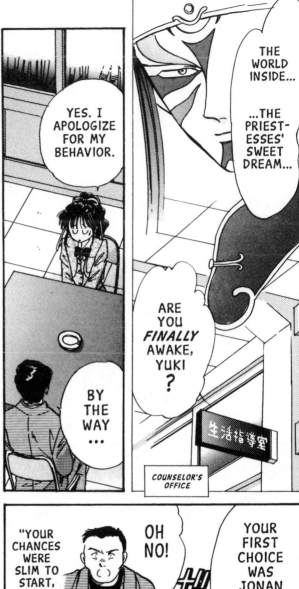

THE WORLD INSIDE...
...THE PRIESTESSES' SWEET DREAM...
ARE YOU FINALLY AWAKE, YUKI ?
YES. I APOLOGIZE FOR MY BEHAVIOR.
BY THE WAY...
生活指導室
COUNSELOR'S OFFICE
YOUR FIRST CHOICE WAS JONAN HIGH SCHOOL, RIGHT?
OH NO!
"YOUR CHANCES WERE SLIM TO START, BUT NOW..."
.....
......
.....

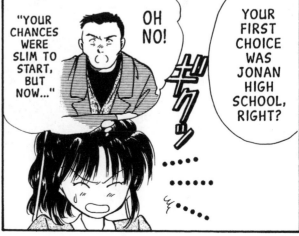

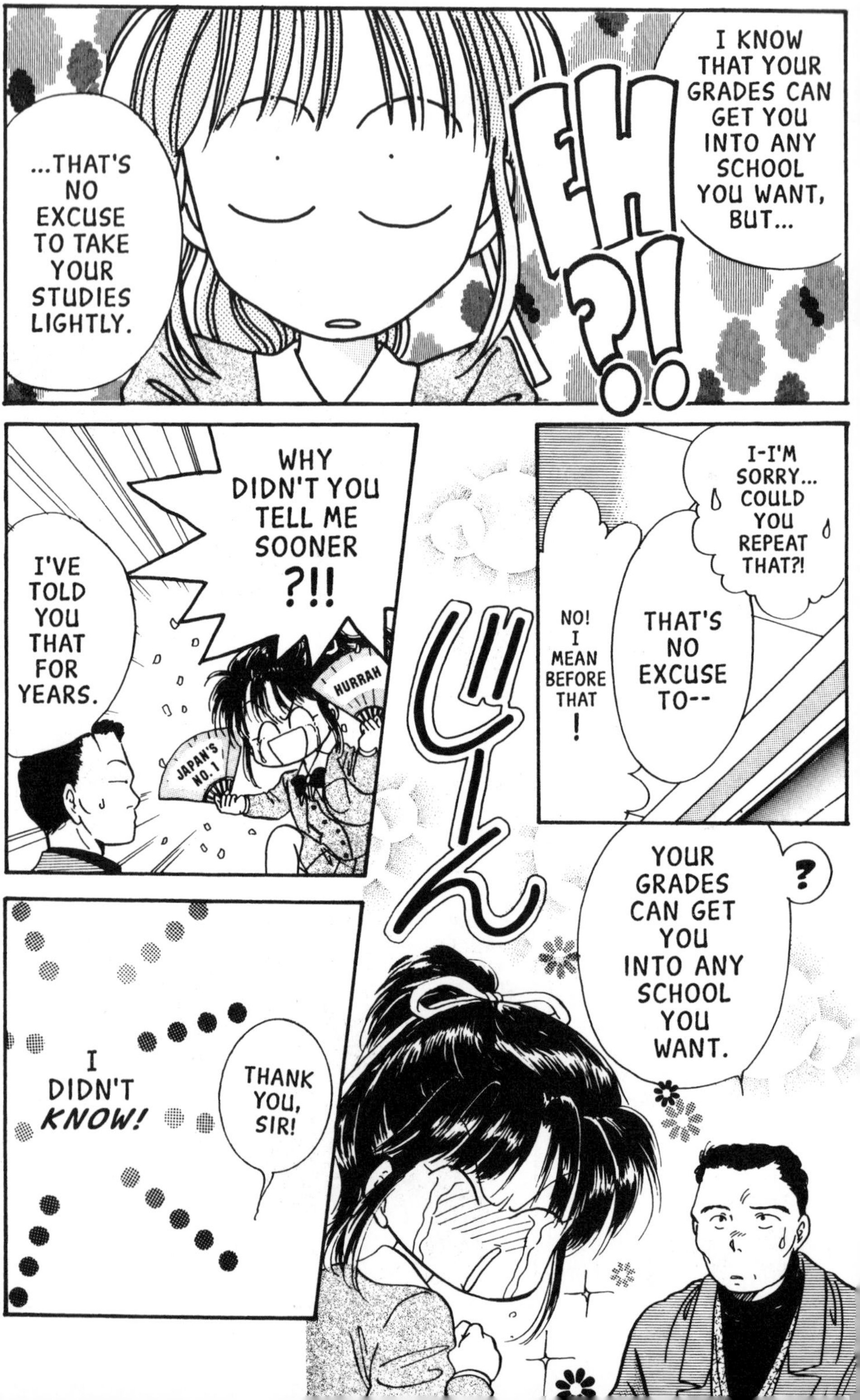
I KNOW THAT YOUR GRADES CAN GET YOU INTO ANY SCHOOL YOU WANT, BUT...
EH ?!
...THAT'S NO EXCUSE TO TAKE YOUR STUDIES LIGHTLY.
I-I'M SORRY... COULD YOU REPEAT THAT?!
THAT'S NO EXCUSE TO--
NO! I MEAN BEFORE THAT!
YOUR GRADES CAN GET YOU INTO ANY SCHOOL YOU WANT.
?
じ〜ん
THANK YOU, SIR!
I DIDN'T KNOW!
WHY DIDN'T YOU TELL ME SOONER ?!!
HURRAH
JAPAN'S NO. 1
I'VE TOLD YOU THAT FOR YEARS.

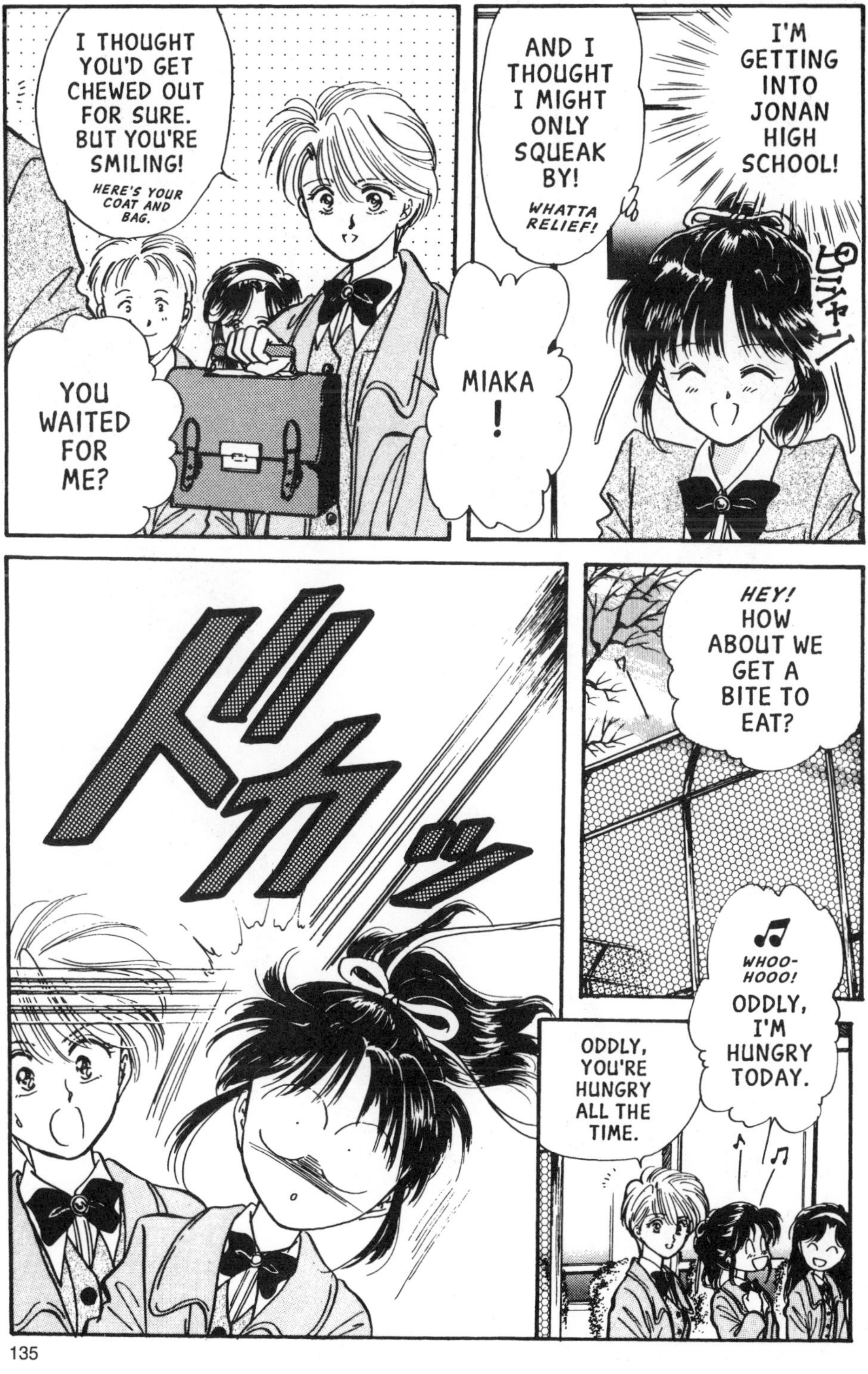
I'M GETTING INTO JONAN HIGH SCHOOL!
AND I THOUGHT I MIGHT ONLY SQUEAK BY!
WHATTA RELIEF!
MIAKA!
I THOUGHT YOU'D GET CHEWED OUT FOR SURE. BUT YOU'RE SMILING!
HERE'S YOUR COAT AND BAG.
YOU WAITED FOR ME?
HEY! HOW ABOUT WE GET A BITE TO EAT?
♫ WHOO-HOOO!
ODDLY, I'M HUNGRY TODAY.
ODDLY, YOU'RE HUNGRY ALL THE TIME.
ドカッ

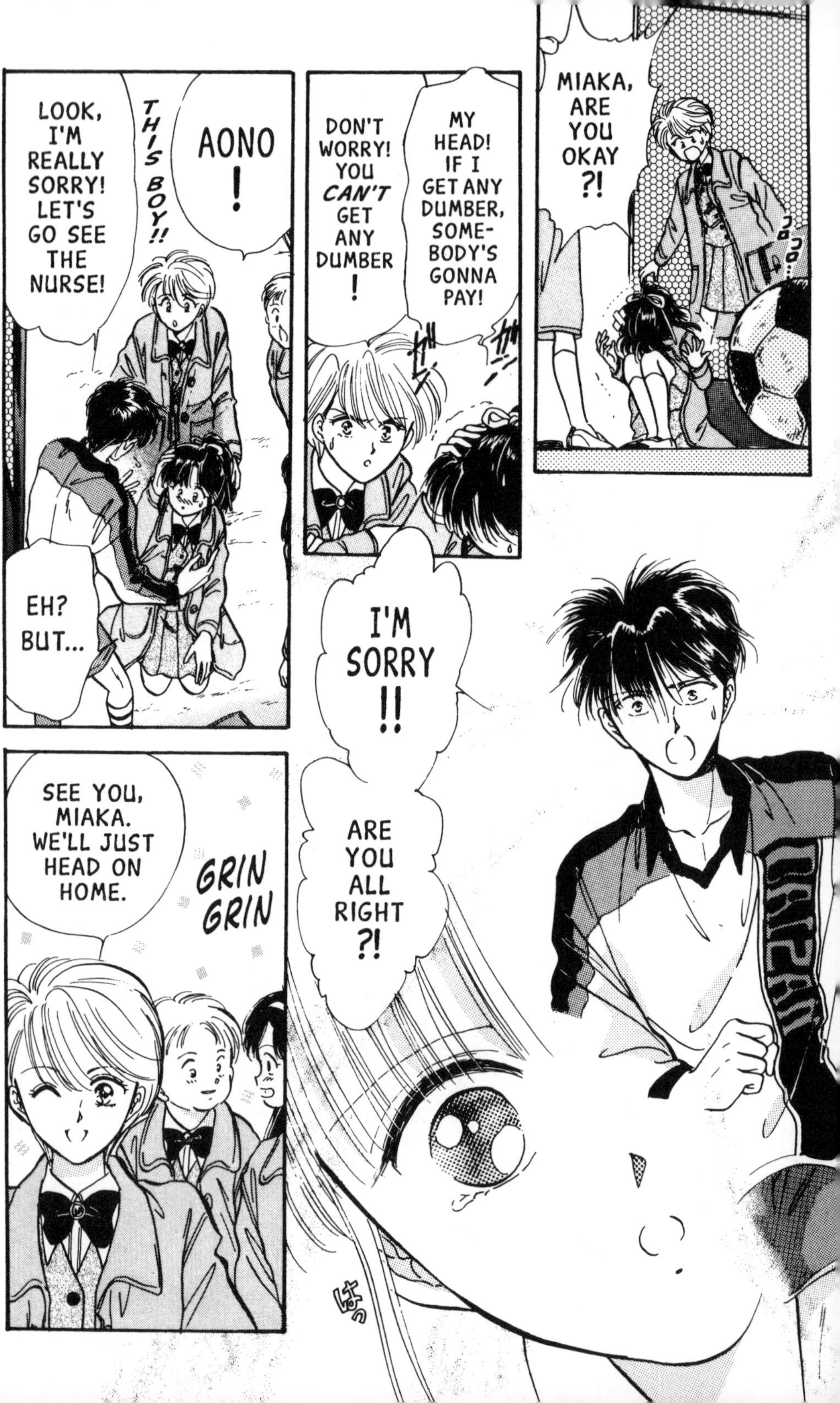
MIAKA, ARE YOU OKAY ?!
MY HEAD! IF I GET ANY DUMBER, SOME-BODY'S GONNA PAY!
DON'T WORRY! YOU *CAN'T* GET ANY DUMBER !
I'M SORRY !!
ARE YOU ALL RIGHT ?!
AONO !
THIS BOY!!
LOOK, I'M REALLY SORRY! LET'S GO SEE THE NURSE!
EH? BUT...
SEE YOU, MIAKA. WE'LL JUST HEAD ON HOME.
GRIN GRIN

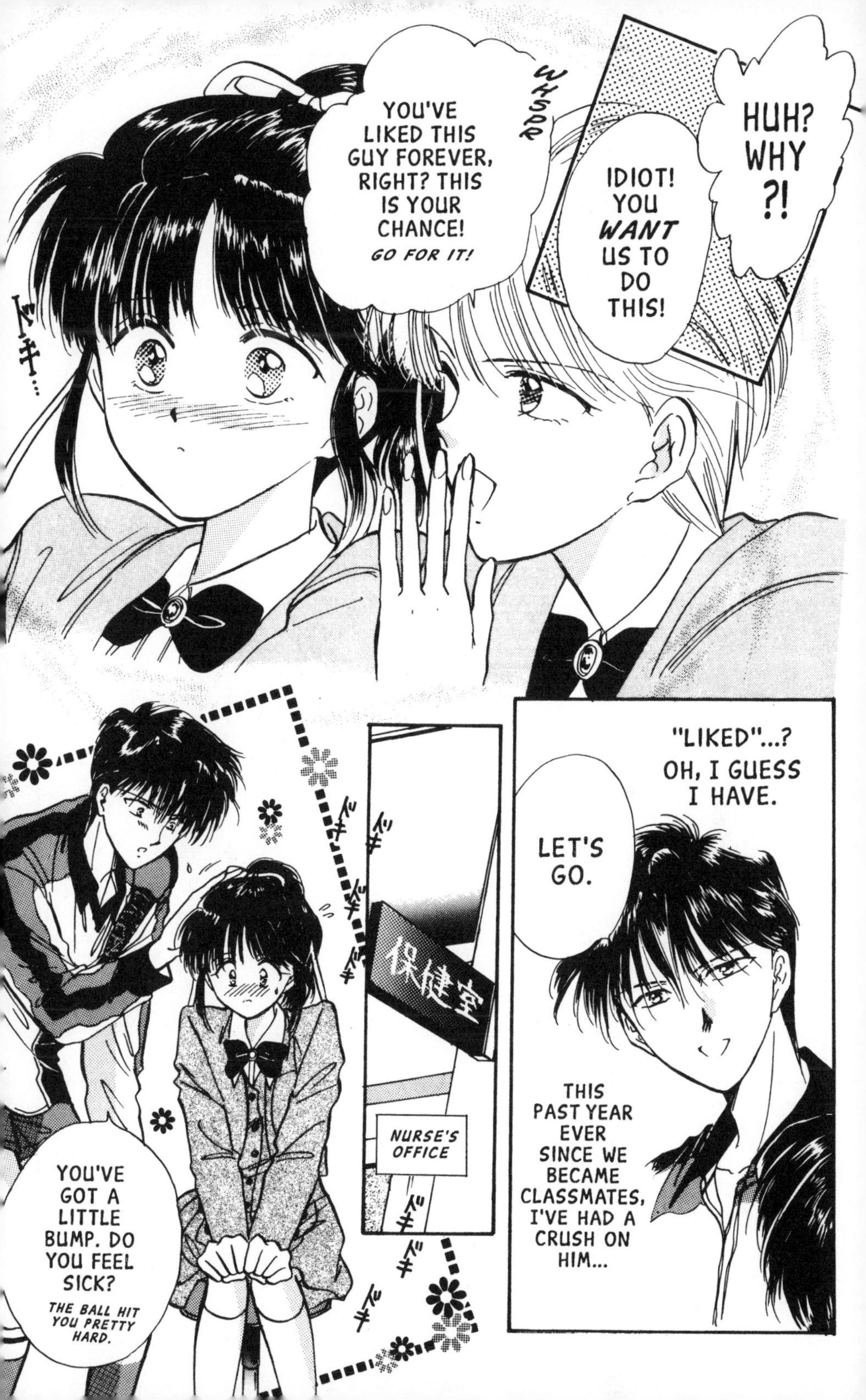
HUH? WHY?!
IDIOT! YOU *WANT* US TO DO THIS!
YOU'VE LIKED THIS GUY FOREVER, RIGHT? THIS IS YOUR CHANCE!
GO FOR IT!
WHSPR
"LIKED"...? OH, I GUESS I HAVE.
LET'S GO.
THIS PAST YEAR EVER SINCE WE BECAME CLASSMATES, I'VE HAD A CRUSH ON HIM...
保健室
NURSE'S OFFICE
YOU'VE GOT A LITTLE BUMP. DO YOU FEEL SICK?
THE BALL HIT YOU PRETTY HARD.

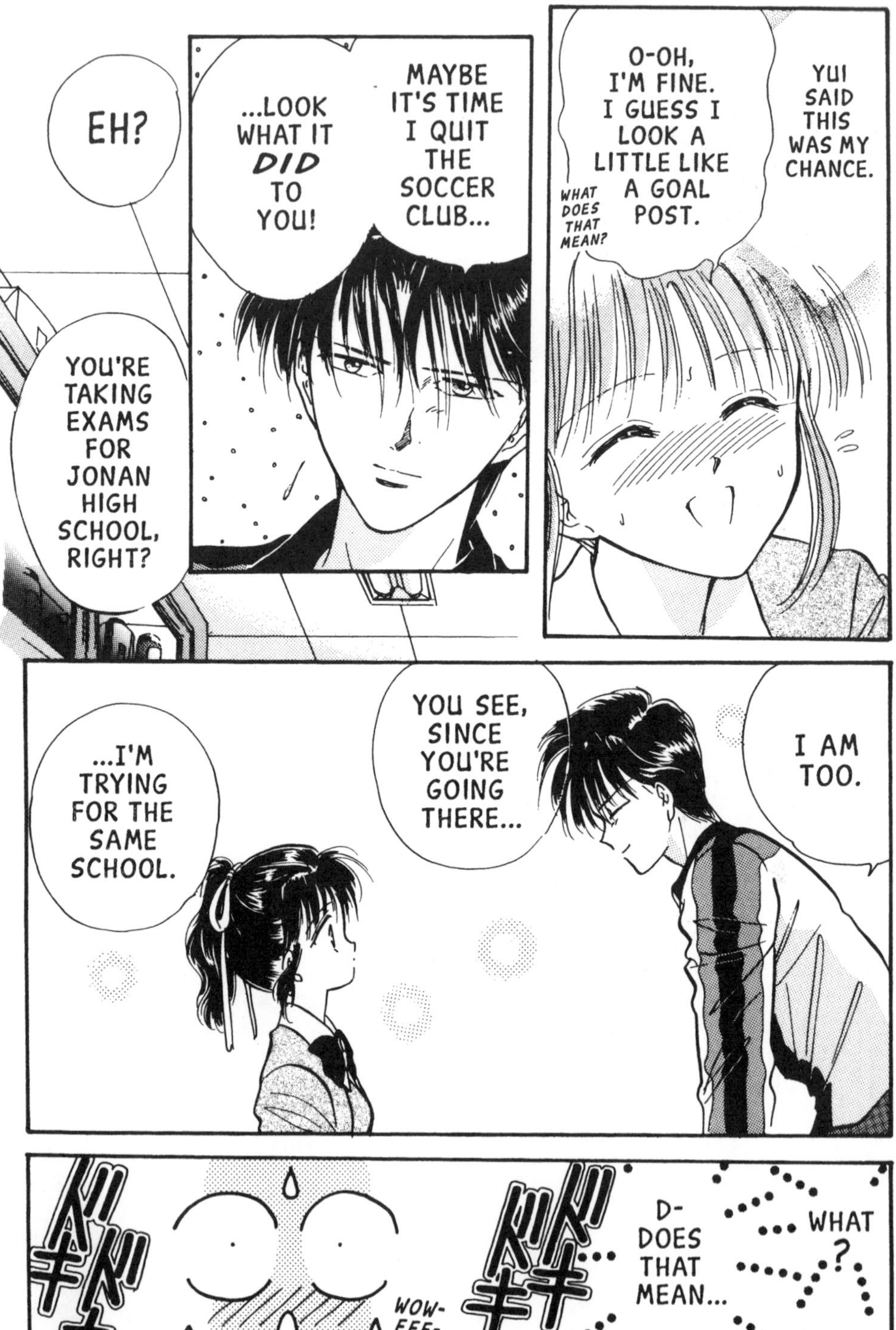
YUI SAID THIS WAS MY CHANCE.
O-OH, I'M FINE. I GUESS I LOOK A LITTLE LIKE A GOAL POST.
WHAT DOES THAT MEAN?
MAYBE IT'S TIME I QUIT THE SOCCER CLUB...
...LOOK WHAT IT DID TO YOU!
EH?
YOU'RE TAKING EXAMS FOR JONAN HIGH SCHOOL, RIGHT?
I AM TOO.
YOU SEE, SINCE YOU'RE GOING THERE...
...I'M TRYING FOR THE SAME SCHOOL.
WHAT?
D-DOES THAT MEAN...
WOW-EEE-EEE!

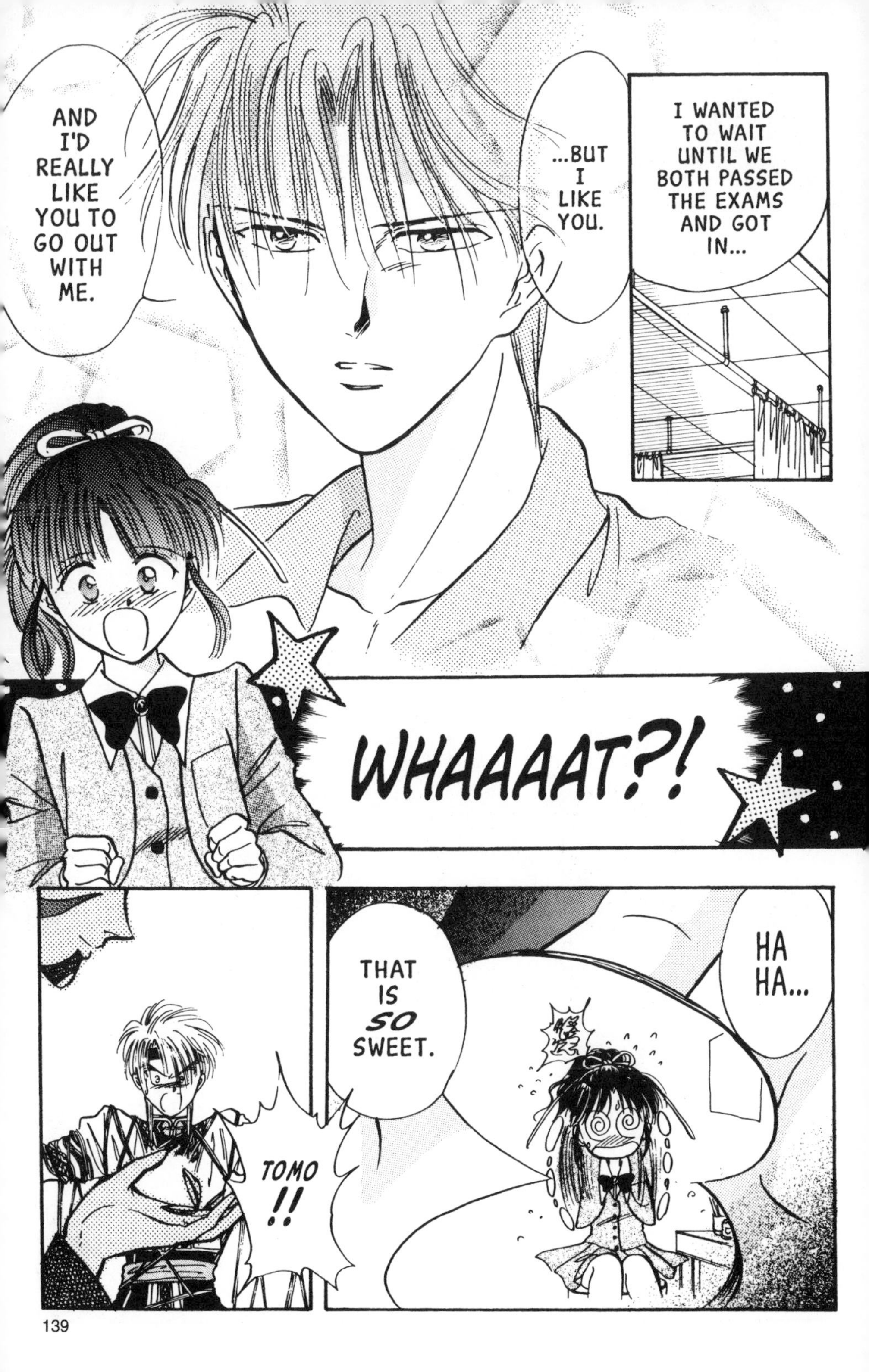
I WANTED TO WAIT UNTIL WE BOTH PASSED THE EXAMS AND GOT IN...
...BUT I LIKE YOU.
AND I'D REALLY LIKE YOU TO GO OUT WITH ME.
WHAAAAT?!
HA HA...
THAT IS *SO* SWEET.
TOMO!!

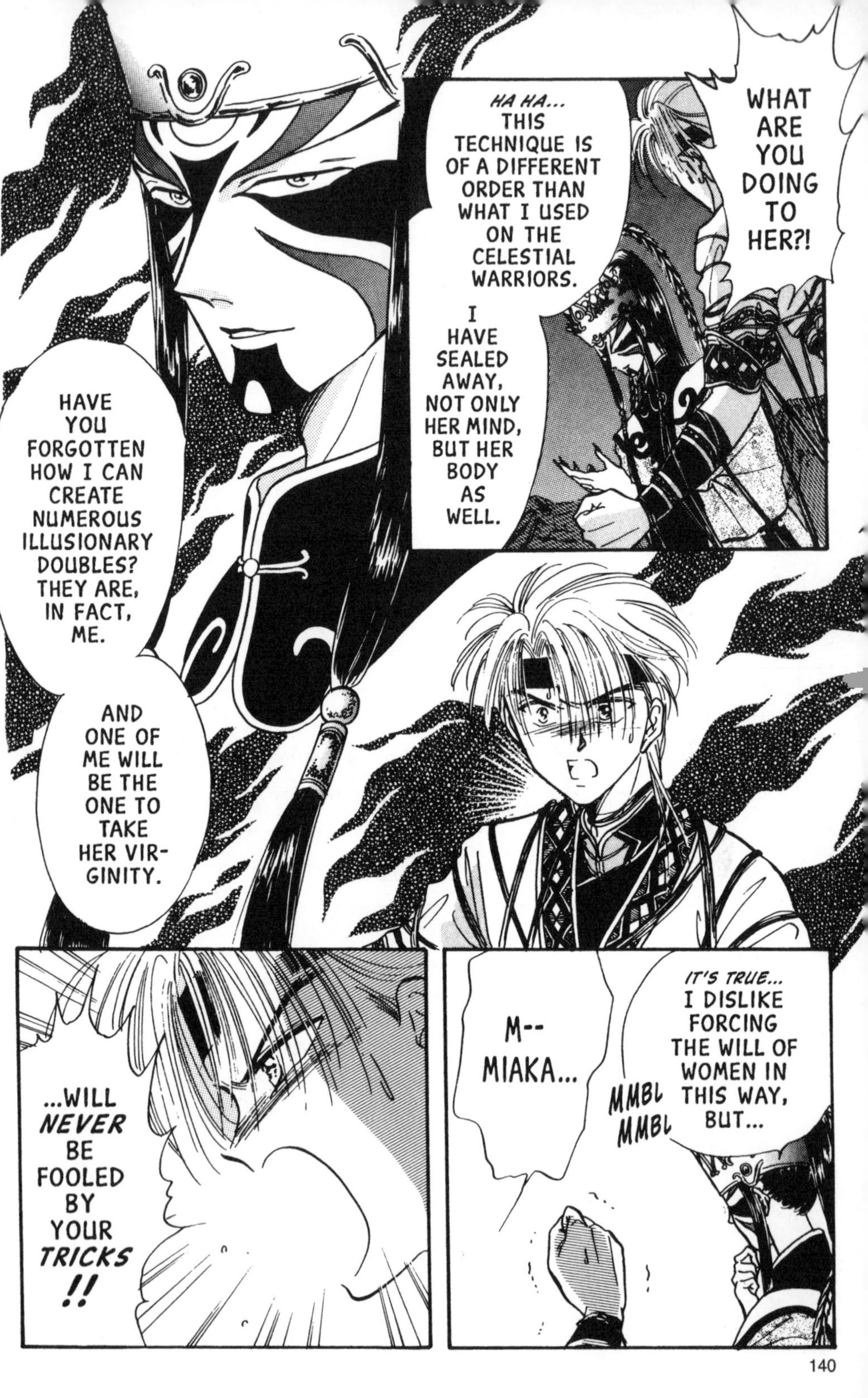

WHAT ARE YOU DOING TO HER?!
HA HA... THIS TECHNIQUE IS OF A DIFFERENT ORDER THAN WHAT I USED ON THE CELESTIAL WARRIORS.
I HAVE SEALED AWAY, NOT ONLY HER MIND, BUT HER BODY AS WELL.
HAVE YOU FORGOTTEN HOW I CAN CREATE NUMEROUS ILLUSIONARY DOUBLES? THEY ARE, IN FACT, ME.
AND ONE OF ME WILL BE THE ONE TO TAKE HER VIRGINITY.
IT'S TRUE... I DISLIKE FORCING THE WILL OF WOMEN IN THIS WAY, BUT...
MMBL MMBL
M-- MIAKA...
...WILL NEVER BE FOOLED BY YOUR TRICKS!!

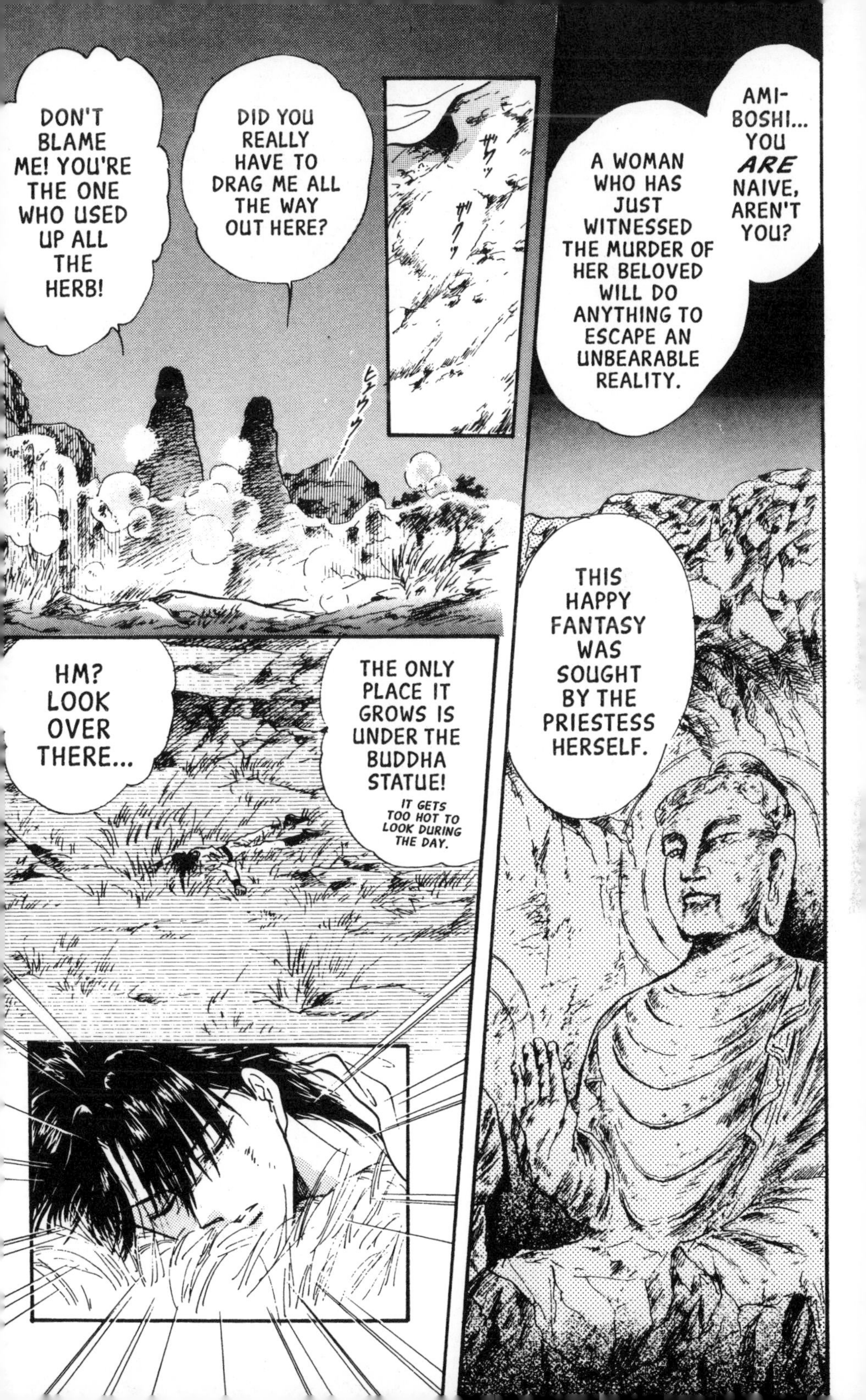
AMI-BOSHI... YOU *ARE* NAIVE, AREN'T YOU?
A WOMAN WHO HAS JUST WITNESSED THE MURDER OF HER BELOVED WILL DO ANYTHING TO ESCAPE AN UNBEARABLE REALITY.
THIS HAPPY FANTASY WAS SOUGHT BY THE PRIESTESS HERSELF.
DID YOU REALLY HAVE TO DRAG ME ALL THE WAY OUT HERE?
DON'T BLAME ME! YOU'RE THE ONE WHO USED UP ALL THE HERB!
THE ONLY PLACE IT GROWS IS UNDER THE BUDDHA STATUE!
IT GETS TOO HOT TO LOOK DURING THE DAY.
HM? LOOK OVER THERE...

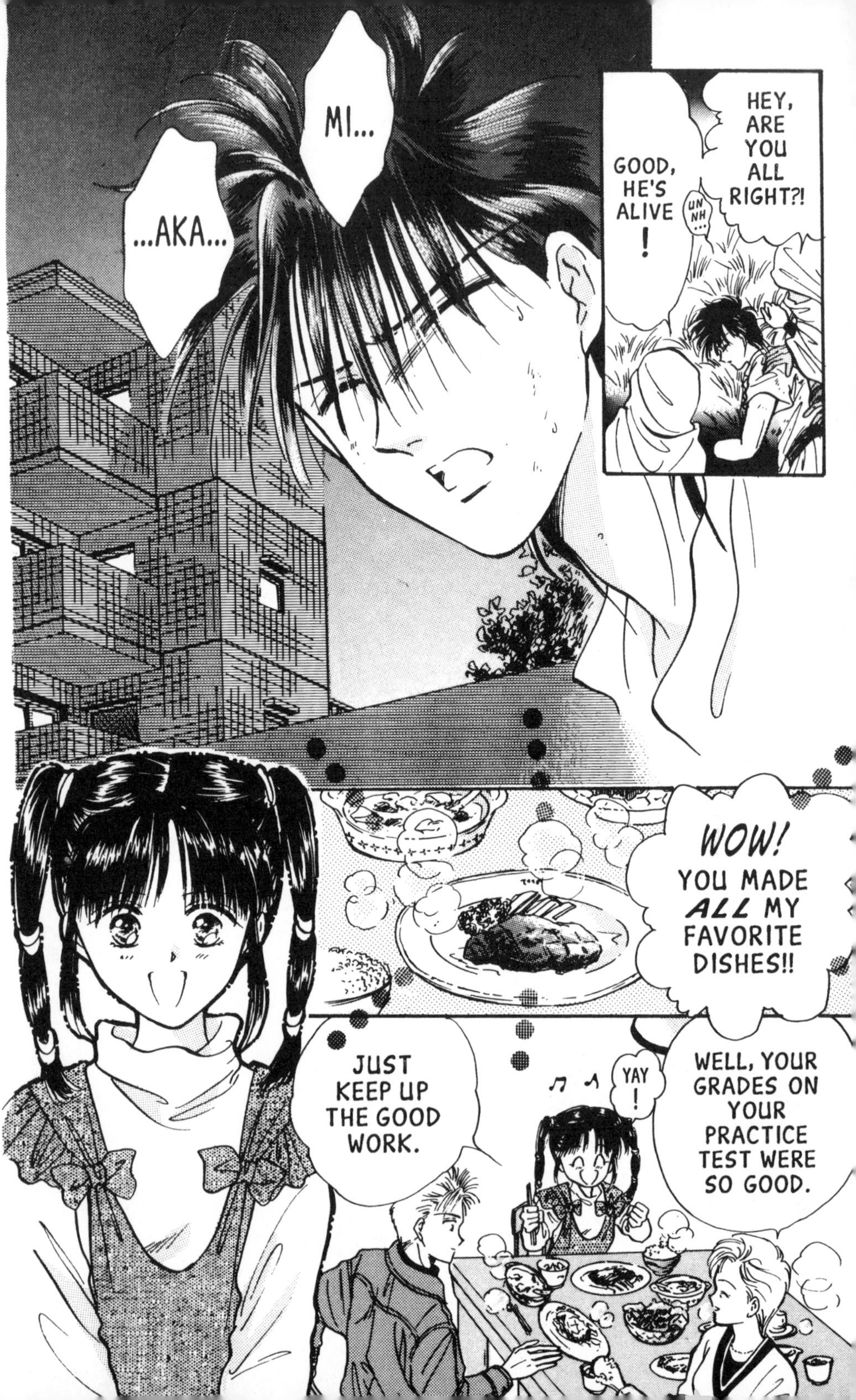
HEY, ARE YOU ALL RIGHT?!
UN NH...
GOOD, HE'S ALIVE!
MI...
...AKA...
WOW! YOU MADE ALL MY FAVORITE DISHES!!
WELL, YOUR GRADES ON YOUR PRACTICE TEST WERE SO GOOD.
YAY!
JUST KEEP UP THE GOOD WORK.

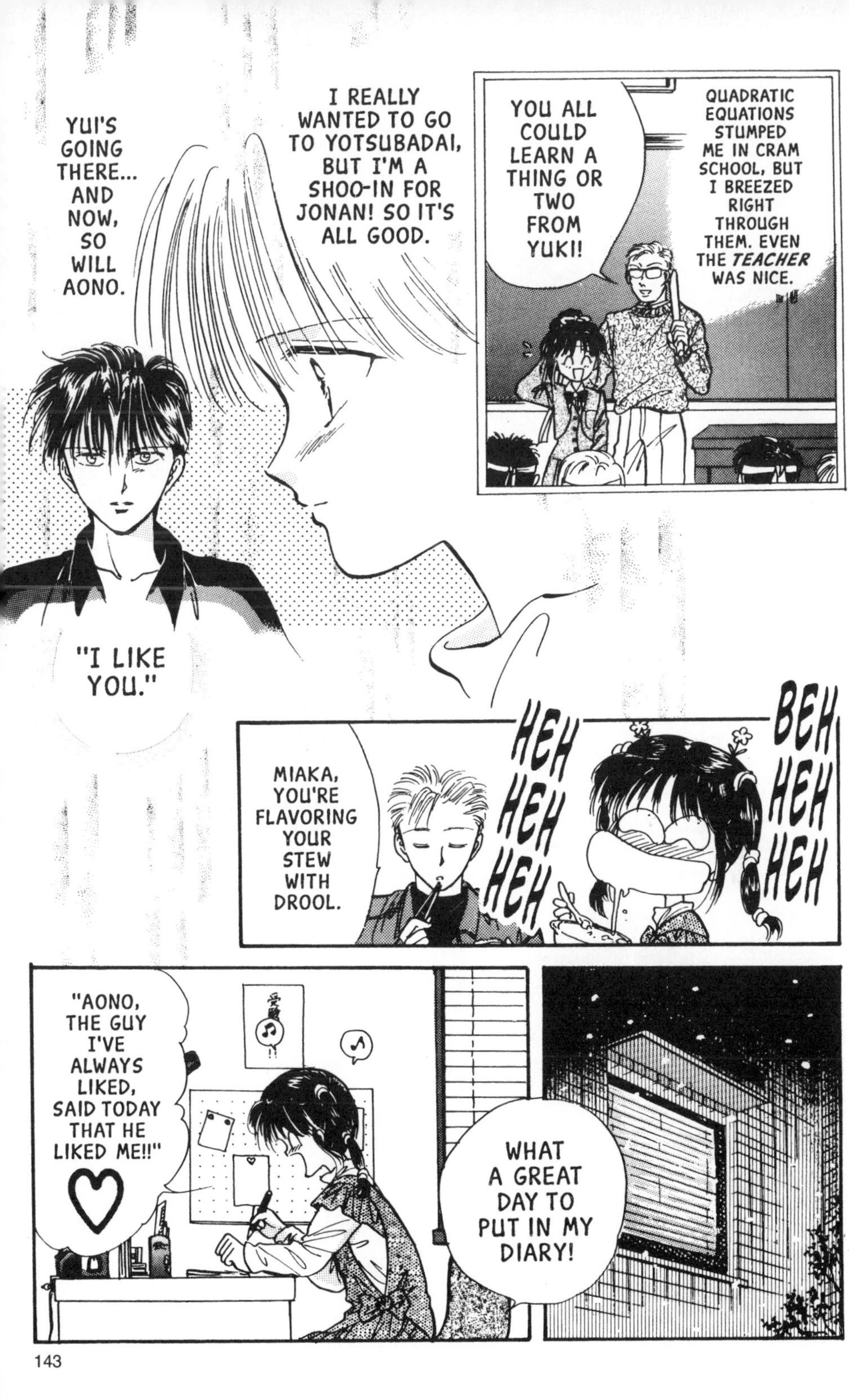
QUADRATIC EQUATIONS STUMPED ME IN CRAM SCHOOL, BUT I BREEZED RIGHT THROUGH THEM. EVEN THE *TEACHER* WAS NICE.
YOU ALL COULD LEARN A THING OR TWO FROM YUKI!
I REALLY WANTED TO GO TO YOTSUBADAI, BUT I'M A SHOO-IN FOR JONAN! SO IT'S ALL GOOD.
YUI'S GOING THERE... AND NOW, SO WILL AONO.
"I LIKE YOU."
BEH HEH HEH HEH
HEH HEH HEH HEH
MIAKA, YOU'RE FLAVORING YOUR STEW WITH DROOL.
"AONO, THE GUY I'VE ALWAYS LIKED, SAID TODAY THAT HE LIKED ME!!"
WHAT A GREAT DAY TO PUT IN MY DIARY!

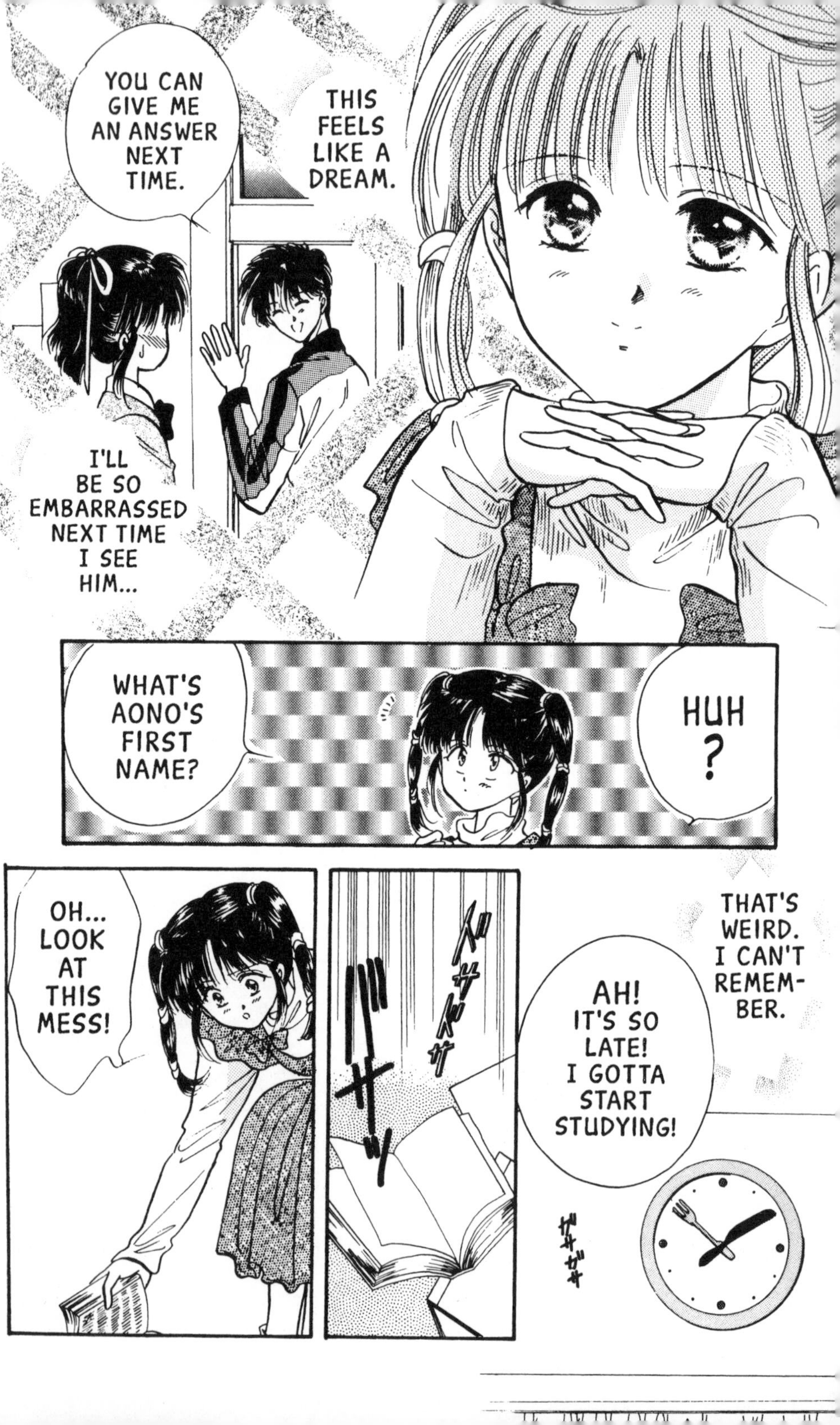
THIS FEELS LIKE A DREAM.
YOU CAN GIVE ME AN ANSWER NEXT TIME.
I'LL BE SO EMBARRASSED NEXT TIME I SEE HIM...
HUH?
WHAT'S AONO'S FIRST NAME?
THAT'S WEIRD. I CAN'T REMEMBER.
AH! IT'S SO LATE! I GOTTA START STUDYING!
OH... LOOK AT THIS MESS!

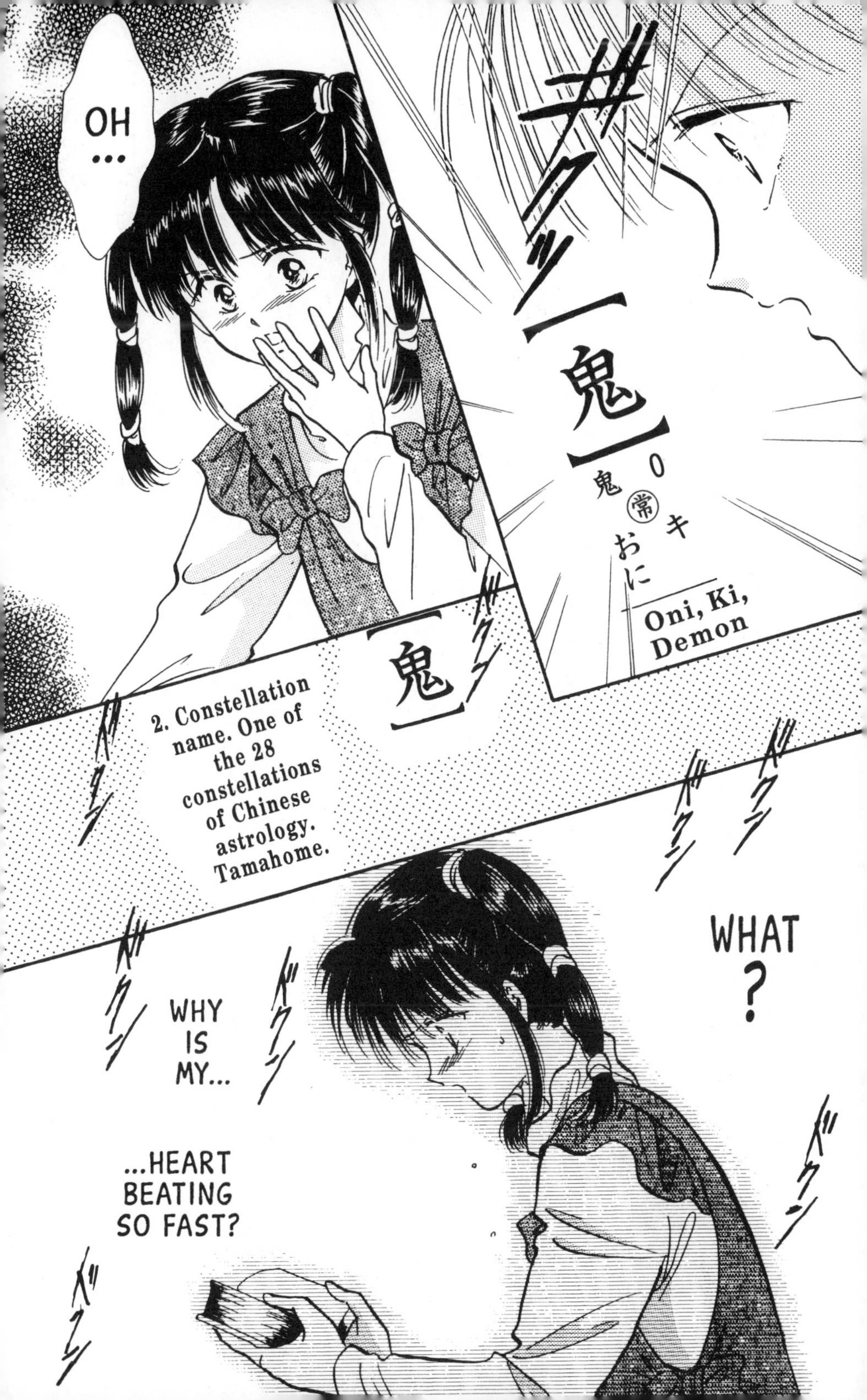

「鬼」
鬼 常 キ おに
Oni, Ki, Demon
OH...
「鬼」
2. Constellation name. One of the 28 constellations of Chinese astrology. Tamahome.
WHAT?
WHY IS MY...
...HEART BEATING SO FAST?

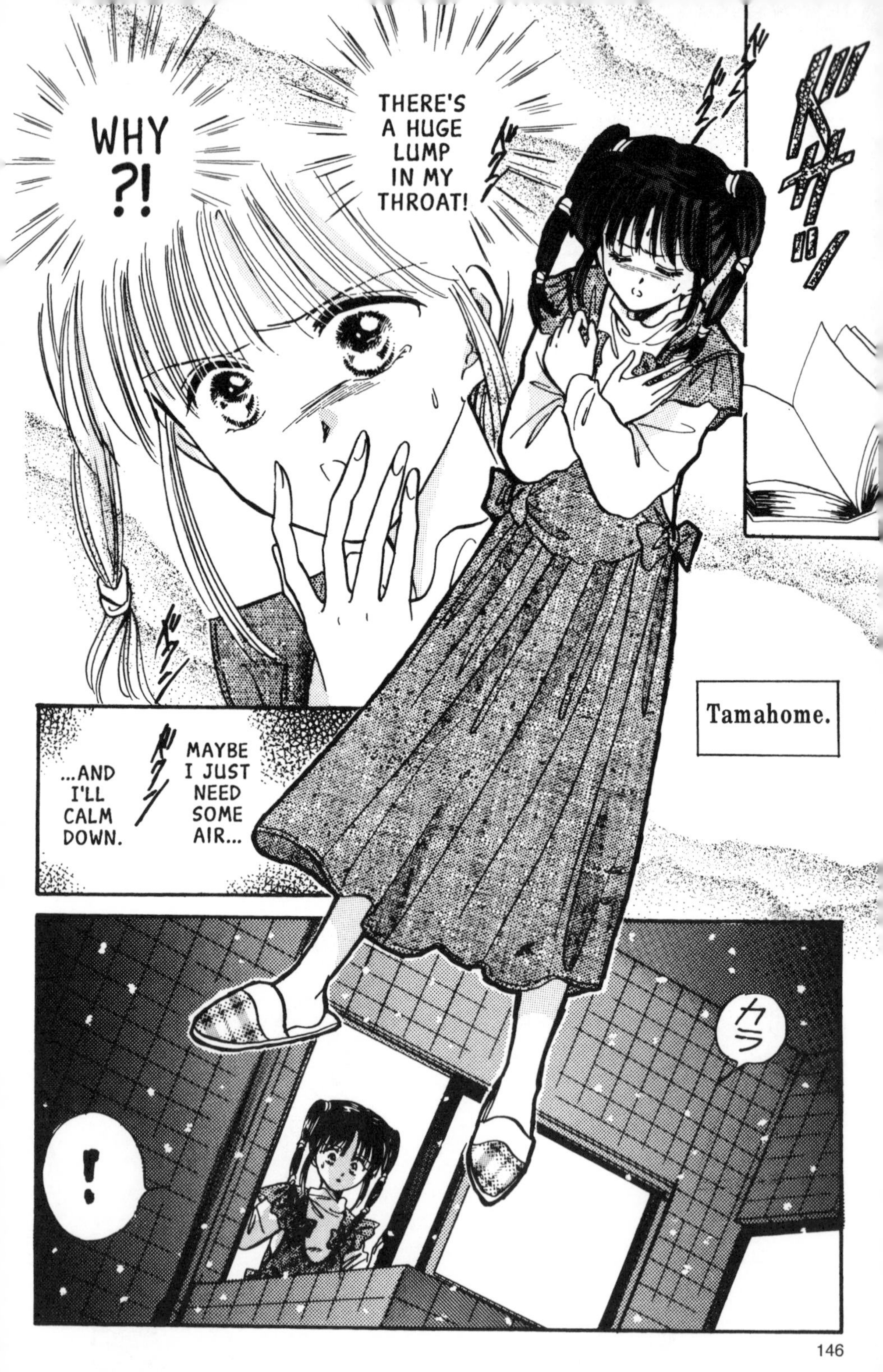
THERE'S A HUGE LUMP IN MY THROAT!
WHY ?!
Tamahome.
MAYBE I JUST NEED SOME AIR...
...AND I'LL CALM DOWN.
カラ
!

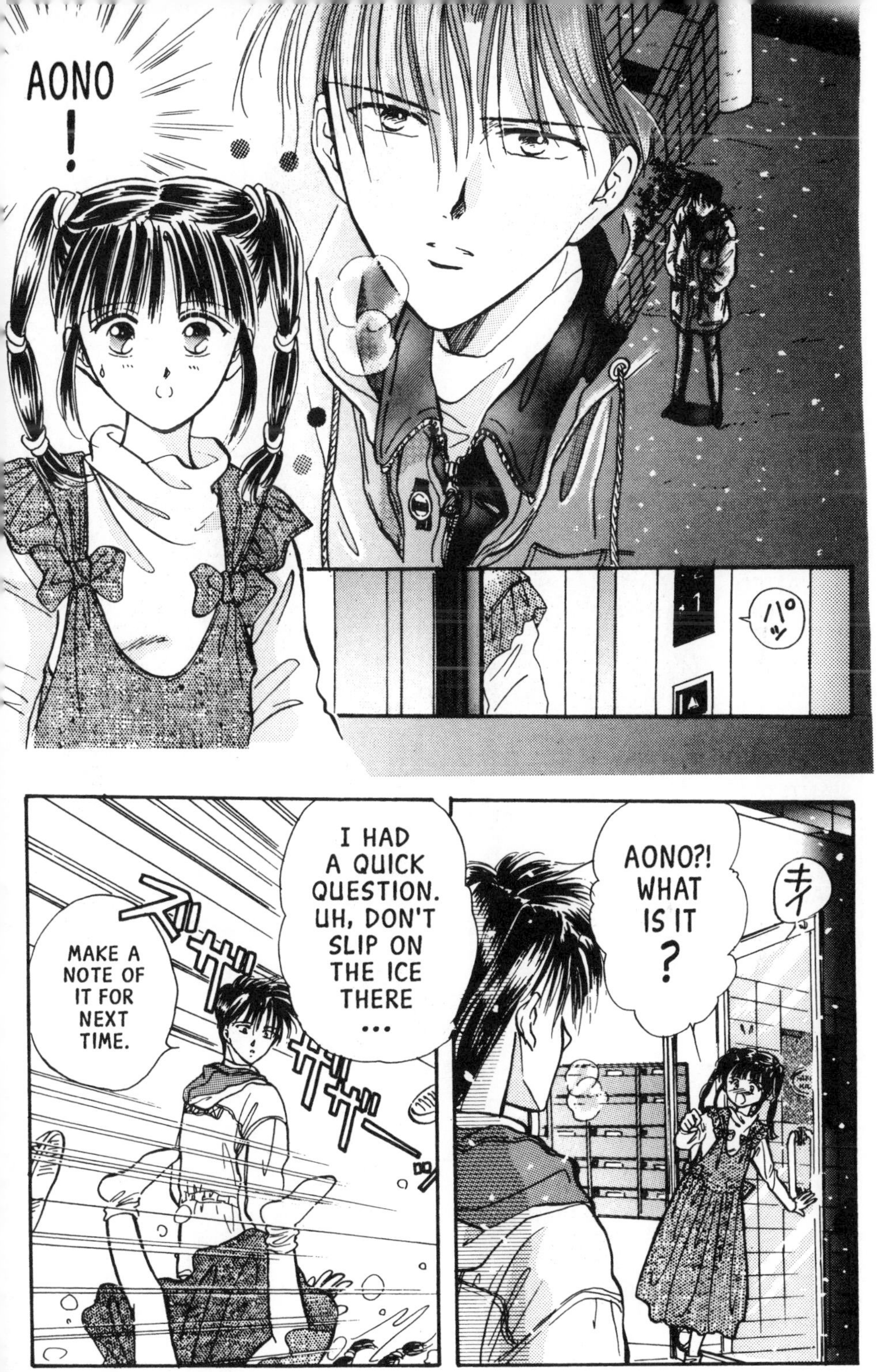
AONO!
パッ
キイ
AONO?! WHAT IS IT?
I HAD A QUICK QUESTION. UH, DON'T SLIP ON THE ICE THERE...
MAKE A NOTE OF IT FOR NEXT TIME.

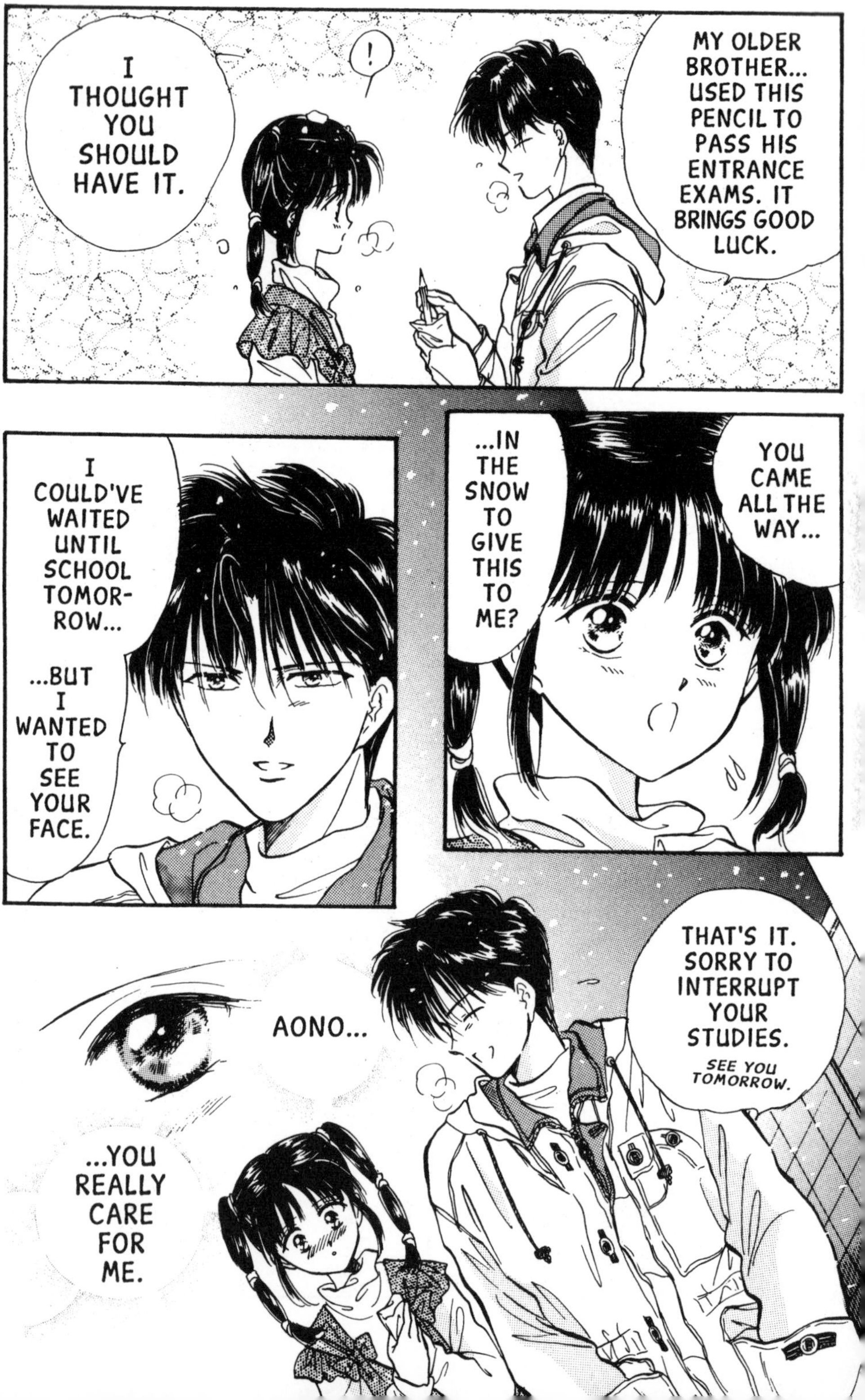
MY OLDER BROTHER... USED THIS PENCIL TO PASS HIS ENTRANCE EXAMS. IT BRINGS GOOD LUCK.
!
I THOUGHT YOU SHOULD HAVE IT.
YOU CAME ALL THE WAY...
...IN THE SNOW TO GIVE THIS TO ME?
I COULD'VE WAITED UNTIL SCHOOL TOMORROW...
...BUT I WANTED TO SEE YOUR FACE.
THAT'S IT. SORRY TO INTERRUPT YOUR STUDIES.
SEE YOU TOMORROW.
AONO...
...YOU REALLY CARE FOR ME.

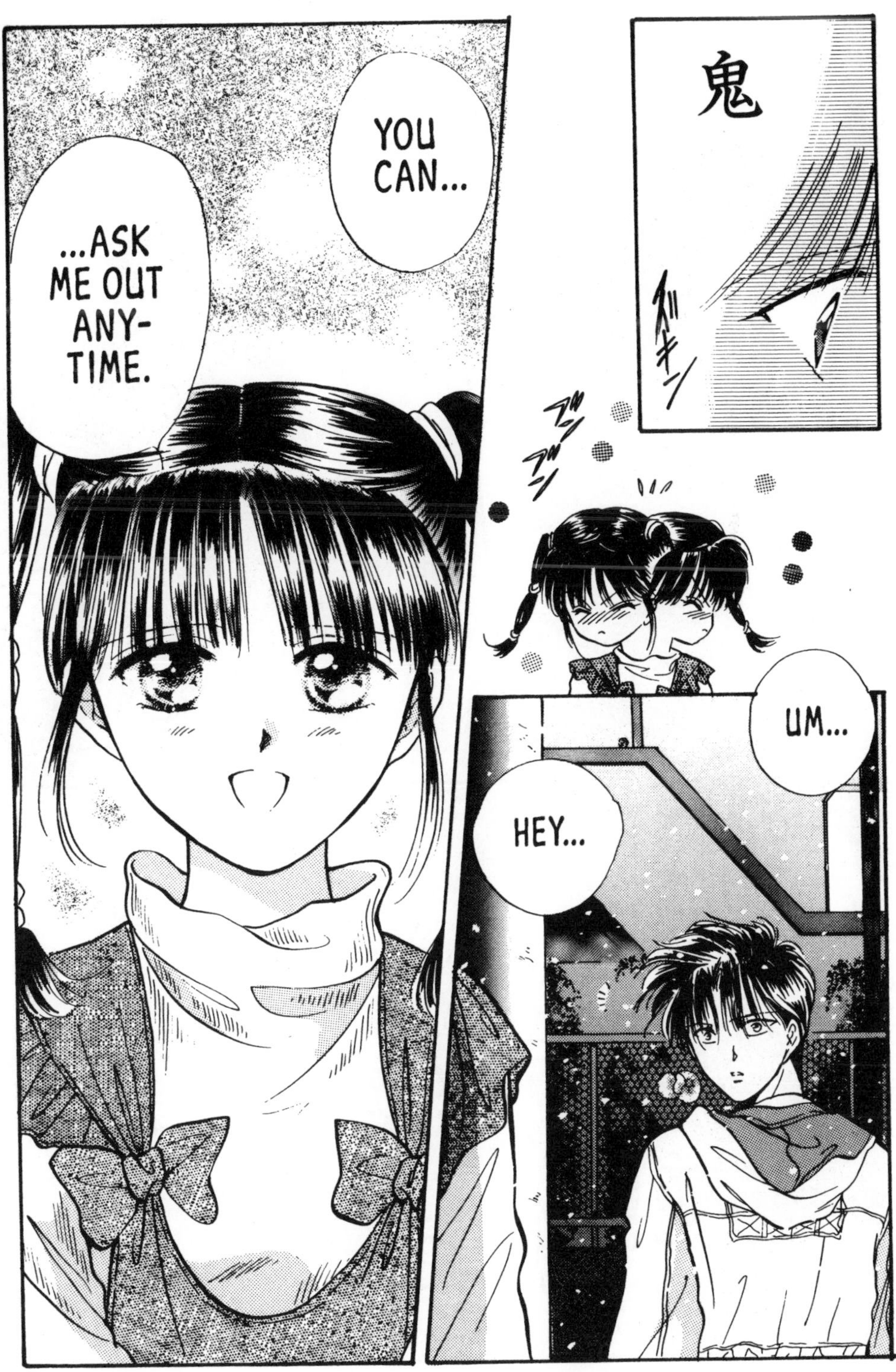
鬼
ブン ブン
UM...
HEY...
YOU CAN...
...ASK ME OUT ANY-TIME.

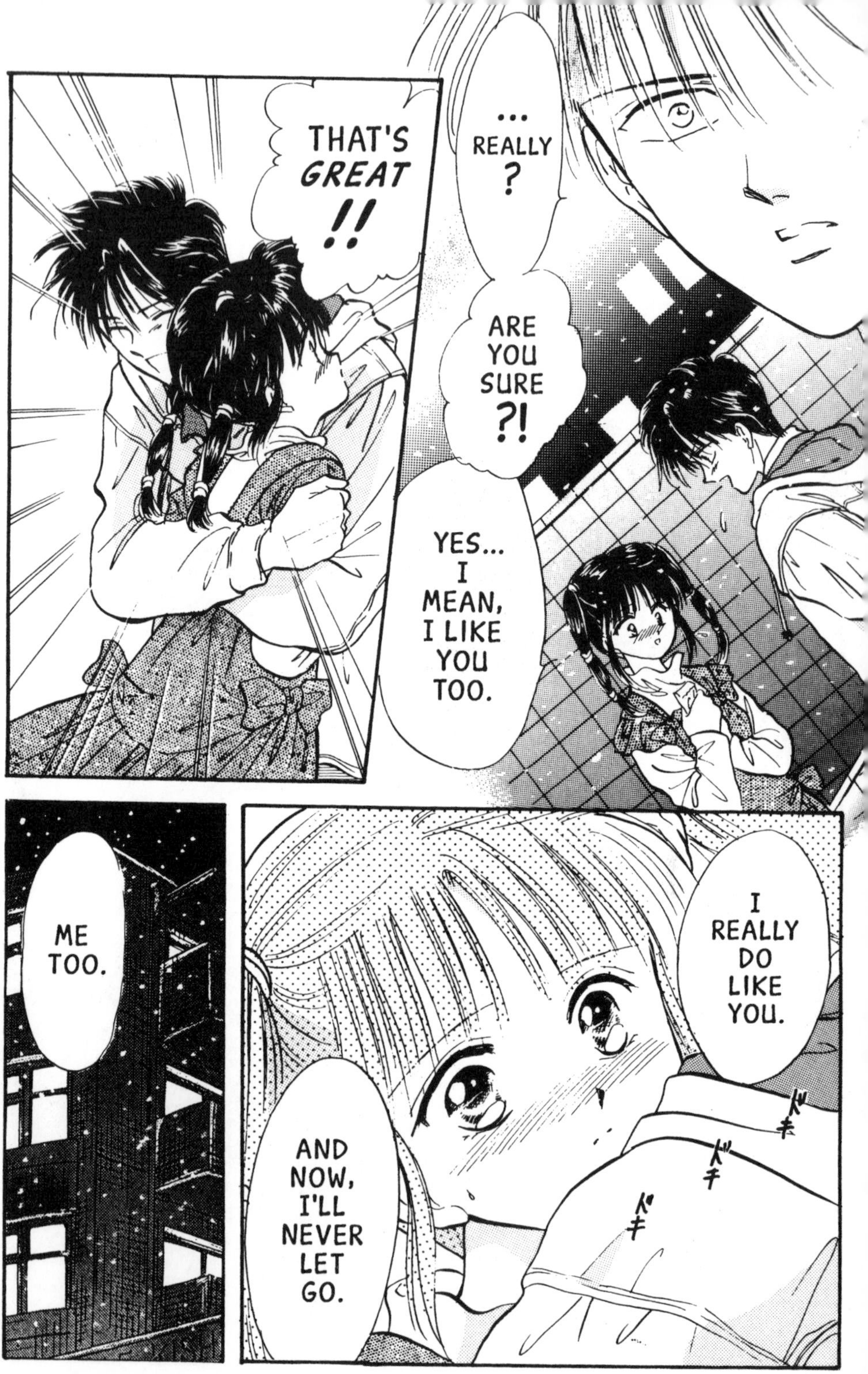
... REALLY ?
ARE YOU SURE ?!
YES... I MEAN, I LIKE YOU TOO.
THAT'S *GREAT* !!
I REALLY DO LIKE YOU.
ドキ
ドキ
ドキ
AND NOW, I'LL NEVER LET GO.
ME TOO.

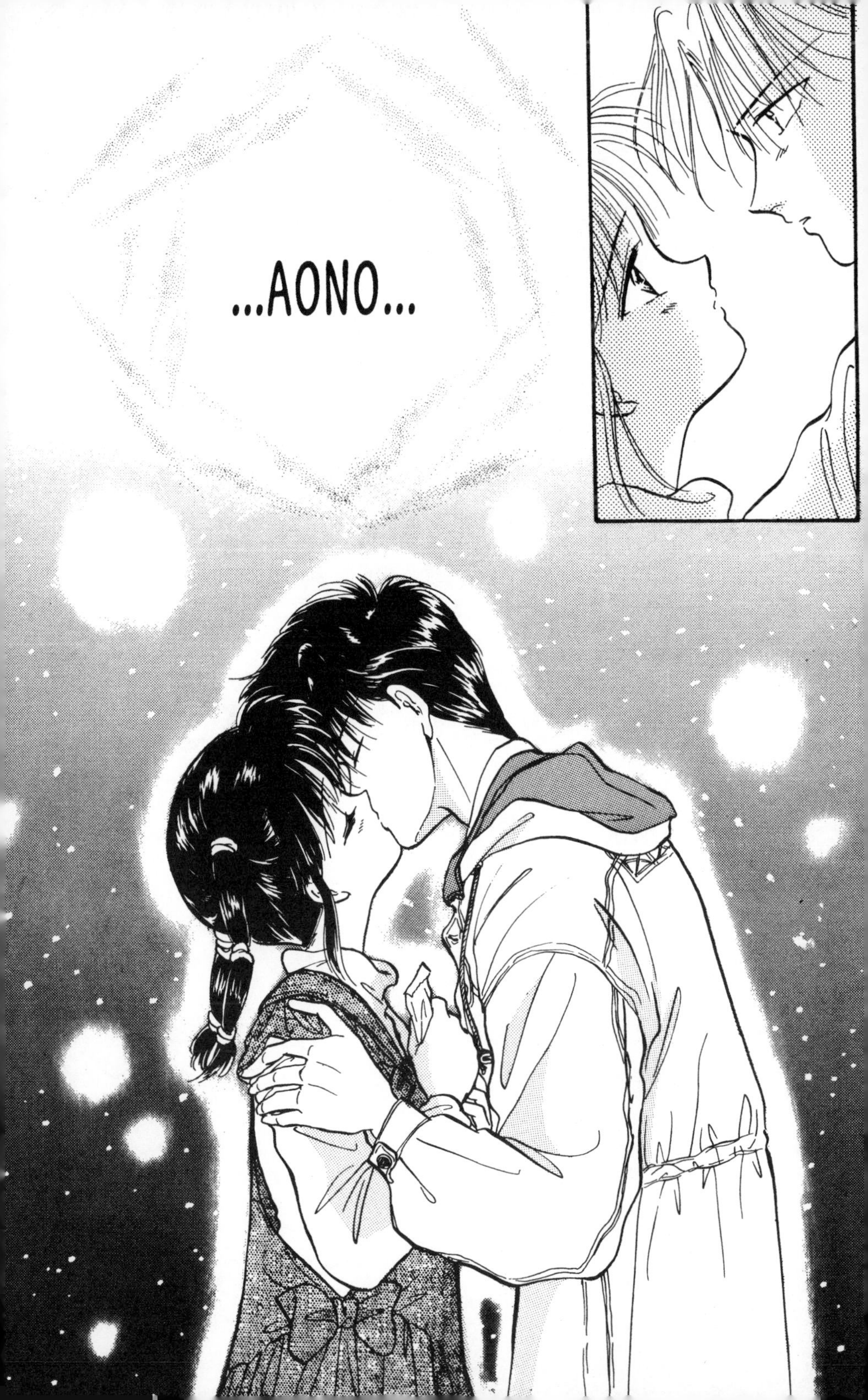
...AONO...

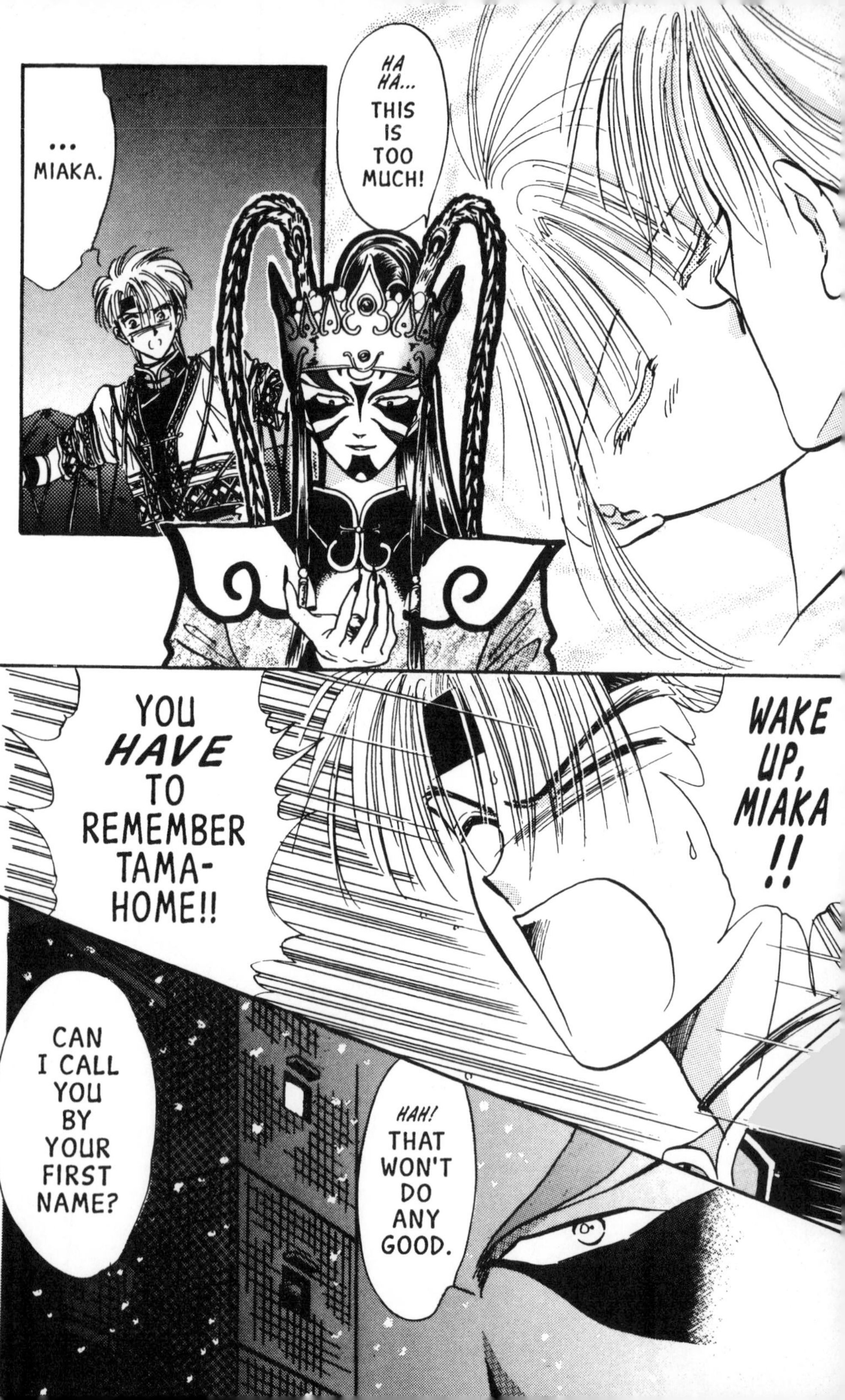
HA HA... THIS IS TOO MUCH!
... MIAKA.
WAKE UP, MIAKA!!
YOU HAVE TO REMEMBER TAMA-HOME!!
HAH! THAT WON'T DO ANY GOOD.
CAN I CALL YOU BY YOUR FIRST NAME?

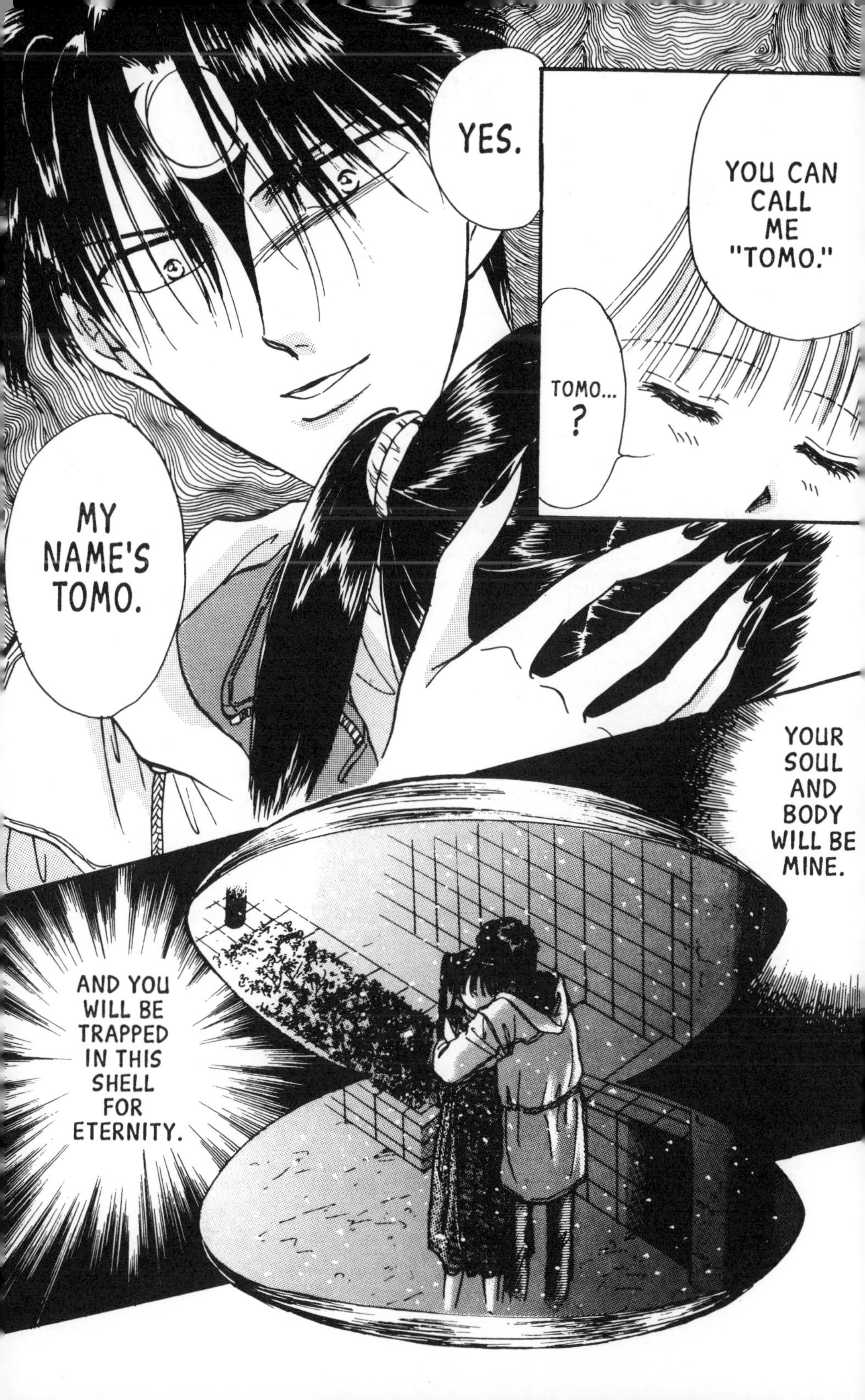
YOU CAN CALL ME "TOMO."
TOMO... ?
YES.
MY NAME'S TOMO.
YOUR SOUL AND BODY WILL BE MINE.
AND YOU WILL BE TRAPPED IN THIS SHELL FOR ETERNITY.

What's So Fushigi About *Fushigi Yūgi* #2

Hey, the name keeps on changing!

Q1: I know Miaka has spare clothes, but what is Yui doing about her clothes?
A: Yui has very nimble fingers. I'm sure she can sew her own underwear using silk-like fabrics! She probably has her uniform washed every night.

Q2: Is Tomo gay? I mean the outfit...
A: Yep. (To be blunt.) Tomo is homosexual. Furthermore, he's in love with Nakago! ☺ His criticisms of Nakago may be an expression of love. "Why," you ask. He just ended up this way. Those of you who know Chinese opera might've realized that I had the opera in mind for his character. The feathers are also from it. In fact, they might be even more gaudy in the actual opera.
After I first drew Tomo, I saw *Farewell My Concubine*, and there was that scene where the female impersonator lead is in love with the male protagonist during the performance of "Front and Back." Which might make you think, "so it's a movie about gay guys." No, not at all!! The drama's much deeper than that. What a great movie! Really! Then there was also *M Butterfly* (about a man who doesn't realize the woman he falls for is in fact a man), and then this Chinese opera...

Personally, a gay theme is no different from a straight theme for me. Those factors were simply in the atmosphere when I came up with Tomo. But ever since Fushigi began, assistant after assistant would not stop talking about it! ☺ With characters like this, I guess it's only natural. What does ya thinks, Olive Oyl? I guess everyone just got into it.
And so Tomo got his look and personality. By the way, I had the same kind of question with regard to Nakago (refer to left comic). Although he isn't gay, he wouldn't let gender stand in his way if he is attracted to someone. It seems natural if you think of it as attraction between people rather than attraction between the sexes.
That's what I thought after seeing Farewell My Concubine.

SPECIAL STRIP
What's So Fushigi About *Fushigi Yūgi*, Special Edition

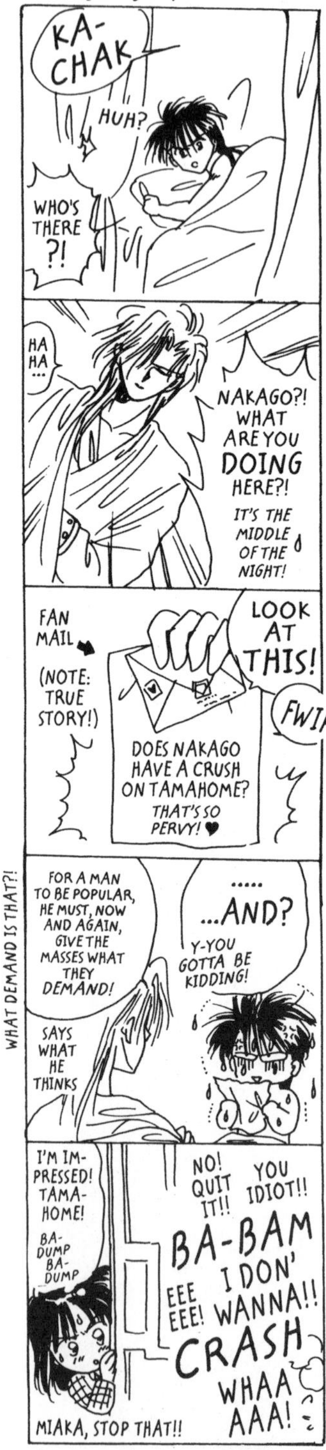
KA-CHAK
HUH?
WHO'S THERE ?!
NAKAGO?! WHAT ARE YOU DOING HERE?!
IT'S THE MIDDLE OF THE NIGHT!
HA HA...
LOOK AT THIS!
FWIP
FAN MAIL
(NOTE: TRUE STORY!)
DOES NAKAGO HAVE A CRUSH ON TAMAHOME? THAT'S SO PERVY! ♥
.....
...AND?
Y-YOU GOTTA BE KIDDING!
FOR A MAN TO BE POPULAR, HE MUST, NOW AND AGAIN, GIVE THE MASSES WHAT THEY DEMAND!
SAYS WHAT HE THINKS
WHAT DEMAND IS THAT?!
YOU IDIOT!!
NO! QUIT IT!!
I'M IMPRESSED! TAMAHOME!
BA-BAM
I DON' WANNA!!
EEE EEE!
BA-DUMP BA-DUMP
CRASH
WHAA AAA!
MIAKA, STOP THAT!!

There must be dojinshi like this! ☺ I heard there was one for Tasuki and Nuriko. I'd like to see it!

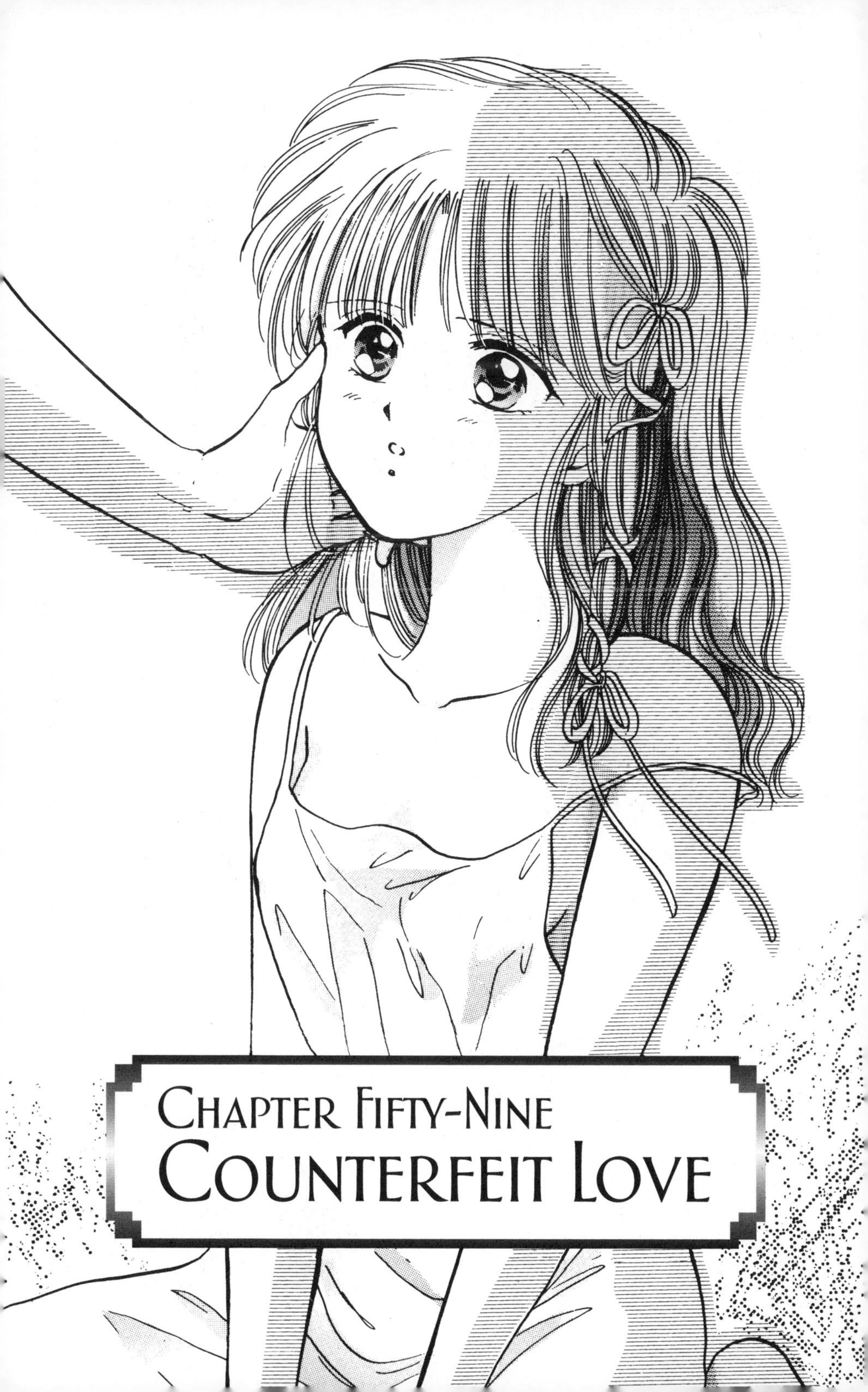
CHAPTER FIFTY-NINE
COUNTERFEIT LOVE

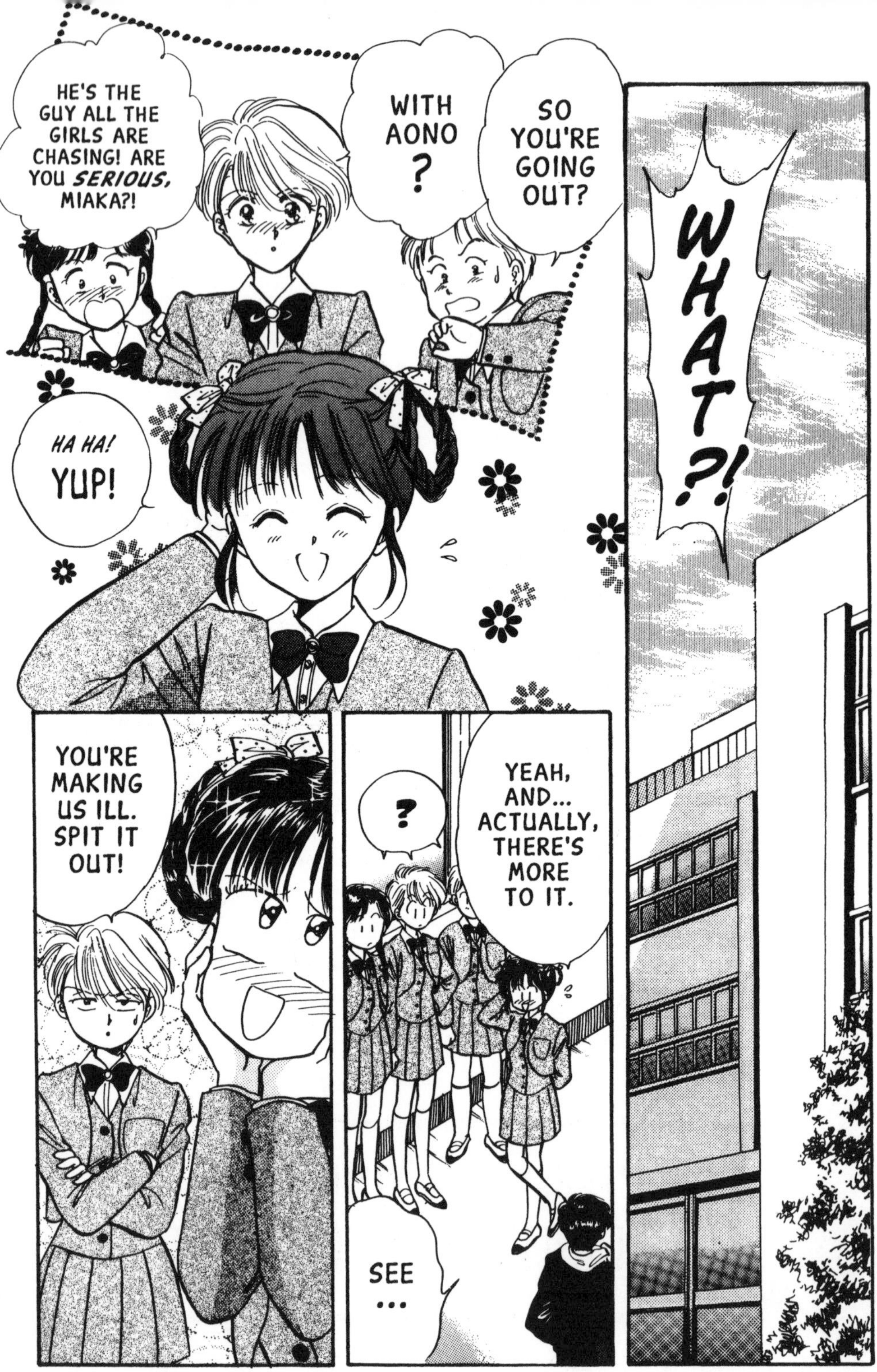
WHAT?!
SO YOU'RE GOING OUT?
WITH AONO?
HE'S THE GUY ALL THE GIRLS ARE CHASING! ARE YOU *SERIOUS,* MIAKA?!
HA HA! YUP!
YEAH, AND... ACTUALLY, THERE'S MORE TO IT.
?
SEE...
YOU'RE MAKING US ILL. SPIT IT OUT!

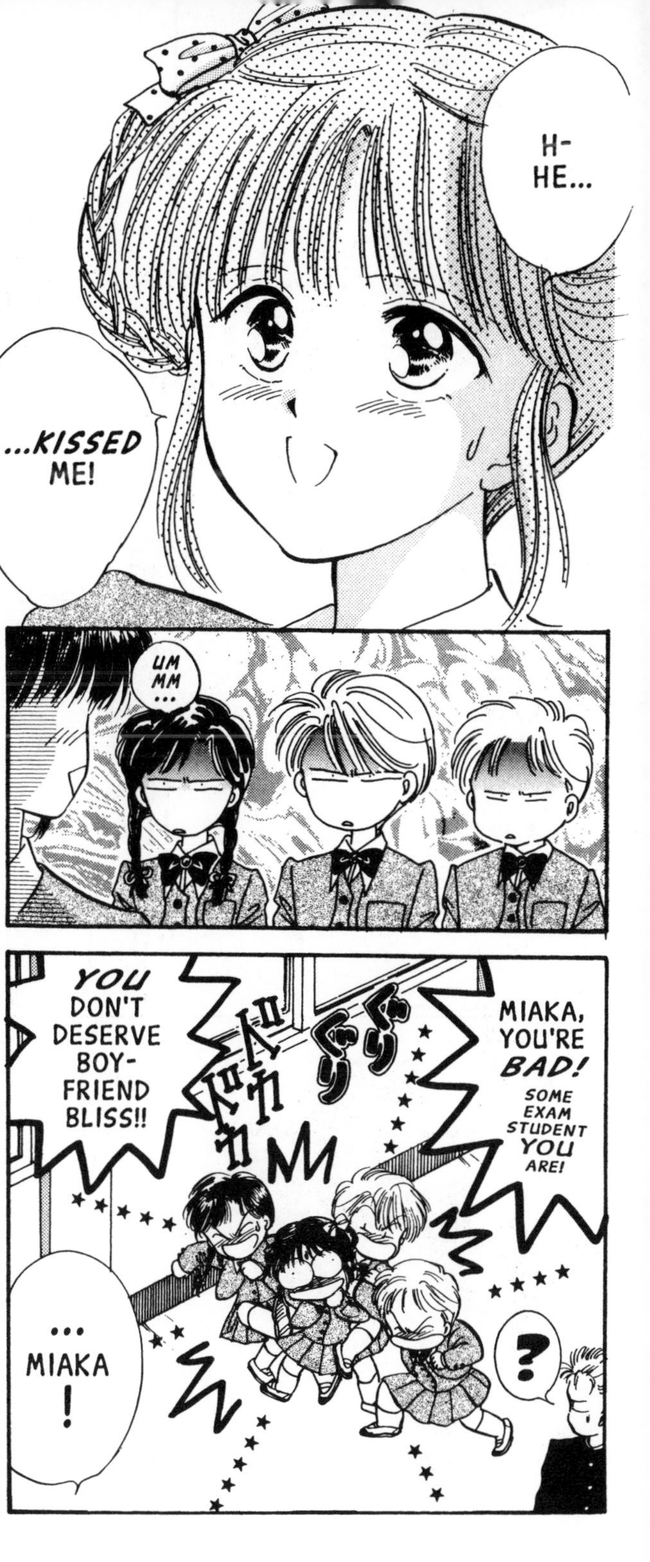
H- HE...
...KISSED ME!
UM MM ...
MIAKA, YOU'RE BAD!
SOME EXAM STUDENT YOU ARE!
YOU DON'T DESERVE BOY-FRIEND BLISS!!
?
... MIAKA !

And because of that... I was so nervous I started sweating! (My entire body was drenched!) My voice broke. Blood rushed to my head. I almost fainted. I just totally clammed up...and couldn't even talk to them!! Dammit!! It was so sad and pathetic. I really missed my chance!
I couldn't even look at them. Why am I so shy?! Argh!! If I could only be more social!! B-but no!! Readers who know anime and voice actors must know what I'm talking about!! I mean voice actors are like superstars!!!
I would recall the voice of the character from the anime that I watched all through high school, and I'd realize, "S-so this person did..." There was no way I could start up a conversation. But finally a reporter from Animate arranged for a short interview with myself along with Mr. Seki, Mr. Matsumoto, Ms. Hidaka, and Ms. Yamazaki... "Wow, we're actually breathing the same air in the same room!" Am I a sickie or WHAT?! ☺ I actually sat next to Ms. Hidaka! She actually shook my hand. She actually shook my hand!! Pant, pant, pant. She seemed so cheerful and kind.
She and Ms. Yamazaki told me they had bought my graphic novels, and I almost burst out crying. Sniff, sniff... But I was so shy, I couldn't watch and had my back to them. I'm such an idiot! (During the entire time they were recording!) That's right! I hear that if you send in the survey form that comes with the CD, you'll get an autographed sign card with the signatures of all 12 voice actors and Yuu Watase! Really?! They must be copies... One of them might be real! (I have one displayed in my room!♫) I'm acting like a junior high school girl!!

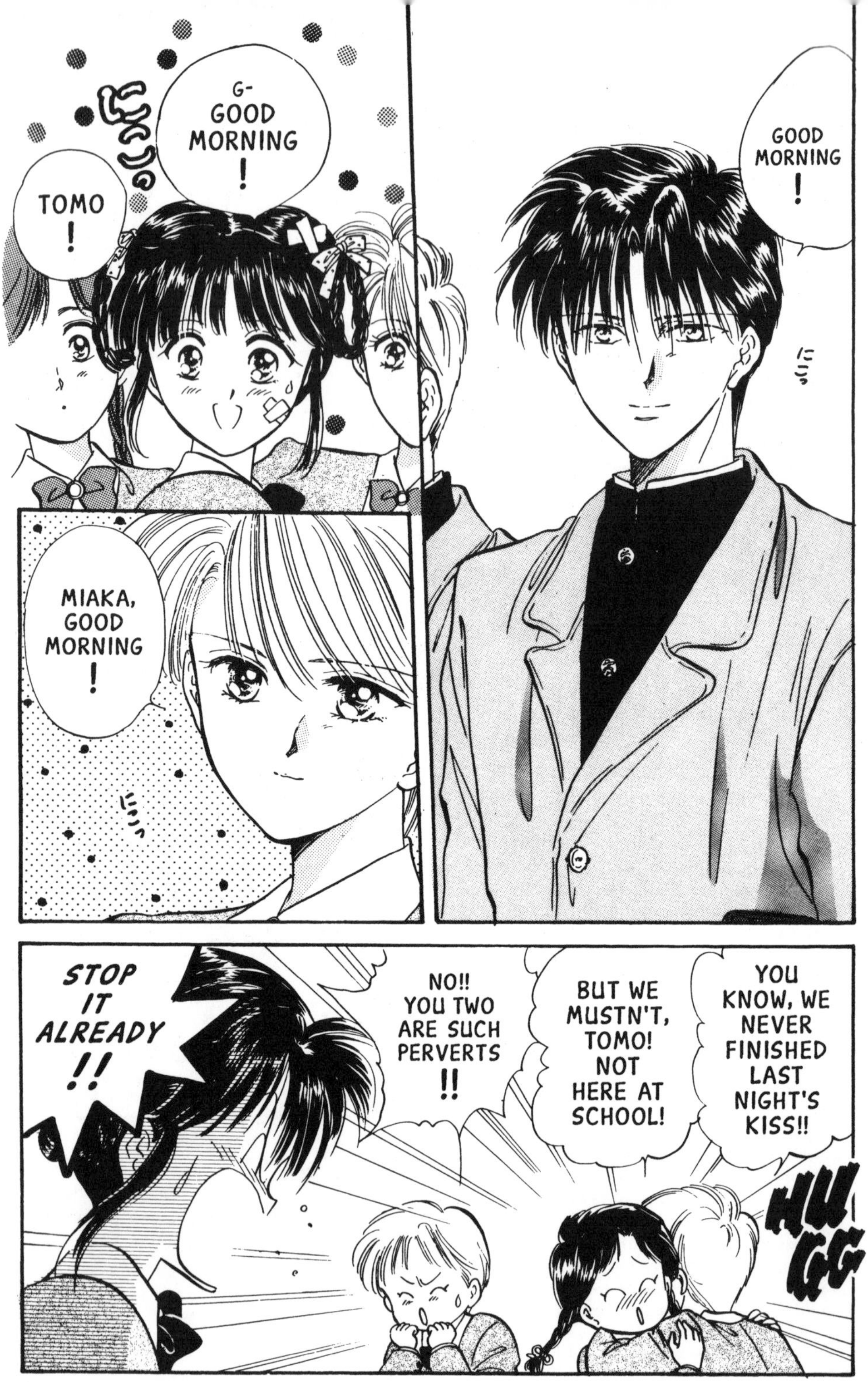
GOOD MORNING!
G- GOOD MORNING!
TOMO!
MIAKA, GOOD MORNING!
YOU KNOW, WE NEVER FINISHED LAST NIGHT'S KISS!!
BUT WE MUSTN'T, TOMO! NOT HERE AT SCHOOL!
NO!! YOU TWO ARE SUCH PERVERTS!!
STOP IT ALREADY!!
HUGG

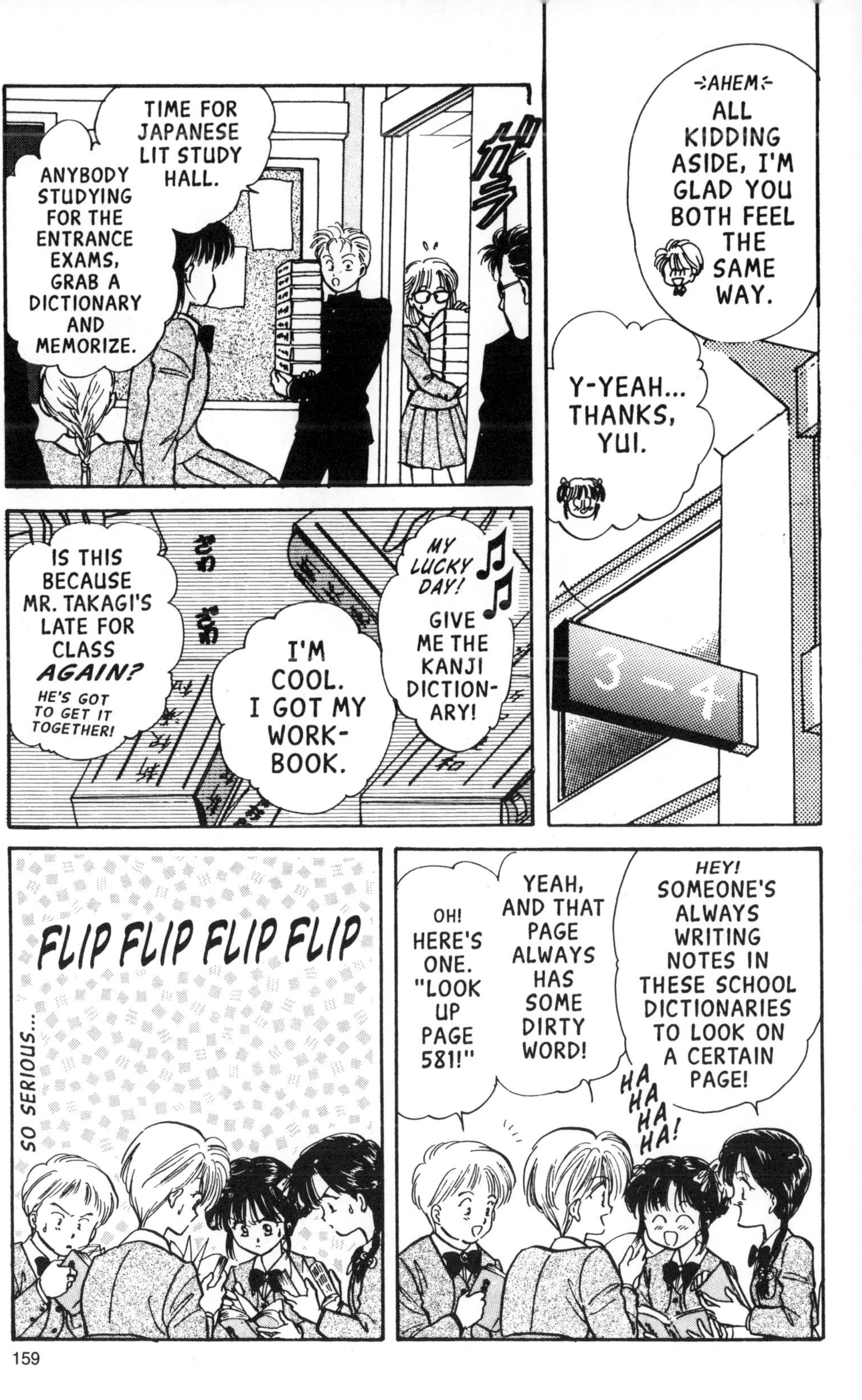
-AHEM-
ALL KIDDING ASIDE, I'M GLAD YOU BOTH FEEL THE SAME WAY.
Y-YEAH... THANKS, YUI.
3-4
ガラ
TIME FOR JAPANESE LIT STUDY HALL.
ANYBODY STUDYING FOR THE ENTRANCE EXAMS, GRAB A DICTIONARY AND MEMORIZE.
MY LUCKY DAY!
GIVE ME THE KANJI DICTIONARY!
I'M COOL. I GOT MY WORK-BOOK.
IS THIS BECAUSE MR. TAKAGI'S LATE FOR CLASS AGAIN?
HE'S GOT TO GET IT TOGETHER!
HEY! SOMEONE'S ALWAYS WRITING NOTES IN THESE SCHOOL DICTIONARIES TO LOOK ON A CERTAIN PAGE!
YEAH, AND THAT PAGE ALWAYS HAS SOME DIRTY WORD!
OH! HERE'S ONE. "LOOK UP PAGE 581!"
HA HA HA HA!
FLIP FLIP FLIP FLIP
SO SERIOUS...

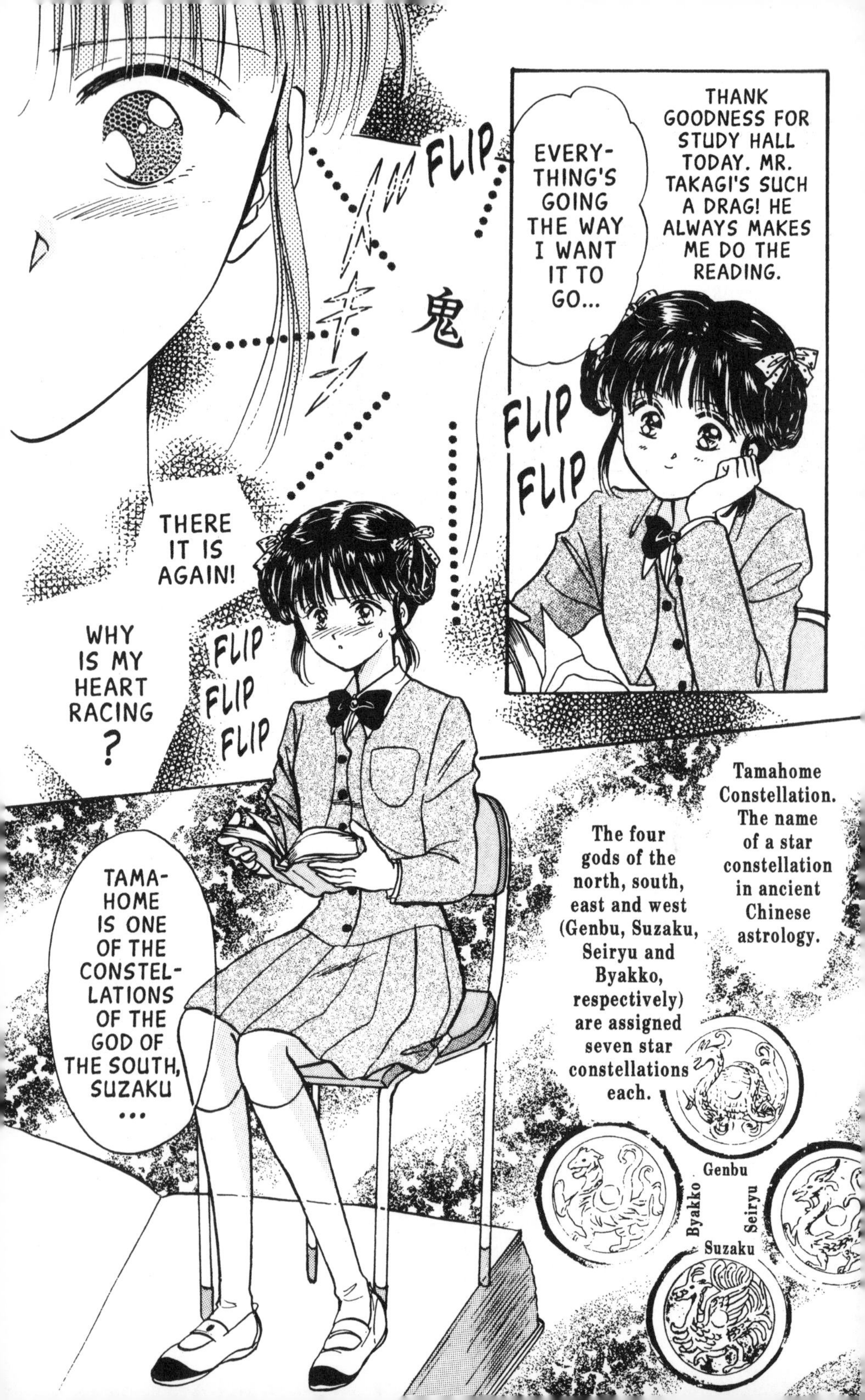

THANK GOODNESS FOR STUDY HALL TODAY. MR. TAKAGI'S SUCH A DRAG! HE ALWAYS MAKES ME DO THE READING.
EVERY-THING'S GOING THE WAY I WANT IT TO GO...
FLIP FLIP
FLIP
鬼
THERE IT IS AGAIN!
WHY IS MY HEART RACING ?
FLIP FLIP FLIP
Tamahome Constellation. The name of a star constellation in ancient Chinese astrology.
The four gods of the north, south, east and west (Genbu, Suzaku, Seiryu and Byakko, respectively) are assigned seven star constellations each.
Genbu
Seiryu
Byakko
Suzaku
TAMA-HOME IS ONE OF THE CONSTEL-LATIONS OF THE GOD OF THE SOUTH, SUZAKU ...

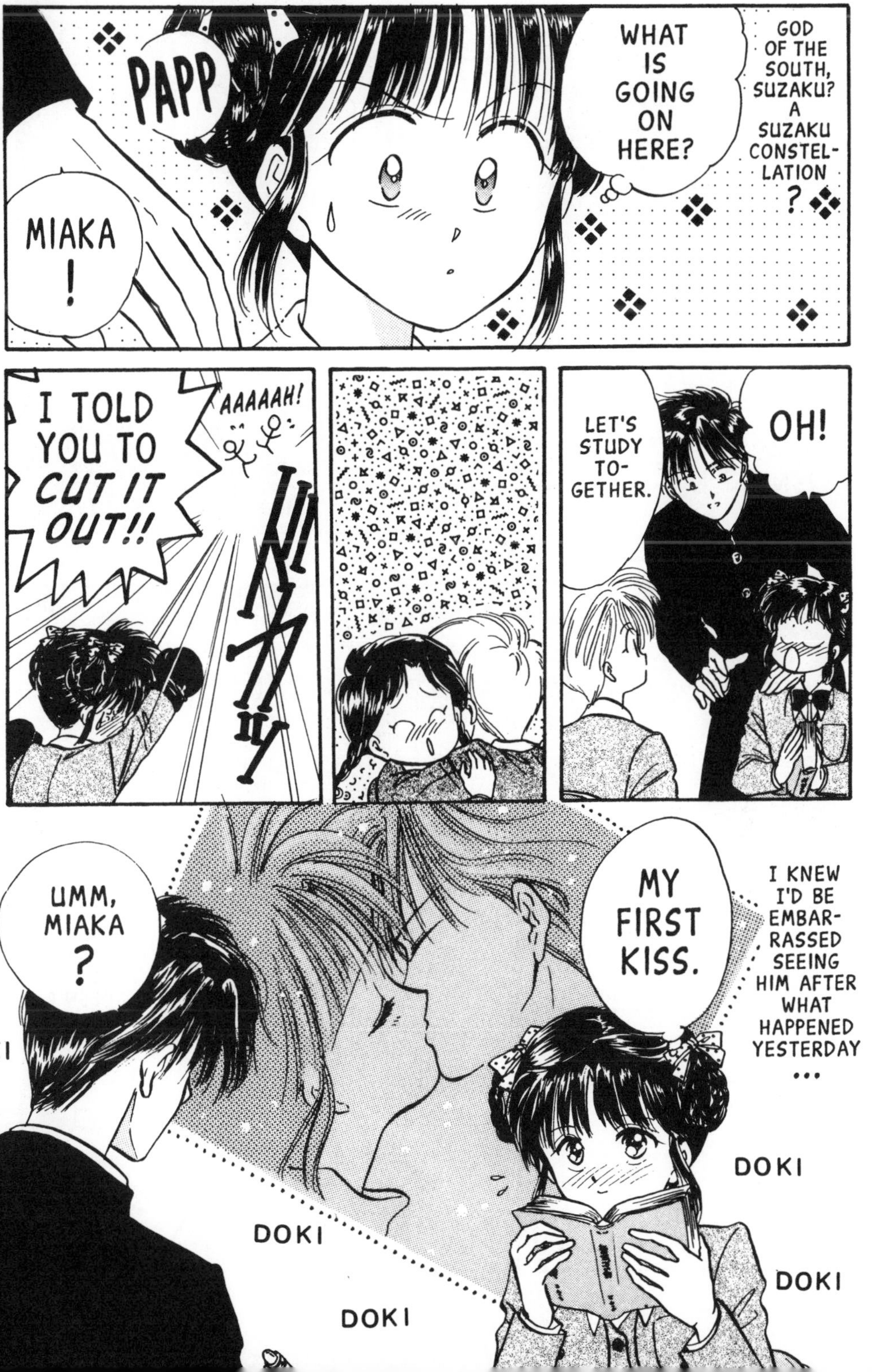
GOD OF THE SOUTH, SUZAKU? A SUZAKU CONSTEL-LATION ?
WHAT IS GOING ON HERE?
PAPP
MIAKA !
OH!
LET'S STUDY TO-GETHER.
AAAAAH!
I TOLD YOU TO *CUT IT OUT!!*
I KNEW I'D BE EMBAR-RASSED SEEING HIM AFTER WHAT HAPPENED YESTERDAY ...
MY FIRST KISS.
UMM, MIAKA ?
DOKI
DOKI
DOKI
DOKI
KI

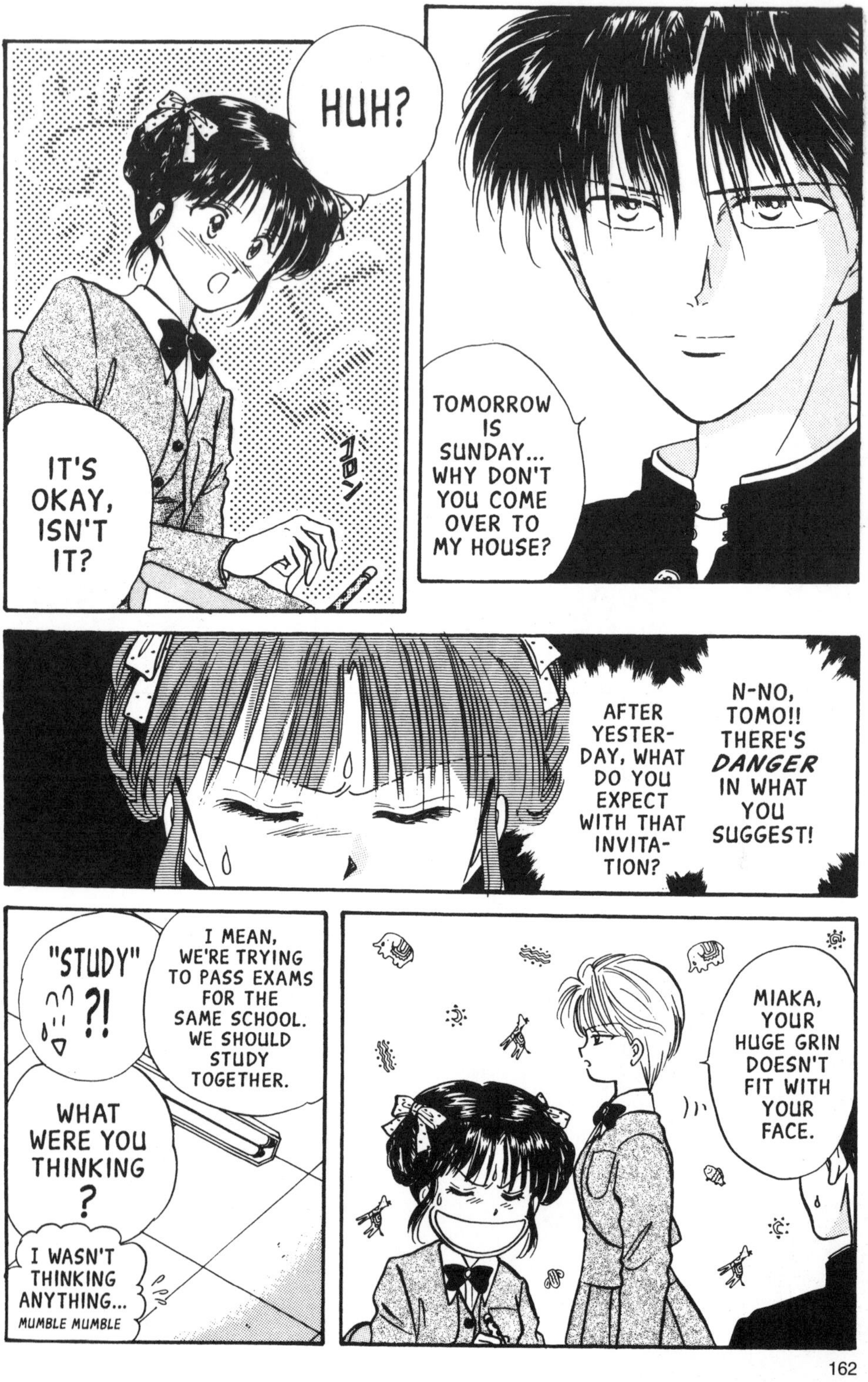
TOMORROW IS SUNDAY... WHY DON'T YOU COME OVER TO MY HOUSE?
HUH?
IT'S OKAY, ISN'T IT?
N-NO, TOMO!! THERE'S *DANGER* IN WHAT YOU SUGGEST!
AFTER YESTER-DAY, WHAT DO YOU EXPECT WITH THAT INVITA-TION?
MIAKA, YOUR HUGE GRIN DOESN'T FIT WITH YOUR FACE.
I MEAN, WE'RE TRYING TO PASS EXAMS FOR THE SAME SCHOOL. WE SHOULD STUDY TOGETHER.
"STUDY" ?!
WHAT WERE YOU THINKING ?
I WASN'T THINKING ANYTHING...
MUMBLE MUMBLE

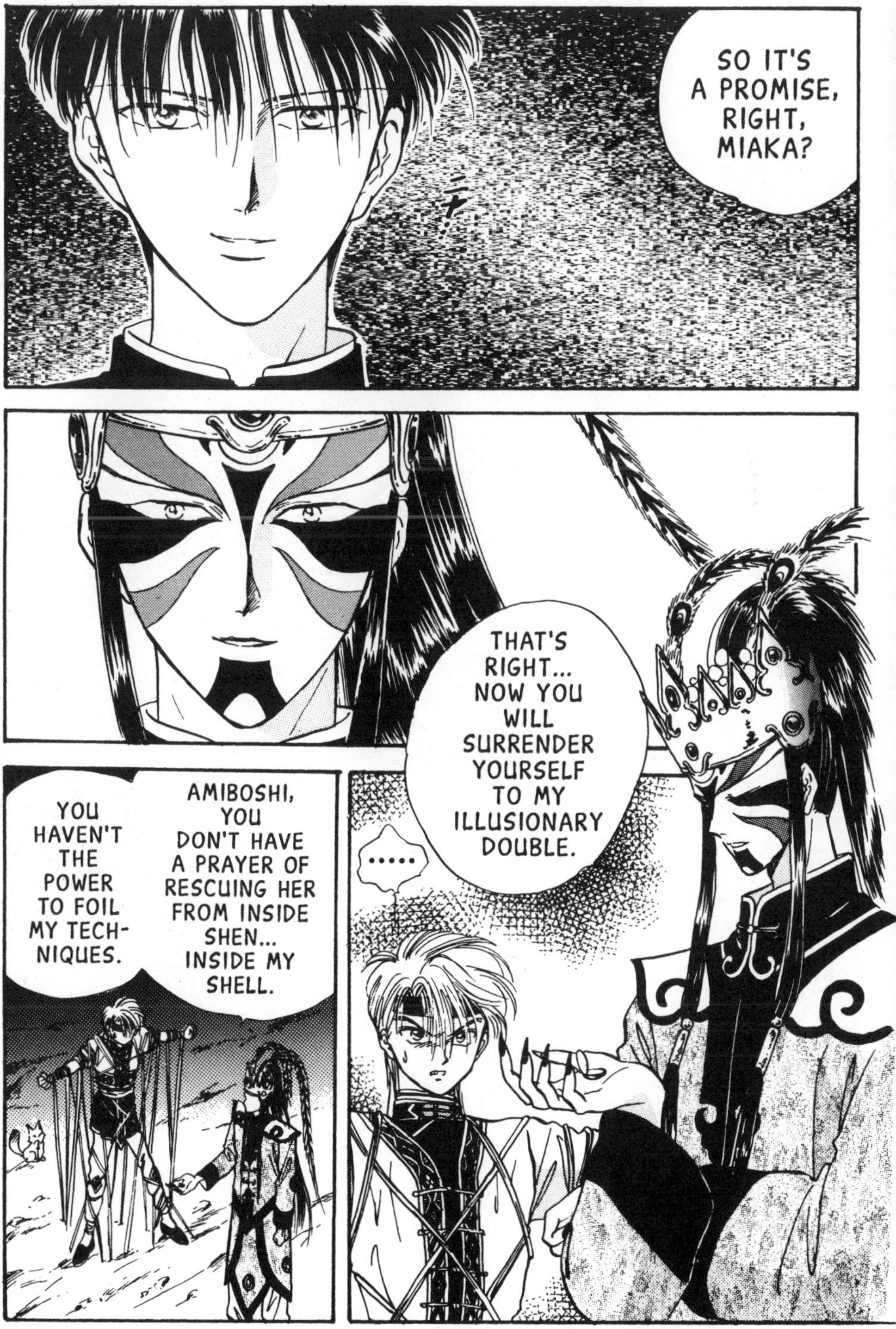
SO IT'S A PROMISE, RIGHT, MIAKA?
THAT'S RIGHT... NOW YOU WILL SURRENDER YOURSELF TO MY ILLUSIONARY DOUBLE.
.....
AMIBOSHI, YOU DON'T HAVE A PRAYER OF RESCUING HER FROM INSIDE SHEN... INSIDE MY SHELL.
YOU HAVEN'T THE POWER TO FOIL MY TECH-NIQUES.

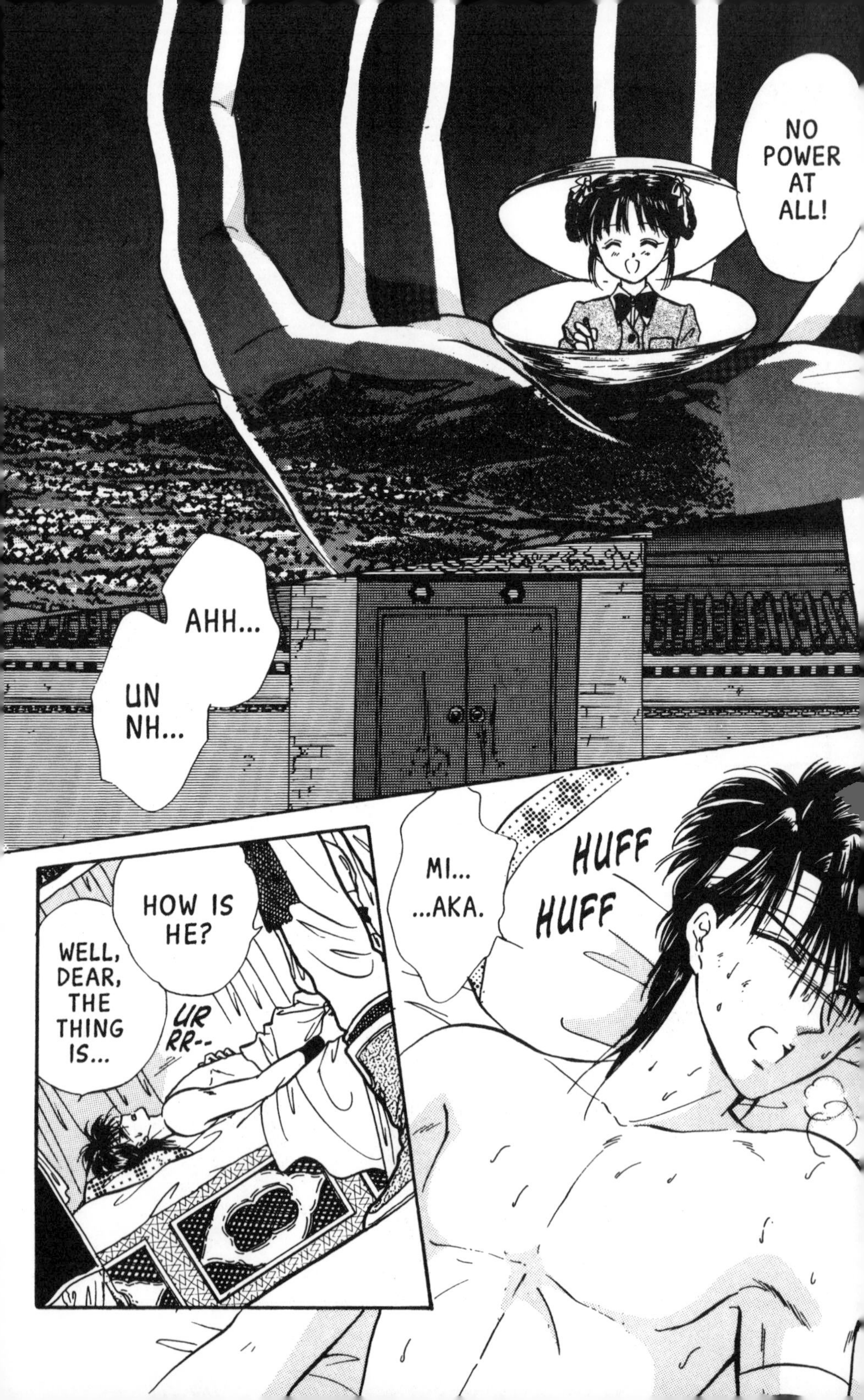
NO POWER AT ALL!
AHH...
UN NH...
HUFF HUFF
MI... ...AKA.
HOW IS HE?
WELL, DEAR, THE THING IS...
URRR--

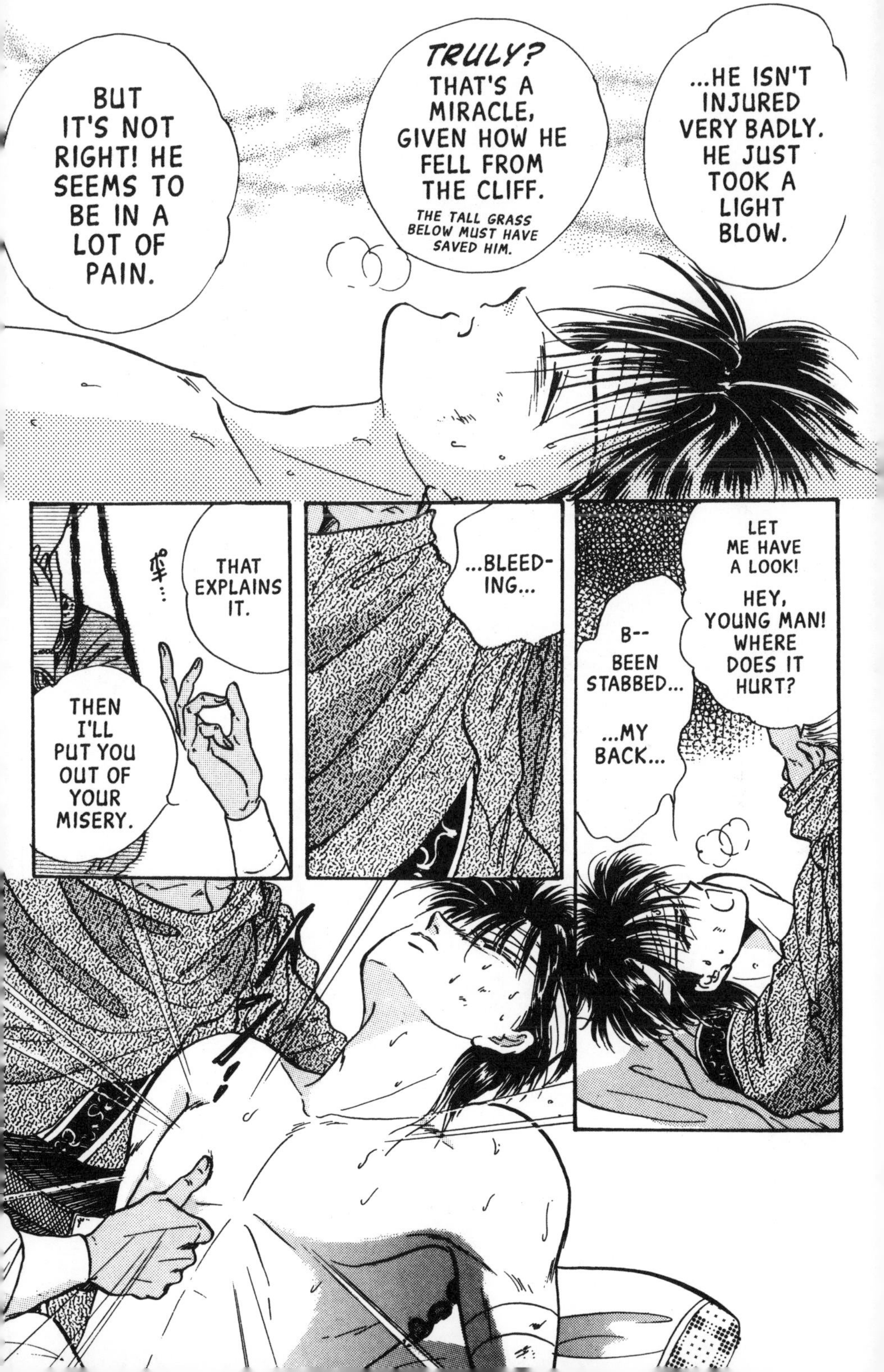
...HE ISN'T INJURED VERY BADLY. HE JUST TOOK A LIGHT BLOW.
TRULY? THAT'S A MIRACLE, GIVEN HOW HE FELL FROM THE CLIFF.
THE TALL GRASS BELOW MUST HAVE SAVED HIM.
BUT IT'S NOT RIGHT! HE SEEMS TO BE IN A LOT OF PAIN.
LET ME HAVE A LOOK!
HEY, YOUNG MAN! WHERE DOES IT HURT?
B-- BEEN STABBED...
...MY BACK...
...BLEED-ING...
THAT EXPLAINS IT.
ポキ...
THEN I'LL PUT YOU OUT OF YOUR MISERY.

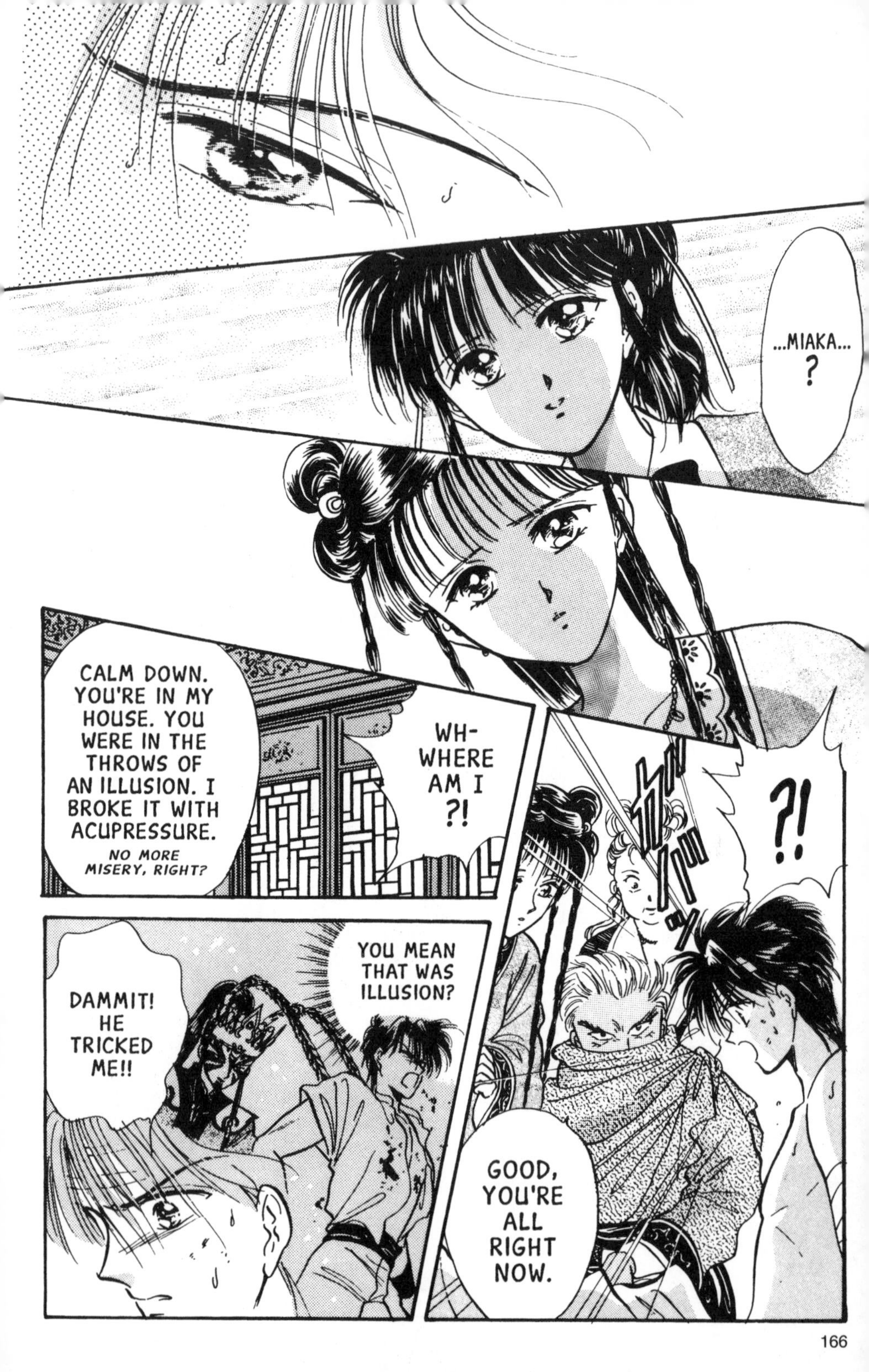
...MIAKA... ?
?!
GOOD, YOU'RE ALL RIGHT NOW.
WH- WHERE AM I ?!
CALM DOWN. YOU'RE IN MY HOUSE. YOU WERE IN THE THROWS OF AN ILLUSION. I BROKE IT WITH ACUPRESSURE.
NO MORE MISERY, RIGHT?
YOU MEAN THAT WAS ILLUSION?
DAMMIT! HE TRICKED ME!!

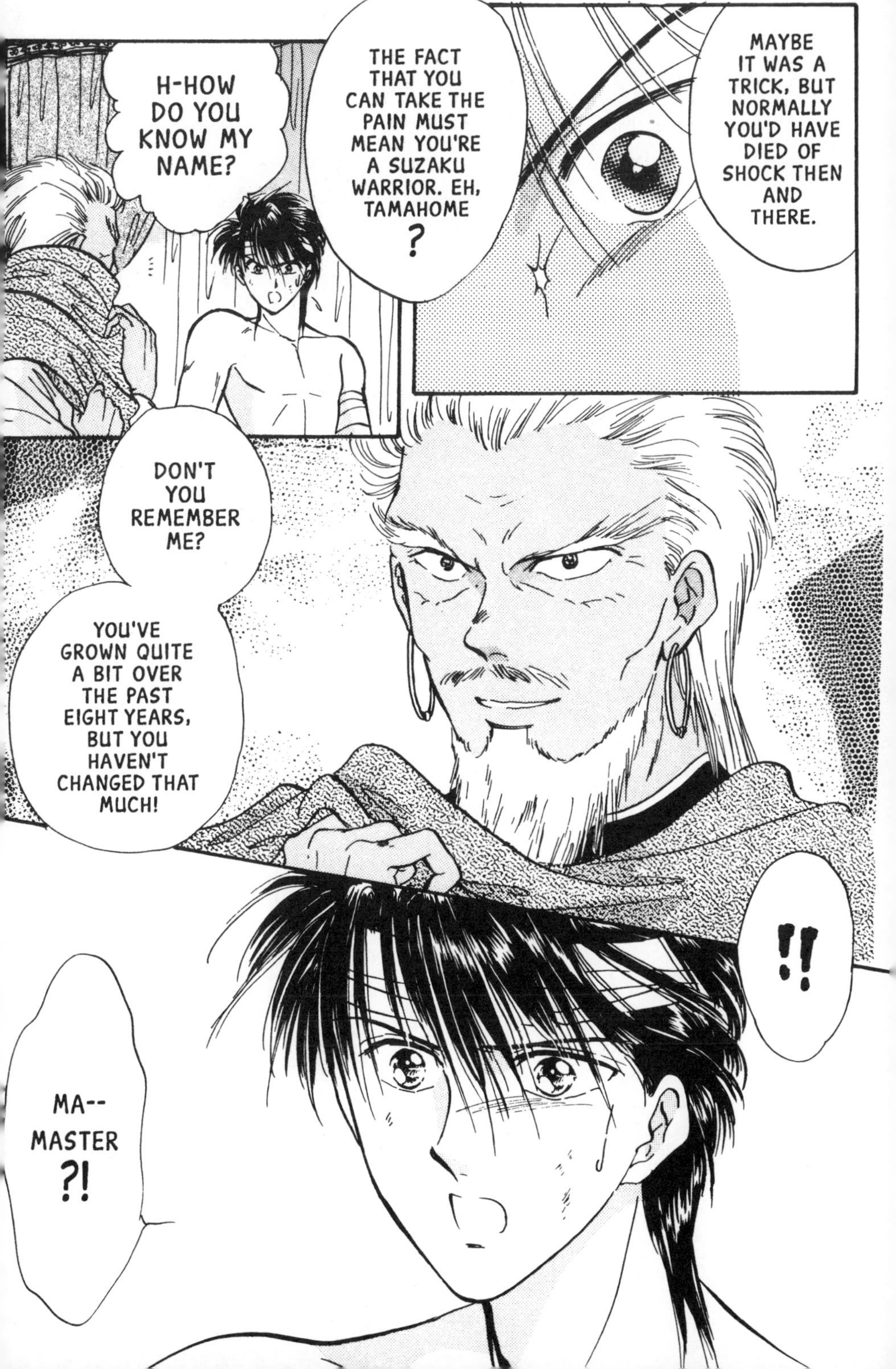
MAYBE IT WAS A TRICK, BUT NORMALLY YOU'D HAVE DIED OF SHOCK THEN AND THERE.
THE FACT THAT YOU CAN TAKE THE PAIN MUST MEAN YOU'RE A SUZAKU WARRIOR. EH, TAMAHOME?
H-HOW DO YOU KNOW MY NAME?
DON'T YOU REMEMBER ME?
YOU'VE GROWN QUITE A BIT OVER THE PAST EIGHT YEARS, BUT YOU HAVEN'T CHANGED THAT MUCH!
!!
MA--MASTER?!

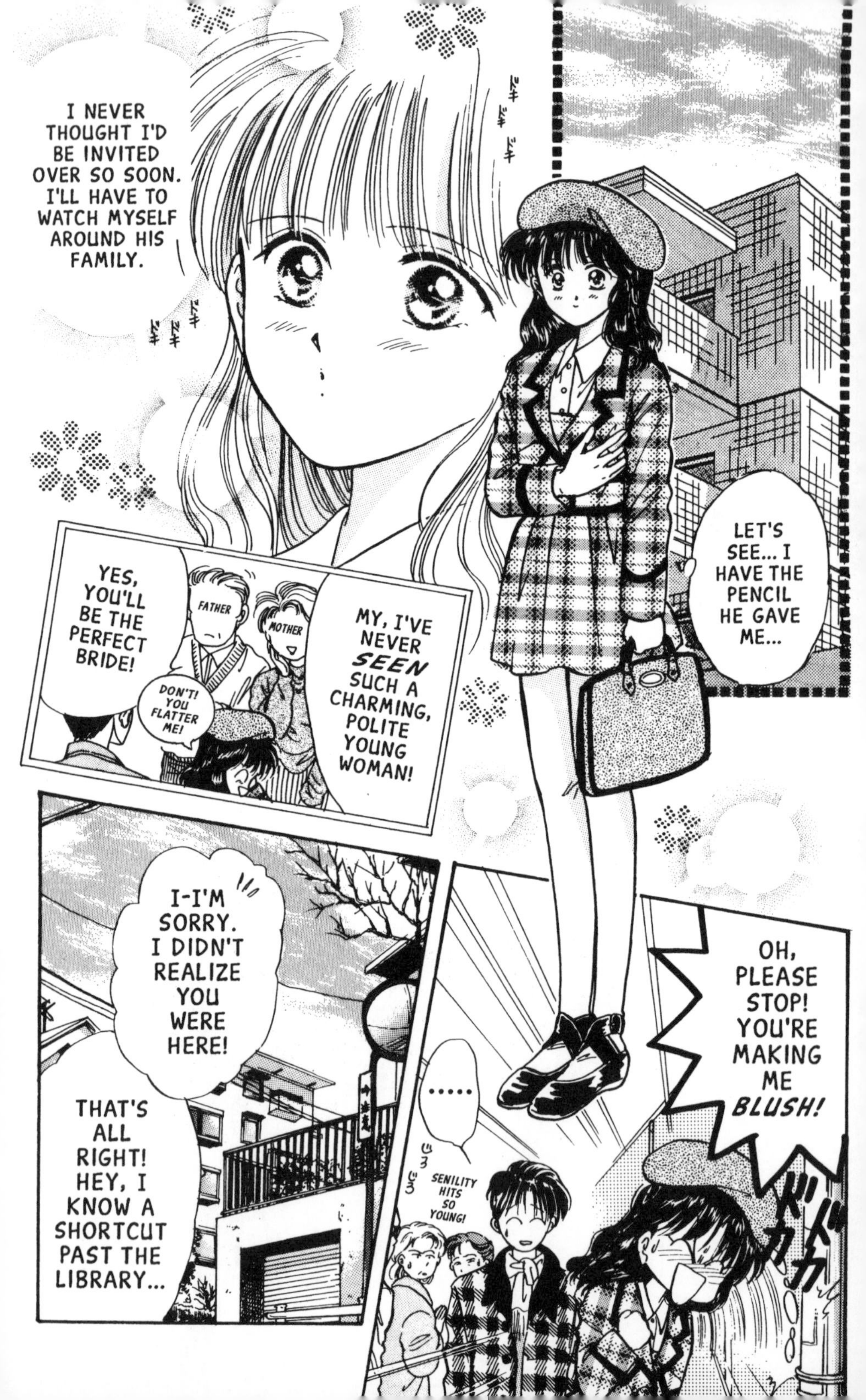
LET'S SEE... I HAVE THE PENCIL HE GAVE ME...
ドキ ドキ ドキ
I NEVER THOUGHT I'D BE INVITED OVER SO SOON. I'LL HAVE TO WATCH MYSELF AROUND HIS FAMILY.
ドキ ドキ ドキ
MY, I'VE NEVER *SEEN* SUCH A CHARMING, POLITE YOUNG WOMAN!
MOTHER
FATHER
YES, YOU'LL BE THE PERFECT BRIDE!
DON'T! YOU FLATTER ME!
OH, PLEASE STOP! YOU'RE MAKING ME *BLUSH!*
......
SENILITY HITS SO YOUNG!
I-I'M SORRY. I DIDN'T REALIZE YOU WERE HERE!
THAT'S ALL RIGHT! HEY, I KNOW A SHORTCUT PAST THE LIBRARY...

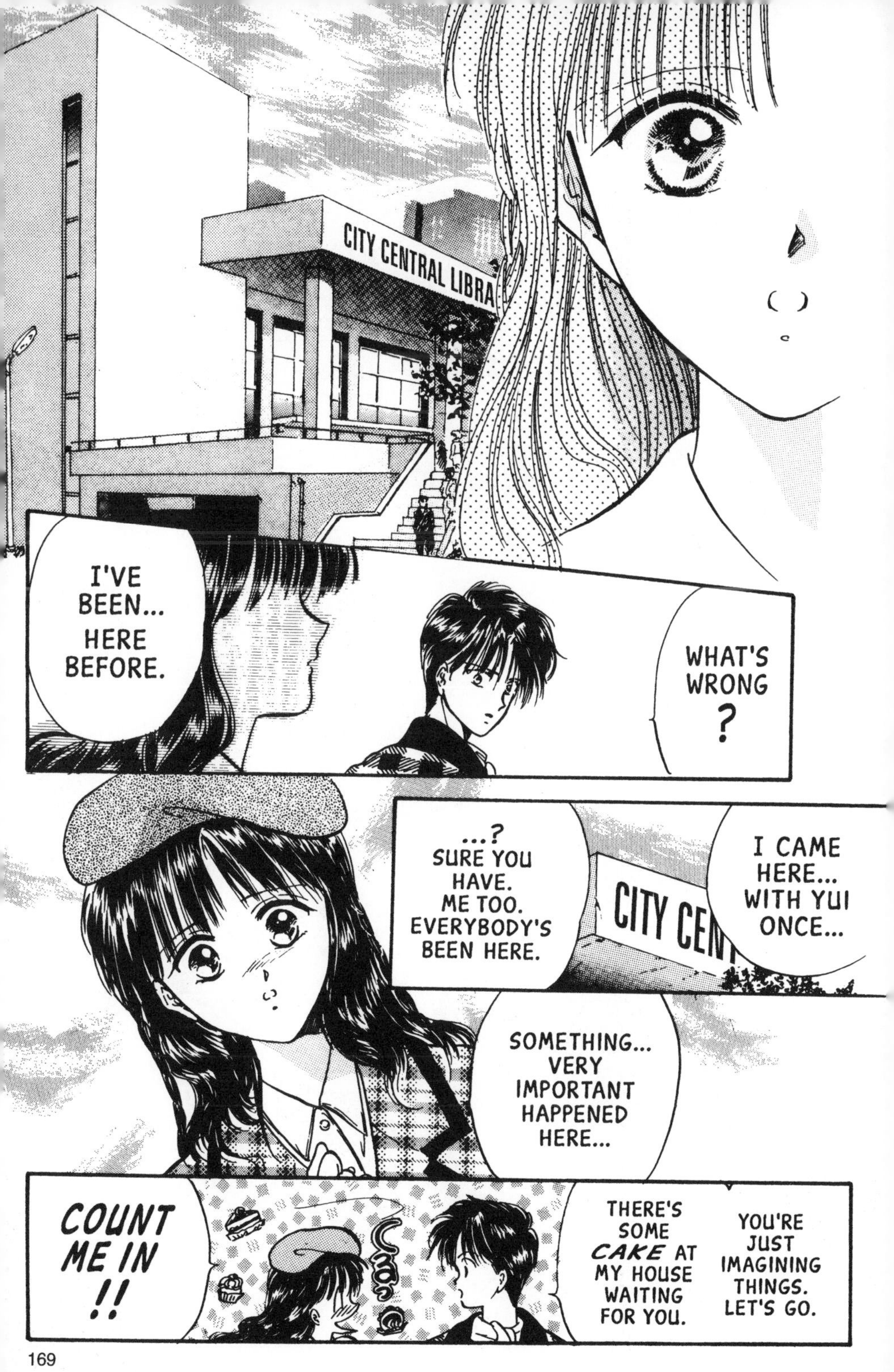
CITY CENTRAL LIBRA
WHAT'S WRONG ?
I'VE BEEN... HERE BEFORE.
I CAME HERE... WITH YUI ONCE...
...? SURE YOU HAVE. ME TOO. EVERYBODY'S BEEN HERE.
CITY CEN
SOMETHING... VERY IMPORTANT HAPPENED HERE...
YOU'RE JUST IMAGINING THINGS. LET'S GO.
THERE'S SOME *CAKE* AT MY HOUSE WAITING FOR YOU.
COUNT ME IN !!

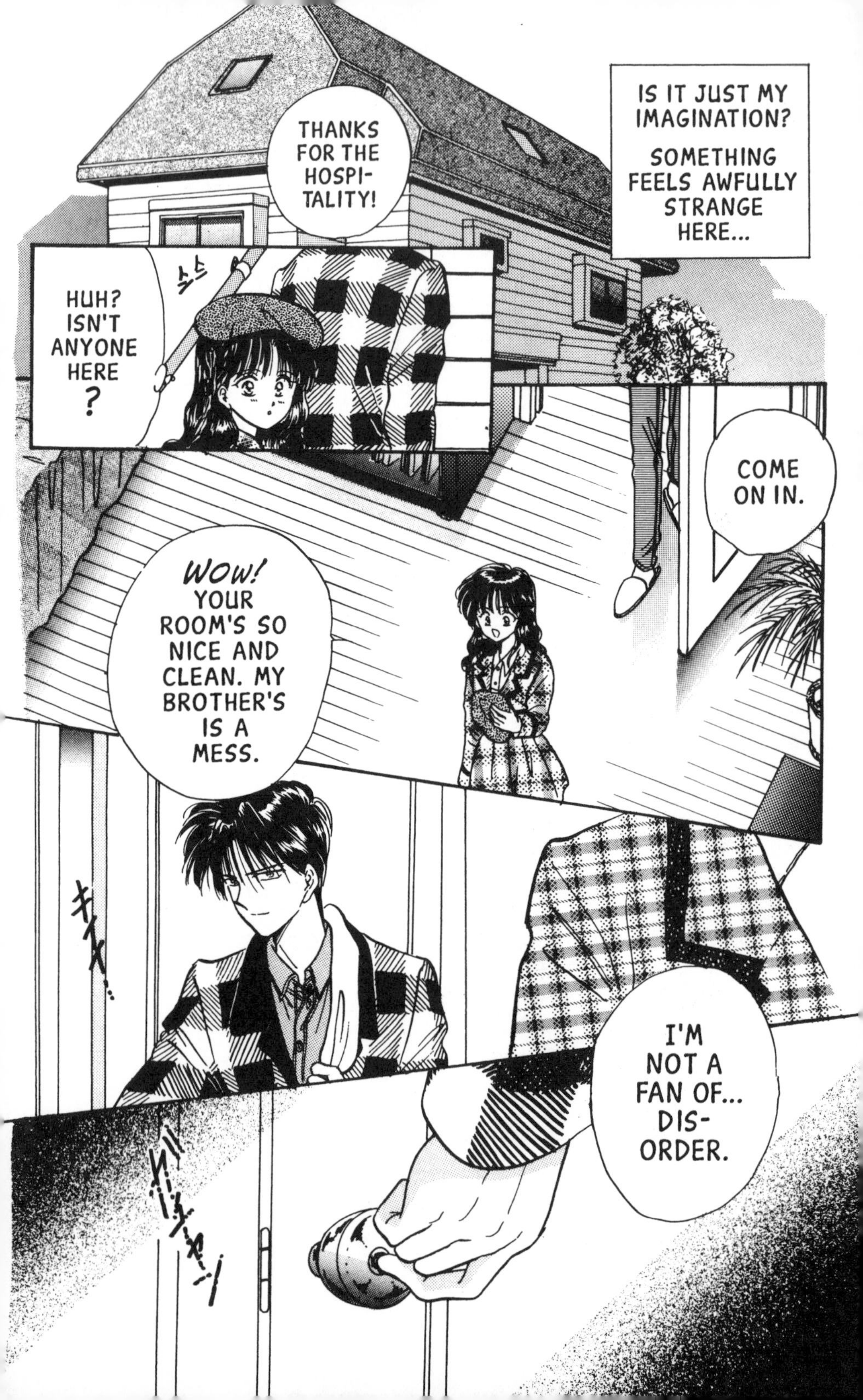
IS IT JUST MY IMAGINATION?
SOMETHING FEELS AWFULLY STRANGE HERE...
THANKS FOR THE HOSPI-TALITY!
HUH? ISN'T ANYONE HERE ?
COME ON IN.
WOW! YOUR ROOM'S SO NICE AND CLEAN. MY BROTHER'S IS A MESS.
I'M NOT A FAN OF... DIS-ORDER.

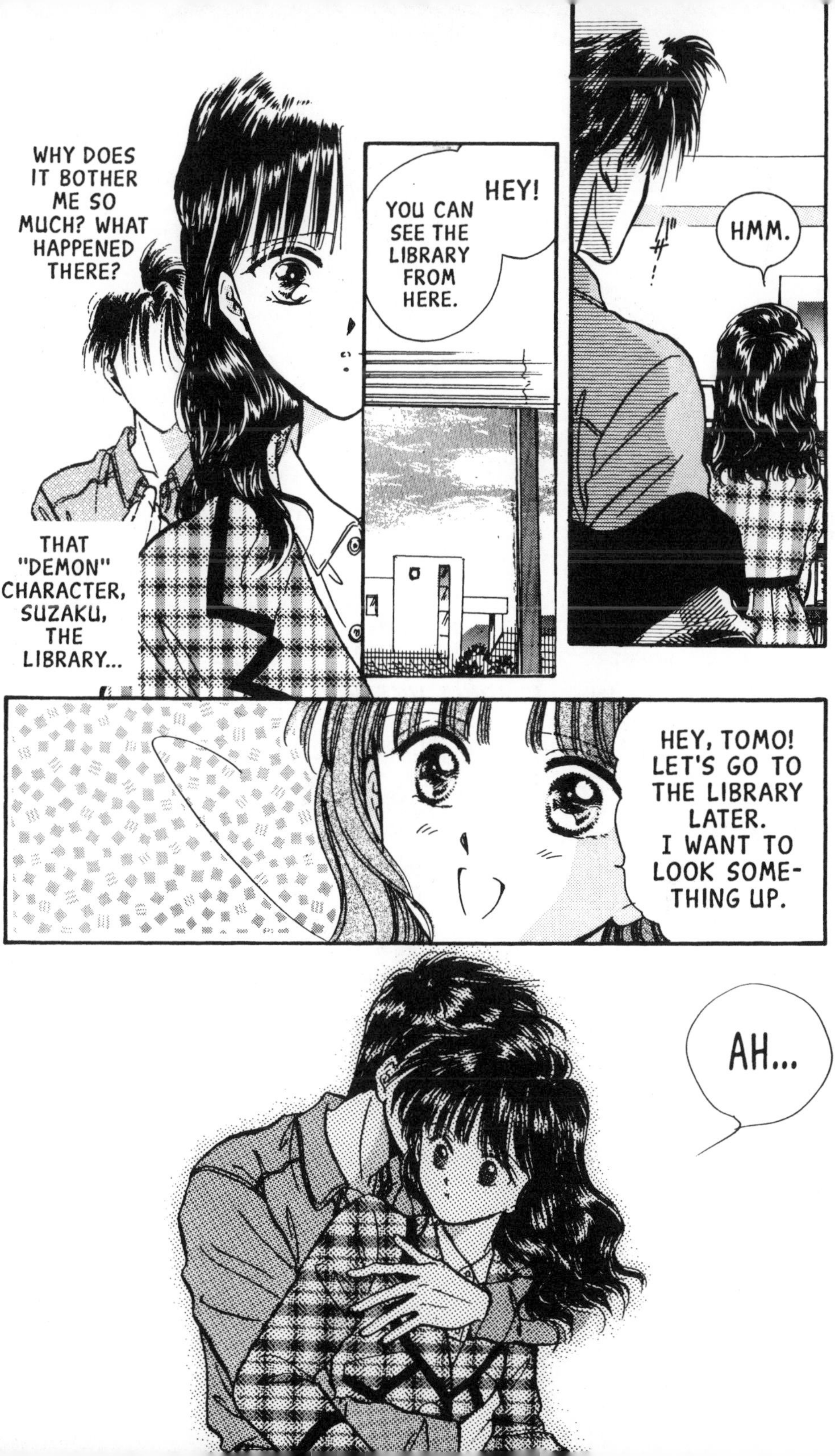
HMM.
HEY! YOU CAN SEE THE LIBRARY FROM HERE.
WHY DOES IT BOTHER ME SO MUCH? WHAT HAPPENED THERE?
THAT "DEMON" CHARACTER, SUZAKU, THE LIBRARY...
HEY, TOMO! LET'S GO TO THE LIBRARY LATER. I WANT TO LOOK SOME-THING UP.
AH...

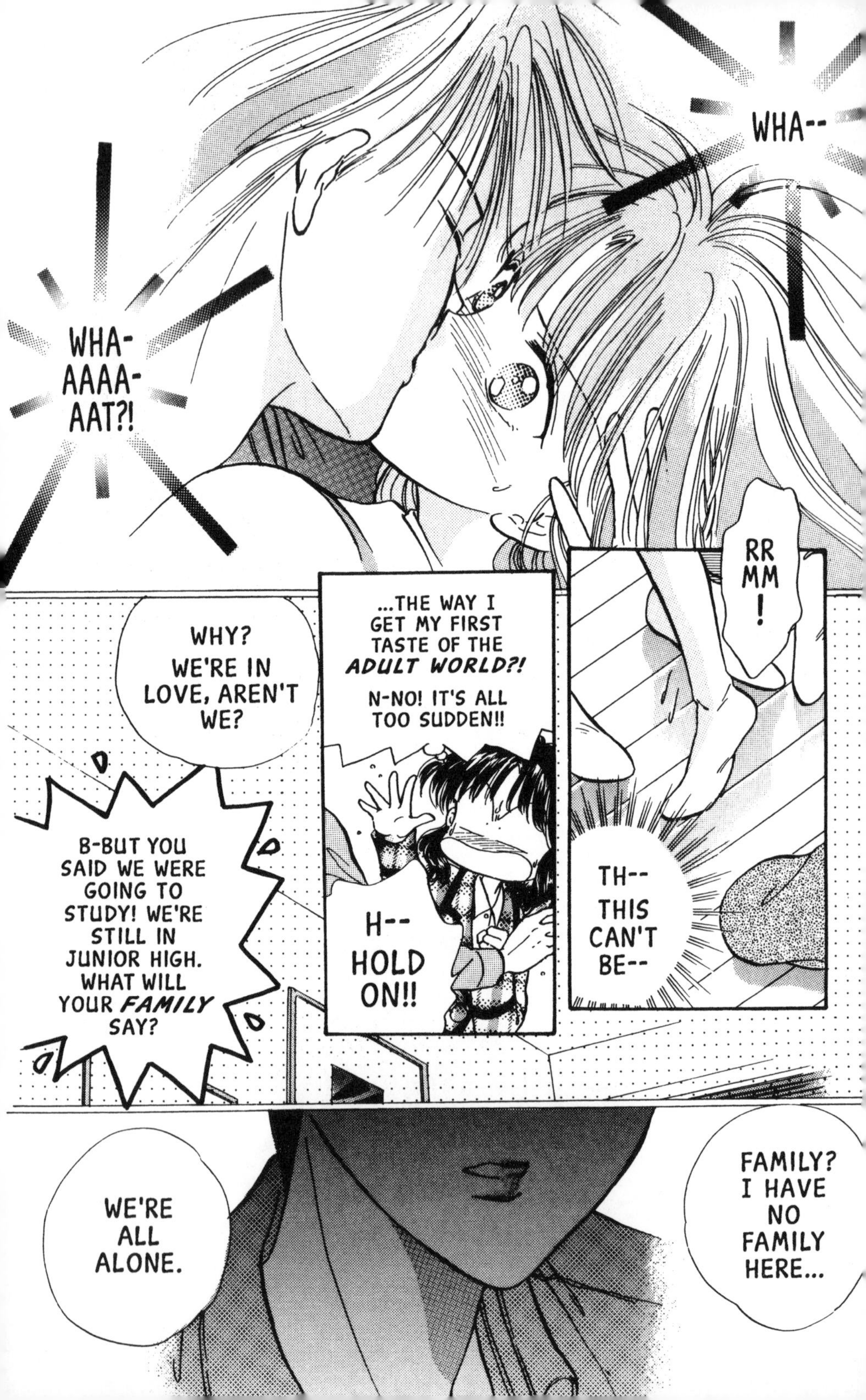
WHA--
WHA-AAAA-AAT?!
RRMM!
TH-- THIS CAN'T BE--
...THE WAY I GET MY FIRST TASTE OF THE *ADULT WORLD?!*
N-NO! IT'S ALL TOO SUDDEN!!
H-- HOLD ON!!
WHY? WE'RE IN LOVE, AREN'T WE?
B-BUT YOU SAID WE WERE GOING TO STUDY! WE'RE STILL IN JUNIOR HIGH. WHAT WILL YOUR *FAMILY* SAY?
FAMILY? I HAVE NO FAMILY HERE...
WE'RE ALL ALONE.

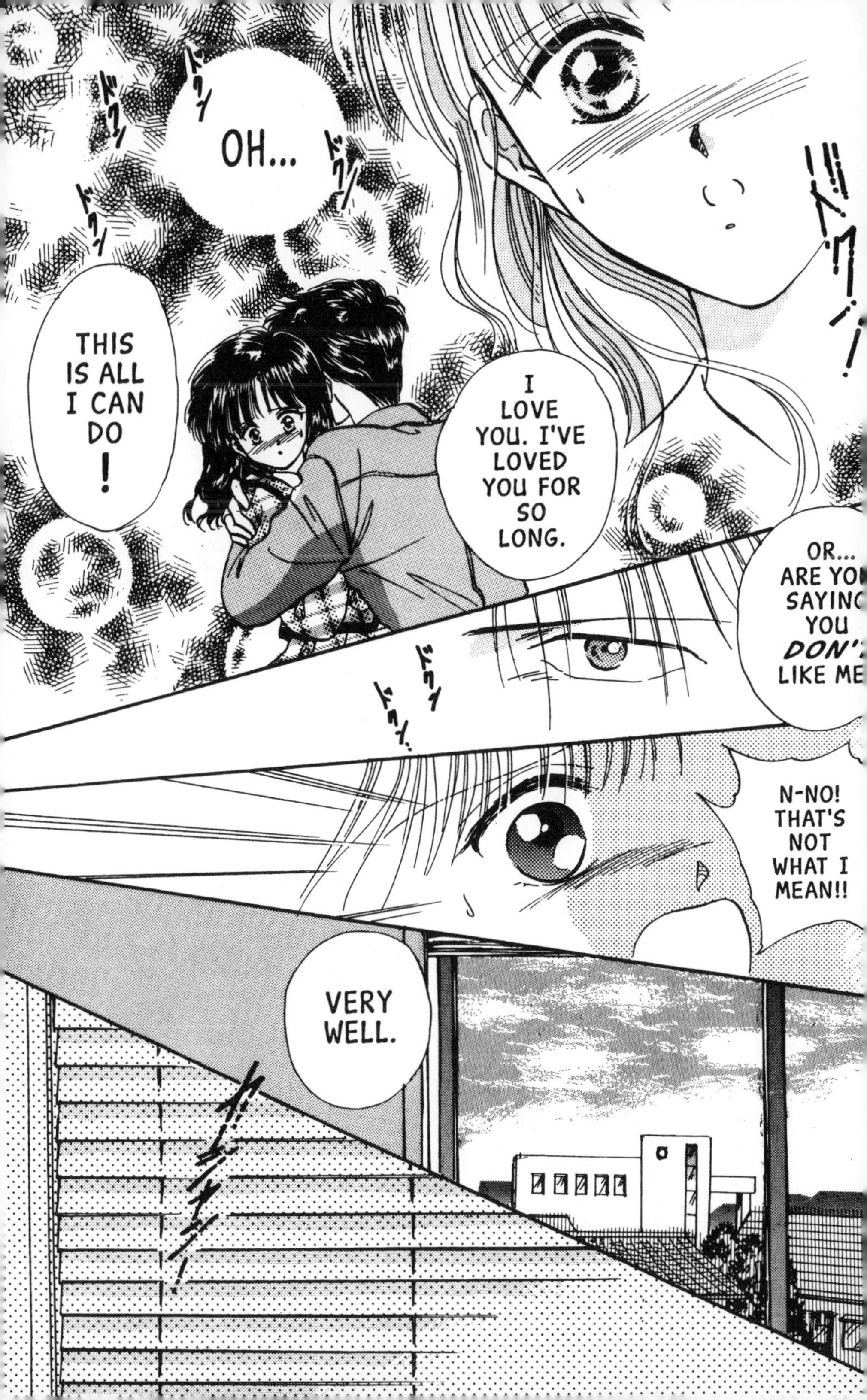
OH...
I LOVE YOU. I'VE LOVED YOU FOR SO LONG.
THIS IS ALL I CAN DO!
OR... ARE YO SAYIN YOU DON' LIKE ME
N-NO! THAT'S NOT WHAT I MEAN!!
VERY WELL.

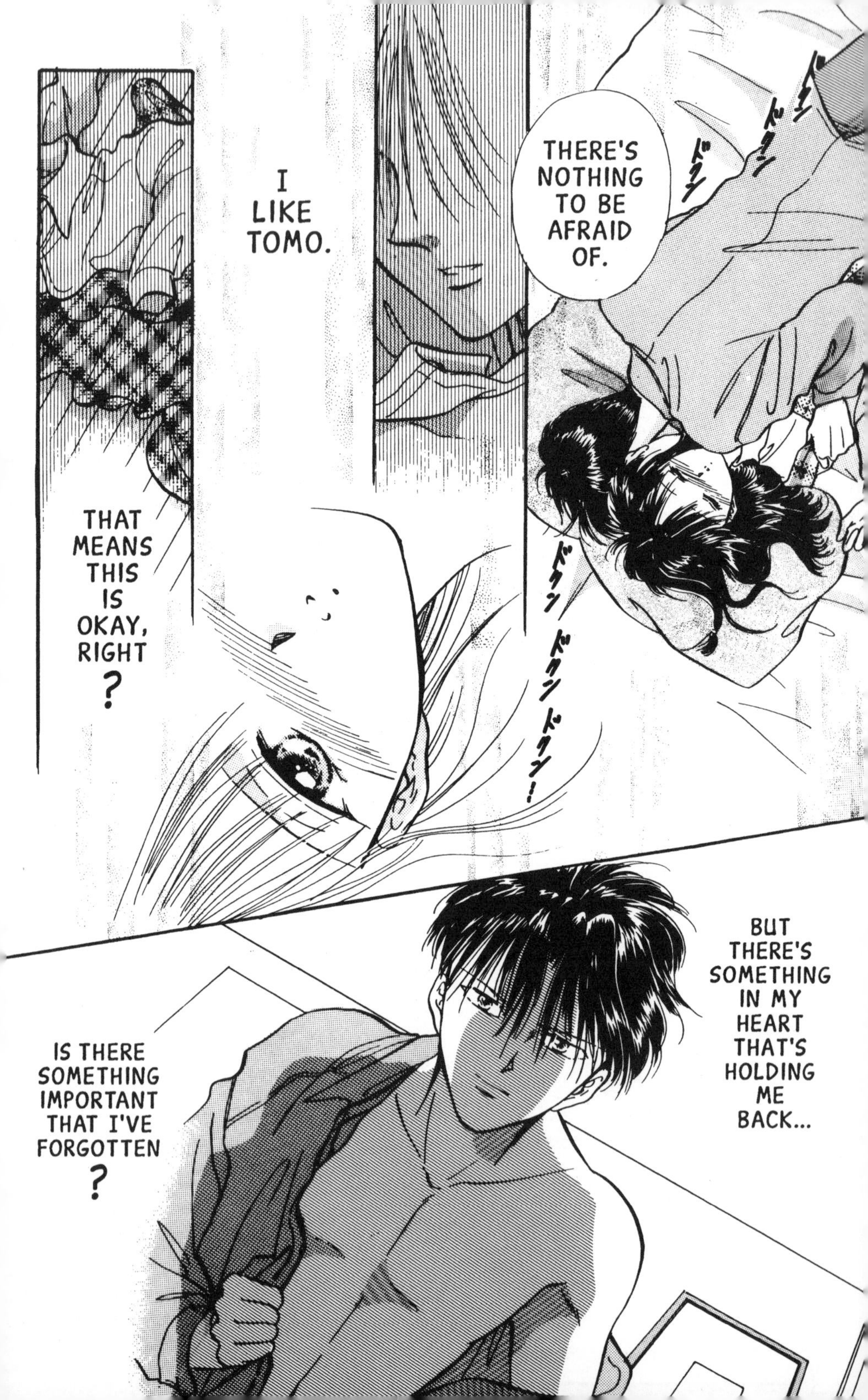

ドクン ドクン
THERE'S NOTHING TO BE AFRAID OF.
ドクン ドクン ドクン!
I LIKE TOMO.
THAT MEANS THIS IS OKAY, RIGHT?
BUT THERE'S SOMETHING IN MY HEART THAT'S HOLDING ME BACK...
IS THERE SOMETHING IMPORTANT THAT I'VE FORGOTTEN?

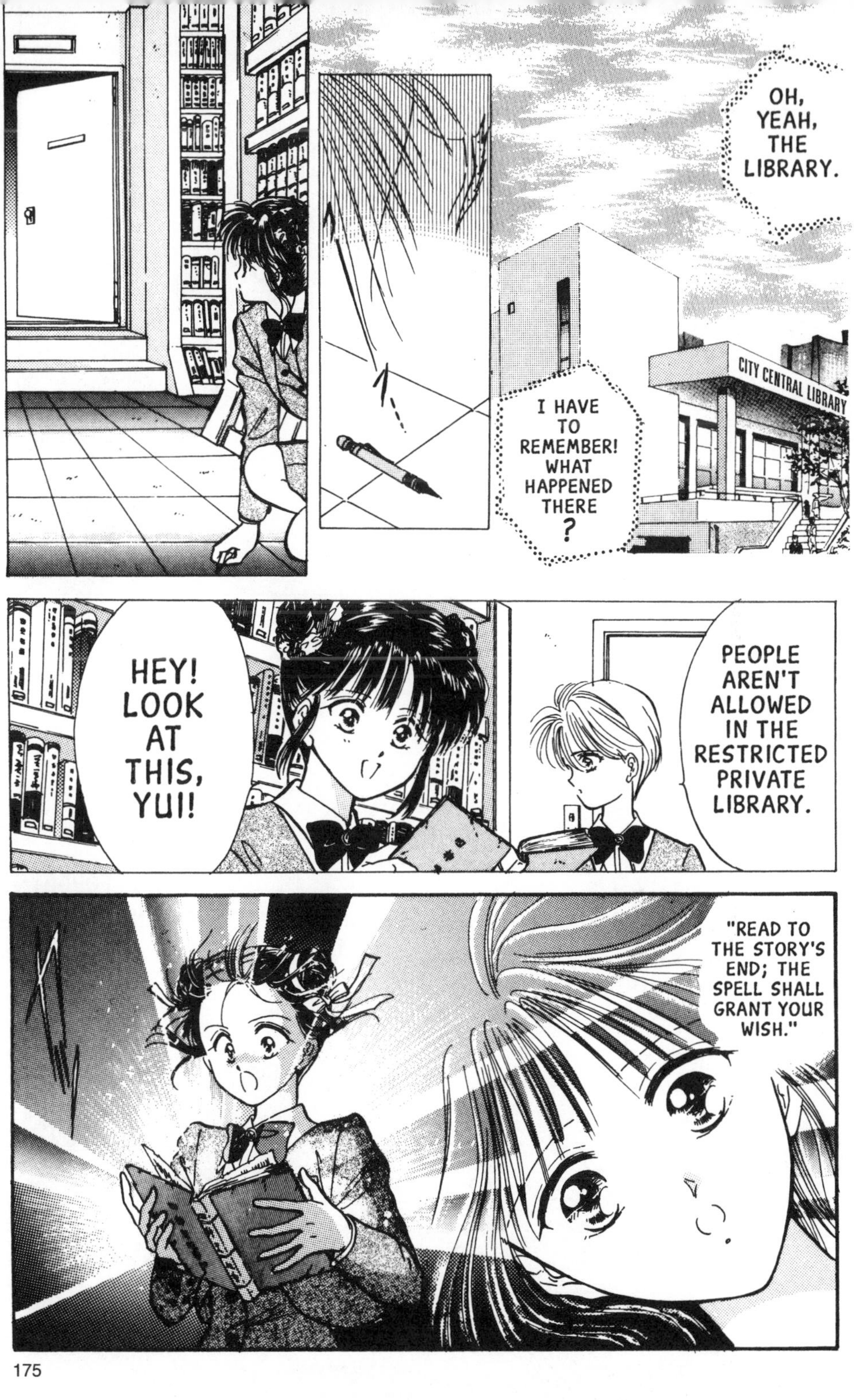
OH, YEAH, THE LIBRARY.
CITY CENTRAL LIBRARY
I HAVE TO REMEMBER! WHAT HAPPENED THERE?
PEOPLE AREN'T ALLOWED IN THE RESTRICTED PRIVATE LIBRARY.
HEY! LOOK AT THIS, YUI!
"READ TO THE STORY'S END; THE SPELL SHALL GRANT YOUR WISH."

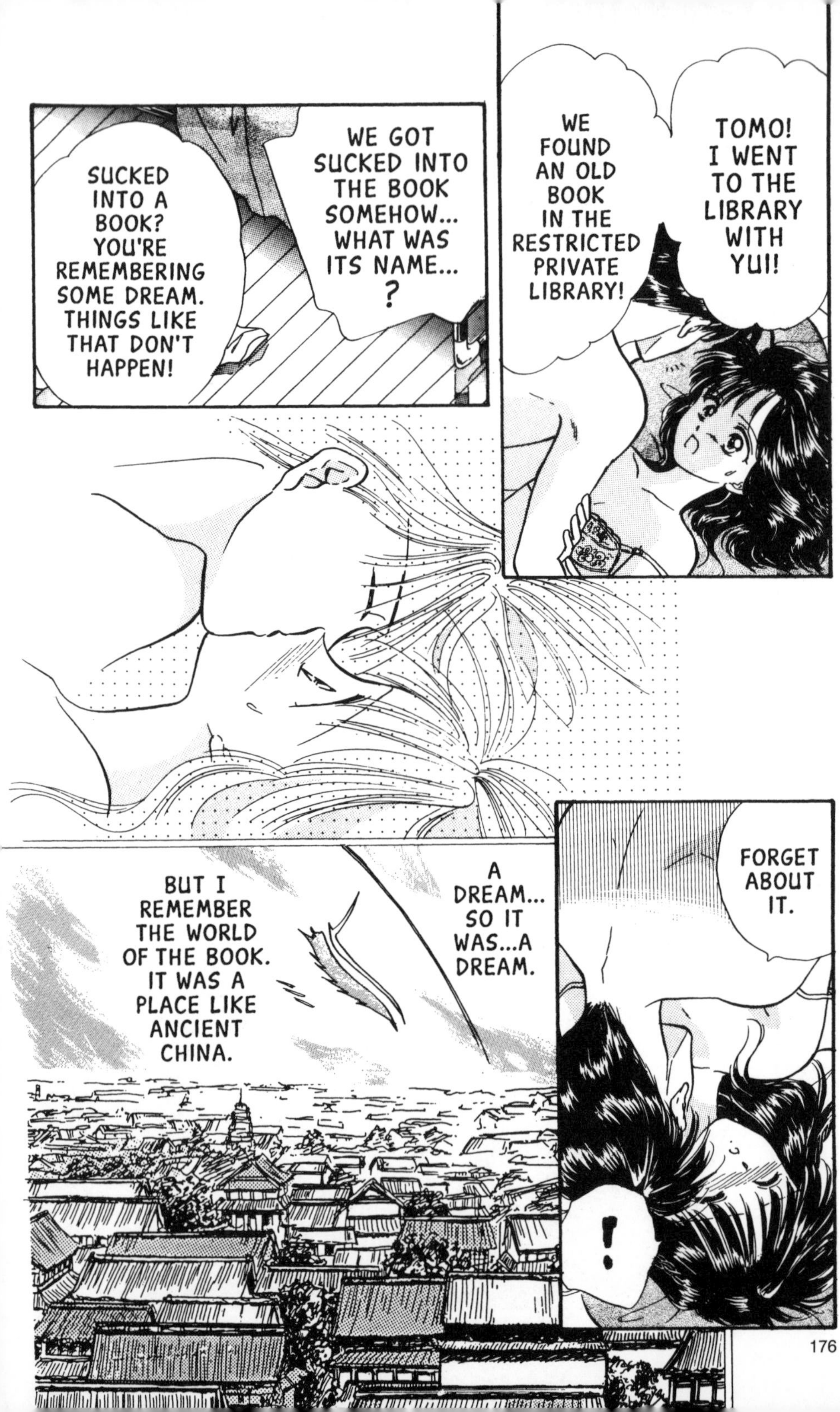
TOMO! I WENT TO THE LIBRARY WITH YUI!
WE FOUND AN OLD BOOK IN THE RESTRICTED PRIVATE LIBRARY!
WE GOT SUCKED INTO THE BOOK SOMEHOW... WHAT WAS ITS NAME... ?
SUCKED INTO A BOOK? YOU'RE REMEMBERING SOME DREAM. THINGS LIKE THAT DON'T HAPPEN!
FORGET ABOUT IT.
!
A DREAM... SO IT WAS...A DREAM.
BUT I REMEMBER THE WORLD OF THE BOOK. IT WAS A PLACE LIKE ANCIENT CHINA.

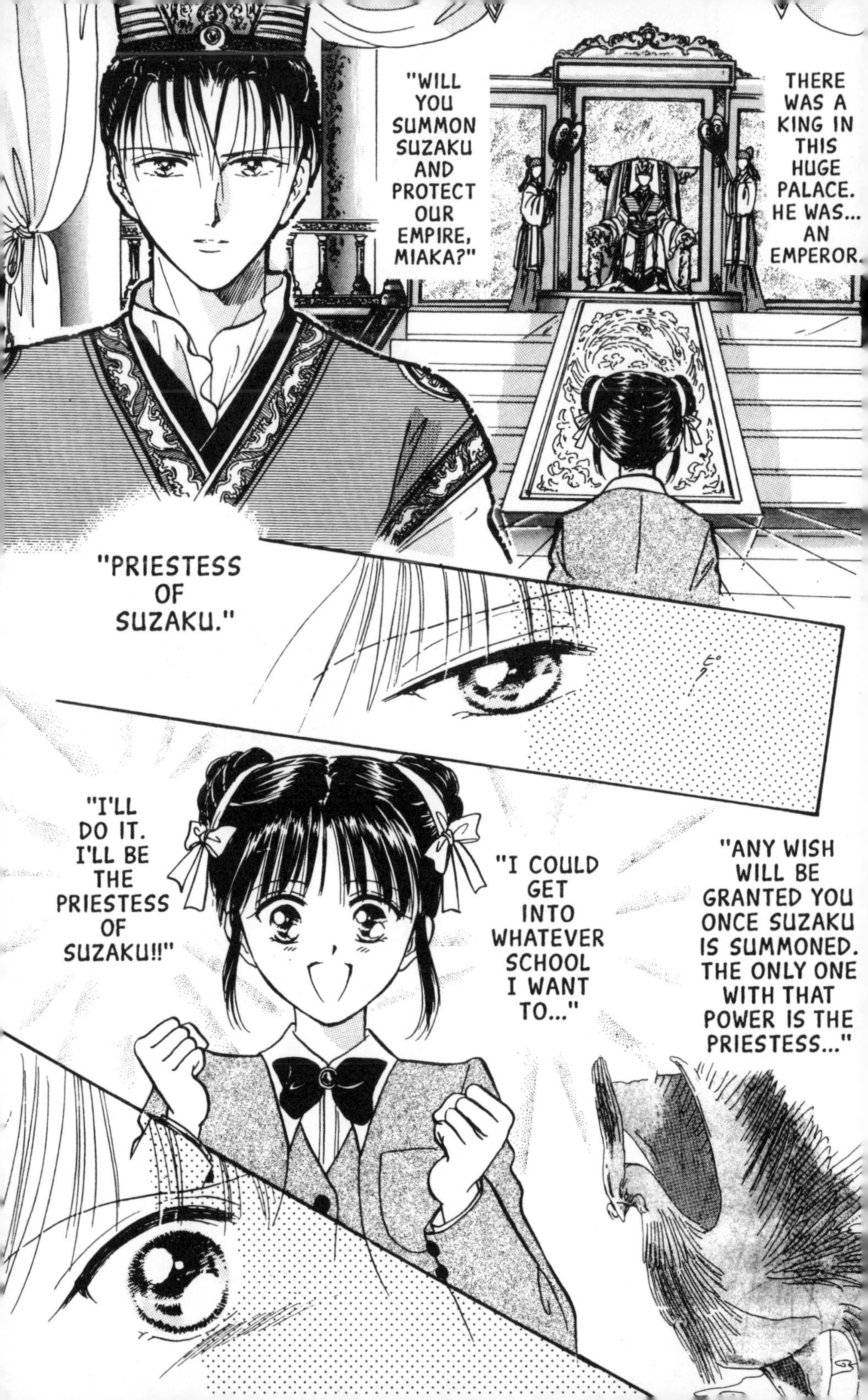
THERE WAS A KING IN THIS HUGE PALACE. HE WAS... AN EMPEROR.
"WILL YOU SUMMON SUZAKU AND PROTECT OUR EMPIRE, MIAKA?"
"PRIESTESS OF SUZAKU."
"ANY WISH WILL BE GRANTED YOU ONCE SUZAKU IS SUMMONED. THE ONLY ONE WITH THAT POWER IS THE PRIESTESS..."
"I COULD GET INTO WHATEVER SCHOOL I WANT TO..."
"I'LL DO IT. I'LL BE THE PRIESTESS OF SUZAKU!!"

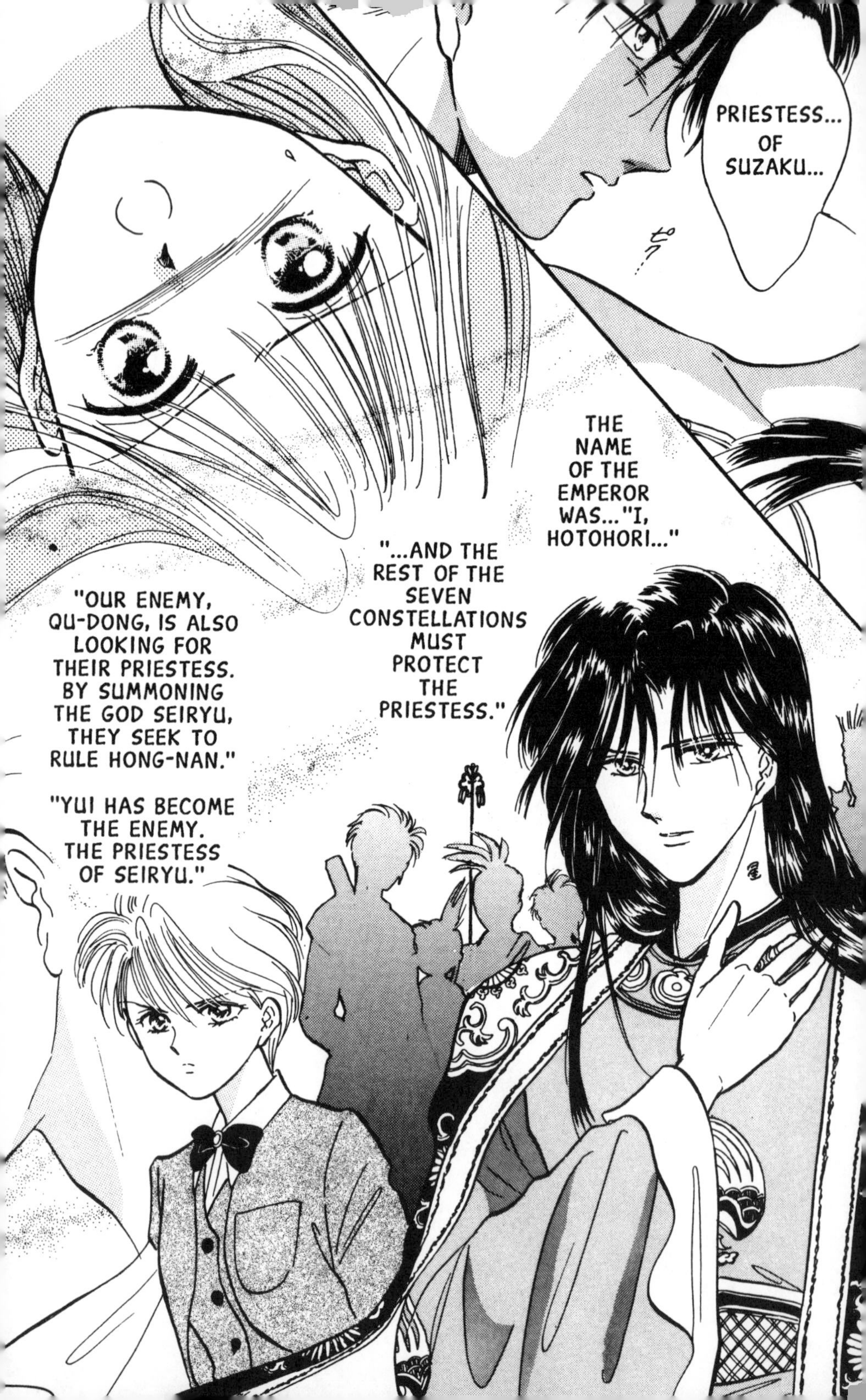
PRIESTESS... OF SUZAKU...
THE NAME OF THE EMPEROR WAS..."I, HOTOHORI..."
"...AND THE REST OF THE SEVEN CONSTELLATIONS MUST PROTECT THE PRIESTESS."
"OUR ENEMY, QU-DONG, IS ALSO LOOKING FOR THEIR PRIESTESS. BY SUMMONING THE GOD SEIRYU, THEY SEEK TO RULE HONG-NAN."
"YUI HAS BECOME THE ENEMY. THE PRIESTESS OF SEIRYU."

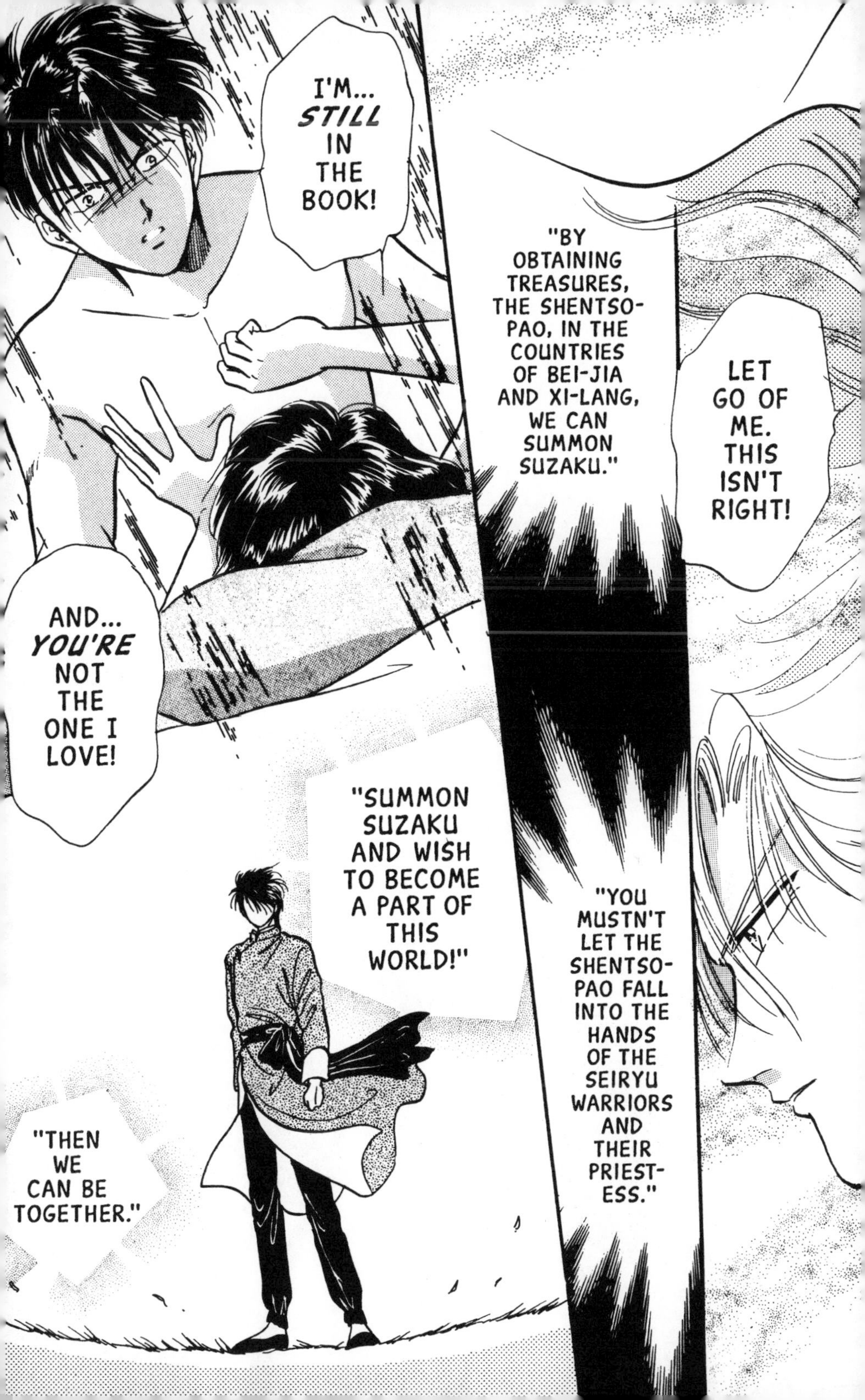
LET GO OF ME. THIS ISN'T RIGHT!
"BY OBTAINING TREASURES, THE SHENTSO-PAO, IN THE COUNTRIES OF BEI-JIA AND XI-LANG, WE CAN SUMMON SUZAKU."
"YOU MUSTN'T LET THE SHENTSO-PAO FALL INTO THE HANDS OF THE SEIRYU WARRIORS AND THEIR PRIEST-ESS."
I'M... *STILL* IN THE BOOK!
AND... *YOU'RE* NOT THE ONE I LOVE!
"SUMMON SUZAKU AND WISH TO BECOME A PART OF THIS WORLD!"
"THEN WE CAN BE TOGETHER."

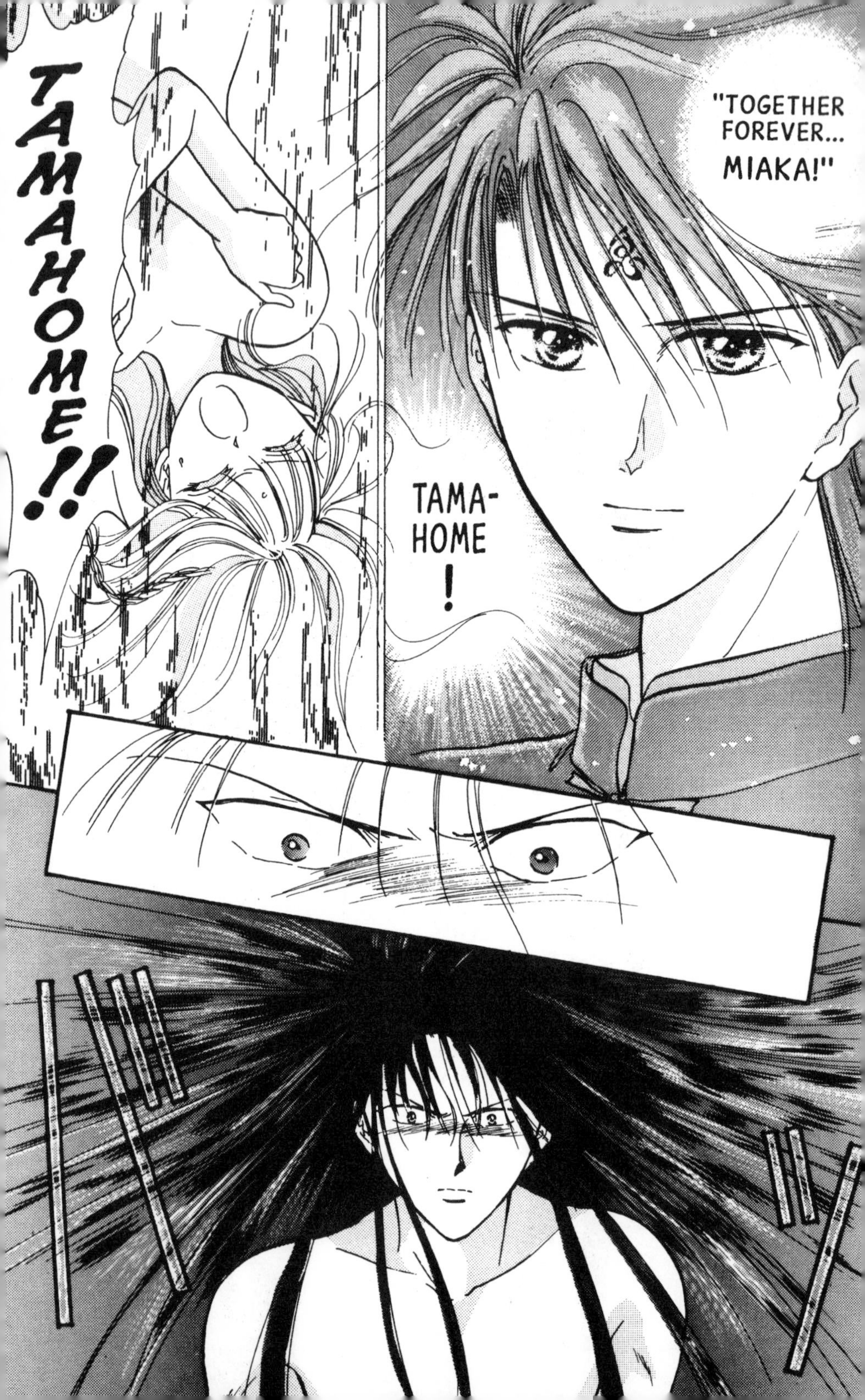
"TOGETHER FOREVER... MIAKA!"
TAMA-HOME!
TAMAHOME!!

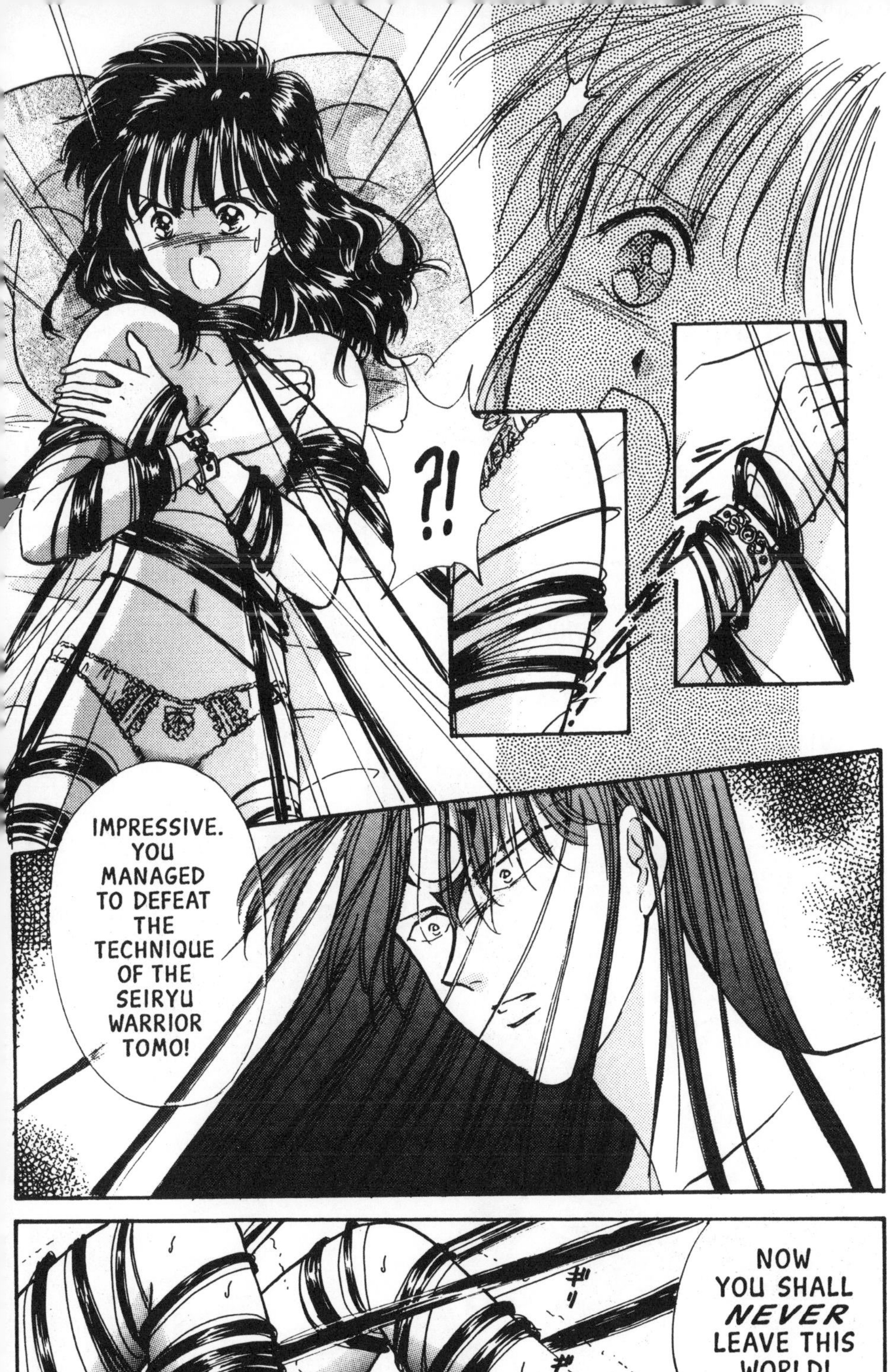
?!
IMPRESSIVE. YOU MANAGED TO DEFEAT THE TECHNIQUE OF THE SEIRYU WARRIOR TOMO!
NOW YOU SHALL *NEVER* LEAVE THIS WORLD!

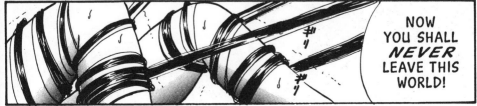

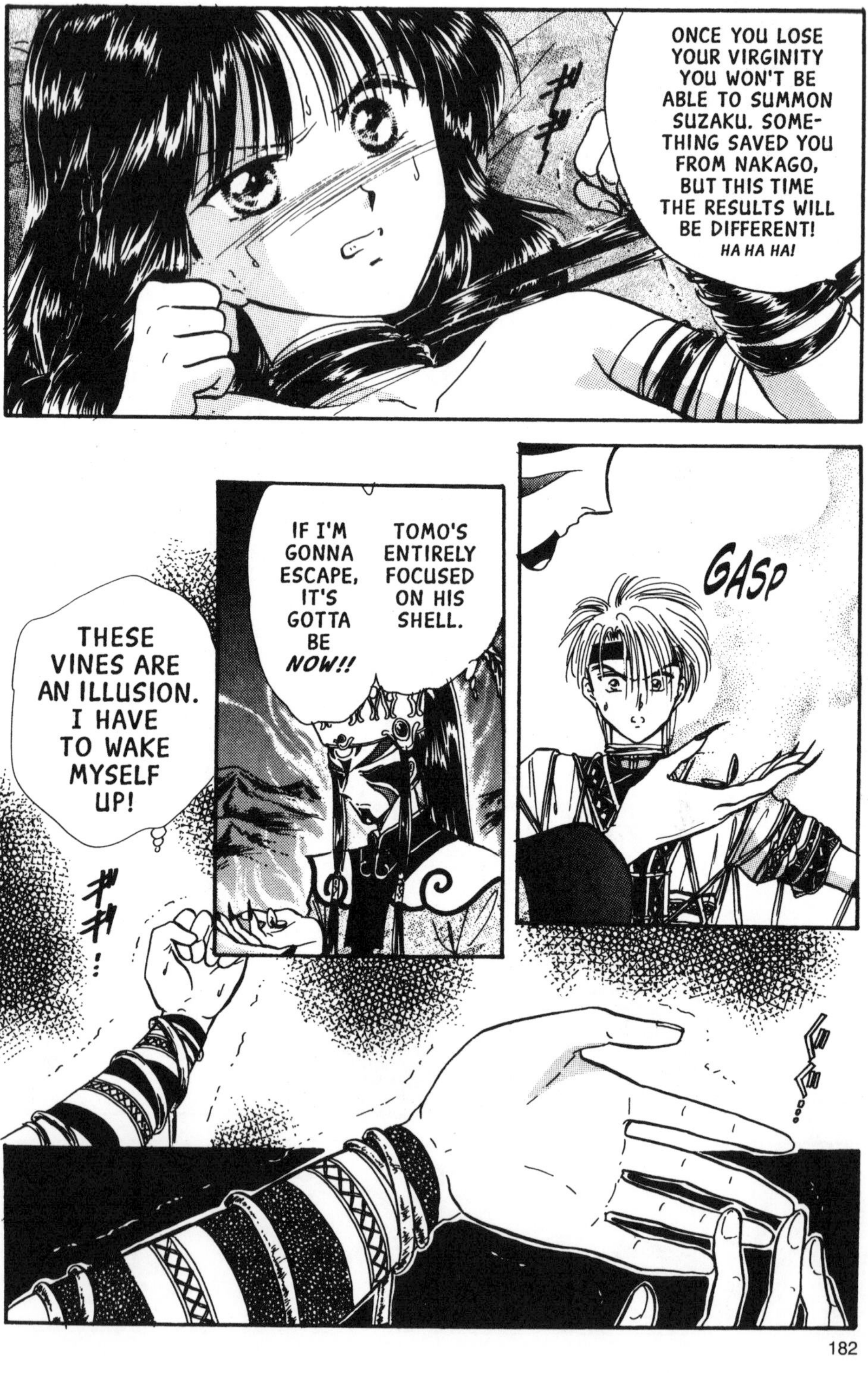
ONCE YOU LOSE YOUR VIRGINITY YOU WON'T BE ABLE TO SUMMON SUZAKU. SOMETHING SAVED YOU FROM NAKAGO, BUT THIS TIME THE RESULTS WILL BE DIFFERENT!
HA HA HA!
GASP
TOMO'S ENTIRELY FOCUSED ON HIS SHELL.
IF I'M GONNA ESCAPE, IT'S GOTTA BE NOW!!
THESE VINES ARE AN ILLUSION. I HAVE TO WAKE MYSELF UP!

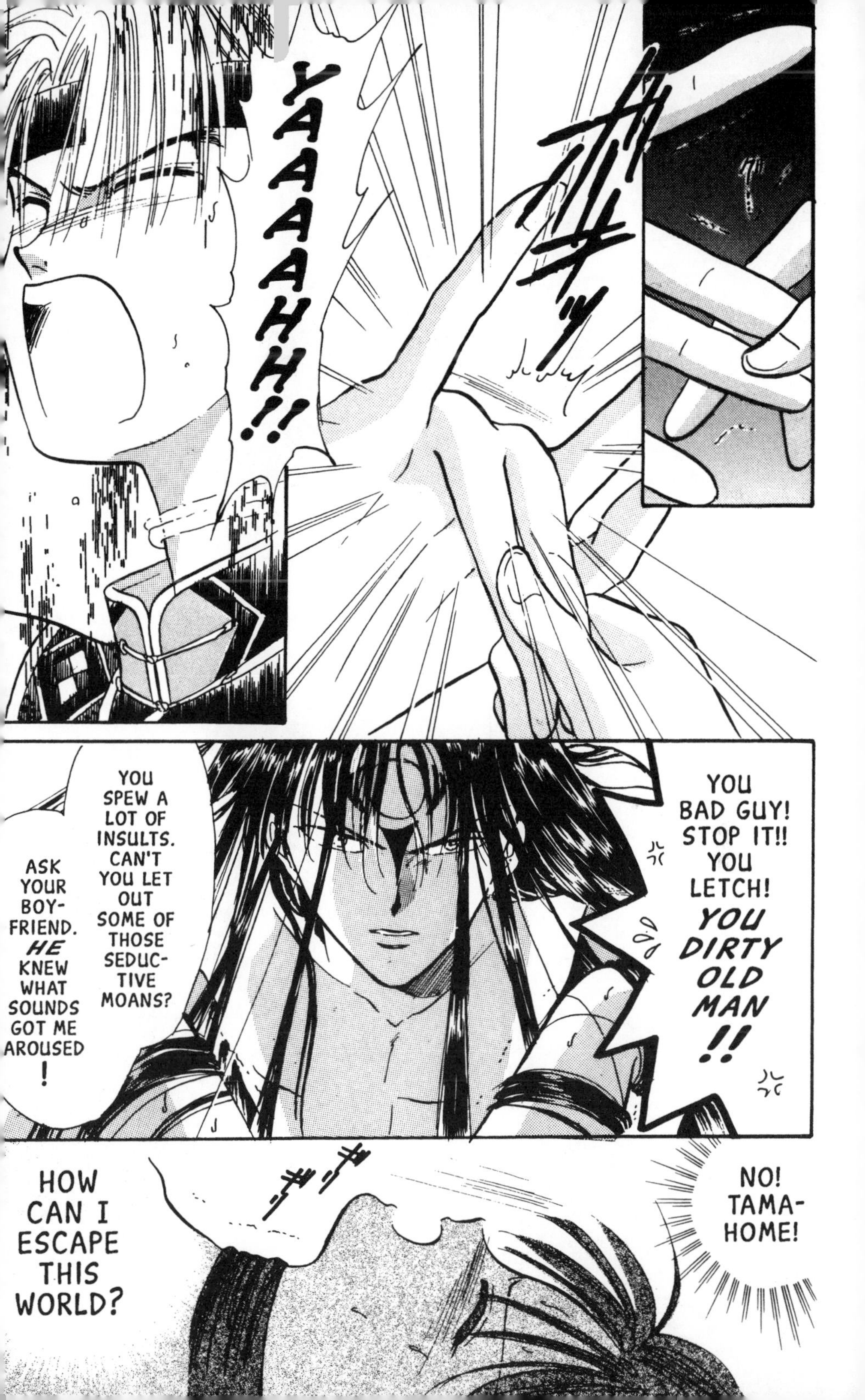
YAAAAAHH!!
YOU BAD GUY! STOP IT!! YOU LETCH! *YOU DIRTY OLD MAN!!*
YOU SPEW A LOT OF INSULTS. CAN'T YOU LET OUT SOME OF THOSE SEDUC-TIVE MOANS?
ASK YOUR BOY-FRIEND. *HE* KNEW WHAT SOUNDS GOT ME AROUSED!
NO! TAMA-HOME!
HOW CAN I ESCAPE THIS WORLD?

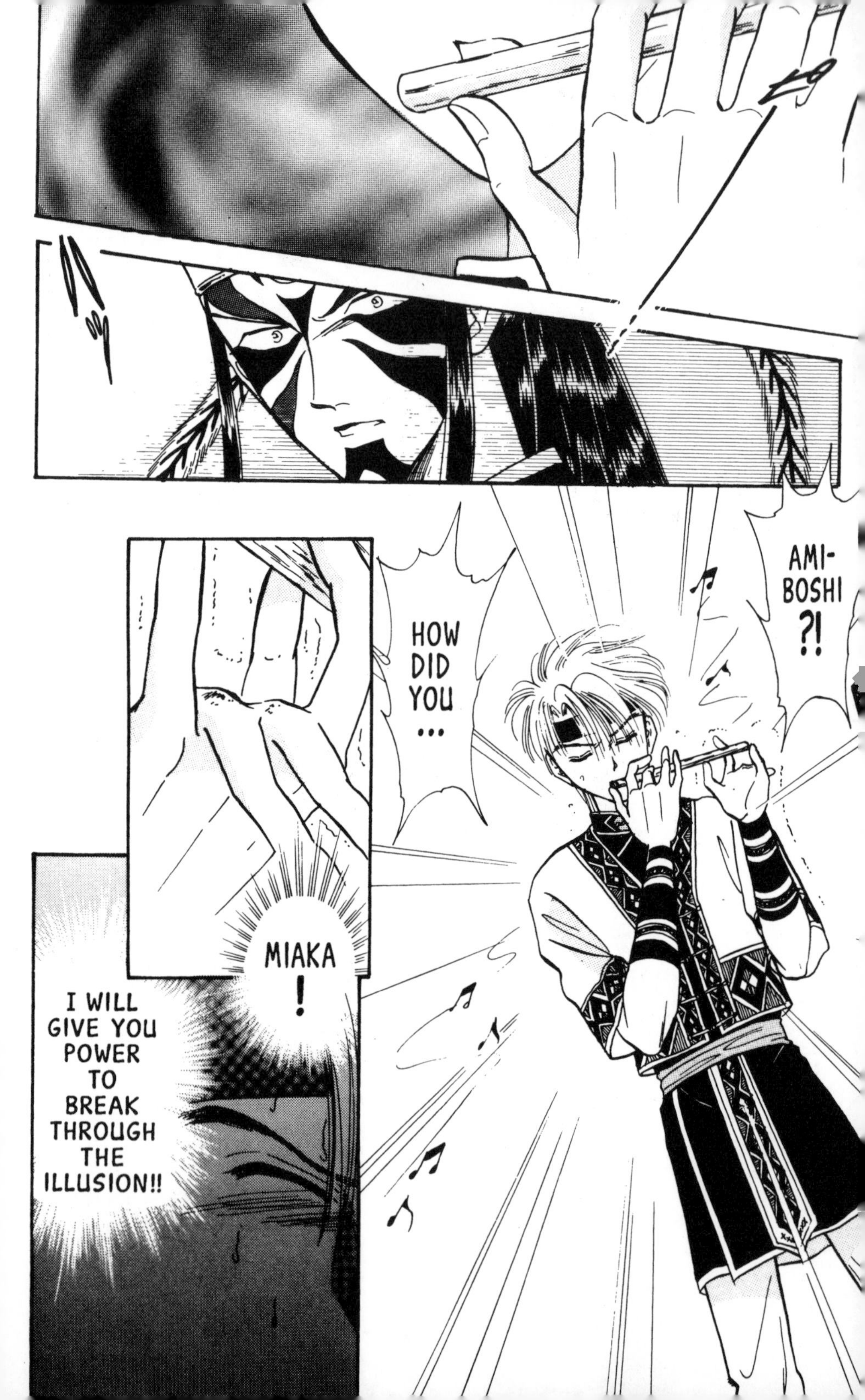

AMI-BOSHI ?!
HOW DID YOU...
MIAKA!
I WILL GIVE YOU POWER TO BREAK THROUGH THE ILLUSION!!

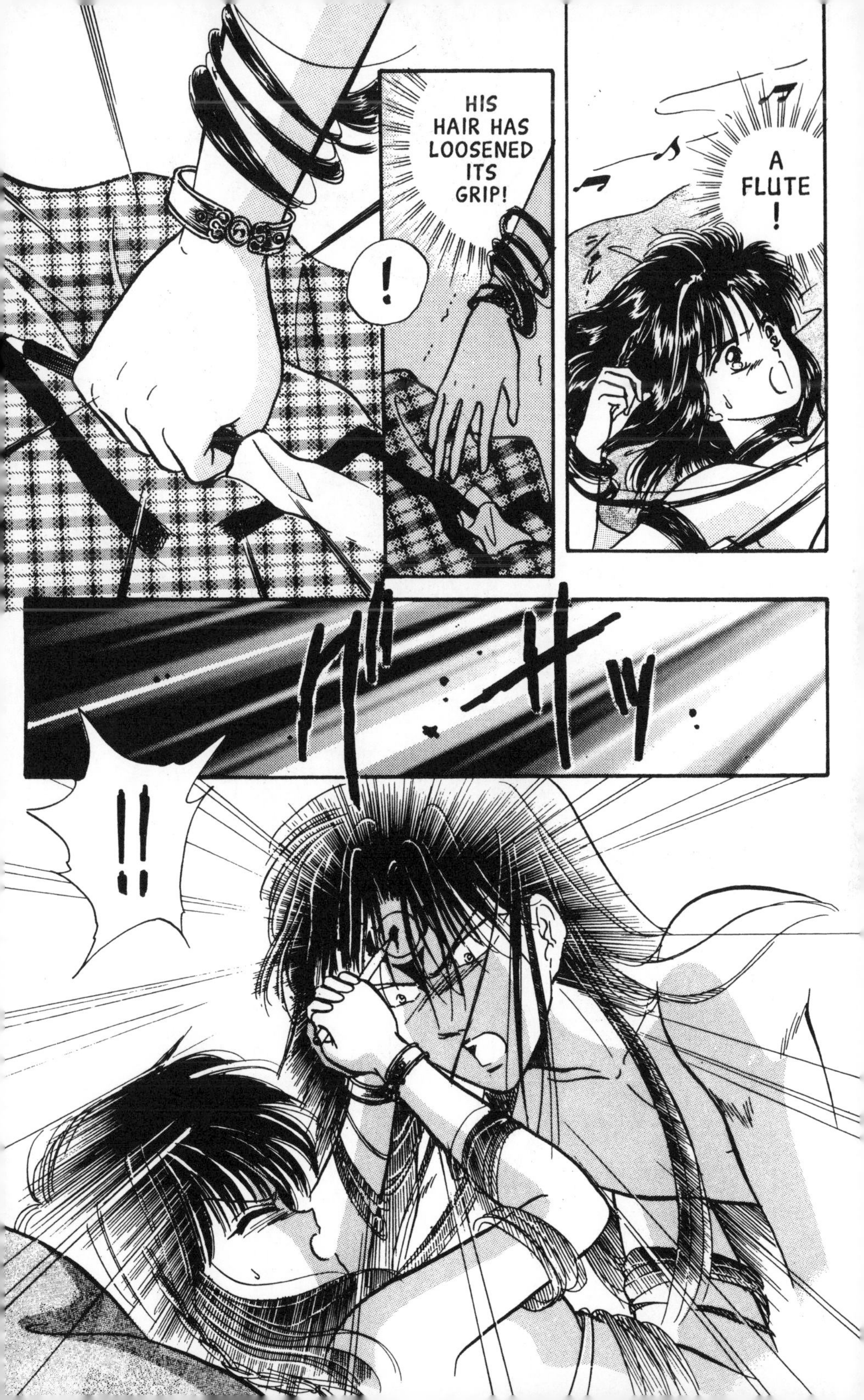
A FLUTE!
HIS HAIR HAS LOOSENED ITS GRIP!
!
!!

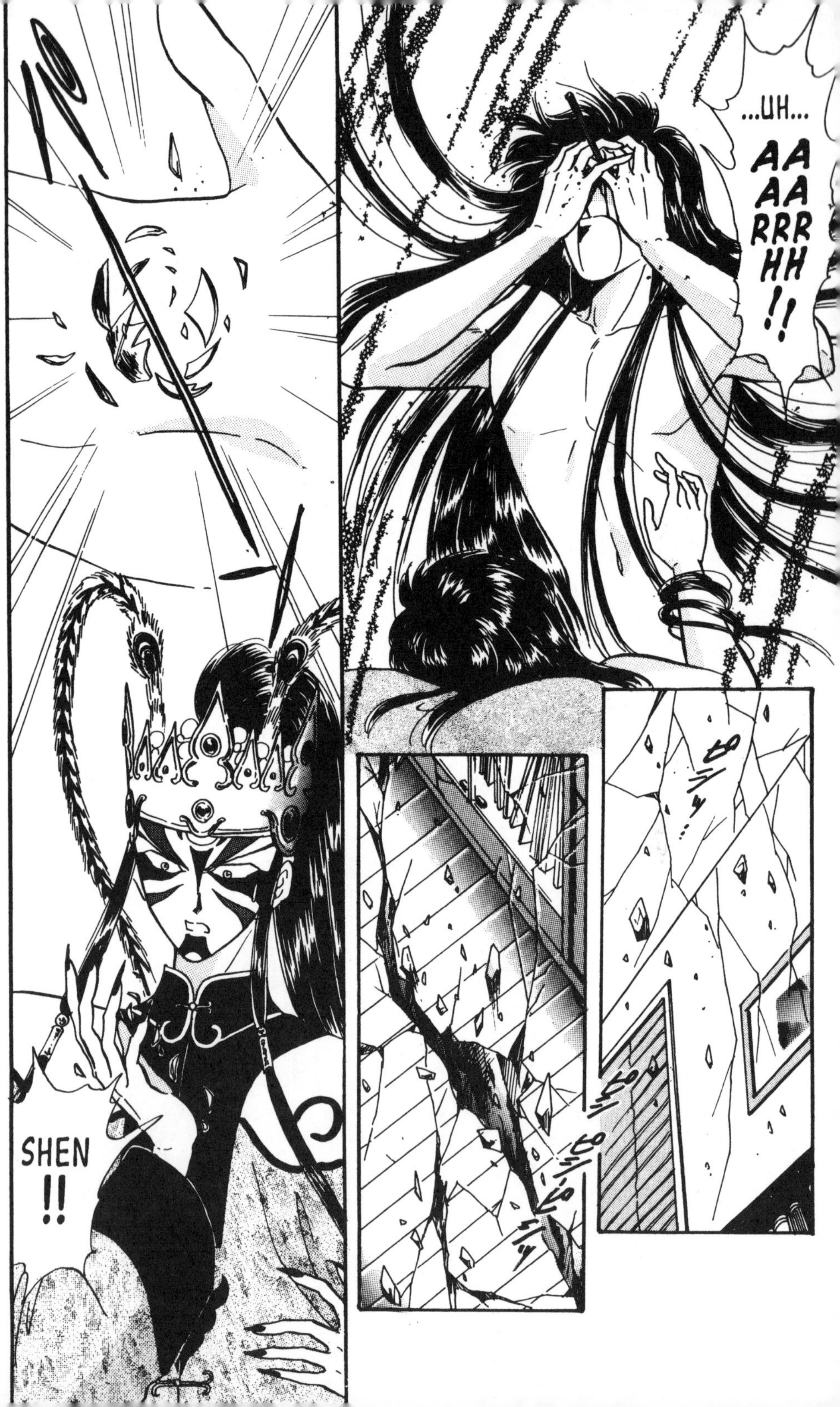
...UH...
AAAARRRHH!!
SHEN!!

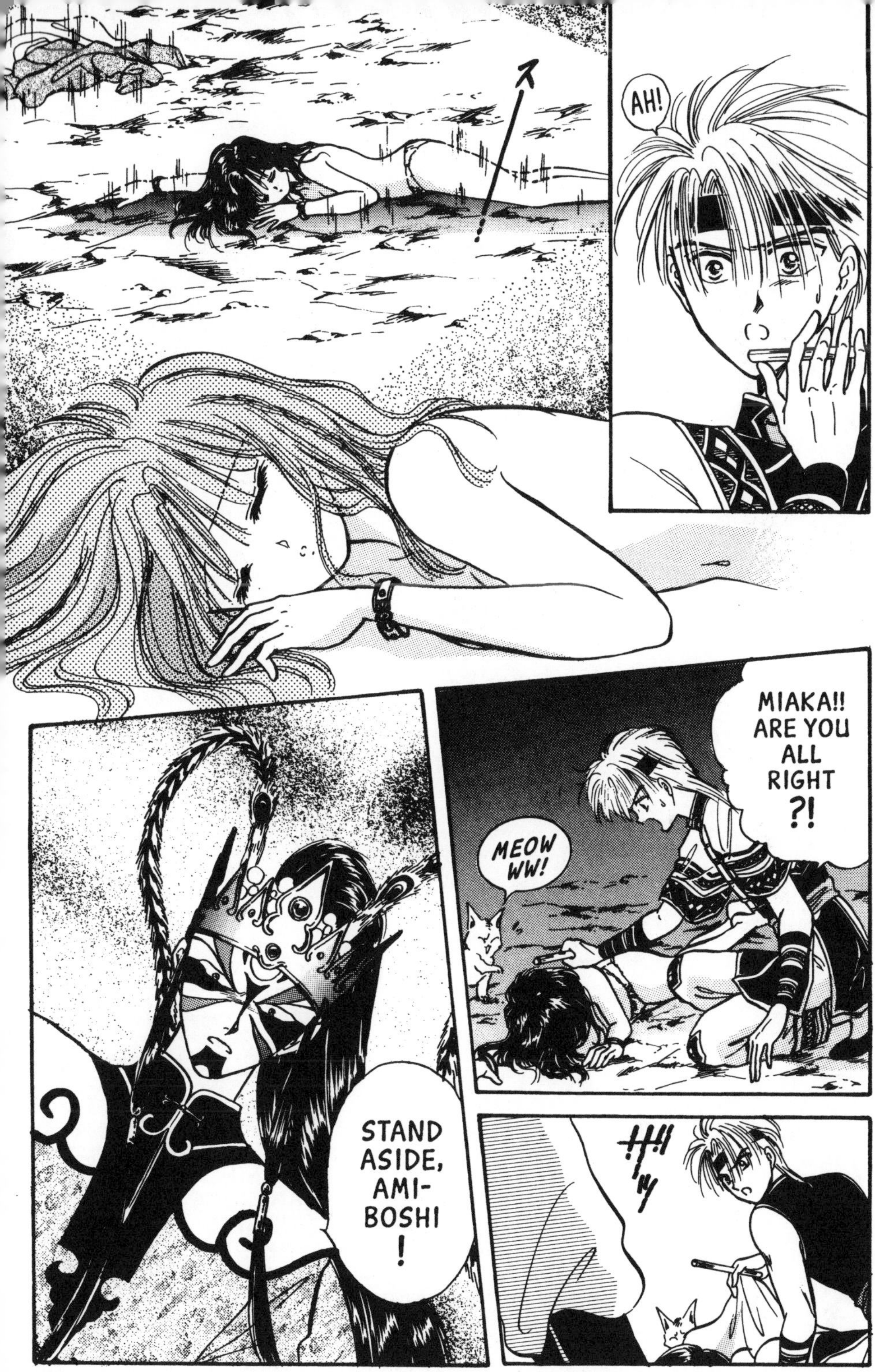
AH!
MIAKA!! ARE YOU ALL RIGHT?!
MEOWWW!
STAND ASIDE, AMIBOSHI!

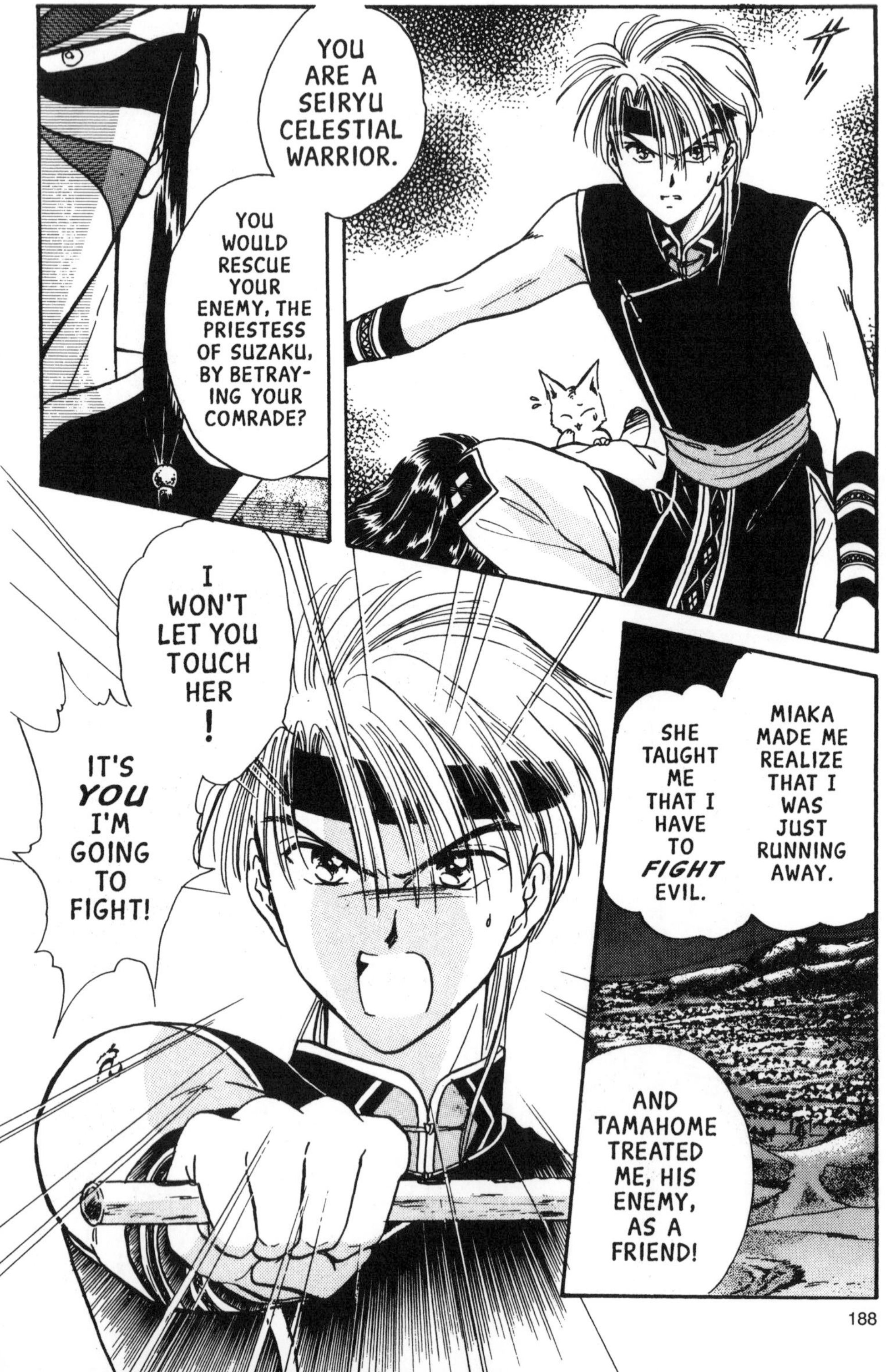
YOU ARE A SEIRYU CELESTIAL WARRIOR.
YOU WOULD RESCUE YOUR ENEMY, THE PRIESTESS OF SUZAKU, BY BETRAY-ING YOUR COMRADE?
MIAKA MADE ME REALIZE THAT I WAS JUST RUNNING AWAY.
SHE TAUGHT ME THAT I HAVE TO *FIGHT* EVIL.
AND TAMAHOME TREATED ME, HIS ENEMY, AS A FRIEND!
I WON'T LET YOU TOUCH HER!
IT'S *YOU* I'M GOING TO FIGHT!

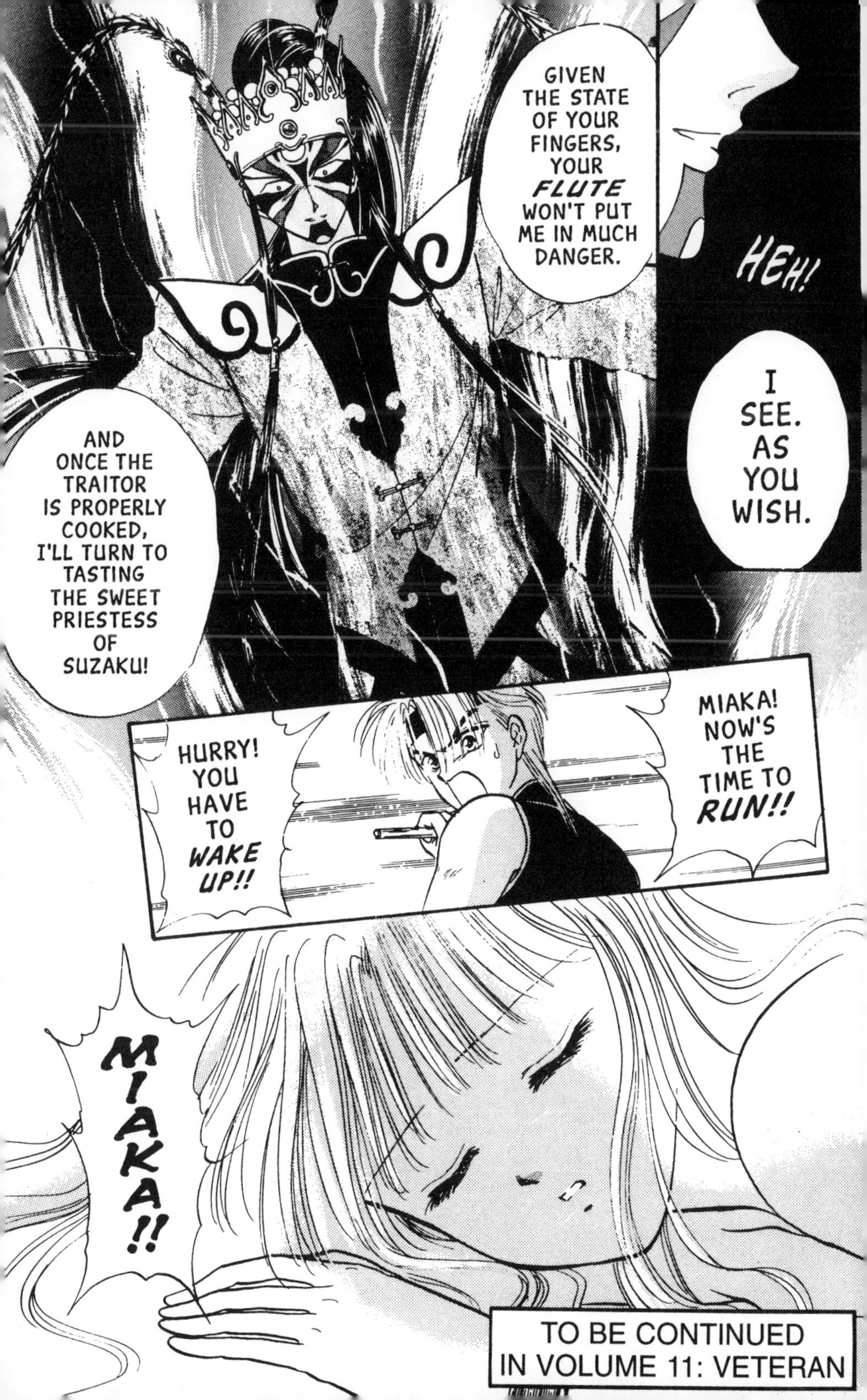
HEH!
I SEE. AS YOU WISH.
GIVEN THE STATE OF YOUR FINGERS, YOUR FLUTE WON'T PUT ME IN MUCH DANGER.
AND ONCE THE TRAITOR IS PROPERLY COOKED, I'LL TURN TO TASTING THE SWEET PRIESTESS OF SUZAKU!
MIAKA! NOW'S THE TIME TO RUN!!
HURRY! YOU HAVE TO WAKE UP!!
MIAKA!!
TO BE CONTINUED IN VOLUME 11: VETERAN

FUSHIGI YÛGI
Volume 11: **Veteran**

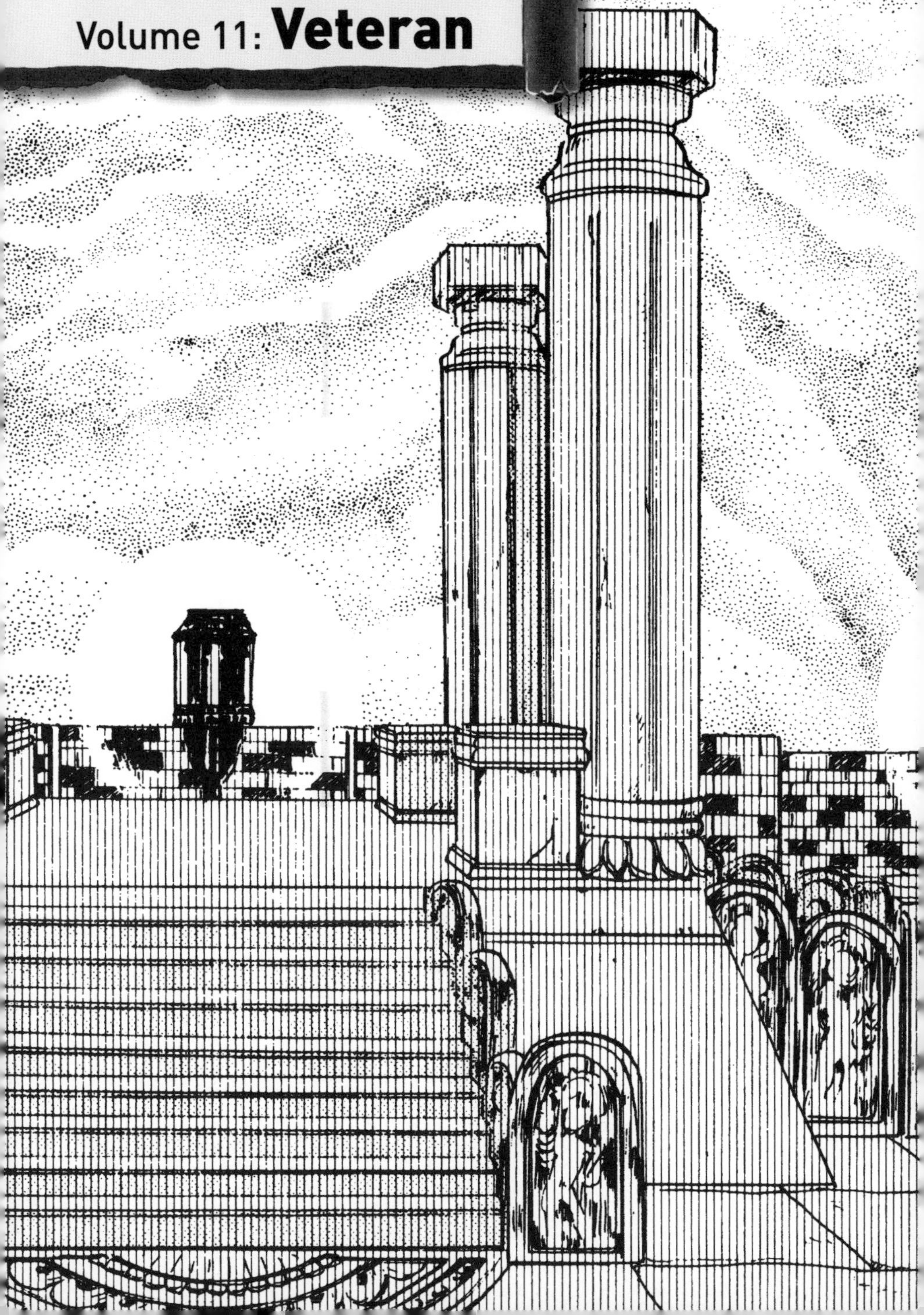

Chapter Sixty
Ray of Resurrection

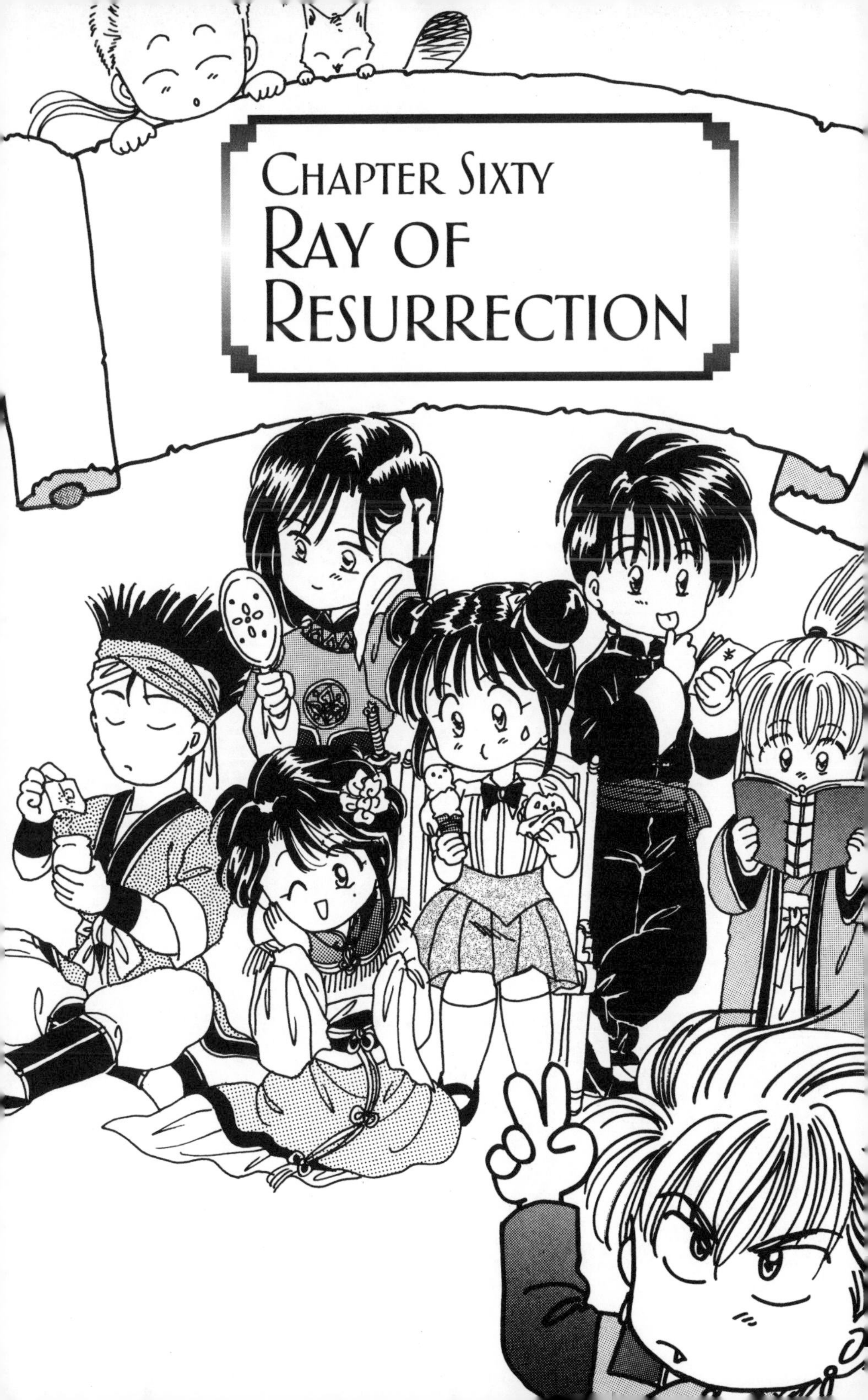

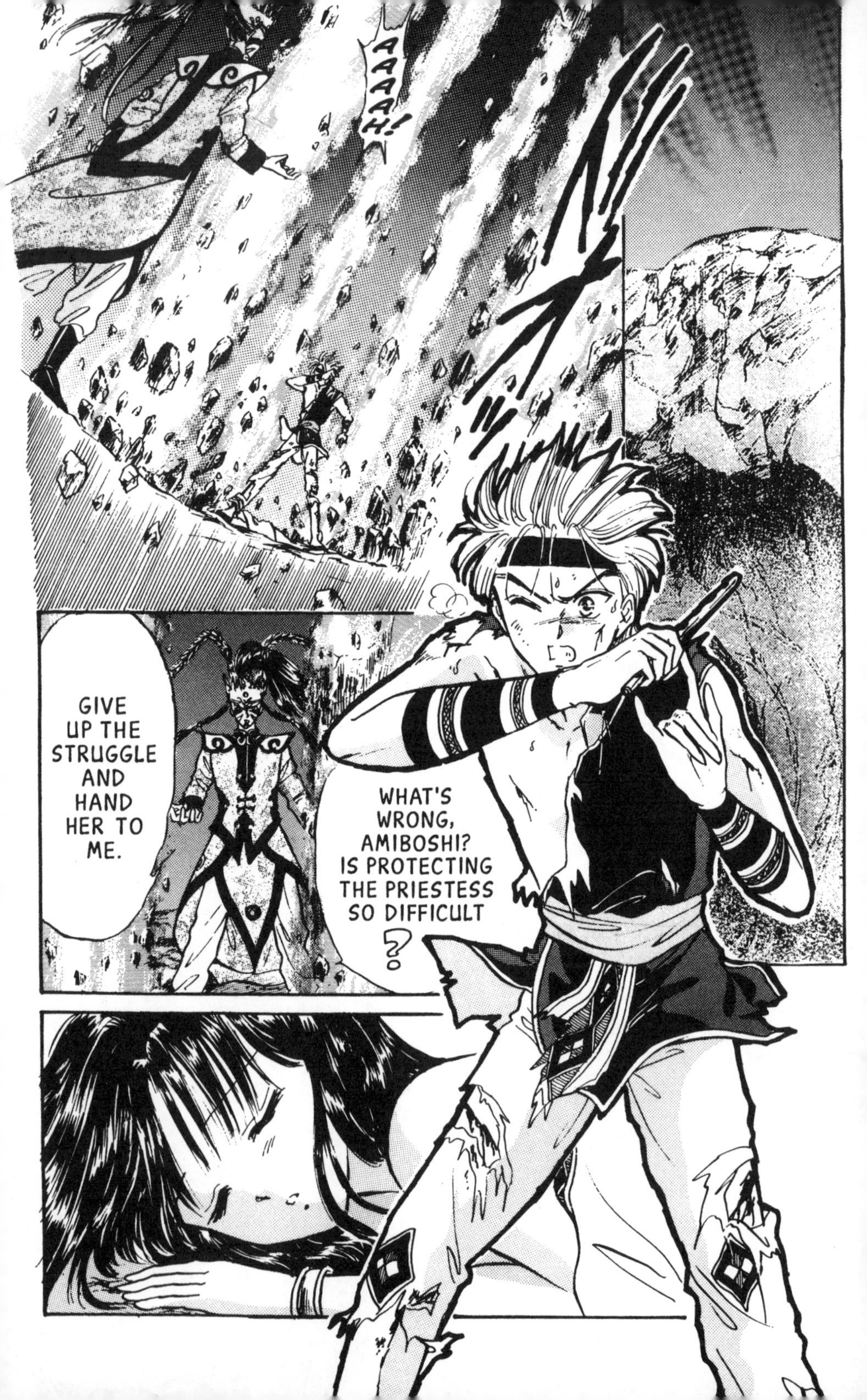
AAAAAH!
WHAT'S WRONG, AMIBOSHI? IS PROTECTING THE PRIESTESS SO DIFFICULT?
GIVE UP THE STRUGGLE AND HAND HER TO ME.

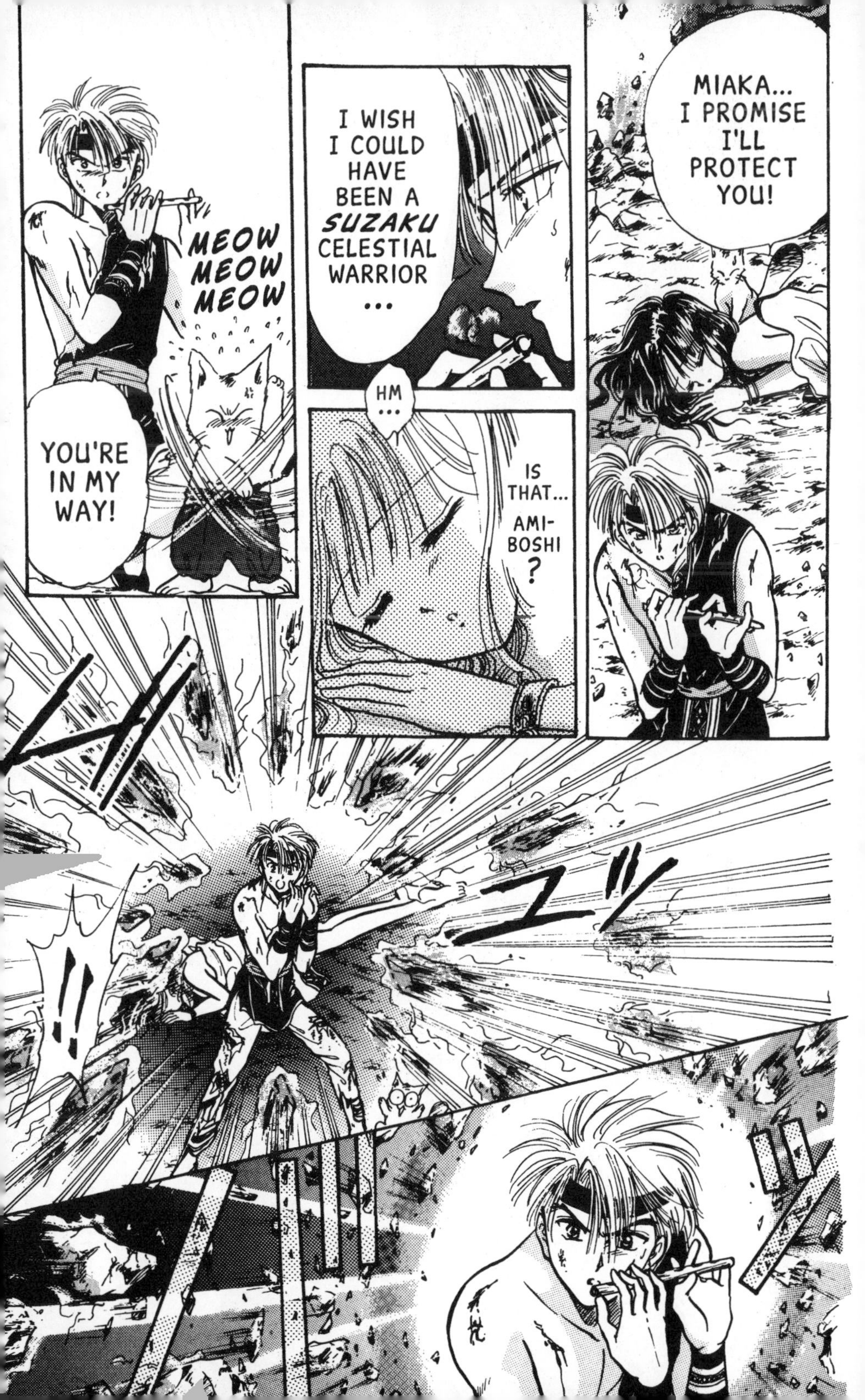
MIAKA... I PROMISE I'LL PROTECT YOU!
I WISH I COULD HAVE BEEN A *SUZAKU* CELESTIAL WARRIOR ...
HM ...
IS THAT... AMI-BOSHI ?
MEOW MEOW MEOW
YOU'RE IN MY WAY!
!!

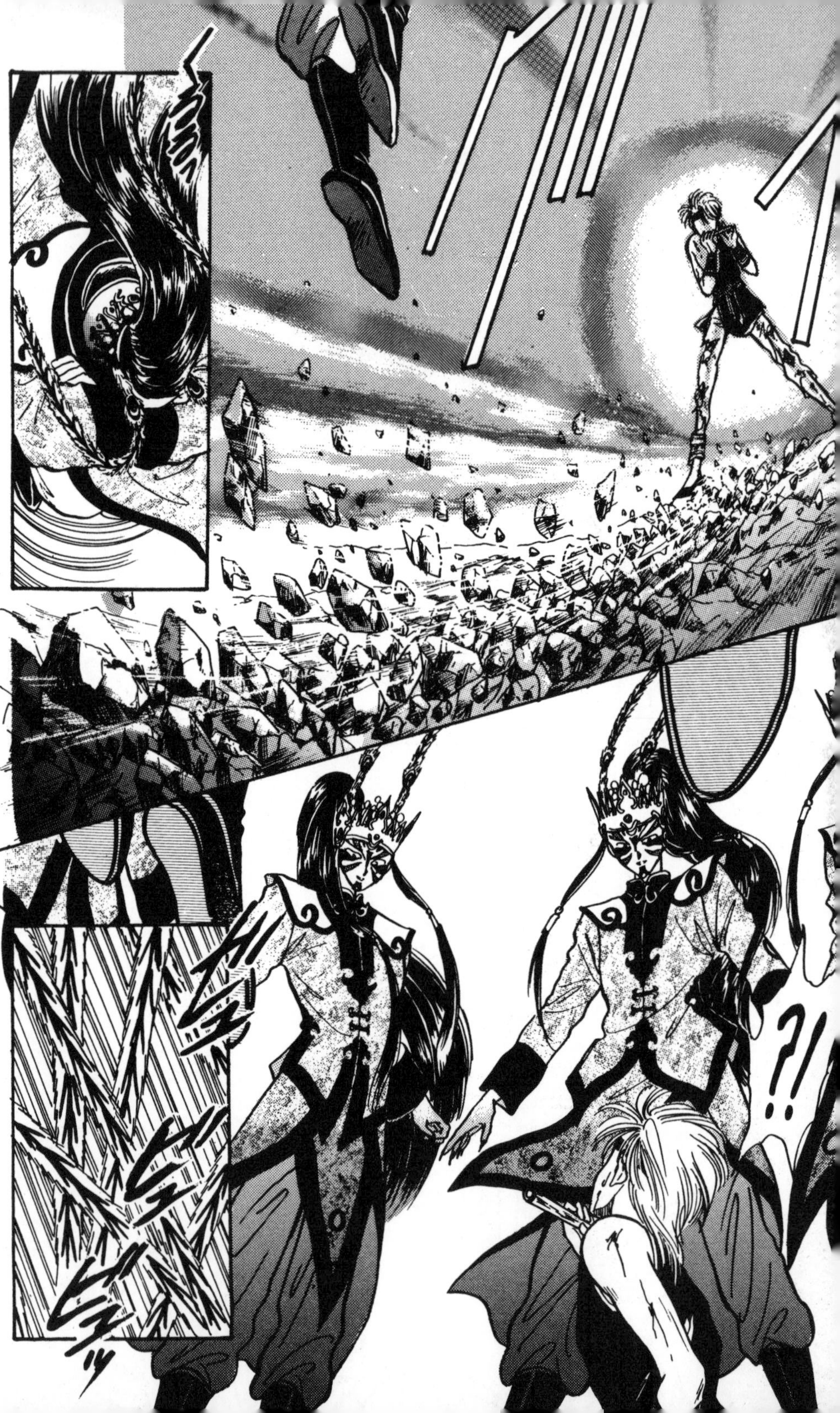
?!!

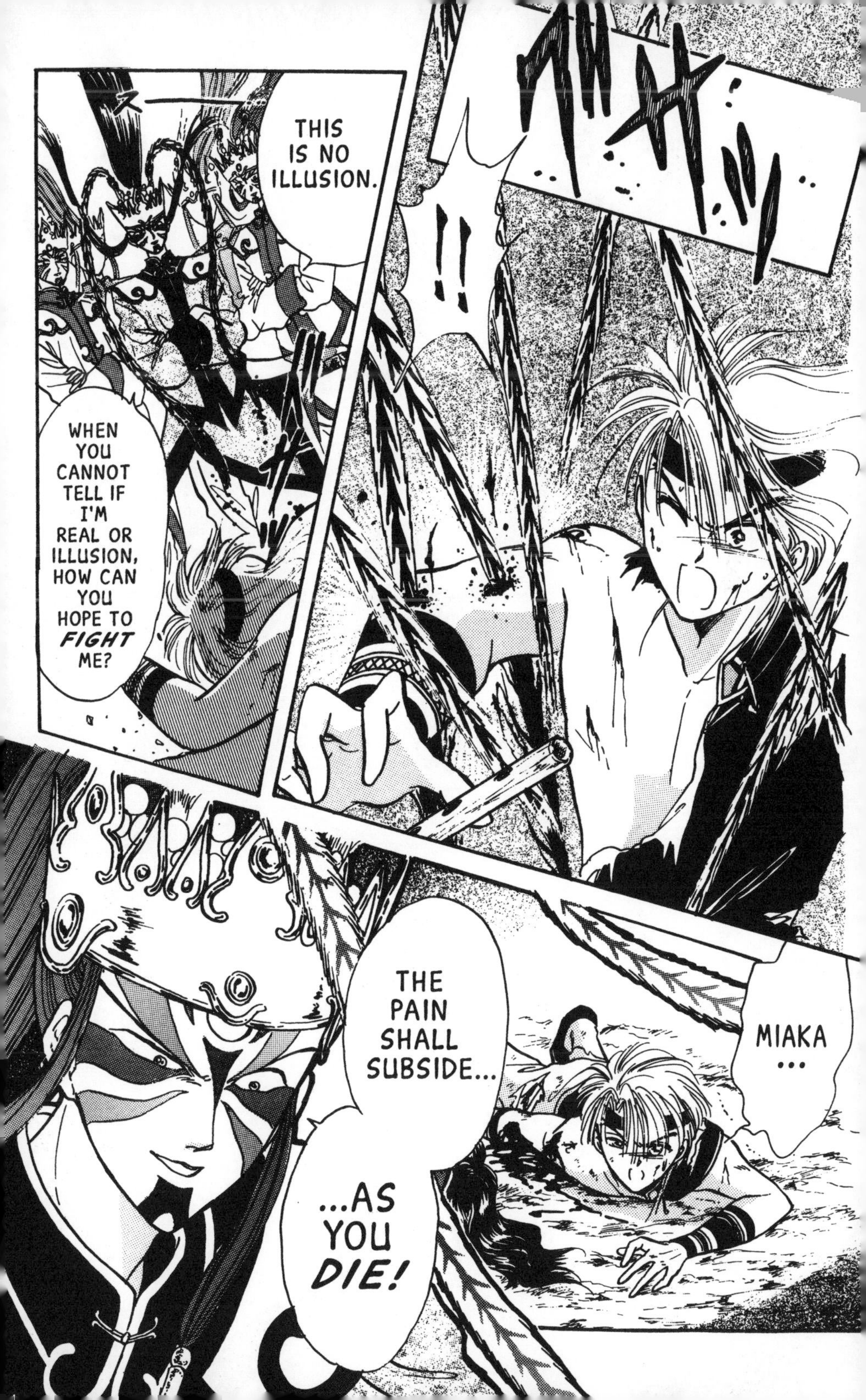
!!
THIS IS NO ILLUSION.
WHEN YOU CANNOT TELL IF I'M REAL OR ILLUSION, HOW CAN YOU HOPE TO *FIGHT* ME?
MIAKA...
THE PAIN SHALL SUBSIDE...
...AS YOU *DIE!*

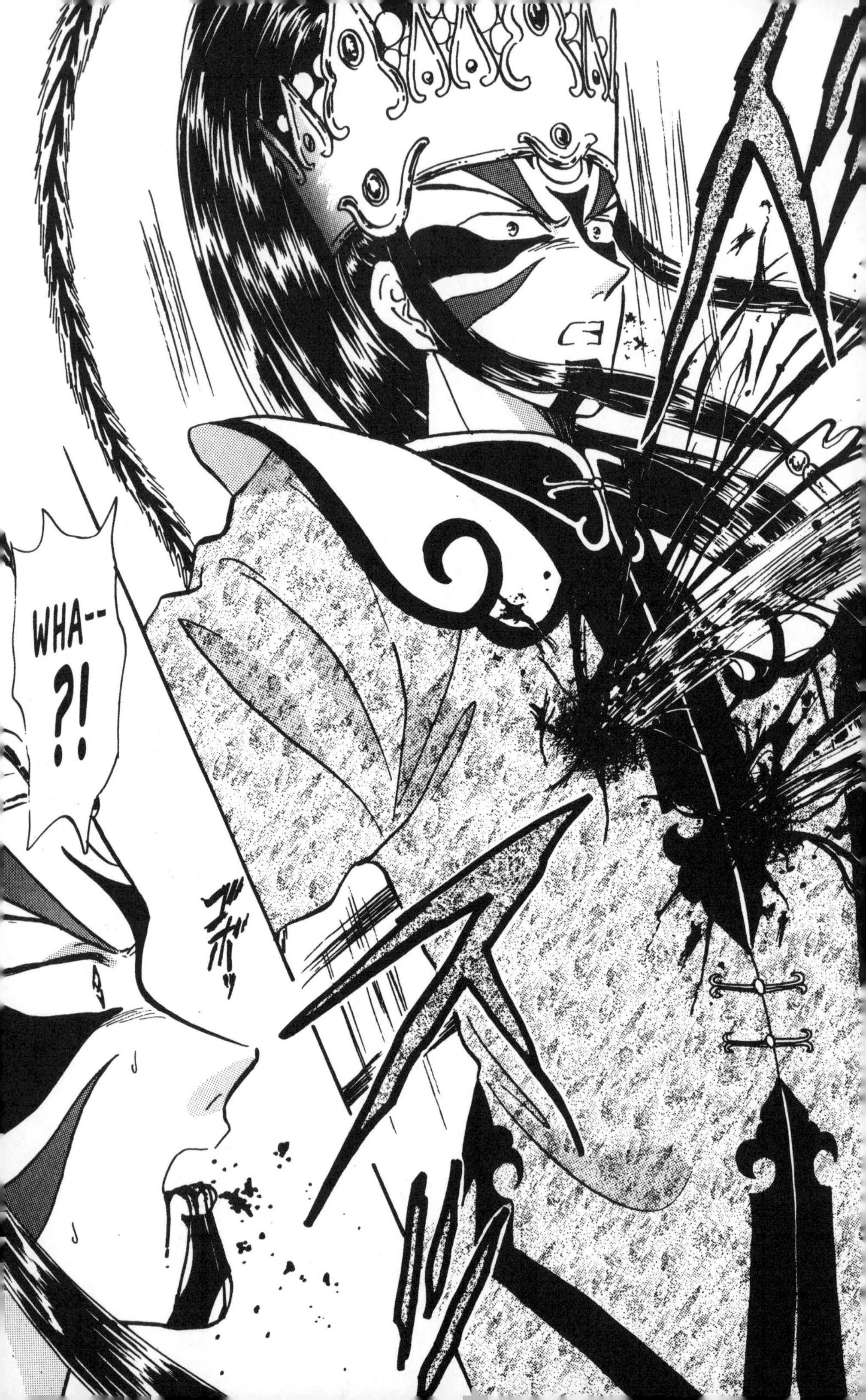
WHA-- ?!

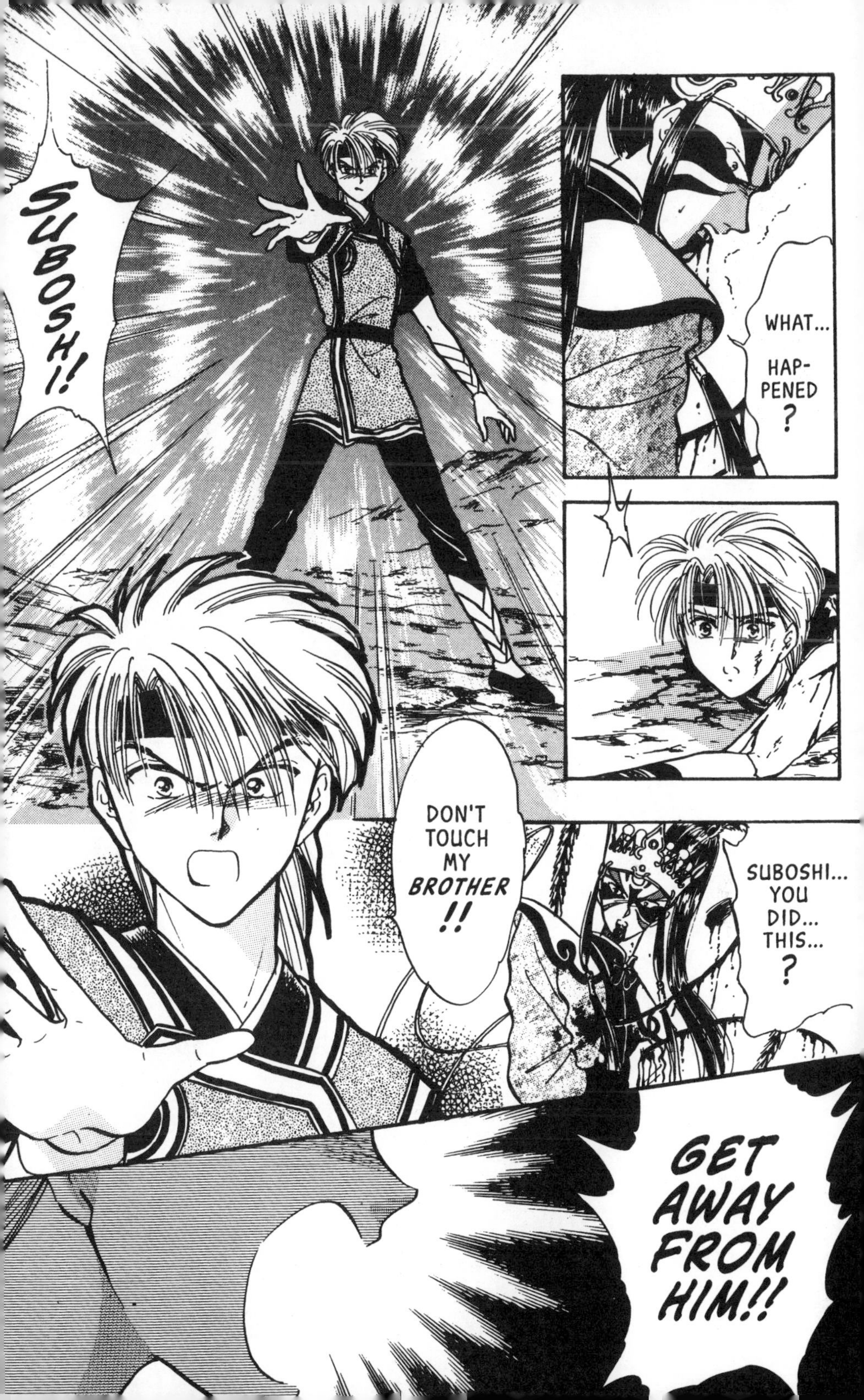
WHAT... HAPPENED?
SUBOSHI!!
SUBOSHI... YOU DID... THIS...?
DON'T TOUCH MY *BROTHER*!!
GET AWAY FROM HIM!!

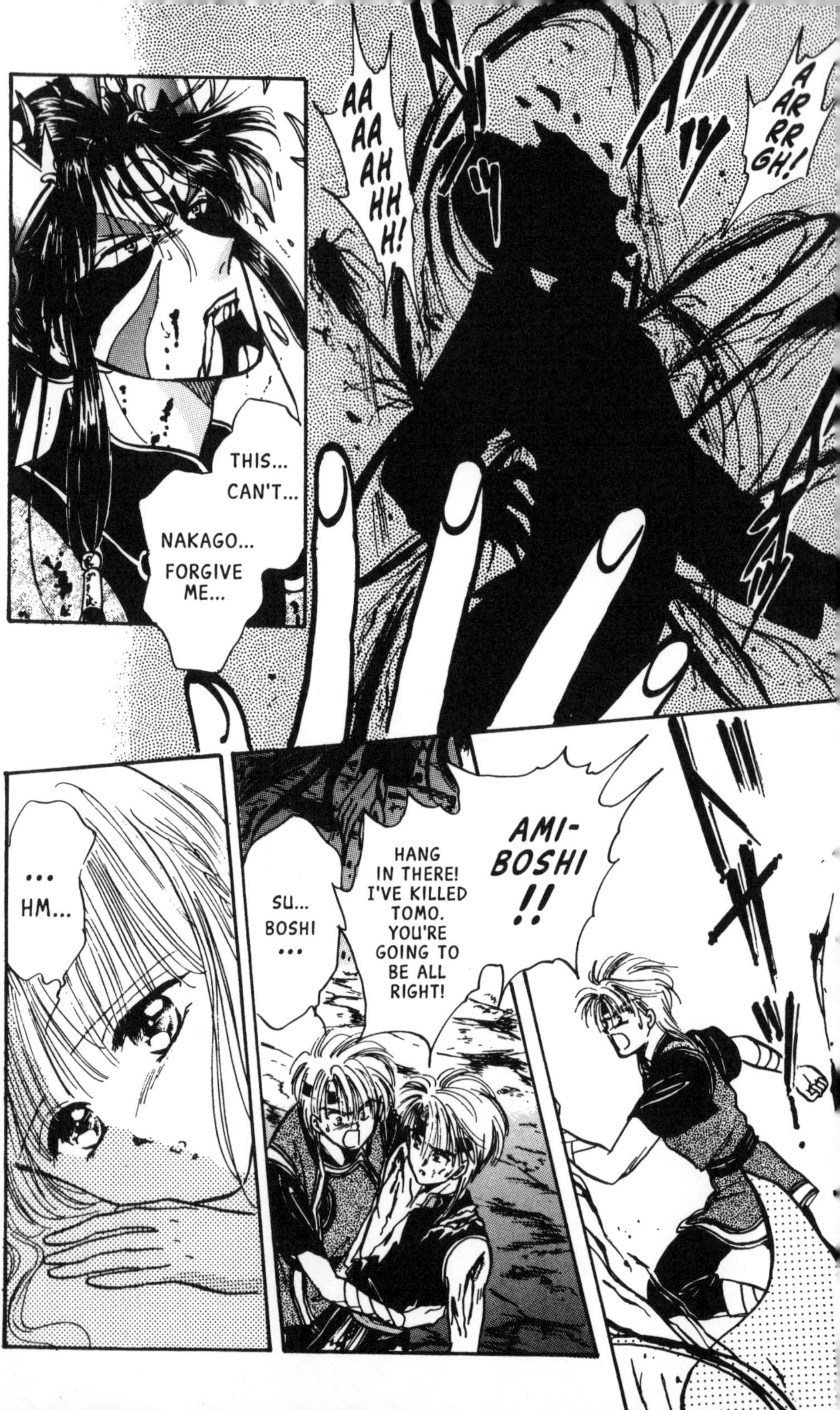
AARRRGH!
AAAAAHHHH!
THIS... CAN'T...
NAKAGO... FORGIVE ME...
AMI-BOSHI!!
HANG IN THERE! I'VE KILLED TOMO. YOU'RE GOING TO BE ALL RIGHT!
SU... BOSHI...
... HM...

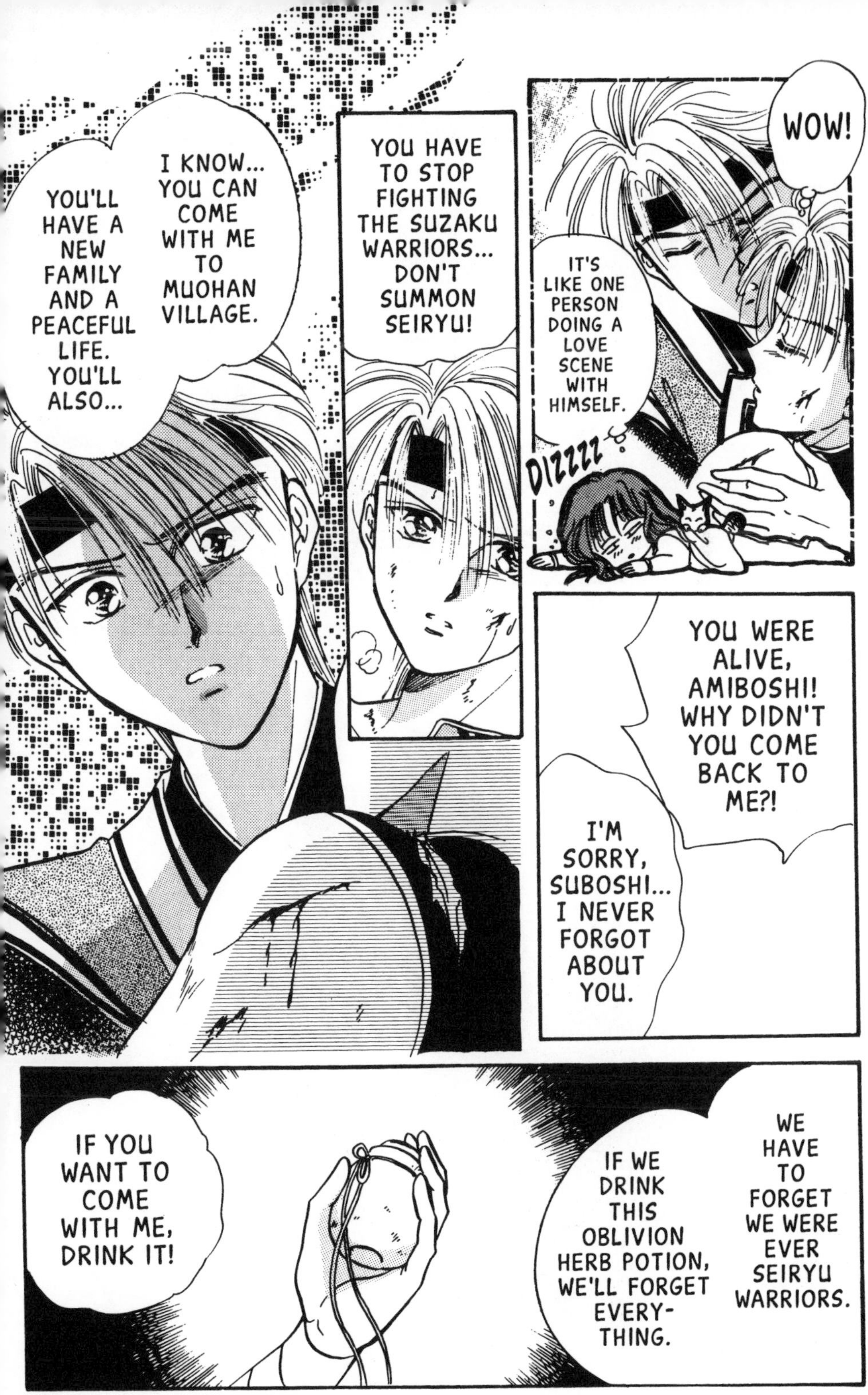
WOW!
IT'S LIKE ONE PERSON DOING A LOVE SCENE WITH HIMSELF.
DIZZZZ
YOU WERE ALIVE, AMIBOSHI! WHY DIDN'T YOU COME BACK TO ME?!
I'M SORRY, SUBOSHI... I NEVER FORGOT ABOUT YOU.
YOU HAVE TO STOP FIGHTING THE SUZAKU WARRIORS... DON'T SUMMON SEIRYU!
I KNOW... YOU CAN COME WITH ME TO MUOHAN VILLAGE.
YOU'LL HAVE A NEW FAMILY AND A PEACEFUL LIFE. YOU'LL ALSO...
WE HAVE TO FORGET WE WERE EVER SEIRYU WARRIORS.
IF WE DRINK THIS OBLIVION HERB POTION, WE'LL FORGET EVERY-THING.
IF YOU WANT TO COME WITH ME, DRINK IT!

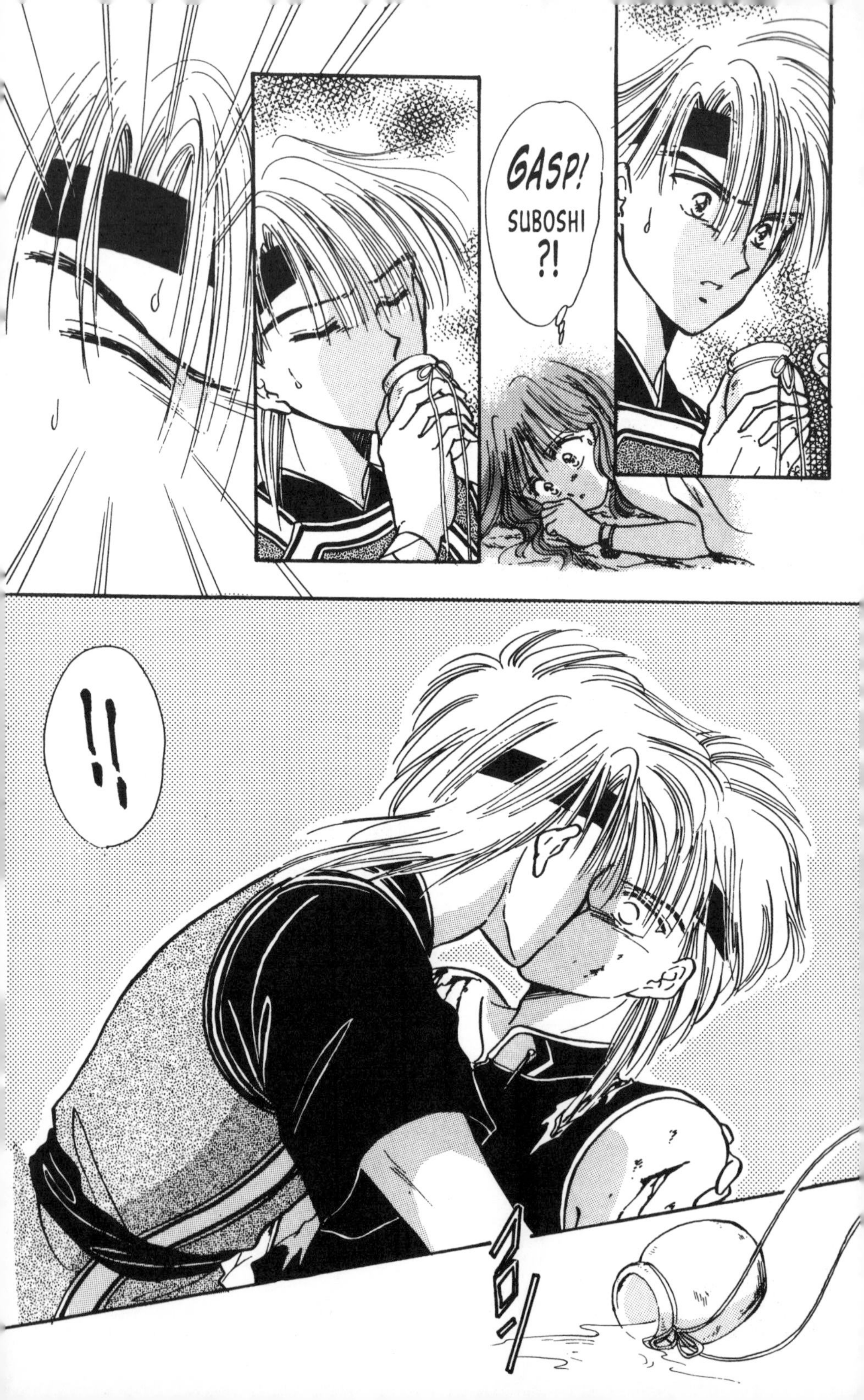
GASP! SUBOSHI ?!
!!

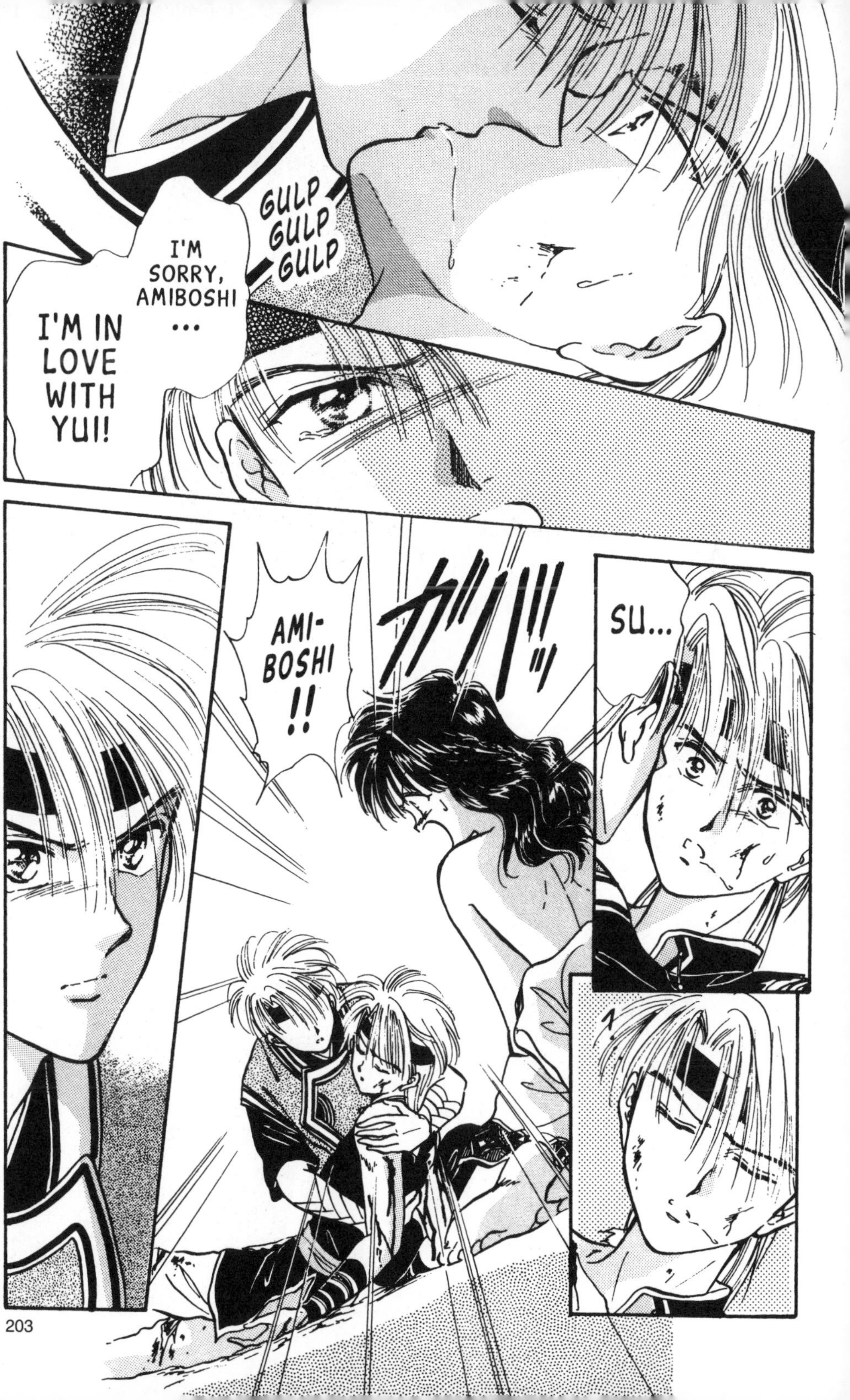
GULP GULP GULP
I'M SORRY, AMIBOSHI...
I'M IN LOVE WITH YUI!
SU...
ガバッ
AMI-BOSHI!!

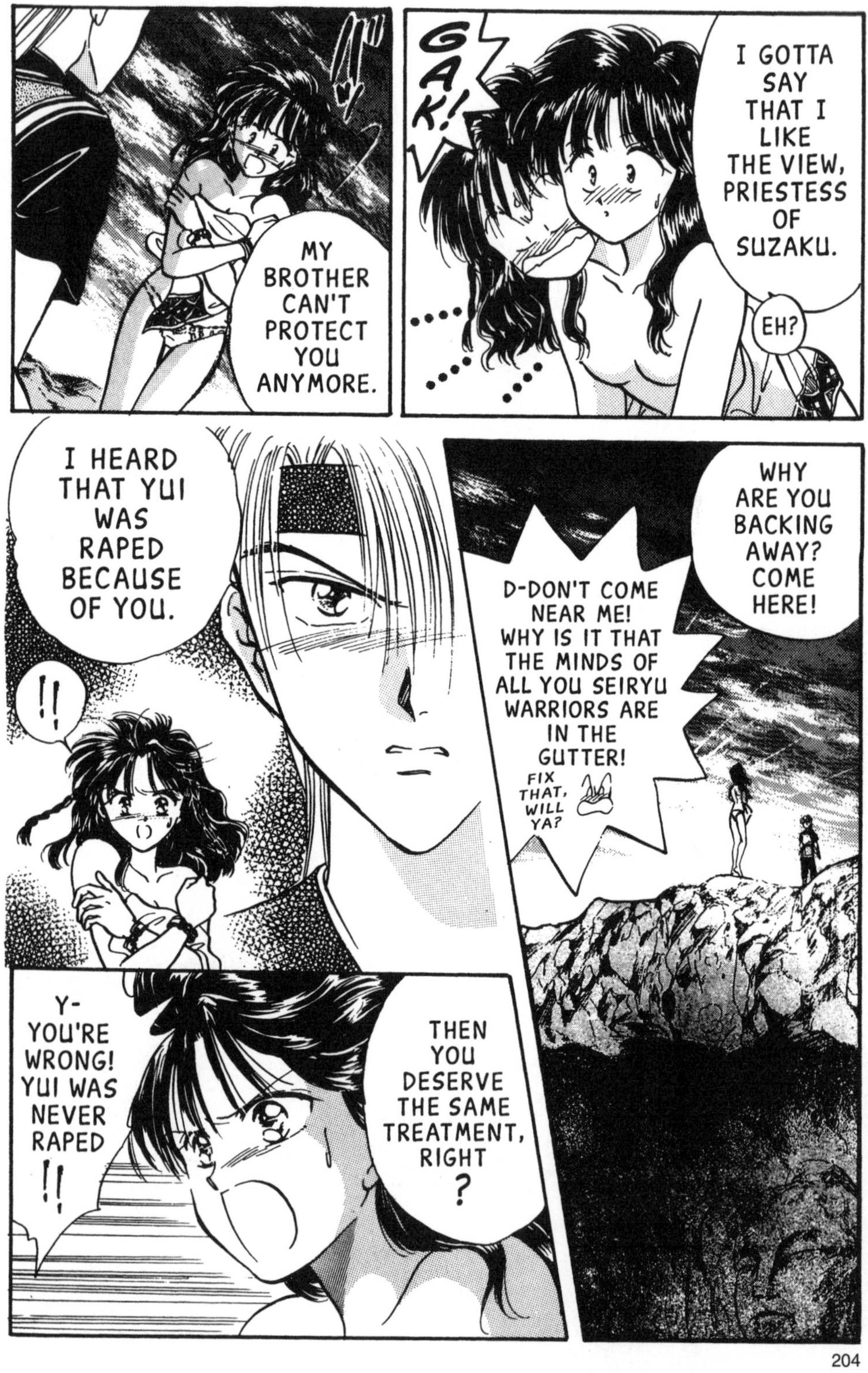
I GOTTA SAY THAT I LIKE THE VIEW, PRIESTESS OF SUZAKU.
GAK!
EH?
....
MY BROTHER CAN'T PROTECT YOU ANYMORE.
WHY ARE YOU BACKING AWAY? COME HERE!
D-DON'T COME NEAR ME! WHY IS IT THAT THE MINDS OF ALL YOU SEIRYU WARRIORS ARE IN THE GUTTER!
FIX THAT, WILL YA?
I HEARD THAT YUI WAS RAPED BECAUSE OF YOU.
!!
THEN YOU DESERVE THE SAME TREATMENT, RIGHT ?
Y-YOU'RE WRONG! YUI WAS NEVER RAPED !!

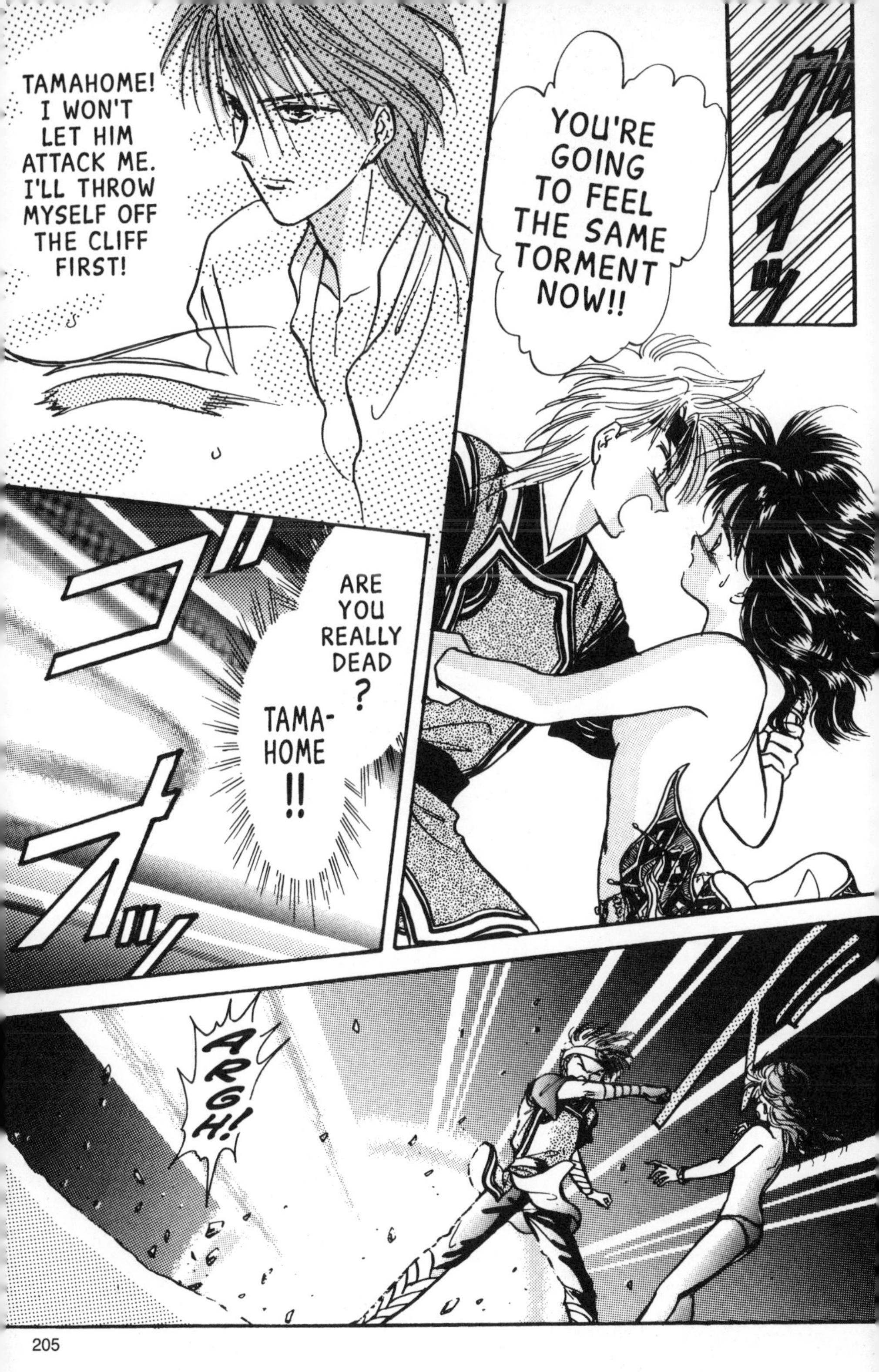
YOU'RE GOING TO FEEL THE SAME TORMENT NOW!!
TAMAHOME! I WON'T LET HIM ATTACK ME. I'LL THROW MYSELF OFF THE CLIFF FIRST!
ARE YOU REALLY DEAD?
TAMA-HOME!!
ARGH!

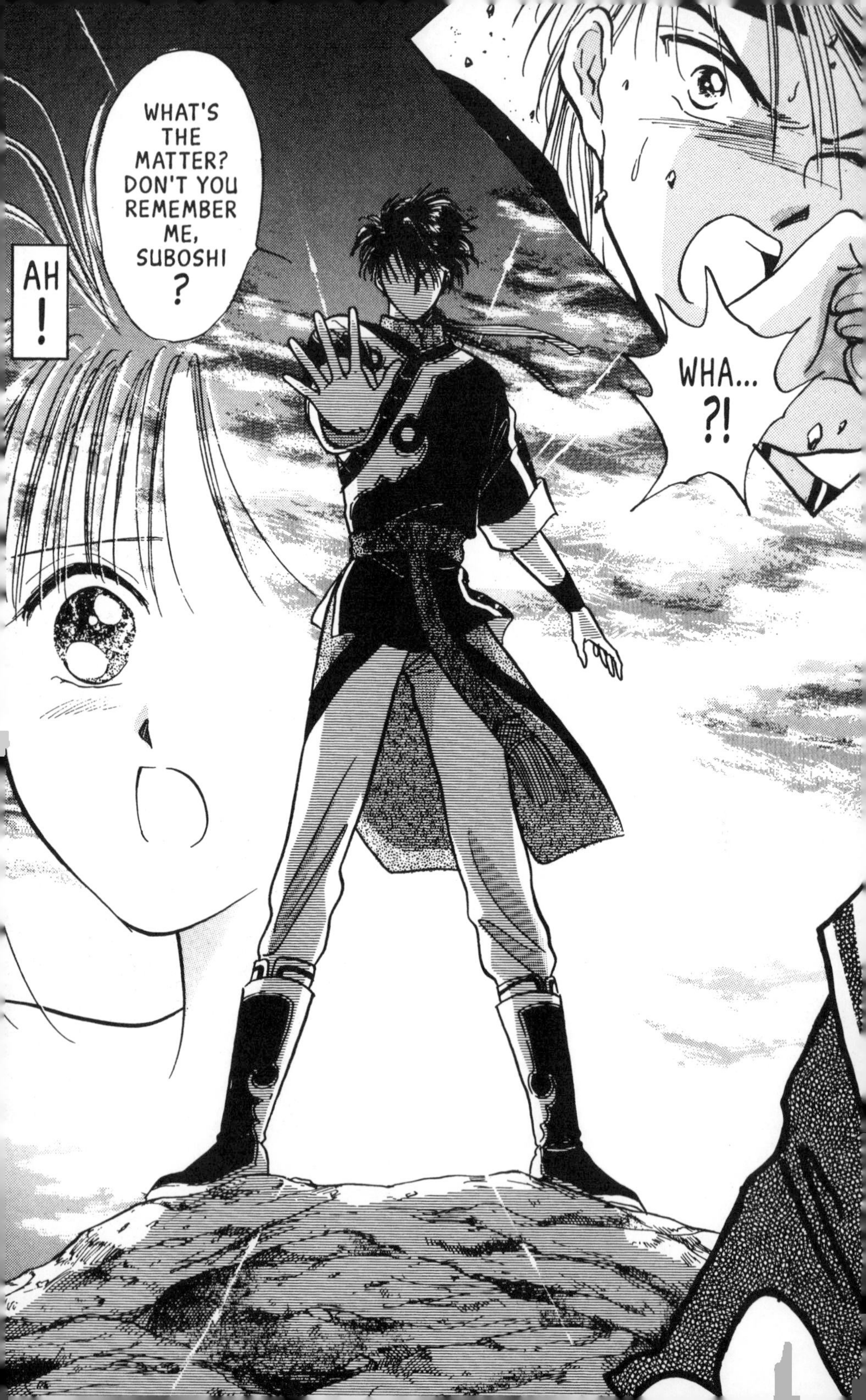
WHA... ?!
WHAT'S THE MATTER? DON'T YOU REMEMBER ME, SUBOSHI ?
AH !

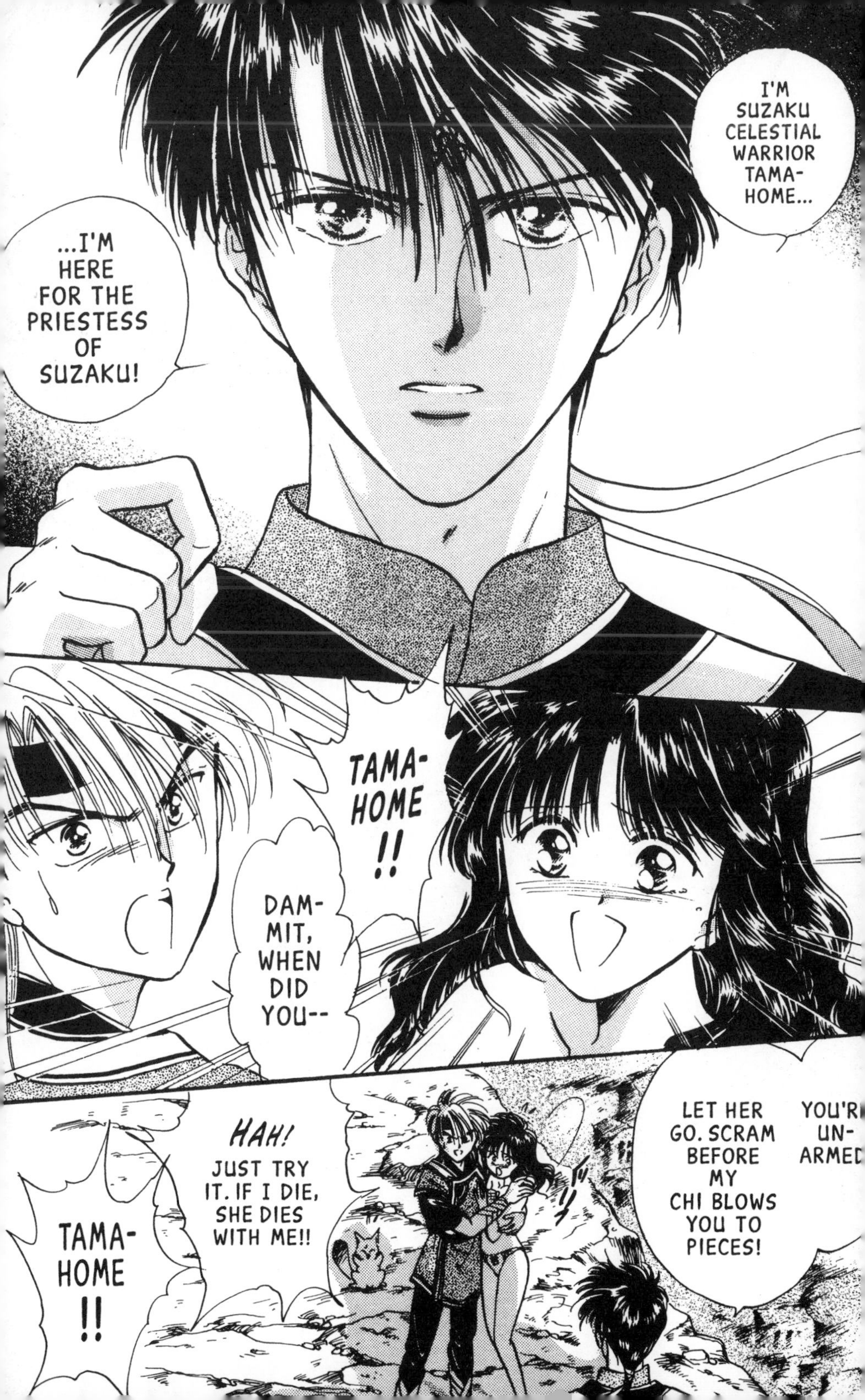

I'M SUZAKU CELESTIAL WARRIOR TAMA-HOME...
...I'M HERE FOR THE PRIESTESS OF SUZAKU!
TAMA-HOME!!
DAM-MIT, WHEN DID YOU--
YOU'R UN-ARMED
LET HER GO. SCRAM BEFORE MY CHI BLOWS YOU TO PIECES!
HAH!
JUST TRY IT. IF I DIE, SHE DIES WITH ME!!
TAMA-HOME!!

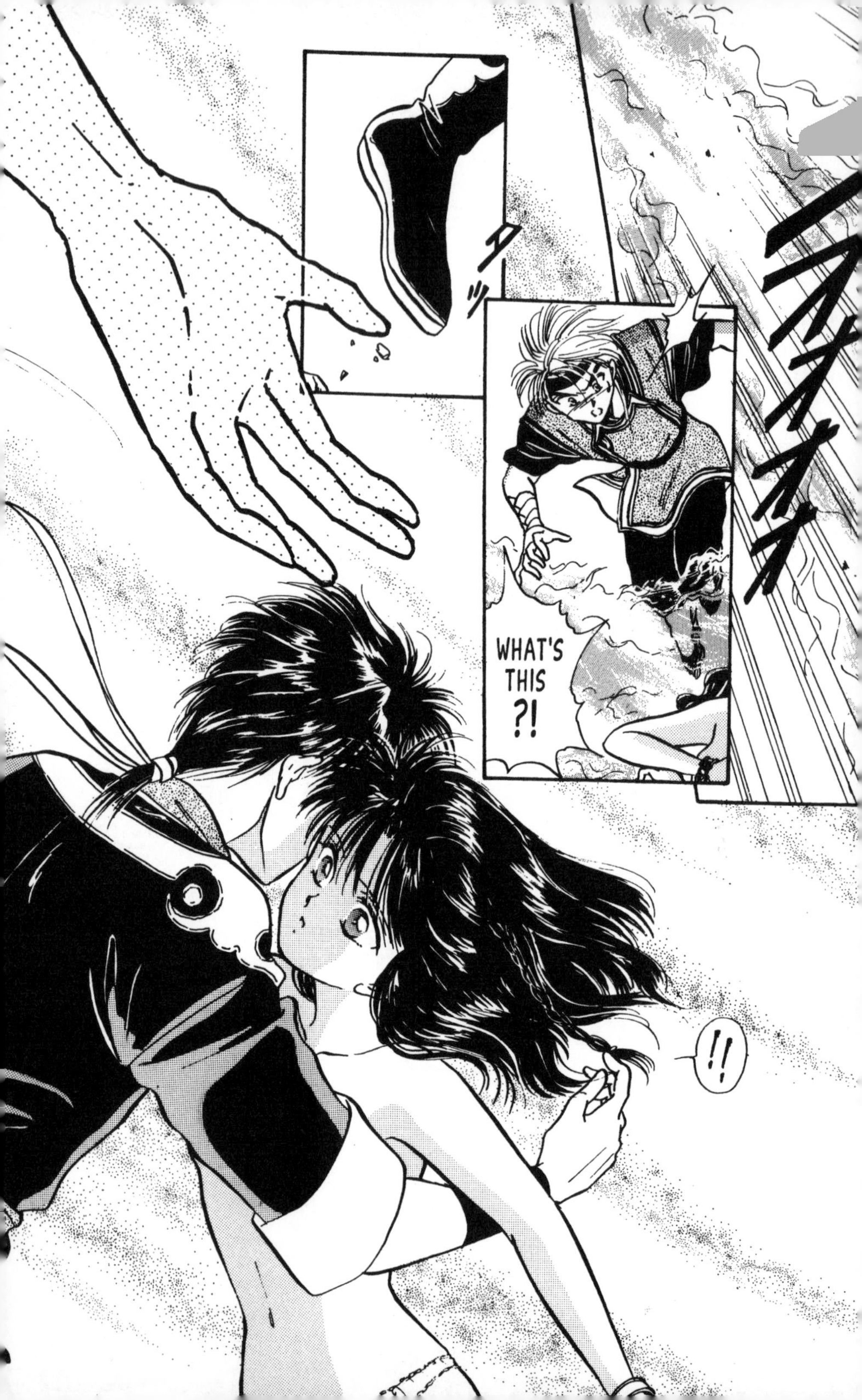
WHAT'S THIS ?!
!!

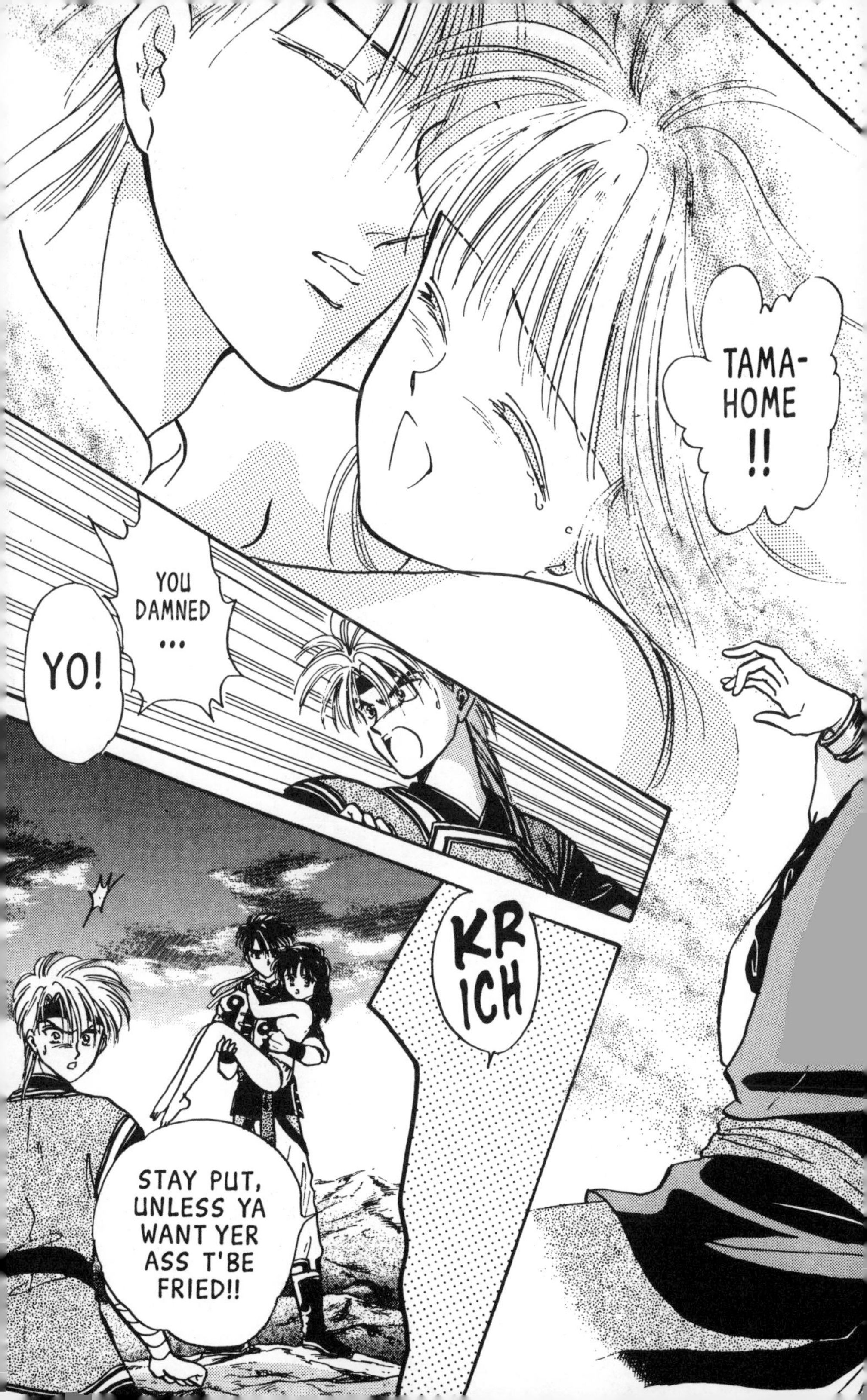
TAMA-HOME!!
YOU DAMNED...
YO!
KRICH
STAY PUT, UNLESS YA WANT YER ASS T'BE FRIED!!

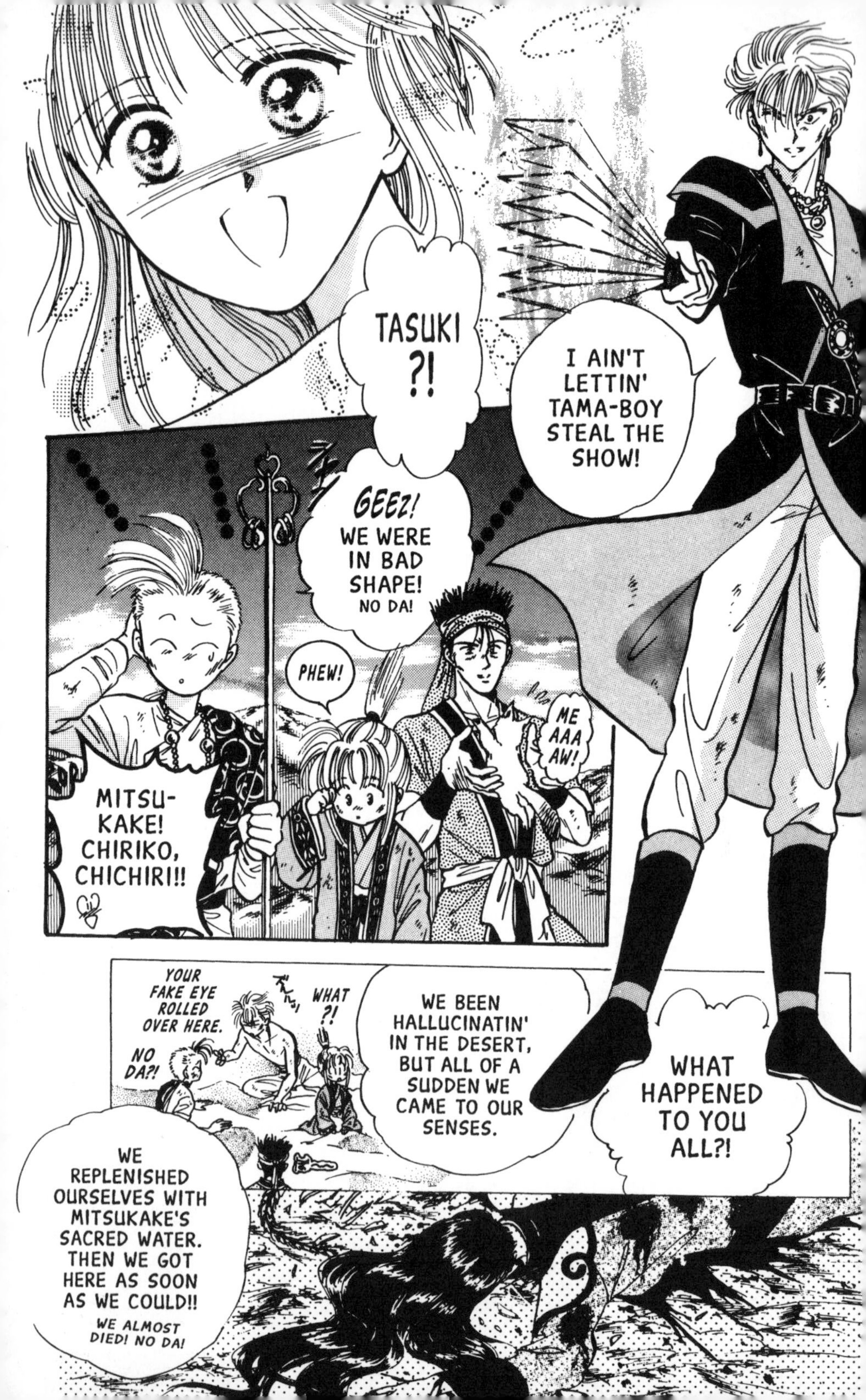

TASUKI ?!
I AIN'T LETTIN' TAMA-BOY STEAL THE SHOW!
GEEZ! WE WERE IN BAD SHAPE! NO DA!
PHEW!
MEAAAAW!
MITSUKAKE! CHIRIKO, CHICHIRI!!
WHAT HAPPENED TO YOU ALL?!
WE BEEN HALLUCINATIN' IN THE DESERT, BUT ALL OF A SUDDEN WE CAME TO OUR SENSES.
WHAT ?!
YOUR FAKE EYE ROLLED OVER HERE.
NO DA?!
WE REPLENISHED OURSELVES WITH MITSUKAKE'S SACRED WATER. THEN WE GOT HERE AS SOON AS WE COULD!!
WE ALMOST DIED! NO DA!

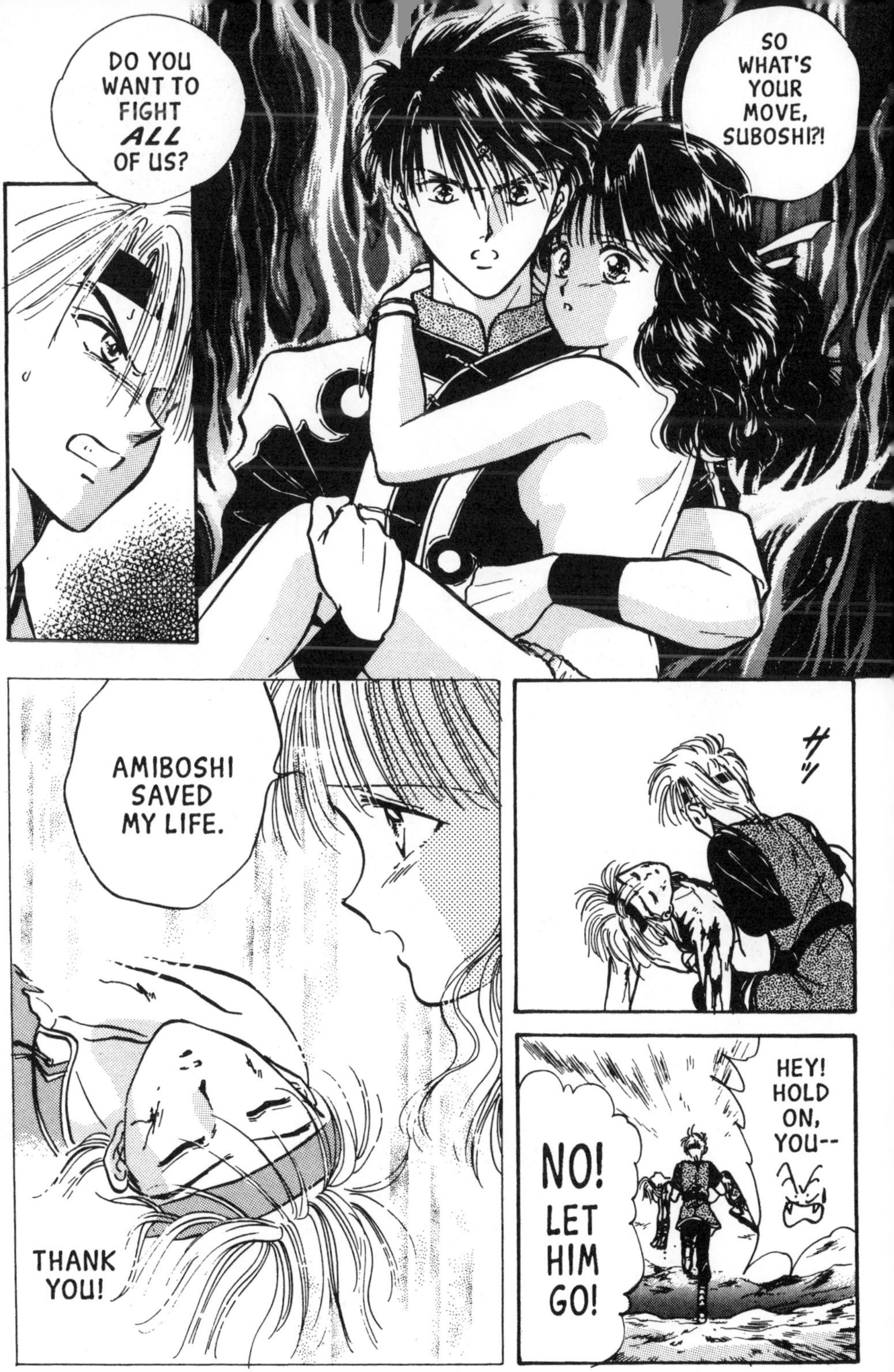
SO WHAT'S YOUR MOVE, SUBOSHI?!
DO YOU WANT TO FIGHT ALL OF US?
ザッ
HEY! HOLD ON, YOU--
NO! LET HIM GO!
AMIBOSHI SAVED MY LIFE.
THANK YOU!

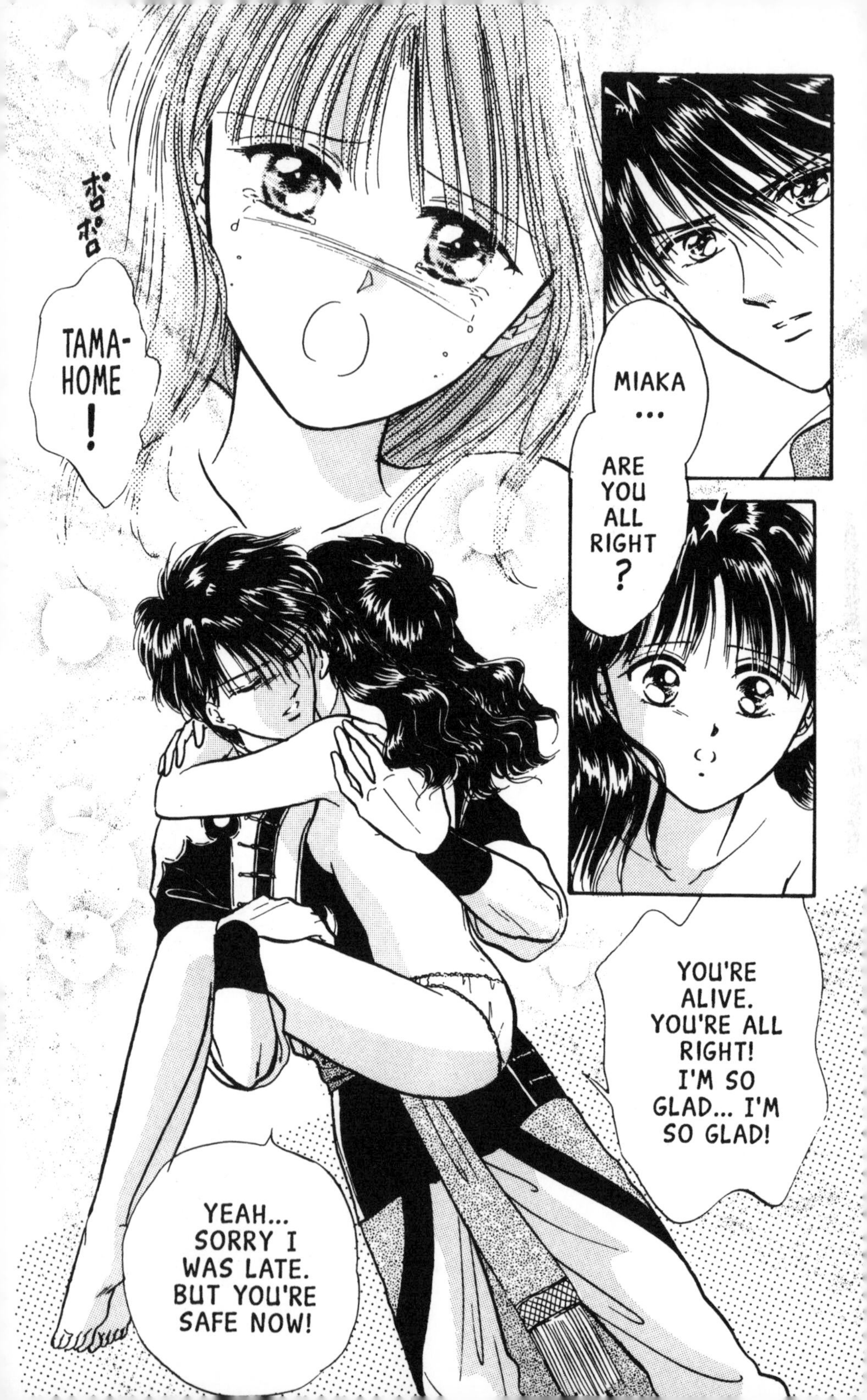
MIAKA... ARE YOU ALL RIGHT?
ポロポロ
TAMA-HOME!
YOU'RE ALIVE. YOU'RE ALL RIGHT! I'M SO GLAD... I'M SO GLAD!
YEAH... SORRY I WAS LATE. BUT YOU'RE SAFE NOW!

Hello, hello! This is Yuu Watase. Right now we're listening to Chopin. We're really into classical music these days. Speaking of music, have you had the chance to listen to CD Book 2? The first song, "Journey of Encounters," and the BGM has a Chinese sound. I'm so into it. Of course, I love all the songs! *Mr. Honda and Mr. Kajiwara from 135 are singing on the demo tape.* ♥♥♥ *How lucky can I get?!*

Nuriko's song might seem like a love song, but in fact, it's about death. Amiboshi was so sexy (his voice, that is). *And Chichiri's is so cute!!*

I also want to thank all you fans who came to the signing event in Fukuoka. Thanks for all the letters and presents. Oh yeah! The emcee at the signing asked me whether this was my first time to Kyushu, and I was so nervous I said "Yes!" but after returning to my hotel, I realized I'd already traveled to Nagasaki with a friend of mine. I was appalled! "I'm so stupid... I've even been to Huis Ten Bosch!" I... I lied! I'm so sorry!

Oh! One more thing! I'm having a book signing in Kyoto in November (1994). So, fans over there, please come by. *Honest, I've never been to Kyoto! But it's been too long since I've been back to Osaka! I miss it so much!*

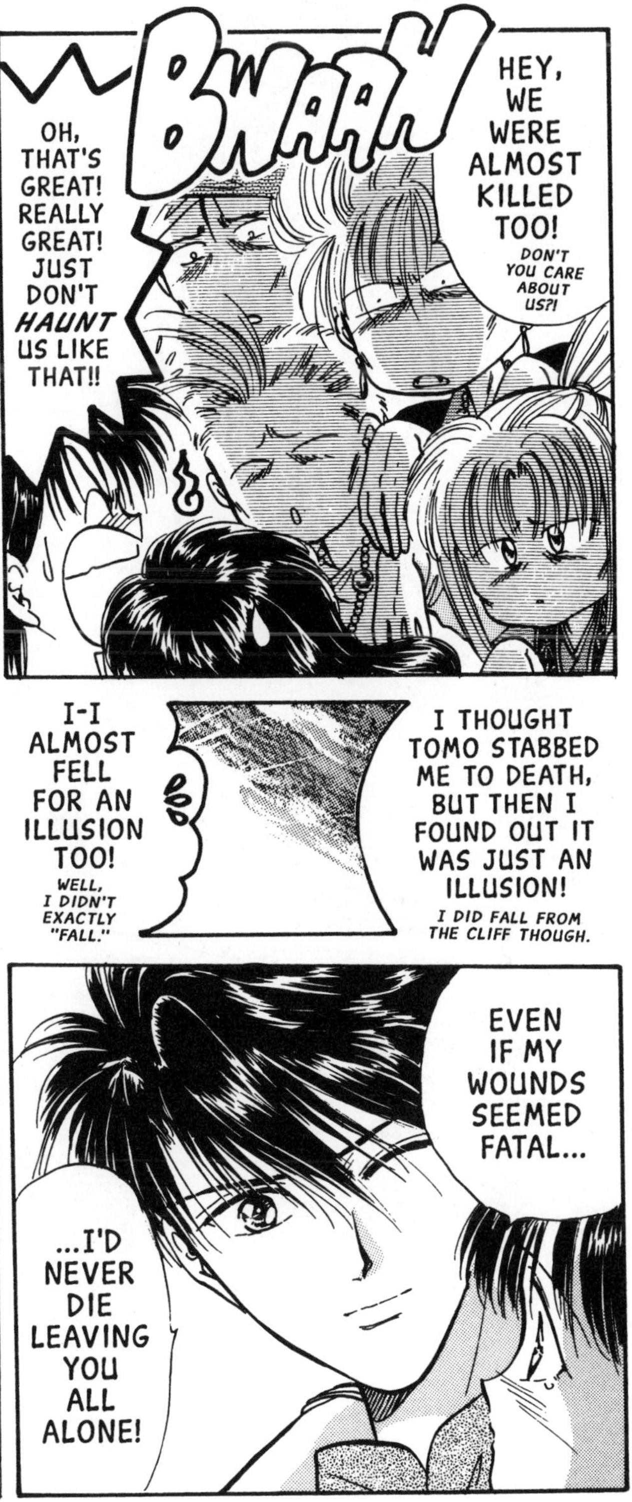
BWAAAH
HEY, WE WERE ALMOST KILLED TOO!
DON'T YOU CARE ABOUT US?!
OH, THAT'S GREAT! REALLY GREAT! JUST DON'T HAUNT US LIKE THAT!!
I THOUGHT TOMO STABBED ME TO DEATH, BUT THEN I FOUND OUT IT WAS JUST AN ILLUSION!
I DID FALL FROM THE CLIFF THOUGH.
I-I ALMOST FELL FOR AN ILLUSION TOO!
WELL, I DIDN'T EXACTLY "FALL."
EVEN IF MY WOUNDS SEEMED FATAL...
...I'D NEVER DIE LEAVING YOU ALL ALONE!

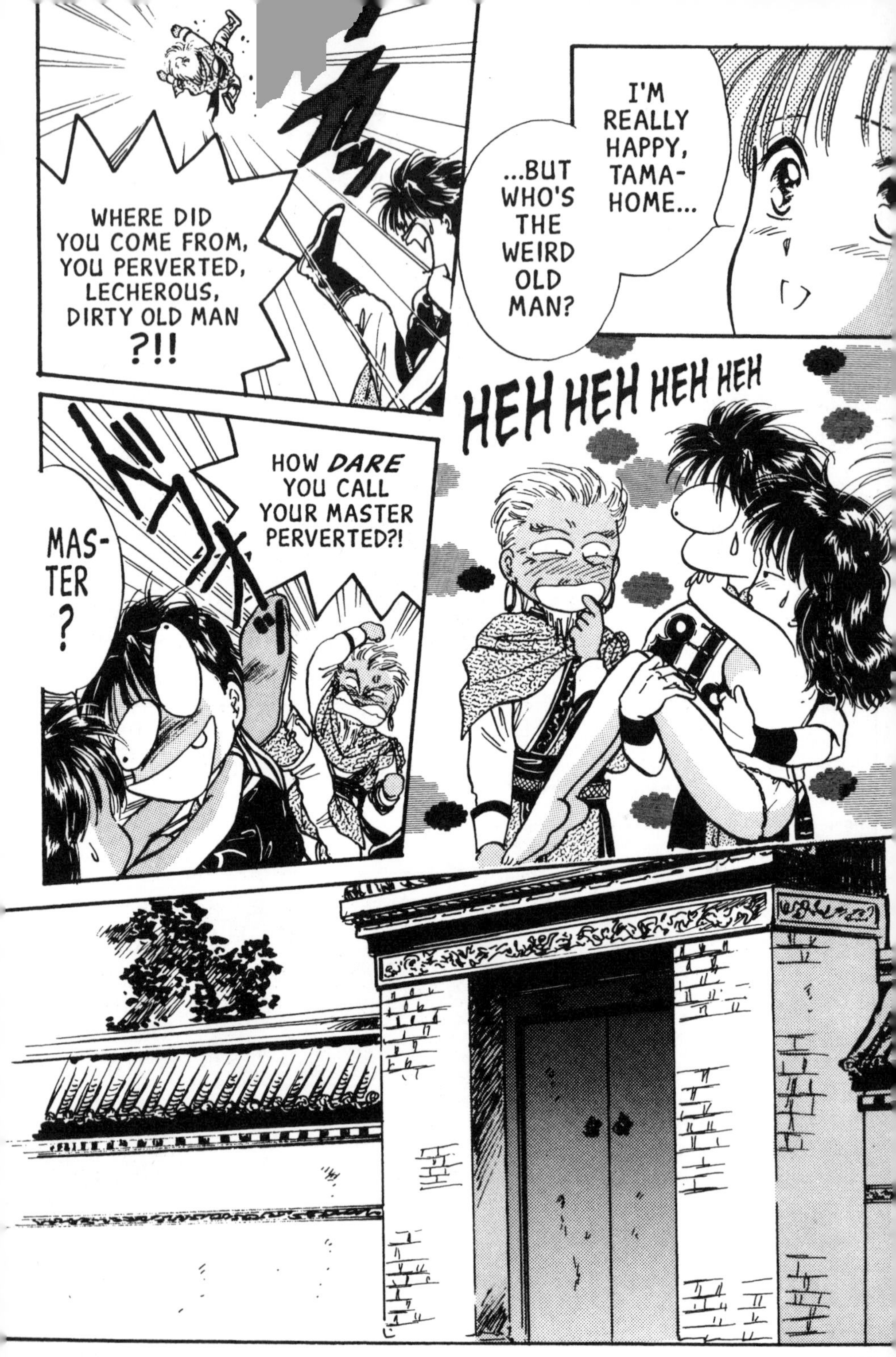
I'M REALLY HAPPY, TAMA-HOME...
...BUT WHO'S THE WEIRD OLD MAN?
WHERE DID YOU COME FROM, YOU PERVERTED, LECHEROUS, DIRTY OLD MAN ?!!
HEH HEH HEH HEH
HOW *DARE* YOU CALL YOUR MASTER PERVERTED?!
MAS-TER ?

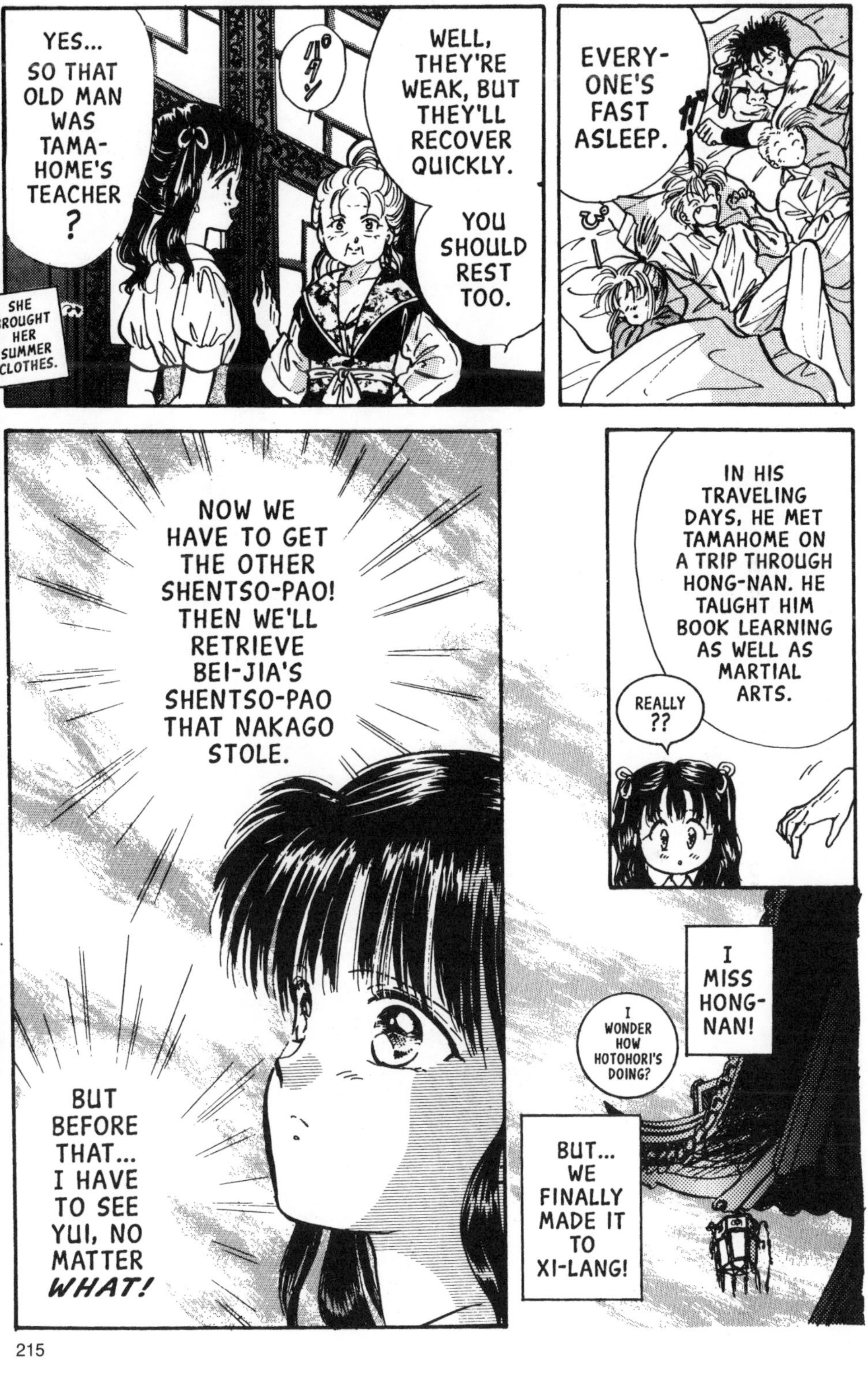
EVERYONE'S FAST ASLEEP.
WELL, THEY'RE WEAK, BUT THEY'LL RECOVER QUICKLY.
YOU SHOULD REST TOO.
パタン
YES... SO THAT OLD MAN WAS TAMAHOME'S TEACHER?
SHE BROUGHT HER SUMMER CLOTHES.
IN HIS TRAVELING DAYS, HE MET TAMAHOME ON A TRIP THROUGH HONG-NAN. HE TAUGHT HIM BOOK LEARNING AS WELL AS MARTIAL ARTS.
REALLY??
I MISS HONG-NAN!
I WONDER HOW HOTOHORI'S DOING?
BUT... WE FINALLY MADE IT TO XI-LANG!
NOW WE HAVE TO GET THE OTHER SHENTSO-PAO! THEN WE'LL RETRIEVE BEI-JIA'S SHENTSO-PAO THAT NAKAGO STOLE.
BUT BEFORE THAT... I HAVE TO SEE YUI, NO MATTER *WHAT!*

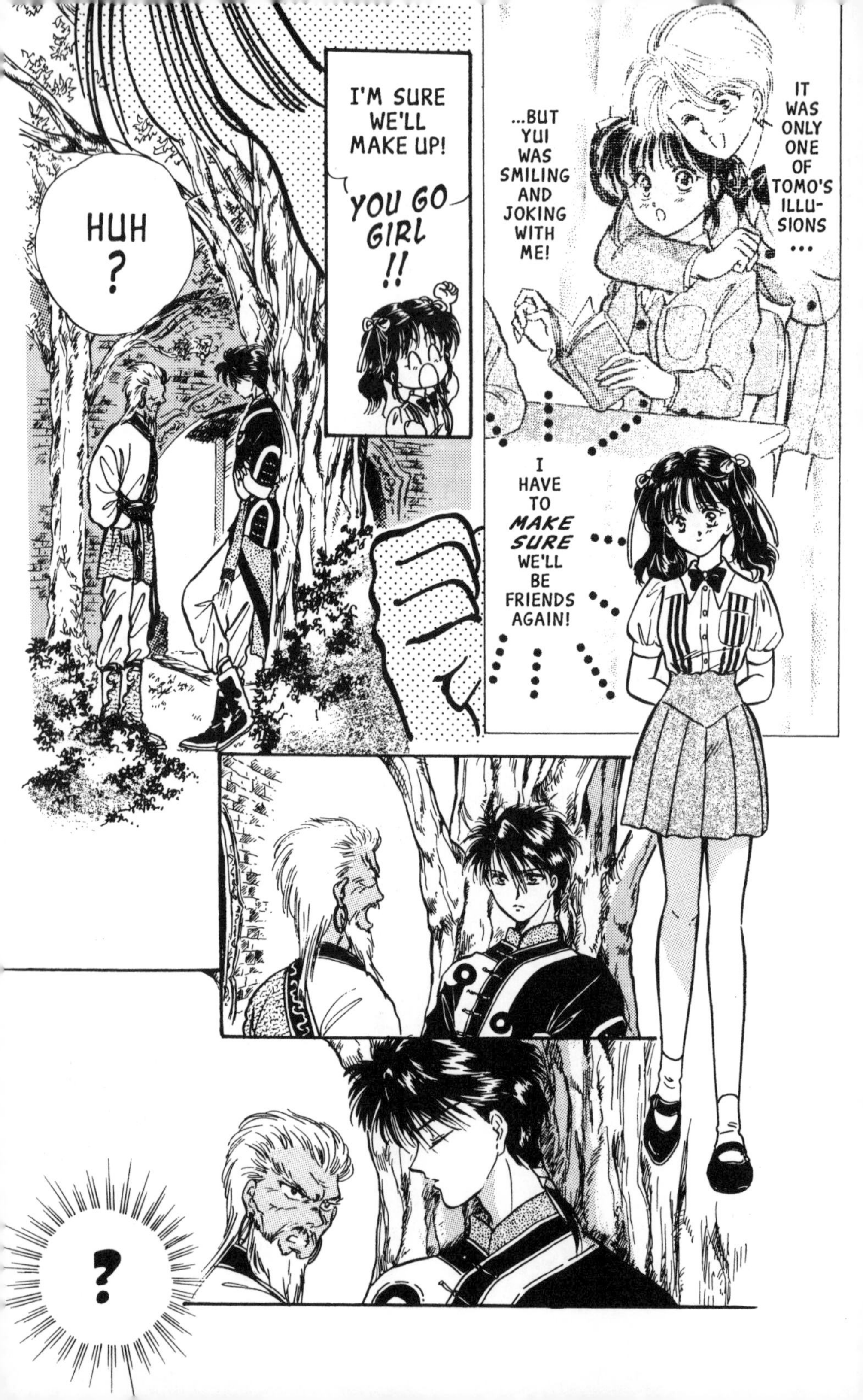
IT WAS ONLY ONE OF TOMO'S ILLUSIONS...
...BUT YUI WAS SMILING AND JOKING WITH ME!
I HAVE TO MAKE SURE WE'LL BE FRIENDS AGAIN!
I'M SURE WE'LL MAKE UP!
YOU GO GIRL!!
HUH?
?

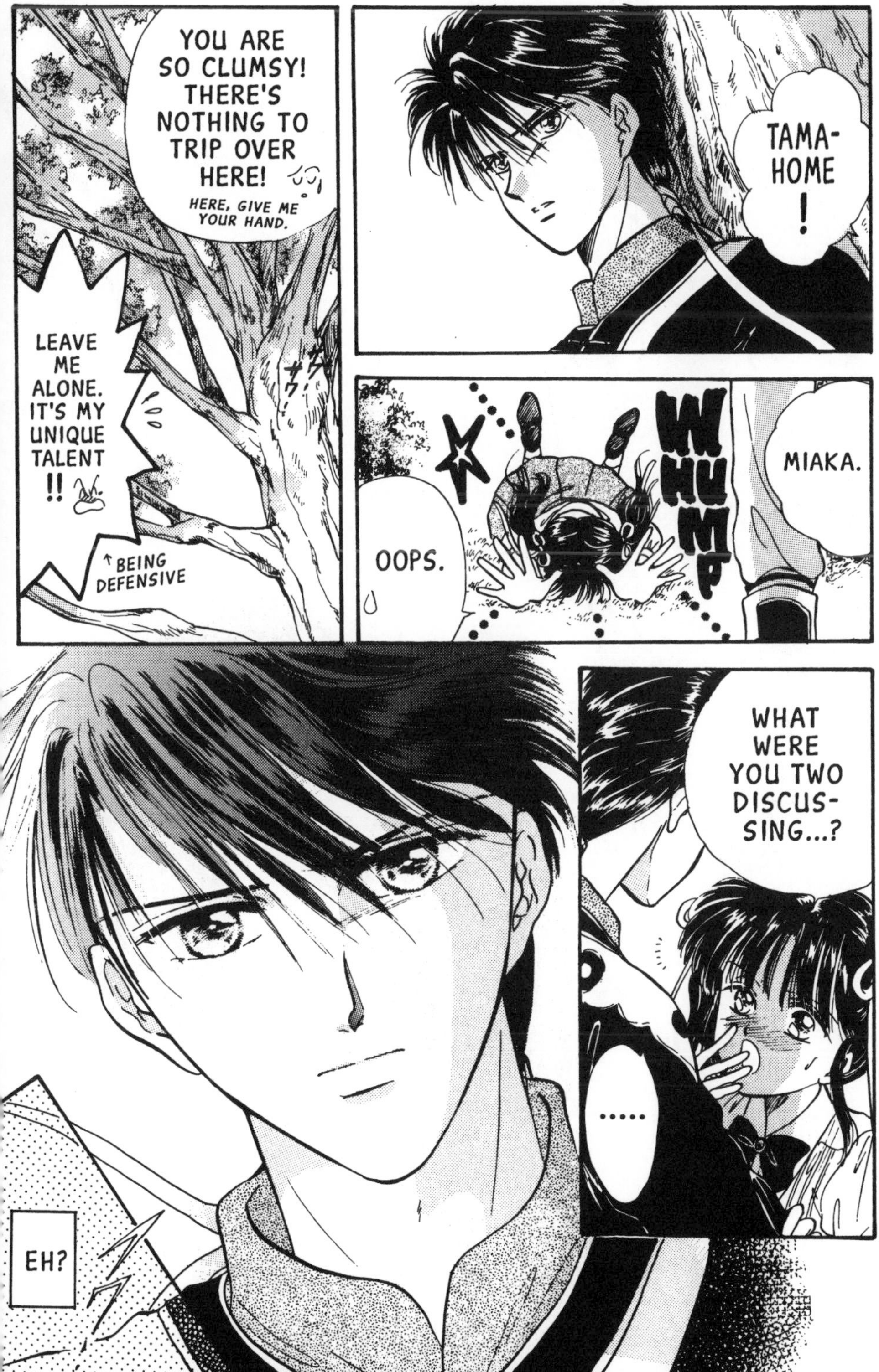
TAMA-HOME !
MIAKA.
WHUMP
OOPS.
YOU ARE SO CLUMSY! THERE'S NOTHING TO TRIP OVER HERE!
HERE, GIVE ME YOUR HAND.
LEAVE ME ALONE. IT'S MY UNIQUE TALENT !!
↑ BEING DEFENSIVE
WHAT WERE YOU TWO DISCUSSING...?
.....
EH?

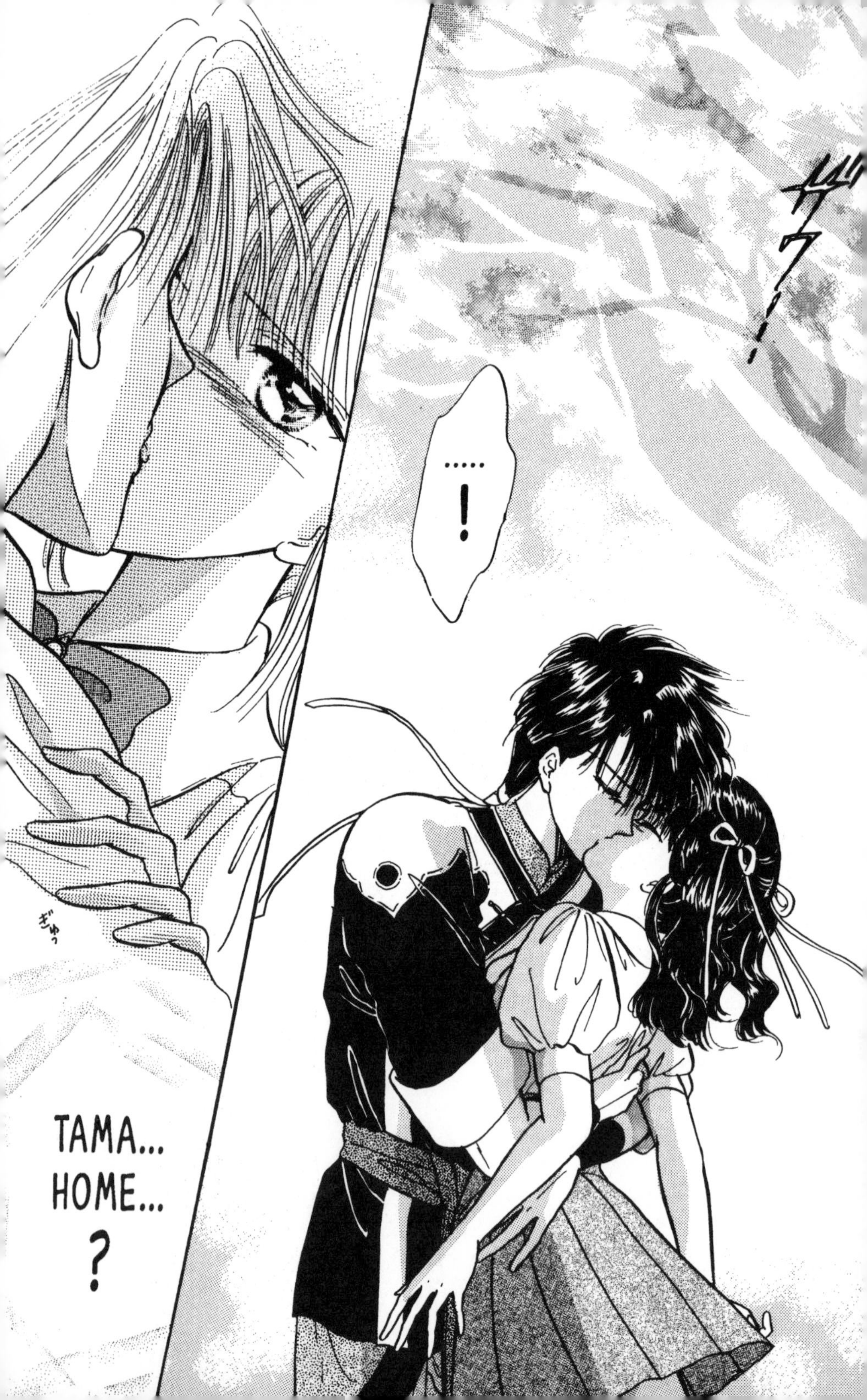
ザワ—!!
.....!
ぎゅっ
TAMA... HOME... ?

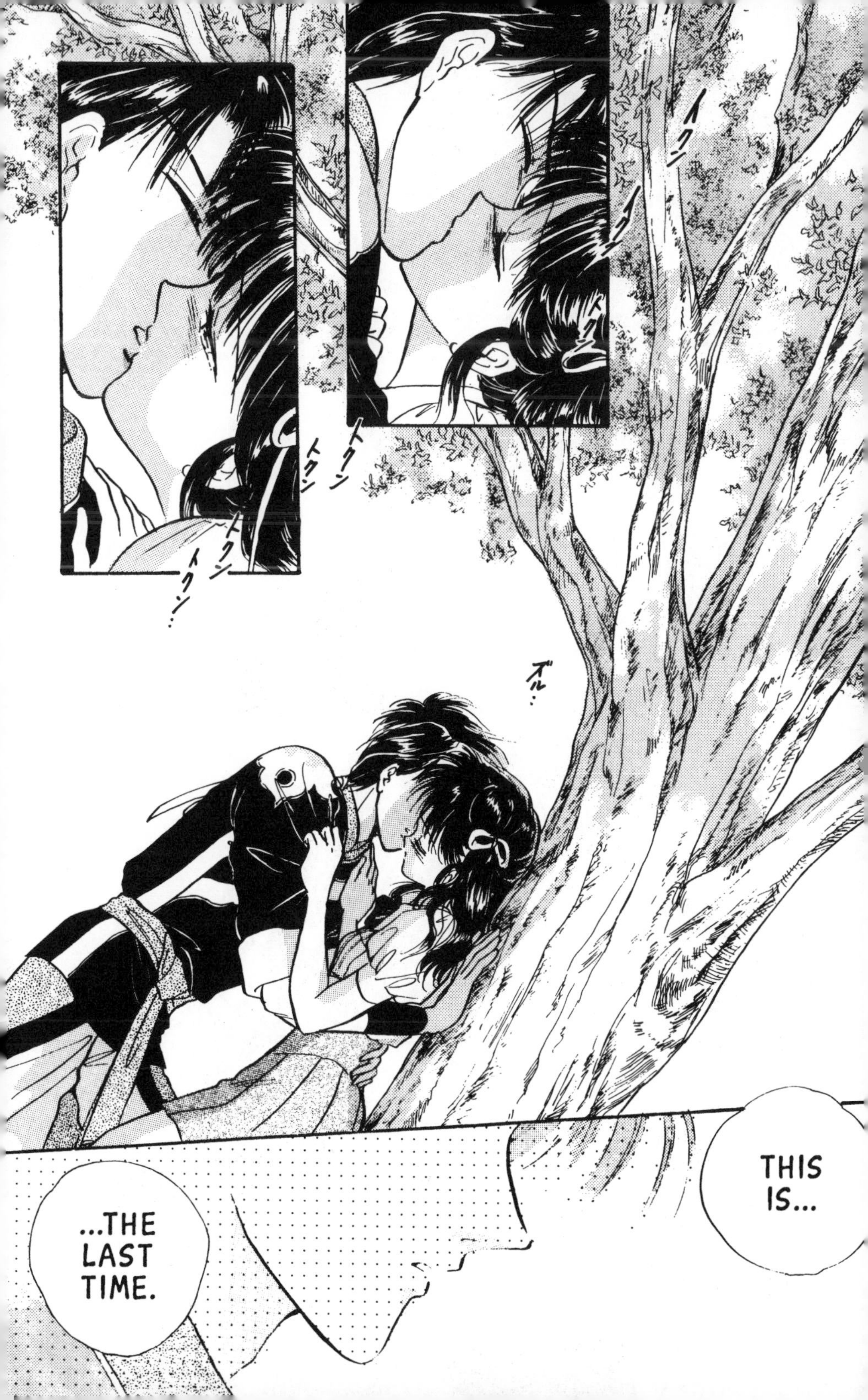
トクン トクン
トクン トクン
トクン トクン…
ズル…
THIS IS...
...THE LAST TIME.

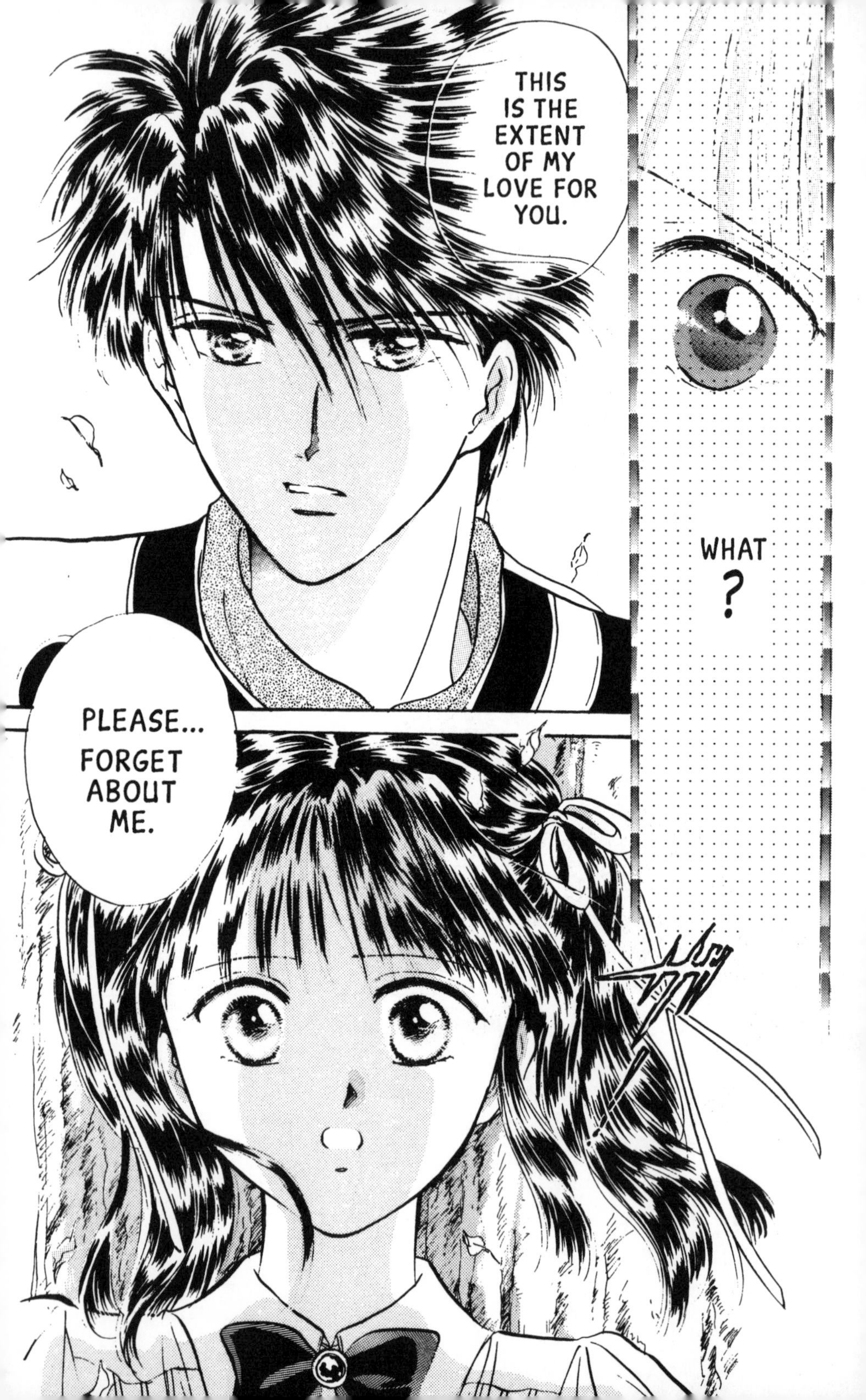
WHAT ?
THIS IS THE EXTENT OF MY LOVE FOR YOU.
PLEASE... FORGET ABOUT ME.

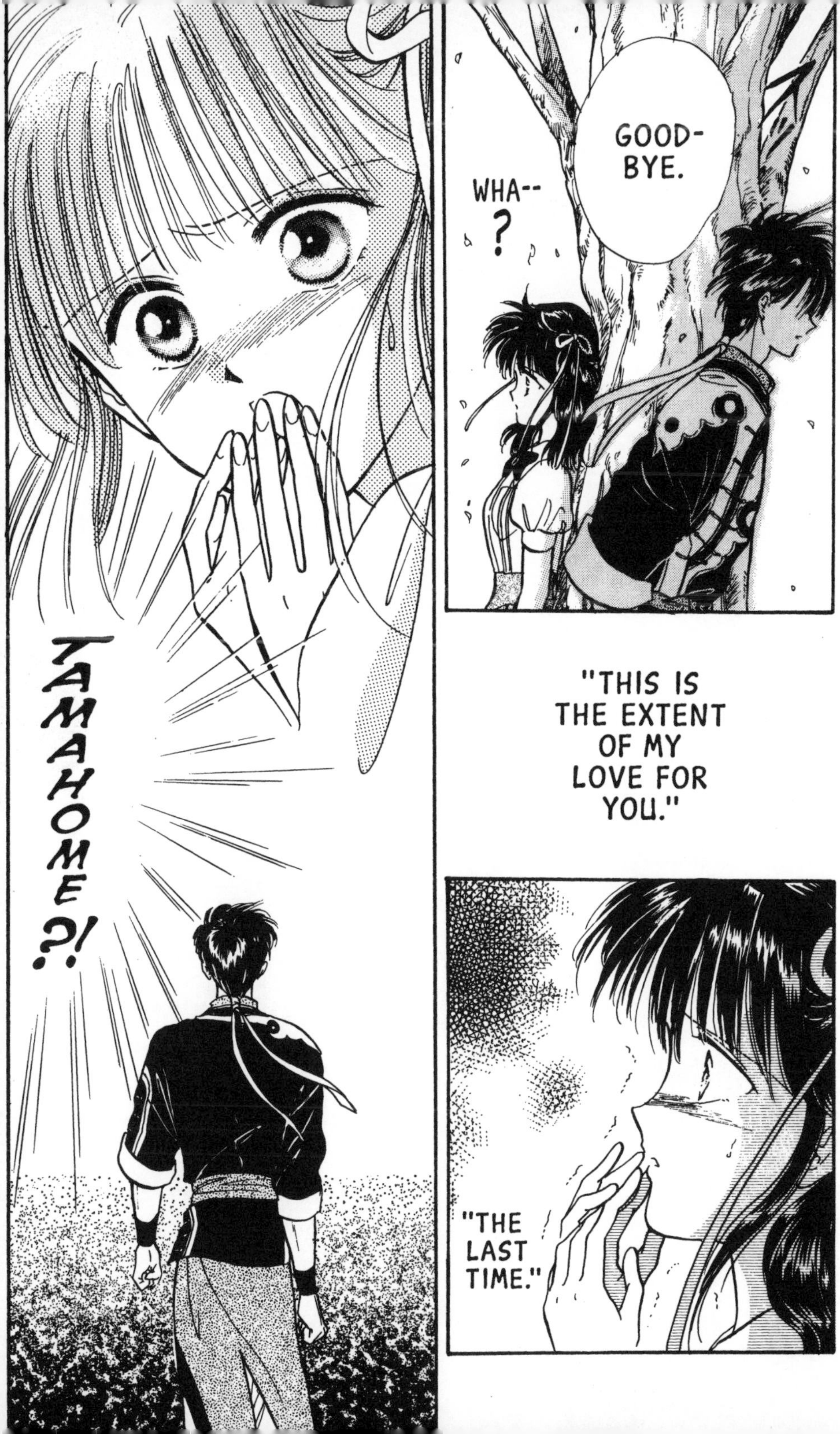
GOOD-BYE.
WHA-- ?
"THIS IS THE EXTENT OF MY LOVE FOR YOU."
"THE LAST TIME."
TAMAHOME?!

Chapter Sixty-One
A Sad Fate

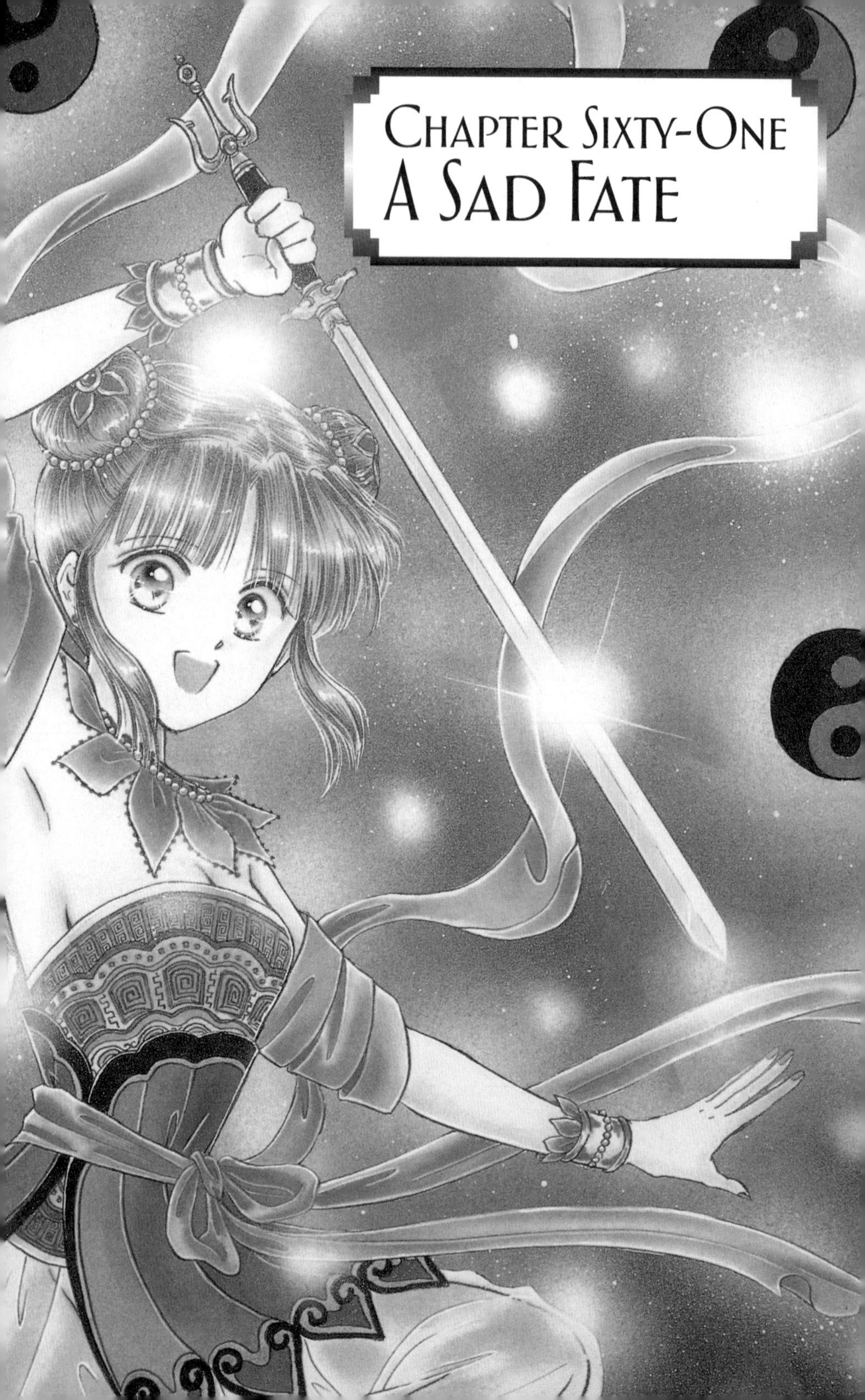

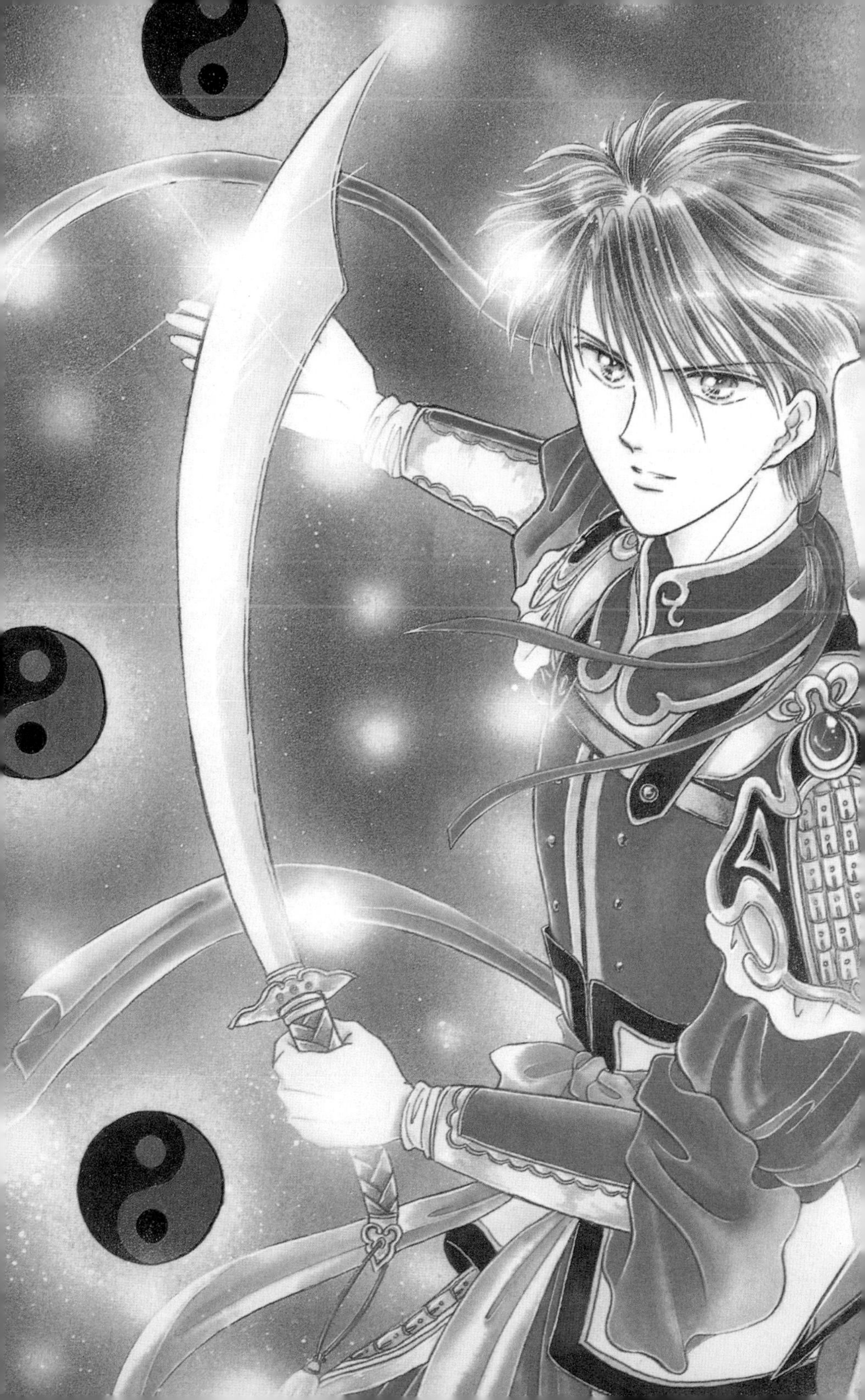

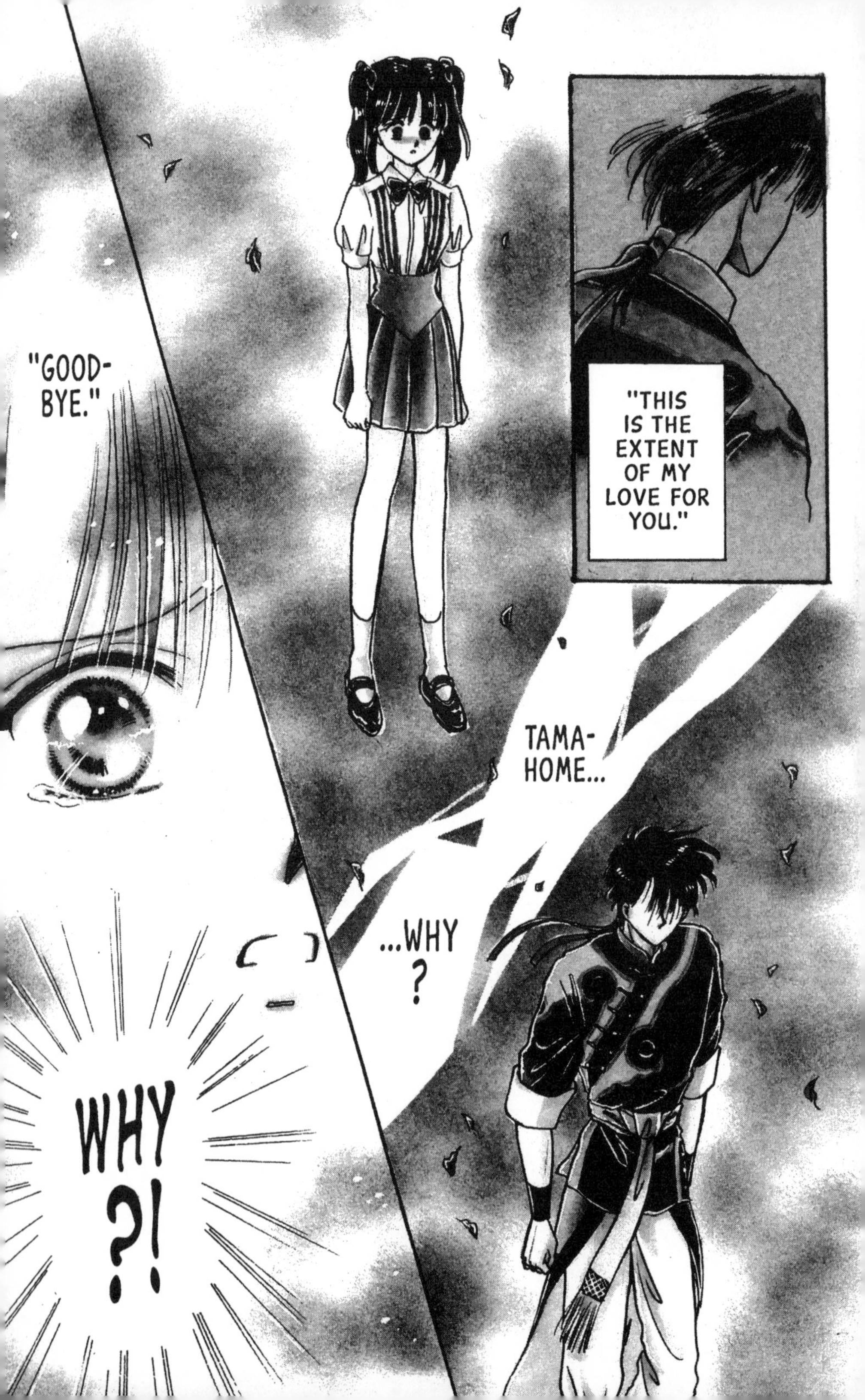
"THIS IS THE EXTENT OF MY LOVE FOR YOU."
TAMA-HOME...
...WHY?
"GOOD-BYE."
WHY?!

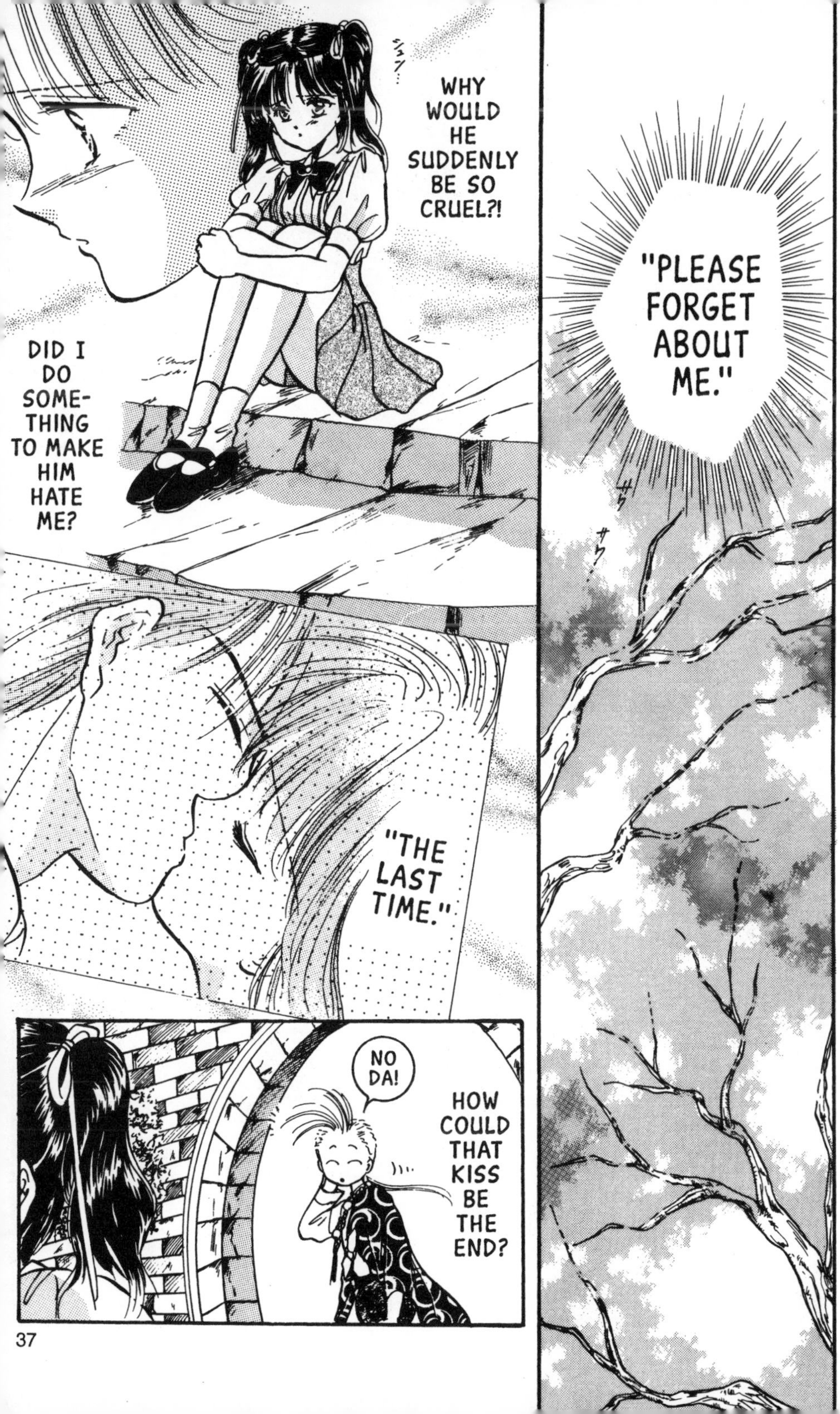
"PLEASE FORGET ABOUT ME."
WHY WOULD HE SUDDENLY BE SO CRUEL?!
DID I DO SOME-THING TO MAKE HIM HATE ME?
"THE LAST TIME."
NO DA!
HOW COULD THAT KISS BE THE END?

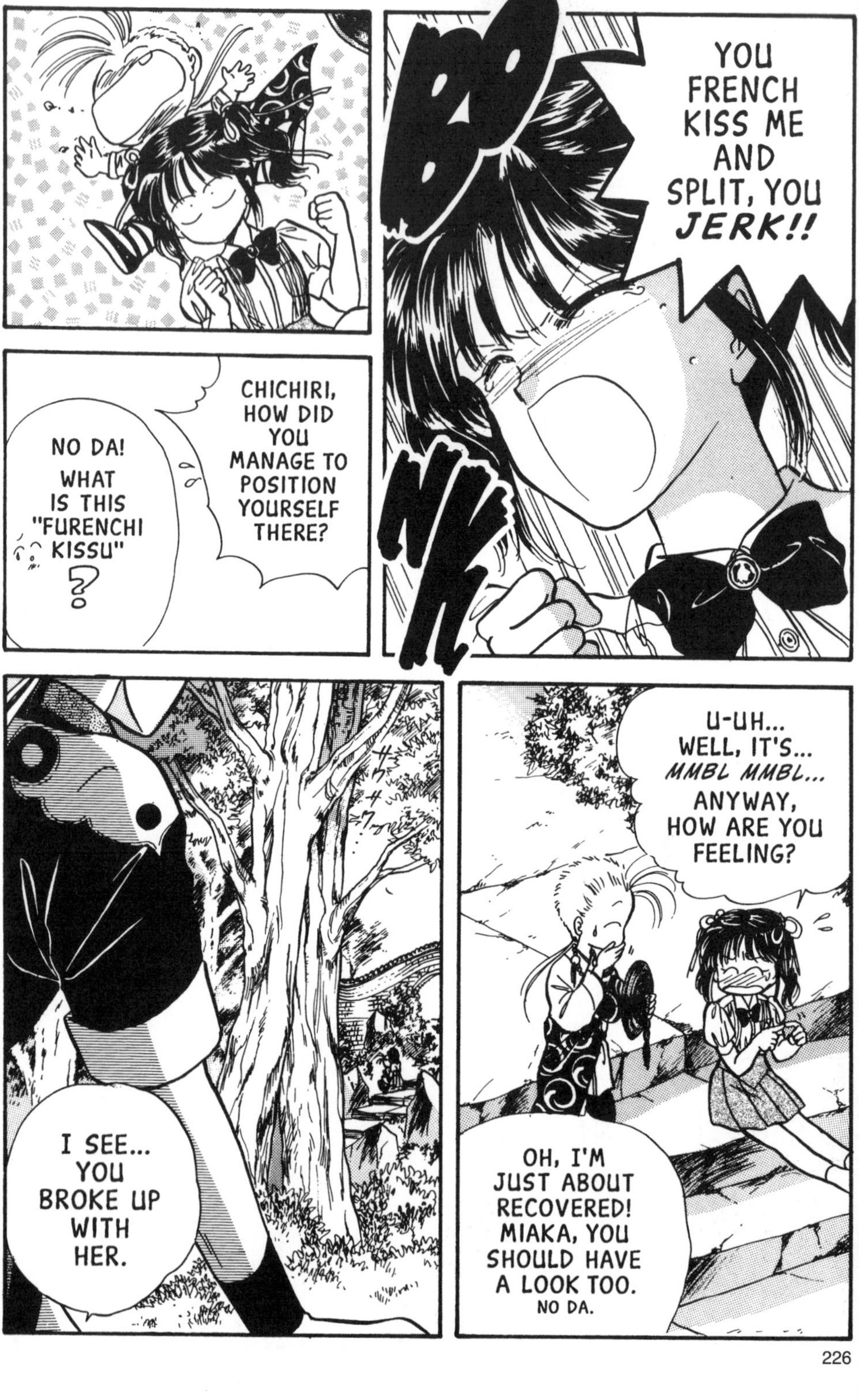
YOU FRENCH KISS ME AND SPLIT, YOU JERK!!
CHICHIRI, HOW DID YOU MANAGE TO POSITION YOURSELF THERE?
NO DA! WHAT IS THIS "FURENCHI KISSU" ?
U-UH... WELL, IT'S... MMBL MMBL... ANYWAY, HOW ARE YOU FEELING?
OH, I'M JUST ABOUT RECOVERED! MIAKA, YOU SHOULD HAVE A LOOK TOO. NO DA.
I SEE... YOU BROKE UP WITH HER.

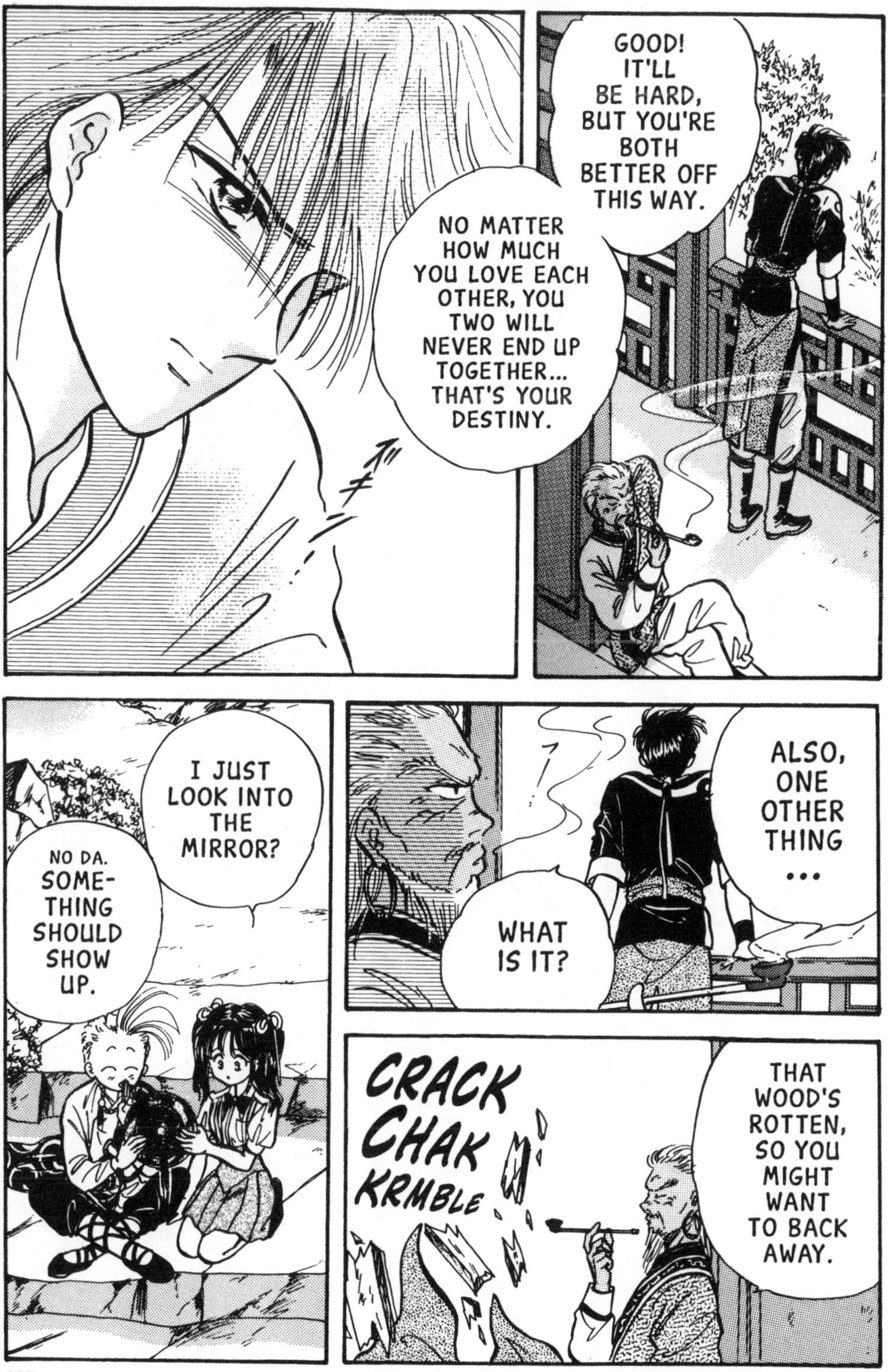
GOOD! IT'LL BE HARD, BUT YOU'RE BOTH BETTER OFF THIS WAY.
NO MATTER HOW MUCH YOU LOVE EACH OTHER, YOU TWO WILL NEVER END UP TOGETHER... THAT'S YOUR DESTINY.
ALSO, ONE OTHER THING...
WHAT IS IT?
THAT WOOD'S ROTTEN, SO YOU MIGHT WANT TO BACK AWAY.
CRACK
CHAK
KRMBLE
I JUST LOOK INTO THE MIRROR?
NO DA. SOME-THING SHOULD SHOW UP.

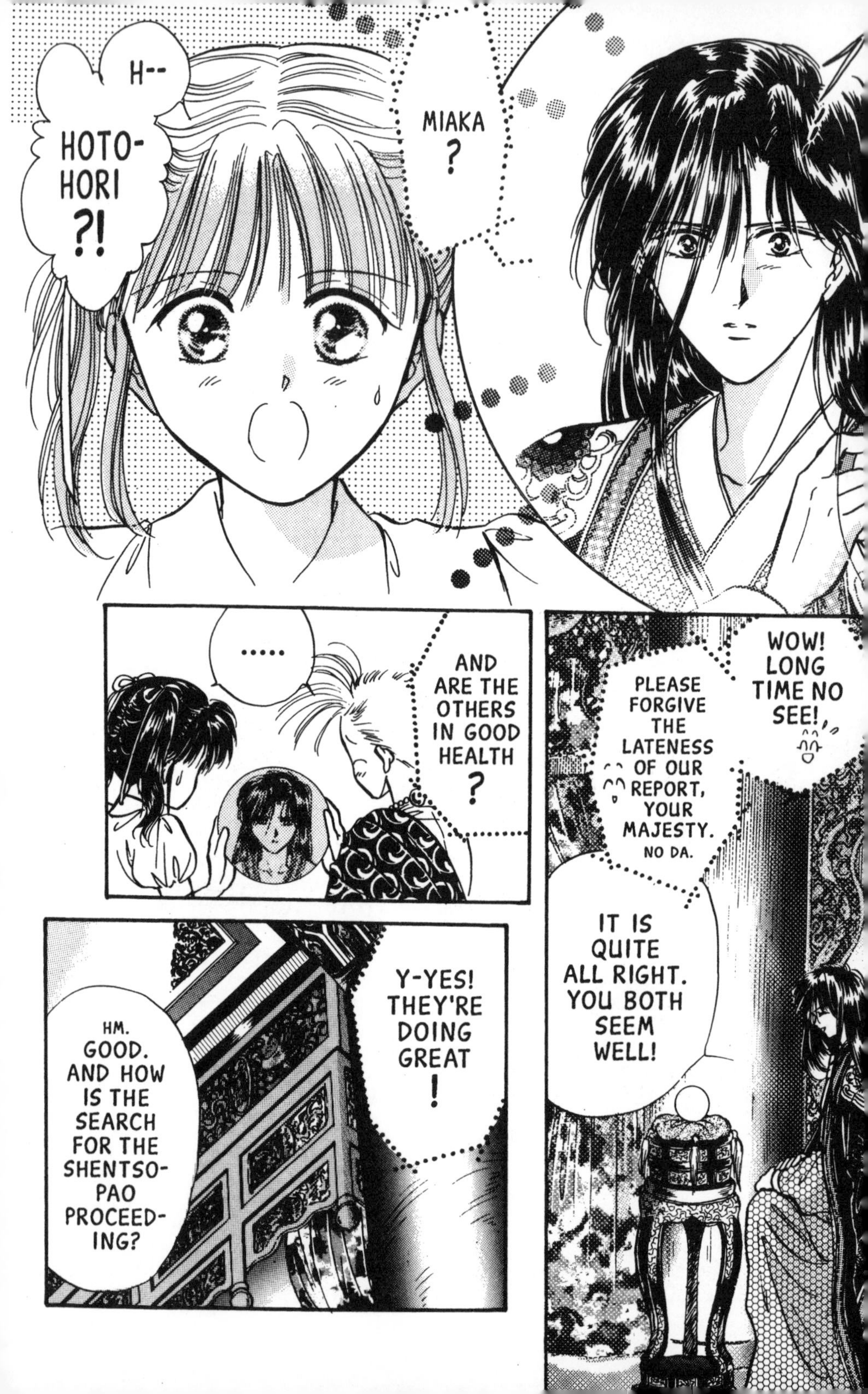
MIAKA?
H-- HOTO-HORI?!
WOW! LONG TIME NO SEE!
PLEASE FORGIVE THE LATENESS OF OUR REPORT, YOUR MAJESTY. NO DA.
IT IS QUITE ALL RIGHT. YOU BOTH SEEM WELL!
AND ARE THE OTHERS IN GOOD HEALTH?
.....
Y-YES! THEY'RE DOING GREAT!
HM. GOOD. AND HOW IS THE SEARCH FOR THE SHENTSO-PAO PROCEED-ING?

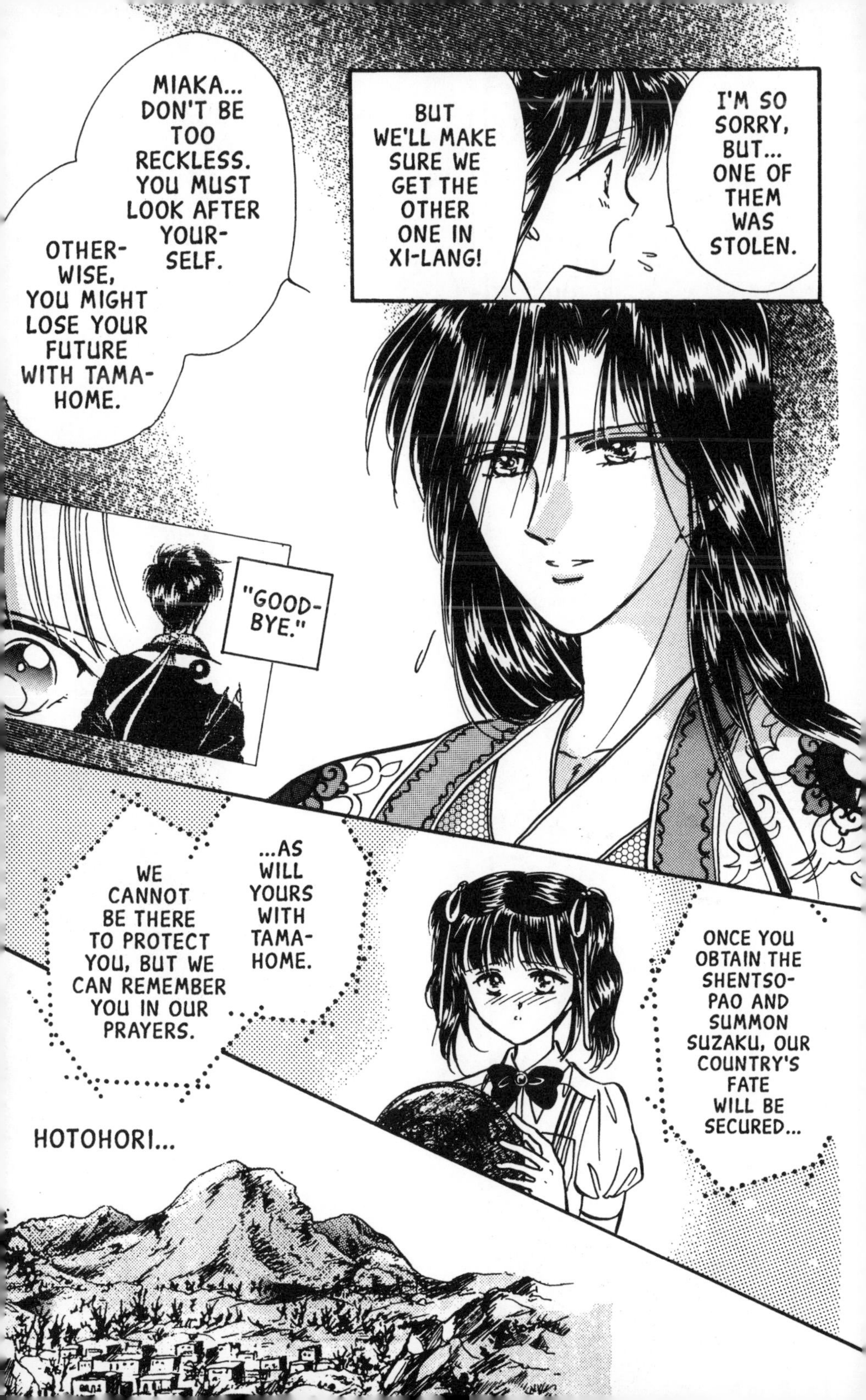
I'M SO SORRY, BUT... ONE OF THEM WAS STOLEN.
BUT WE'LL MAKE SURE WE GET THE OTHER ONE IN XI-LANG!
MIAKA... DON'T BE TOO RECKLESS. YOU MUST LOOK AFTER YOURSELF.
OTHERWISE, YOU MIGHT LOSE YOUR FUTURE WITH TAMAHOME.
"GOOD-BYE."
ONCE YOU OBTAIN THE SHENTSO-PAO AND SUMMON SUZAKU, OUR COUNTRY'S FATE WILL BE SECURED...
...AS WILL YOURS WITH TAMAHOME.
WE CANNOT BE THERE TO PROTECT YOU, BUT WE CAN REMEMBER YOU IN OUR PRAYERS.
HOTOHORI...

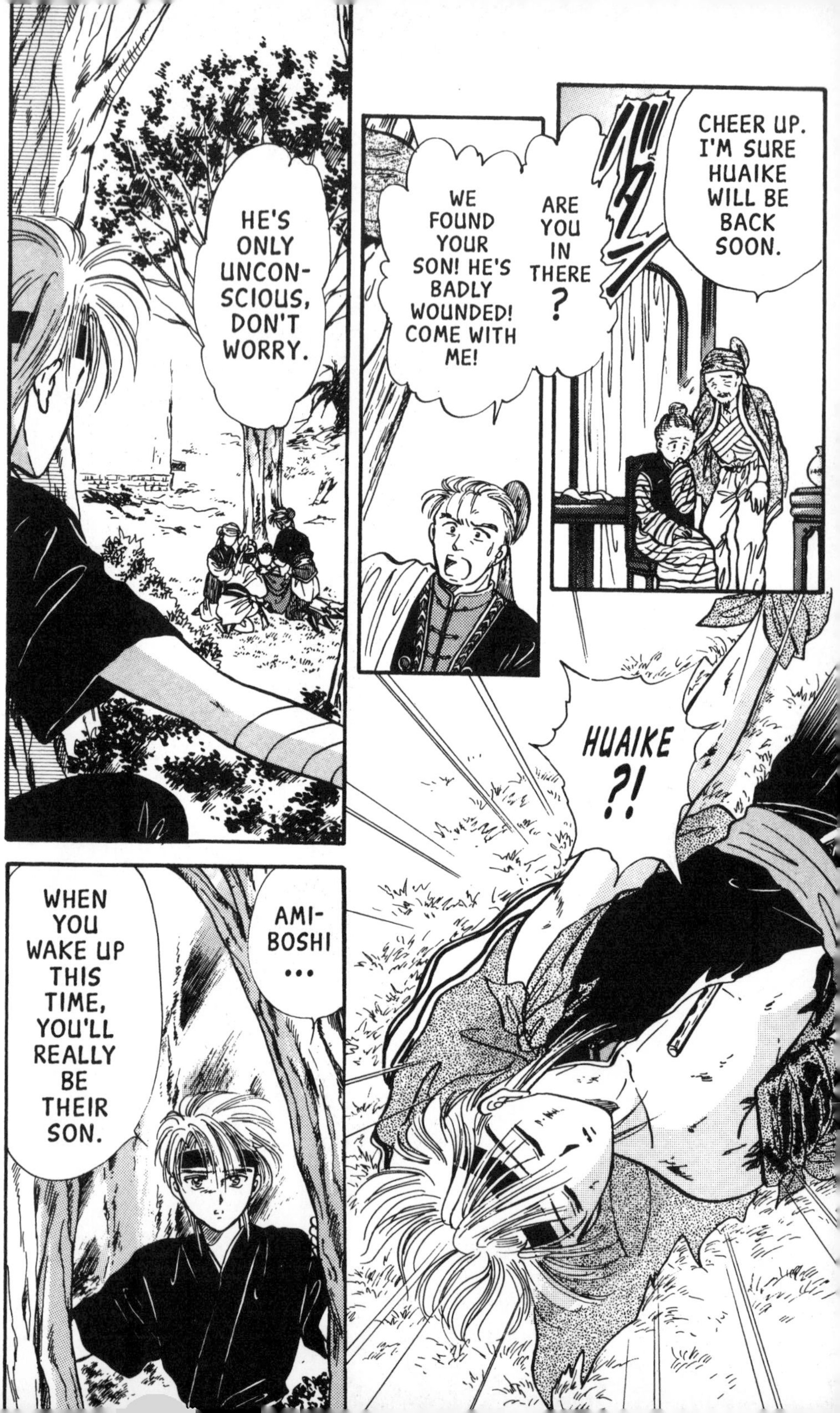
CHEER UP. I'M SURE HUAIKE WILL BE BACK SOON.
ARE YOU IN THERE?
WE FOUND YOUR SON! HE'S BADLY WOUNDED! COME WITH ME!
HUAIKE?!
HE'S ONLY UNCONSCIOUS, DON'T WORRY.
AMIBOSHI...
WHEN YOU WAKE UP THIS TIME, YOU'LL REALLY BE THEIR SON.

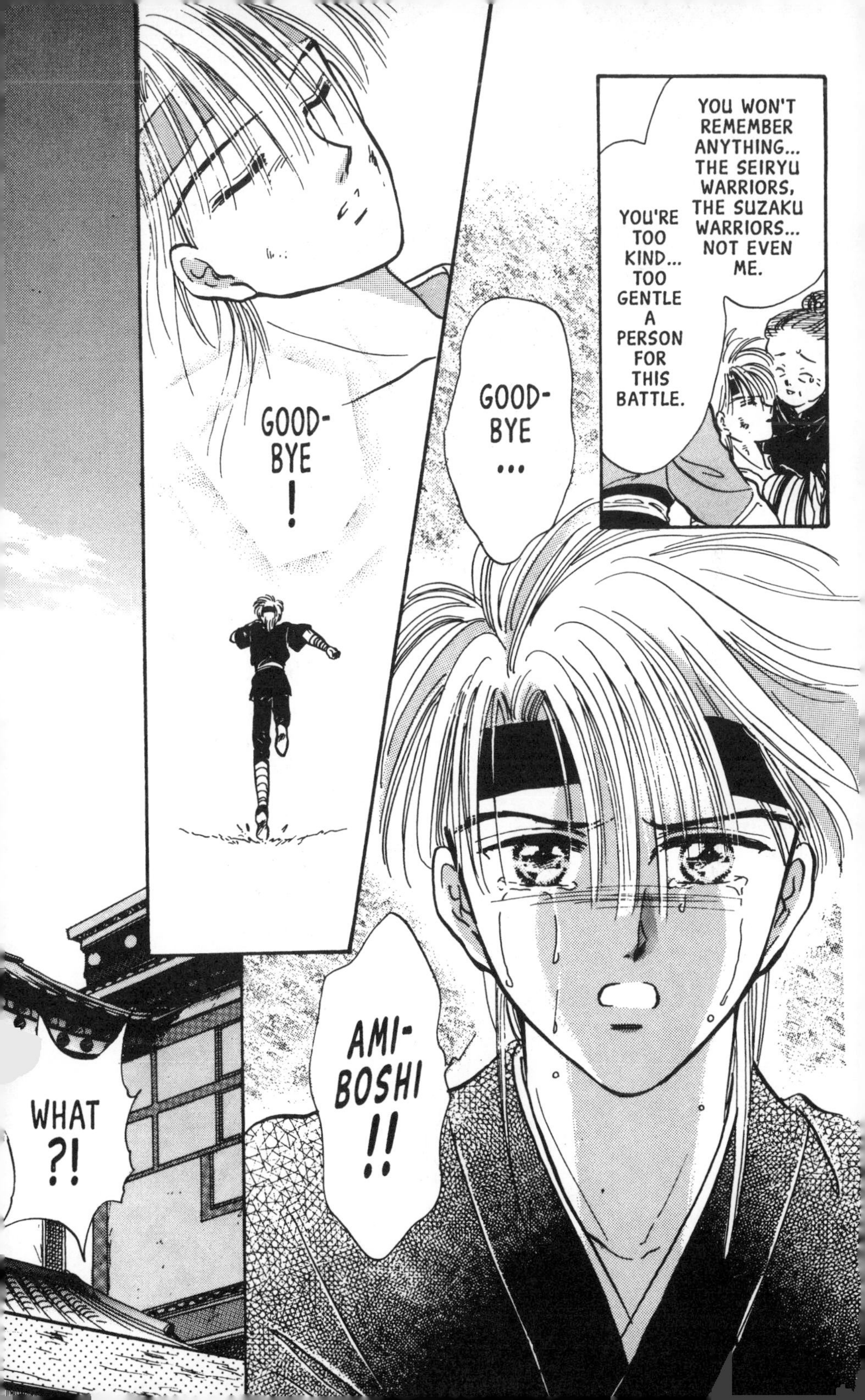
YOU WON'T REMEMBER ANYTHING... THE SEIRYU WARRIORS, THE SUZAKU WARRIORS... NOT EVEN ME.
YOU'RE TOO KIND... TOO GENTLE A PERSON FOR THIS BATTLE.
GOOD-BYE...
GOOD-BYE!
AMI-BOSHI!!
WHAT?!

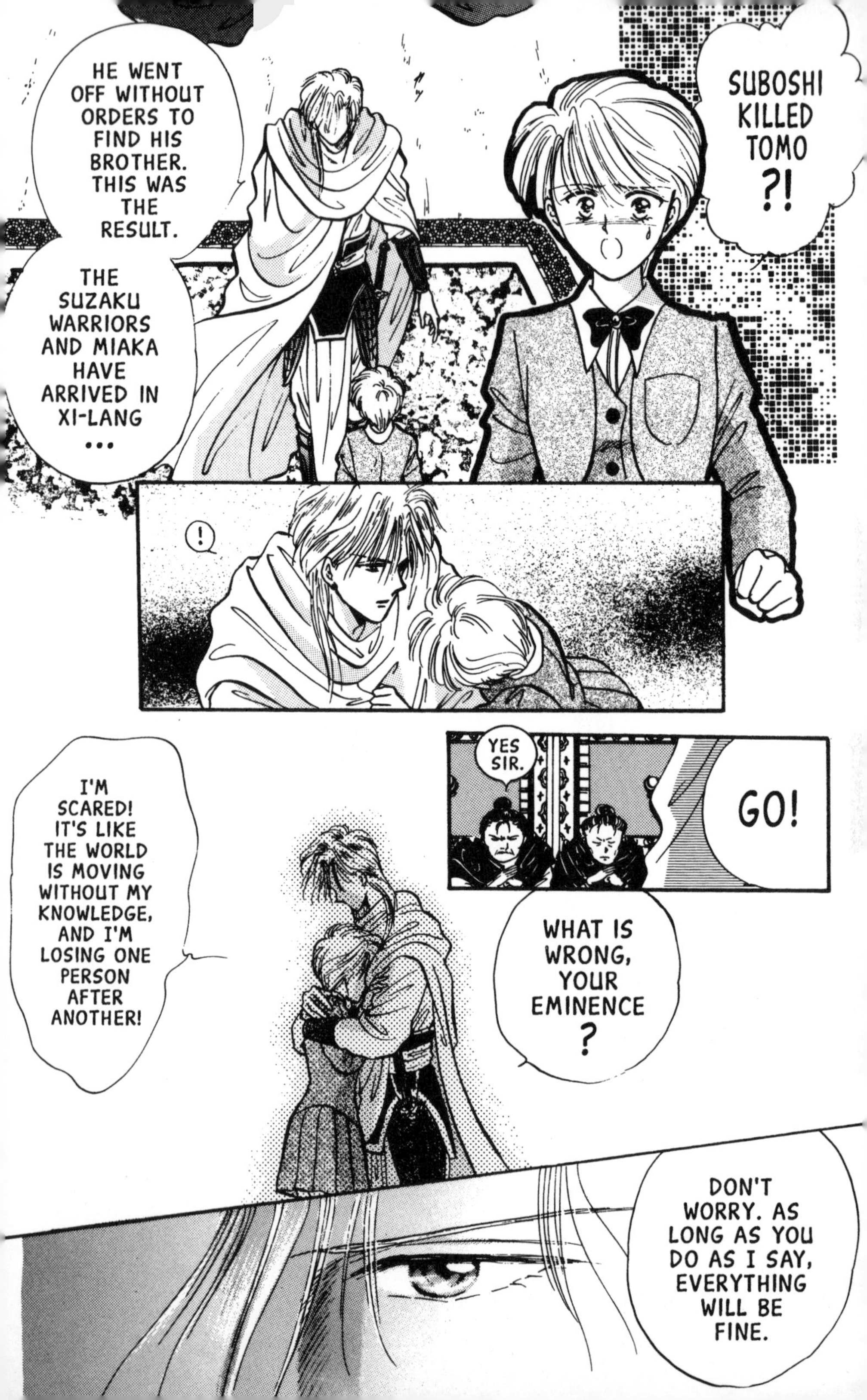
SUBOSHI KILLED TOMO?!
HE WENT OFF WITHOUT ORDERS TO FIND HIS BROTHER. THIS WAS THE RESULT.
THE SUZAKU WARRIORS AND MIAKA HAVE ARRIVED IN XI-LANG...
!
GO!
YES SIR.
WHAT IS WRONG, YOUR EMINENCE?
I'M SCARED! IT'S LIKE THE WORLD IS MOVING WITHOUT MY KNOWLEDGE, AND I'M LOSING ONE PERSON AFTER ANOTHER!
DON'T WORRY. AS LONG AS YOU DO AS I SAY, EVERYTHING WILL BE FINE.

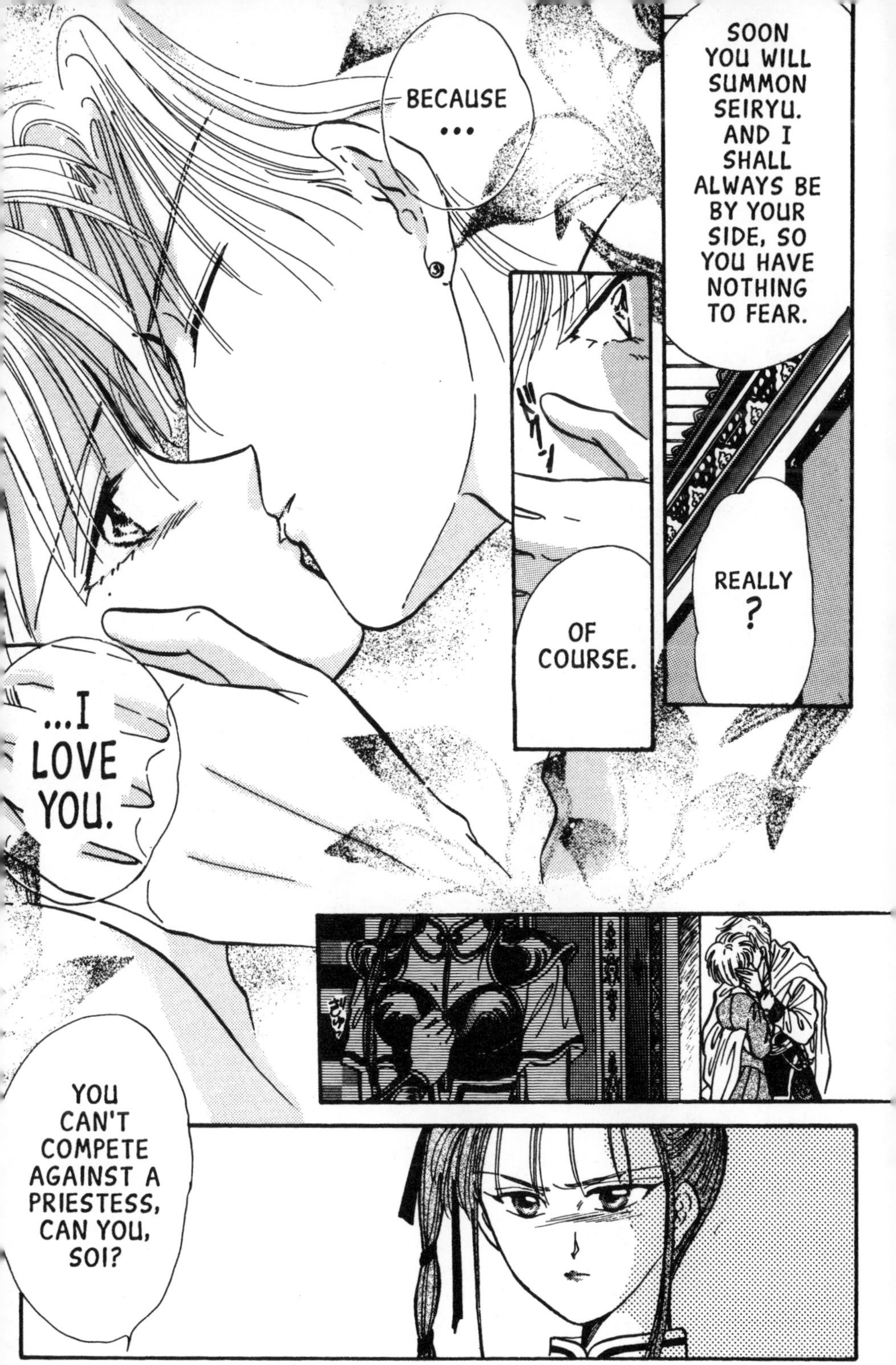
SOON YOU WILL SUMMON SEIRYU. AND I SHALL ALWAYS BE BY YOUR SIDE, SO YOU HAVE NOTHING TO FEAR.
REALLY?
OF COURSE.
BECAUSE...
...I LOVE YOU.
YOU CAN'T COMPETE AGAINST A PRIESTESS, CAN YOU, SOI?

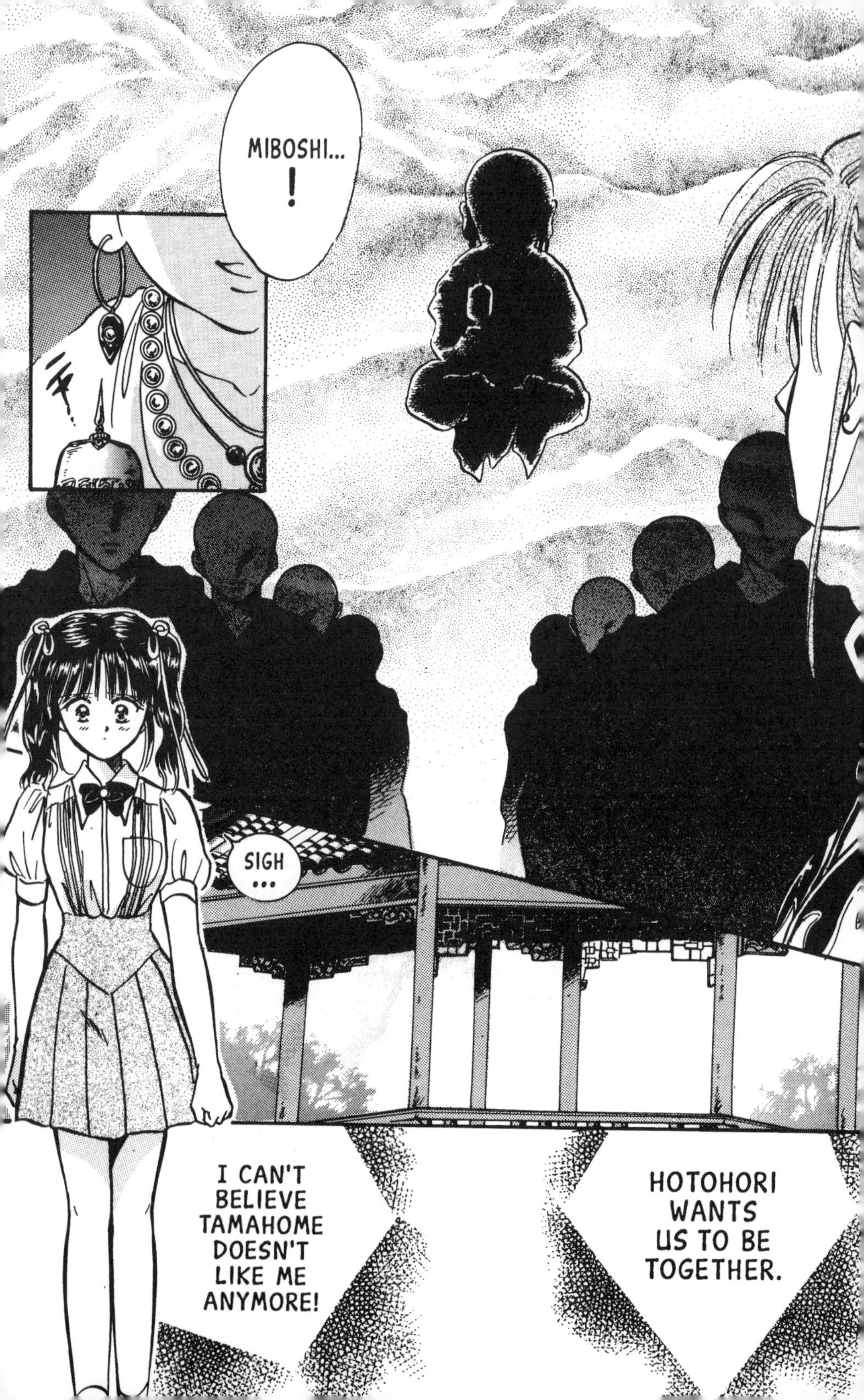
MIBOSHI... !
SIGH ...
HOTOHORI WANTS US TO BE TOGETHER.
I CAN'T BELIEVE TAMAHOME DOESN'T LIKE ME ANYMORE!

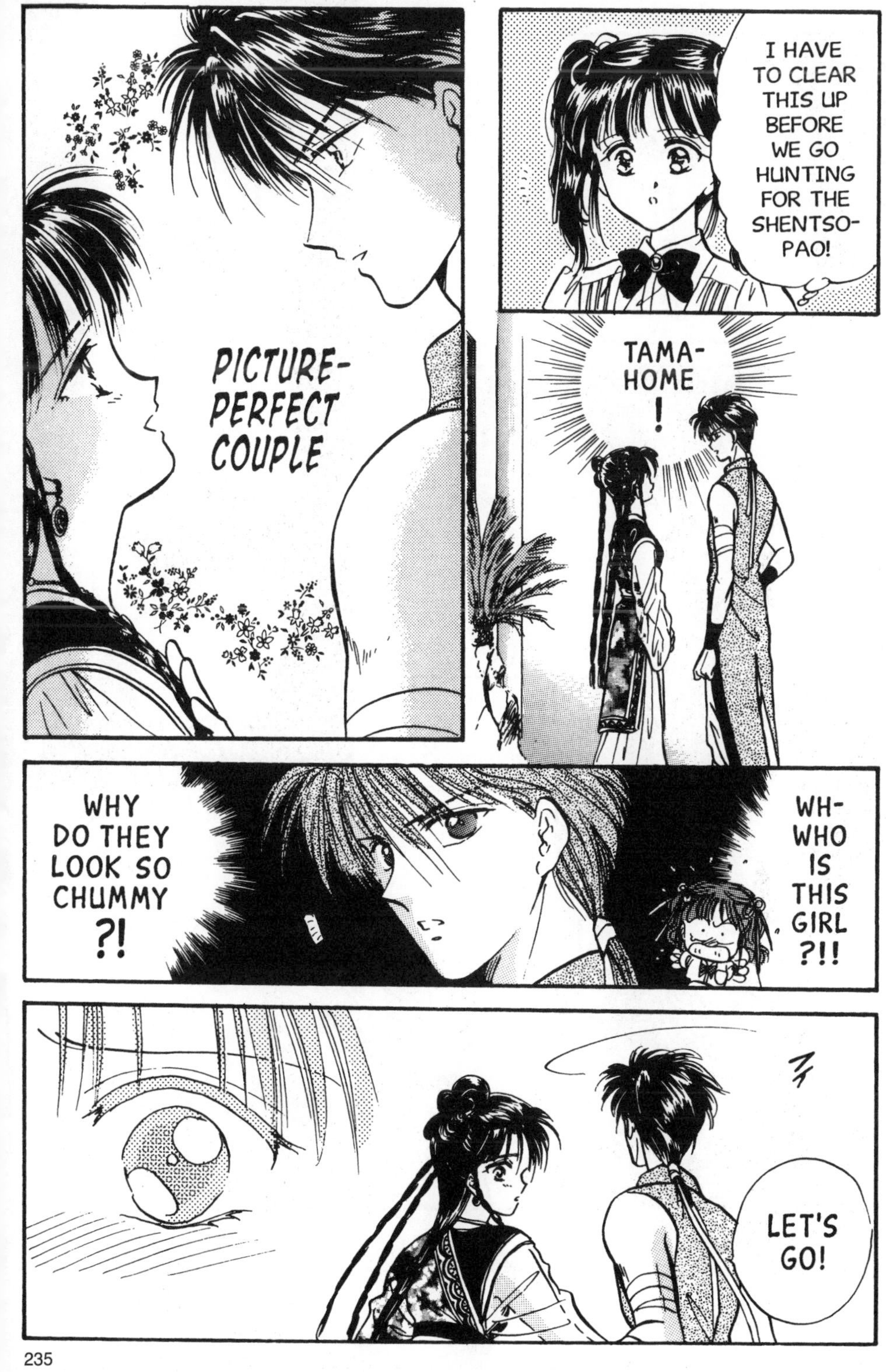
I HAVE TO CLEAR THIS UP BEFORE WE GO HUNTING FOR THE SHENTSO-PAO!
TAMA-HOME!
PICTURE-PERFECT COUPLE
WH-WHO IS THIS GIRL?!!
WHY DO THEY LOOK SO CHUMMY?!
LET'S GO!

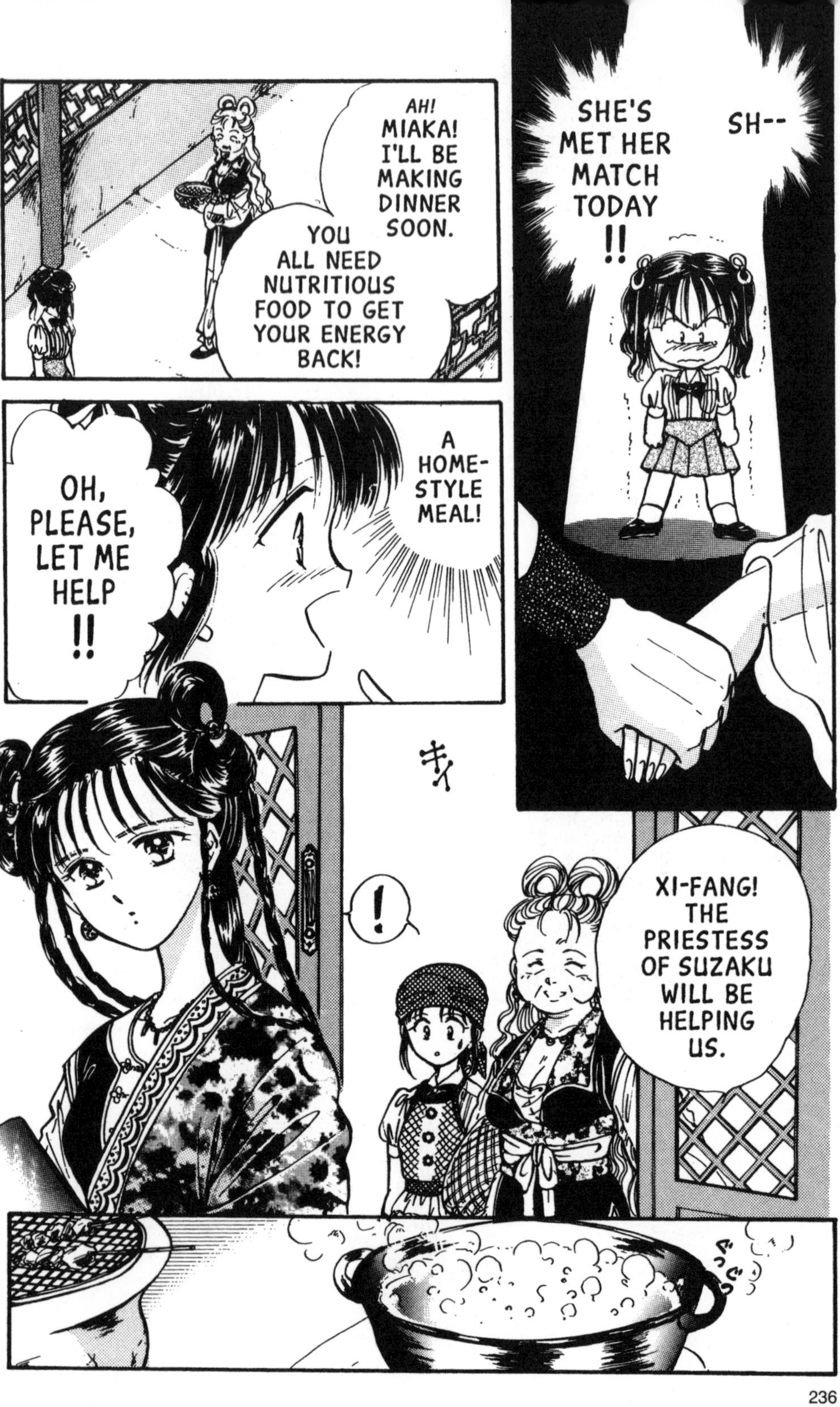
SH--
SHE'S MET HER MATCH TODAY!!
AH! MIAKA! I'LL BE MAKING DINNER SOON.
YOU ALL NEED NUTRITIOUS FOOD TO GET YOUR ENERGY BACK!
A HOME-STYLE MEAL!
OH, PLEASE, LET ME HELP!!
XI-FANG! THE PRIESTESS OF SUZAKU WILL BE HELPING US.
!

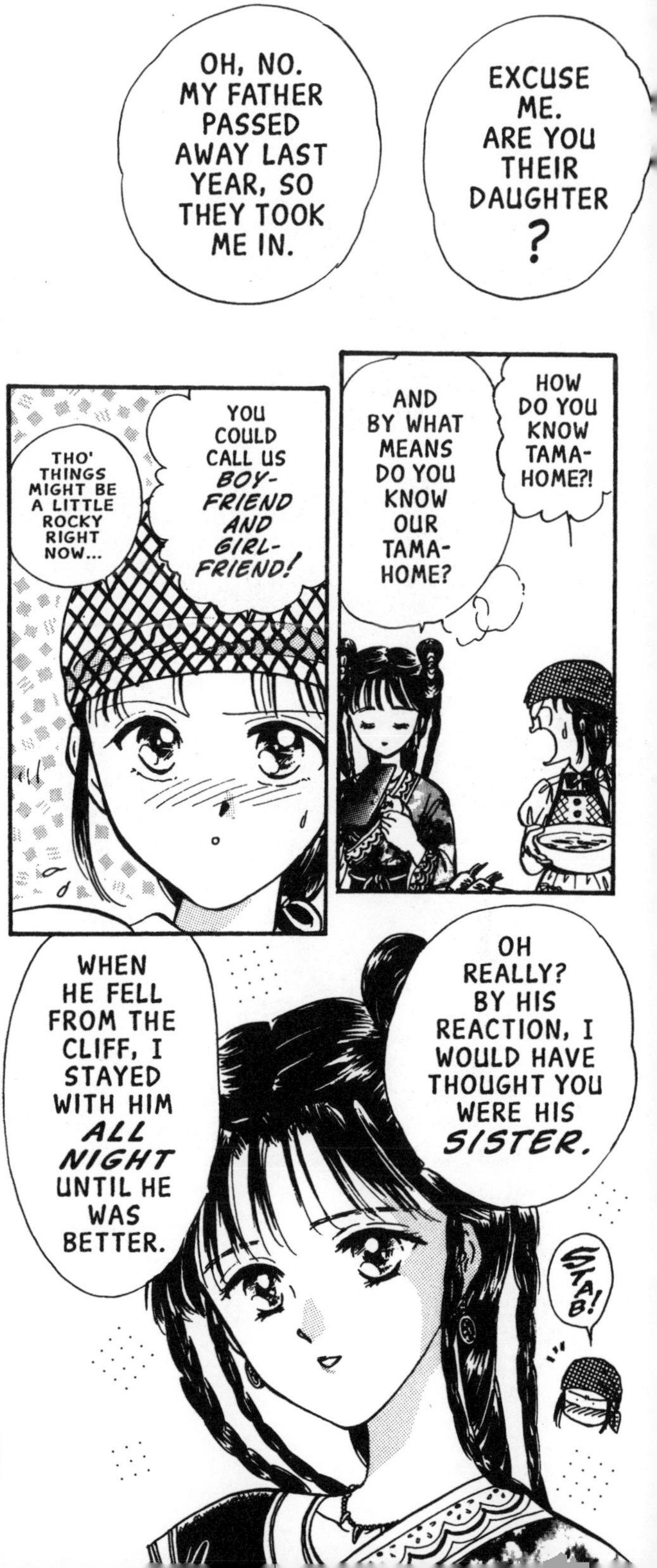
EXCUSE ME. ARE YOU THEIR DAUGHTER?
OH, NO. MY FATHER PASSED AWAY LAST YEAR, SO THEY TOOK ME IN.
HOW DO YOU KNOW TAMAHOME?!
AND BY WHAT MEANS DO YOU KNOW OUR TAMAHOME?
YOU COULD CALL US *BOYFRIEND AND GIRLFRIEND!*
THO' THINGS MIGHT BE A LITTLE ROCKY RIGHT NOW...
OH REALLY? BY HIS REACTION, I WOULD HAVE THOUGHT YOU WERE HIS *SISTER.*
WHEN HE FELL FROM THE CLIFF, I STAYED WITH HIM *ALL NIGHT* UNTIL HE WAS BETTER.
STAB!

Now, what shall we talk about?
How about the stories behind how the characters developed?
First, Miaka. I think you all have your own ideas about her, but the basic color I had in mind for her was white, pure white. I wanted to depict a girl who was honest, pure and innocent. A kid who is doing her best to cope with every situation she encounters, but her naiveté can work against her too. She hesitates, and even gets self-destructive at times. Some readers have complained about this, but no one can be perfect. People feel depressed and try to run away, but in the end she says, "I'll do my best!" Watching her you might think, "Oh, no! Don't go there, Miaka!!" but she has to deal with her own obstacles and find her way back to the right path in order to make up with Yui and be with Tamahome. Yui and Miaka's falling out might have been because of misunderstanding, but if it were me, and Yui went that far, I'd have gotten angry and cut her off! Wouldn't you? ☺
However, what is a friend but knowing the good parts and the bad parts, and loving them just the same.
Miaka loves Yui. For Miaka it's not a question of choosing love over friendship.
It's way beyond that. She has such a big heart.

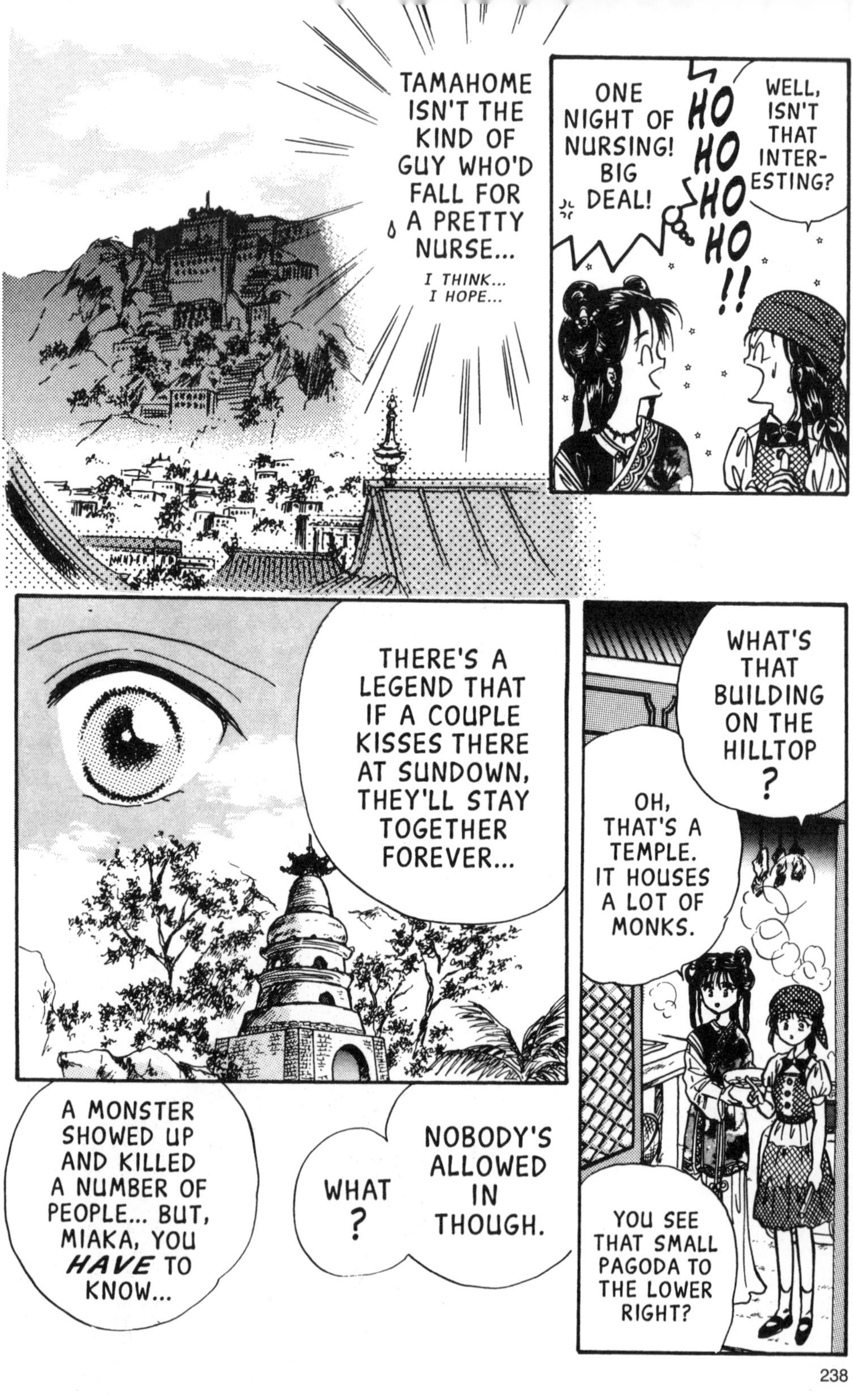
WELL, ISN'T THAT INTER-ESTING?
HO HO HO HO!!
ONE NIGHT OF NURSING! BIG DEAL!
TAMAHOME ISN'T THE KIND OF GUY WHO'D FALL FOR A PRETTY NURSE...
I THINK... I HOPE...
WHAT'S THAT BUILDING ON THE HILLTOP?
OH, THAT'S A TEMPLE. IT HOUSES A LOT OF MONKS.
YOU SEE THAT SMALL PAGODA TO THE LOWER RIGHT?
THERE'S A LEGEND THAT IF A COUPLE KISSES THERE AT SUNDOWN, THEY'LL STAY TOGETHER FOREVER...
NOBODY'S ALLOWED IN THOUGH.
WHAT?
A MONSTER SHOWED UP AND KILLED A NUMBER OF PEOPLE... BUT, MIAKA, YOU ***HAVE*** TO KNOW...

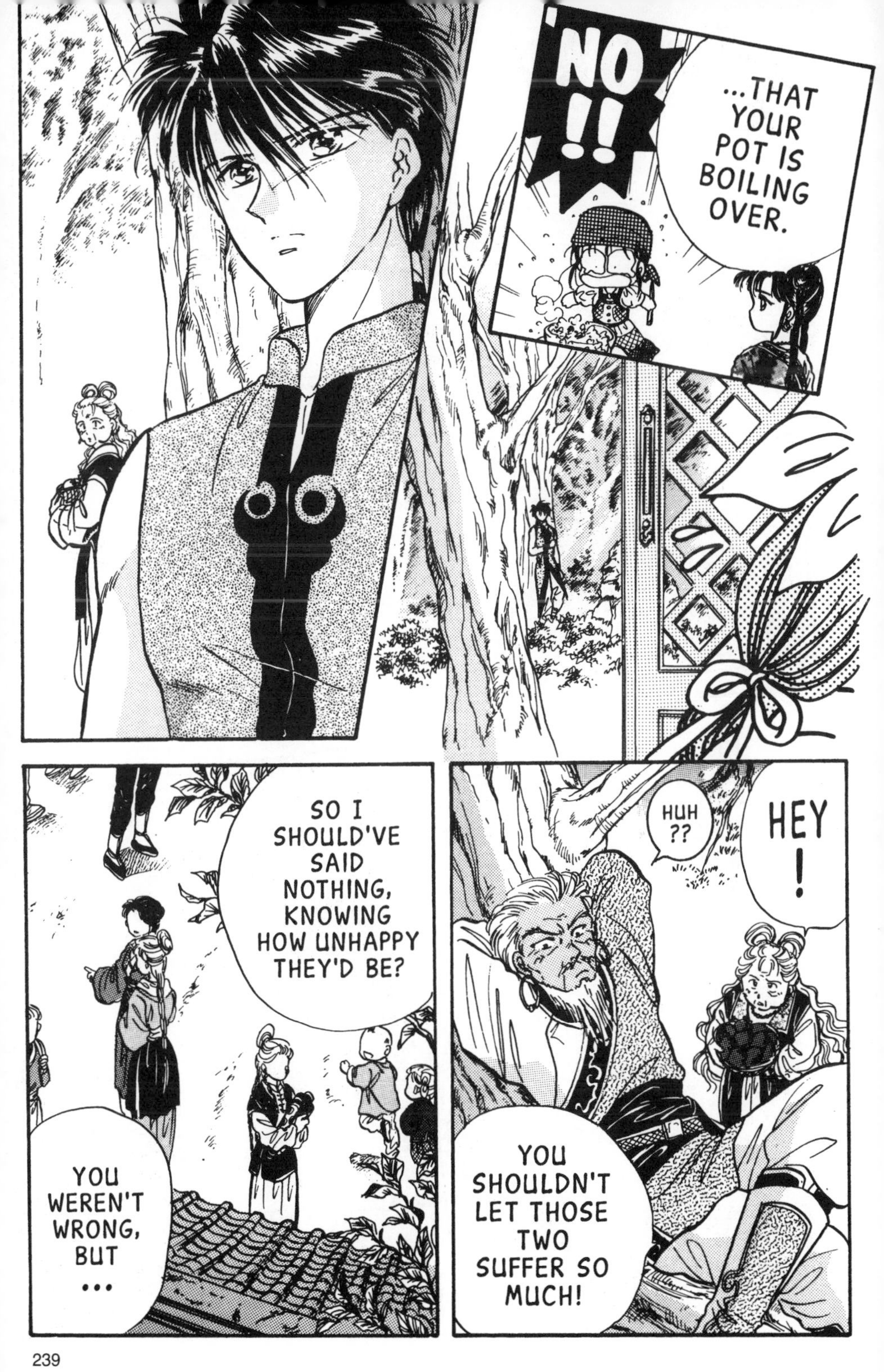
...THAT YOUR POT IS BOILING OVER.
NO !!
HEY !
HUH ??
YOU SHOULDN'T LET THOSE TWO SUFFER SO MUCH!
SO I SHOULD'VE SAID NOTHING, KNOWING HOW UNHAPPY THEY'D BE?
YOU WEREN'T WRONG, BUT ...

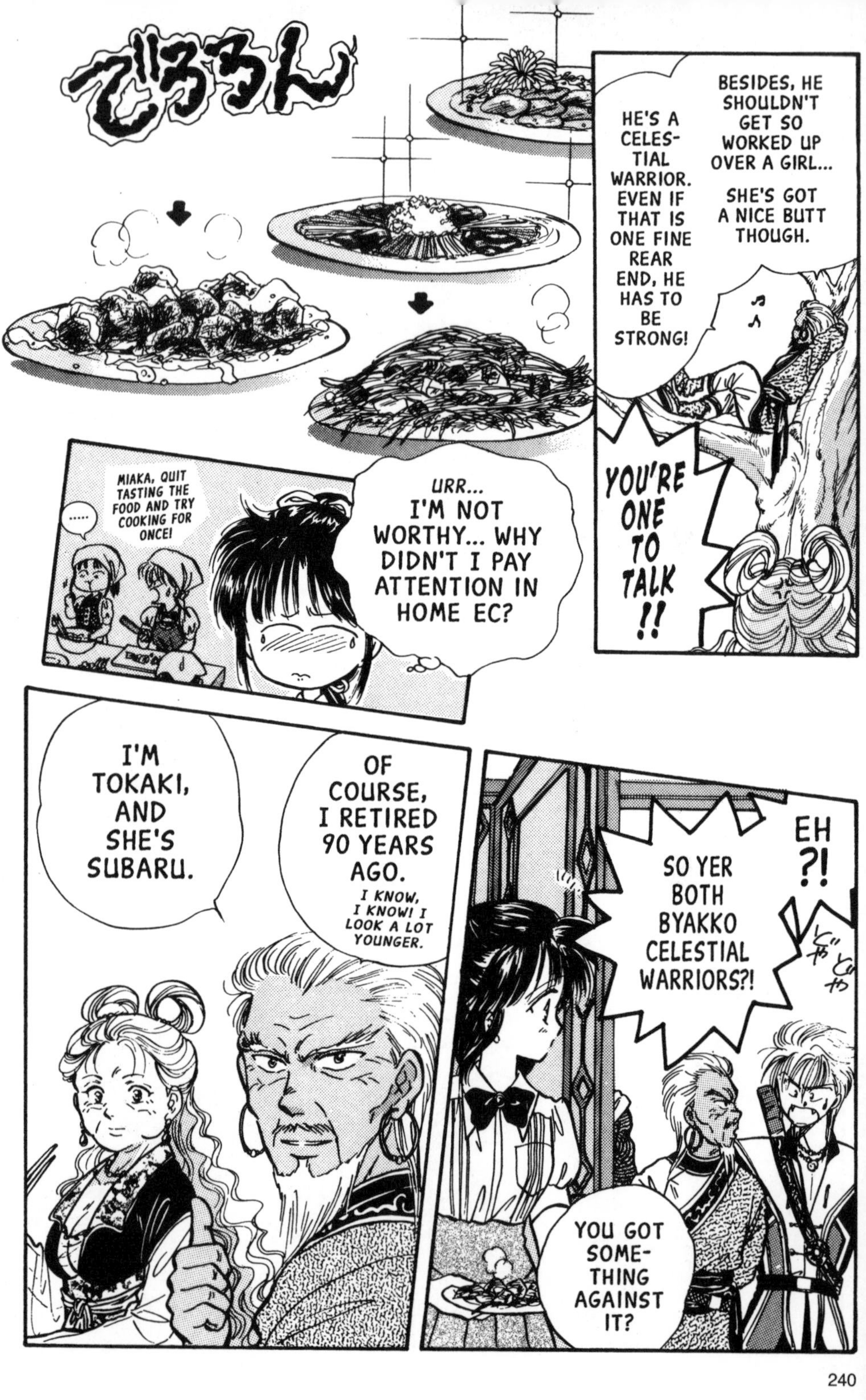
BESIDES, HE SHOULDN'T GET SO WORKED UP OVER A GIRL... SHE'S GOT A NICE BUTT THOUGH.
HE'S A CELESTIAL WARRIOR. EVEN IF THAT IS ONE FINE REAR END, HE HAS TO BE STRONG!
♪ ♪
YOU'RE ONE TO TALK!!
でろろん
URR... I'M NOT WORTHY... WHY DIDN'T I PAY ATTENTION IN HOME EC?
MIAKA, QUIT TASTING THE FOOD AND TRY COOKING FOR ONCE!
.....
EH?!
SO YER BOTH BYAKKO CELESTIAL WARRIORS?!
YOU GOT SOMETHING AGAINST IT?
OF COURSE, I RETIRED 90 YEARS AGO.
I KNOW, I KNOW! I LOOK A LOT YOUNGER.
I'M TOKAKI, AND SHE'S SUBARU.

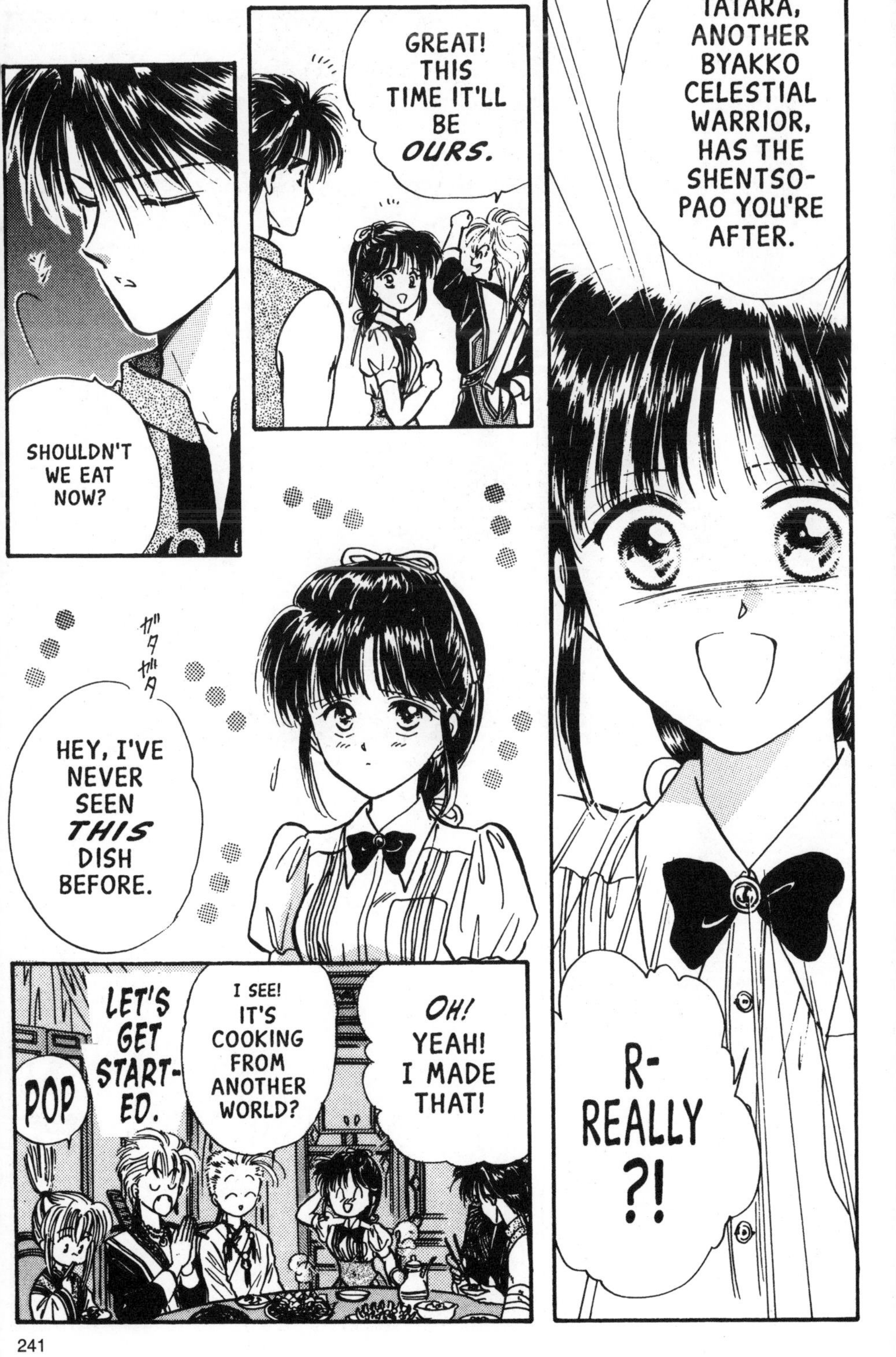
TATARA, ANOTHER BYAKKO CELESTIAL WARRIOR, HAS THE SHENTSO-PAO YOU'RE AFTER.
R-REALLY?!
GREAT! THIS TIME IT'LL BE *OURS.*
SHOULDN'T WE EAT NOW?
ガタガタ
HEY, I'VE NEVER SEEN *THIS* DISH BEFORE.
OH! YEAH! I MADE THAT!
I SEE! IT'S COOKING FROM ANOTHER WORLD?
LET'S GET START-ED.
POP

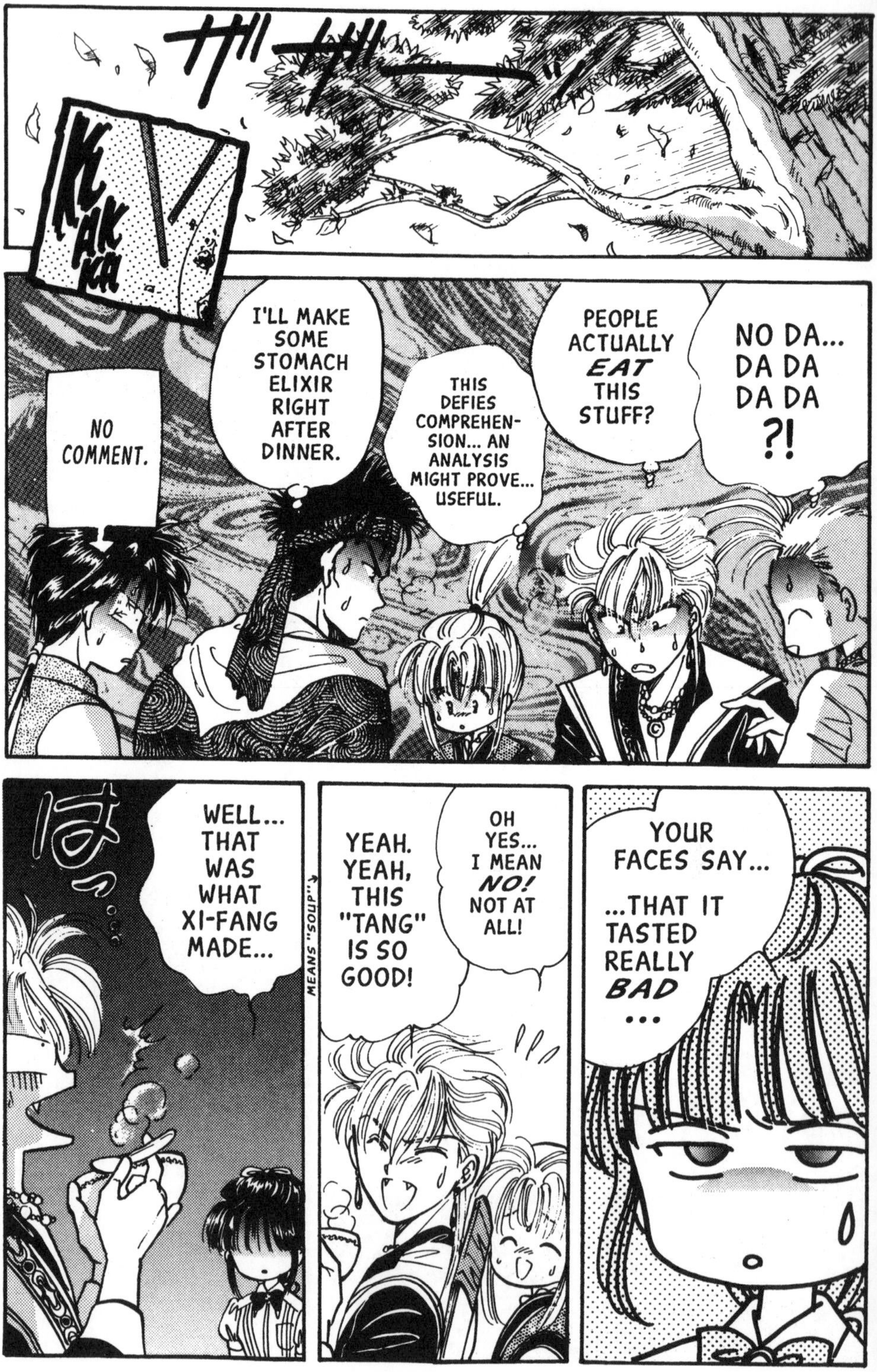
ザザーーッ
KLAKKA
NO DA... DA DA DA DA ?!
PEOPLE ACTUALLY EAT THIS STUFF?
THIS DEFIES COMPREHENSION... AN ANALYSIS MIGHT PROVE... USEFUL.
I'LL MAKE SOME STOMACH ELIXIR RIGHT AFTER DINNER.
NO COMMENT.
YOUR FACES SAY...
...THAT IT TASTED REALLY BAD...
OH YES... I MEAN NO! NOT AT ALL!
YEAH. YEAH, THIS "TANG" IS SO GOOD!
MEANS "SOUP"
WELL... THAT WAS WHAT XI-FANG MADE...
はっ

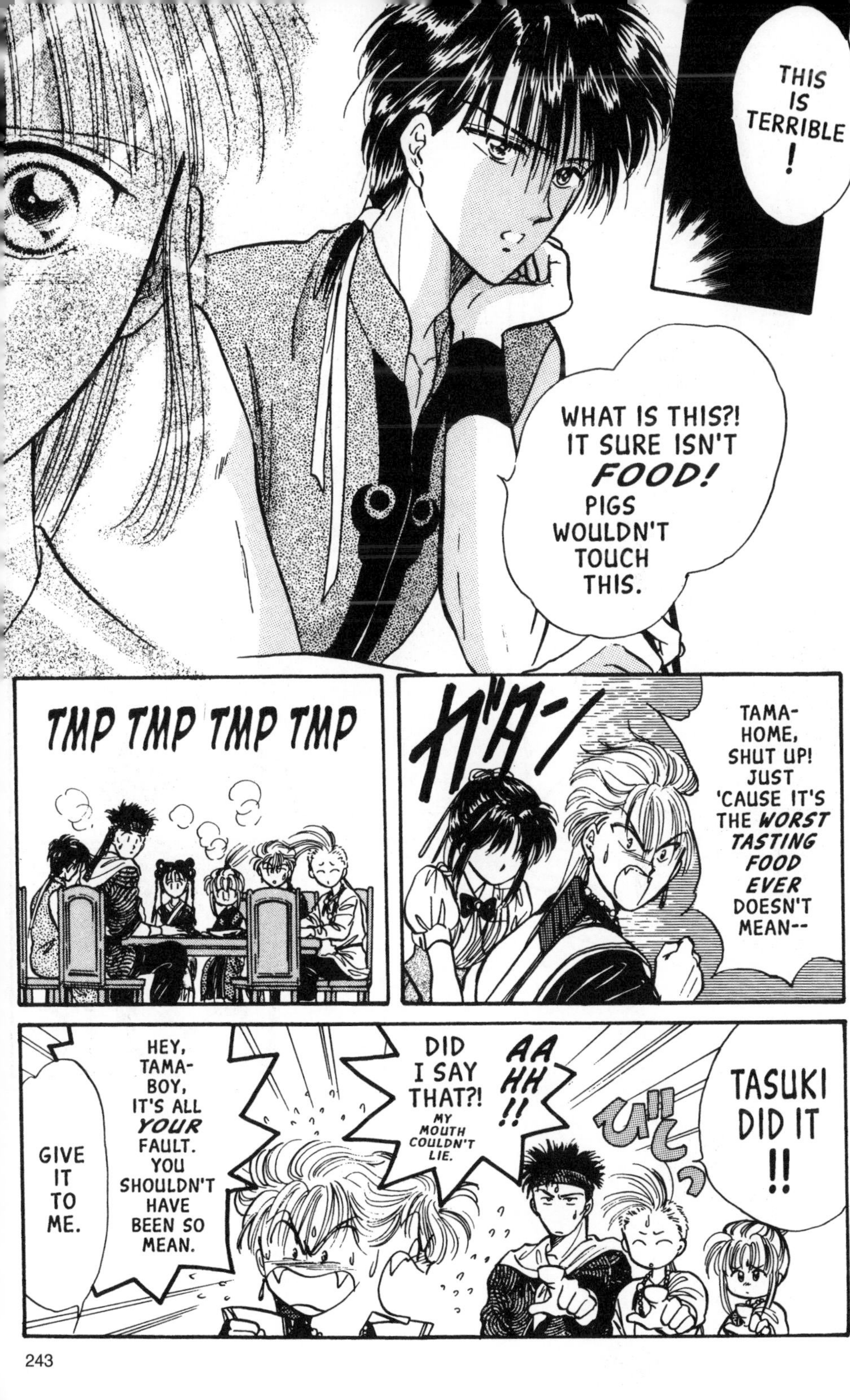
THIS IS TERRIBLE!
WHAT IS THIS?! IT SURE ISN'T FOOD! PIGS WOULDN'T TOUCH THIS.
ガターン
TAMA-HOME, SHUT UP! JUST 'CAUSE IT'S THE WORST TASTING FOOD EVER DOESN'T MEAN--
TMP TMP TMP TMP
TASUKI DID IT !!
びくっ
AAHH!!
DID I SAY THAT?!
MY MOUTH COULDN'T LIE.
HEY, TAMA-BOY, IT'S ALL YOUR FAULT. YOU SHOULDN'T HAVE BEEN SO MEAN.
GIVE IT TO ME.

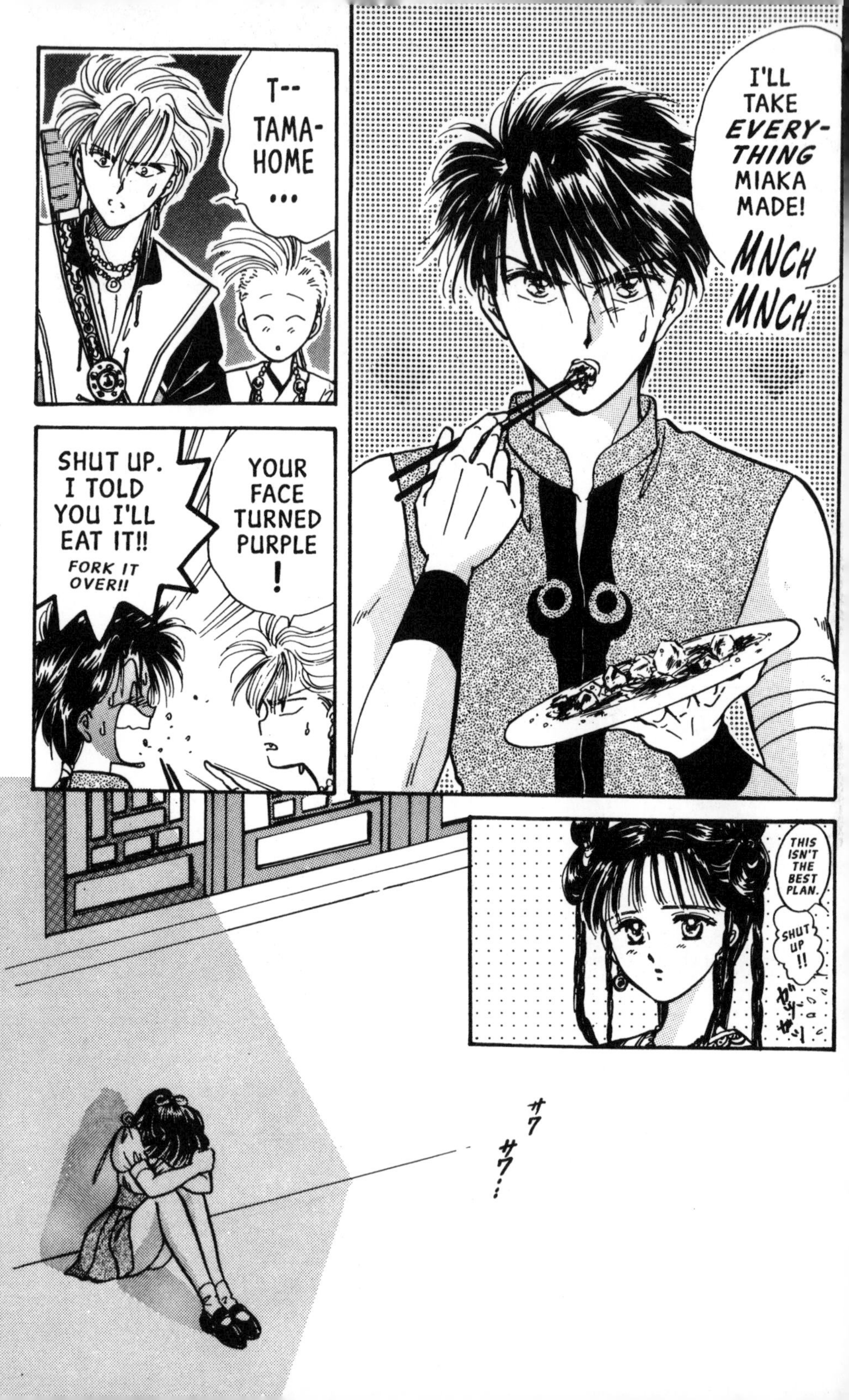
I'LL TAKE EVERYTHING MIAKA MADE!
MNCH MNCH
T-- TAMA-HOME ...
YOUR FACE TURNED PURPLE!
SHUT UP. I TOLD YOU I'LL EAT IT!!
FORK IT OVER!!
THIS ISN'T THE BEST PLAN.
SHUT UP!!
サワ サワ‥

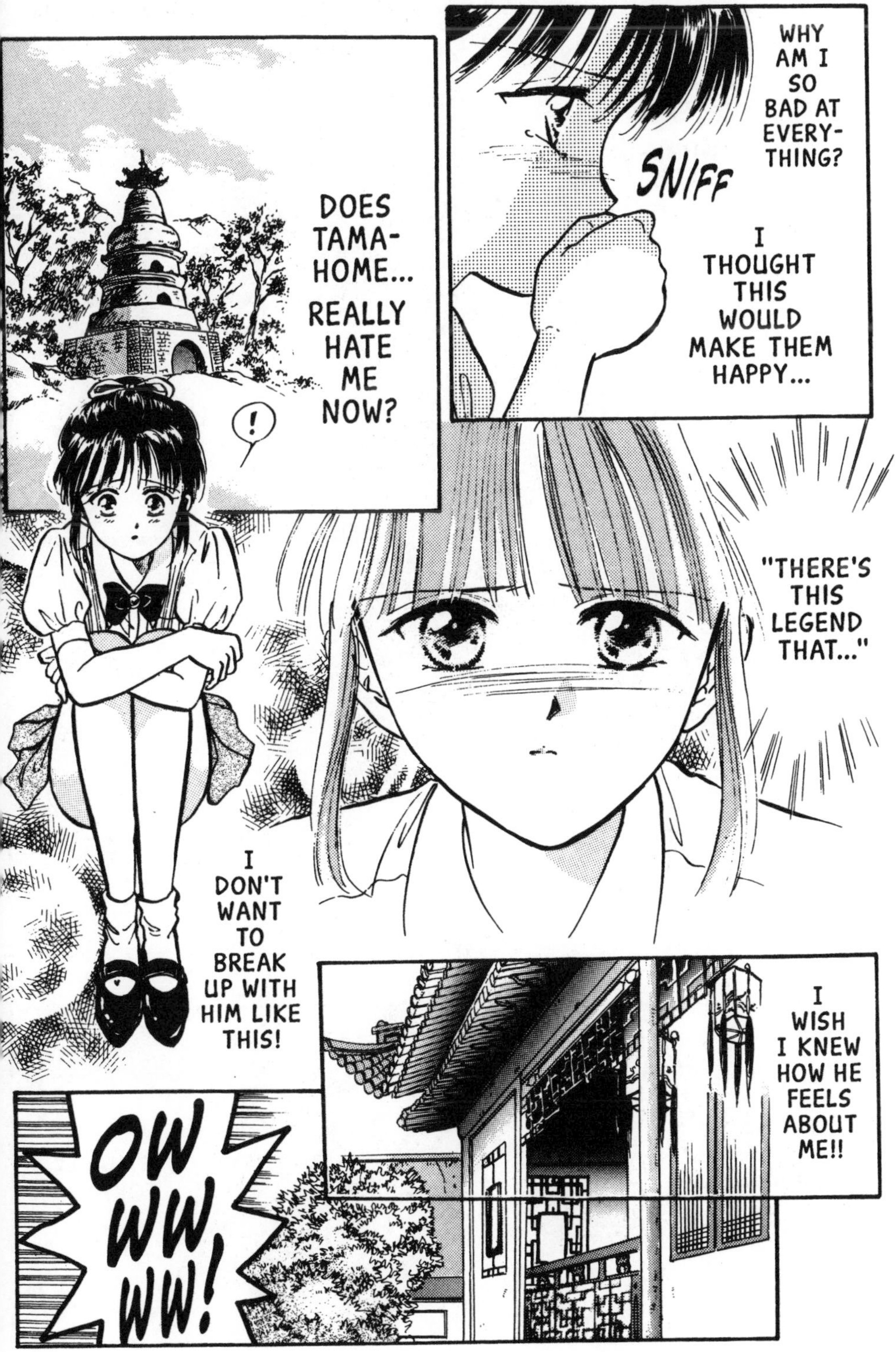
WHY AM I SO BAD AT EVERY-THING?
SNIFF
I THOUGHT THIS WOULD MAKE THEM HAPPY...
DOES TAMA-HOME...
REALLY HATE ME NOW?
!
"THERE'S THIS LEGEND THAT..."
I DON'T WANT TO BREAK UP WITH HIM LIKE THIS!
I WISH I KNEW HOW HE FEELS ABOUT ME!!
OW WW WW!

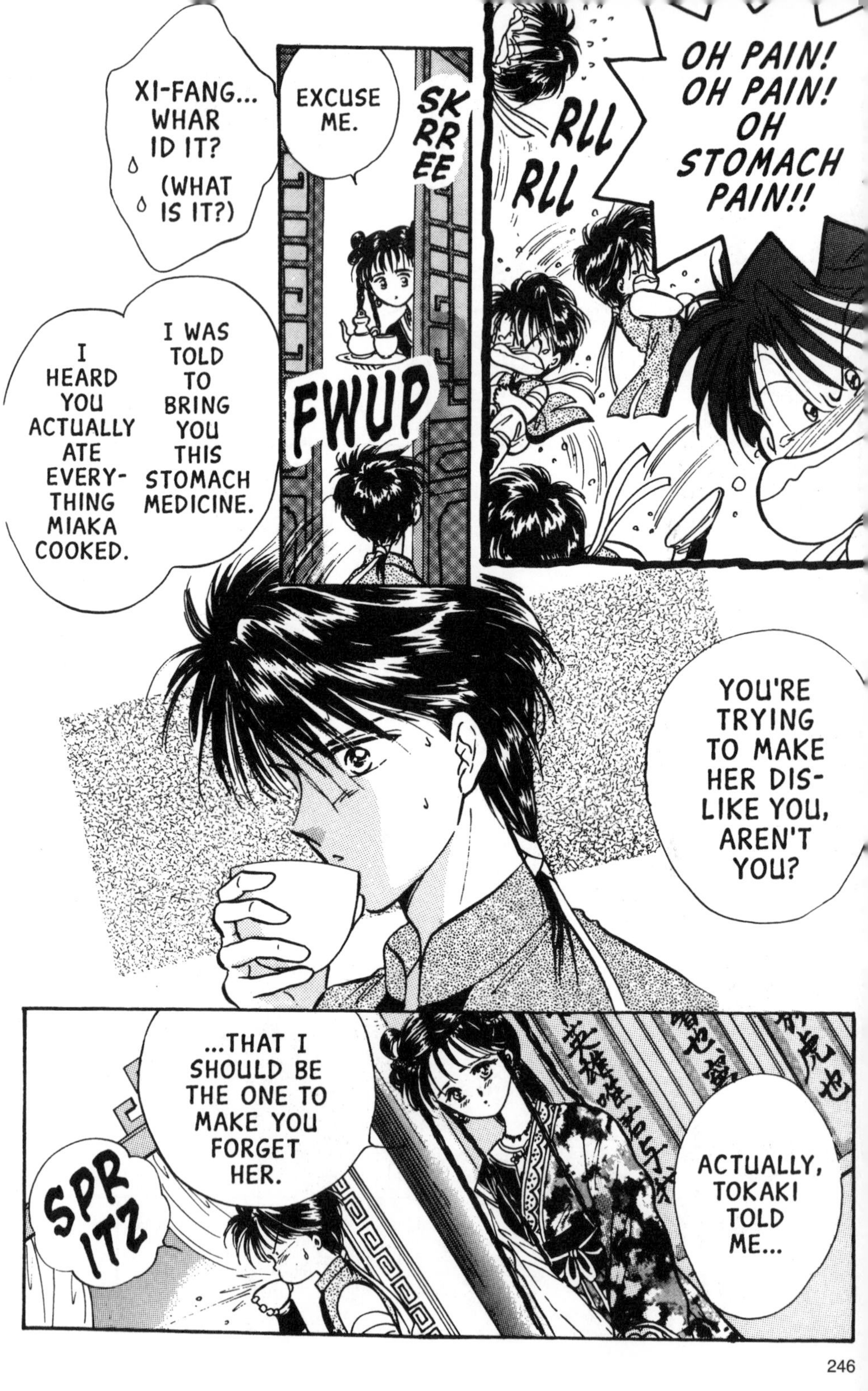
OH PAIN! OH PAIN! OH STOMACH PAIN!!
RLL RLL
SKRREE
EXCUSE ME.
XI-FANG... WHAR ID IT? (WHAT IS IT?)
FWUP
I WAS TOLD TO BRING YOU THIS STOMACH MEDICINE.
I HEARD YOU ACTUALLY ATE EVERYTHING MIAKA COOKED.
YOU'RE TRYING TO MAKE HER DISLIKE YOU, AREN'T YOU?
ACTUALLY, TOKAKI TOLD ME...
...THAT I SHOULD BE THE ONE TO MAKE YOU FORGET HER.
SPRITZ

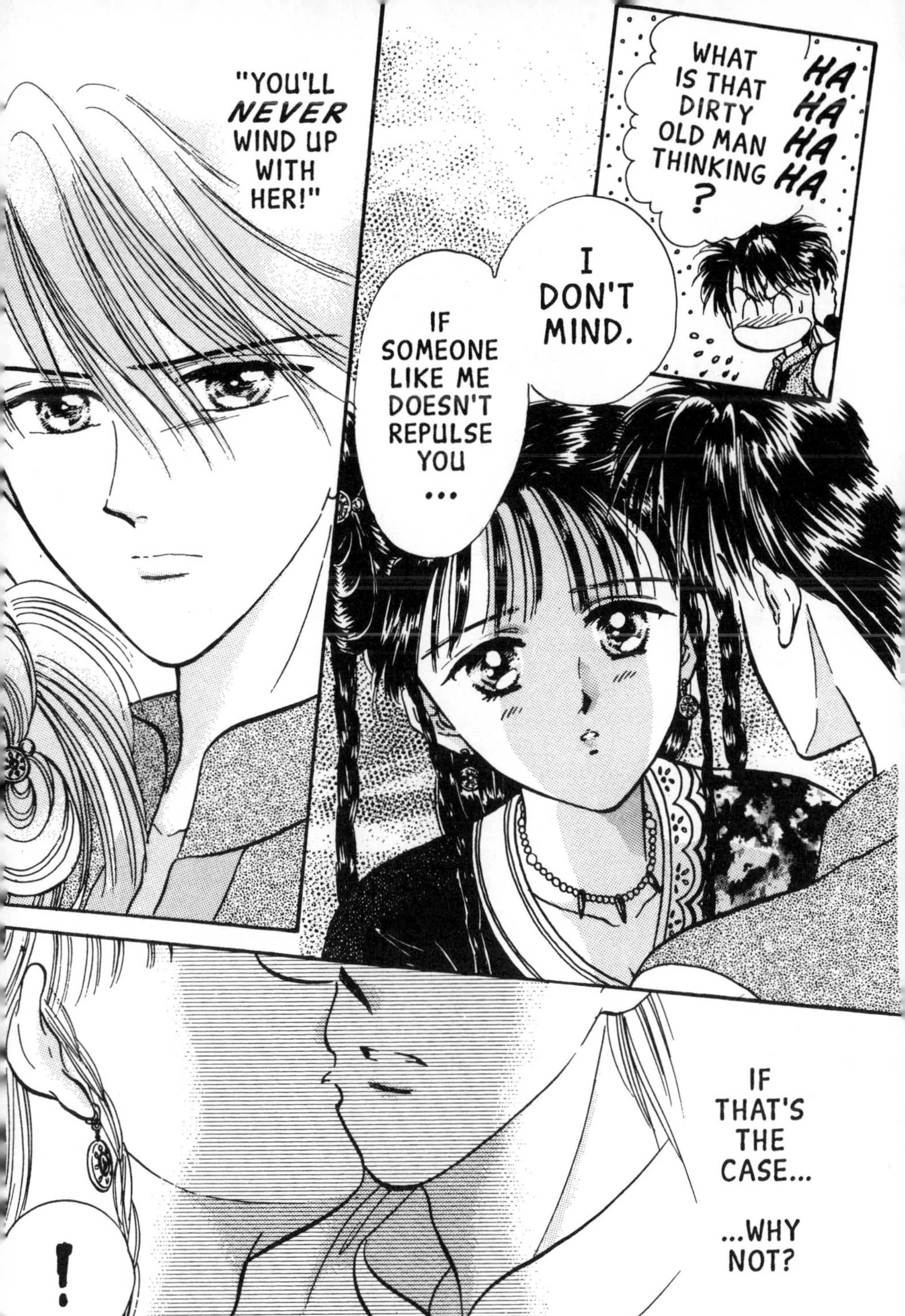
WHAT IS THAT DIRTY OLD MAN THINKING?
HA HA HA HA
I DON'T MIND.
IF SOMEONE LIKE ME DOESN'T REPULSE YOU...
"YOU'LL *NEVER* WIND UP WITH HER!"
IF THAT'S THE CASE...
...WHY NOT?
!

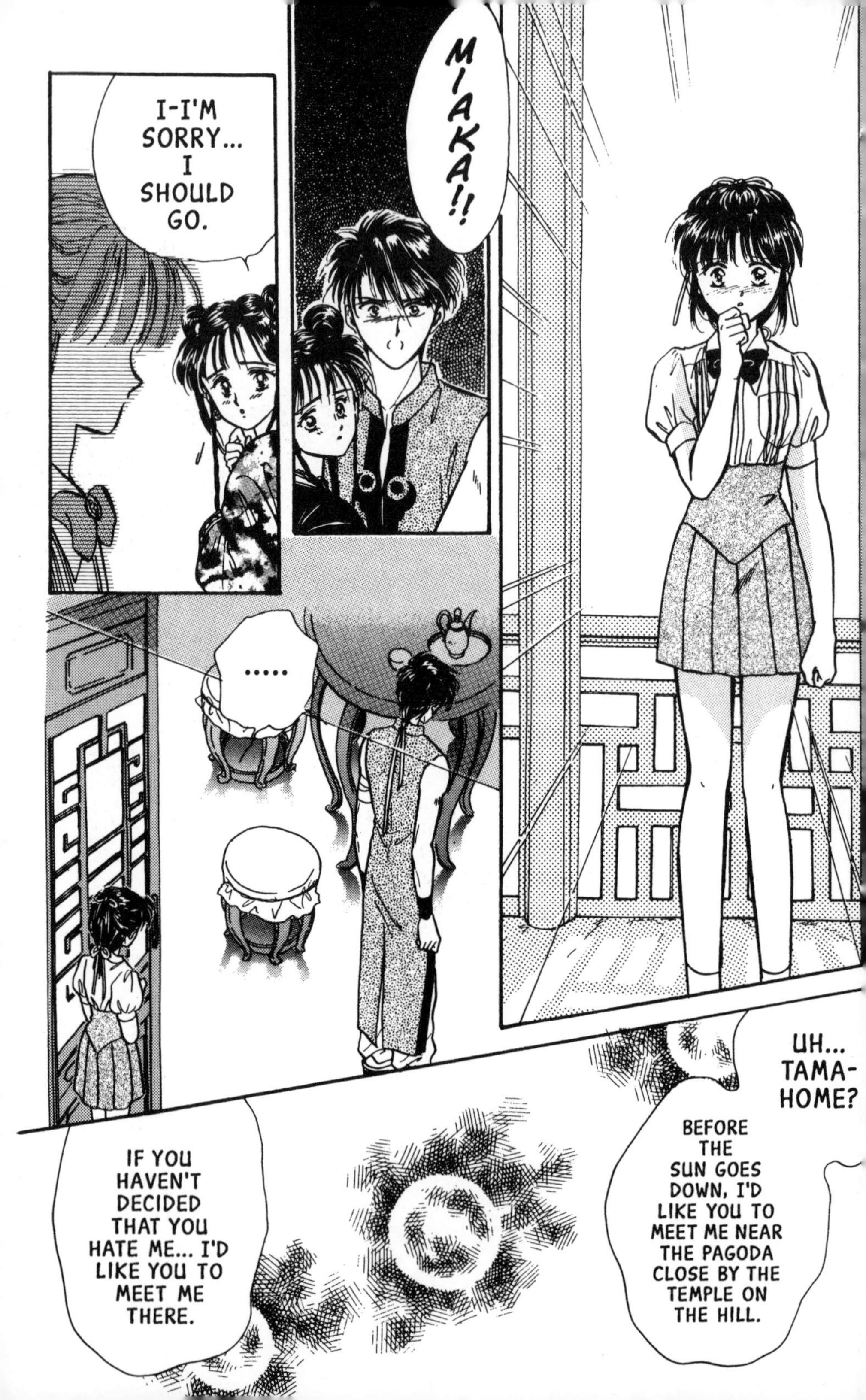
MIAKA!!
I-I'M SORRY... I SHOULD GO.
.....
UH... TAMA-HOME?
BEFORE THE SUN GOES DOWN, I'D LIKE YOU TO MEET ME NEAR THE PAGODA CLOSE BY THE TEMPLE ON THE HILL.
IF YOU HAVEN'T DECIDED THAT YOU HATE ME... I'D LIKE YOU TO MEET ME THERE.

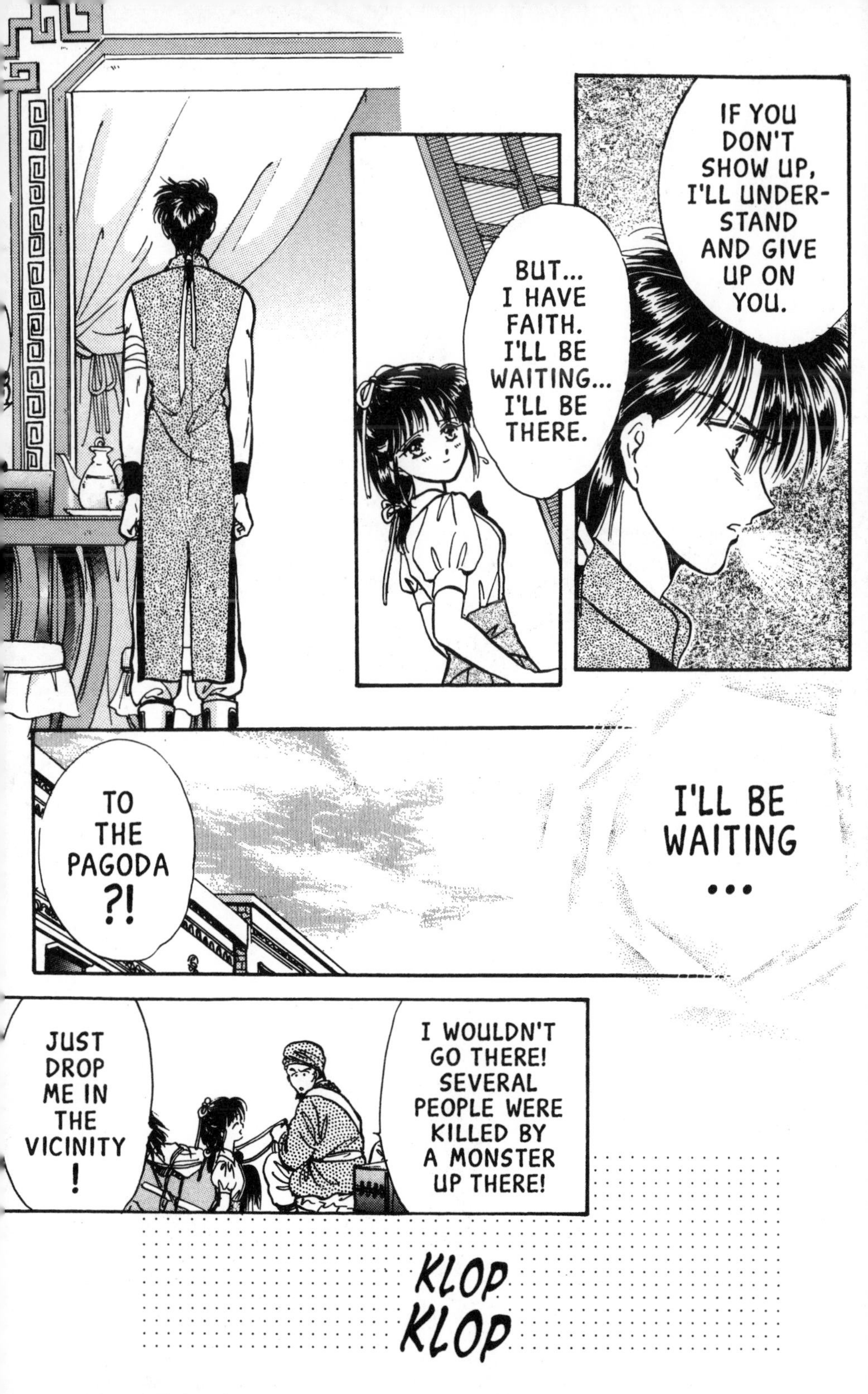
IF YOU DON'T SHOW UP, I'LL UNDER- STAND AND GIVE UP ON YOU.
BUT... I HAVE FAITH. I'LL BE WAITING... I'LL BE THERE.
I'LL BE WAITING ...
TO THE PAGODA ?!
I WOULDN'T GO THERE! SEVERAL PEOPLE WERE KILLED BY A MONSTER UP THERE!
JUST DROP ME IN THE VICINITY !
KLOP KLOP

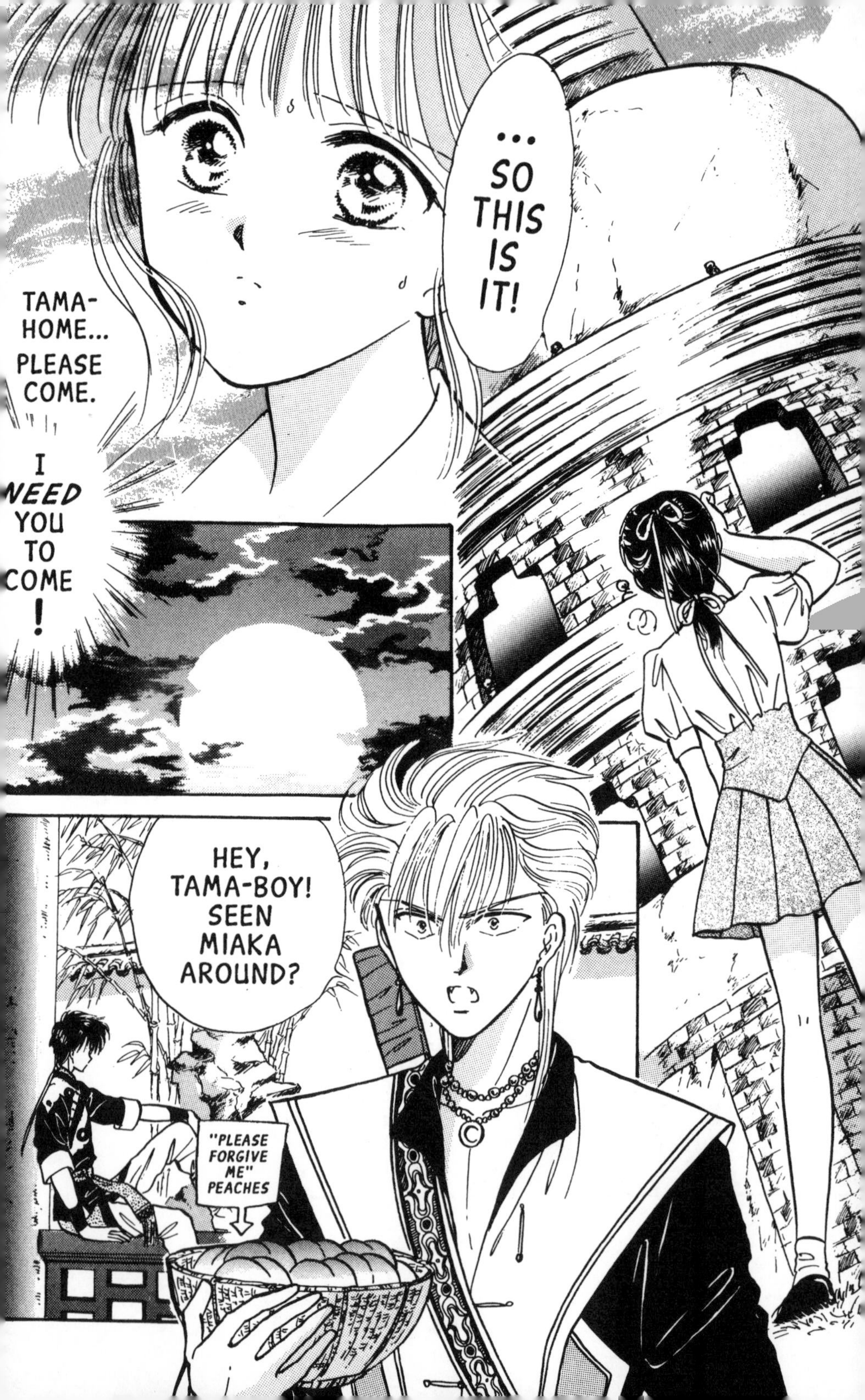
...SO THIS IS IT!
TAMA-HOME... PLEASE COME.
I *NEED* YOU TO COME!
HEY, TAMA-BOY! SEEN MIAKA AROUND?
"PLEASE FORGIVE ME" PEACHES

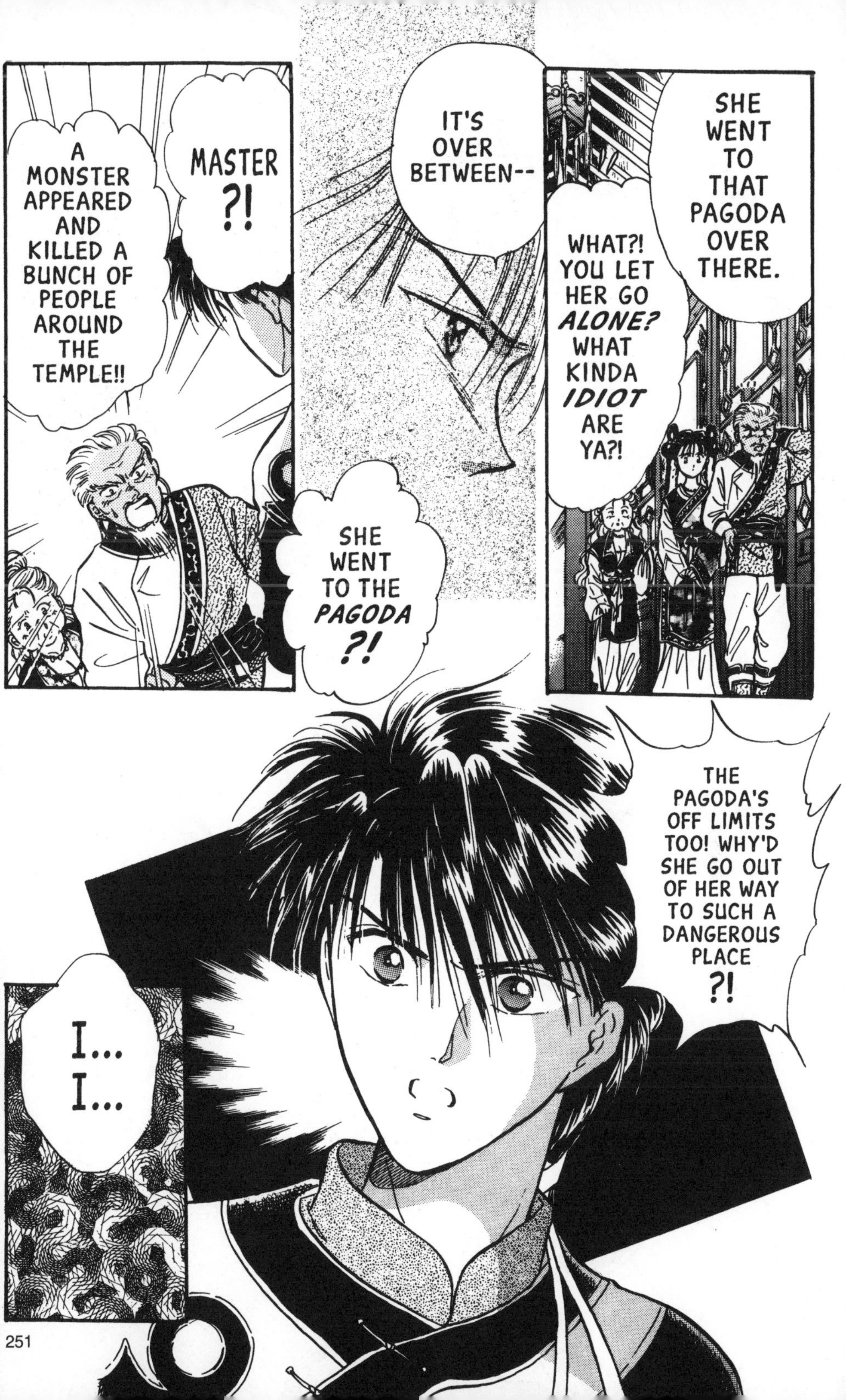
SHE WENT TO THAT PAGODA OVER THERE.
WHAT?! YOU LET HER GO *ALONE?* WHAT KINDA *IDIOT* ARE YA?!
IT'S OVER BETWEEN--
SHE WENT TO THE *PAGODA* ?!
MASTER ?!
A MONSTER APPEARED AND KILLED A BUNCH OF PEOPLE AROUND THE TEMPLE!!
THE PAGODA'S OFF LIMITS TOO! WHY'D SHE GO OUT OF HER WAY TO SUCH A DANGEROUS PLACE ?!
I... I...

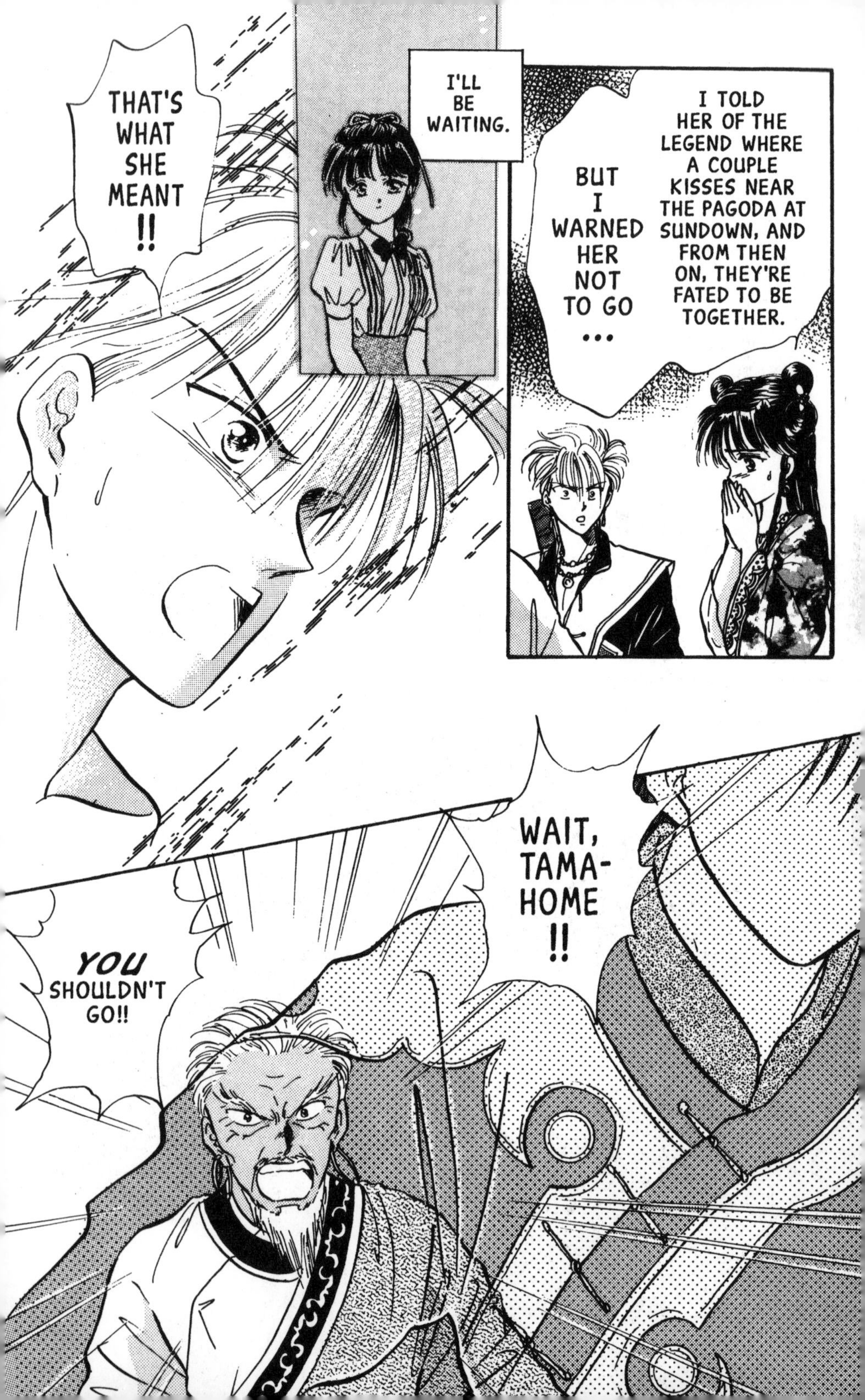
I TOLD HER OF THE LEGEND WHERE A COUPLE KISSES NEAR THE PAGODA AT SUNDOWN, AND FROM THEN ON, THEY'RE FATED TO BE TOGETHER.
BUT I WARNED HER NOT TO GO ...
I'LL BE WAITING.
THAT'S WHAT SHE MEANT !!
WAIT, TAMA-HOME !!
YOU SHOULDN'T GO!!

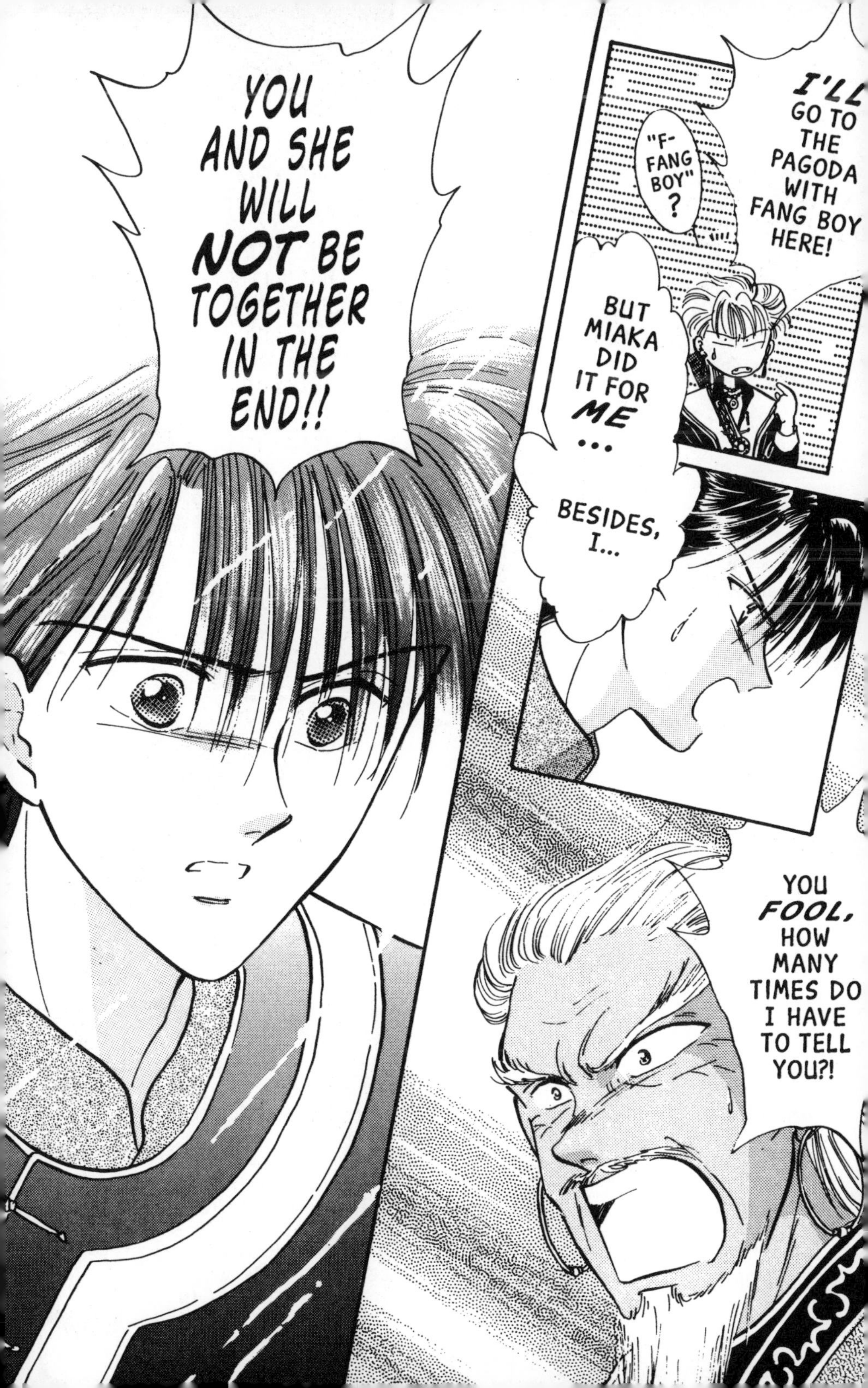
I'LL GO TO THE PAGODA WITH FANG BOY HERE!
"F-FANG BOY"?
BUT MIAKA DID IT FOR ME...
BESIDES, I...
YOU FOOL, HOW MANY TIMES DO I HAVE TO TELL YOU?!
YOU AND SHE WILL NOT BE TOGETHER IN THE END!!

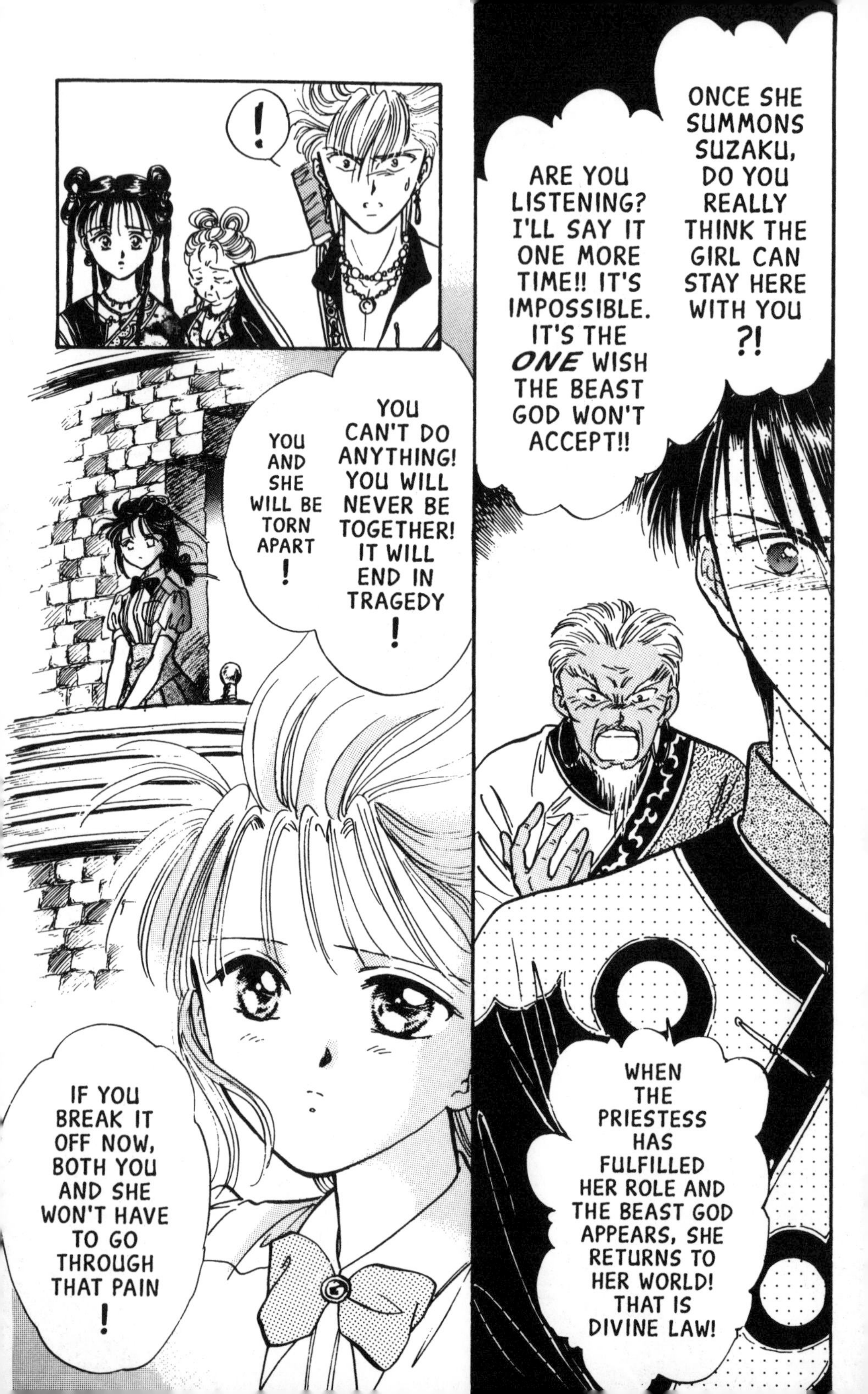

ONCE SHE SUMMONS SUZAKU, DO YOU REALLY THINK THE GIRL CAN STAY HERE WITH YOU ?!
ARE YOU LISTENING? I'LL SAY IT ONE MORE TIME!! IT'S IMPOSSIBLE. IT'S THE *ONE* WISH THE BEAST GOD WON'T ACCEPT!!
WHEN THE PRIESTESS HAS FULFILLED HER ROLE AND THE BEAST GOD APPEARS, SHE RETURNS TO HER WORLD! THAT IS DIVINE LAW!
!
YOU CAN'T DO ANYTHING! YOU WILL NEVER BE TOGETHER! IT WILL END IN TRAGEDY !
YOU AND SHE WILL BE TORN APART !
IF YOU BREAK IT OFF NOW, BOTH YOU AND SHE WON'T HAVE TO GO THROUGH THAT PAIN !

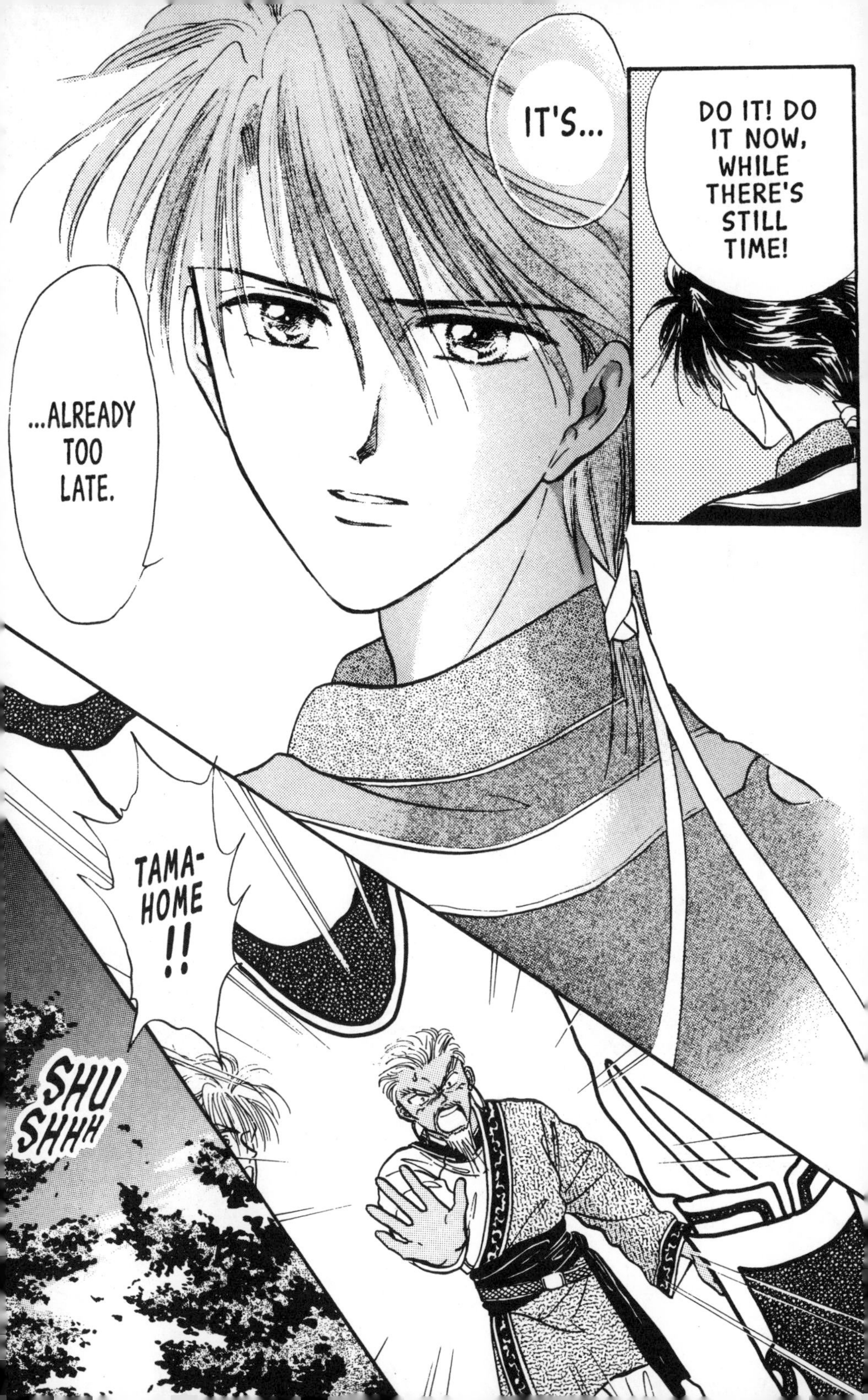
DO IT! DO IT NOW, WHILE THERE'S STILL TIME!
IT'S...
...ALREADY TOO LATE.
TAMA-HOME!!
SHUSHHH

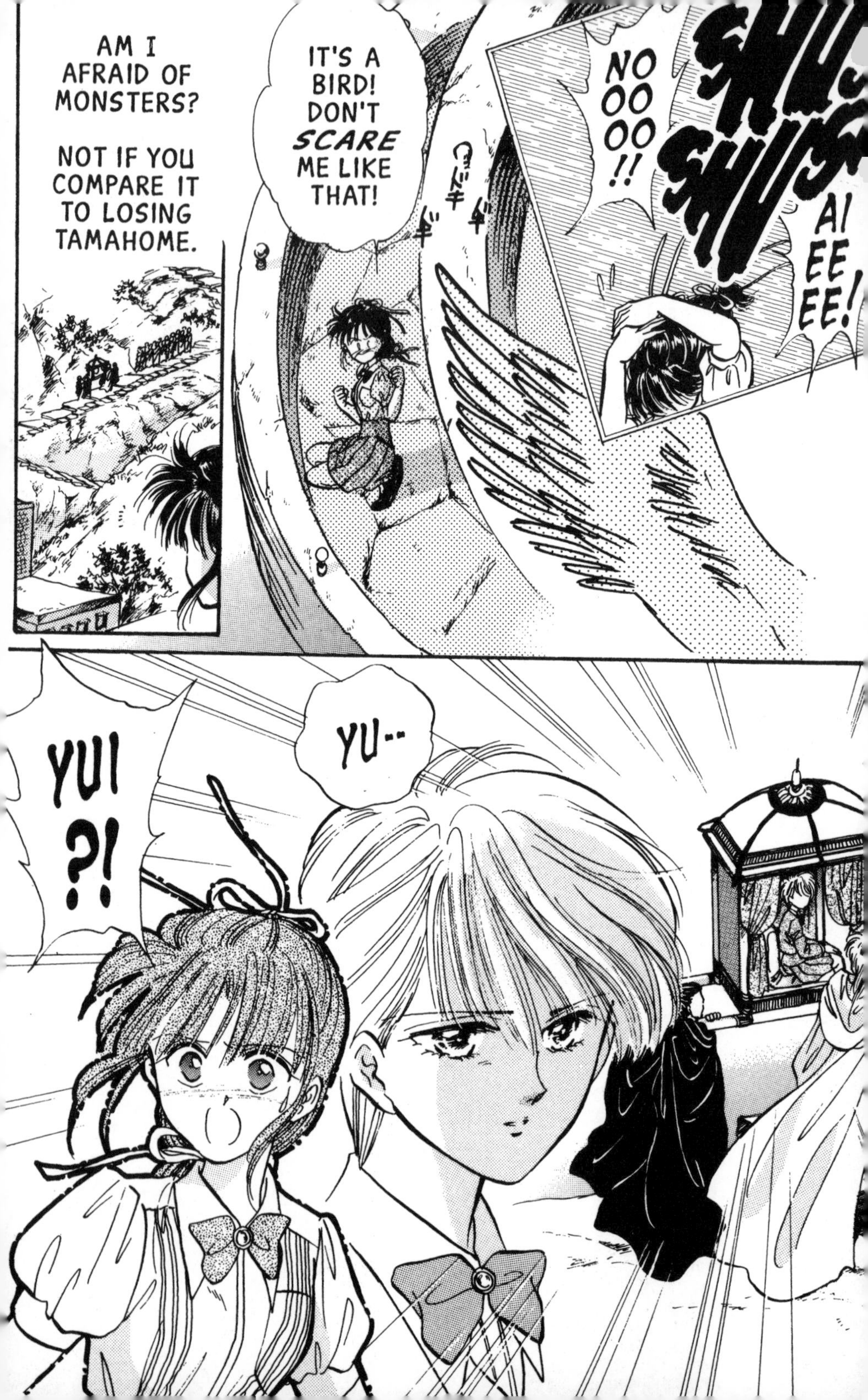
SHU SHU
NOOOOOO!!
AIEEEE!
IT'S A BIRD! DON'T *SCARE* ME LIKE THAT!
AM I AFRAID OF MONSTERS?
NOT IF YOU COMPARE IT TO LOSING TAMAHOME.
YU--
YUI?!

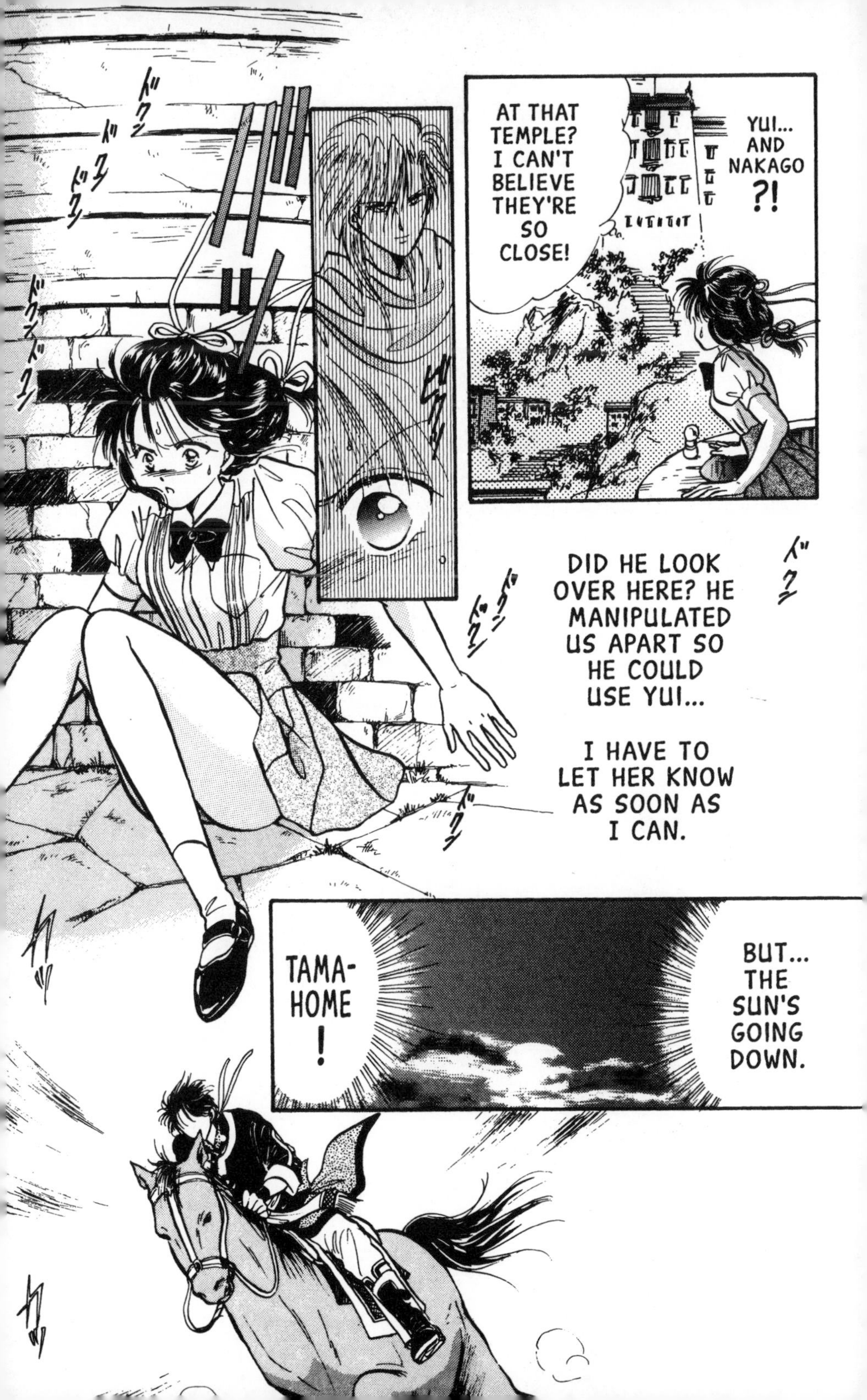
YUI... AND NAKAGO ?!
AT THAT TEMPLE? I CAN'T BELIEVE THEY'RE SO CLOSE!
DID HE LOOK OVER HERE? HE MANIPULATED US APART SO HE COULD USE YUI...
I HAVE TO LET HER KNOW AS SOON AS I CAN.
BUT... THE SUN'S GOING DOWN.
TAMA-HOME !

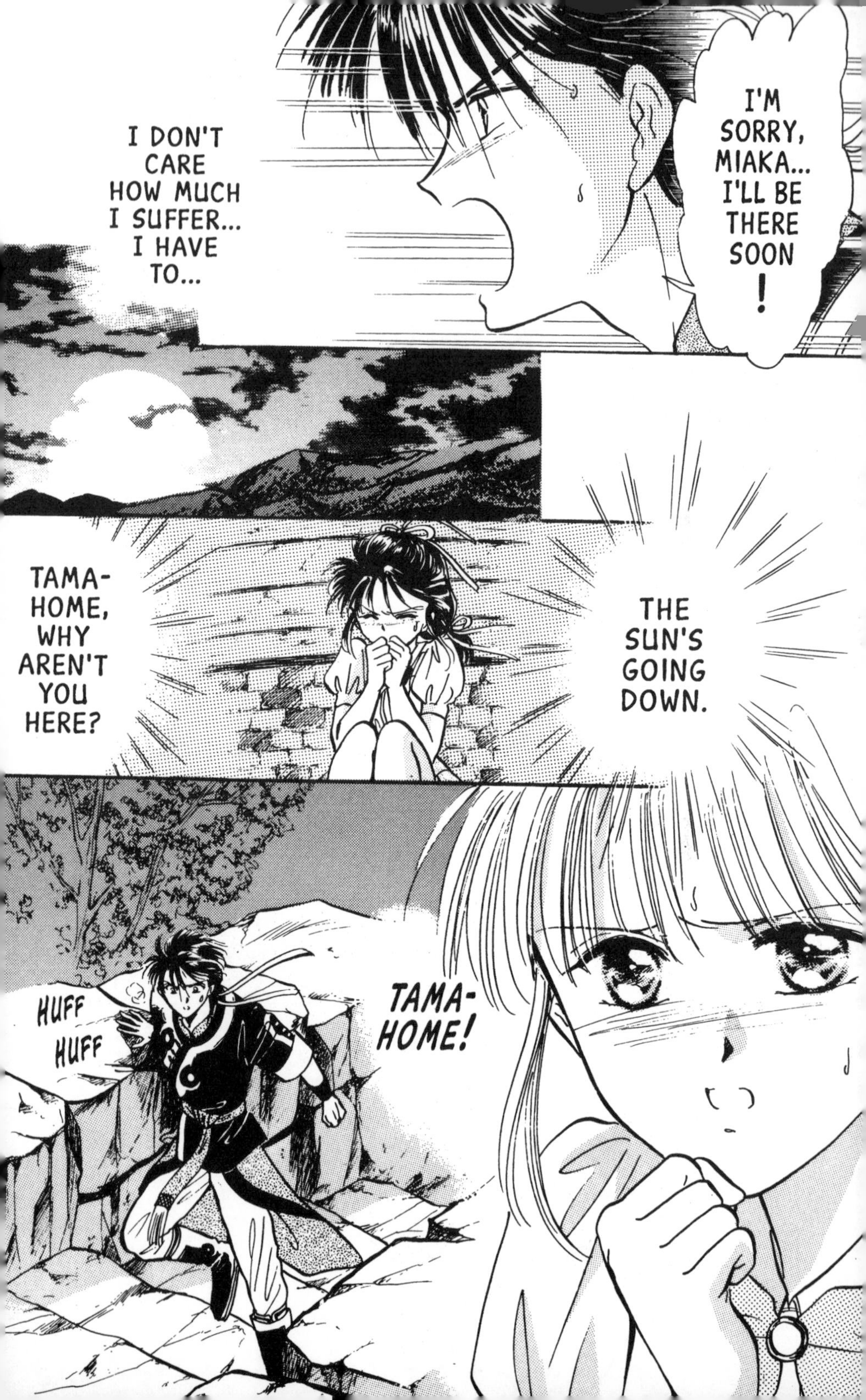

I'M SORRY, MIAKA... I'LL BE THERE SOON!
I DON'T CARE HOW MUCH I SUFFER... I HAVE TO...
THE SUN'S GOING DOWN.
TAMA-HOME, WHY AREN'T YOU HERE?
TAMA-HOME!
HUFF HUFF

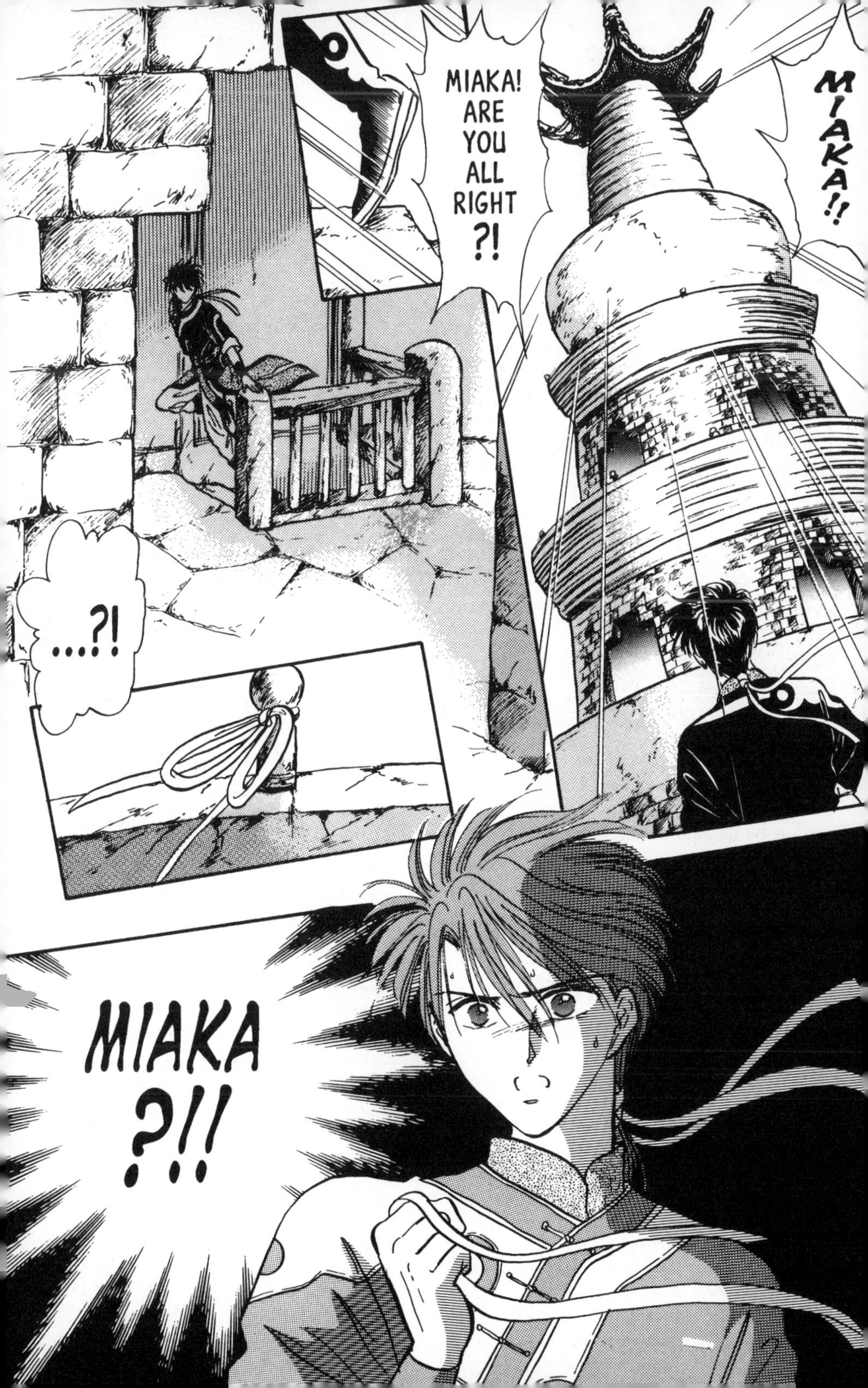
MIAKA!!
MIAKA! ARE YOU ALL RIGHT ?!
...?!
MIAKA ?!!

(VIRGO)※

WU JUN-JIA
武俊角

(VIRGO)※

WU GANG-DE
武亢徳

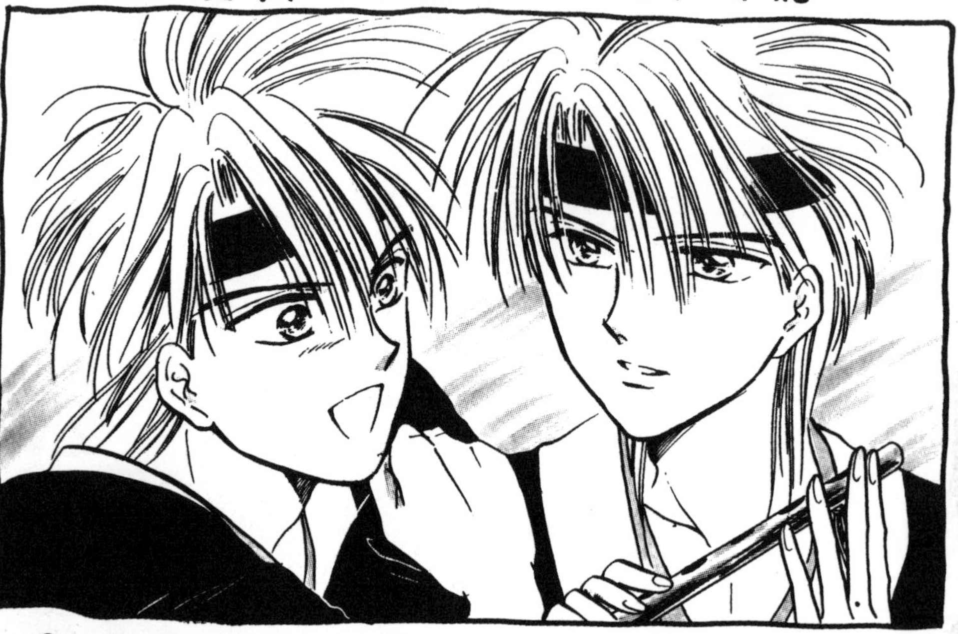

SUBOSHI

- Birthplace: Same as right side.
- Age: Same as right side.
- Family: Younger of the twins.
- Height: Same as right side.
- Blood Type: Same as right side.
- Talents: He can use a secret weapon (a weapon that doesn't look like a weapon) called the Ryusei-Sui, and control it with his will (actually there is no other way that it can be a weapon).
- The exact opposite of his brother, he's fierce, and if he gets an idea stuck in his head, he won't listen to reason--he'll just rush in like a madman. They lost their parents at a very young age and had a very tough childhood, so he's very much bonded with his brother (to the point where it goes too far). The bond is so strong that he would not hesitate to kill for his brother. Yui was the first person besides his brother to show him any tenderness and he quickly fell in love (first love) with her. It's because of Yui that he feels anger toward Miaka and jealousy toward Tamahome.

AMIBOSHI

- Birthplace: The village of Tian-Ling in the Shan-Yun province of Qu-Dong.
- Age: 15
- Family: Elder of twin brothers who lost their parents in a civil war.
- Height: 168 cm (5' 6")
- Blood Type: A
- Talents: Can emit chi through his mouth and channel it through a flute to control people's will.
- Tranquil and reserved, but at times he can be single-minded and merciless. Before the events of the book, he was a kind young man determined to judiciously protect his younger brother. And for that reason, he was faced with a dilemma and the pain of choosing between the Seiryu warriors and the Suzaku warriors.

I forgot to put in Nakago's constellation in the last volume! óóó

⇦ HERE IT IS.

(SCORPIO)

※The constellations for Amiboshi and Suboshi combined to make Virgo.

Chapter Sixty-Two
The Unbreakable Wall

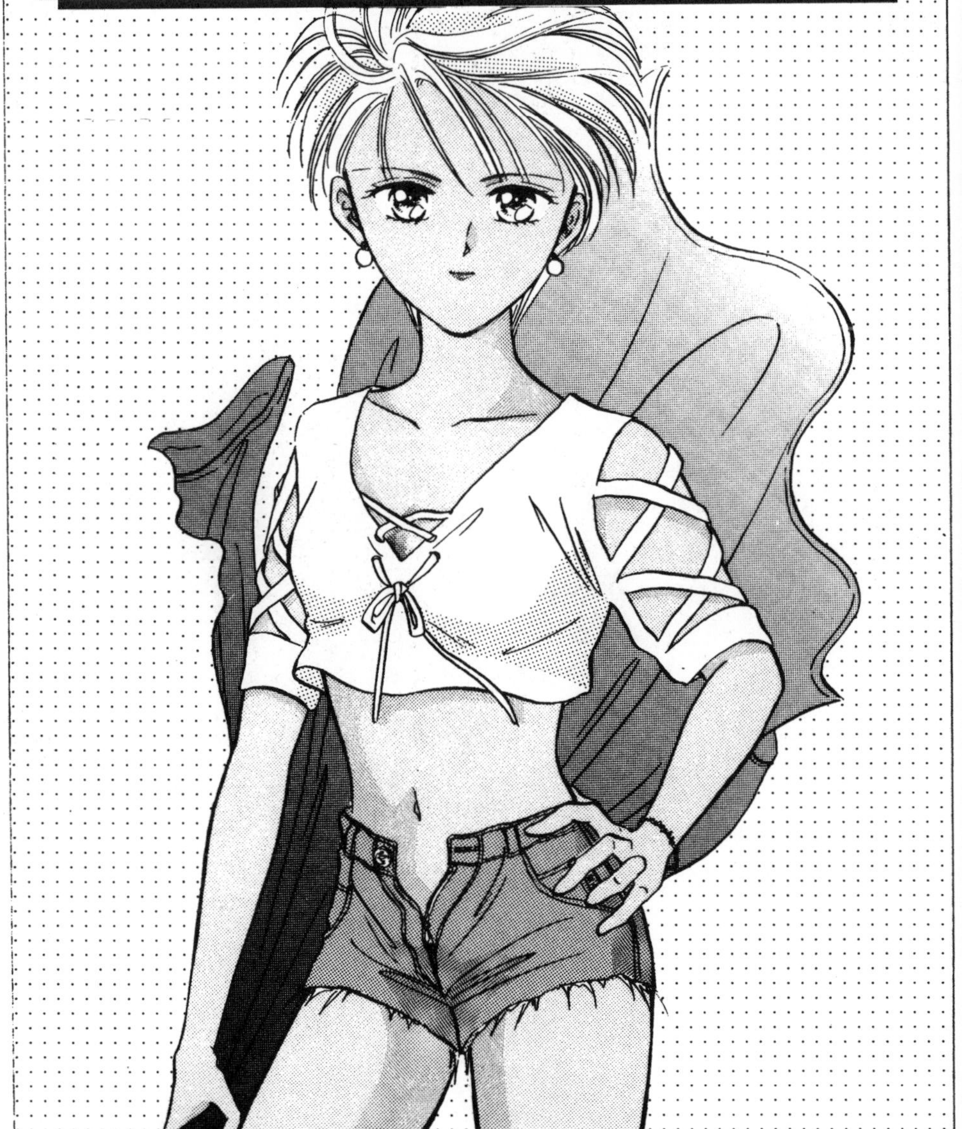

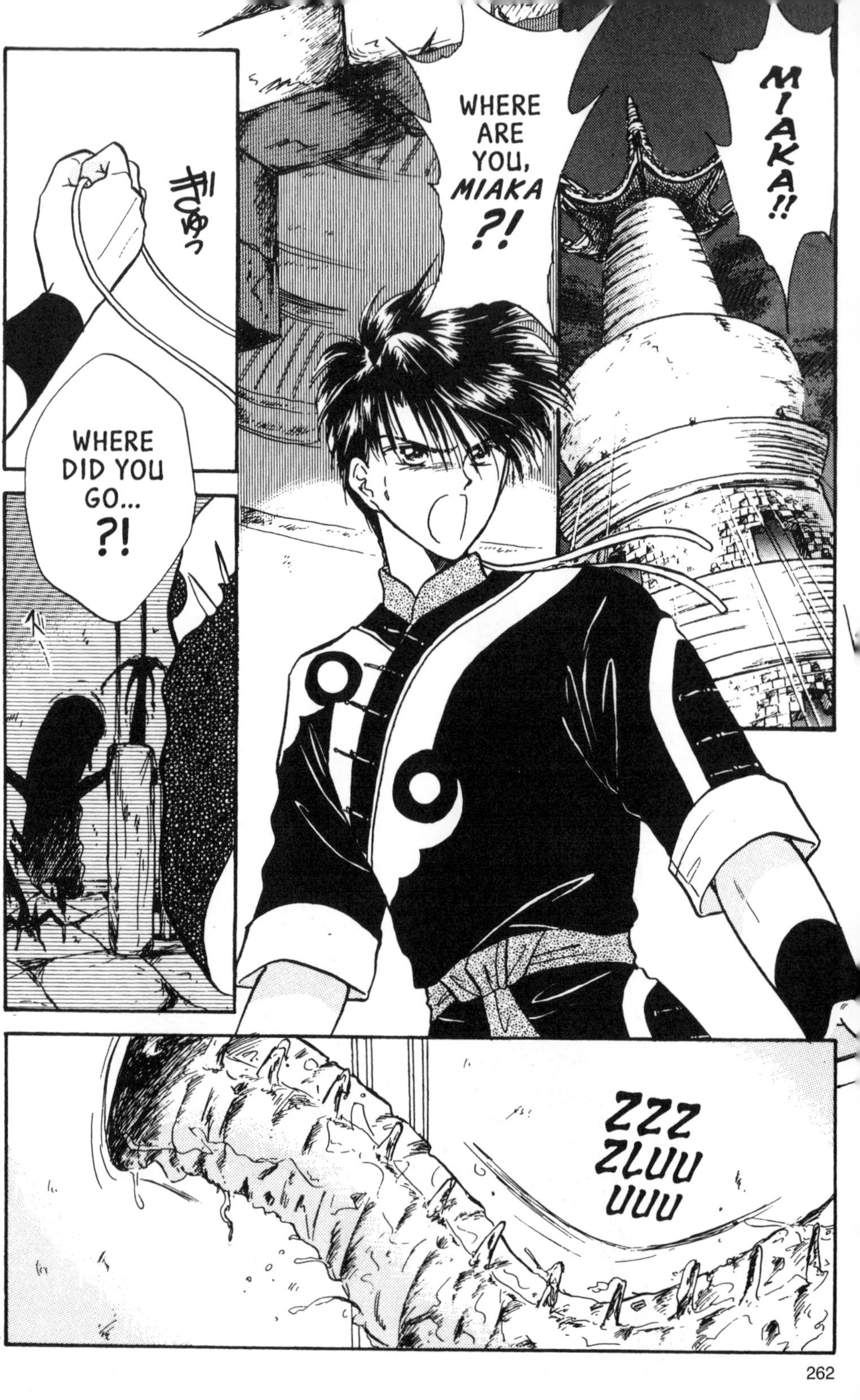
MIAKA!!
WHERE ARE YOU, MIAKA?!
ぎゅっ
WHERE DID YOU GO...?!
ZZZ ZLUUU UUU

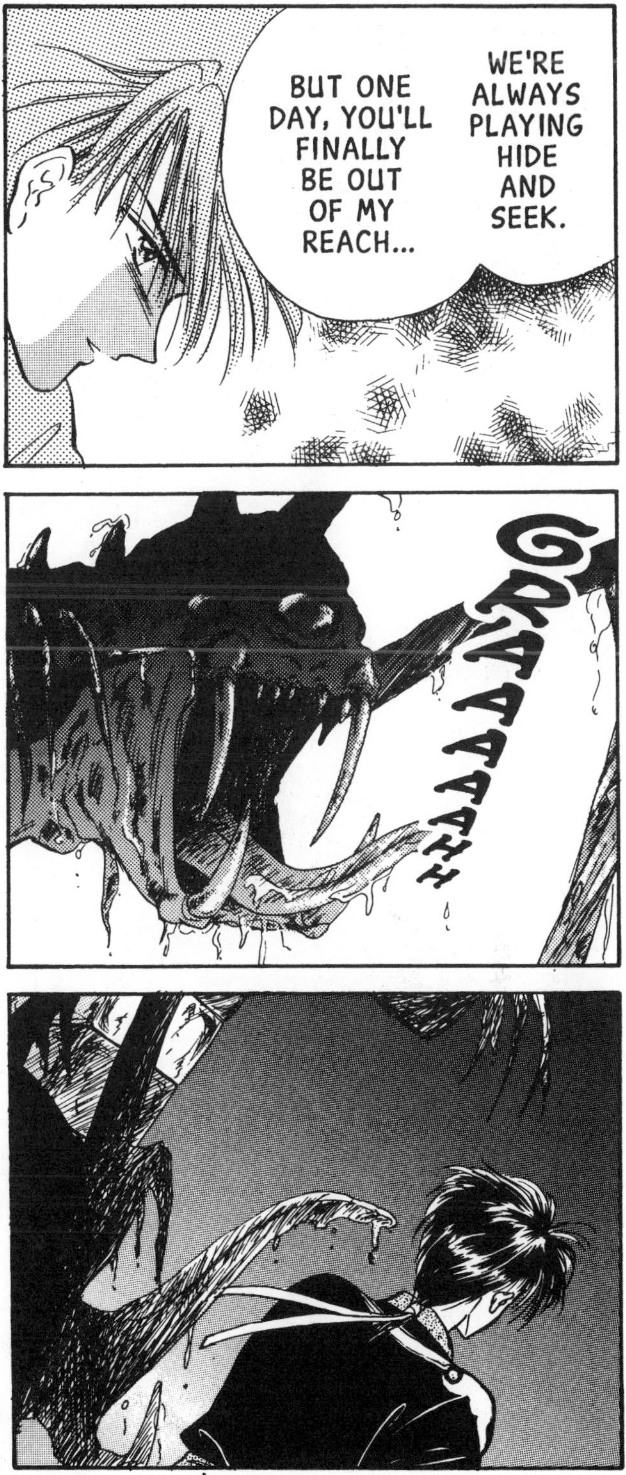
WE'RE ALWAYS PLAYING HIDE AND SEEK.
BUT ONE DAY, YOU'LL FINALLY BE OUT OF MY REACH...
GRAAAAAHH

Next is Tamahome. His character has changed significantly since before I started drawing the manga. Unaware of love, he discovers it for the first time in his life upon meeting Miaka. S-so, she's his first love! I drew Tamahome when I was 18 (before I was published), and when I worked on the short story "Heart ni Jewel" (A Jewel for the Heart), I found my old sketches for him. So he goes way back! (Oh, so does Hotohori!) He can be a clown, but at the same time he has a dark side. So he's a little complicated. (I thought he was completely different from Manato in *Prepubescence*, which I was working on at the time.) He's strong yet vulnerable. He protects himself by protecting others. That's about it. According to the CD booklet listener-response surveys, he was ranked No. 1 in the favorite-character category. (Although these were just the initial results. Miaka ranked No. 4, but in the *Shojo Comic* survey she was No. 1!!) I'm not saying he's my personal type, but he's someone you want to hug and pat on the head. I wonder why?!

Hotohori! Readers go to both extremes over him. The younger readers don't seem to like him. I wonder if they relate more to Tamahome. But the ones who really like Hotohori send in letters that ramble on about him and nothing else. I mean, he's a nice guy. He's dedicated. He graciously withdrew from pursuing Miaka. Some might accuse him of going after her in volume 6, but that's not a fair interpretation... Of course I have to defend him! I'm so sorry for him!

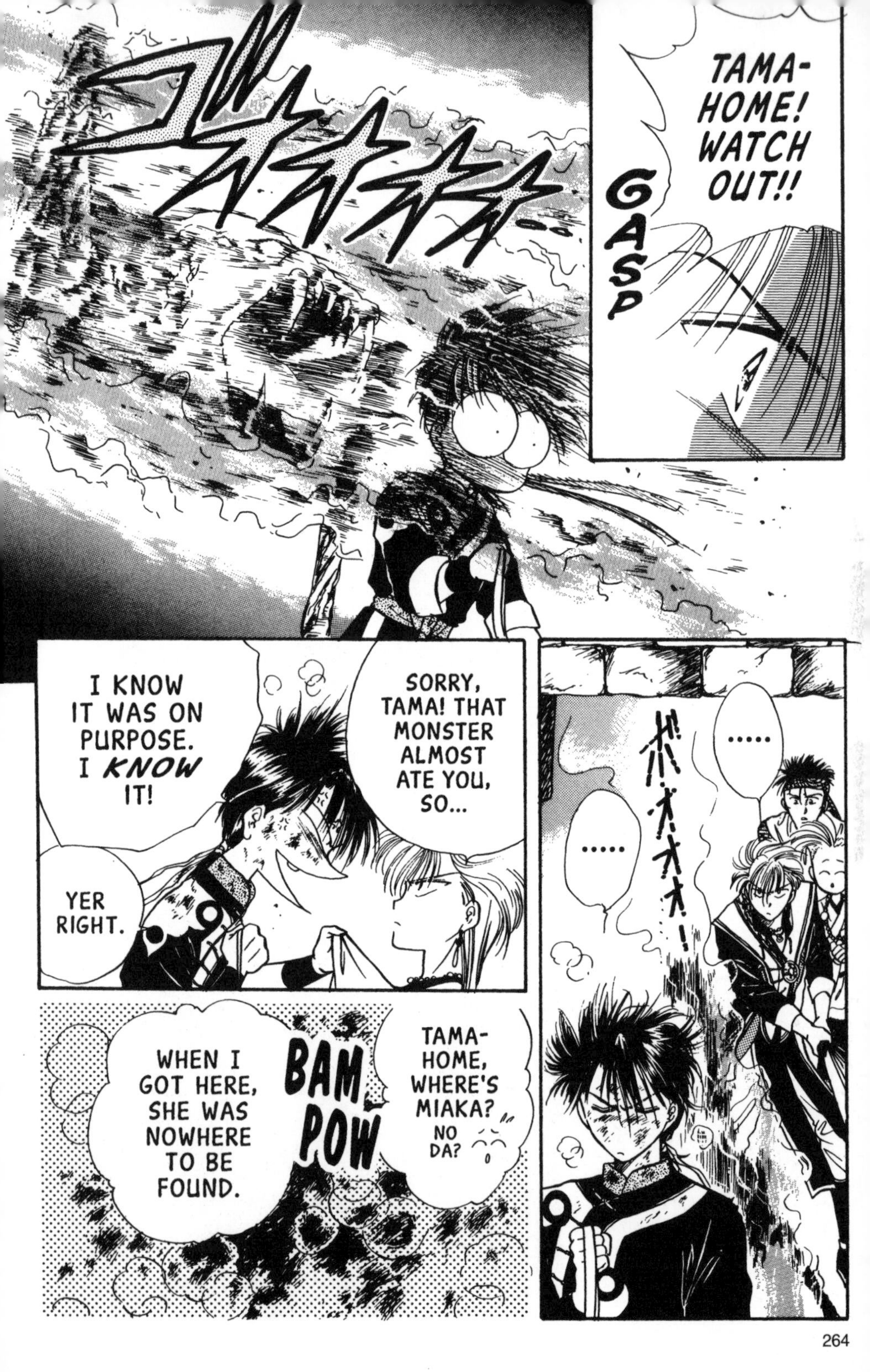
TAMA-HOME! WATCH OUT!!
GASP
.....
.....
SORRY, TAMA! THAT MONSTER ALMOST ATE YOU, SO...
I KNOW IT WAS ON PURPOSE. I *KNOW* IT!
YER RIGHT.
TAMA-HOME, WHERE'S MIAKA?
NO DA?
BAM POW
WHEN I GOT HERE, SHE WAS NOWHERE TO BE FOUND.

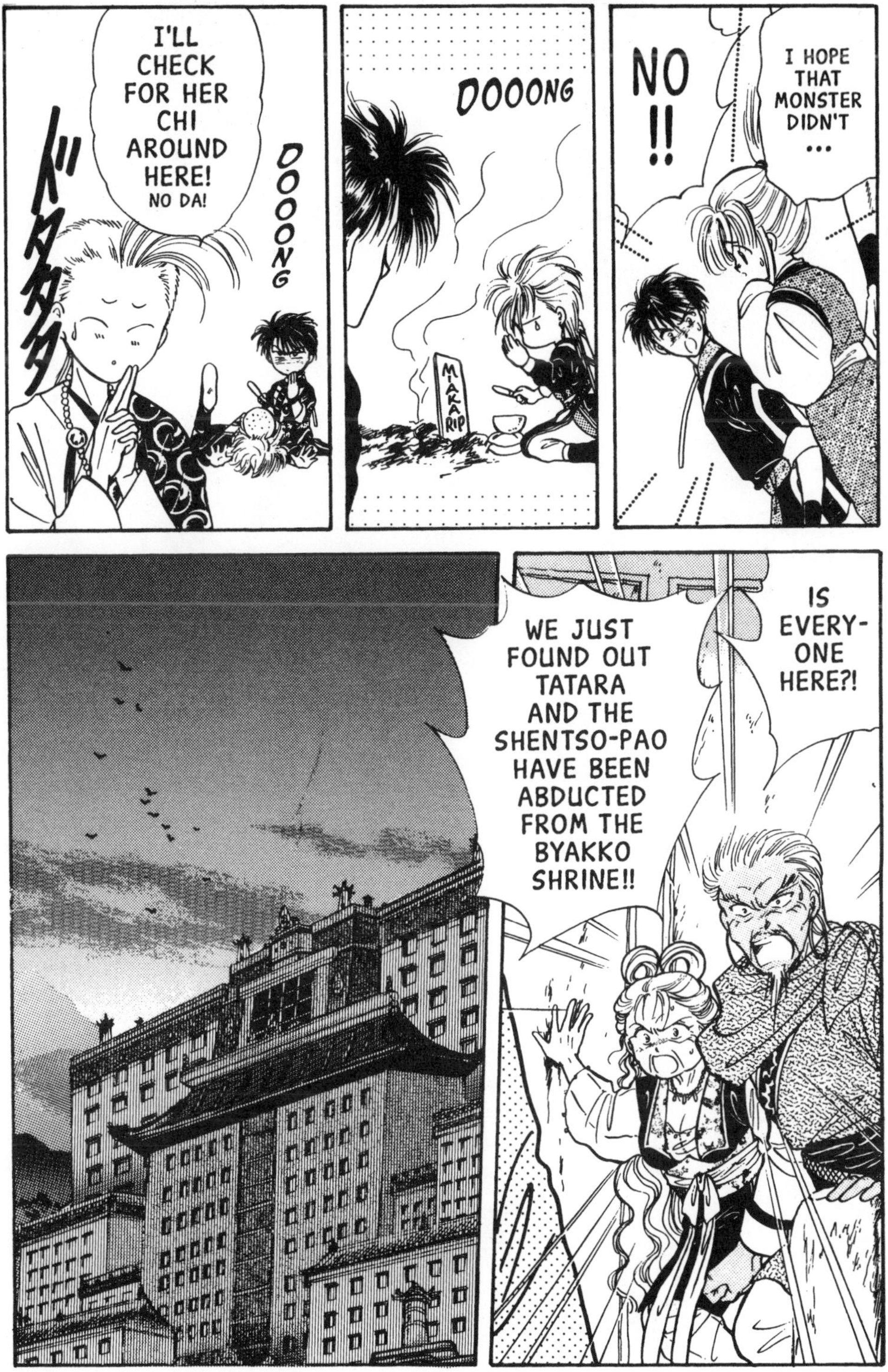
I HOPE THAT MONSTER DIDN'T ...
NO !!
DOOONG
MIAKA RIP
I'LL CHECK FOR HER CHI AROUND HERE! NO DA!
DOOOOONG
ドタタタタ
IS EVERY-ONE HERE?!
WE JUST FOUND OUT TATARA AND THE SHENTSO-PAO HAVE BEEN ABDUCTED FROM THE BYAKKO SHRINE!!

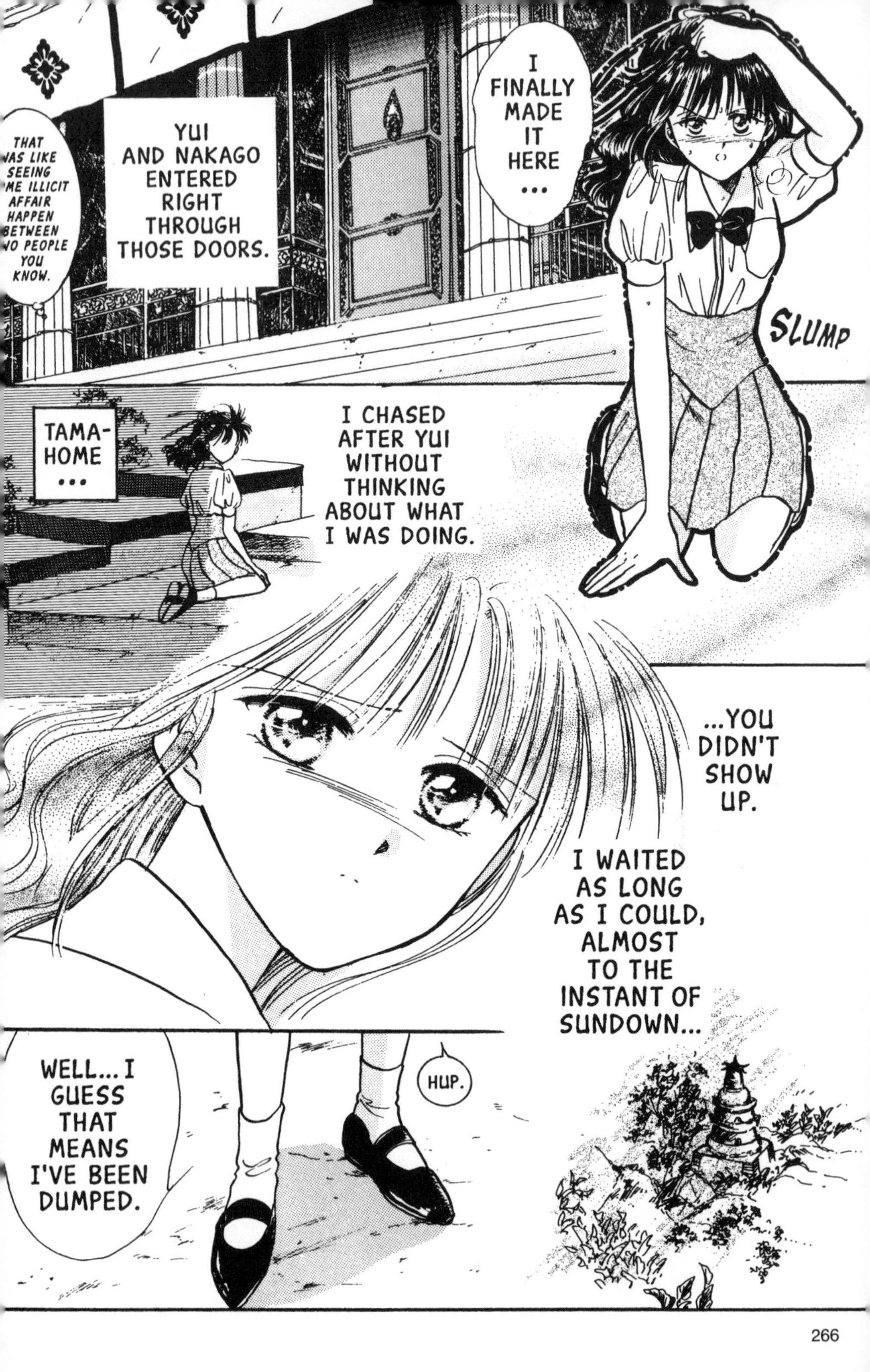
I FINALLY MADE IT HERE...
SLUMP
YUI AND NAKAGO ENTERED RIGHT THROUGH THOSE DOORS.
THAT WAS LIKE SEEING ME ILLICIT AFFAIR HAPPEN BETWEEN WO PEOPLE YOU KNOW.
I CHASED AFTER YUI WITHOUT THINKING ABOUT WHAT I WAS DOING.
TAMA-HOME...
...YOU DIDN'T SHOW UP.
I WAITED AS LONG AS I COULD, ALMOST TO THE INSTANT OF SUNDOWN...
HUP.
WELL... I GUESS THAT MEANS I'VE BEEN DUMPED.

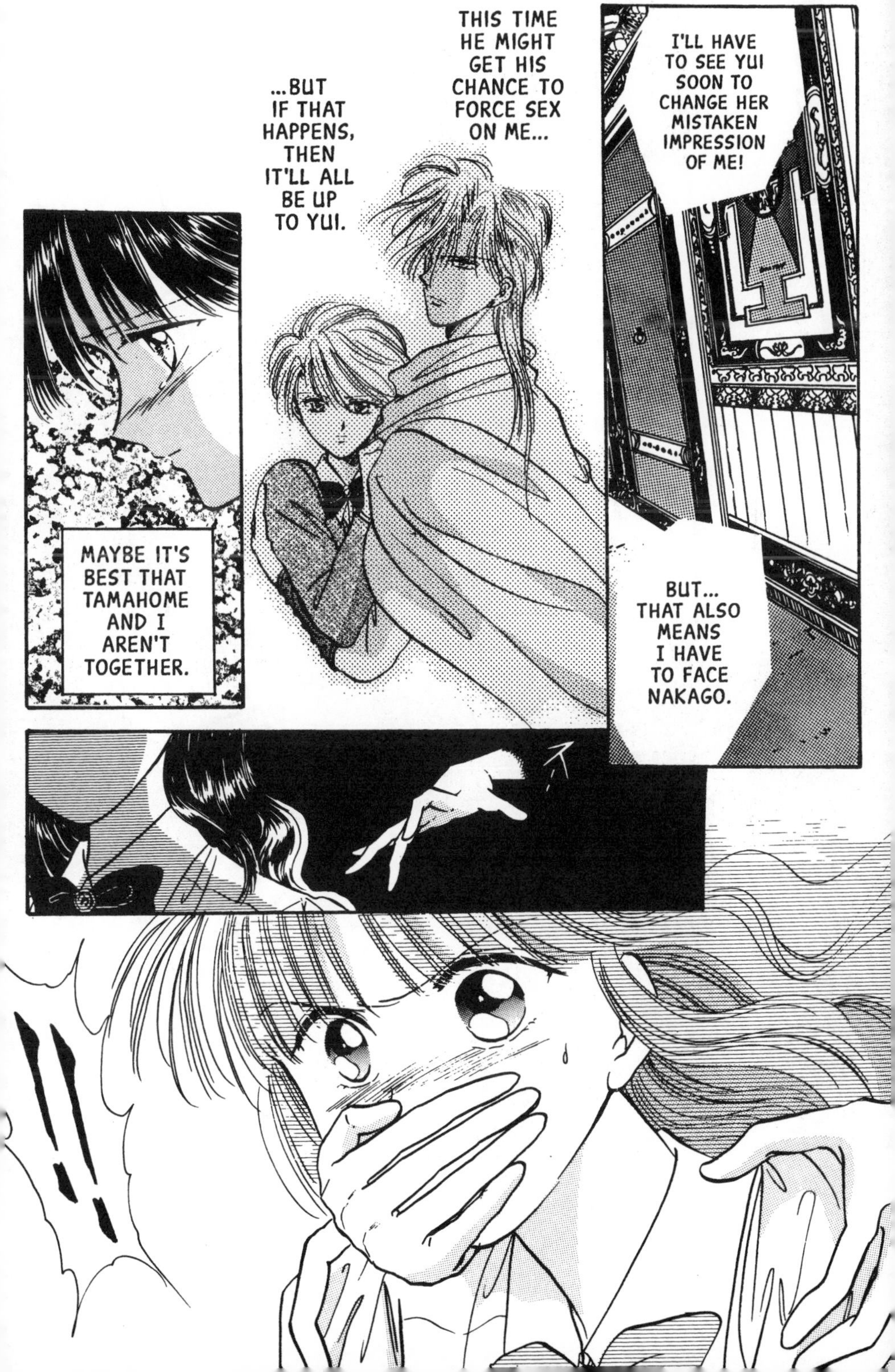
I'LL HAVE TO SEE YUI SOON TO CHANGE HER MISTAKEN IMPRESSION OF ME!
BUT... THAT ALSO MEANS I HAVE TO FACE NAKAGO.
THIS TIME HE MIGHT GET HIS CHANCE TO FORCE SEX ON ME...
...BUT IF THAT HAPPENS, THEN IT'LL ALL BE UP TO YUI.
MAYBE IT'S BEST THAT TAMAHOME AND I AREN'T TOGETHER.
!!

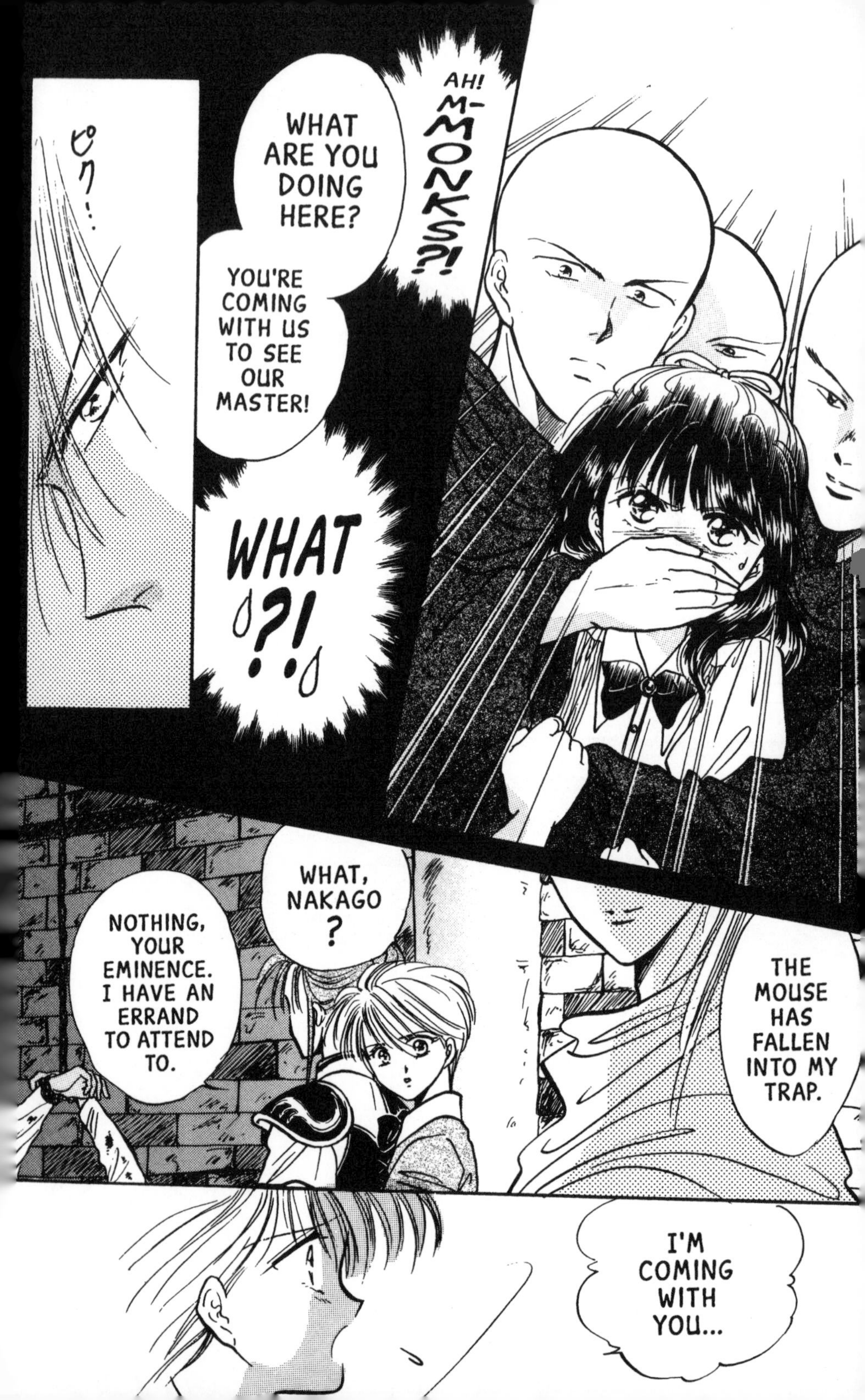
AH! M-MONKS?!
WHAT ARE YOU DOING HERE?
YOU'RE COMING WITH US TO SEE OUR MASTER!
WHAT?!
ピク…
THE MOUSE HAS FALLEN INTO MY TRAP.
WHAT, NAKAGO?
NOTHING, YOUR EMINENCE. I HAVE AN ERRAND TO ATTEND TO.
I'M COMING WITH YOU...

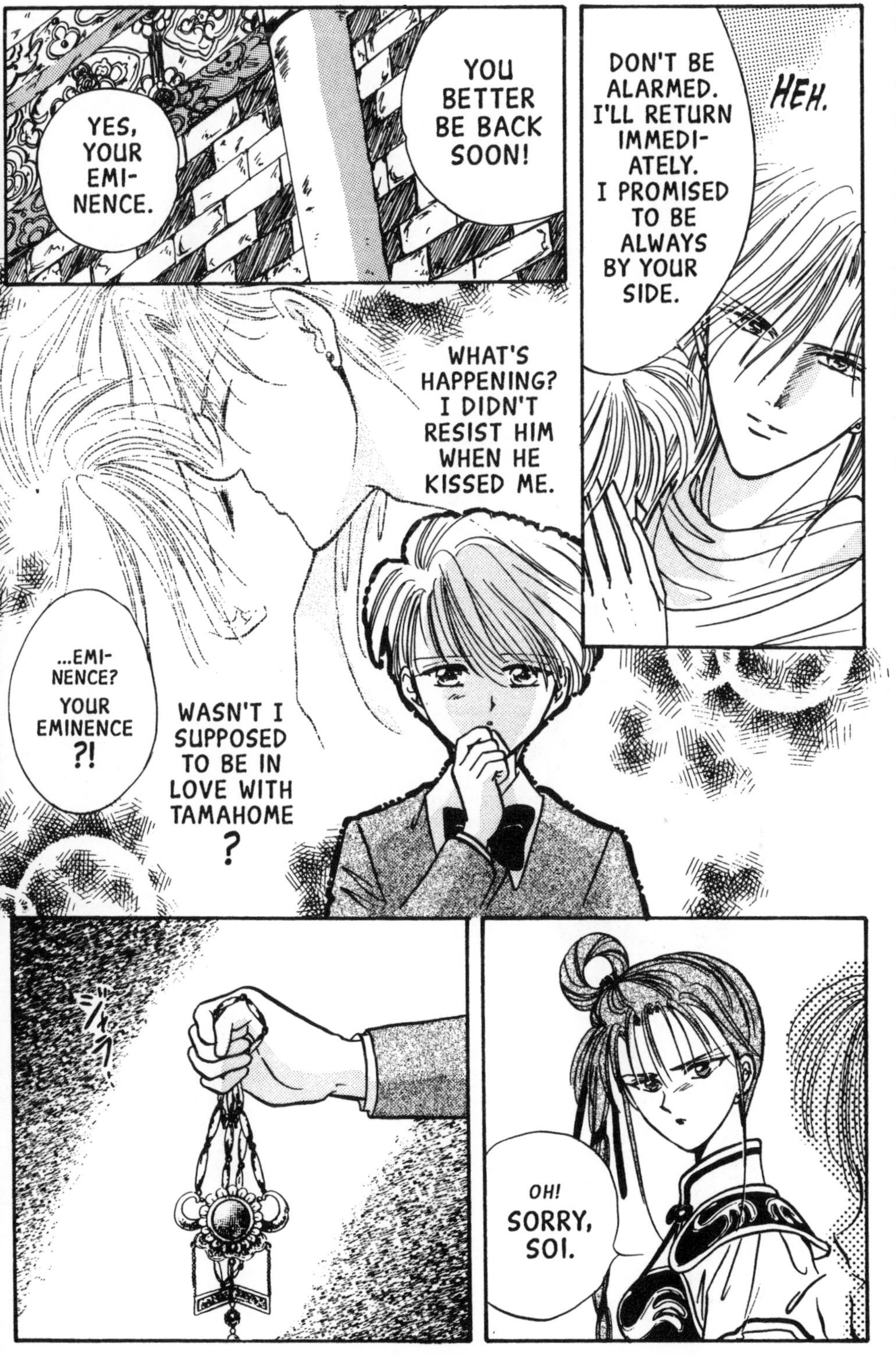
DON'T BE ALARMED. I'LL RETURN IMMEDI-ATELY. I PROMISED TO BE ALWAYS BY YOUR SIDE.
HEH.
YOU BETTER BE BACK SOON!
YES, YOUR EMI-NENCE.
WHAT'S HAPPENING? I DIDN'T RESIST HIM WHEN HE KISSED ME.
WASN'T I SUPPOSED TO BE IN LOVE WITH TAMAHOME ?
...EMI-NENCE? YOUR EMINENCE ?!
OH! SORRY, SOI.

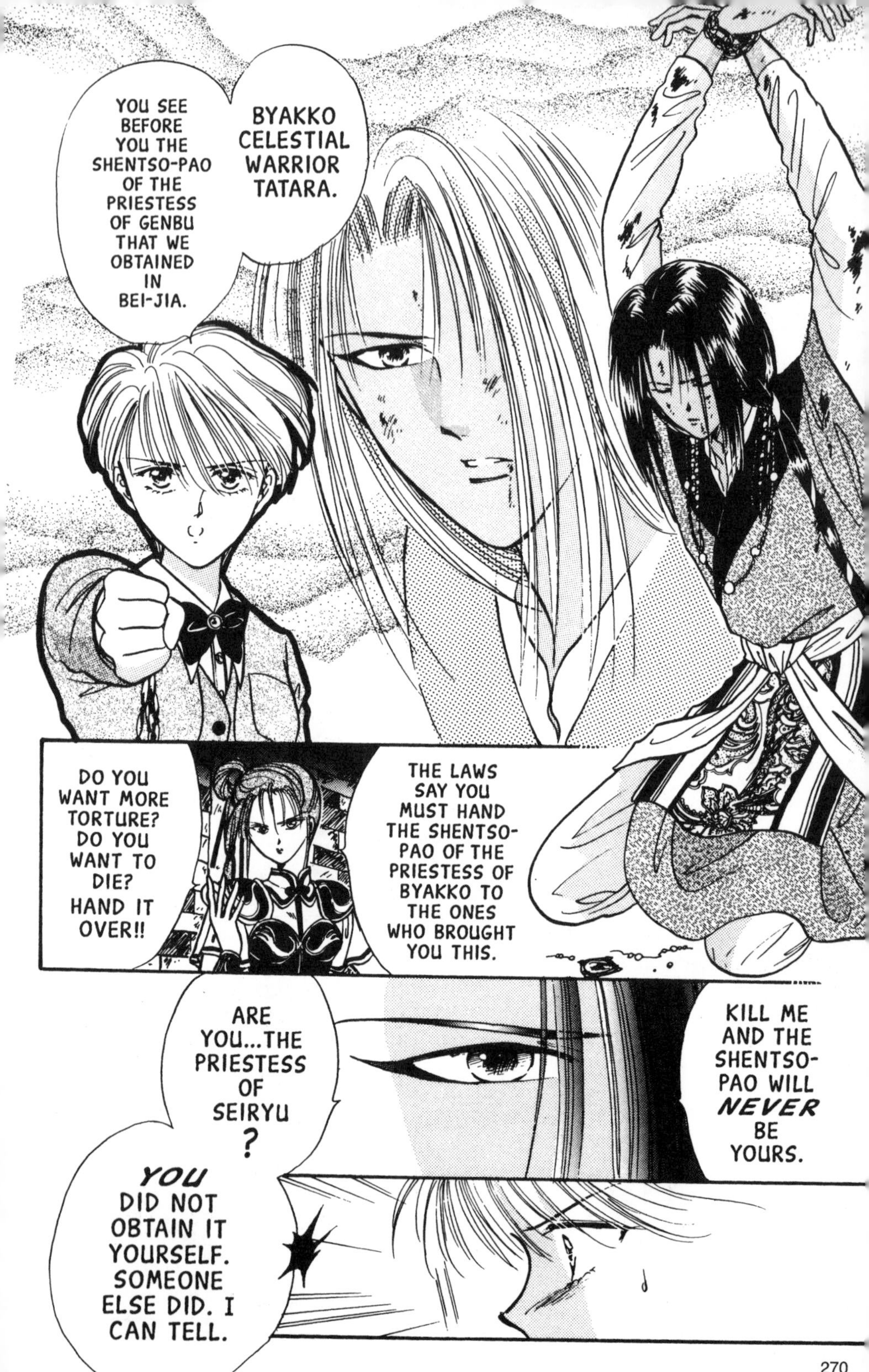
BYAKKO CELESTIAL WARRIOR TATARA.
YOU SEE BEFORE YOU THE SHENTSO-PAO OF THE PRIESTESS OF GENBU THAT WE OBTAINED IN BEI-JIA.
THE LAWS SAY YOU MUST HAND THE SHENTSO-PAO OF THE PRIESTESS OF BYAKKO TO THE ONES WHO BROUGHT YOU THIS.
DO YOU WANT MORE TORTURE? DO YOU WANT TO DIE? HAND IT OVER!!
KILL ME AND THE SHENTSO-PAO WILL *NEVER* BE YOURS.
ARE YOU...THE PRIESTESS OF SEIRYU?
YOU DID NOT OBTAIN IT YOURSELF. SOMEONE ELSE DID. I CAN TELL.

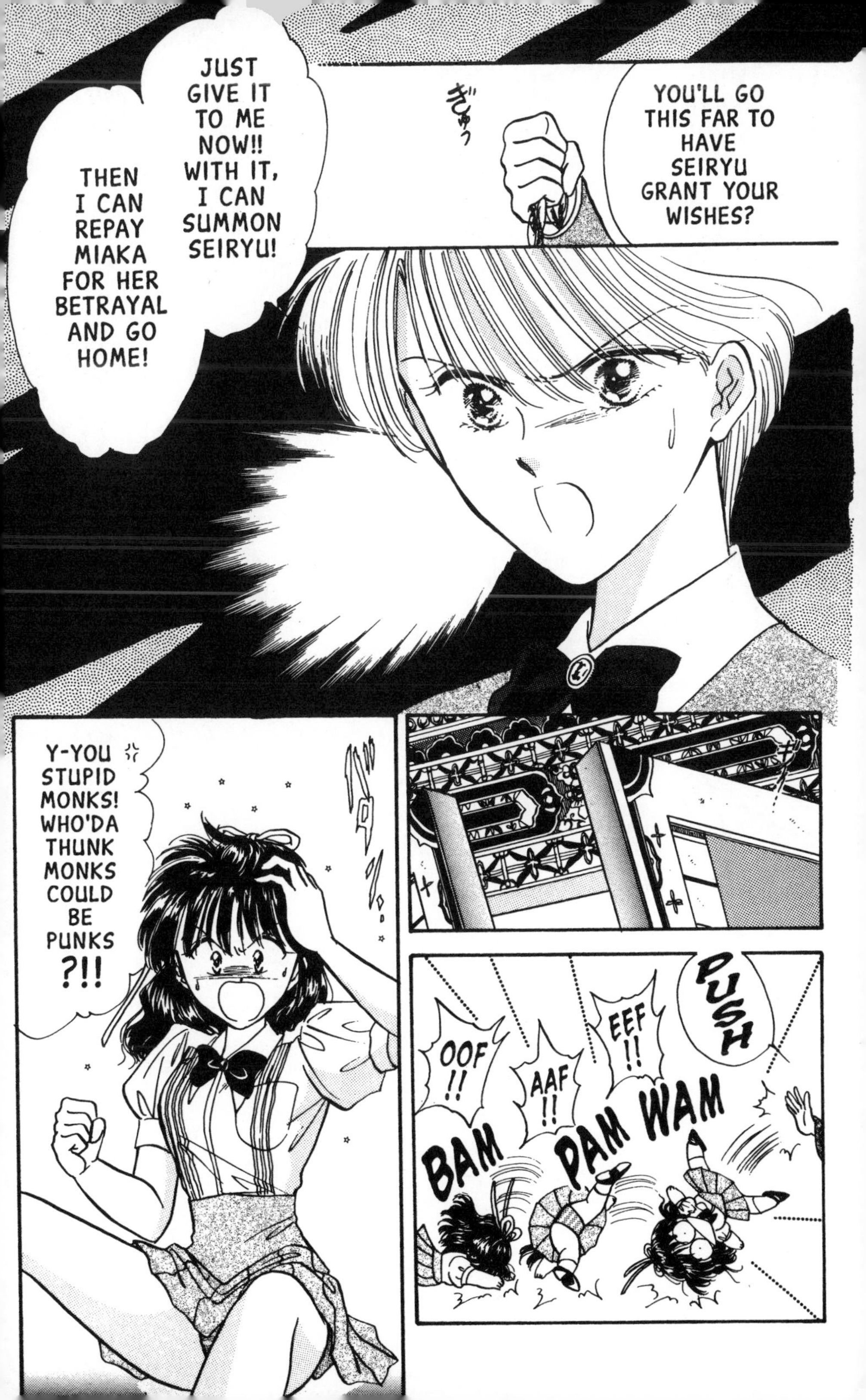

ぎゅっ
YOU'LL GO THIS FAR TO HAVE SEIRYU GRANT YOUR WISHES?
JUST GIVE IT TO ME NOW!! WITH IT, I CAN SUMMON SEIRYU!
THEN I CAN REPAY MIAKA FOR HER BETRAYAL AND GO HOME!
PUSH
EEF !!
AAF !!
OOF !!
WAM
PAM
BAM
Y-YOU STUPID MONKS! WHO'DA THUNK MONKS COULD BE PUNKS ?!!

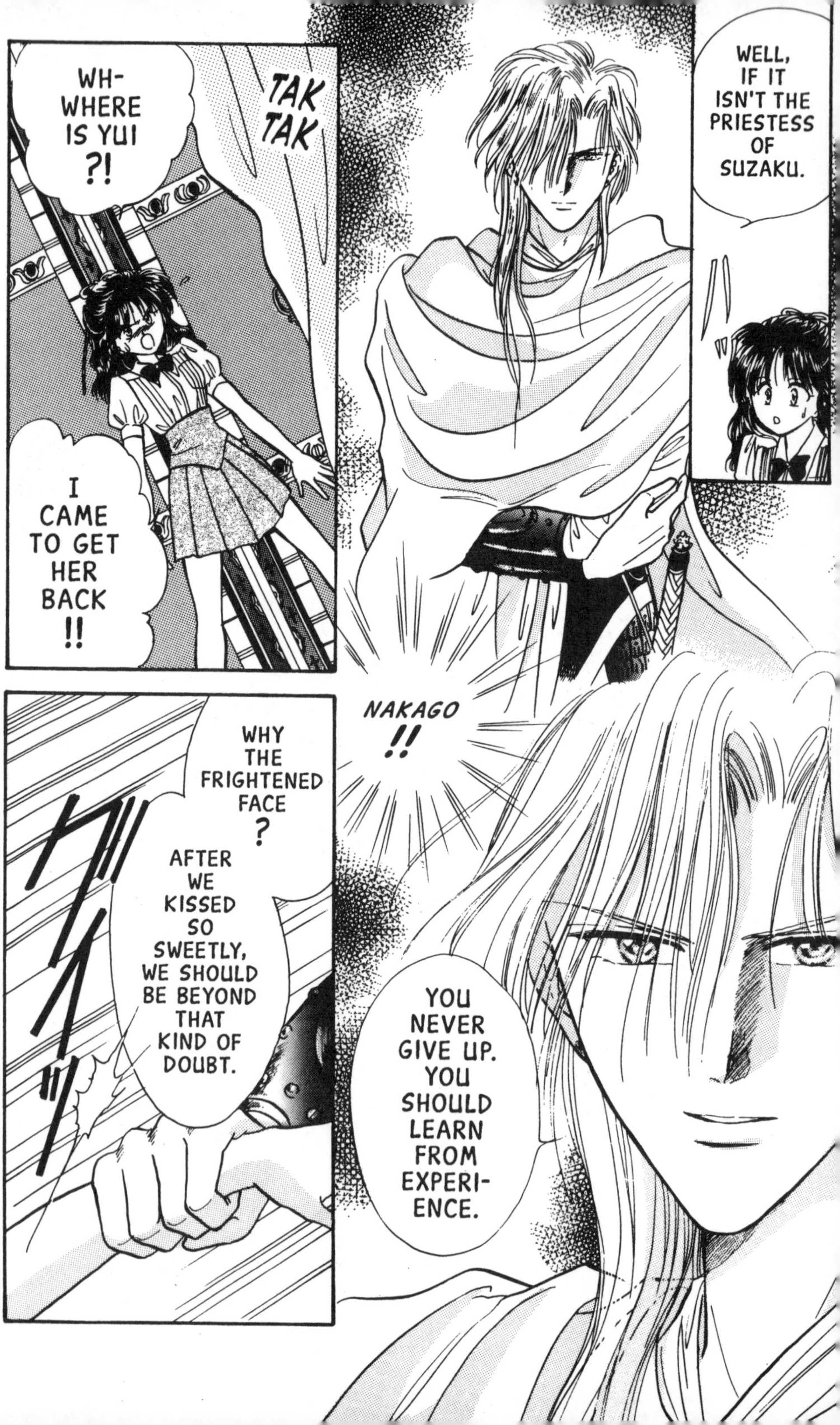

WELL, IF IT ISN'T THE PRIESTESS OF SUZAKU.
TAK TAK
WH-WHERE IS YUI ?!
I CAME TO GET HER BACK !!
NAKAGO !!
YOU NEVER GIVE UP. YOU SHOULD LEARN FROM EXPERI-ENCE.
WHY THE FRIGHTENED FACE ?
AFTER WE KISSED SO SWEETLY, WE SHOULD BE BEYOND THAT KIND OF DOUBT.

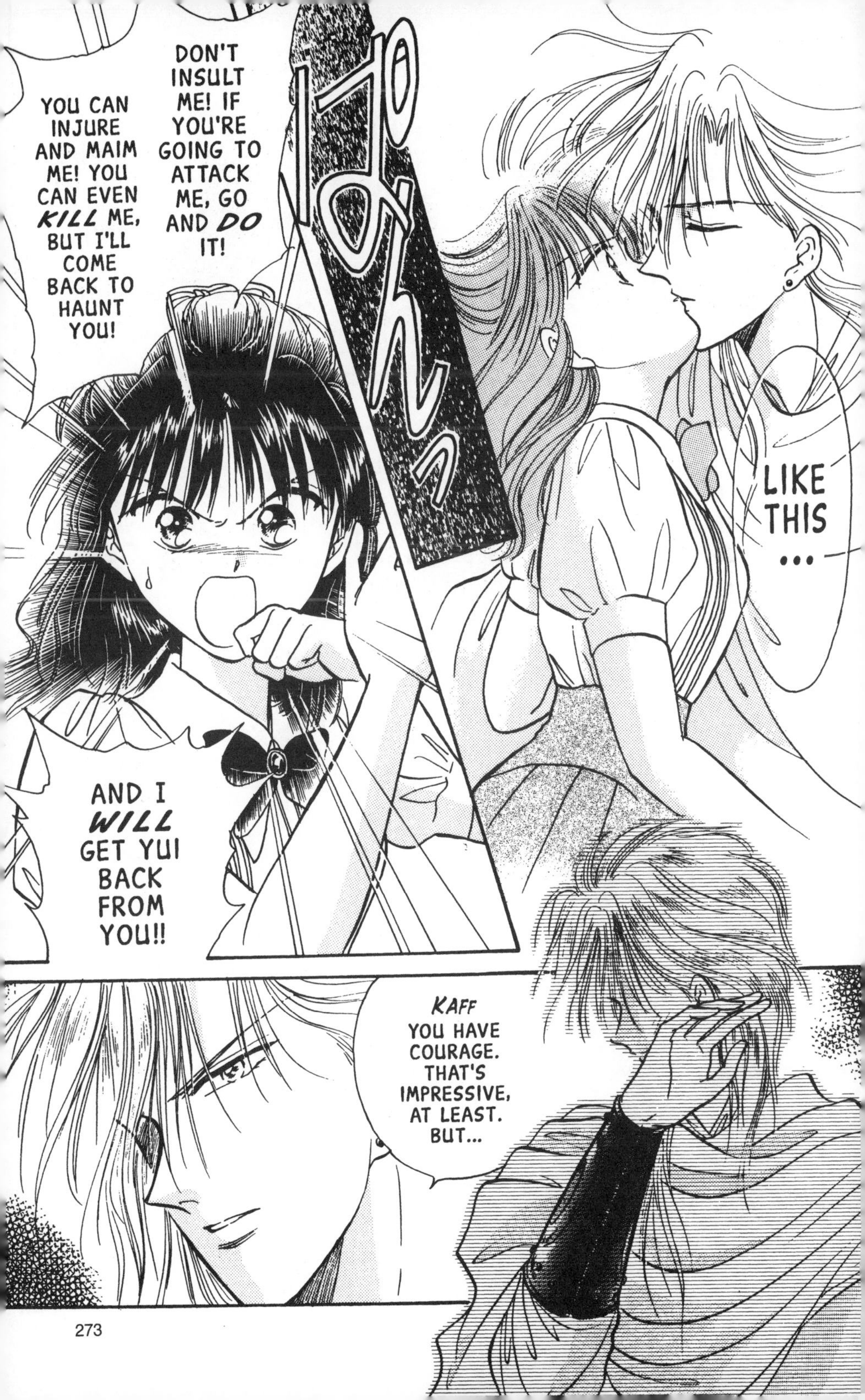
LIKE THIS...
DON'T INSULT ME! IF YOU'RE GOING TO ATTACK ME, GO AND *DO* IT!
YOU CAN INJURE AND MAIM ME! YOU CAN EVEN *KILL* ME, BUT I'LL COME BACK TO HAUNT YOU!
AND I *WILL* GET YUI BACK FROM YOU!!
KAFF YOU HAVE COURAGE. THAT'S IMPRESSIVE, AT LEAST. BUT...

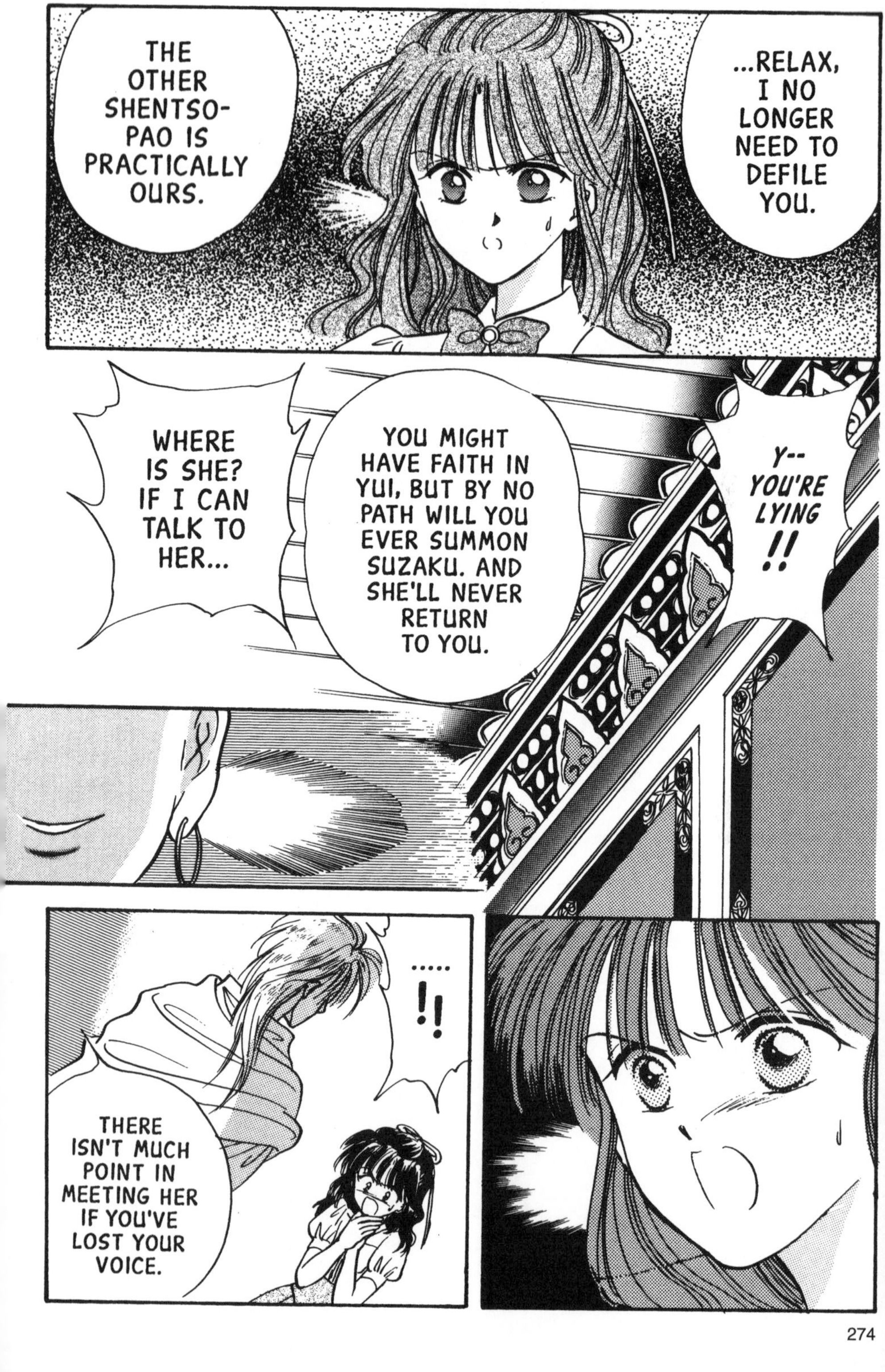
...RELAX, I NO LONGER NEED TO DEFILE YOU.
THE OTHER SHENTSO-PAO IS PRACTICALLY OURS.
Y-- YOU'RE LYING!!
WHERE IS SHE? IF I CAN TALK TO HER...
YOU MIGHT HAVE FAITH IN YUI, BUT BY NO PATH WILL YOU EVER SUMMON SUZAKU. AND SHE'LL NEVER RETURN TO YOU.
......!!
THERE ISN'T MUCH POINT IN MEETING HER IF YOU'VE LOST YOUR VOICE.

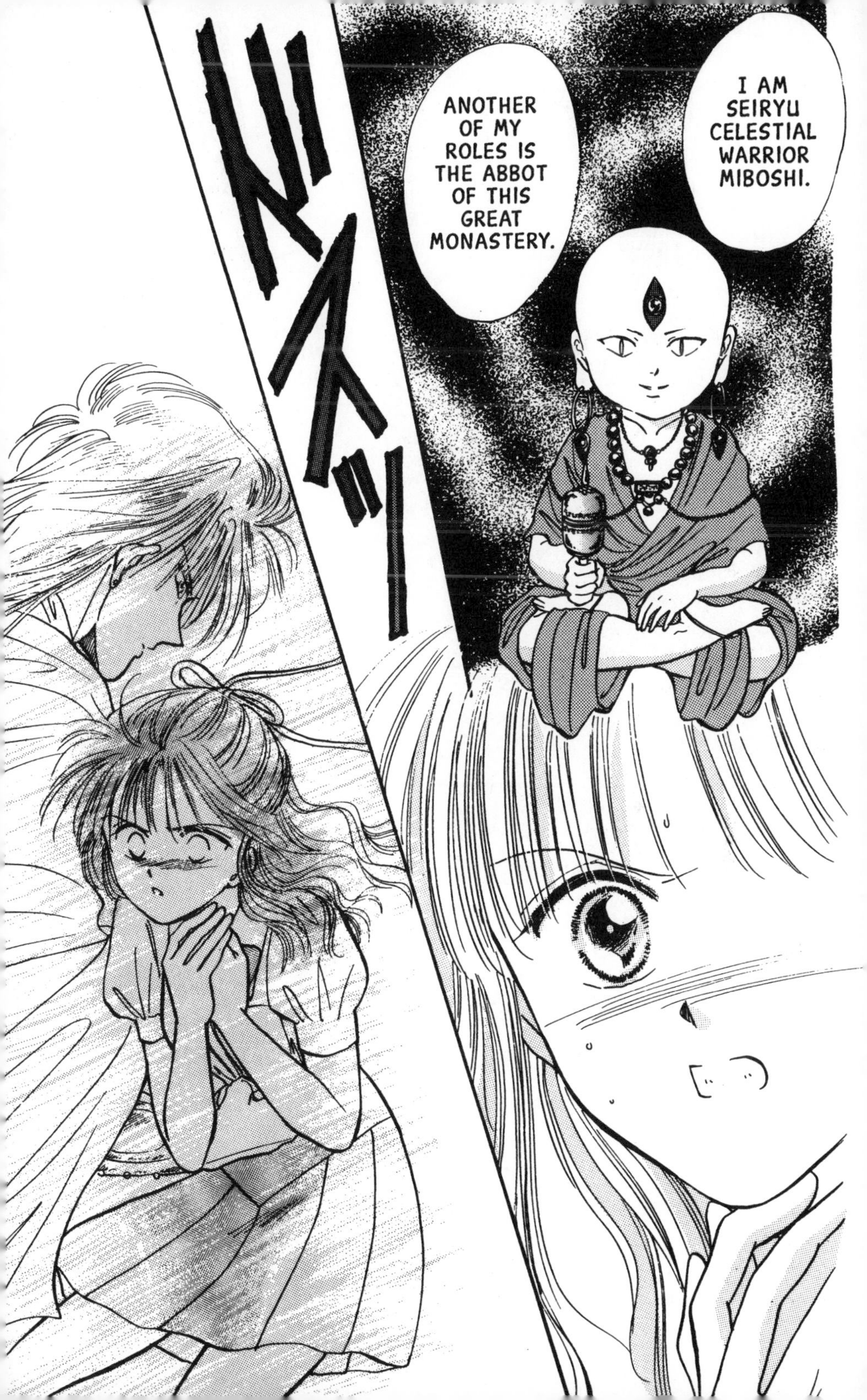
I AM SEIRYU CELESTIAL WARRIOR MIBOSHI.
ANOTHER OF MY ROLES IS THE ABBOT OF THIS GREAT MONASTERY.

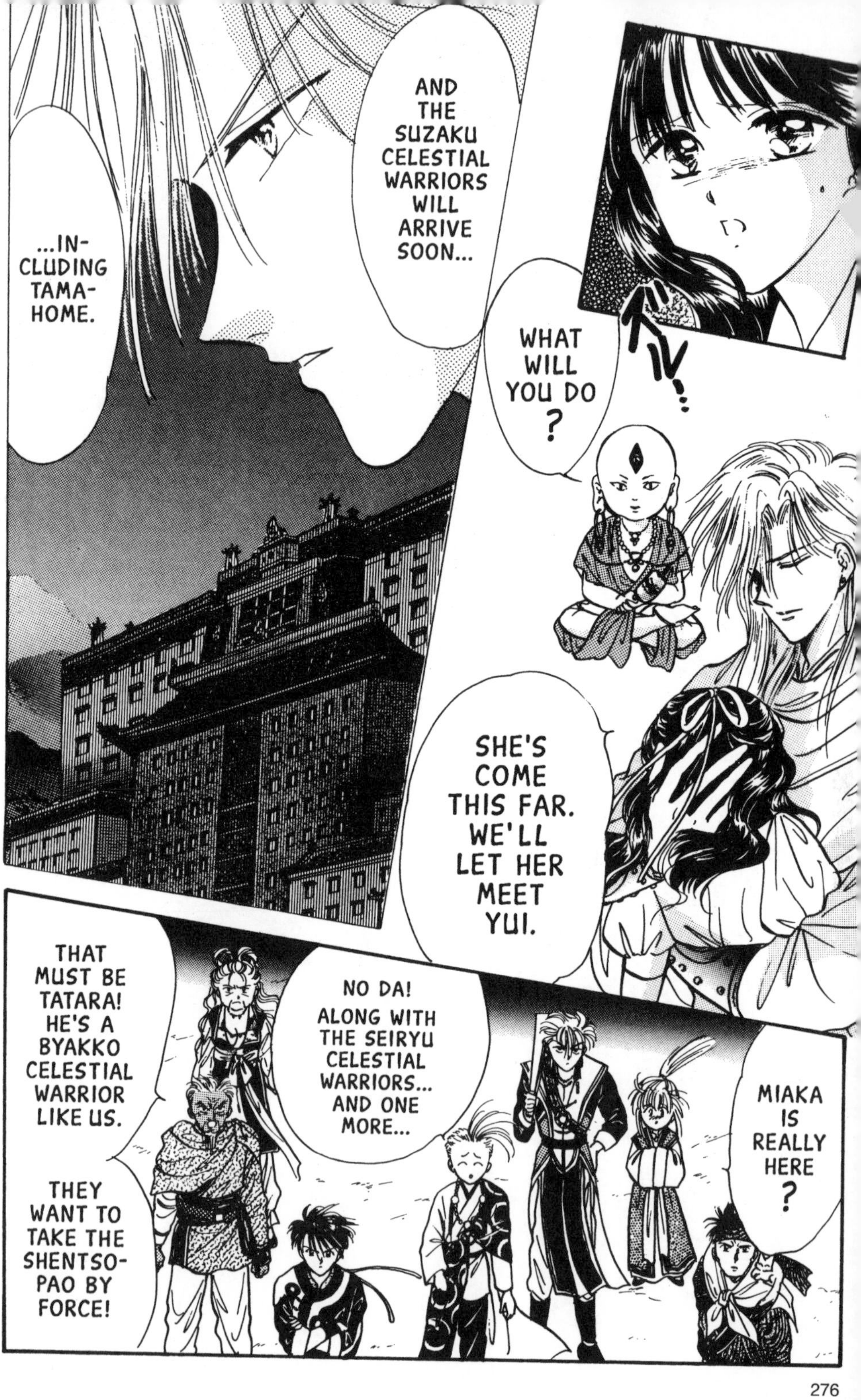

WHAT WILL YOU DO?
SHE'S COME THIS FAR. WE'LL LET HER MEET YUI.
AND THE SUZAKU CELESTIAL WARRIORS WILL ARRIVE SOON...
...INCLUDING TAMAHOME.
MIAKA IS REALLY HERE?
NO DA! ALONG WITH THE SEIRYU CELESTIAL WARRIORS... AND ONE MORE...
THAT MUST BE TATARA! HE'S A BYAKKO CELESTIAL WARRIOR LIKE US.
THEY WANT TO TAKE THE SHENTSO-PAO BY FORCE!

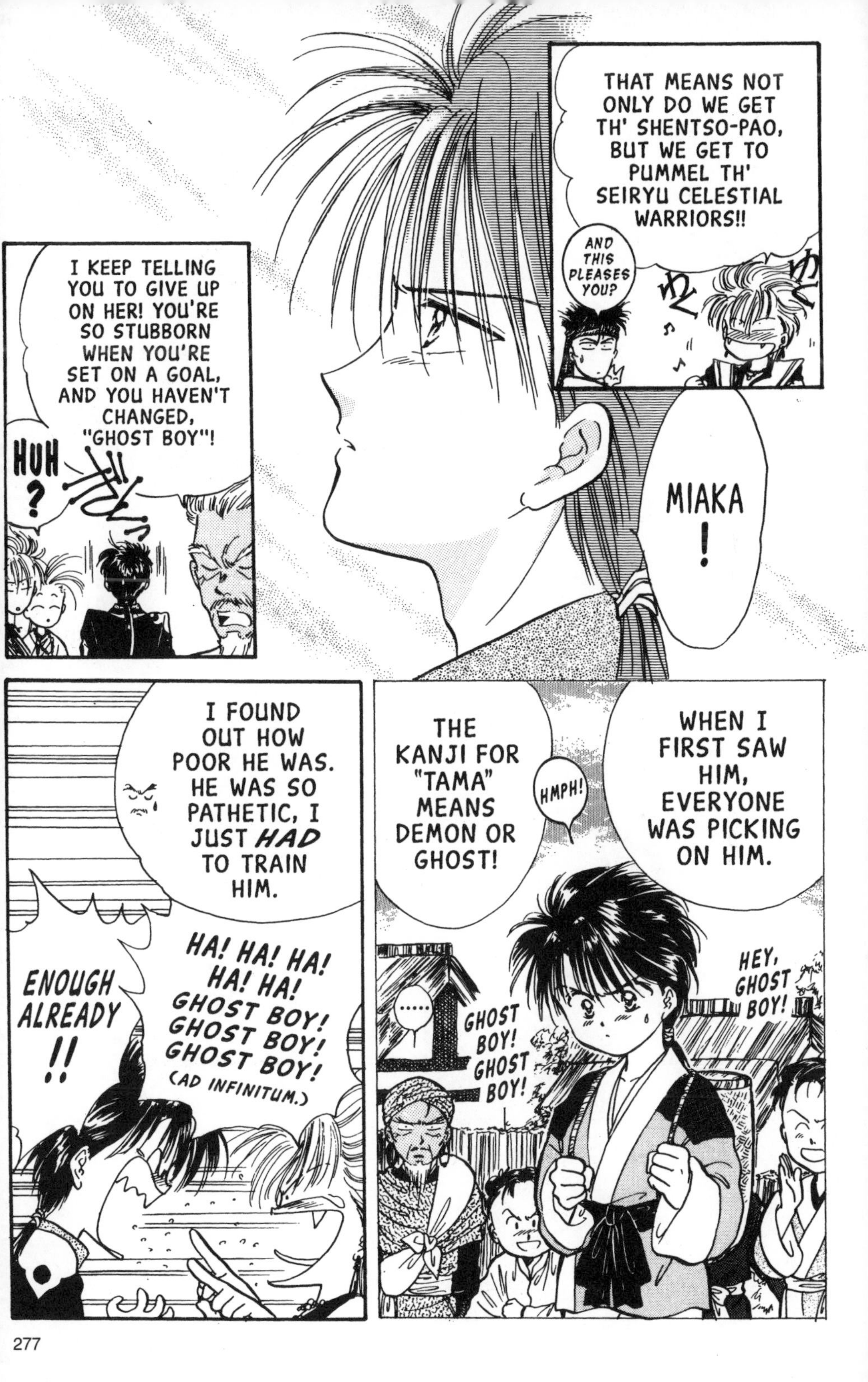

THAT MEANS NOT ONLY DO WE GET TH' SHENTSO-PAO, BUT WE GET TO PUMMEL TH' SEIRYU CELESTIAL WARRIORS!!
AND THIS PLEASES YOU?
MIAKA!
I KEEP TELLING YOU TO GIVE UP ON HER! YOU'RE SO STUBBORN WHEN YOU'RE SET ON A GOAL, AND YOU HAVEN'T CHANGED, "GHOST BOY"!
HUH?
WHEN I FIRST SAW HIM, EVERYONE WAS PICKING ON HIM.
HMPH!
THE KANJI FOR "TAMA" MEANS DEMON OR GHOST!
HEY, GHOST BOY!
GHOST BOY! GHOST BOY!
......
I FOUND OUT HOW POOR HE WAS. HE WAS SO PATHETIC, I JUST *HAD* TO TRAIN HIM.
HA! HA! HA! HA! HA! GHOST BOY! GHOST BOY! GHOST BOY! (AD INFINITUM.)
ENOUGH ALREADY!!

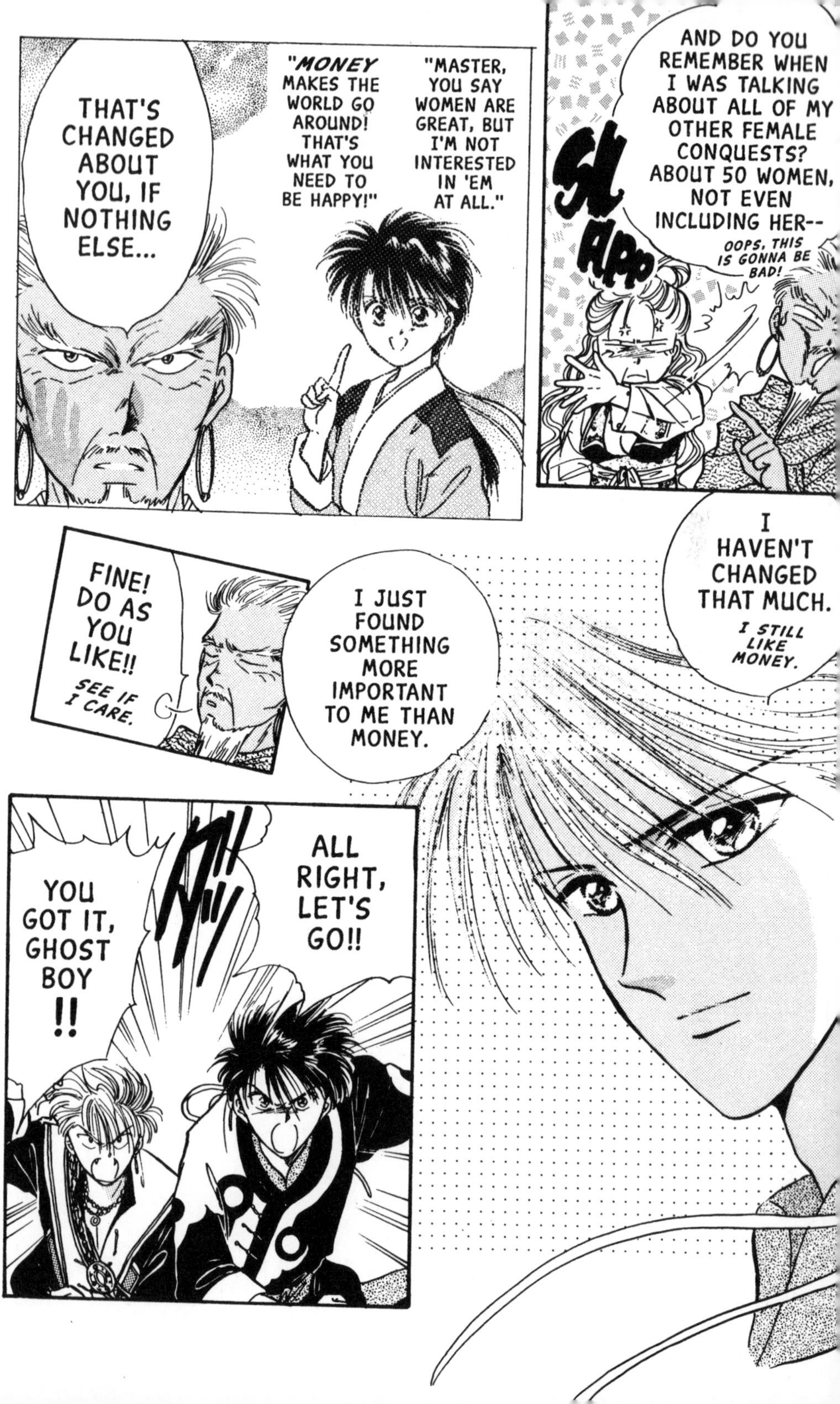
AND DO YOU REMEMBER WHEN I WAS TALKING ABOUT ALL OF MY OTHER FEMALE CONQUESTS? ABOUT 50 WOMEN, NOT EVEN INCLUDING HER--
OOPS, THIS IS GONNA BE BAD!
SLAPP
"MASTER, YOU SAY WOMEN ARE GREAT, BUT I'M NOT INTERESTED IN 'EM AT ALL."
"MONEY MAKES THE WORLD GO AROUND! THAT'S WHAT YOU NEED TO BE HAPPY!"
THAT'S CHANGED ABOUT YOU, IF NOTHING ELSE...
I HAVEN'T CHANGED THAT MUCH.
I STILL LIKE MONEY.
I JUST FOUND SOMETHING MORE IMPORTANT TO ME THAN MONEY.
FINE! DO AS YOU LIKE!!
SEE IF I CARE.
ALL RIGHT, LET'S GO!!
YOU GOT IT, GHOST BOY!!

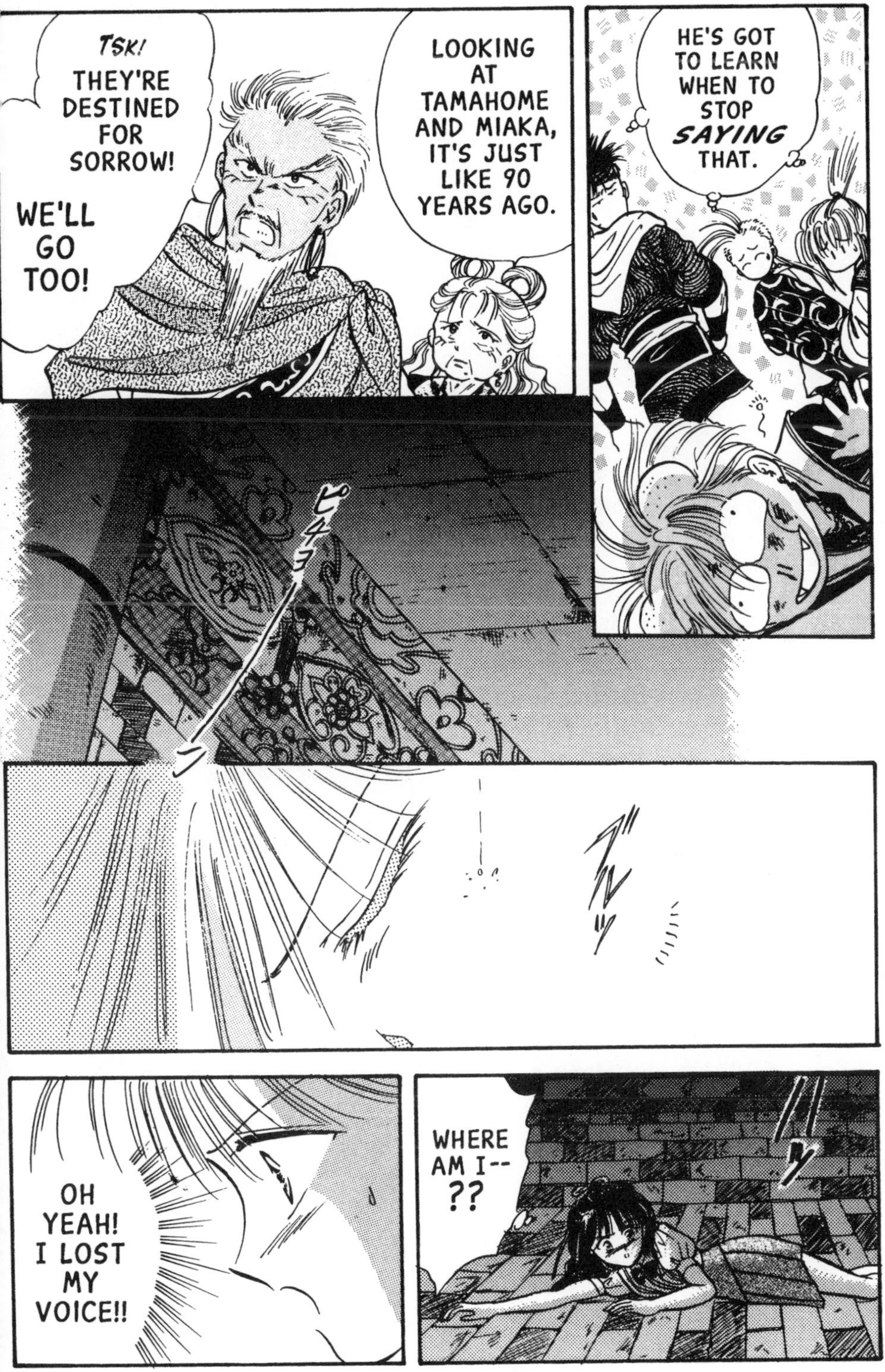
HE'S GOT TO LEARN WHEN TO STOP SAYING THAT.
LOOKING AT TAMAHOME AND MIAKA, IT'S JUST LIKE 90 YEARS AGO.
TSK! THEY'RE DESTINED FOR SORROW!
WE'LL GO TOO!
WHERE AM I--??
OH YEAH! I LOST MY VOICE!!

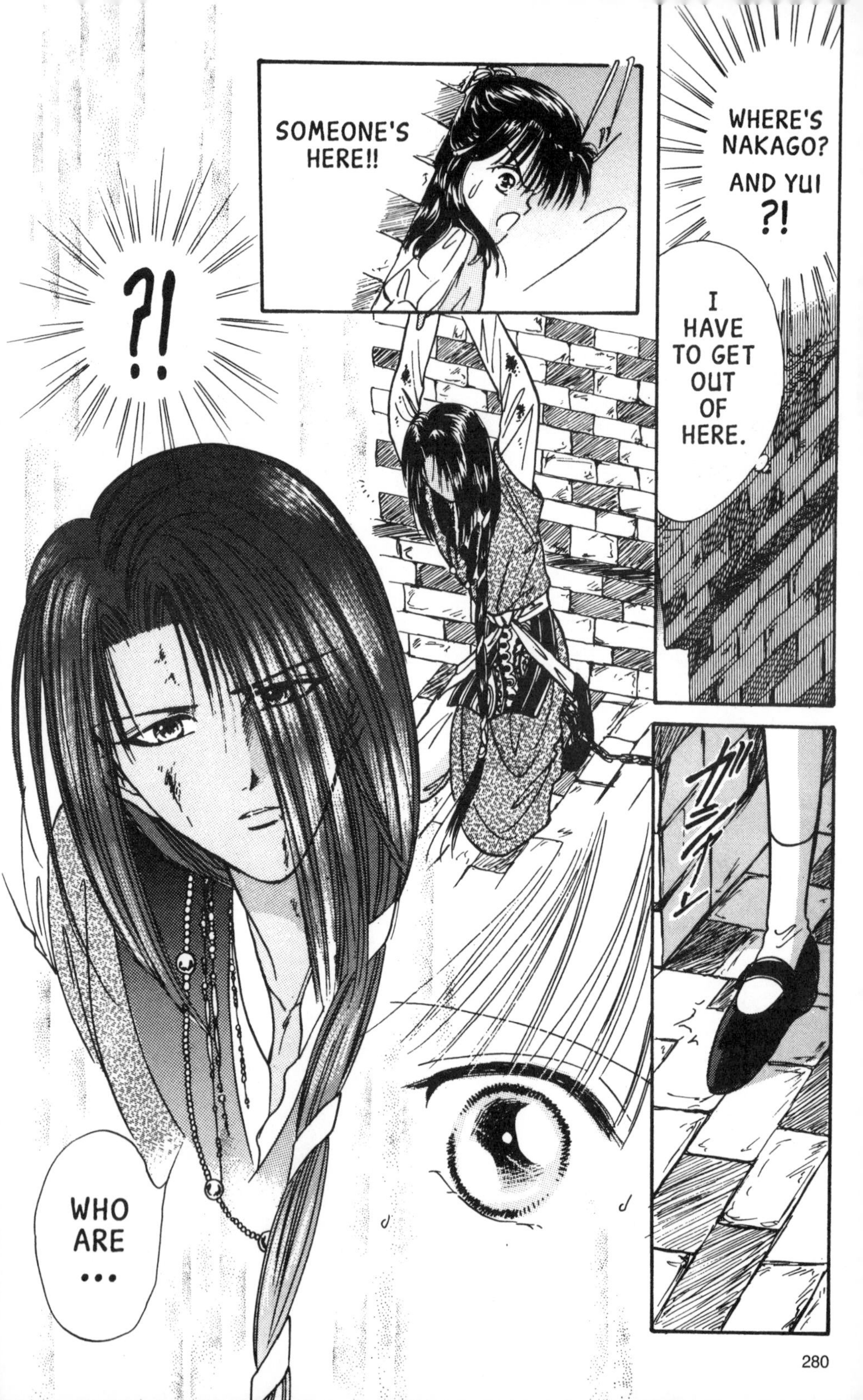
WHERE'S NAKAGO?
AND YUI ?!
I HAVE TO GET OUT OF HERE.
SOMEONE'S HERE!!
?!
WHO ARE ...

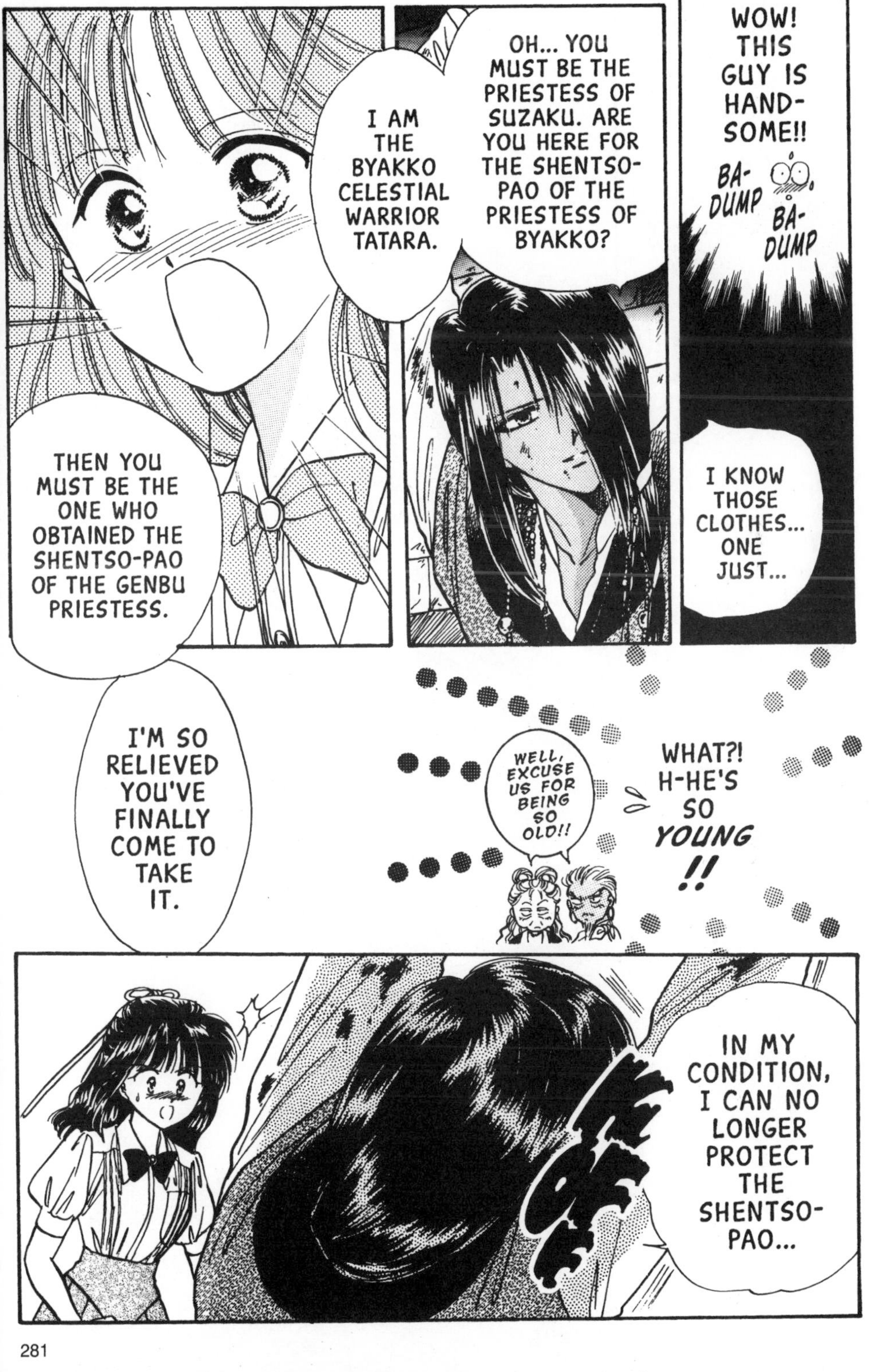

WOW! THIS GUY IS HANDSOME!!
BA-DUMP BA-DUMP
I KNOW THOSE CLOTHES... ONE JUST...
OH... YOU MUST BE THE PRIESTESS OF SUZAKU. ARE YOU HERE FOR THE SHENTSO-PAO OF THE PRIESTESS OF BYAKKO?
I AM THE BYAKKO CELESTIAL WARRIOR TATARA.
THEN YOU MUST BE THE ONE WHO OBTAINED THE SHENTSO-PAO OF THE GENBU PRIESTESS.
WHAT?! H-HE'S SO YOUNG!!
WELL, EXCUSE US FOR BEING SO OLD!!
I'M SO RELIEVED YOU'VE FINALLY COME TO TAKE IT.
IN MY CONDITION, I CAN NO LONGER PROTECT THE SHENTSO-PAO...

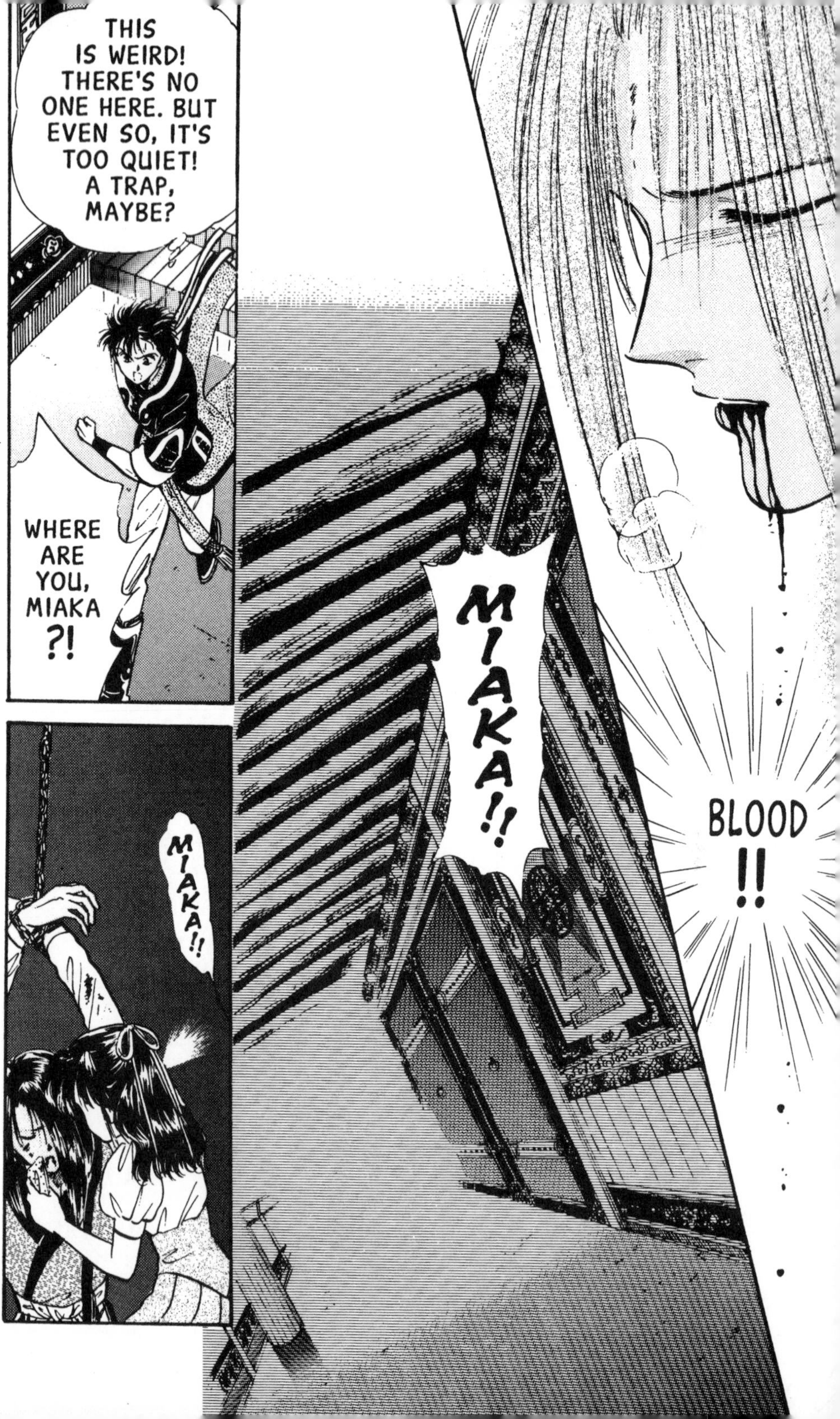
BLOOD !!
MIAKA!!
THIS IS WEIRD! THERE'S NO ONE HERE. BUT EVEN SO, IT'S TOO QUIET! A TRAP, MAYBE?
WHERE ARE YOU, MIAKA ?!
MIAKA!!

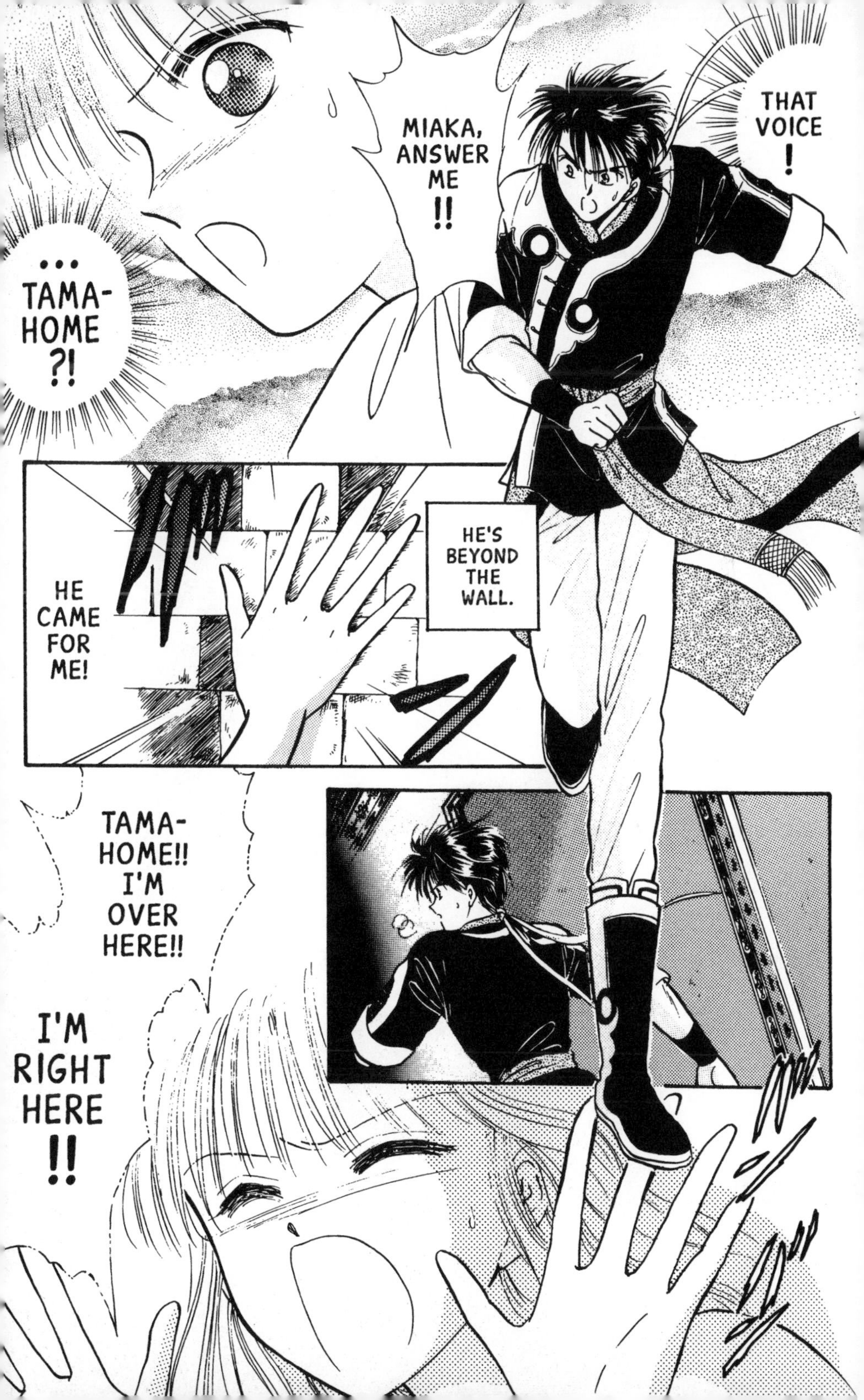
THAT VOICE!
MIAKA, ANSWER ME!!
...TAMA-HOME?!
HE'S BEYOND THE WALL.
HE CAME FOR ME!
TAMA-HOME!! I'M OVER HERE!!
I'M RIGHT HERE!!

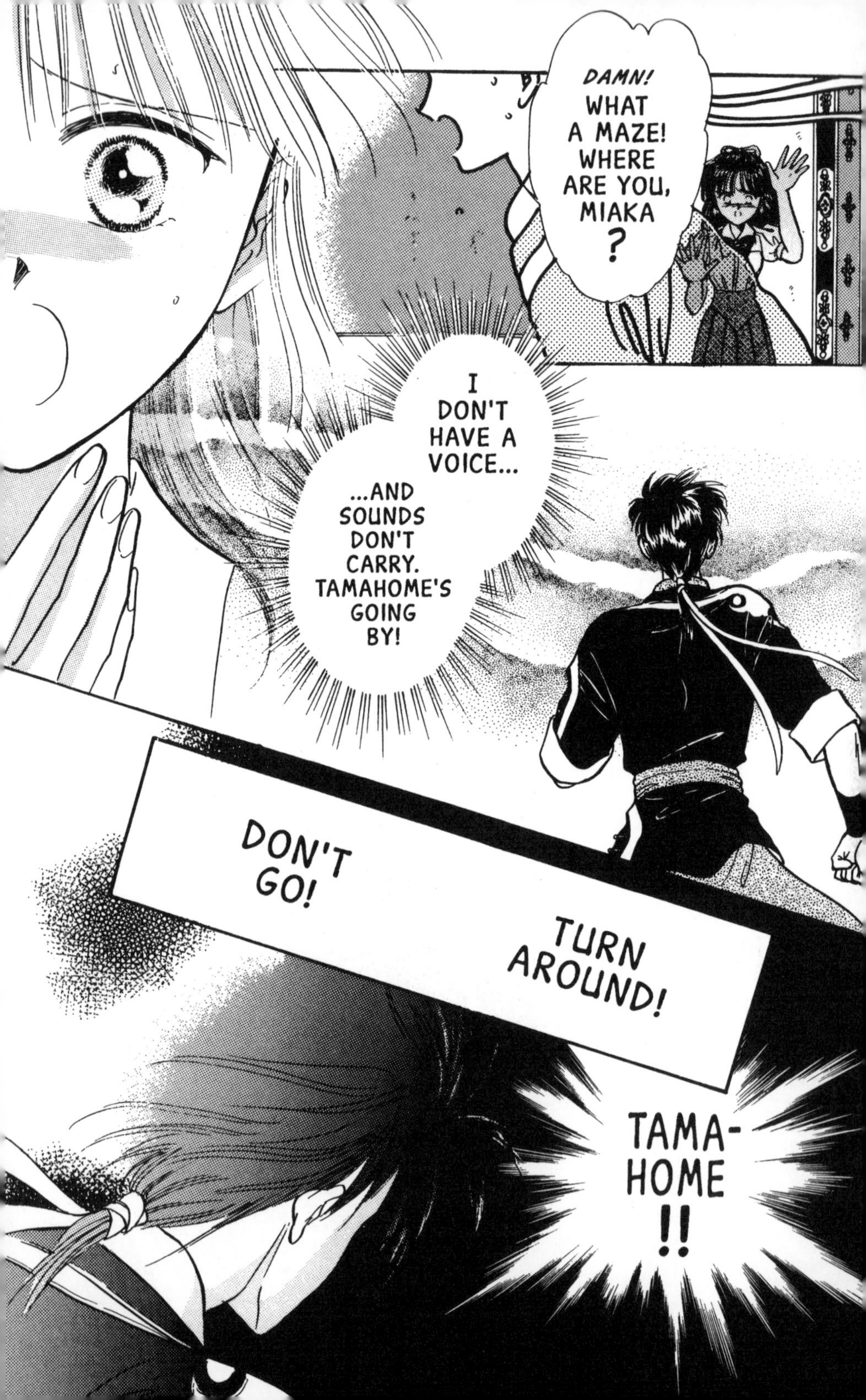
DAMN! WHAT A MAZE! WHERE ARE YOU, MIAKA?
I DON'T HAVE A VOICE...
...AND SOUNDS DON'T CARRY. TAMAHOME'S GOING BY!
DON'T GO!
TURN AROUND!
TAMA-HOME!!

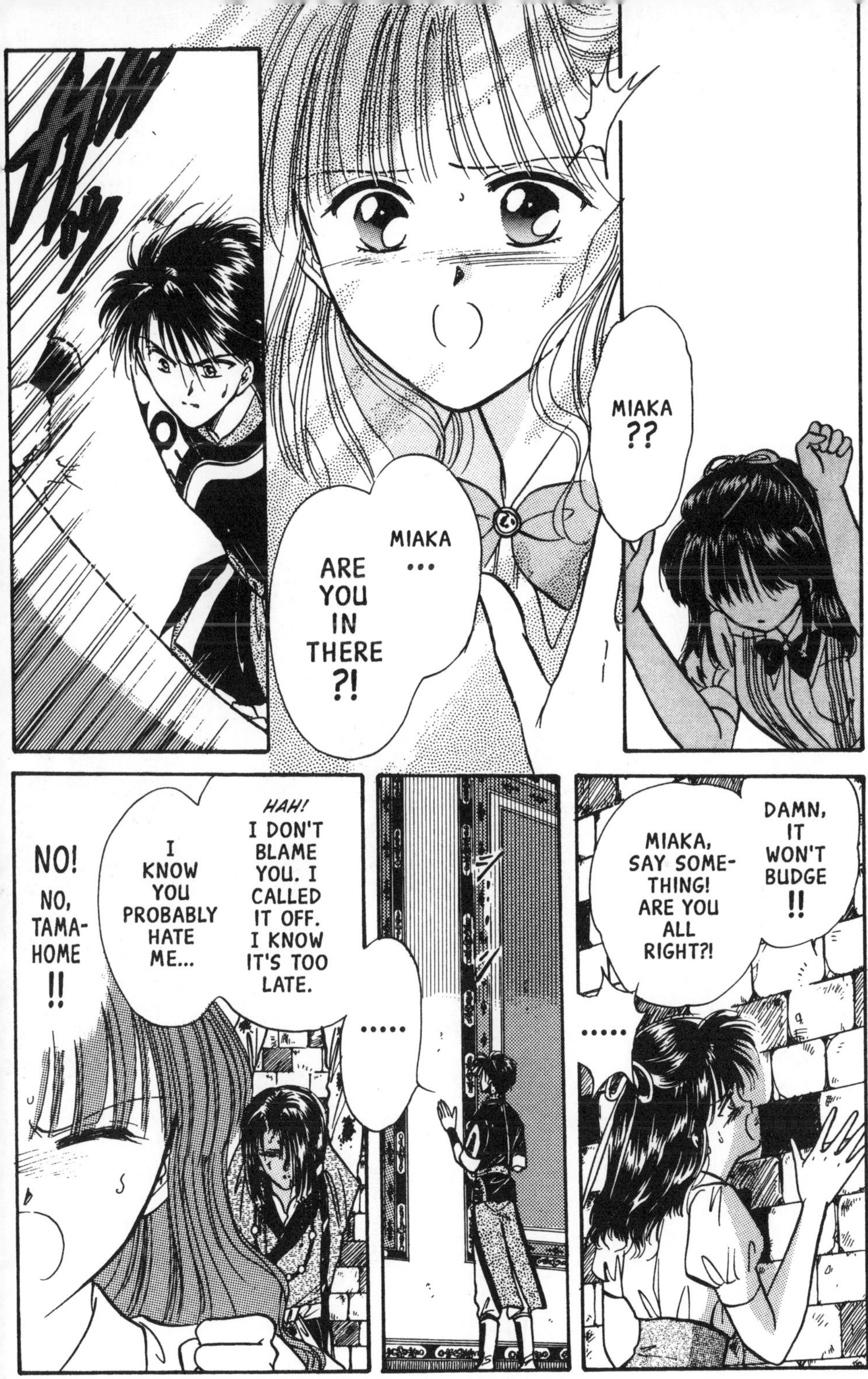
MIAKA ??
MIAKA... ARE YOU IN THERE ?!
DAMN, IT WON'T BUDGE !!
MIAKA, SAY SOME-THING! ARE YOU ALL RIGHT?!
.....
.....
HAH! I DON'T BLAME YOU. I CALLED IT OFF. I KNOW IT'S TOO LATE.
I KNOW YOU PROBABLY HATE ME...
NO! NO, TAMA-HOME !!

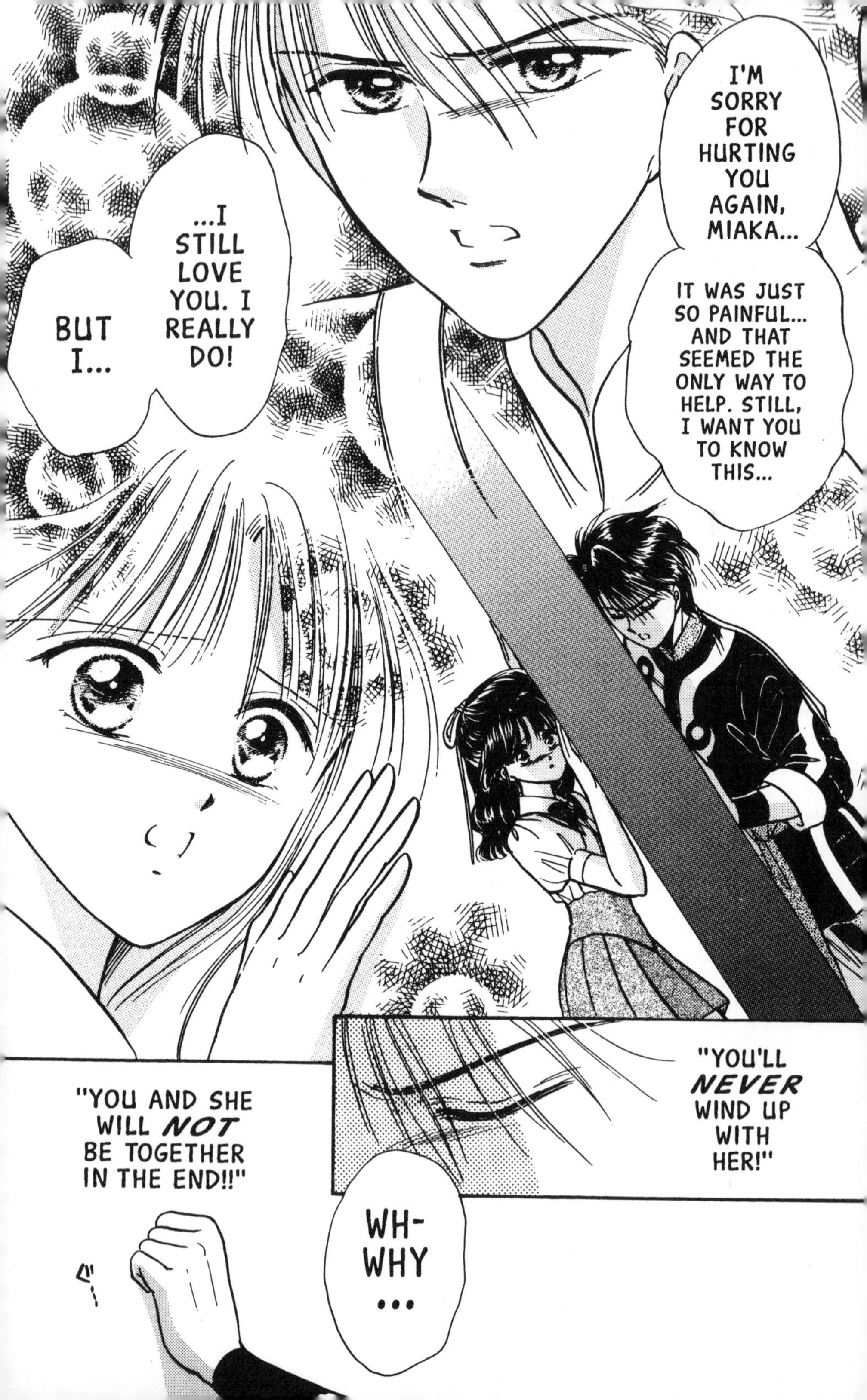
I'M SORRY FOR HURTING YOU AGAIN, MIAKA...
IT WAS JUST SO PAINFUL... AND THAT SEEMED THE ONLY WAY TO HELP. STILL, I WANT YOU TO KNOW THIS...
...I STILL LOVE YOU. I REALLY DO!
BUT I...
"YOU'LL *NEVER* WIND UP WITH HER!"
"YOU AND SHE WILL *NOT* BE TOGETHER IN THE END!!"
WH-WHY...

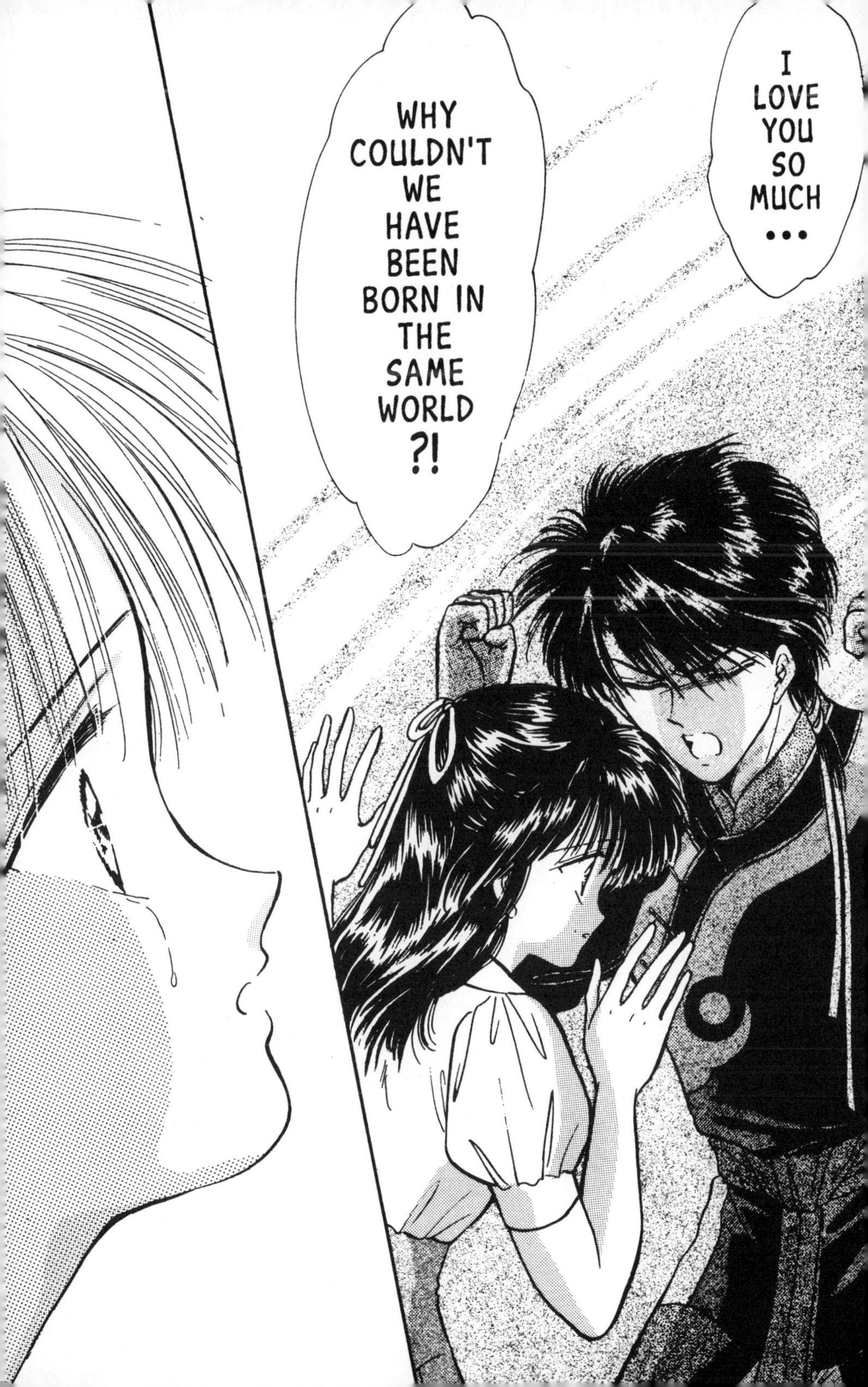
I LOVE YOU SO MUCH...
WHY COULDN'T WE HAVE BEEN BORN IN THE SAME WORLD?!

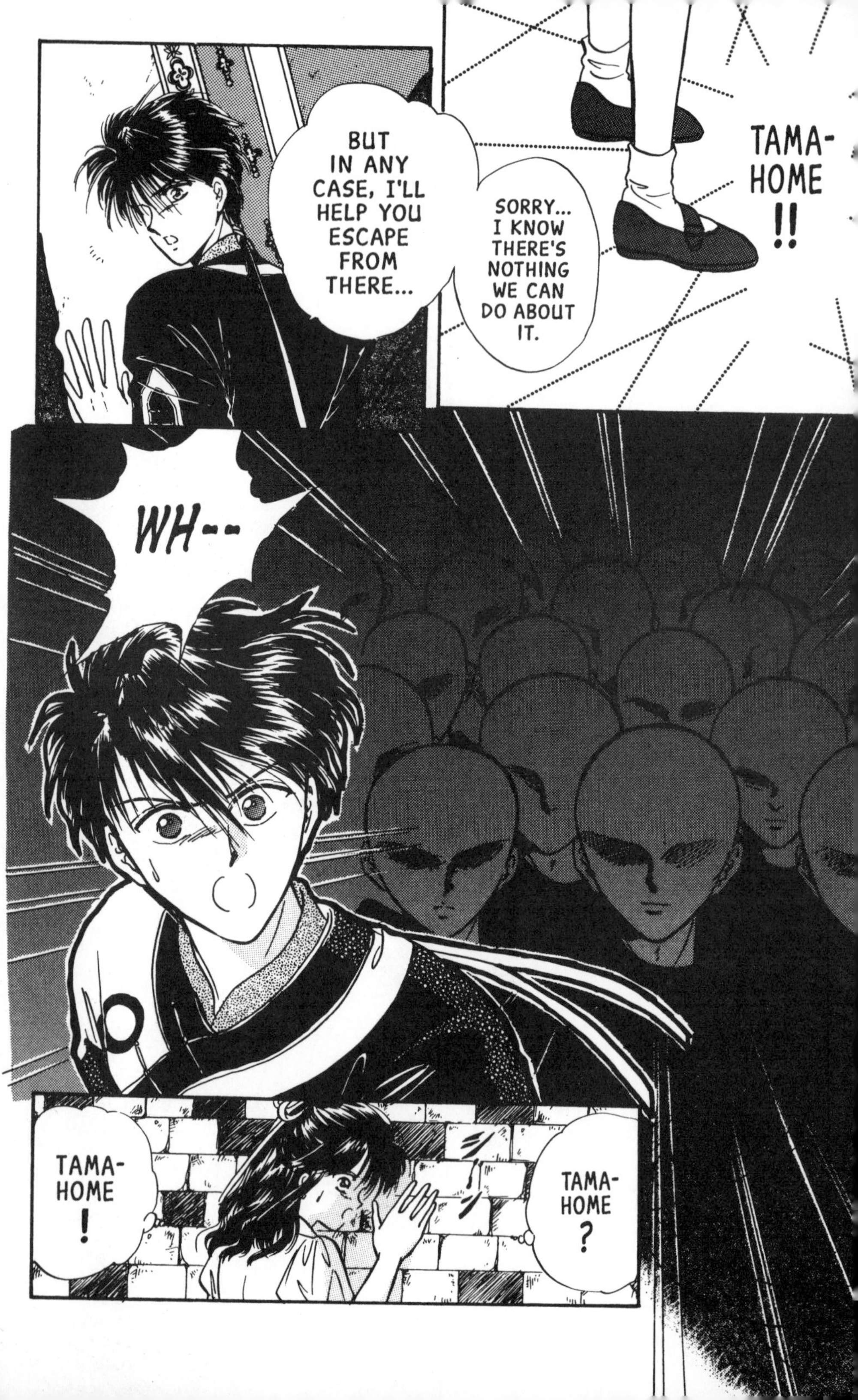
TAMA-HOME!!
SORRY... I KNOW THERE'S NOTHING WE CAN DO ABOUT IT.
BUT IN ANY CASE, I'LL HELP YOU ESCAPE FROM THERE...
WH--
TAMA-HOME?
TAMA-HOME!

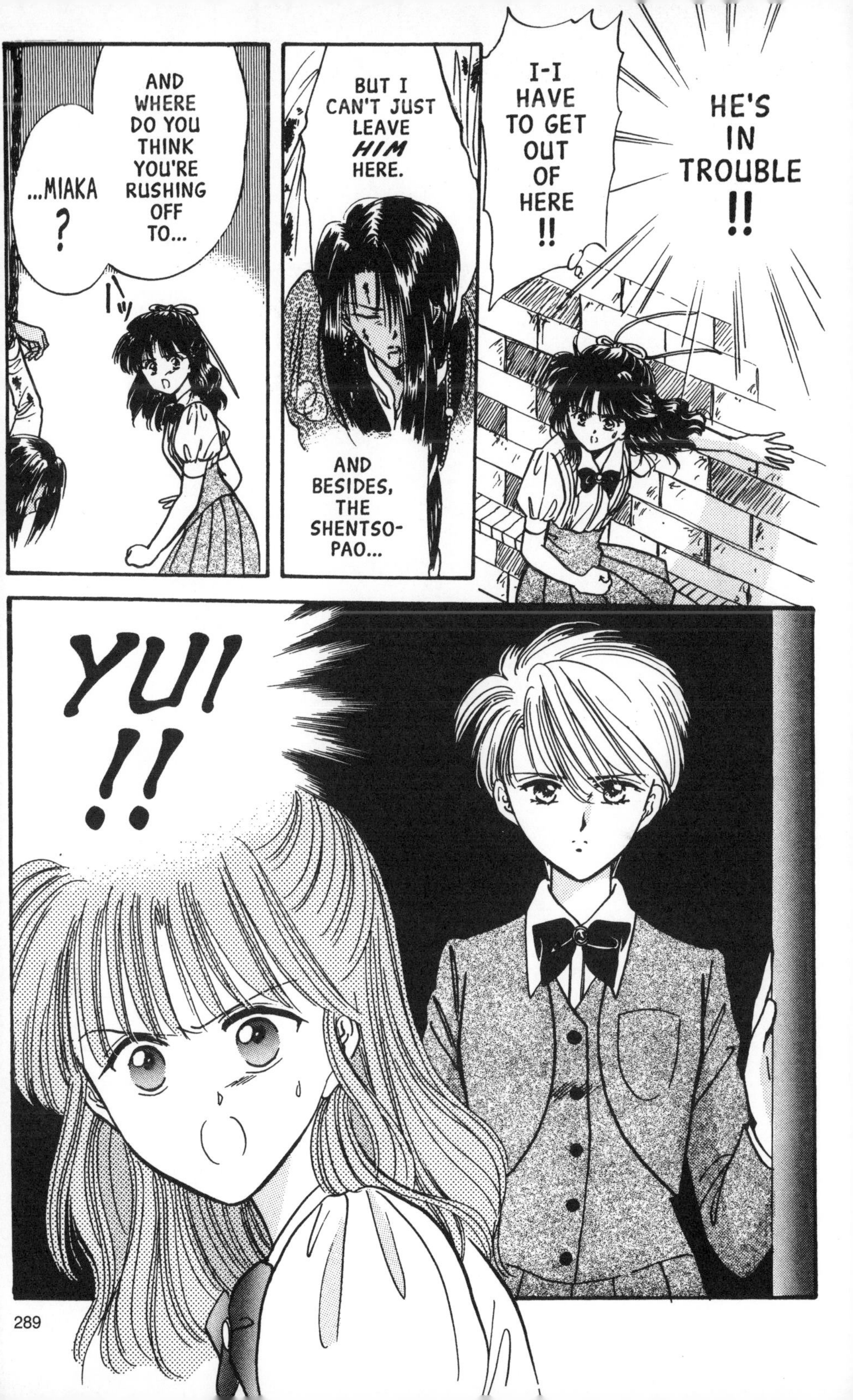
HE'S IN TROUBLE!!
I-I HAVE TO GET OUT OF HERE!!
BUT I CAN'T JUST LEAVE *HIM* HERE.
AND BESIDES, THE SHENTSO-PAO...
AND WHERE DO YOU THINK YOU'RE RUSHING OFF TO...
...MIAKA?
YUI!!

Chapter Sixty-Three
The Truth Revealed

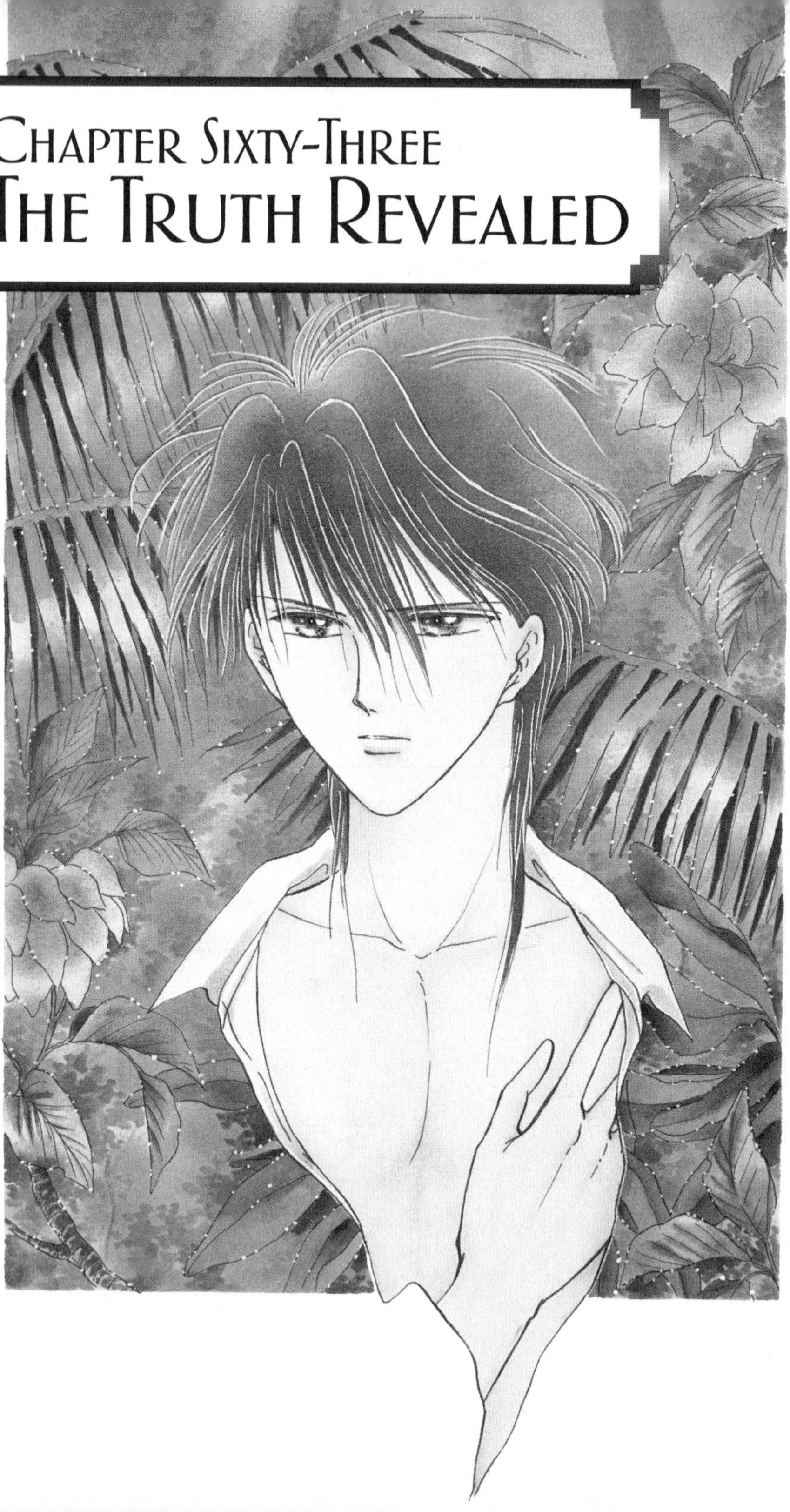

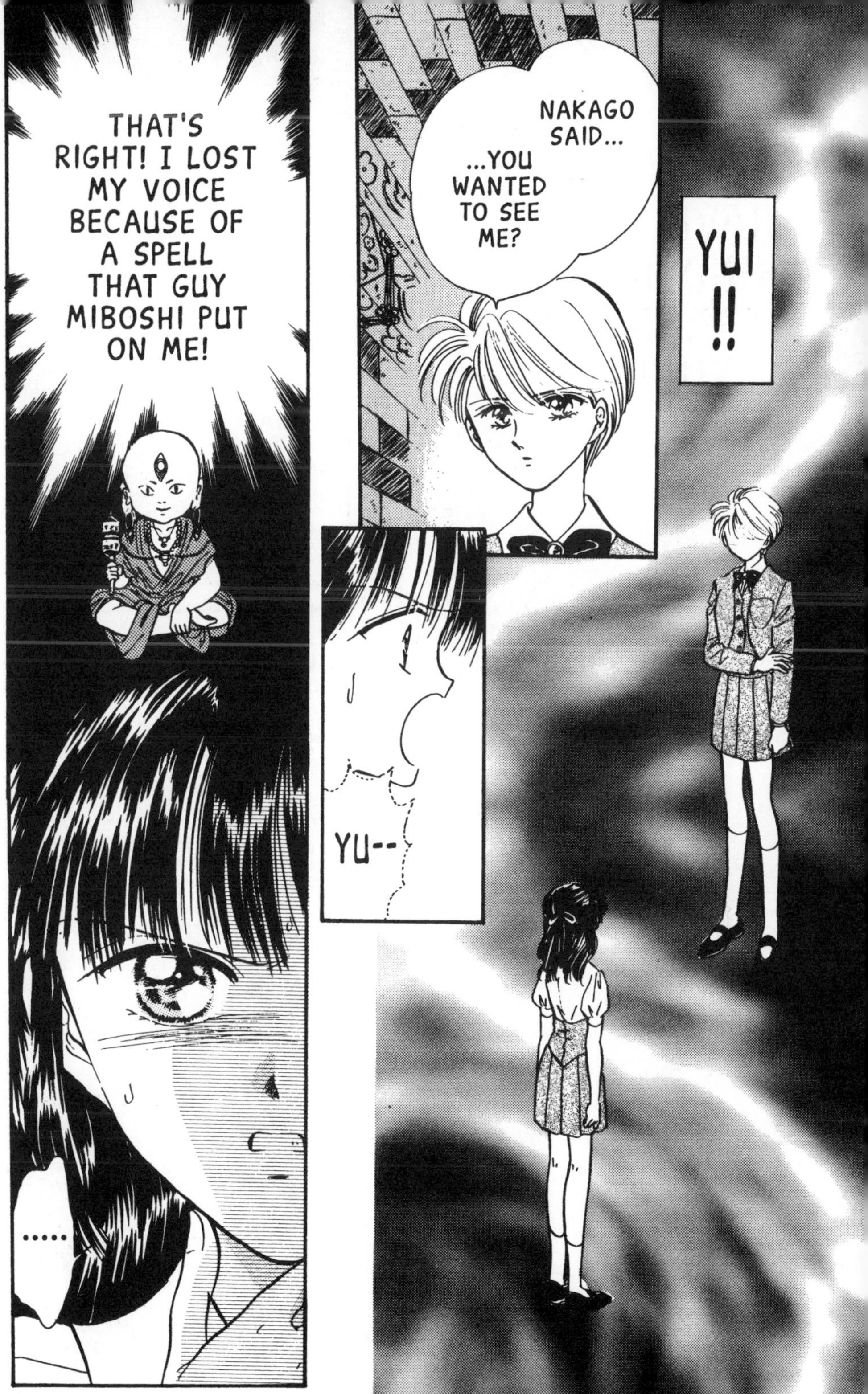
YUI !!
NAKAGO SAID...
...YOU WANTED TO SEE ME?
THAT'S RIGHT! I LOST MY VOICE BECAUSE OF A SPELL THAT GUY MIBOSHI PUT ON ME!
YU--
.....

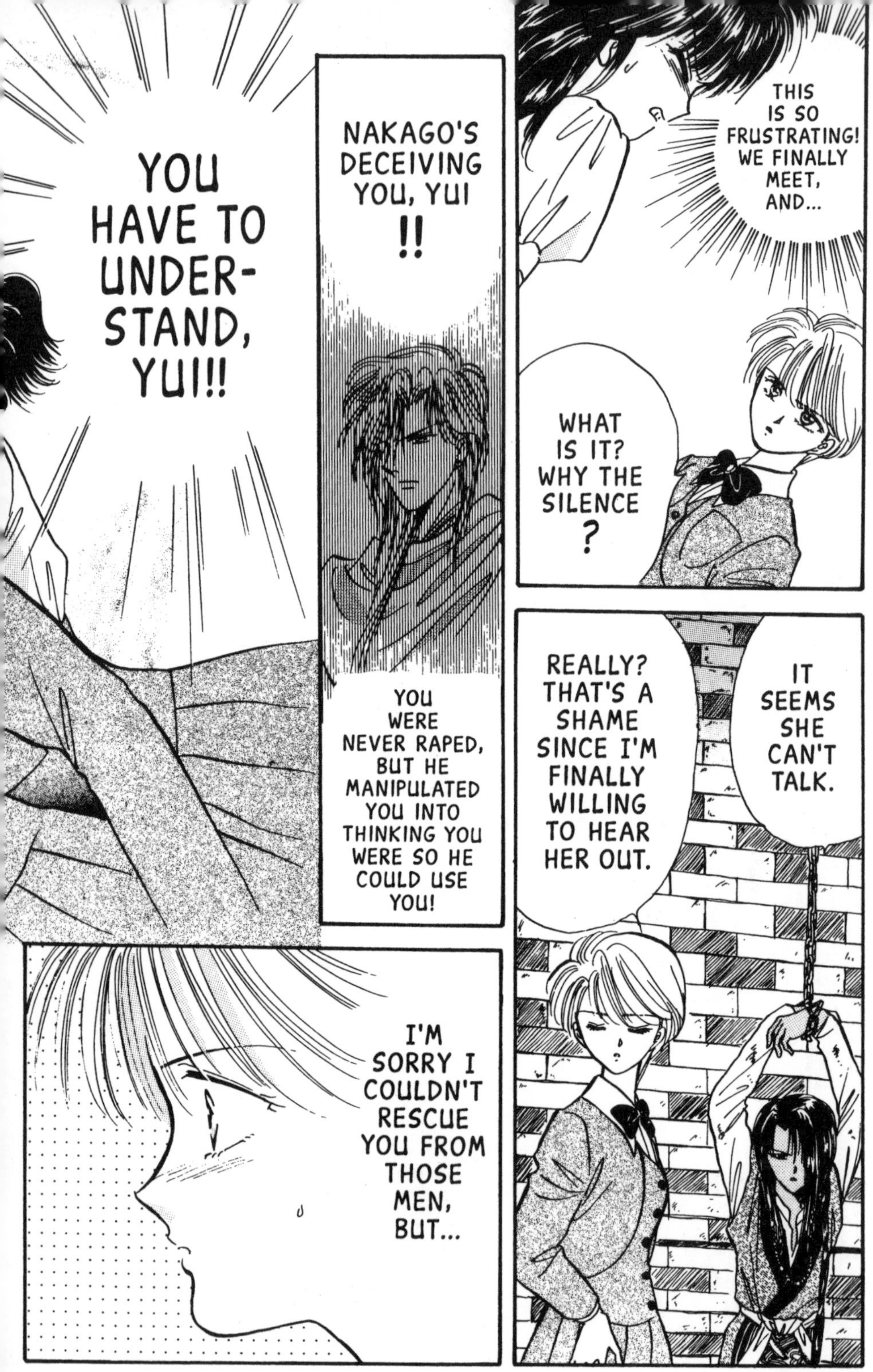
THIS IS SO FRUSTRATING! WE FINALLY MEET, AND...
WHAT IS IT? WHY THE SILENCE?
IT SEEMS SHE CAN'T TALK.
REALLY? THAT'S A SHAME SINCE I'M FINALLY WILLING TO HEAR HER OUT.
NAKAGO'S DECEIVING YOU, YUI!!
YOU WERE NEVER RAPED, BUT HE MANIPULATED YOU INTO THINKING YOU WERE SO HE COULD USE YOU!
YOU HAVE TO UNDER-STAND, YUI!!
I'M SORRY I COULDN'T RESCUE YOU FROM THOSE MEN, BUT...

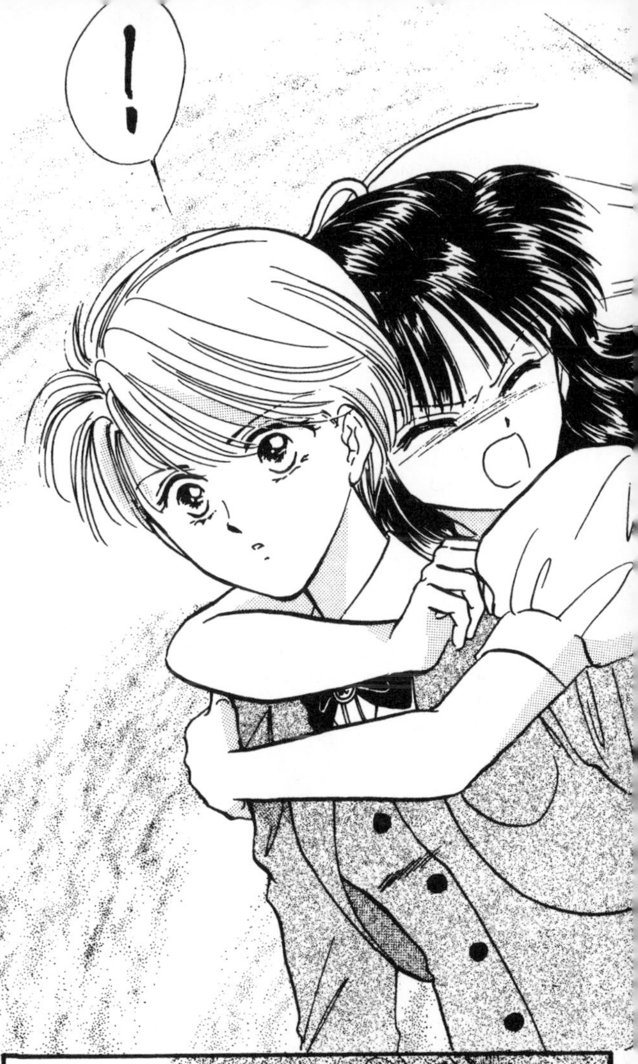
!

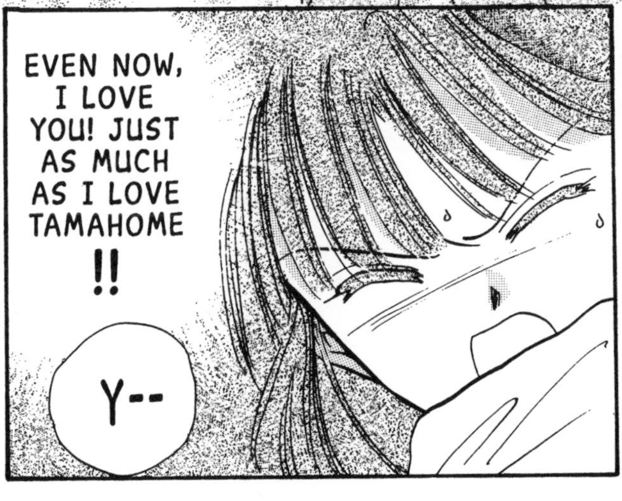
EVEN NOW, I LOVE YOU! JUST AS MUCH AS I LOVE TAMAHOME !!
Y--

Maybe Hotohori's meant for older readers like high school students. 💧 But when *Fushigi Yûgi* was covered in a magazine column, they said that Hotohori was much more popular than Tamahome! (Nuriko was popular too.) Go, Hotohori! If I were to get married, he'd be my first choice!! When I first came up with him at the age of 18, I hadn't decided whether the story would be set in Japan or China. But the earliest versions had him as a prince. Then one day, when we began the serial, my editor said, "Let's just go for it and make him emperor." That also limited his actions.

Although Nuriko passed away a while ago, he's still popular. No. 3 in the CD booklet survey! Readers from Taiwan requested that I bring him back to life. Sorry, but...

His homosexuality was conceived for comic relief, but it ended up being a very good concept. It added character. With Hotohori, I had in mind a man who had the beauty of a woman, but for Nuriko, he basically is a woman... At first, I made his body totally masculine. He was tall and manly. I have the drawings. But that would have made him into "just another cross dresser." So I just decided, "Make him look like Hibari-kun!" (from the manga *Stop Hibari-kun*) and he ended up that way. Come to think of it, if Nuriko loved Hotohori, it would seem like homosexual love, but he loved him as a woman. It's not so much gay as transsexual. In other words, he's kind of like a big sister (?) you could turn to who would understand both men's and women's feelings.

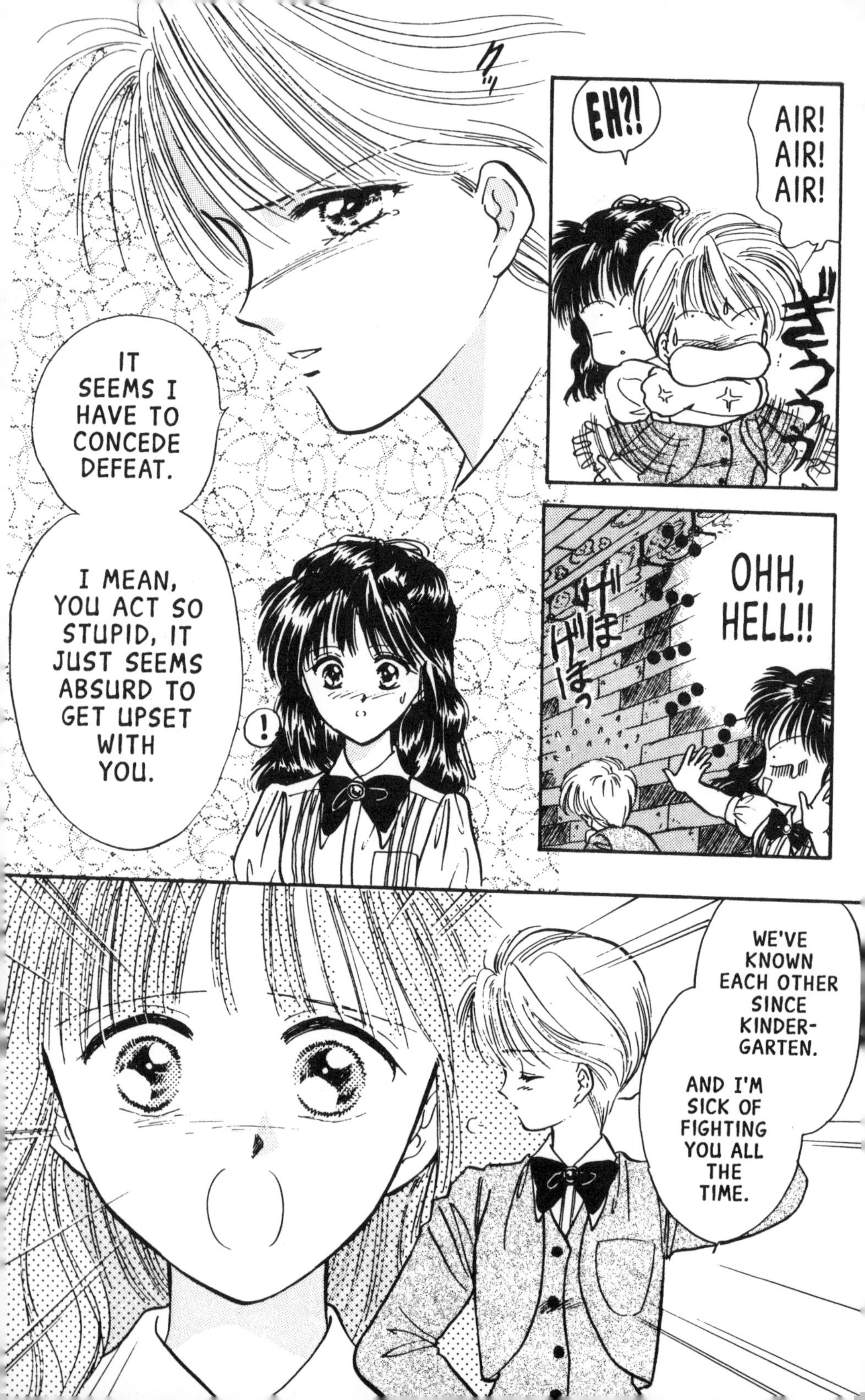
AIR! AIR! AIR!
EH?!
OHH, HELL!!
げほげほっ
IT SEEMS I HAVE TO CONCEDE DEFEAT.
I MEAN, YOU ACT SO STUPID, IT JUST SEEMS ABSURD TO GET UPSET WITH YOU.
!
WE'VE KNOWN EACH OTHER SINCE KINDER-GARTEN.
AND I'M SICK OF FIGHTING YOU ALL THE TIME.

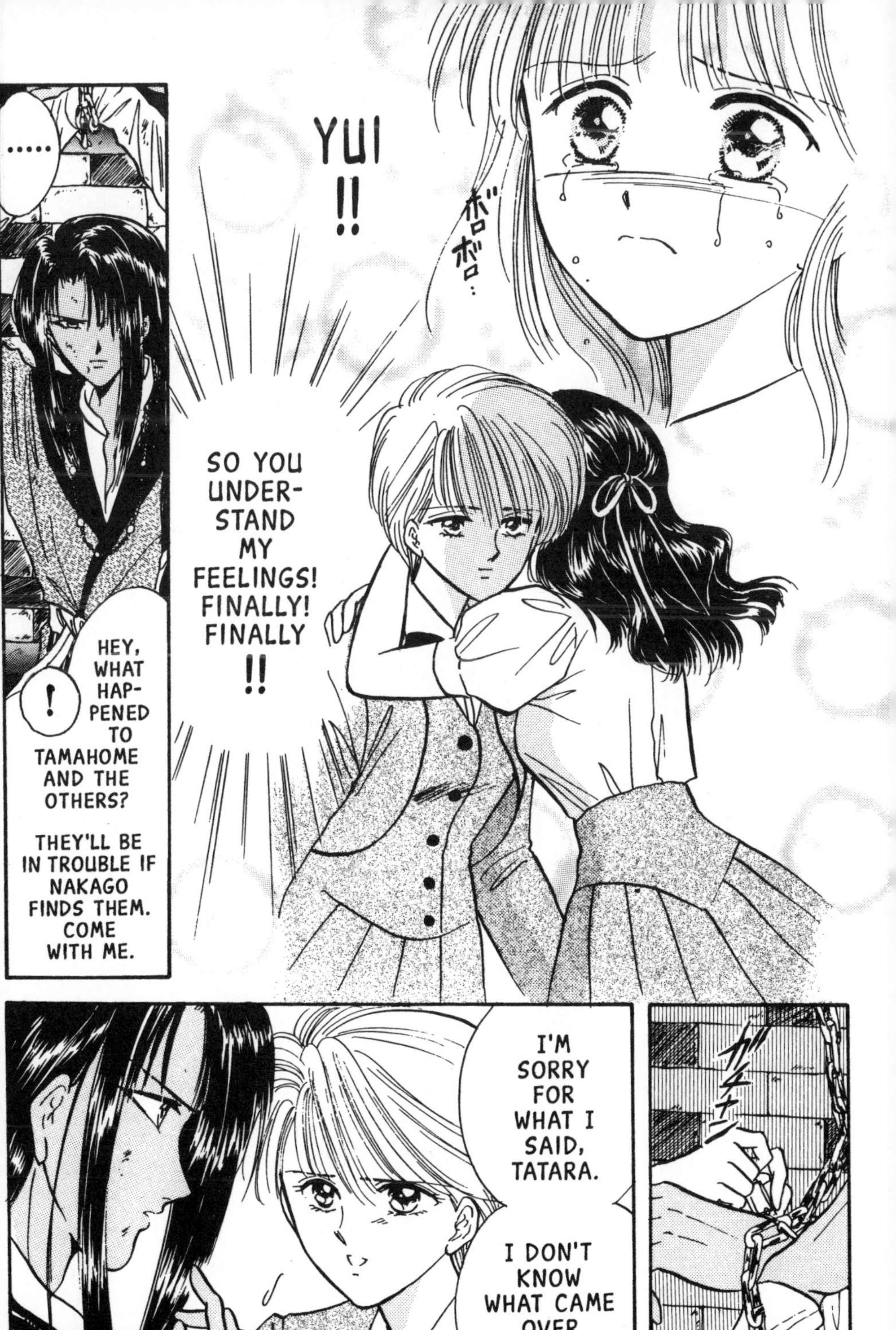
YUI!!
SO YOU UNDERSTAND MY FEELINGS! FINALLY! FINALLY!!
......
!
HEY, WHAT HAPPENED TO TAMAHOME AND THE OTHERS?
THEY'LL BE IN TROUBLE IF NAKAGO FINDS THEM. COME WITH ME.
I'M SORRY FOR WHAT I SAID, TATARA.
I DON'T KNOW WHAT CAME OVER ME.

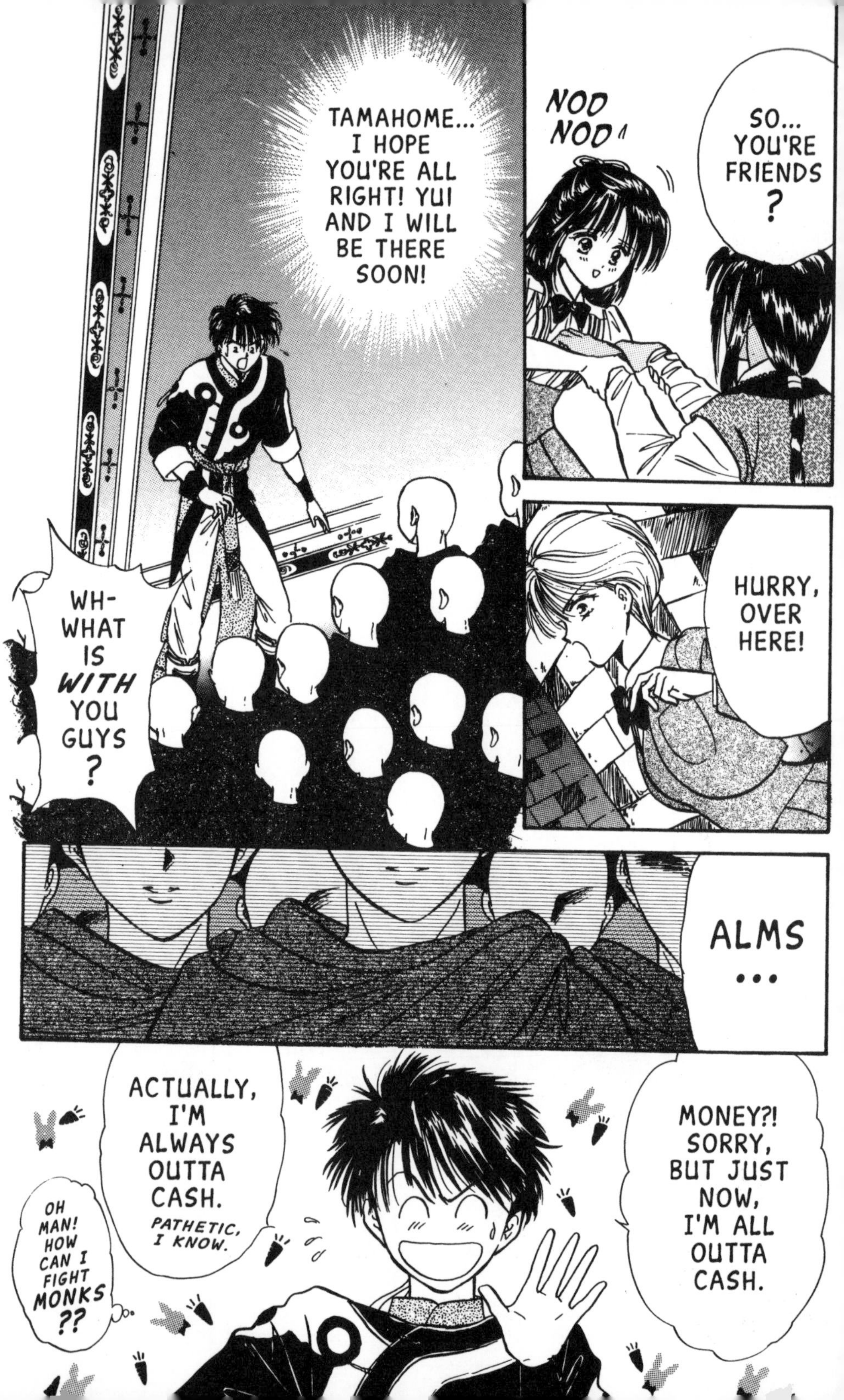
SO... YOU'RE FRIENDS?
NOD NOD
HURRY, OVER HERE!
TAMAHOME... I HOPE YOU'RE ALL RIGHT! YUI AND I WILL BE THERE SOON!
WH-WHAT IS *WITH* YOU GUYS?
ALMS...
MONEY?! SORRY, BUT JUST NOW, I'M ALL OUTTA CASH.
ACTUALLY, I'M ALWAYS OUTTA CASH.
PATHETIC, I KNOW.
OH MAN! HOW CAN I FIGHT MONKS??

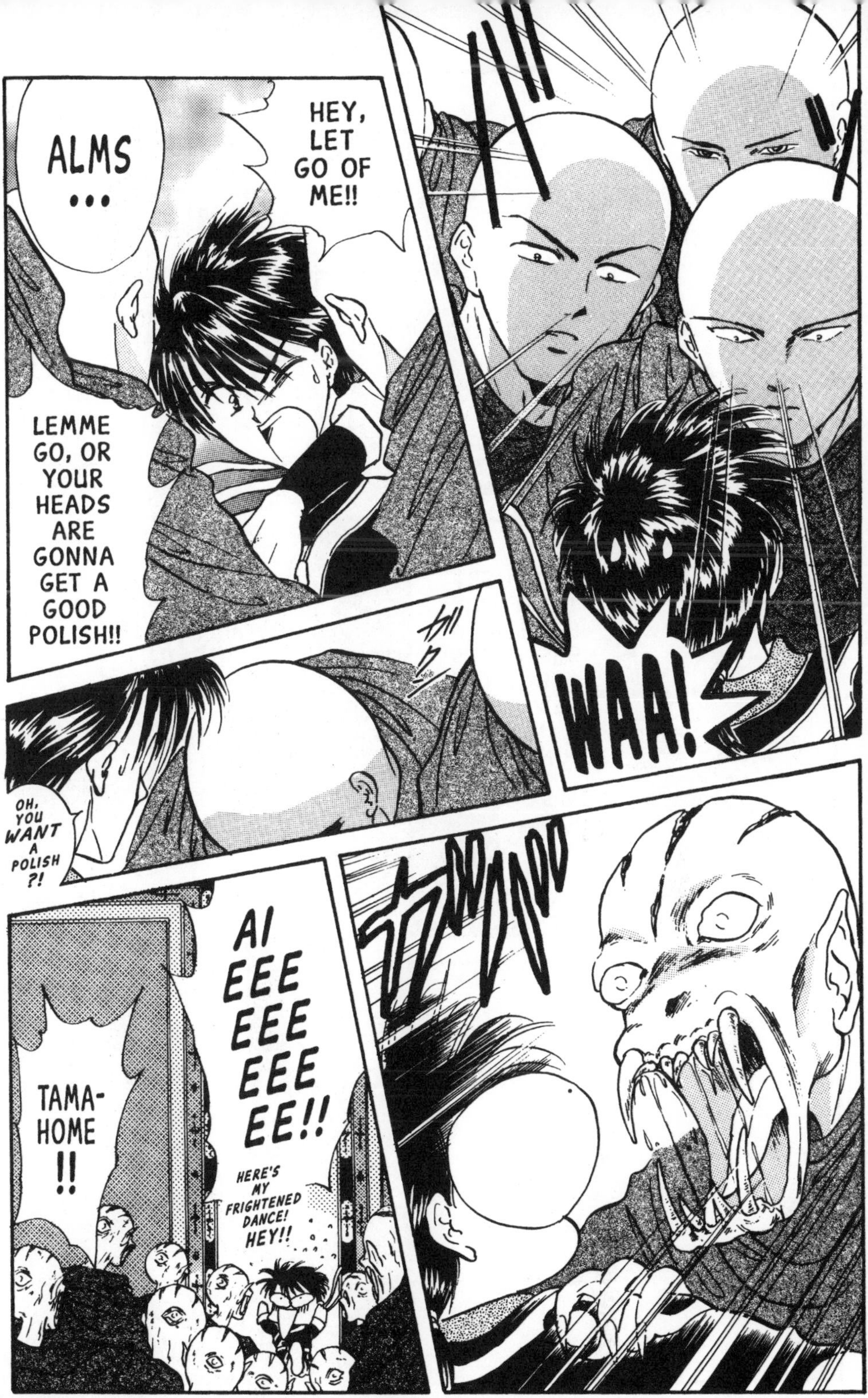
WAA!
HEY, LET GO OF ME!!
ALMS...
LEMME GO, OR YOUR HEADS ARE GONNA GET A GOOD POLISH!!
OH, YOU WANT A POLISH?!
AI EEE EEE EEE EE!!
HERE'S MY FRIGHTENED DANCE! HEY!!
TAMA-HOME!!

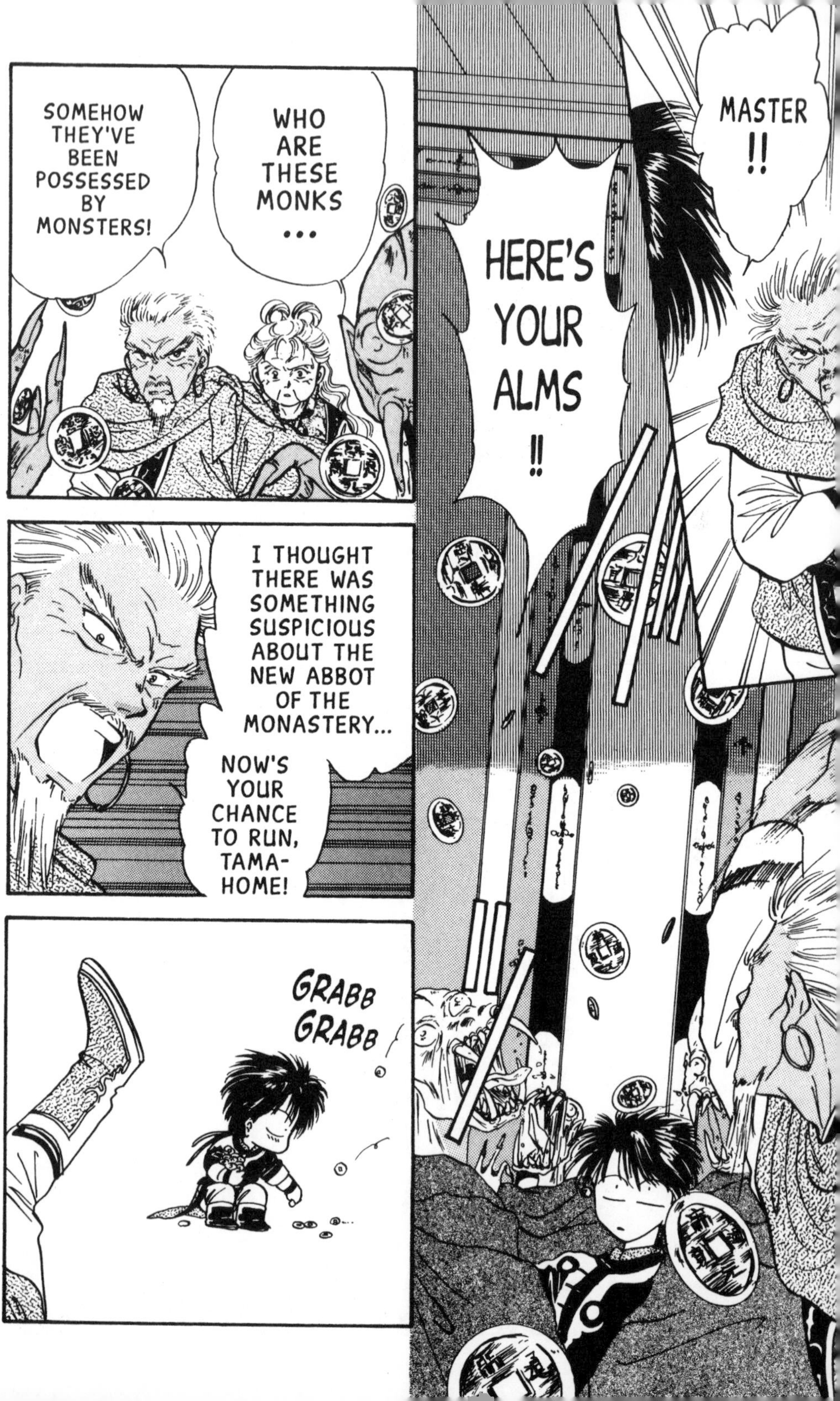
MASTER !!
HERE'S YOUR ALMS !!
WHO ARE THESE MONKS ...
SOMEHOW THEY'VE BEEN POSSESSED BY MONSTERS!
I THOUGHT THERE WAS SOMETHING SUSPICIOUS ABOUT THE NEW ABBOT OF THE MONASTERY...
NOW'S YOUR CHANCE TO RUN, TAMA-HOME!
GRABB GRABB

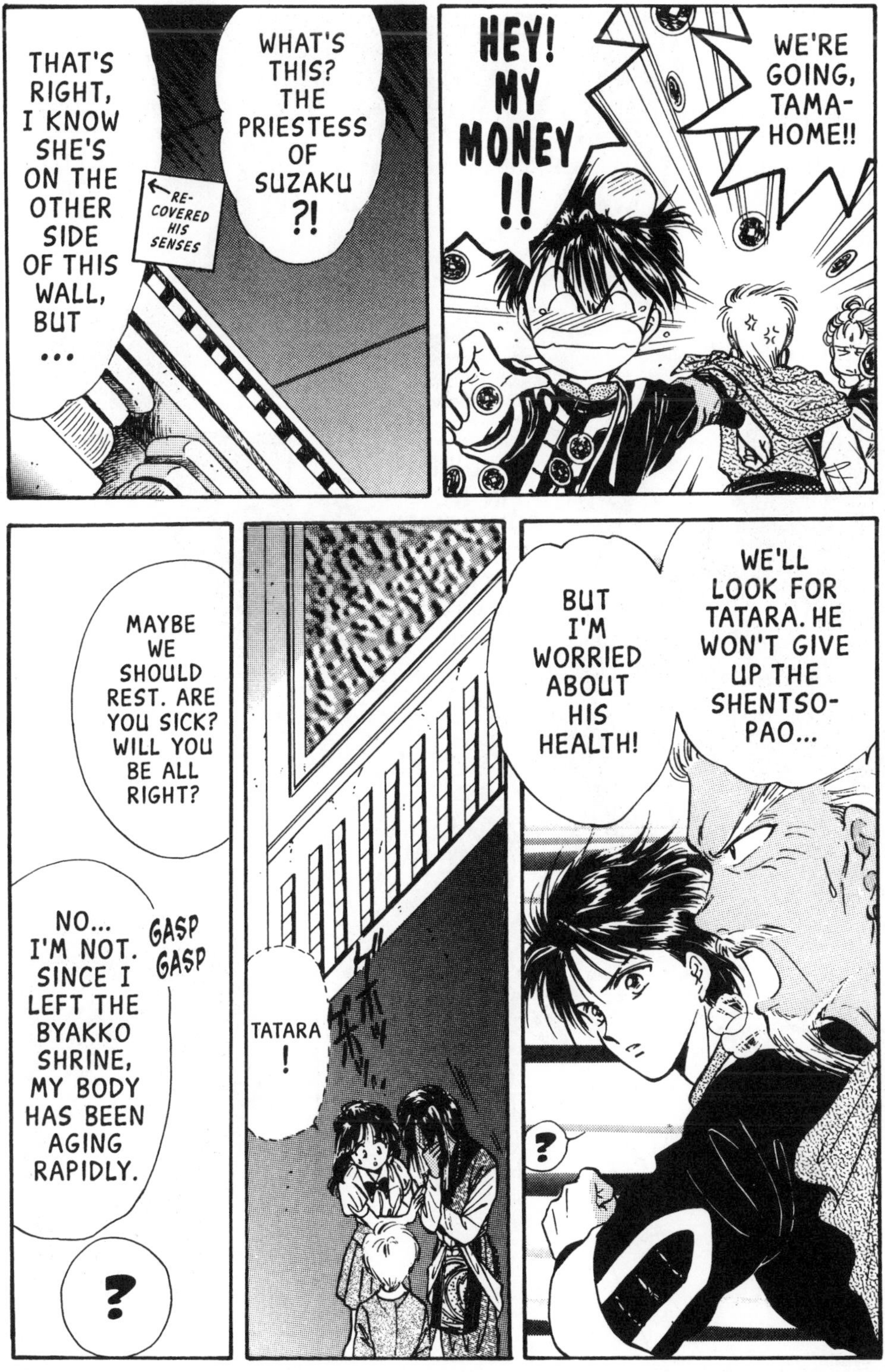
WE'RE GOING, TAMA-HOME!!
HEY! MY MONEY!!
WHAT'S THIS? THE PRIESTESS OF SUZAKU?!
THAT'S RIGHT, I KNOW SHE'S ON THE OTHER SIDE OF THIS WALL, BUT...
← RE-COVERED HIS SENSES
WE'LL LOOK FOR TATARA. HE WON'T GIVE UP THE SHENTSO-PAO...
BUT I'M WORRIED ABOUT HIS HEALTH!
?
TATARA!
MAYBE WE SHOULD REST. ARE YOU SICK? WILL YOU BE ALL RIGHT?
NO... I'M NOT. SINCE I LEFT THE BYAKKO SHRINE, MY BODY HAS BEEN AGING RAPIDLY.
GASP GASP
?

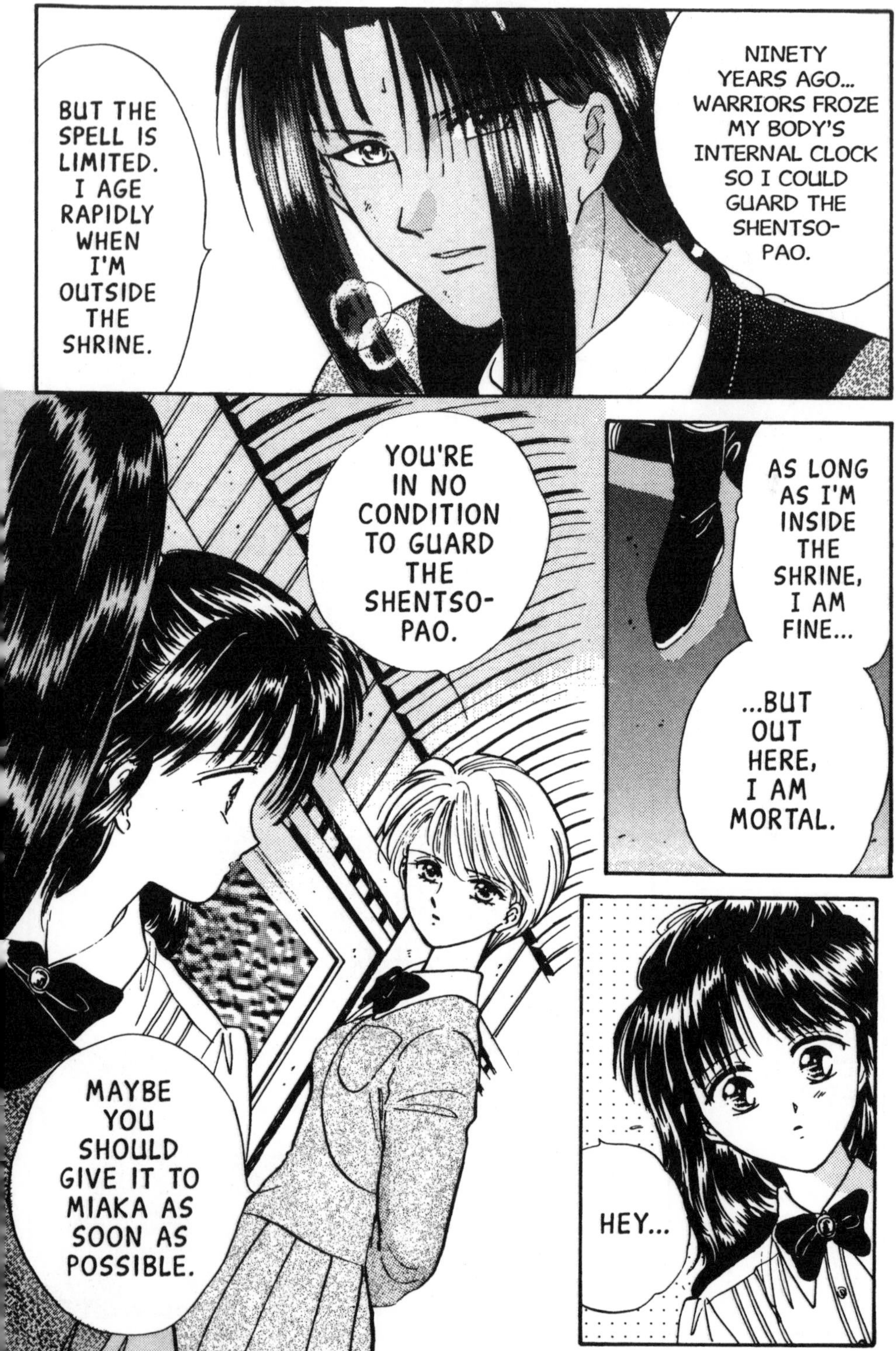
NINETY YEARS AGO... WARRIORS FROZE MY BODY'S INTERNAL CLOCK SO I COULD GUARD THE SHENTSO-PAO.
BUT THE SPELL IS LIMITED. I AGE RAPIDLY WHEN I'M OUTSIDE THE SHRINE.
AS LONG AS I'M INSIDE THE SHRINE, I AM FINE...
...BUT OUT HERE, I AM MORTAL.
HEY...
YOU'RE IN NO CONDITION TO GUARD THE SHENTSO-PAO.
MAYBE YOU SHOULD GIVE IT TO MIAKA AS SOON AS POSSIBLE.

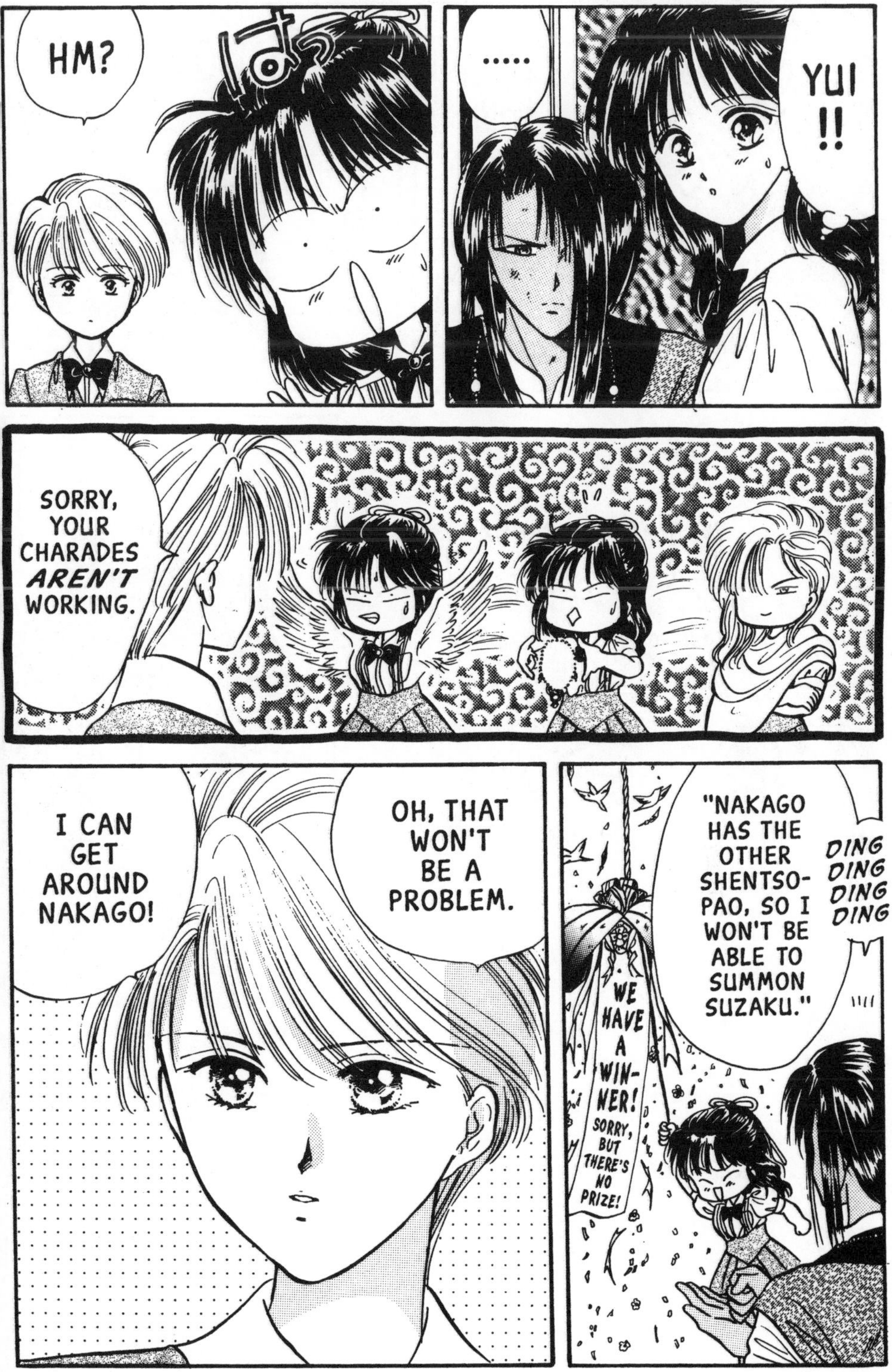
YUI !!
.....
はっ
HM?
SORRY, YOUR CHARADES *AREN'T* WORKING.
"NAKAGO HAS THE OTHER SHENTSO-PAO, SO I WON'T BE ABLE TO SUMMON SUZAKU."
DING DING DING DING
WE HAVE A WIN-NER!
SORRY, BUT THERE'S NO PRIZE!
OH, THAT WON'T BE A PROBLEM.
I CAN GET AROUND NAKAGO!

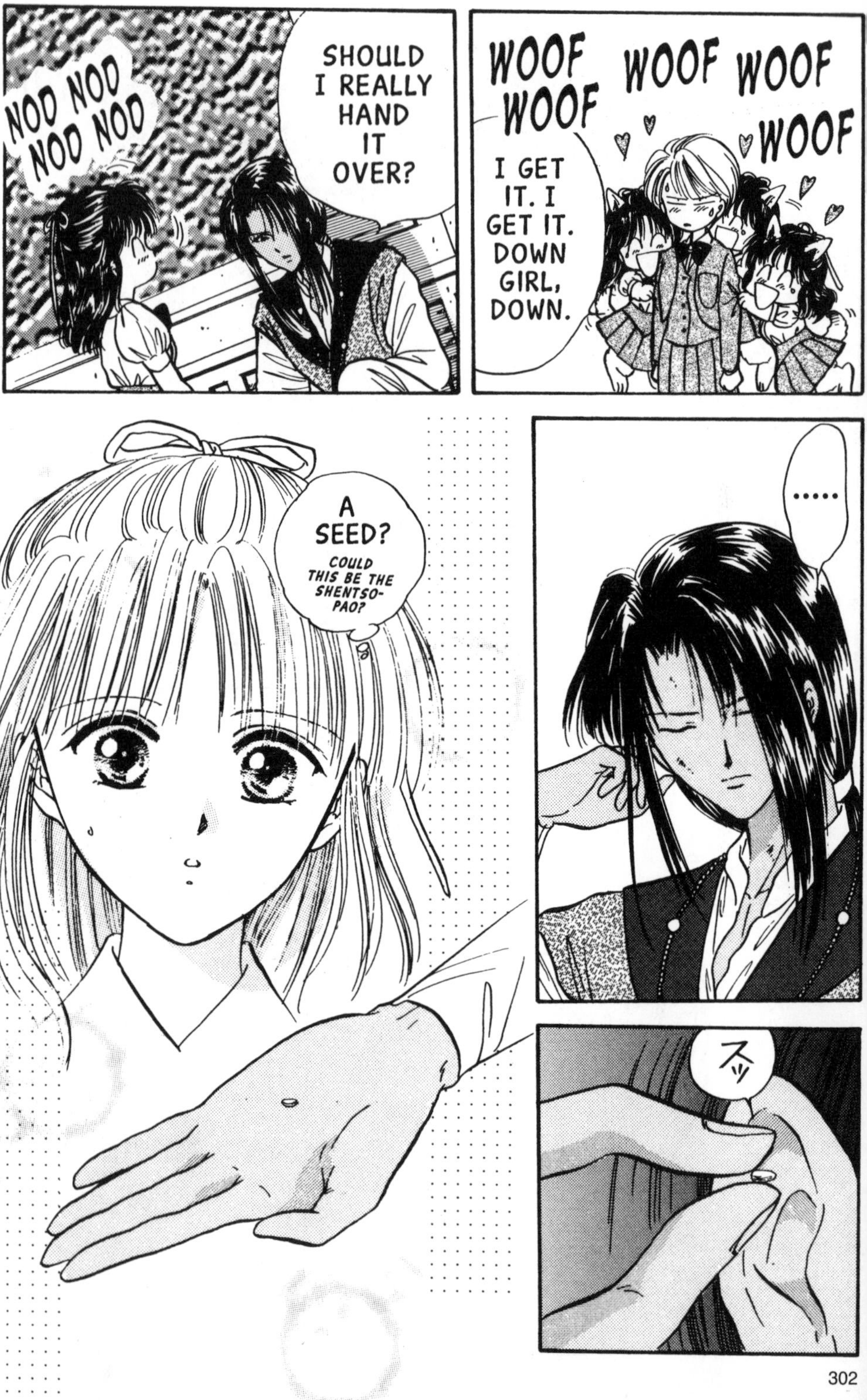
WOOF WOOF WOOF
WOOF WOOF WOOF
I GET IT. I GET IT. DOWN GIRL, DOWN.
SHOULD I REALLY HAND IT OVER?
NOD NOD NOD NOD
.....
スッ
A SEED?
COULD THIS BE THE SHENTSO-PAO?

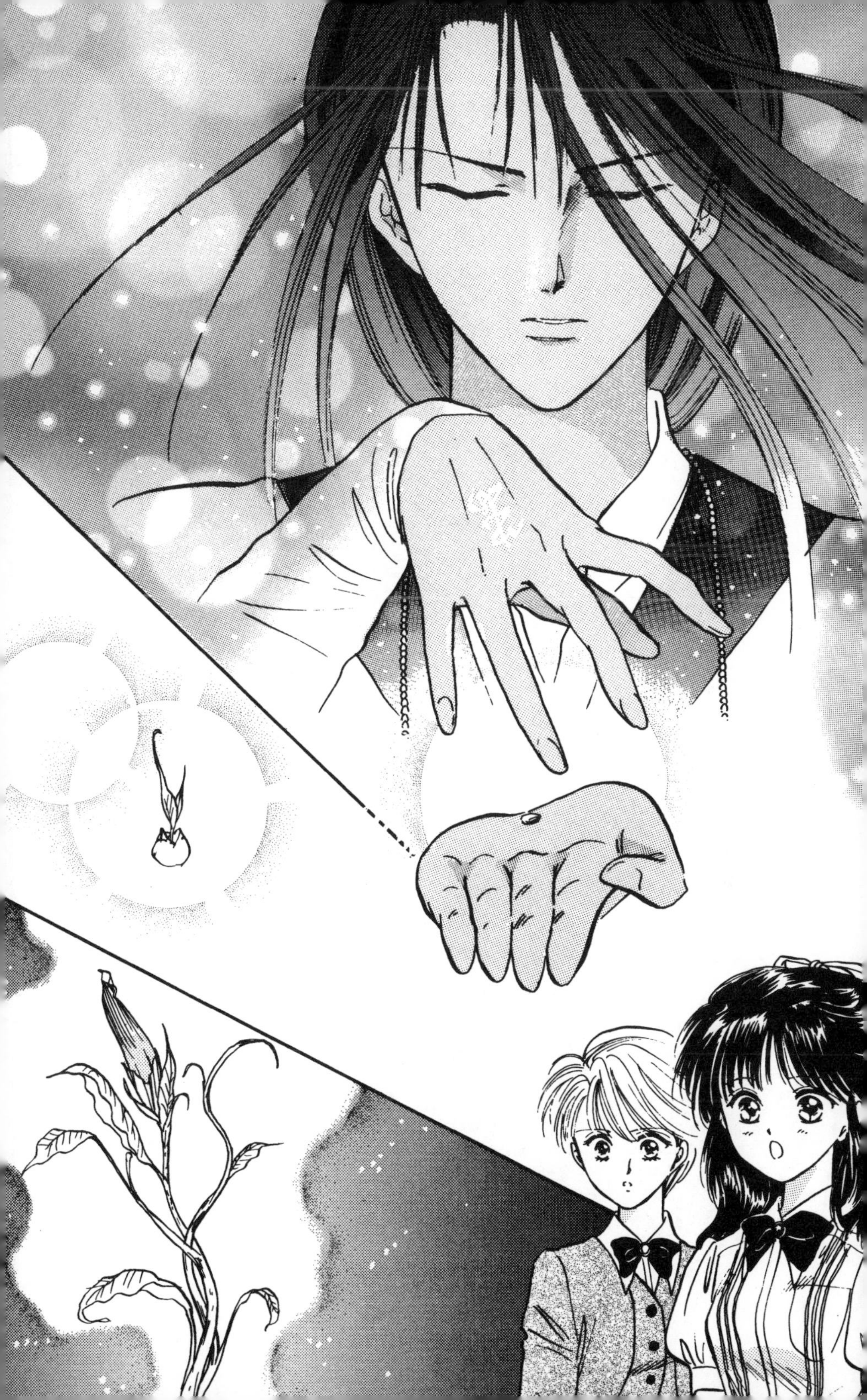

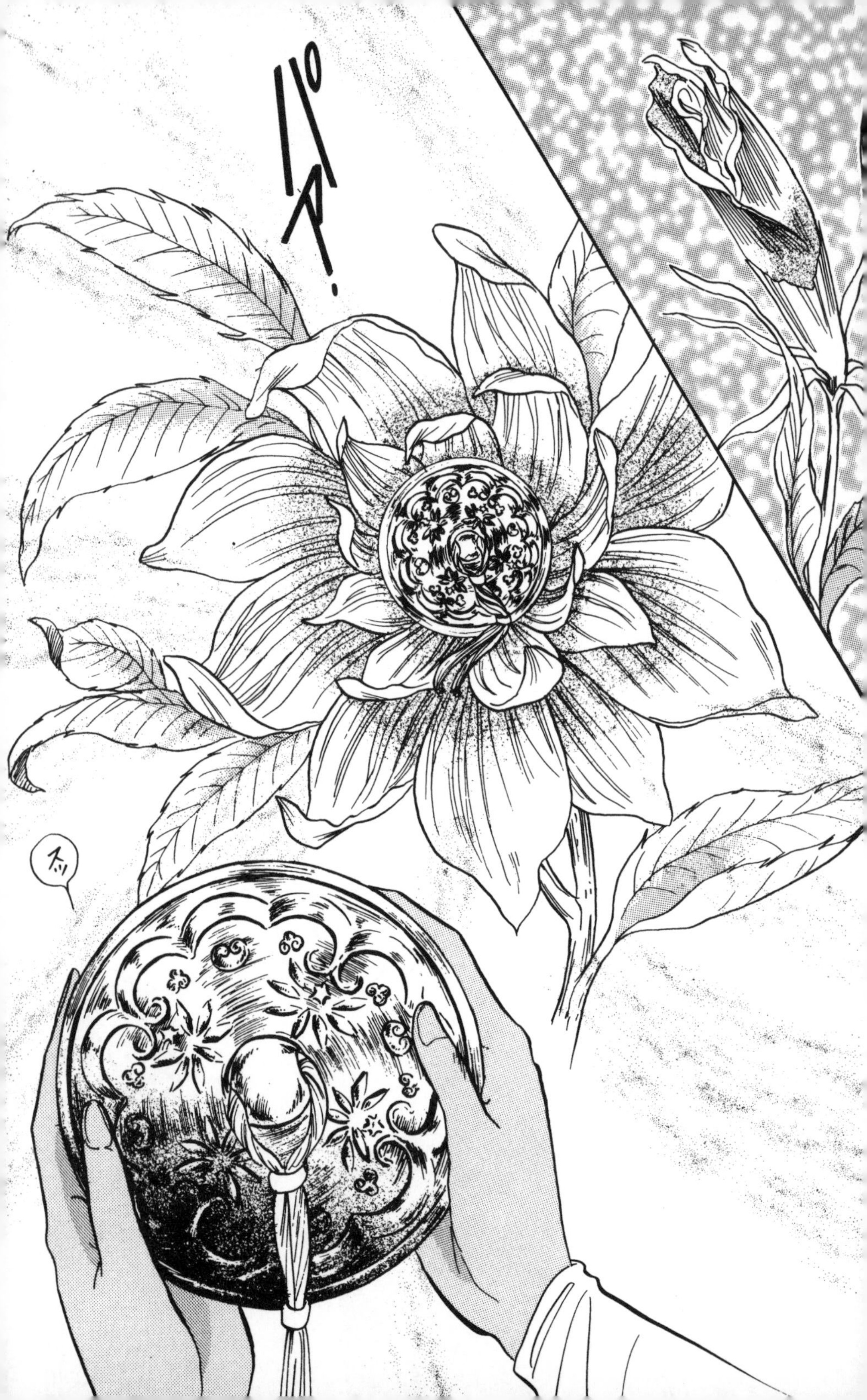
パァ!
スッ

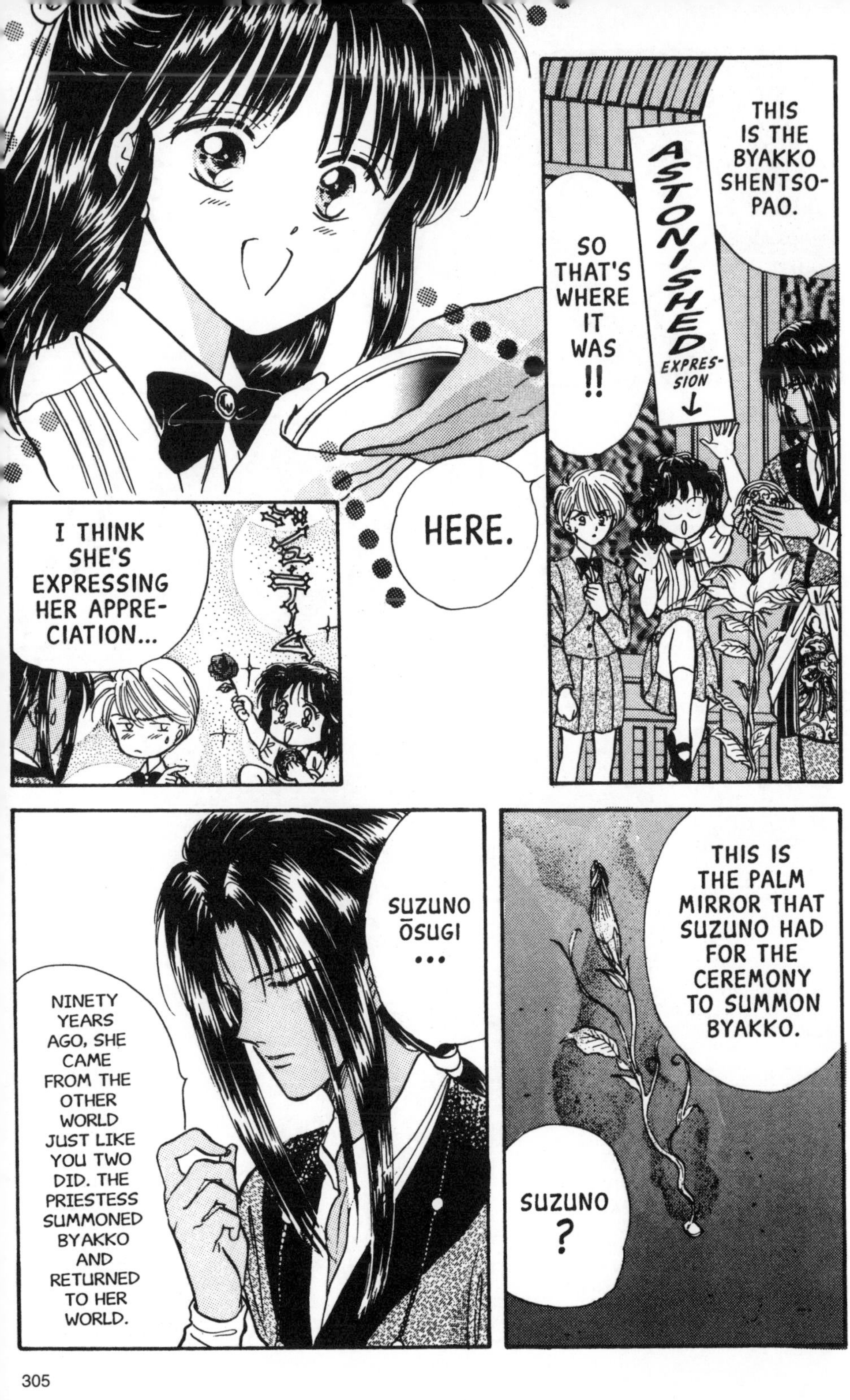
THIS IS THE BYAKKO SHENTSO-PAO.
ASTONISHED EXPRESSION ↓
SO THAT'S WHERE IT WAS!!
HERE.
I THINK SHE'S EXPRESSING HER APPRECIATION...
THIS IS THE PALM MIRROR THAT SUZUNO HAD FOR THE CEREMONY TO SUMMON BYAKKO.
SUZUNO?
SUZUNO ŌSUGI...
NINETY YEARS AGO, SHE CAME FROM THE OTHER WORLD JUST LIKE YOU TWO DID. THE PRIESTESS SUMMONED BYAKKO AND RETURNED TO HER WORLD.

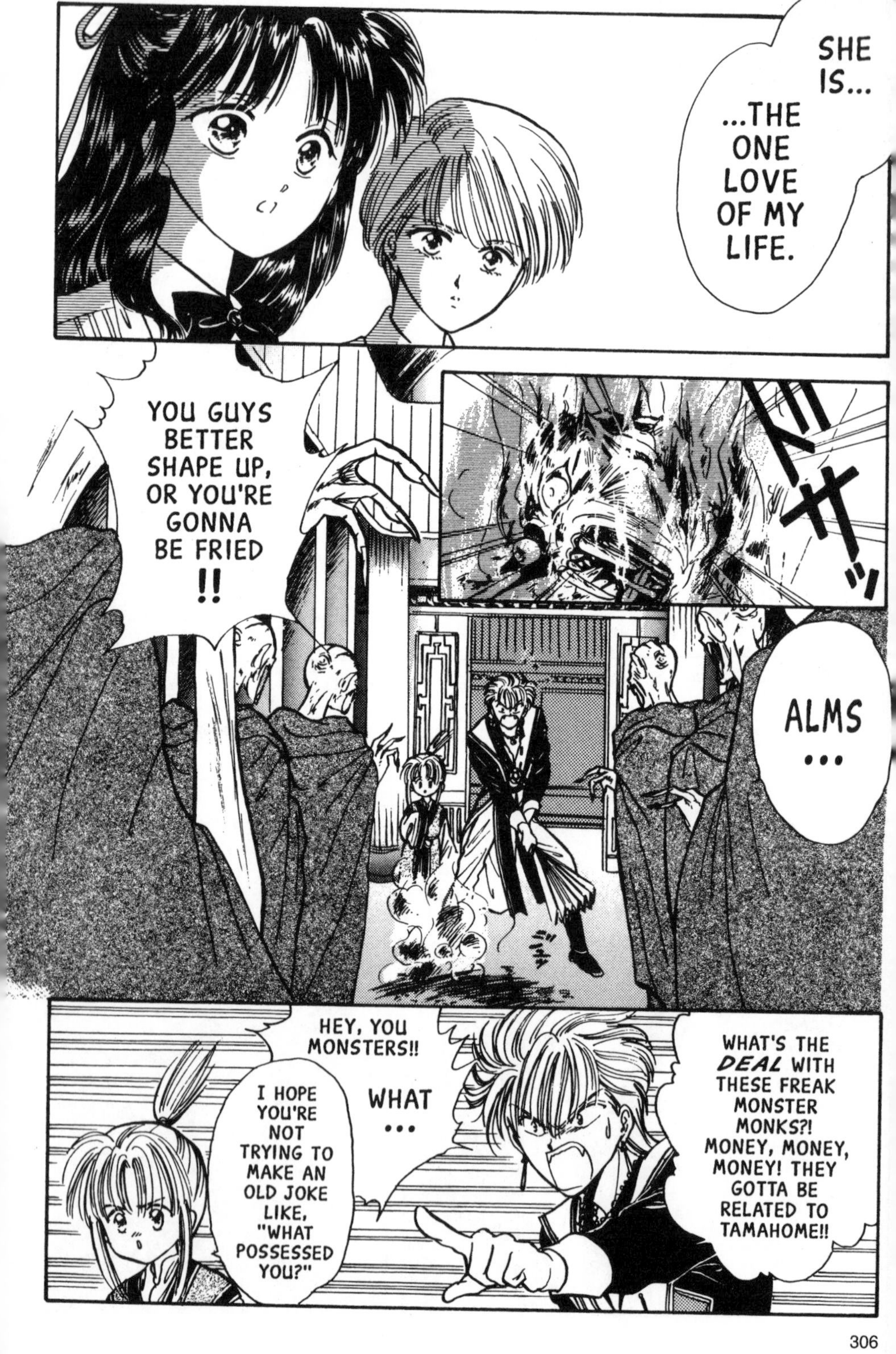

SHE IS... ...THE ONE LOVE OF MY LIFE.
ALMS...
YOU GUYS BETTER SHAPE UP, OR YOU'RE GONNA BE FRIED!!
WHAT'S THE DEAL WITH THESE FREAK MONSTER MONKS?! MONEY, MONEY, MONEY! THEY GOTTA BE RELATED TO TAMAHOME!!
HEY, YOU MONSTERS!!
WHAT...
I HOPE YOU'RE NOT TRYING TO MAKE AN OLD JOKE LIKE, "WHAT POSSESSED YOU?"

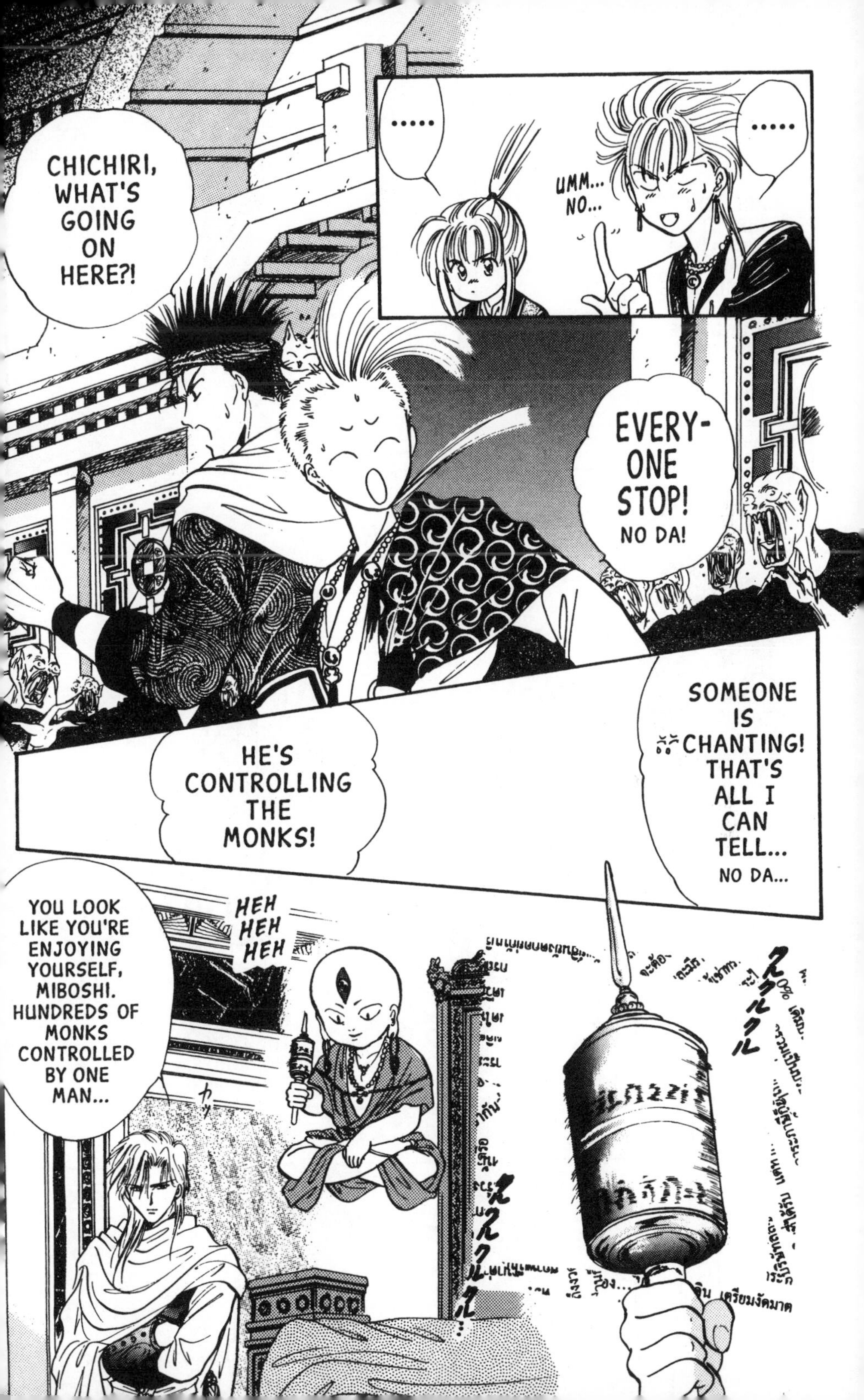
.....
UMM... NO...
.....
CHICHIRI, WHAT'S GOING ON HERE?!
EVERY-ONE STOP! NO DA!
SOMEONE IS CHANTING! THAT'S ALL I CAN TELL... NO DA...
HE'S CONTROLLING THE MONKS!
HEH HEH HEH
YOU LOOK LIKE YOU'RE ENJOYING YOURSELF, MIBOSHI. HUNDREDS OF MONKS CONTROLLED BY ONE MAN...

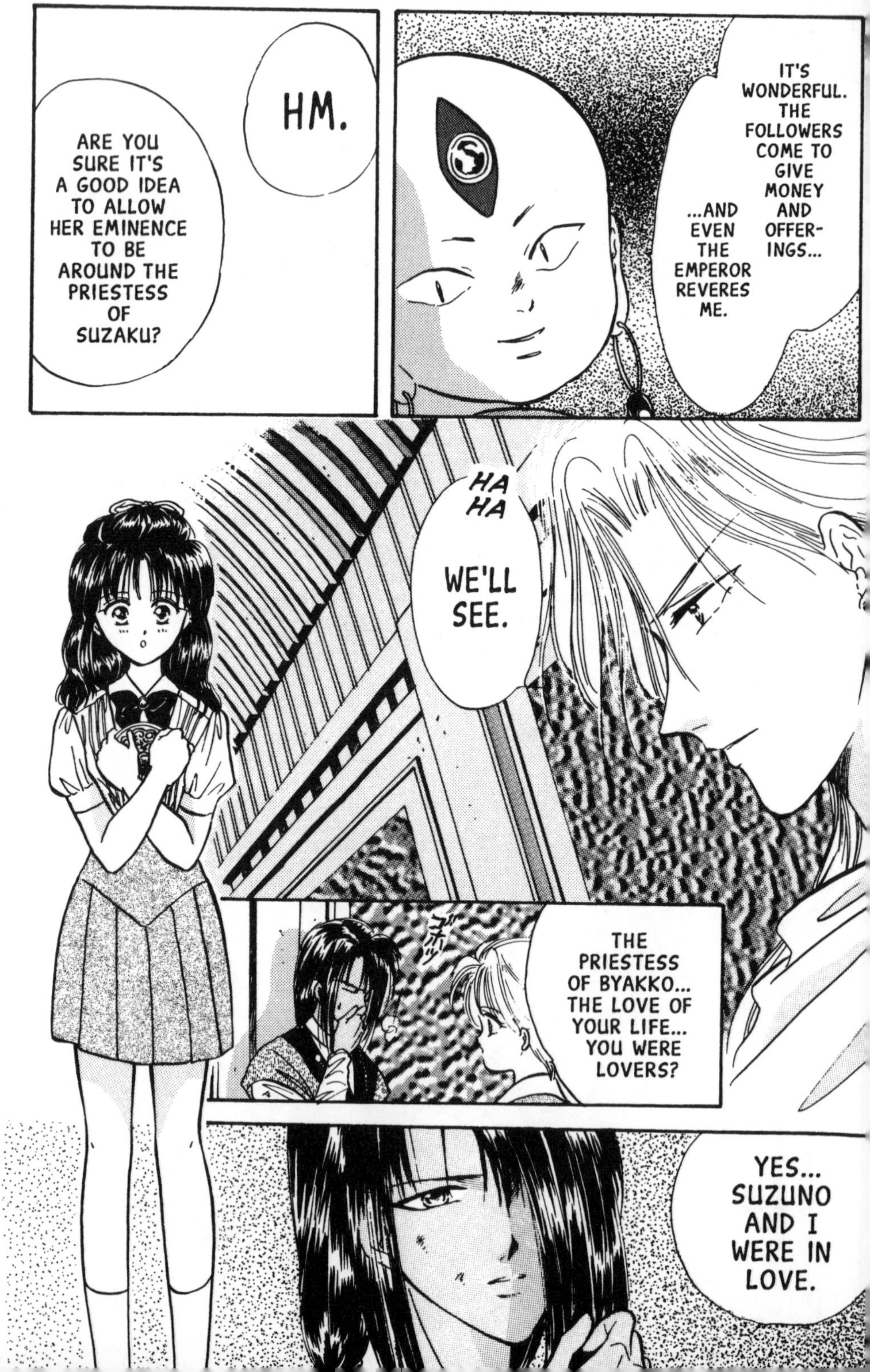
IT'S WONDERFUL. THE FOLLOWERS COME TO GIVE MONEY AND OFFERINGS...
...AND EVEN THE EMPEROR REVERES ME.
HM.
ARE YOU SURE IT'S A GOOD IDEA TO ALLOW HER EMINENCE TO BE AROUND THE PRIESTESS OF SUZAKU?
HA HA
WE'LL SEE.
THE PRIESTESS OF BYAKKO... THE LOVE OF YOUR LIFE... YOU WERE LOVERS?
ゴホッ
YES... SUZUNO AND I WERE IN LOVE.

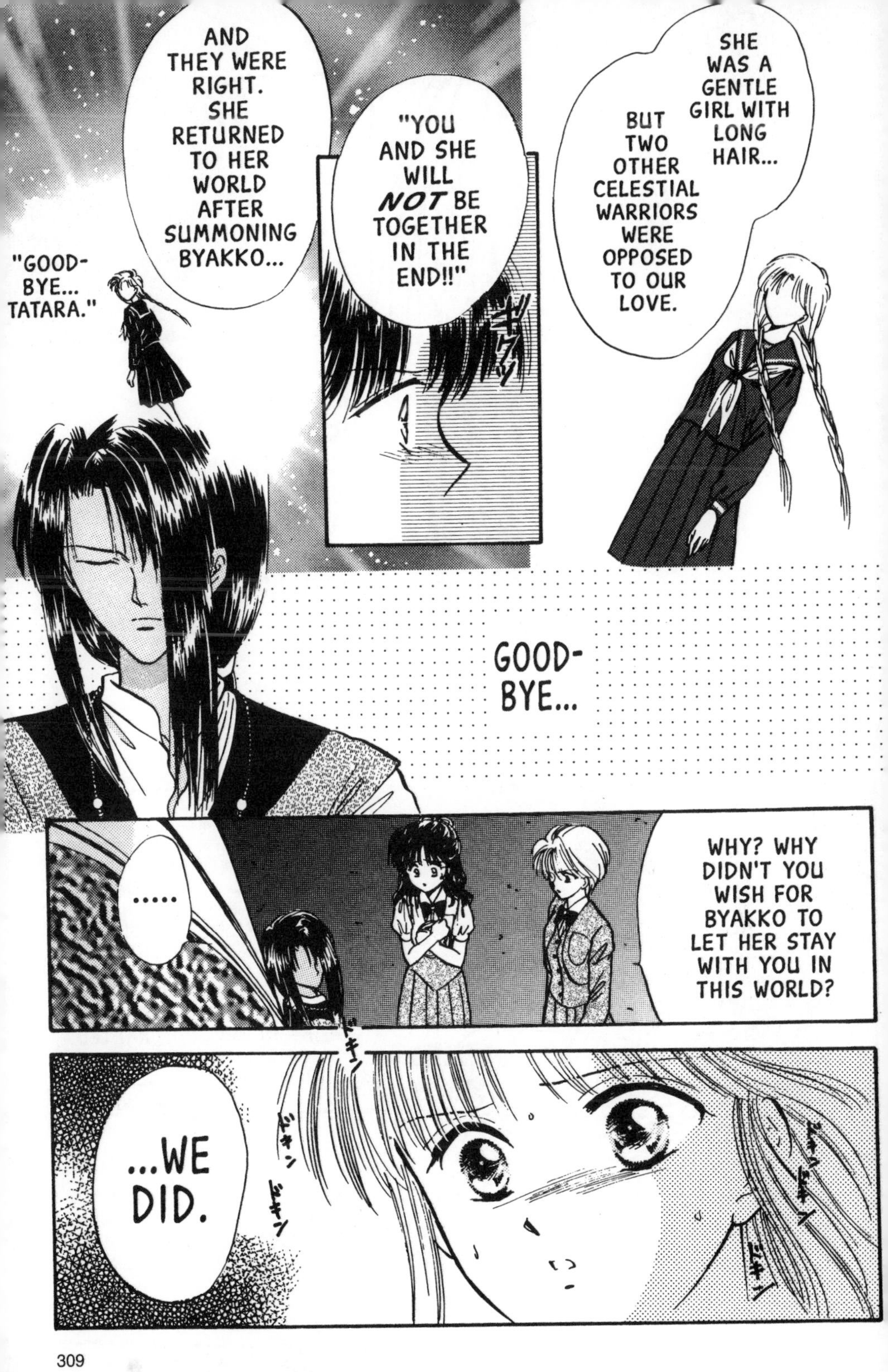
SHE WAS A GENTLE GIRL WITH LONG HAIR...
BUT TWO OTHER CELESTIAL WARRIORS WERE OPPOSED TO OUR LOVE.
"YOU AND SHE WILL *NOT* BE TOGETHER IN THE END!!"
AND THEY WERE RIGHT. SHE RETURNED TO HER WORLD AFTER SUMMONING BYAKKO...
"GOOD-BYE... TATARA."
GOOD-BYE...
WHY? WHY DIDN'T YOU WISH FOR BYAKKO TO LET HER STAY WITH YOU IN THIS WORLD?
.....
...WE DID.

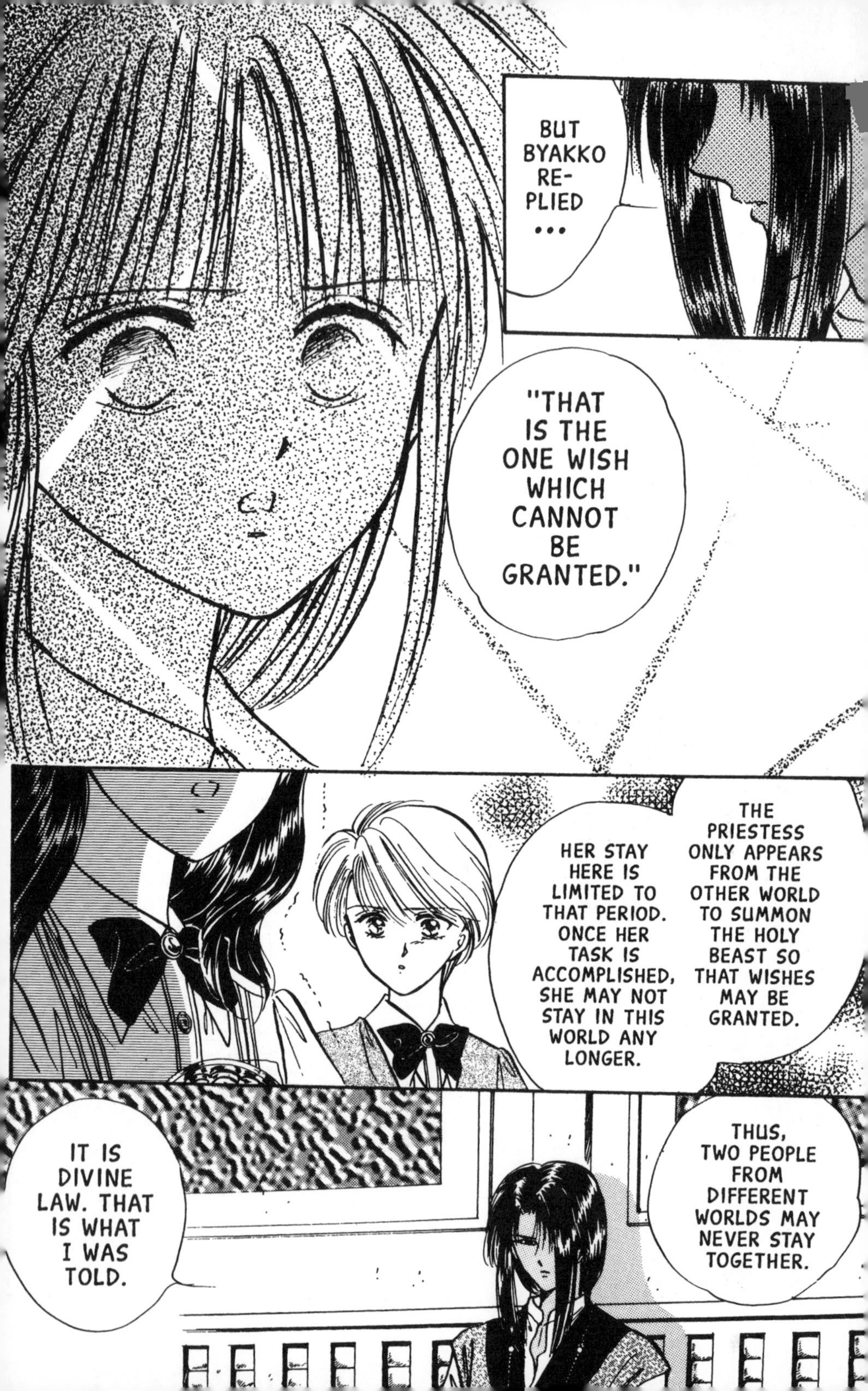
BUT BYAKKO RE-PLIED ...
"THAT IS THE ONE WISH WHICH CANNOT BE GRANTED."
THE PRIESTESS ONLY APPEARS FROM THE OTHER WORLD TO SUMMON THE HOLY BEAST SO THAT WISHES MAY BE GRANTED.
HER STAY HERE IS LIMITED TO THAT PERIOD. ONCE HER TASK IS ACCOMPLISHED, SHE MAY NOT STAY IN THIS WORLD ANY LONGER.
THUS, TWO PEOPLE FROM DIFFERENT WORLDS MAY NEVER STAY TOGETHER.
IT IS DIVINE LAW. THAT IS WHAT I WAS TOLD.

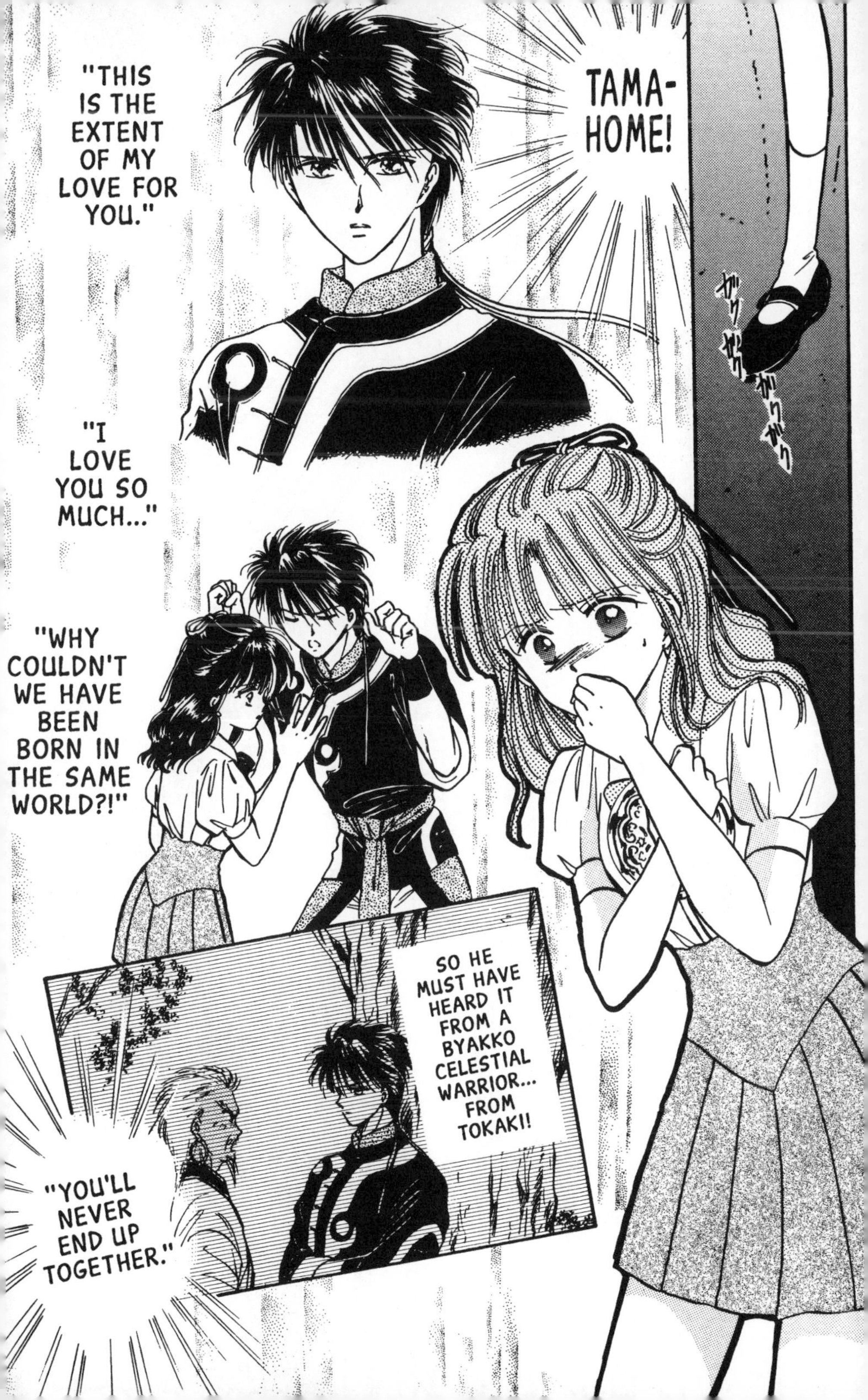
TAMA-HOME!
"THIS IS THE EXTENT OF MY LOVE FOR YOU."
"I LOVE YOU SO MUCH..."
"WHY COULDN'T WE HAVE BEEN BORN IN THE SAME WORLD?!"
SO HE MUST HAVE HEARD IT FROM A BYAKKO CELESTIAL WARRIOR... FROM TOKAKI!
"YOU'LL NEVER END UP TOGETHER."

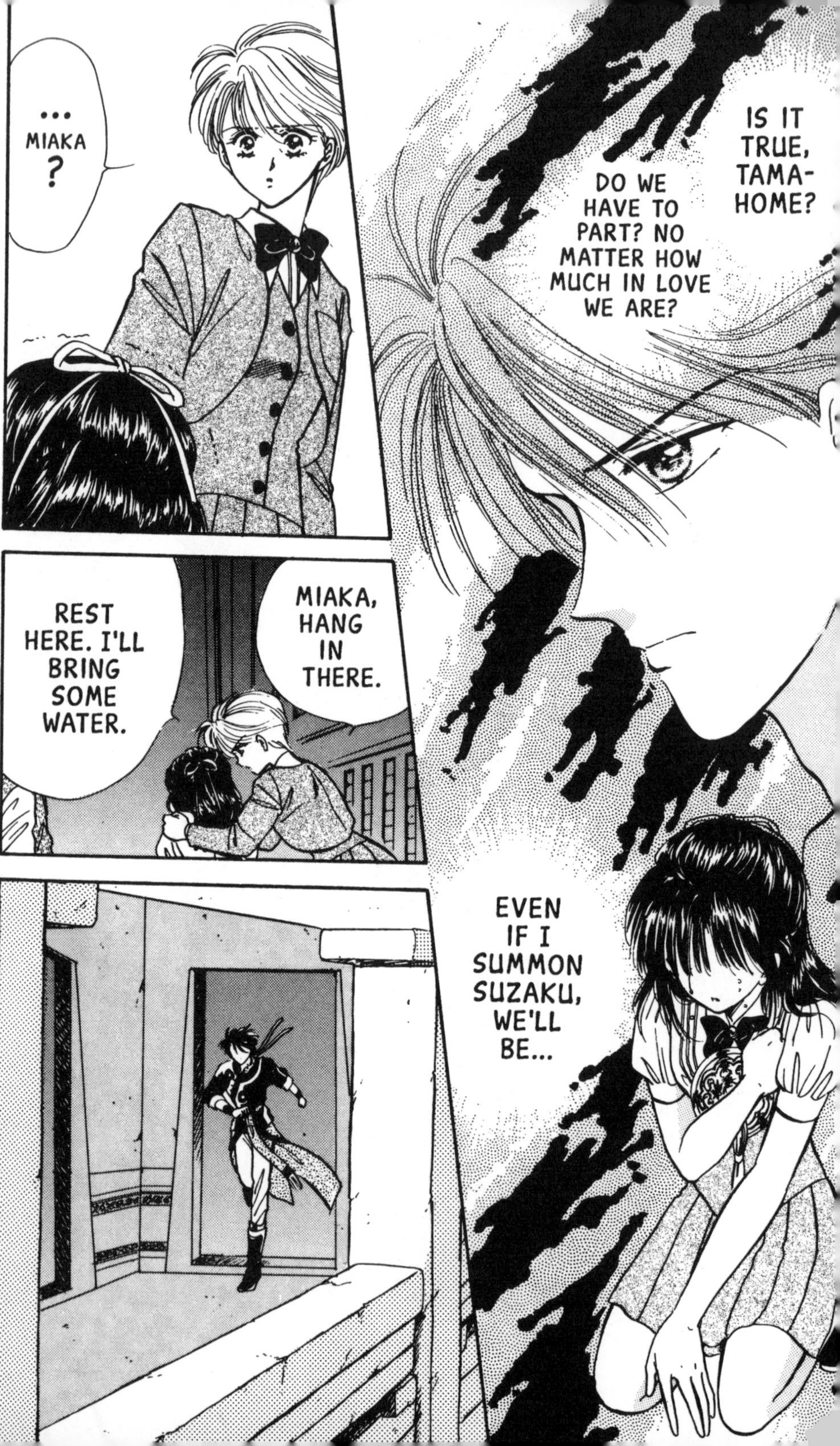
IS IT TRUE, TAMA-HOME?
DO WE HAVE TO PART? NO MATTER HOW MUCH IN LOVE WE ARE?
EVEN IF I SUMMON SUZAKU, WE'LL BE...
...MIAKA?
MIAKA, HANG IN THERE.
REST HERE. I'LL BRING SOME WATER.

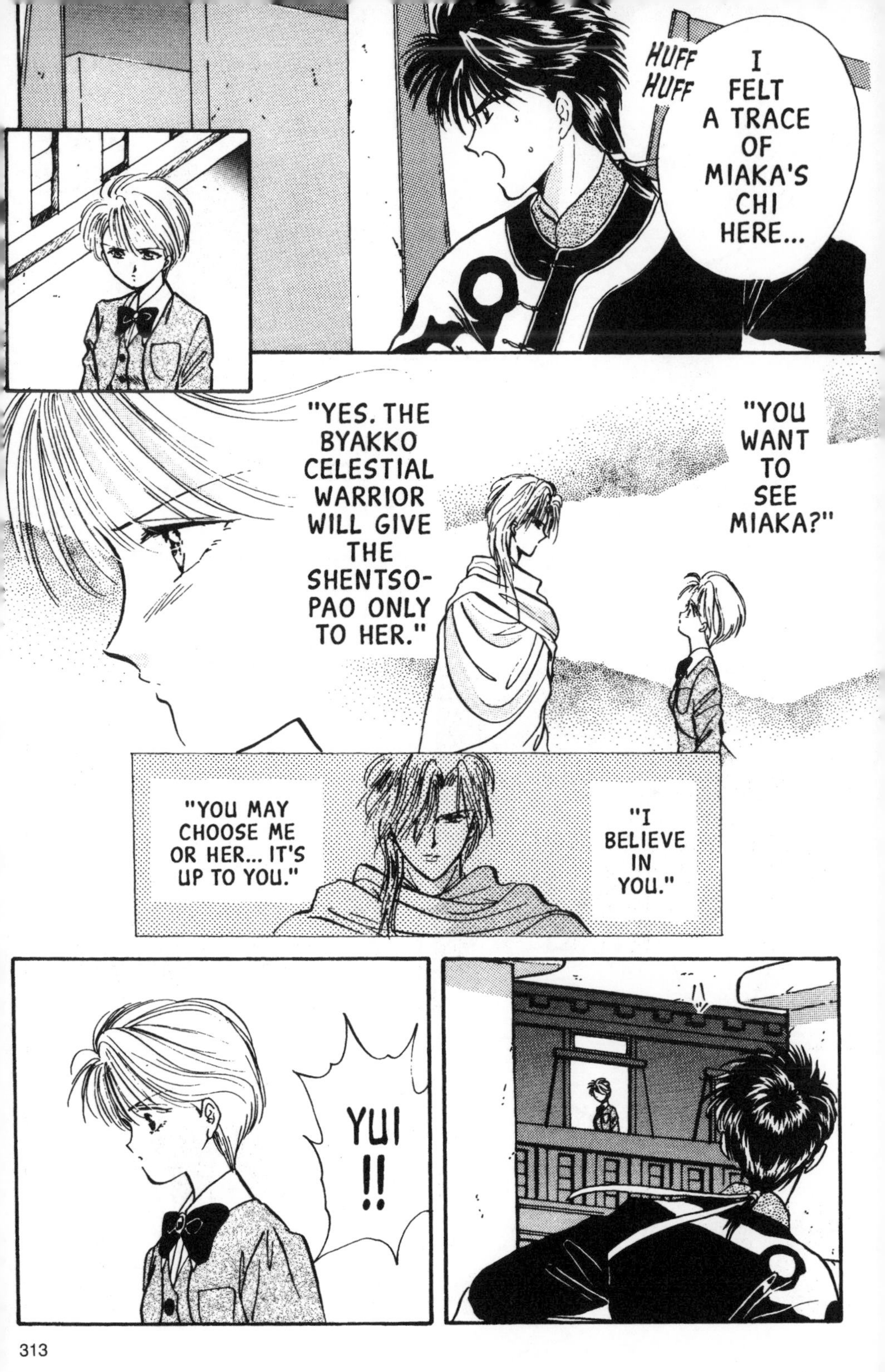
HUFF HUFF
I FELT A TRACE OF MIAKA'S CHI HERE...
"YOU WANT TO SEE MIAKA?"
"YES. THE BYAKKO CELESTIAL WARRIOR WILL GIVE THE SHENTSO-PAO ONLY TO HER."
"I BELIEVE IN YOU."
"YOU MAY CHOOSE ME OR HER... IT'S UP TO YOU."
YUI !!

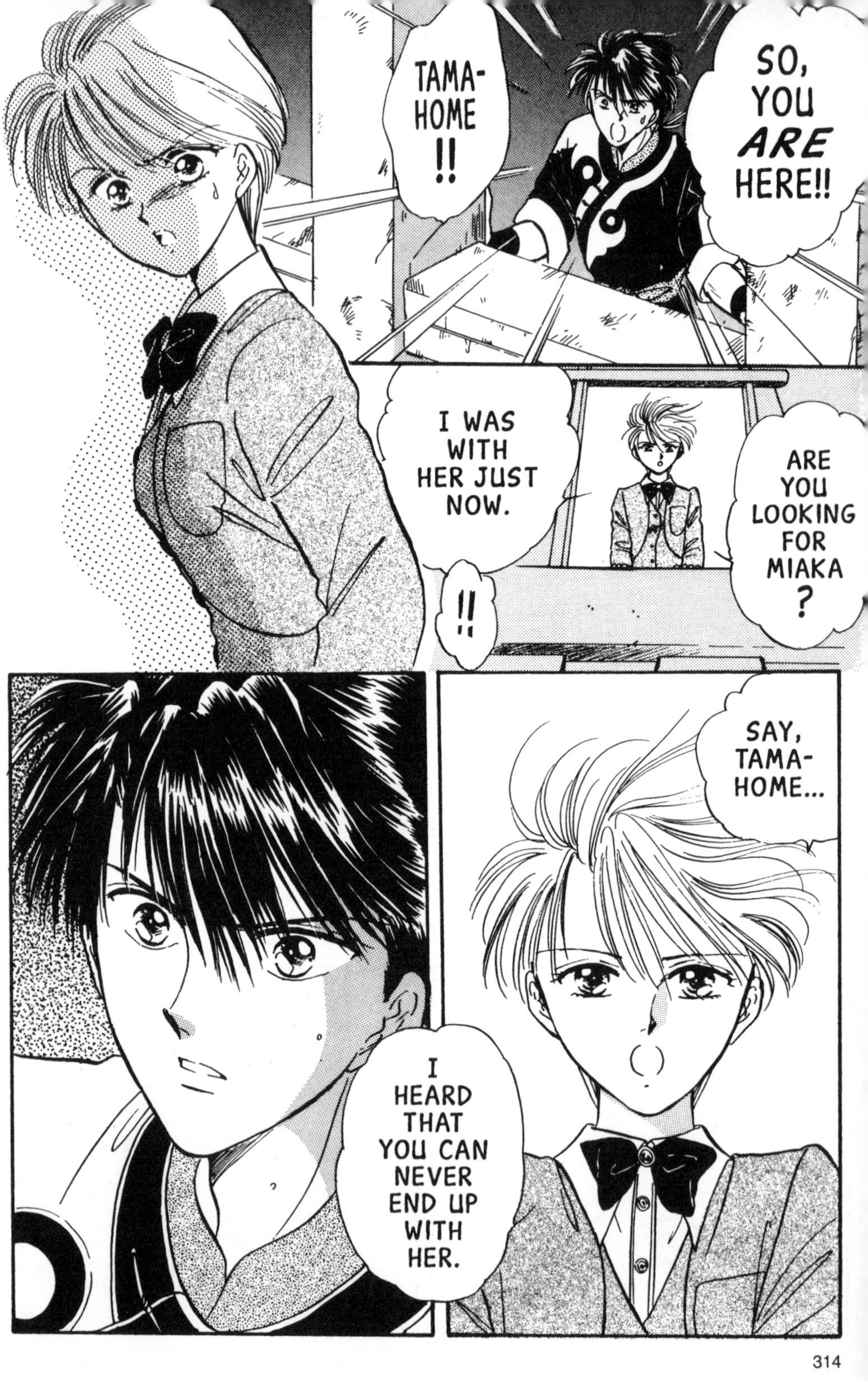
SO, YOU ARE HERE!!
TAMA-HOME!!
ARE YOU LOOKING FOR MIAKA?
I WAS WITH HER JUST NOW.
!!
SAY, TAMA-HOME...
I HEARD THAT YOU CAN NEVER END UP WITH HER.

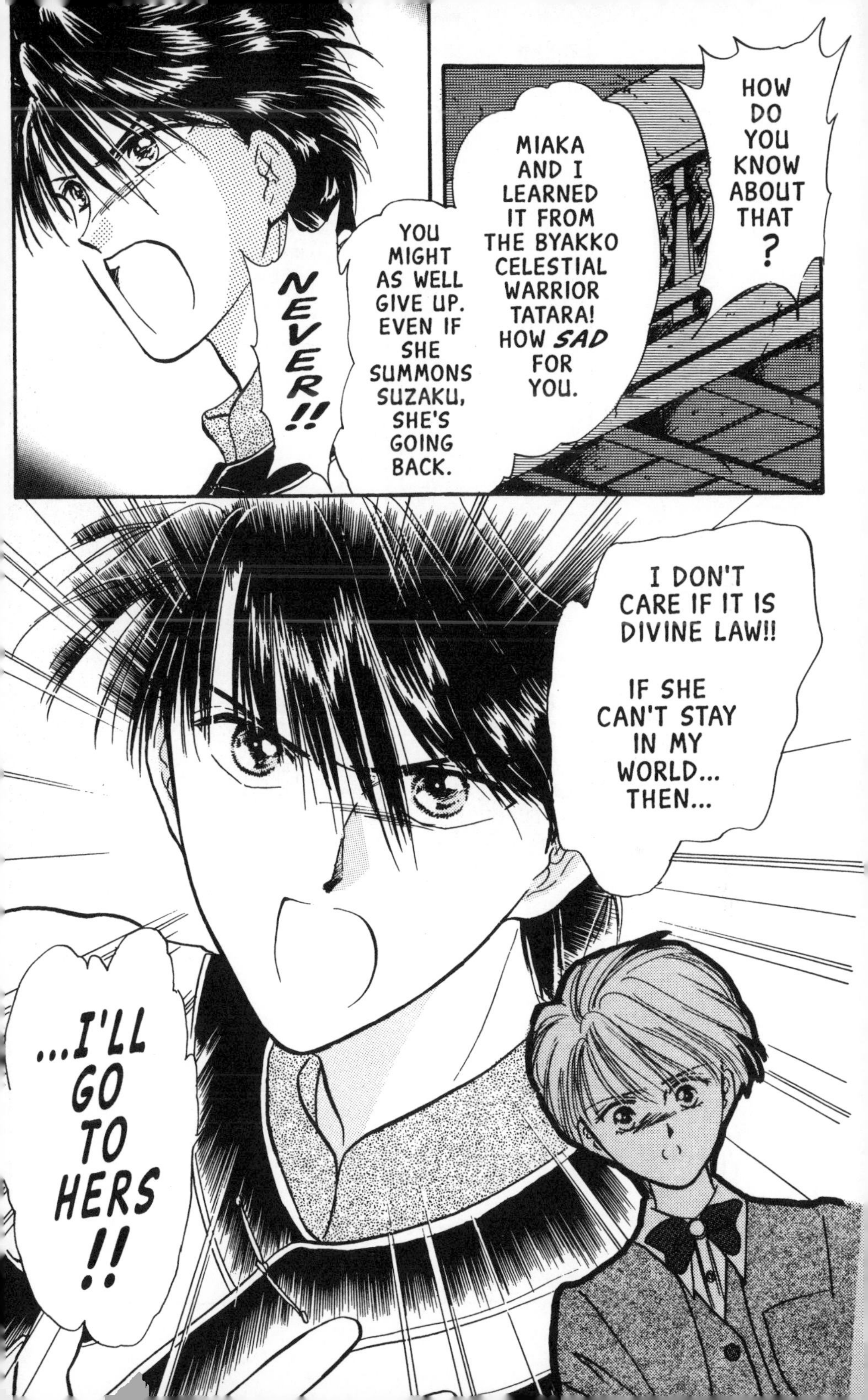
HOW DO YOU KNOW ABOUT THAT?
MIAKA AND I LEARNED IT FROM THE BYAKKO CELESTIAL WARRIOR TATARA! HOW SAD FOR YOU.
YOU MIGHT AS WELL GIVE UP. EVEN IF SHE SUMMONS SUZAKU, SHE'S GOING BACK.
NEVER!!
I DON'T CARE IF IT IS DIVINE LAW!!
IF SHE CAN'T STAY IN MY WORLD... THEN...
...I'LL GO TO HERS!!

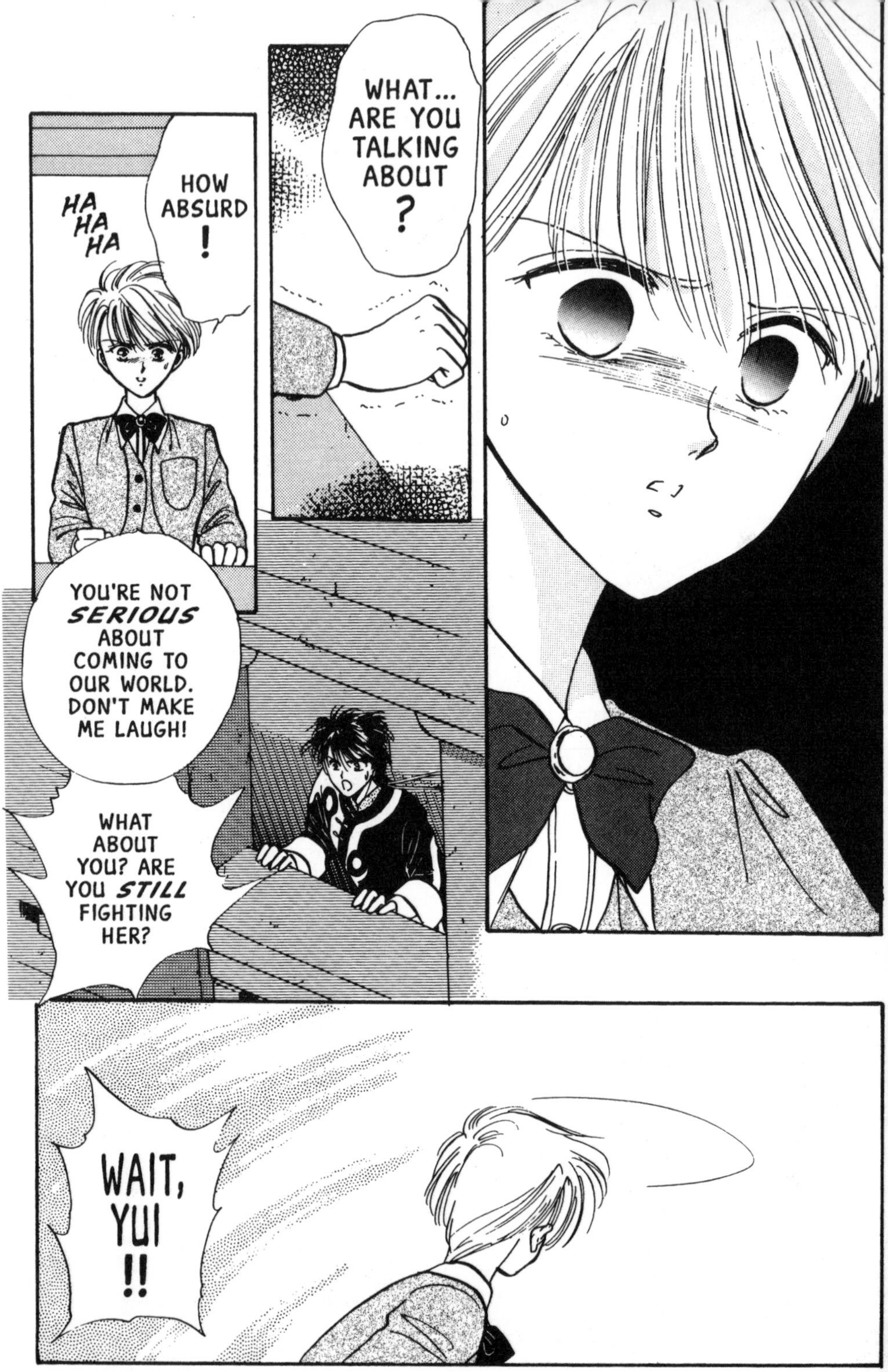
WHAT... ARE YOU TALKING ABOUT?
HA HA HA
HOW ABSURD!
YOU'RE NOT SERIOUS ABOUT COMING TO OUR WORLD. DON'T MAKE ME LAUGH!
WHAT ABOUT YOU? ARE YOU STILL FIGHTING HER?
WAIT, YUI!!

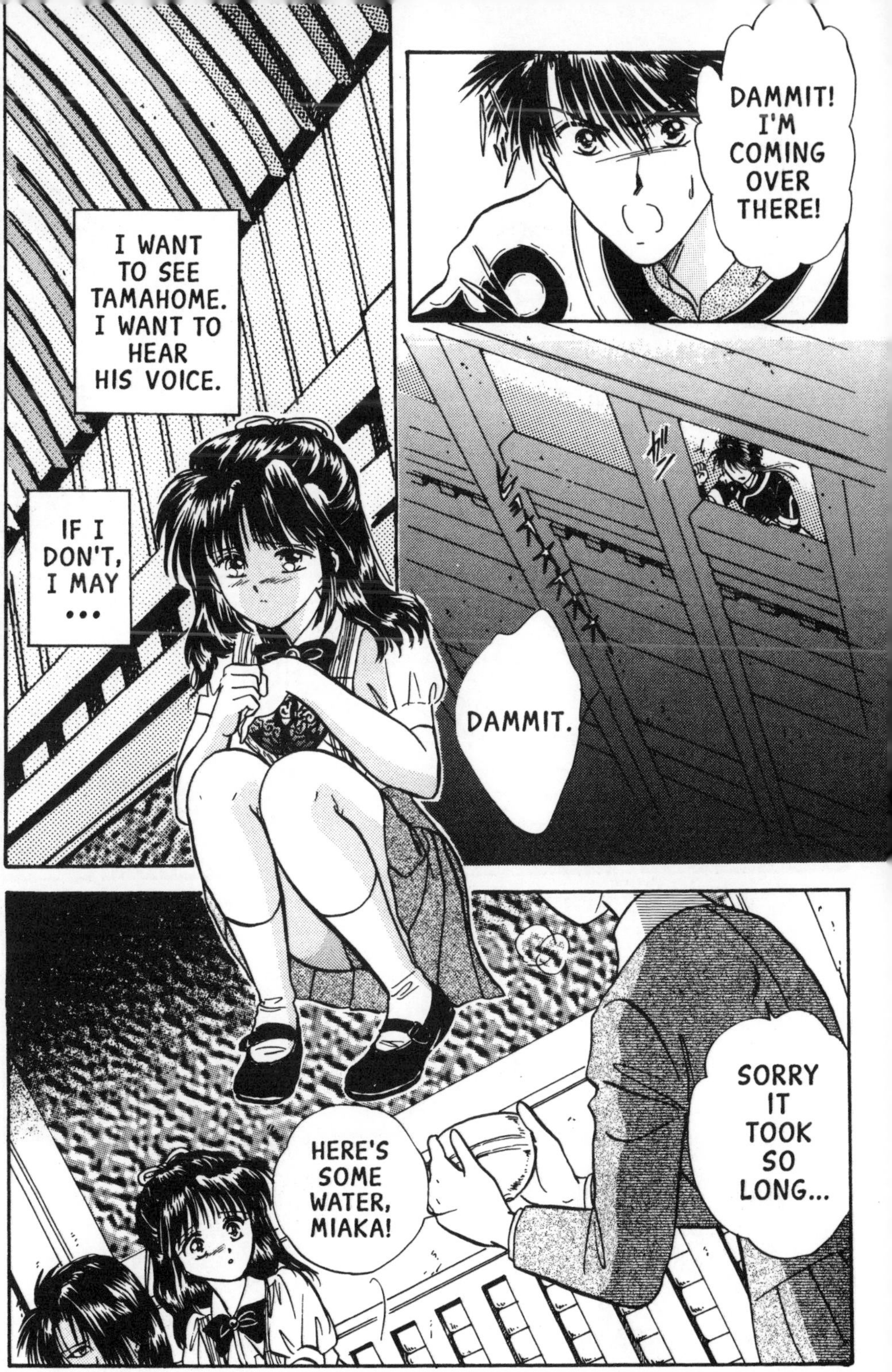
DAMMIT! I'M COMING OVER THERE!
DAMMIT.
I WANT TO SEE TAMAHOME. I WANT TO HEAR HIS VOICE.
IF I DON'T, I MAY ...
SORRY IT TOOK SO LONG...
HERE'S SOME WATER, MIAKA!

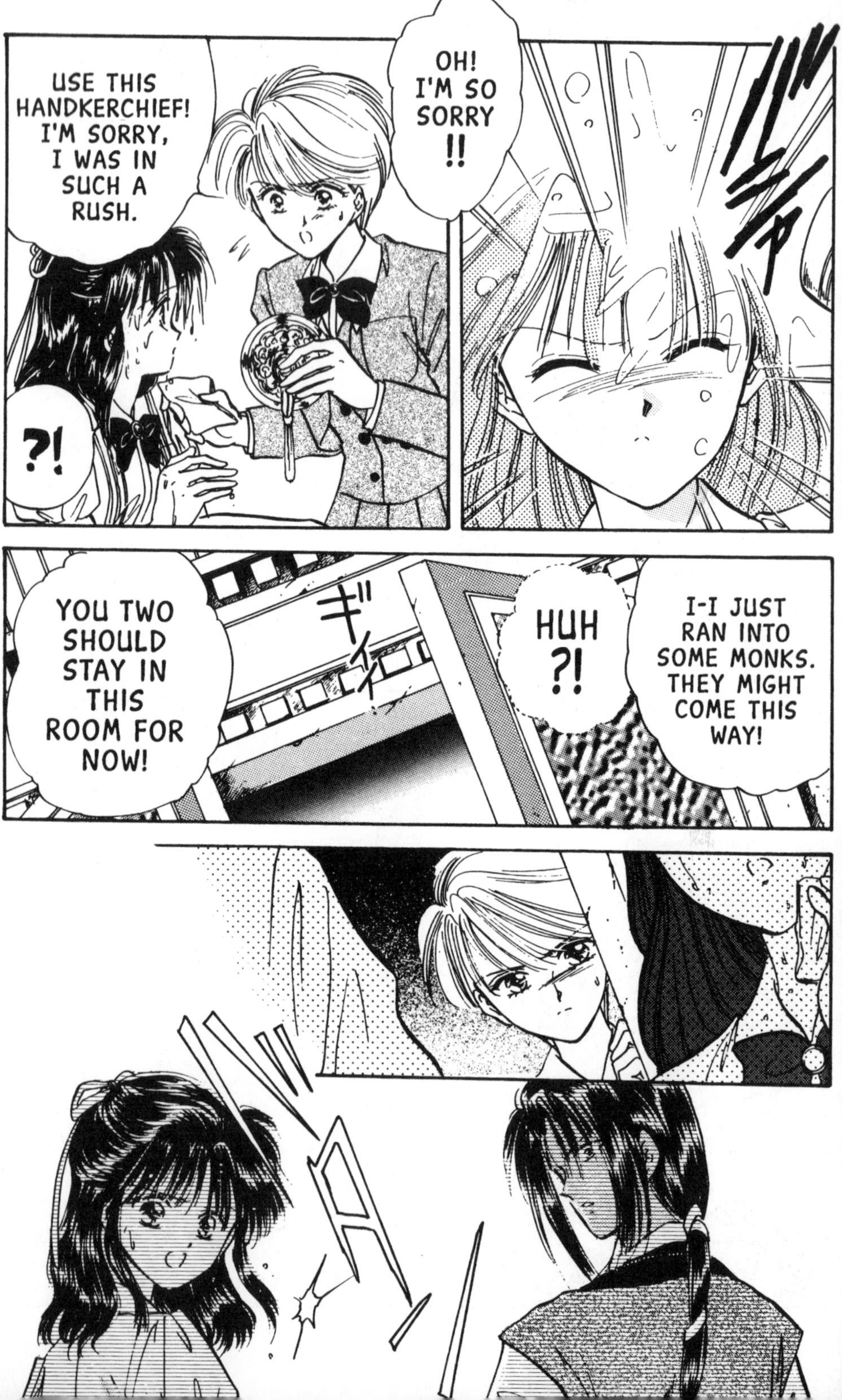
OH! I'M SO SORRY !!
USE THIS HANDKERCHIEF! I'M SORRY, I WAS IN SUCH A RUSH.
?!
I-I JUST RAN INTO SOME MONKS. THEY MIGHT COME THIS WAY!
HUH ?!
ギイ
YOU TWO SHOULD STAY IN THIS ROOM FOR NOW!

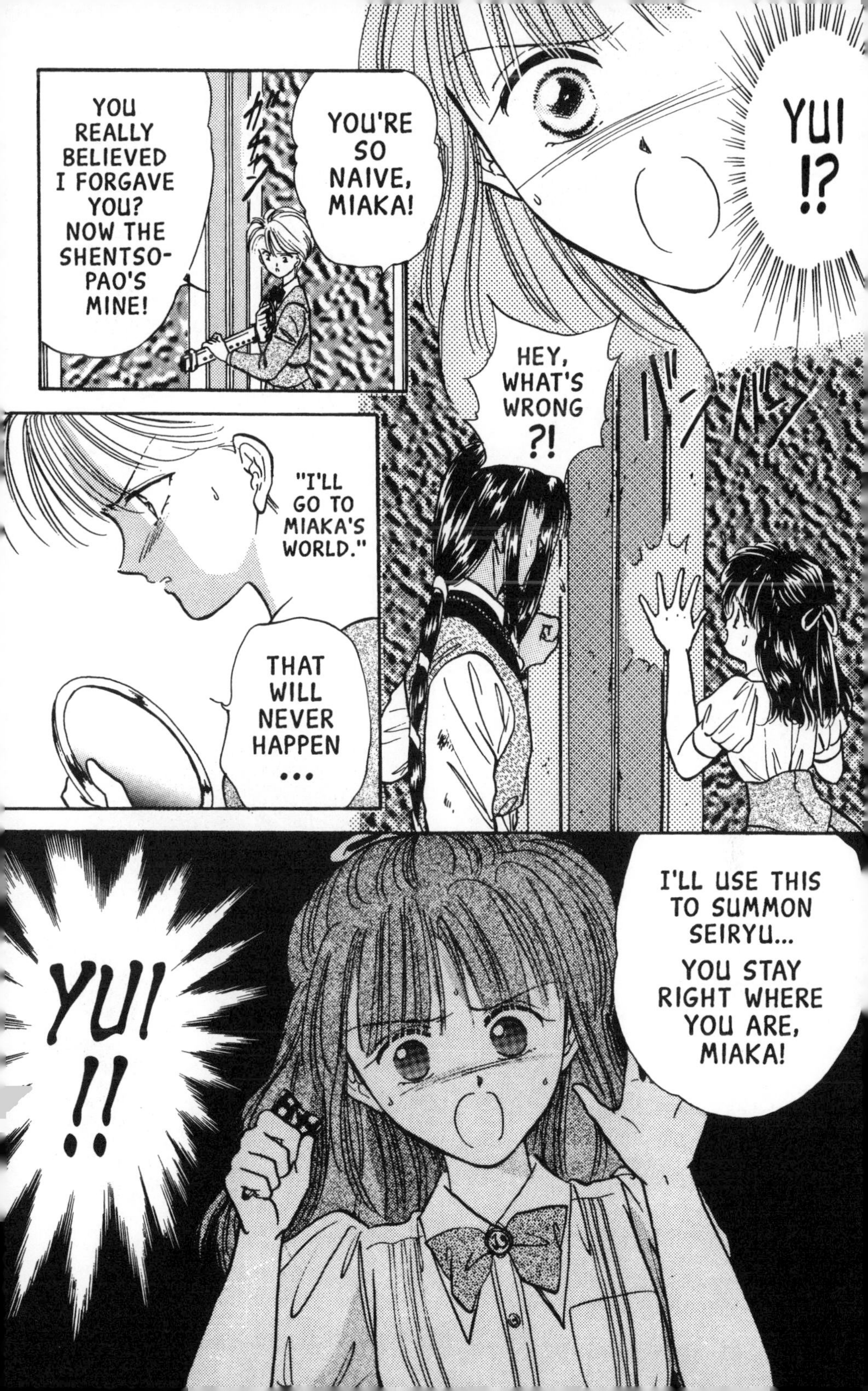
YUI !?
HEY, WHAT'S WRONG ?!
YOU'RE SO NAIVE, MIAKA!
YOU REALLY BELIEVED I FORGAVE YOU? NOW THE SHENTSO-PAO'S MINE!
"I'LL GO TO MIAKA'S WORLD."
THAT WILL NEVER HAPPEN...
I'LL USE THIS TO SUMMON SEIRYU... YOU STAY RIGHT WHERE YOU ARE, MIAKA!
YUI !!

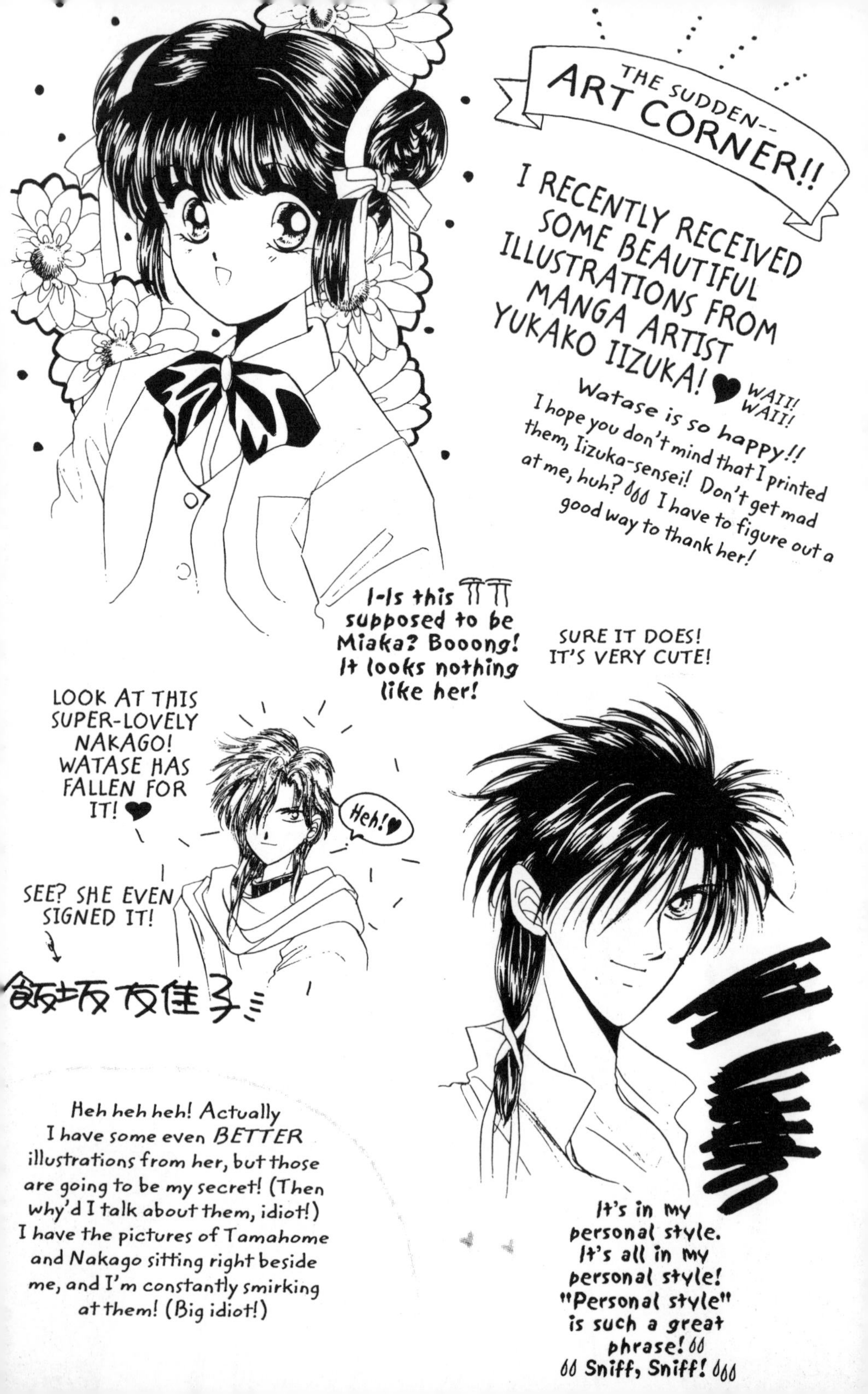
THE SUDDEN--
ART CORNER!!
I RECENTLY RECEIVED SOME BEAUTIFUL ILLUSTRATIONS FROM MANGA ARTIST YUKAKO IIZUKA! ♥
WAII! WAII!
Watase is so happy!! I hope you don't mind that I printed them, Iizuka-sensei! Don't get mad at me, huh? I have to figure out a good way to thank her!
I-Is this supposed to be Miaka? Booong! It looks nothing like her!
SURE IT DOES! IT'S VERY CUTE!
LOOK AT THIS SUPER-LOVELY NAKAGO! WATASE HAS FALLEN FOR IT! ♥
Heh! ♥
SEE? SHE EVEN SIGNED IT!
飯坂友佳子
Heh heh heh! Actually I have some even BETTER illustrations from her, but those are going to be my secret! (Then why'd I talk about them, idiot!) I have the pictures of Tamahome and Nakago sitting right beside me, and I'm constantly smirking at them! (Big idiot!)
It's in my personal style. It's all in my personal style! "Personal style" is such a great phrase!
Sniff, Sniff!

QUIZ!!

The bottom scene occurs one second after the top scene. How many items have changed?

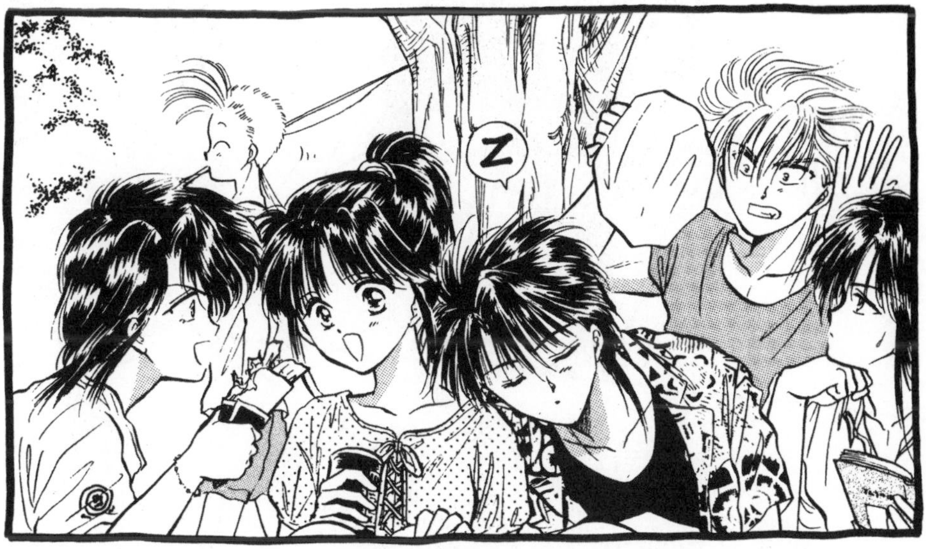
Z

Chapter Sixty-Four
Imminent Parting

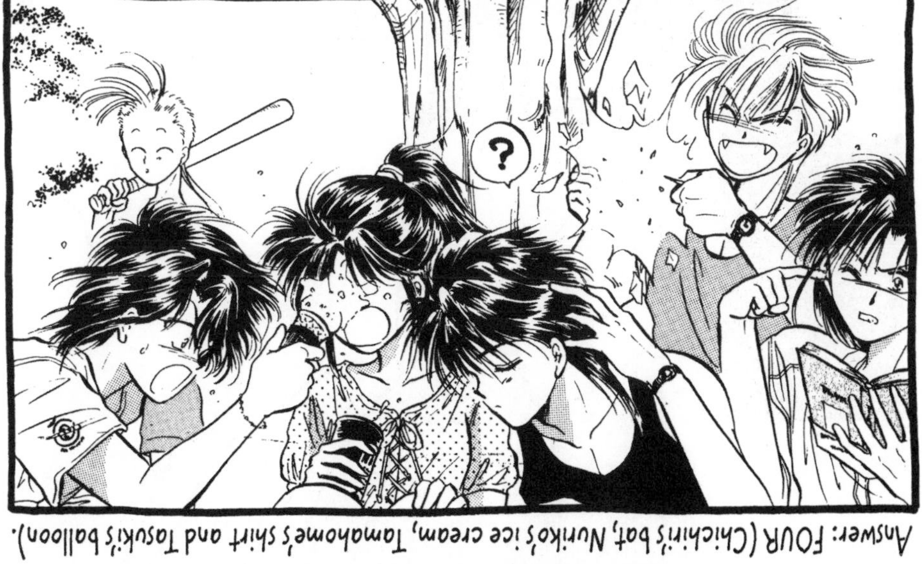
?

Answer: FOUR (Chichiri's bat, Nuriko's ice cream, Tamahome's shirt and Tasuki's balloon).

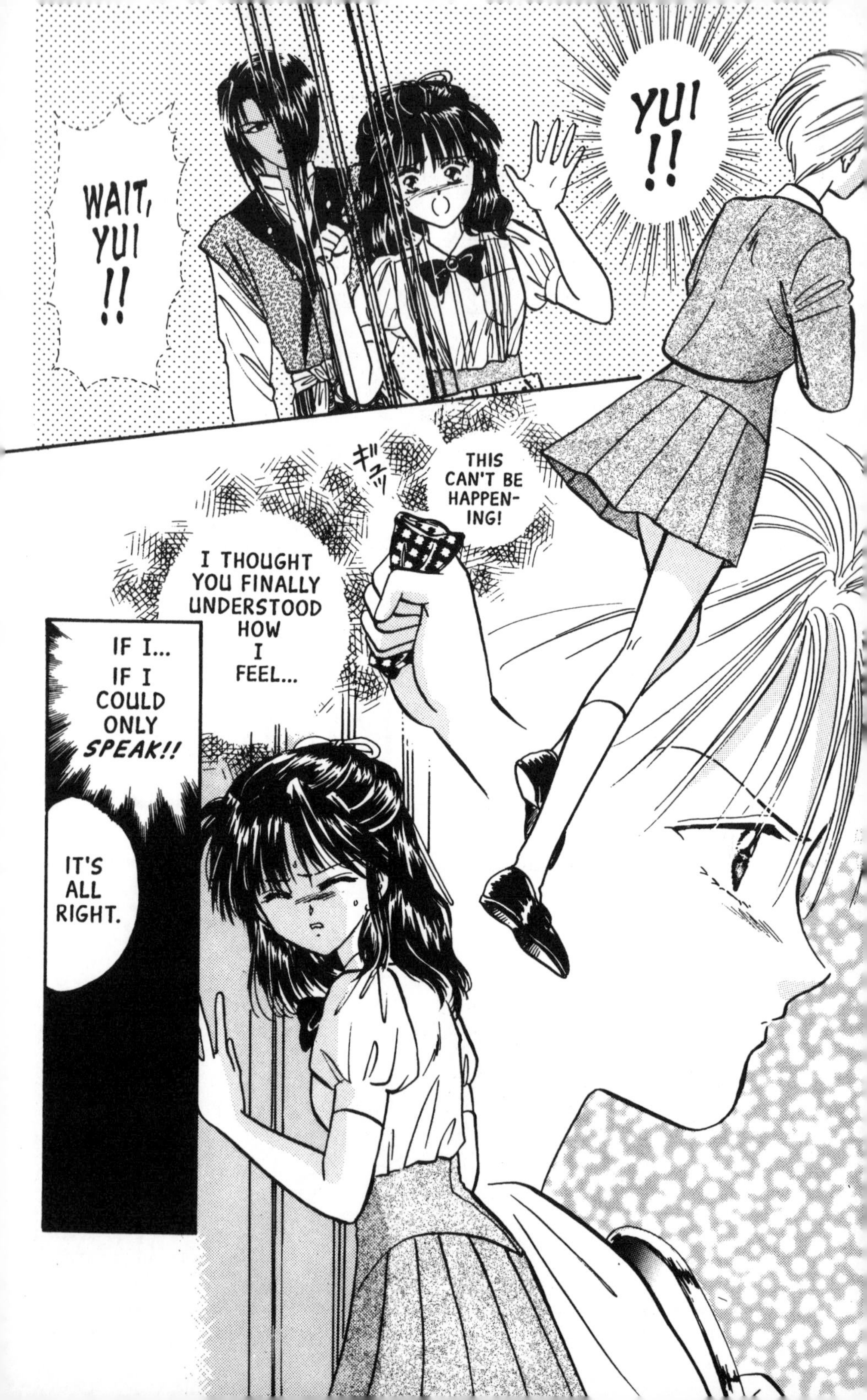
YUI!!
WAIT, YUI!!
ギュッ
THIS CAN'T BE HAPPEN-ING!
I THOUGHT YOU FINALLY UNDERSTOOD HOW I FEEL...
IF I... IF I COULD ONLY *SPEAK!!*
IT'S ALL RIGHT.

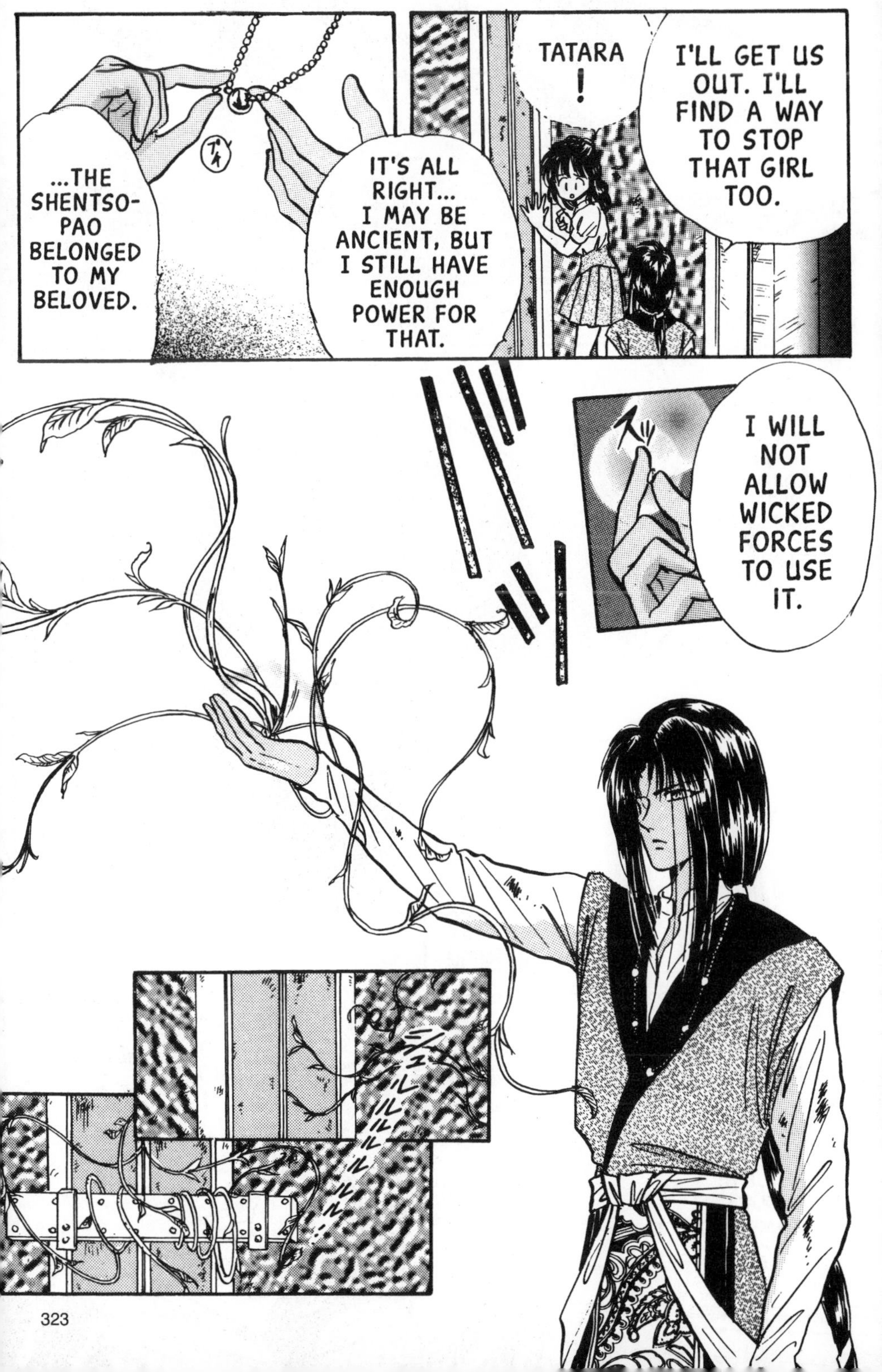
TATARA !
I'LL GET US OUT. I'LL FIND A WAY TO STOP THAT GIRL TOO.
IT'S ALL RIGHT... I MAY BE ANCIENT, BUT I STILL HAVE ENOUGH POWER FOR THAT.
...THE SHENTSO-PAO BELONGED TO MY BELOVED.
I WILL NOT ALLOW WICKED FORCES TO USE IT.

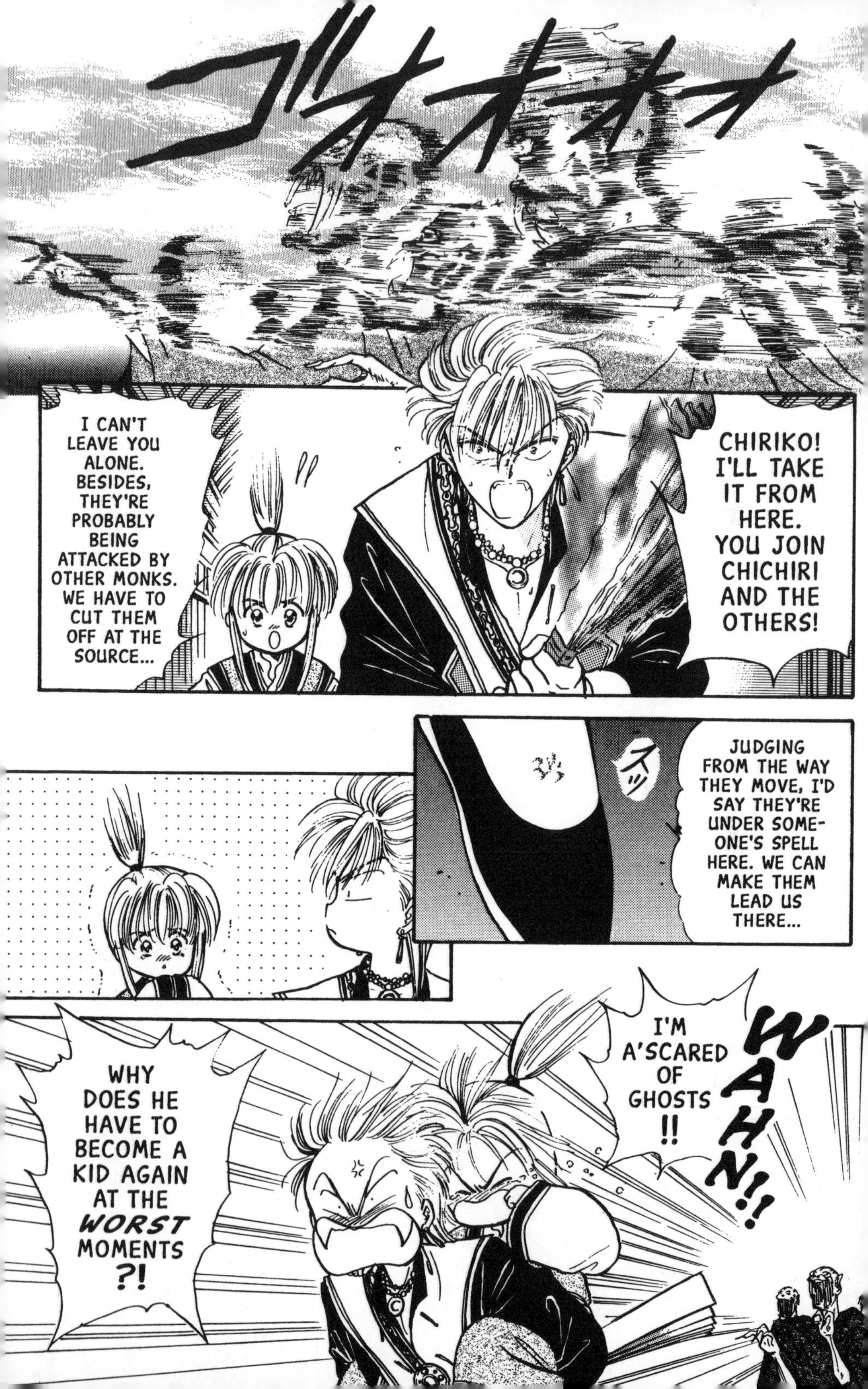
ゴオオオ
CHIRIKO! I'LL TAKE IT FROM HERE. YOU JOIN CHICHIRI AND THE OTHERS!
I CAN'T LEAVE YOU ALONE. BESIDES, THEY'RE PROBABLY BEING ATTACKED BY OTHER MONKS. WE HAVE TO CUT THEM OFF AT THE SOURCE...
JUDGING FROM THE WAY THEY MOVE, I'D SAY THEY'RE UNDER SOME-ONE'S SPELL HERE. WE CAN MAKE THEM LEAD US THERE...
スッ
WAHN!!
I'M A'SCARED OF GHOSTS!!
WHY DOES HE HAVE TO BECOME A KID AGAIN AT THE *WORST* MOMENTS?!

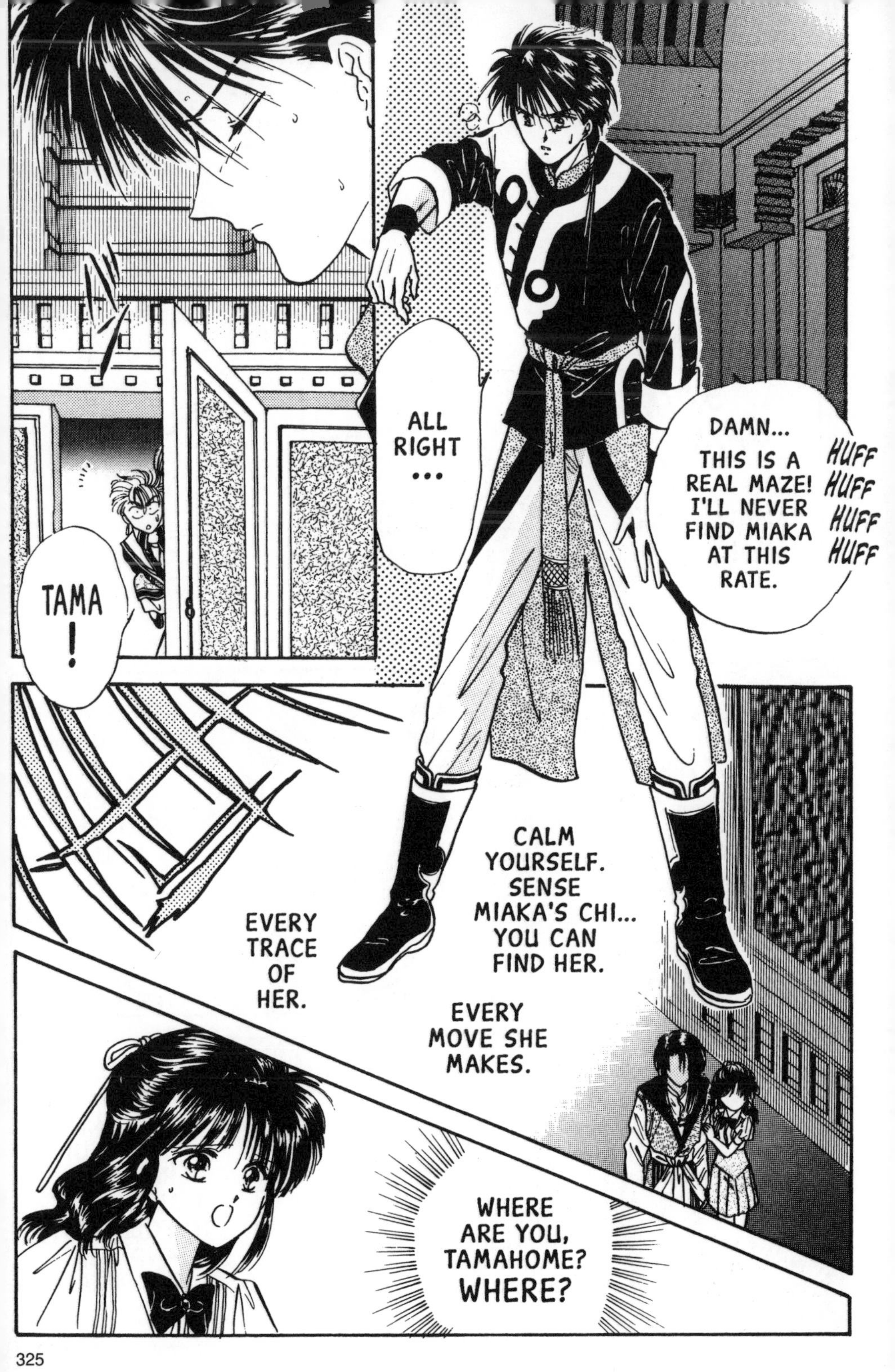
DAMN... THIS IS A REAL MAZE! I'LL NEVER FIND MIAKA AT THIS RATE.
HUFF HUFF HUFF HUFF
ALL RIGHT ...
TAMA!
CALM YOURSELF. SENSE MIAKA'S CHI... YOU CAN FIND HER.
EVERY TRACE OF HER.
EVERY MOVE SHE MAKES.
WHERE ARE YOU, TAMAHOME? WHERE?

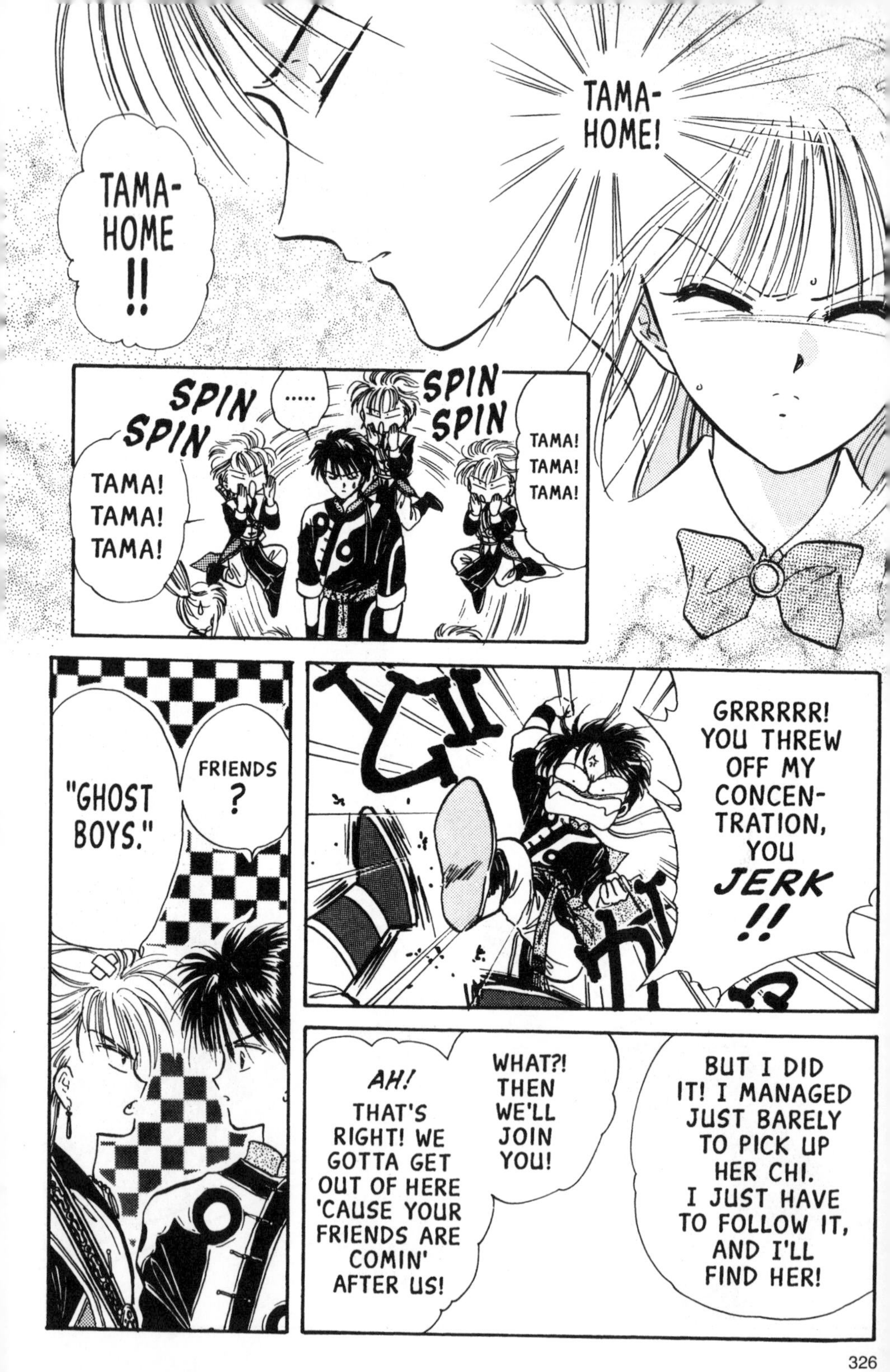
TAMA-HOME!
TAMA-HOME !!
TAMA! TAMA! TAMA!
SPIN SPIN
.....
SPIN SPIN
TAMA! TAMA! TAMA!
GRRRRRR! YOU THREW OFF MY CONCENTRATION, YOU JERK !!
BUT I DID IT! I MANAGED JUST BARELY TO PICK UP HER CHI. I JUST HAVE TO FOLLOW IT, AND I'LL FIND HER!
WHAT?! THEN WE'LL JOIN YOU!
AH! THAT'S RIGHT! WE GOTTA GET OUT OF HERE 'CAUSE YOUR FRIENDS ARE COMIN' AFTER US!
FRIENDS ?
"GHOST BOYS."

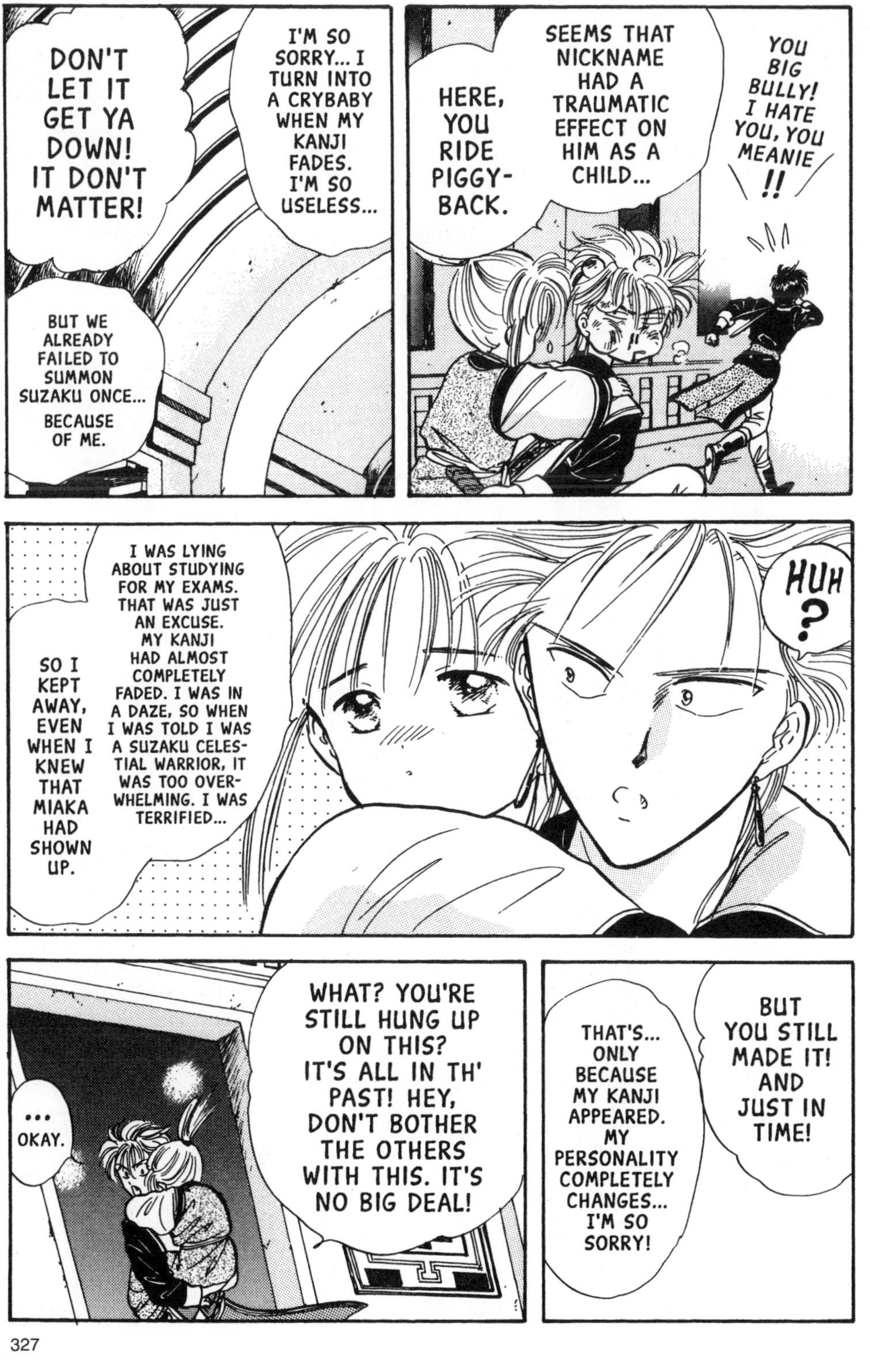
YOU BIG BULLY! I HATE YOU, YOU MEANIE!!
SEEMS THAT NICKNAME HAD A TRAUMATIC EFFECT ON HIM AS A CHILD...
HERE, YOU RIDE PIGGY-BACK.
I'M SO SORRY... I TURN INTO A CRYBABY WHEN MY KANJI FADES. I'M SO USELESS...
DON'T LET IT GET YA DOWN! IT DON'T MATTER!
BUT WE ALREADY FAILED TO SUMMON SUZAKU ONCE... BECAUSE OF ME.
HUH?
I WAS LYING ABOUT STUDYING FOR MY EXAMS. THAT WAS JUST AN EXCUSE. MY KANJI HAD ALMOST COMPLETELY FADED. I WAS IN A DAZE, SO WHEN I WAS TOLD I WAS A SUZAKU CELESTIAL WARRIOR, IT WAS TOO OVERWHELMING. I WAS TERRIFIED...
SO I KEPT AWAY, EVEN WHEN I KNEW THAT MIAKA HAD SHOWN UP.
BUT YOU STILL MADE IT! AND JUST IN TIME!
THAT'S... ONLY BECAUSE MY KANJI APPEARED. MY PERSONALITY COMPLETELY CHANGES... I'M SO SORRY!
WHAT? YOU'RE STILL HUNG UP ON THIS? IT'S ALL IN TH' PAST! HEY, DON'T BOTHER THE OTHERS WITH THIS. IT'S NO BIG DEAL!
...OKAY.

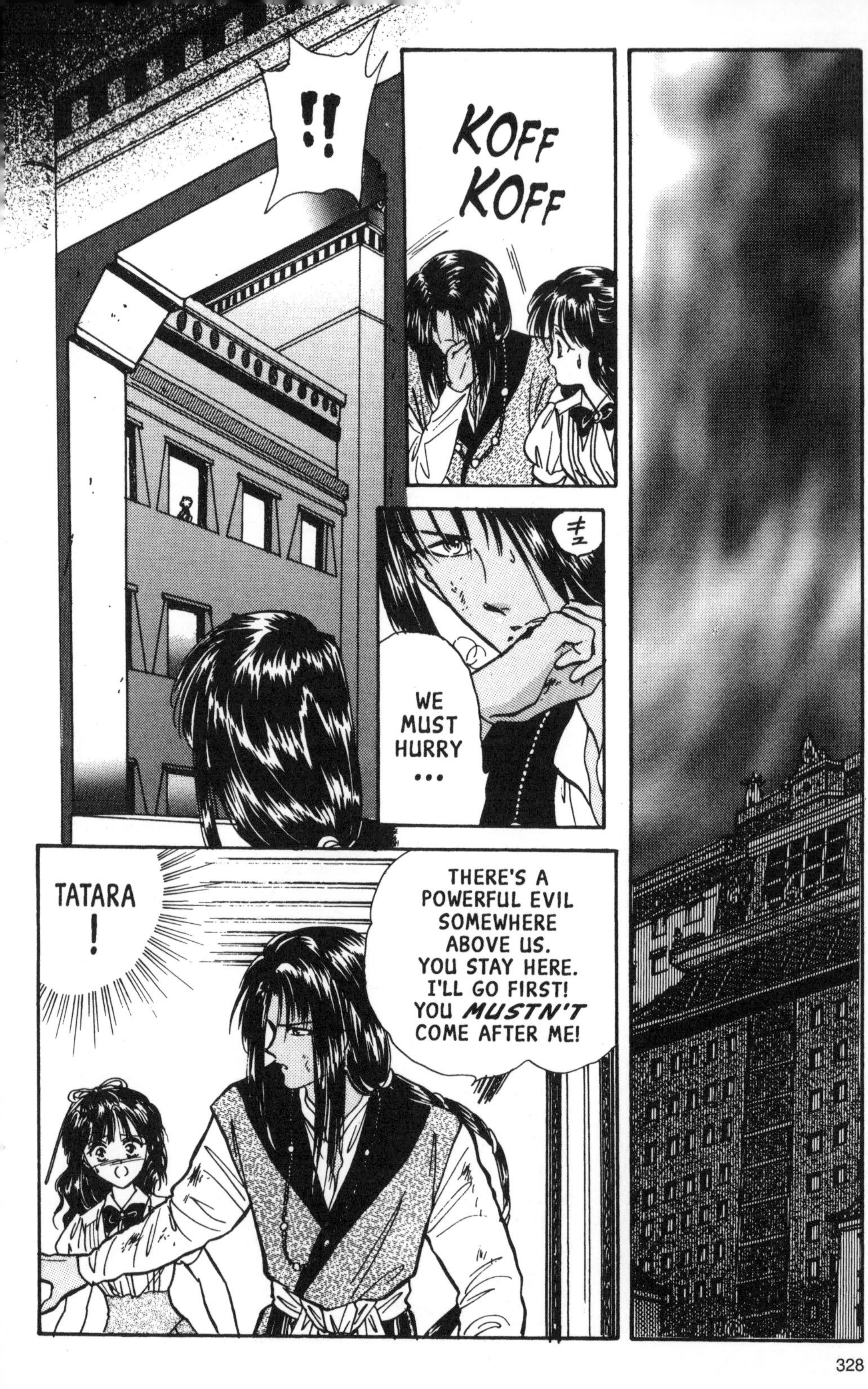
KOFF KOFF
キュ
WE MUST HURRY...
!!
TATARA!
THERE'S A POWERFUL EVIL SOMEWHERE ABOVE US. YOU STAY HERE. I'LL GO FIRST! YOU *MUSTN'T* COME AFTER ME!

Next is the No. 2 character in the CD survey, Tasuki. His Kansai dialect is a humorous touch. I wanted him to be different from the others. I had a wolf boy in mind, so his hairstyle and fangs were all part of that. It wouldn't have been interesting if he was just another handsome guy, a variation on "Tama" and "Hori." Still, my concept design for him changed several times. His personality was totally different in the first version, and the idea was that he was supposed to be a childhood friend of Tamahome's. The mountain bandit idea came to me because I wanted him to stand out from the usual cast of characters like farmer (peasant), emperor, monk, or doctor. There's one in Suikoden. And his harisen (fan) was another touch. I wanted something like the Basho harisen in Saiyuki, and then I was like, "speaking of Osaka," I came up with the idea of his accent. By the way, although you don't see it very often, Tasuki's a very fast runner. *Really!* You know how he just swept Miaka away when he first appeared. He's a strong fighter. He's not limited to just one strength like the other celestial warriors. He's incredibly strong in all regards.

I really wanted Chichiri to be very unique. He's based on the draft I did when I first came up with the story. I wanted someone lighthearted. Because he's a priest, he should be bald, but I ended up giving him an odd hairstyle. I claimed he had a Mohawk in volume 4, but it isn't really. It's just that he has very long bangs.

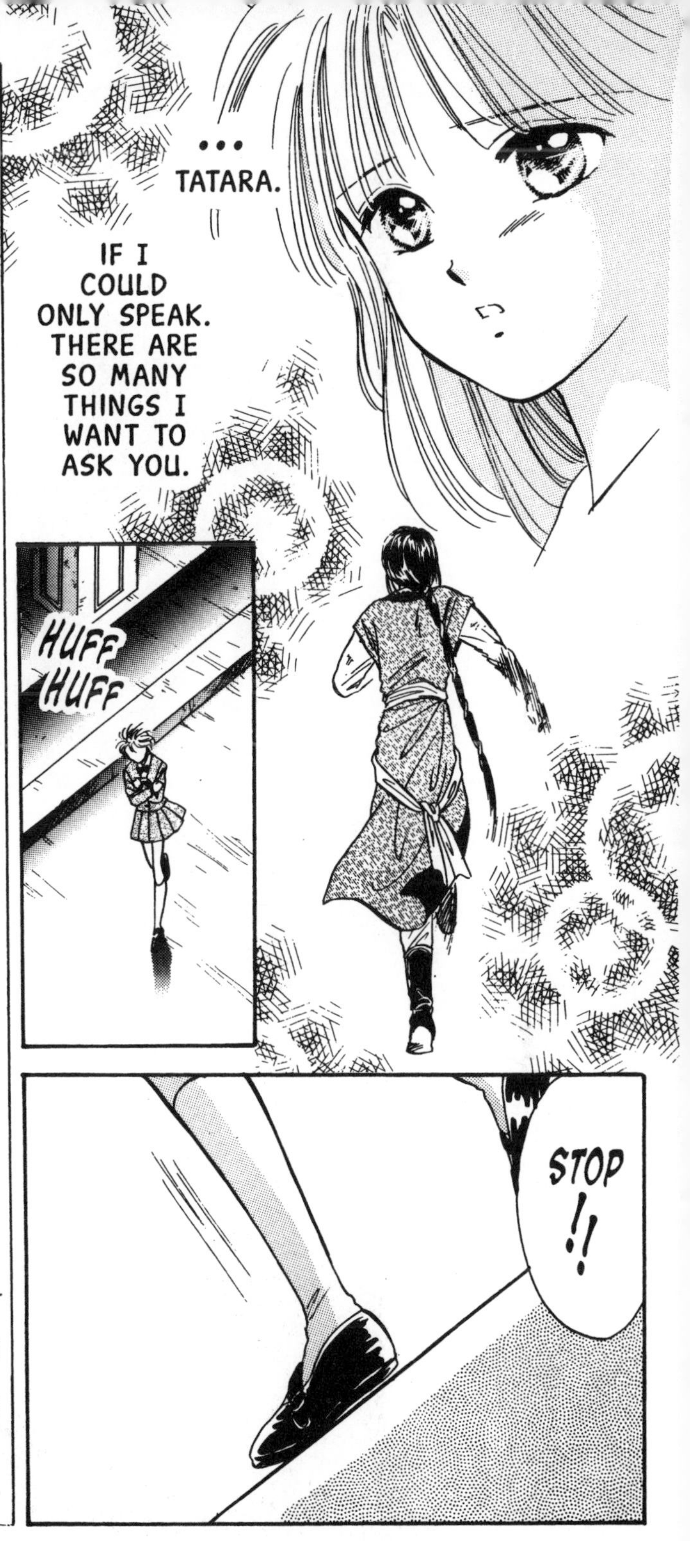
... TATARA.
IF I COULD ONLY SPEAK. THERE ARE SO MANY THINGS I WANT TO ASK YOU.
HUFF HUFF
STOP !!

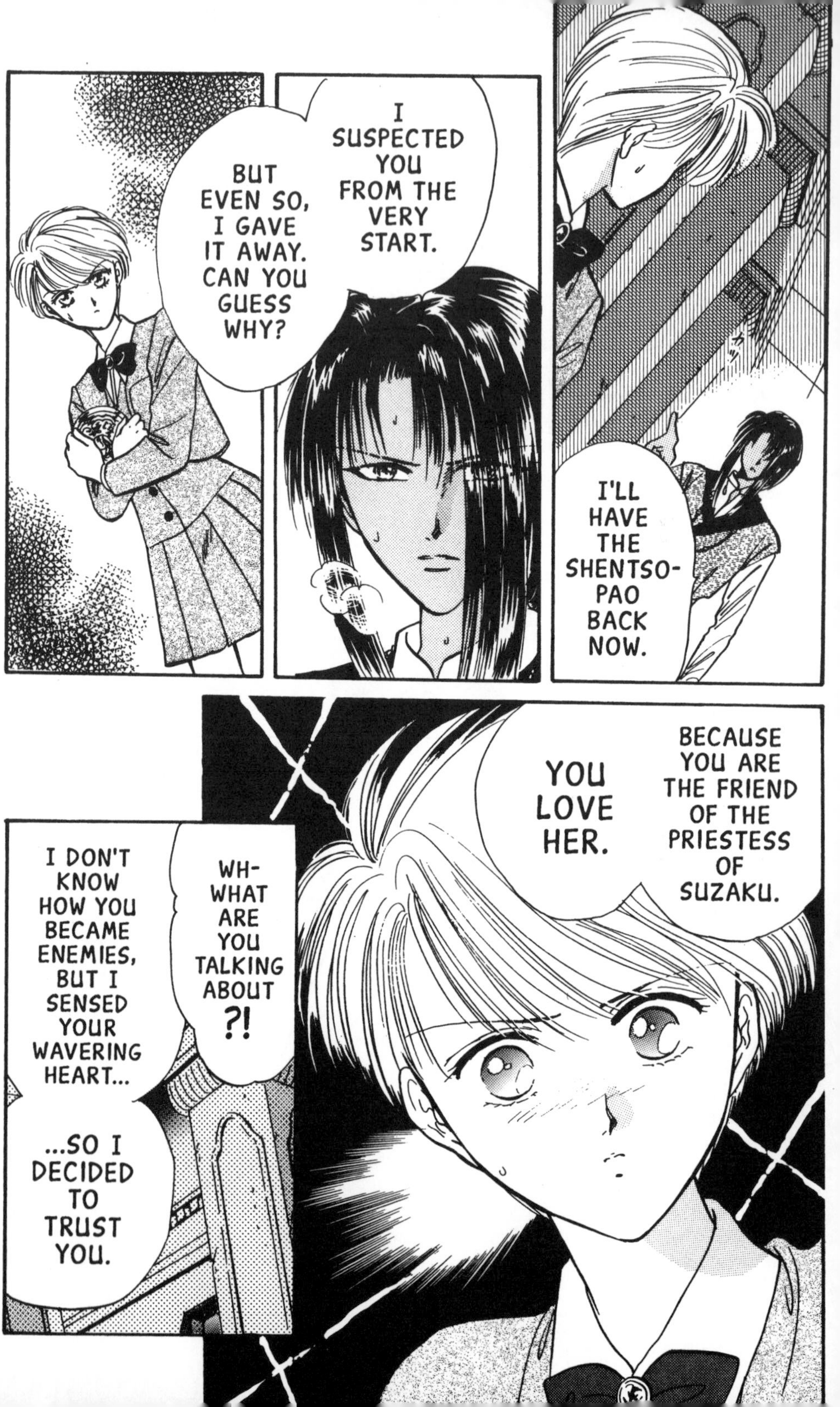
I'LL HAVE THE SHENTSO-PAO BACK NOW.
I SUSPECTED YOU FROM THE VERY START.
BUT EVEN SO, I GAVE IT AWAY. CAN YOU GUESS WHY?
BECAUSE YOU ARE THE FRIEND OF THE PRIESTESS OF SUZAKU.
YOU LOVE HER.
WH-WHAT ARE YOU TALKING ABOUT?!
I DON'T KNOW HOW YOU BECAME ENEMIES, BUT I SENSED YOUR WAVERING HEART...
...SO I DECIDED TO TRUST YOU.

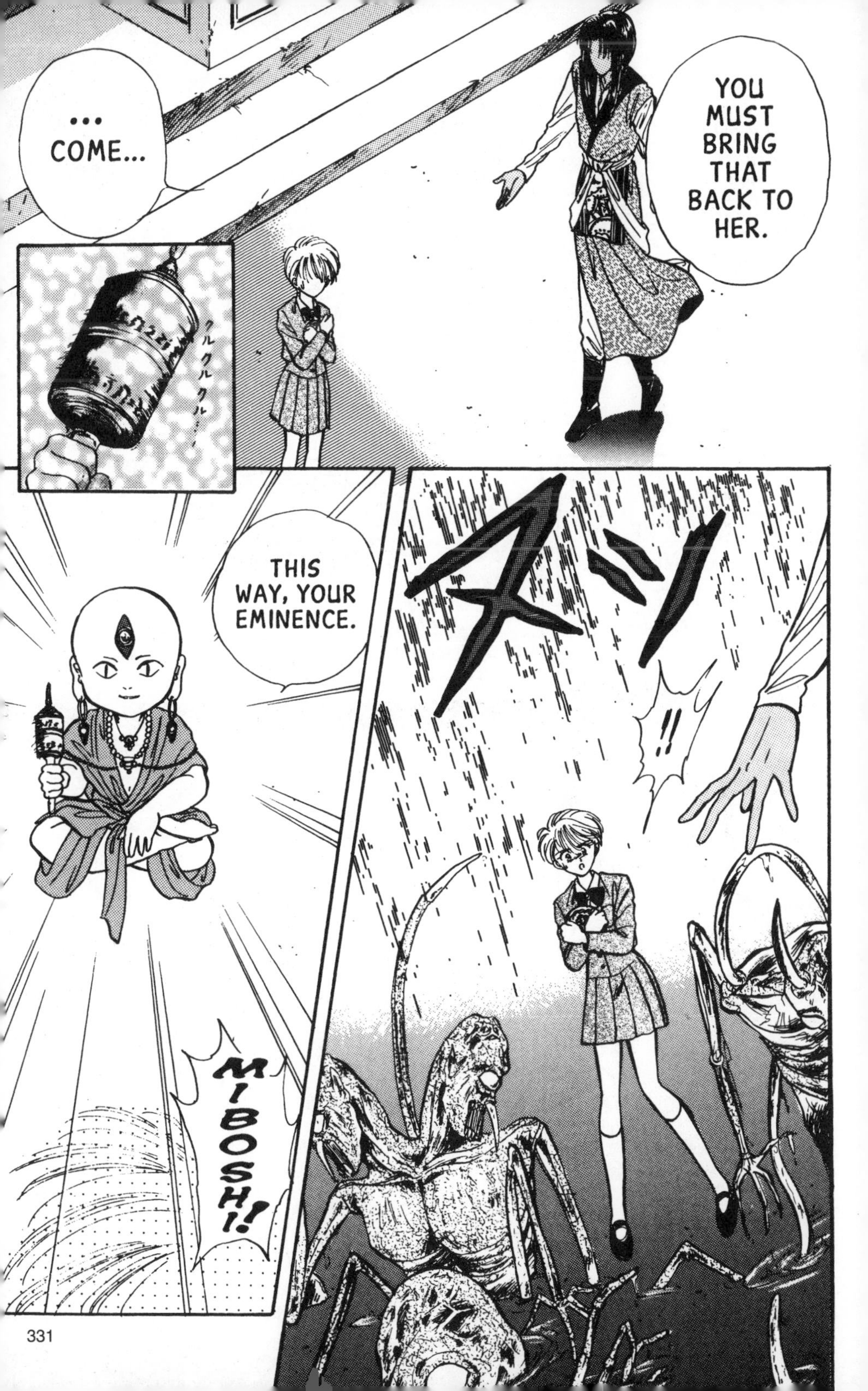
YOU MUST BRING THAT BACK TO HER.
... COME...
クルクルクル…
スッ
!!
THIS WAY, YOUR EMINENCE.
MIBOSHI!!

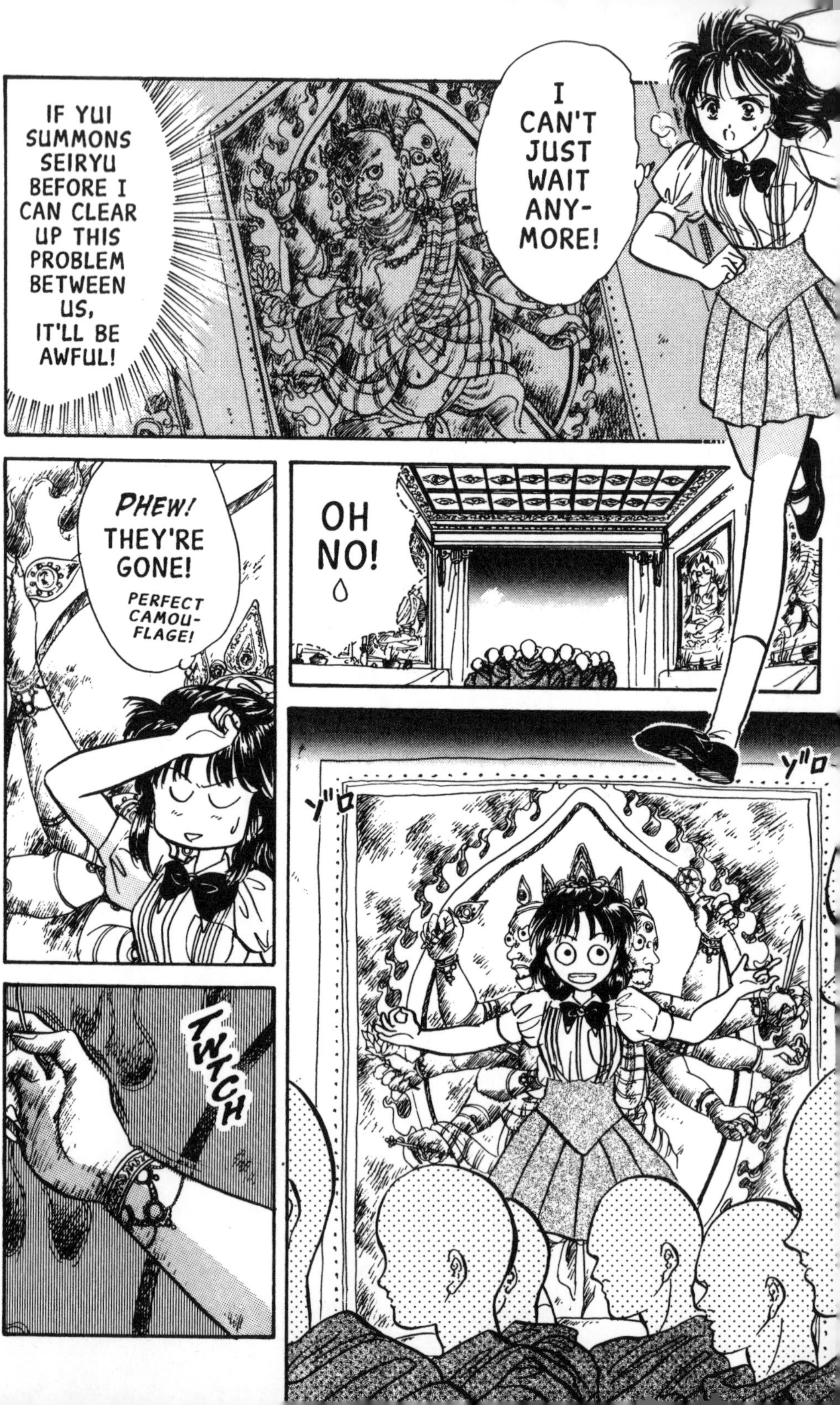
I CAN'T JUST WAIT ANYMORE!
IF YUI SUMMONS SEIRYU BEFORE I CAN CLEAR UP THIS PROBLEM BETWEEN US, IT'LL BE AWFUL!
OH NO!
PHEW! THEY'RE GONE!
PERFECT CAMOUFLAGE!
ゾロ
ゾロ
TWITCH

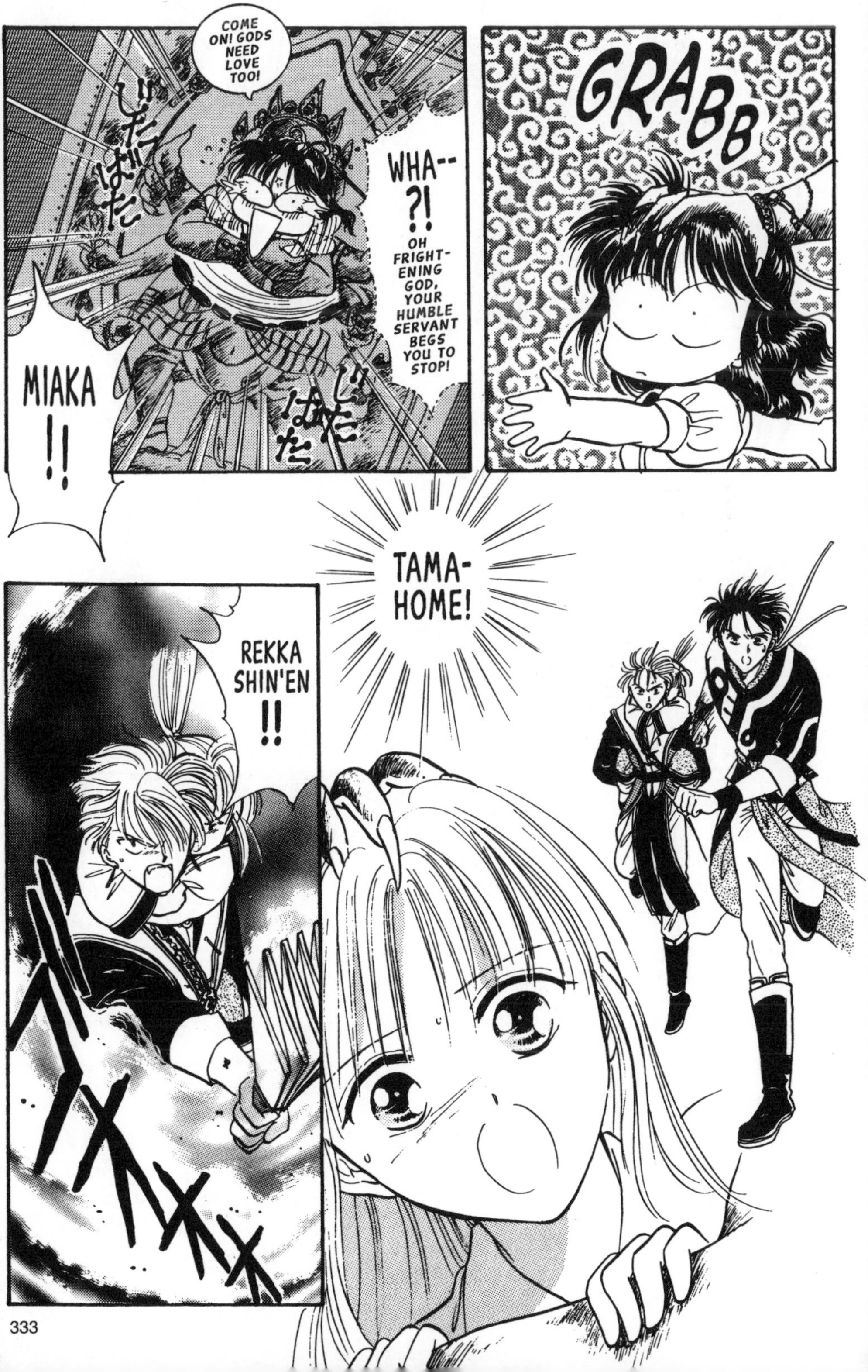
GRABB
COME ON! GODS NEED LOVE TOO!
WHA-- ?!
OH FRIGHTENING GOD, YOUR HUMBLE SERVANT BEGS YOU TO STOP!
MIAKA !!
TAMA-HOME!
REKKA SHIN'EN !!

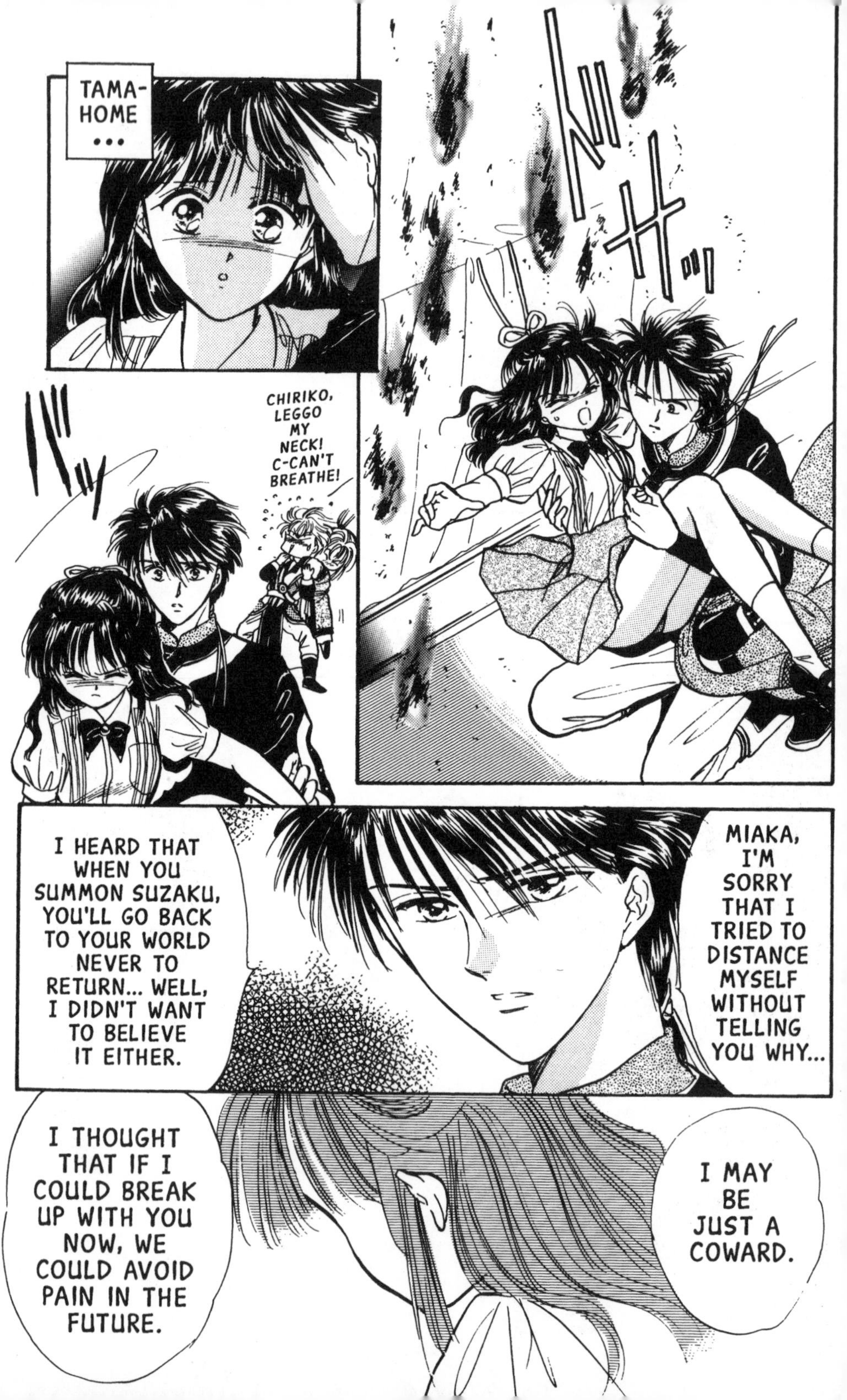
TAMA-HOME...
CHIRIKO, LEGGO MY NECK! C-CAN'T BREATHE!
MIAKA, I'M SORRY THAT I TRIED TO DISTANCE MYSELF WITHOUT TELLING YOU WHY...
I HEARD THAT WHEN YOU SUMMON SUZAKU, YOU'LL GO BACK TO YOUR WORLD NEVER TO RETURN... WELL, I DIDN'T WANT TO BELIEVE IT EITHER.
I MAY BE JUST A COWARD.
I THOUGHT THAT IF I COULD BREAK UP WITH YOU NOW, WE COULD AVOID PAIN IN THE FUTURE.

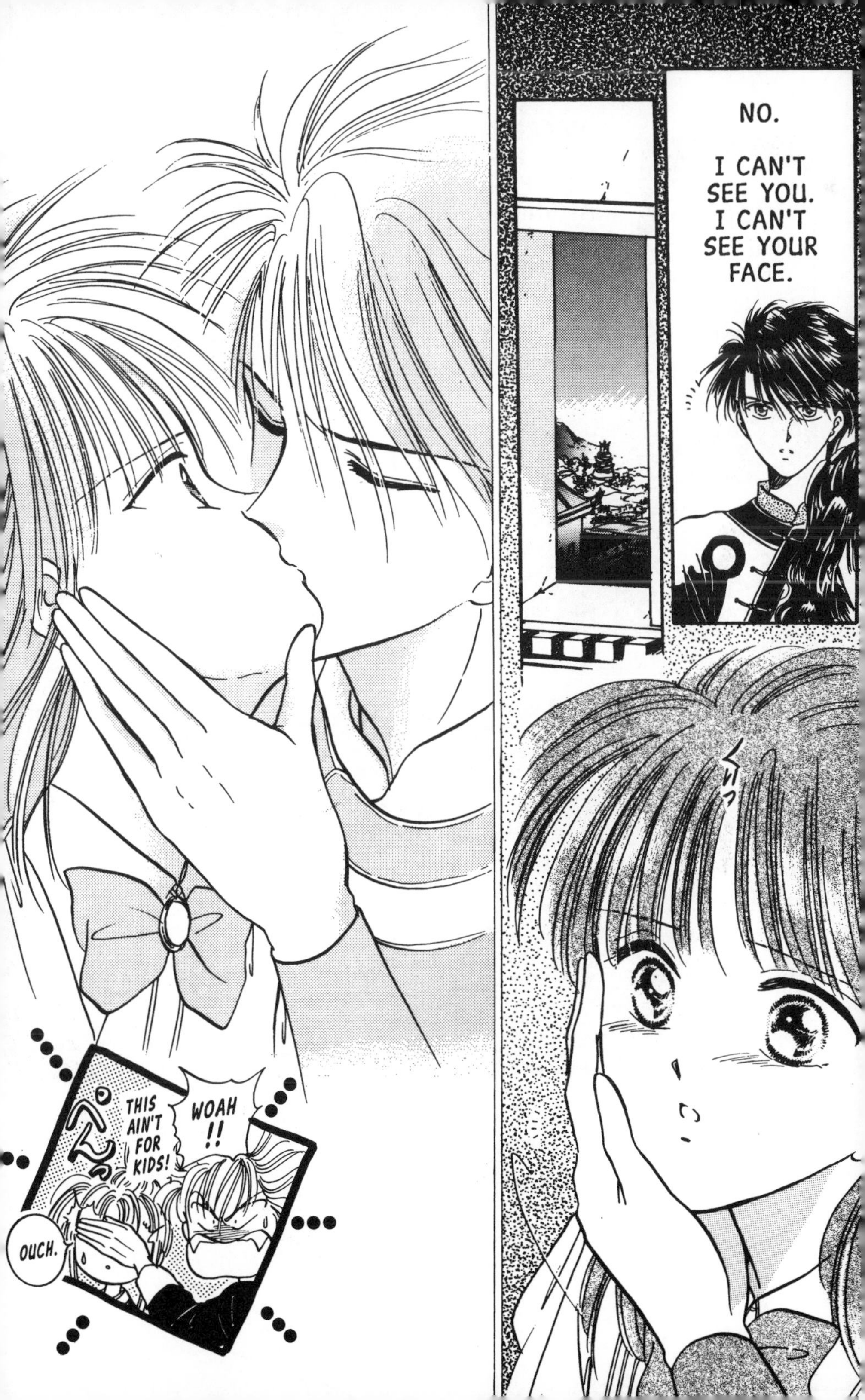
NO.
I CAN'T SEE YOU. I CAN'T SEE YOUR FACE.
WOAH !!
THIS AIN'T FOR KIDS!
OUCH.

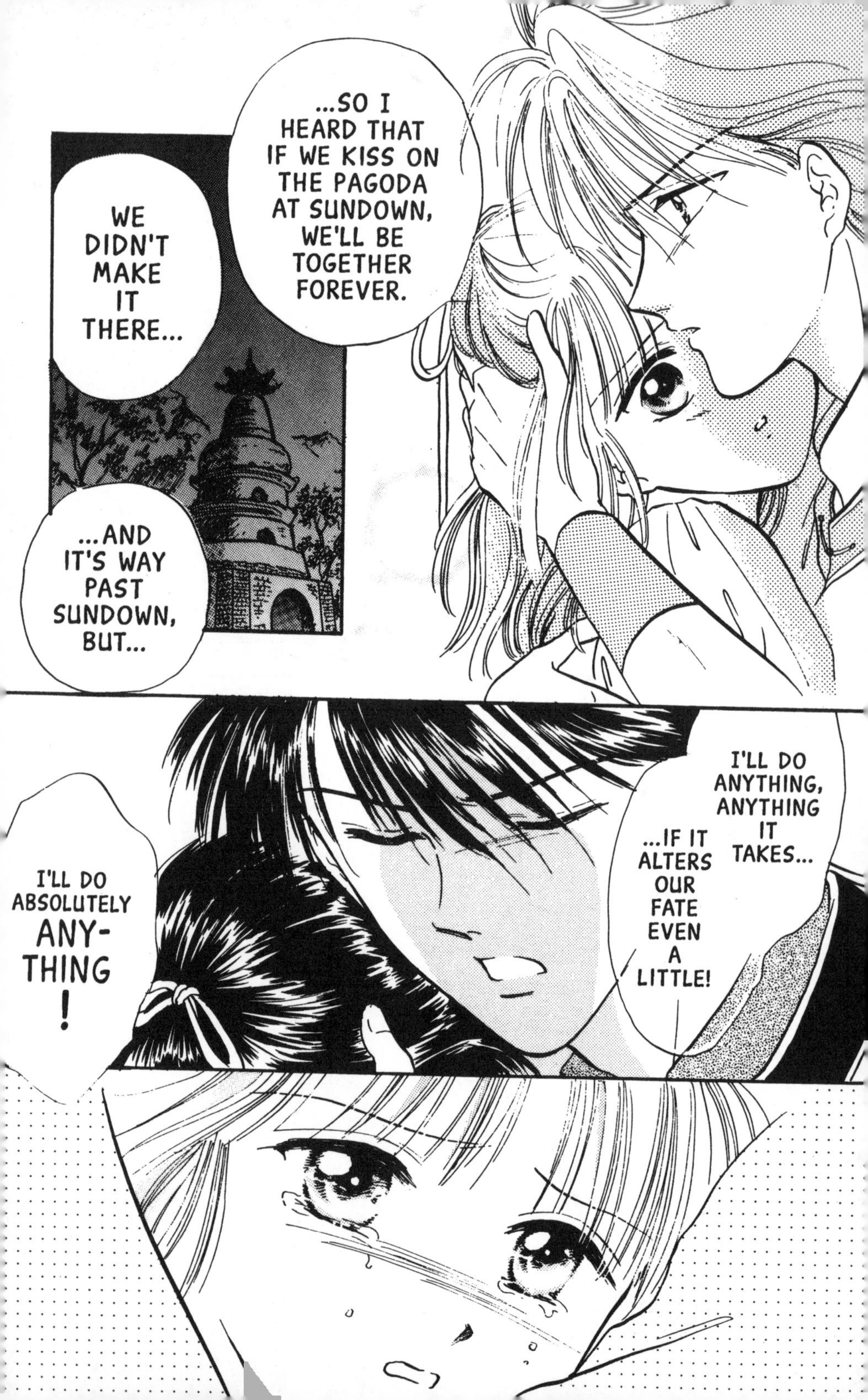
...SO I HEARD THAT IF WE KISS ON THE PAGODA AT SUNDOWN, WE'LL BE TOGETHER FOREVER.
WE DIDN'T MAKE IT THERE...
...AND IT'S WAY PAST SUNDOWN, BUT...
I'LL DO ANYTHING, ANYTHING IT TAKES...
...IF IT ALTERS OUR FATE EVEN A LITTLE!
I'LL DO ABSOLUTELY ANY-THING!

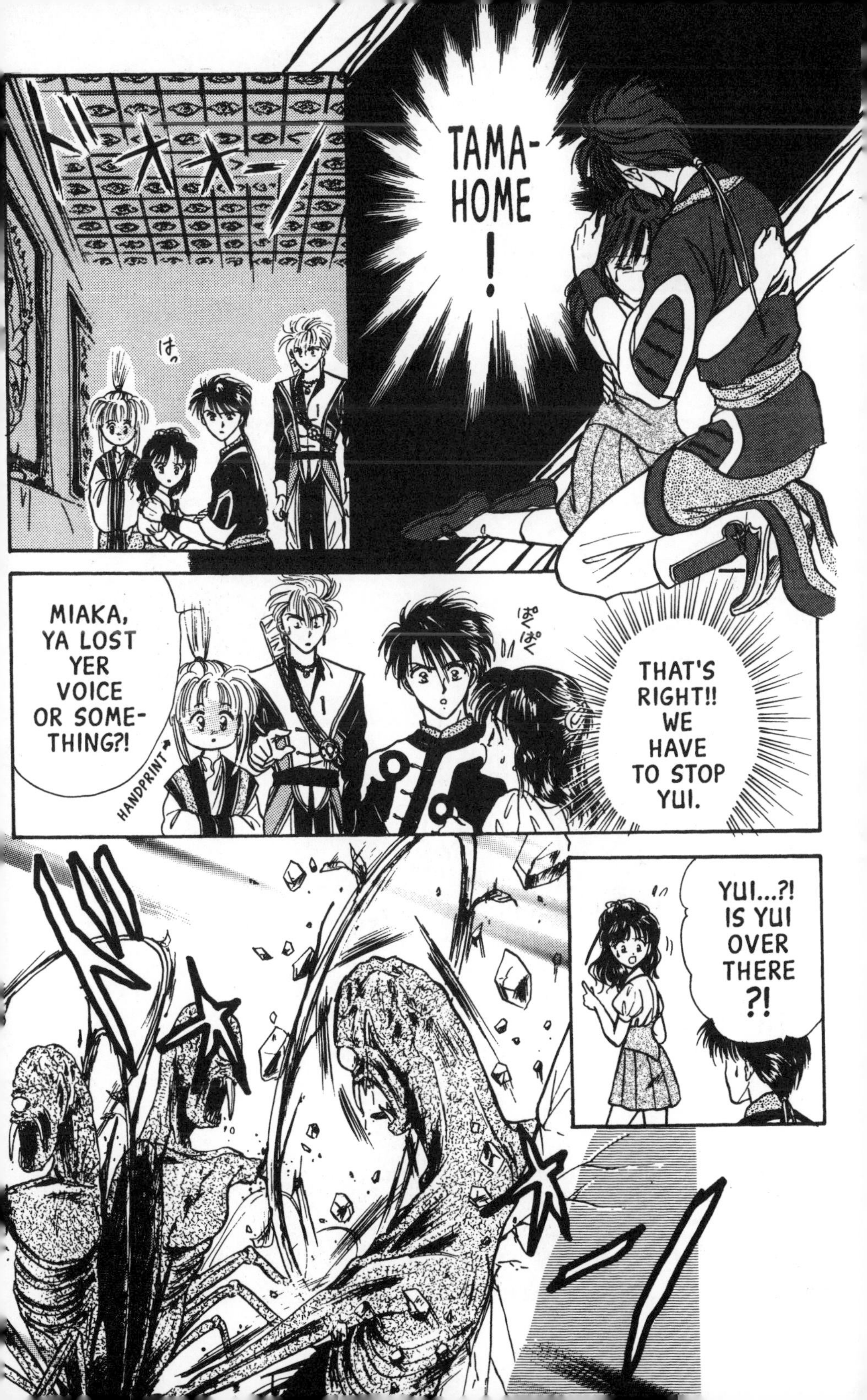
TAMA-HOME !
はっ
THAT'S RIGHT!! WE HAVE TO STOP YUI.
ぱくぱく
MIAKA, YA LOST YER VOICE OR SOME-THING?!
HANDPRINT
YUI...?! IS YUI OVER THERE ?!

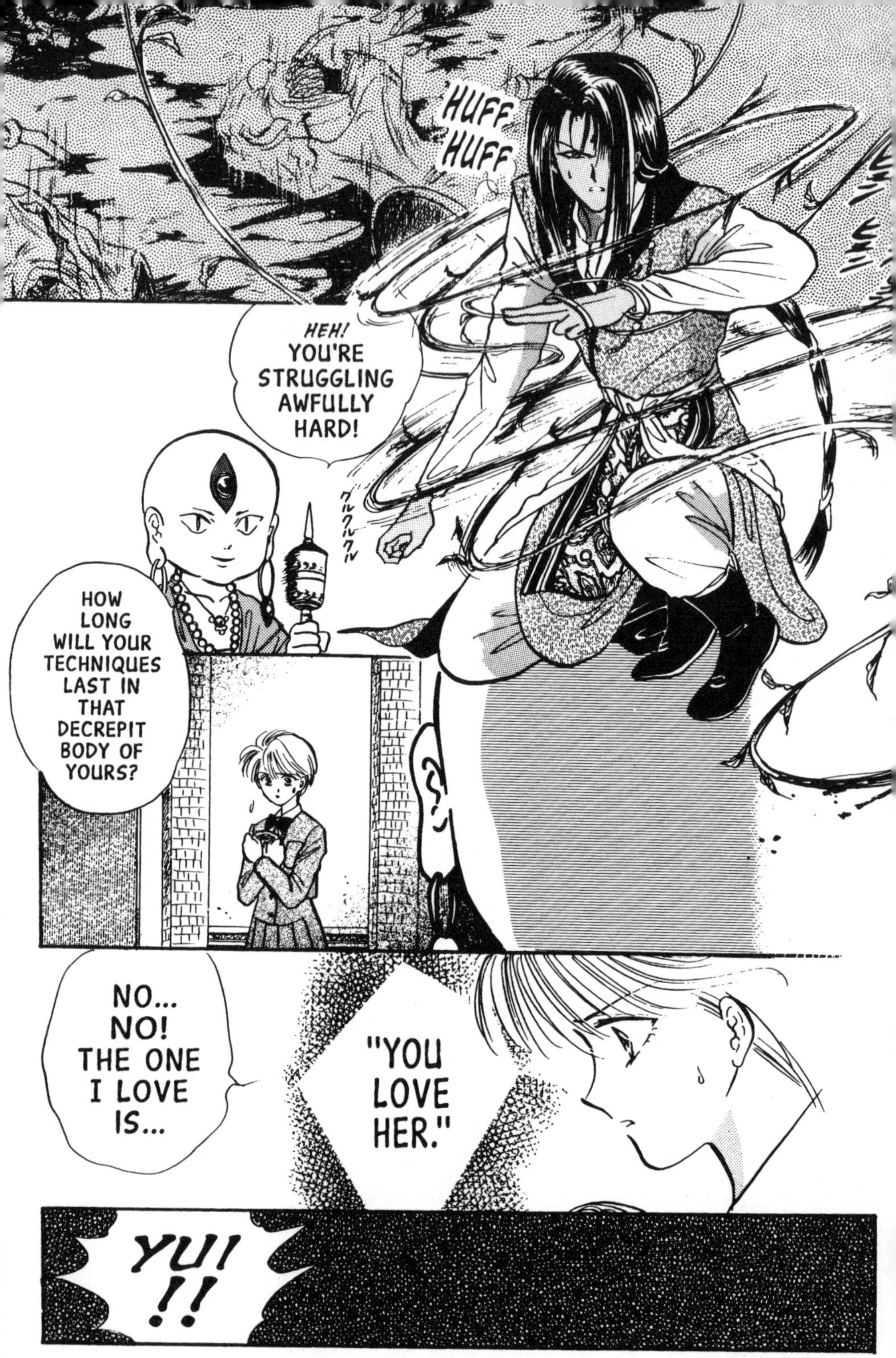
HUFF HUFF
HEH! YOU'RE STRUGGLING AWFULLY HARD!
HOW LONG WILL YOUR TECHNIQUES LAST IN THAT DECREPIT BODY OF YOURS?
"YOU LOVE HER."
NO... NO! THE ONE I LOVE IS...
YUI!!

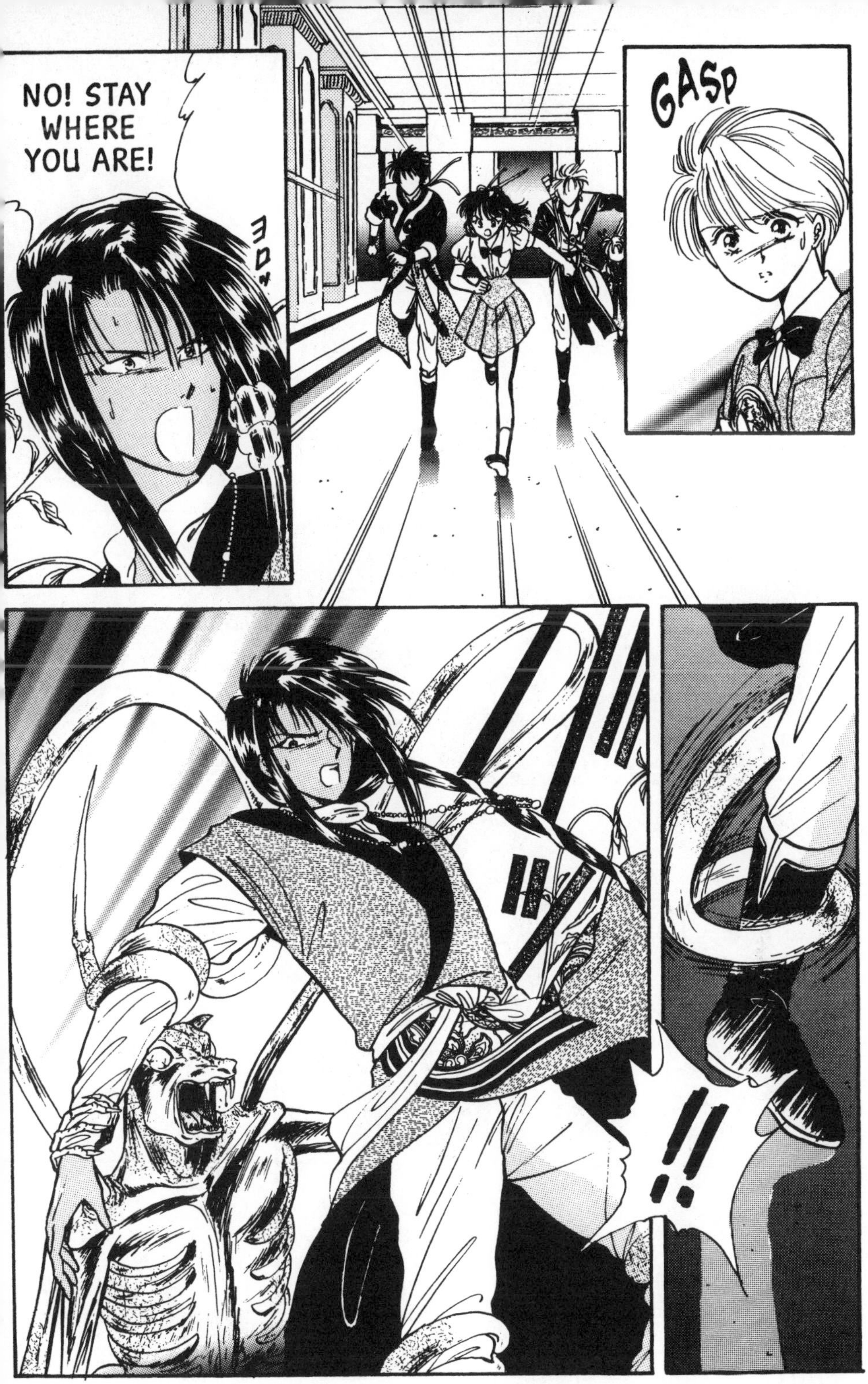
GASP
NO! STAY WHERE YOU ARE!
ヨロッ
!!

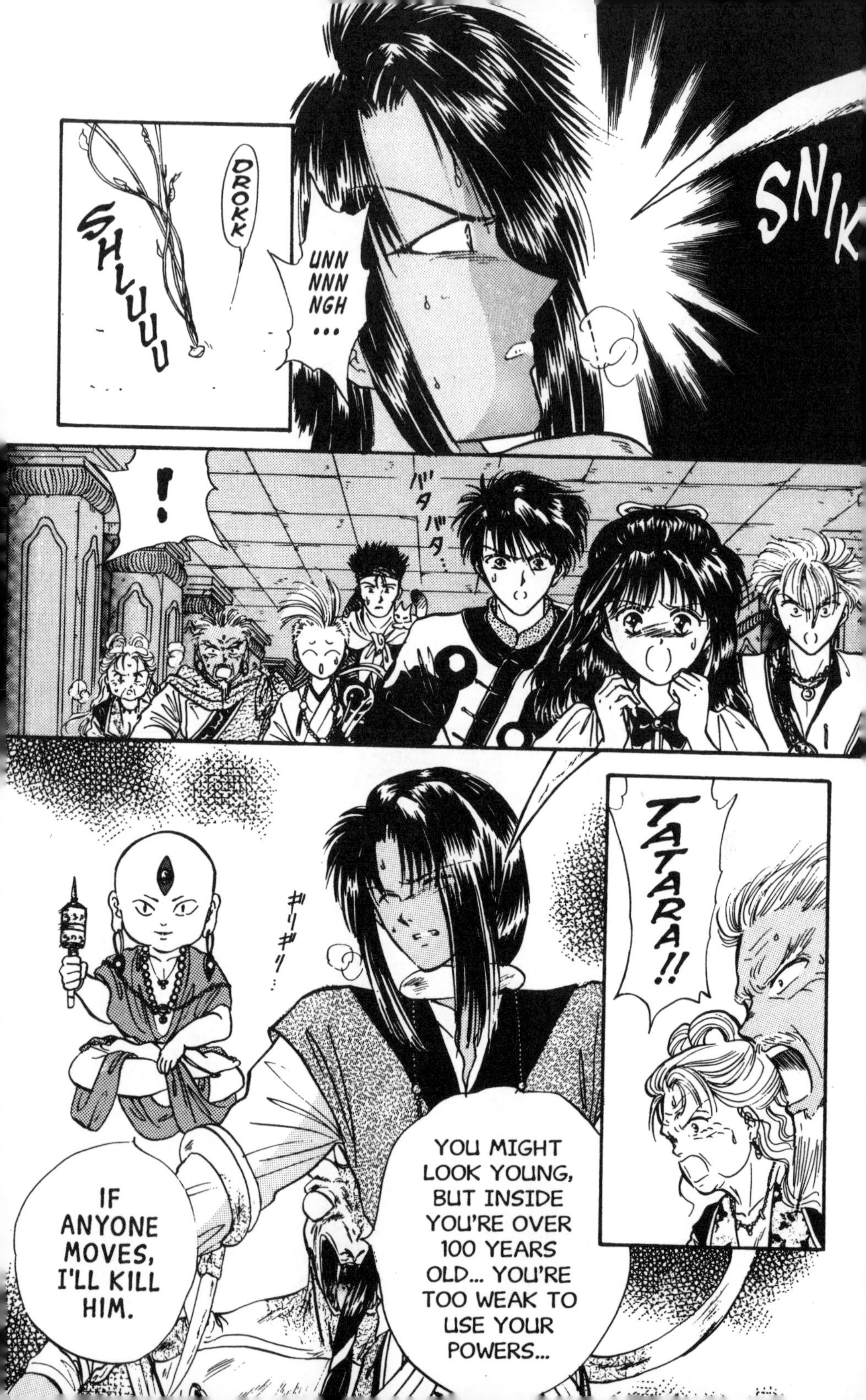

SNIK
UNN NNN NGH...
OROKK
SHLUUU...
バタバタ...
!
TATARA!!
ギリギリ...
YOU MIGHT LOOK YOUNG, BUT INSIDE YOU'RE OVER 100 YEARS OLD... YOU'RE TOO WEAK TO USE YOUR POWERS...
IF ANYONE MOVES, I'LL KILL HIM.

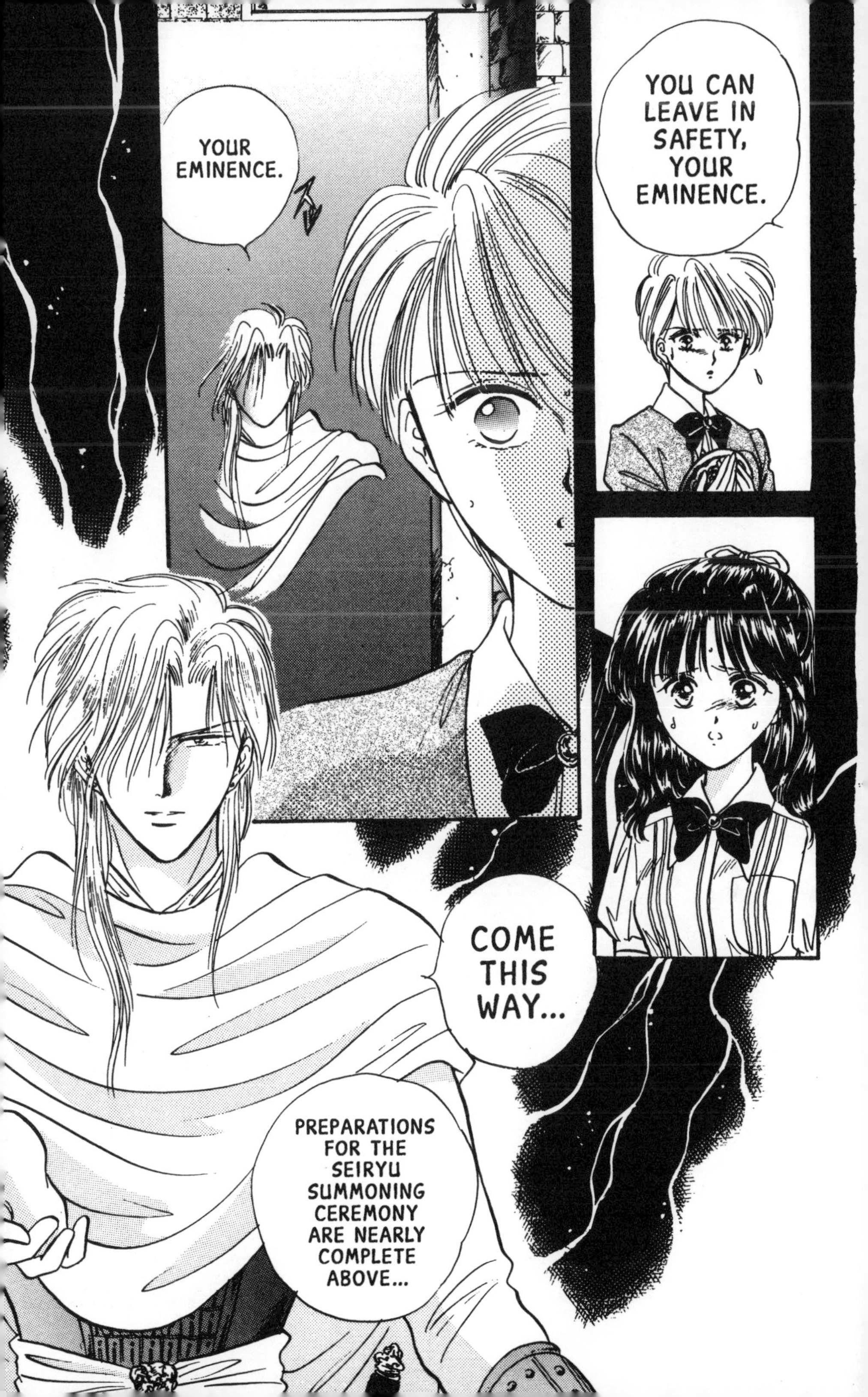
YOU CAN LEAVE IN SAFETY, YOUR EMINENCE.
YOUR EMINENCE.
COME THIS WAY...
PREPARATIONS FOR THE SEIRYU SUMMONING CEREMONY ARE NEARLY COMPLETE ABOVE...

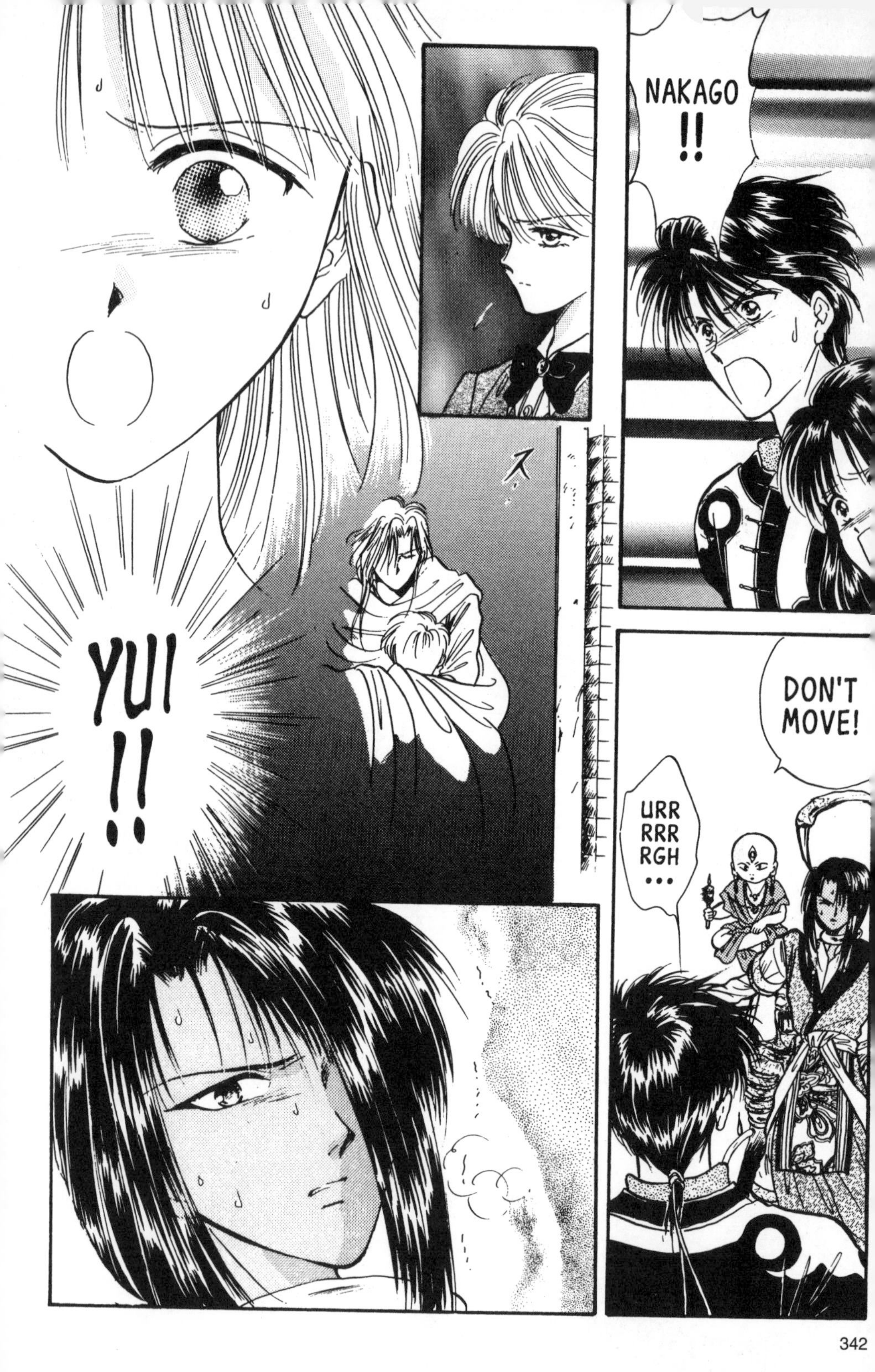
NAKAGO !!
YUI !!
ス
DON'T MOVE!
URR RRR RGH ...

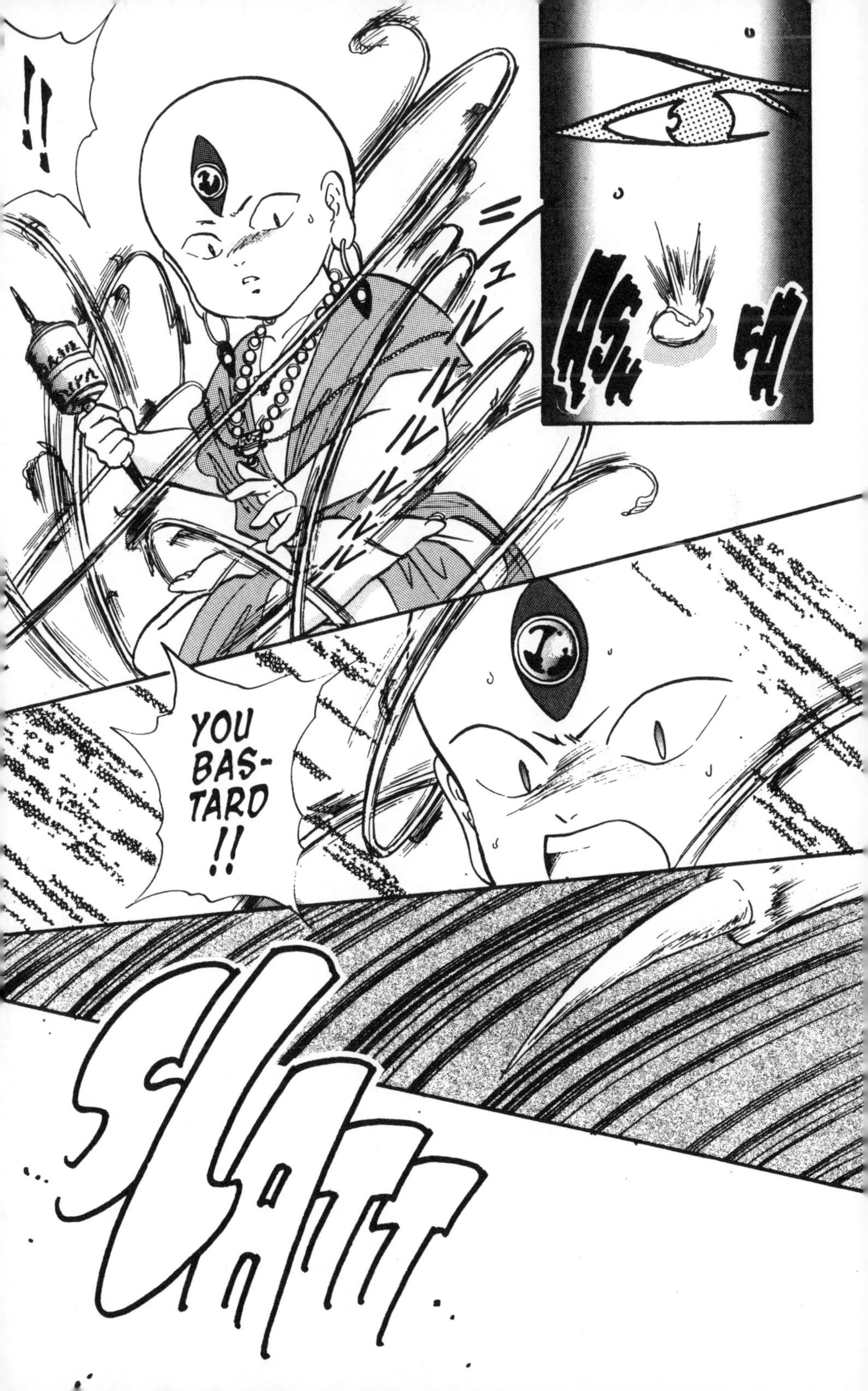
!!
YOU BASTARD!!

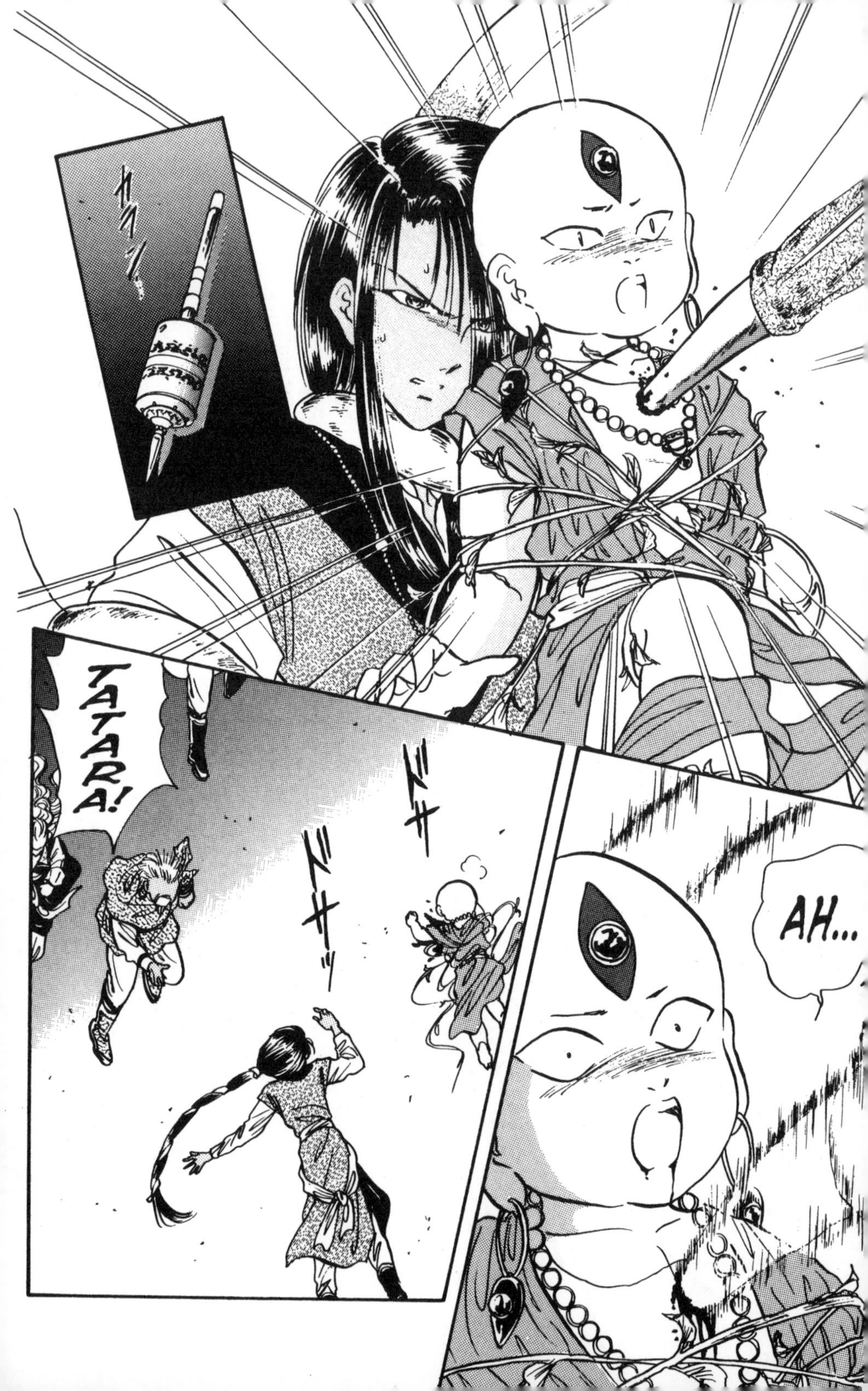
カラン…
AH...
ドキ
ドキッ
TATARA!

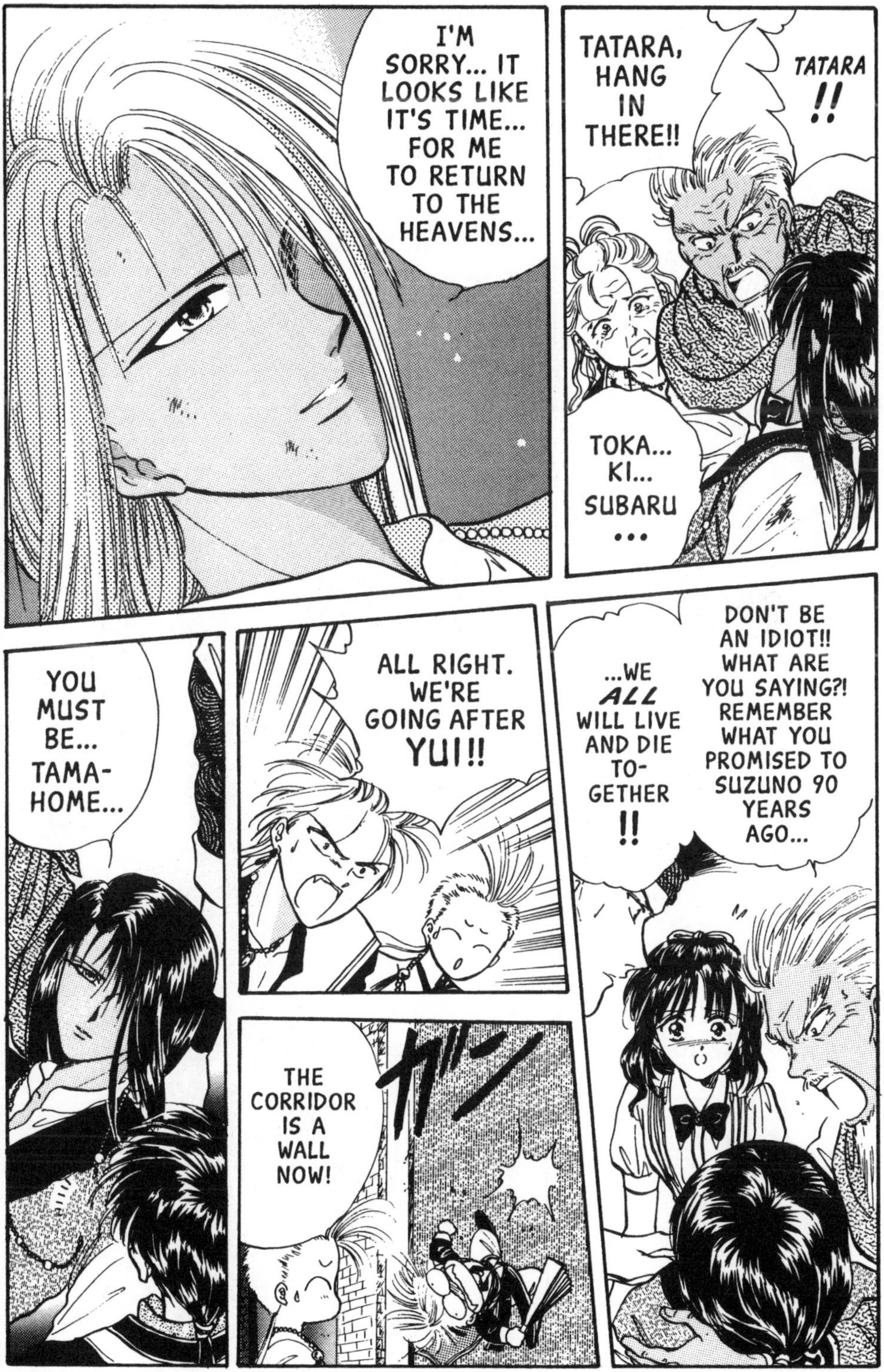
TATARA !!
TATARA, HANG IN THERE!!
TOKA... KI... SUBARU...
I'M SORRY... IT LOOKS LIKE IT'S TIME... FOR ME TO RETURN TO THE HEAVENS...
DON'T BE AN IDIOT!! WHAT ARE YOU SAYING?! REMEMBER WHAT YOU PROMISED TO SUZUNO 90 YEARS AGO...
...WE ALL WILL LIVE AND DIE TOGETHER !!
ALL RIGHT. WE'RE GOING AFTER YUI!!
ガン
THE CORRIDOR IS A WALL NOW!
YOU MUST BE... TAMAHOME...

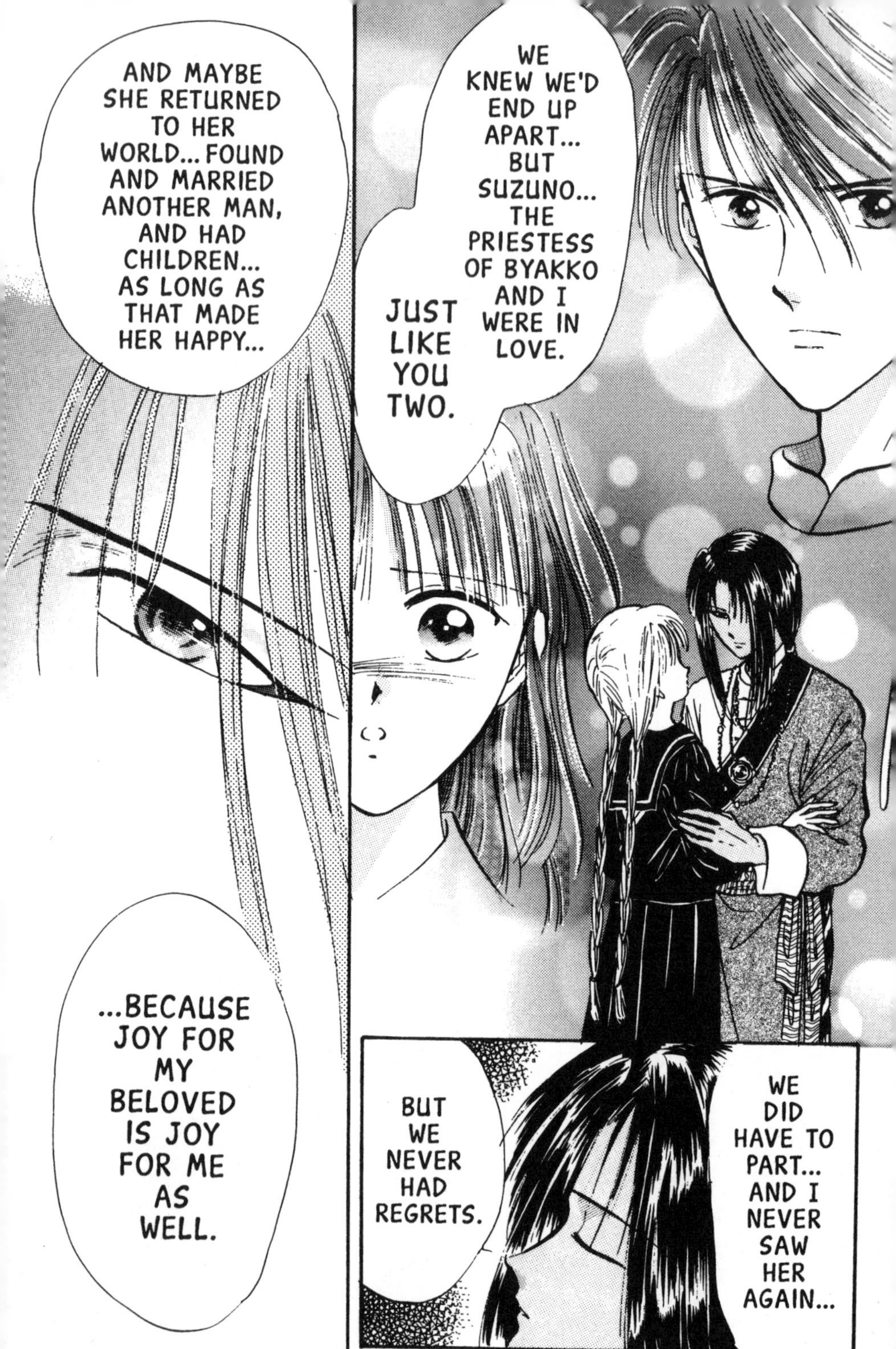
WE KNEW WE'D END UP APART... BUT SUZUNO... THE PRIESTESS OF BYAKKO AND I WERE IN LOVE.
JUST LIKE YOU TWO.
WE DID HAVE TO PART... AND I NEVER SAW HER AGAIN...
BUT WE NEVER HAD REGRETS.
AND MAYBE SHE RETURNED TO HER WORLD... FOUND AND MARRIED ANOTHER MAN, AND HAD CHILDREN... AS LONG AS THAT MADE HER HAPPY...
...BECAUSE JOY FOR MY BELOVED IS JOY FOR ME AS WELL.

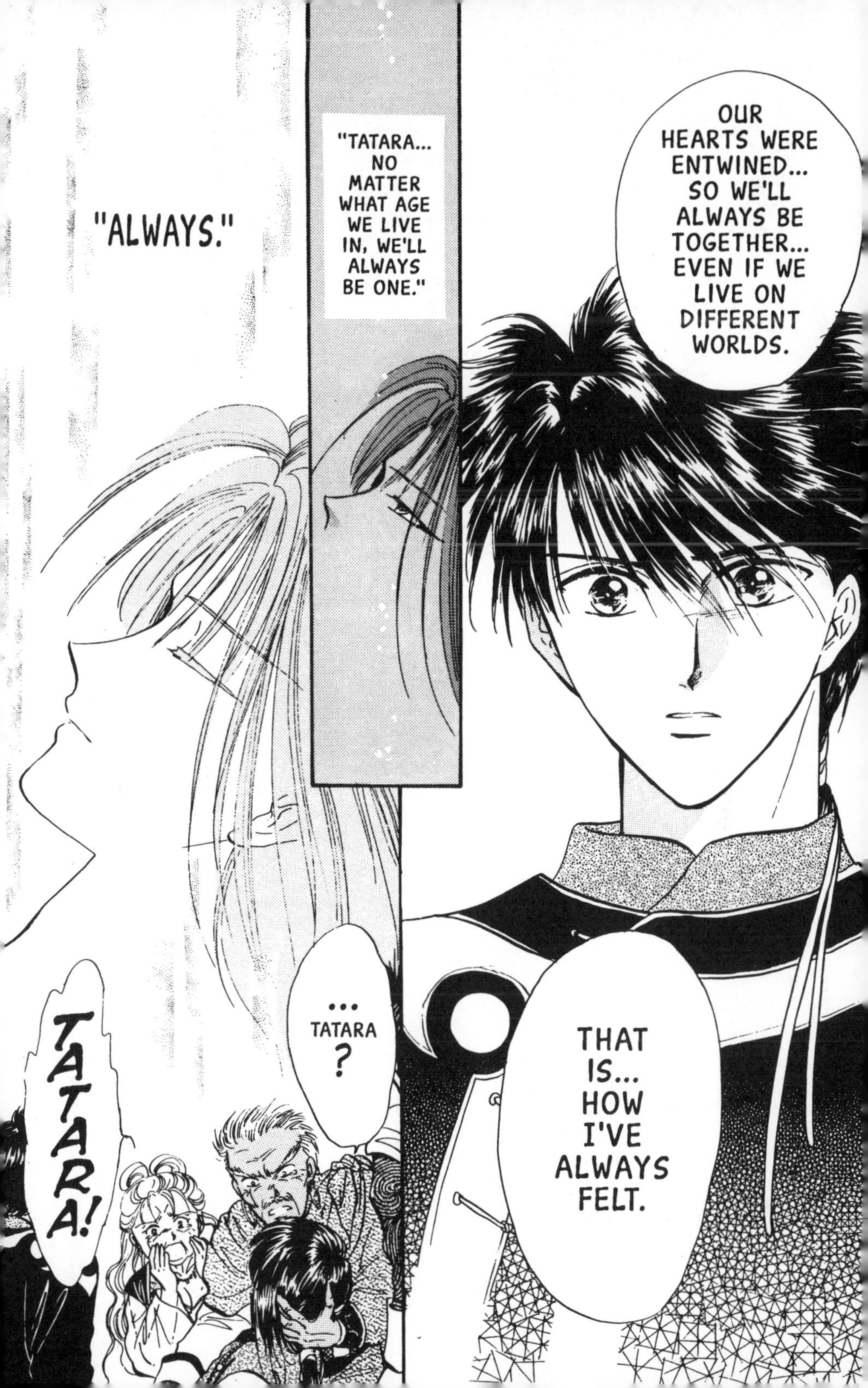
OUR HEARTS WERE ENTWINED... SO WE'LL ALWAYS BE TOGETHER... EVEN IF WE LIVE ON DIFFERENT WORLDS.
"TATARA... NO MATTER WHAT AGE WE LIVE IN, WE'LL ALWAYS BE ONE."
"ALWAYS."
THAT IS... HOW I'VE ALWAYS FELT.
...TATARA?
TATARA!

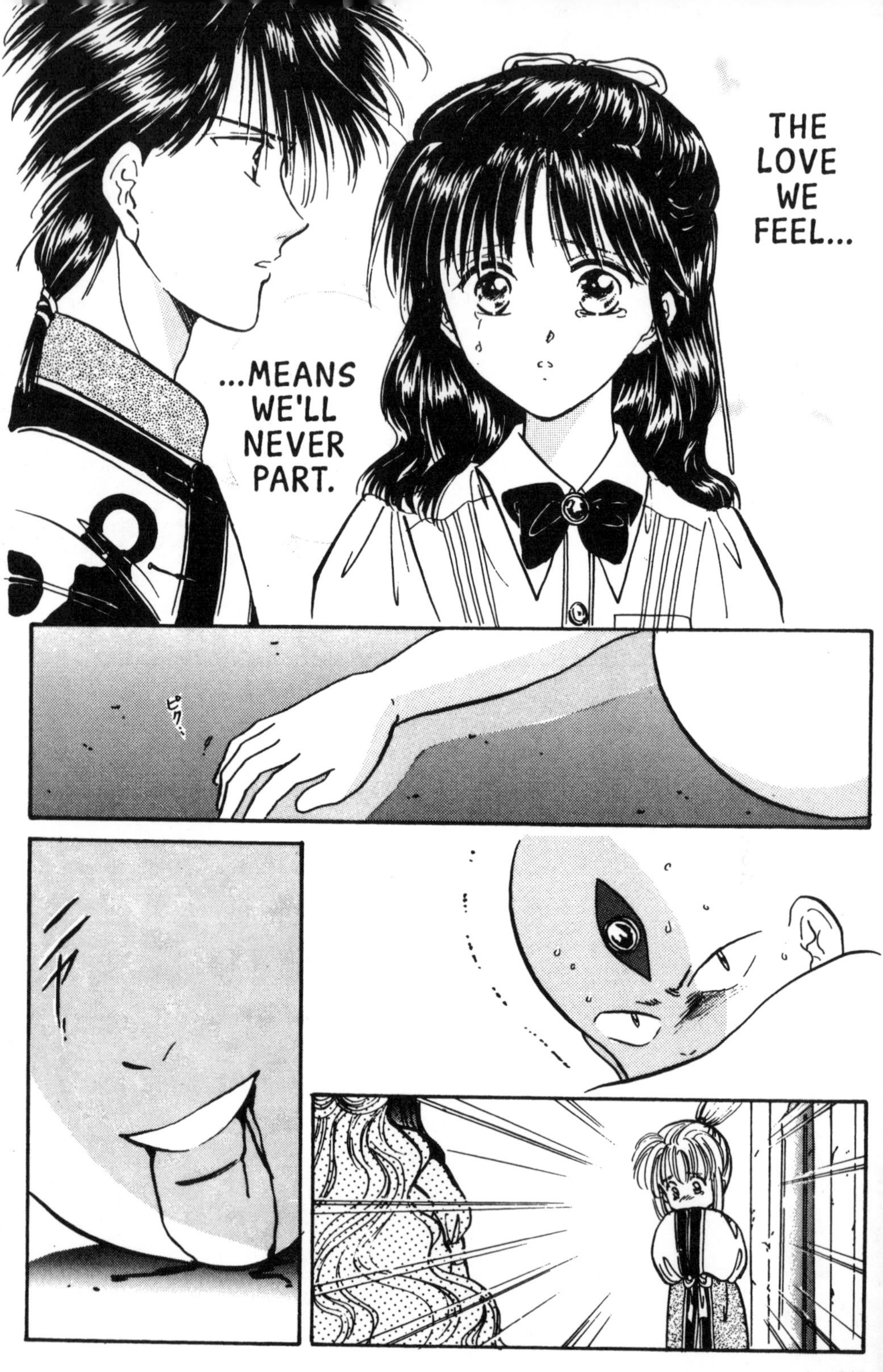
THE LOVE WE FEEL...
...MEANS WE'LL NEVER PART.

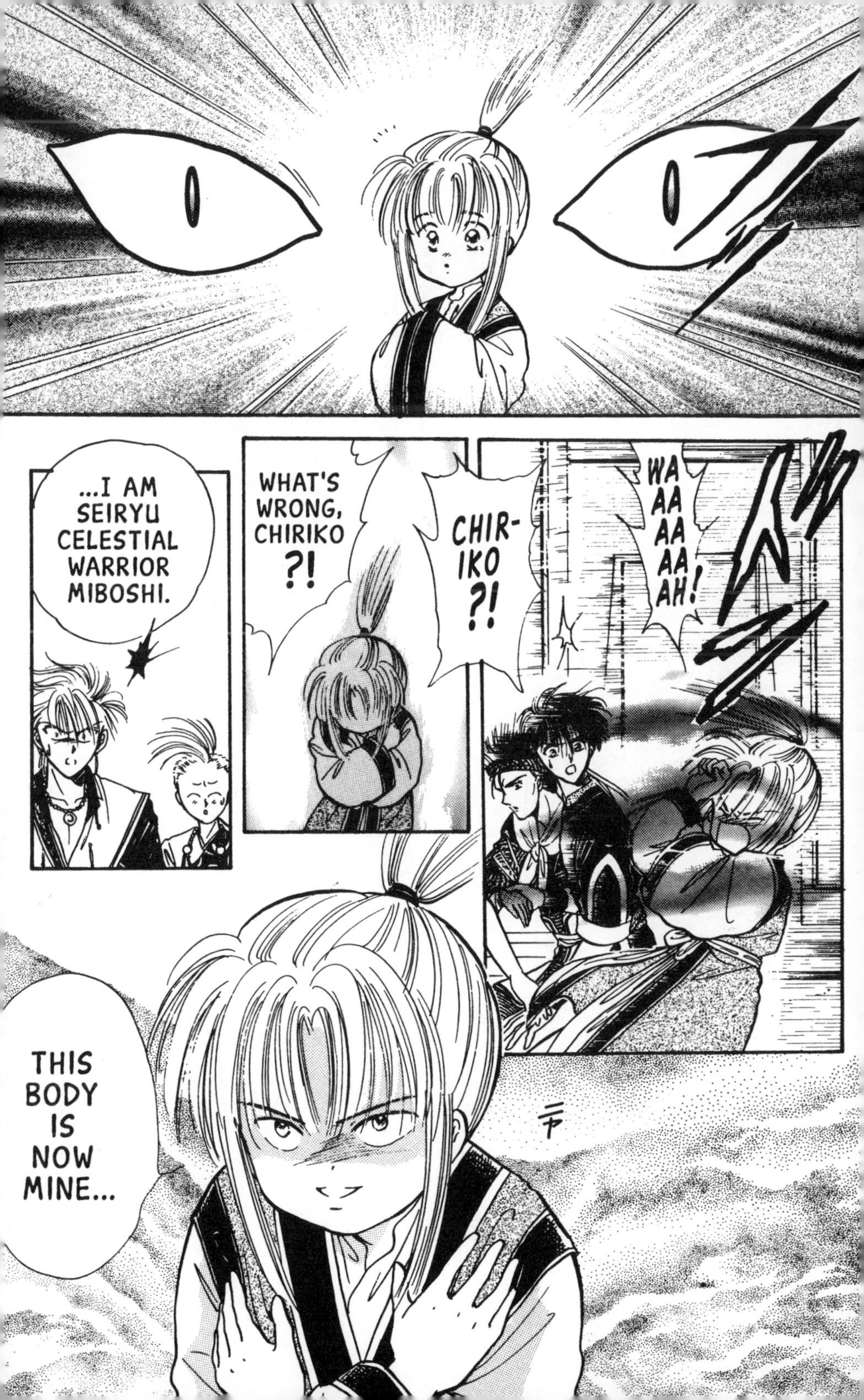
WAAAAAAAAAH!
CHIR-IKO?!
WHAT'S WRONG, CHIRIKO?!
...I AM SEIRYU CELESTIAL WARRIOR MIBOSHI.
THIS BODY IS NOW MINE...

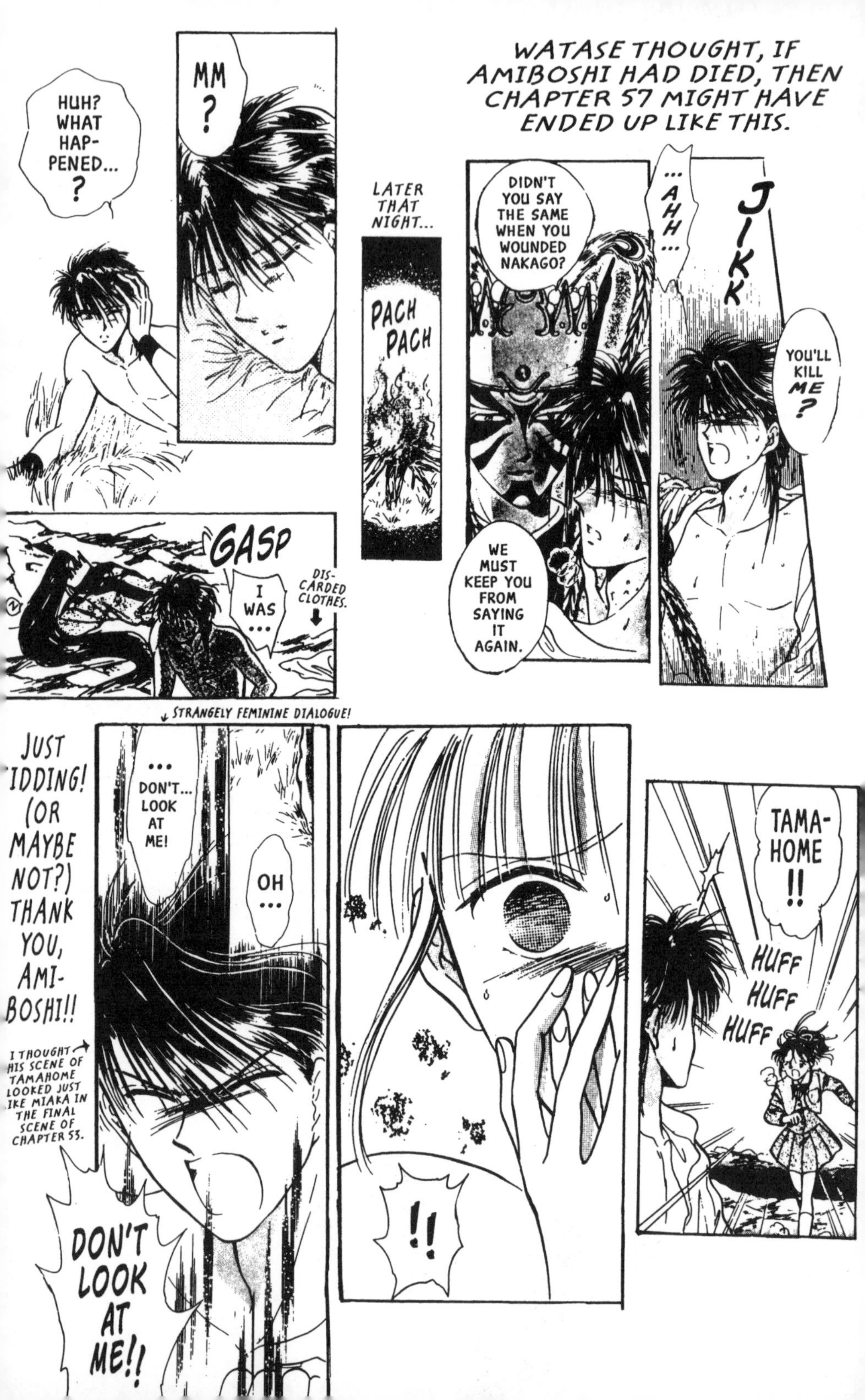
WATASE THOUGHT, IF AMIBOSHI HAD DIED, THEN CHAPTER 57 MIGHT HAVE ENDED UP LIKE THIS.
JIKK
...AHH...
YOU'LL KILL ME?
DIDN'T YOU SAY THE SAME WHEN YOU WOUNDED NAKAGO?
WE MUST KEEP YOU FROM SAYING IT AGAIN.
LATER THAT NIGHT...
PACH PACH
MM ?
HUH? WHAT HAP-PENED... ?
GASP
I WAS...
DIS-CARDED CLOTHES.
TAMA-HOME !!
HUFF HUFF HUFF
!!
STRANGELY FEMININE DIALOGUE!
... DON'T... LOOK AT ME!
OH ...
DON'T LOOK AT ME!!
JUST IDDING! (OR MAYBE NOT?) THANK YOU, AMI-BOSHI!!
I THOUGHT HIS SCENE OF TAMAHOME LOOKED JUST IKE MIAKA IN THE FINAL SCENE OF CHAPTER 53.

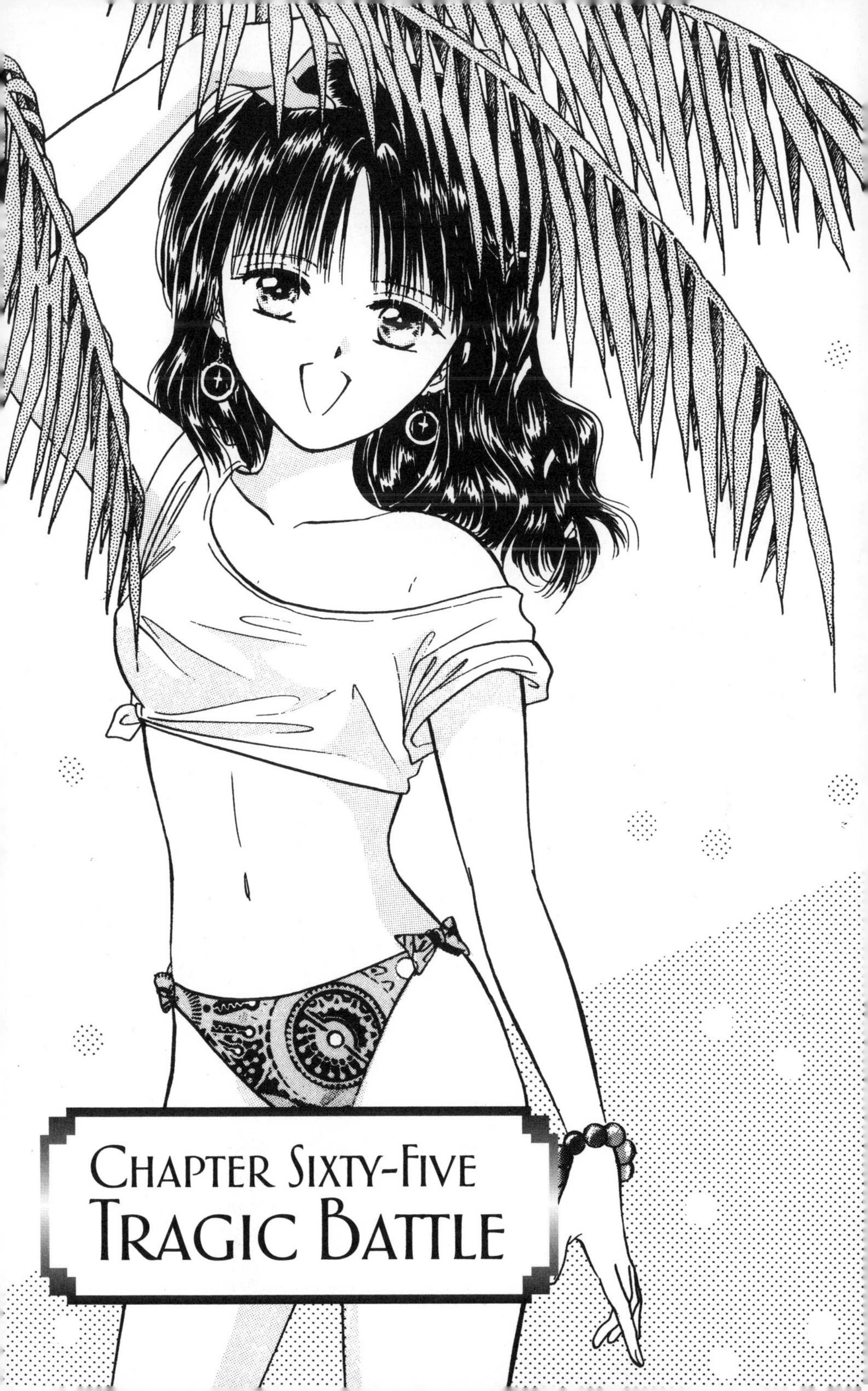
Chapter Sixty-Five
Tragic Battle

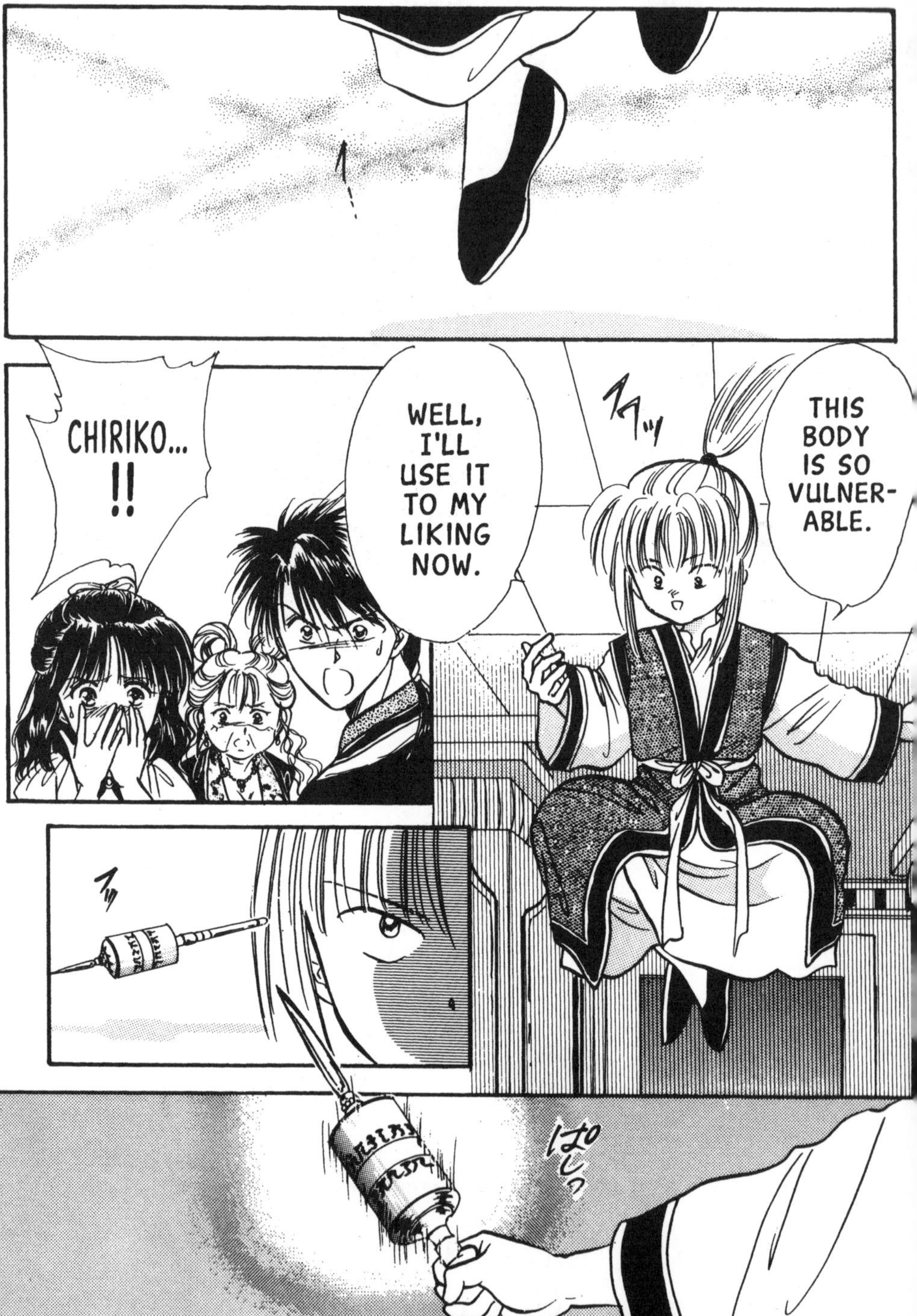
スゥッ
THIS BODY IS SO VULNER- ABLE.
WELL, I'LL USE IT TO MY LIKING NOW.
CHIRIKO... !!
フッ
ぱしっ

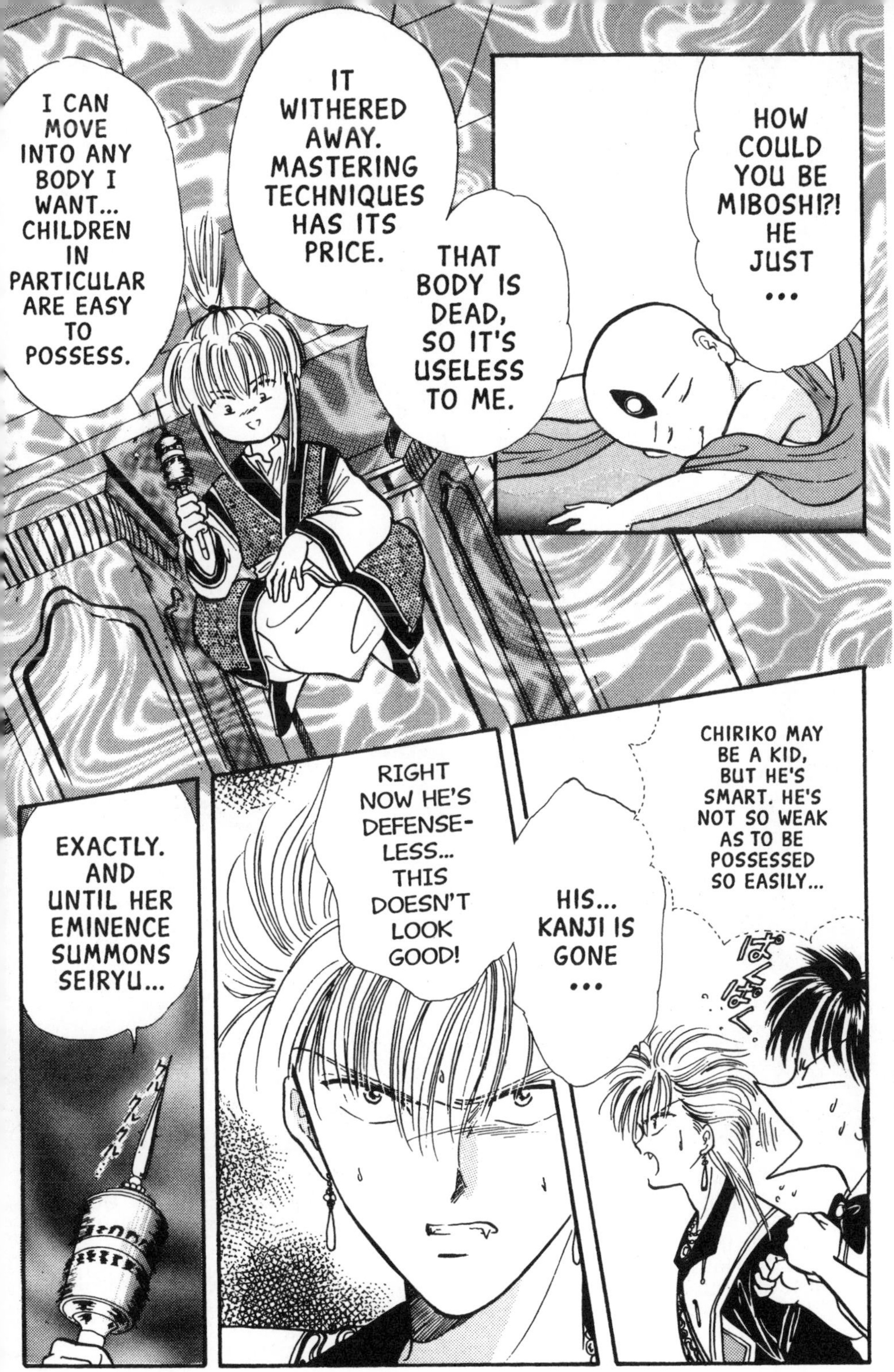
HOW COULD YOU BE MIBOSHI?! HE JUST ...
THAT BODY IS DEAD, SO IT'S USELESS TO ME.
IT WITHERED AWAY. MASTERING TECHNIQUES HAS ITS PRICE.
I CAN MOVE INTO ANY BODY I WANT... CHILDREN IN PARTICULAR ARE EASY TO POSSESS.
CHIRIKO MAY BE A KID, BUT HE'S SMART. HE'S NOT SO WEAK AS TO BE POSSESSED SO EASILY...
ぱくぱく
HIS... KANJI IS GONE ...
RIGHT NOW HE'S DEFENSE-LESS... THIS DOESN'T LOOK GOOD!
EXACTLY. AND UNTIL HER EMINENCE SUMMONS SEIRYU...

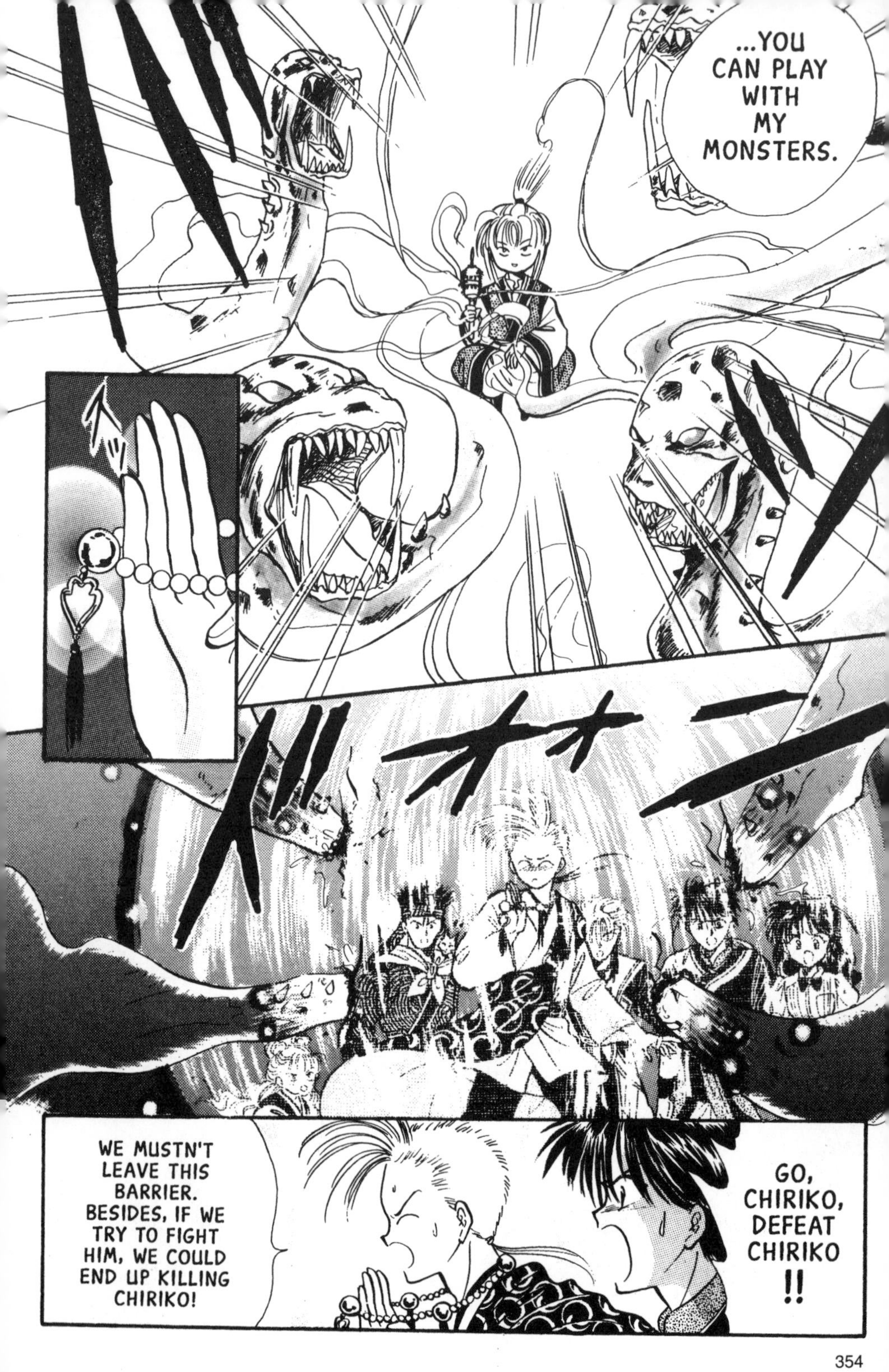
...YOU CAN PLAY WITH MY MONSTERS.
GO, CHIRIKO, DEFEAT CHIRIKO!!
WE MUSTN'T LEAVE THIS BARRIER. BESIDES, IF WE TRY TO FIGHT HIM, WE COULD END UP KILLING CHIRIKO!

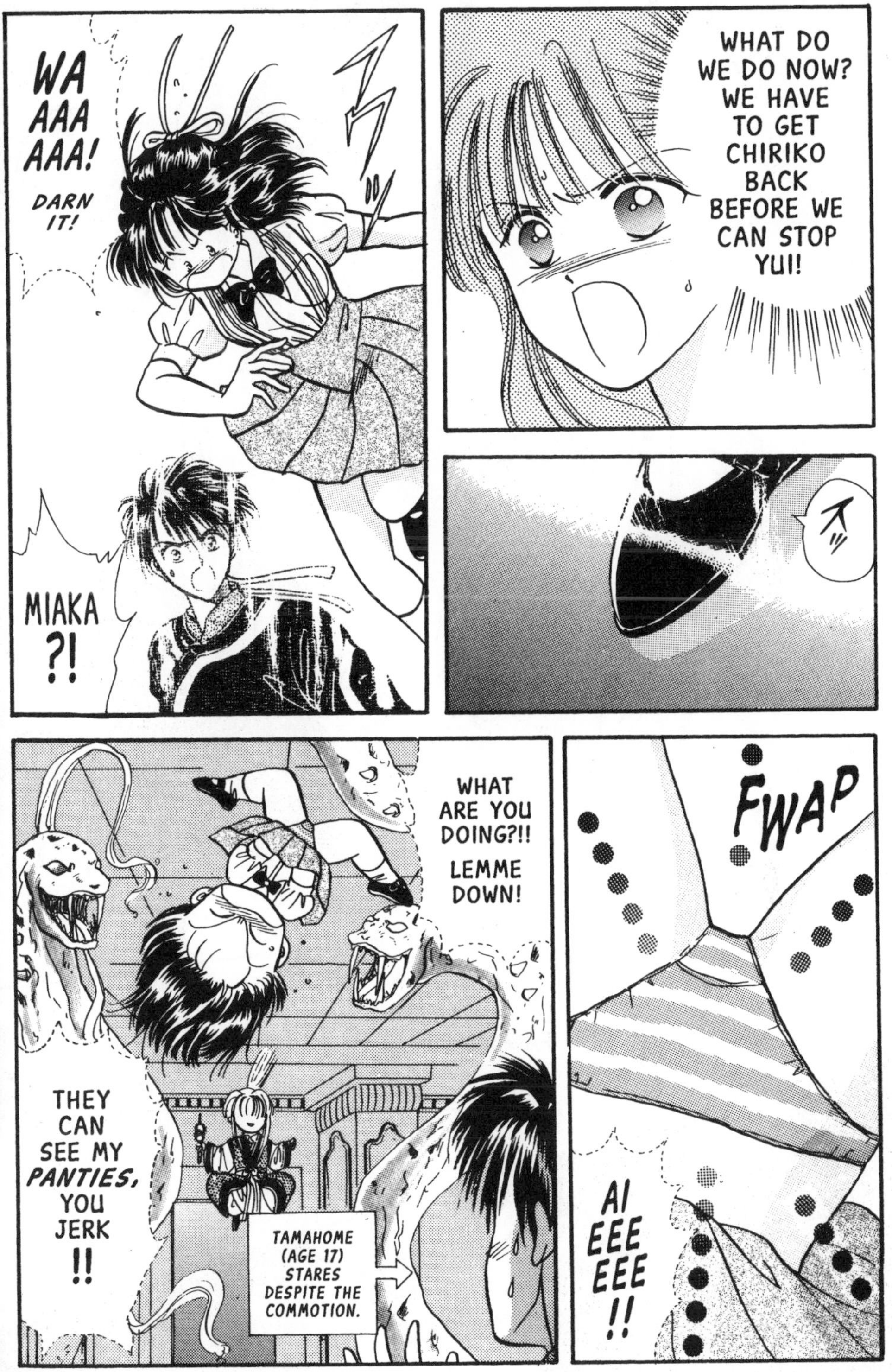
WHAT DO WE DO NOW? WE HAVE TO GET CHIRIKO BACK BEFORE WE CAN STOP YUI!
スッ
WA AAA AAA!
DARN IT!
MIAKA ?!
FWAP
AI EEE EEE !!
WHAT ARE YOU DOING?!!
LEMME DOWN!
THEY CAN SEE MY *PANTIES,* YOU JERK !!
TAMAHOME (AGE 17) STARES DESPITE THE COMMOTION.

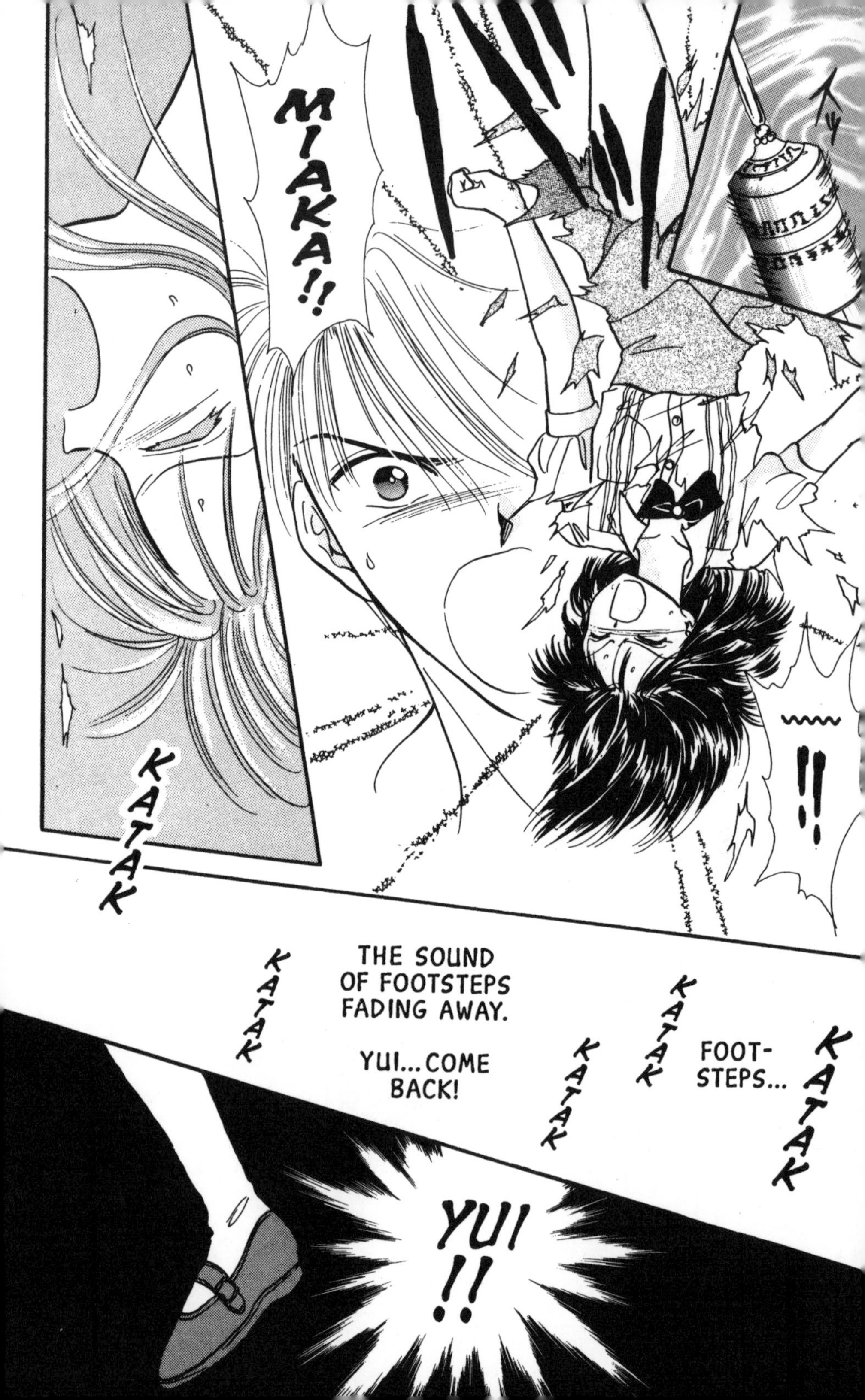

!!
MIAKA!!
KATAK
KATAK
FOOT-STEPS...
KATAK
KATAK
THE SOUND OF FOOTSTEPS FADING AWAY.
YUI...COME BACK!
KATAK
YUI!!

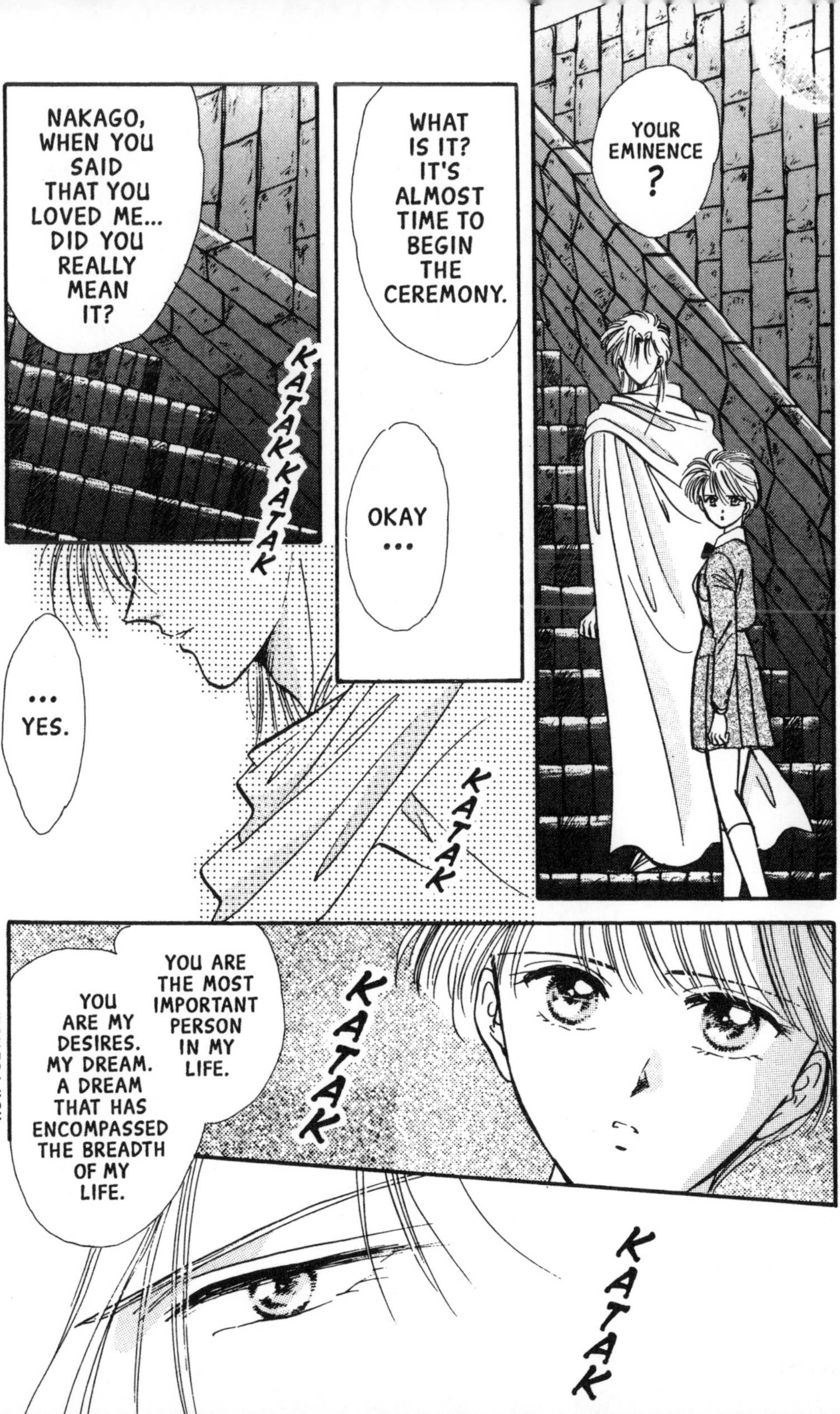

YOUR EMINENCE ?
WHAT IS IT? IT'S ALMOST TIME TO BEGIN THE CEREMONY.
OKAY ...
NAKAGO, WHEN YOU SAID THAT YOU LOVED ME... DID YOU REALLY MEAN IT?
KATAKKATAK
... YES.
KATAK
KATAK
YOU ARE THE MOST IMPORTANT PERSON IN MY LIFE.
YOU ARE MY DESIRES. MY DREAM. A DREAM THAT HAS ENCOMPASSED THE BREADTH OF MY LIFE.
HOW POETIC...
KATAK

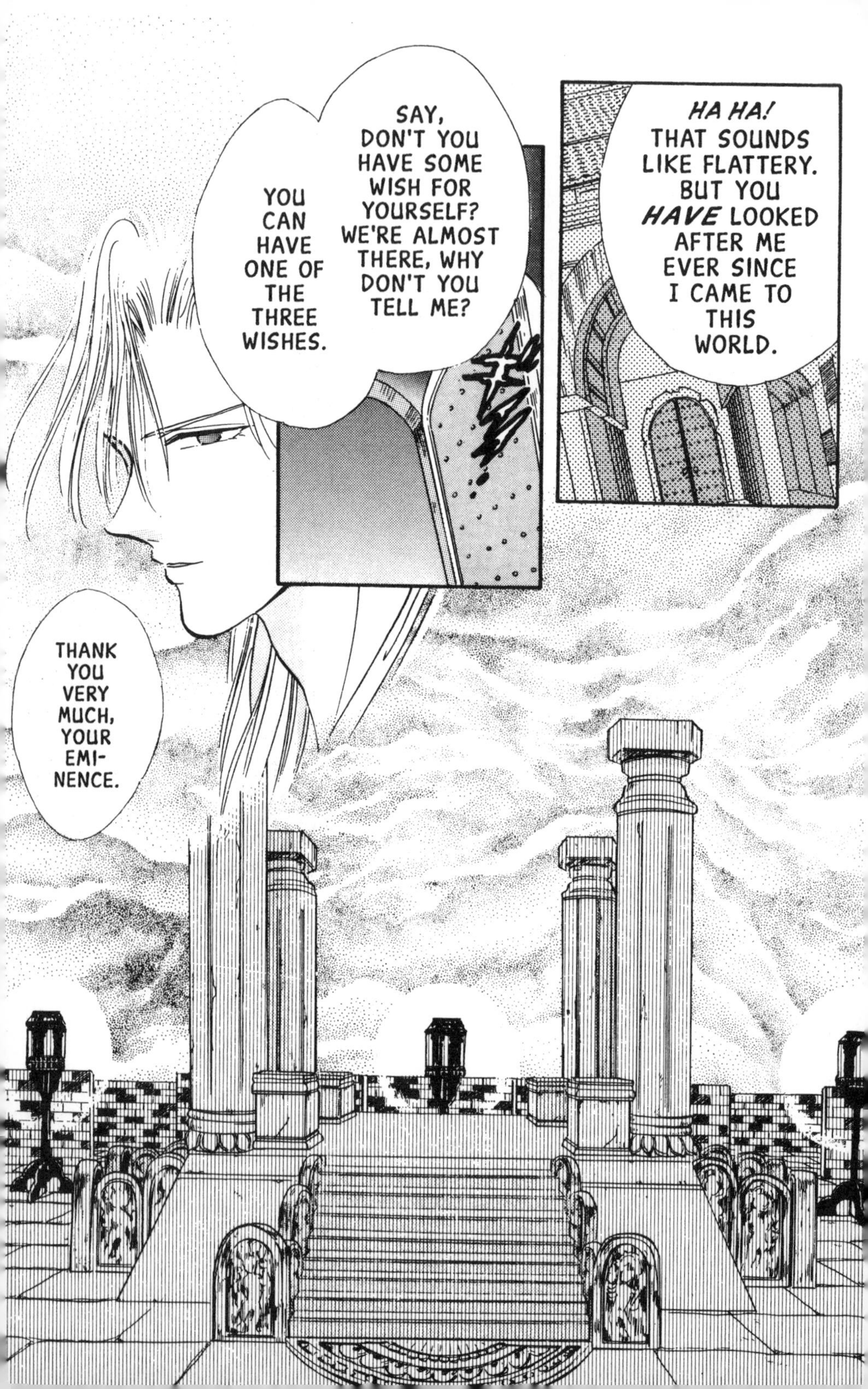
HA HA! THAT SOUNDS LIKE FLATTERY. BUT YOU HAVE LOOKED AFTER ME EVER SINCE I CAME TO THIS WORLD.
SAY, DON'T YOU HAVE SOME WISH FOR YOURSELF? WE'RE ALMOST THERE, WHY DON'T YOU TELL ME?
YOU CAN HAVE ONE OF THE THREE WISHES.
THANK YOU VERY MUCH, YOUR EMINENCE.

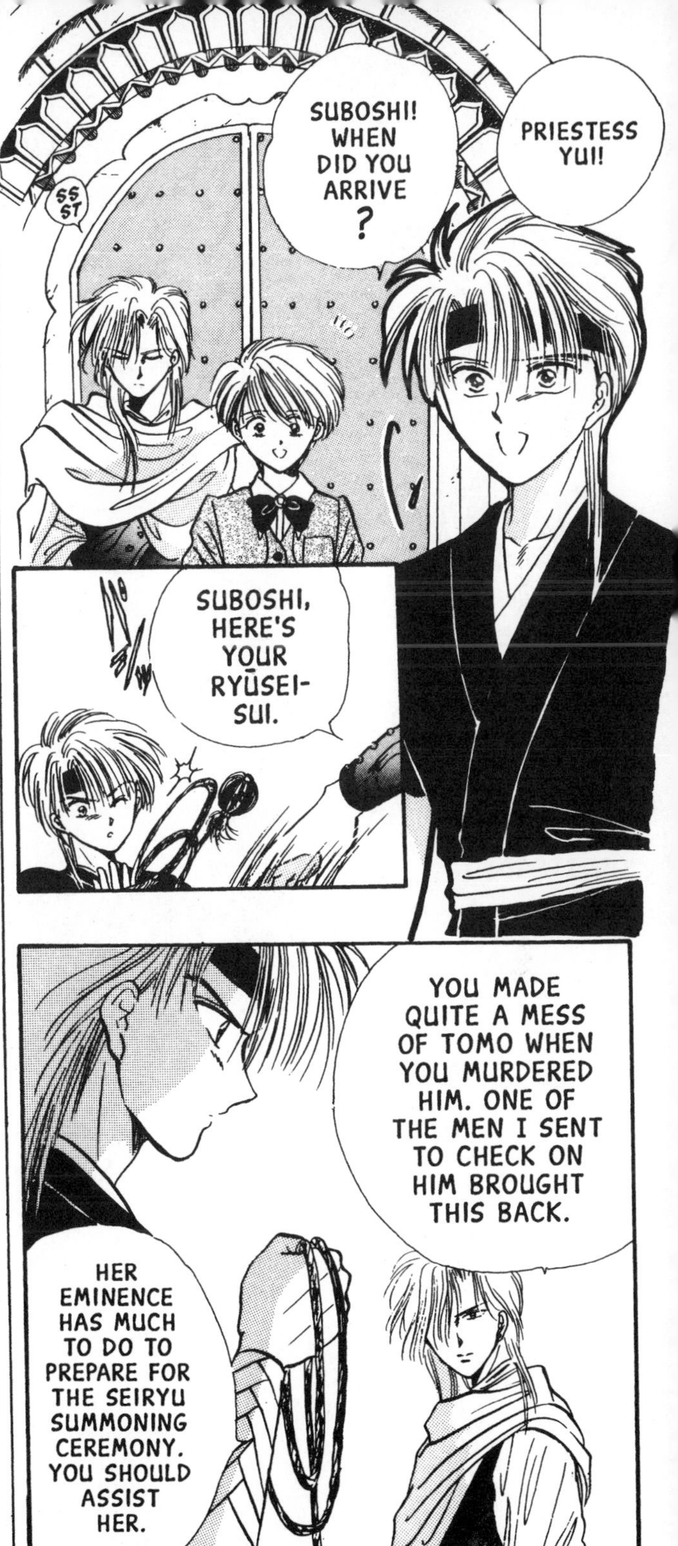
PRIESTESS YUI!
SUBOSHI! WHEN DID YOU ARRIVE?
SSST
SUBOSHI, HERE'S YOUR RYŪSEI-SUI.
YOU MADE QUITE A MESS OF TOMO WHEN YOU MURDERED HIM. ONE OF THE MEN I SENT TO CHECK ON HIM BROUGHT THIS BACK.
HER EMINENCE HAS MUCH TO DO TO PREPARE FOR THE SEIRYU SUMMONING CEREMONY. YOU SHOULD ASSIST HER.

I knew that Chichiri's face would be a mask from the very start. I wanted him to be totally serious when the situation called for it, but at the same time be relaxed and not too concerned with the world. I bet the tone of his voice changes accordingly. I have to say, the times when he suddenly gets small are really popular.

Hey, I only managed to cover six of the warriors!! Well, that's about it for this volume. I'll continue this in volume 12. I'll cover the Seiryu celestial warriors too! Don't you want me to? Weeell, I will! I get the occasional fan mail where someone asks me why I have to pick on Miaka so much. I'm not so interested in picking on her as I am in showing her rise above her challenges. I guess it's all right for some people to have a protagonist who doesn't have to suffer...someone who's always nurtured...where everything works out fine. But I wanted Miaka to be challenged.
I mean, reality is hard! So I'm hoping my readers will be encouraged to do their best once they see her trying hard too. My readers are always supporting me, but I'm also trying to encourage my readers as well.
...since I can't respond to your letters.

Now, the 1995 calendar will be out in November. This time, there'll be five new drawings. That's one less than last time, but in exchange, I plan to draw a whole lot of new pictures for a book of illustrations! Also, the second novelization of *Prepubescence* will be out in November. Like the previous one, all the illustrations will be new. I hope you get a chance to pick one up.
See you.

'94 9/5

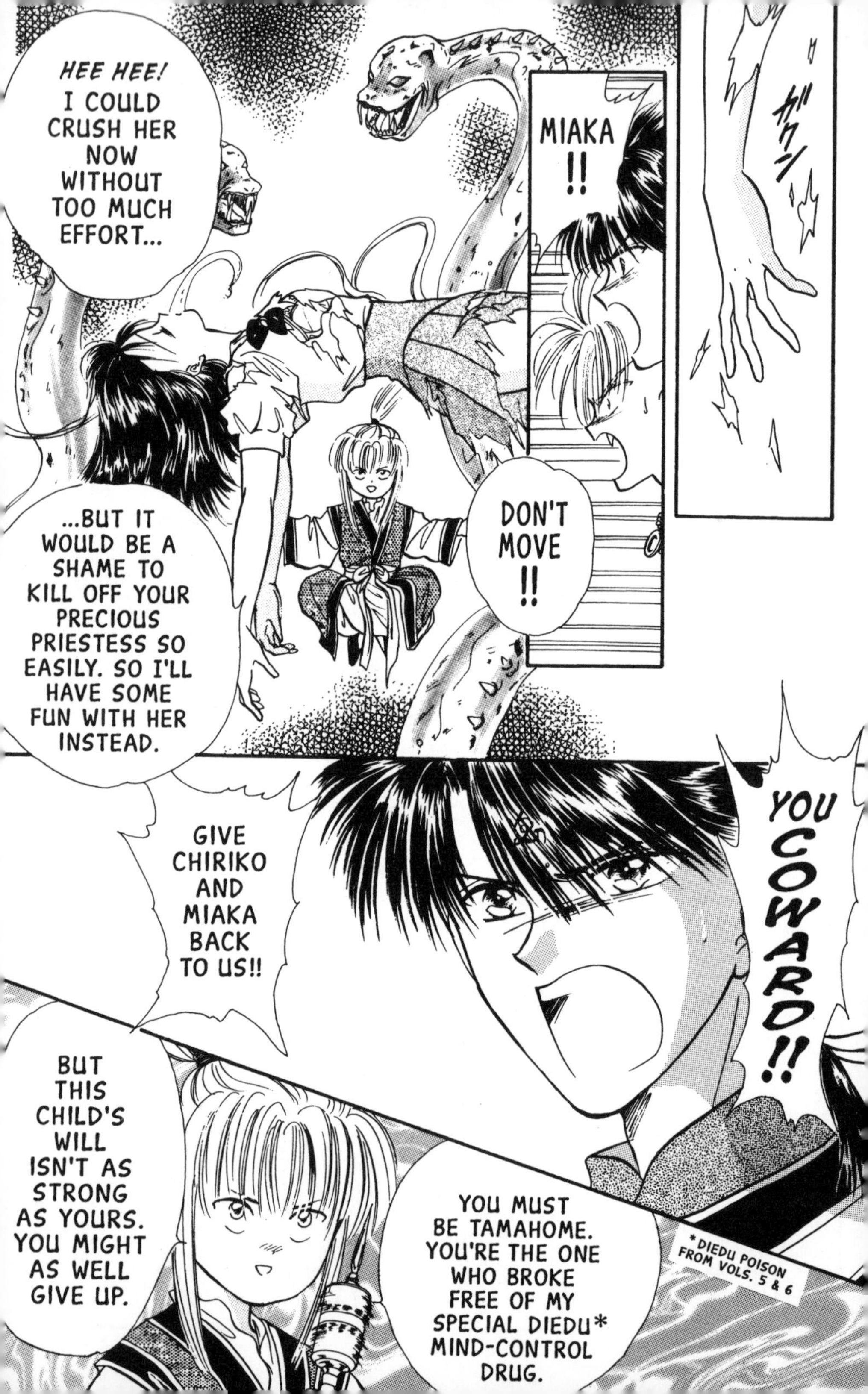
MIAKA !!
DON'T MOVE !!
HEE HEE! I COULD CRUSH HER NOW WITHOUT TOO MUCH EFFORT...
...BUT IT WOULD BE A SHAME TO KILL OFF YOUR PRECIOUS PRIESTESS SO EASILY. SO I'LL HAVE SOME FUN WITH HER INSTEAD.
YOU COWARD!!
GIVE CHIRIKO AND MIAKA BACK TO US!!
YOU MUST BE TAMAHOME. YOU'RE THE ONE WHO BROKE FREE OF MY SPECIAL DIEDU* MIND-CONTROL DRUG.
*DIEDU POISON FROM VOLS. 5 & 6
BUT THIS CHILD'S WILL ISN'T AS STRONG AS YOURS. YOU MIGHT AS WELL GIVE UP.

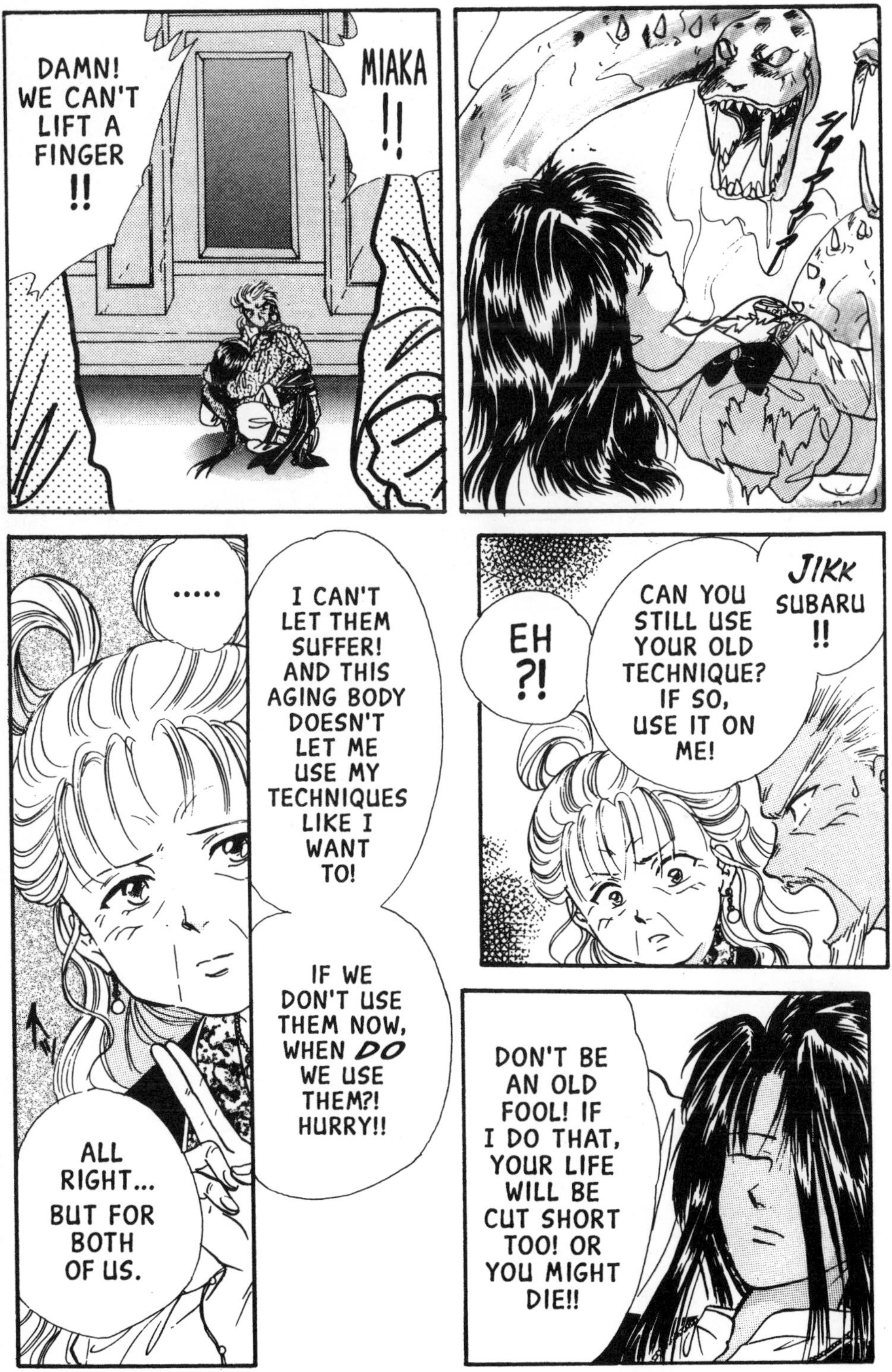

MIAKA!!
DAMN! WE CAN'T LIFT A FINGER!!
JIKK
SUBARU!!
CAN YOU STILL USE YOUR OLD TECHNIQUE? IF SO, USE IT ON ME!
EH?!
DON'T BE AN OLD FOOL! IF I DO THAT, YOUR LIFE WILL BE CUT SHORT TOO! OR YOU MIGHT DIE!!
I CAN'T LET THEM SUFFER! AND THIS AGING BODY DOESN'T LET ME USE MY TECHNIQUES LIKE I WANT TO!
.....
IF WE DON'T USE THEM NOW, WHEN *DO* WE USE THEM?! HURRY!!
ALL RIGHT... BUT FOR BOTH OF US.

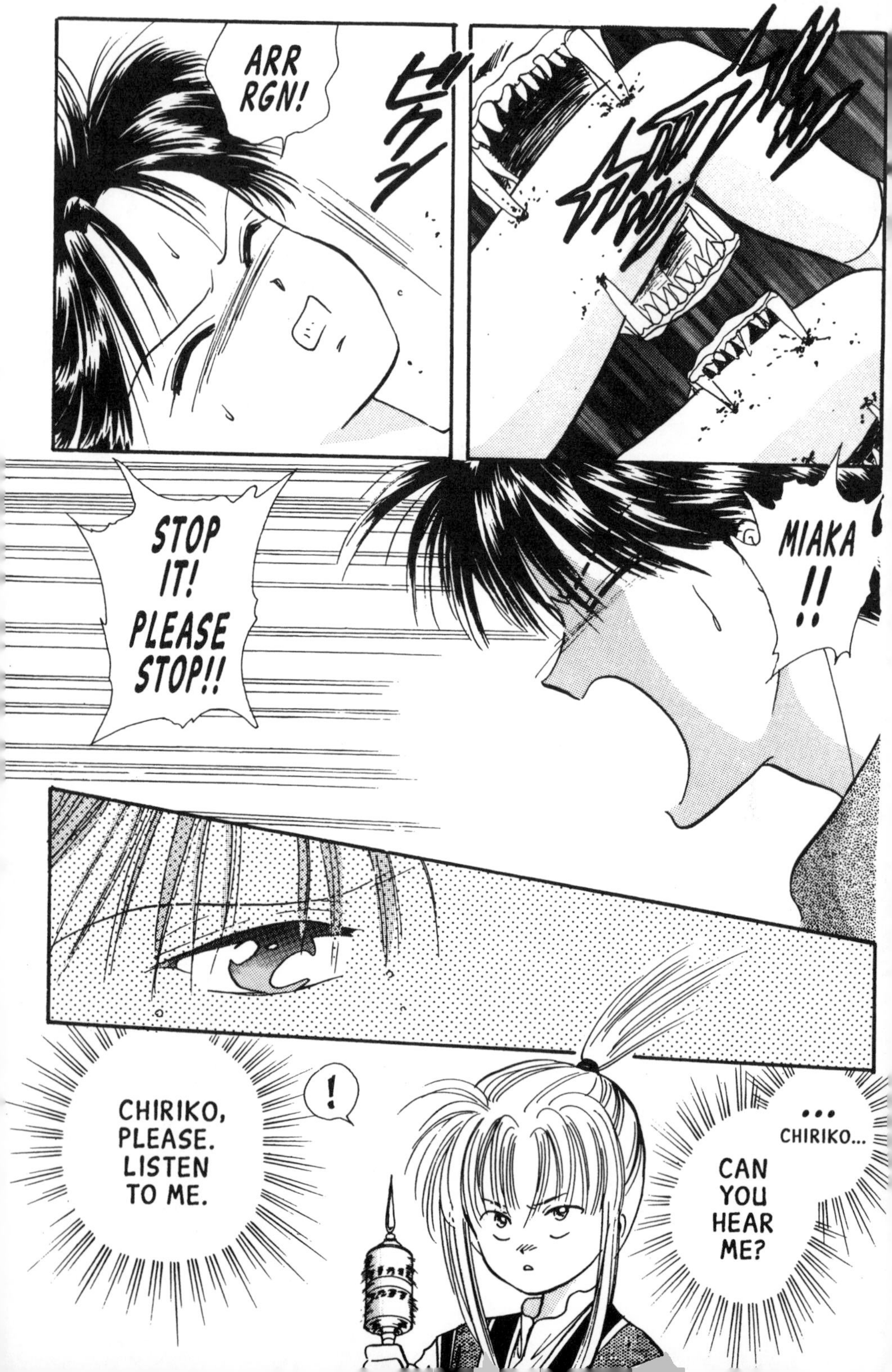
ARR RGN!
MIAKA!!
STOP IT! PLEASE STOP!!
...CHIRIKO...
CAN YOU HEAR ME?
!
CHIRIKO, PLEASE. LISTEN TO ME.

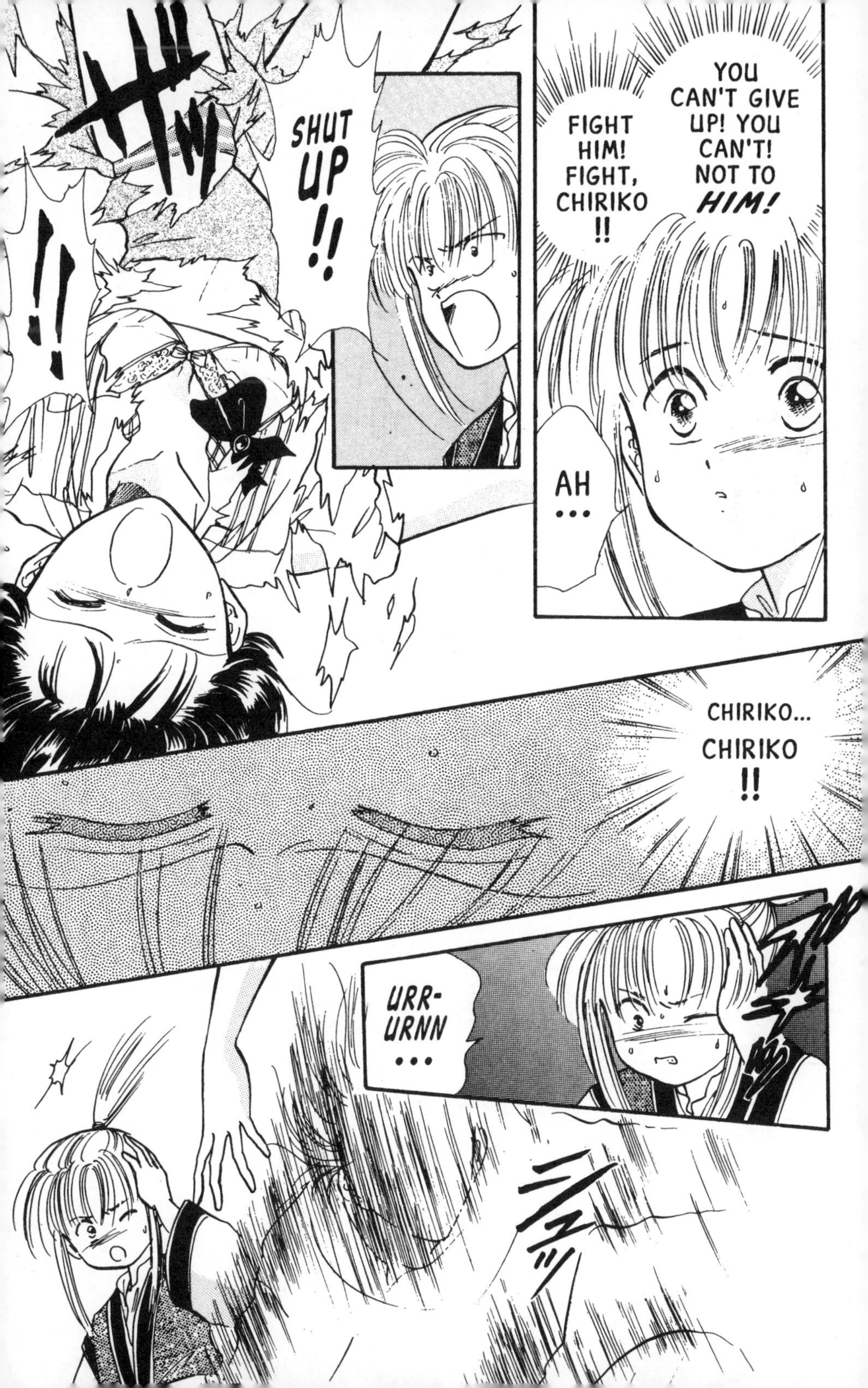
YOU CAN'T GIVE UP! YOU CAN'T! NOT TO *HIM!*
FIGHT HIM! FIGHT, CHIRIKO!!
AH...
SHUT UP!!
!!
CHIRIKO... CHIRIKO!!
URR-URNN...

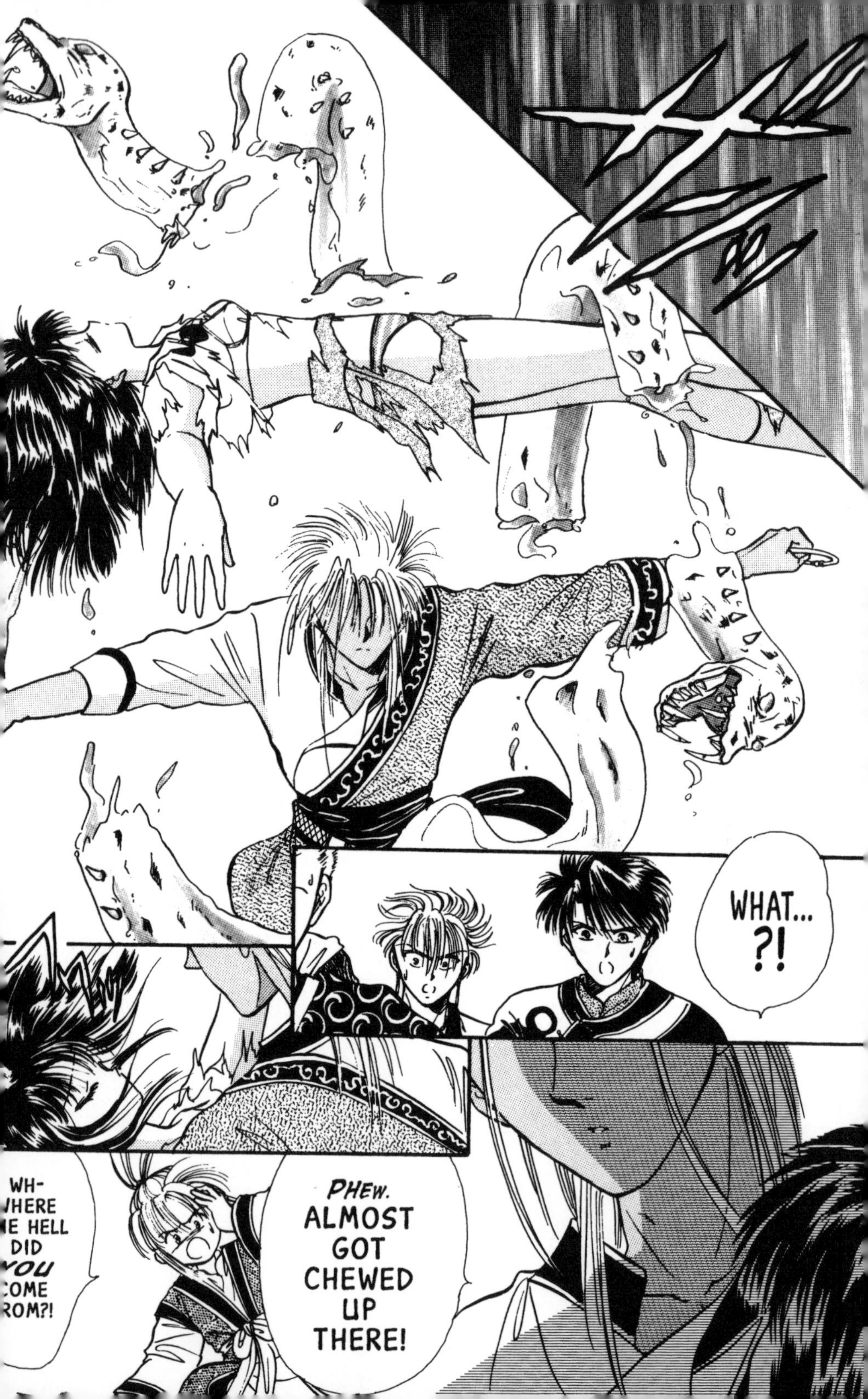
WHAT... ?!
PHEW. ALMOST GOT CHEWED UP THERE!
WH- WHERE E HELL DID YOU COME ROM?!

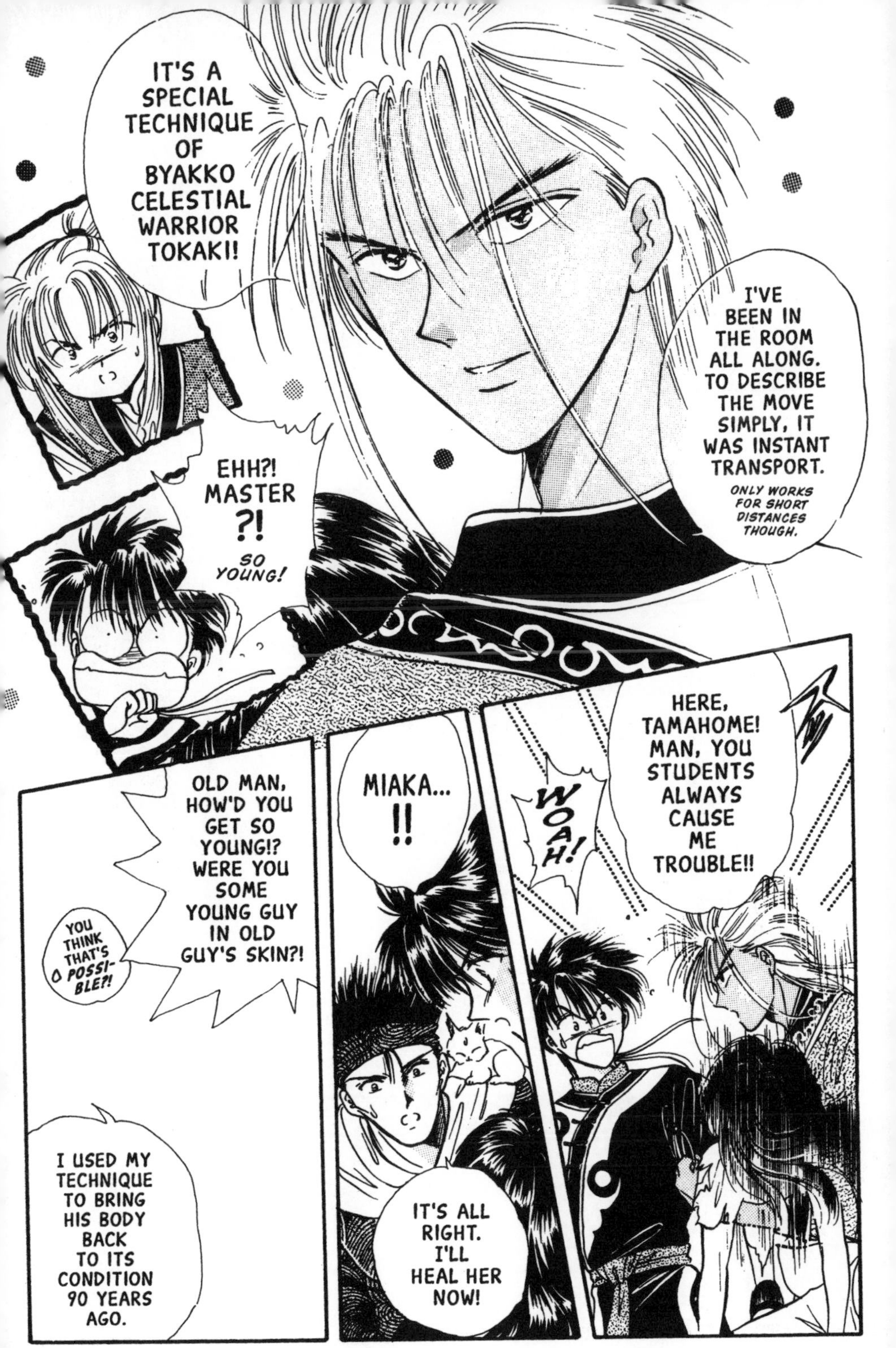
I'VE BEEN IN THE ROOM ALL ALONG. TO DESCRIBE THE MOVE SIMPLY, IT WAS INSTANT TRANSPORT.
ONLY WORKS FOR SHORT DISTANCES THOUGH.
IT'S A SPECIAL TECHNIQUE OF BYAKKO CELESTIAL WARRIOR TOKAKI!
EHH?! MASTER ?!
SO YOUNG!
HERE, TAMAHOME! MAN, YOU STUDENTS ALWAYS CAUSE ME TROUBLE!!
WOAH!
MIAKA... !!
IT'S ALL RIGHT. I'LL HEAL HER NOW!
OLD MAN, HOW'D YOU GET SO YOUNG!? WERE YOU SOME YOUNG GUY IN OLD GUY'S SKIN?!
YOU THINK THAT'S POSSIBLE?!
I USED MY TECHNIQUE TO BRING HIS BODY BACK TO ITS CONDITION 90 YEARS AGO.

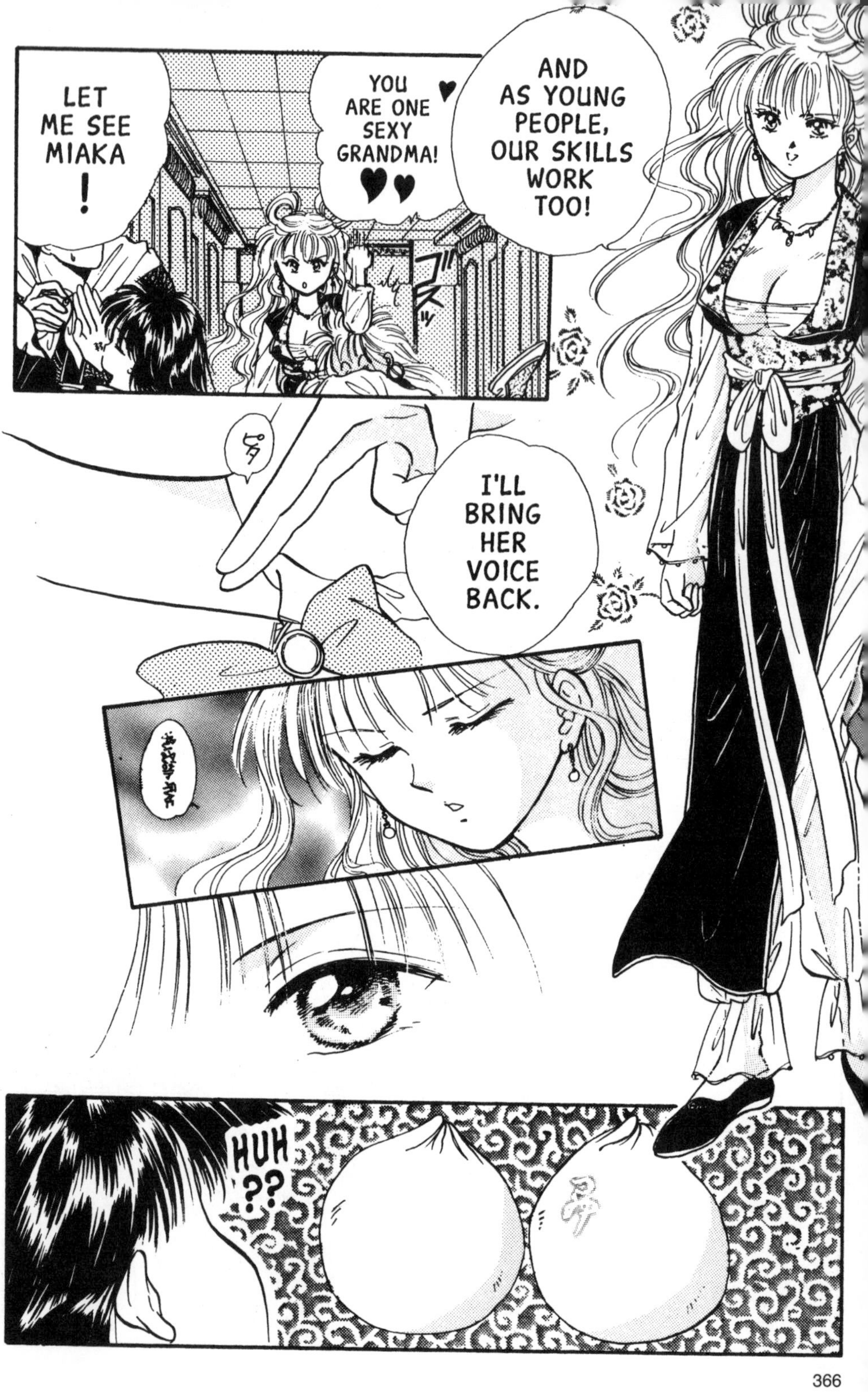
AND AS YOUNG PEOPLE, OUR SKILLS WORK TOO!
YOU ARE ONE SEXY GRANDMA!
LET ME SEE MIAKA!
ピタ
I'LL BRING HER VOICE BACK.
HUH ??

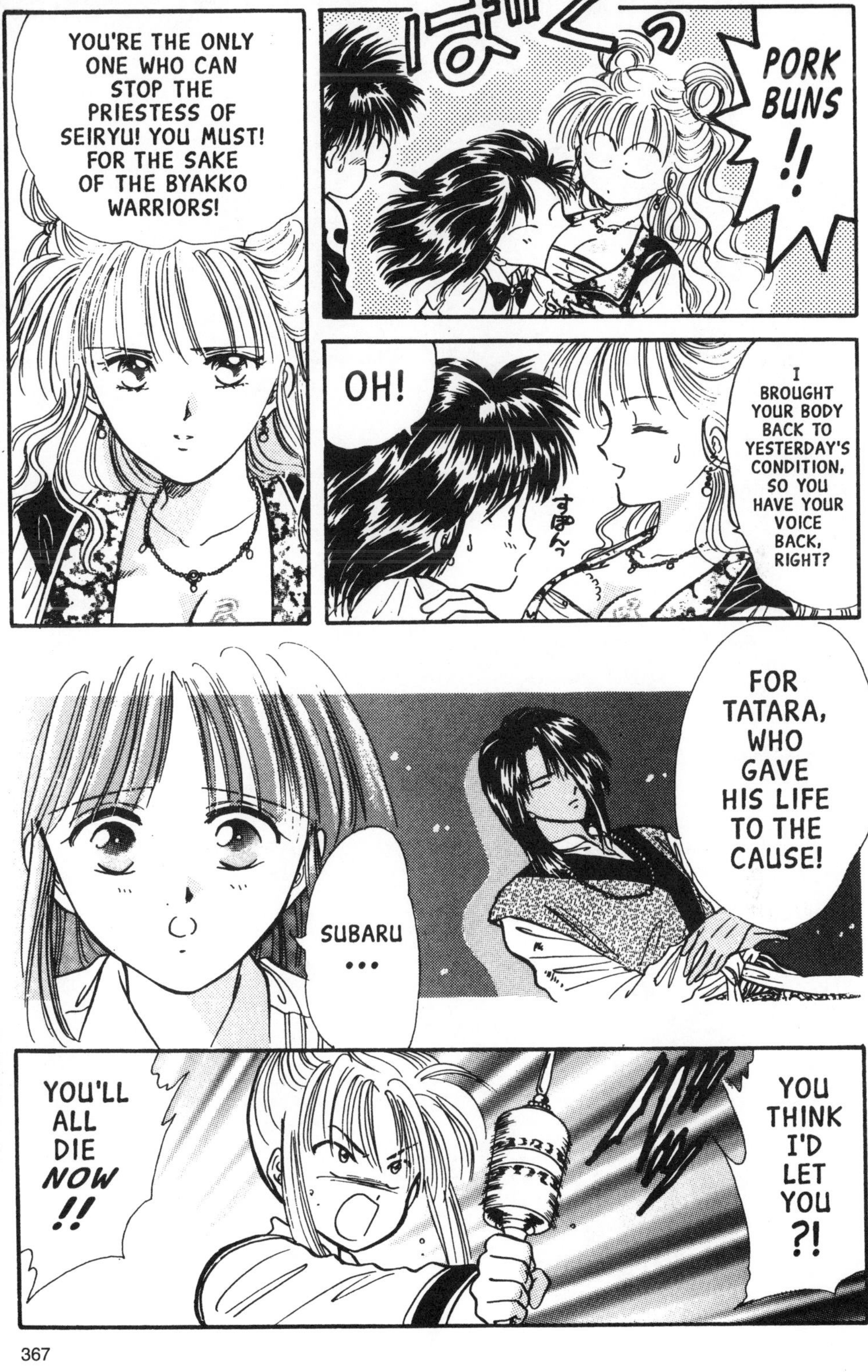
ばくっ
PORK BUNS!!
I BROUGHT YOUR BODY BACK TO YESTERDAY'S CONDITION, SO YOU HAVE YOUR VOICE BACK, RIGHT?
すぽんっ
OH!
YOU'RE THE ONLY ONE WHO CAN STOP THE PRIESTESS OF SEIRYU! YOU MUST! FOR THE SAKE OF THE BYAKKO WARRIORS!
FOR TATARA, WHO GAVE HIS LIFE TO THE CAUSE!
SUBARU...
YOU THINK I'D LET YOU?!
YOU'LL ALL DIE NOW!!

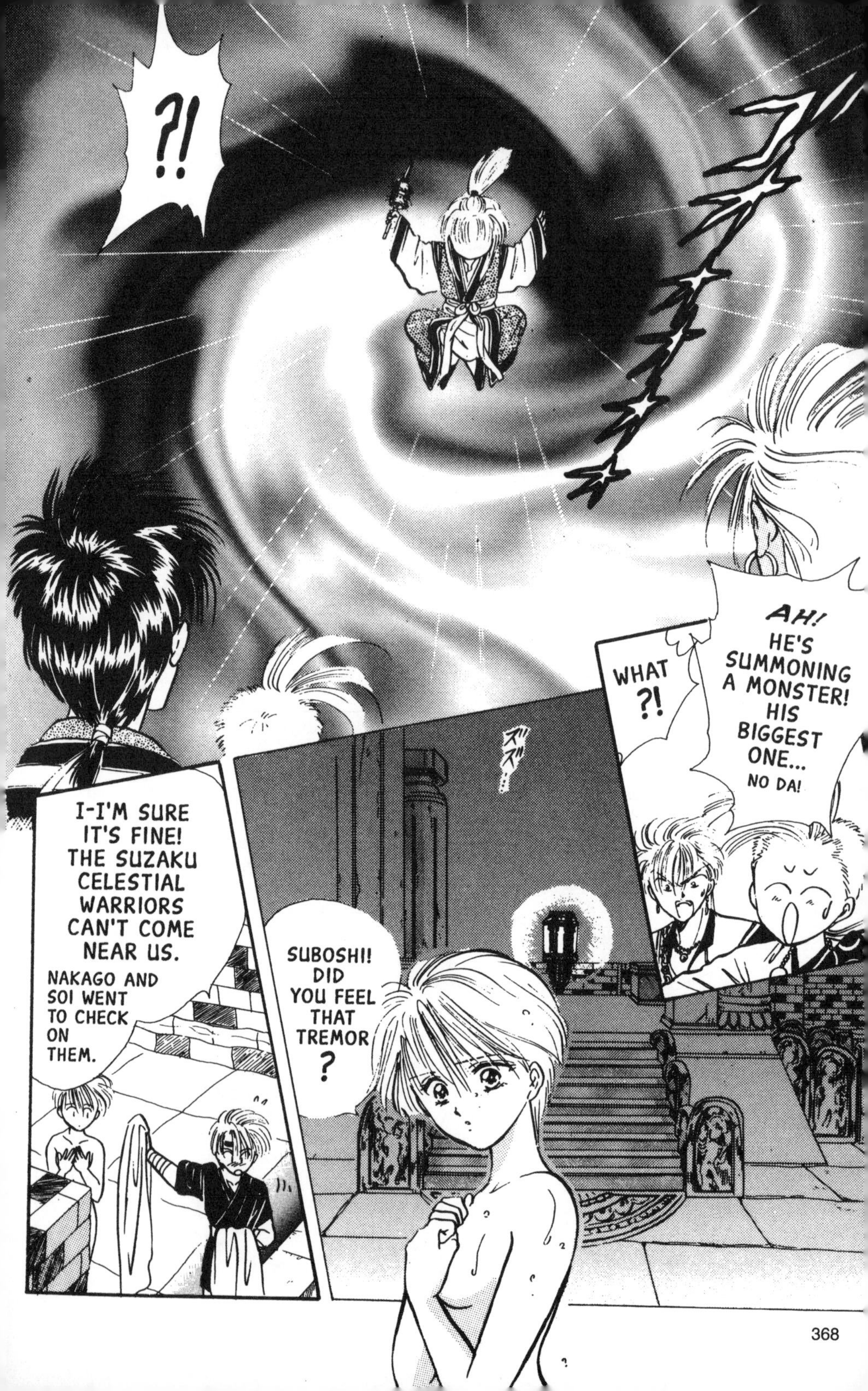
?!
AH! HE'S SUMMONING A MONSTER! HIS BIGGEST ONE... NO DA!
WHAT ?!
SUBOSHI! DID YOU FEEL THAT TREMOR ?
I-I'M SURE IT'S FINE! THE SUZAKU CELESTIAL WARRIORS CAN'T COME NEAR US.
NAKAGO AND SOI WENT TO CHECK ON THEM.

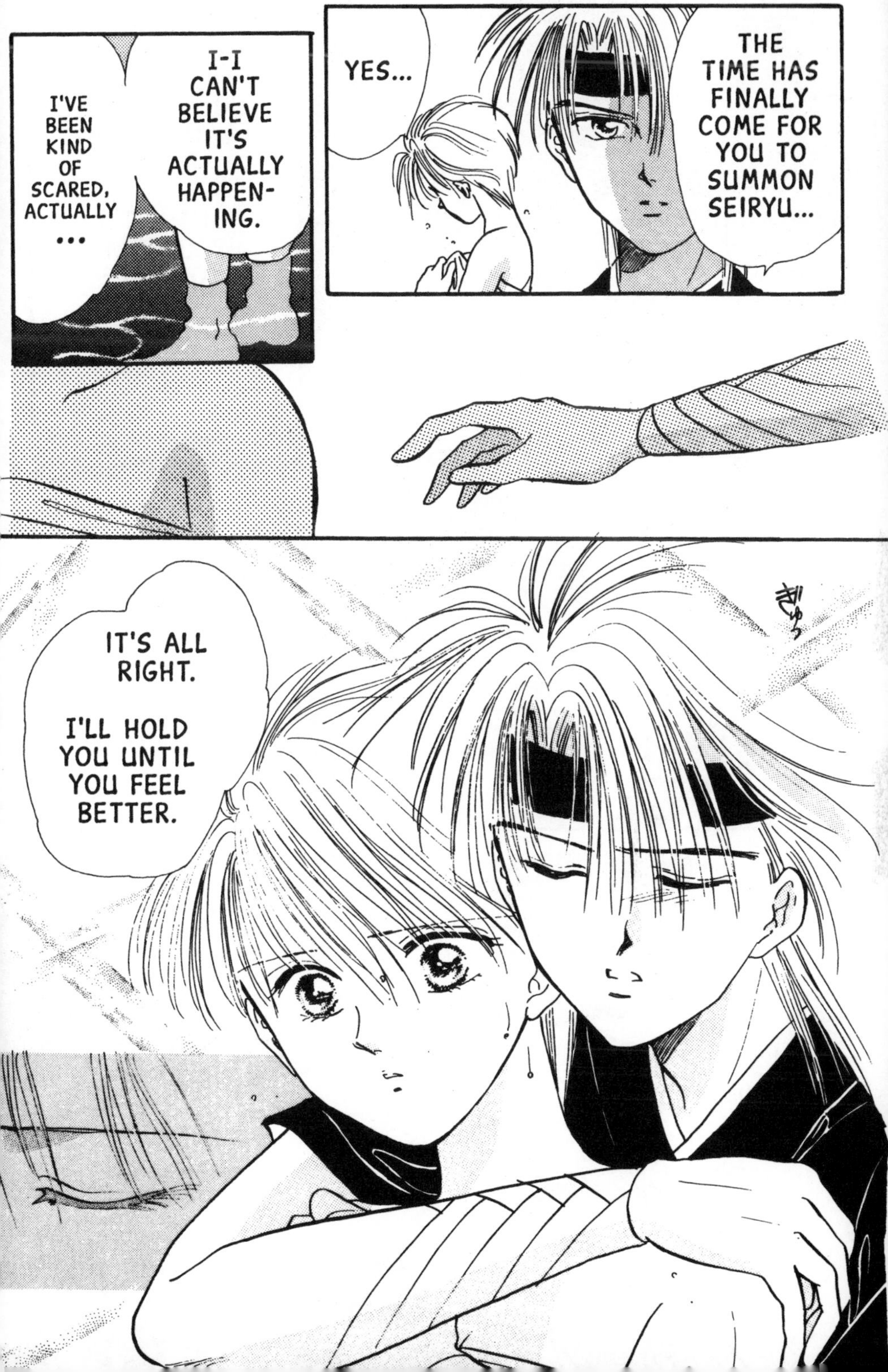
THE TIME HAS FINALLY COME FOR YOU TO SUMMON SEIRYU...
YES...
I-I CAN'T BELIEVE IT'S ACTUALLY HAPPENING.
I'VE BEEN KIND OF SCARED, ACTUALLY...
ぎゅっ
IT'S ALL RIGHT.
I'LL HOLD YOU UNTIL YOU FEEL BETTER.

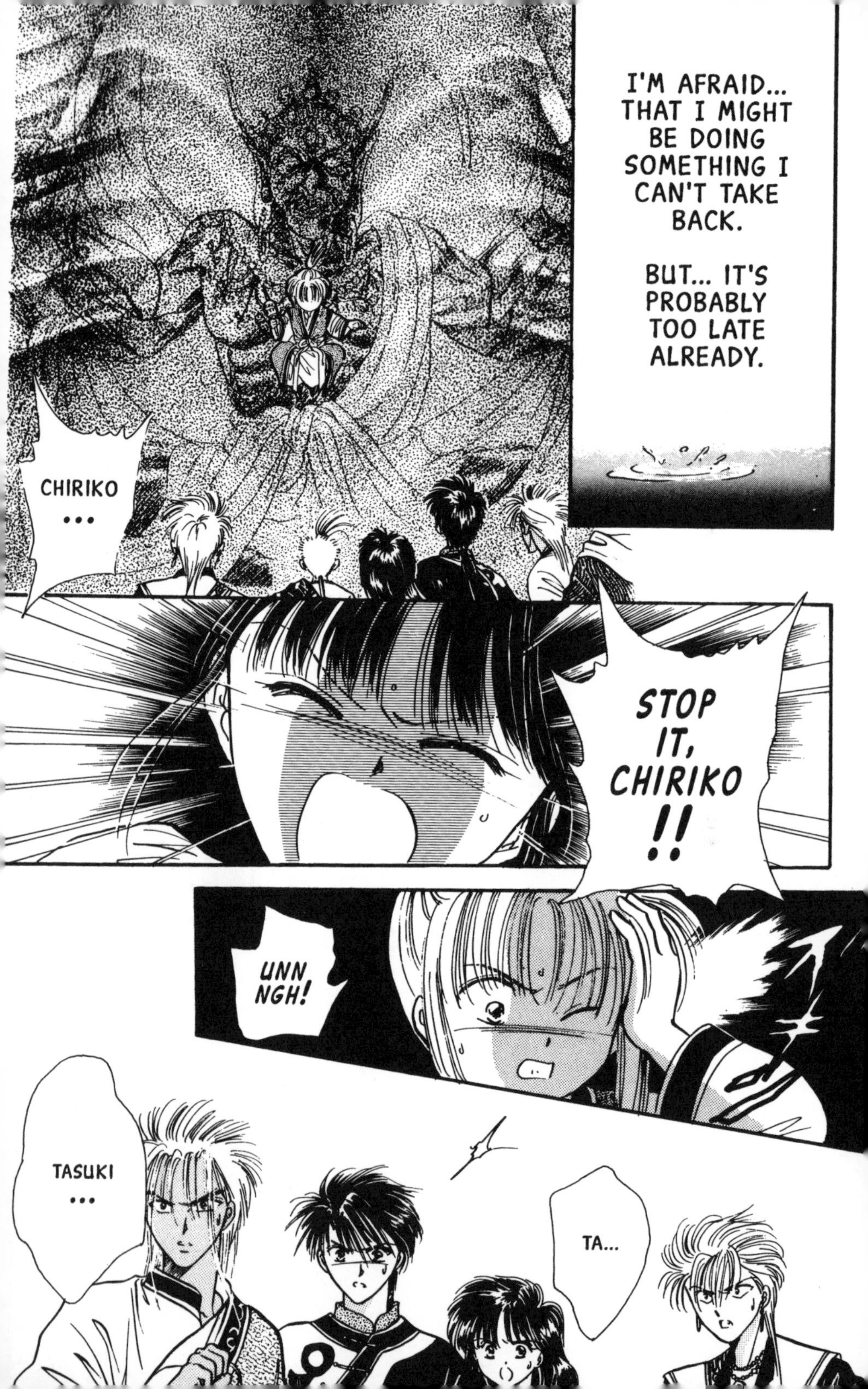
I'M AFRAID... THAT I MIGHT BE DOING SOMETHING I CAN'T TAKE BACK.
BUT... IT'S PROBABLY TOO LATE ALREADY.
CHIRIKO ...
STOP IT, CHIRIKO !!
UNN NGH!
TA...
TASUKI ...

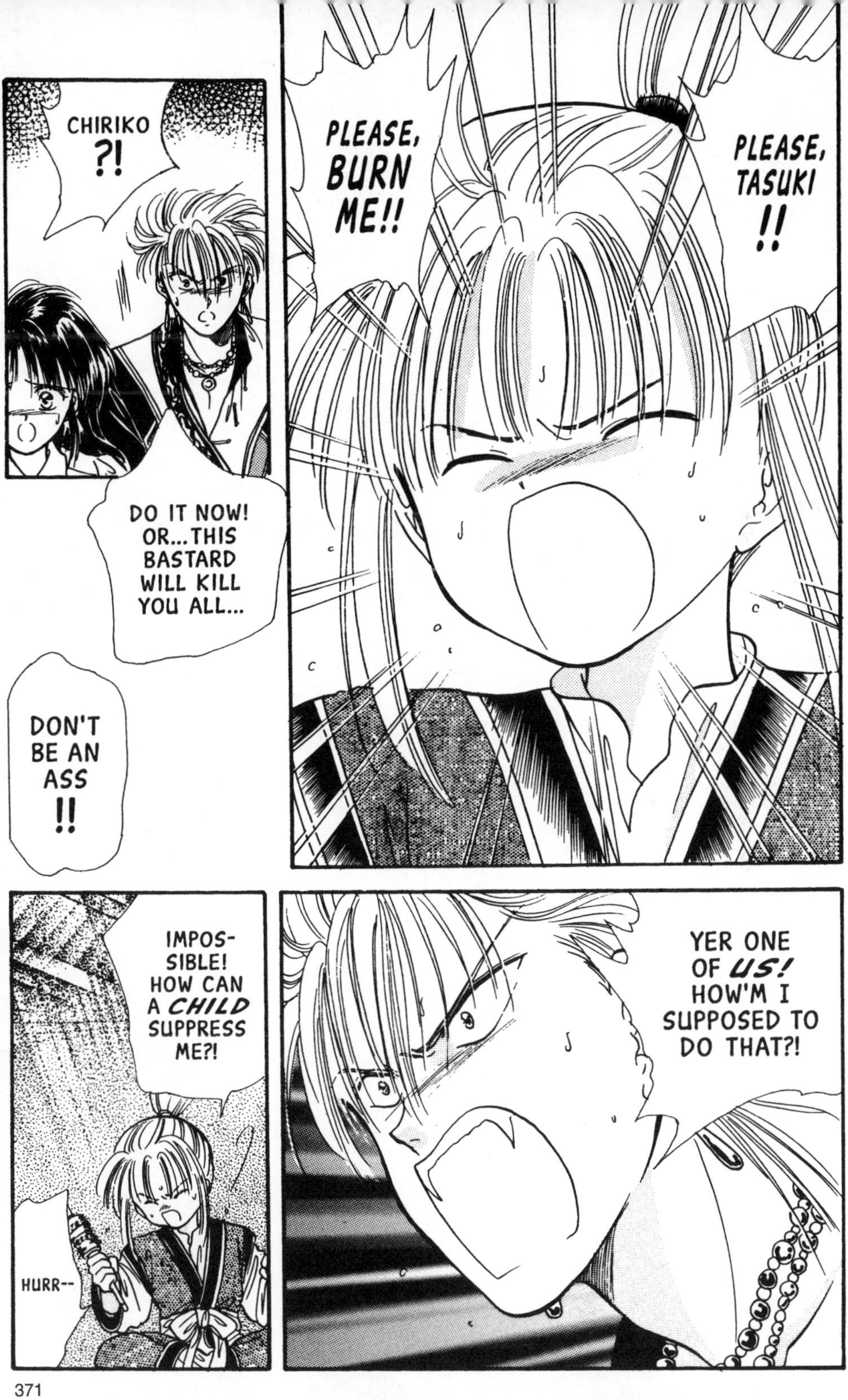
PLEASE, TASUKI!!
PLEASE, BURN ME!!
CHIRIKO?!
DO IT NOW! OR...THIS BASTARD WILL KILL YOU ALL...
DON'T BE AN ASS!!
YER ONE OF *US!* HOW'M I SUPPOSED TO DO THAT?!
IMPOS-SIBLE! HOW CAN A *CHILD* SUPPRESS ME?!
HURR--

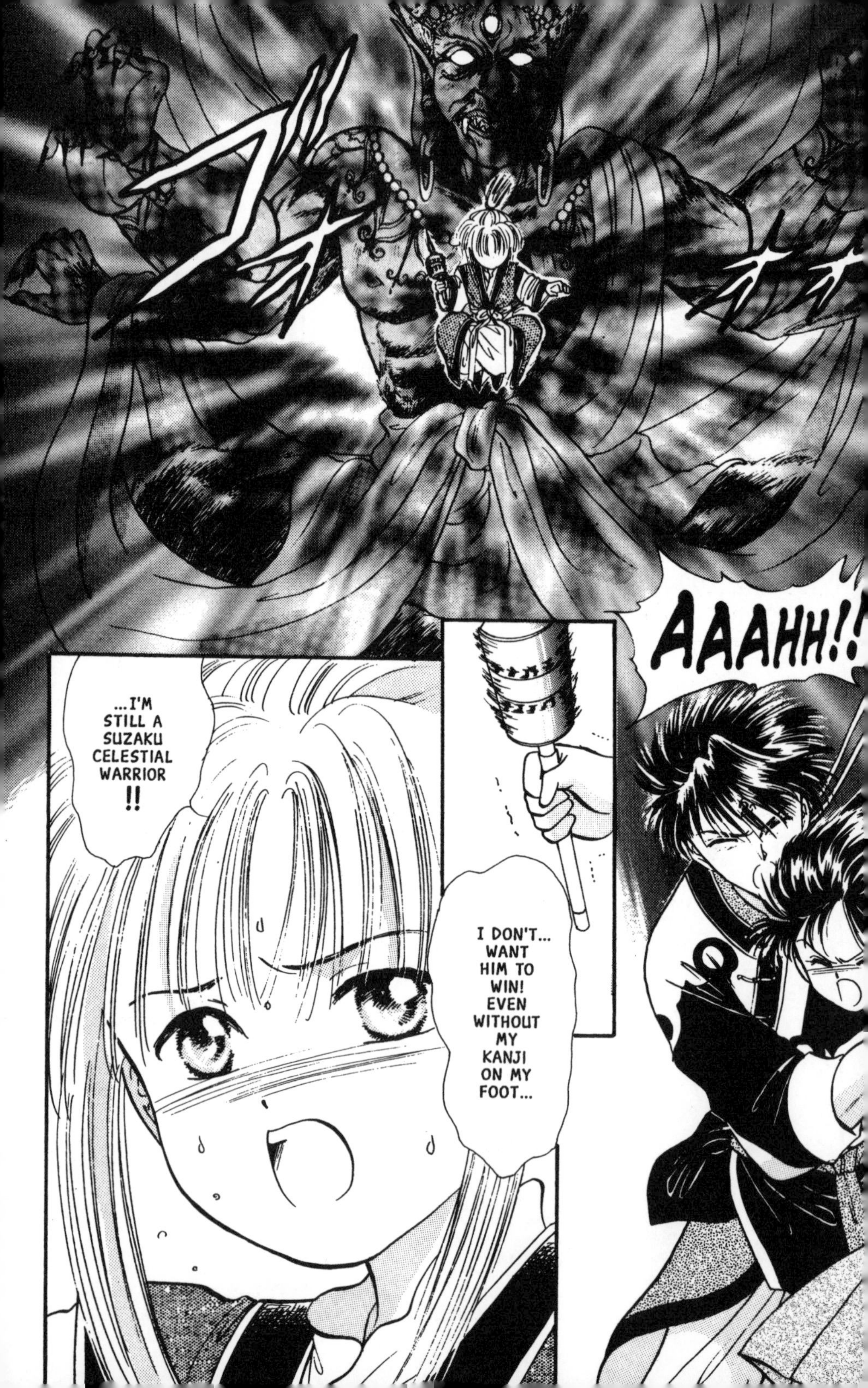
AAAHH!!
I DON'T... WANT HIM TO WIN! EVEN WITHOUT MY KANJI ON MY FOOT...
...I'M STILL A SUZAKU CELESTIAL WARRIOR!!

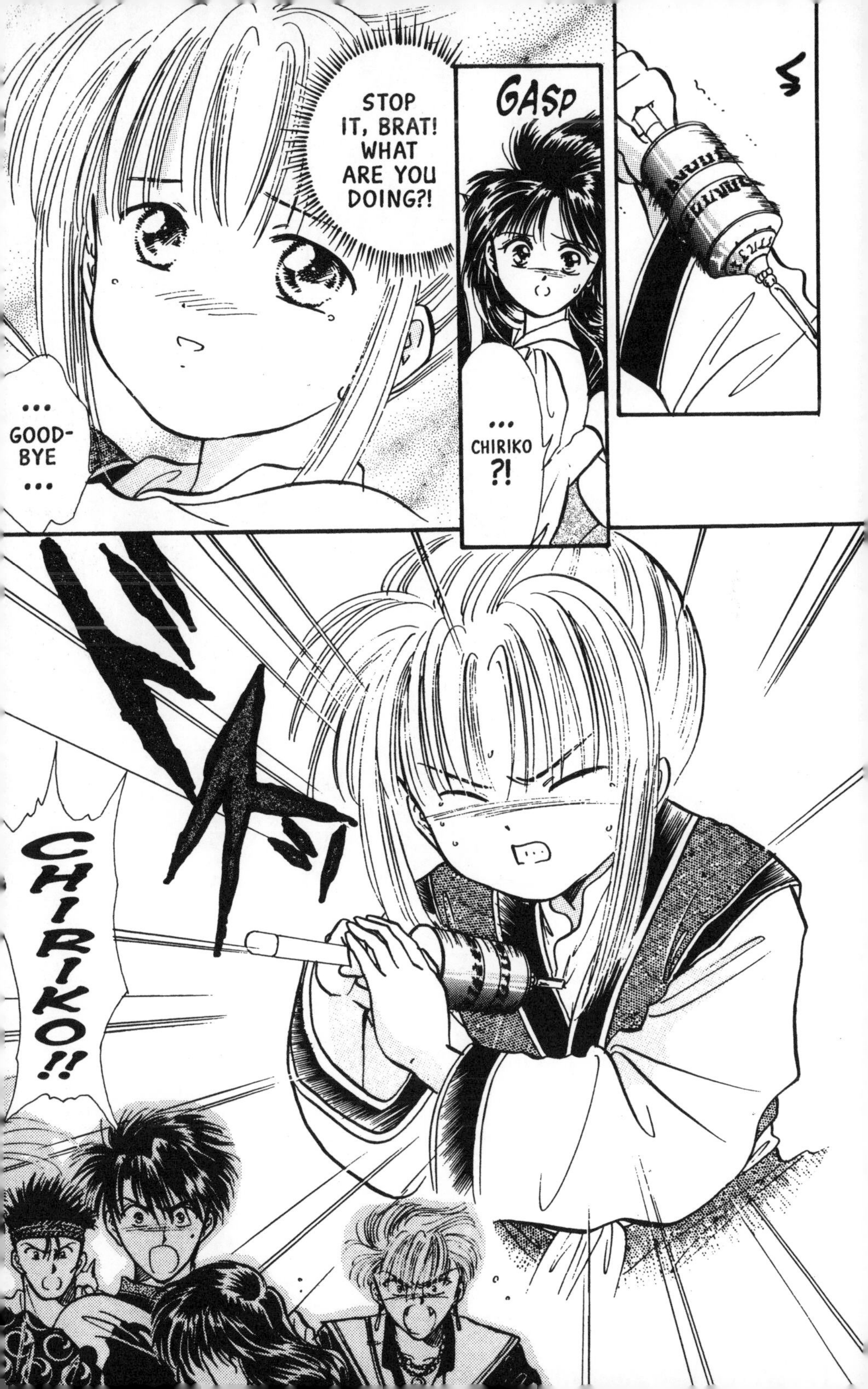
GASP
...CHIRIKO?!
STOP IT, BRAT! WHAT ARE YOU DOING?!
...GOOD-BYE...
CHIRIKO!!

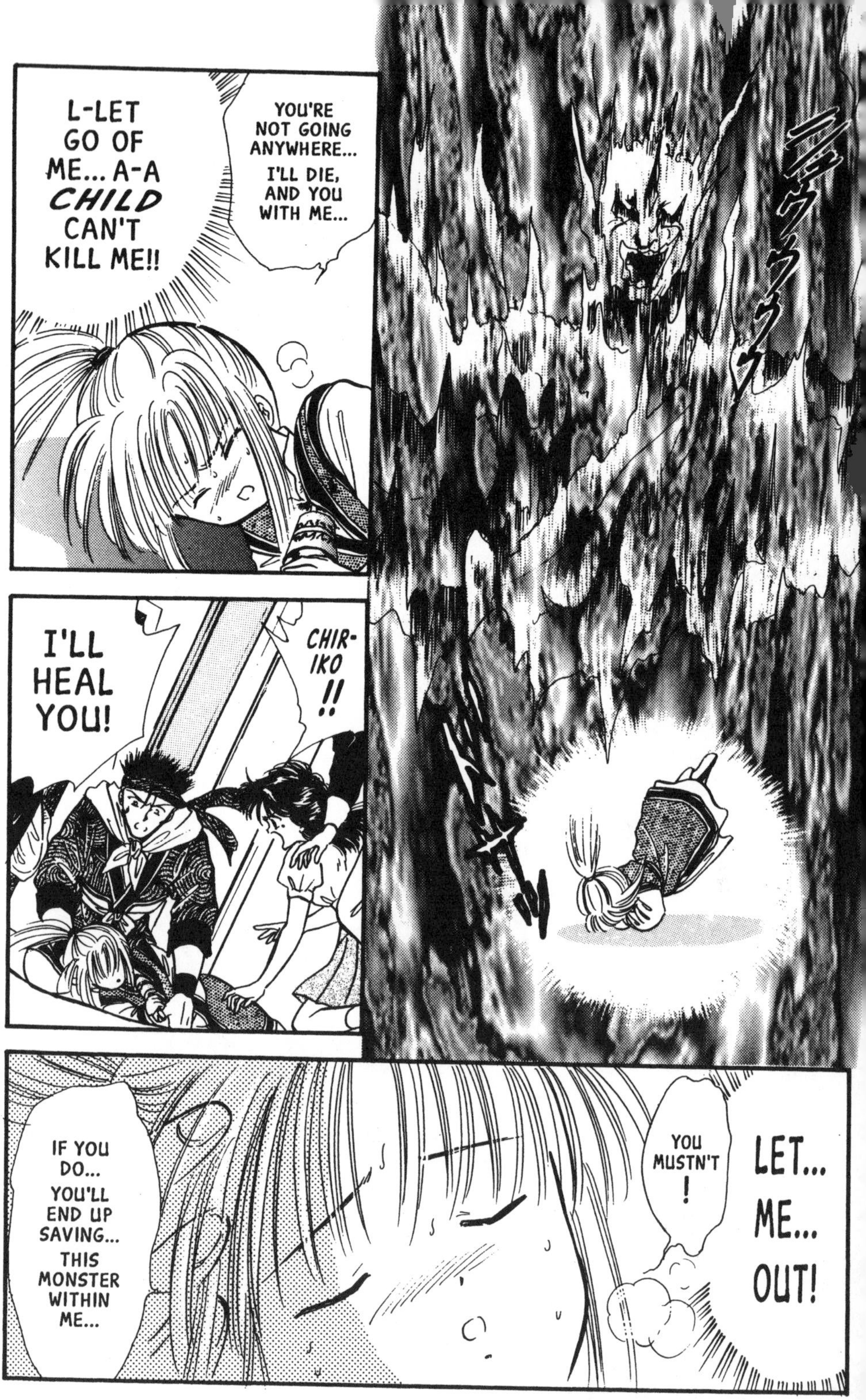
YOU'RE NOT GOING ANYWHERE... I'LL DIE, AND YOU WITH ME...
L-LET GO OF ME... A-A CHILD CAN'T KILL ME!!
CHIRI-KO!!
I'LL HEAL YOU!
LET... ME... OUT!
YOU MUSTN'T!
IF YOU DO... YOU'LL END UP SAVING... THIS MONSTER WITHIN ME...

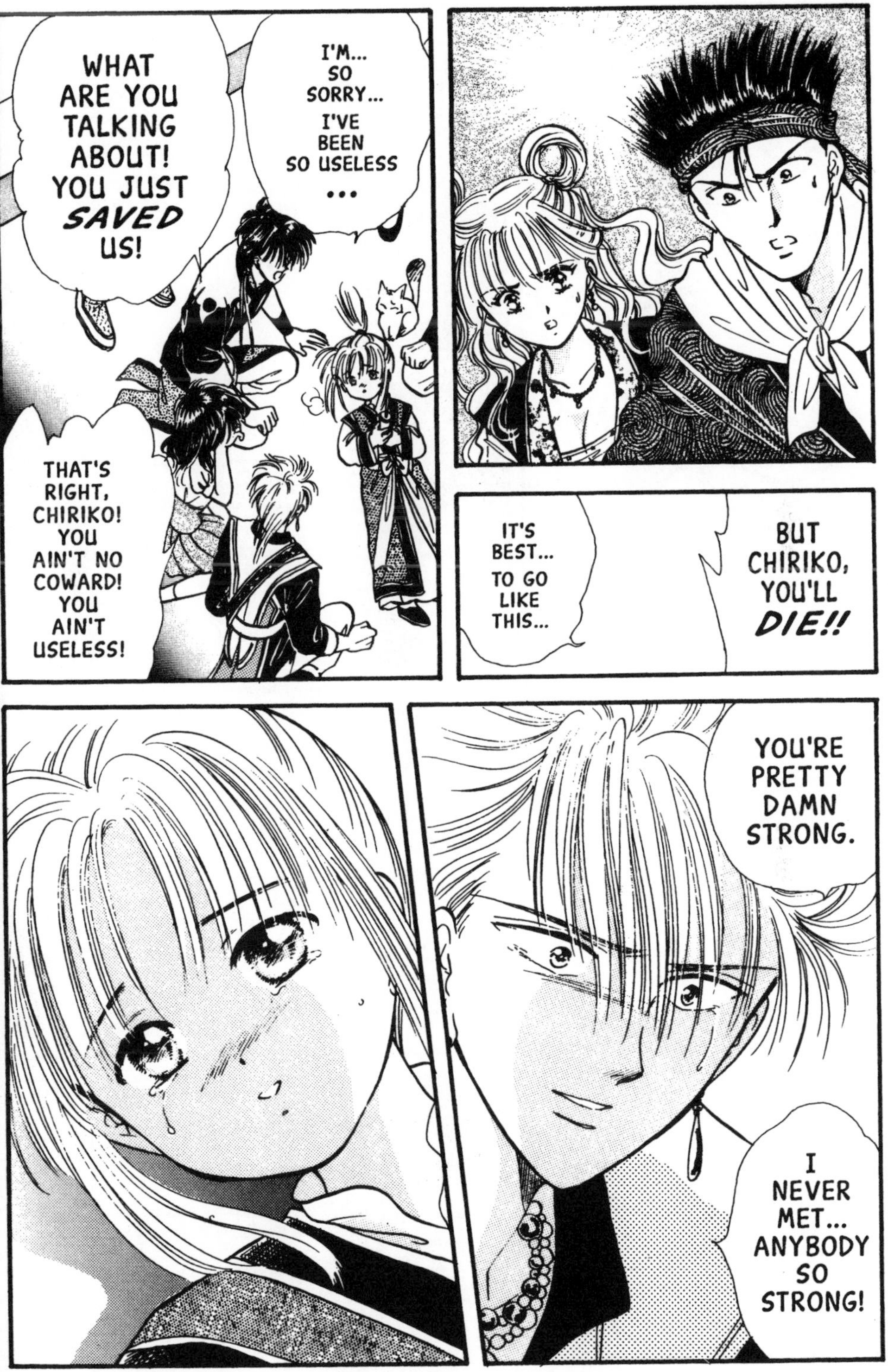
BUT CHIRIKO, YOU'LL DIE!!
IT'S BEST... TO GO LIKE THIS...
I'M... SO SORRY... I'VE BEEN SO USELESS...
WHAT ARE YOU TALKING ABOUT! YOU JUST SAVED US!
THAT'S RIGHT, CHIRIKO! YOU AIN'T NO COWARD! YOU AIN'T USELESS!
YOU'RE PRETTY DAMN STRONG.
I NEVER MET... ANYBODY SO STRONG!

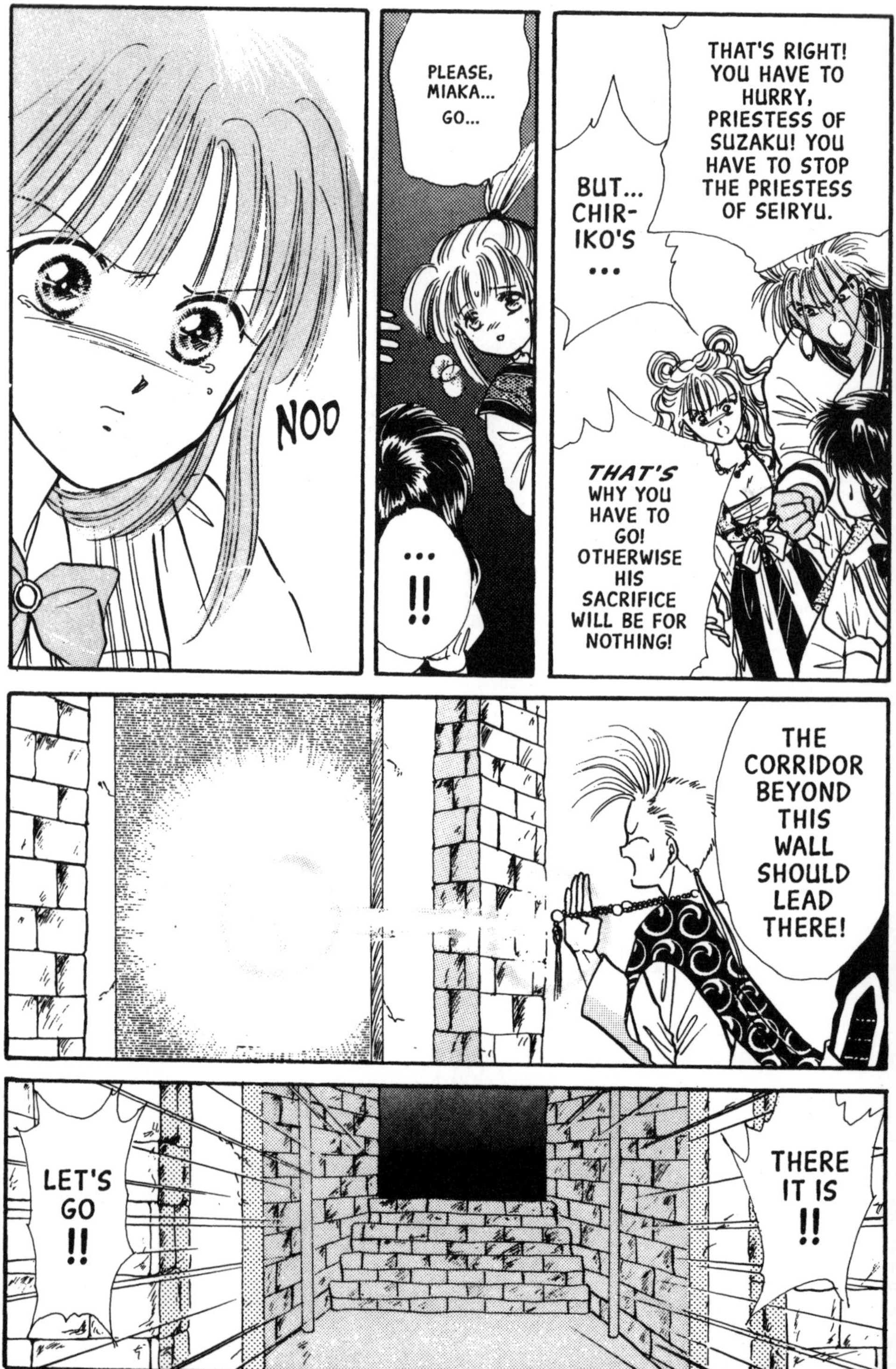
THAT'S RIGHT! YOU HAVE TO HURRY, PRIESTESS OF SUZAKU! YOU HAVE TO STOP THE PRIESTESS OF SEIRYU.
BUT... CHIRIKO'S...
THAT'S WHY YOU HAVE TO GO! OTHERWISE HIS SACRIFICE WILL BE FOR NOTHING!
PLEASE, MIAKA... GO...
...!!
NOD
THE CORRIDOR BEYOND THIS WALL SHOULD LEAD THERE!
THERE IT IS!!
LET'S GO!!

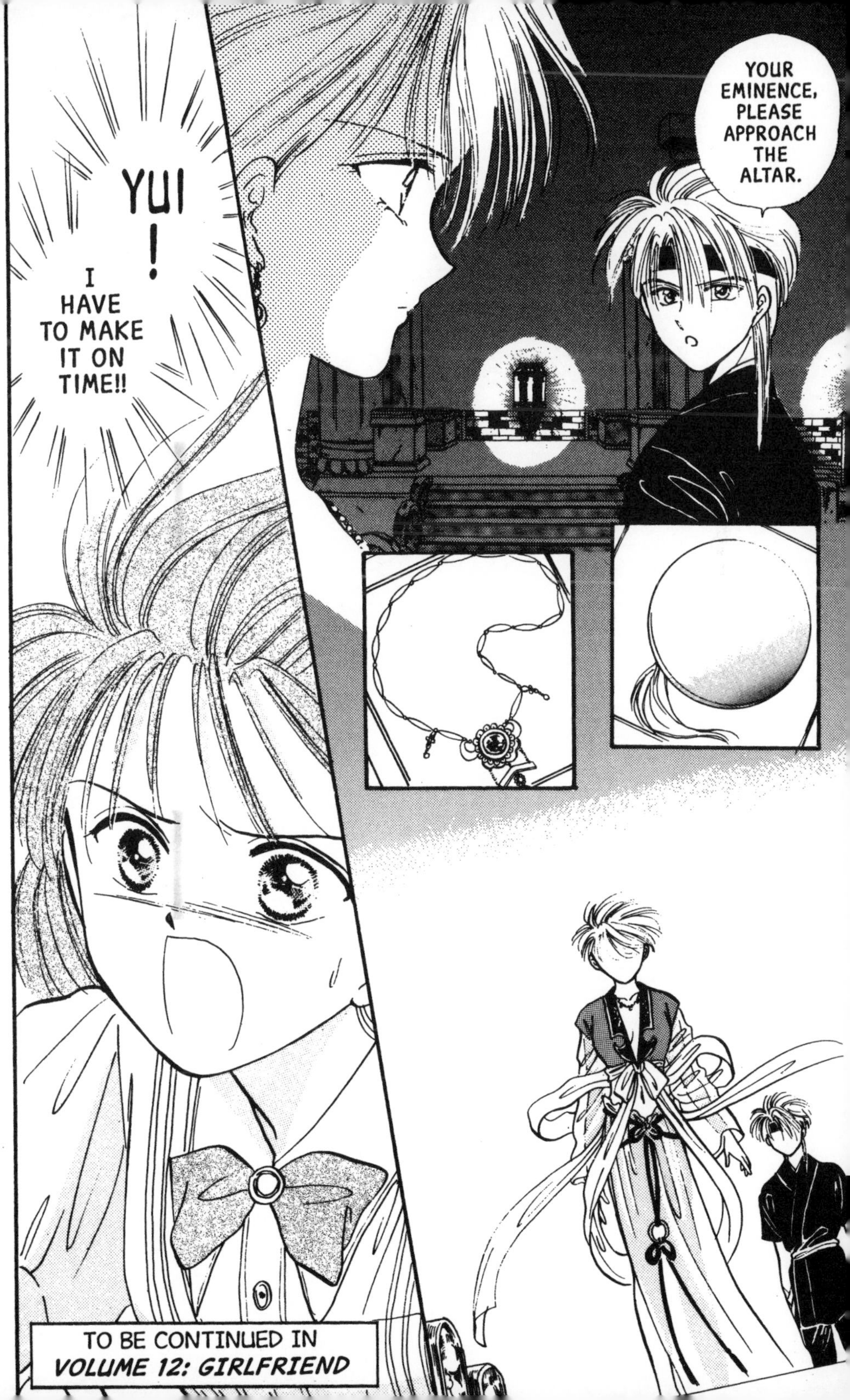
YOUR EMINENCE, PLEASE APPROACH THE ALTAR.
YUI!
I HAVE TO MAKE IT ON TIME!!
TO BE CONTINUED IN *VOLUME 12: GIRLFRIEND*

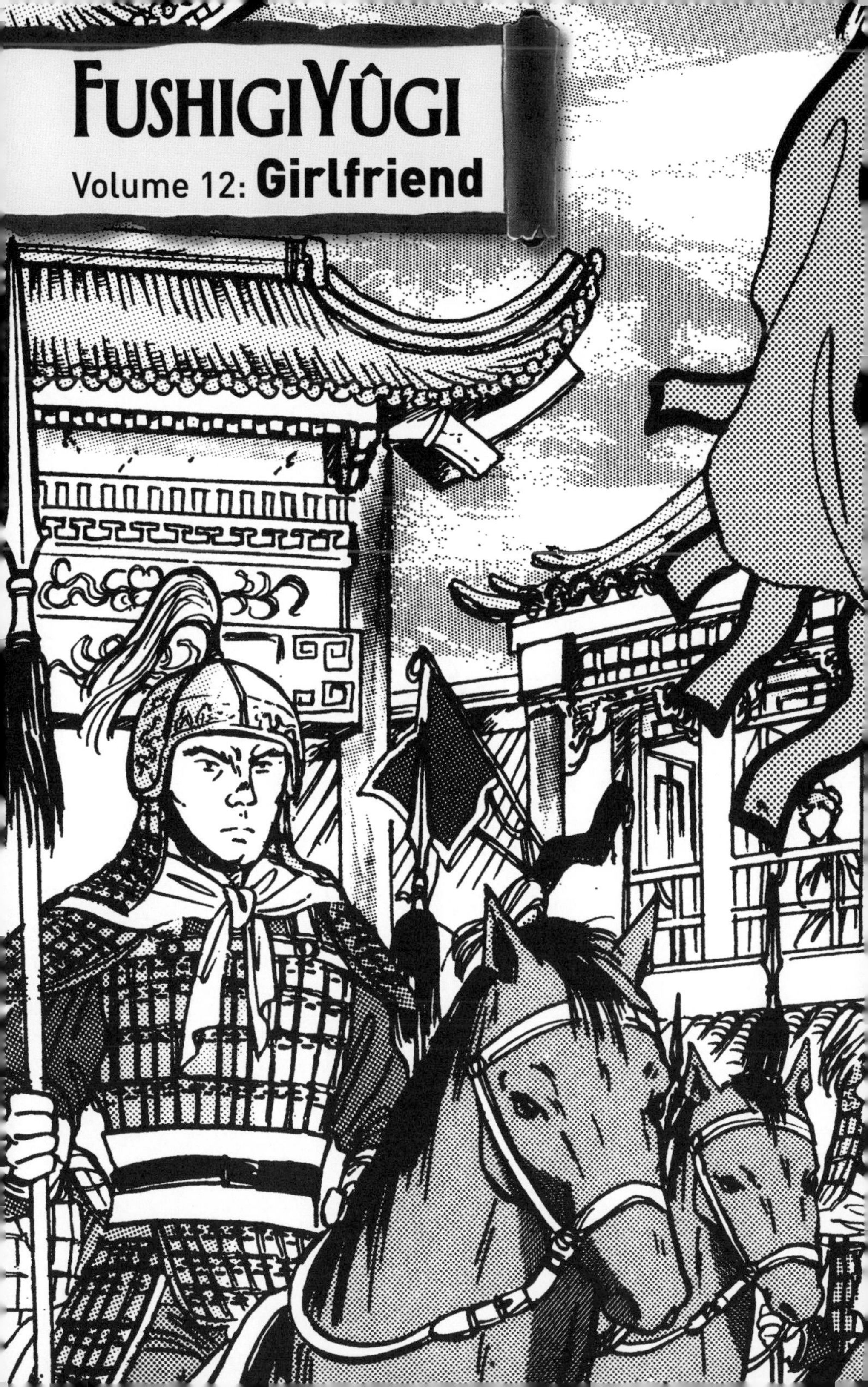
FUSHIGI YÛGI
Volume 12: Girlfriend

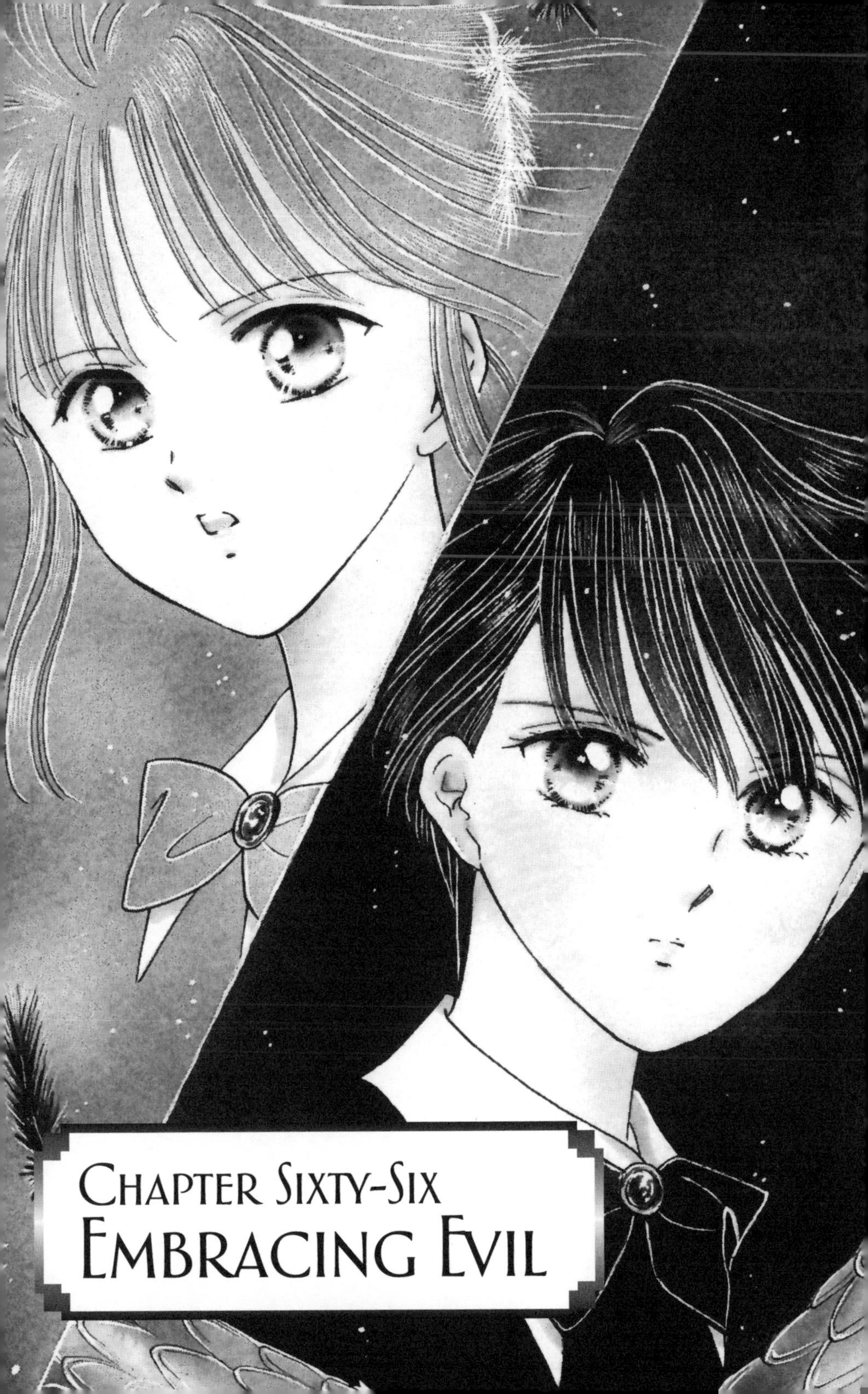
Chapter Sixty-Six
Embracing Evil

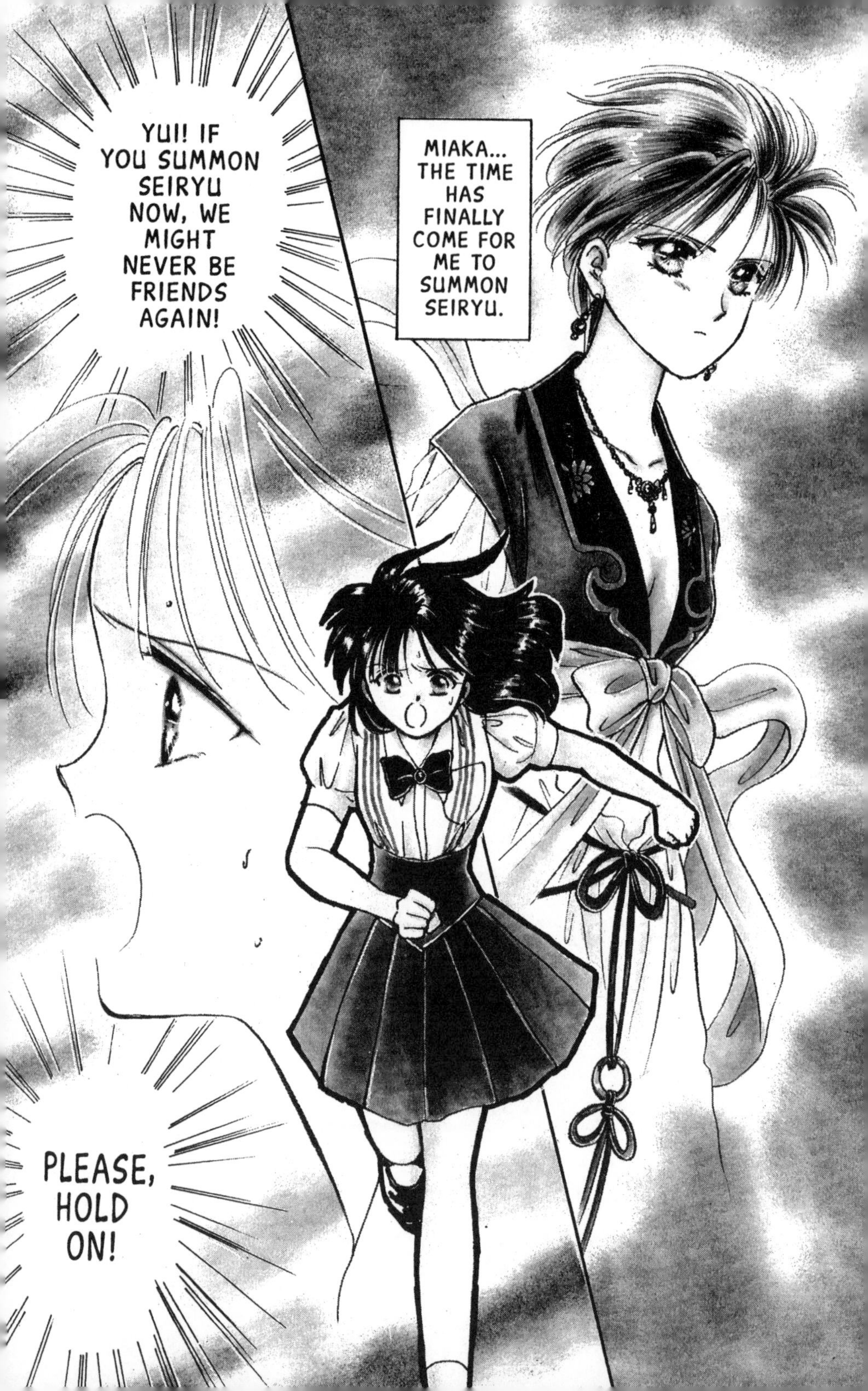
MIAKA... THE TIME HAS FINALLY COME FOR ME TO SUMMON SEIRYU.
YUI! IF YOU SUMMON SEIRYU NOW, WE MIGHT NEVER BE FRIENDS AGAIN!
PLEASE, HOLD ON!

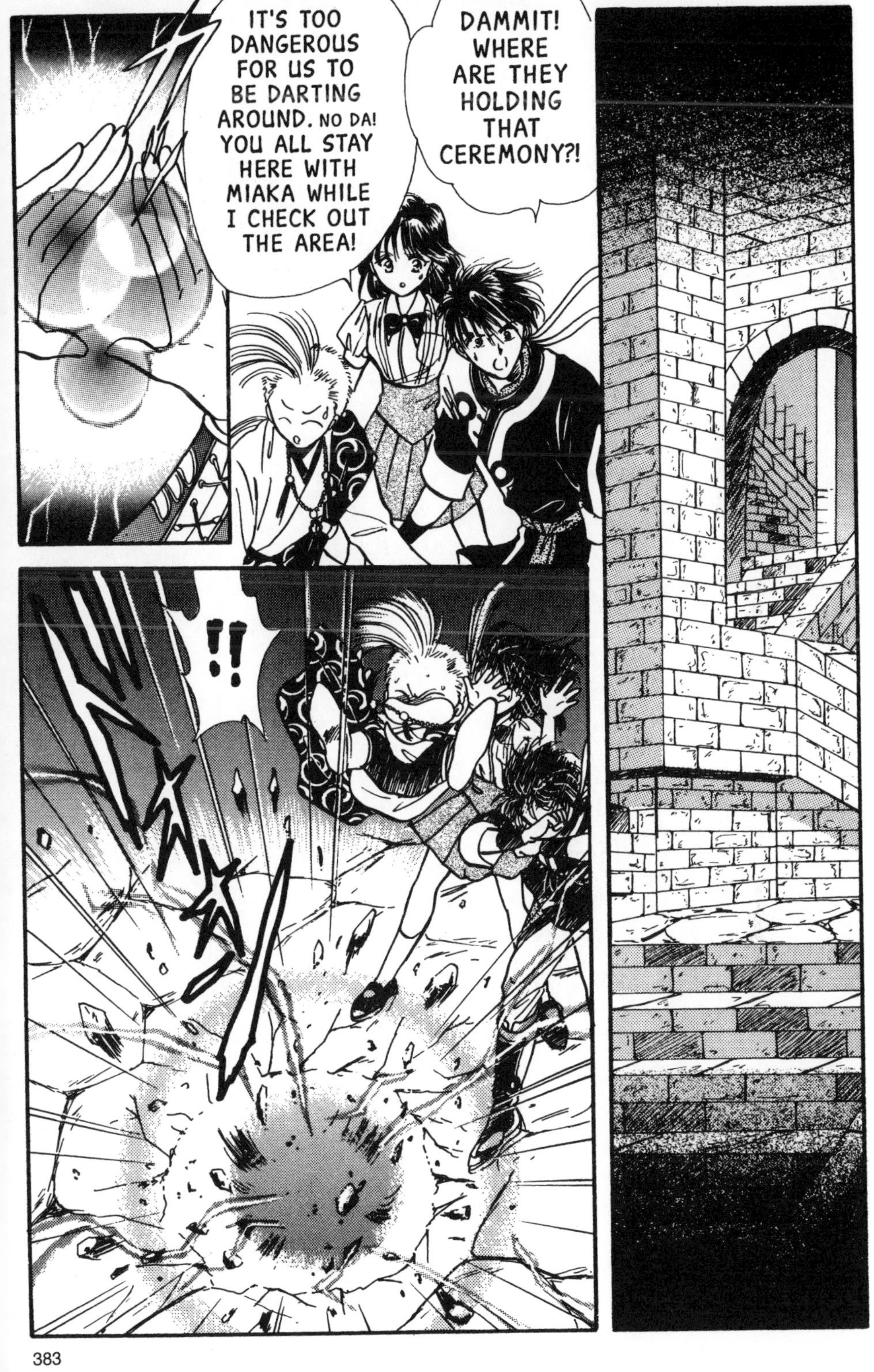
DAMMIT! WHERE ARE THEY HOLDING THAT CEREMONY?!
IT'S TOO DANGEROUS FOR US TO BE DARTING AROUND. NO DA! YOU ALL STAY HERE WITH MIAKA WHILE I CHECK OUT THE AREA!
!!

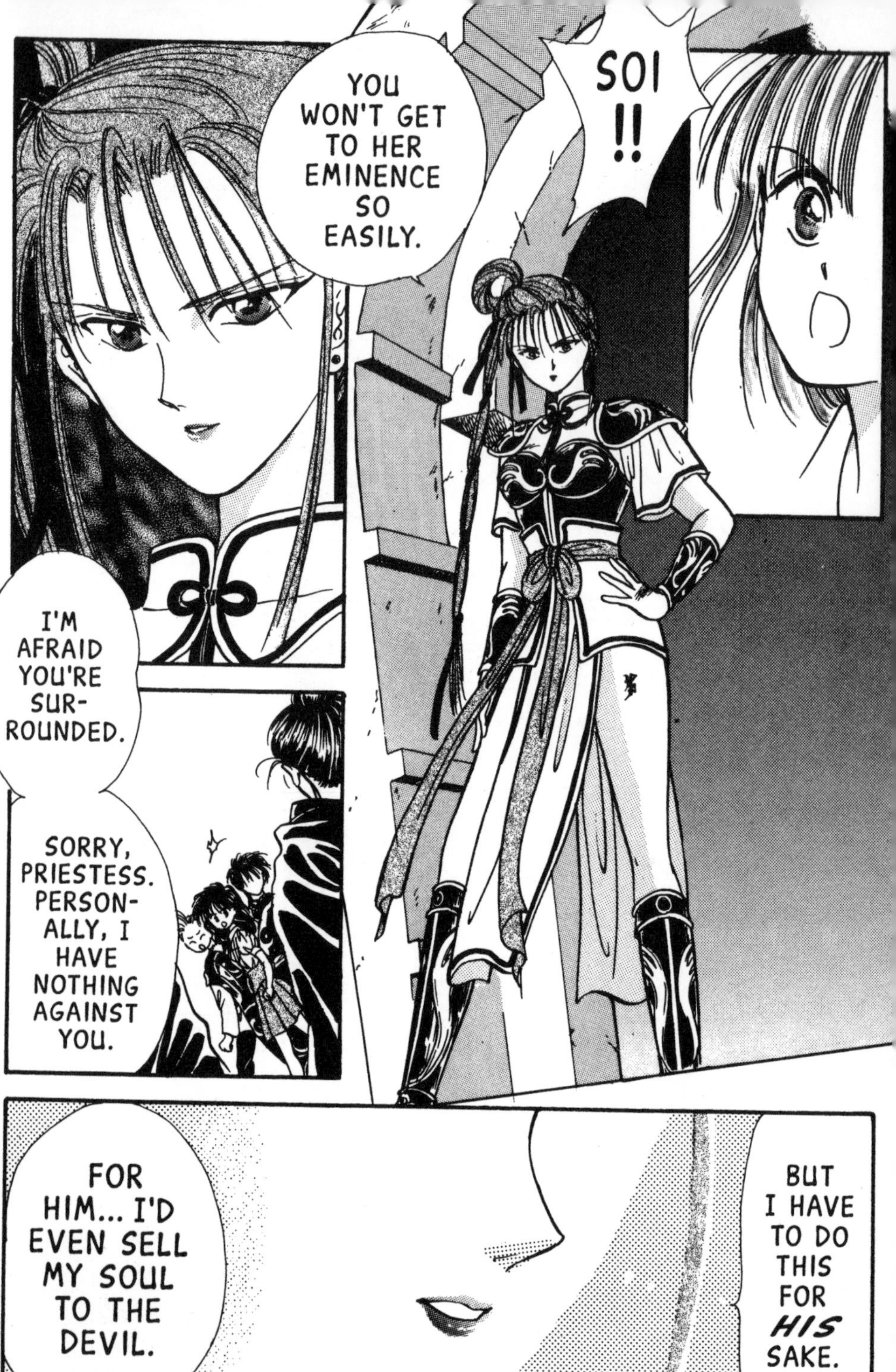
SOI !!
YOU WON'T GET TO HER EMINENCE SO EASILY.
I'M AFRAID YOU'RE SUR-ROUNDED.
SORRY, PRIESTESS. PERSON-ALLY, I HAVE NOTHING AGAINST YOU.
BUT I HAVE TO DO THIS FOR *HIS* SAKE.
FOR HIM... I'D EVEN SELL MY SOUL TO THE DEVIL.

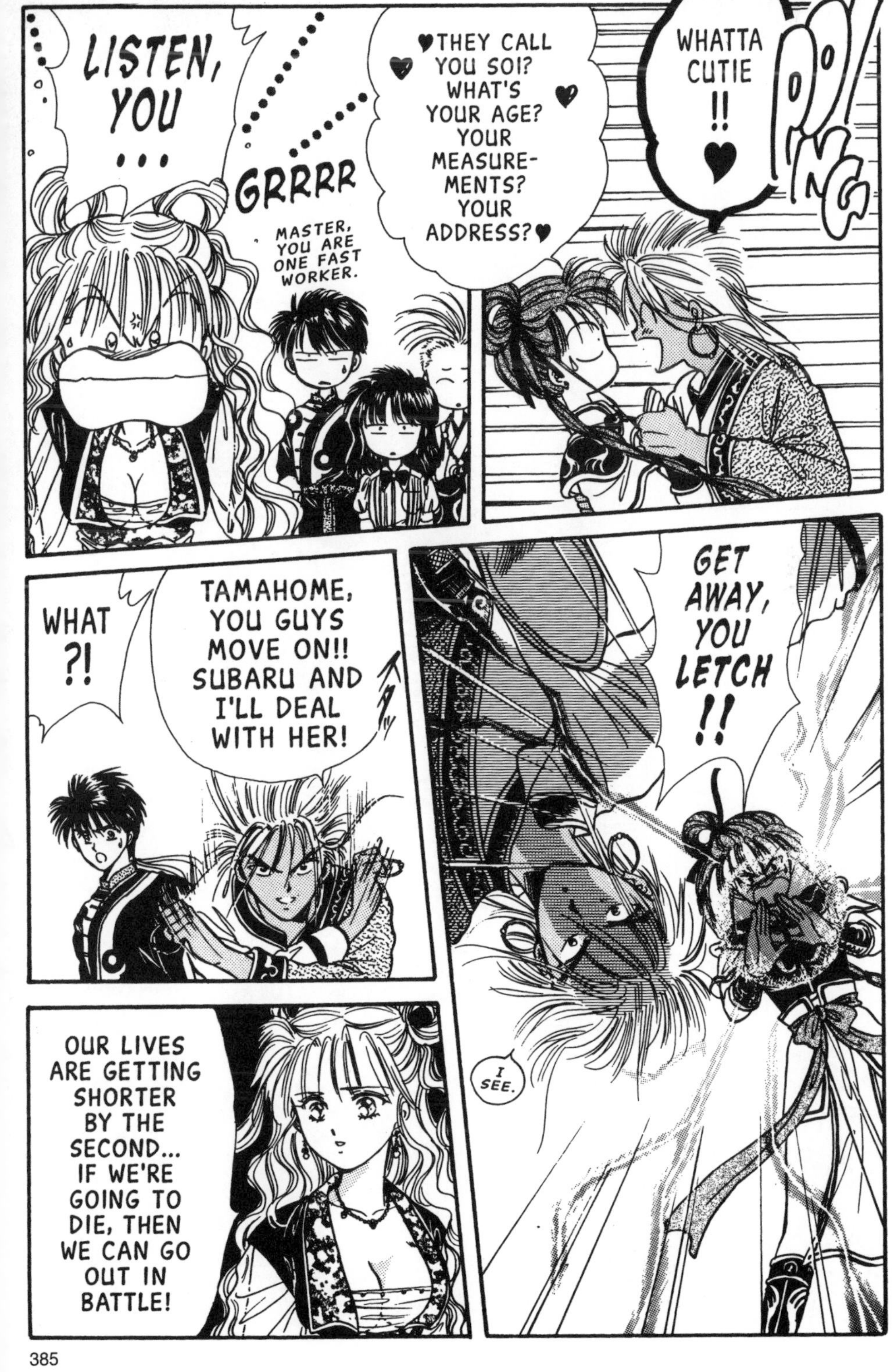
WHATTA CUTIE !! ♥
POING
♥THEY CALL YOU SOI? WHAT'S YOUR AGE? YOUR MEASUREMENTS? YOUR ADDRESS?♥
LISTEN, YOU ...
GRRRR
MASTER, YOU ARE ONE FAST WORKER.
GET AWAY, YOU LETCH !!
I SEE.
TAMAHOME, YOU GUYS MOVE ON!! SUBARU AND I'LL DEAL WITH HER!
WHAT ?!
OUR LIVES ARE GETTING SHORTER BY THE SECOND... IF WE'RE GOING TO DIE, THEN WE CAN GO OUT IN BATTLE!

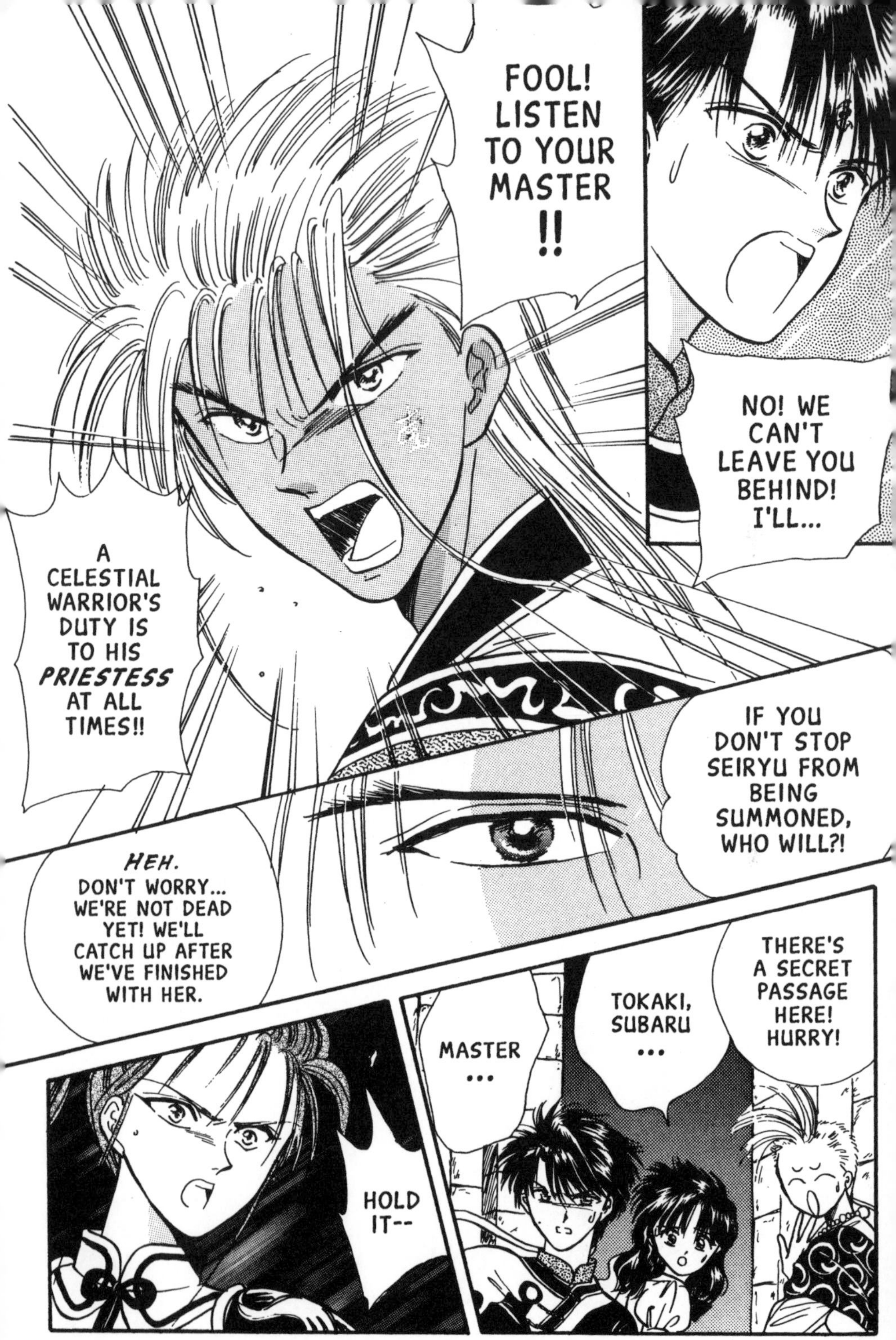
NO! WE CAN'T LEAVE YOU BEHIND! I'LL...
FOOL! LISTEN TO YOUR MASTER !!
A CELESTIAL WARRIOR'S DUTY IS TO HIS *PRIESTESS* AT ALL TIMES!!
IF YOU DON'T STOP SEIRYU FROM BEING SUMMONED, WHO WILL?!
HEH. DON'T WORRY... WE'RE NOT DEAD YET! WE'LL CATCH UP AFTER WE'VE FINISHED WITH HER.
THERE'S A SECRET PASSAGE HERE! HURRY!
TOKAKI, SUBARU ...
MASTER ...
HOLD IT--

NO YOU DON'T.
!
WHAT DO YOU SAY WE HAVE A WOMEN'S FIGHT...?
YOU SENILE HAG.
WHAT WAS THAT?! I MAY HAVE A FEW MONTHS ON YOU, BUT AT LEAST I'VE LEARNED HOW TO DRESS WITH STYLE!
AND YOU!! GIVE YOU A FEW YEARS, AND SEE HOW THE WRINKLES SPREAD!
HAH! THAT DOESN'T CHANGE THE FACT THAT YOU'RE A HAG! I'M THE ONE WITH THE GOOD SKIN HERE. PLUS I DON'T HAVE TO PRETEND I'M 19.
..... WHEN I SAID FIGHTING, I DIDN'T MEAN ARGUING!

Hello, it's me Watase. I pulled an all-nighter, so I'm really exhausted! Lately, I've been pulling them several nights in a row. I've got dark rings under my eyes. Now, Positive attitude here! Let's continue with my comments on the characters...
Oh, wait, before that, I want to thank all the fans who came to my book signing in Kyoto. At the "Comic One-Point Lesson," the participants bombarded me with questions like "Who does Nakago really love?" "What's Tasuki's history with women?" "Who was the murderer of Chichiri's best friend?" I managed to respond to all of them, but I have to say they probed deeply. Also, thanks for all the gifts. The mini-Tama doll (Tamahome) someone made for me is now the idol of the entire staff here. He's super cute. Now if we only had one of Nakago. If we had all the characters covered we could play "house" with them!! My secret wish(?)

To continue... Regarding Mitsukake, I wanted someone macho. Someone you'd take one look at and say, "Wow, he's a man's man." I bet he'd be a really good husband. He's kind and calm. Many times I've wished I could just snuggle up against his back... (so large and inviting, a "snuggable" back!) I added the cat to emphasize his kindness. Big man with a kitty. Nice pair.

Speaking of pairs, I came up with Chiriko as a character to contrast with Mitsukake. The big man has to be paired up with a little kid. Of course, Chiriko has to be smart, but it turns out he's got a split personality. When his character appears, and he's wise, he can't recall being a dazed child.

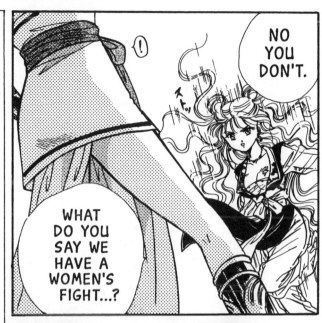

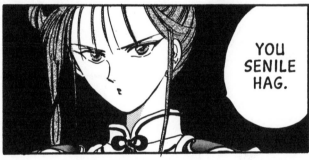

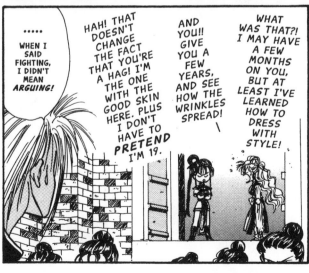

To be continued →

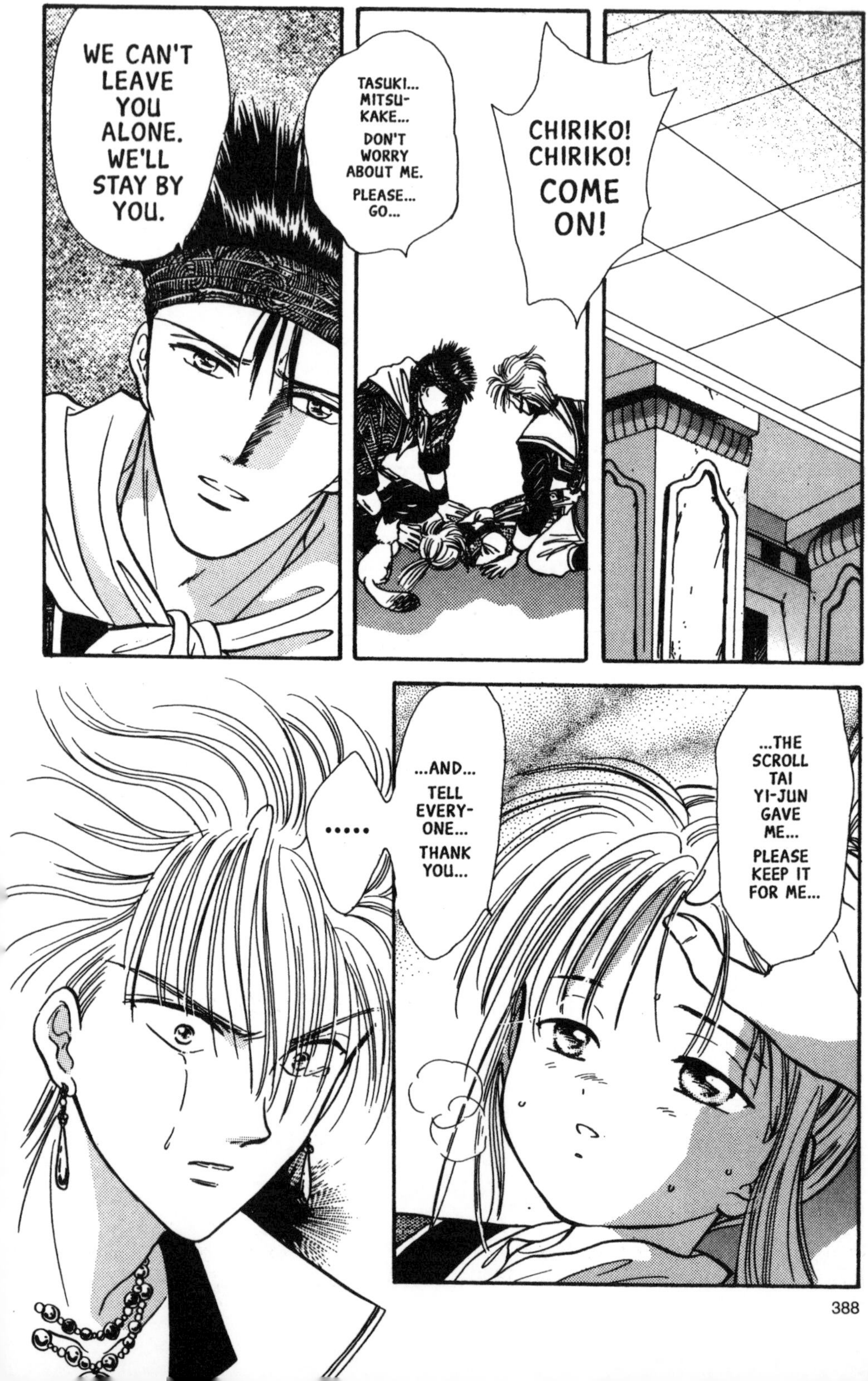
CHIRIKO! CHIRIKO! COME ON!
TASUKI... MITSU-KAKE... DON'T WORRY ABOUT ME. PLEASE... GO...
WE CAN'T LEAVE YOU ALONE. WE'LL STAY BY YOU.
...THE SCROLL TAI YI-JUN GAVE ME... PLEASE KEEP IT FOR ME...
...AND... TELL EVERY-ONE... THANK YOU...
.....

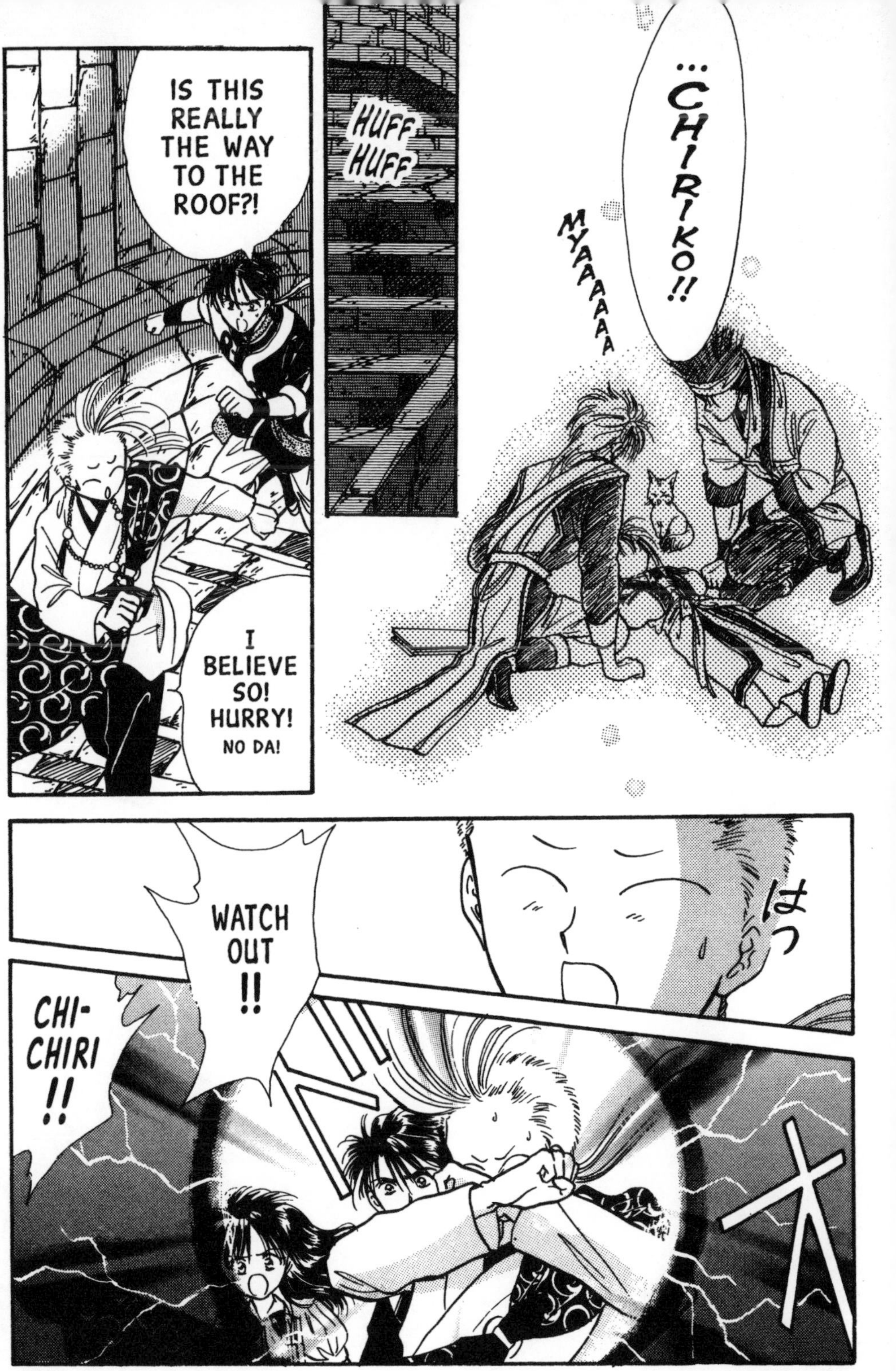
...CHIRIKO!!
MYAAAAAA
HUFF HUFF
IS THIS REALLY THE WAY TO THE ROOF?!
I BELIEVE SO! HURRY! NO DA!
はっ
WATCH OUT!!
CHI-CHIRI!!

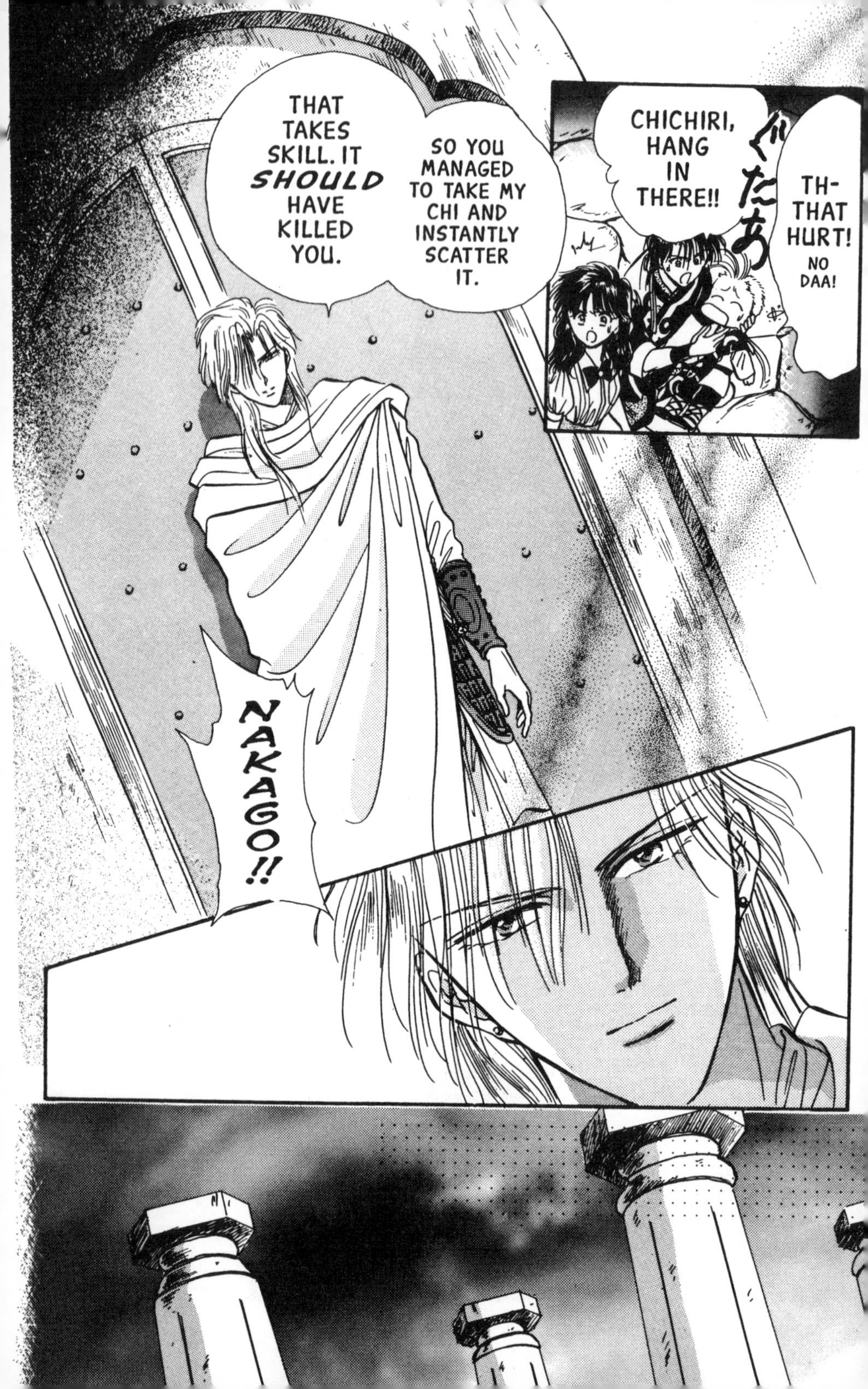
TH-THAT HURT! NO DAA!
ぐたあ
CHICHIRI, HANG IN THERE!!
SO YOU MANAGED TO TAKE MY CHI AND INSTANTLY SCATTER IT.
THAT TAKES SKILL. IT *SHOULD* HAVE KILLED YOU.
NAKAGO!!

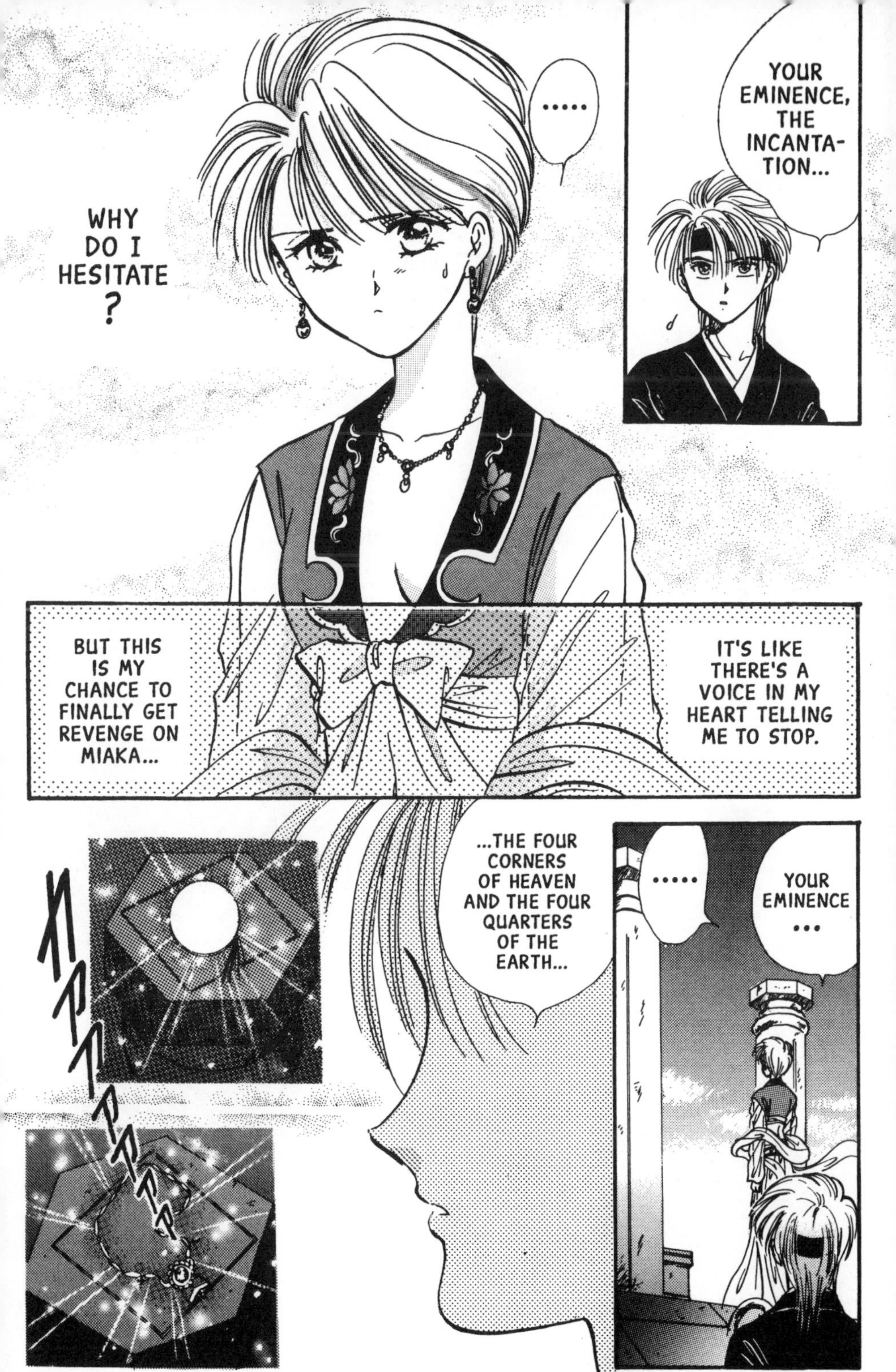
YOUR EMINENCE, THE INCANTATION...
.....
WHY DO I HESITATE ?
IT'S LIKE THERE'S A VOICE IN MY HEART TELLING ME TO STOP.
BUT THIS IS MY CHANCE TO FINALLY GET REVENGE ON MIAKA...
YOUR EMINENCE ...
.....
...THE FOUR CORNERS OF HEAVEN AND THE FOUR QUARTERS OF THE EARTH...

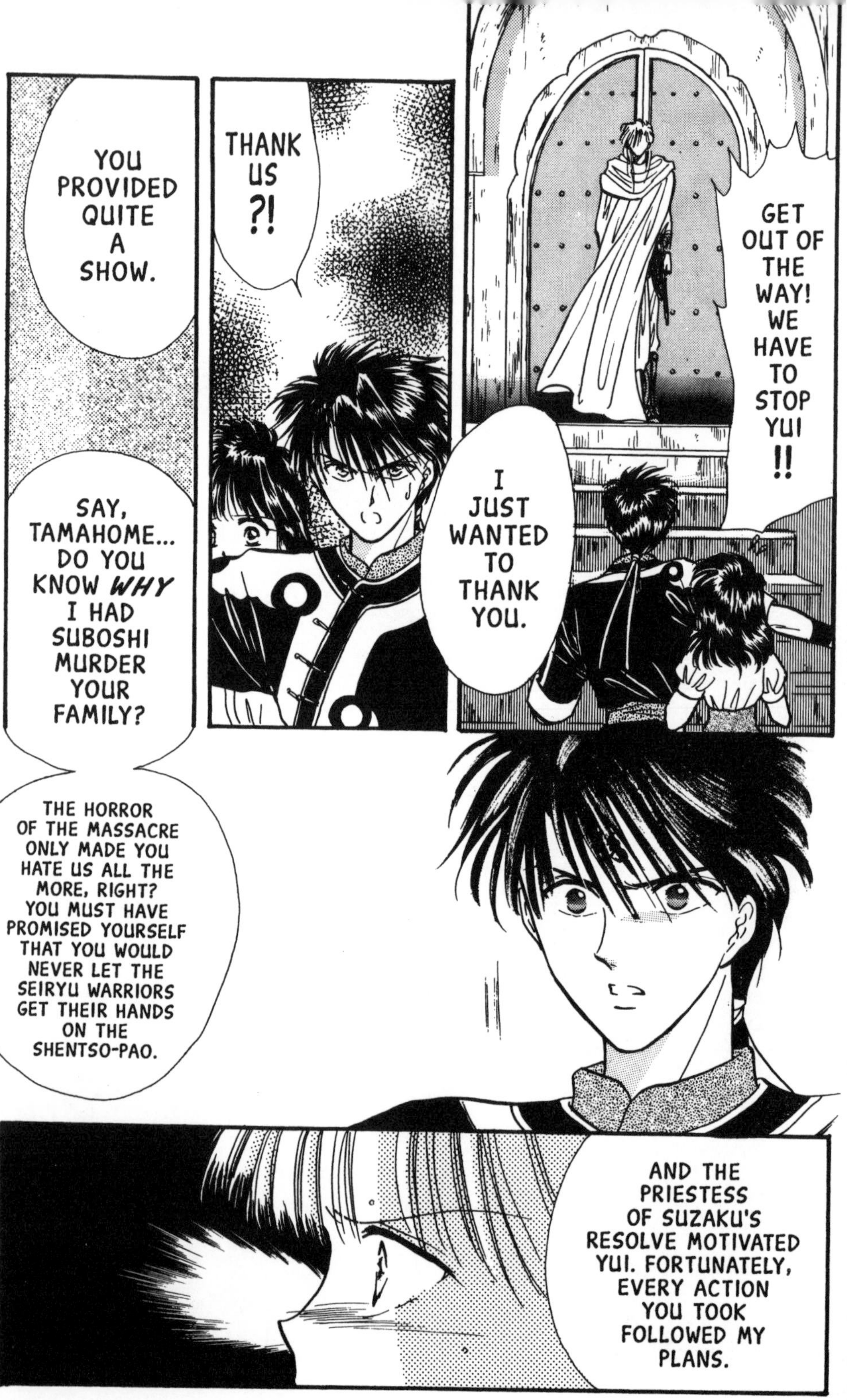
GET OUT OF THE WAY! WE HAVE TO STOP YUI!!
I JUST WANTED TO THANK YOU.
THANK US?!
YOU PROVIDED QUITE A SHOW.
SAY, TAMAHOME... DO YOU KNOW *WHY* I HAD SUBOSHI MURDER YOUR FAMILY?
THE HORROR OF THE MASSACRE ONLY MADE YOU HATE US ALL THE MORE, RIGHT? YOU MUST HAVE PROMISED YOURSELF THAT YOU WOULD NEVER LET THE SEIRYU WARRIORS GET THEIR HANDS ON THE SHENTSO-PAO.
AND THE PRIESTESS OF SUZAKU'S RESOLVE MOTIVATED YUI. FORTUNATELY, EVERY ACTION YOU TOOK FOLLOWED MY PLANS.

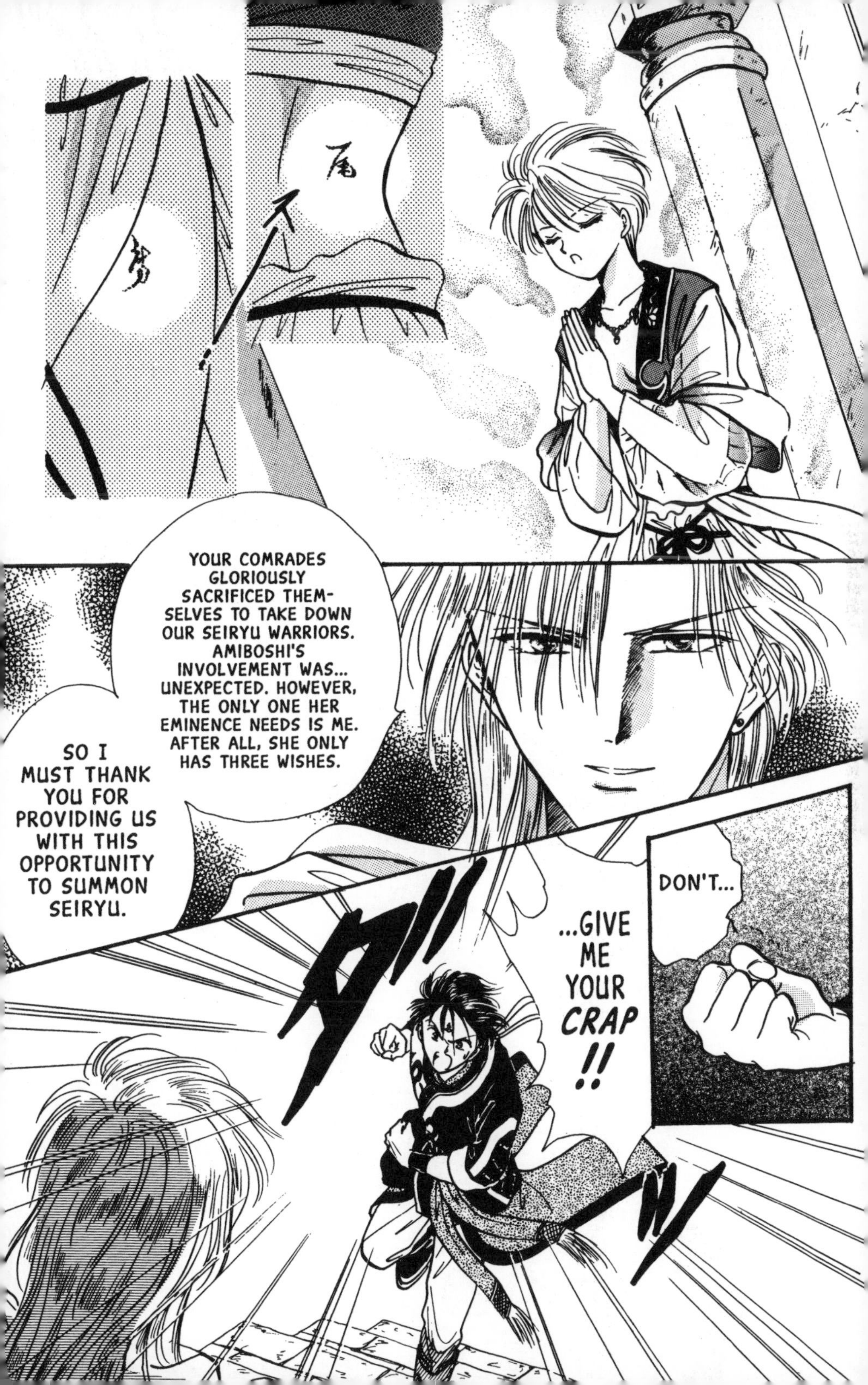
YOUR COMRADES GLORIOUSLY SACRIFICED THEM-SELVES TO TAKE DOWN OUR SEIRYU WARRIORS. AMIBOSHI'S INVOLVEMENT WAS... UNEXPECTED. HOWEVER, THE ONLY ONE HER EMINENCE NEEDS IS ME. AFTER ALL, SHE ONLY HAS THREE WISHES.
SO I MUST THANK YOU FOR PROVIDING US WITH THIS OPPORTUNITY TO SUMMON SEIRYU.
DON'T...
...GIVE ME YOUR *CRAP* !!

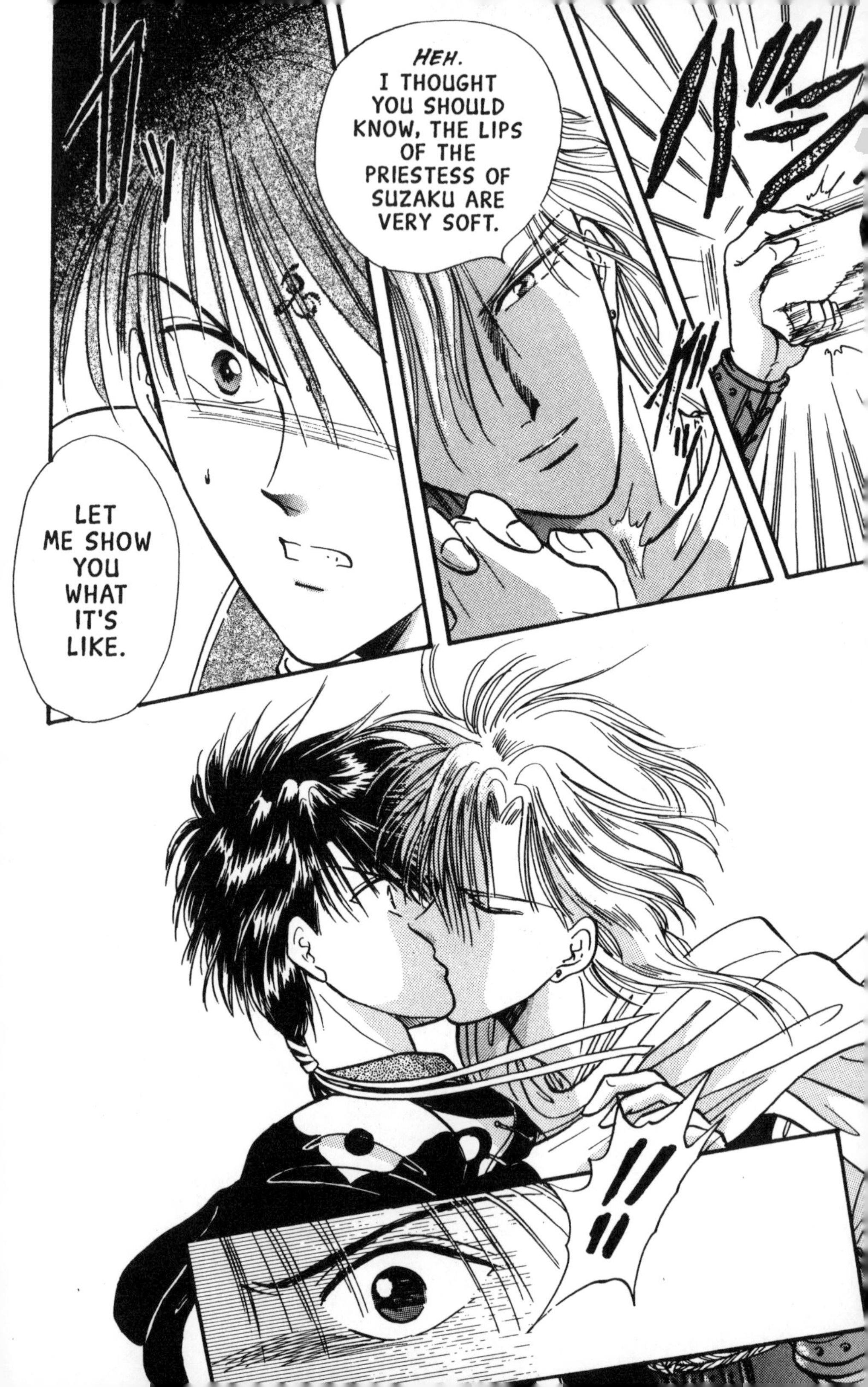
HEH.
I THOUGHT YOU SHOULD KNOW, THE LIPS OF THE PRIESTESS OF SUZAKU ARE VERY SOFT.
LET ME SHOW YOU WHAT IT'S LIKE.

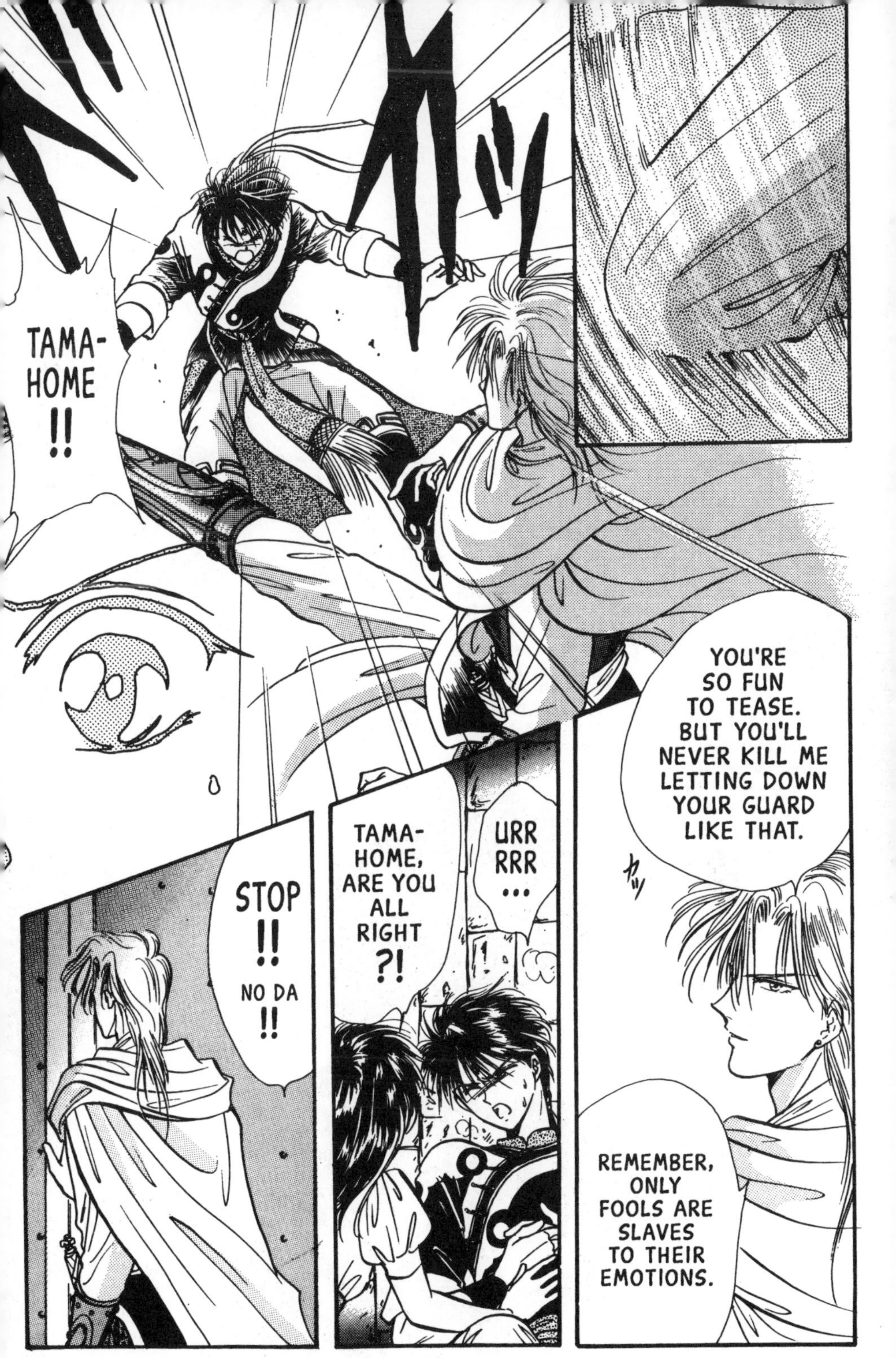
TAMA-HOME!!
YOU'RE SO FUN TO TEASE. BUT YOU'LL NEVER KILL ME LETTING DOWN YOUR GUARD LIKE THAT.
カッ
REMEMBER, ONLY FOOLS ARE SLAVES TO THEIR EMOTIONS.
URR RRR...
TAMA-HOME, ARE YOU ALL RIGHT?!
STOP!! NO DA!!

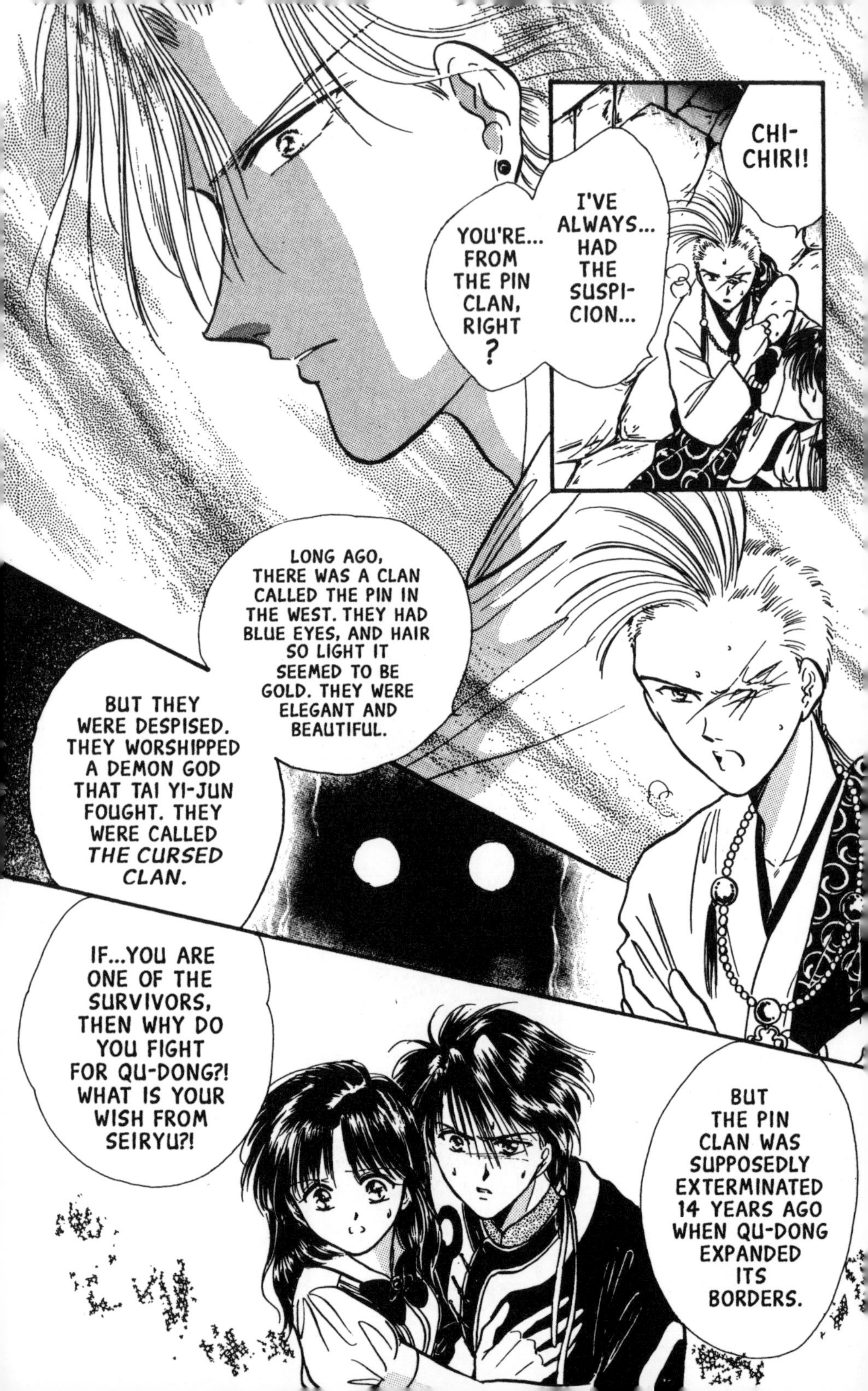
CHI-CHIRI!
I'VE ALWAYS... HAD THE SUSPICION...
YOU'RE... FROM THE PIN CLAN, RIGHT?
LONG AGO, THERE WAS A CLAN CALLED THE PIN IN THE WEST. THEY HAD BLUE EYES, AND HAIR SO LIGHT IT SEEMED TO BE GOLD. THEY WERE ELEGANT AND BEAUTIFUL.
BUT THEY WERE DESPISED. THEY WORSHIPPED A DEMON GOD THAT TAI YI-JUN FOUGHT. THEY WERE CALLED *THE CURSED CLAN*.
BUT THE PIN CLAN WAS SUPPOSEDLY EXTERMINATED 14 YEARS AGO WHEN QU-DONG EXPANDED ITS BORDERS.
IF...YOU ARE ONE OF THE SURVIVORS, THEN WHY DO YOU FIGHT FOR QU-DONG?! WHAT IS YOUR WISH FROM SEIRYU?!

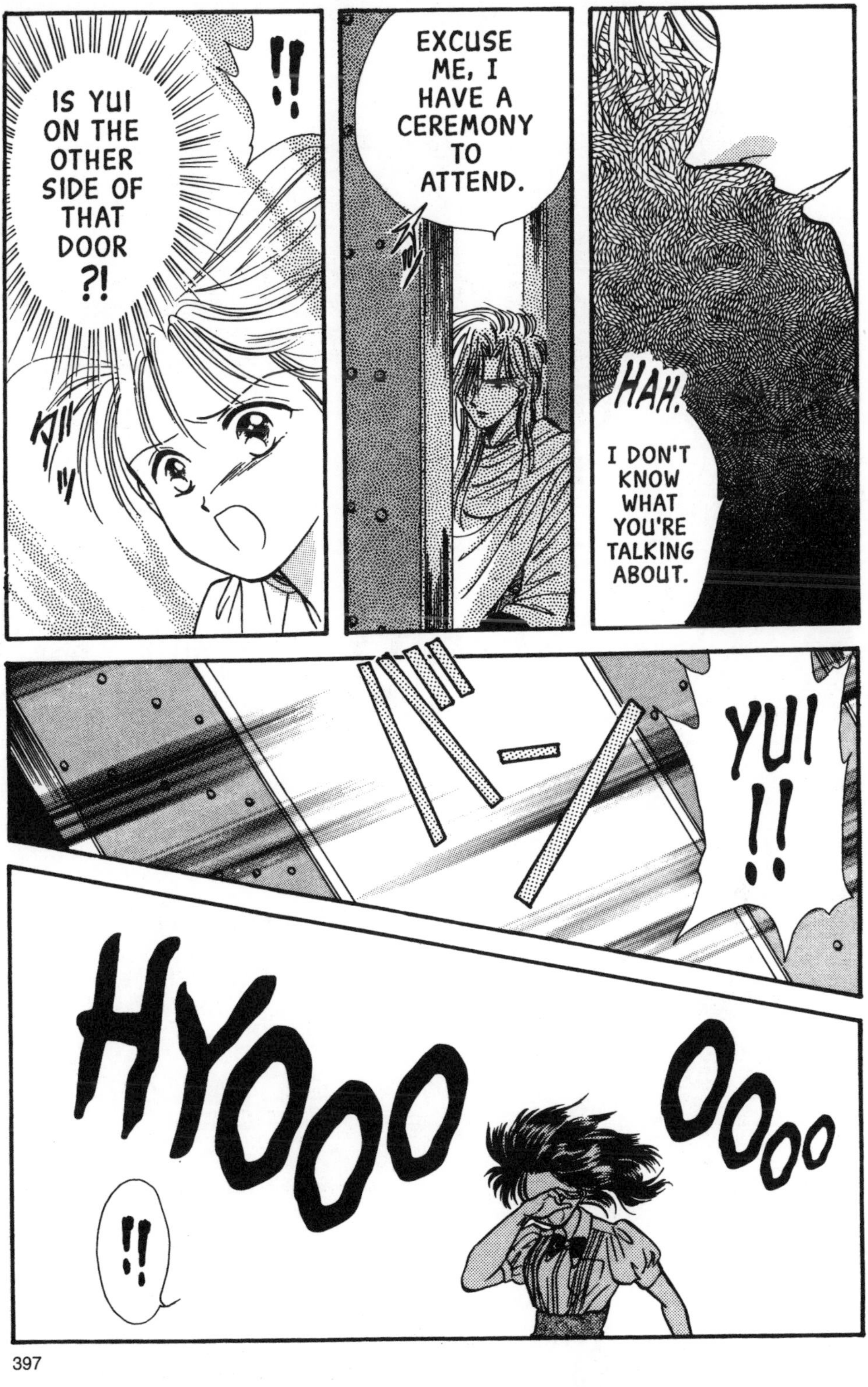
HAH.
I DON'T KNOW WHAT YOU'RE TALKING ABOUT.
EXCUSE ME, I HAVE A CEREMONY TO ATTEND.
!!
IS YUI ON THE OTHER SIDE OF THAT DOOR?!
YUI!!
HYOOO
OOOO
!!

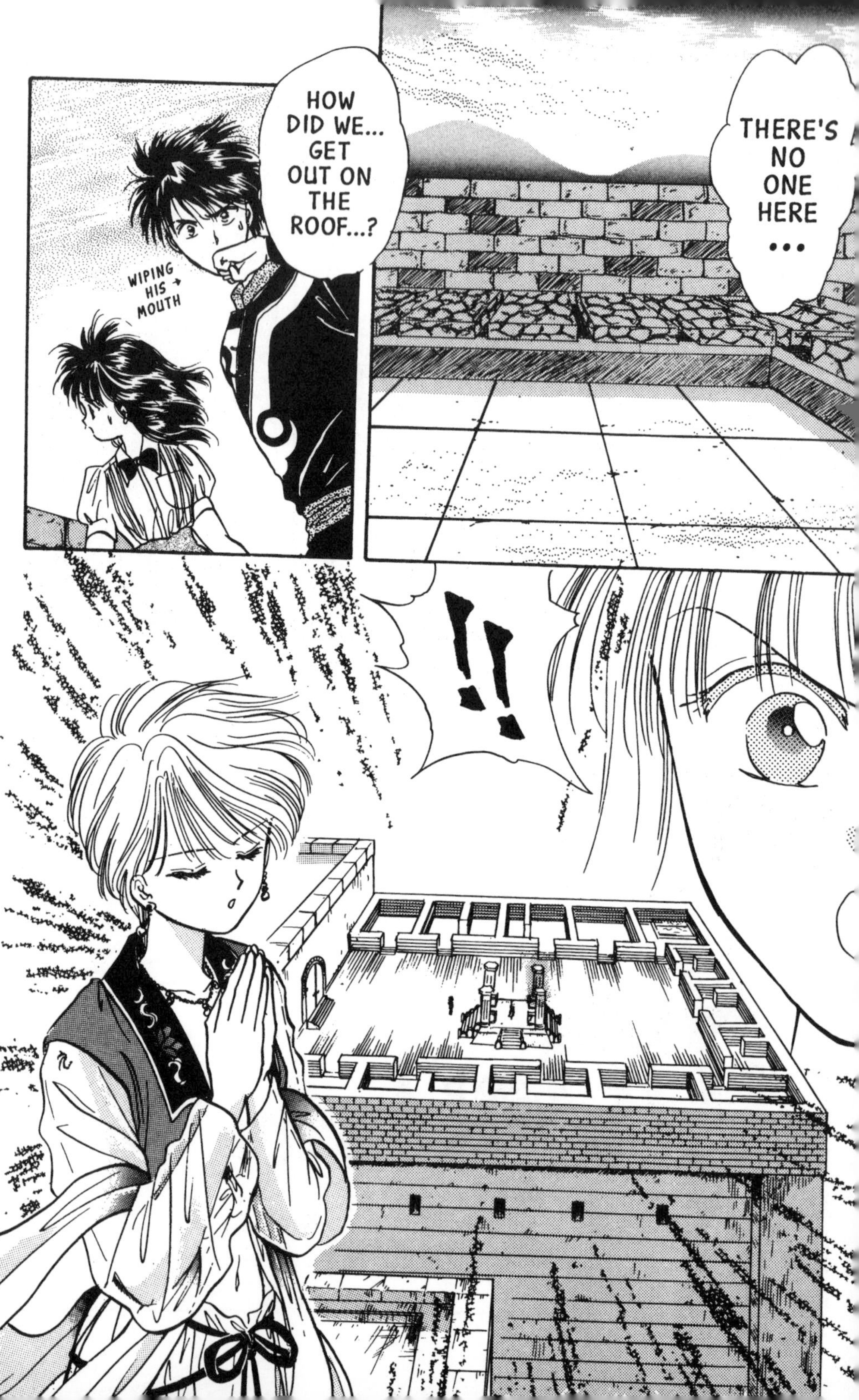
THERE'S NO ONE HERE ...
HOW DID WE... GET OUT ON THE ROOF...?
WIPING HIS → MOUTH
!!

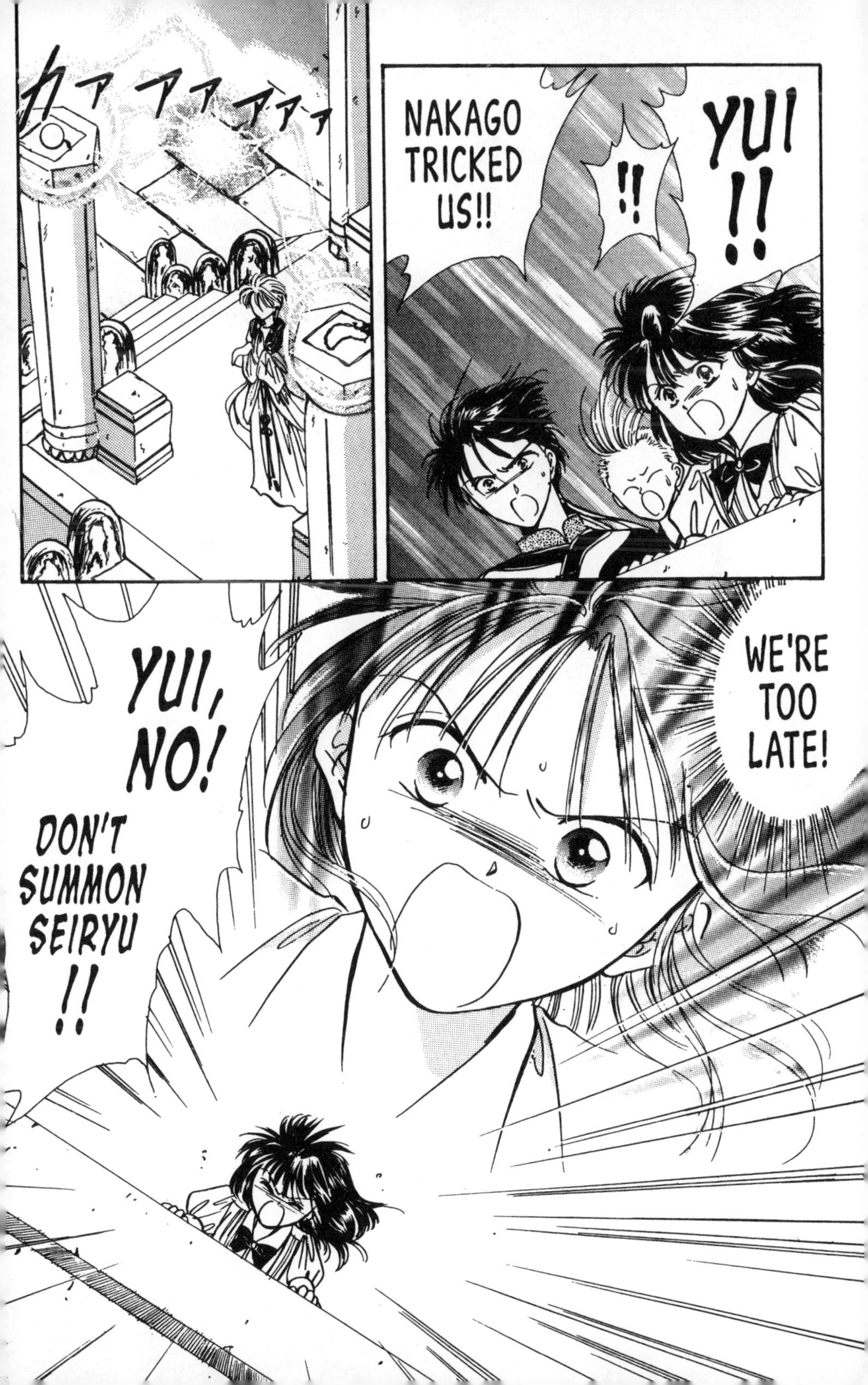
YUI!!
!!
NAKAGO TRICKED US!!
カァアアァァ
WE'RE TOO LATE!
YUI, NO!
DON'T SUMMON SEIRYU!!

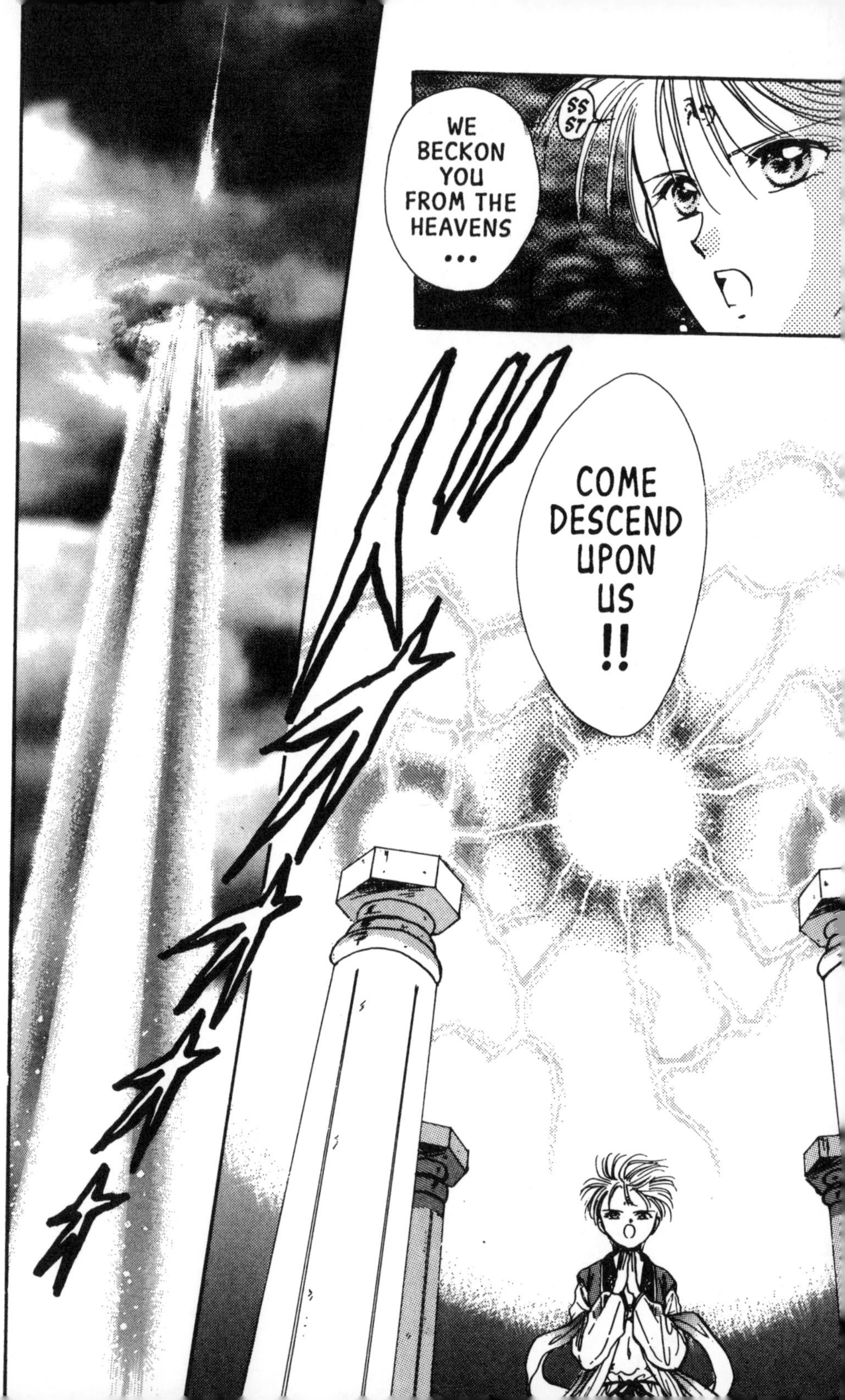
SS ST
WE BECKON YOU FROM THE HEAVENS ...
COME DESCEND UPON US !!

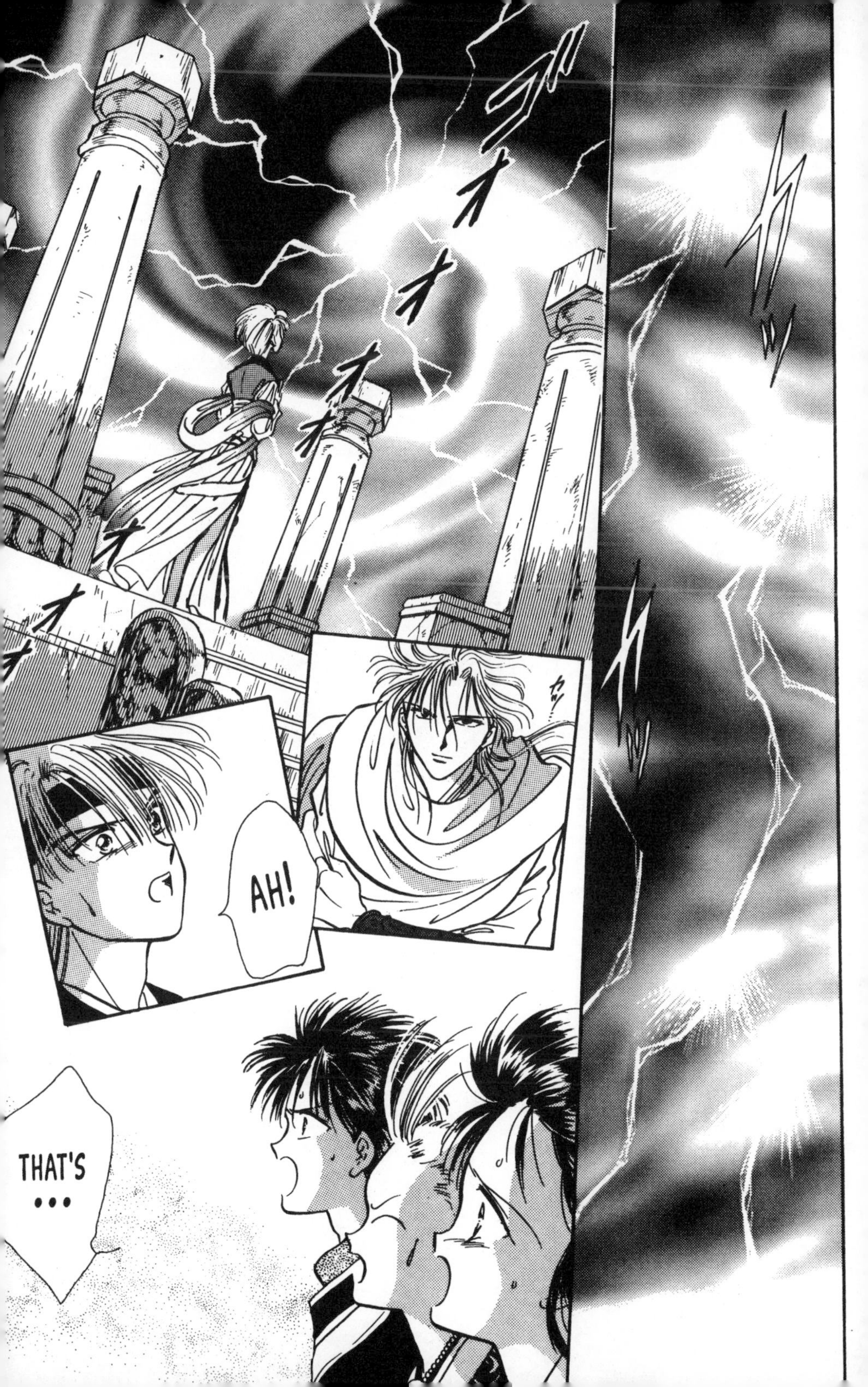
AH!
THAT'S ...

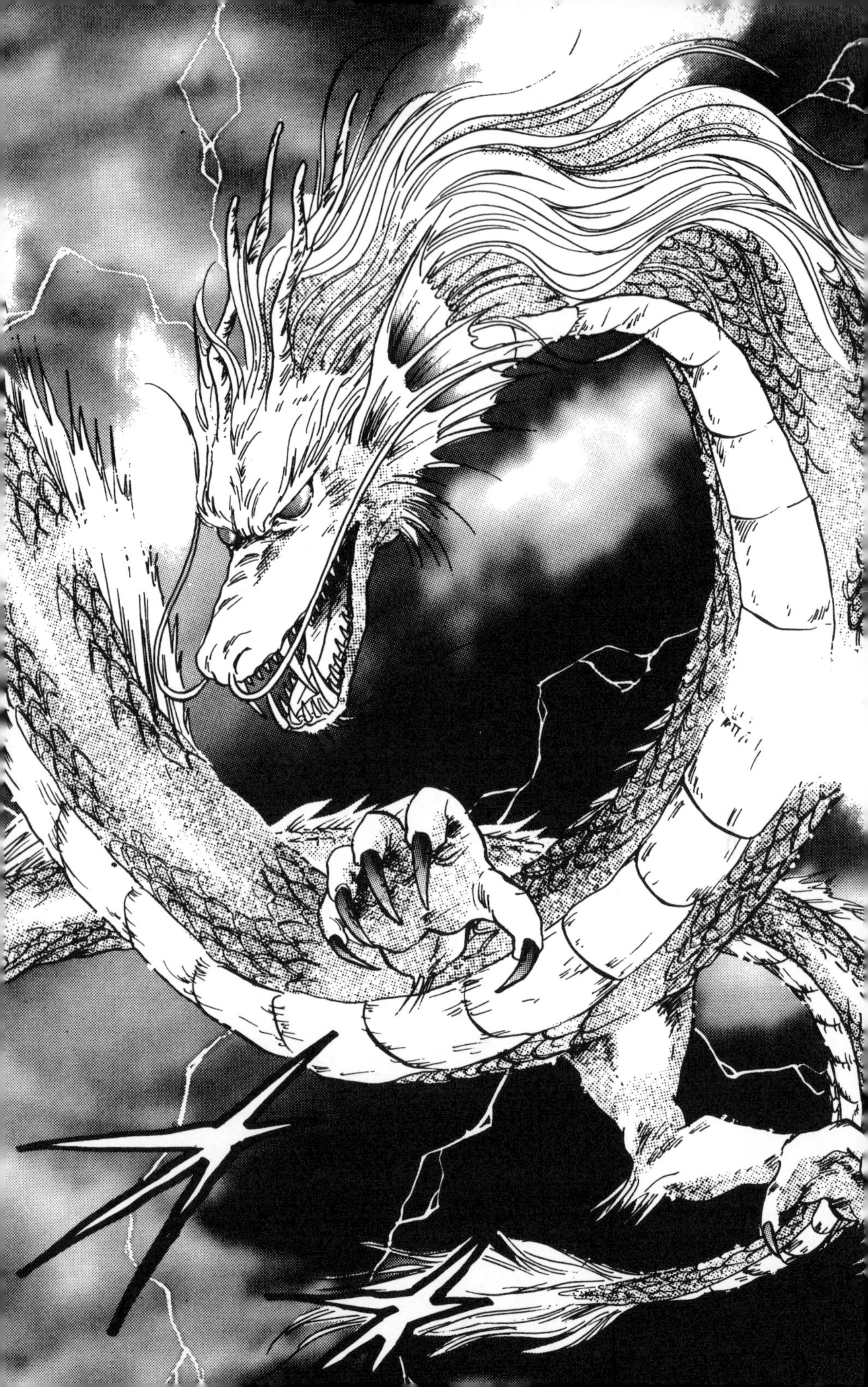

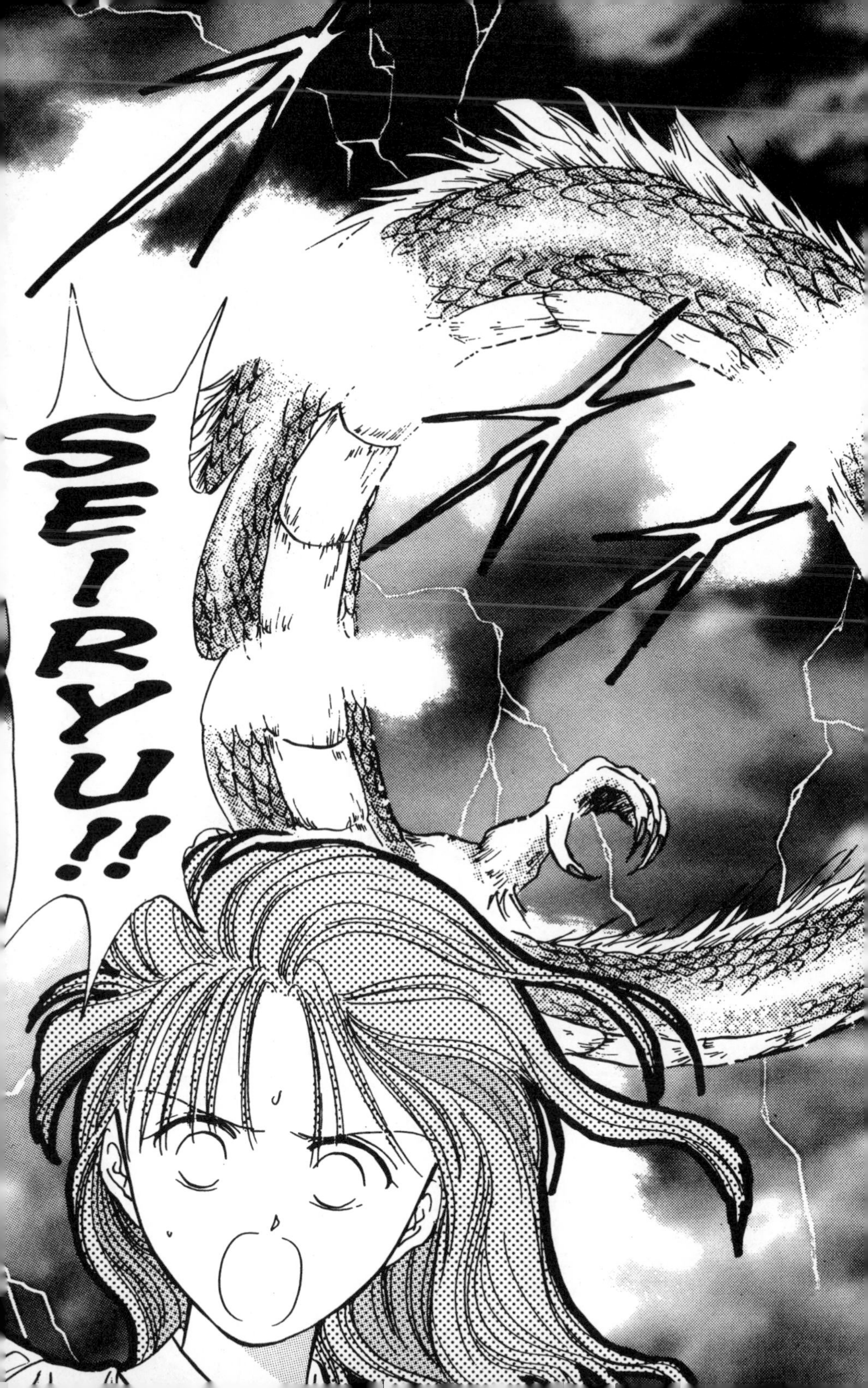
SEIRYU!!

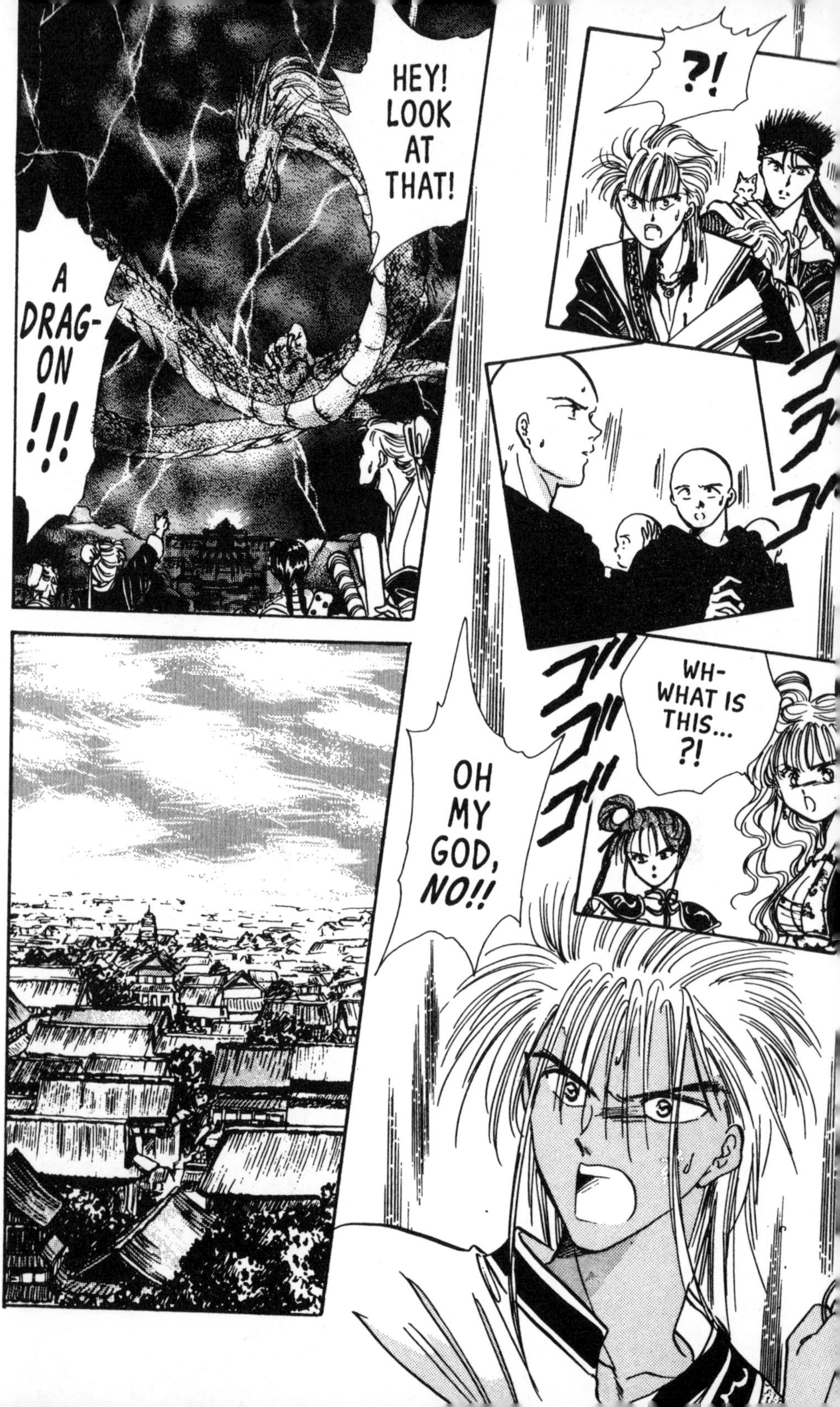
?!
WH-WHAT IS THIS...?!
HEY! LOOK AT THAT!
A DRAG-ON!!!
OH MY GOD, NO!!

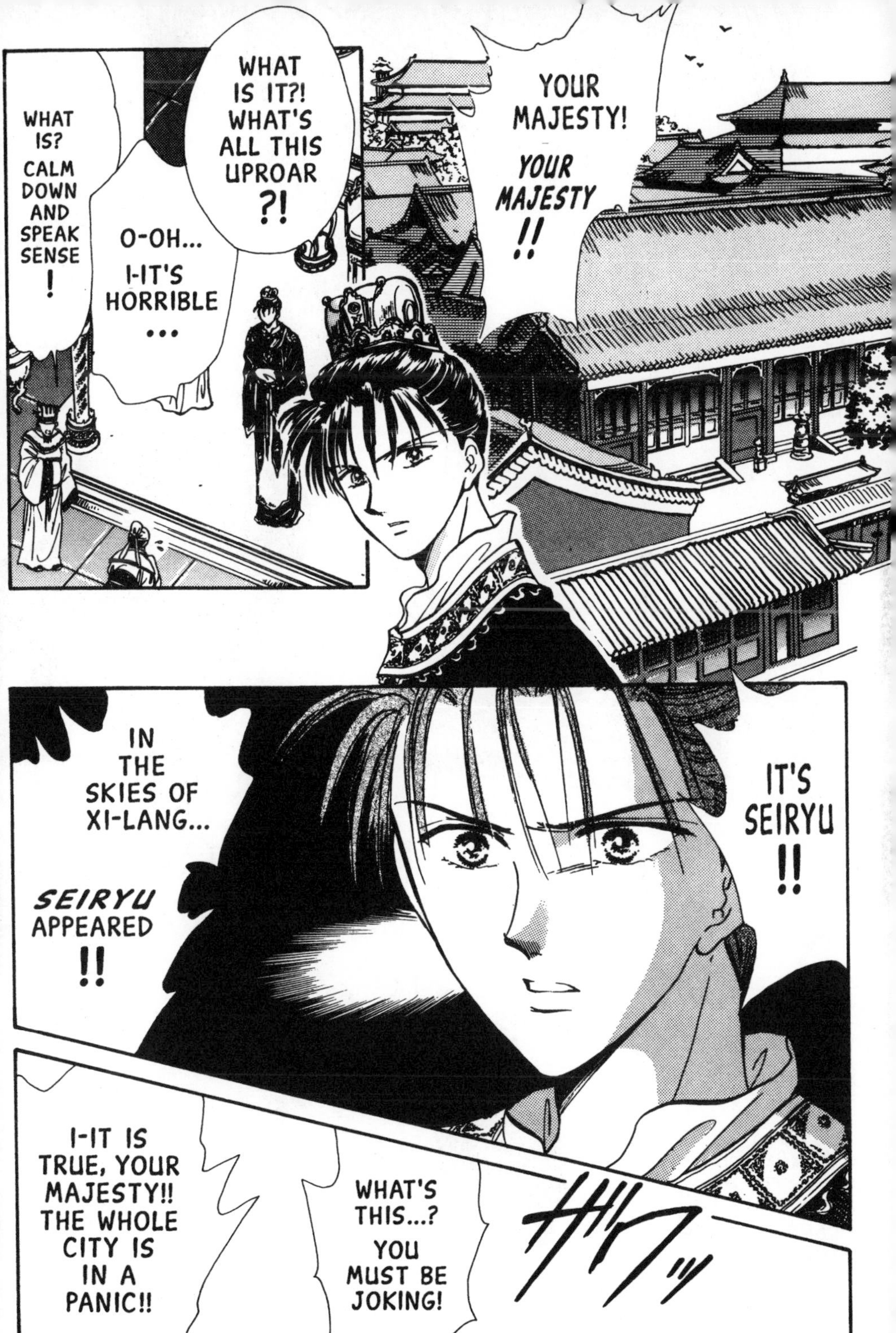
YOUR MAJESTY!
YOUR MAJESTY!!
WHAT IS IT?! WHAT'S ALL THIS UPROAR?!
O-OH... I-IT'S HORRIBLE...
WHAT IS? CALM DOWN AND SPEAK SENSE!
IT'S SEIRYU!!
IN THE SKIES OF XI-LANG...
SEIRYU APPEARED!!
WHAT'S THIS...? YOU MUST BE JOKING!
I-IT IS TRUE, YOUR MAJESTY!! THE WHOLE CITY IS IN A PANIC!!

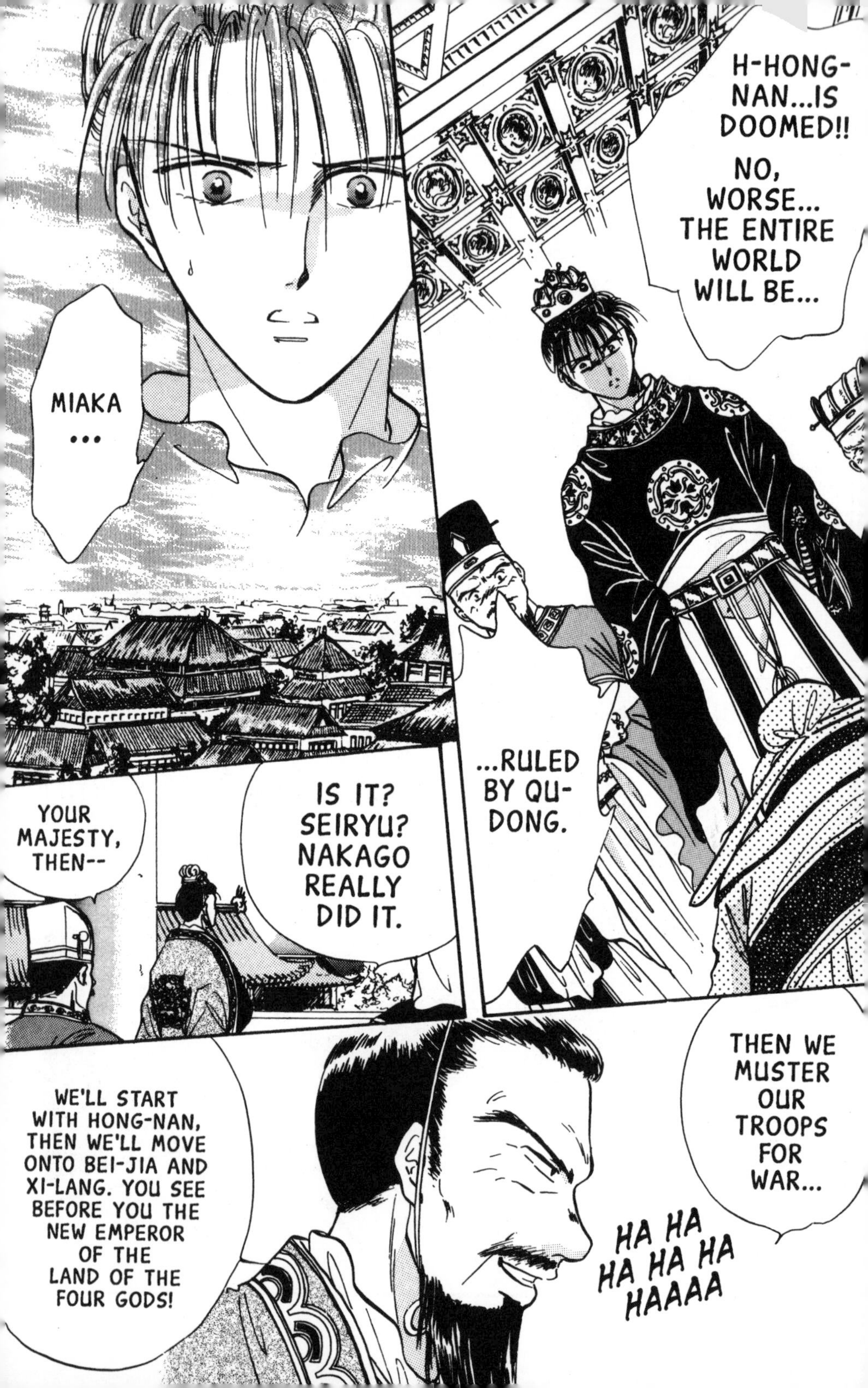
H-HONG-NAN...IS DOOMED!!
NO, WORSE... THE ENTIRE WORLD WILL BE...
...RULED BY QU-DONG.
MIAKA ...
IS IT? SEIRYU? NAKAGO REALLY DID IT.
YOUR MAJESTY, THEN--
THEN WE MUSTER OUR TROOPS FOR WAR...
WE'LL START WITH HONG-NAN, THEN WE'LL MOVE ONTO BEI-JIA AND XI-LANG. YOU SEE BEFORE YOU THE NEW EMPEROR OF THE LAND OF THE FOUR GODS!
HA HA HA HA HA HAAAA

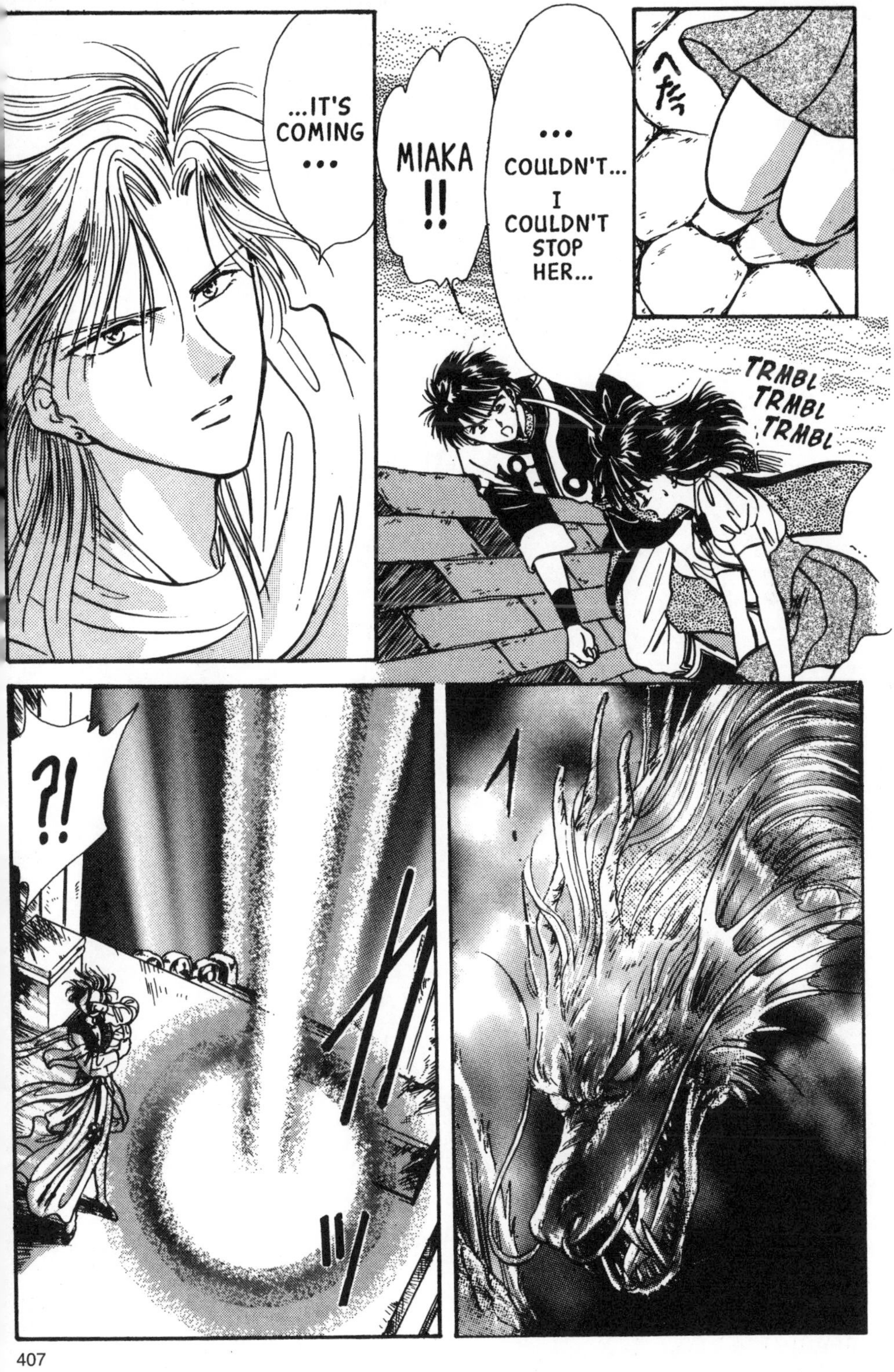
へたっ
... COULDN'T... I COULDN'T STOP HER...
MIAKA !!
TRMBL TRMBL TRMBL
...IT'S COMING ...
!
?!

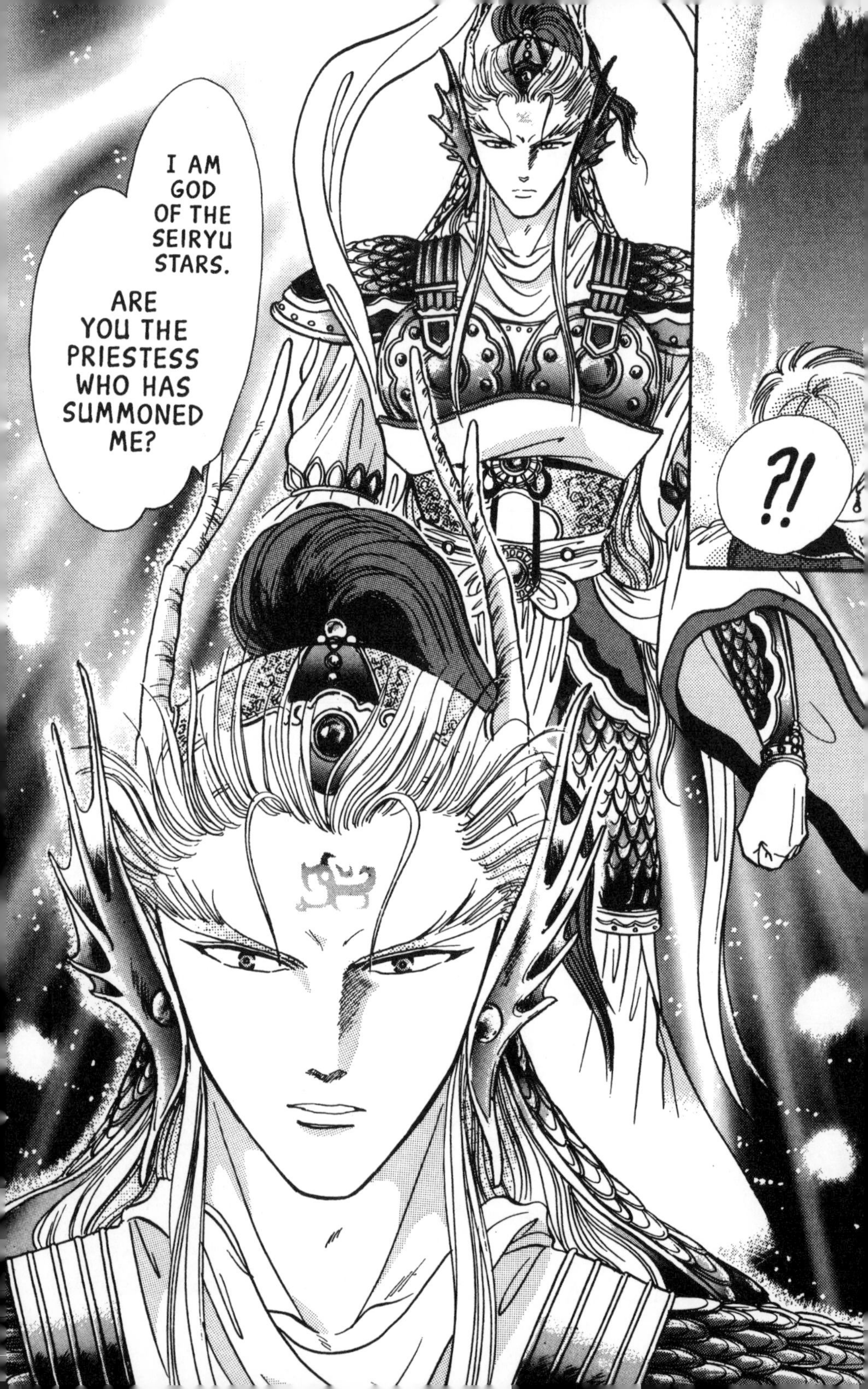
?!
I AM GOD OF THE SEIRYU STARS.
ARE YOU THE PRIESTESS WHO HAS SUMMONED ME?

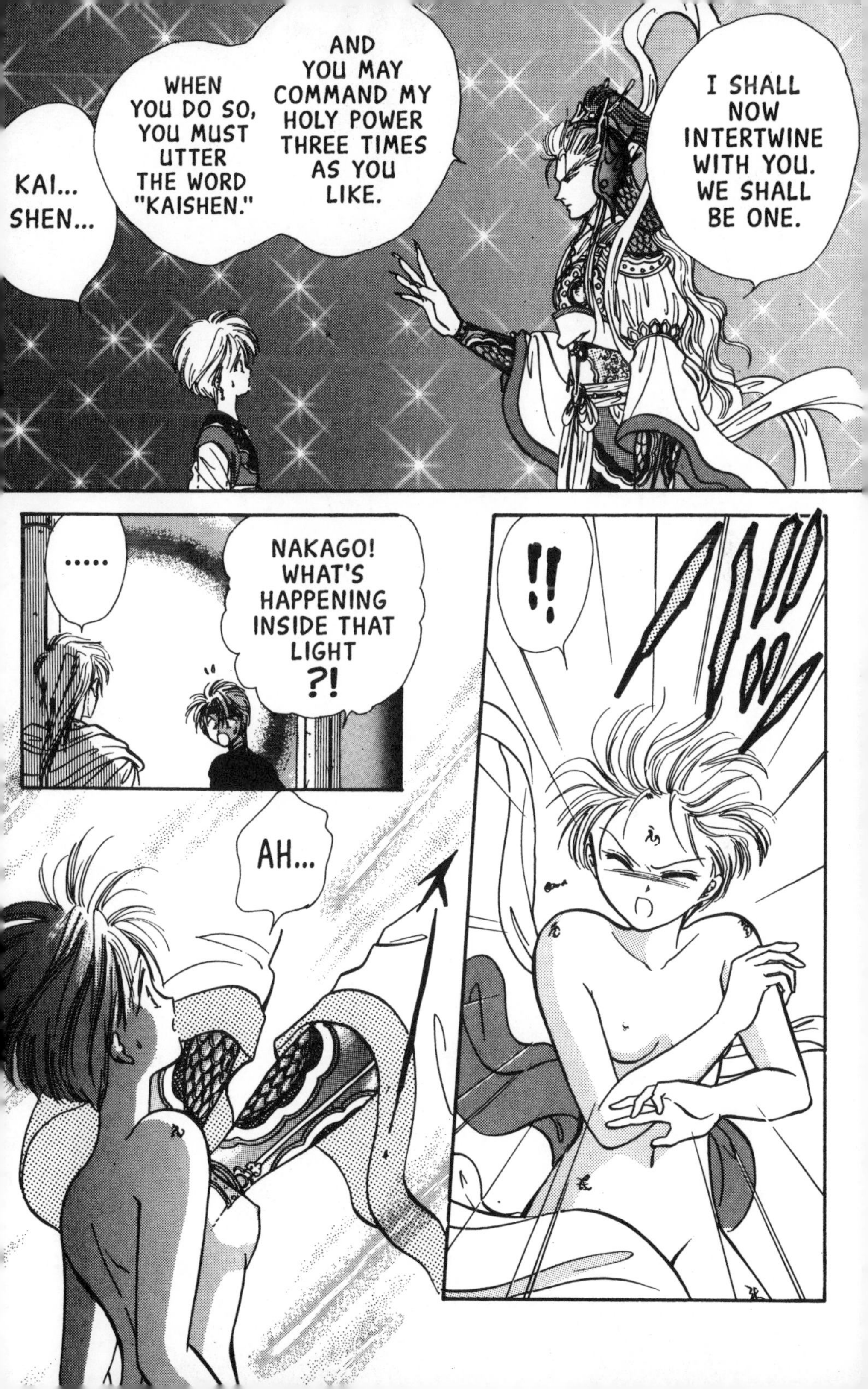
I SHALL NOW INTERTWINE WITH YOU. WE SHALL BE ONE.
AND YOU MAY COMMAND MY HOLY POWER THREE TIMES AS YOU LIKE.
WHEN YOU DO SO, YOU MUST UTTER THE WORD "KAISHEN."
KAI... SHEN...
!!
NAKAGO! WHAT'S HAPPENING INSIDE THAT LIGHT ?!
.....
AH...

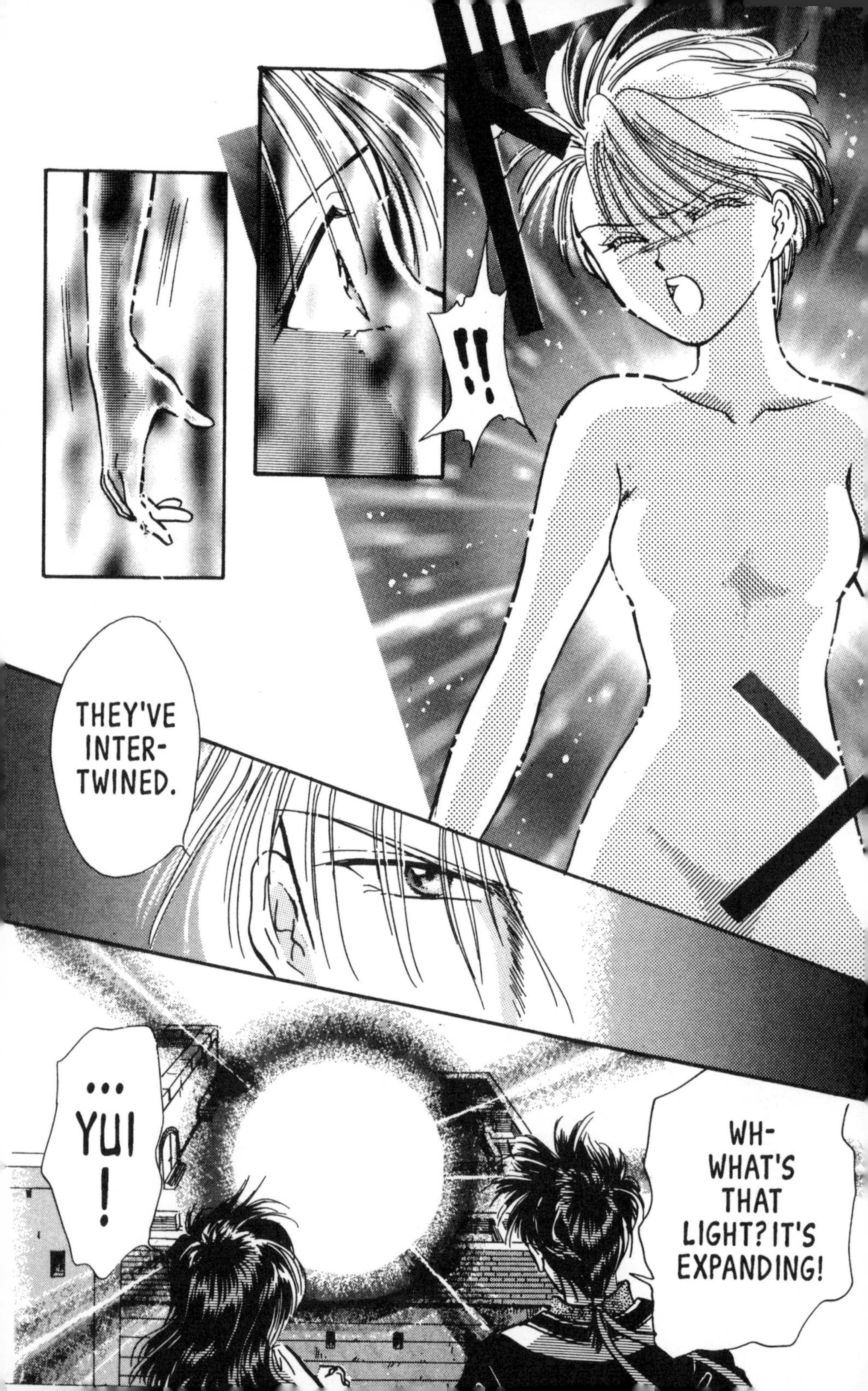
!!
THEY'VE INTER-TWINED.
WH-WHAT'S THAT LIGHT? IT'S EXPANDING!
...YUI!

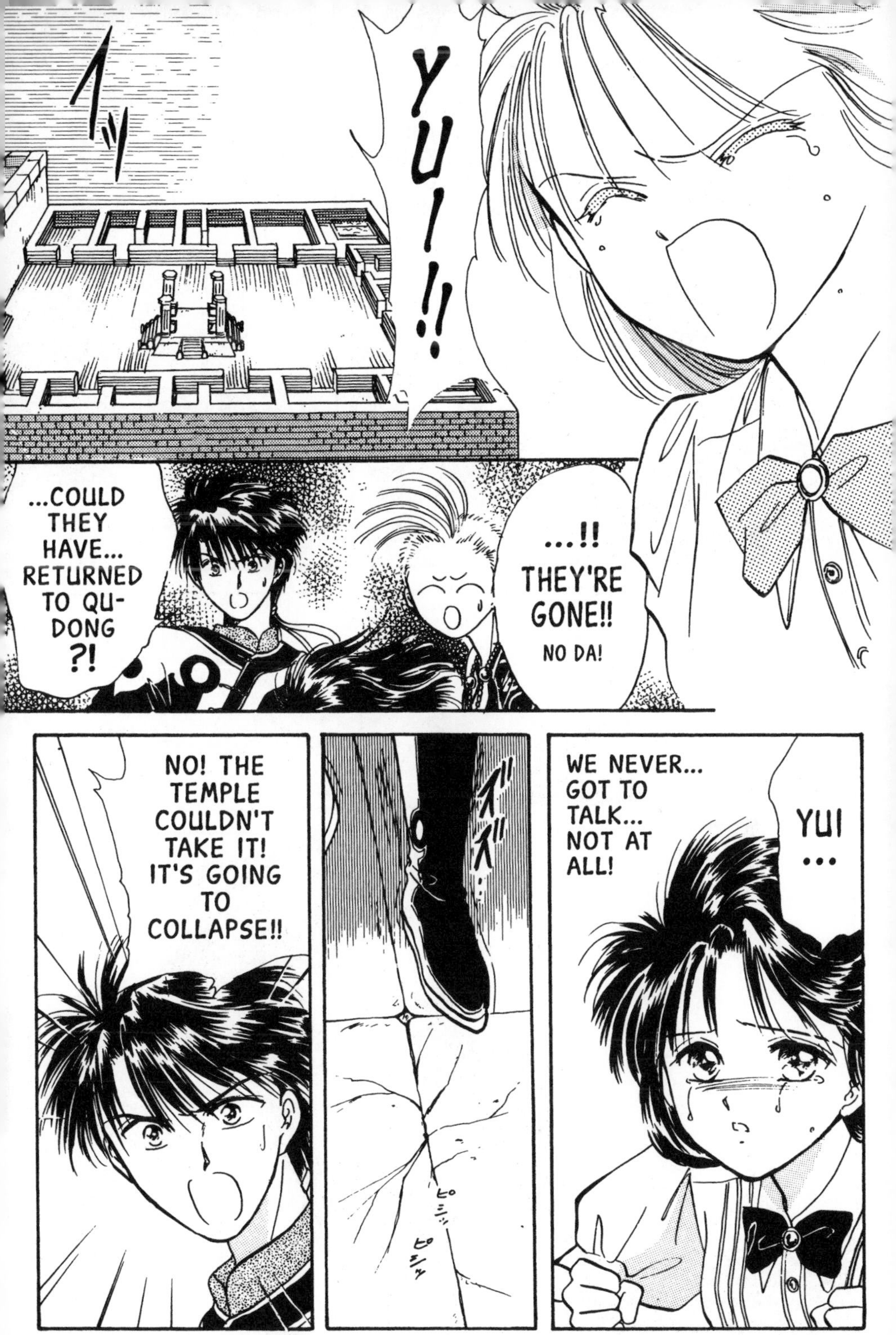
YUI!!!
...!! THEY'RE GONE!! NO DA!
...COULD THEY HAVE... RETURNED TO QU-DONG ?!
YUI...
WE NEVER... GOT TO TALK... NOT AT ALL!
NO! THE TEMPLE COULDN'T TAKE IT! IT'S GOING TO COLLAPSE!!

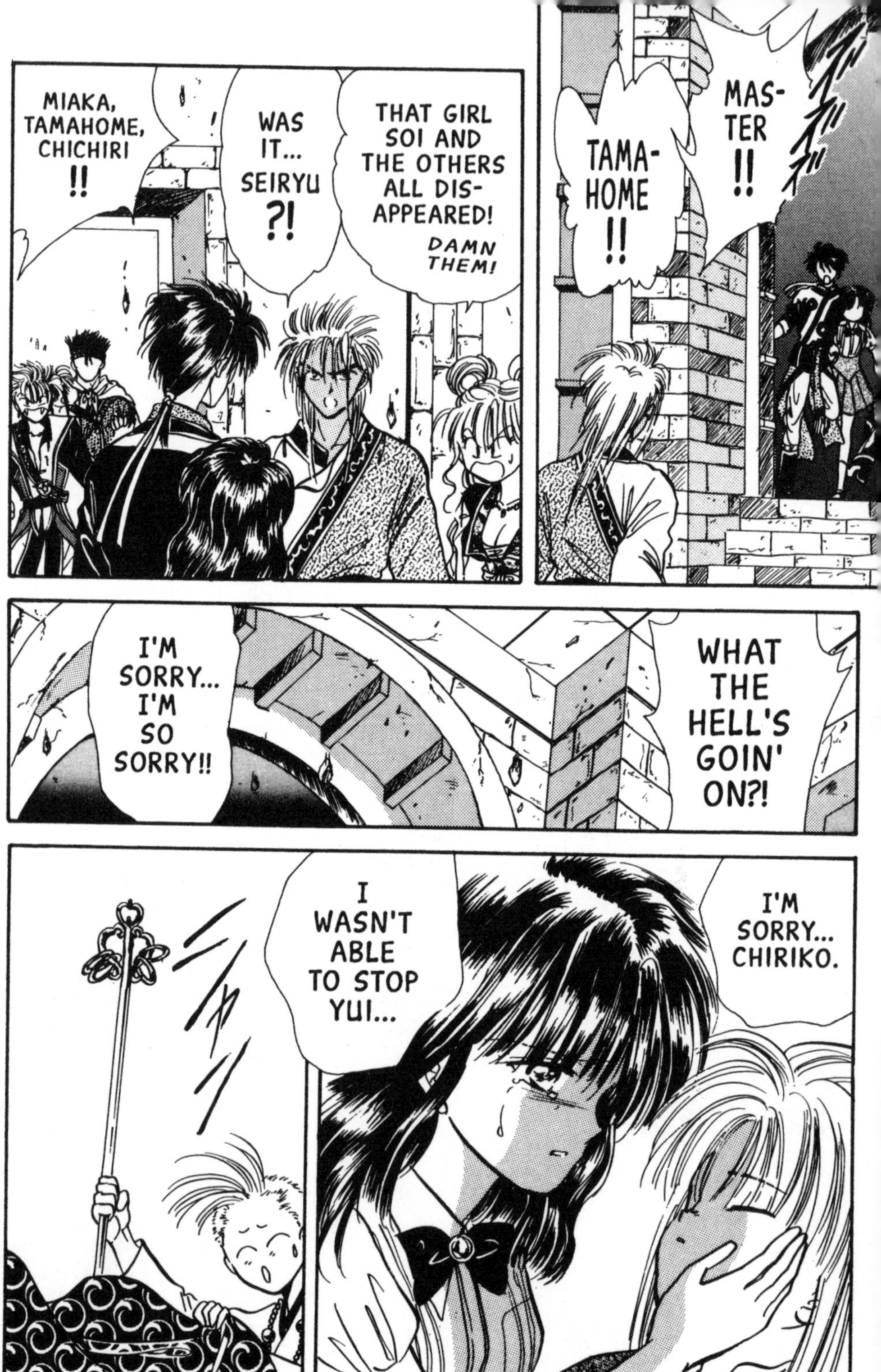
MASTER!!
TAMAHOME!!
THAT GIRL SOI AND THE OTHERS ALL DISAPPEARED!
DAMN THEM!
WAS IT... SEIRYU?!
MIAKA, TAMAHOME, CHICHIRI!!
WHAT THE HELL'S GOIN' ON?!
I'M SORRY... I'M SO SORRY!!
I'M SORRY... CHIRIKO.
I WASN'T ABLE TO STOP YUI...

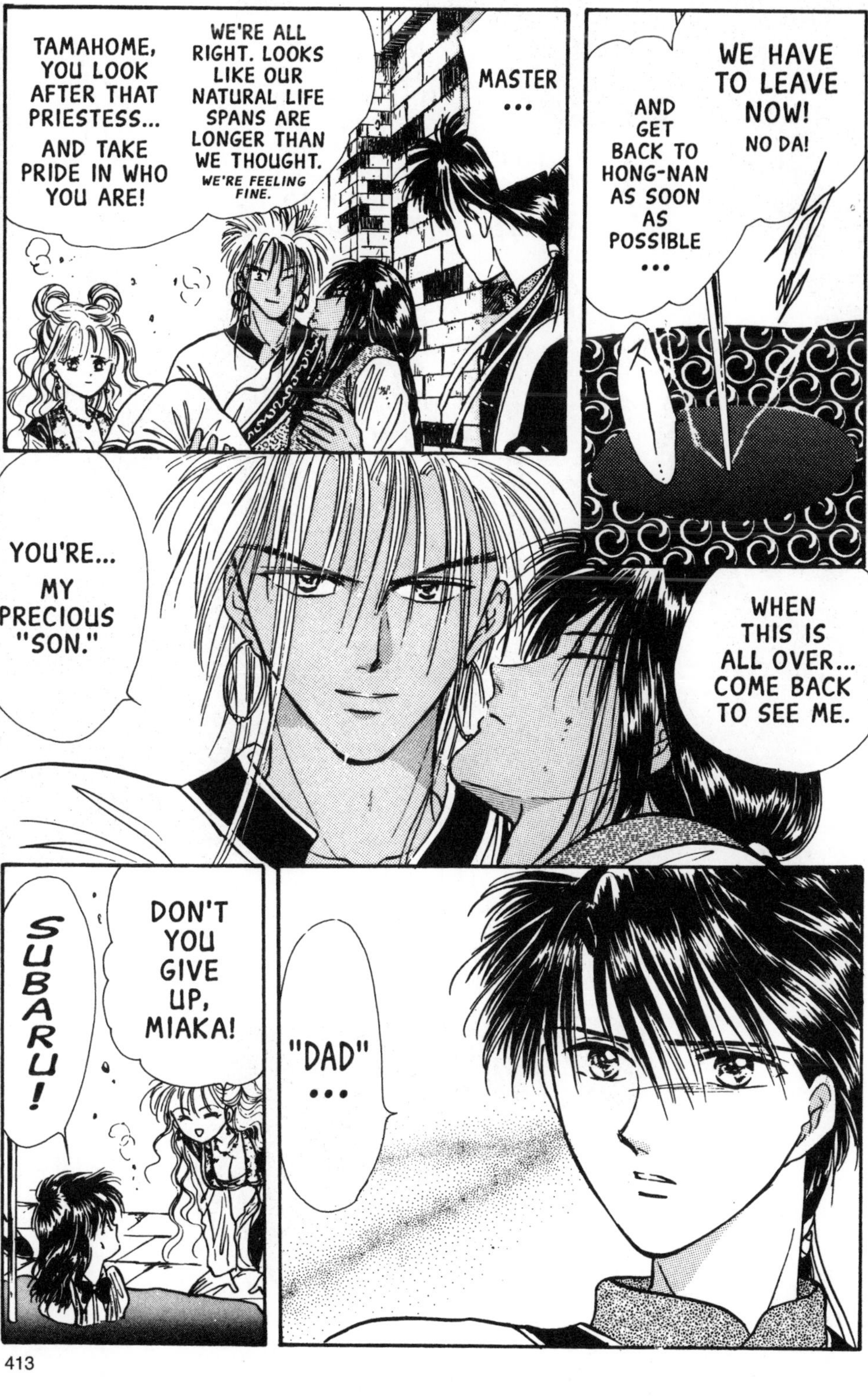
WE HAVE TO LEAVE NOW! NO DA!
AND GET BACK TO HONG-NAN AS SOON AS POSSIBLE...
MASTER...
WE'RE ALL RIGHT. LOOKS LIKE OUR NATURAL LIFE SPANS ARE LONGER THAN WE THOUGHT. WE'RE FEELING FINE.
TAMAHOME, YOU LOOK AFTER THAT PRIESTESS... AND TAKE PRIDE IN WHO YOU ARE!
WHEN THIS IS ALL OVER... COME BACK TO SEE ME.
YOU'RE... MY PRECIOUS "SON."
"DAD"...
DON'T YOU GIVE UP, MIAKA!
SUBARU!

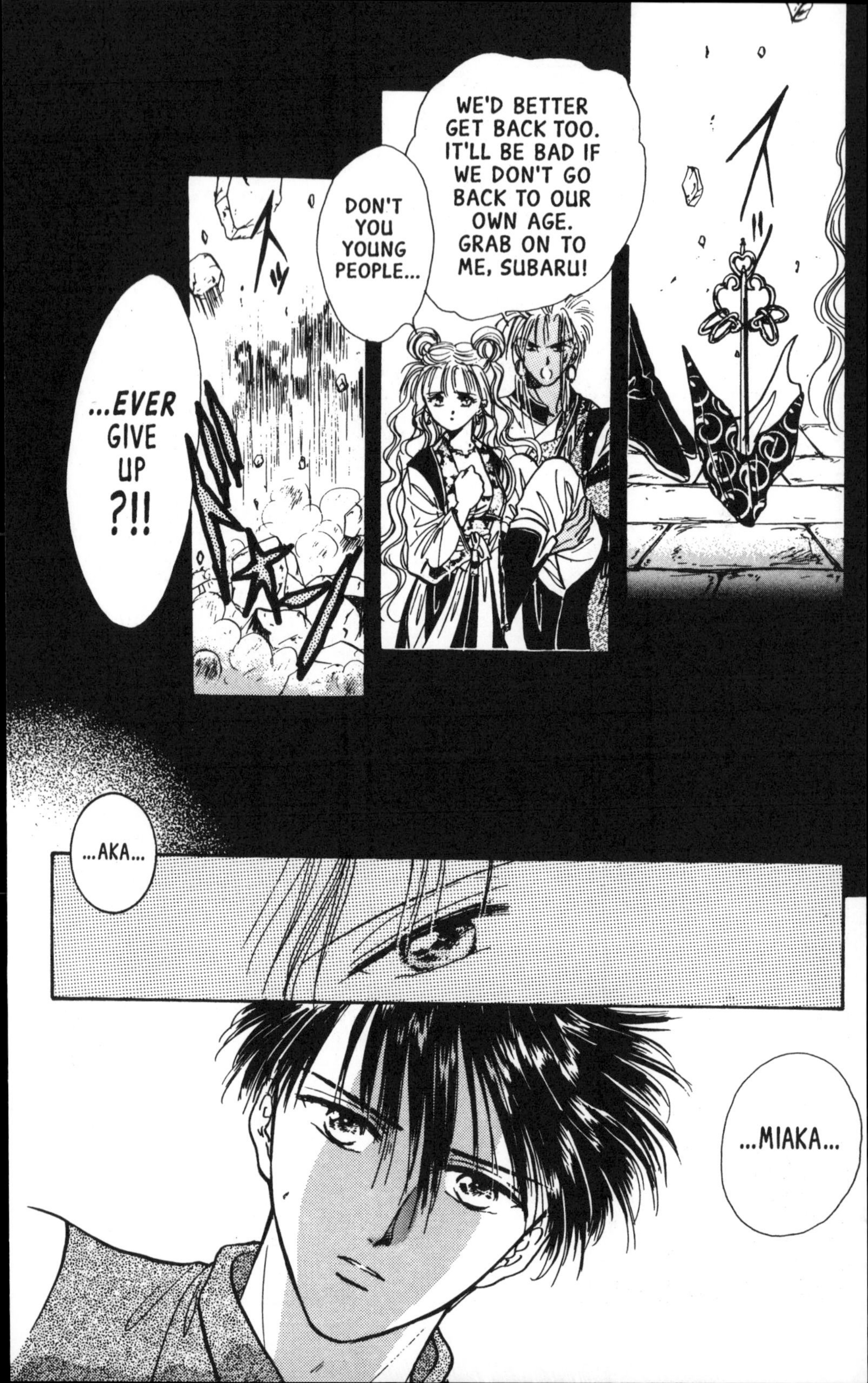
WE'D BETTER GET BACK TOO. IT'LL BE BAD IF WE DON'T GO BACK TO OUR OWN AGE. GRAB ON TO ME, SUBARU!
DON'T YOU YOUNG PEOPLE...
...EVER GIVE UP ?!!
...AKA...
...MIAKA...

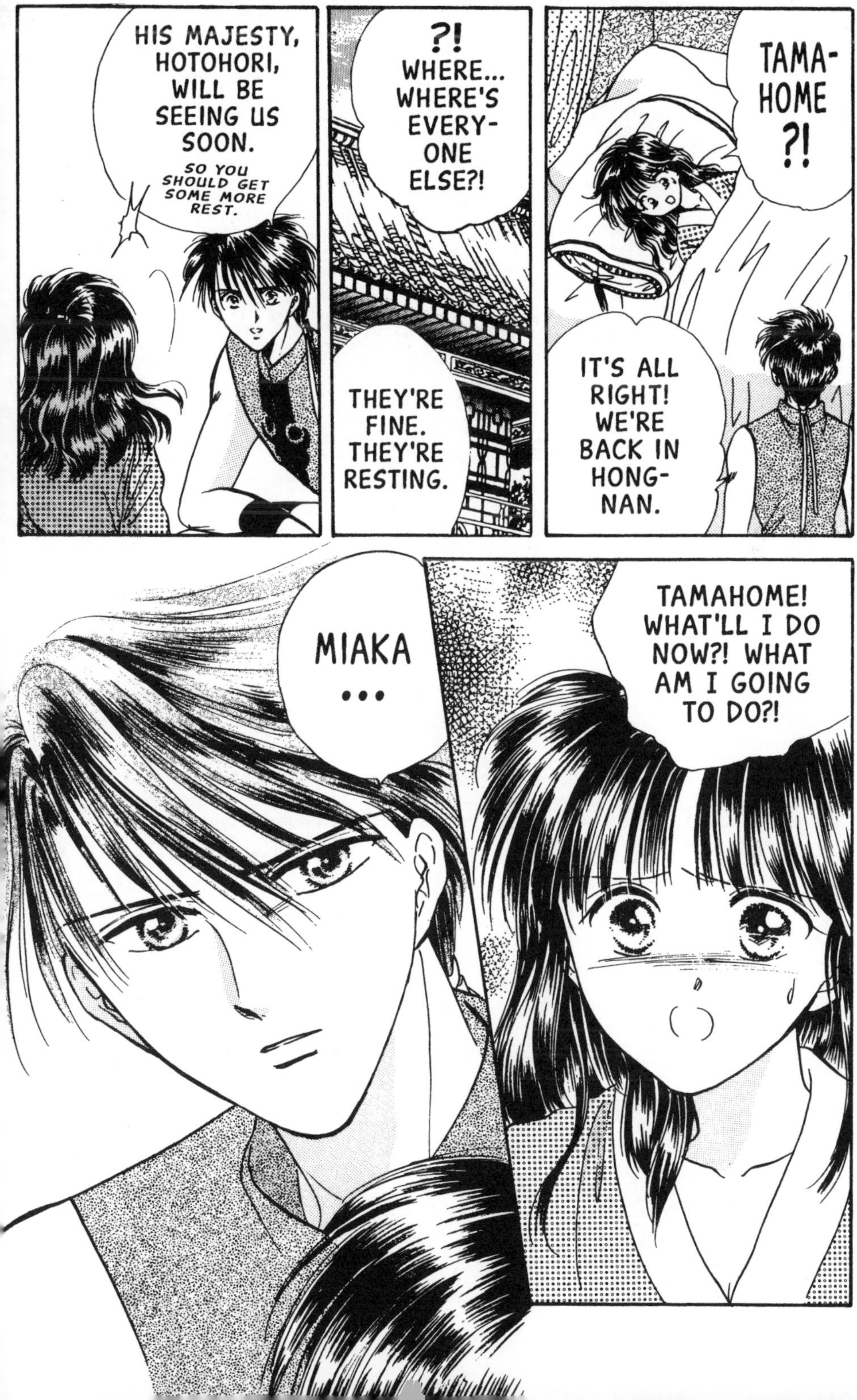
TAMA-HOME?!
IT'S ALL RIGHT! WE'RE BACK IN HONG-NAN.
?! WHERE... WHERE'S EVERY-ONE ELSE?!
THEY'RE FINE. THEY'RE RESTING.
HIS MAJESTY, HOTOHORI, WILL BE SEEING US SOON.
SO YOU SHOULD GET SOME MORE REST.
TAMAHOME! WHAT'LL I DO NOW?! WHAT AM I GOING TO DO?!
MIAKA...

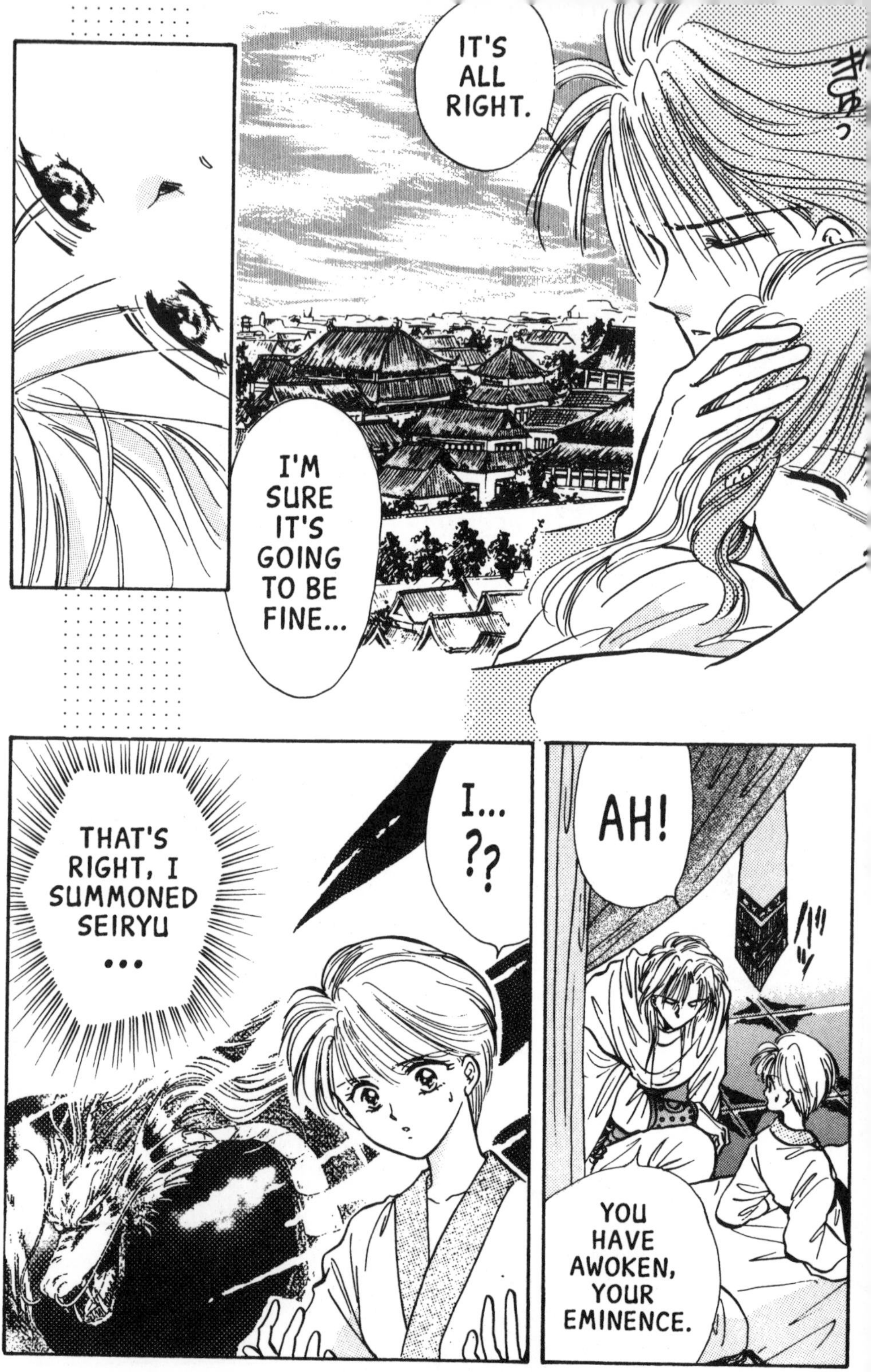
ぎゅっ
IT'S ALL RIGHT.
I'M SURE IT'S GOING TO BE FINE...
AH!
バッ
YOU HAVE AWOKEN, YOUR EMINENCE.
I... ??
THAT'S RIGHT, I SUMMONED SEIRYU...

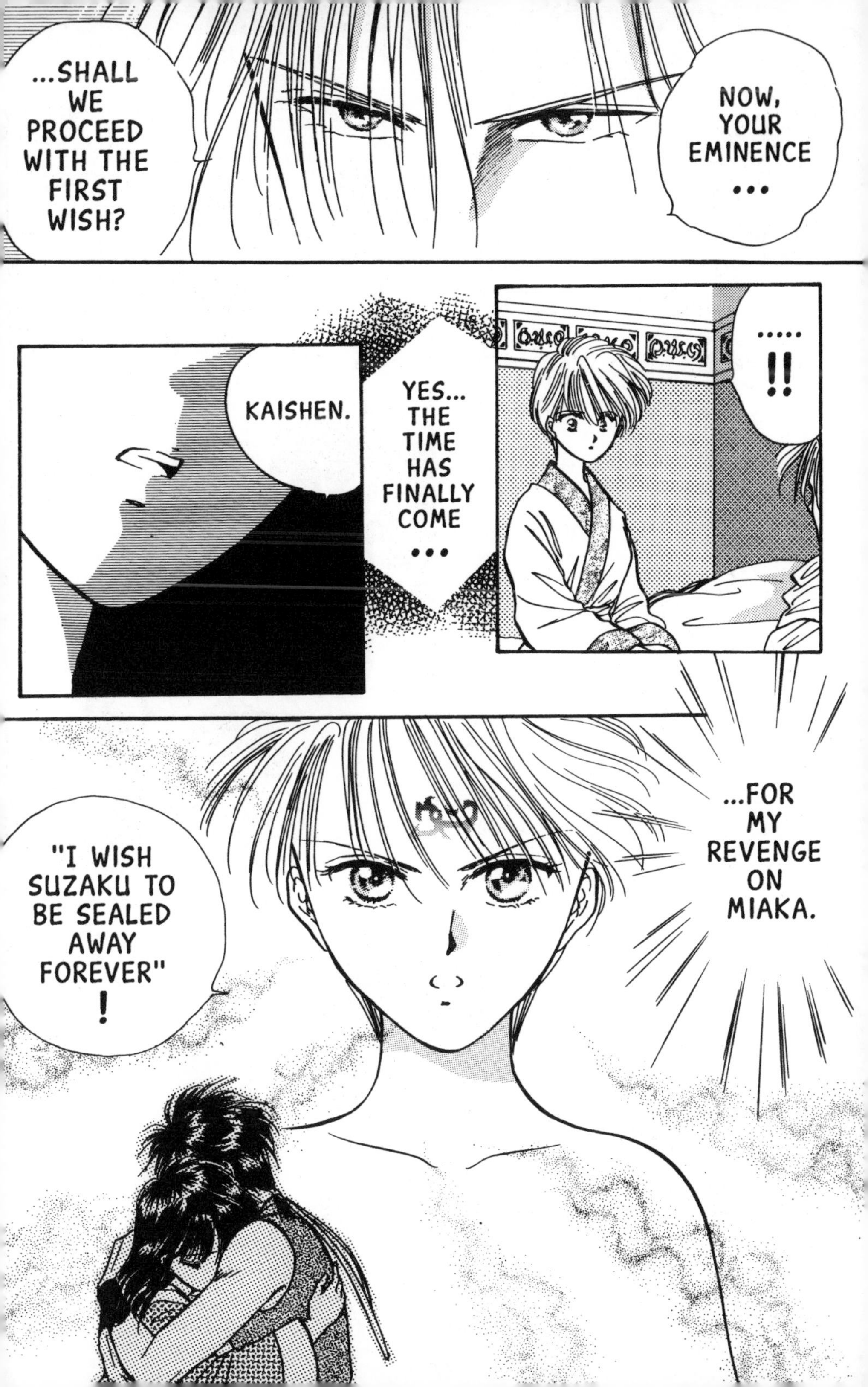
NOW, YOUR EMINENCE ...
...SHALL WE PROCEED WITH THE FIRST WISH?
..... !!
YES... THE TIME HAS FINALLY COME ...
KAISHEN.
...FOR MY REVENGE ON MIAKA.
"I WISH SUZAKU TO BE SEALED AWAY FOREVER" !

ふ[illegible]ぎ悪戯

FUSHIGI AKUGI (10)

THE MALICIOUS PLAY

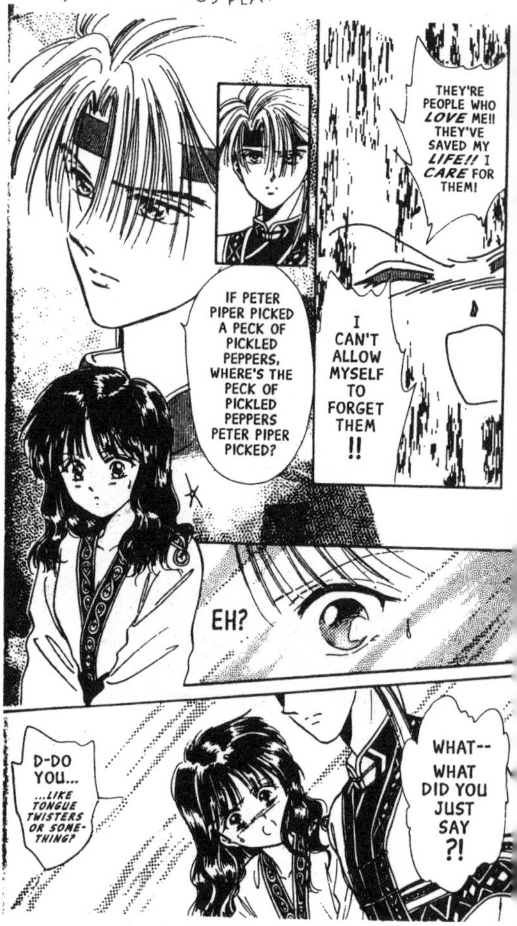
THEY'RE PEOPLE WHO LOVE ME!! THEY'VE SAVED MY LIFE!! I CARE FOR THEM!
I CAN'T ALLOW MYSELF TO FORGET THEM !!
IF PETER PIPER PICKED A PECK OF PICKLED PEPPERS, WHERE'S THE PECK OF PICKLED PEPPERS PETER PIPER PICKED?
EH?
WHAT-- WHAT DID YOU JUST SAY ?!
D-DO YOU... ...LIKE TONGUE TWISTERS OR SOMETHING?

By Mio Akita → (age 15). Congratulations! It's really a good joke where you only have to change a few words of dialog! And I'm surprised how well she knew the tongue twister! I only know about half of it! But I wonder if you would get it if you don't know it's a tongue twister...

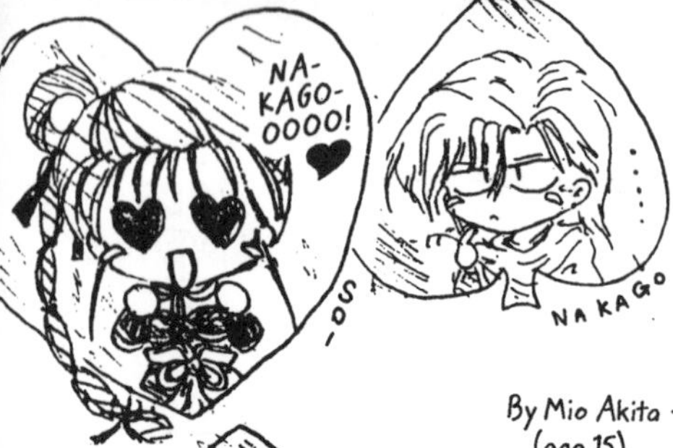
NA-KAGO-OOOO!
NAKAGO

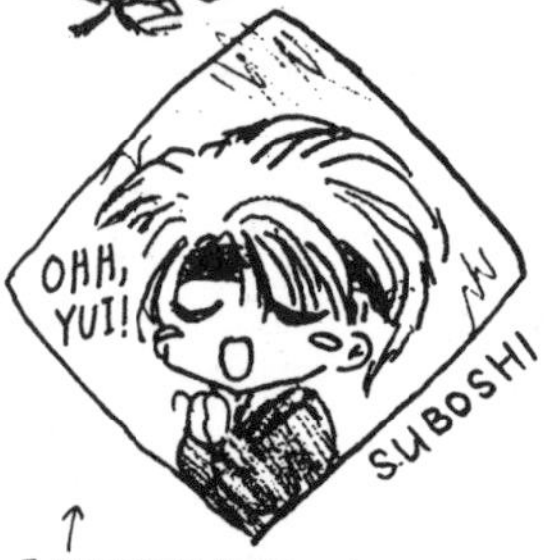
OHH, YUI!
SUBOSHI

↑
3 ILLUSTRATIONS
By Ms. Ono, who's apparently a Seiryu Celestial warrior fan.

I wonder if the Celestial Club is still putting out its "Fushigi" dojinshi.

I had Ms. Iizaka draw Tasuki and Tatara. Thank you so much!

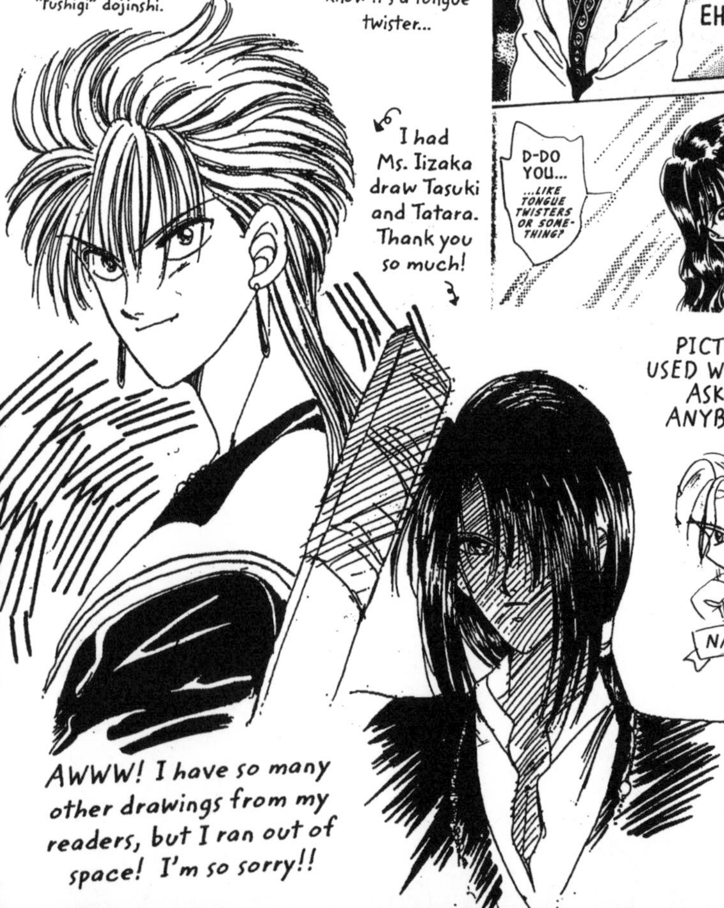

AWWW! I have so many other drawings from my readers, but I ran out of space! I'm so sorry!!

PICTURES USED WITHOUT ASKING ANYBODY!

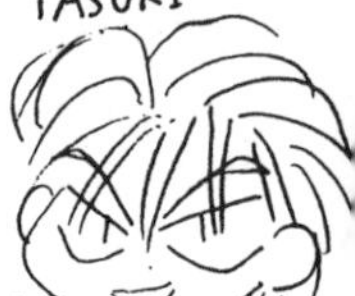
TASUKI

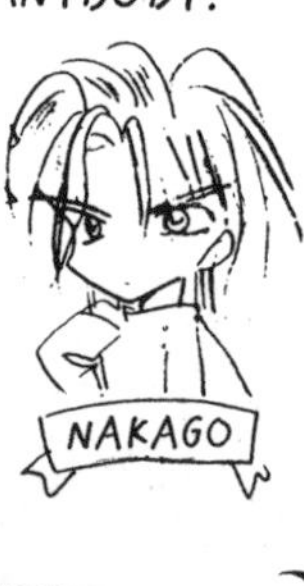
NAKAGO

These are by Maki-san, a devoted reader.

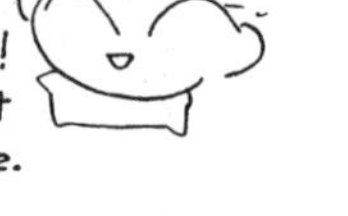
CHICHIRI

Tee hee! He's just too cute.

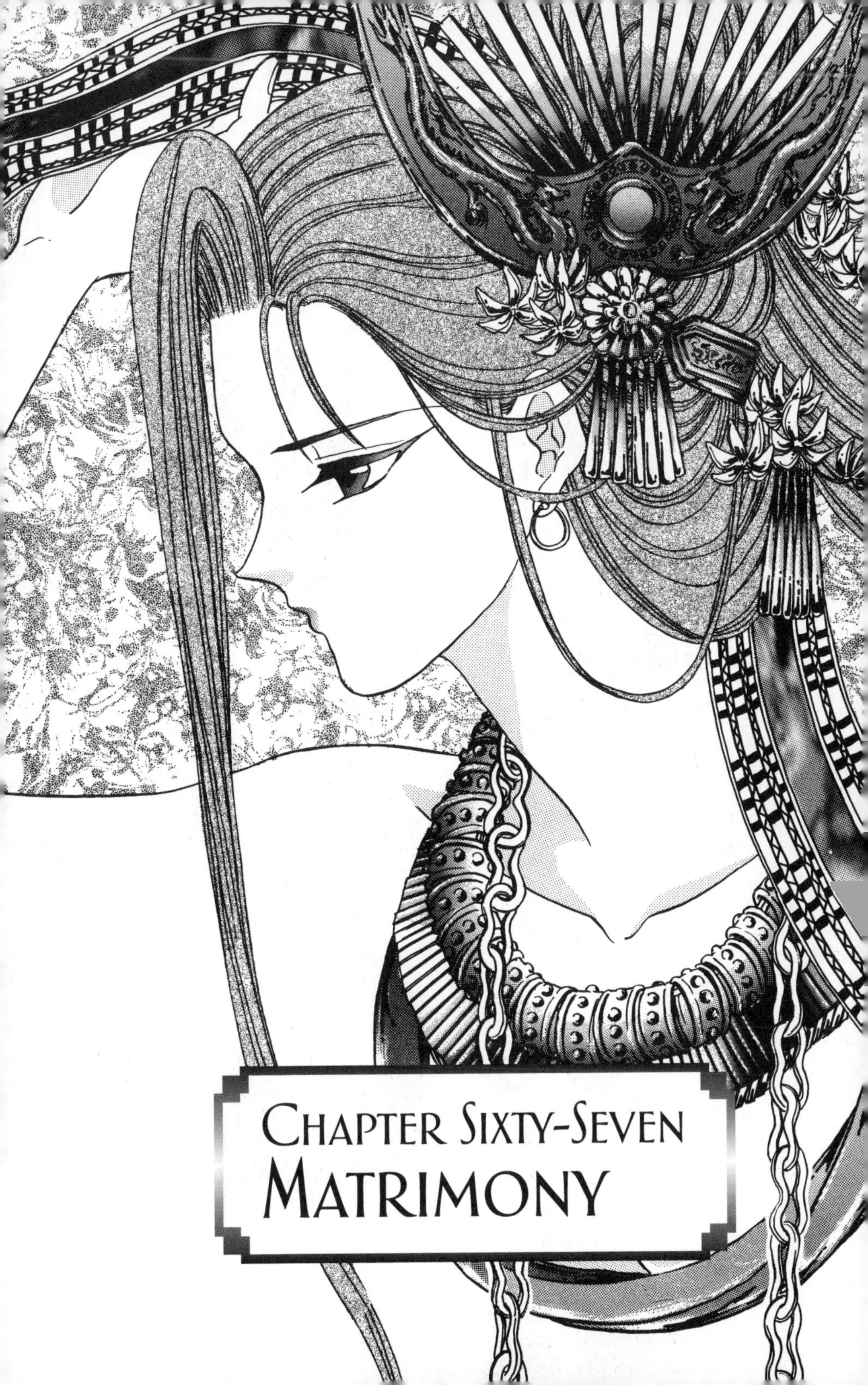
CHAPTER SIXTY-SEVEN
MATRIMONY

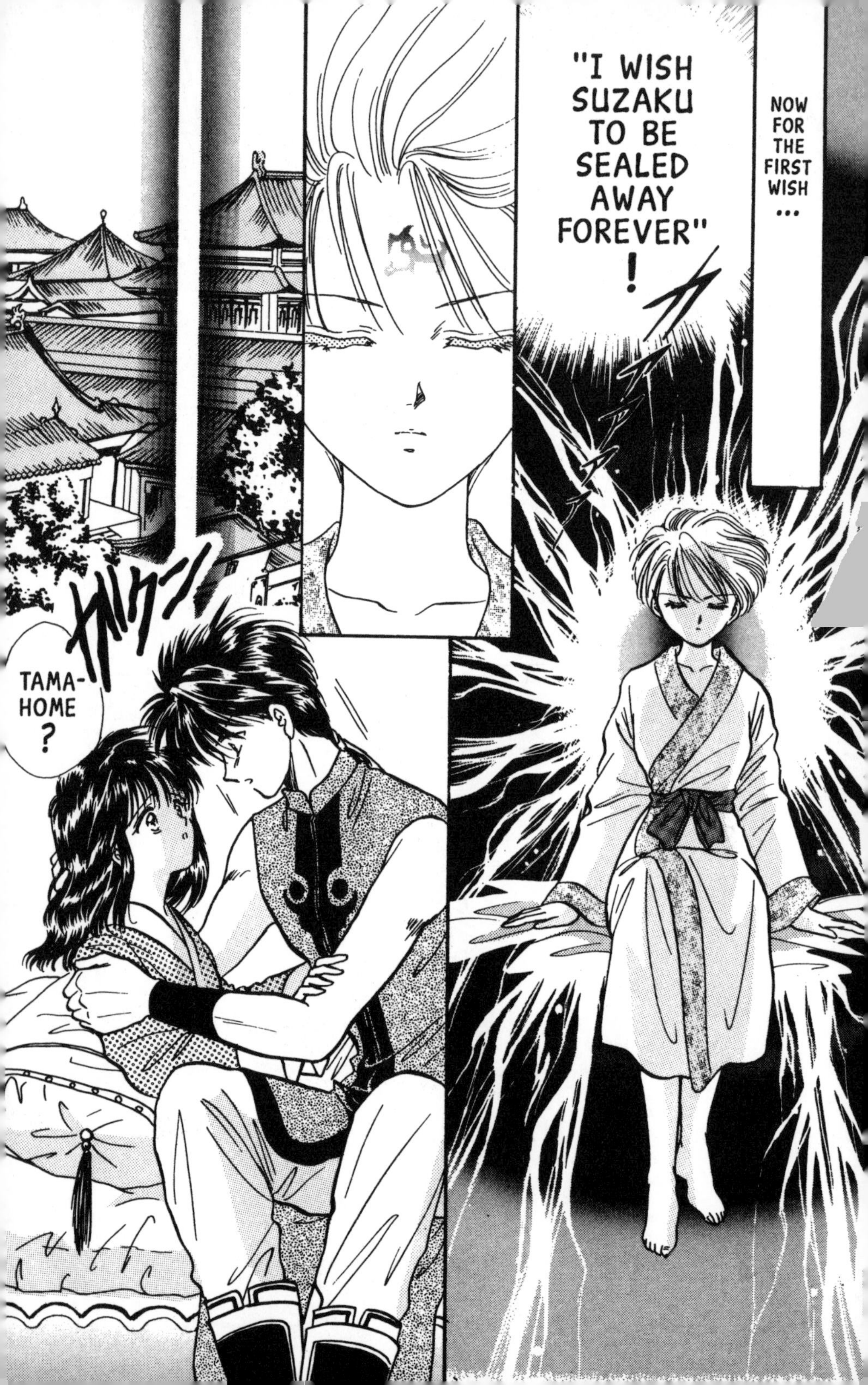
NOW FOR THE FIRST WISH...
"I WISH SUZAKU TO BE SEALED AWAY FOREVER"!
TAMA-HOME?

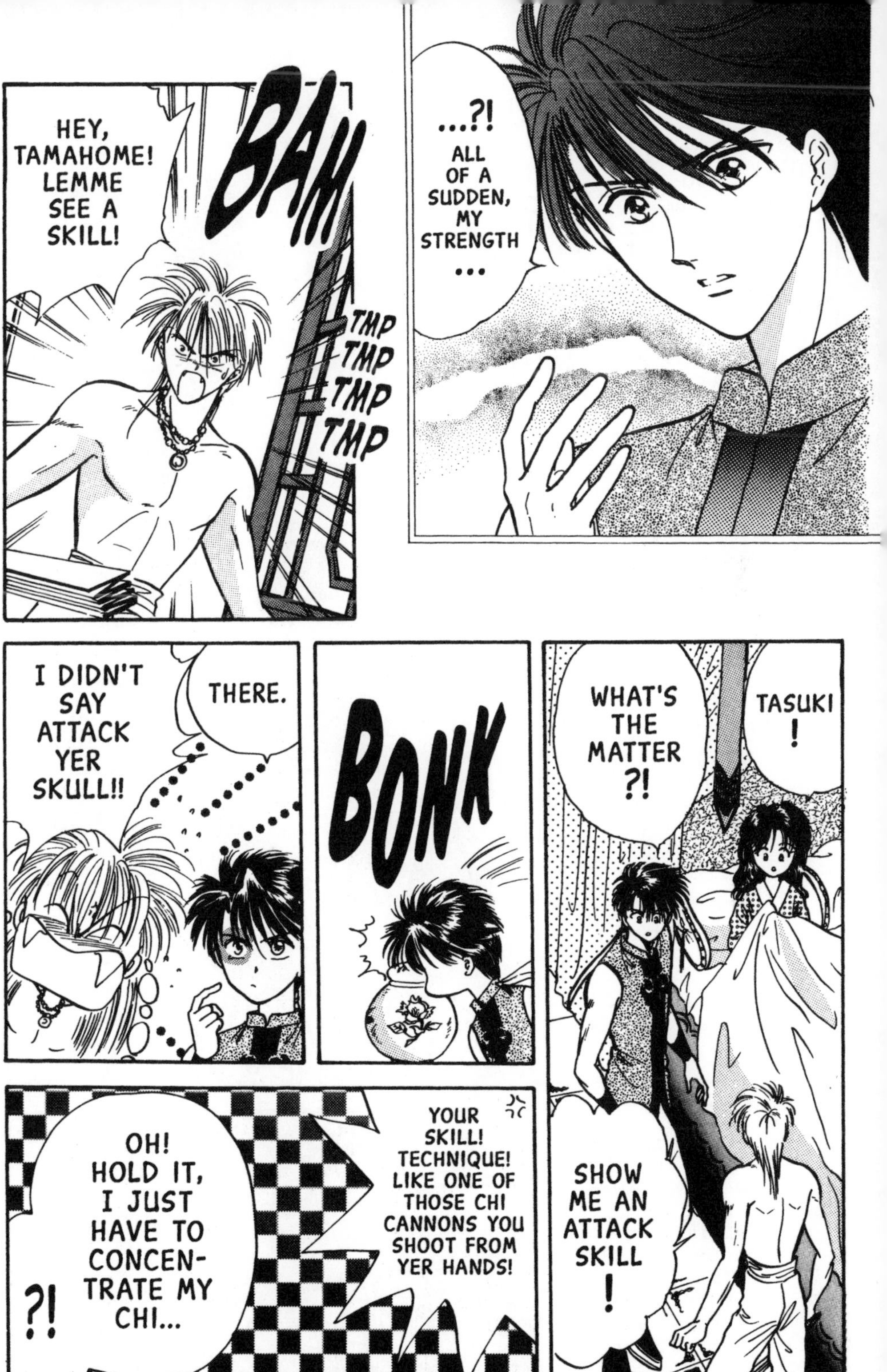
...?!
ALL OF A SUDDEN, MY STRENGTH...
BAM
HEY, TAMAHOME! LEMME SEE A SKILL!
TMP TMP TMP TMP
TASUKI!
WHAT'S THE MATTER?!
SHOW ME AN ATTACK SKILL!
BONK
THERE.
I DIDN'T SAY ATTACK YER SKULL!!
YOUR SKILL! TECHNIQUE! LIKE ONE OF THOSE CHI CANNONS YOU SHOOT FROM YER HANDS!
OH! HOLD IT, I JUST HAVE TO CONCEN-TRATE MY CHI...
?!

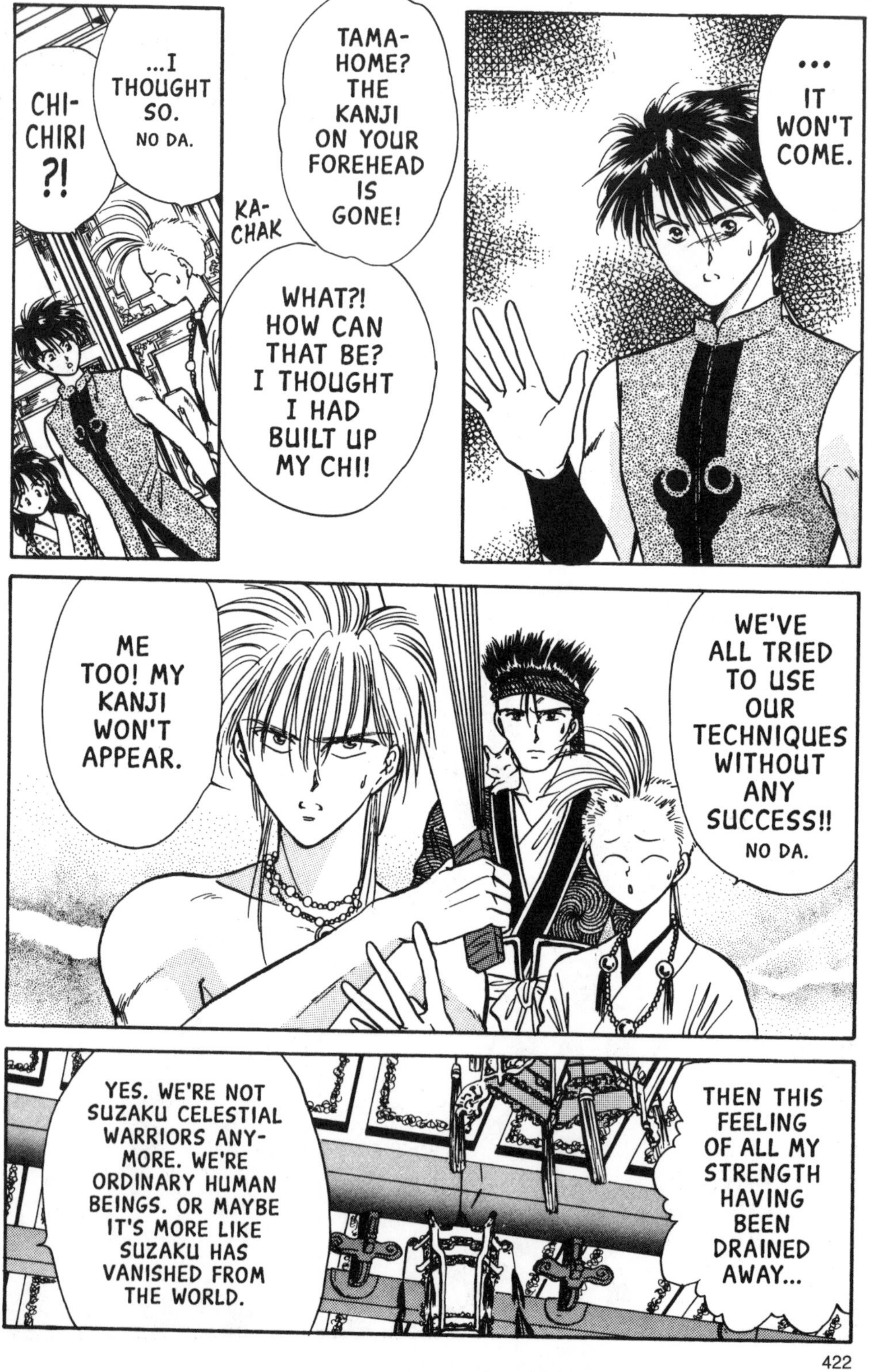

... IT WON'T COME.
TAMA-HOME? THE KANJI ON YOUR FOREHEAD IS GONE!
KA-CHAK
WHAT?! HOW CAN THAT BE? I THOUGHT I HAD BUILT UP MY CHI!
...I THOUGHT SO. NO DA.
CHI-CHIRI?!
WE'VE ALL TRIED TO USE OUR TECHNIQUES WITHOUT ANY SUCCESS!! NO DA.
ME TOO! MY KANJI WON'T APPEAR.
THEN THIS FEELING OF ALL MY STRENGTH HAVING BEEN DRAINED AWAY...
YES. WE'RE NOT SUZAKU CELESTIAL WARRIORS ANY-MORE. WE'RE ORDINARY HUMAN BEINGS. OR MAYBE IT'S MORE LIKE SUZAKU HAS VANISHED FROM THE WORLD.

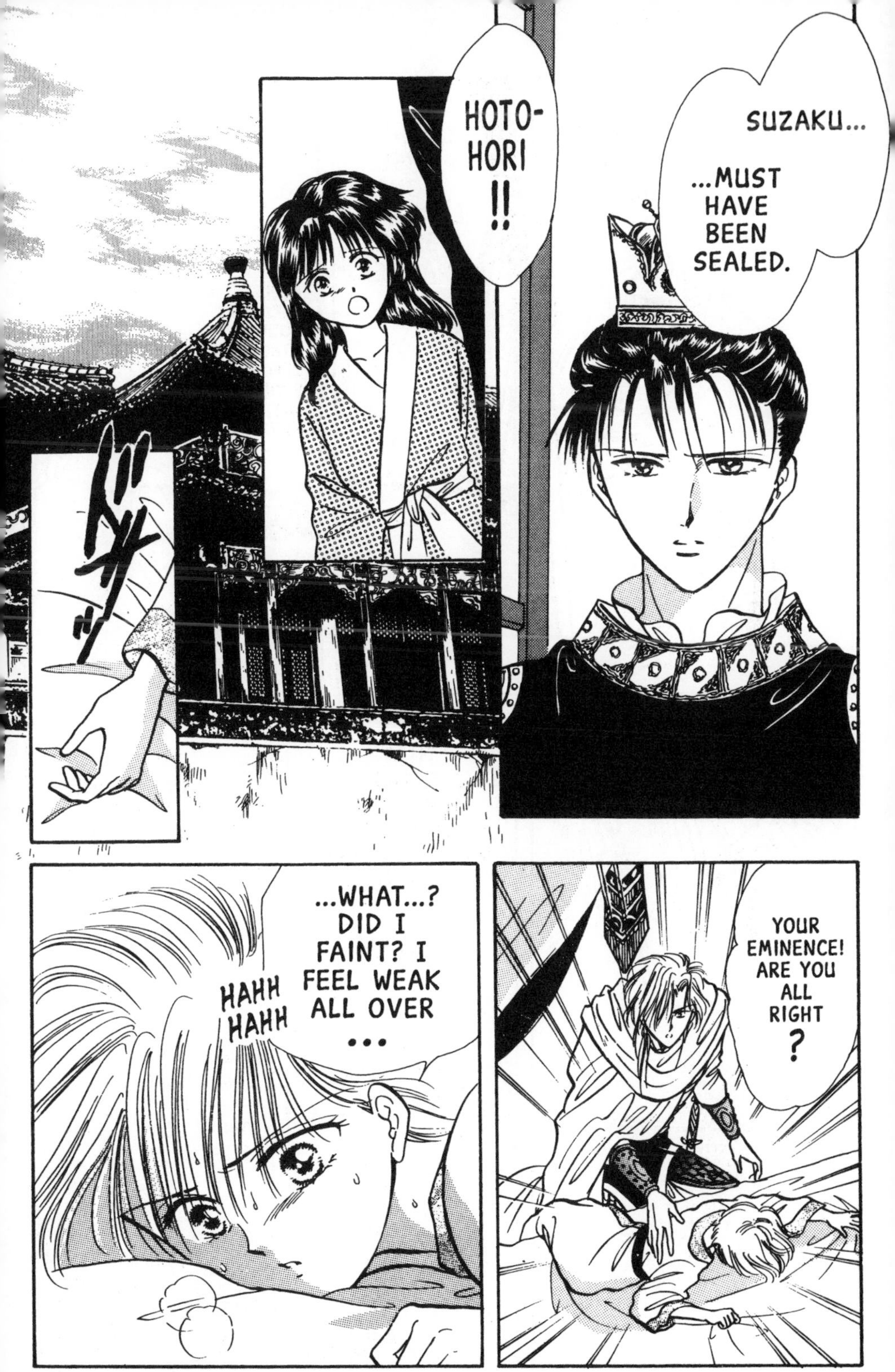
SUZAKU...
...MUST HAVE BEEN SEALED.
HOTO-HORI !!
YOUR EMINENCE! ARE YOU ALL RIGHT ?
...WHAT...? DID I FAINT? I FEEL WEAK ALL OVER ...
HAHH HAHH

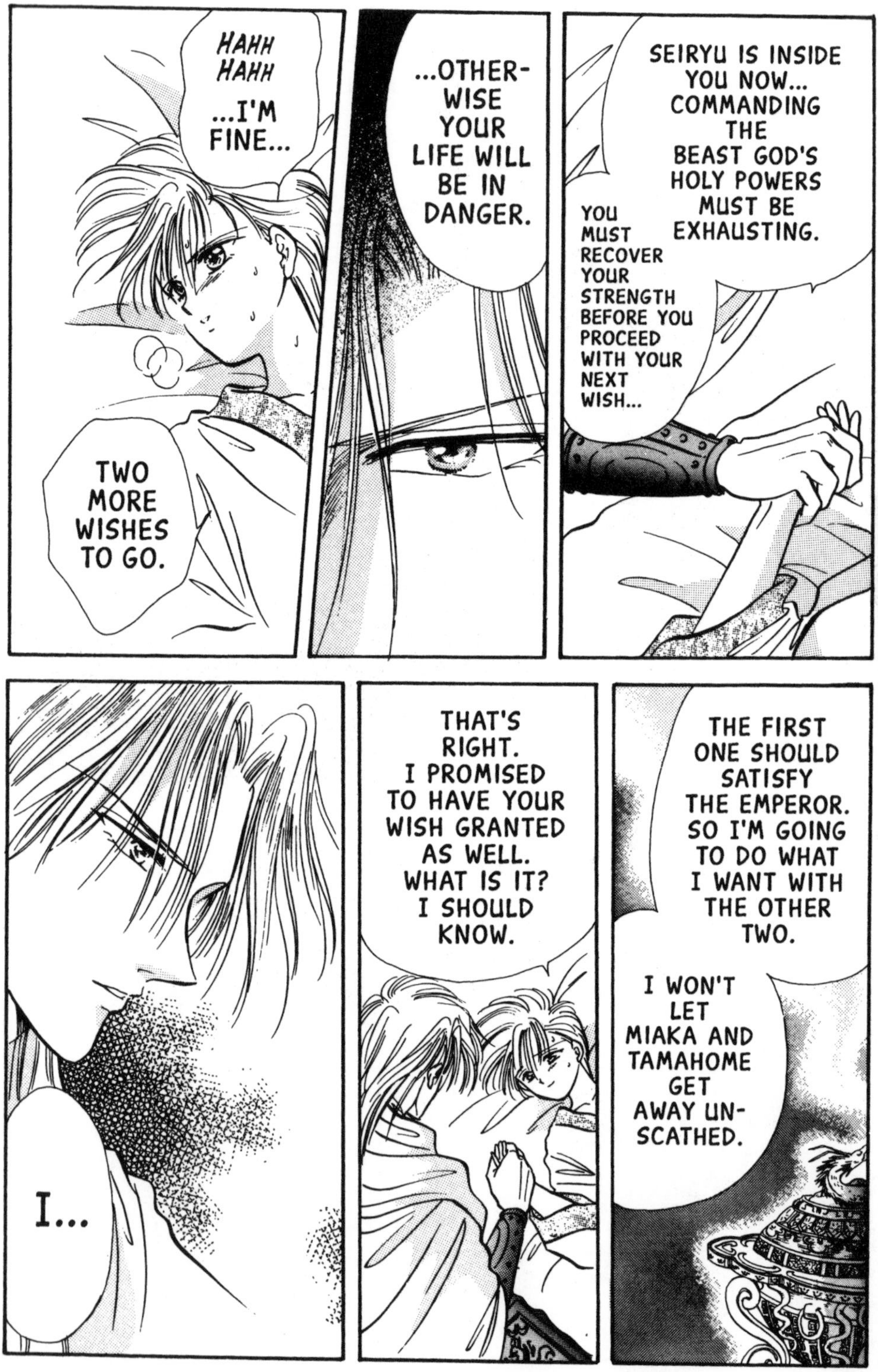
SEIRYU IS INSIDE YOU NOW... COMMANDING THE BEAST GOD'S HOLY POWERS MUST BE EXHAUSTING.
YOU MUST RECOVER YOUR STRENGTH BEFORE YOU PROCEED WITH YOUR NEXT WISH...
...OTHER-WISE YOUR LIFE WILL BE IN DANGER.
HAHH HAHH
...I'M FINE...
TWO MORE WISHES TO GO.
THE FIRST ONE SHOULD SATISFY THE EMPEROR. SO I'M GOING TO DO WHAT I WANT WITH THE OTHER TWO.
I WON'T LET MIAKA AND TAMAHOME GET AWAY UN-SCATHED.
THAT'S RIGHT. I PROMISED TO HAVE YOUR WISH GRANTED AS WELL. WHAT IS IT? I SHOULD KNOW.
I...

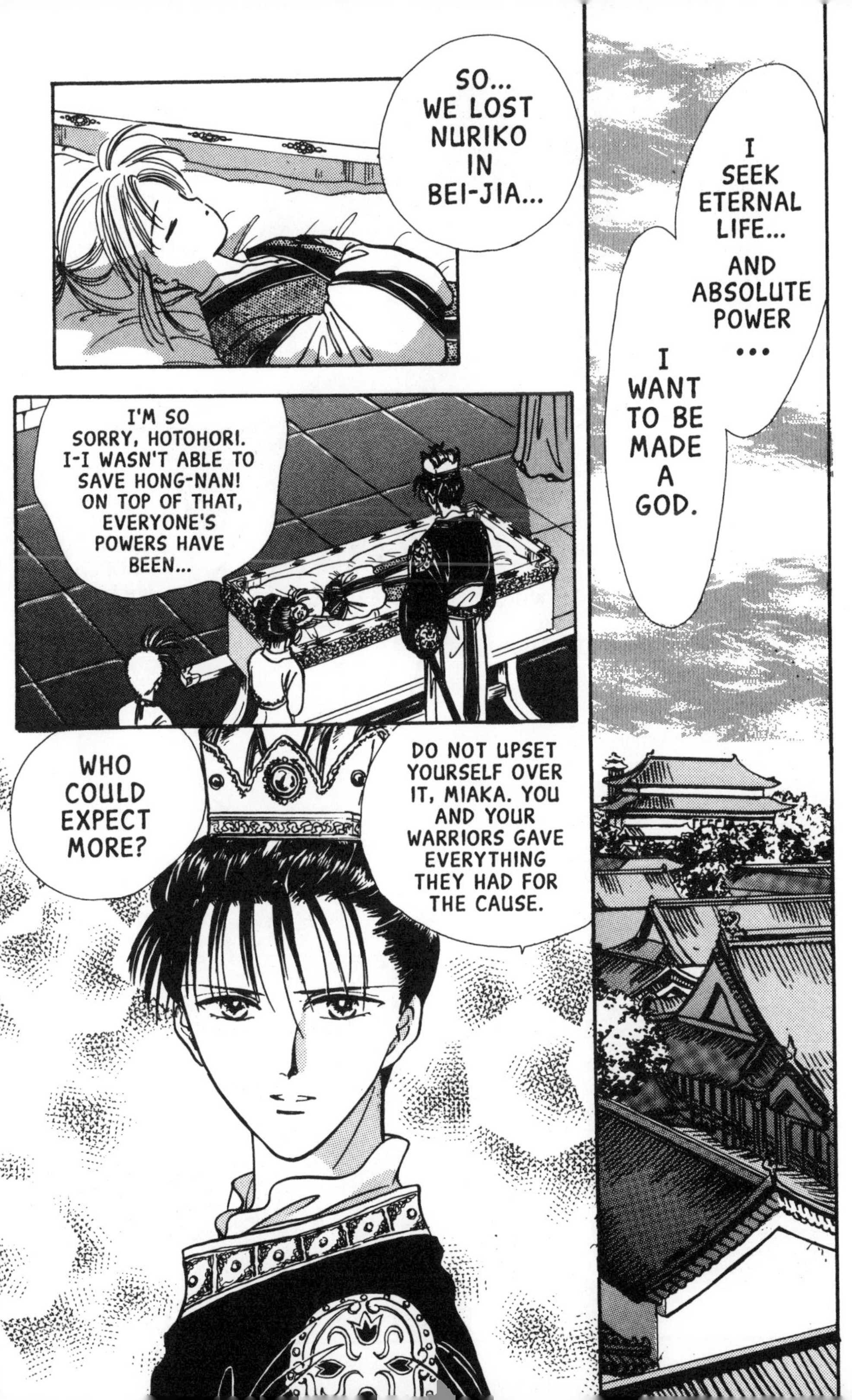
I SEEK ETERNAL LIFE... AND ABSOLUTE POWER ...
I WANT TO BE MADE A GOD.
SO... WE LOST NURIKO IN BEI-JIA...
I'M SO SORRY, HOTOHORI. I-I WASN'T ABLE TO SAVE HONG-NAN! ON TOP OF THAT, EVERYONE'S POWERS HAVE BEEN...
DO NOT UPSET YOURSELF OVER IT, MIAKA. YOU AND YOUR WARRIORS GAVE EVERYTHING THEY HAD FOR THE CAUSE.
WHO COULD EXPECT MORE?

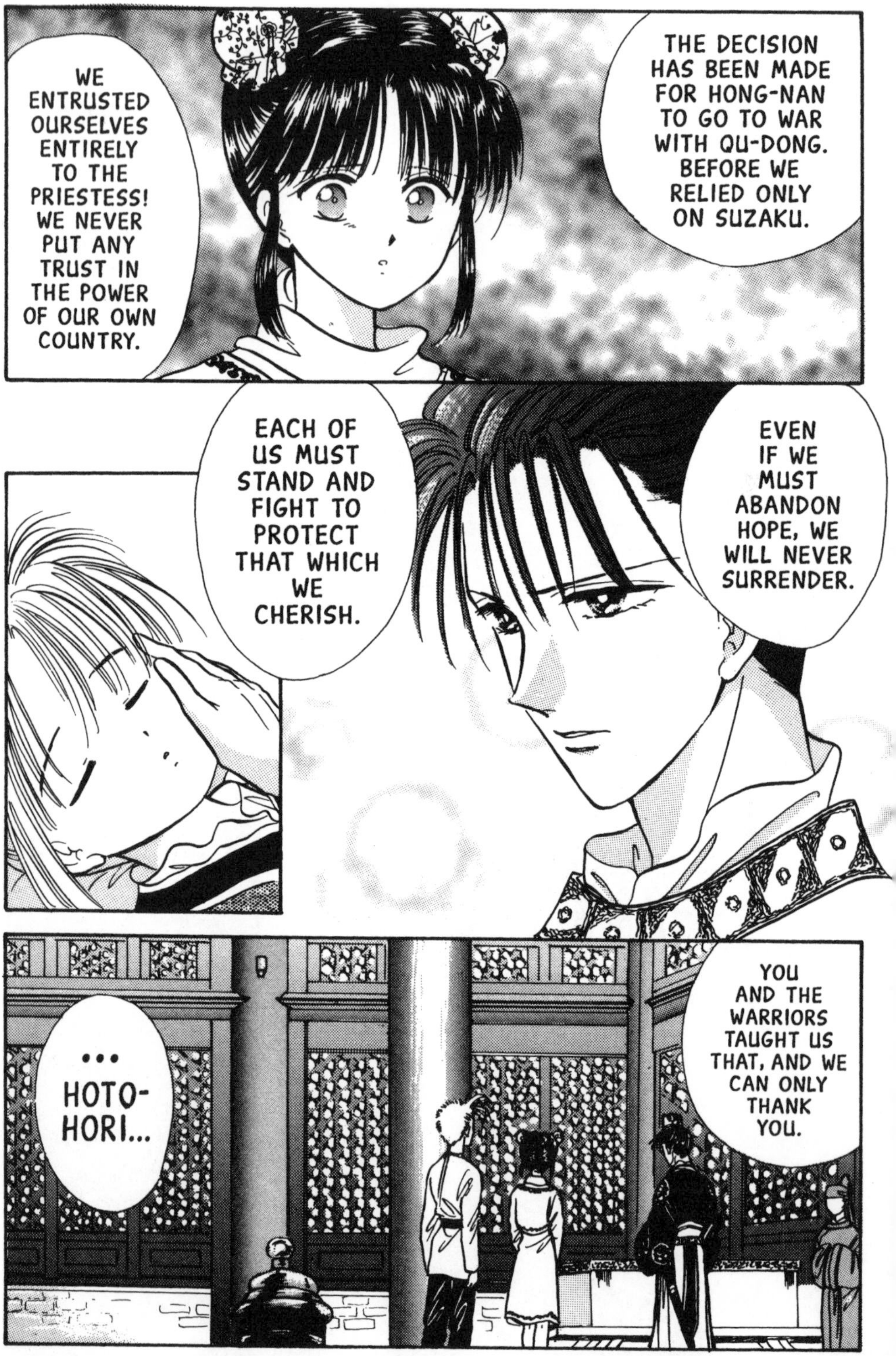
THE DECISION HAS BEEN MADE FOR HONG-NAN TO GO TO WAR WITH QU-DONG. BEFORE WE RELIED ONLY ON SUZAKU.
WE ENTRUSTED OURSELVES ENTIRELY TO THE PRIESTESS! WE NEVER PUT ANY TRUST IN THE POWER OF OUR OWN COUNTRY.
EVEN IF WE MUST ABANDON HOPE, WE WILL NEVER SURRENDER.
EACH OF US MUST STAND AND FIGHT TO PROTECT THAT WHICH WE CHERISH.
YOU AND THE WARRIORS TAUGHT US THAT, AND WE CAN ONLY THANK YOU.
... HOTO-HORI...

When he's a crybaby without his kanji, he can recall his wise self. So that must've been hard on him. The real Chiriko might in fact be the spacey one... By the way, I think I'm like Chiriko. I don't resemble him in terms of his height or intelligence, but when it comes to manga it's like I'm in a trance. My mind can't concentrate on anything else... No, really! They actually call me spacey. I swear, it's like I'm a different person. *Scary!*

Now, on to the Seiryu celestial warriors. *Hmm, hmm...*
Nakago! The first Seiryu I came up with. I made him (look like a) blond to contrast him against Tamahome... his greatest rival. The "armor" also just came to me, so that became his outfit. And that's when he became a general. Come to think of it now, I think that armor protecting his "heart" represents his personality. But I didn't expect him to be so active in the story. He even kisses Tama! He was doing it to spite Miaka's and Tama's relationship. That feeling comes as naturally to him as eating, so he doesn't have to think twice about it. But I'm glad he's become popular lately. I like him! His foolishness is cute. Manato from *Pre-pubescence* used to be my favorite male character, but to be honest, Nakago's right up there with him. Basically, though, I like them all.

Amiboshi's very popular. According to the CD survey, he was ranked at No. 5. I got a lot of flack when he betrayed the Suzaku Warriors. (Or was it because he supposedly died?) *At the time...*

YAH!
HAH!
HYAAH!
IT AIN'T NO GOOD!! MY HARISEN JUST WON'T *WORK* ANYMORE!
HUFF HUFF
SO EVERY POWER WE GOT AS SUZAKU CELESTIAL WARRIORS HAS BEEN STRIPPED FROM US.
AND I ONLY RECENTLY PERFECTED THE CHI ATTACK FROM WHEN TAI YI-JUN GAVE US THE POWER BOOST!

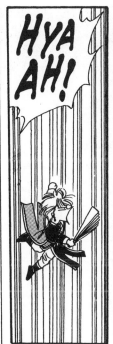

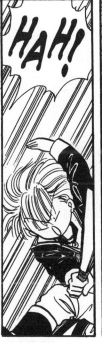

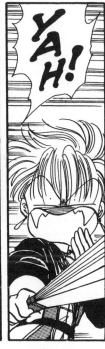

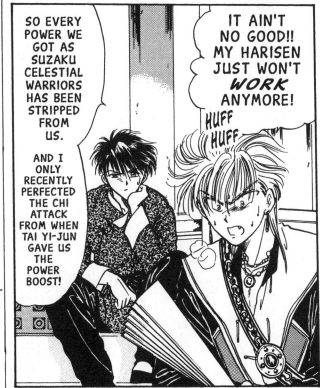

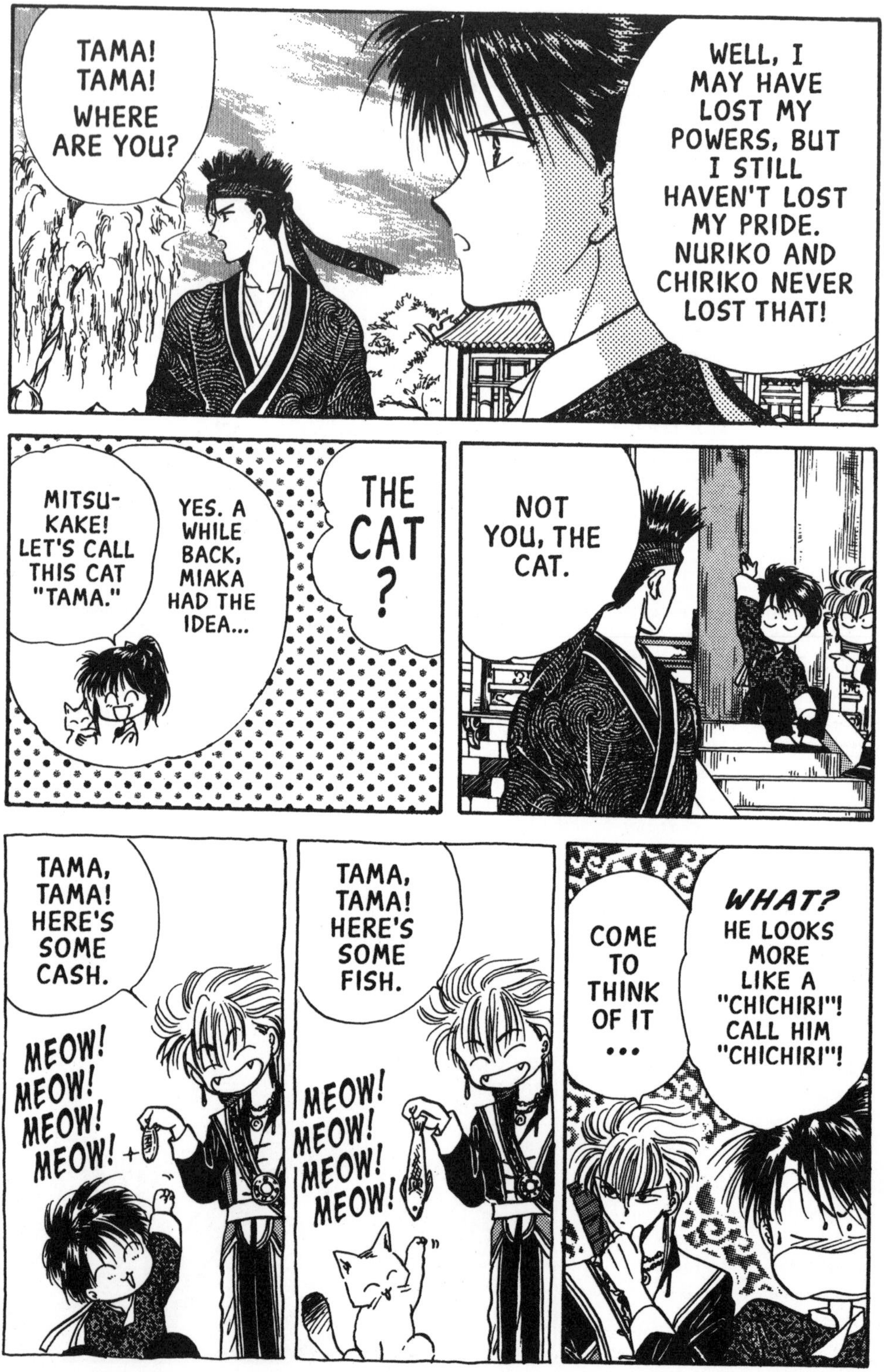
WELL, I MAY HAVE LOST MY POWERS, BUT I STILL HAVEN'T LOST MY PRIDE. NURIKO AND CHIRIKO NEVER LOST THAT!
TAMA! TAMA! WHERE ARE YOU?
NOT YOU, THE CAT.
THE CAT?
YES. A WHILE BACK, MIAKA HAD THE IDEA...
MITSU-KAKE! LET'S CALL THIS CAT "TAMA."
WHAT? HE LOOKS MORE LIKE A "CHICHIRI"! CALL HIM "CHICHIRI"!
COME TO THINK OF IT...
TAMA, TAMA! HERE'S SOME FISH.
MEOW! MEOW! MEOW! MEOW!
TAMA, TAMA! HERE'S SOME CASH.
MEOW! MEOW! MEOW! MEOW!

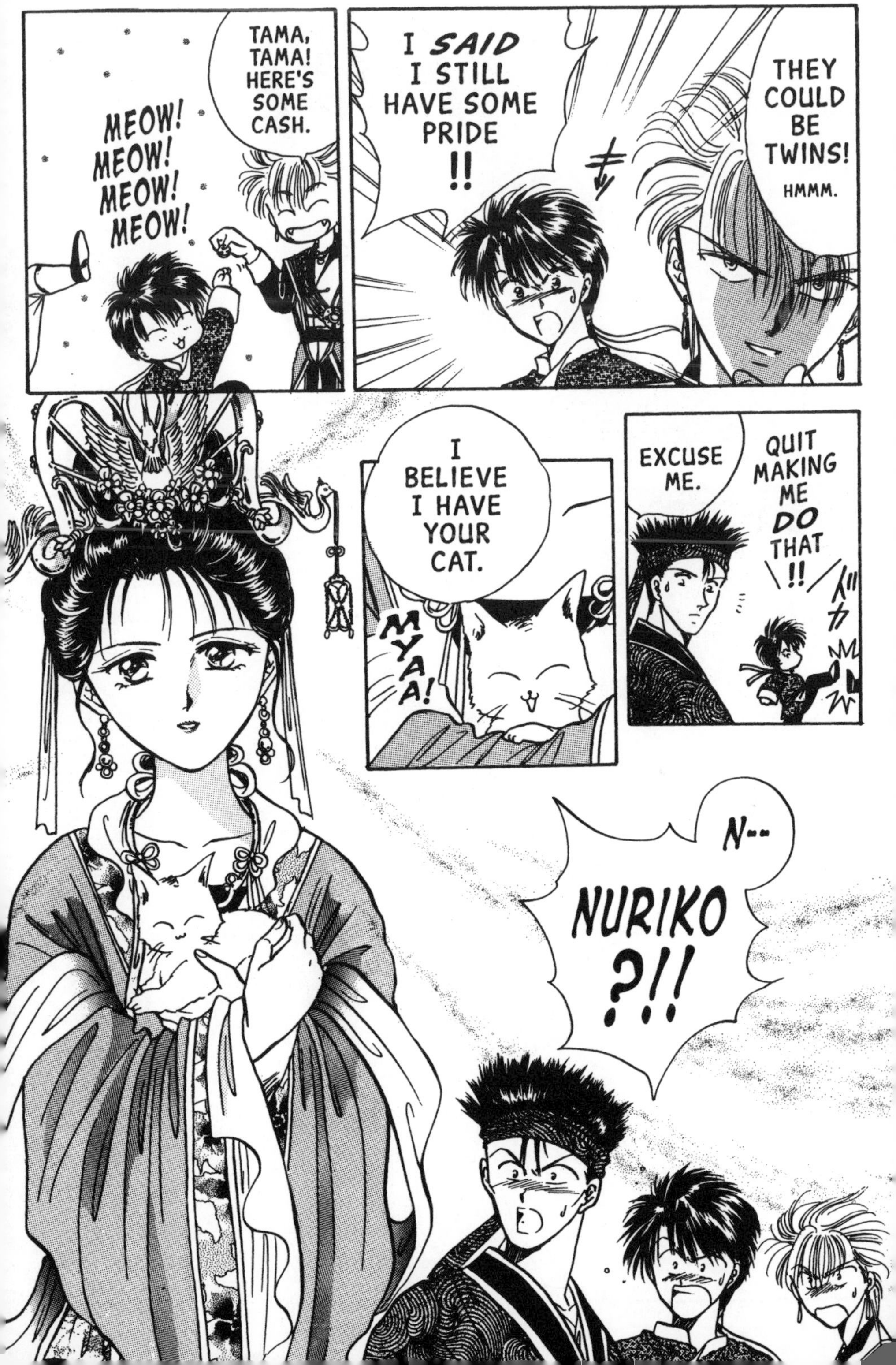
THEY COULD BE TWINS!
HMMM.
I SAID I STILL HAVE SOME PRIDE!!
TAMA, TAMA! HERE'S SOME CASH.
MEOW! MEOW! MEOW! MEOW!
EXCUSE ME.
QUIT MAKING ME DO THAT!!
I BELIEVE I HAVE YOUR CAT.
MYAA!
N--
NURIKO?!!

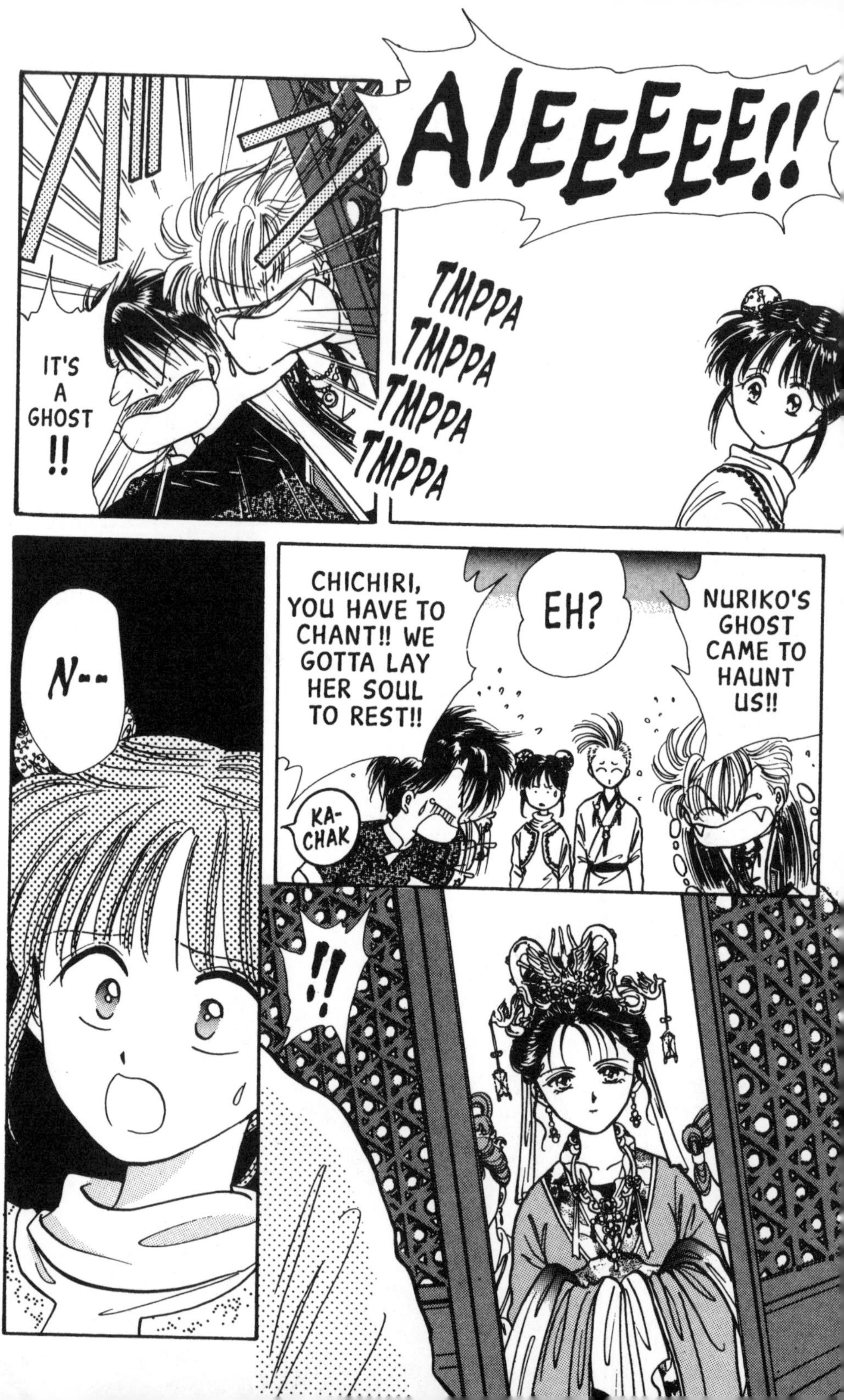
AIEEEEEE!!
TMPPA
TMPPA
TMPPA
TMPPA
IT'S A GHOST !!
NURIKO'S GHOST CAME TO HAUNT US!!
EH?
CHICHIRI, YOU HAVE TO CHANT!! WE GOTTA LAY HER SOUL TO REST!!
KA-CHAK
!!
N--

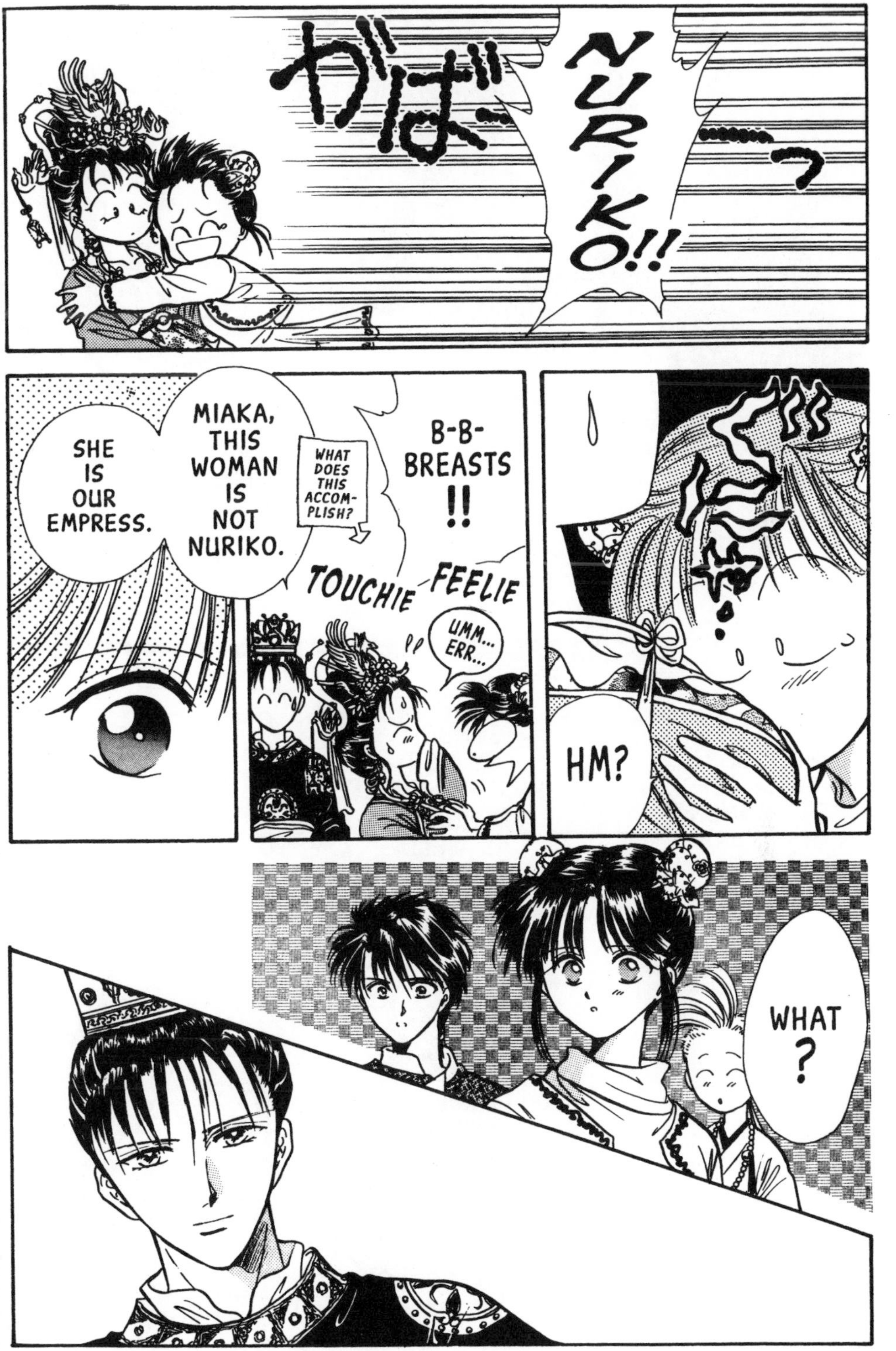
NURIKO!!
がばーっ
HM?
B-B-BREASTS!!
WHAT DOES THIS ACCOMPLISH?
TOUCHIE FEELIE
UMM... ERR...
MIAKA, THIS WOMAN IS NOT NURIKO.
SHE IS OUR EMPRESS.
WHAT?

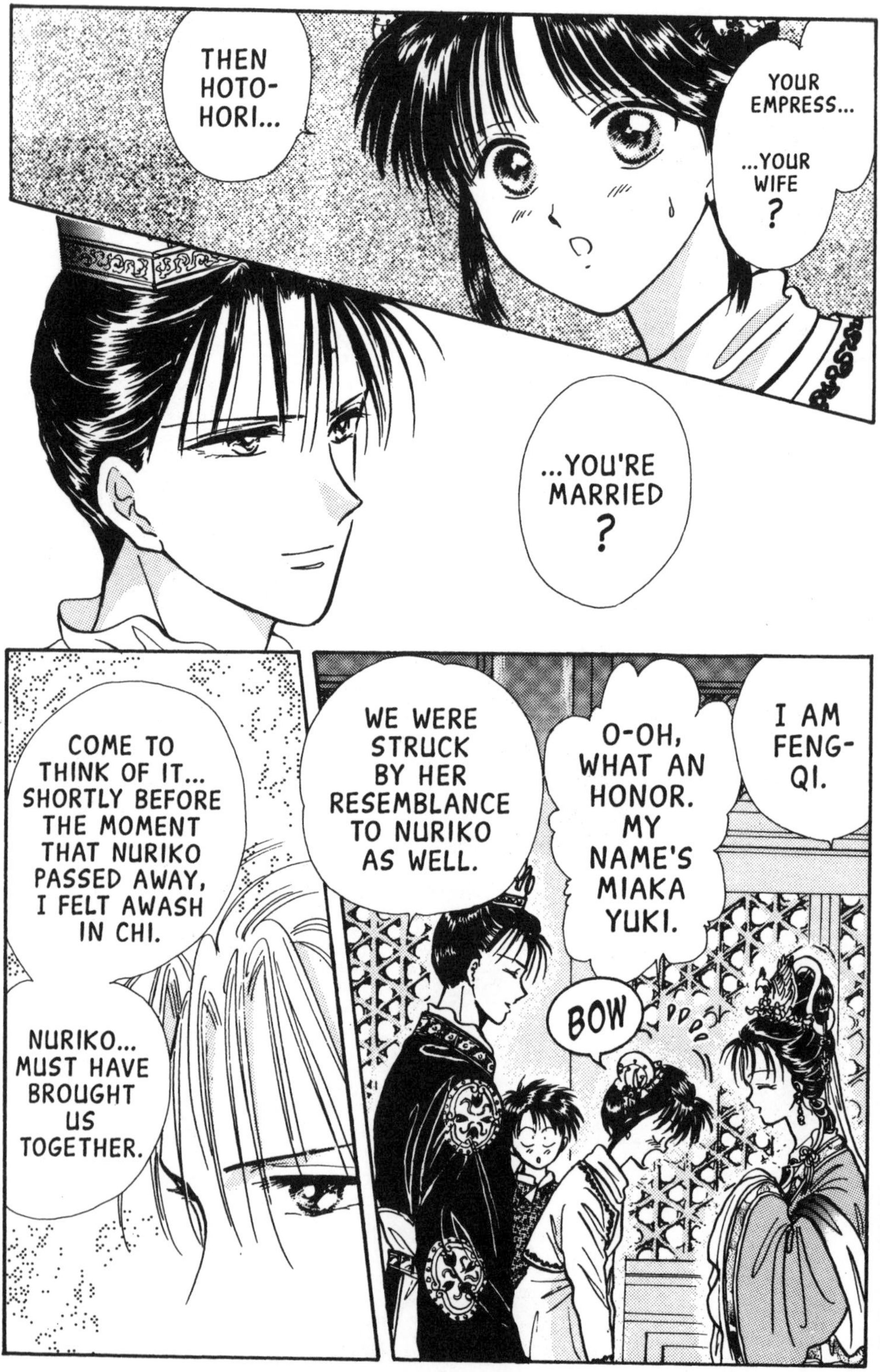
YOUR EMPRESS... ...YOUR WIFE ?
THEN HOTOHORI...
...YOU'RE MARRIED ?
I AM FENG-QI.
O-OH, WHAT AN HONOR. MY NAME'S MIAKA YUKI.
BOW
WE WERE STRUCK BY HER RESEMBLANCE TO NURIKO AS WELL.
COME TO THINK OF IT... SHORTLY BEFORE THE MOMENT THAT NURIKO PASSED AWAY, I FELT AWASH IN CHI.
NURIKO... MUST HAVE BROUGHT US TOGETHER.

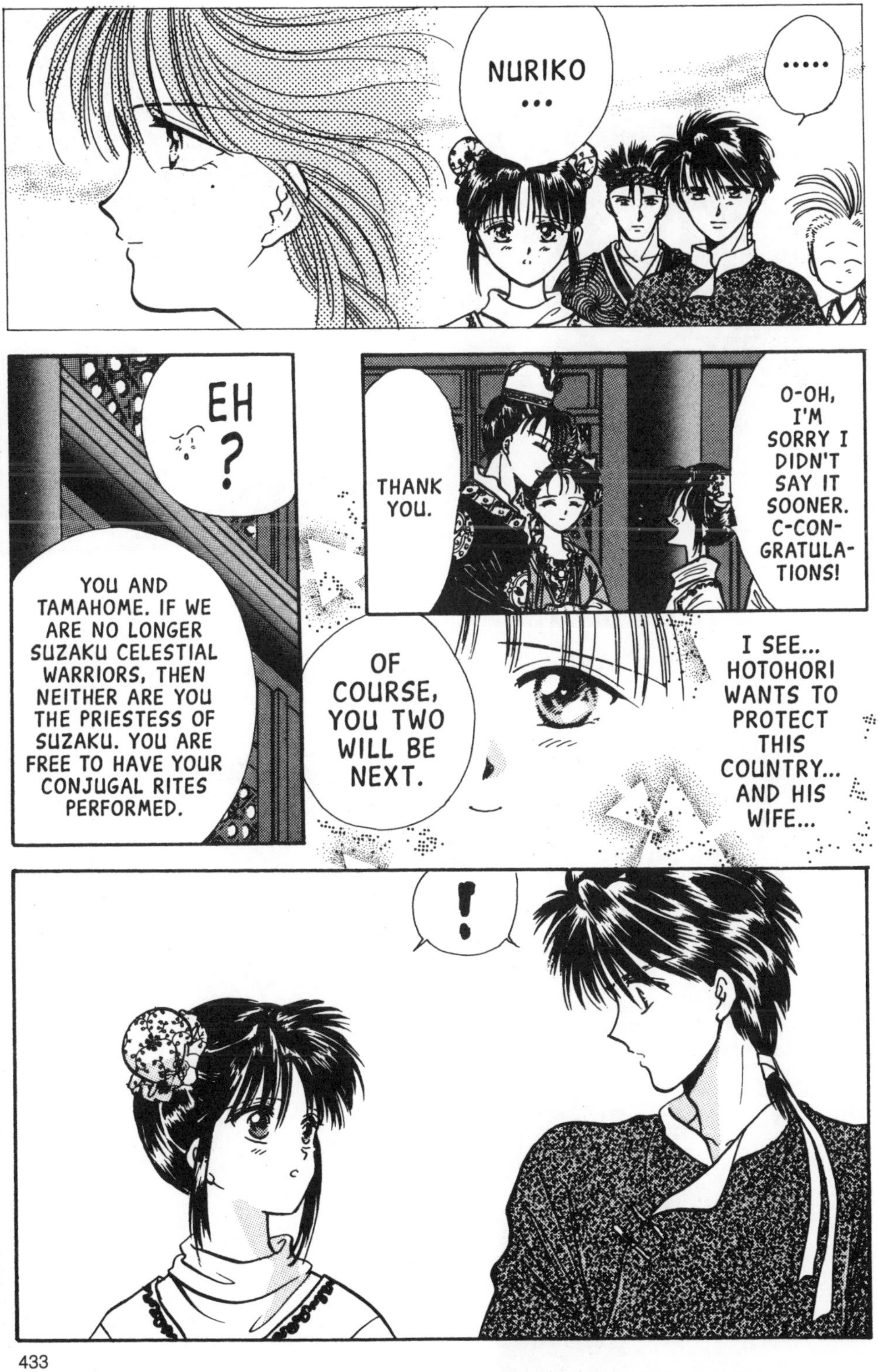
.....
NURIKO ...
O-OH, I'M SORRY I DIDN'T SAY IT SOONER. C-CONGRATULATIONS!
THANK YOU.
I SEE... HOTOHORI WANTS TO PROTECT THIS COUNTRY... AND HIS WIFE...
OF COURSE, YOU TWO WILL BE NEXT.
EH ?
YOU AND TAMAHOME. IF WE ARE NO LONGER SUZAKU CELESTIAL WARRIORS, THEN NEITHER ARE YOU THE PRIESTESS OF SUZAKU. YOU ARE FREE TO HAVE YOUR CONJUGAL RITES PERFORMED.
!

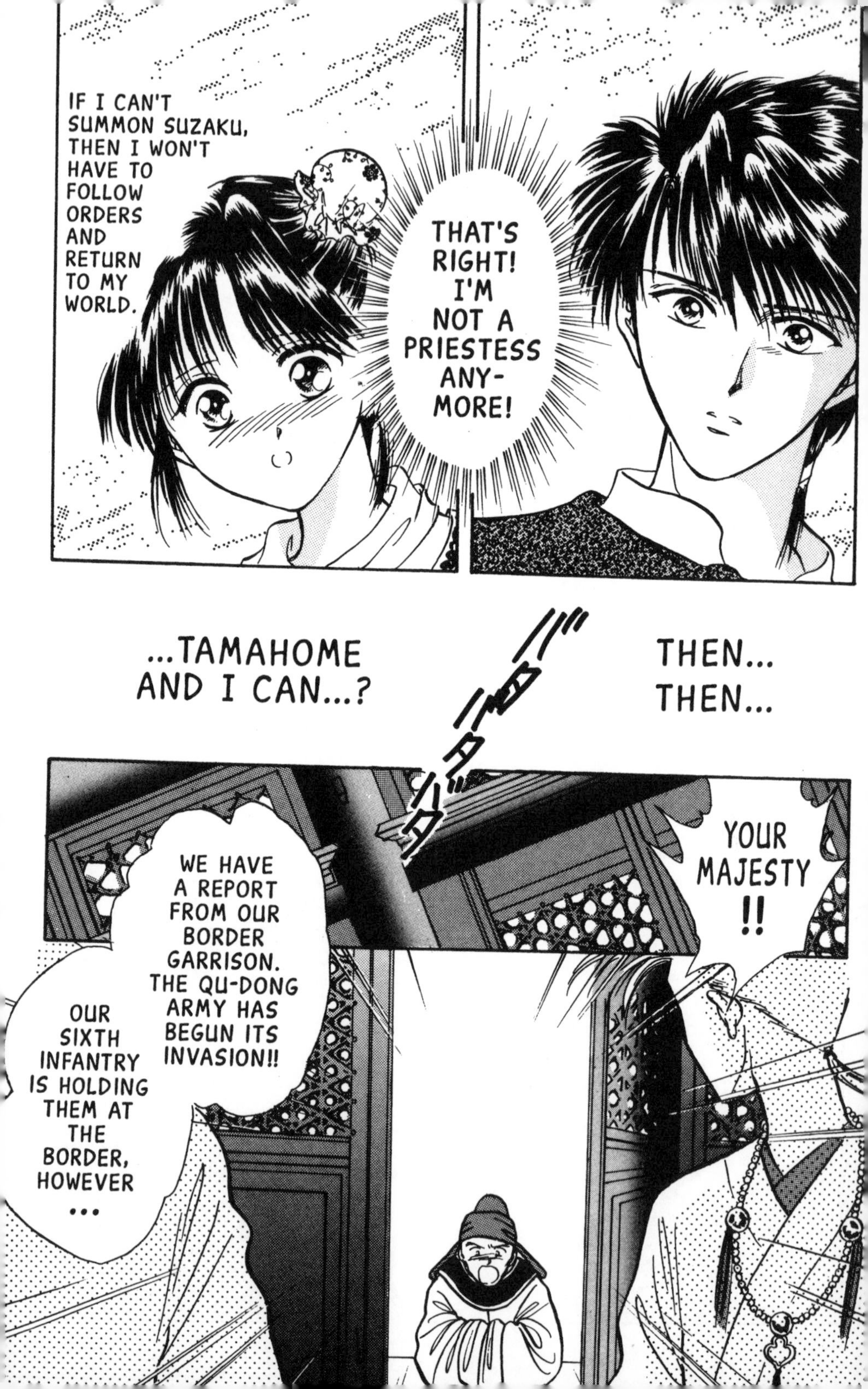
IF I CAN'T SUMMON SUZAKU, THEN I WON'T HAVE TO FOLLOW ORDERS AND RETURN TO MY WORLD.
THAT'S RIGHT! I'M NOT A PRIESTESS ANY-MORE!
THEN... THEN...
...TAMAHOME AND I CAN...?
YOUR MAJESTY!!
WE HAVE A REPORT FROM OUR BORDER GARRISON. THE QU-DONG ARMY HAS BEGUN ITS INVASION!!
OUR SIXTH INFANTRY IS HOLDING THEM AT THE BORDER, HOWEVER...

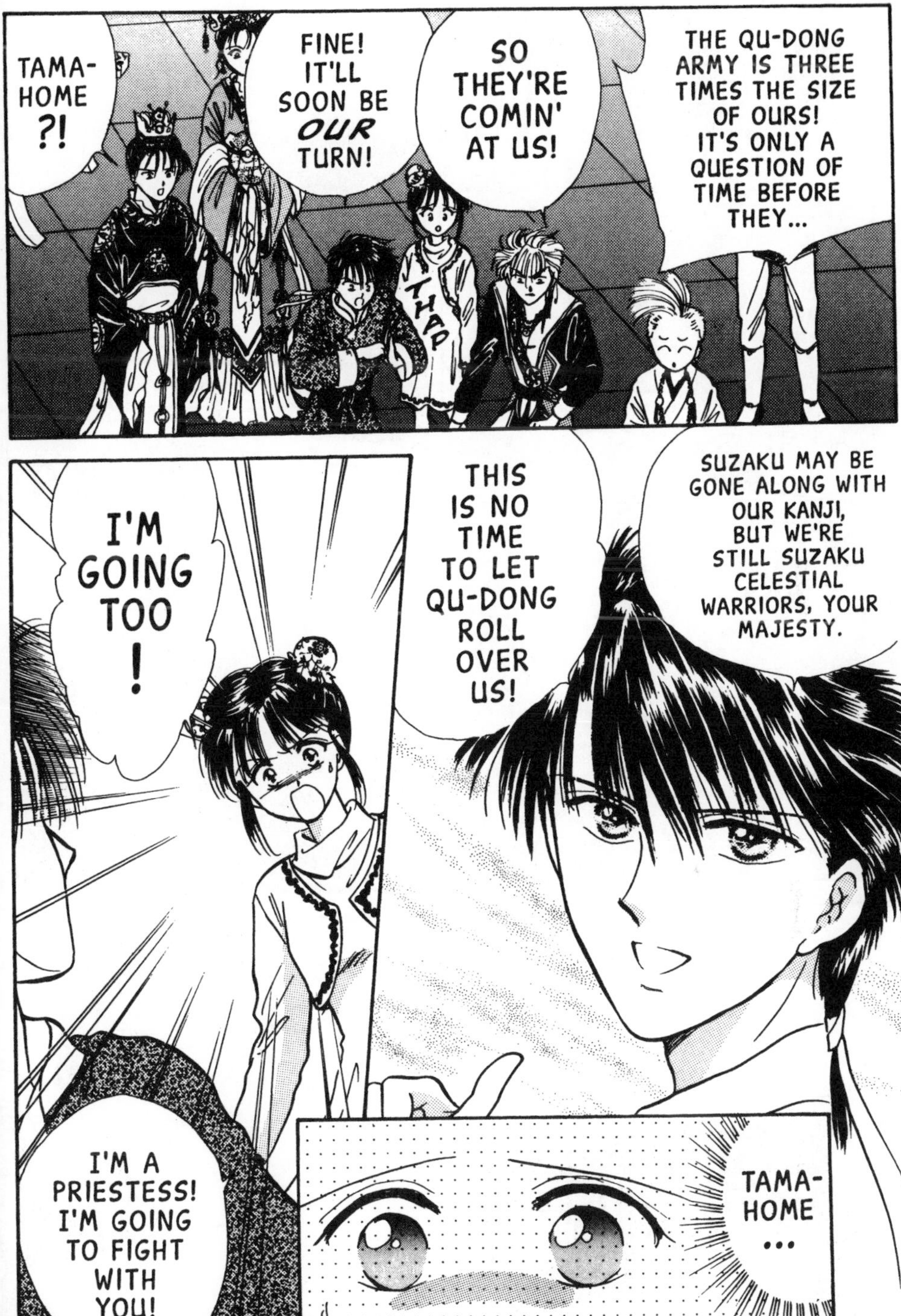

THE QU-DONG ARMY IS THREE TIMES THE SIZE OF OURS! IT'S ONLY A QUESTION OF TIME BEFORE THEY...
SO THEY'RE COMIN' AT US!
FINE! IT'LL SOON BE *OUR* TURN!
THAP
TAMA-HOME ?!
SUZAKU MAY BE GONE ALONG WITH OUR KANJI, BUT WE'RE STILL SUZAKU CELESTIAL WARRIORS, YOUR MAJESTY.
THIS IS NO TIME TO LET QU-DONG ROLL OVER US!
TAMA-HOME ...
I'M GOING TOO !
I'M A PRIESTESS! I'M GOING TO FIGHT WITH YOU!

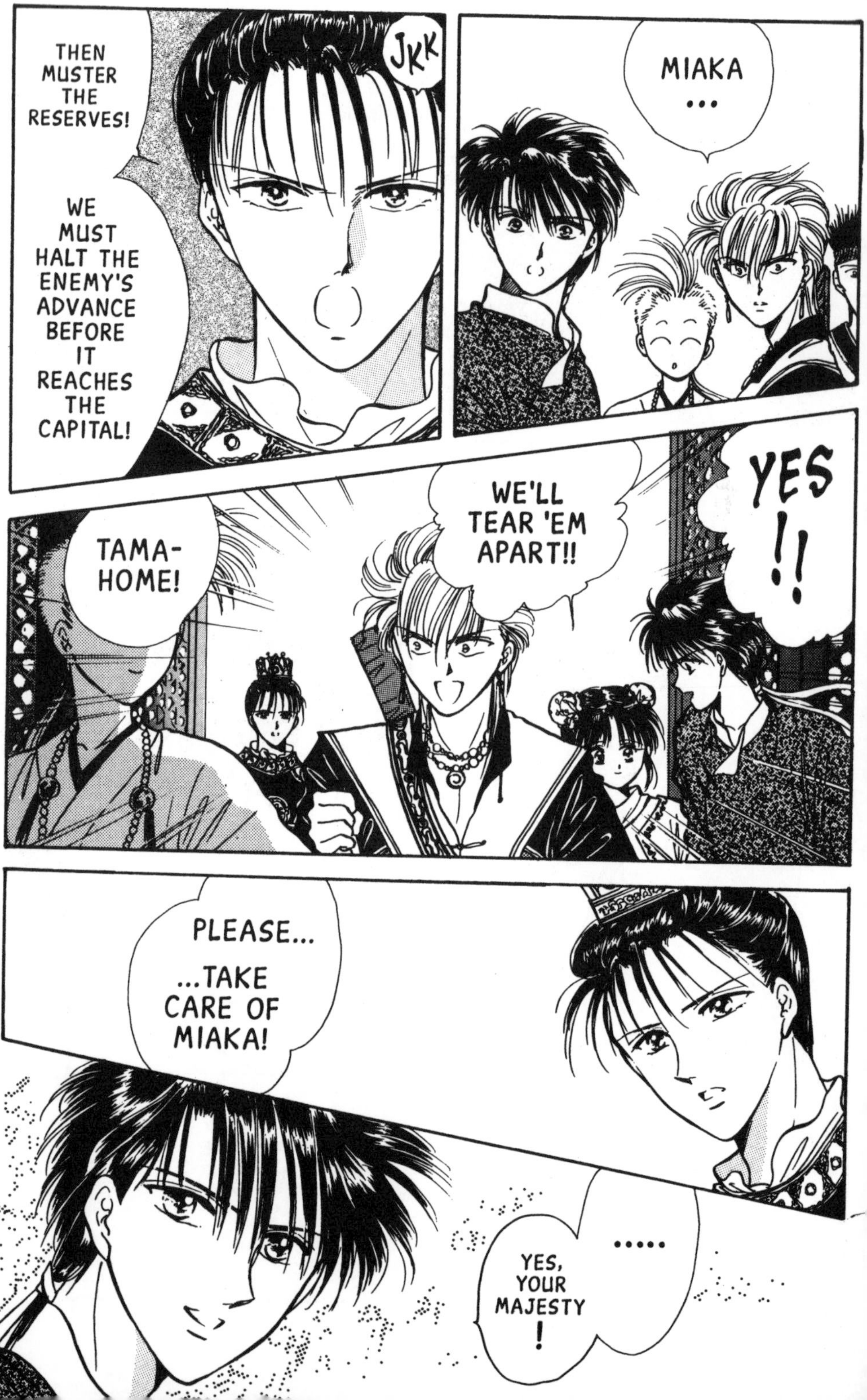
MIAKA ...
JKK
THEN MUSTER THE RESERVES!
WE MUST HALT THE ENEMY'S ADVANCE BEFORE IT REACHES THE CAPITAL!
YES !!
WE'LL TEAR 'EM APART!!
TAMA-HOME!
PLEASE...
...TAKE CARE OF MIAKA!
.....
YES, YOUR MAJESTY !

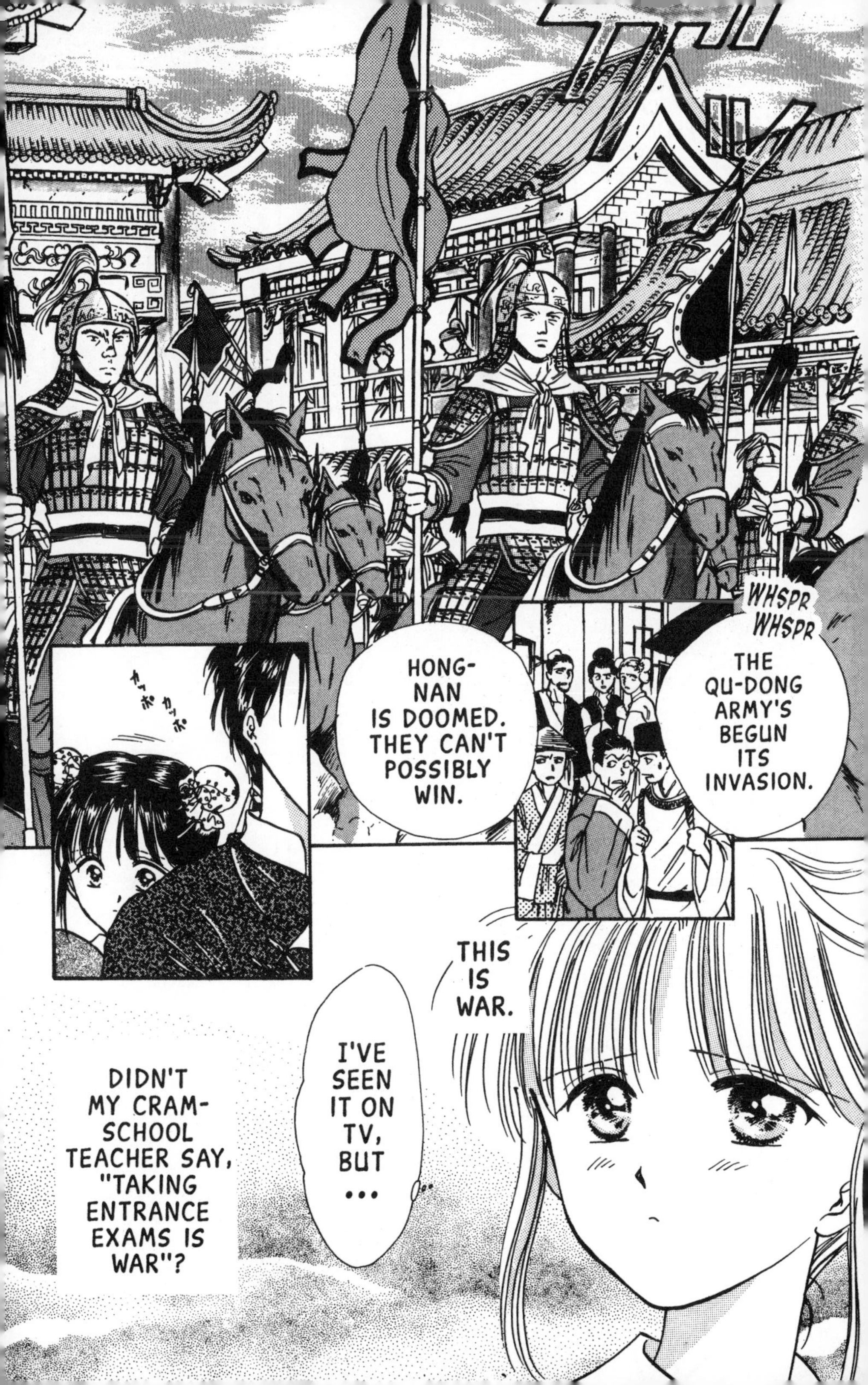
WHSPR WHSPR
THE QU-DONG ARMY'S BEGUN ITS INVASION.
HONG-NAN IS DOOMED. THEY CAN'T POSSIBLY WIN.
THIS IS WAR.
I'VE SEEN IT ON TV, BUT ...
DIDN'T MY CRAM-SCHOOL TEACHER SAY, "TAKING ENTRANCE EXAMS IS WAR"?

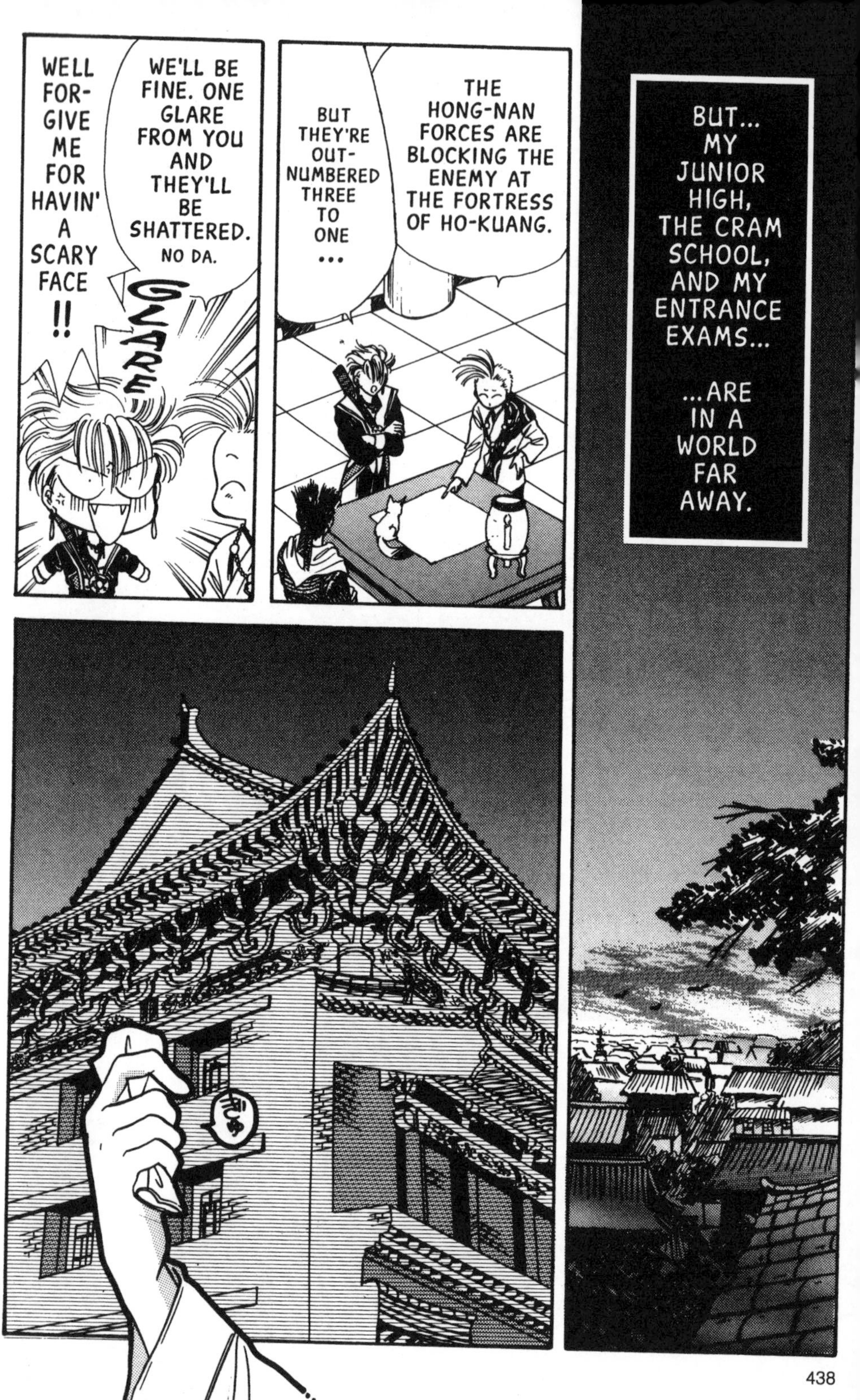
BUT... MY JUNIOR HIGH, THE CRAM SCHOOL, AND MY ENTRANCE EXAMS...
...ARE IN A WORLD FAR AWAY.
THE HONG-NAN FORCES ARE BLOCKING THE ENEMY AT THE FORTRESS OF HO-KUANG.
BUT THEY'RE OUT-NUMBERED THREE TO ONE...
WE'LL BE FINE. ONE GLARE FROM YOU AND THEY'LL BE SHATTERED. NO DA.
GLARE
WELL FORGIVE ME FOR HAVIN' A SCARY FACE!!

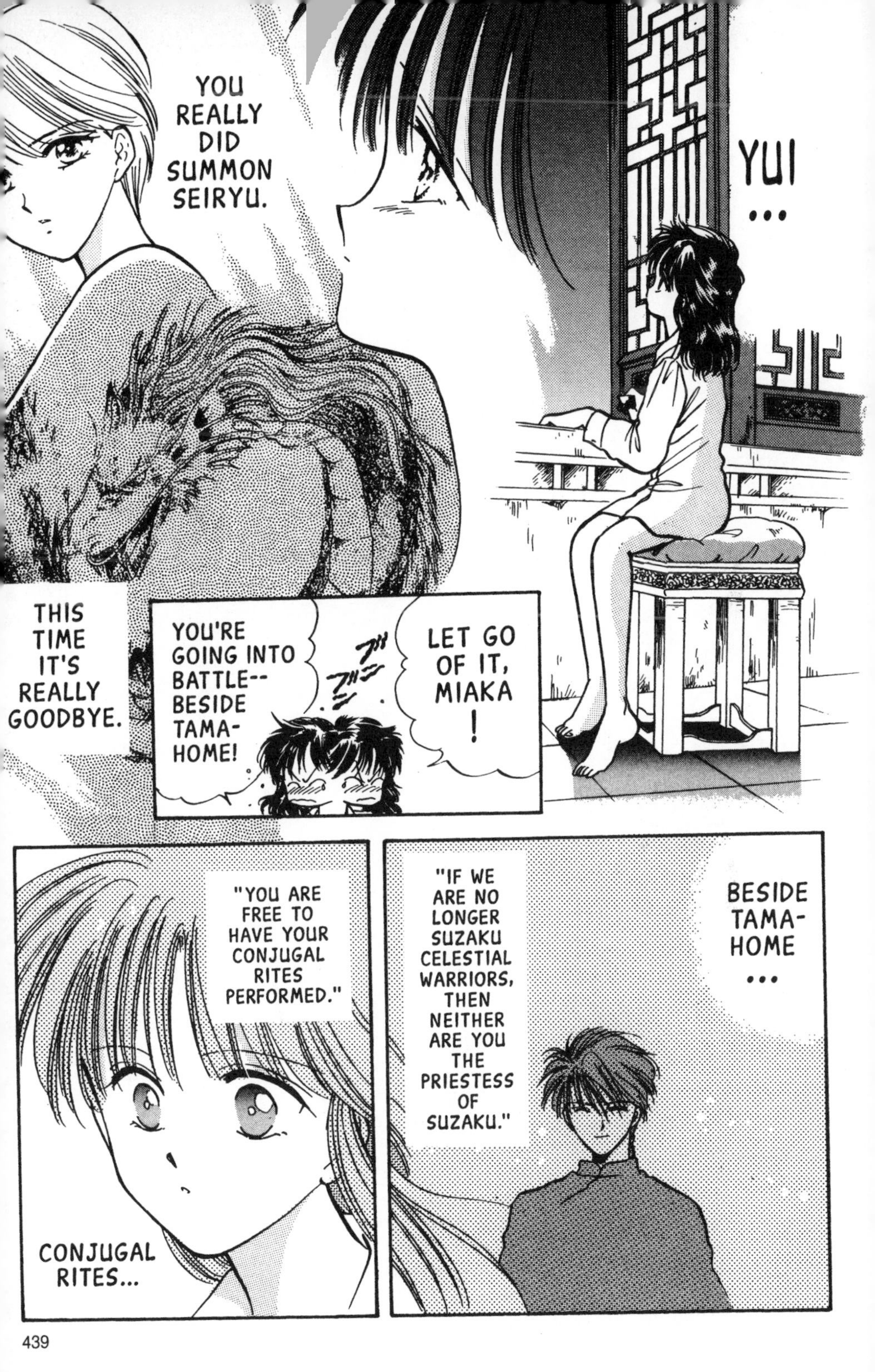
YUI...
YOU REALLY DID SUMMON SEIRYU.
THIS TIME IT'S REALLY GOODBYE.
LET GO OF IT, MIAKA!
YOU'RE GOING INTO BATTLE-- BESIDE TAMA-HOME!
BESIDE TAMA-HOME...
"IF WE ARE NO LONGER SUZAKU CELESTIAL WARRIORS, THEN NEITHER ARE YOU THE PRIESTESS OF SUZAKU."
"YOU ARE FREE TO HAVE YOUR CONJUGAL RITES PERFORMED."
CONJUGAL RITES...

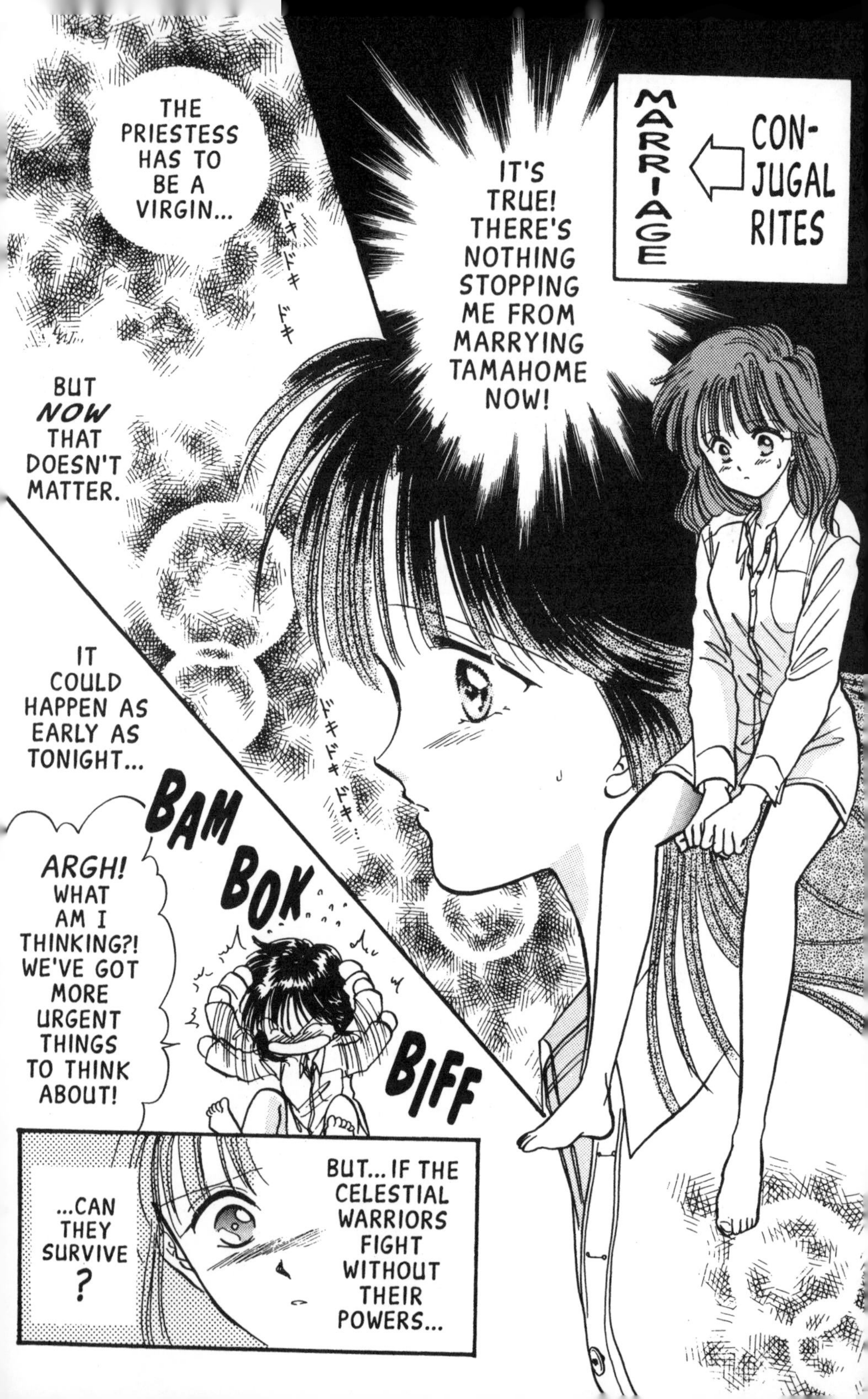
IT'S TRUE! THERE'S NOTHING STOPPING ME FROM MARRYING TAMAHOME NOW!
CONJUGAL RITES
MARRIAGE
THE PRIESTESS HAS TO BE A VIRGIN...
ドキドキ ドキ
BUT *NOW* THAT DOESN'T MATTER.
IT COULD HAPPEN AS EARLY AS TONIGHT...
ドキドキドキ…
BAM
BOK
BIFF
ARGH! WHAT AM I THINKING?! WE'VE GOT MORE URGENT THINGS TO THINK ABOUT!
BUT... IF THE CELESTIAL WARRIORS FIGHT WITHOUT THEIR POWERS...
...CAN THEY SURVIVE ?

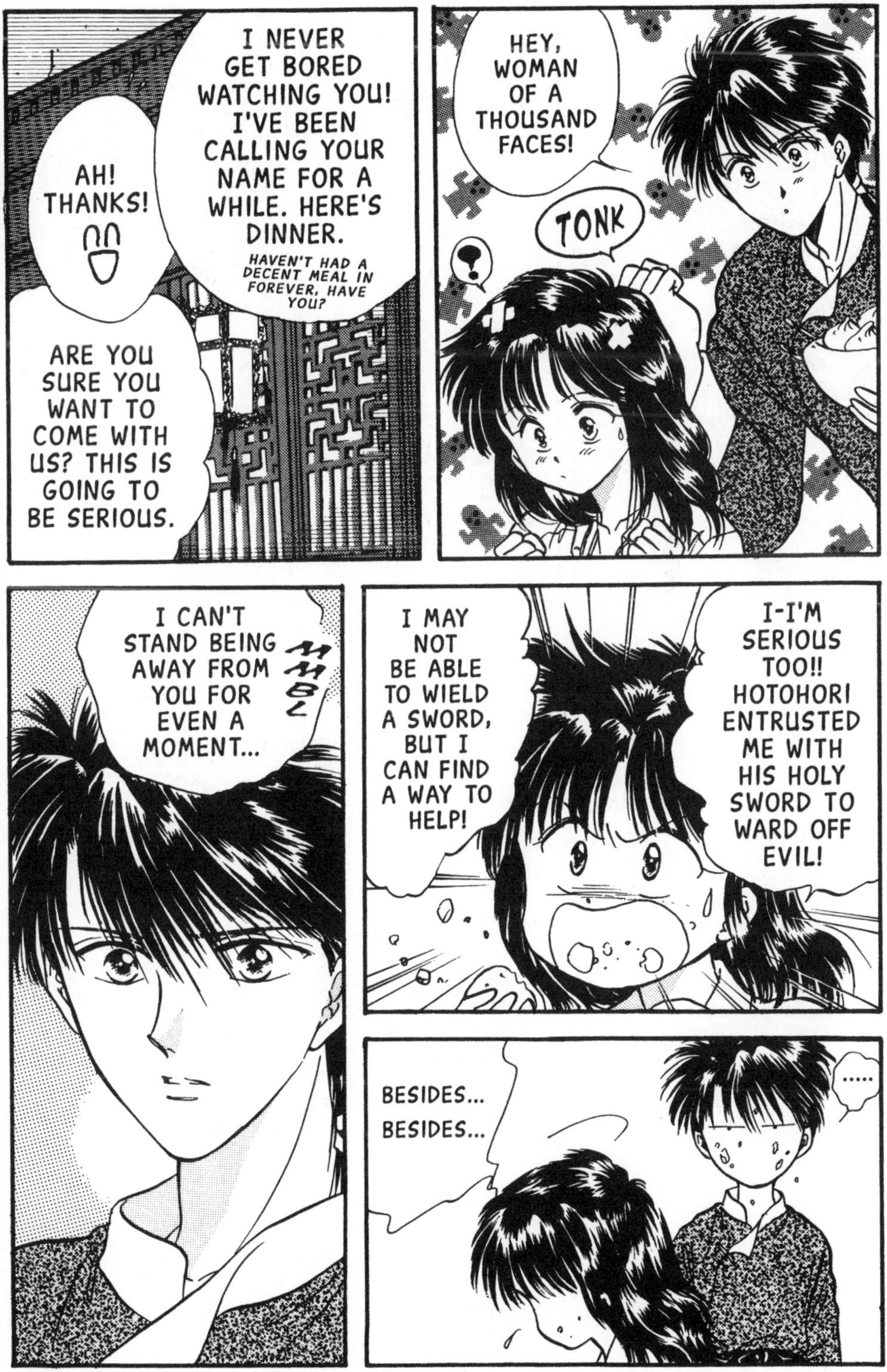
HEY, WOMAN OF A THOUSAND FACES!
TONK
!
I NEVER GET BORED WATCHING YOU! I'VE BEEN CALLING YOUR NAME FOR A WHILE. HERE'S DINNER.
HAVEN'T HAD A DECENT MEAL IN FOREVER, HAVE YOU?
AH! THANKS!
ARE YOU SURE YOU WANT TO COME WITH US? THIS IS GOING TO BE SERIOUS.
I-I'M SERIOUS TOO!! HOTOHORI ENTRUSTED ME WITH HIS HOLY SWORD TO WARD OFF EVIL!
I MAY NOT BE ABLE TO WIELD A SWORD, BUT I CAN FIND A WAY TO HELP!
.....
BESIDES... BESIDES...
I CAN'T STAND BEING AWAY FROM YOU FOR EVEN A MOMENT...
MMBL

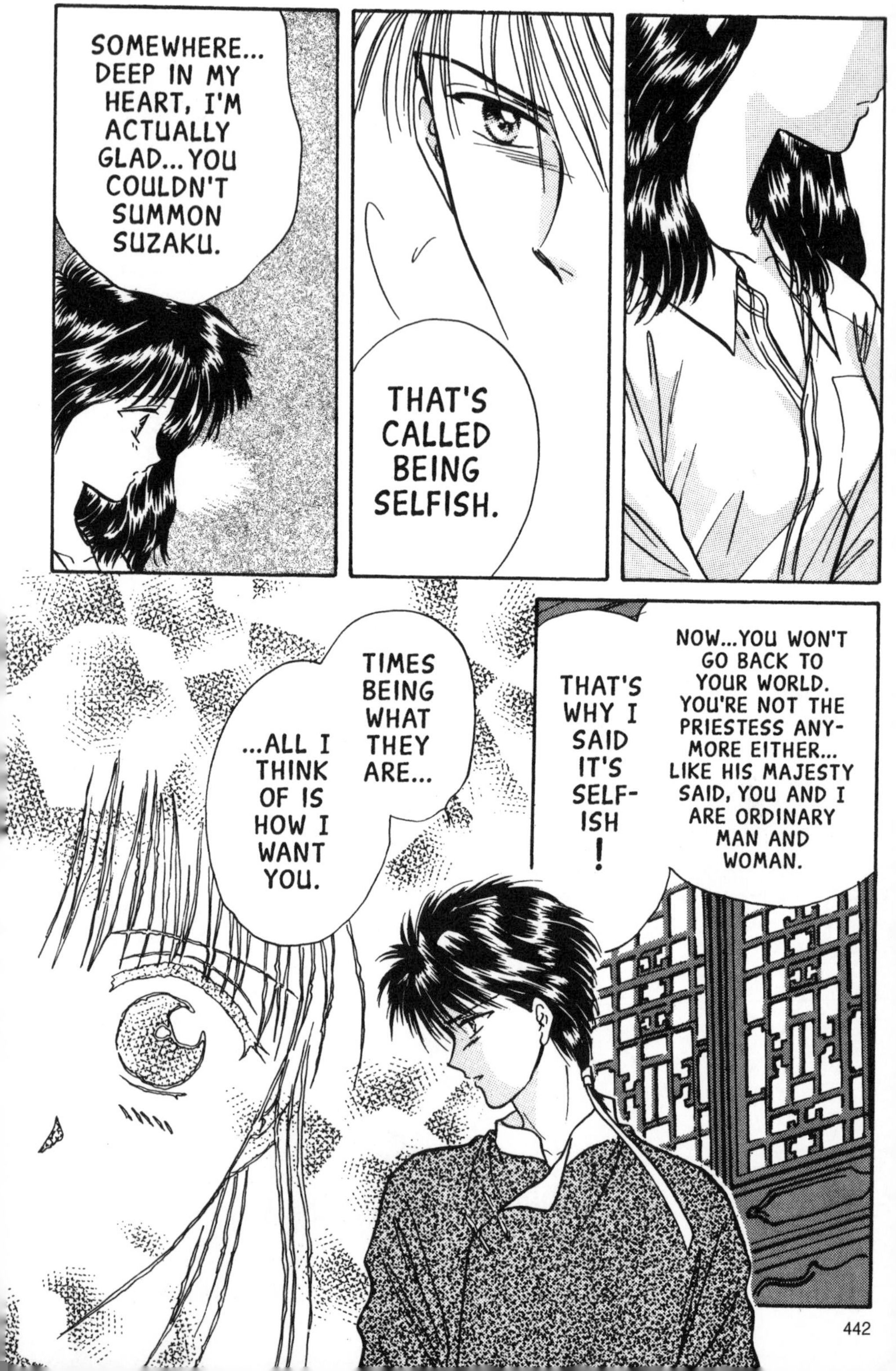
THAT'S CALLED BEING SELFISH.
SOMEWHERE... DEEP IN MY HEART, I'M ACTUALLY GLAD... YOU COULDN'T SUMMON SUZAKU.
NOW... YOU WON'T GO BACK TO YOUR WORLD. YOU'RE NOT THE PRIESTESS ANY-MORE EITHER... LIKE HIS MAJESTY SAID, YOU AND I ARE ORDINARY MAN AND WOMAN.
THAT'S WHY I SAID IT'S SELF-ISH!
TIMES BEING WHAT THEY ARE...
...ALL I THINK OF IS HOW I WANT YOU.

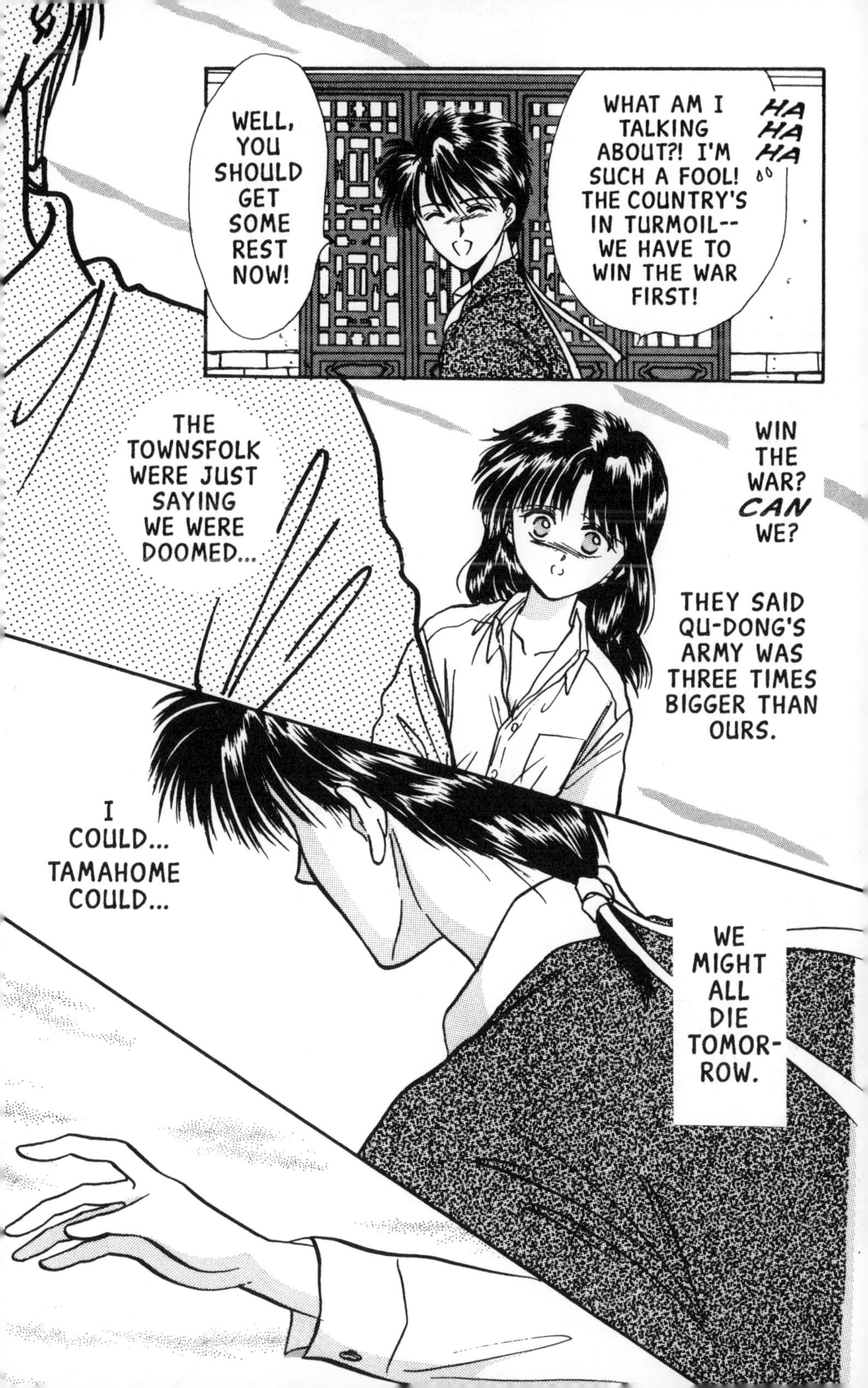
WHAT AM I TALKING ABOUT?! I'M SUCH A FOOL! THE COUNTRY'S IN TURMOIL-- WE HAVE TO WIN THE WAR FIRST!
HA HA HA
WELL, YOU SHOULD GET SOME REST NOW!
WIN THE WAR? CAN WE?
THE TOWNSFOLK WERE JUST SAYING WE WERE DOOMED...
THEY SAID QU-DONG'S ARMY WAS THREE TIMES BIGGER THAN OURS.
WE MIGHT ALL DIE TOMOR-ROW.
I COULD... TAMAHOME COULD...

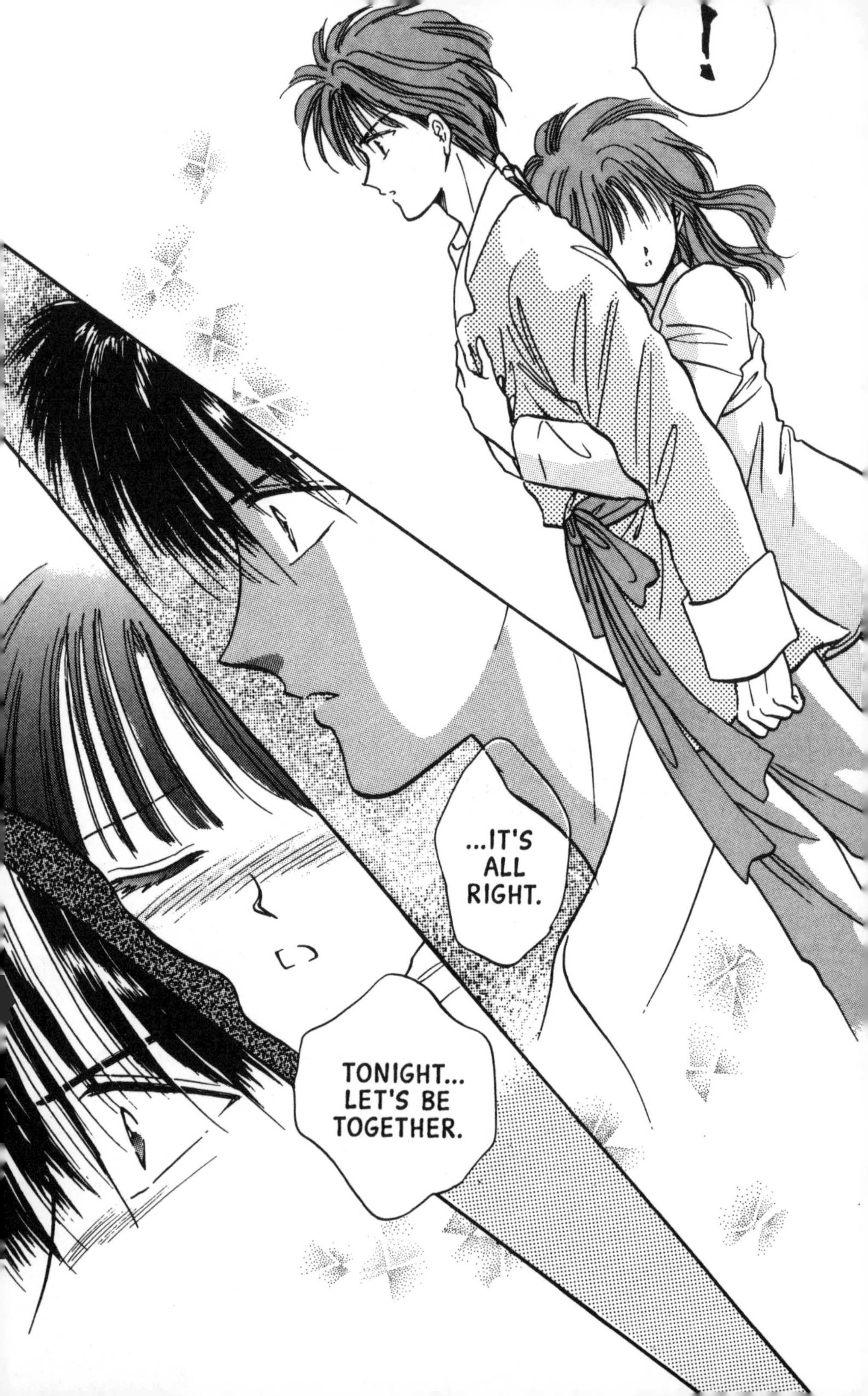
!
...IT'S ALL RIGHT.
TONIGHT... LET'S BE TOGETHER.

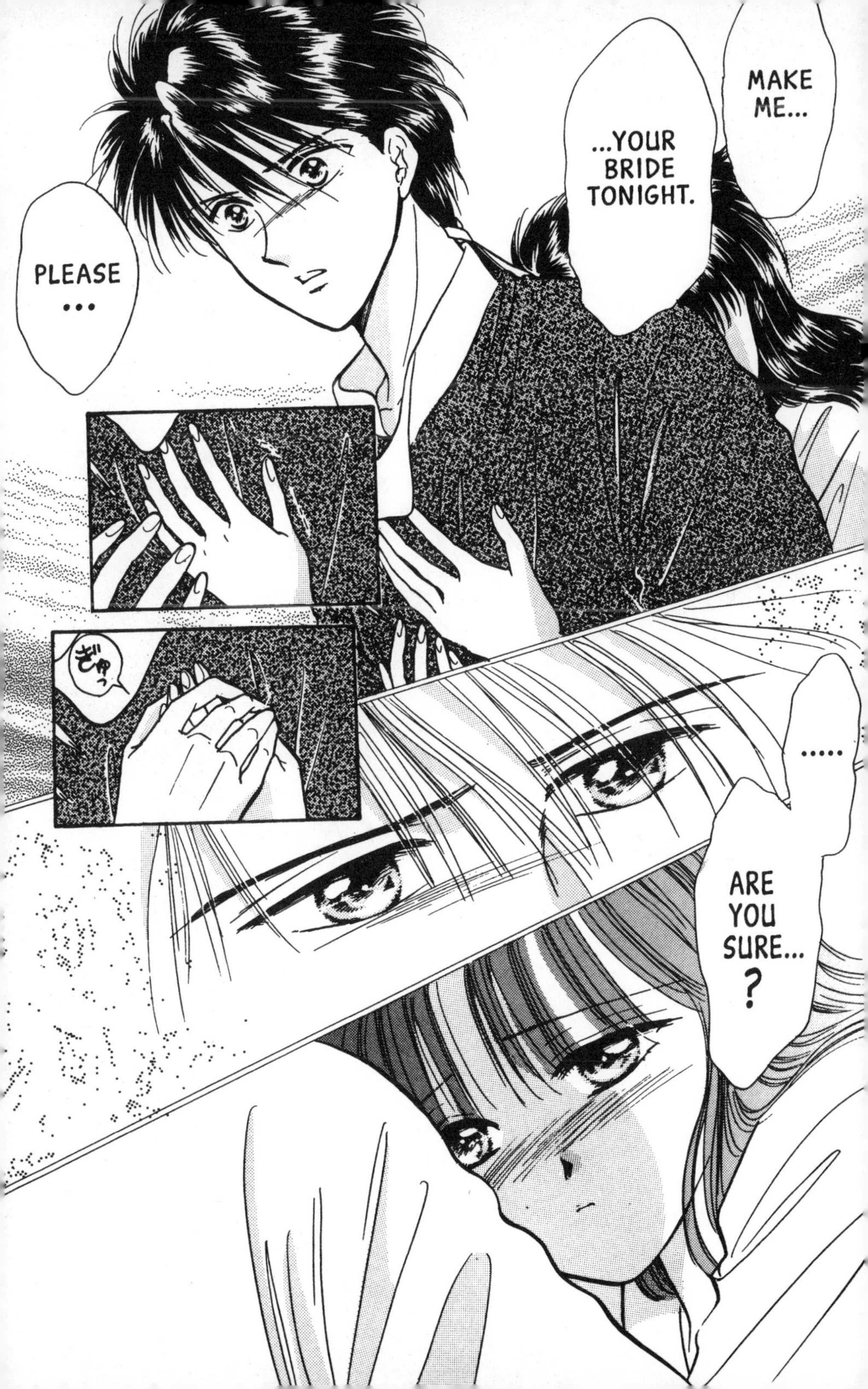
MAKE ME...
...YOUR BRIDE TONIGHT.
PLEASE ...
ぎゅっ
.....
ARE YOU SURE...?

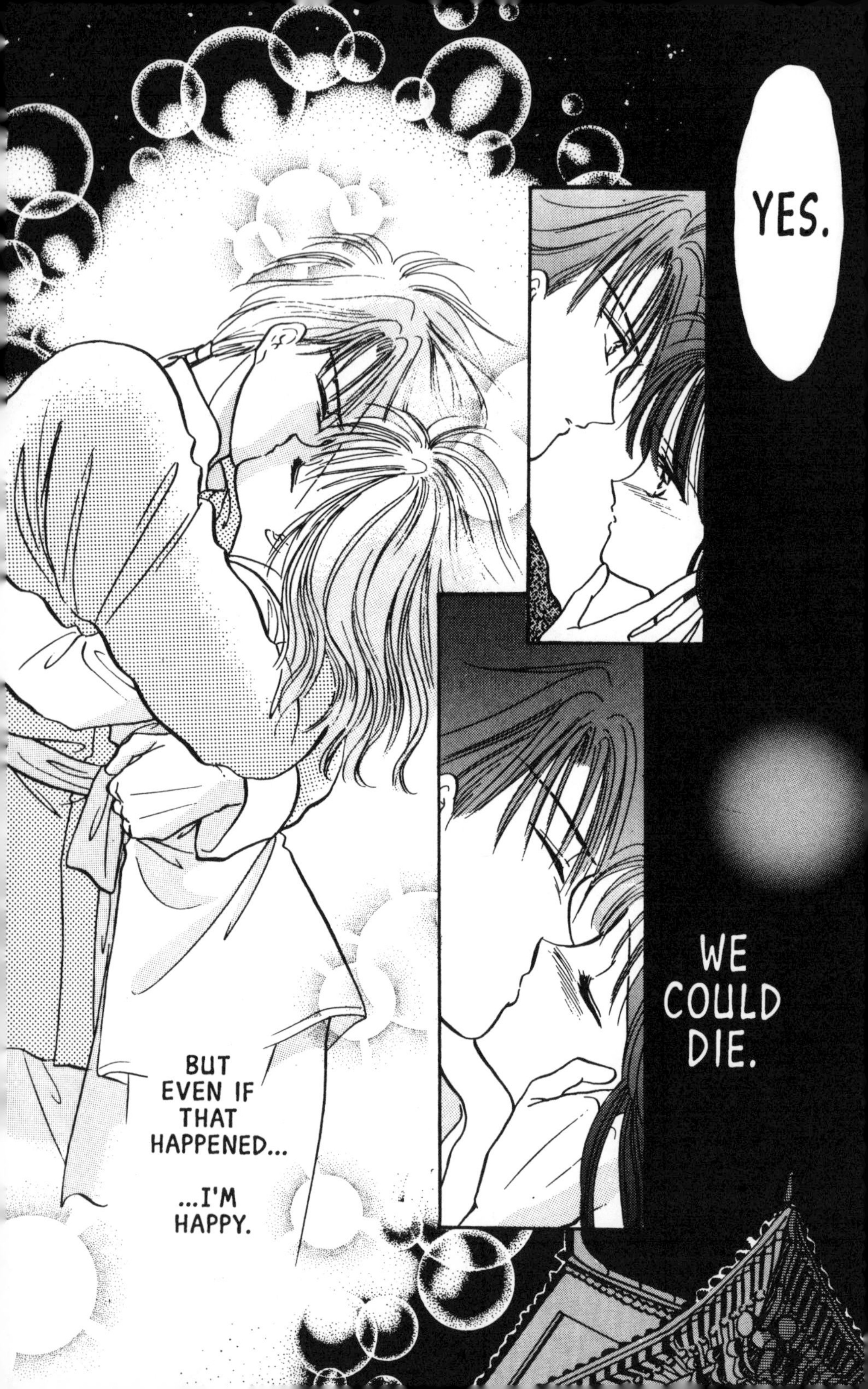
YES.
WE COULD DIE.
BUT EVEN IF THAT HAPPENED...
...I'M HAPPY.

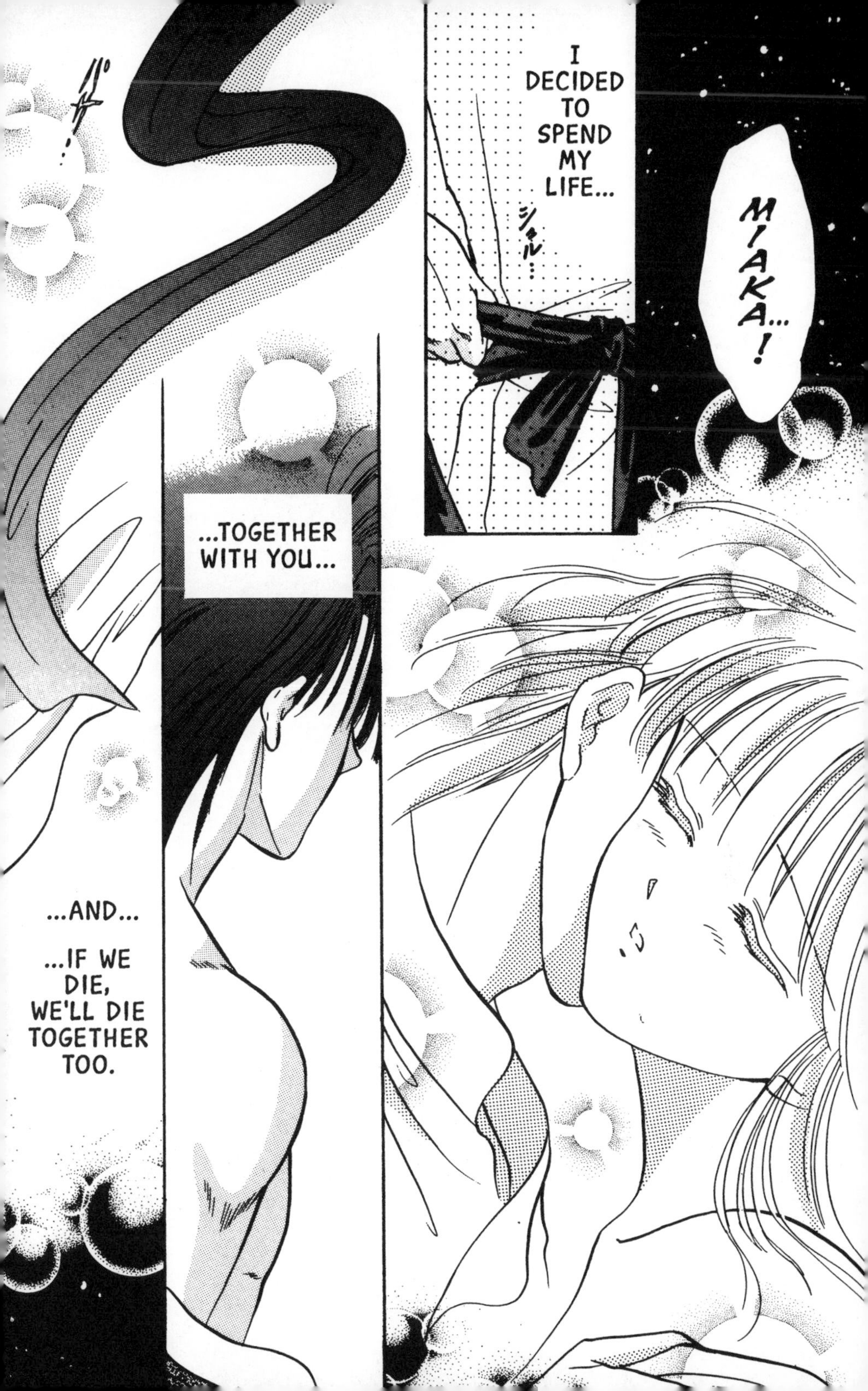
MIAKA...!
I DECIDED TO SPEND MY LIFE...
シュル…
...TOGETHER WITH YOU...
パサ…
...AND...
...IF WE DIE, WE'LL DIE TOGETHER TOO.

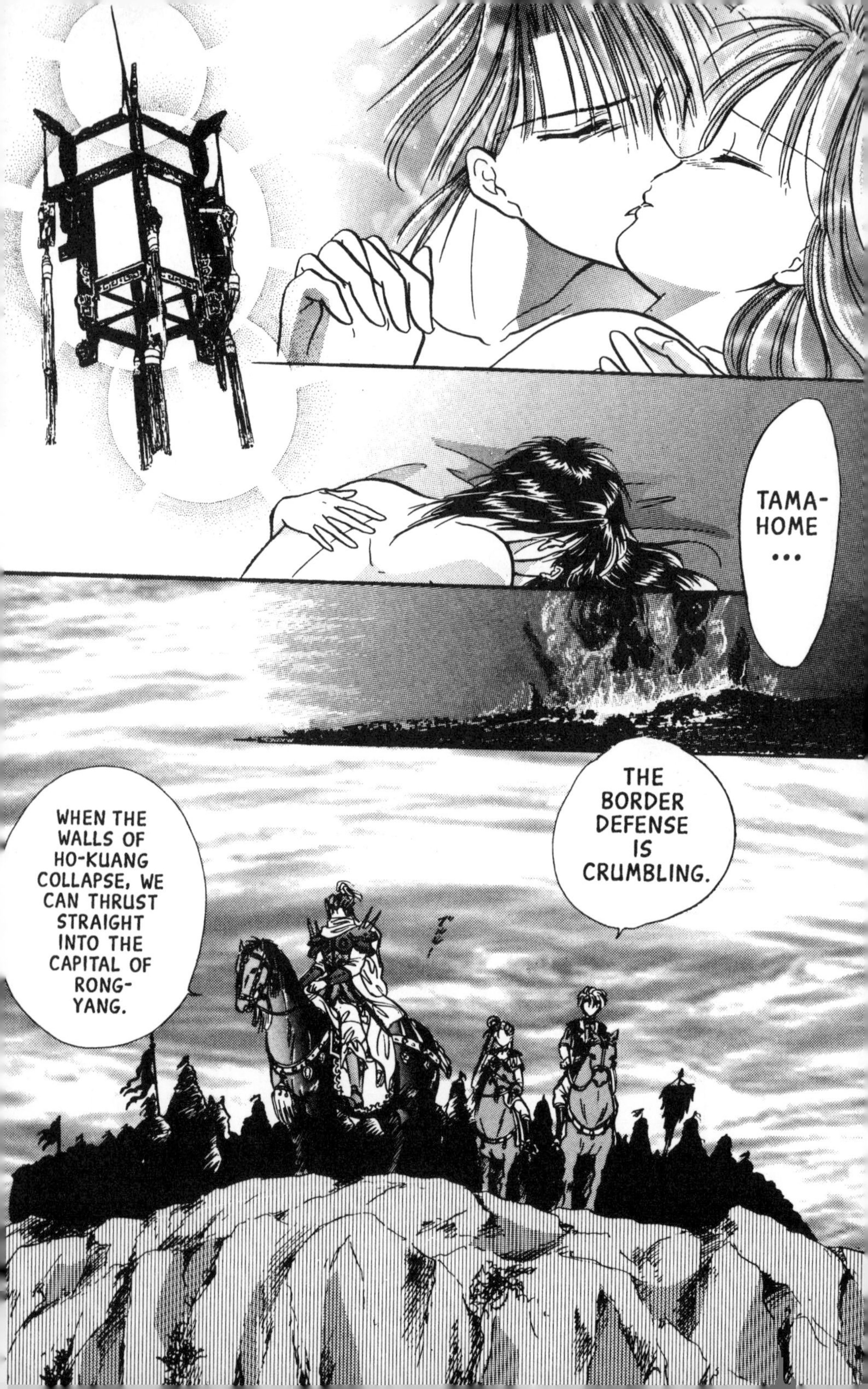
TAMA-HOME...
THE BORDER DEFENSE IS CRUMBLING.
WHEN THE WALLS OF HO-KUANG COLLAPSE, WE CAN THRUST STRAIGHT INTO THE CAPITAL OF RONG-YANG.

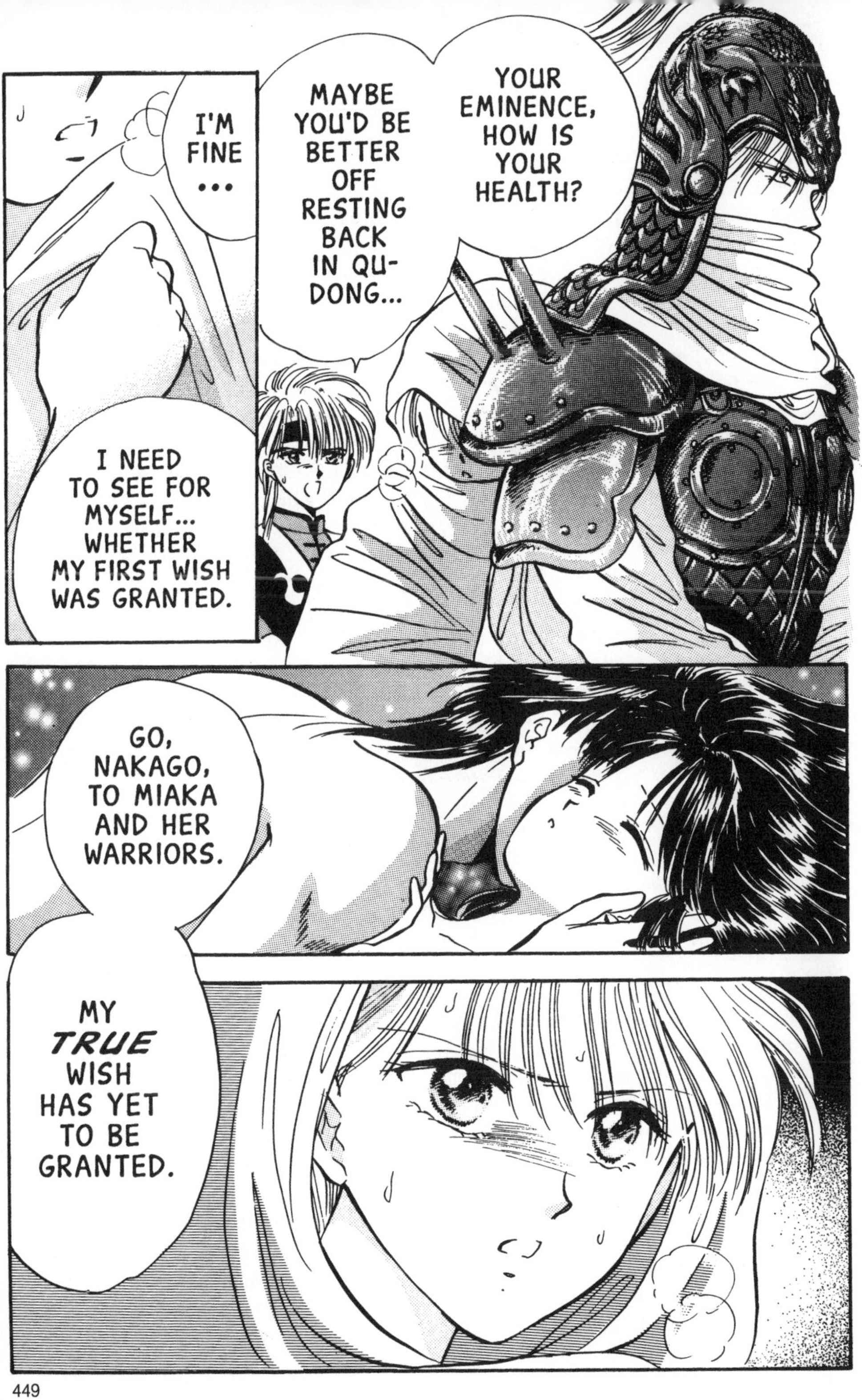
YOUR EMINENCE, HOW IS YOUR HEALTH?
MAYBE YOU'D BE BETTER OFF RESTING BACK IN QU-DONG...
I'M FINE...
I NEED TO SEE FOR MYSELF... WHETHER MY FIRST WISH WAS GRANTED.
GO, NAKAGO, TO MIAKA AND HER WARRIORS.
MY *TRUE* WISH HAS YET TO BE GRANTED.

FUSHIGI YŪGI "?"s PART 4

Q1: Are the celestial warriors' Chinese kanji (characters) always visible on their skin?

A: Not always. They show up when the warrior's chi is elevated. Once they're used to using their chi, they can make it appear by their own will. By the way, the colors for the celestial warriors' characters are also symbolic, Suzaku's being red and Seiryu's blue. Also, the font changed to *sōshotai* ("grass writing") after the warriors powered up. (I changed it 'cause it looks cool!)

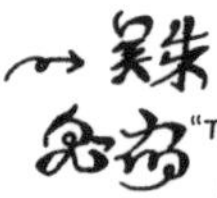

"MIAKA" LOOKS LIKE THIS.

"TAMAHOME" LOOKS LIKE THIS.

Q2: How does time pass for Miaka and Yui in the book? Are they growing up?

A: Time moves at the same rate for them as it does in the real world. Even if the characters in the book age over the course of many years, if it's only been a couple days in the real world, that's all that Miaka and Yui age. So having a change of clothes and underwear isn't that crucial for the girls, because in reality, they're only wearing their clothes for a couple days. So, "that time of the month" isn't an issue, either. If they'd spent a hundred years in the book, then maybe the day would come in the real world, but... Tamahome would be an old man by then.

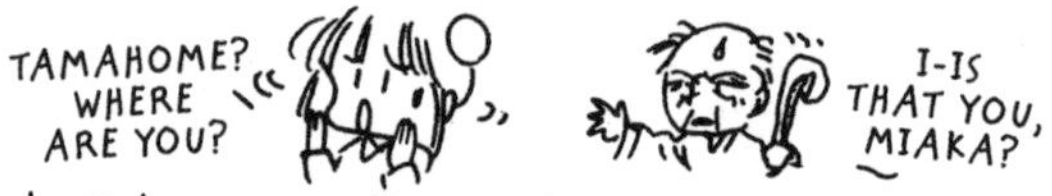
TAMAHOME? WHERE ARE YOU?
I-IS THAT YOU, MIAKA?

Q3: How is it that the celestial warriors all come from the same generation? Aren't there any who've died or ones that haven't been born yet?

A: It's destiny. (Quite simply.) There wouldn't be much point in them being so scattered over generations. The appearance of the Priestess would lose its significance. The Priestess and celestial warriors have a combined destiny.

Q4: Did Tasuki ever have a girlfriend?

A: No. His older sisters picked on him, so he left, yelling, "I'm outta here!" and became a woman-hating delinquent. But he has had experience with women. As a bandit, he had to "take the pressure off," and so he has been to the pleasure quarters with Knei-Gong.

Q5: Why doesn't Tai Yi-Jun show up on the Seiryu side?

A: Tai Yi-Jun (the Emperor of the Heavens) imparts wisdom to celestial warriors, but this isn't the case with the Seiryu because they've allied themselves with the demon worshipped by Nakago. Just as Tai Yi-Jun claimed, the beautiful Daichi-san Mountain only appears like a barren rocky bluff when the wicked see it. Those with negative chi cannot even discern the existence of Tai Yi-Jun. By the way, Tai Yi-Jun assumes the guise of an old woman for humans.

Q6: Warning from a Nuriko fan! Many of her drawings are missing her mole!!

A: The moles were lost in the printing process because they were so small. I made sure she always had one in the original art. Also, there's a typographical error for Suboshi (in the Japanese original) where the word "*masaka*" ("that can't be") was mistakenly spelled "mamaka." This occurred in the layout process -- I wrote them correctly in the original. So please let those slide.

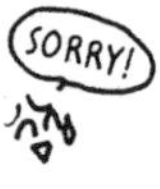
SORRY!

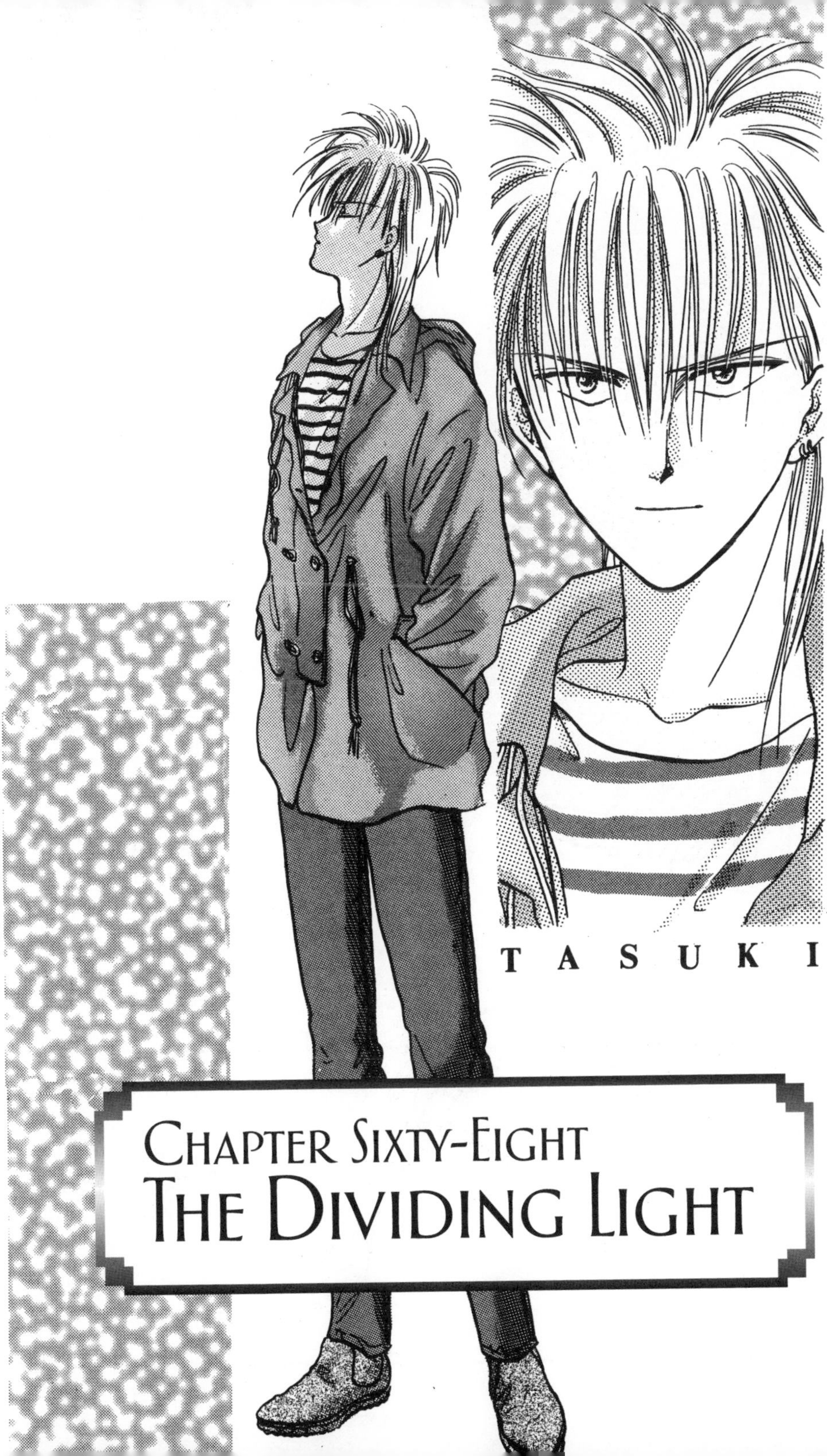
TASUKI

Chapter Sixty-Eight
The Dividing Light

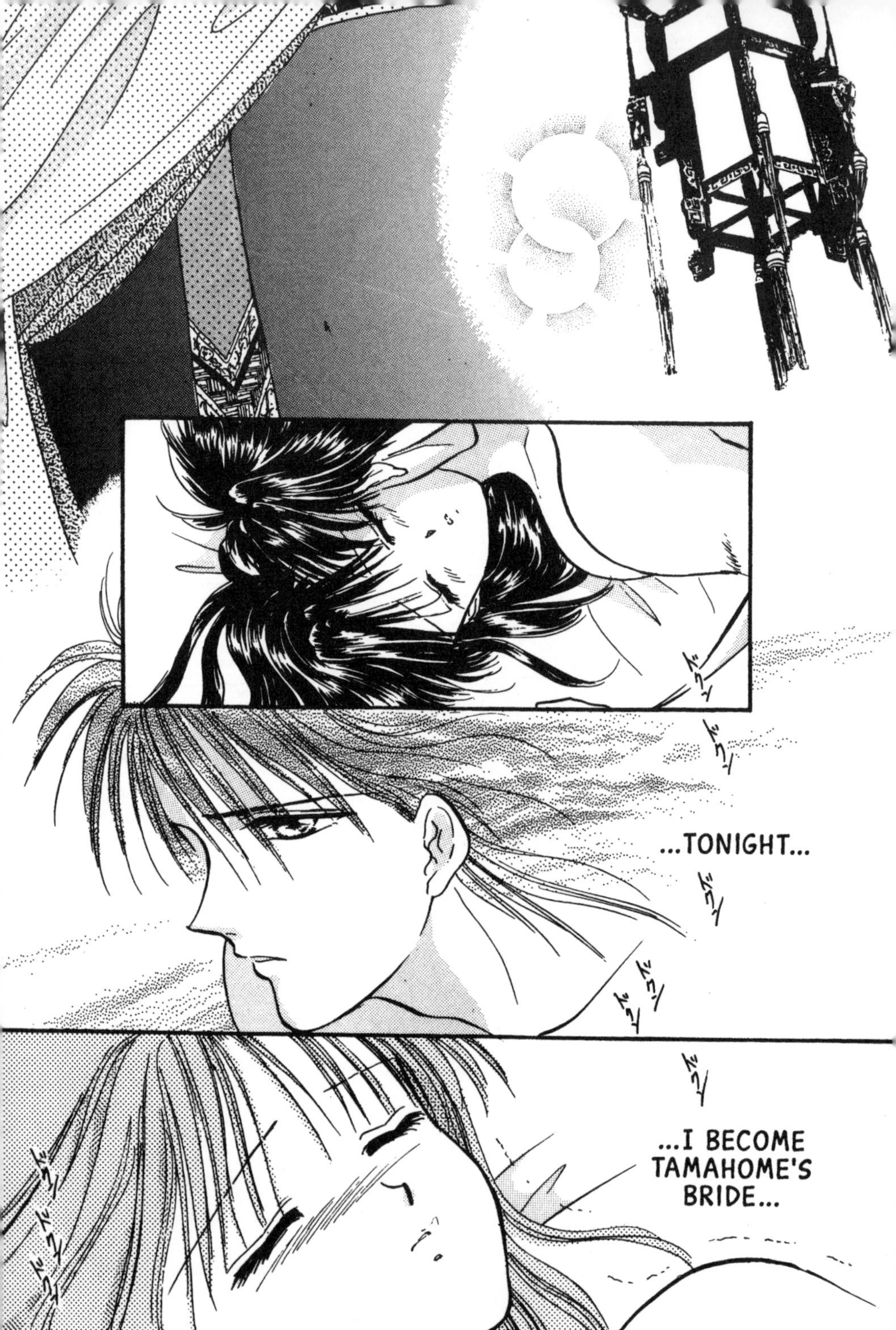

...TONIGHT...
...I BECOME TAMAHOME'S BRIDE...

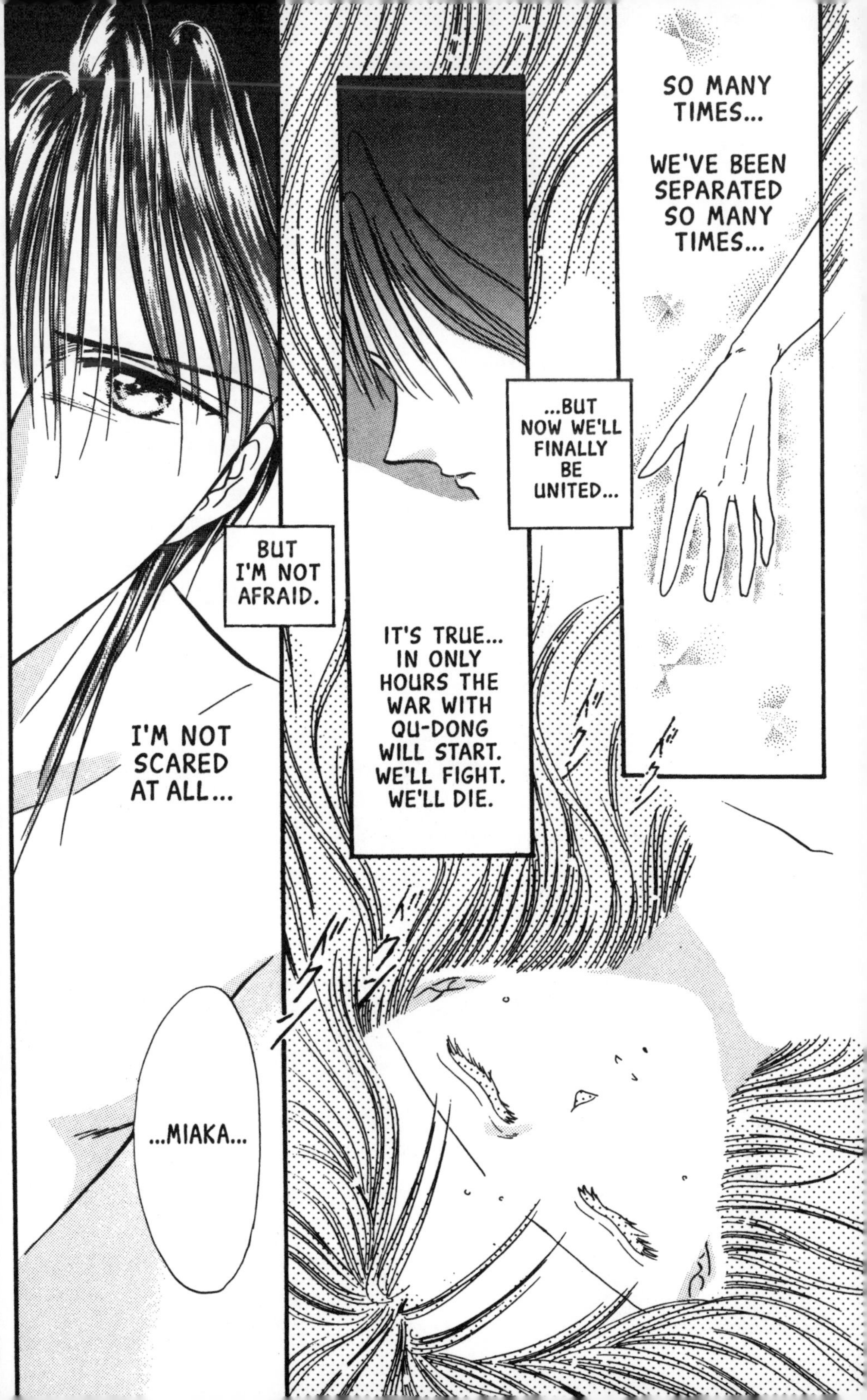
SO MANY TIMES...
WE'VE BEEN SEPARATED SO MANY TIMES...
...BUT NOW WE'LL FINALLY BE UNITED...
IT'S TRUE... IN ONLY HOURS THE WAR WITH QU-DONG WILL START. WE'LL FIGHT. WE'LL DIE.
BUT I'M NOT AFRAID.
I'M NOT SCARED AT ALL...
...MIAKA...

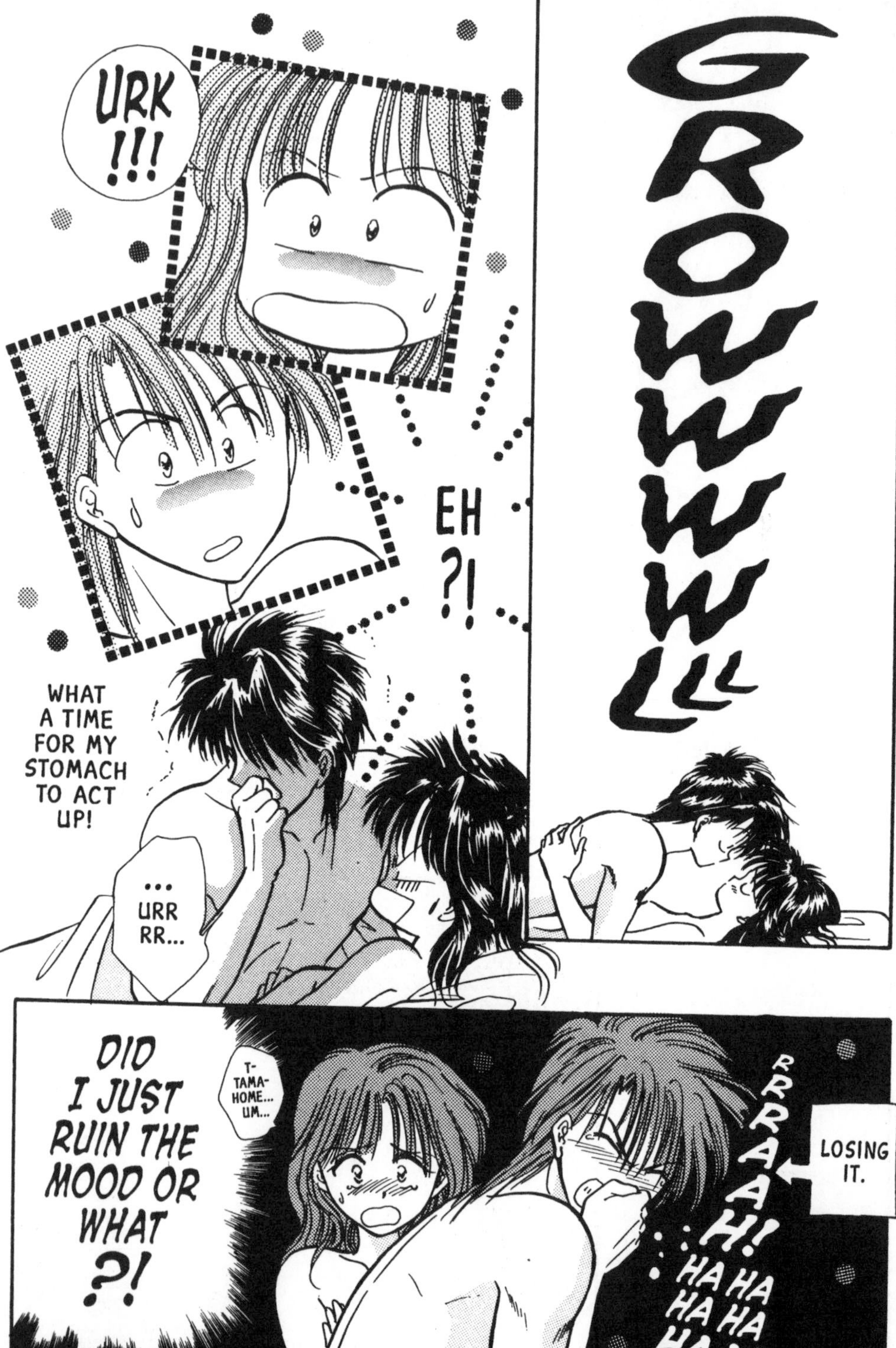
GROWWWWL
URK!!!
EH?!
WHAT A TIME FOR MY STOMACH TO ACT UP!
...URRRR...
LOSING IT.
RRRAAAH! HA HA HA HA HAA!
T-TAMAHOME... UM...
DID I JUST RUIN THE MOOD OR WHAT?!

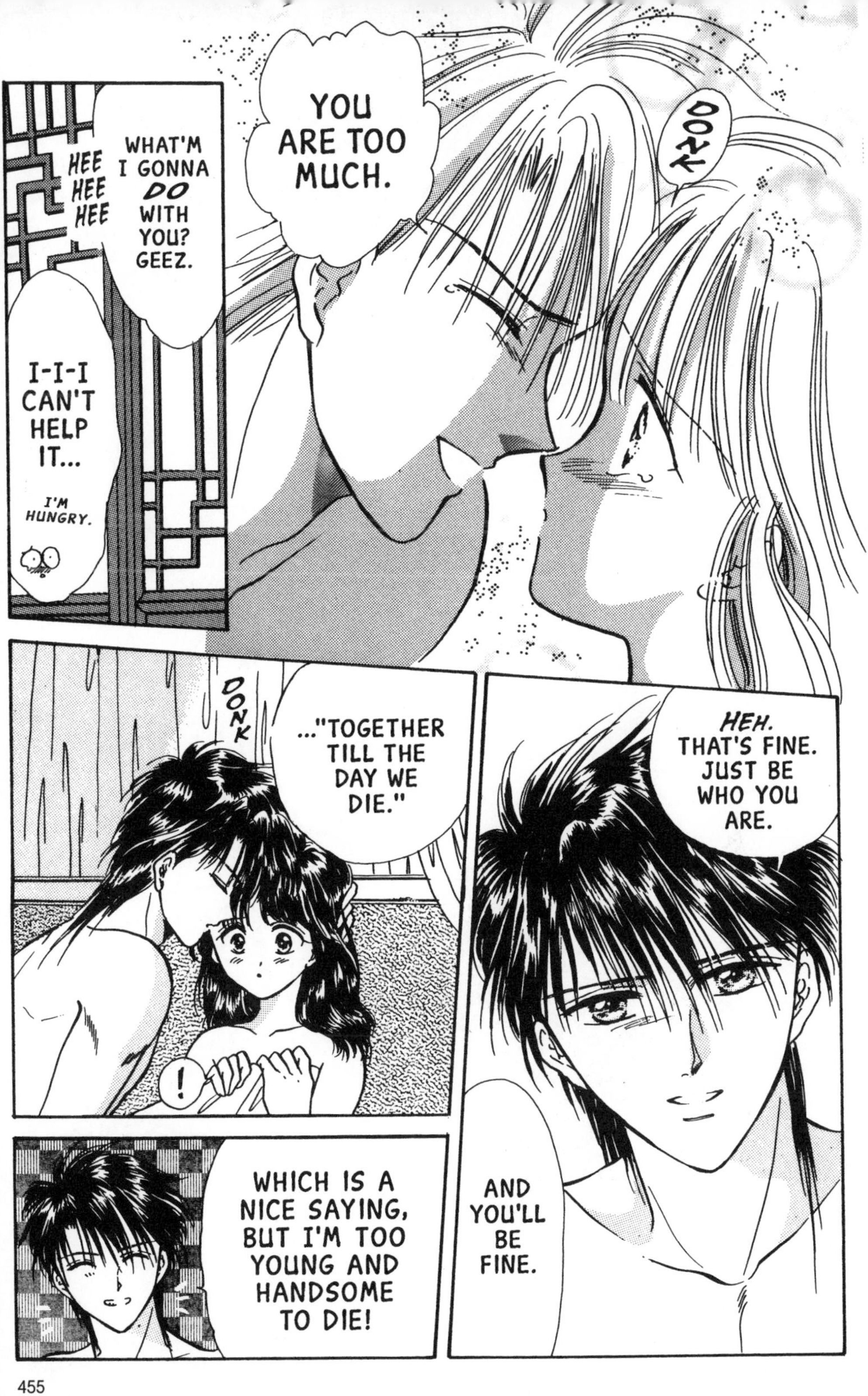
DONK
YOU ARE TOO MUCH.
WHAT'M I GONNA DO WITH YOU? GEEZ.
HEE HEE HEE
I-I-I CAN'T HELP IT...
I'M HUNGRY.
HEH. THAT'S FINE. JUST BE WHO YOU ARE.
AND YOU'LL BE FINE.
DONK
..."TOGETHER TILL THE DAY WE DIE."
!
WHICH IS A NICE SAYING, BUT I'M TOO YOUNG AND HANDSOME TO DIE!

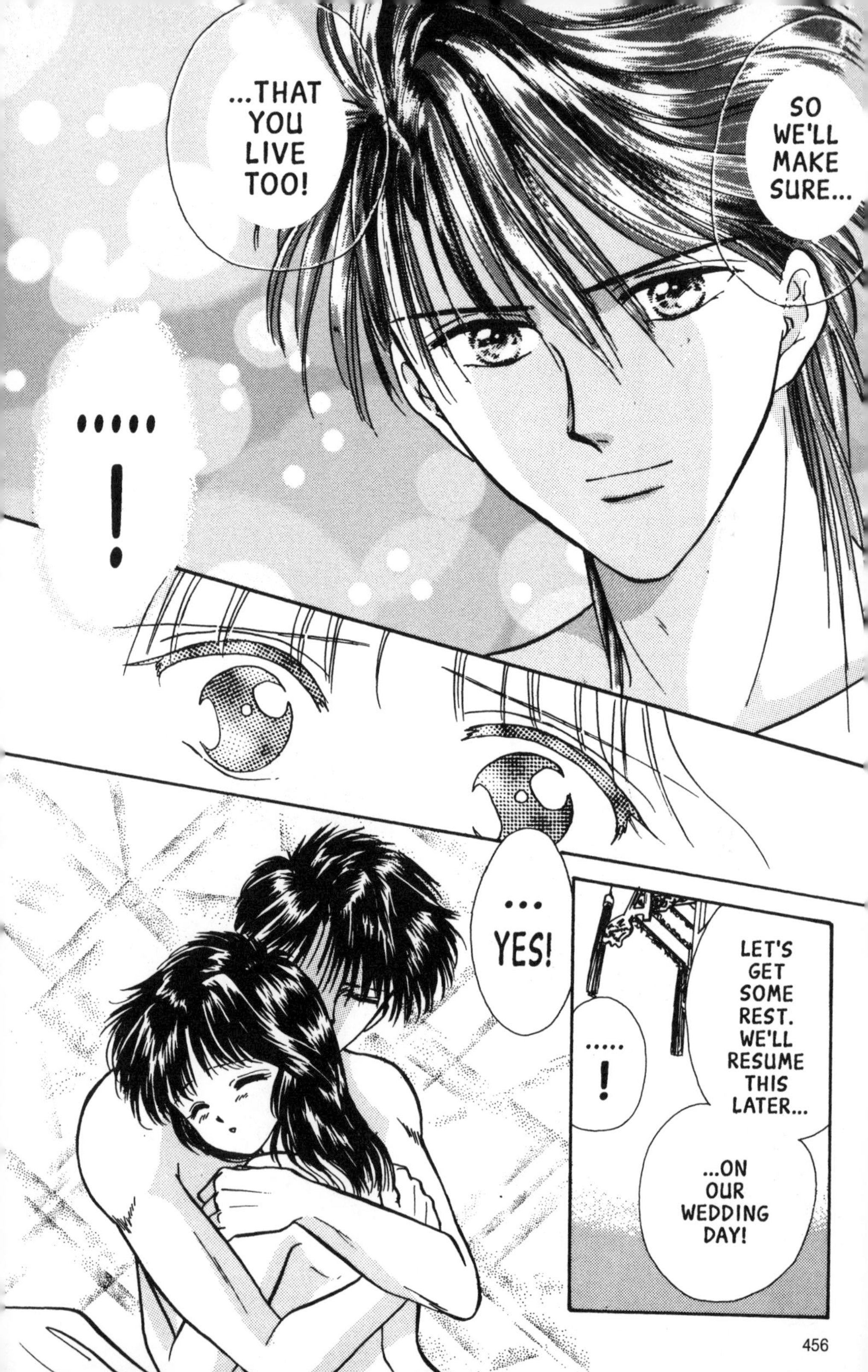
SO WE'LL MAKE SURE...
...THAT YOU LIVE TOO!
.....!
LET'S GET SOME REST. WE'LL RESUME THIS LATER...
...ON OUR WEDDING DAY!
.....!
... YES!

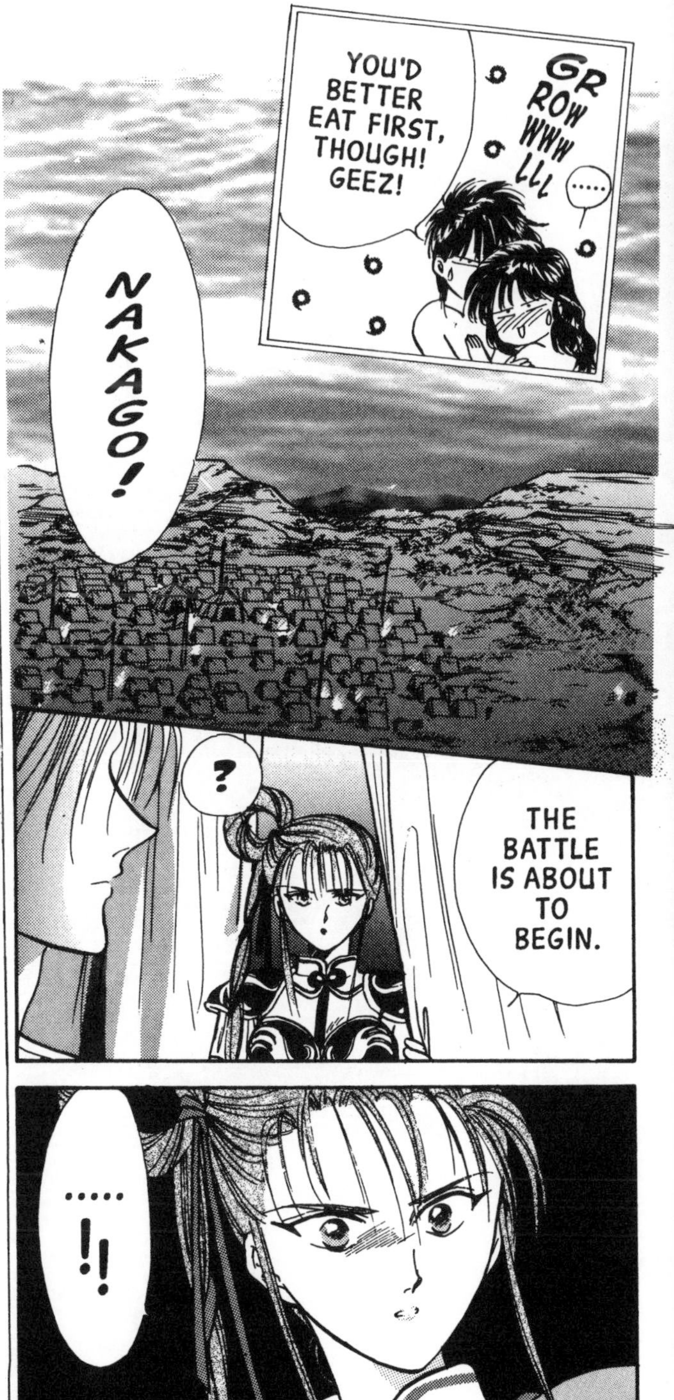
GRROWWWWLLL
YOU'D BETTER EAT FIRST, THOUGH! GEEZ!
.....
NAKAGO!
THE BATTLE IS ABOUT TO BEGIN.
?
.....
!!

But it turns out Amiboshi was having second thoughts during the ceremony. When Amiboshi and Miaka met the second time, and the village was attacked, he used his chi and his flute to annihilate the Qu-Dong soldiers and protect Miaka. He could have used that power at the ceremony, but he didn't. I also don't think his feelings for Miaka are romantic. *I think.* It's just that both of them are caring in the same way... He must have really been moved by what Miaka said to him right before he fell into the river. You know, that weird phase you go through right before falling in love? I think that's what it felt like for him.
By the way, he holds the flute in his left hand when he releases his chi. But when he plays it normally, it's in his right hand. He's ambidextrous.

Suboshi is identical to Amiboshi. *They're twins.* But Suboshi can rub some people the wrong way. He has an extreme personality. *He's too loyal!* He's a nice kid who'll fight to the death with anyone who threatens or attacks his older brother. He started out being a caring brother, but now, his feelings could almost be considered incestuous... Well, there's only an element of that, so I guess it's all right. *Of course it's not!* Suboshi's the only extreme one. Amiboshi's normal after all.
It's true that Suboshi has a crush on Yui. They're actually the same age, but Yui is mentally more mature...
I don't know how I came up with the idea that Suboshi and Amiboshi would be twins. They're exactly identical, but some readers have claimed, "I can see the difference in their eyes and their aura." That's true. Suboshi does have a look that's entirely absent from Amiboshi.
A difference in personality.
In any case, the illustration in volume 10 caused quite a stir...
I didn't mean it to be so sexual...

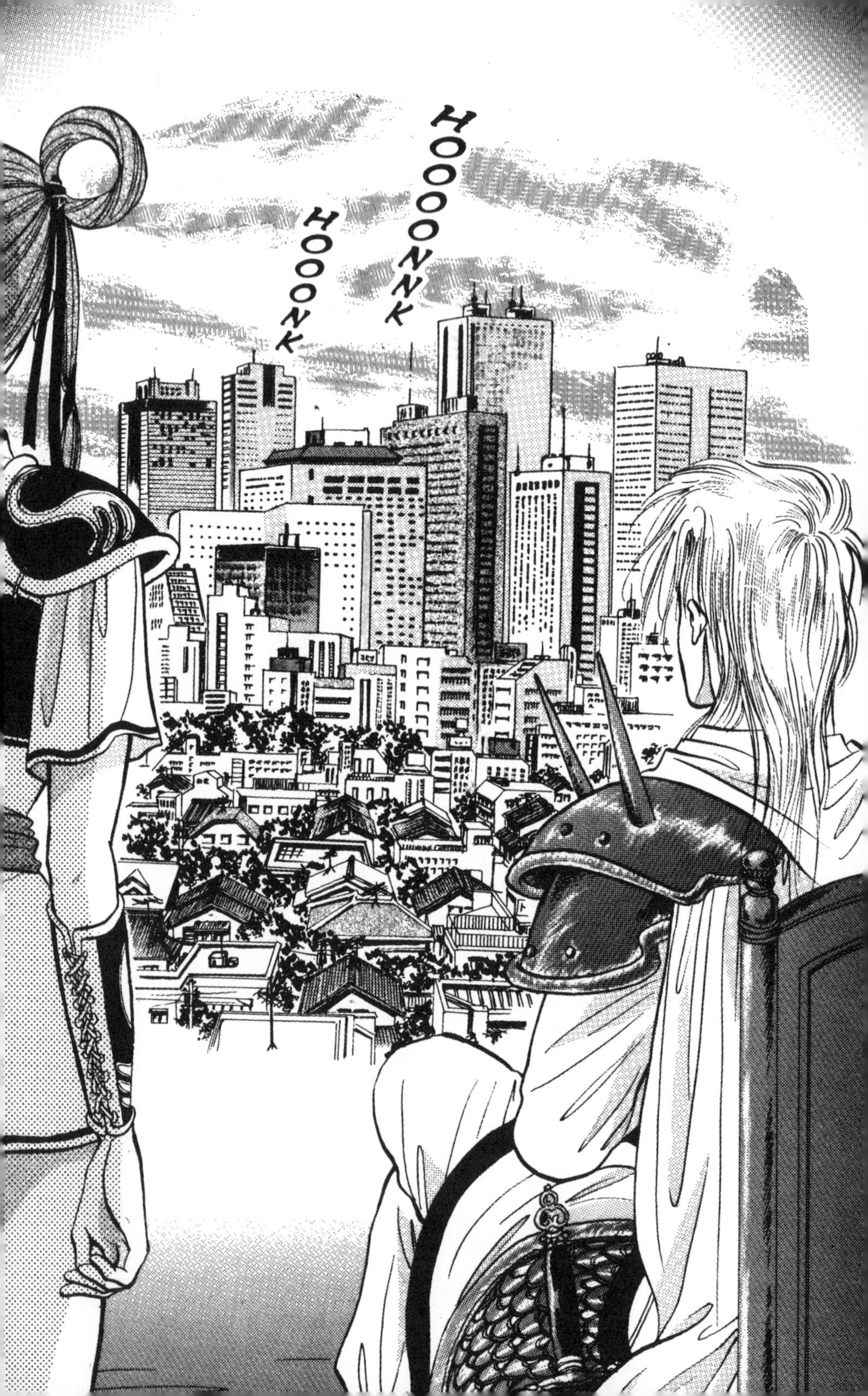
HOOOOONNK
HOOOONK

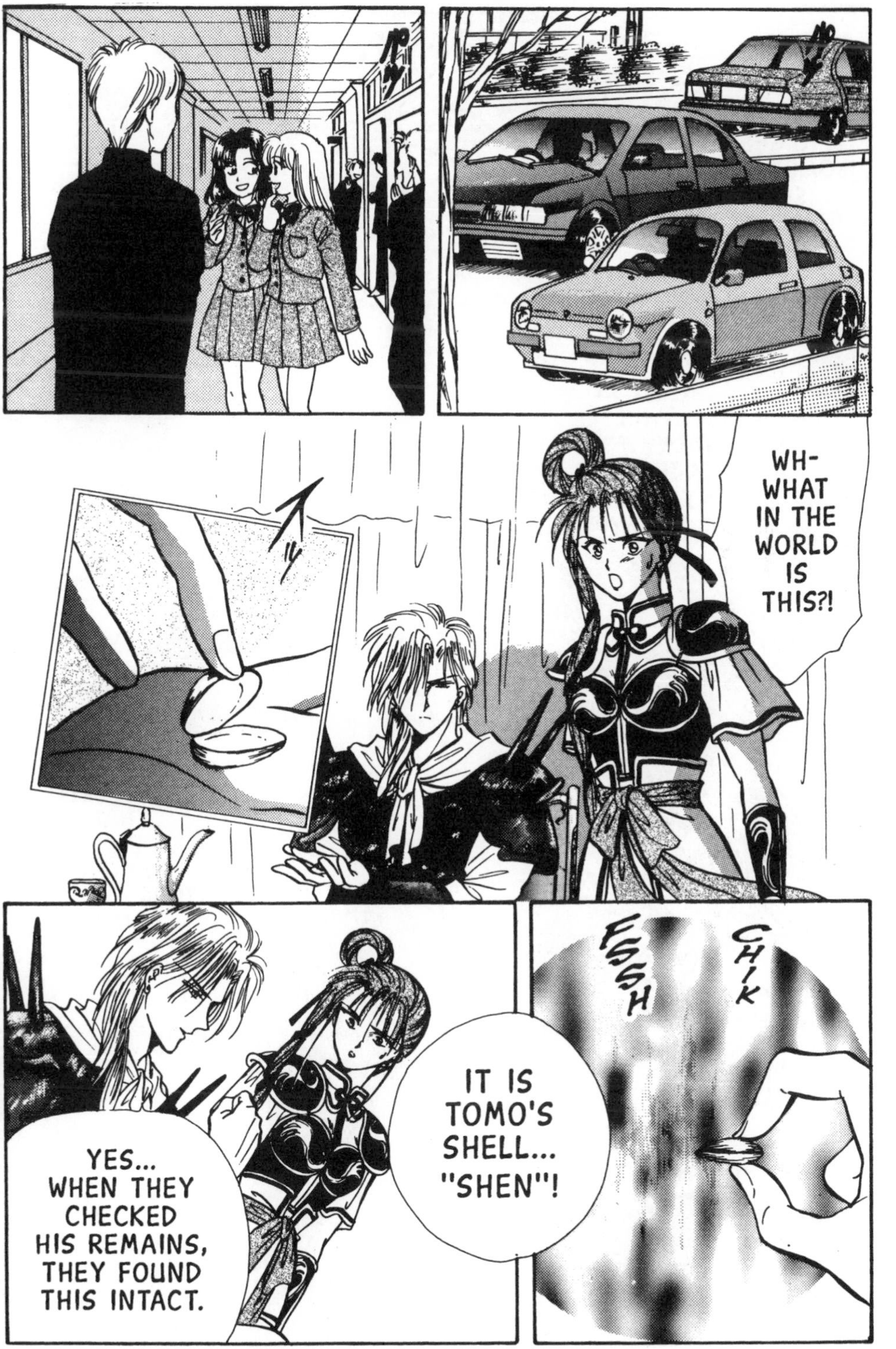
WH- WHAT IN THE WORLD IS THIS?!
CHIK
FSSH
IT IS TOMO'S SHELL... "SHEN"!
YES... WHEN THEY CHECKED HIS REMAINS, THEY FOUND THIS INTACT.

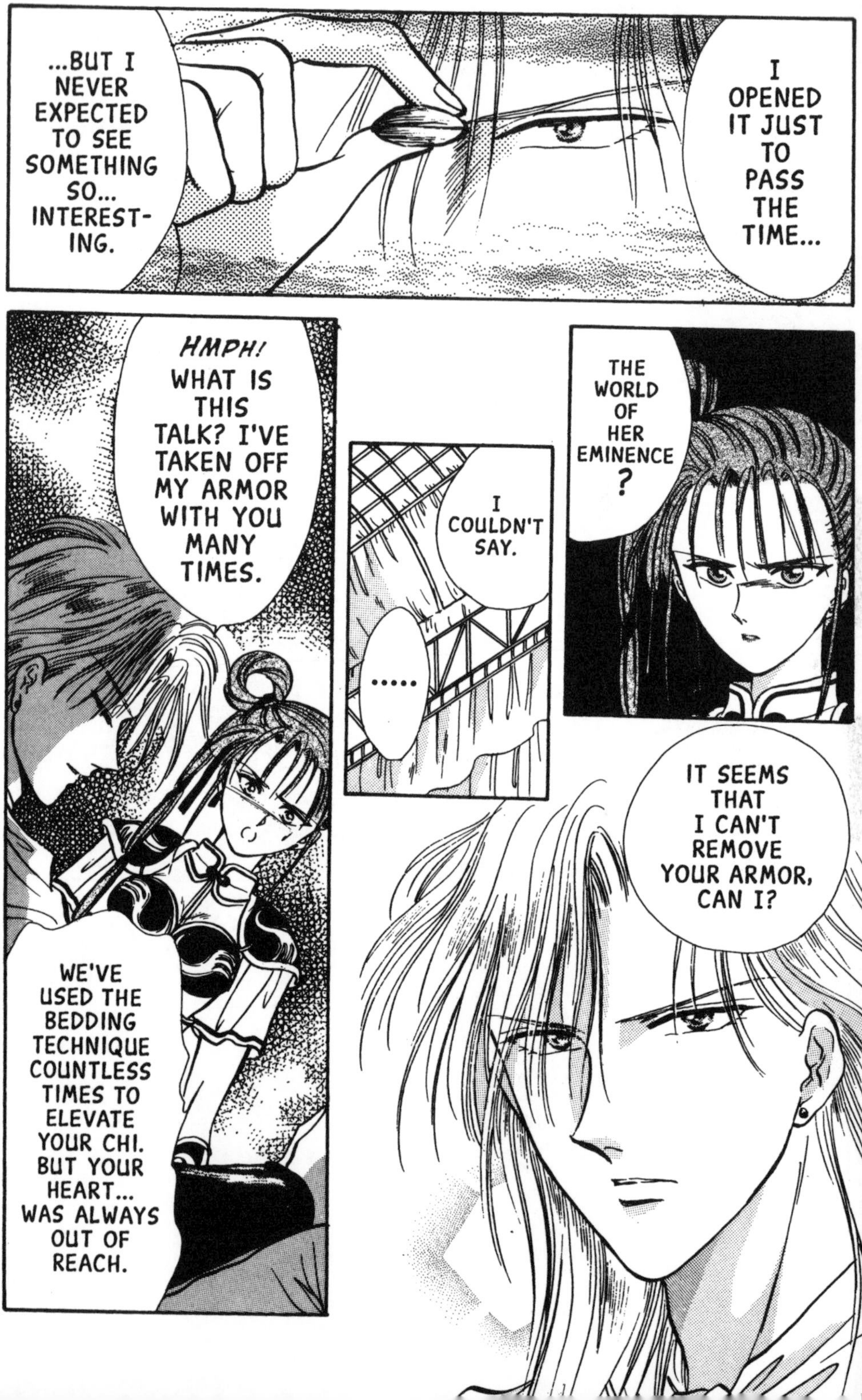
I OPENED IT JUST TO PASS THE TIME...
...BUT I NEVER EXPECTED TO SEE SOMETHING SO... INTEREST-ING.
THE WORLD OF HER EMINENCE?
I COULDN'T SAY.
......
IT SEEMS THAT I CAN'T REMOVE YOUR ARMOR, CAN I?
HMPH! WHAT IS THIS TALK? I'VE TAKEN OFF MY ARMOR WITH YOU MANY TIMES.
WE'VE USED THE BEDDING TECHNIQUE COUNTLESS TIMES TO ELEVATE YOUR CHI. BUT YOUR HEART... WAS ALWAYS OUT OF REACH.

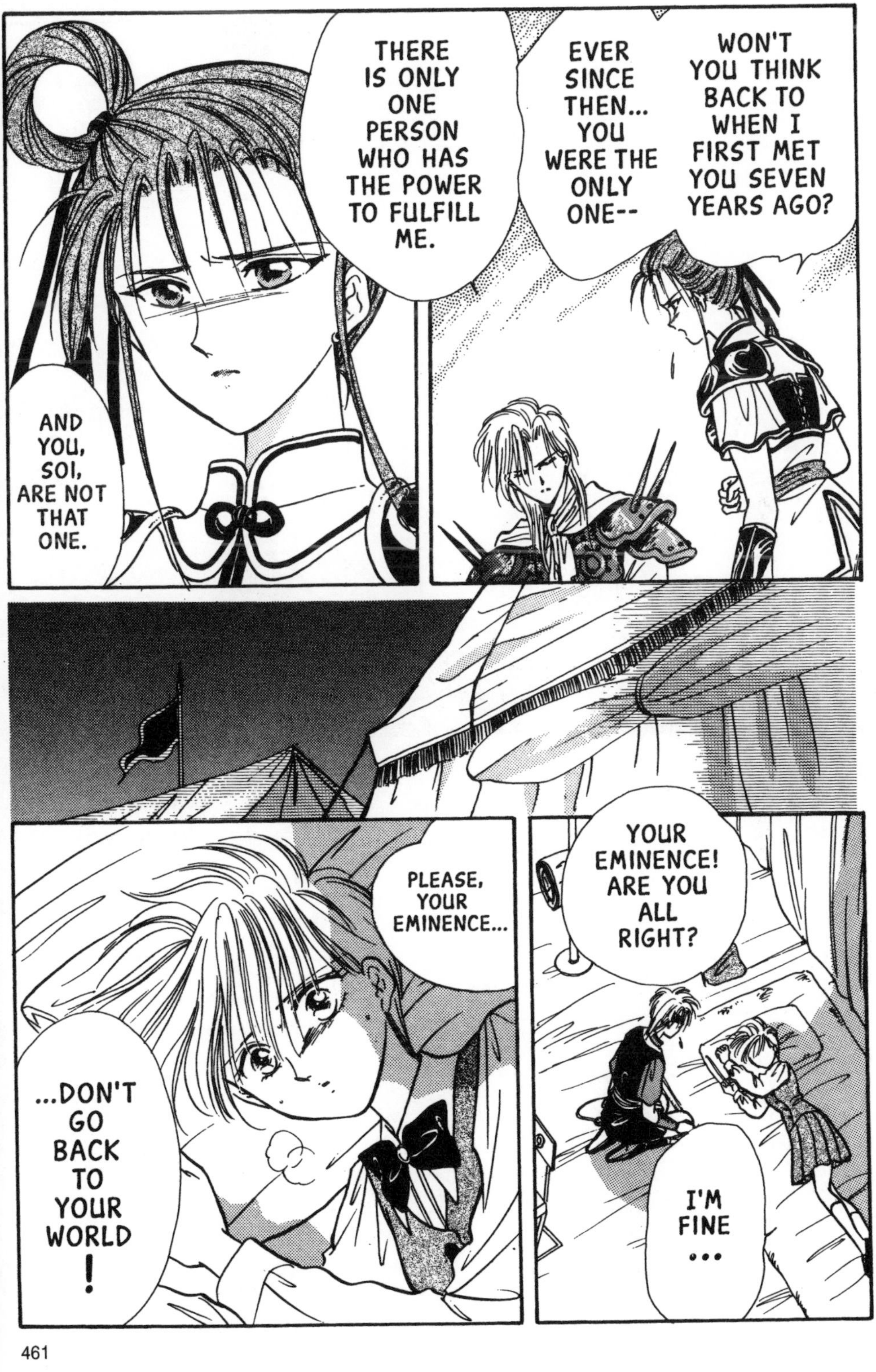
WON'T YOU THINK BACK TO WHEN I FIRST MET YOU SEVEN YEARS AGO?
EVER SINCE THEN... YOU WERE THE ONLY ONE--
THERE IS ONLY ONE PERSON WHO HAS THE POWER TO FULFILL ME.
AND YOU, SOI, ARE NOT THAT ONE.
YOUR EMINENCE! ARE YOU ALL RIGHT?
I'M FINE...
PLEASE, YOUR EMINENCE...
...DON'T GO BACK TO YOUR WORLD!

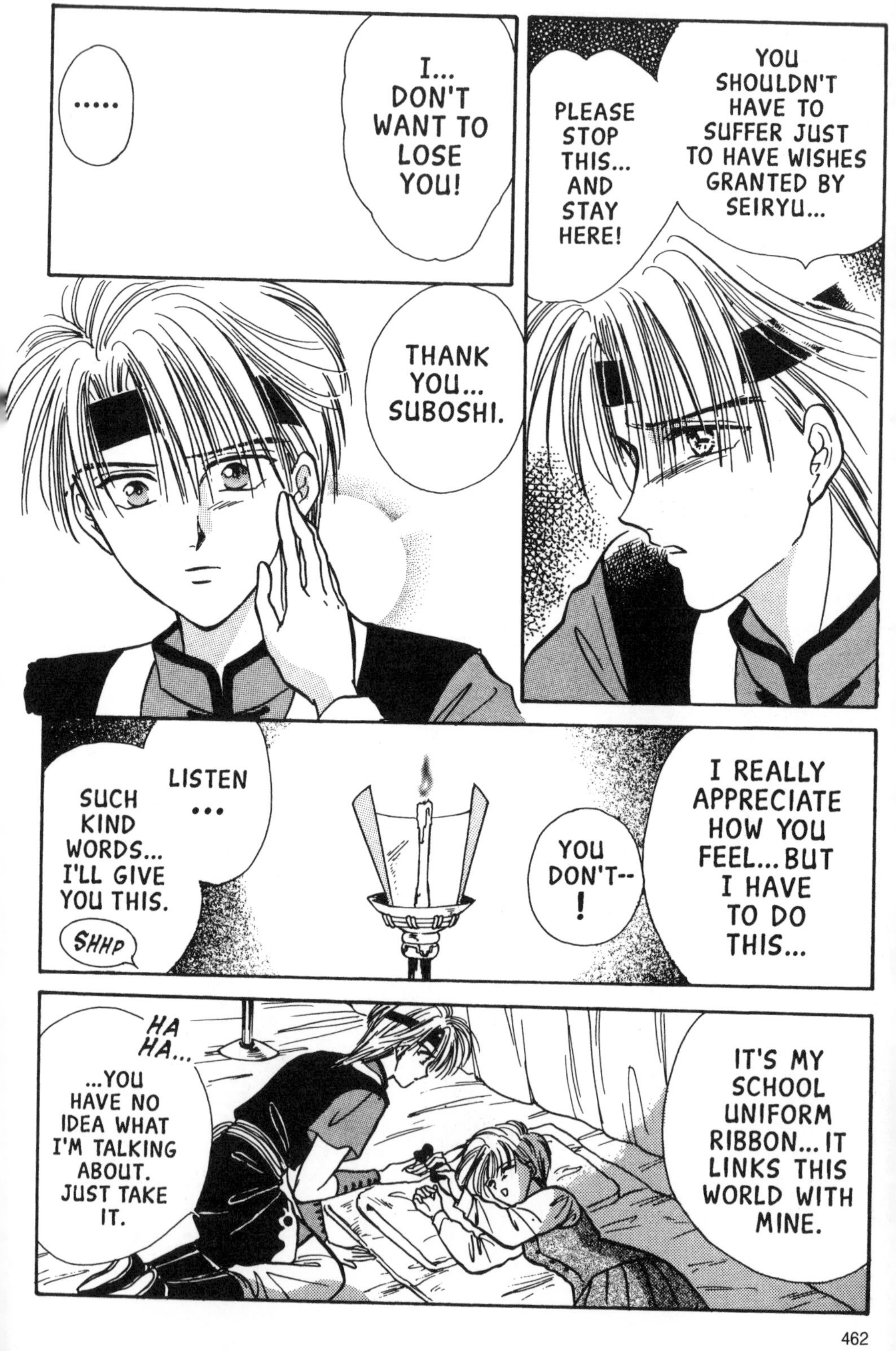
YOU SHOULDN'T HAVE TO SUFFER JUST TO HAVE WISHES GRANTED BY SEIRYU...
PLEASE STOP THIS... AND STAY HERE!
I... DON'T WANT TO LOSE YOU!
......
THANK YOU... SUBOSHI.
I REALLY APPRECIATE HOW YOU FEEL... BUT I HAVE TO DO THIS...
YOU DON'T--!
LISTEN...
SUCH KIND WORDS... I'LL GIVE YOU THIS.
SHHP
IT'S MY SCHOOL UNIFORM RIBBON... IT LINKS THIS WORLD WITH MINE.
HA HA...
...YOU HAVE NO IDEA WHAT I'M TALKING ABOUT. JUST TAKE IT.

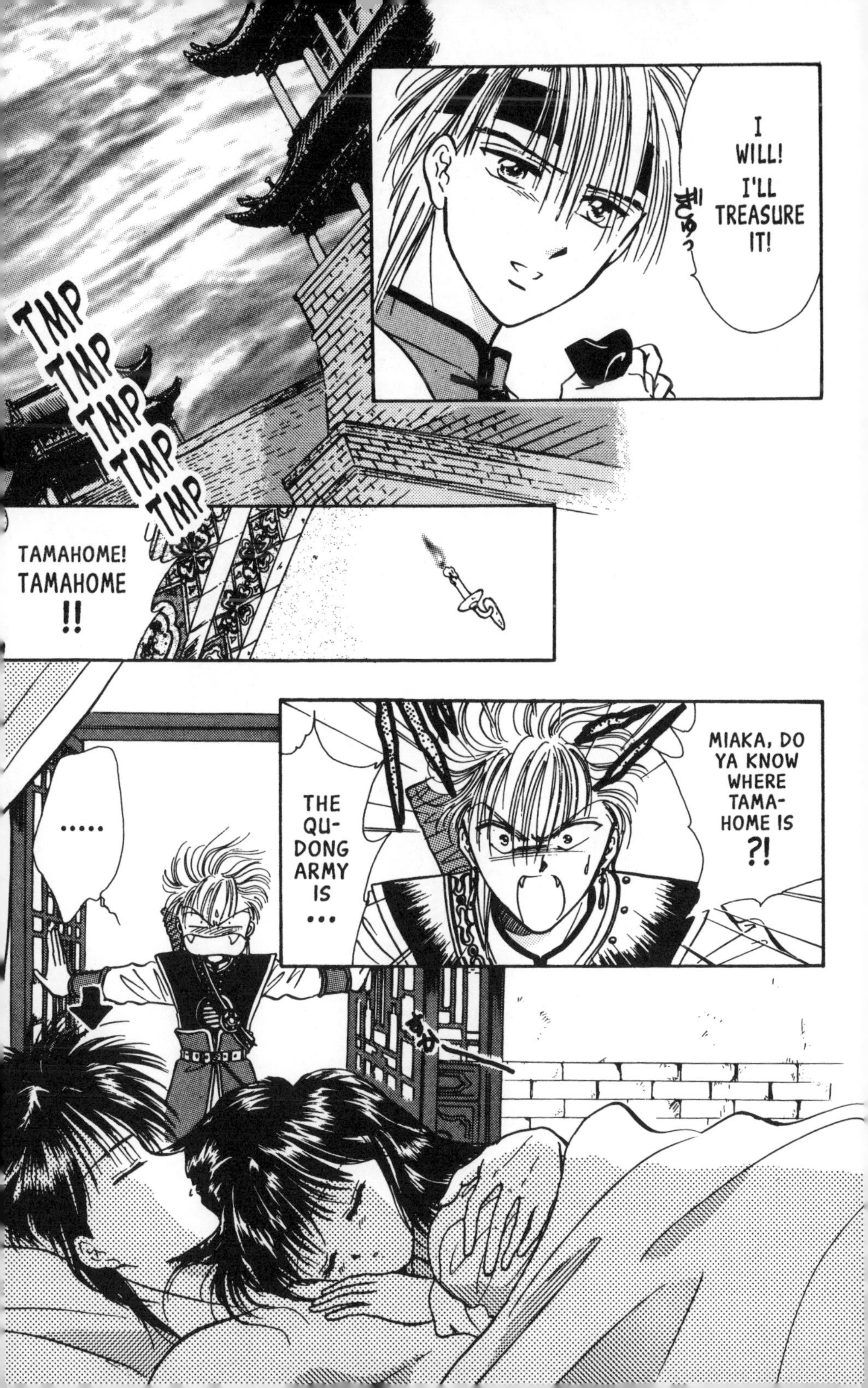
I WILL! I'LL TREASURE IT!
TMP TMP TMP TMP TMP
TAMAHOME! TAMAHOME !!
MIAKA, DO YA KNOW WHERE TAMA-HOME IS ?!
THE QU-DONG ARMY IS ...
.....

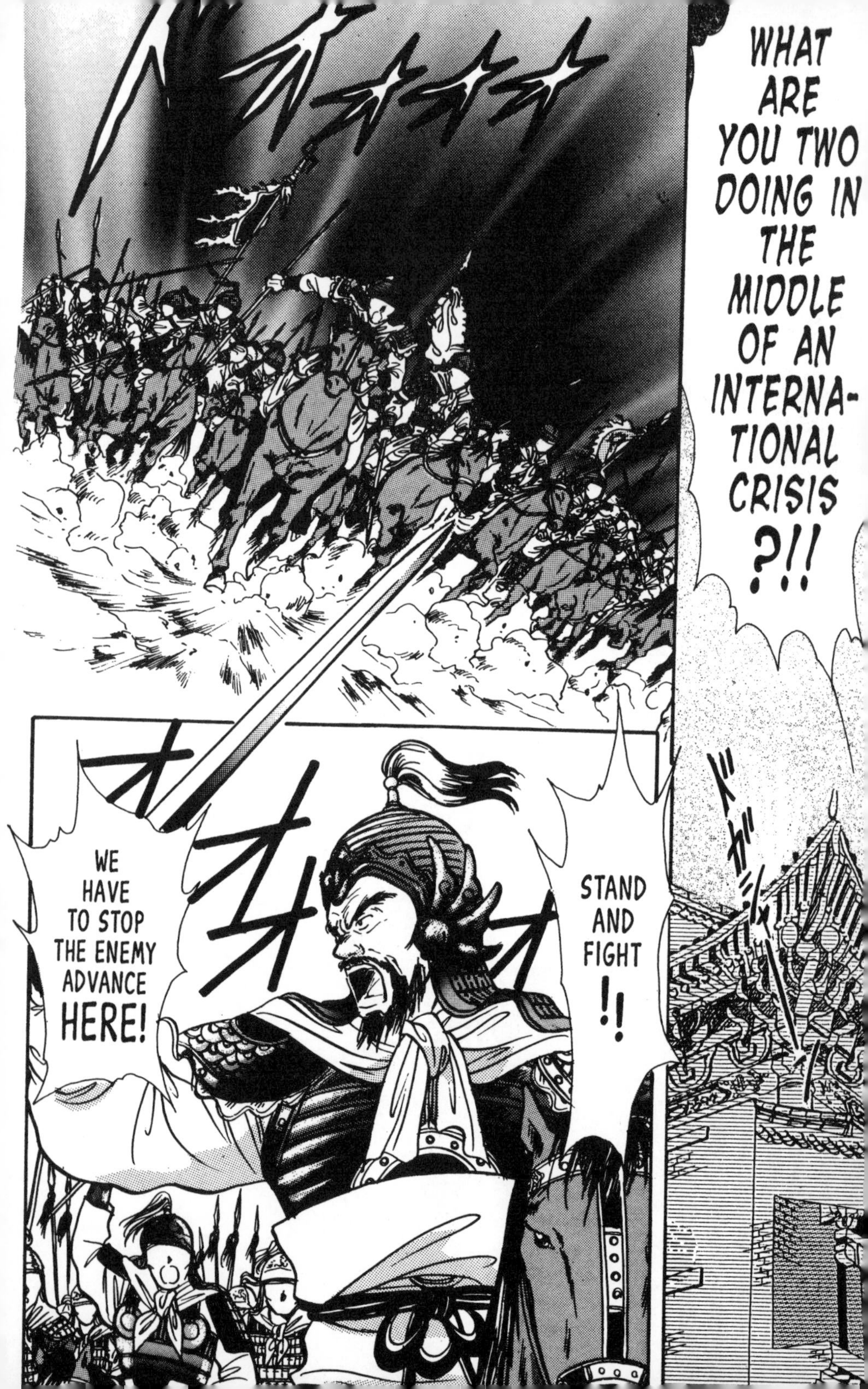
WHAT ARE YOU TWO DOING IN THE MIDDLE OF AN INTERNATIONAL CRISIS?!!
STAND AND FIGHT!!
WE HAVE TO STOP THE ENEMY ADVANCE HERE!

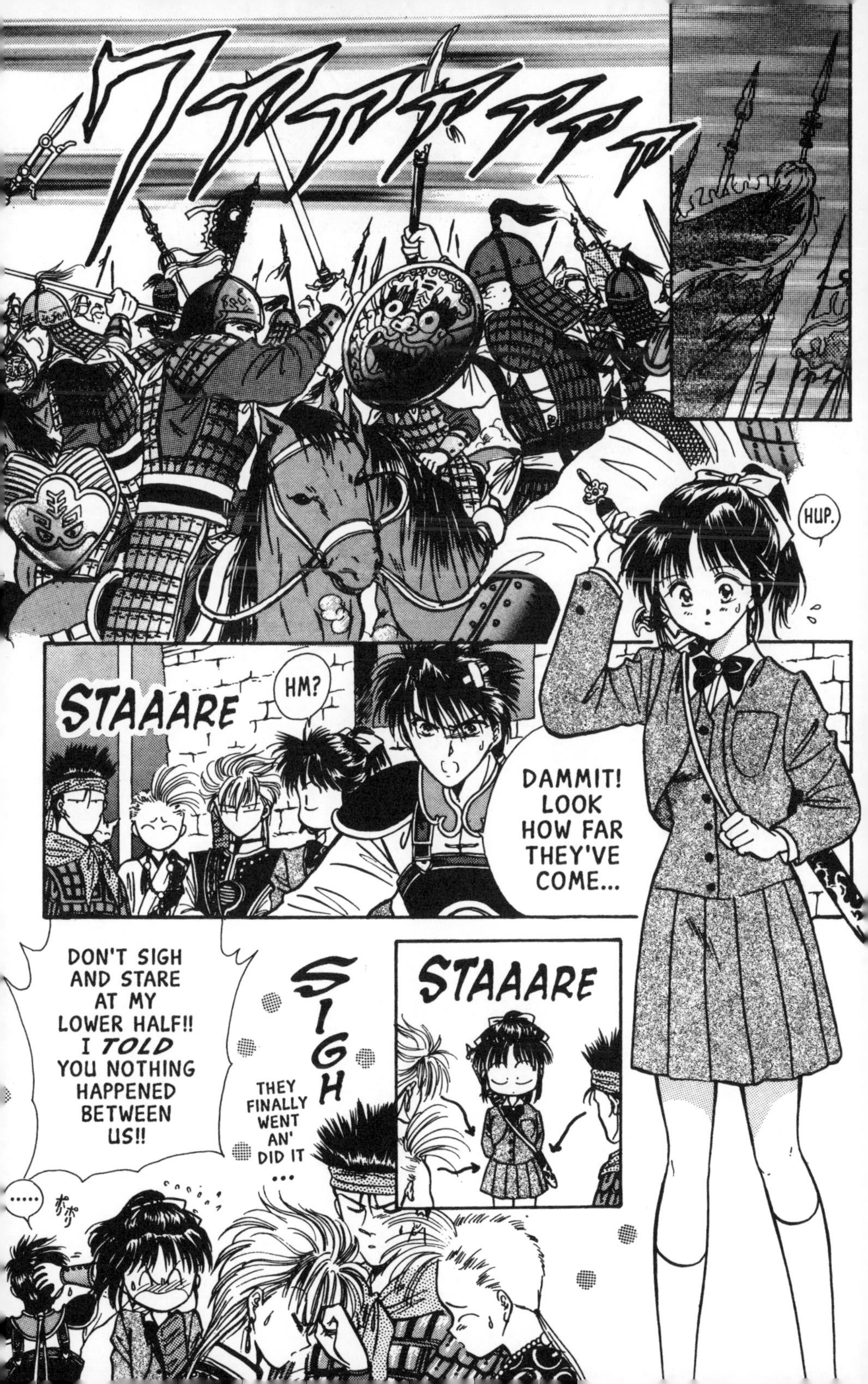
HUP.
DAMMIT! LOOK HOW FAR THEY'VE COME...
HM?
STAAARE
STAAARE
SIGH
THEY FINALLY WENT AN' DID IT...
DON'T SIGH AND STARE AT MY LOWER HALF!! I *TOLD* YOU NOTHING HAPPENED BETWEEN US!!
......

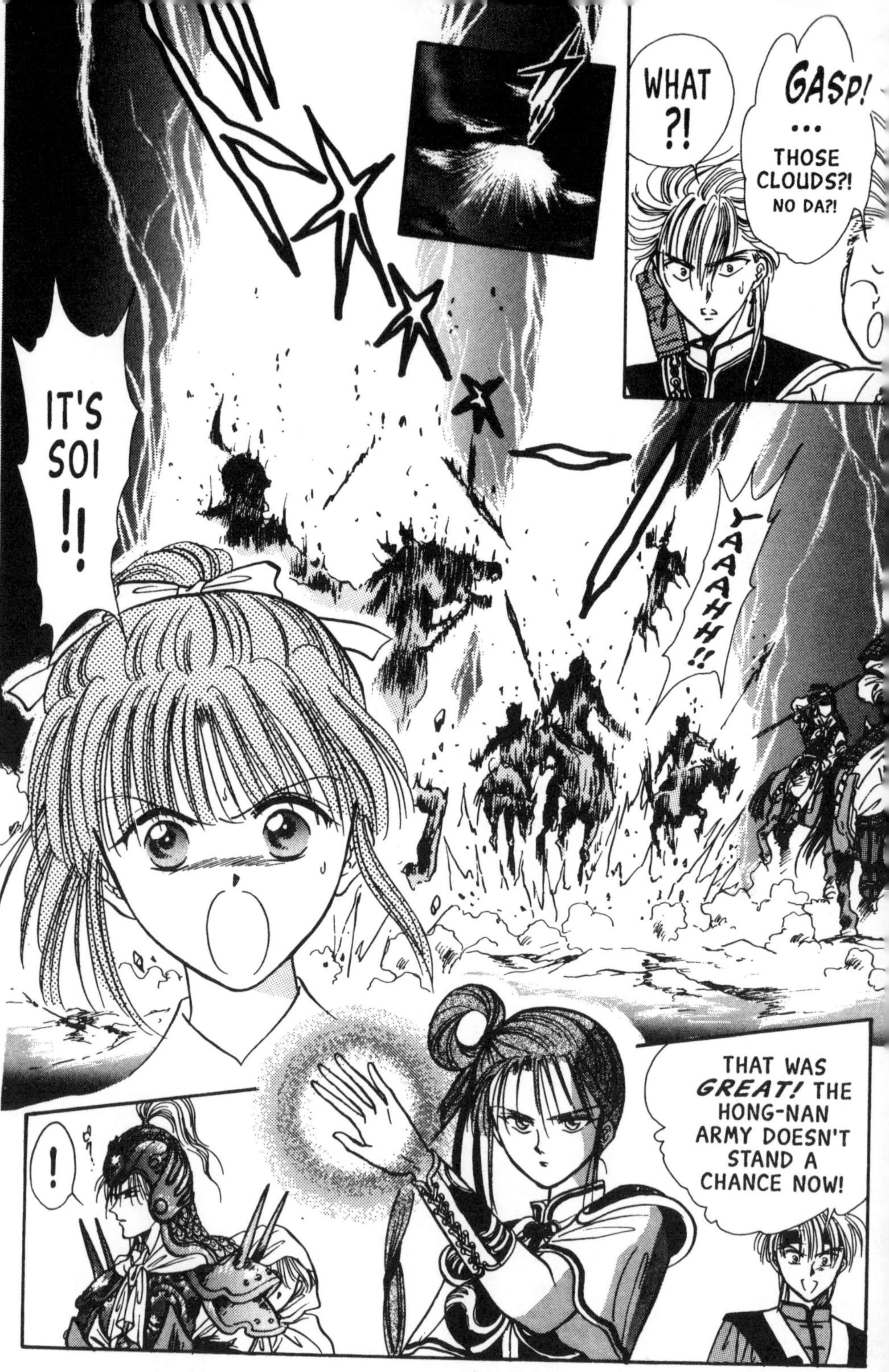
GASP! ... THOSE CLOUDS?! NO DA?!
WHAT ?!
YAAAAHH!!
IT'S SOI !!
THAT WAS GREAT! THE HONG-NAN ARMY DOESN'T STAND A CHANCE NOW!
!

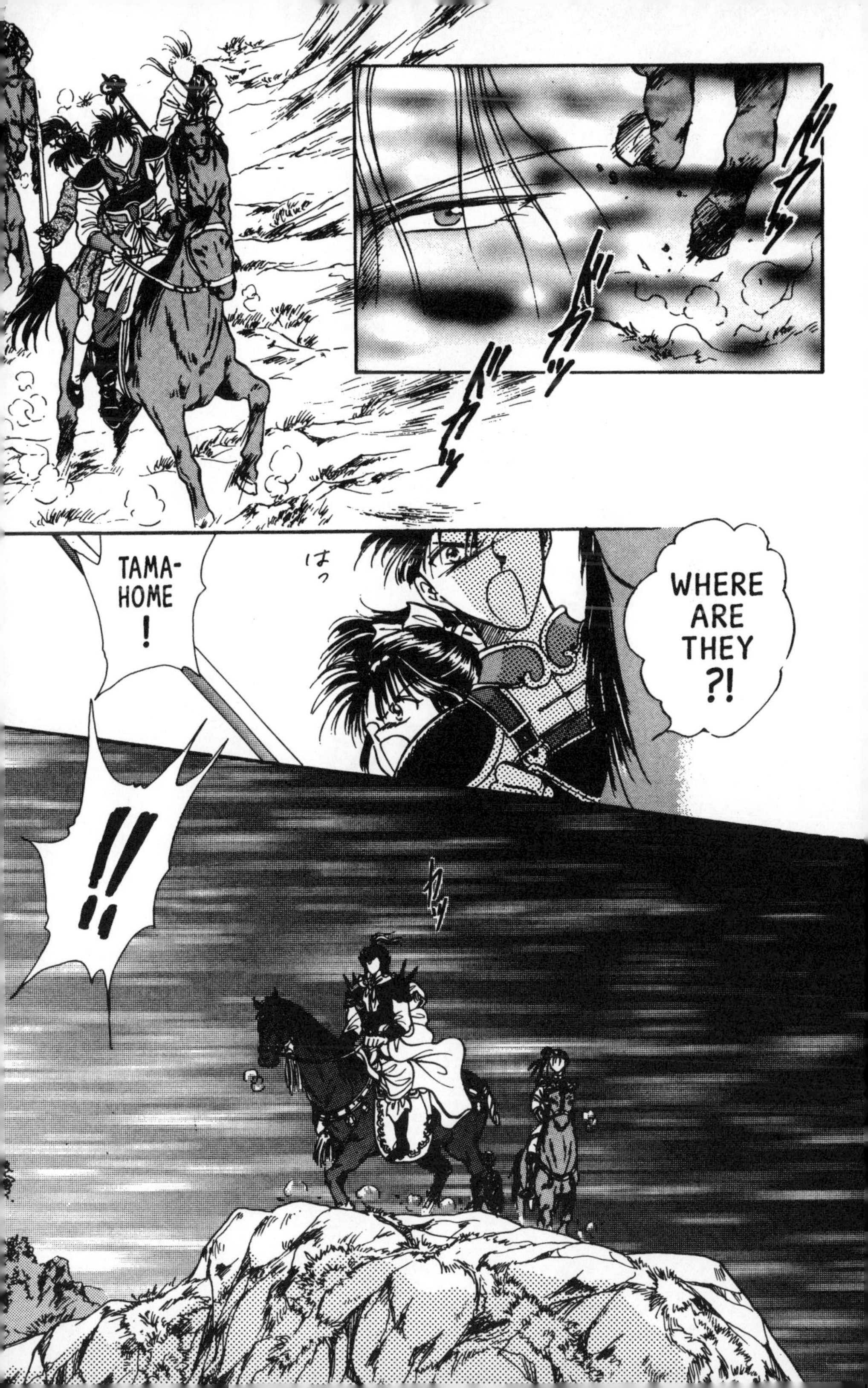
WHERE ARE THEY ?!
はっ
TAMA-HOME !
!!

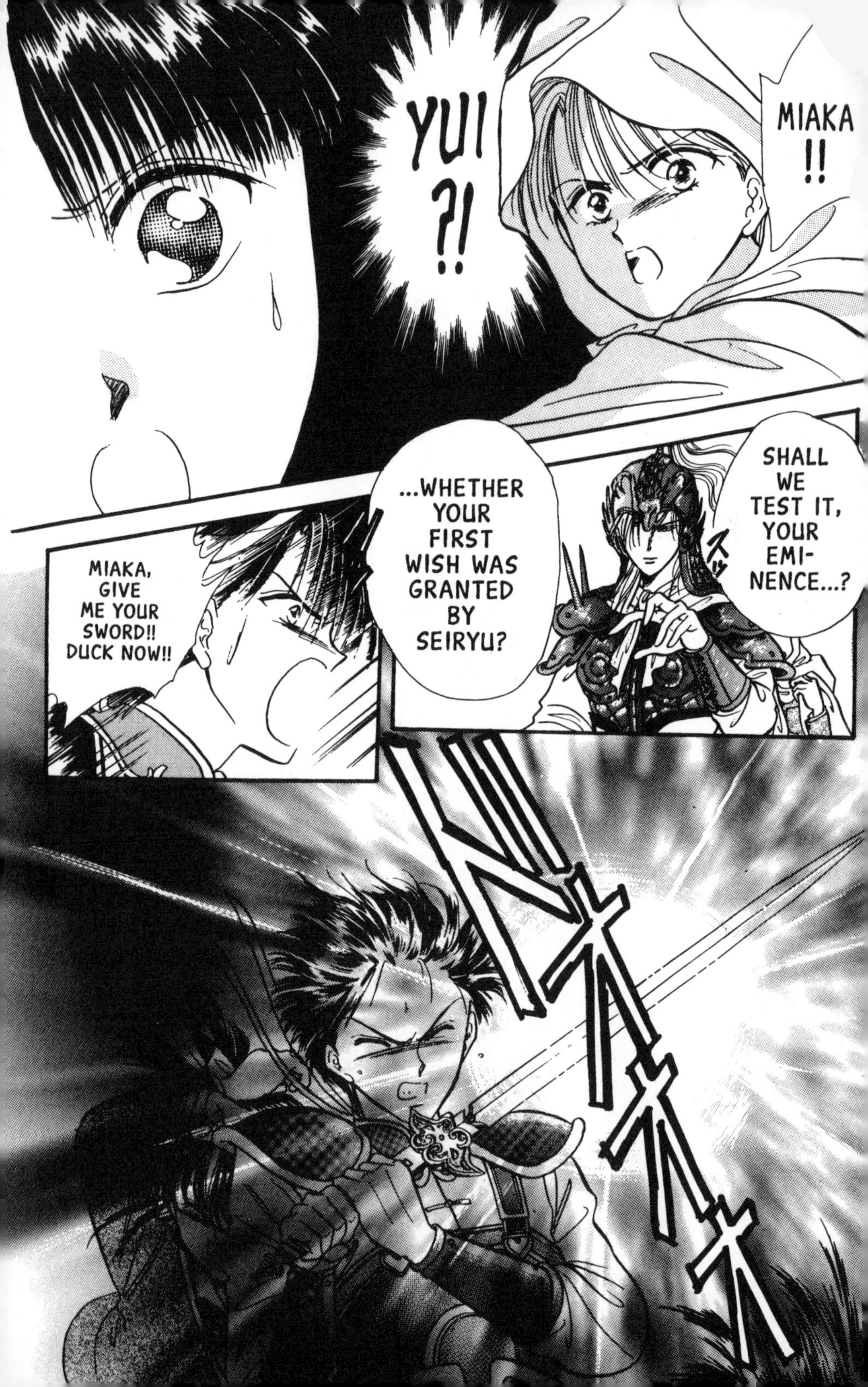
MIAKA !!
YUI ?!
SHALL WE TEST IT, YOUR EMINENCE...?
...WHETHER YOUR FIRST WISH WAS GRANTED BY SEIRYU?
MIAKA, GIVE ME YOUR SWORD!! DUCK NOW!!

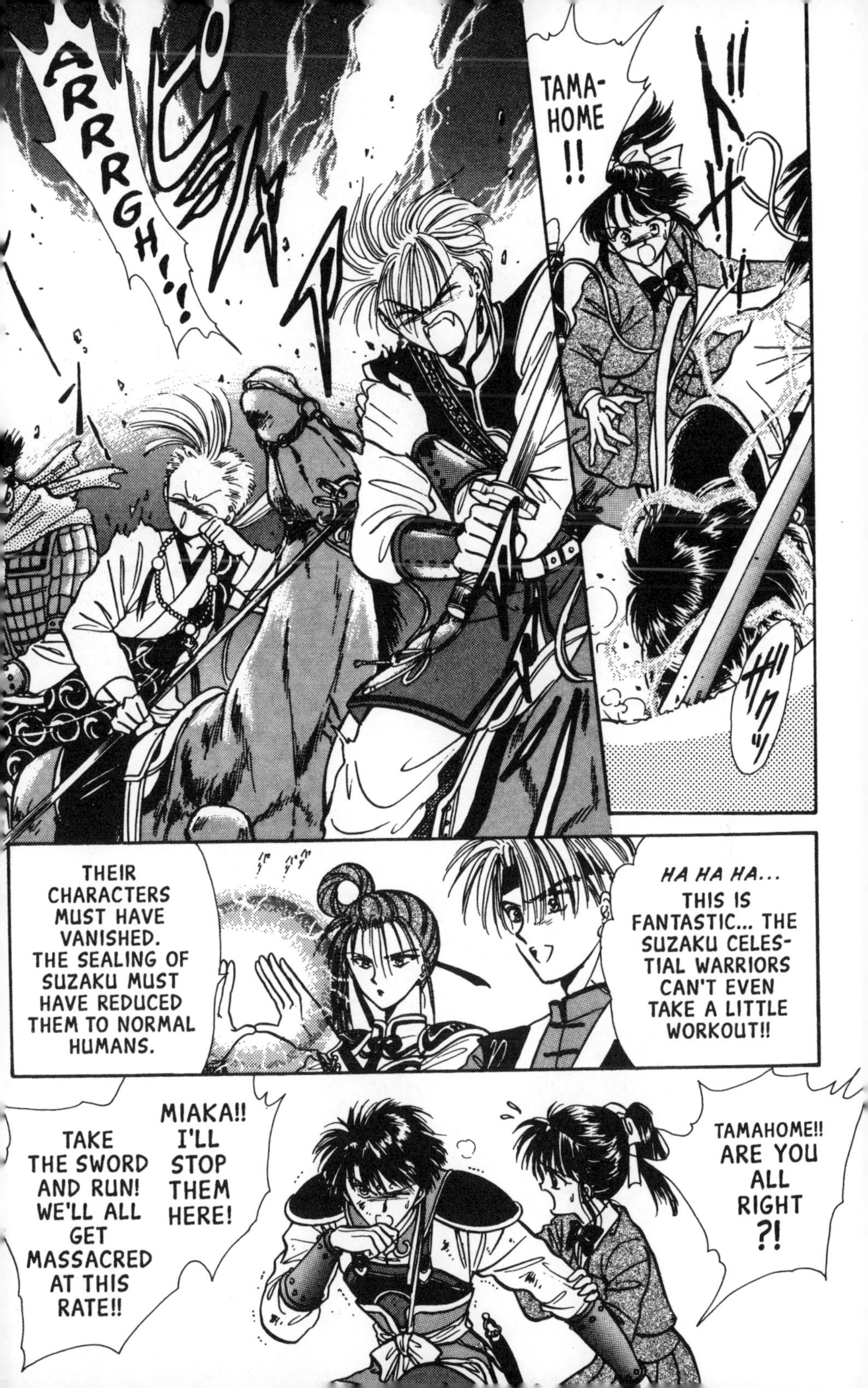
TAMA-HOME!!
ARRRGH!!!
HA HA HA... THIS IS FANTASTIC... THE SUZAKU CELES-TIAL WARRIORS CAN'T EVEN TAKE A LITTLE WORKOUT!!
THEIR CHARACTERS MUST HAVE VANISHED. THE SEALING OF SUZAKU MUST HAVE REDUCED THEM TO NORMAL HUMANS.
TAMAHOME!! ARE YOU ALL RIGHT?!
MIAKA!! I'LL STOP THEM HERE!
TAKE THE SWORD AND RUN! WE'LL ALL GET MASSACRED AT THIS RATE!!

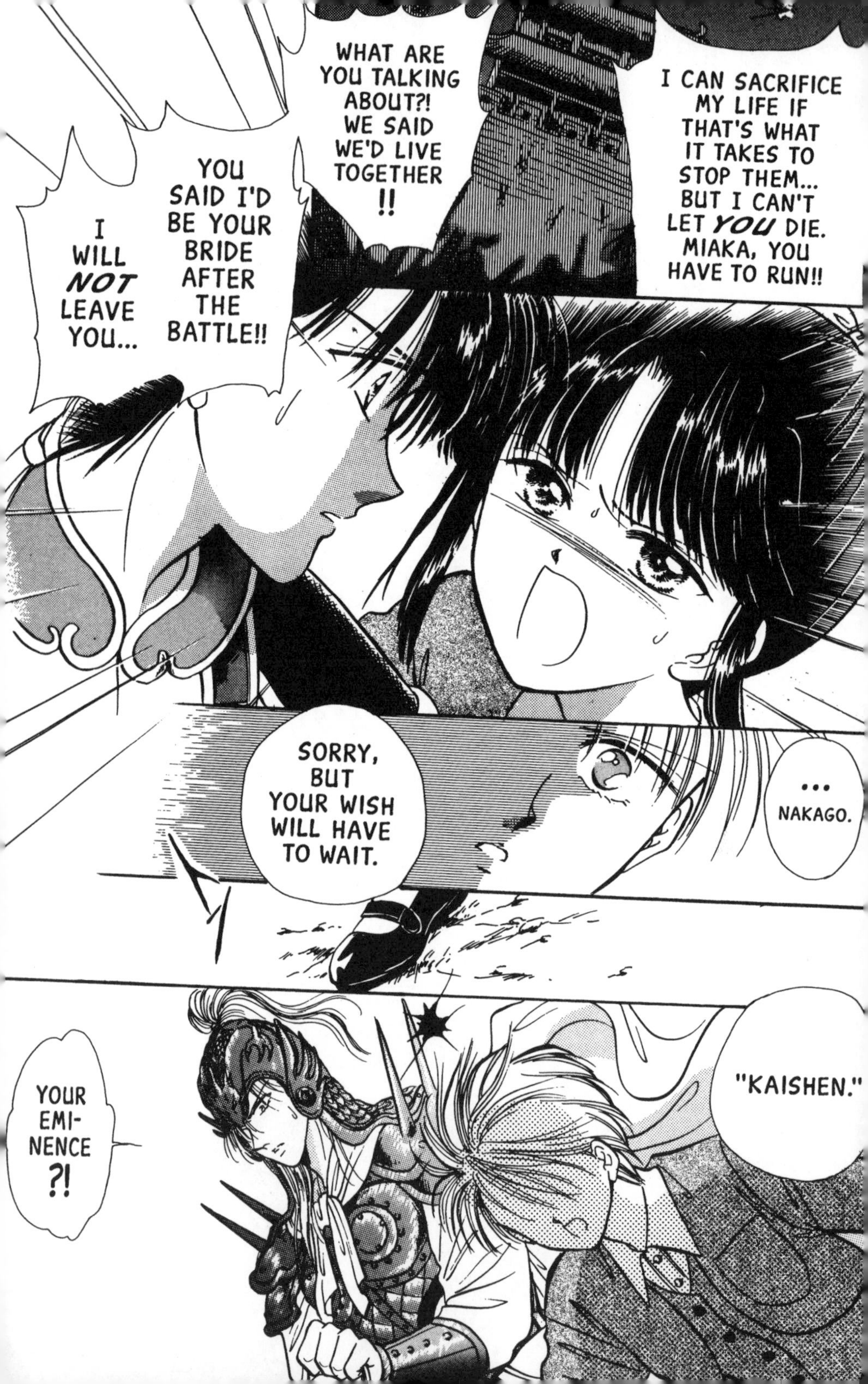
I CAN SACRIFICE MY LIFE IF THAT'S WHAT IT TAKES TO STOP THEM... BUT I CAN'T LET YOU DIE. MIAKA, YOU HAVE TO RUN!!
WHAT ARE YOU TALKING ABOUT?! WE SAID WE'D LIVE TOGETHER!!
YOU SAID I'D BE YOUR BRIDE AFTER THE BATTLE!!
I WILL NOT LEAVE YOU...
... NAKAGO.
SORRY, BUT YOUR WISH WILL HAVE TO WAIT.
"KAISHEN."
YOUR EMI-NENCE?!

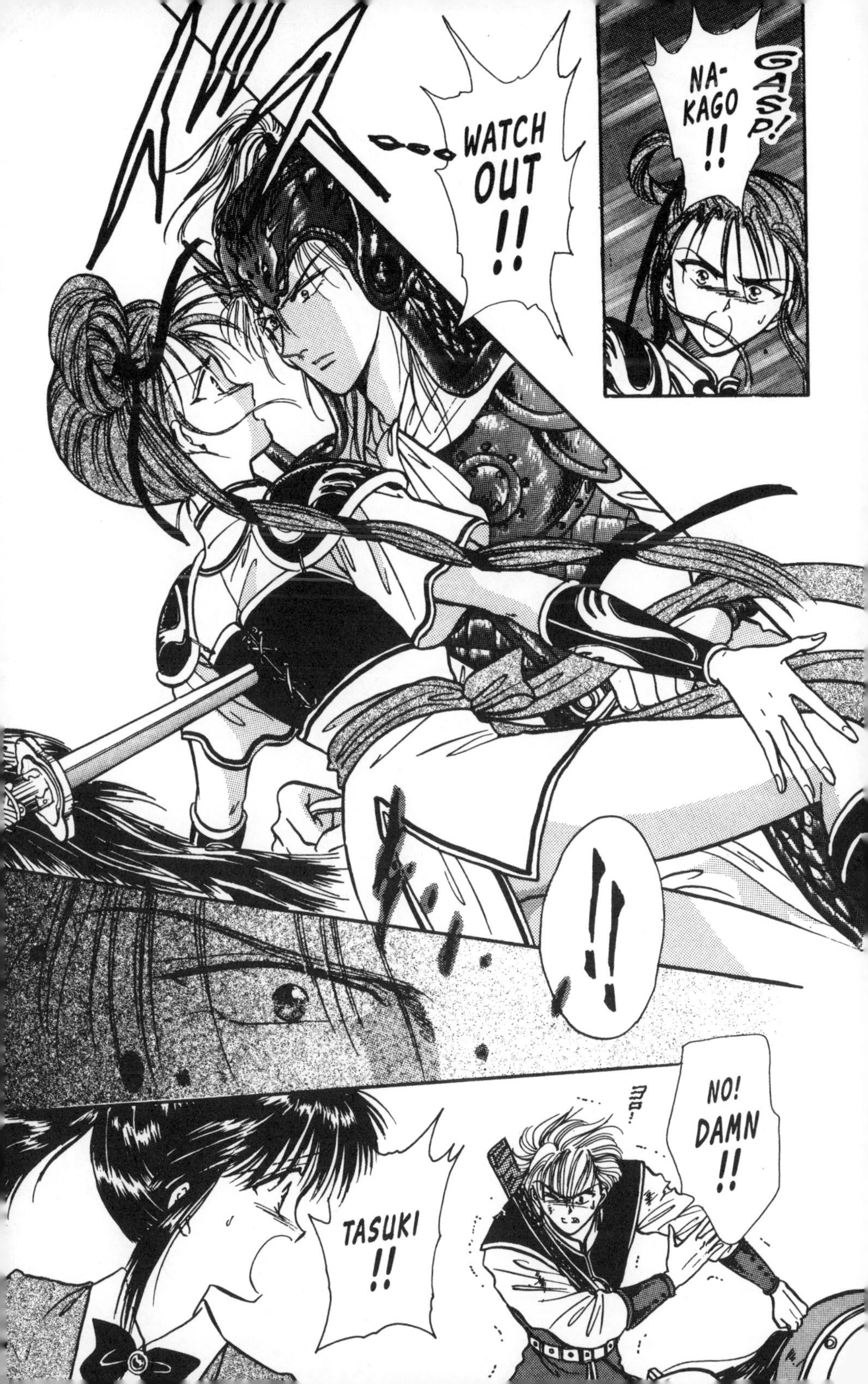
GASP!
NA-KAGO!!
WATCH OUT!!
!!
NO! DAMN!!
TASUKI!!

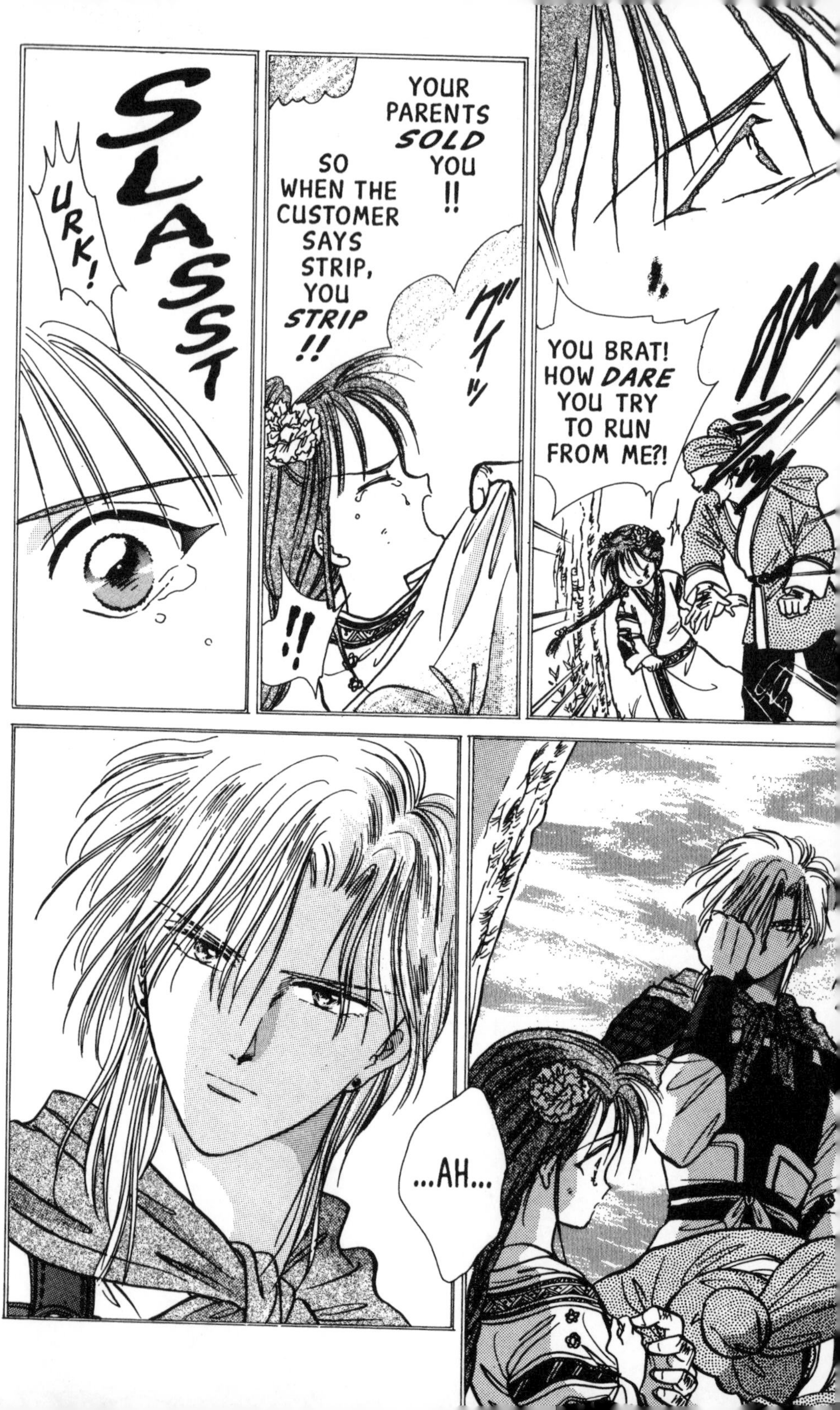
YOU BRAT! HOW *DARE* YOU TRY TO RUN FROM ME?!
YOUR PARENTS *SOLD* YOU !!
SO WHEN THE CUSTOMER SAYS STRIP, YOU *STRIP* !!
グイッ
!!
SLASSST
URK!
...AH...

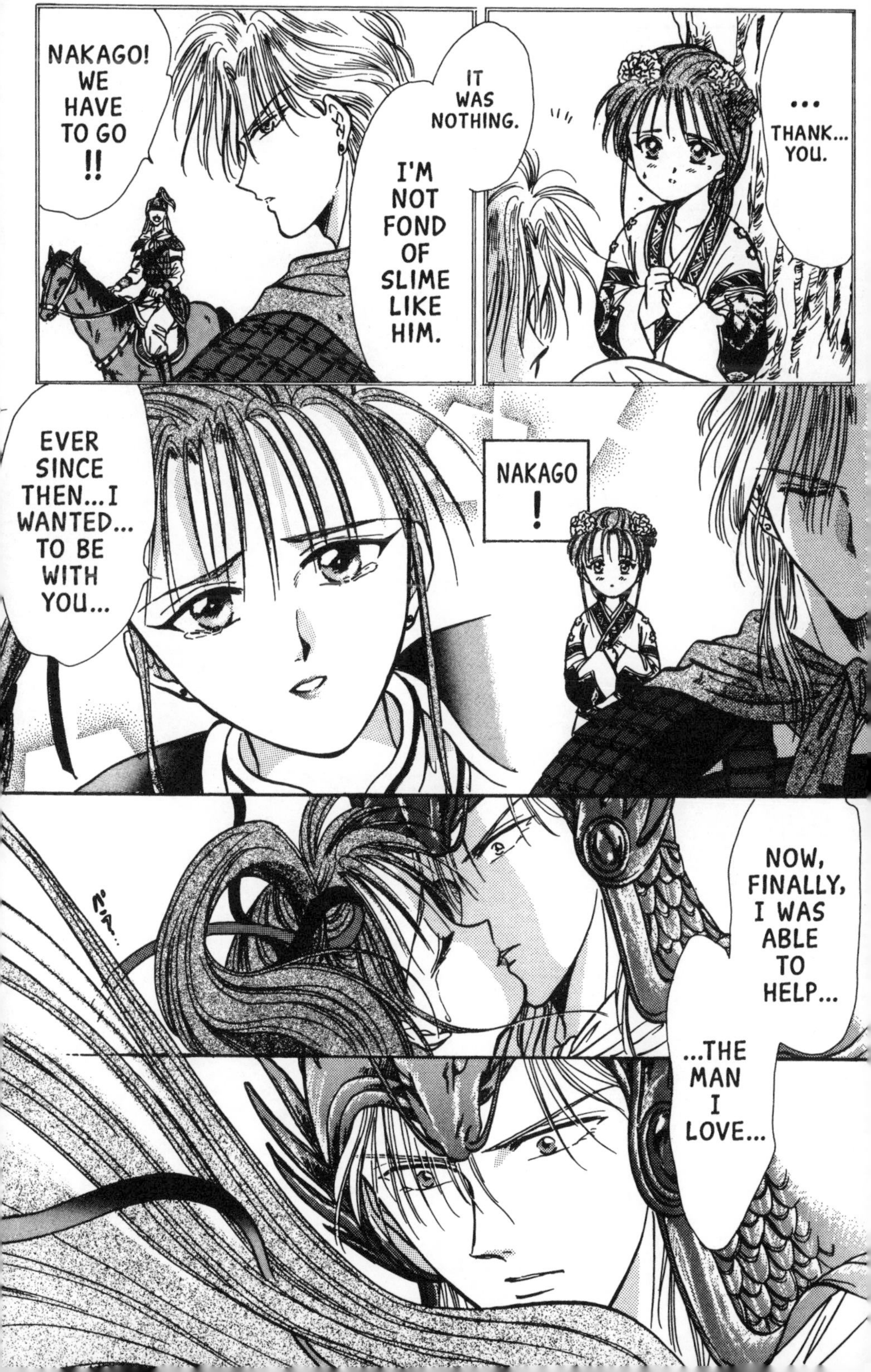
...
THANK... YOU.
IT WAS NOTHING.
I'M NOT FOND OF SLIME LIKE HIM.
NAKAGO! WE HAVE TO GO !!
NAKAGO !
EVER SINCE THEN... I WANTED... TO BE WITH YOU...
NOW, FINALLY, I WAS ABLE TO HELP...
...THE MAN I LOVE...

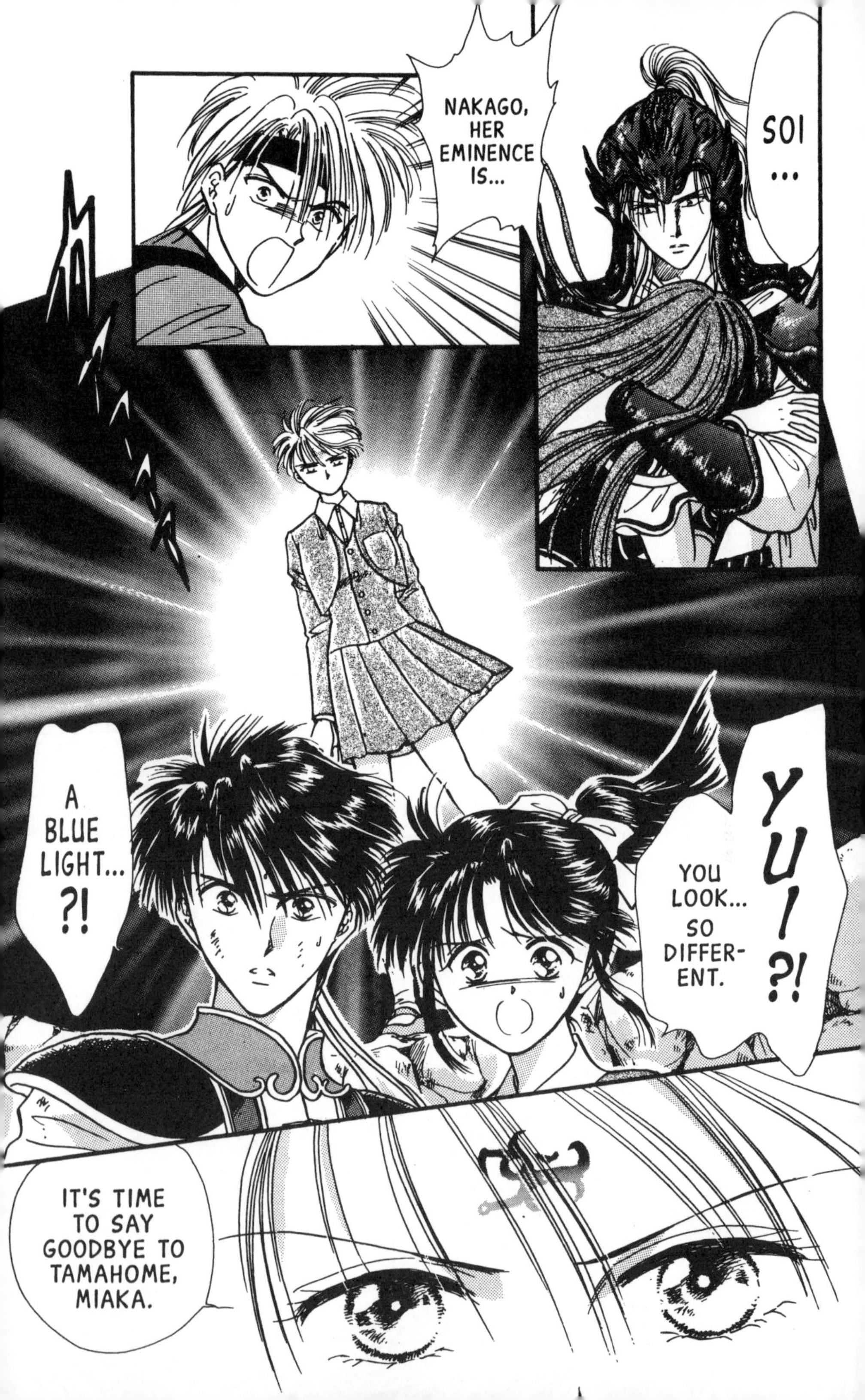
NAKAGO, HER EMINENCE IS...
SOI ...
YUI ?!
YOU LOOK... SO DIFFERENT.
A BLUE LIGHT... ?!
IT'S TIME TO SAY GOODBYE TO TAMAHOME, MIAKA.

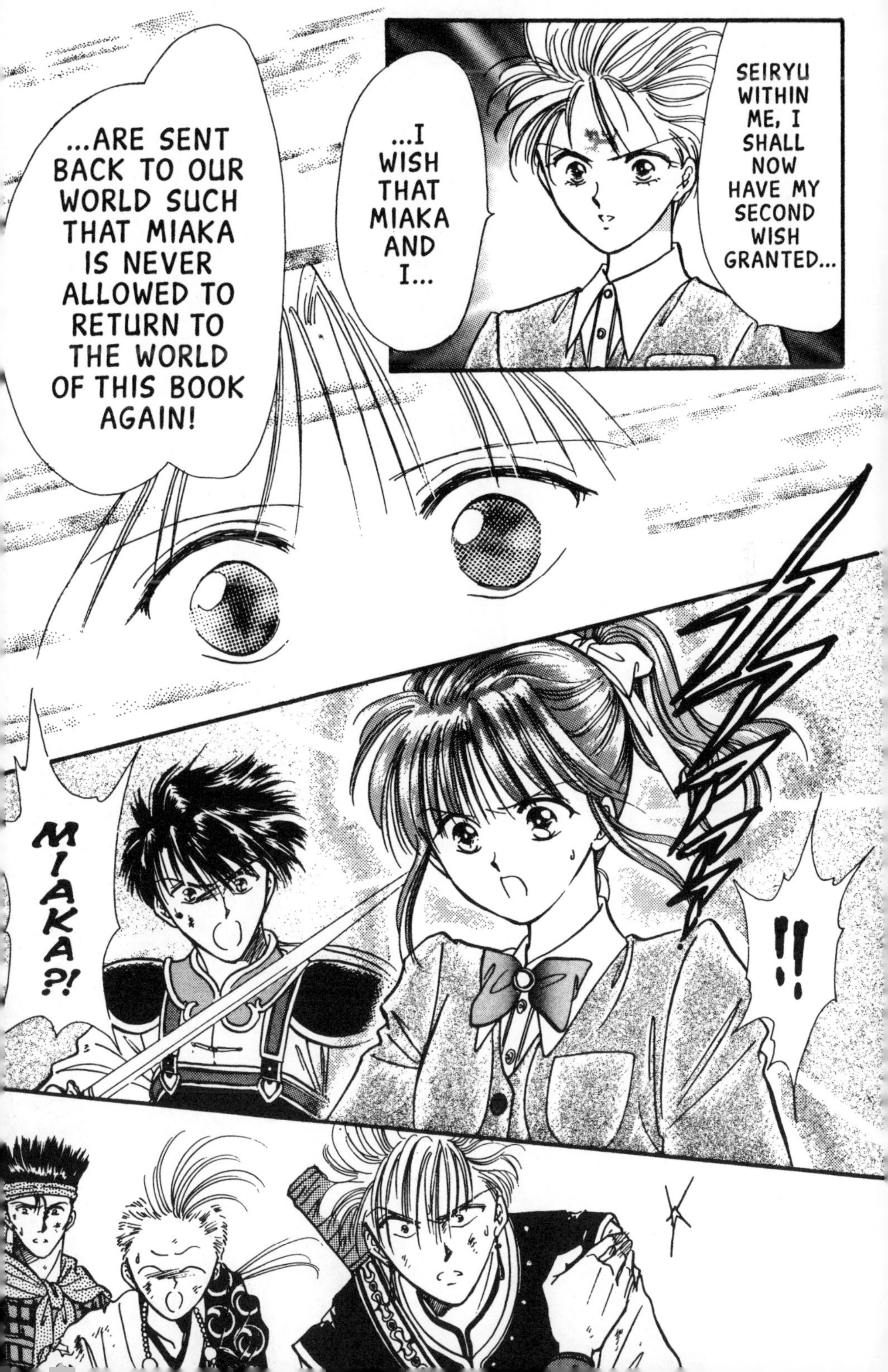
SEIRYU WITHIN ME, I SHALL NOW HAVE MY SECOND WISH GRANTED...
...I WISH THAT MIAKA AND I...
...ARE SENT BACK TO OUR WORLD SUCH THAT MIAKA IS NEVER ALLOWED TO RETURN TO THE WORLD OF THIS BOOK AGAIN!
!!
MIAKA?!

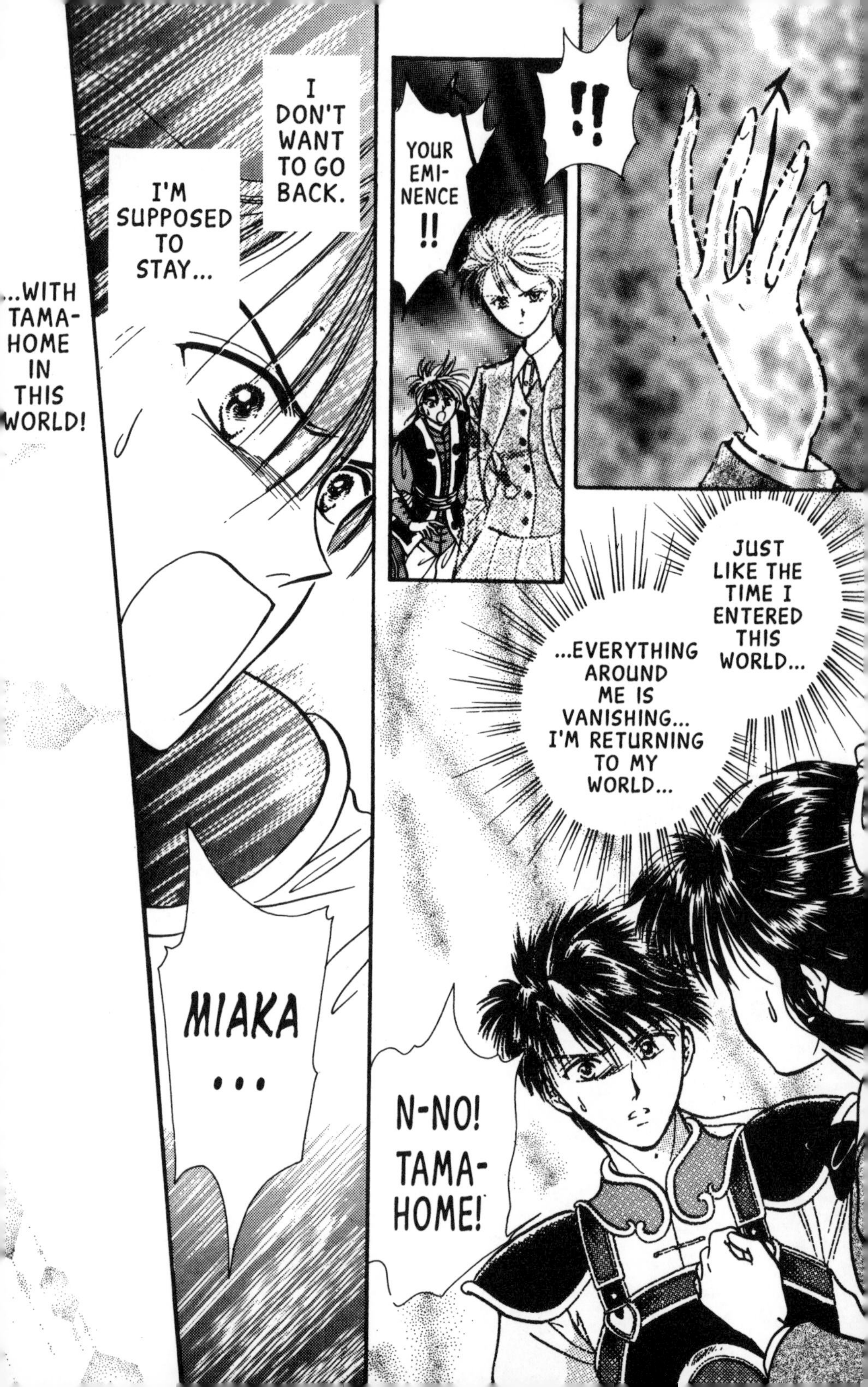
!!
YOUR EMINENCE !!
JUST LIKE THE TIME I ENTERED THIS WORLD...
...EVERYTHING AROUND ME IS VANISHING... I'M RETURNING TO MY WORLD...
N-NO! TAMAHOME!
I DON'T WANT TO GO BACK.
I'M SUPPOSED TO STAY...
...WITH TAMAHOME IN THIS WORLD!
MIAKA...

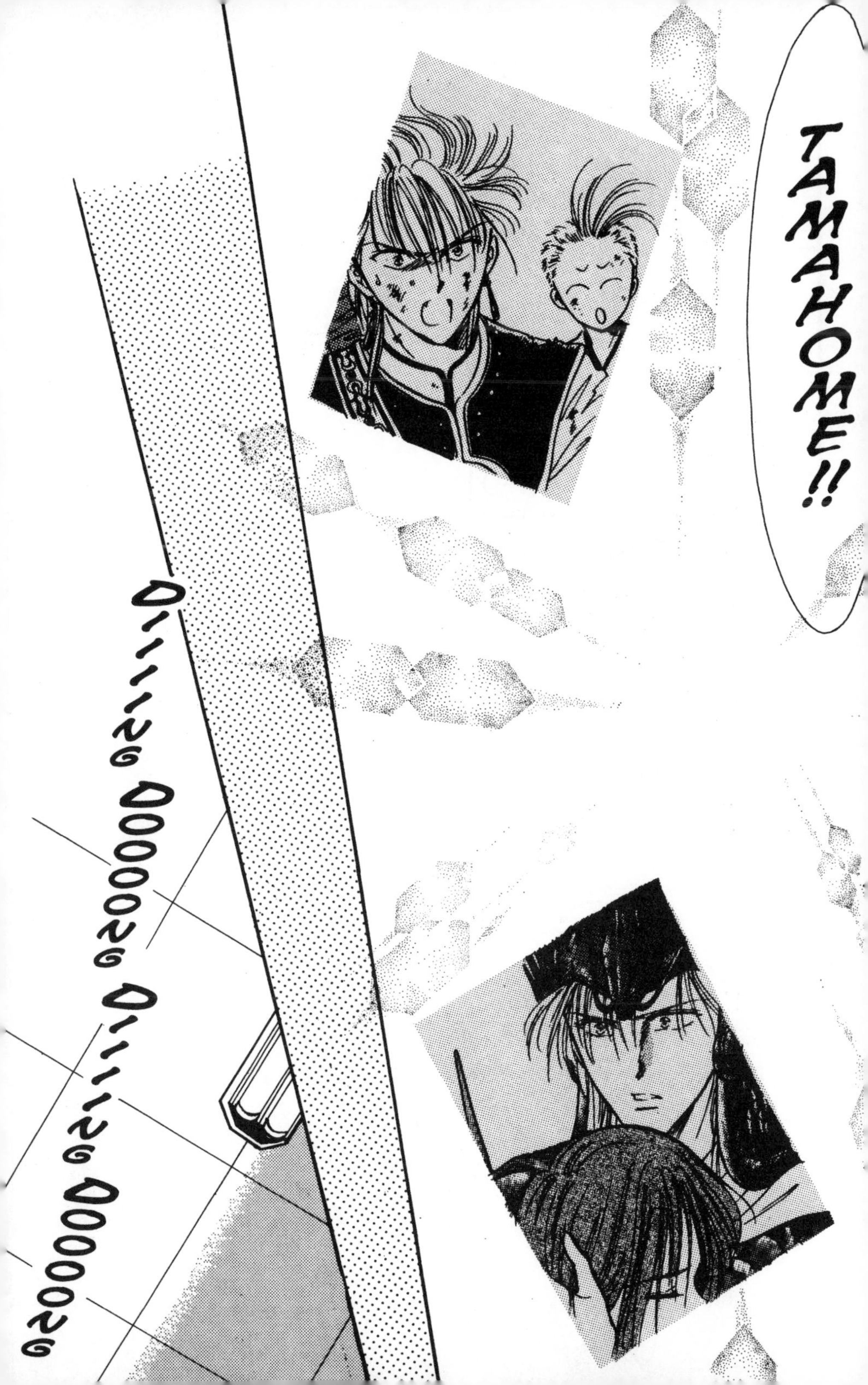
TAMAHOME!!
DOOOOONG DOOOOONG

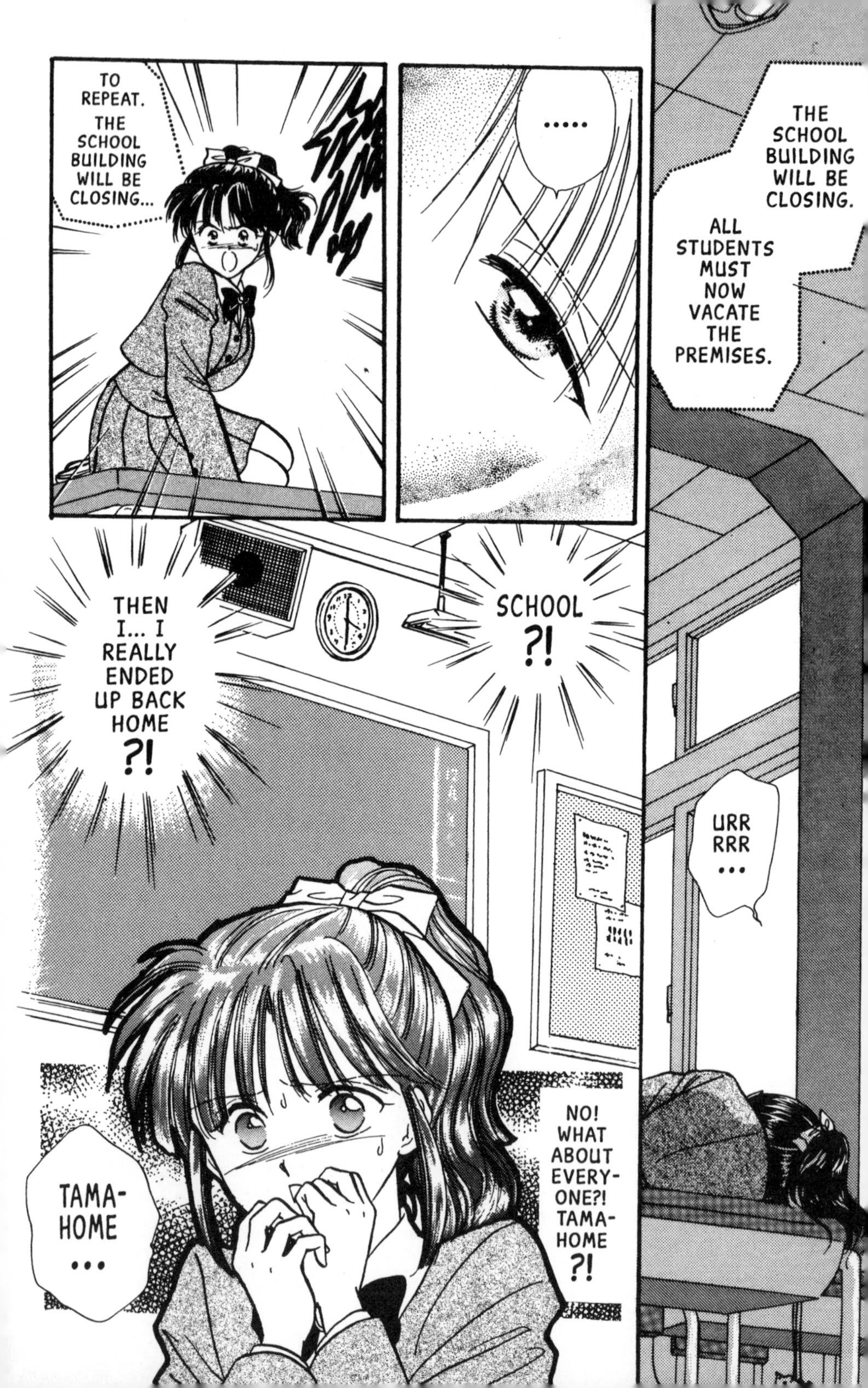
THE SCHOOL BUILDING WILL BE CLOSING.
ALL STUDENTS MUST NOW VACATE THE PREMISES.
URR RRR...
.....
TO REPEAT.
THE SCHOOL BUILDING WILL BE CLOSING...
SCHOOL ?!
THEN I... I REALLY ENDED UP BACK HOME ?!
NO! WHAT ABOUT EVERY-ONE?! TAMA-HOME ?!
TAMA-HOME ...

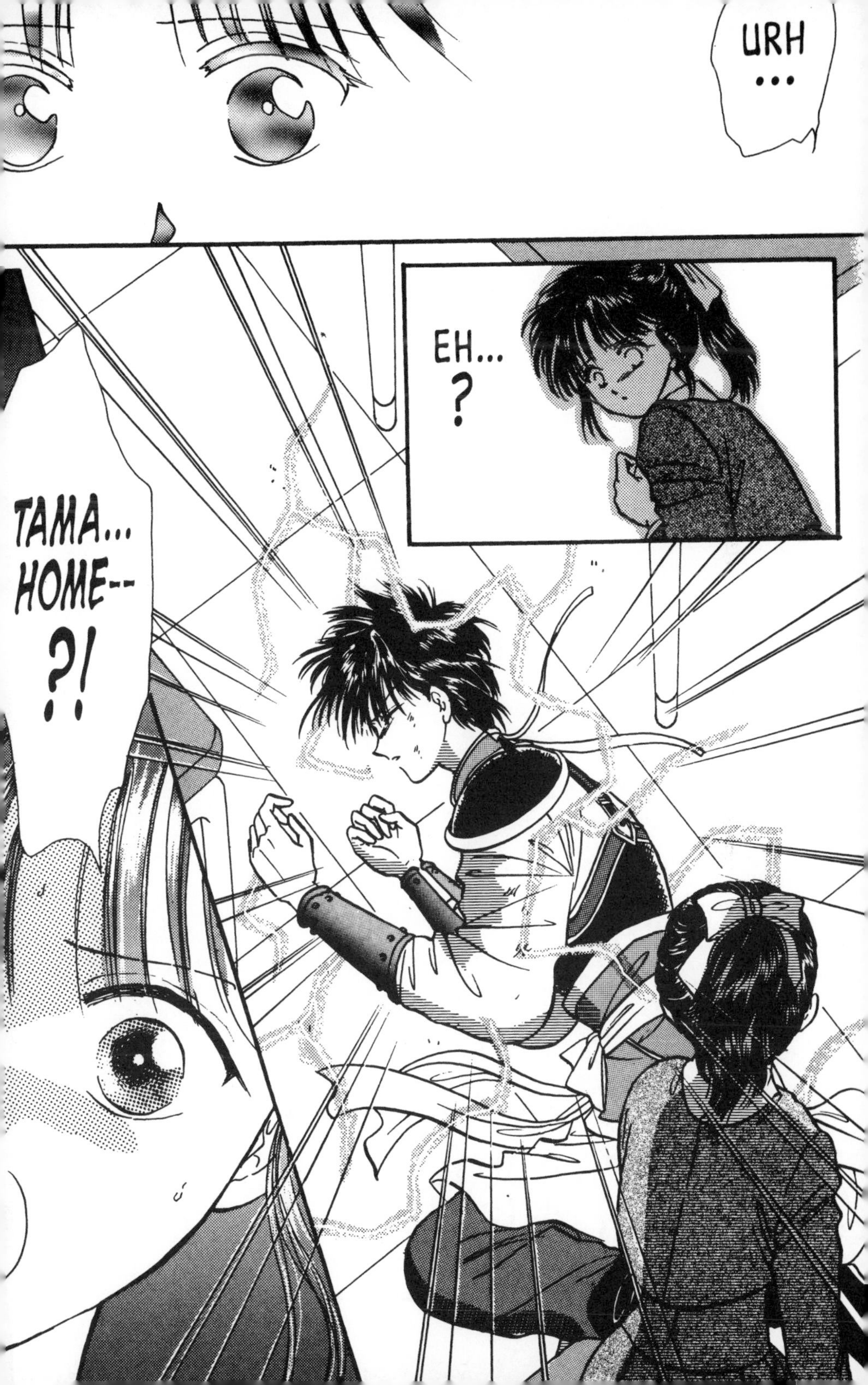
URH ...
EH... ?
TAMA... HOME-- ?!

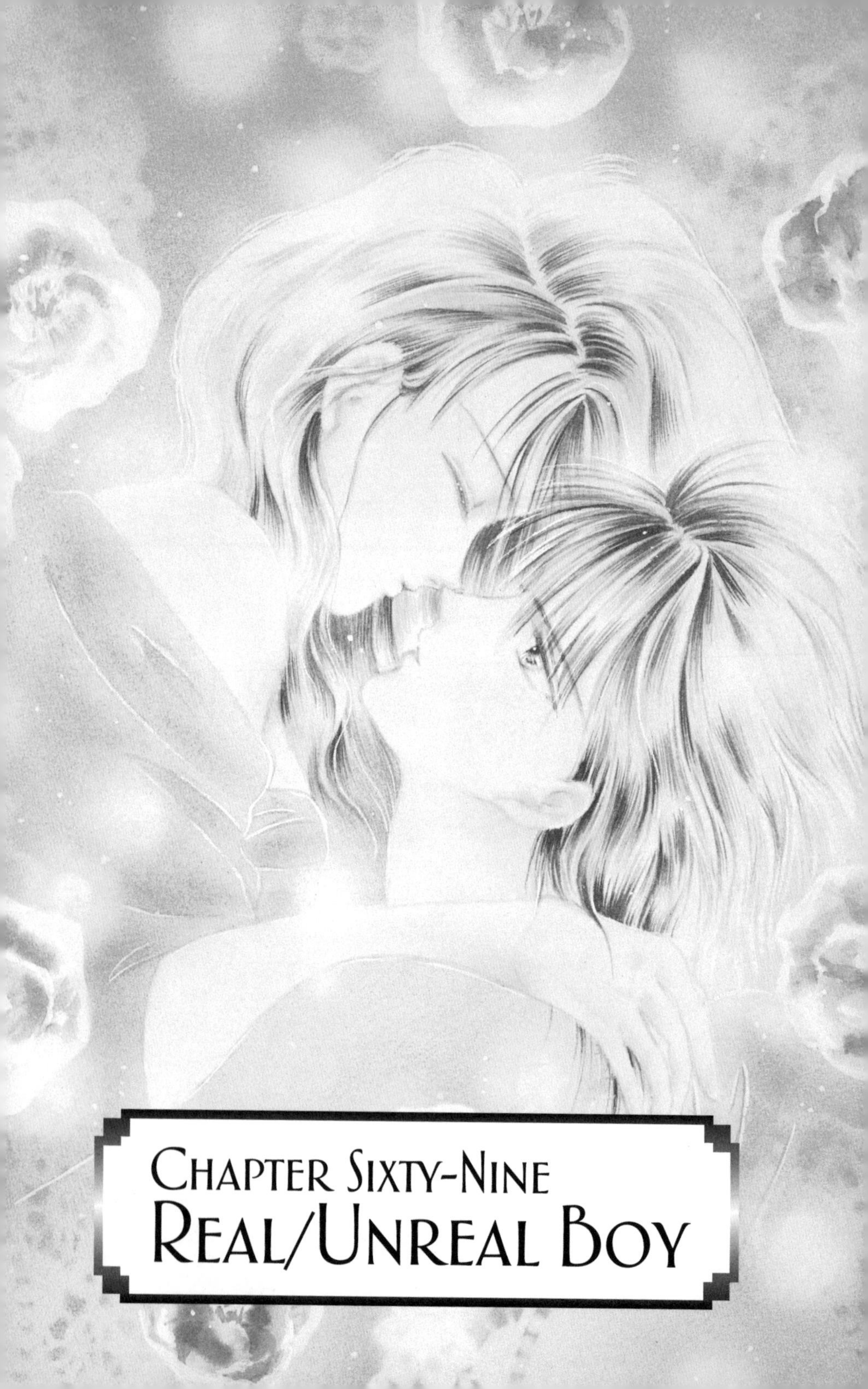

Chapter Sixty-Nine
Real/Unreal Boy

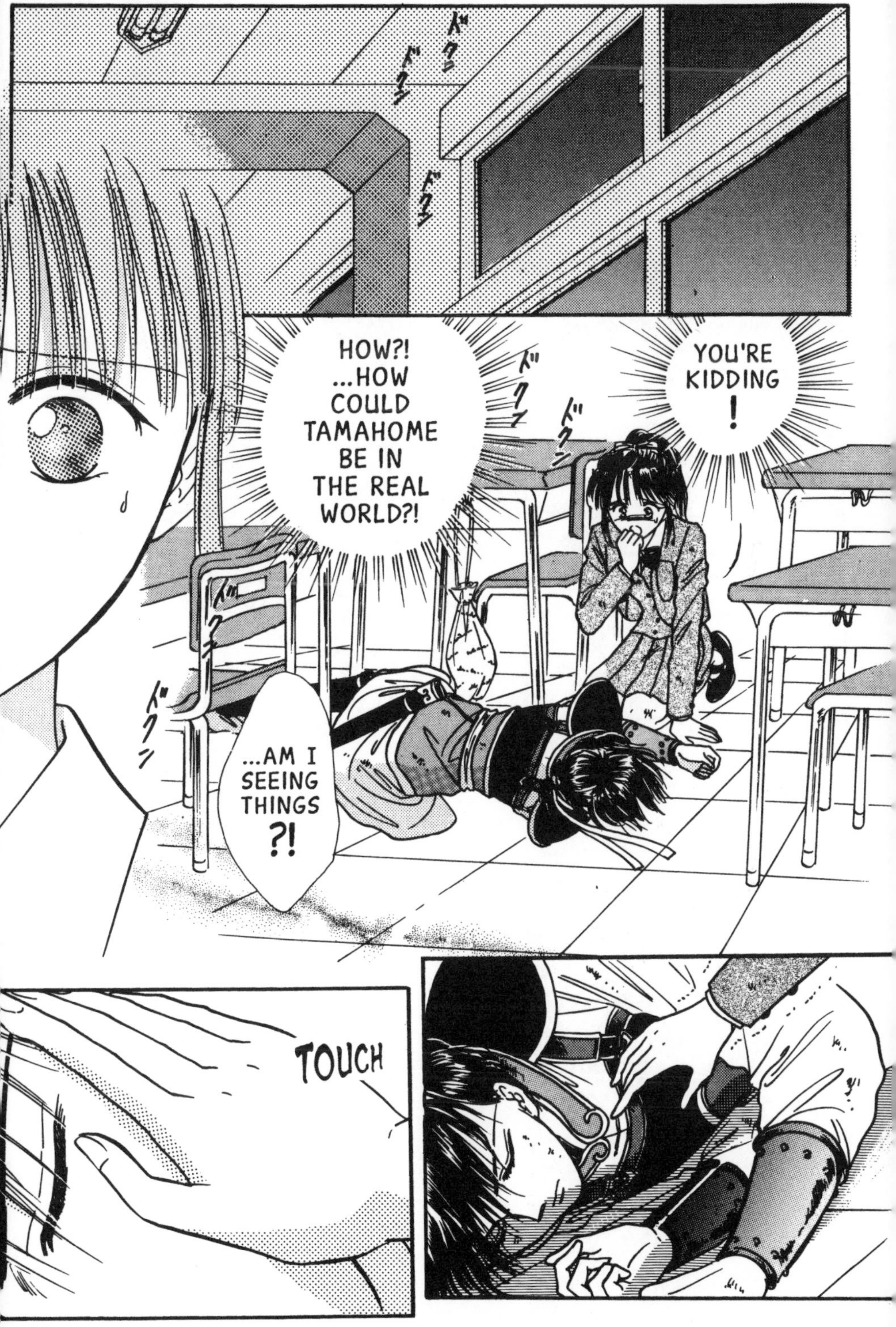
YOU'RE KIDDING!
HOW?! ...HOW COULD TAMAHOME BE IN THE REAL WORLD?!
...AM I SEEING THINGS?!
TOUCH

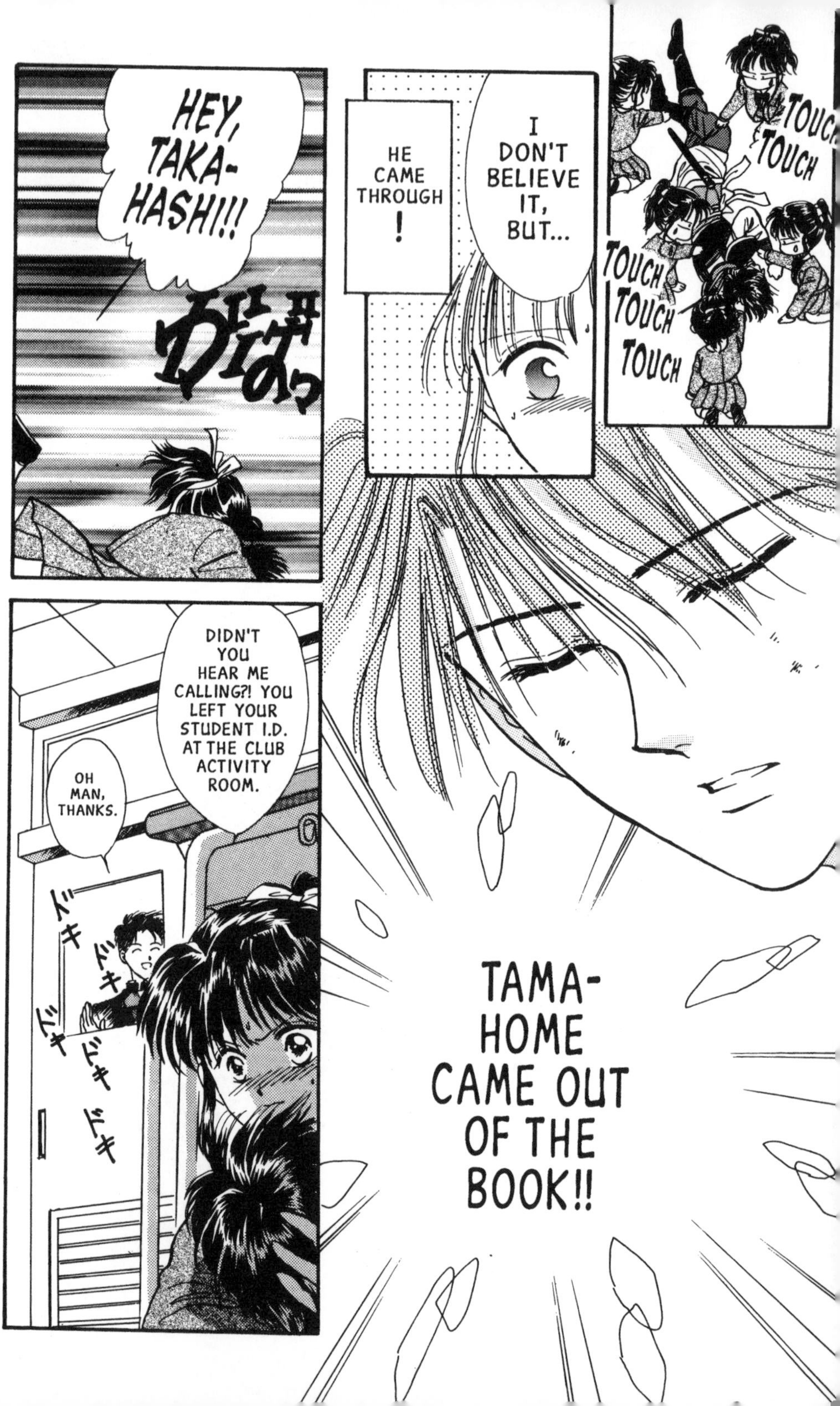
TOUCH TOUCH
TOUCH TOUCH TOUCH
I DON'T BELIEVE IT, BUT...
HE CAME THROUGH!
TAMA-HOME CAME OUT OF THE BOOK!!
HEY, TAKA-HASHI!!!
DIDN'T YOU HEAR ME CALLING?! YOU LEFT YOUR STUDENT I.D. AT THE CLUB ACTIVITY ROOM.
OH MAN, THANKS.
ドキ ドキ ドキ ドキ ドキ

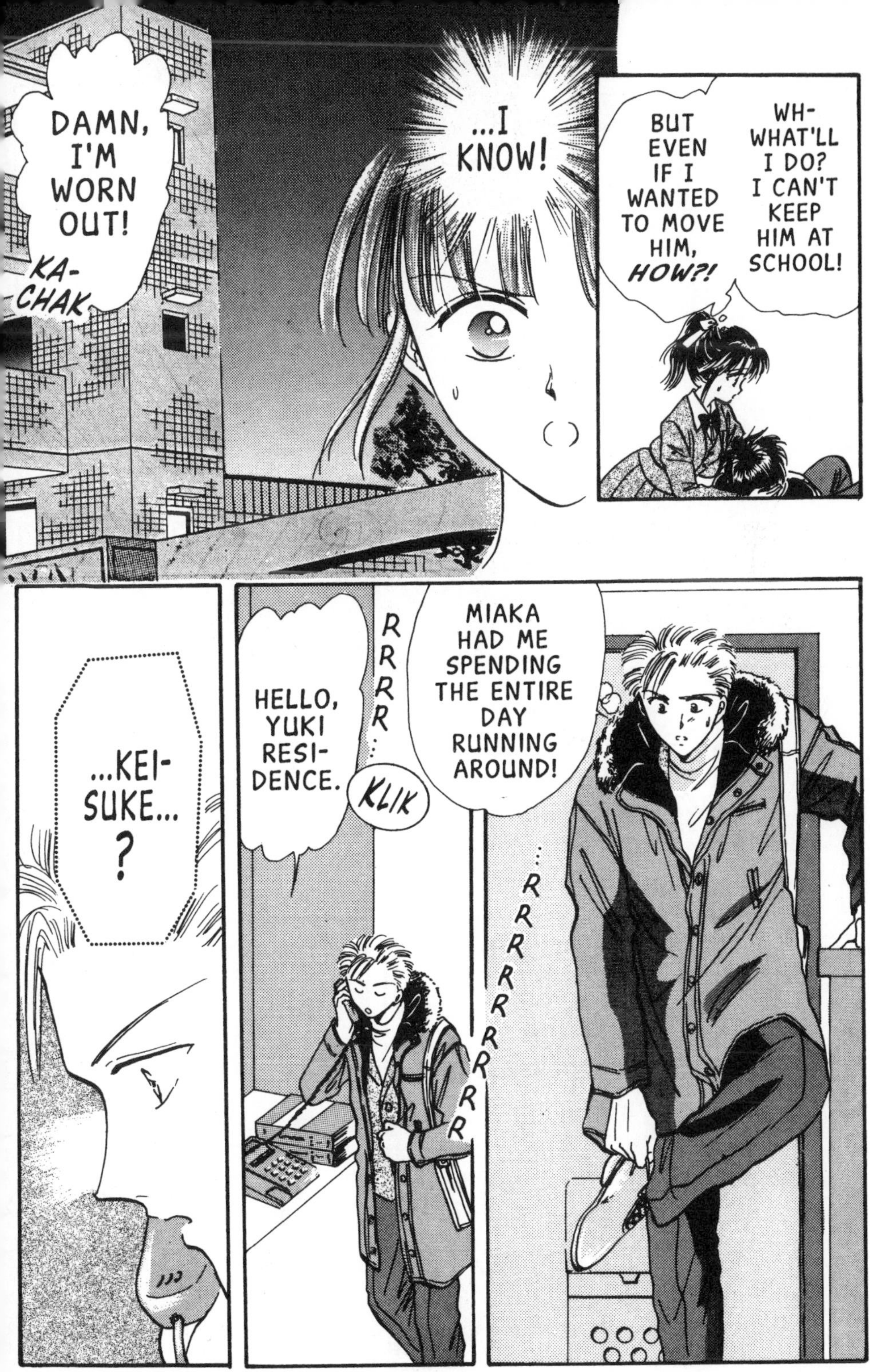
WH-WHAT'LL I DO? I CAN'T KEEP HIM AT SCHOOL!
BUT EVEN IF I WANTED TO MOVE HIM, *HOW?!*
...I KNOW!
DAMN, I'M WORN OUT!
KA-CHAK
MIAKA HAD ME SPENDING THE ENTIRE DAY RUNNING AROUND!
...RRRRRRRRR
RRRR...
KLIK
HELLO, YUKI RESI-DENCE.
...KEI-SUKE...?

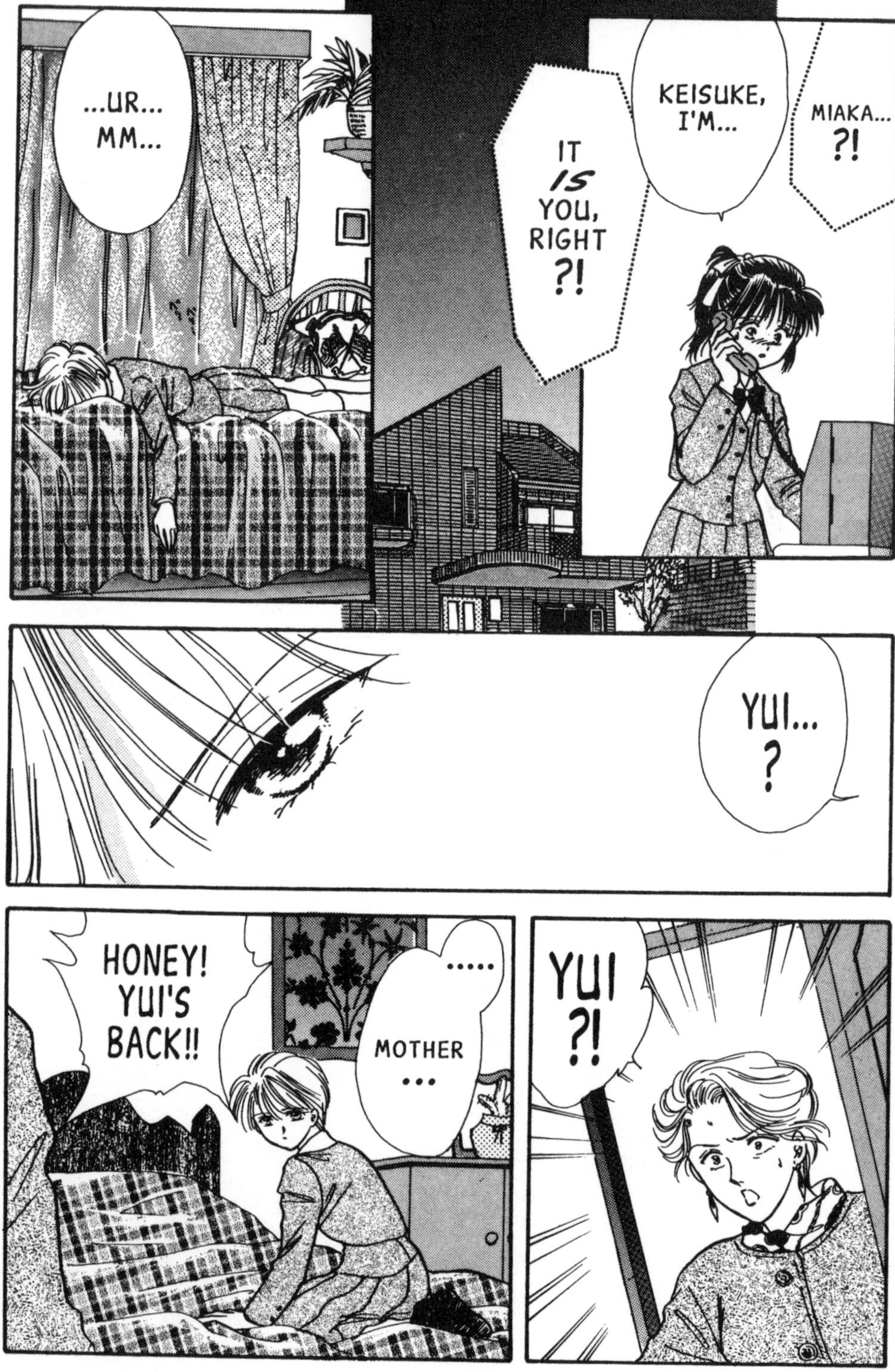
MIAKA... ?!
KEISUKE, I'M...
IT *IS* YOU, RIGHT ?!
...UR... MM...
YUI... ?
YUI ?!
..... MOTHER ...
HONEY! YUI'S BACK!!

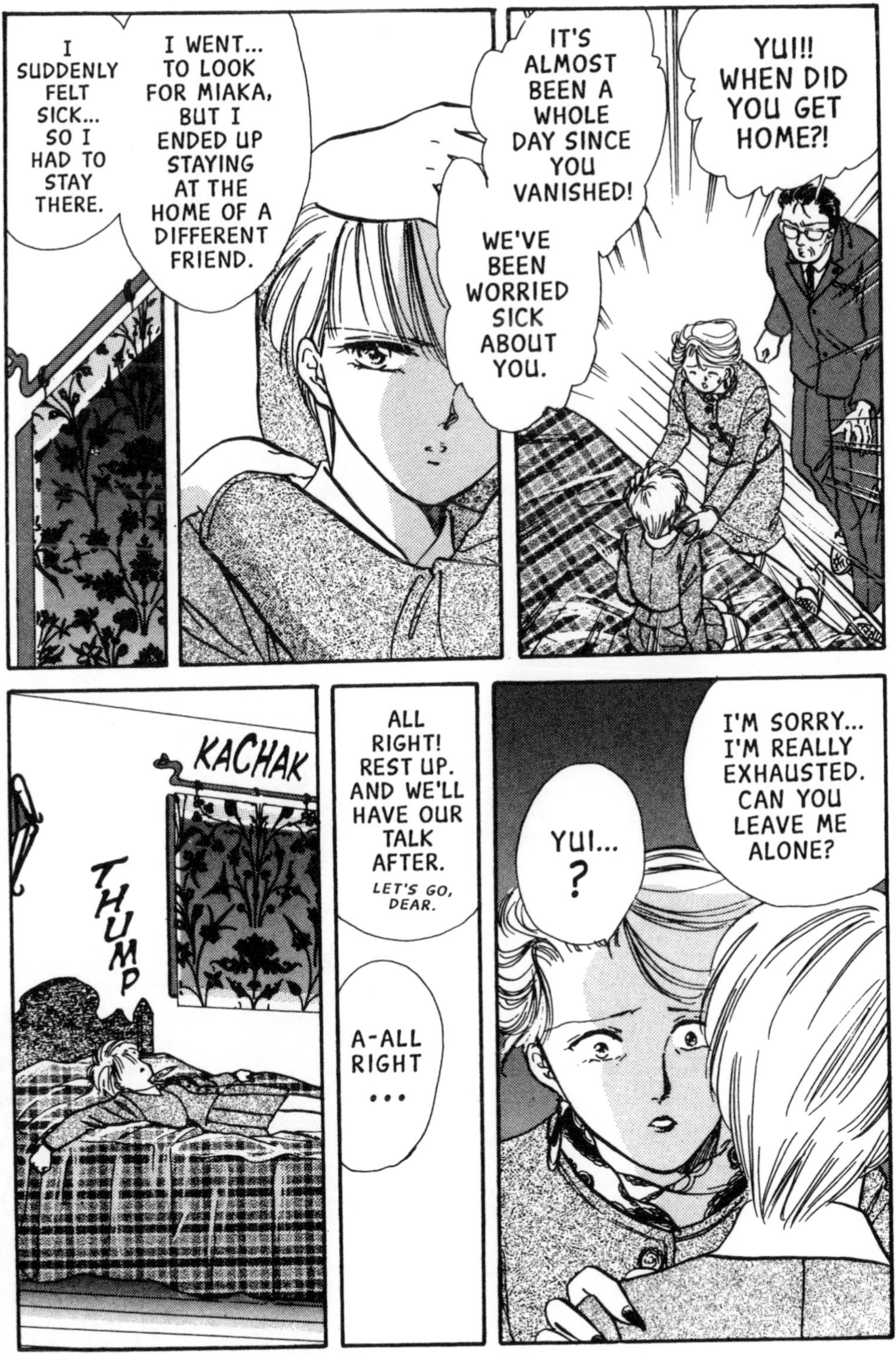
YUI!! WHEN DID YOU GET HOME?!
IT'S ALMOST BEEN A WHOLE DAY SINCE YOU VANISHED!
WE'VE BEEN WORRIED SICK ABOUT YOU.
I WENT... TO LOOK FOR MIAKA, BUT I ENDED UP STAYING AT THE HOME OF A DIFFERENT FRIEND.
I SUDDENLY FELT SICK... SO I HAD TO STAY THERE.
I'M SORRY... I'M REALLY EXHAUSTED. CAN YOU LEAVE ME ALONE?
YUI... ?
ALL RIGHT! REST UP. AND WE'LL HAVE OUR TALK AFTER.
LET'S GO, DEAR.
A-ALL RIGHT ...
KACHAK
THUMP

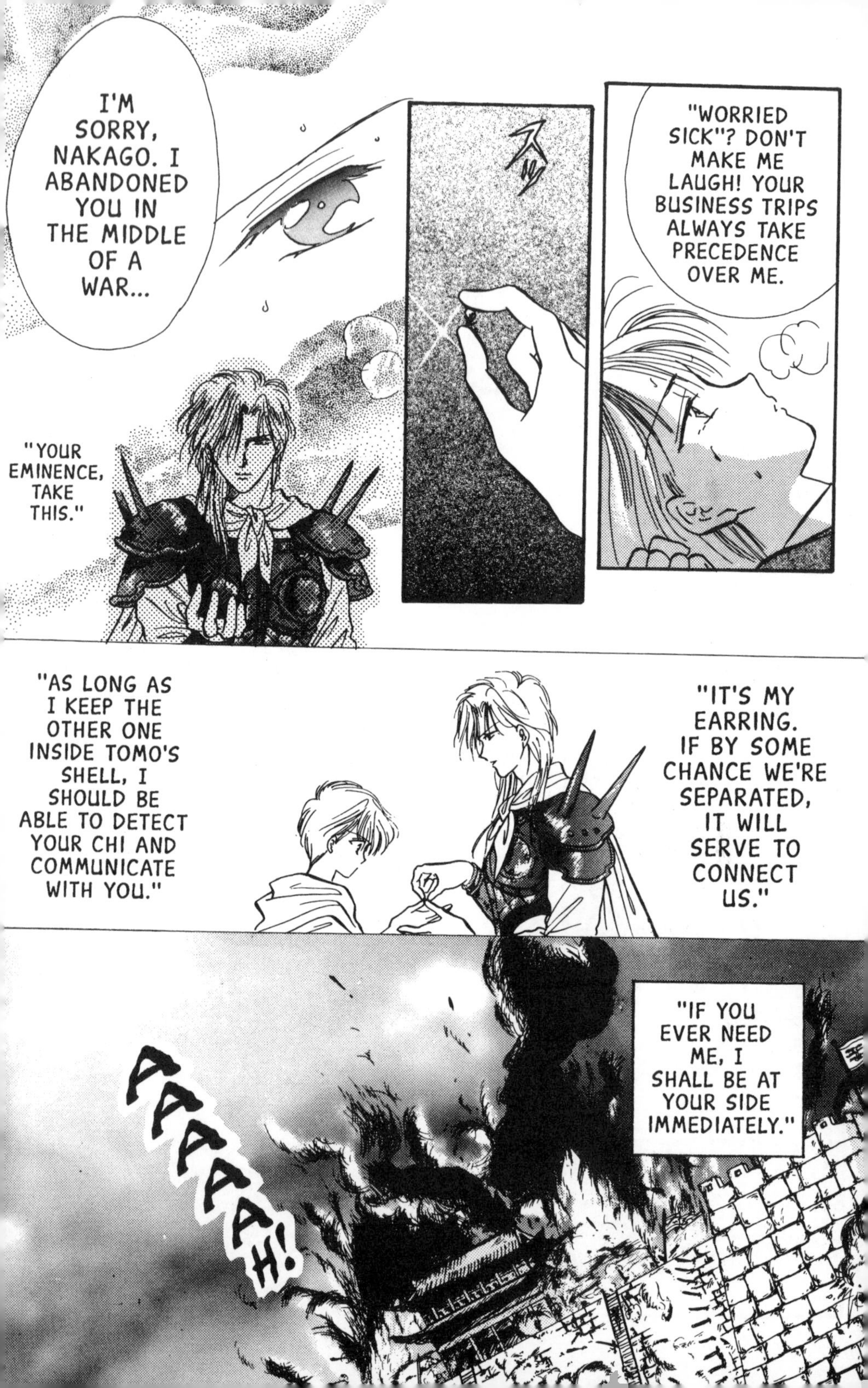
"WORRIED SICK"? DON'T MAKE ME LAUGH! YOUR BUSINESS TRIPS ALWAYS TAKE PRECEDENCE OVER ME.
I'M SORRY, NAKAGO. I ABANDONED YOU IN THE MIDDLE OF A WAR...
"YOUR EMINENCE, TAKE THIS."
"IT'S MY EARRING. IF BY SOME CHANCE WE'RE SEPARATED, IT WILL SERVE TO CONNECT US."
"AS LONG AS I KEEP THE OTHER ONE INSIDE TOMO'S SHELL, I SHOULD BE ABLE TO DETECT YOUR CHI AND COMMUNICATE WITH YOU."
"IF YOU EVER NEED ME, I SHALL BE AT YOUR SIDE IMMEDIATELY."
AAAAAH!

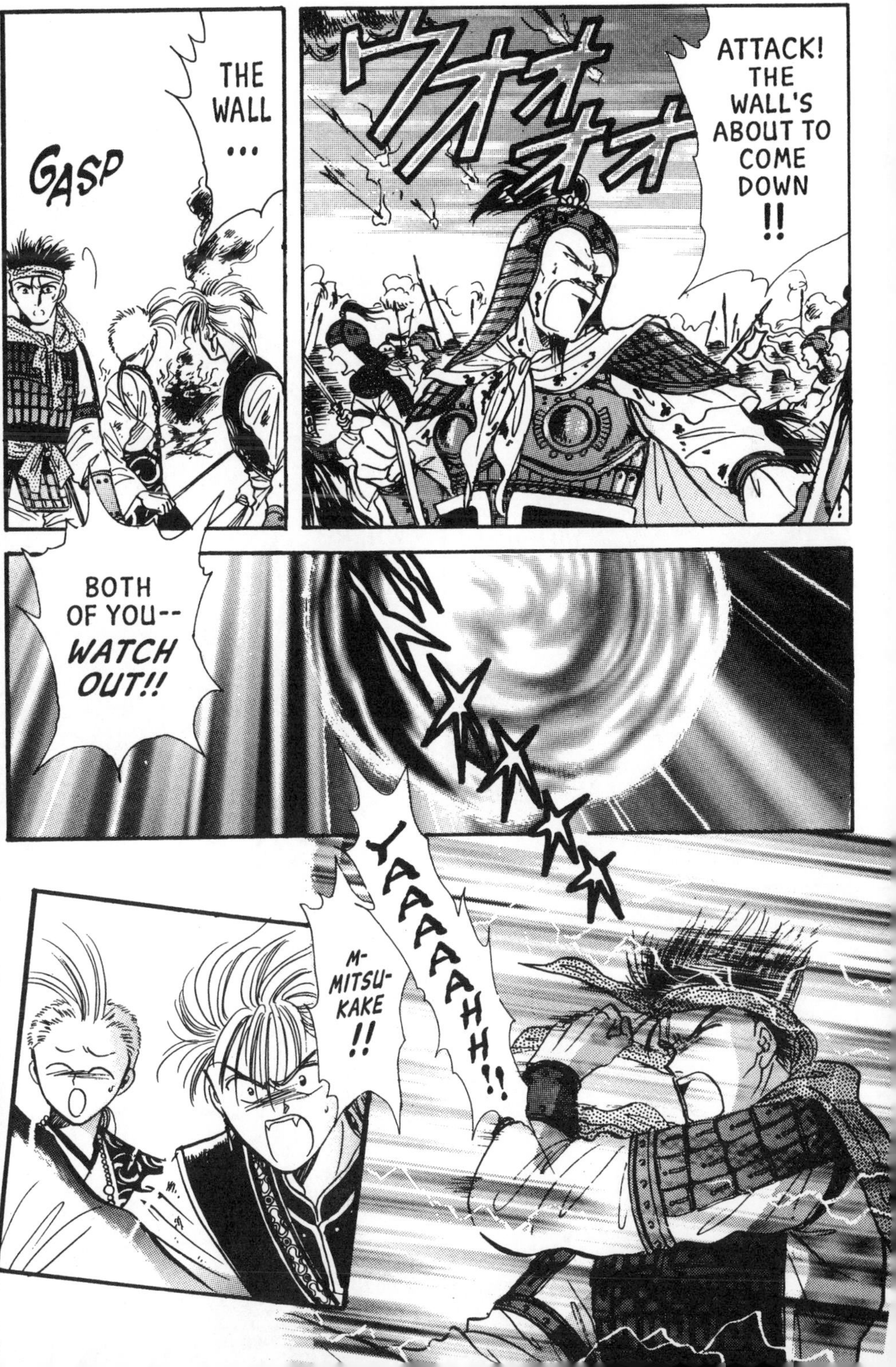
ATTACK! THE WALL'S ABOUT TO COME DOWN !!
THE WALL ...
GASP
BOTH OF YOU-- *WATCH OUT!!*
YAAAAAHH!!
M-MITSU-KAKE !!

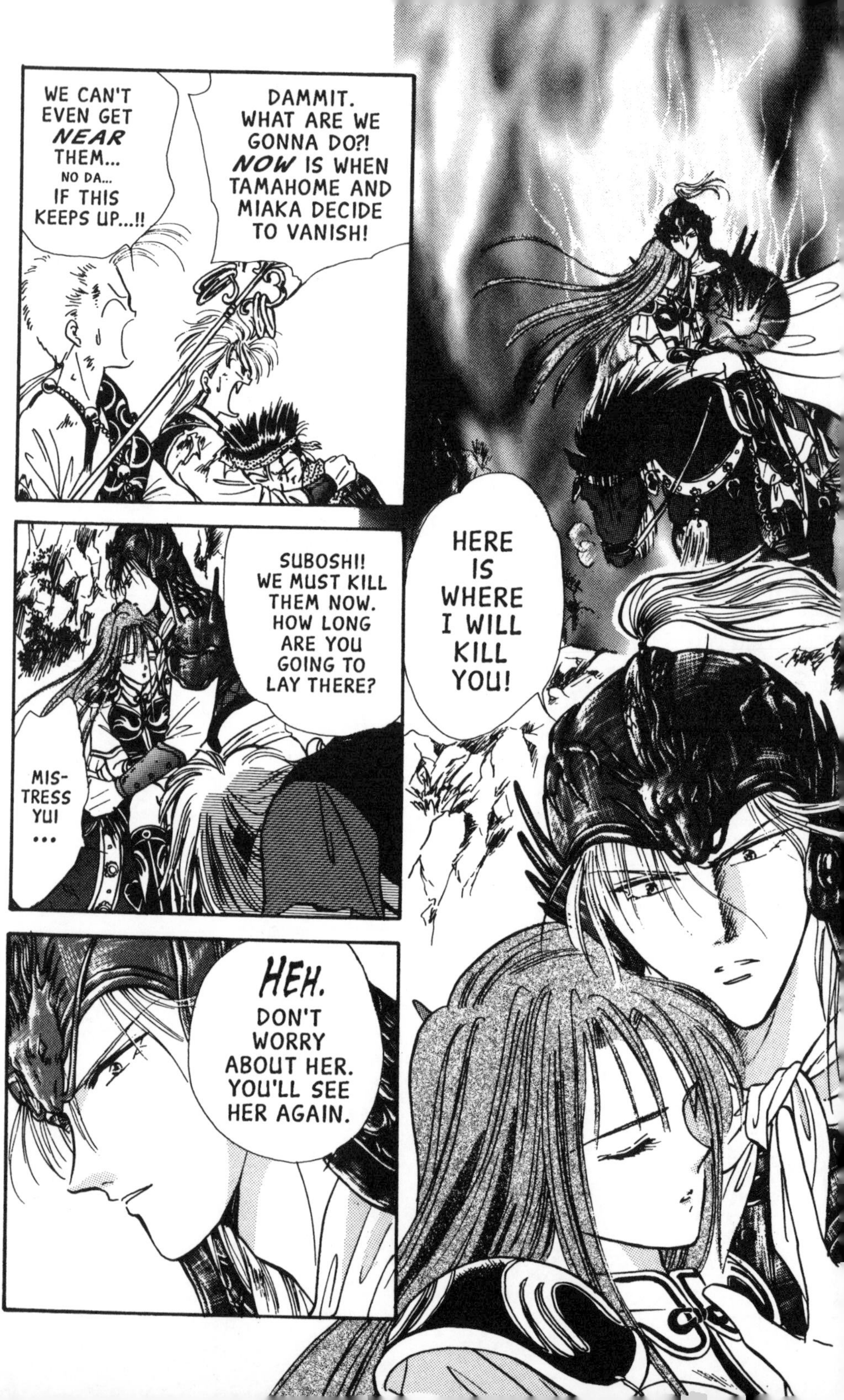
HERE IS WHERE I WILL KILL YOU!
DAMMIT. WHAT ARE WE GONNA DO?! *NOW* IS WHEN TAMAHOME AND MIAKA DECIDE TO VANISH!
WE CAN'T EVEN GET *NEAR* THEM... NO DA... IF THIS KEEPS UP...!!
SUBOSHI! WE MUST KILL THEM NOW. HOW LONG ARE YOU GOING TO LAY THERE?
MISTRESS YUI...
HEH. DON'T WORRY ABOUT HER. YOU'LL SEE HER AGAIN.

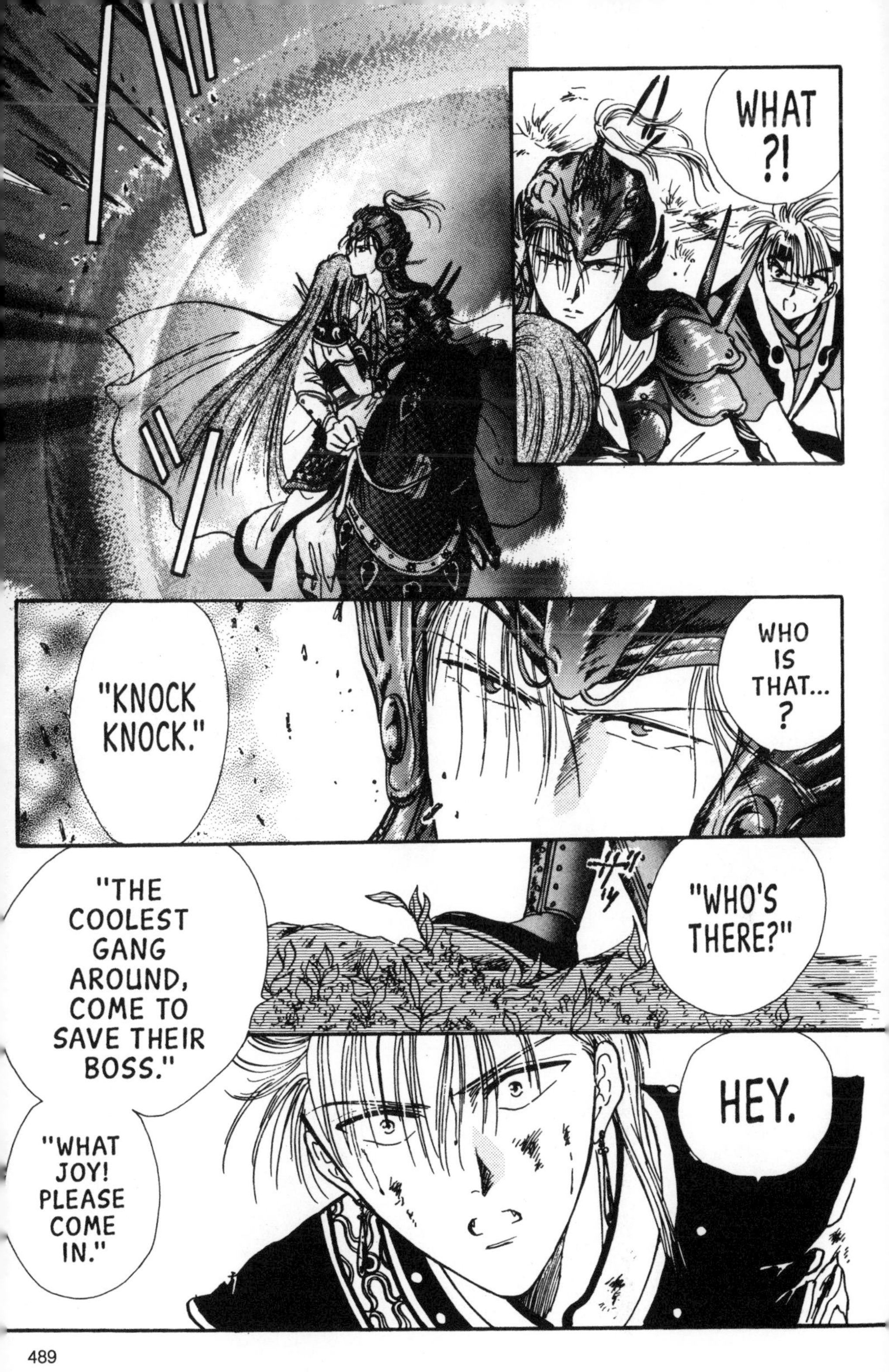
WHAT ?!
WHO IS THAT... ?
"KNOCK KNOCK."
"WHO'S THERE?"
"THE COOLEST GANG AROUND, COME TO SAVE THEIR BOSS."
HEY.
"WHAT JOY! PLEASE COME IN."

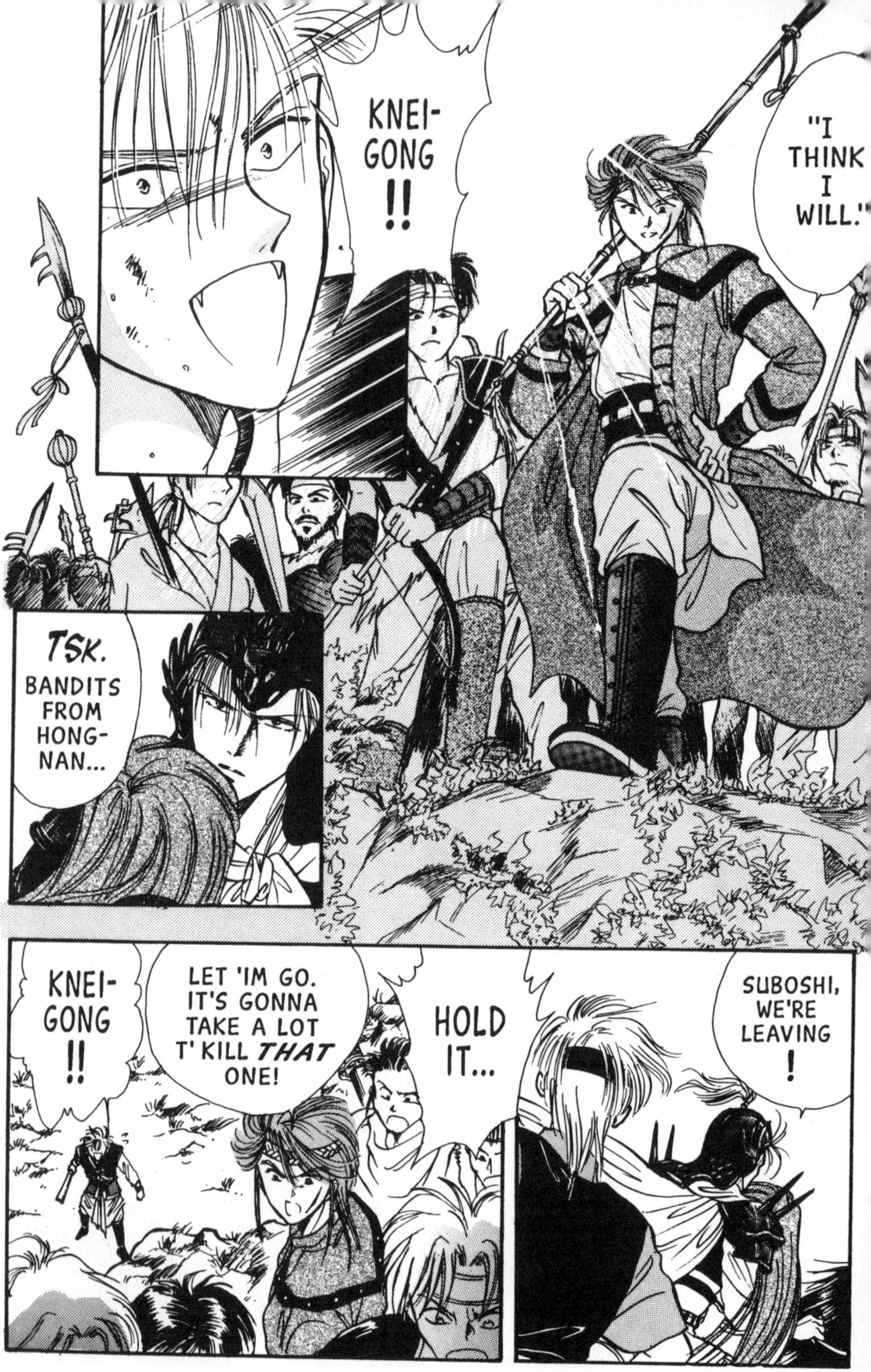
"I THINK I WILL."
KNEI-GONG !!
TSK. BANDITS FROM HONG-NAN...
SUBOSHI, WE'RE LEAVING !
HOLD IT...
LET 'IM GO. IT'S GONNA TAKE A LOT T' KILL *THAT* ONE!
KNEI-GONG !!

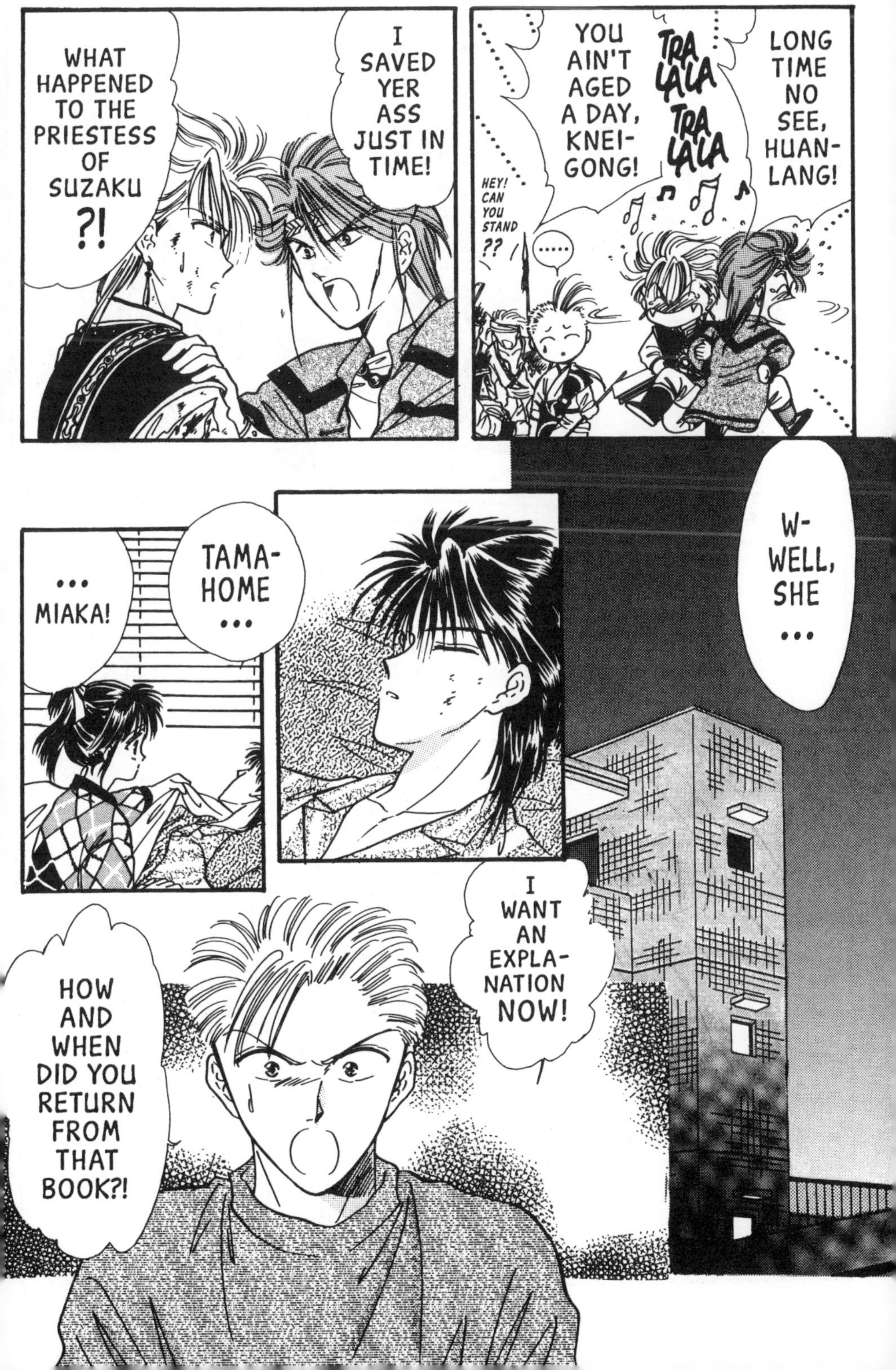
LONG TIME NO SEE, HUAN-LANG!
TRA LA LA TRA LA LA
YOU AIN'T AGED A DAY, KNEI-GONG!
......
HEY! CAN YOU STAND??
I SAVED YER ASS JUST IN TIME!
WHAT HAPPENED TO THE PRIESTESS OF SUZAKU?!
W-WELL, SHE...
TAMA-HOME...
...MIAKA!
I WANT AN EXPLA-NATION NOW!
HOW AND WHEN DID YOU RETURN FROM THAT BOOK?!

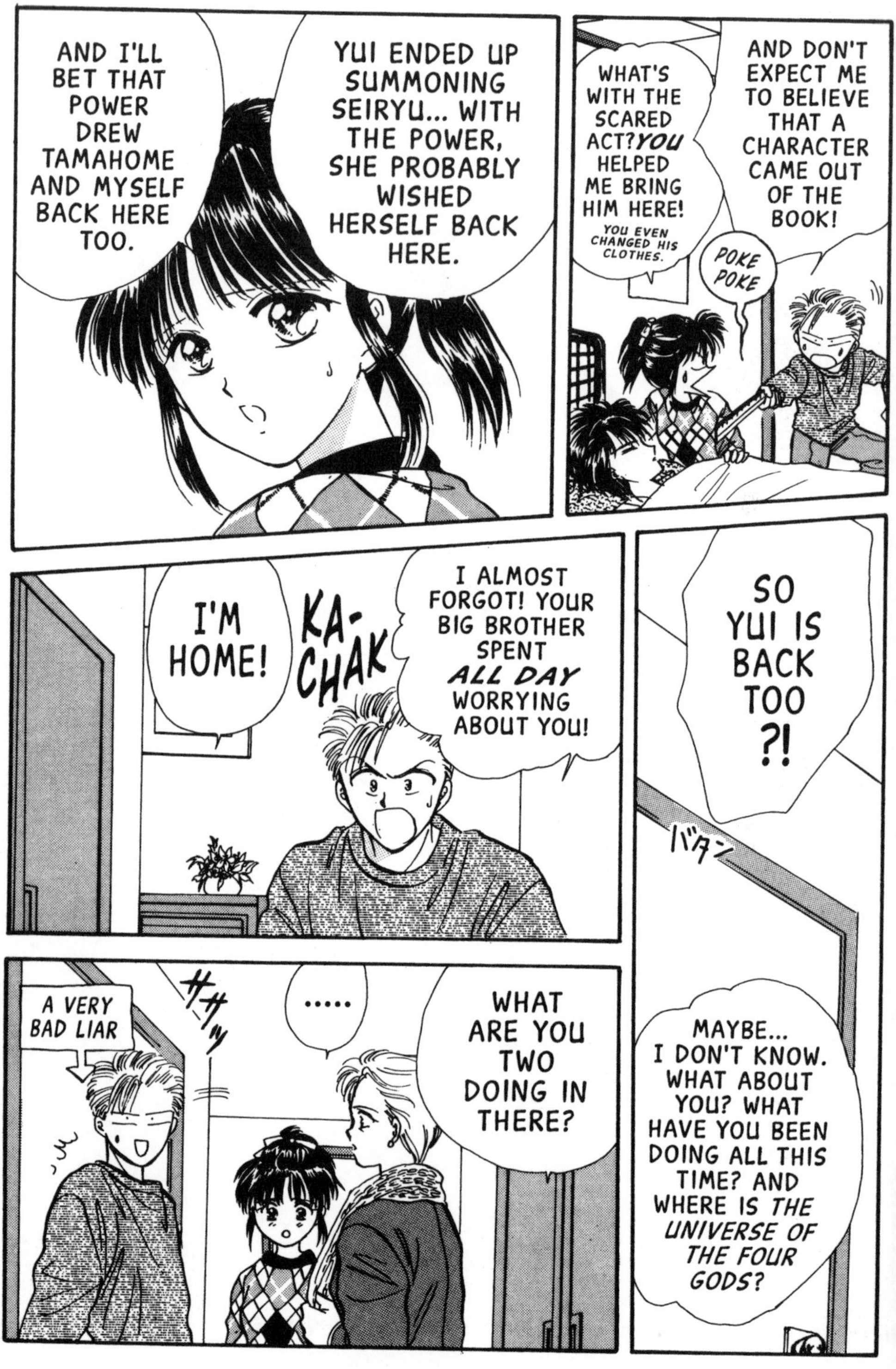
AND DON'T EXPECT ME TO BELIEVE THAT A CHARACTER CAME OUT OF THE BOOK!
WHAT'S WITH THE SCARED ACT? *YOU* HELPED ME BRING HIM HERE!
YOU EVEN CHANGED HIS CLOTHES.
POKE POKE
YUI ENDED UP SUMMONING SEIRYU... WITH THE POWER, SHE PROBABLY WISHED HERSELF BACK HERE.
AND I'LL BET THAT POWER DREW TAMAHOME AND MYSELF BACK HERE TOO.
SO YUI IS BACK TOO ?!
バタン
MAYBE... I DON'T KNOW. WHAT ABOUT YOU? WHAT HAVE YOU BEEN DOING ALL THIS TIME? AND WHERE IS *THE UNIVERSE OF THE FOUR GODS*?
I ALMOST FORGOT! YOUR BIG BROTHER SPENT *ALL DAY* WORRYING ABOUT YOU!
KA-CHAK
I'M HOME!
WHAT ARE YOU TWO DOING IN THERE?
.....
ササッ
A VERY BAD LIAR

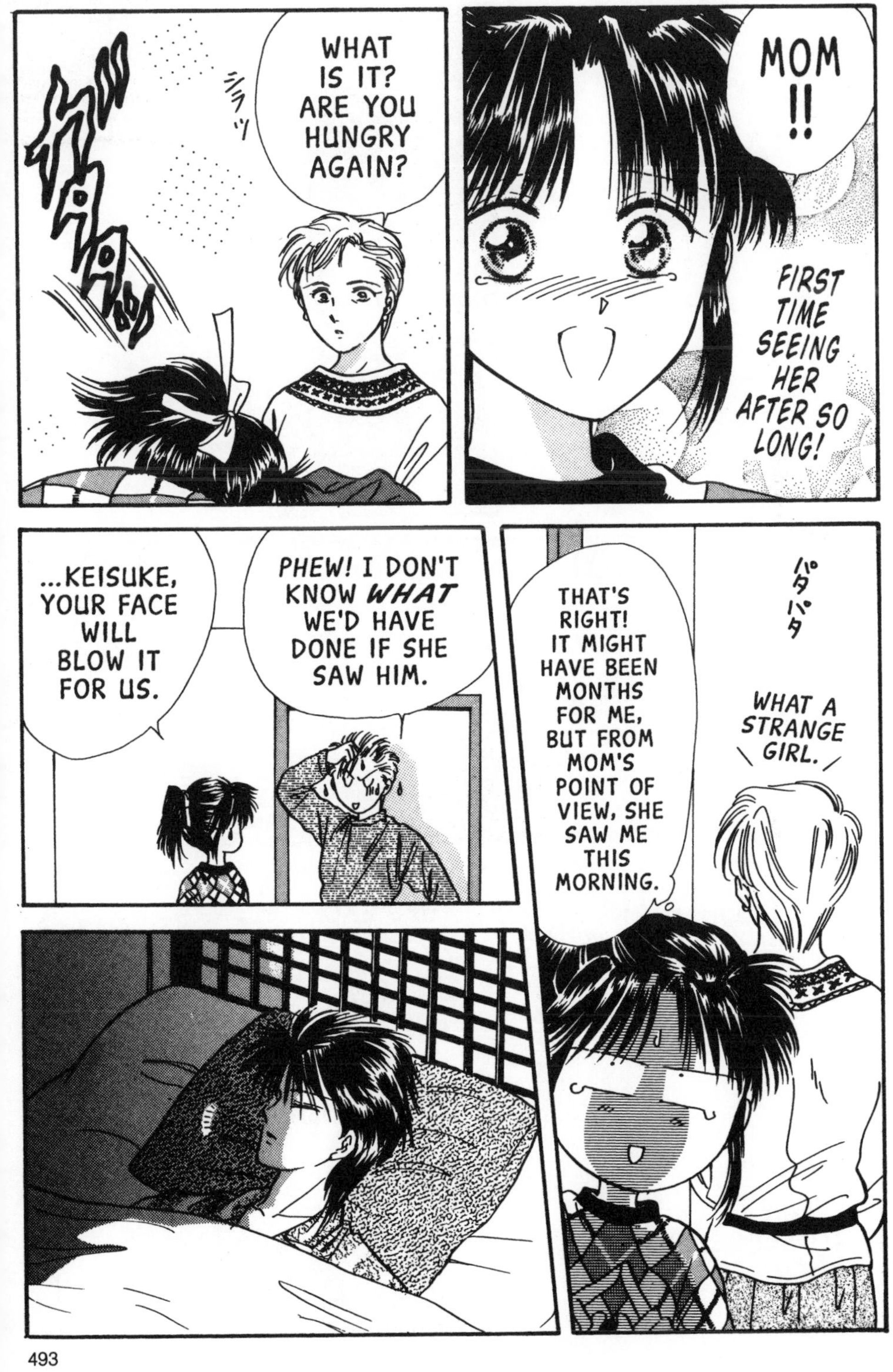
MOM!!
FIRST TIME SEEING HER AFTER SO LONG!
WHAT IS IT? ARE YOU HUNGRY AGAIN?
シラッ
パタパタ
WHAT A STRANGE GIRL.
THAT'S RIGHT! IT MIGHT HAVE BEEN MONTHS FOR ME, BUT FROM MOM'S POINT OF VIEW, SHE SAW ME THIS MORNING.
PHEW! I DON'T KNOW *WHAT* WE'D HAVE DONE IF SHE SAW HIM.
...KEISUKE, YOUR FACE WILL BLOW IT FOR US.

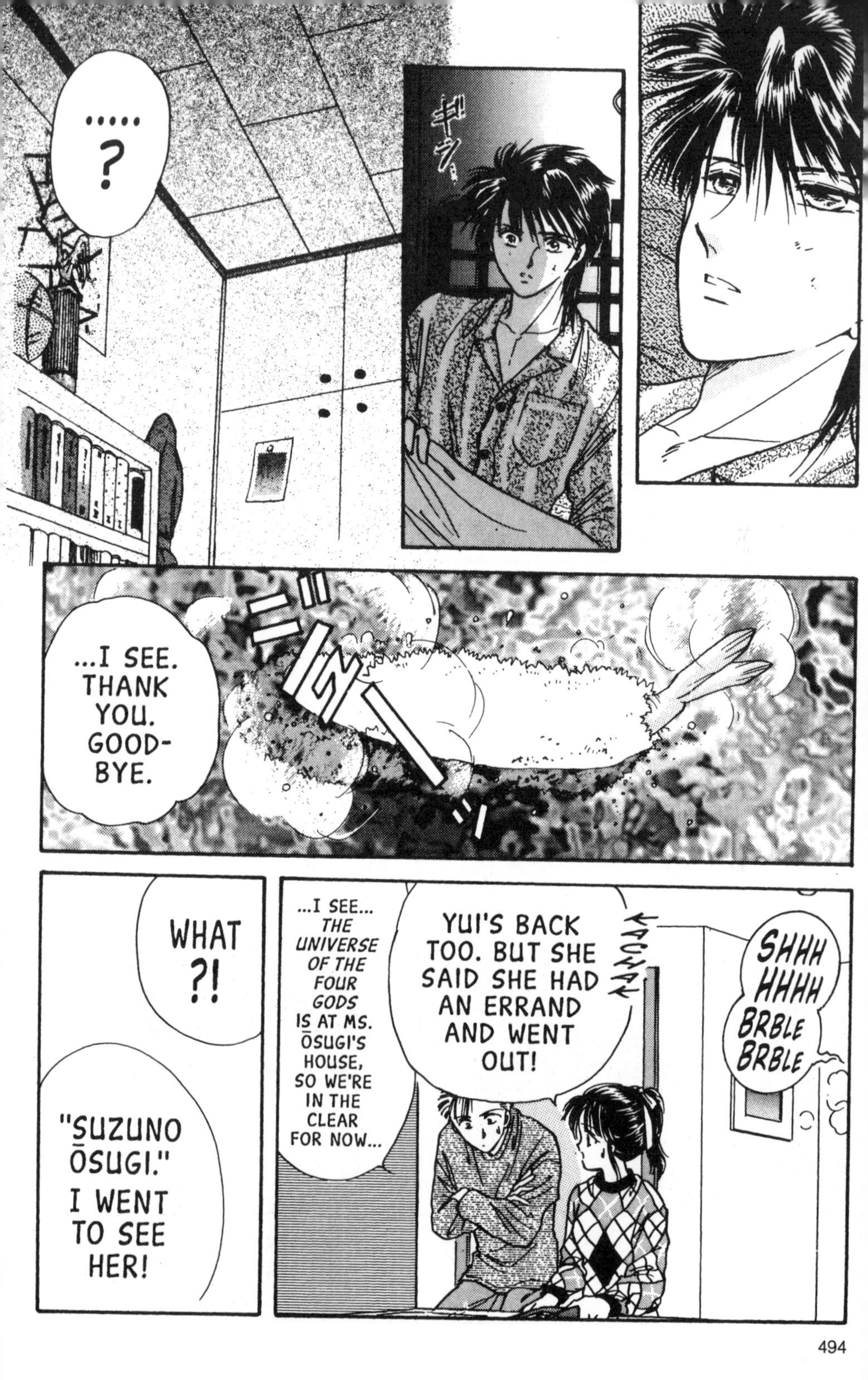
.....
?
...I SEE. THANK YOU. GOOD-BYE.
SHHH HHHH BRBLE BRBLE
KACHAK
YUI'S BACK TOO. BUT SHE SAID SHE HAD AN ERRAND AND WENT OUT!
...I SEE... THE UNIVERSE OF THE FOUR GODS IS AT MS. ŌSUGI'S HOUSE, SO WE'RE IN THE CLEAR FOR NOW...
WHAT?!
"SUZUNO ŌSUGI." I WENT TO SEE HER!

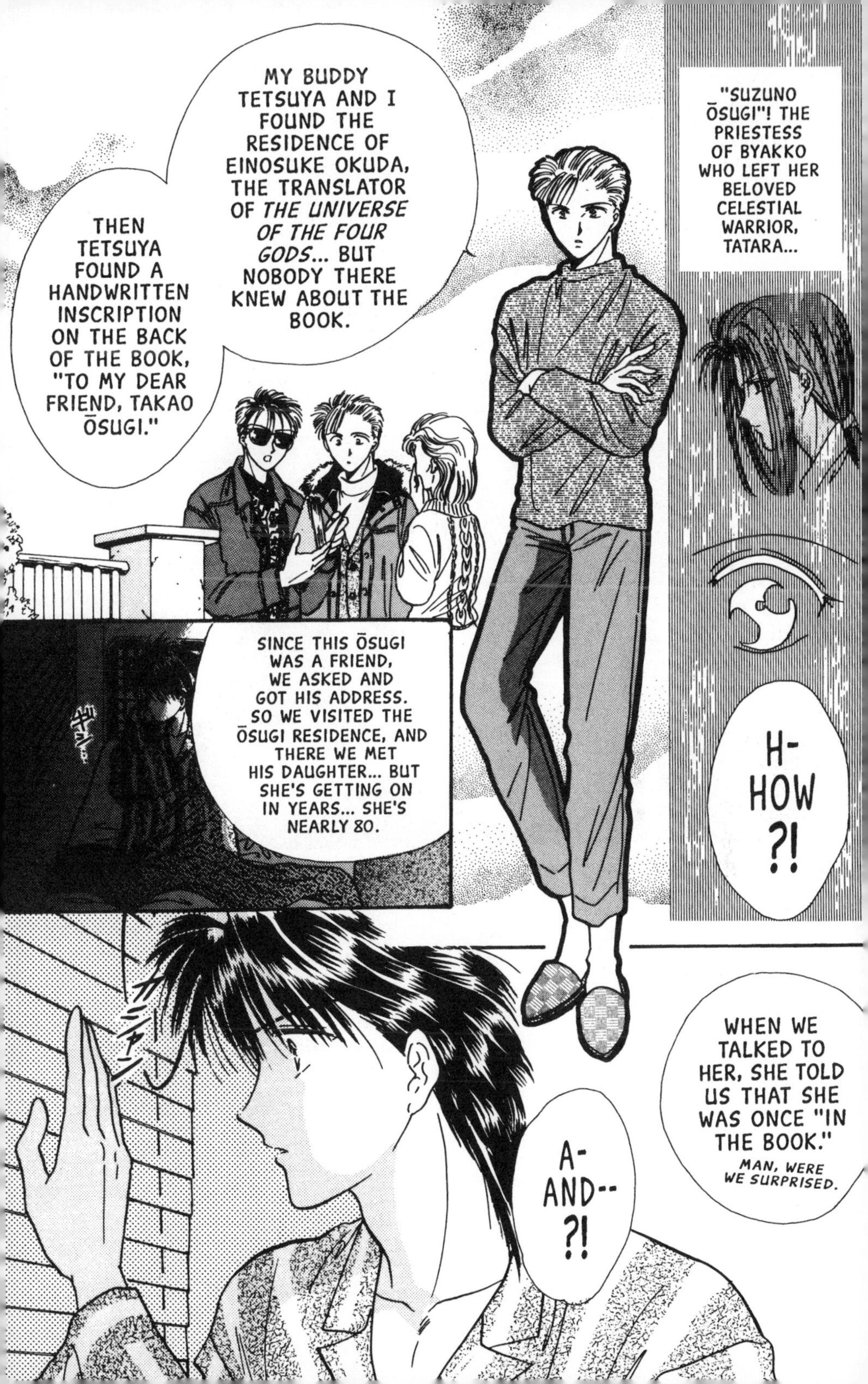
"SUZUNO ŌSUGI"! THE PRIESTESS OF BYAKKO WHO LEFT HER BELOVED CELESTIAL WARRIOR, TATARA...
H-HOW ?!
MY BUDDY TETSUYA AND I FOUND THE RESIDENCE OF EINOSUKE OKUDA, THE TRANSLATOR OF *THE UNIVERSE OF THE FOUR GODS*... BUT NOBODY THERE KNEW ABOUT THE BOOK.
THEN TETSUYA FOUND A HANDWRITTEN INSCRIPTION ON THE BACK OF THE BOOK, "TO MY DEAR FRIEND, TAKAO ŌSUGI."
SINCE THIS ŌSUGI WAS A FRIEND, WE ASKED AND GOT HIS ADDRESS. SO WE VISITED THE ŌSUGI RESIDENCE, AND THERE WE MET HIS DAUGHTER... BUT SHE'S GETTING ON IN YEARS... SHE'S NEARLY 80.
WHEN WE TALKED TO HER, SHE TOLD US THAT SHE WAS ONCE "IN THE BOOK."
MAN, WERE WE SURPRISED.
A-AND-- ?!

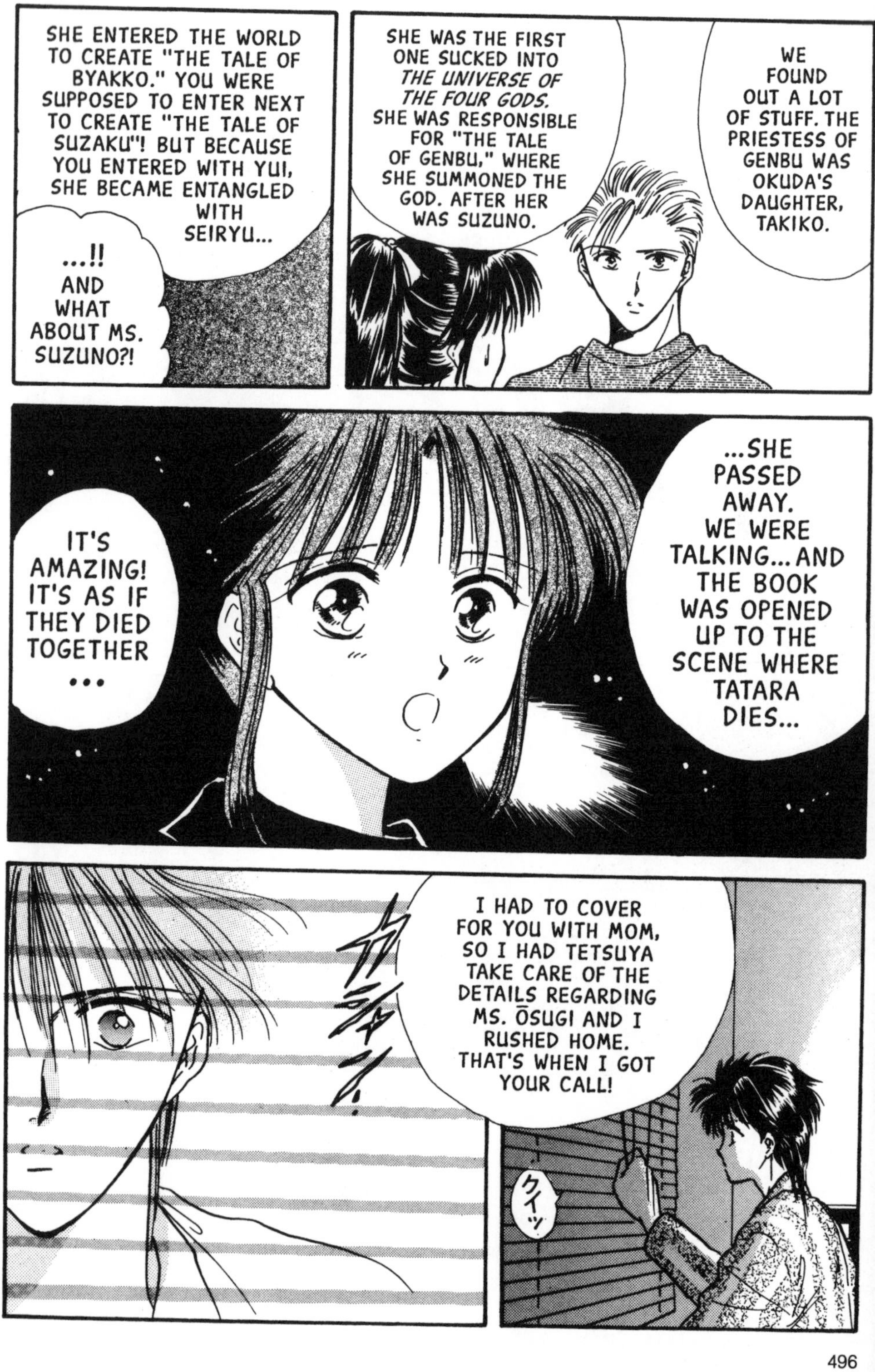
WE FOUND OUT A LOT OF STUFF. THE PRIESTESS OF GENBU WAS OKUDA'S DAUGHTER, TAKIKO.
SHE WAS THE FIRST ONE SUCKED INTO *THE UNIVERSE OF THE FOUR GODS.* SHE WAS RESPONSIBLE FOR "THE TALE OF GENBU," WHERE SHE SUMMONED THE GOD. AFTER HER WAS SUZUNO.
SHE ENTERED THE WORLD TO CREATE "THE TALE OF BYAKKO." YOU WERE SUPPOSED TO ENTER NEXT TO CREATE "THE TALE OF SUZAKU"! BUT BECAUSE YOU ENTERED WITH YUI, SHE BECAME ENTANGLED WITH SEIRYU...
...!! AND WHAT ABOUT MS. SUZUNO?!
...SHE PASSED AWAY. WE WERE TALKING... AND THE BOOK WAS OPENED UP TO THE SCENE WHERE TATARA DIES...
IT'S AMAZING! IT'S AS IF THEY DIED TOGETHER...
I HAD TO COVER FOR YOU WITH MOM, SO I HAD TETSUYA TAKE CARE OF THE DETAILS REGARDING MS. ŌSUGI AND I RUSHED HOME. THAT'S WHEN I GOT YOUR CALL!
クイッ

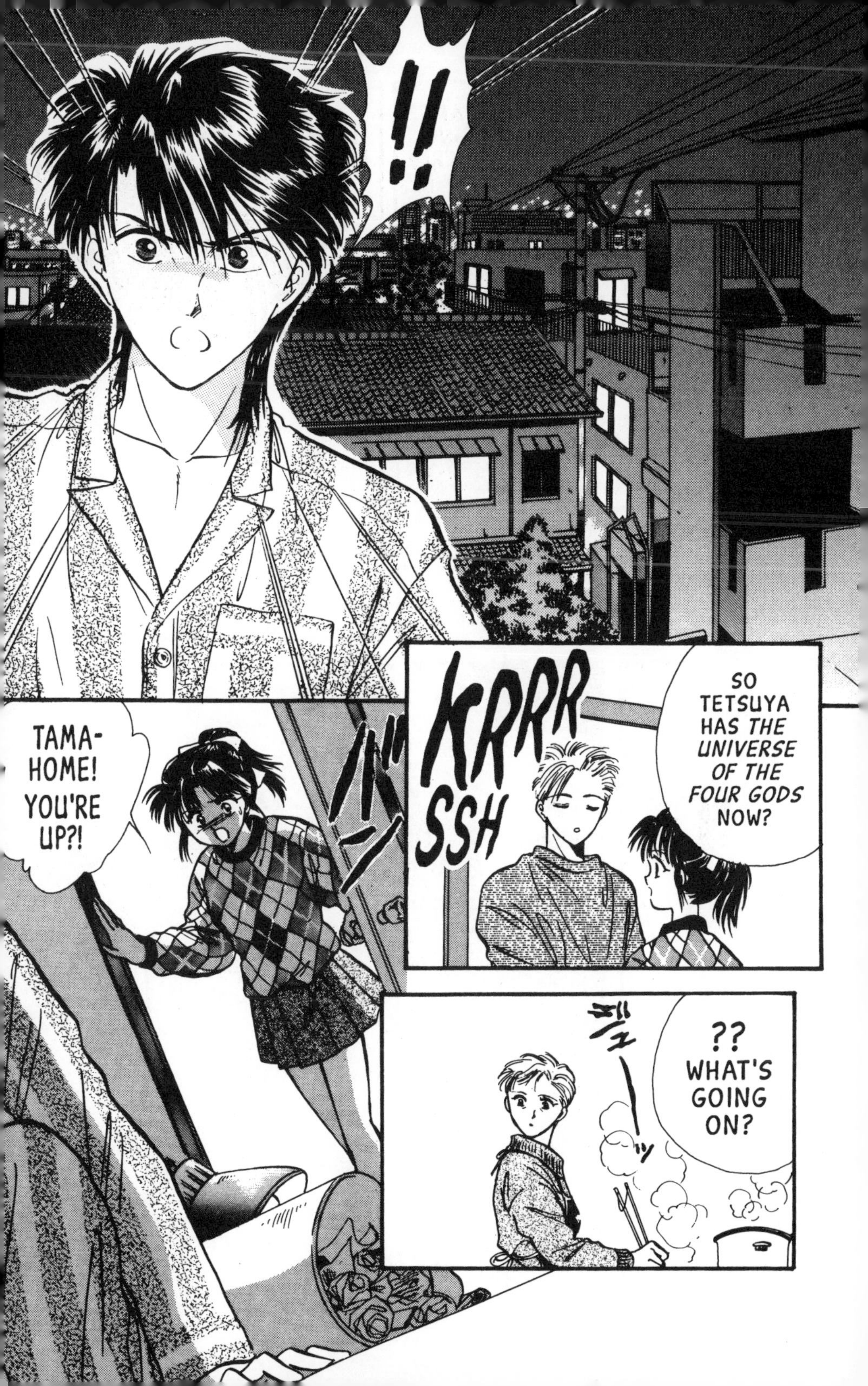
!!
KRRR SSH
SO TETSUYA HAS THE UNIVERSE OF THE FOUR GODS NOW?
?? WHAT'S GOING ON?
TAMA-HOME! YOU'RE UP?!

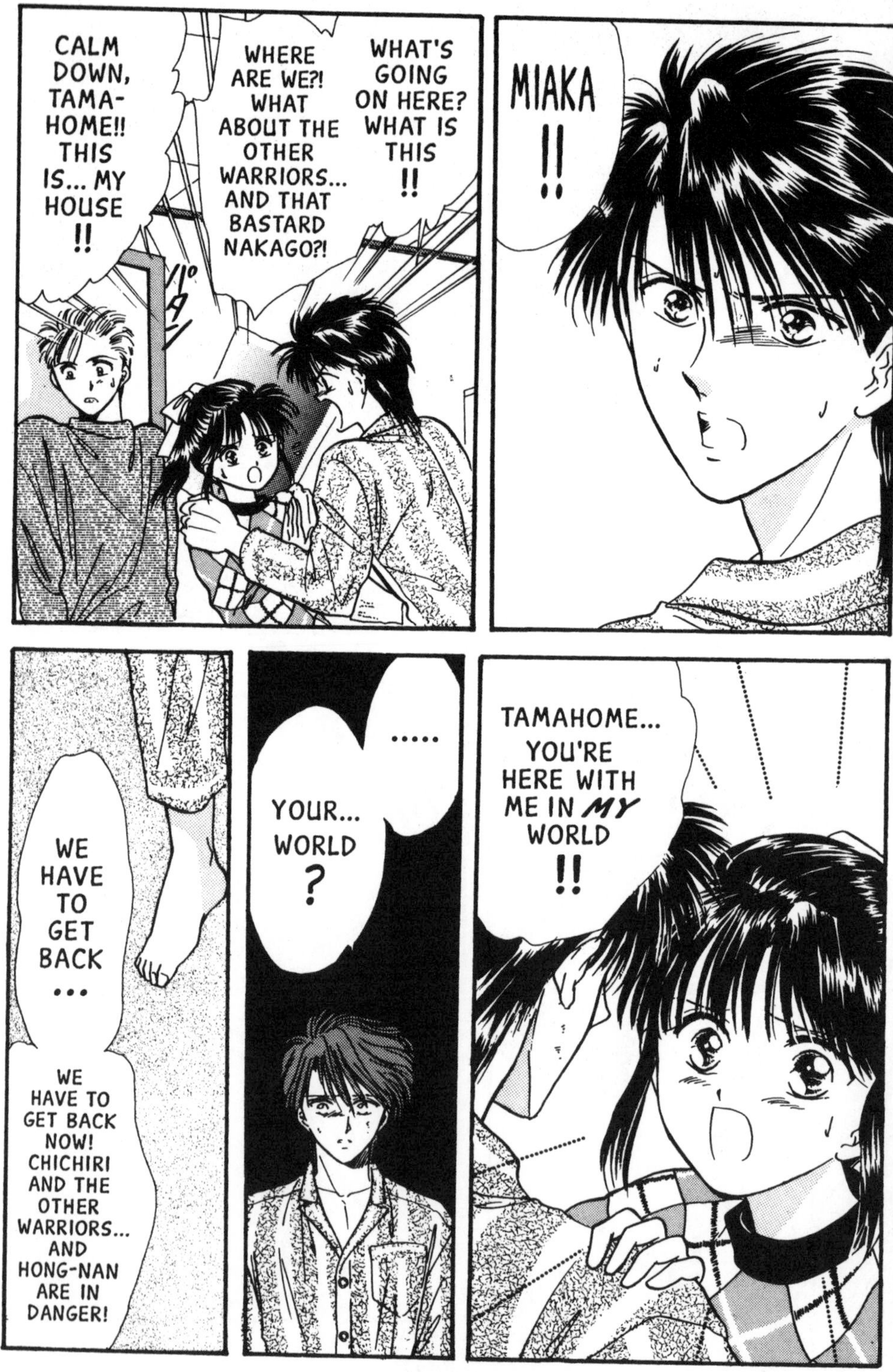
MIAKA !!
WHAT'S GOING ON HERE? WHAT IS THIS !!
WHERE ARE WE?! WHAT ABOUT THE OTHER WARRIORS... AND THAT BASTARD NAKAGO?!
CALM DOWN, TAMA-HOME!! THIS IS... MY HOUSE !!
TAMAHOME... YOU'RE HERE WITH ME IN *MY* WORLD !!
.....
YOUR... WORLD ?
WE HAVE TO GET BACK ...
WE HAVE TO GET BACK NOW! CHICHIRI AND THE OTHER WARRIORS... AND HONG-NAN ARE IN DANGER!

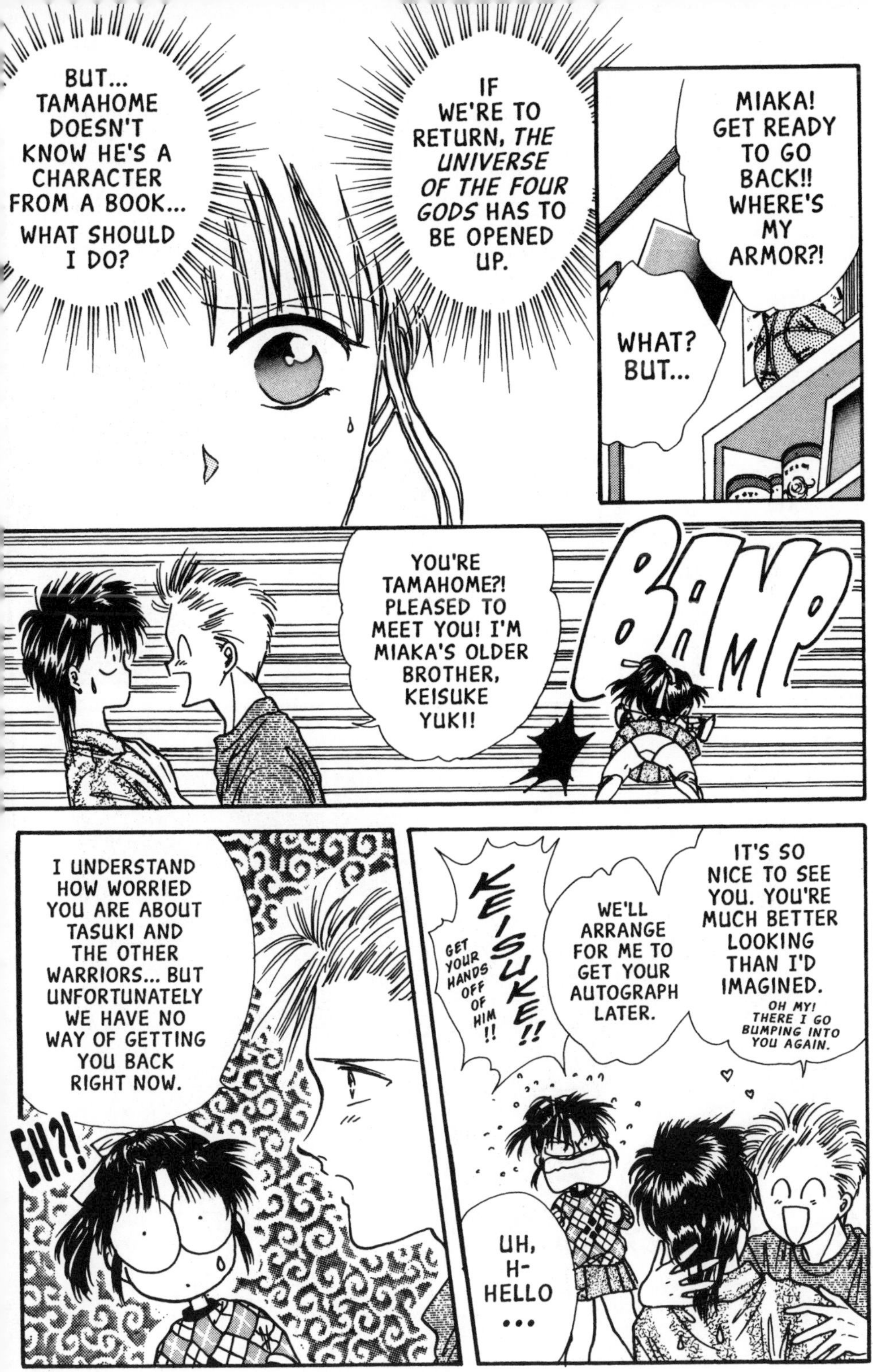
MIAKA! GET READY TO GO BACK!! WHERE'S MY ARMOR?!
WHAT? BUT...
IF WE'RE TO RETURN, *THE UNIVERSE OF THE FOUR GODS* HAS TO BE OPENED UP.
BUT... TAMAHOME DOESN'T KNOW HE'S A CHARACTER FROM A BOOK... WHAT SHOULD I DO?
BAMP
YOU'RE TAMAHOME?! PLEASED TO MEET YOU! I'M MIAKA'S OLDER BROTHER, KEISUKE YUKI!
IT'S SO NICE TO SEE YOU. YOU'RE MUCH BETTER LOOKING THAN I'D IMAGINED.
OH MY! THERE I GO BUMPING INTO YOU AGAIN.
WE'LL ARRANGE FOR ME TO GET YOUR AUTOGRAPH LATER.
KEISUKE!!
GET YOUR HANDS OFF OF HIM!!
UH, H-HELLO...
I UNDERSTAND HOW WORRIED YOU ARE ABOUT TASUKI AND THE OTHER WARRIORS... BUT UNFORTUNATELY WE HAVE NO WAY OF GETTING YOU BACK RIGHT NOW.
EH?!

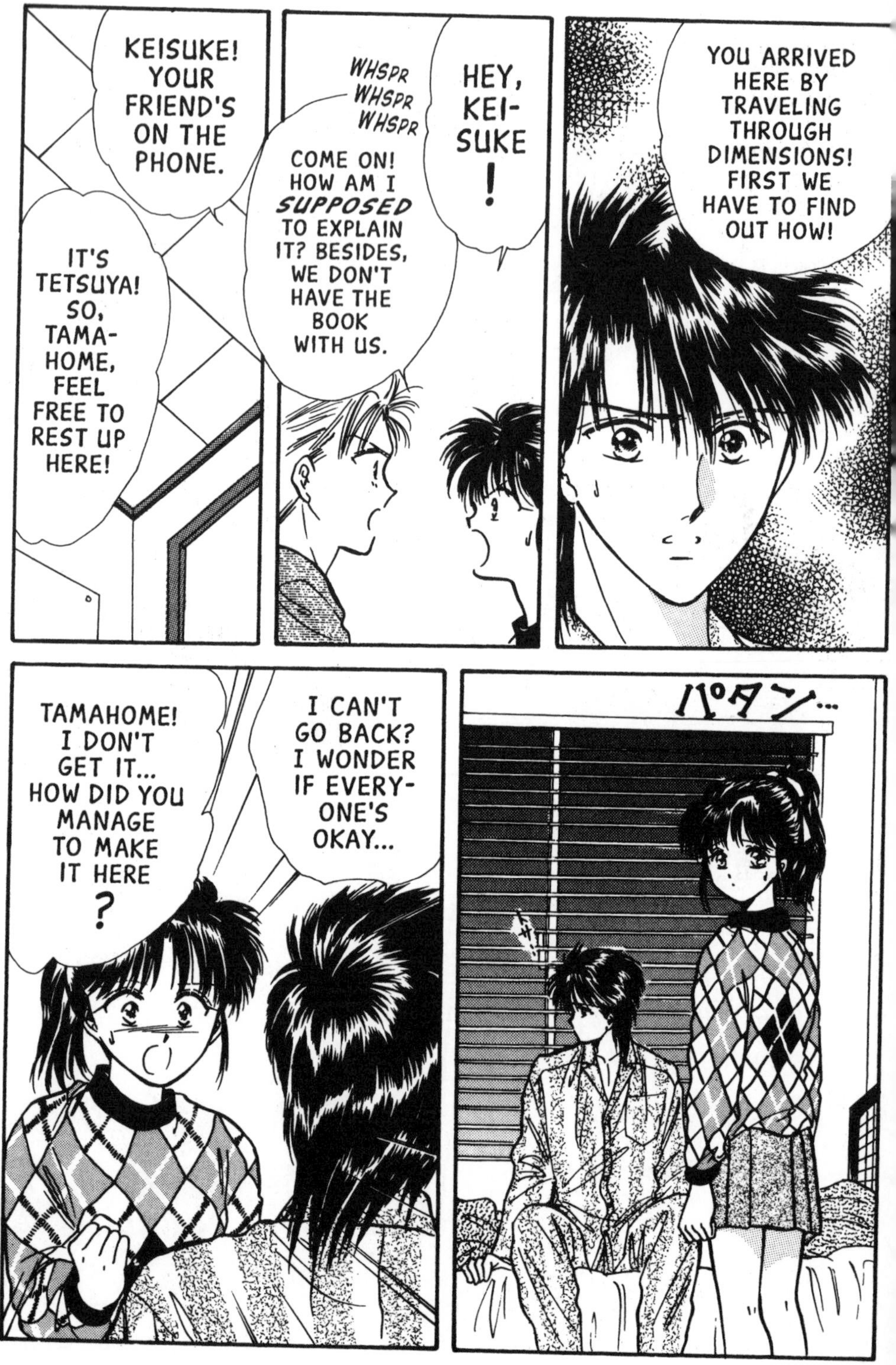
YOU ARRIVED HERE BY TRAVELING THROUGH DIMENSIONS! FIRST WE HAVE TO FIND OUT HOW!
HEY, KEI-SUKE!
WHSPR WHSPR WHSPR
COME ON! HOW AM I SUPPOSED TO EXPLAIN IT? BESIDES, WE DON'T HAVE THE BOOK WITH US.
KEISUKE! YOUR FRIEND'S ON THE PHONE.
IT'S TETSUYA! SO, TAMAHOME, FEEL FREE TO REST UP HERE!
パタン…
I CAN'T GO BACK? I WONDER IF EVERYONE'S OKAY...
TAMAHOME! I DON'T GET IT... HOW DID YOU MANAGE TO MAKE IT HERE?

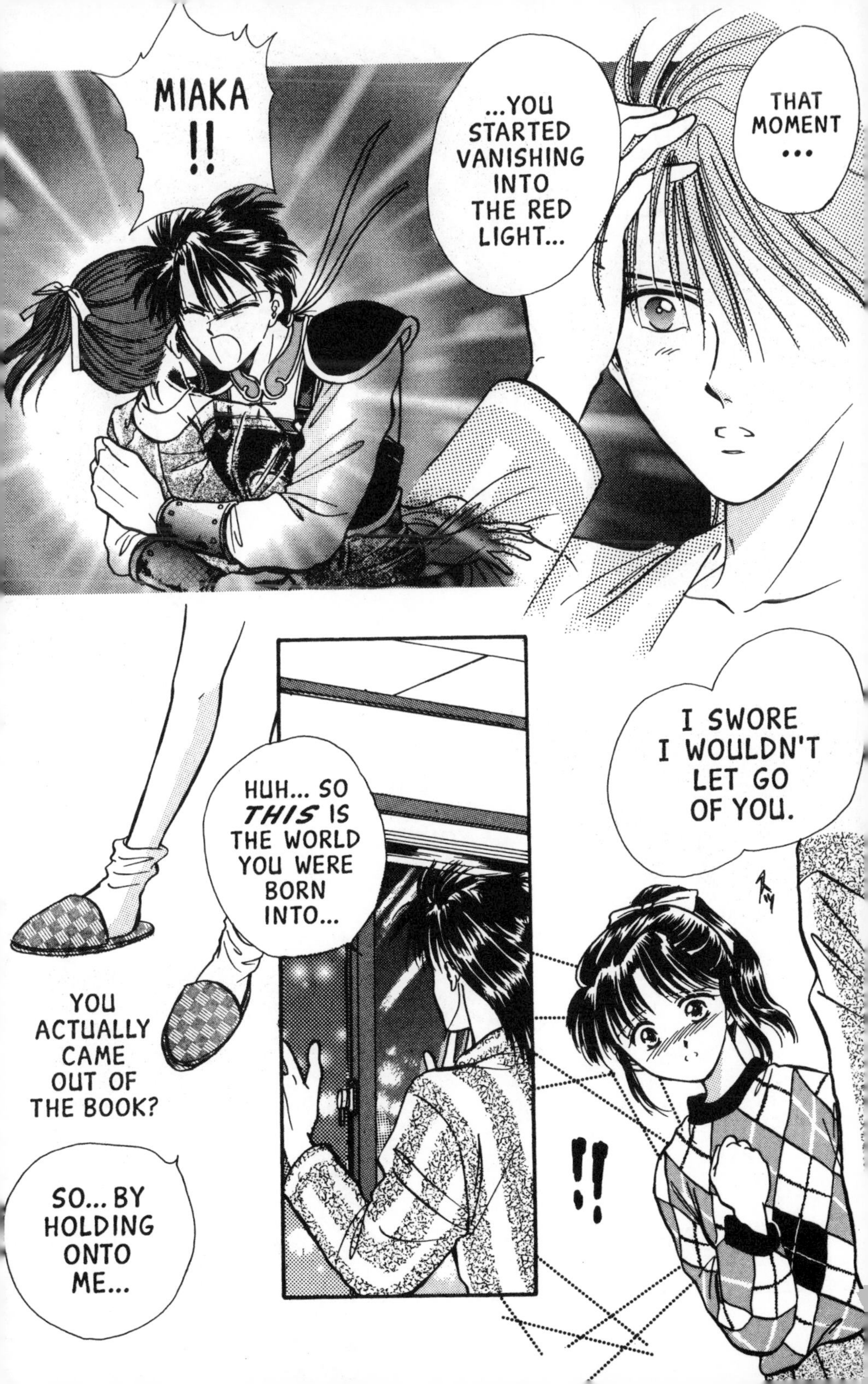
THAT MOMENT...
...YOU STARTED VANISHING INTO THE RED LIGHT...
MIAKA!!
I SWORE I WOULDN'T LET GO OF YOU.
!!
HUH... SO *THIS* IS THE WORLD YOU WERE BORN INTO...
YOU ACTUALLY CAME OUT OF THE BOOK?
SO... BY HOLDING ONTO ME...

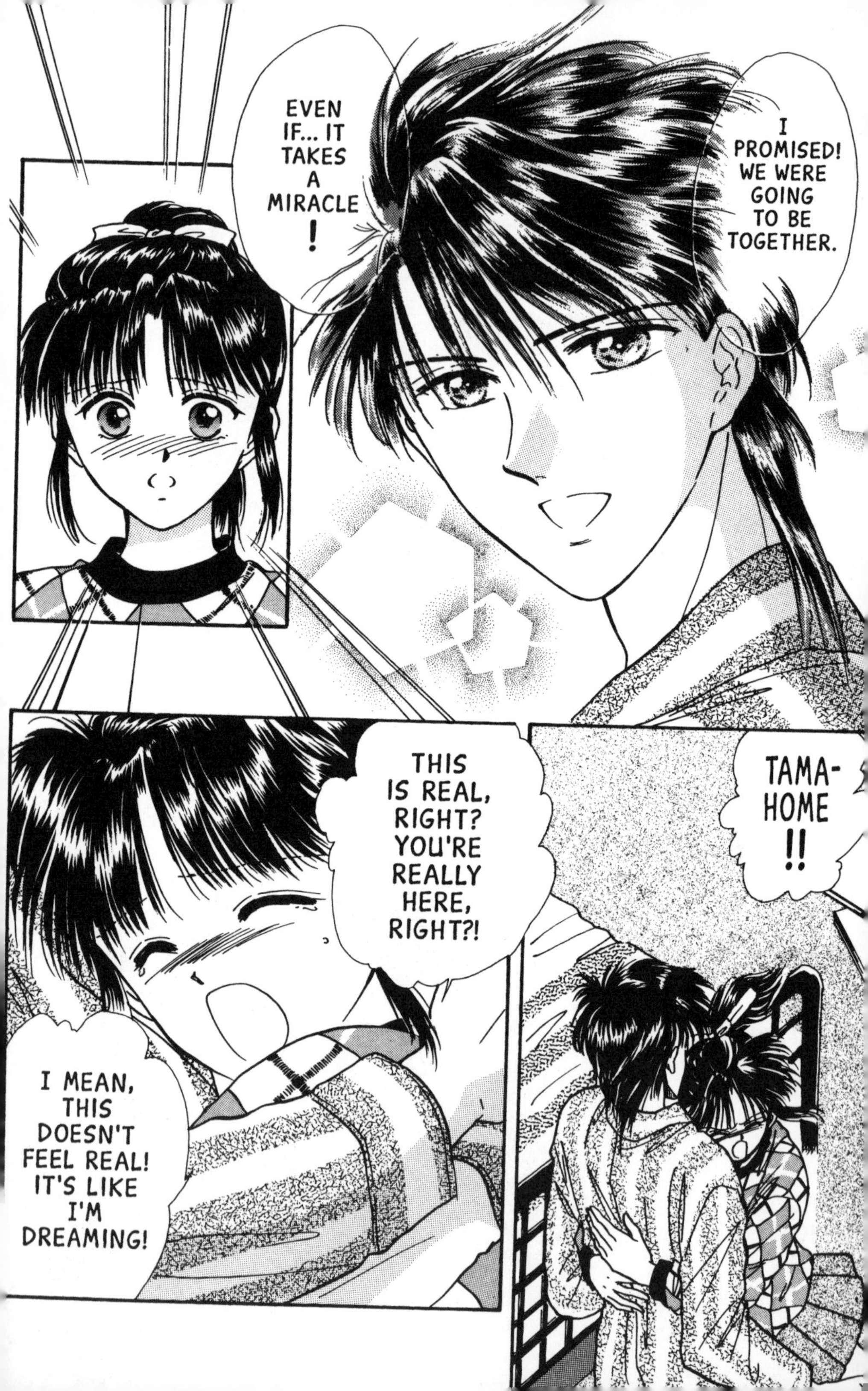
I PROMISED! WE WERE GOING TO BE TOGETHER.
EVEN IF... IT TAKES A MIRACLE!
TAMA-HOME!!
THIS IS REAL, RIGHT? YOU'RE REALLY HERE, RIGHT?!
I MEAN, THIS DOESN'T FEEL REAL! IT'S LIKE I'M DREAMING!

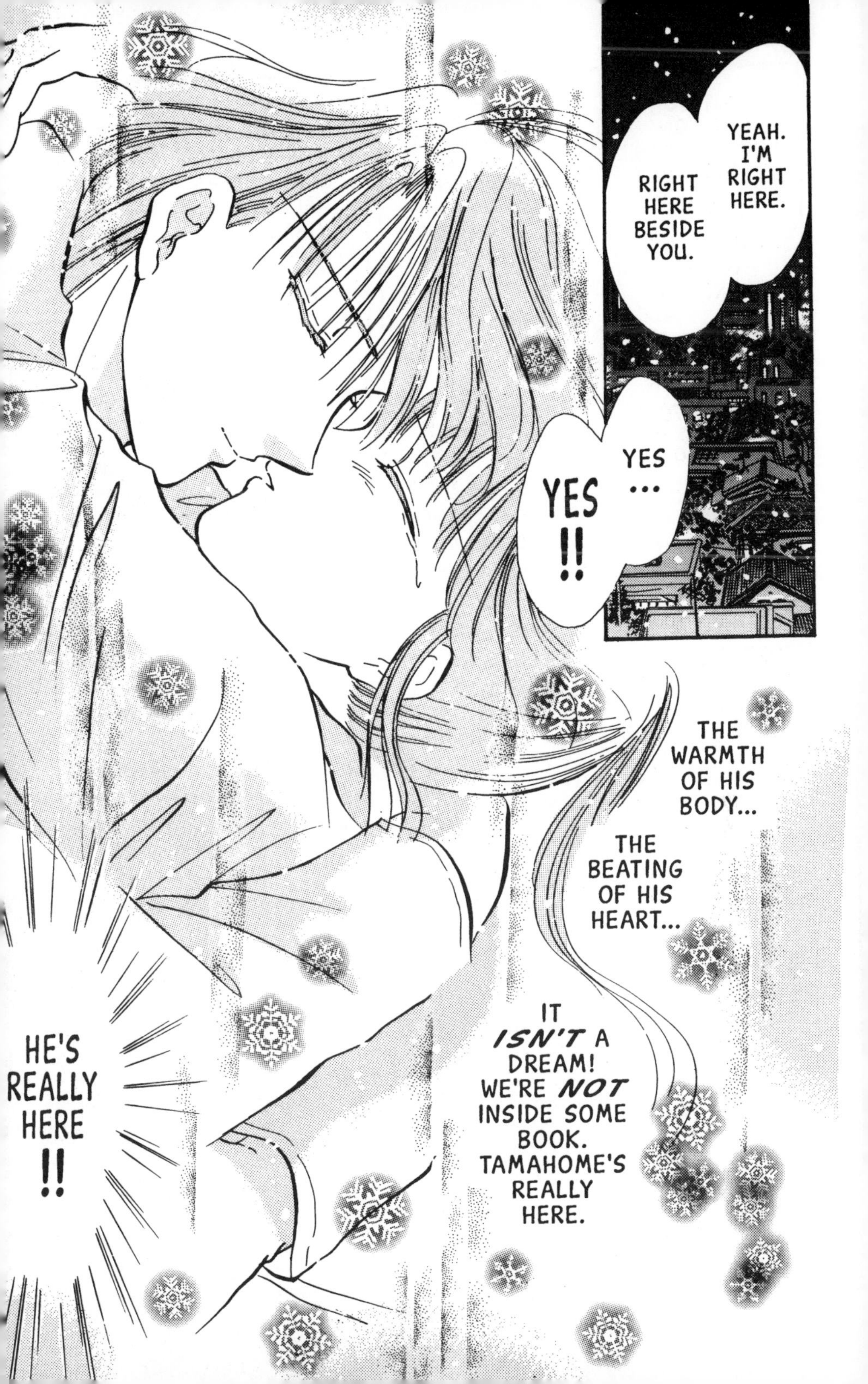
YEAH. I'M RIGHT HERE.
RIGHT HERE BESIDE YOU.
YES...
YES!!
THE WARMTH OF HIS BODY...
THE BEATING OF HIS HEART...
IT *ISN'T* A DREAM! WE'RE *NOT* INSIDE SOME BOOK. TAMAHOME'S REALLY HERE.
HE'S REALLY HERE!!

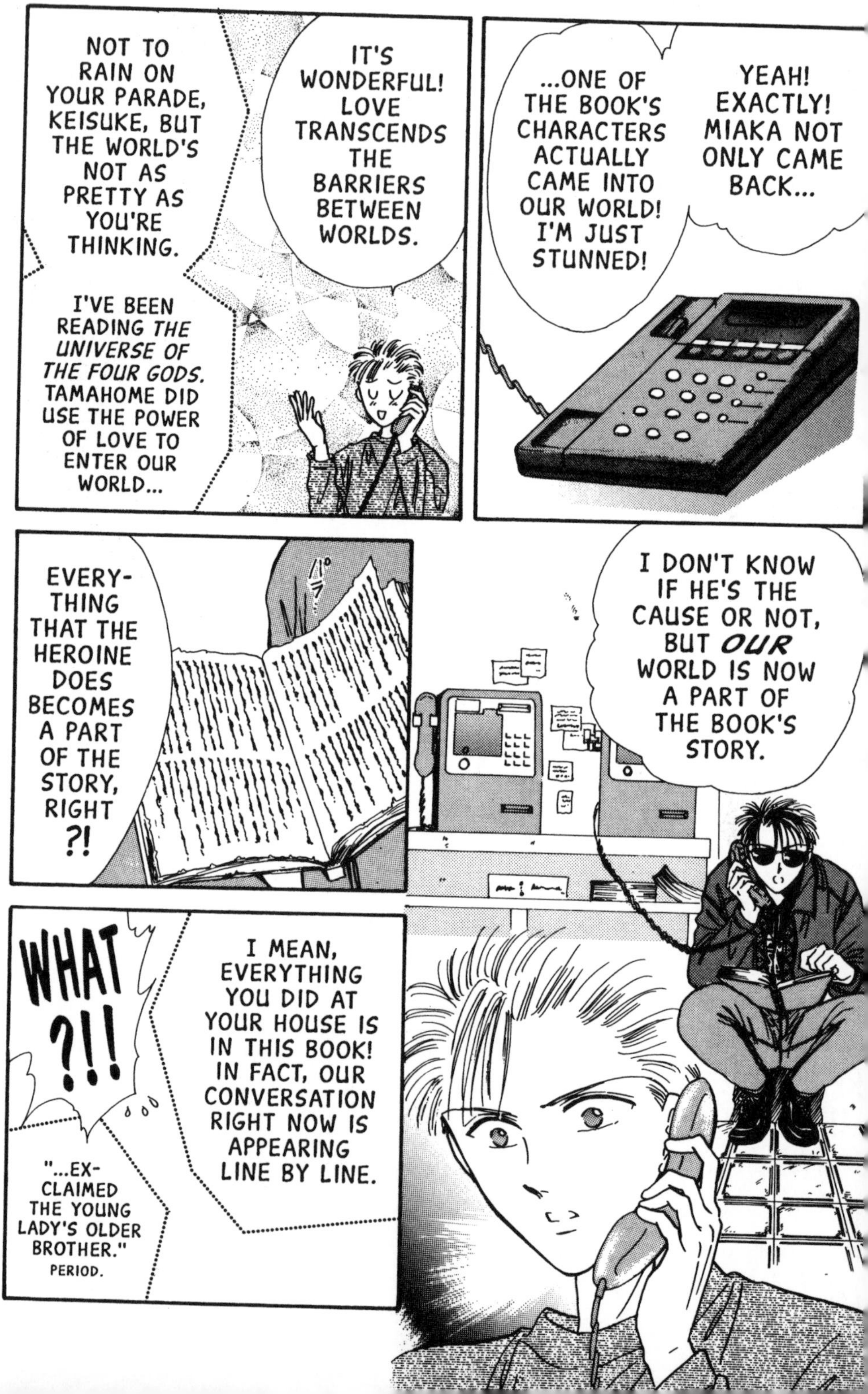
YEAH! EXACTLY! MIAKA NOT ONLY CAME BACK...
...ONE OF THE BOOK'S CHARACTERS ACTUALLY CAME INTO OUR WORLD! I'M JUST STUNNED!
IT'S WONDERFUL! LOVE TRANSCENDS THE BARRIERS BETWEEN WORLDS.
NOT TO RAIN ON YOUR PARADE, KEISUKE, BUT THE WORLD'S NOT AS PRETTY AS YOU'RE THINKING.
I'VE BEEN READING *THE UNIVERSE OF THE FOUR GODS.* TAMAHOME DID USE THE POWER OF LOVE TO ENTER OUR WORLD...
I DON'T KNOW IF HE'S THE CAUSE OR NOT, BUT *OUR* WORLD IS NOW A PART OF THE BOOK'S STORY.
EVERY-THING THAT THE HEROINE DOES BECOMES A PART OF THE STORY, RIGHT?!
I MEAN, EVERYTHING YOU DID AT YOUR HOUSE IS IN THIS BOOK! IN FACT, OUR CONVERSATION RIGHT NOW IS APPEARING LINE BY LINE.
WHAT?!!
"...EX-CLAIMED THE YOUNG LADY'S OLDER BROTHER." PERIOD.

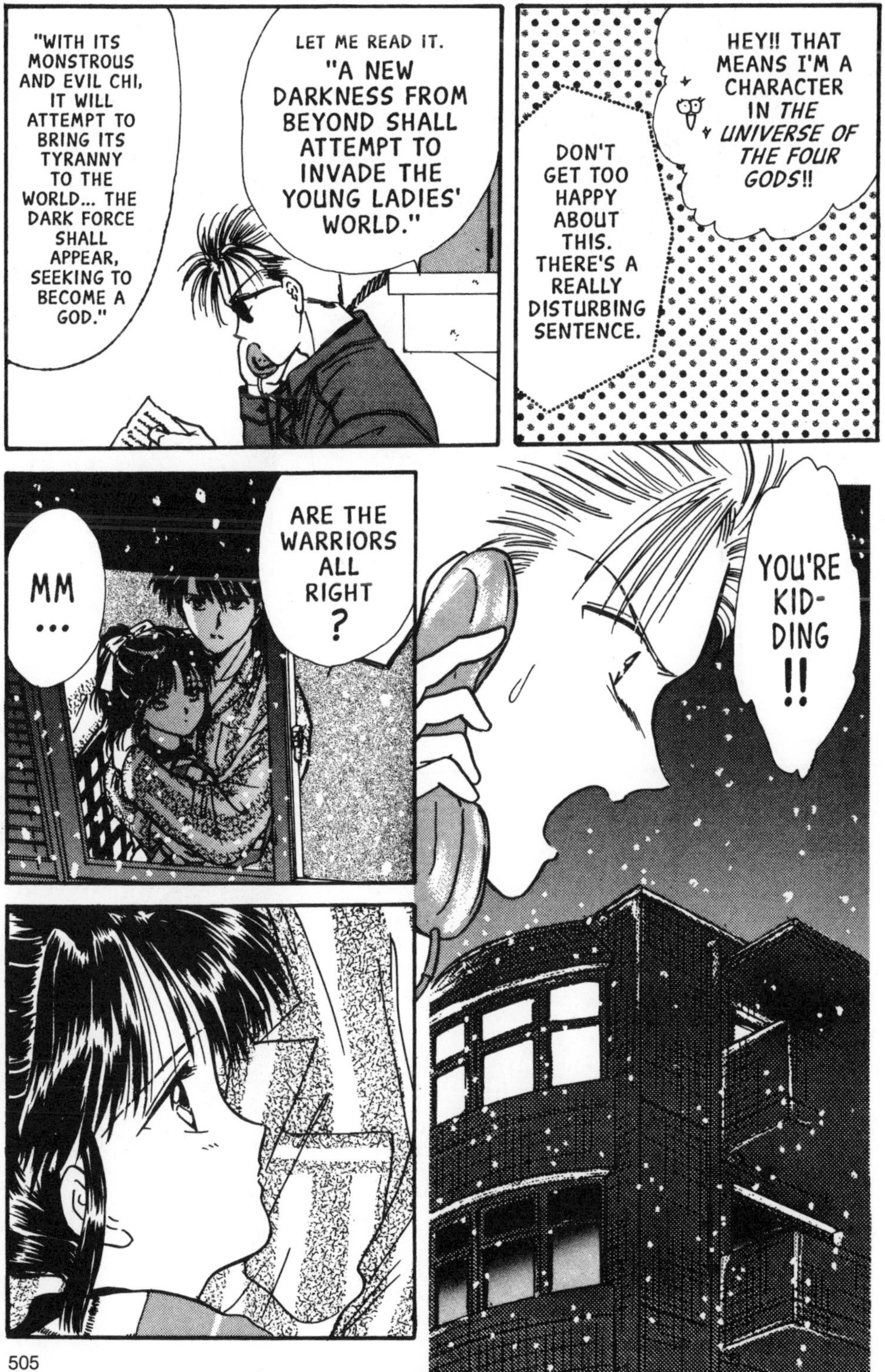
HEY!! THAT MEANS I'M A CHARACTER IN *THE UNIVERSE OF THE FOUR GODS*!!
DON'T GET TOO HAPPY ABOUT THIS. THERE'S A REALLY DISTURBING SENTENCE.
LET ME READ IT. "A NEW DARKNESS FROM BEYOND SHALL ATTEMPT TO INVADE THE YOUNG LADIES' WORLD."
"WITH ITS MONSTROUS AND EVIL CHI, IT WILL ATTEMPT TO BRING ITS TYRANNY TO THE WORLD... THE DARK FORCE SHALL APPEAR, SEEKING TO BECOME A GOD."
YOU'RE KID-DING!!
ARE THE WARRIORS ALL RIGHT?
MM...

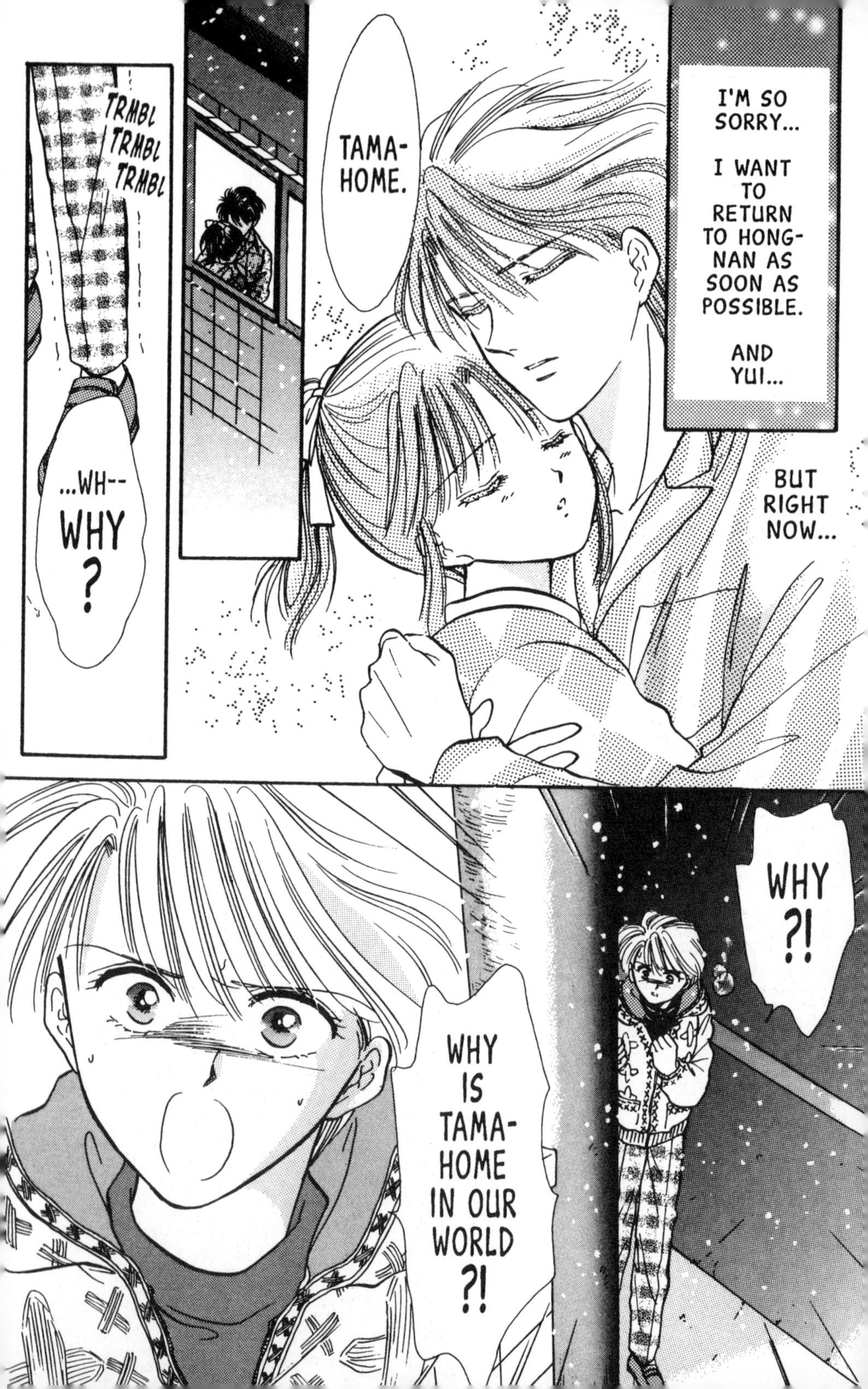
I'M SO SORRY... I WANT TO RETURN TO HONG-NAN AS SOON AS POSSIBLE. AND YUI...
BUT RIGHT NOW...
TAMA-HOME.
TRMBL TRMBL TRMBL
...WH-- WHY ?
WHY ?!
WHY IS TAMA-HOME IN OUR WORLD ?!

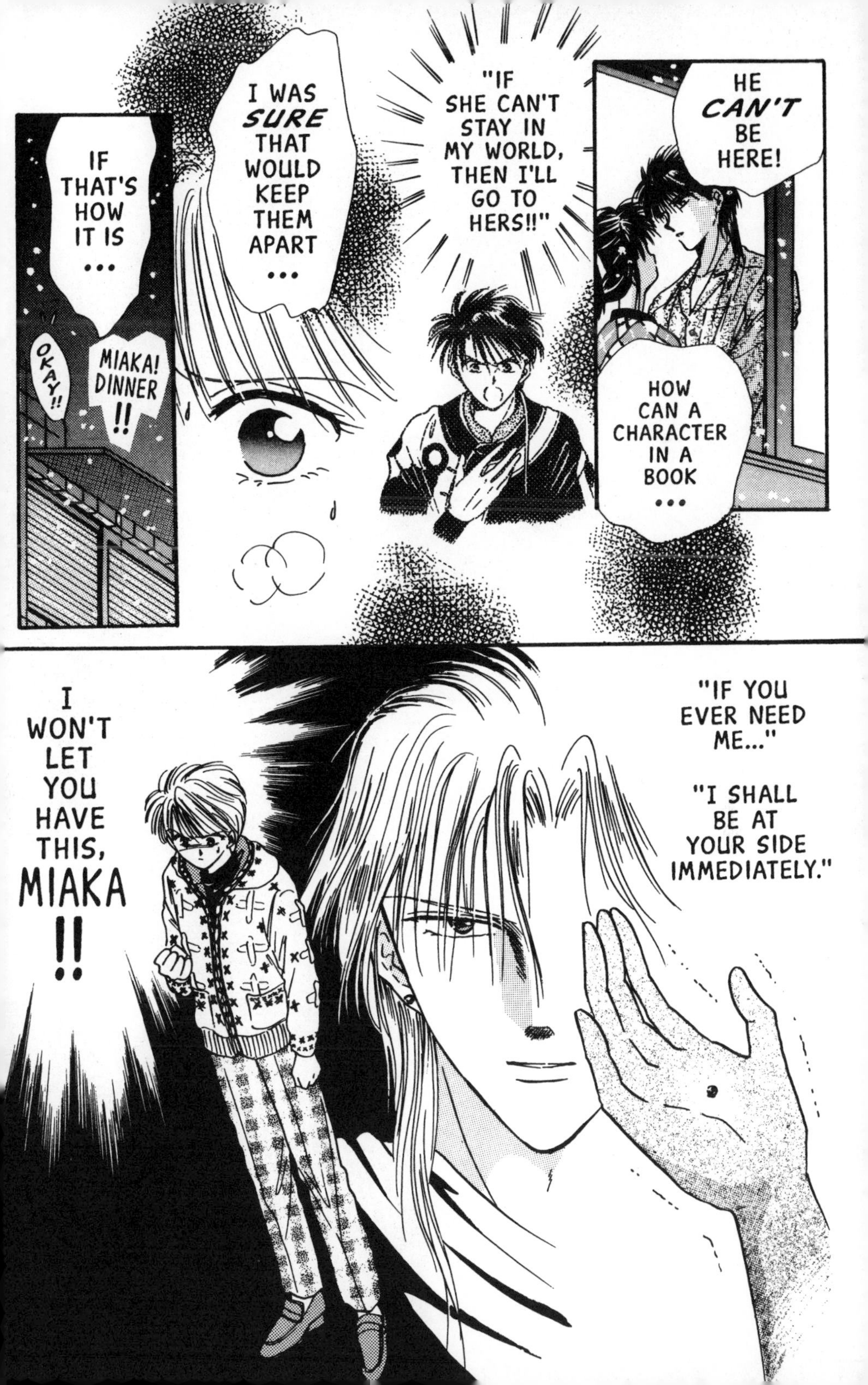
HE *CAN'T* BE HERE!
HOW CAN A CHARACTER IN A BOOK ...
"IF SHE CAN'T STAY IN MY WORLD, THEN I'LL GO TO HERS!!"
I WAS *SURE* THAT WOULD KEEP THEM APART ...
IF THAT'S HOW IT IS ...
MIAKA! DINNER !!
OKAY!!
"IF YOU EVER NEED ME..."
"I SHALL BE AT YOUR SIDE IMMEDIATELY."
I WON'T LET YOU HAVE THIS, MIAKA !!

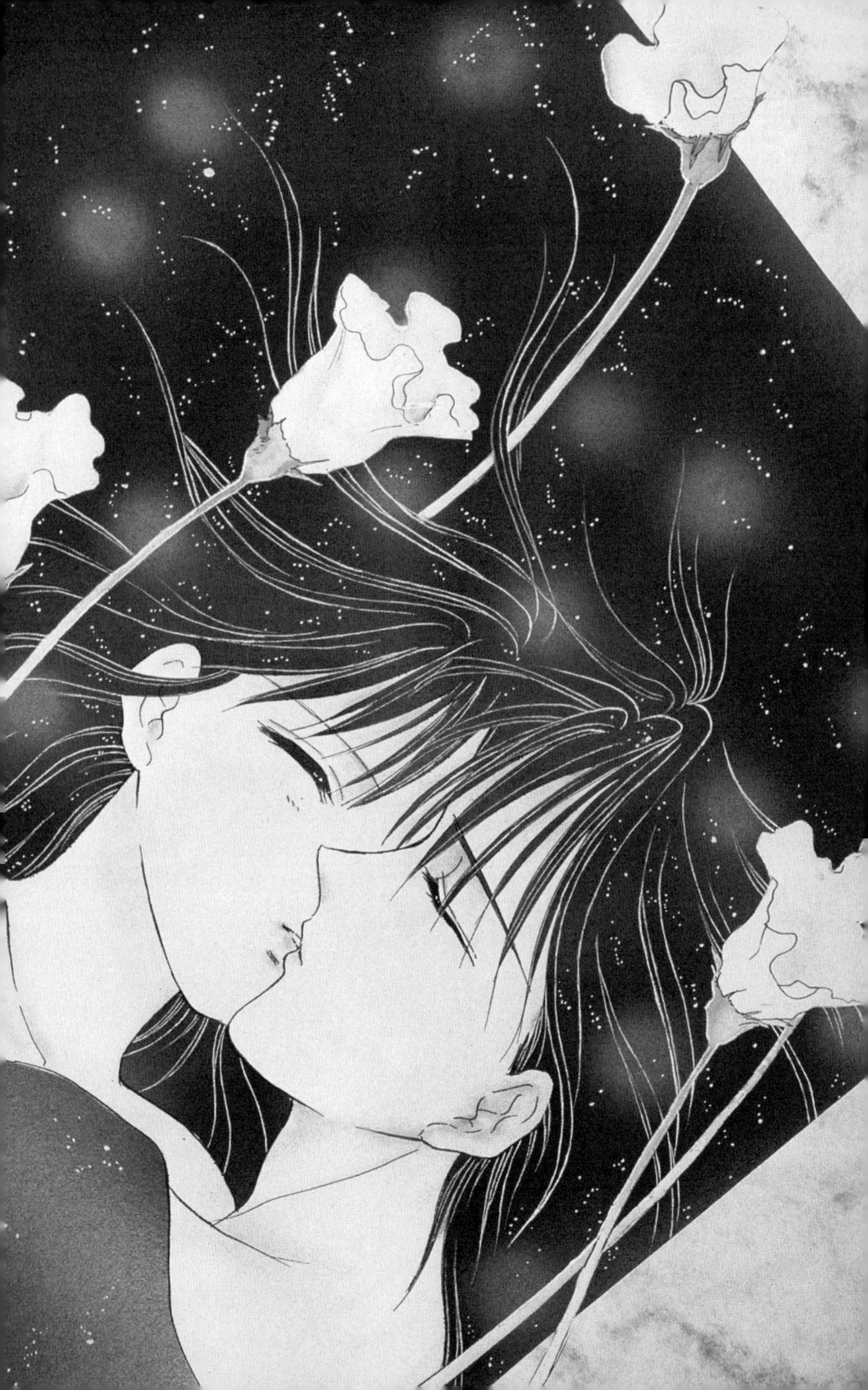

Chapter Seventy
Surge of the Heart

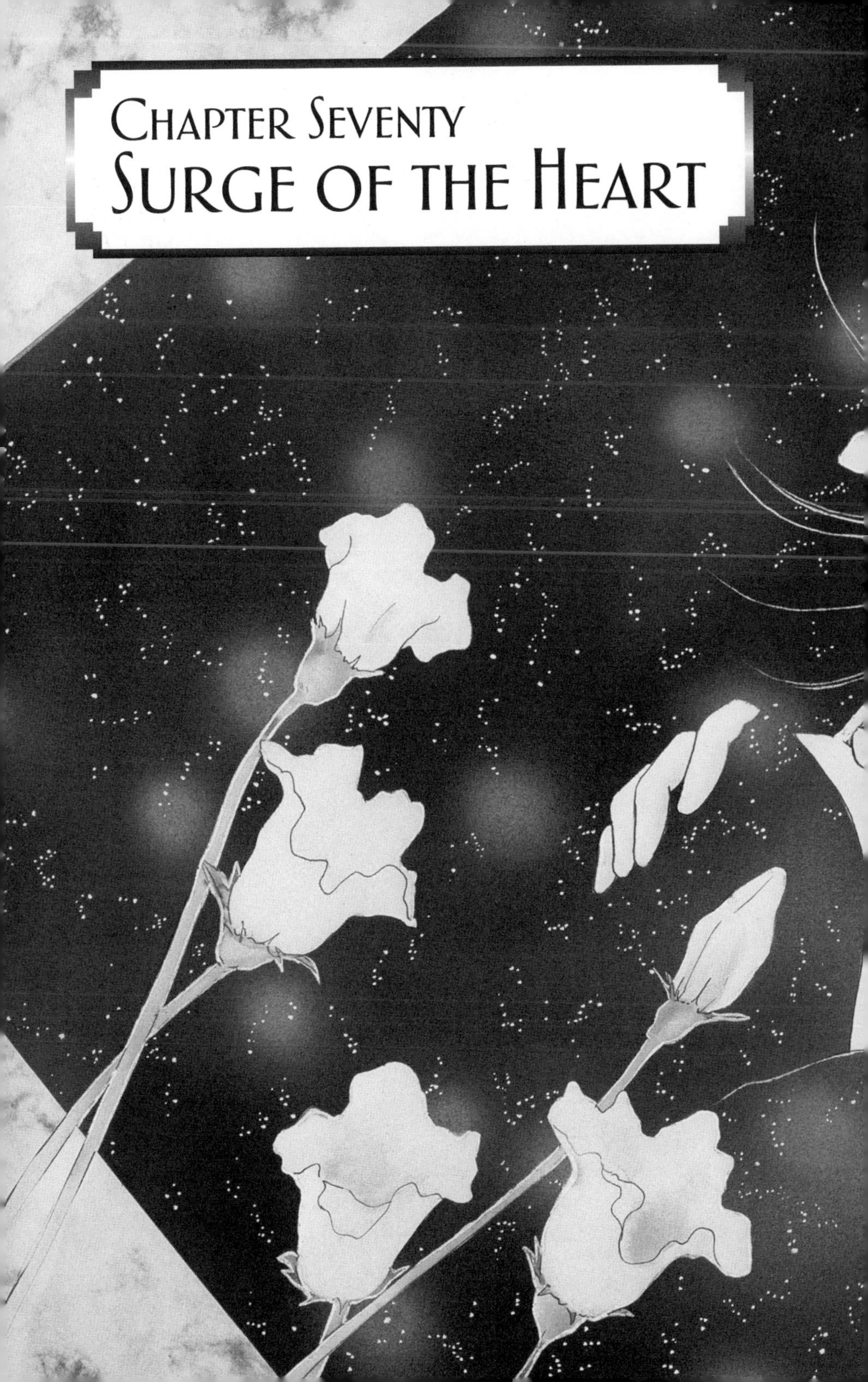

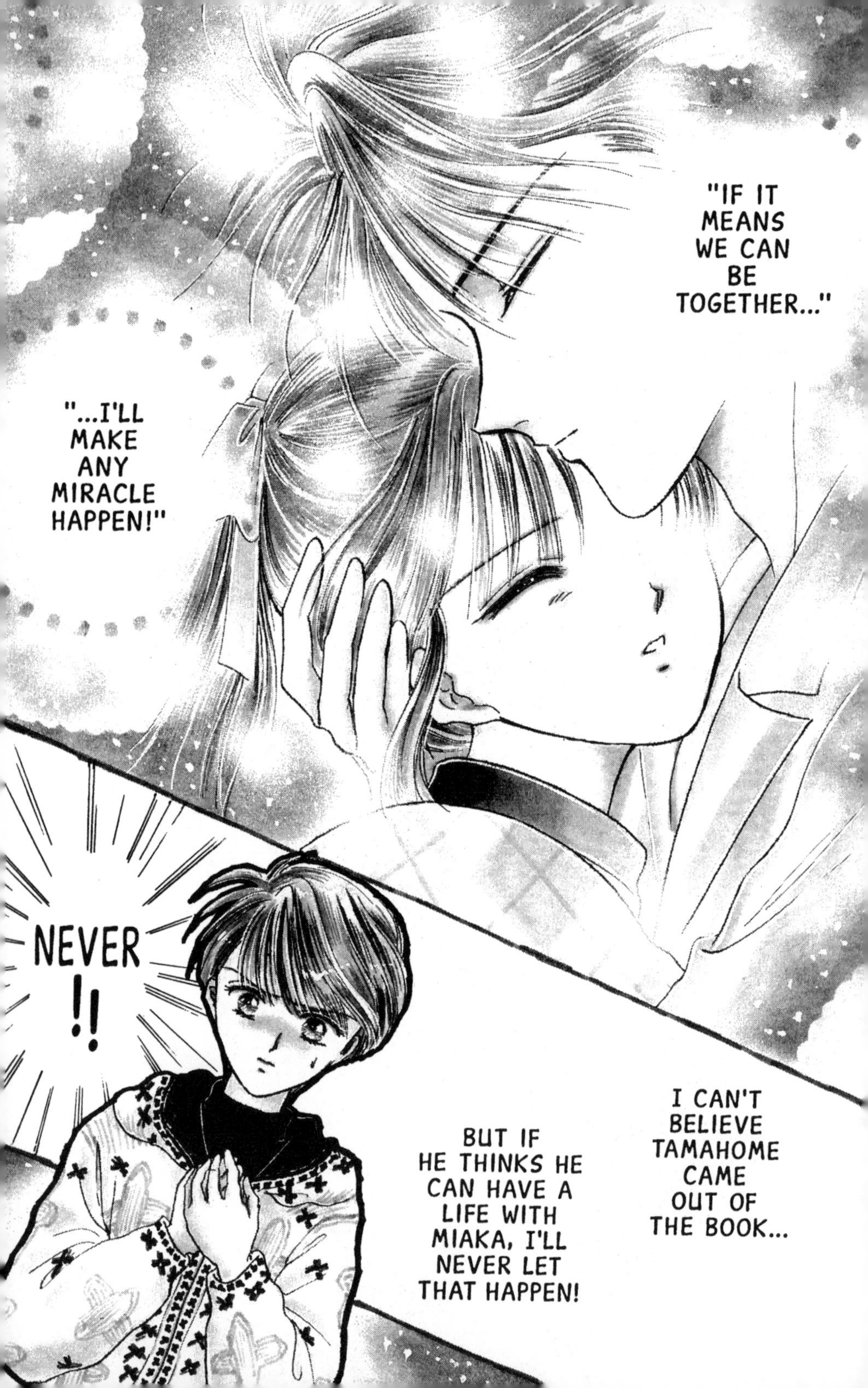
"IF IT MEANS WE CAN BE TOGETHER..."
"...I'LL MAKE ANY MIRACLE HAPPEN!"
I CAN'T BELIEVE TAMAHOME CAME OUT OF THE BOOK...
BUT IF HE THINKS HE CAN HAVE A LIFE WITH MIAKA, I'LL NEVER LET THAT HAPPEN!
NEVER !!

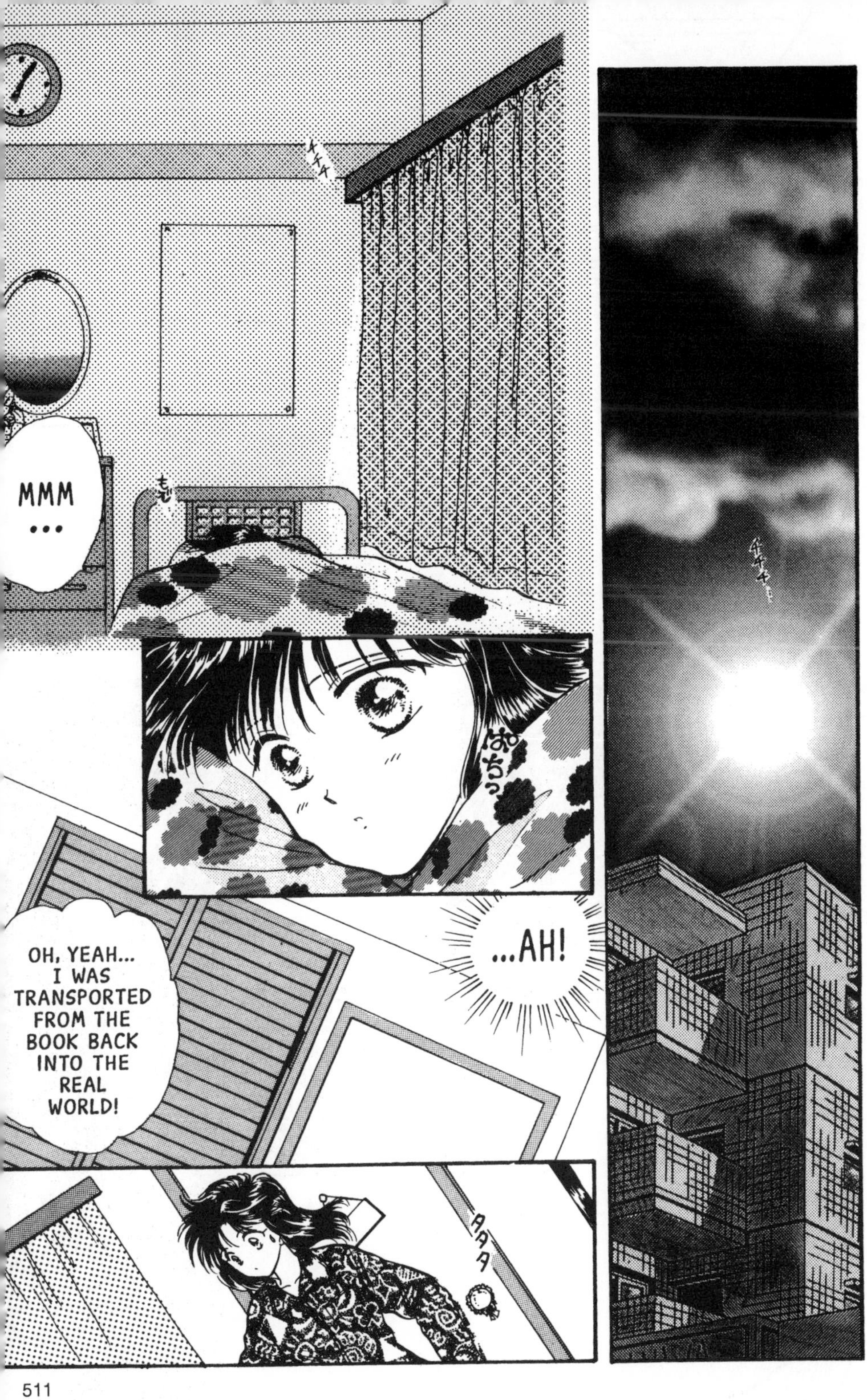
MMM ...
...AH!
OH, YEAH... I WAS TRANSPORTED FROM THE BOOK BACK INTO THE REAL WORLD!

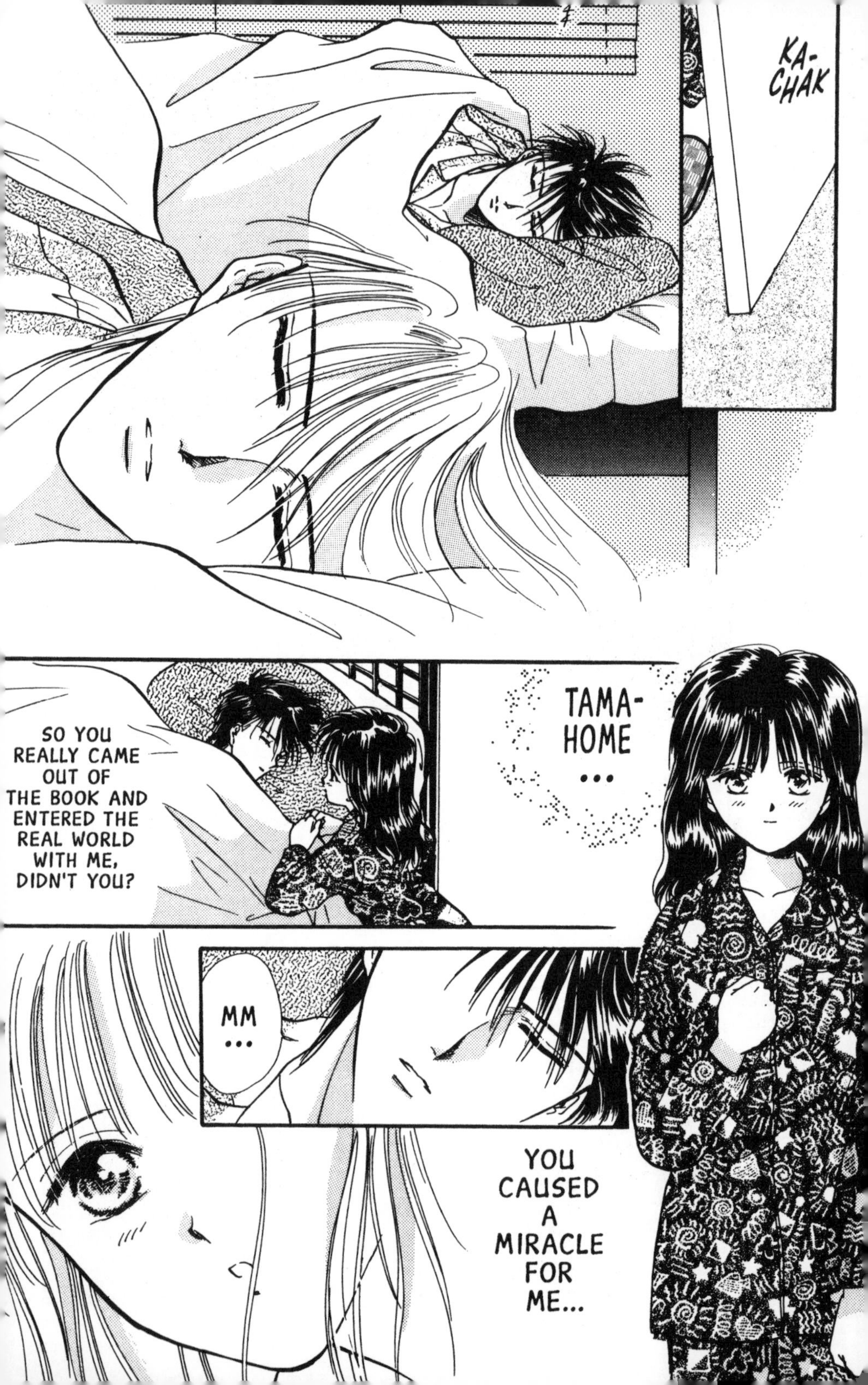
KA-CHAK
TAMA-HOME ...
SO YOU REALLY CAME OUT OF THE BOOK AND ENTERED THE REAL WORLD WITH ME, DIDN'T YOU?
MM ...
YOU CAUSED A MIRACLE FOR ME...

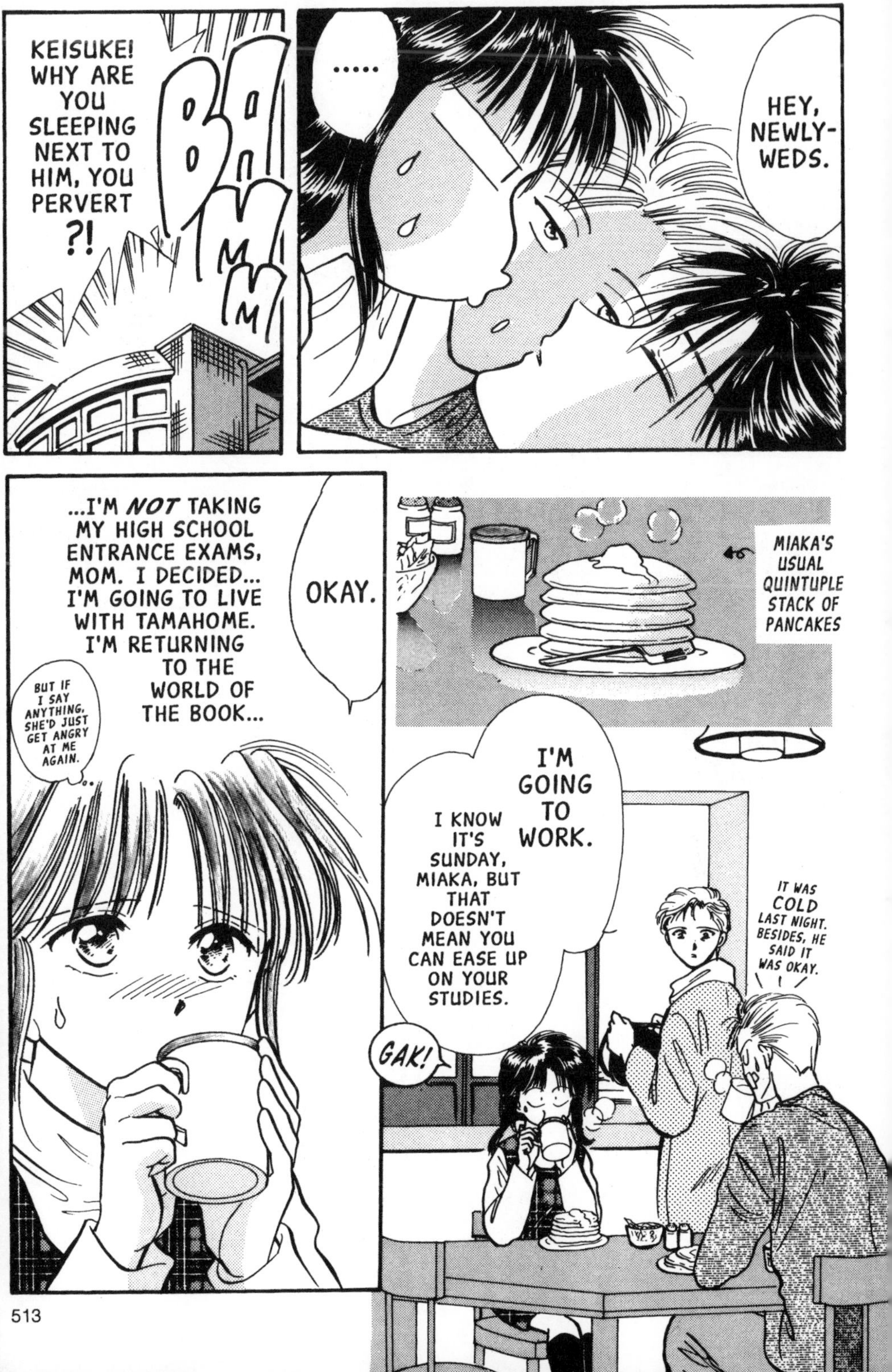
HEY, NEWLYWEDS.
.....
KEISUKE! WHY ARE YOU SLEEPING NEXT TO HIM, YOU PERVERT?!
BAMMM
MIAKA'S USUAL QUINTUPLE STACK OF PANCAKES
I'M GOING TO WORK.
I KNOW IT'S SUNDAY, MIAKA, BUT THAT DOESN'T MEAN YOU CAN EASE UP ON YOUR STUDIES.
IT WAS COLD LAST NIGHT. BESIDES, HE SAID IT WAS OKAY.
GAK!
OKAY.
...I'M NOT TAKING MY HIGH SCHOOL ENTRANCE EXAMS, MOM. I DECIDED... I'M GOING TO LIVE WITH TAMAHOME. I'M RETURNING TO THE WORLD OF THE BOOK...
BUT IF I SAY ANYTHING, SHE'D JUST GET ANGRY AT ME AGAIN.

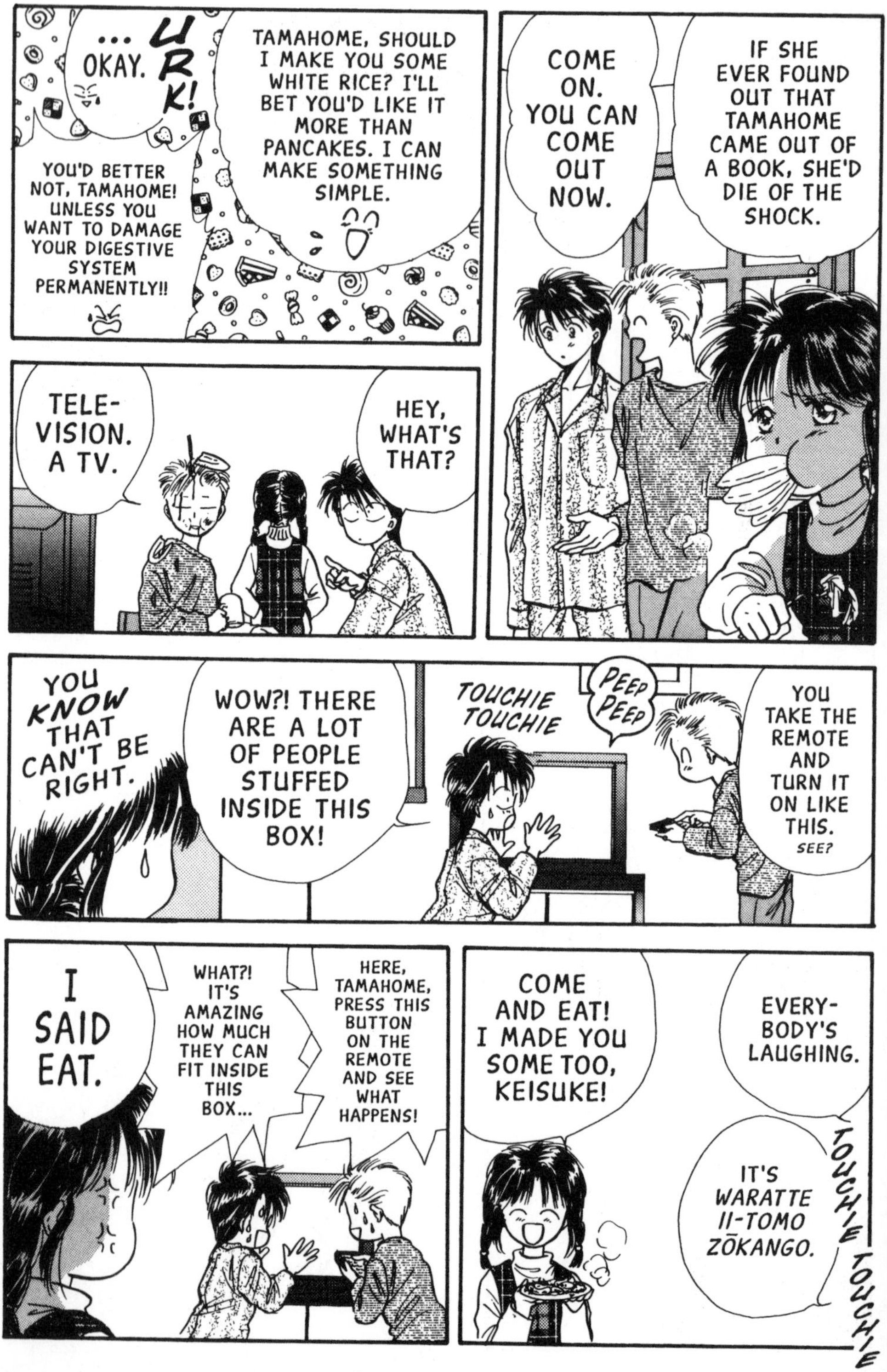
IF SHE EVER FOUND OUT THAT TAMAHOME CAME OUT OF A BOOK, SHE'D DIE OF THE SHOCK.
COME ON. YOU CAN COME OUT NOW.
TAMAHOME, SHOULD I MAKE YOU SOME WHITE RICE? I'LL BET YOU'D LIKE IT MORE THAN PANCAKES. I CAN MAKE SOMETHING SIMPLE.
URK!
...OKAY.
YOU'D BETTER NOT, TAMAHOME! UNLESS YOU WANT TO DAMAGE YOUR DIGESTIVE SYSTEM PERMANENTLY!!
HEY, WHAT'S THAT?
TELE-VISION. A TV.
YOU TAKE THE REMOTE AND TURN IT ON LIKE THIS. SEE?
PEEP PEEP
TOUCHIE TOUCHIE
WOW?! THERE ARE A LOT OF PEOPLE STUFFED INSIDE THIS BOX!
YOU KNOW THAT CAN'T BE RIGHT.
EVERY-BODY'S LAUGHING.
COME AND EAT! I MADE YOU SOME TOO, KEISUKE!
IT'S WARATTE II-TOMO ZŌKANGO.
TOUCHIE TOUCHIE
HERE, TAMAHOME, PRESS THIS BUTTON ON THE REMOTE AND SEE WHAT HAPPENS!
WHAT?! IT'S AMAZING HOW MUCH THEY CAN FIT INSIDE THIS BOX...
I SAID EAT.

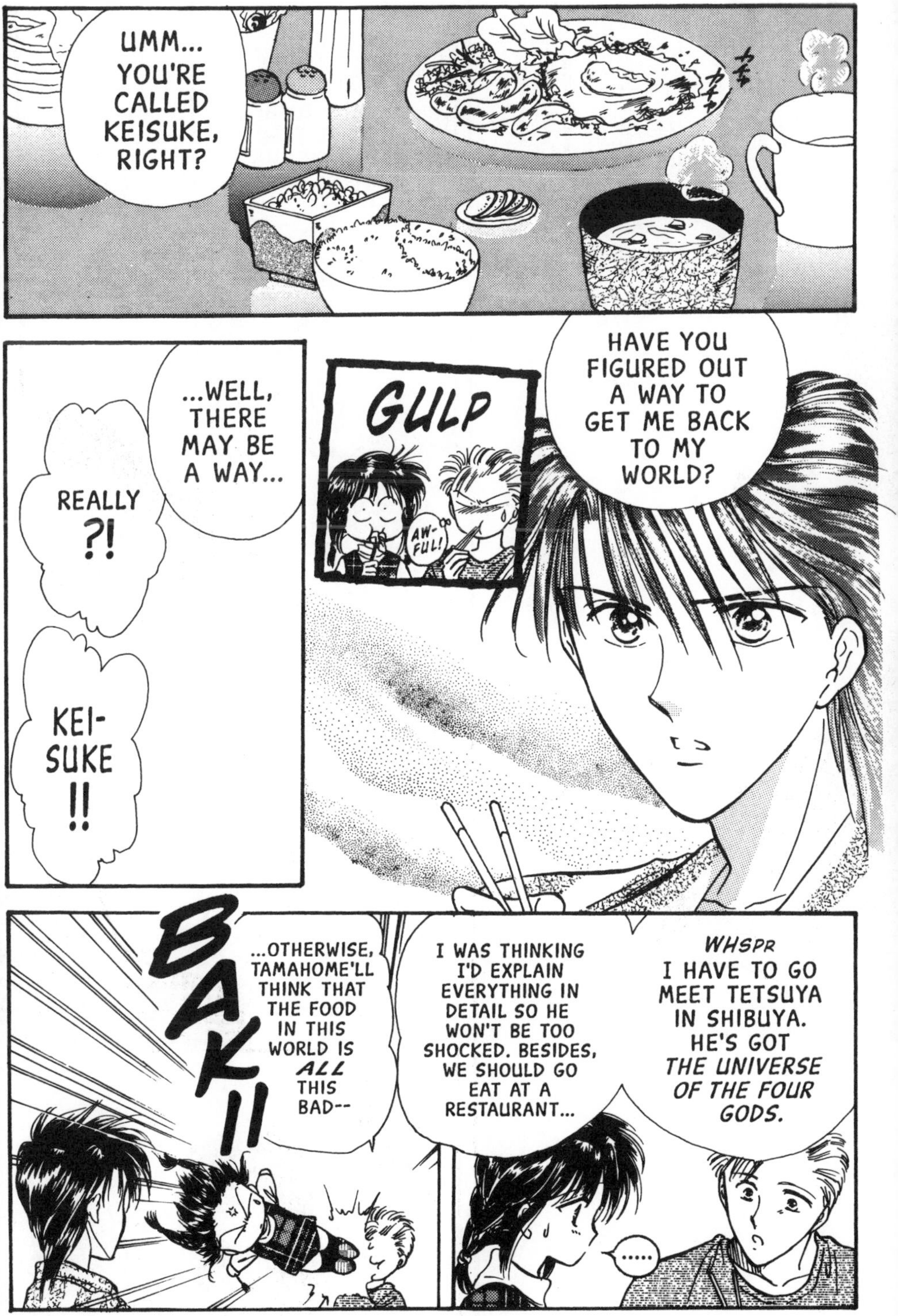
UMM... YOU'RE CALLED KEISUKE, RIGHT?
HAVE YOU FIGURED OUT A WAY TO GET ME BACK TO MY WORLD?
GULP
AW-FUL!
...WELL, THERE MAY BE A WAY...
REALLY ?!
KEI-SUKE !!
WHSPR I HAVE TO GO MEET TETSUYA IN SHIBUYA. HE'S GOT *THE UNIVERSE OF THE FOUR GODS.*
I WAS THINKING I'D EXPLAIN EVERYTHING IN DETAIL SO HE WON'T BE TOO SHOCKED. BESIDES, WE SHOULD GO EAT AT A RESTAURANT...
......
...OTHERWISE, TAMAHOME'LL THINK THAT THE FOOD IN THIS WORLD IS *ALL* THIS BAD--
BAK!!

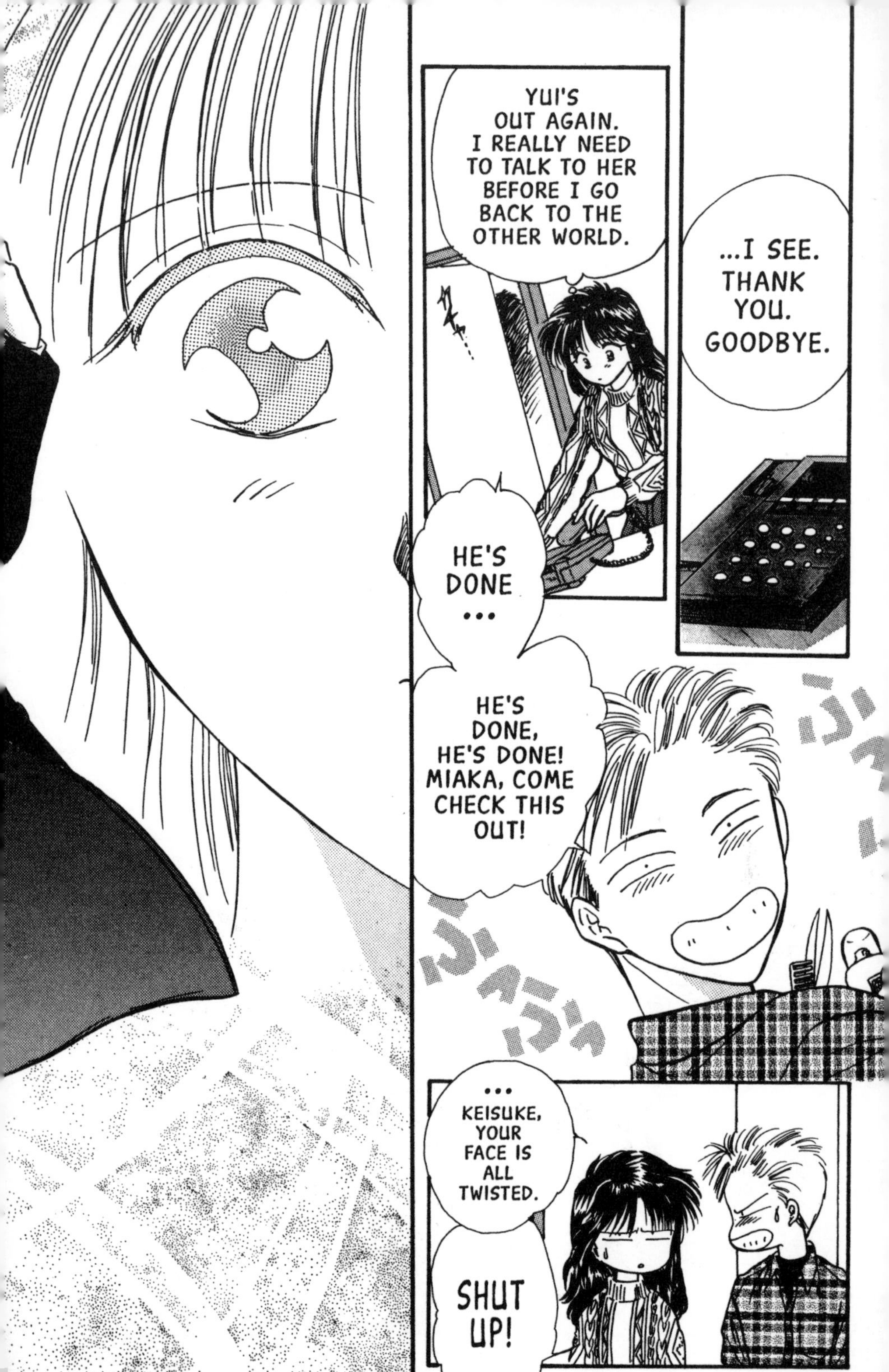
...I SEE. THANK YOU. GOODBYE.
YUI'S OUT AGAIN. I REALLY NEED TO TALK TO HER BEFORE I GO BACK TO THE OTHER WORLD.
HE'S DONE...
HE'S DONE, HE'S DONE! MIAKA, COME CHECK THIS OUT!
...KEISUKE, YOUR FACE IS ALL TWISTED.
SHUT UP!

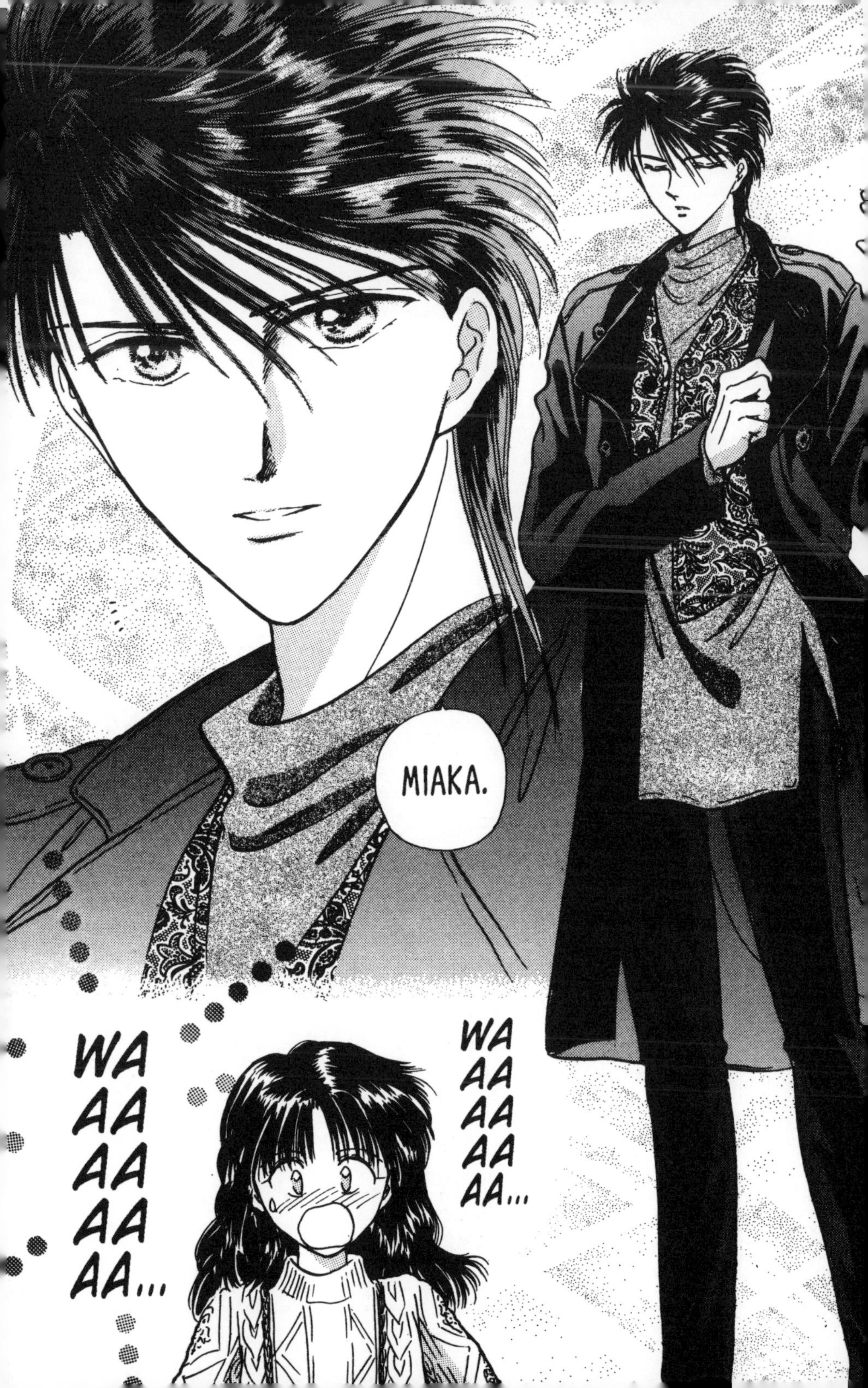
MIAKA.
WA AA AA AA AA...
WA AA AA AA AA AA...

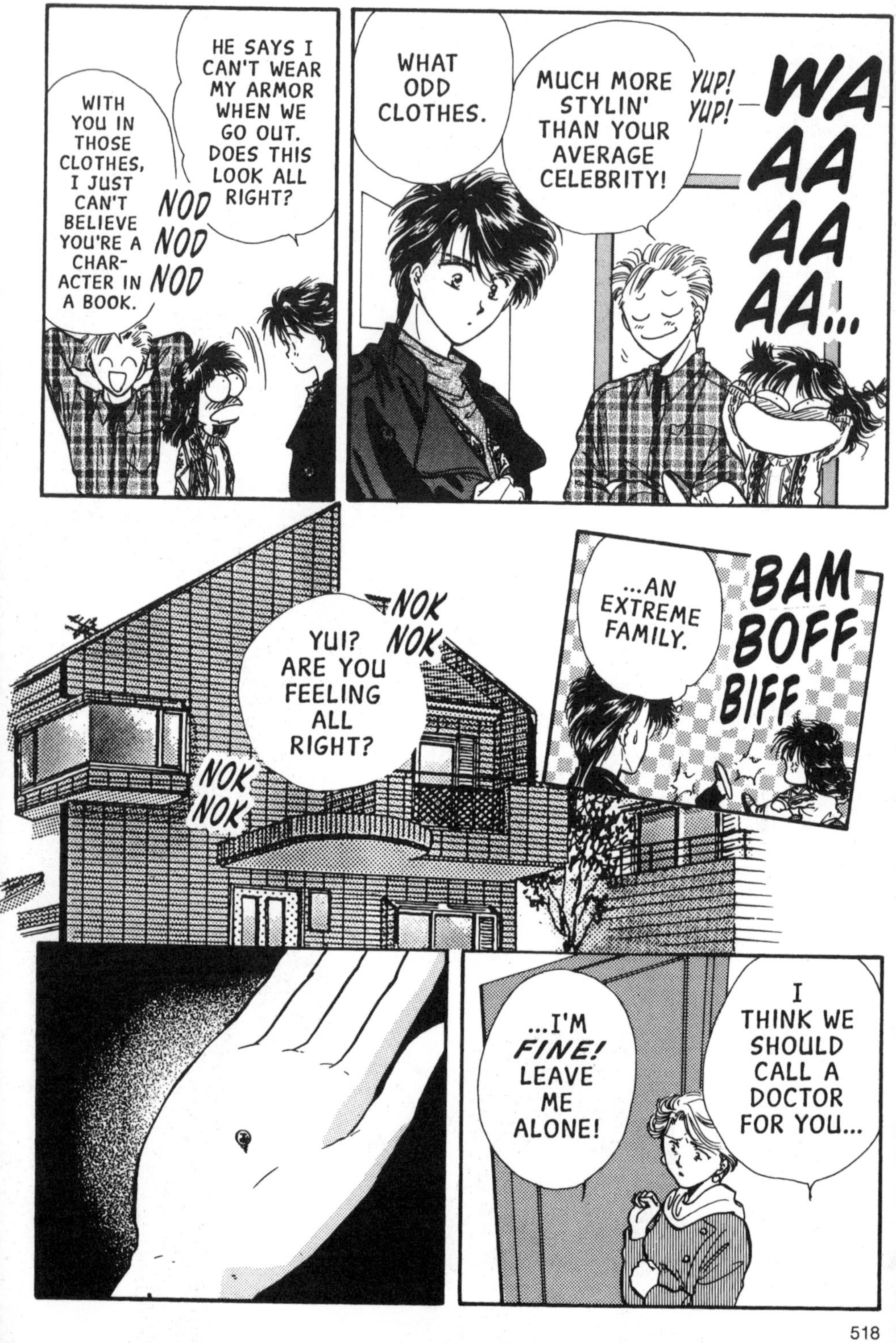
WAAAAAAA...
YUP! YUP!
MUCH MORE STYLIN' THAN YOUR AVERAGE CELEBRITY!
WHAT ODD CLOTHES.
HE SAYS I CAN'T WEAR MY ARMOR WHEN WE GO OUT. DOES THIS LOOK ALL RIGHT?
NOD NOD NOD
WITH YOU IN THOSE CLOTHES, I JUST CAN'T BELIEVE YOU'RE A CHARACTER IN A BOOK.
BAM BOFF BIFF
...AN EXTREME FAMILY.
NOK NOK
YUI? ARE YOU FEELING ALL RIGHT?
NOK NOK
I THINK WE SHOULD CALL A DOCTOR FOR YOU...
...I'M *FINE!* LEAVE ME ALONE!

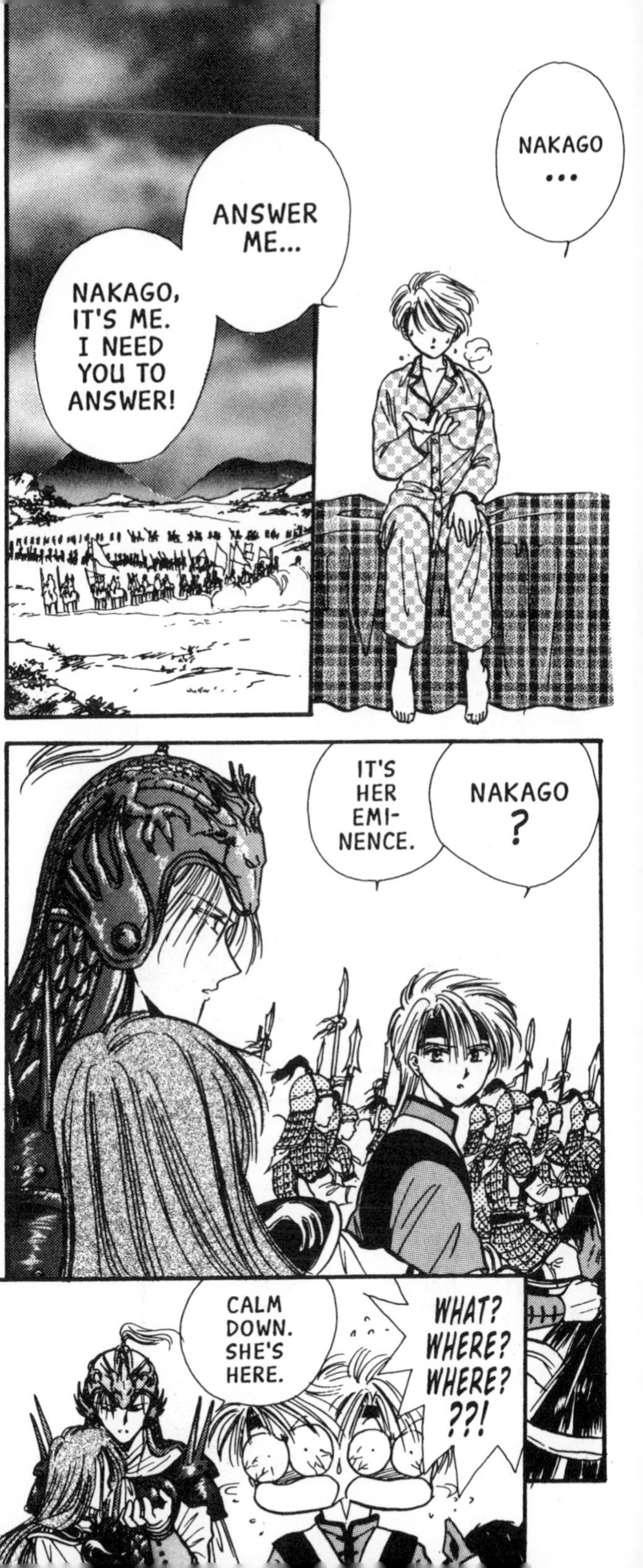
NAKAGO ...
ANSWER ME...
NAKAGO, IT'S ME. I NEED YOU TO ANSWER!
NAKAGO?
IT'S HER EMI-NENCE.
WHAT? WHERE? WHERE? ??!
CALM DOWN. SHE'S HERE.

Soi. With those long, elegant eyes peering out from under her cloak... at first, many readers thought that the character was a handsome boy. But, she's a woman. She's the only female charcter of the Seiryu Celestial Warriors. By the way, the fact that all of the Suzaku warriors are men...there's no significance to it. *I guess Nuriko played the part of a woman.* Soi's character design was really hard! I had to design her three or four times! At first, I tried drawing her as a boyish charac-ter -- a woman in men's clothes to contrast with Nuriko -- but that didn't work. I had so many prob-lems with her hairstyle. I was plan-ning on having her wear armor, but...still nothing. Then one day I came up with those long, elegant eyes, and all of a sudden her hair-style fell into place, and then her armor. She seems really tough because she talks like a man and wears armor, but her lipstick gives away her true feminine nature. She wears makeup for the man she loves. She's wearing a Chinese tribal bride's dress in the title illustration for chapter 67. I'll bet she would have rather stood next to Nakago with that on than her armor.

Tomo. I LOVE TOMO. ♥♥ "I love him because he's so foolish, mischievous, gaudy and gay," came the strange praise from a fan, Golden boy. He didn't come to me until the very last minute. I wanted someone who was mysteri-ous like Chichiri, but I just couldn't come up with him. We had the mil-itary man, the twins, the woman, the beast, and the child...there was nobody left! As the time crunch was getting bad, I went for a walk and caught a glimpse of a store-front sign. Yep, that was when I saw a sign in a Chinese restaurant that had a Chinese-opera mask -- the generic kind you see everywhere. And thus was born this wonderful, unique Chinese-opera gay boy. *I really liked him... Heh.*

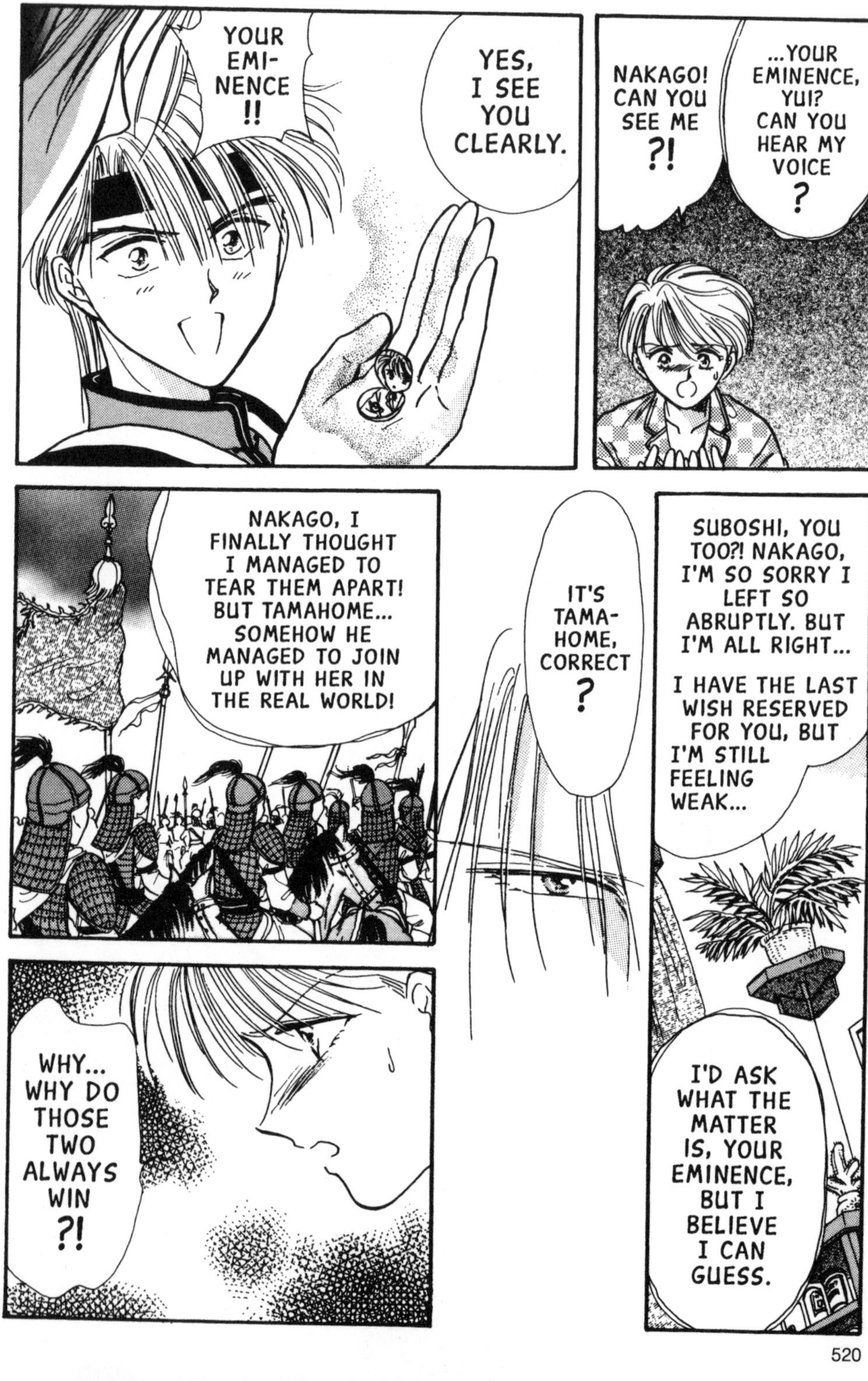
...YOUR EMINENCE, YUI? CAN YOU HEAR MY VOICE ?
NAKAGO! CAN YOU SEE ME ?!
YES, I SEE YOU CLEARLY.
YOUR EMI-NENCE !!
SUBOSHI, YOU TOO?! NAKAGO, I'M SO SORRY I LEFT SO ABRUPTLY. BUT I'M ALL RIGHT...
I HAVE THE LAST WISH RESERVED FOR YOU, BUT I'M STILL FEELING WEAK...
I'D ASK WHAT THE MATTER IS, YOUR EMINENCE, BUT I BELIEVE I CAN GUESS.
IT'S TAMA-HOME, CORRECT ?
NAKAGO, I FINALLY THOUGHT I MANAGED TO TEAR THEM APART! BUT TAMAHOME... SOMEHOW HE MANAGED TO JOIN UP WITH HER IN THE REAL WORLD!
WHY... WHY DO THOSE TWO ALWAYS WIN ?!

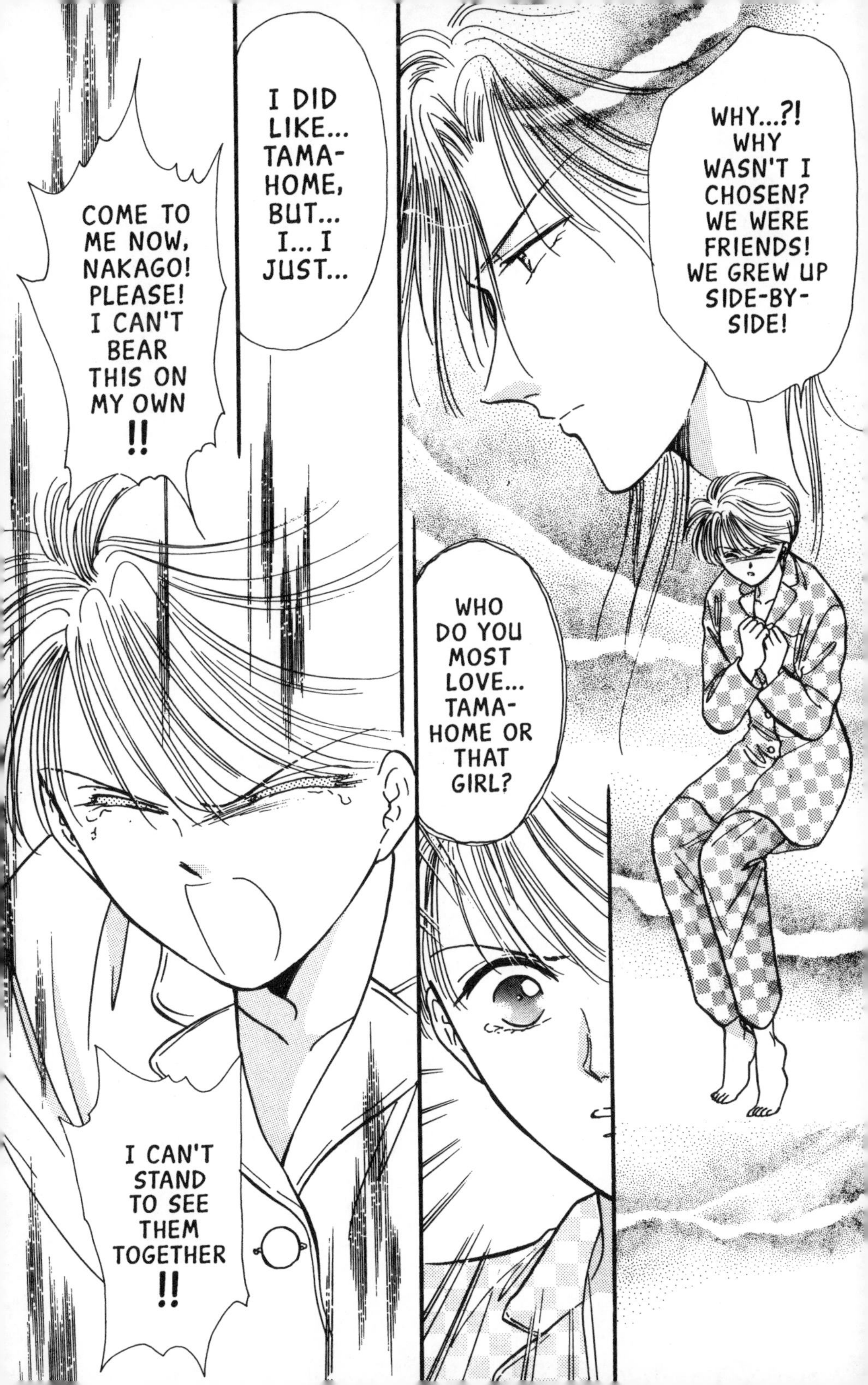
WHY...?! WHY WASN'T I CHOSEN? WE WERE FRIENDS! WE GREW UP SIDE-BY-SIDE!
WHO DO YOU MOST LOVE... TAMA-HOME OR THAT GIRL?
I DID LIKE... TAMA-HOME, BUT... I... I JUST...
COME TO ME NOW, NAKAGO! PLEASE! I CAN'T BEAR THIS ON MY OWN!!
I CAN'T STAND TO SEE THEM TOGETHER!!

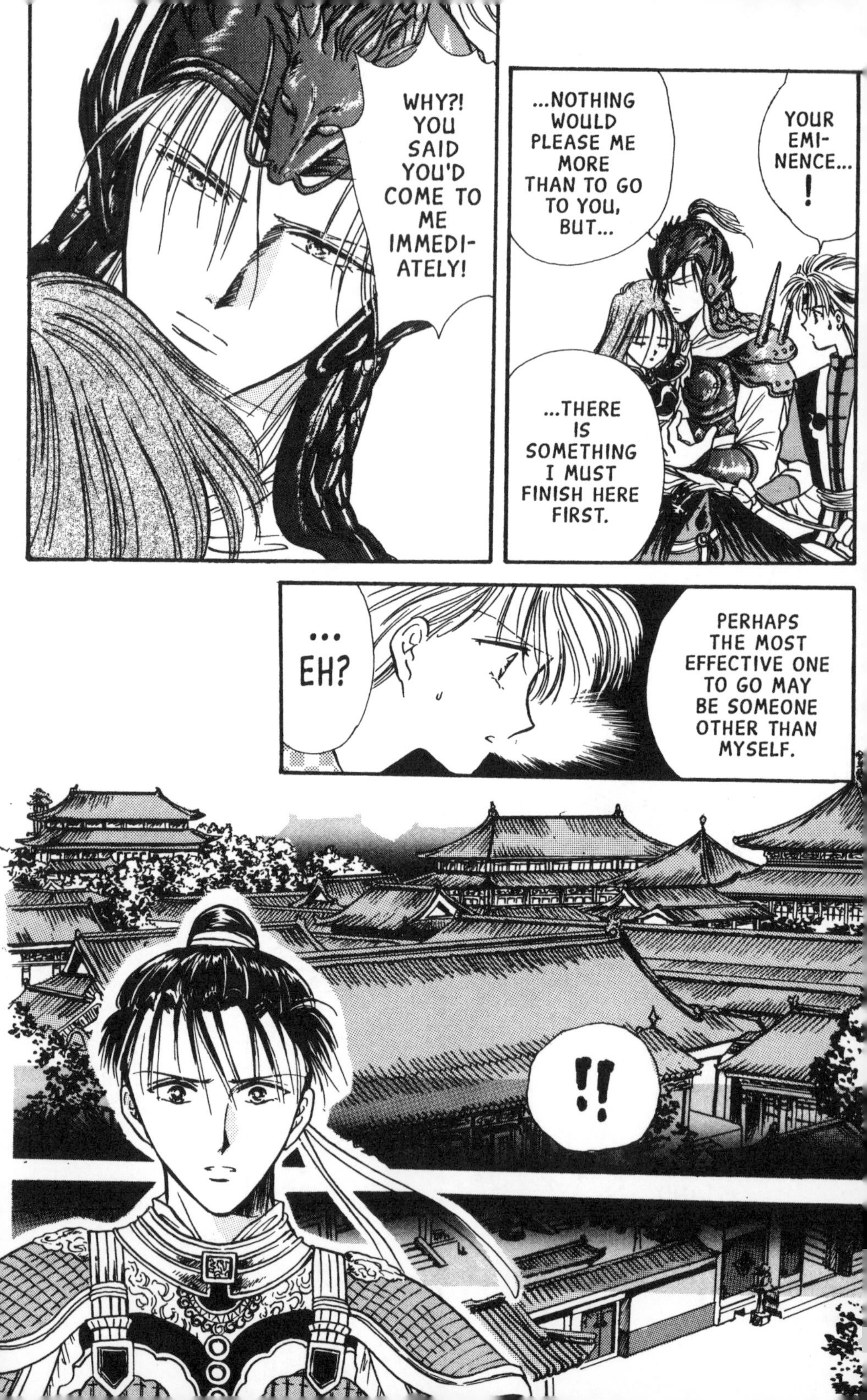
YOUR EMINENCE... !
...NOTHING WOULD PLEASE ME MORE THAN TO GO TO YOU, BUT...
...THERE IS SOMETHING I MUST FINISH HERE FIRST.
WHY?! YOU SAID YOU'D COME TO ME IMMEDIATELY!
PERHAPS THE MOST EFFECTIVE ONE TO GO MAY BE SOMEONE OTHER THAN MYSELF.
... EH?
!!

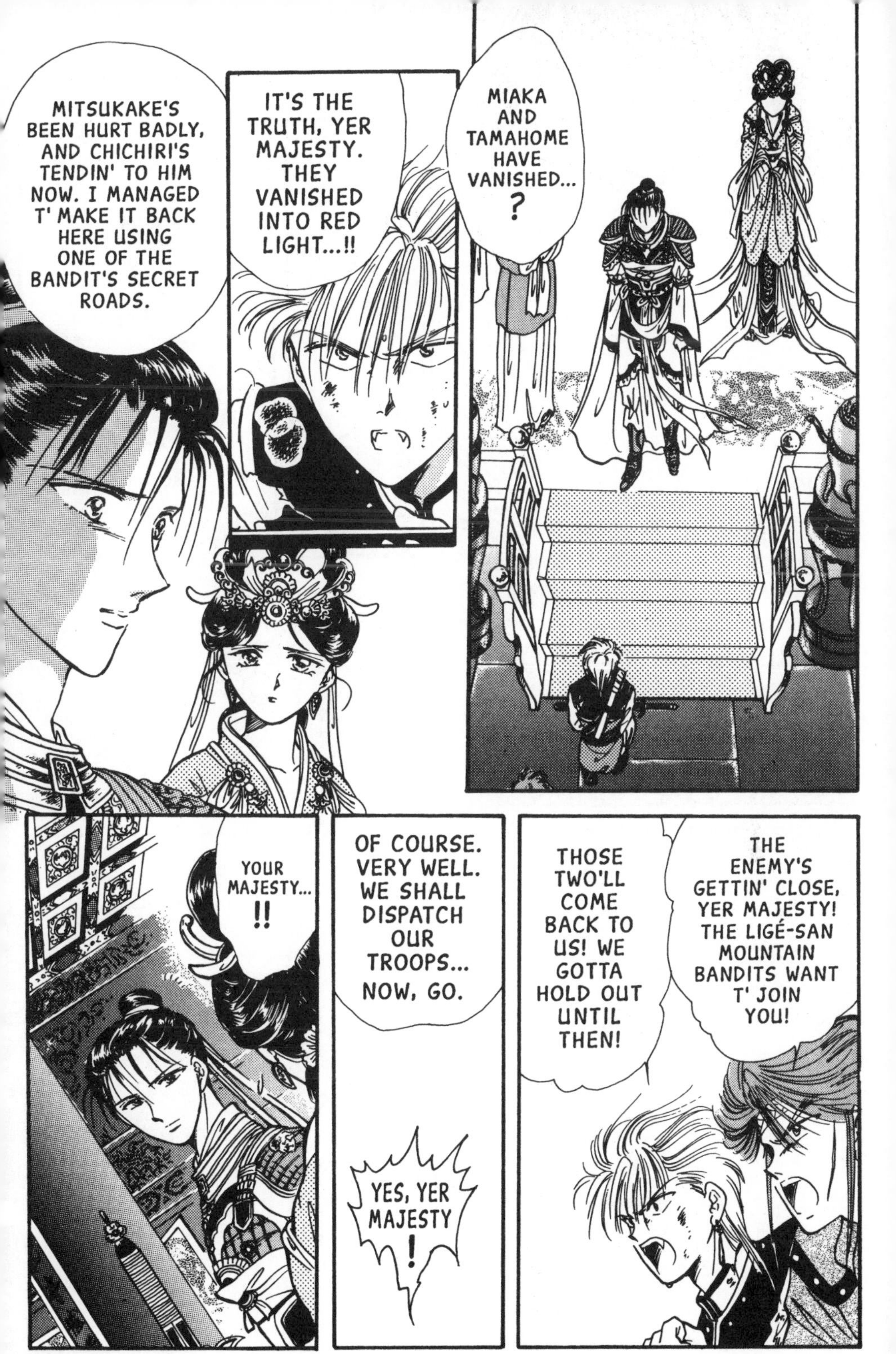
MIAKA AND TAMAHOME HAVE VANISHED...?
IT'S THE TRUTH, YER MAJESTY. THEY VANISHED INTO RED LIGHT...!!
MITSUKAKE'S BEEN HURT BADLY, AND CHICHIRI'S TENDIN' TO HIM NOW. I MANAGED T' MAKE IT BACK HERE USING ONE OF THE BANDIT'S SECRET ROADS.
THE ENEMY'S GETTIN' CLOSE, YER MAJESTY! THE LIGÉ-SAN MOUNTAIN BANDITS WANT T' JOIN YOU!
THOSE TWO'LL COME BACK TO US! WE GOTTA HOLD OUT UNTIL THEN!
OF COURSE. VERY WELL. WE SHALL DISPATCH OUR TROOPS... NOW, GO.
YES, YER MAJESTY!
YOUR MAJESTY...!!

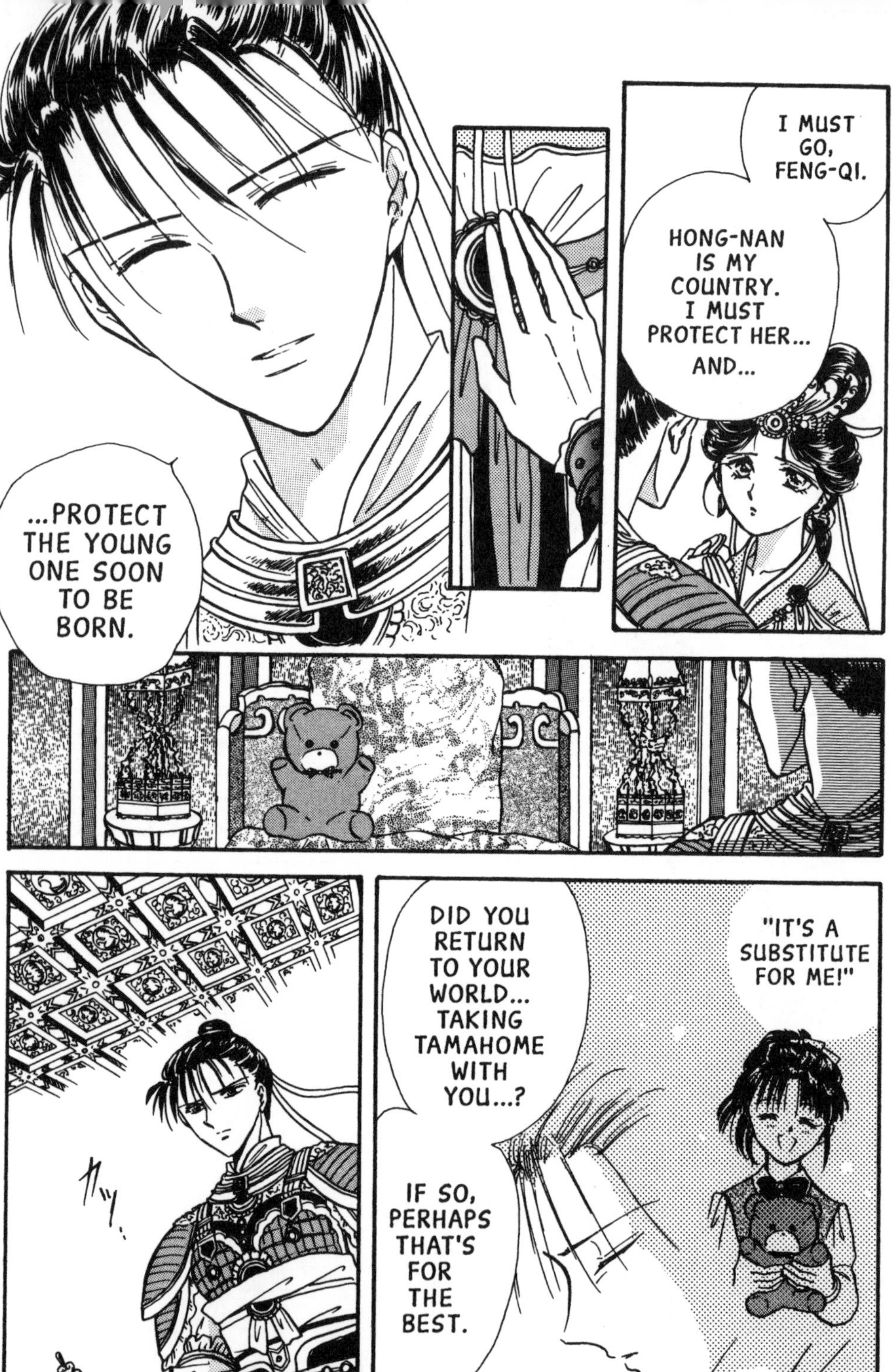
I MUST GO, FENG-QI.
HONG-NAN IS MY COUNTRY. I MUST PROTECT HER... AND...
...PROTECT THE YOUNG ONE SOON TO BE BORN.
"IT'S A SUBSTITUTE FOR ME!"
DID YOU RETURN TO YOUR WORLD... TAKING TAMAHOME WITH YOU...?
IF SO, PERHAPS THAT'S FOR THE BEST.
カッ

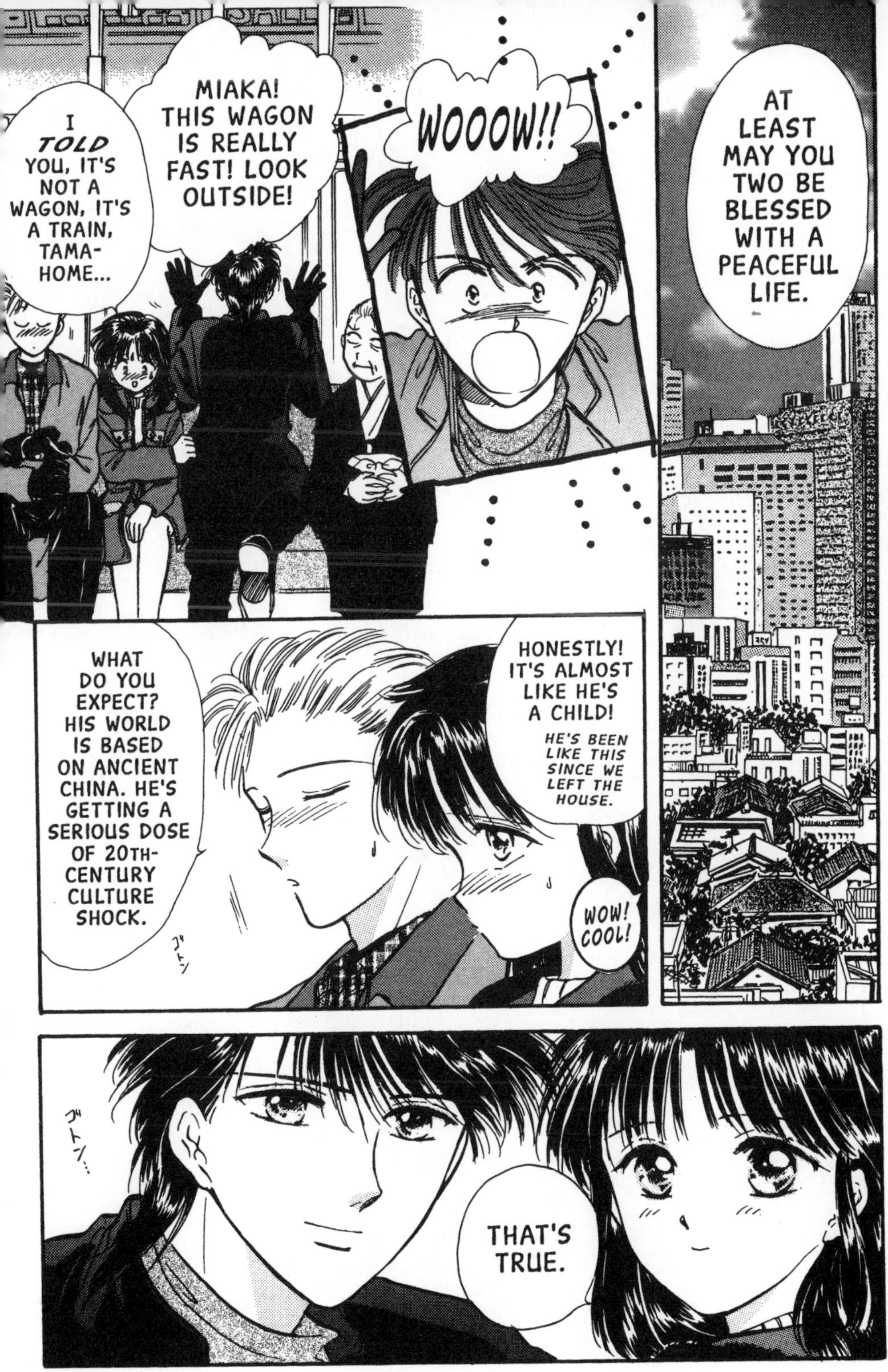
AT LEAST MAY YOU TWO BE BLESSED WITH A PEACEFUL LIFE.
WOOOW!!
MIAKA! THIS WAGON IS REALLY FAST! LOOK OUTSIDE!
I *TOLD* YOU, IT'S NOT A WAGON, IT'S A TRAIN, TAMA-HOME...
HONESTLY! IT'S ALMOST LIKE HE'S A CHILD!
HE'S BEEN LIKE THIS SINCE WE LEFT THE HOUSE.
WOW! COOL!
WHAT DO YOU EXPECT? HIS WORLD IS BASED ON ANCIENT CHINA. HE'S GETTING A SERIOUS DOSE OF 20TH-CENTURY CULTURE SHOCK.
ゴトン
THAT'S TRUE.
ゴトン…

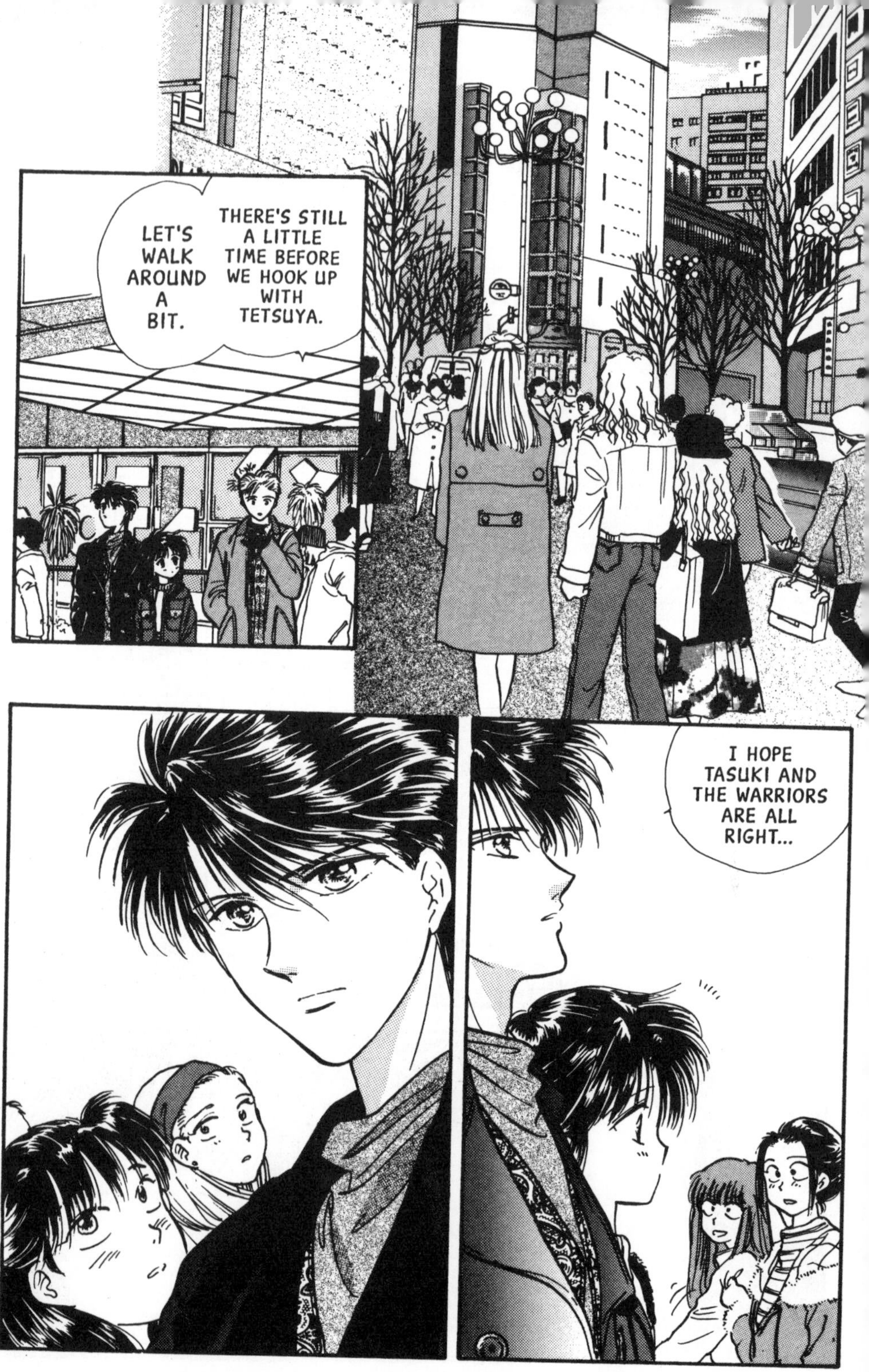
THERE'S STILL A LITTLE TIME BEFORE WE HOOK UP WITH TETSUYA.
LET'S WALK AROUND A BIT.
I HOPE TASUKI AND THE WARRIORS ARE ALL RIGHT...

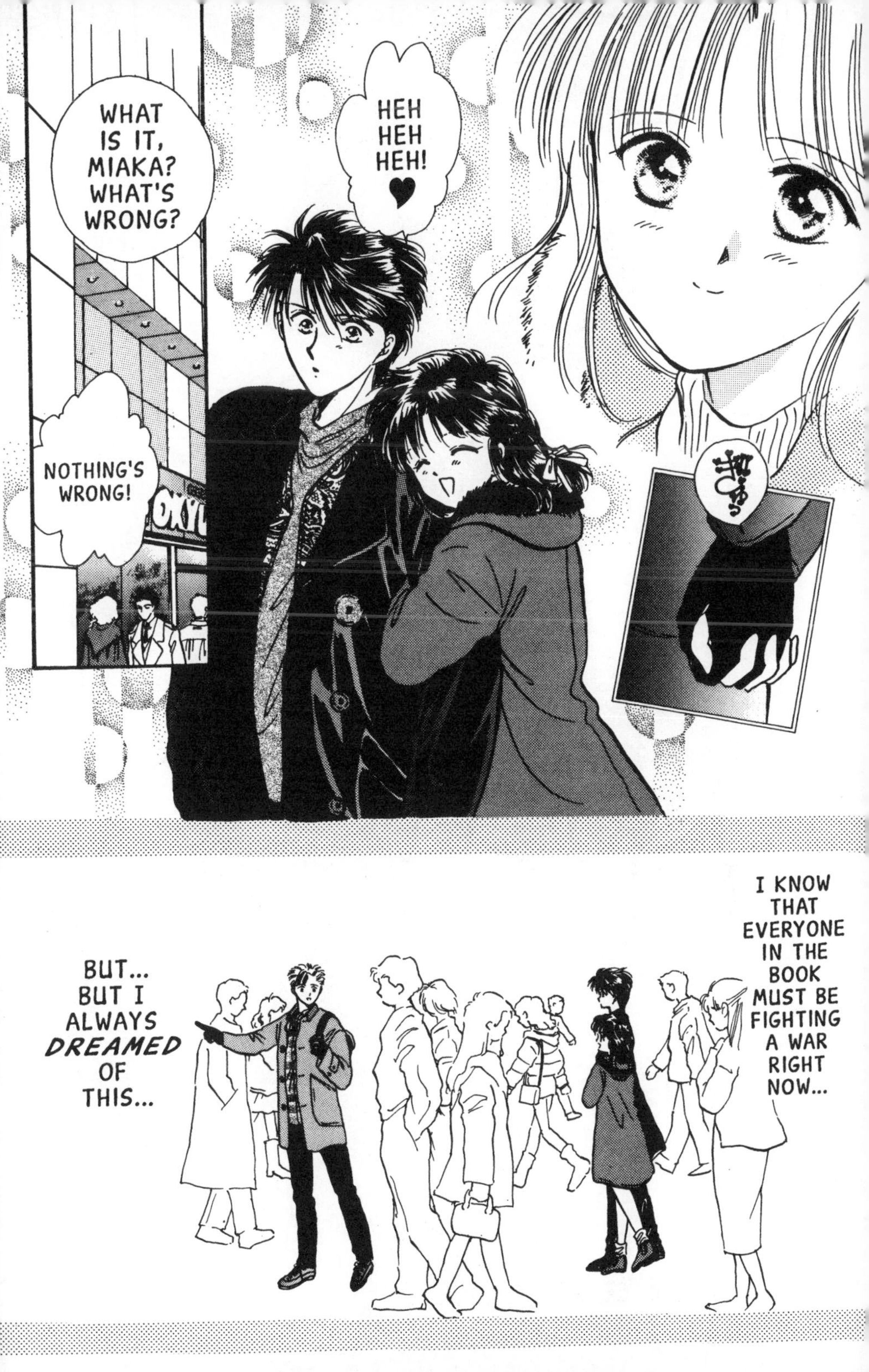
ぎゅっ
HEH HEH HEH! ♥
WHAT IS IT, MIAKA? WHAT'S WRONG?
NOTHING'S WRONG!
I KNOW THAT EVERYONE IN THE BOOK MUST BE FIGHTING A WAR RIGHT NOW...
BUT... BUT I ALWAYS *DREAMED* OF THIS...

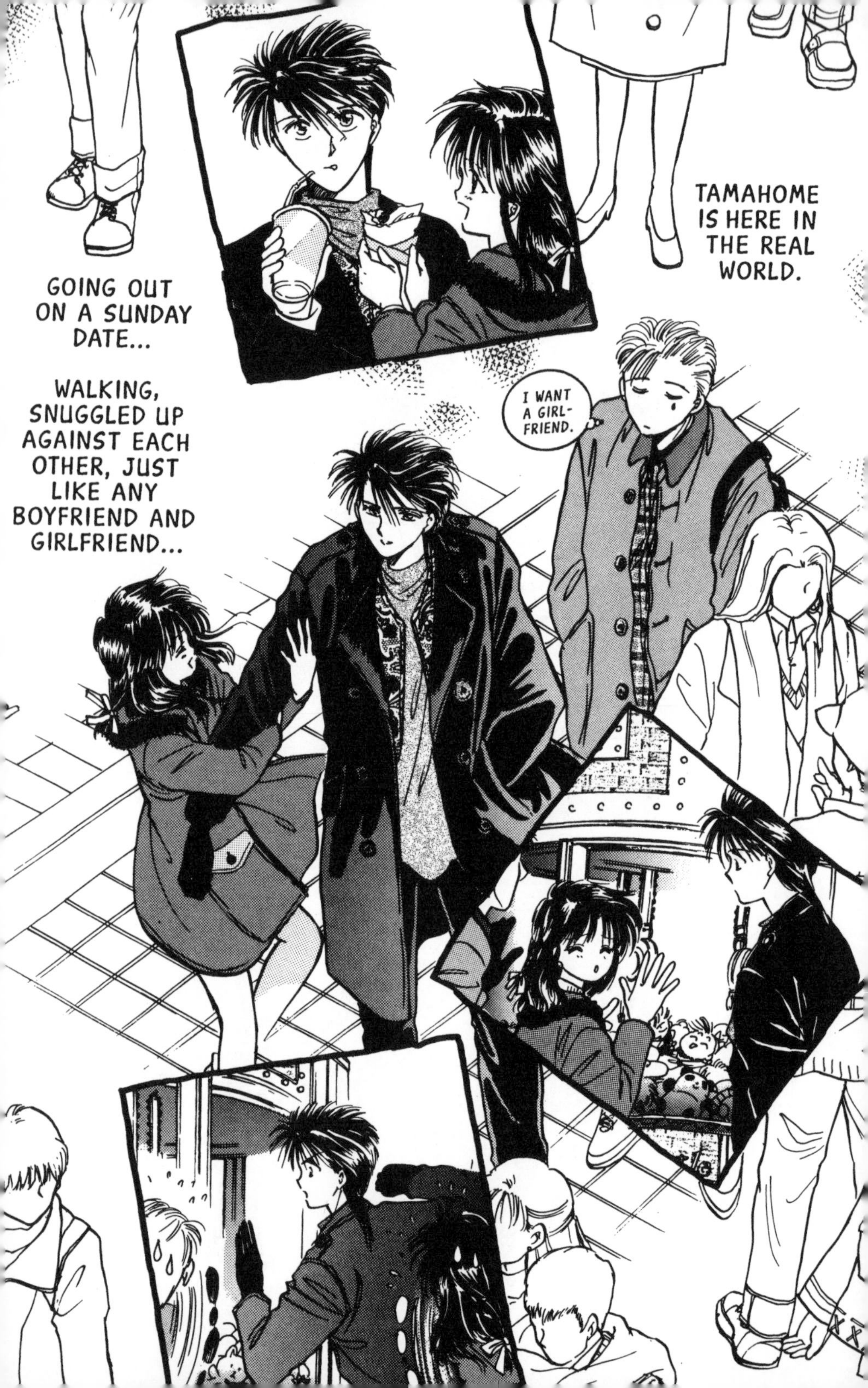
TAMAHOME IS HERE IN THE REAL WORLD.
GOING OUT ON A SUNDAY DATE...
WALKING, SNUGGLED UP AGAINST EACH OTHER, JUST LIKE ANY BOYFRIEND AND GIRLFRIEND...
I WANT A GIRL-FRIEND.

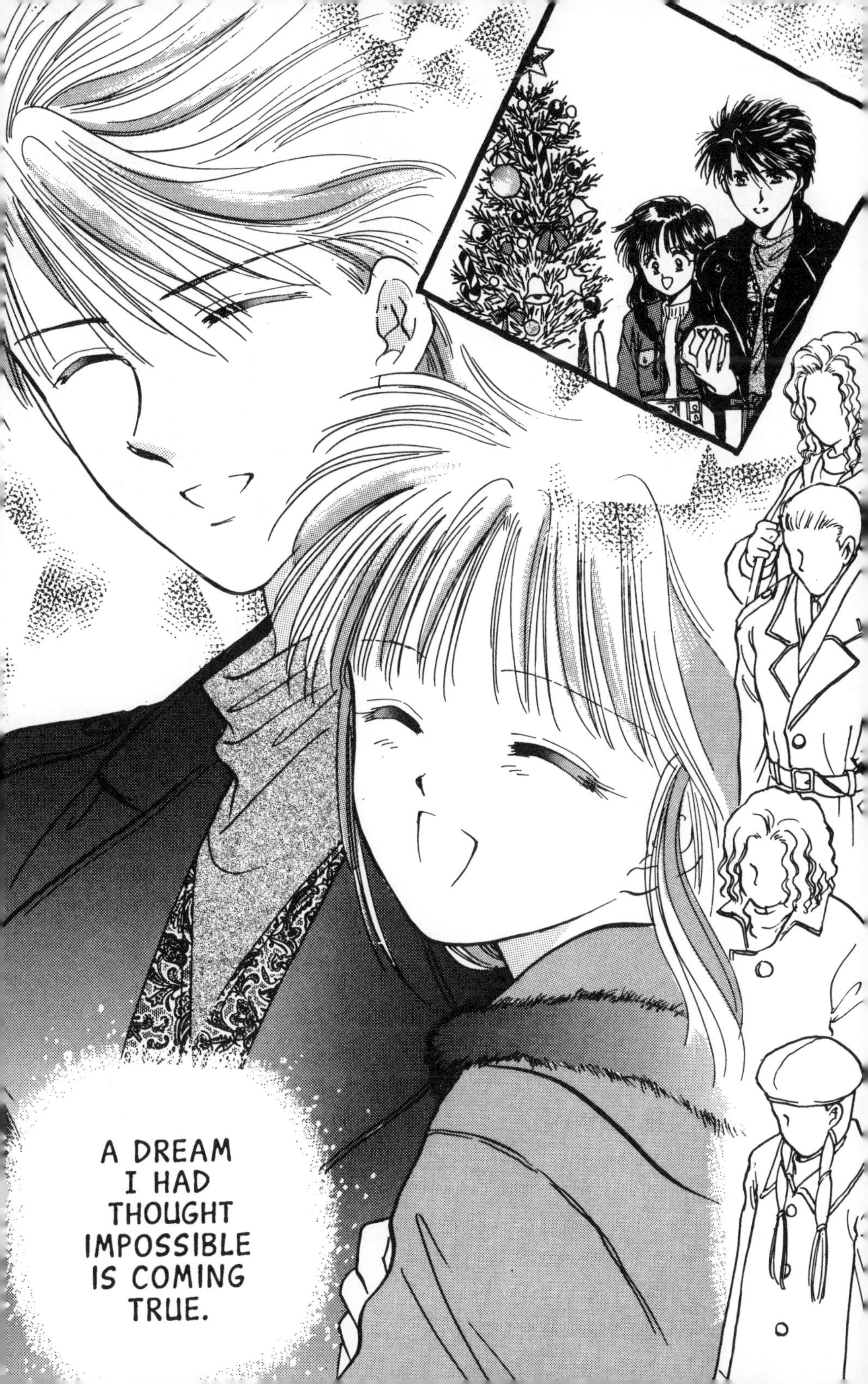
A DREAM I HAD THOUGHT IMPOSSIBLE IS COMING TRUE.

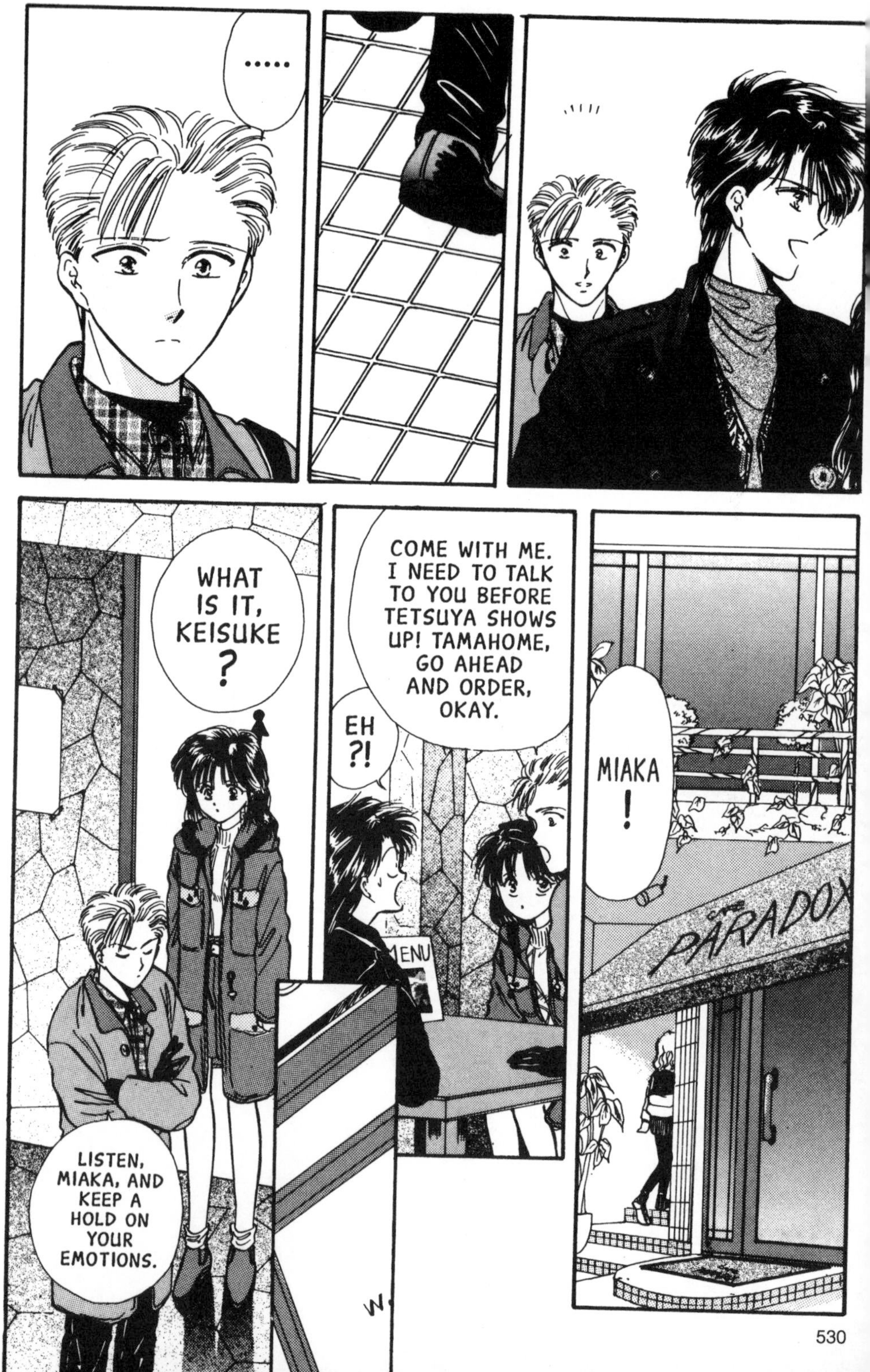
.....
MIAKA!
PARADOX
COME WITH ME. I NEED TO TALK TO YOU BEFORE TETSUYA SHOWS UP! TAMAHOME, GO AHEAD AND ORDER, OKAY.
EH?!
MENU
WHAT IS IT, KEISUKE?
LISTEN, MIAKA, AND KEEP A HOLD ON YOUR EMOTIONS.

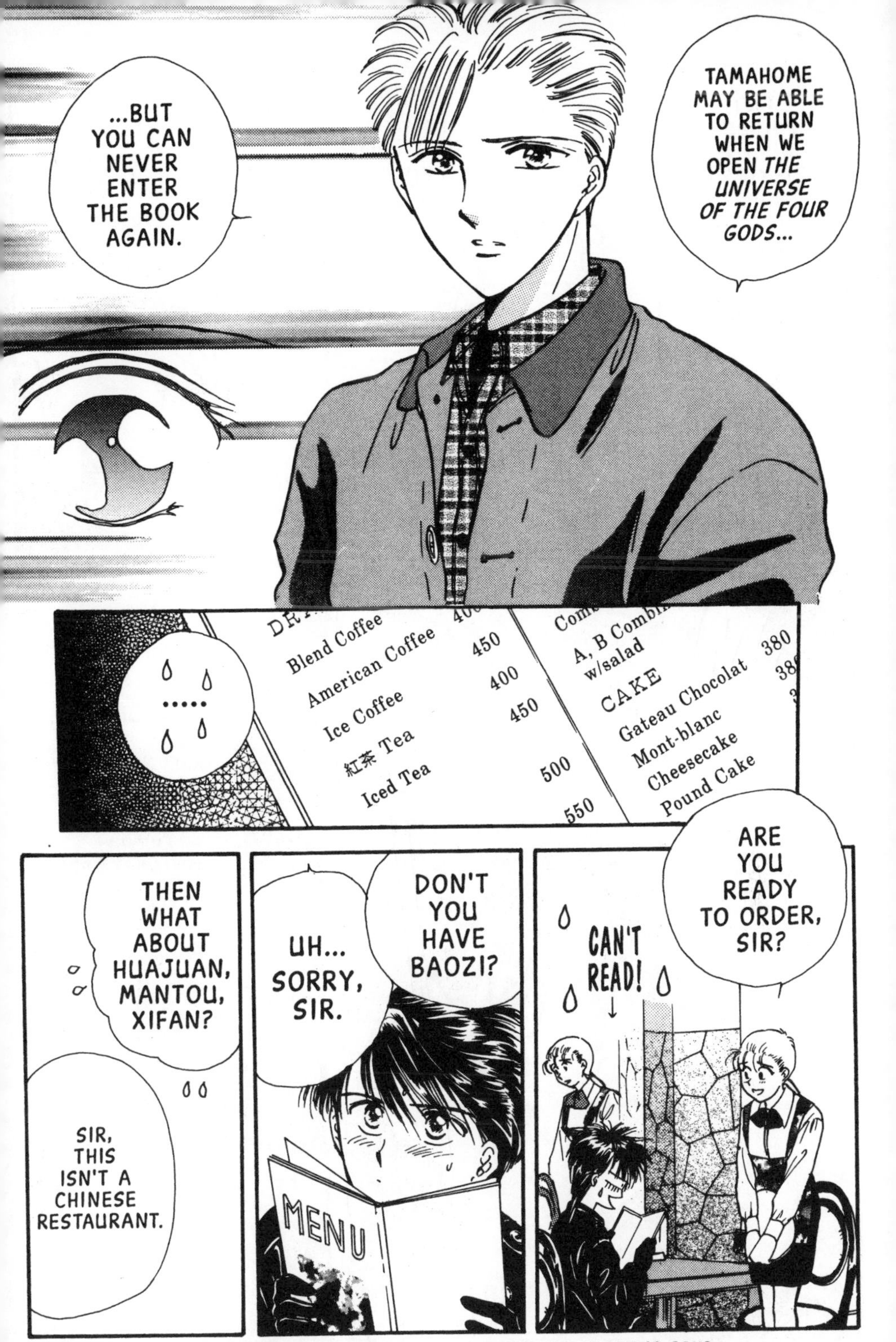
TAMAHOME MAY BE ABLE TO RETURN WHEN WE OPEN *THE UNIVERSE OF THE FOUR GODS*...
...BUT YOU CAN NEVER ENTER THE BOOK AGAIN.
Blend Coffee
American Coffee 450
Ice Coffee 400
紅茶 Tea 450
Iced Tea 500
550
w/salad
CAKE
Gateau Chocolat 380
Mont-blanc
Cheesecake
Pound Cake
ARE YOU READY TO ORDER, SIR?
CAN'T READ!
DON'T YOU HAVE BAOZI?
UH... SORRY, SIR.
MENU
THEN WHAT ABOUT HUAJUAN, MANTOU, XIFAN?
SIR, THIS ISN'T A CHINESE RESTAURANT.

BAOZI, HUAJUAN, AND MANTOU ARE KINDS OF CHINESE BUNS. XIFAN IS SOUP.

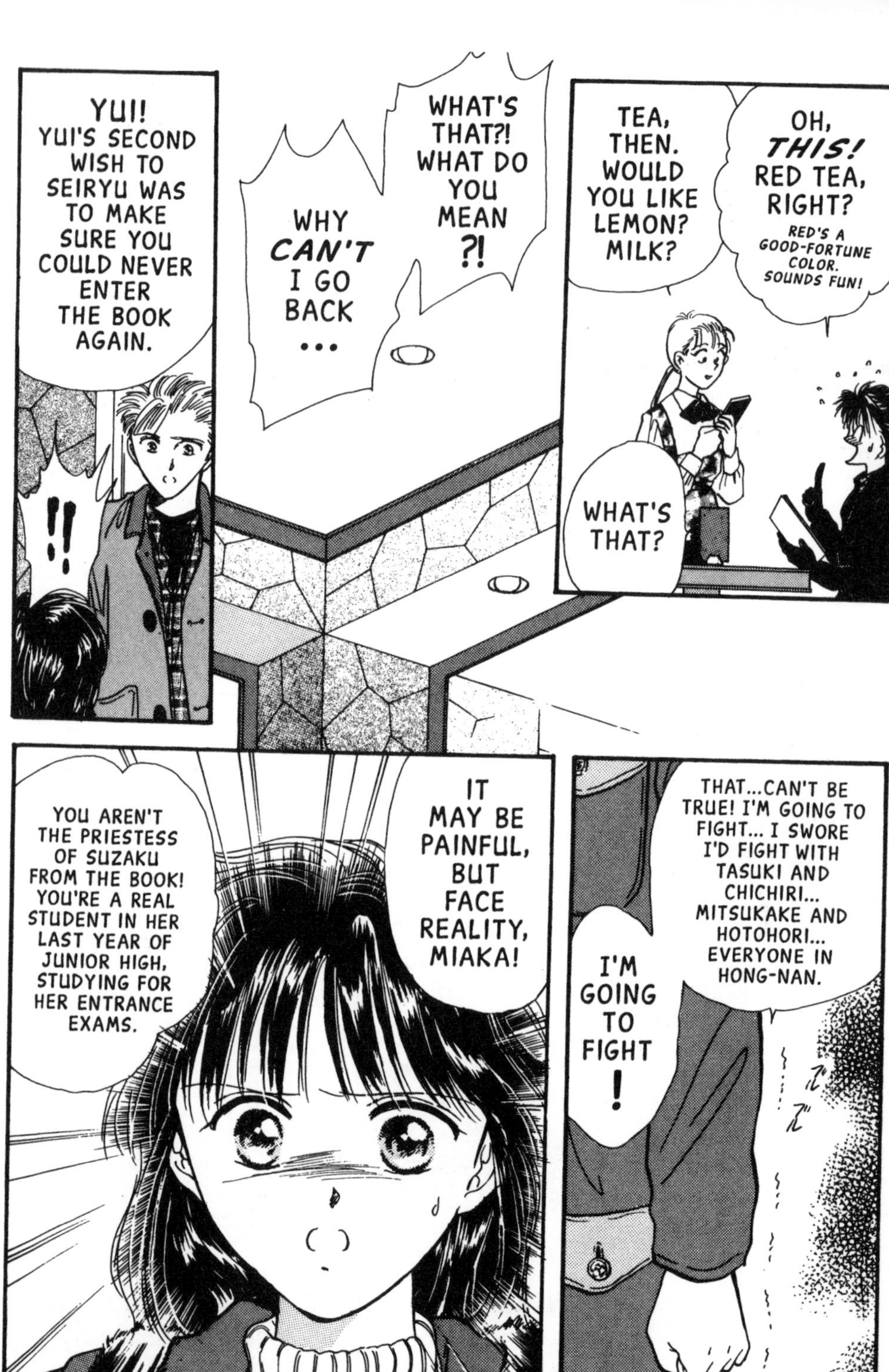
OH, THIS! RED TEA, RIGHT?
RED'S A GOOD-FORTUNE COLOR. SOUNDS FUN!
TEA, THEN. WOULD YOU LIKE LEMON? MILK?
WHAT'S THAT?
WHAT'S THAT?! WHAT DO YOU MEAN?!
WHY CAN'T I GO BACK...
YUI! YUI'S SECOND WISH TO SEIRYU WAS TO MAKE SURE YOU COULD NEVER ENTER THE BOOK AGAIN.
!!
THAT...CAN'T BE TRUE! I'M GOING TO FIGHT... I SWORE I'D FIGHT WITH TASUKI AND CHICHIRI... MITSUKAKE AND HOTOHORI... EVERYONE IN HONG-NAN.
I'M GOING TO FIGHT!
IT MAY BE PAINFUL, BUT FACE REALITY, MIAKA!
YOU AREN'T THE PRIESTESS OF SUZAKU FROM THE BOOK! YOU'RE A REAL STUDENT IN HER LAST YEAR OF JUNIOR HIGH, STUDYING FOR HER ENTRANCE EXAMS.

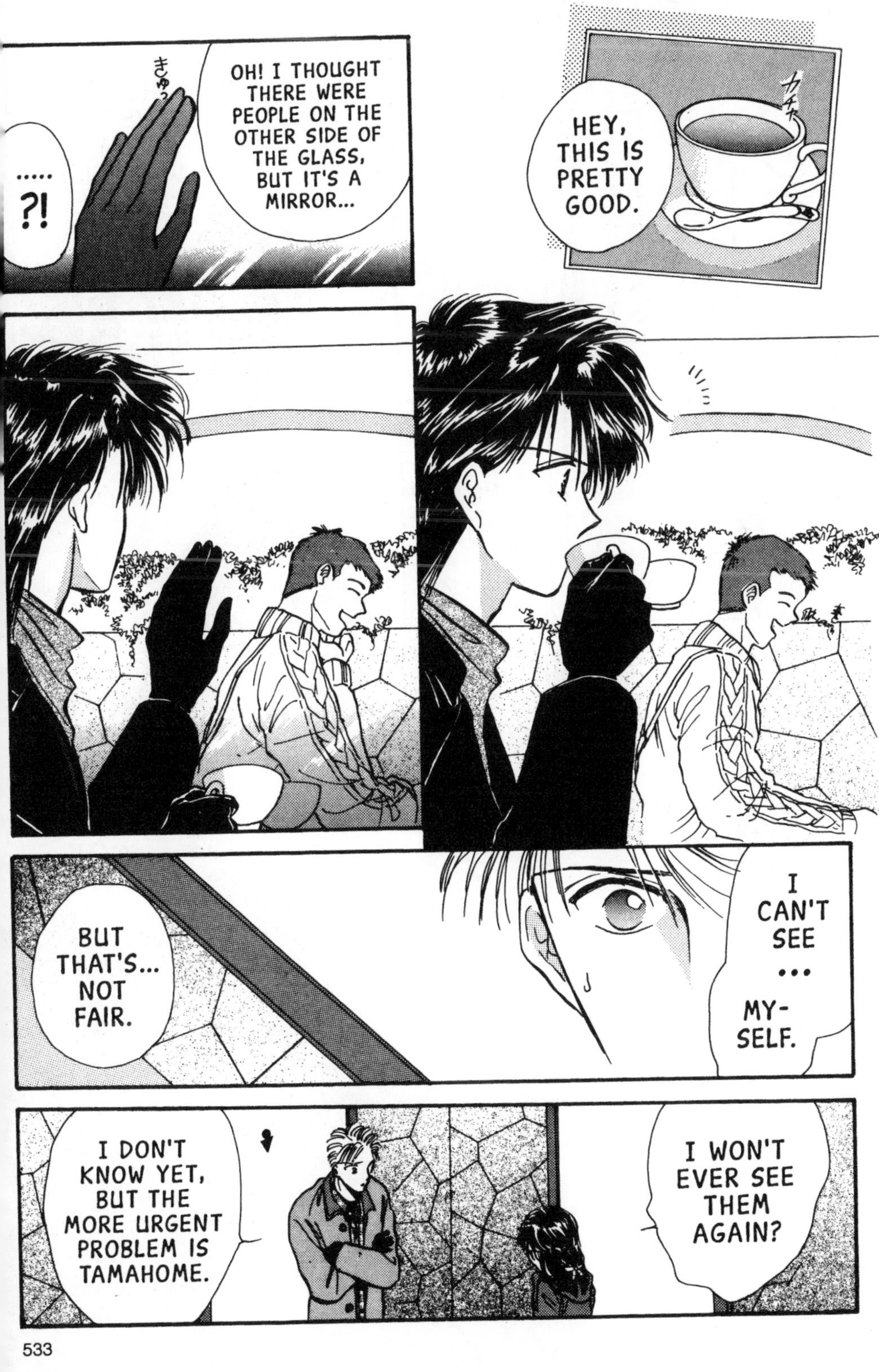
カチャ
HEY, THIS IS PRETTY GOOD.
きゅっ
OH! I THOUGHT THERE WERE PEOPLE ON THE OTHER SIDE OF THE GLASS, BUT IT'S A MIRROR...
..... ?!
I CAN'T SEE ... MY-SELF.
BUT THAT'S... NOT FAIR.
I WON'T EVER SEE THEM AGAIN?
I DON'T KNOW YET, BUT THE MORE URGENT PROBLEM IS TAMAHOME.

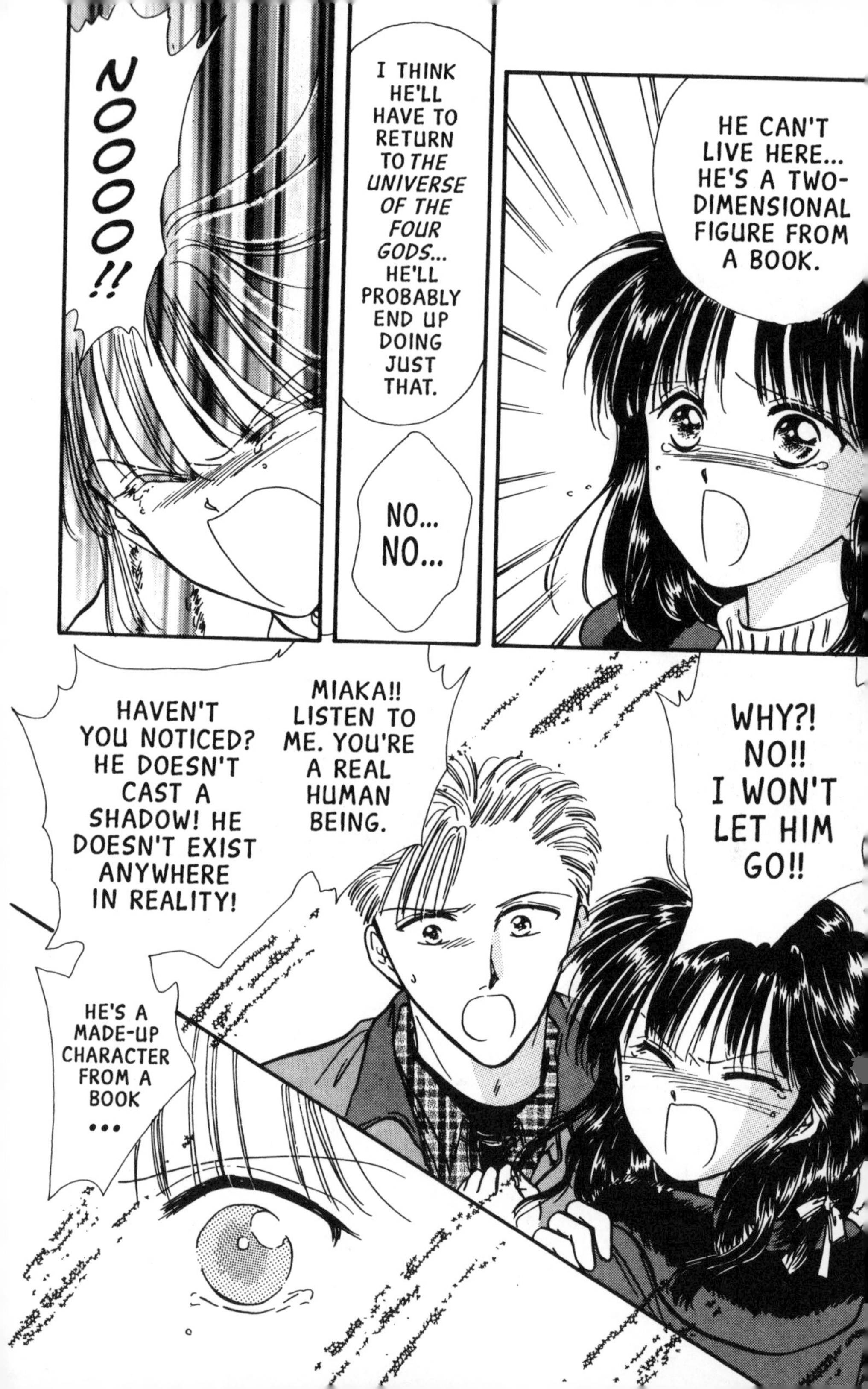
HE CAN'T LIVE HERE... HE'S A TWO-DIMENSIONAL FIGURE FROM A BOOK.
I THINK HE'LL HAVE TO RETURN TO *THE UNIVERSE OF THE FOUR GODS*... HE'LL PROBABLY END UP DOING JUST THAT.
NO... NO...
NOOOOO!!
WHY?! NO!! I WON'T LET HIM GO!!
MIAKA!! LISTEN TO ME. YOU'RE A REAL HUMAN BEING.
HAVEN'T YOU NOTICED? HE DOESN'T CAST A SHADOW! HE DOESN'T EXIST ANYWHERE IN REALITY!
HE'S A MADE-UP CHARACTER FROM A BOOK ...

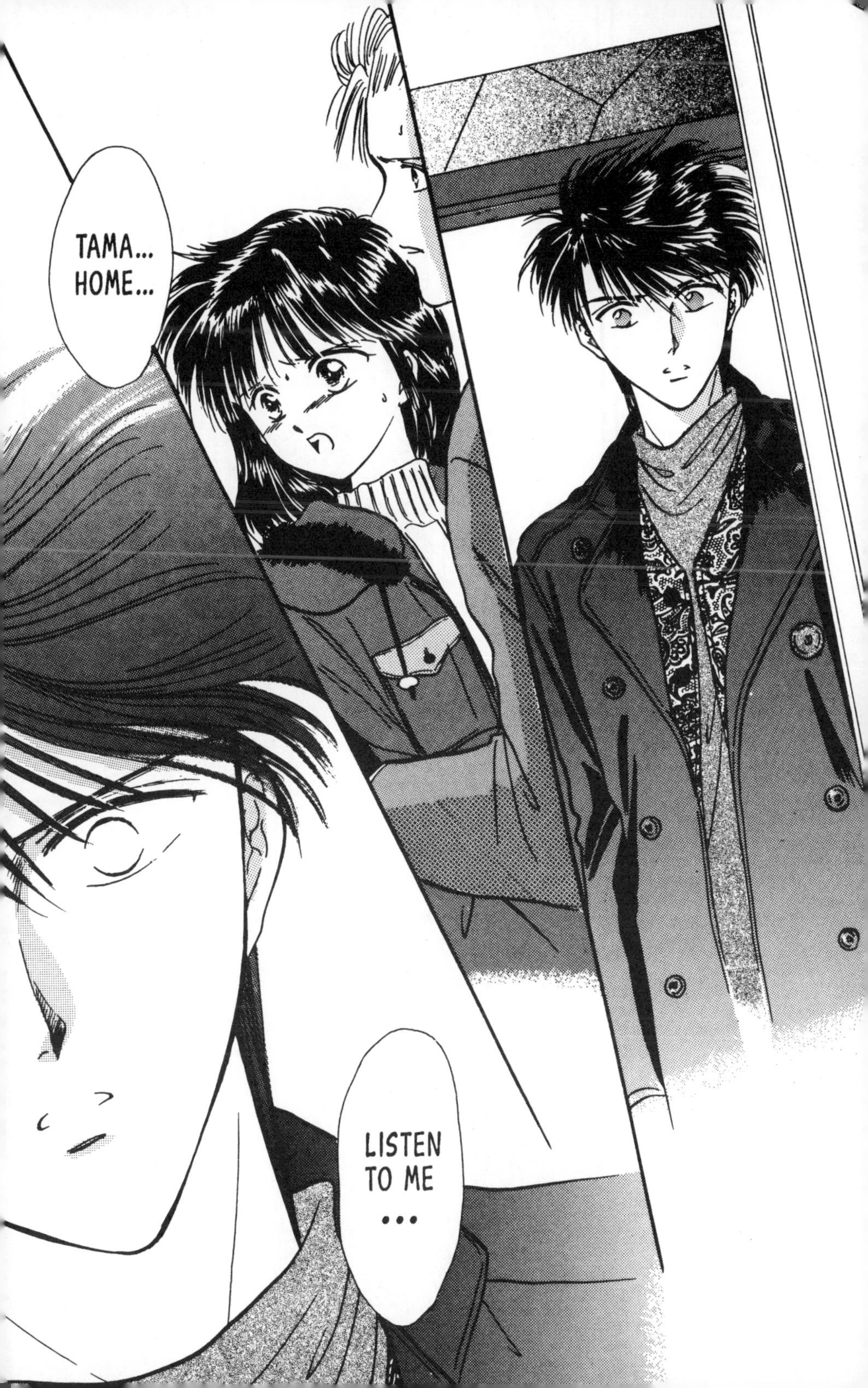
TAMA... HOME...
LISTEN TO ME ...

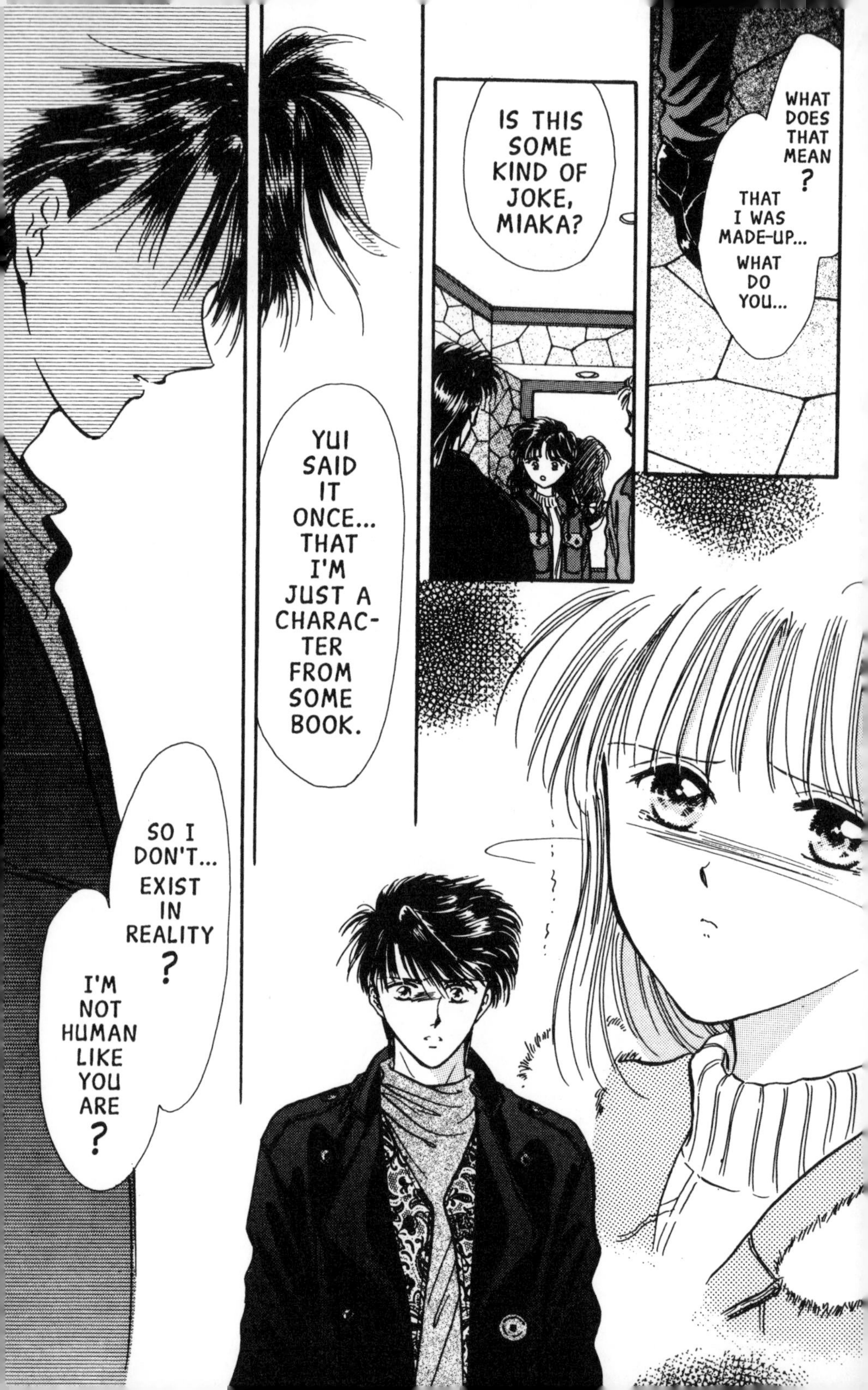
WHAT DOES THAT MEAN?
THAT I WAS MADE-UP... WHAT DO YOU...
IS THIS SOME KIND OF JOKE, MIAKA?
YUI SAID IT ONCE... THAT I'M JUST A CHARAC-TER FROM SOME BOOK.
SO I DON'T... EXIST IN REALITY?
I'M NOT HUMAN LIKE YOU ARE?

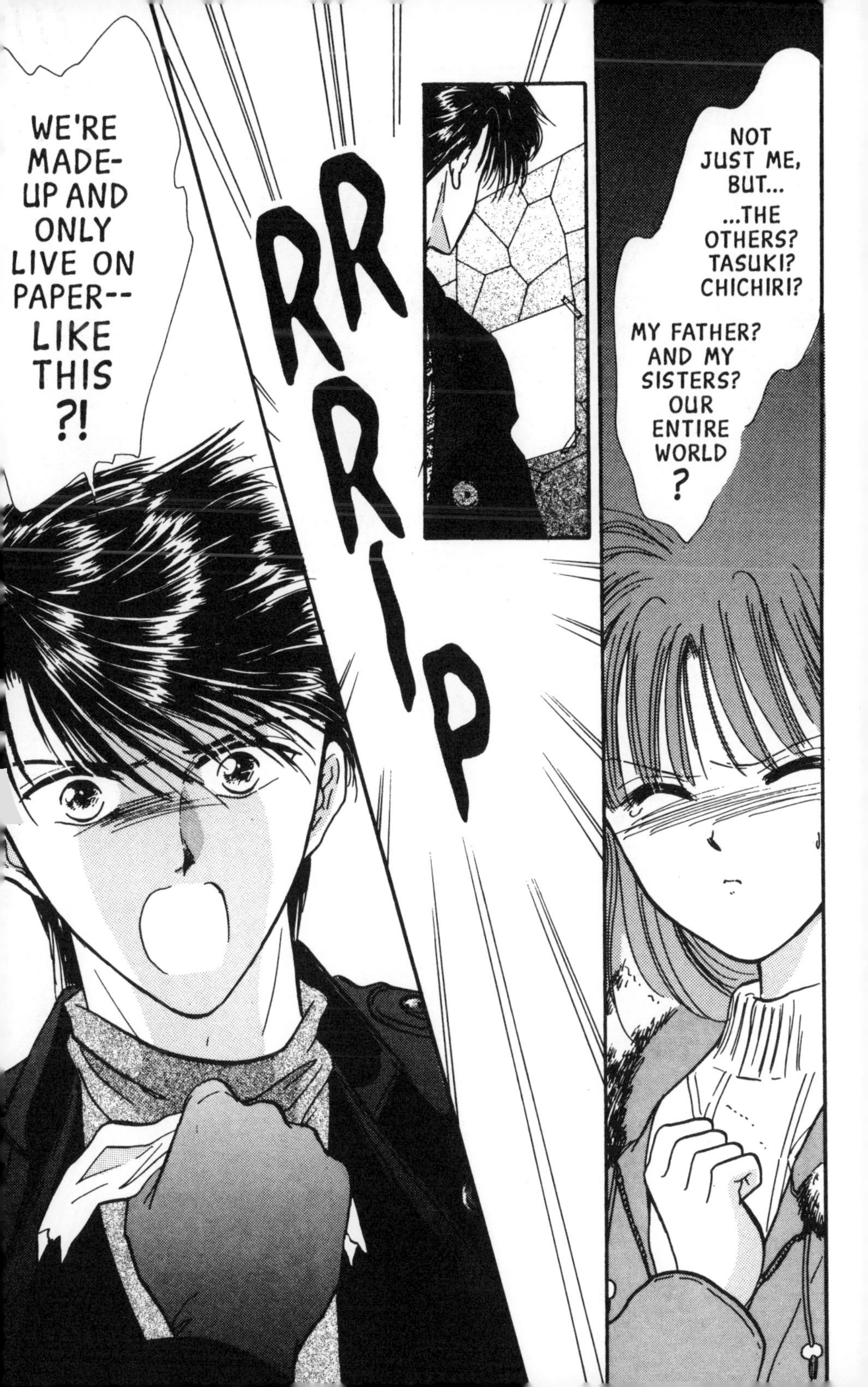
NOT JUST ME, BUT...
...THE OTHERS? TASUKI? CHICHIRI?
MY FATHER? AND MY SISTERS? OUR ENTIRE WORLD ?
RRRIP
WE'RE MADE-UP AND ONLY LIVE ON PAPER-- LIKE THIS ?!

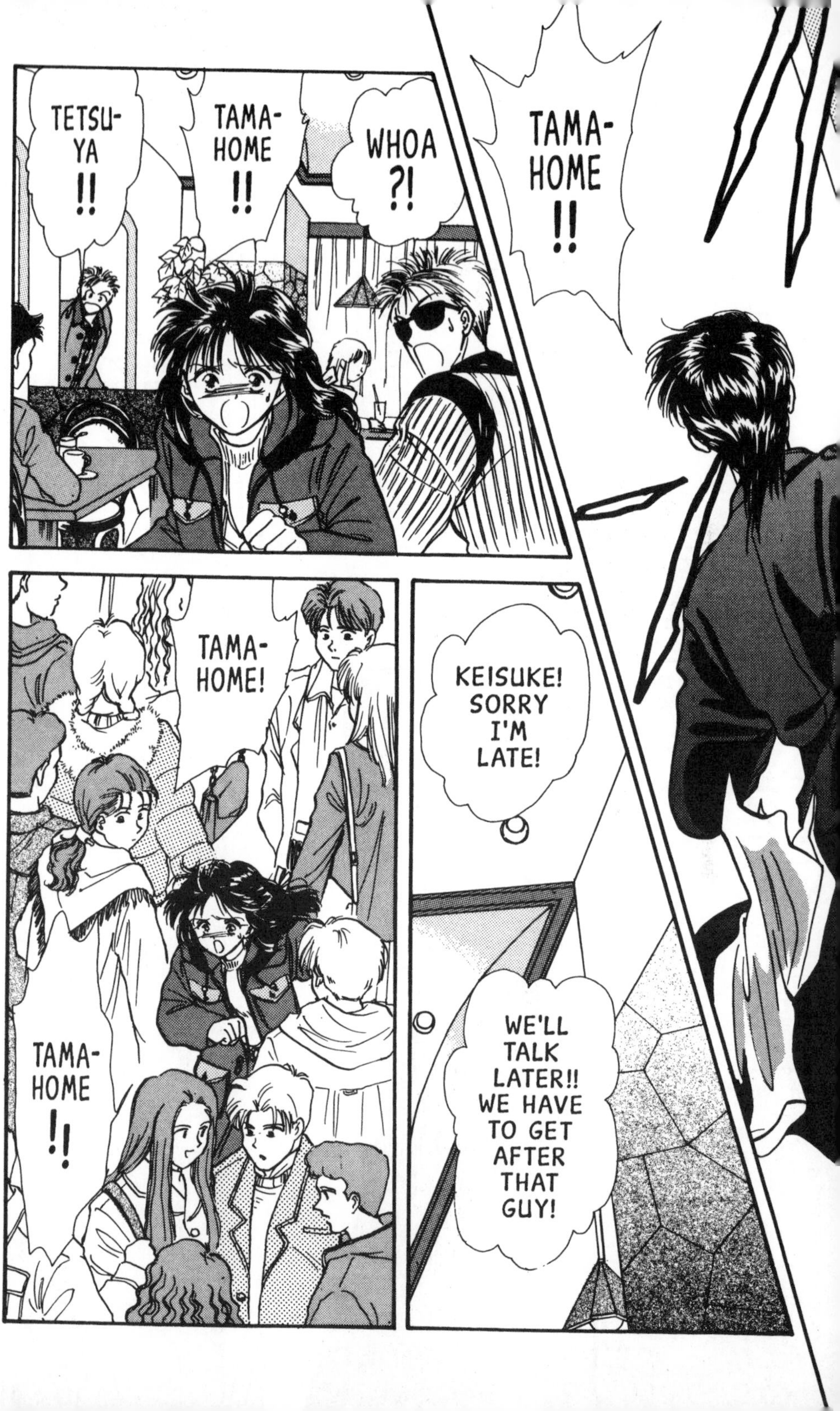
TAMA-
HOME
!!
WHOA
?!
TAMA-
HOME
!!
TETSU-
YA
!!
KEISUKE! SORRY I'M LATE!
WE'LL TALK LATER!! WE HAVE TO GET AFTER THAT GUY!
TAMA-
HOME!
TAMA-
HOME
!!

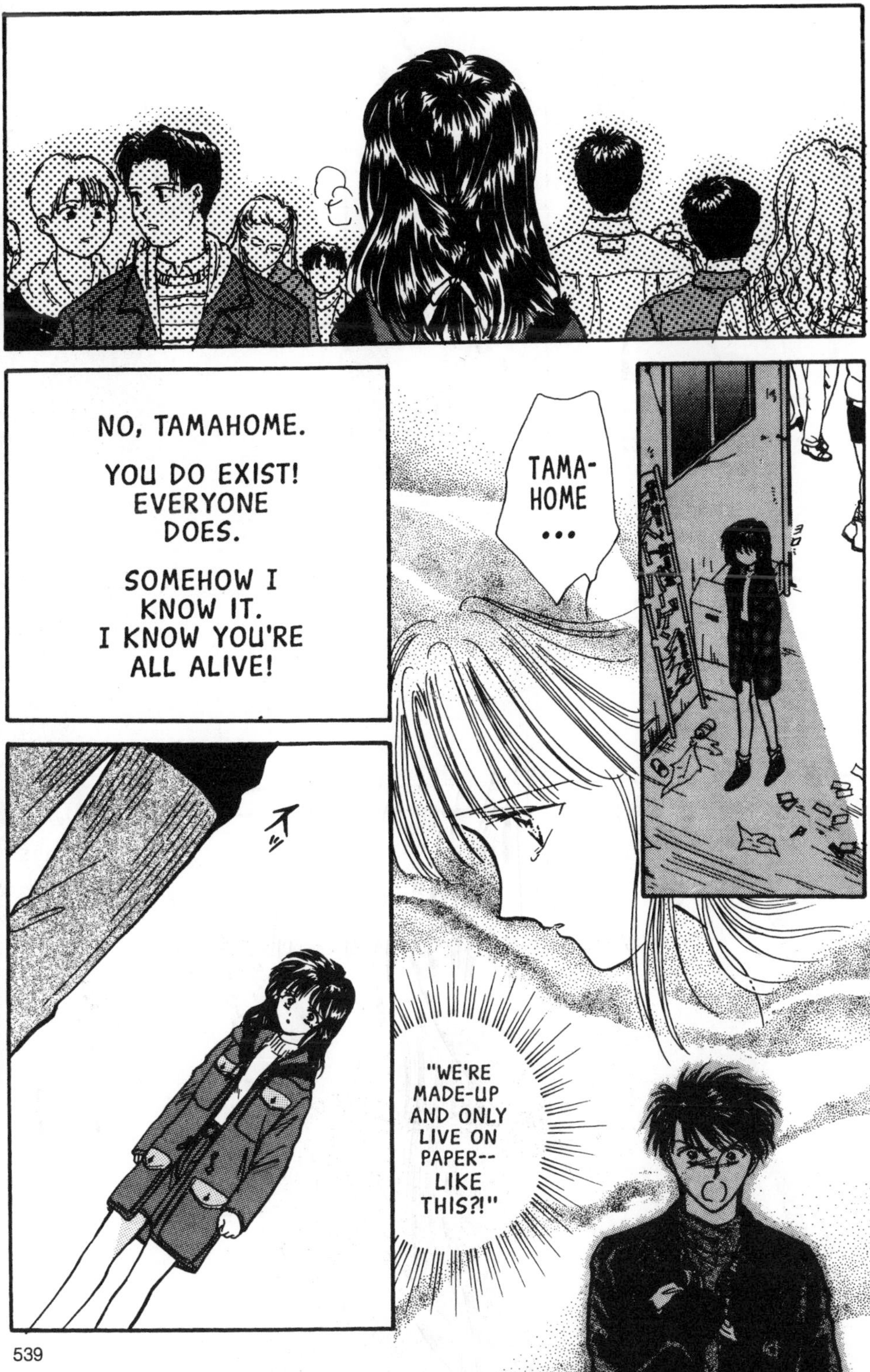
TAMA-HOME...
"WE'RE MADE-UP AND ONLY LIVE ON PAPER--LIKE THIS?!"
NO, TAMAHOME.
YOU DO EXIST! EVERYONE DOES.
SOMEHOW I KNOW IT. I KNOW YOU'RE ALL ALIVE!

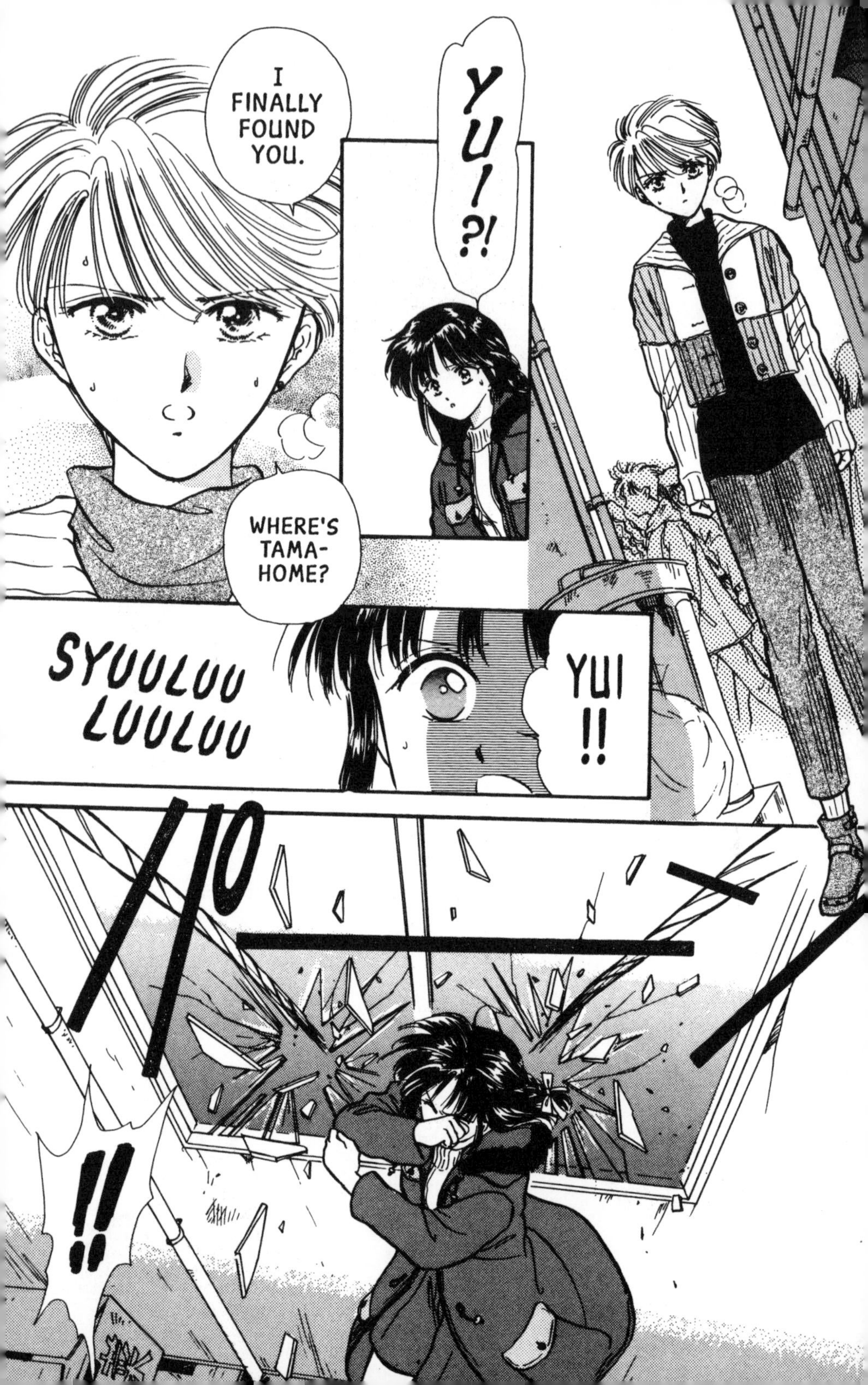
YUI?!
I FINALLY FOUND YOU.
WHERE'S TAMA-HOME?
YUI!!
SYUULUU LUULUU
!!

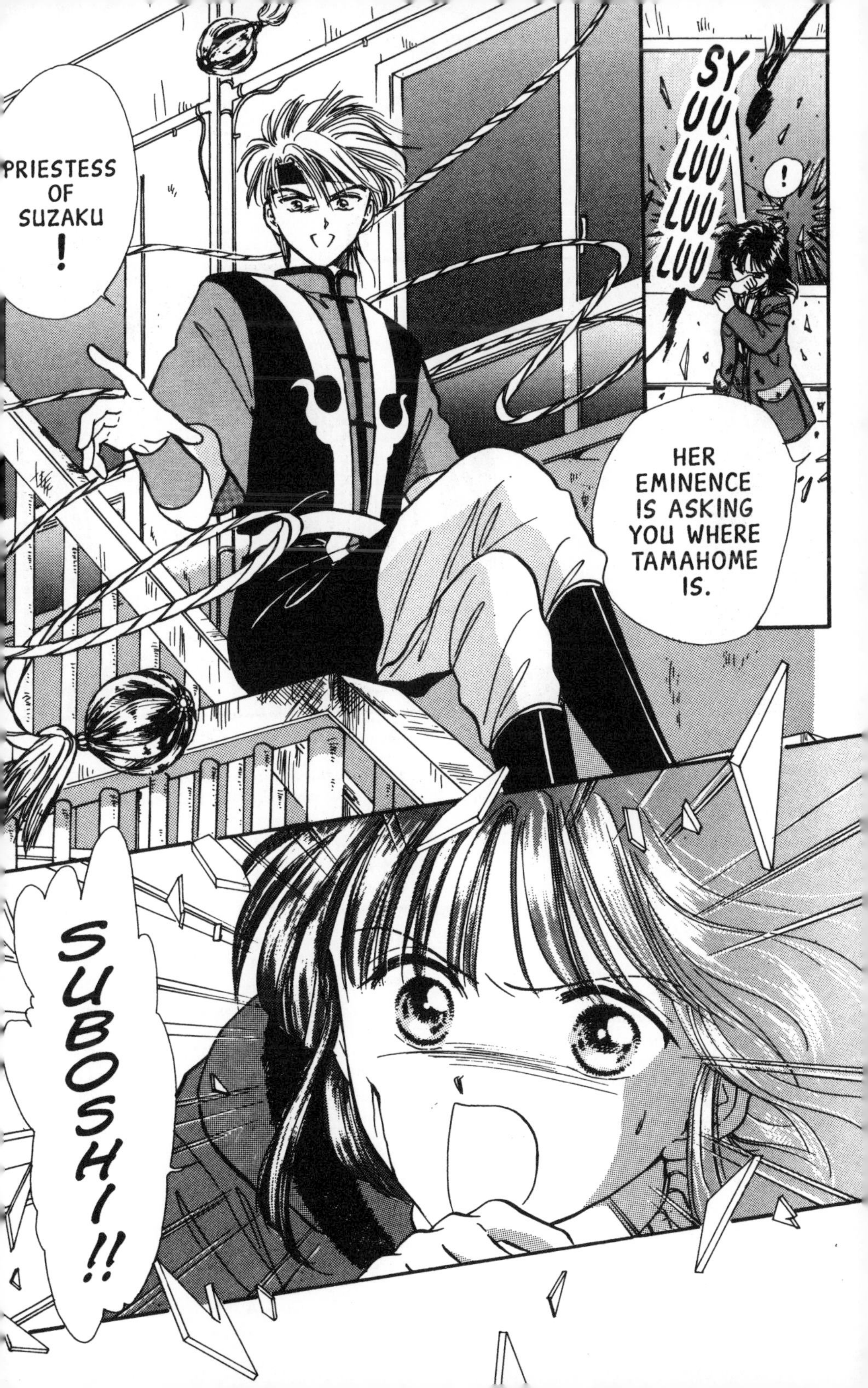
SYUULUULUULUU
!
PRIESTESS OF SUZAKU!
HER EMINENCE IS ASKING YOU WHERE TAMAHOME IS.
SUBOSHI!!

THESE TWO DIDN'T GET ALONG ON ACCOUNT OF NAKAGO.

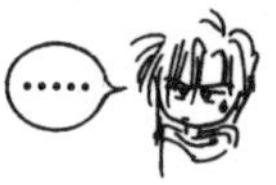

LIBRA

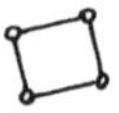

SCORPIO

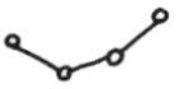

LUO 羅 CHUIN 軍

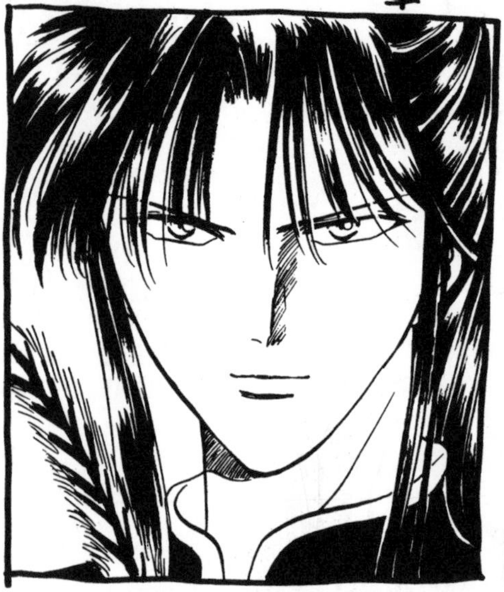

HIS REAL FACE, BACK BY POPULAR DEMAND

T O M O

BAI 白 HUA 花 WAN 婉

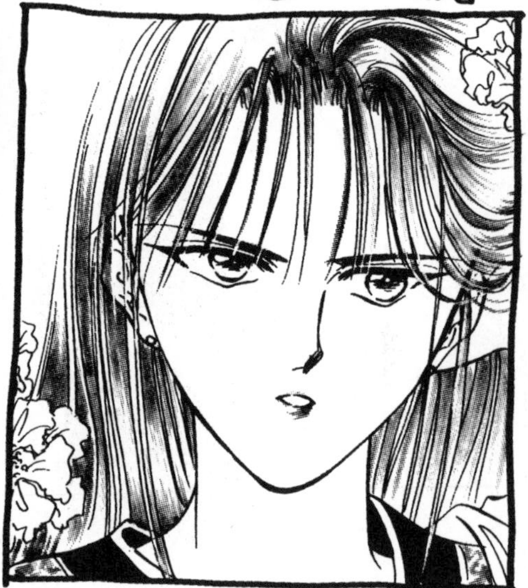

S O I

• He was abandoned as a baby, so his birthplace remains unknown (his real name is unknown too). (His childhood caretaker gave him this name.)

• 21 years old
• Height: 184 cm (6' 0")
• Blood type: AB
• Powers: Hypnosis and illusion using a shell
• Hobbies: Sadism (particularly with men)
⇧ *He rarely actually hurts anyone...*

• He has a very complicated personality. He's pretty harsh and jaded, probably due to the hardships he had to suffer as a child. But he's become a little twisted.
Because his caretaker was a dancer, he learned the art and made a living on it (his makeup and clothes come from the stage). *A street performer really.*
He's very nimble because of this background.
It could be that he was surrounded only by men, or he simply could have been born that way, but he is homosexual. He's in love with Nakago, but because of his jaded personality, he can't be upfront about it. So he usually ends up saying something irritating.
Although he's calm, he has a flaky side too. He doesn't like women, but he can effectively take them on (!) when he needs to.

• Born in the village of Xuan, home of the Ning tribe in the Western region (a satellite country) of Qu-Dong).*

• 19 years old
• Height: 170 cm (5' 7")
• Blood type: O
• Measurements B: 89 W: 56 H: 85 (35, 22, 33)

• Powers: Special Feng shui powers to control lightning, electro-magnetic fields, and Fangzhong (bedding) techniques.

• Because her family was so poor, as a child, she was sold to a brothel and grew up there. She fell in love with Nakago at the age of 12 when she first met him. She knew her love was unrequited, and that she was being used so he could recover and heighten his chi, but that didn't stop her from giving him everything she had.
She is normally bound in armor, speaks like a man, and is formidable as a fighter.
But now, everything she does is, in one way or another, to try to assist Nakago. In fact, she is very feminine and kind. Because of her jealousy toward Yui, she's sympathetic to Miaka.

* Satellite country: A country under the rule of a neighboring major power.

Chapter Seventy-One To Live for You

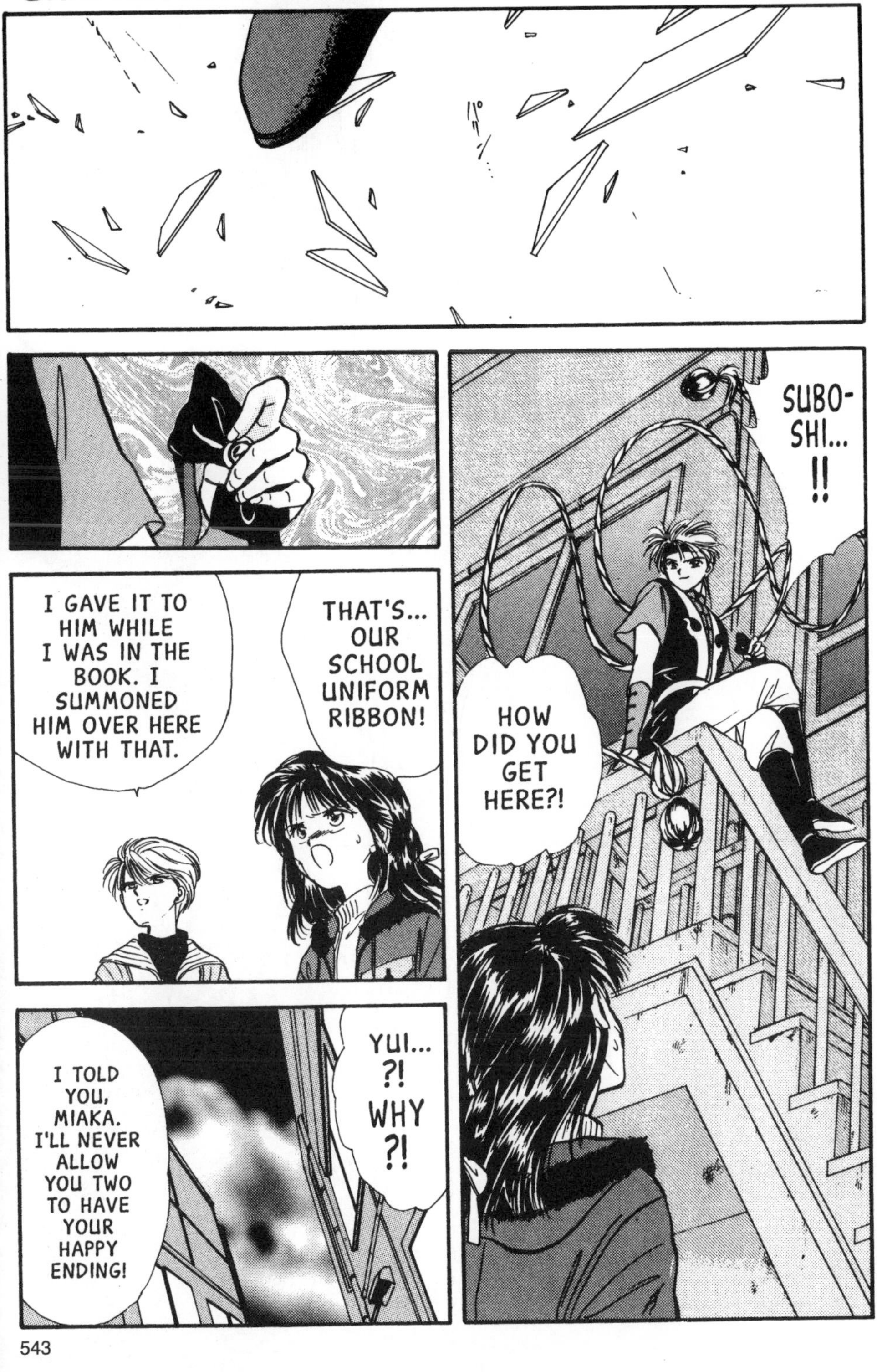
SUBO-SHI... !!
HOW DID YOU GET HERE?!
THAT'S... OUR SCHOOL UNIFORM RIBBON!
I GAVE IT TO HIM WHILE I WAS IN THE BOOK. I SUMMONED HIM OVER HERE WITH THAT.
YUI... ?! WHY ?!
I TOLD YOU, MIAKA. I'LL NEVER ALLOW YOU TWO TO HAVE YOUR HAPPY ENDING!

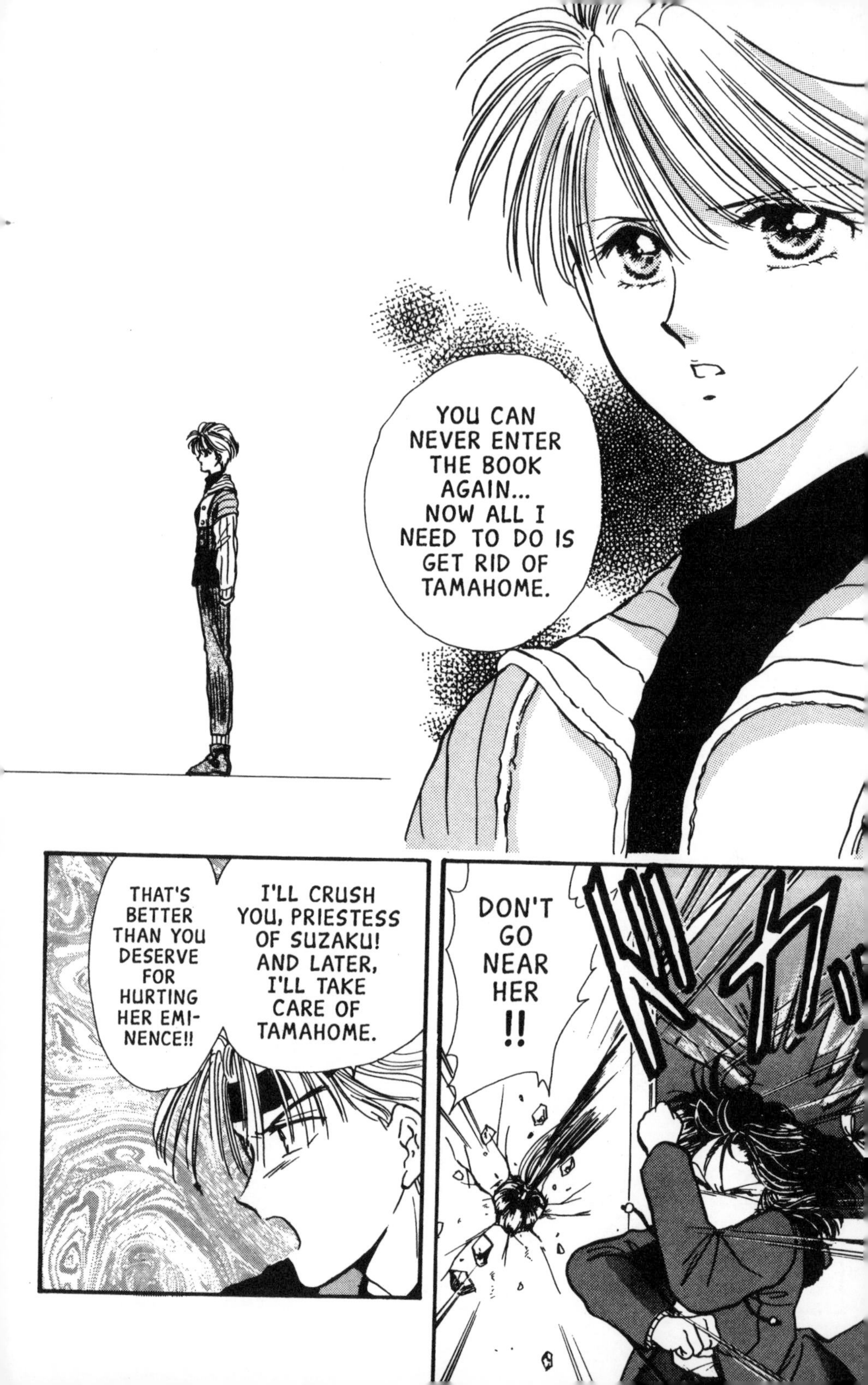
YOU CAN NEVER ENTER THE BOOK AGAIN... NOW ALL I NEED TO DO IS GET RID OF TAMAHOME.
DON'T GO NEAR HER !!
I'LL CRUSH YOU, PRIESTESS OF SUZAKU! AND LATER, I'LL TAKE CARE OF TAMAHOME.
THAT'S BETTER THAN YOU DESERVE FOR HURTING HER EMI-NENCE!!

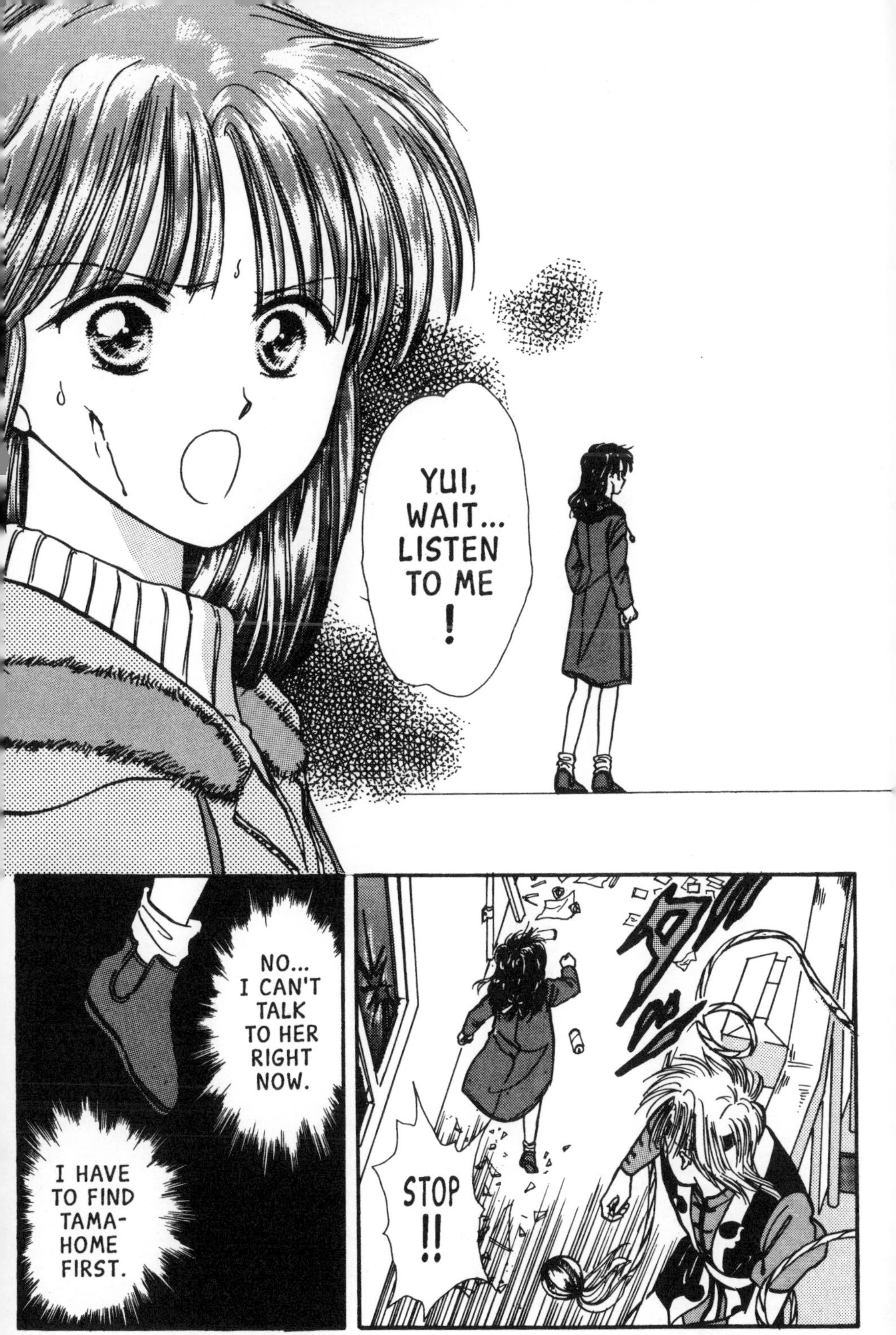
YUI, WAIT... LISTEN TO ME!
STOP!!
NO... I CAN'T TALK TO HER RIGHT NOW.
I HAVE TO FIND TAMA-HOME FIRST.

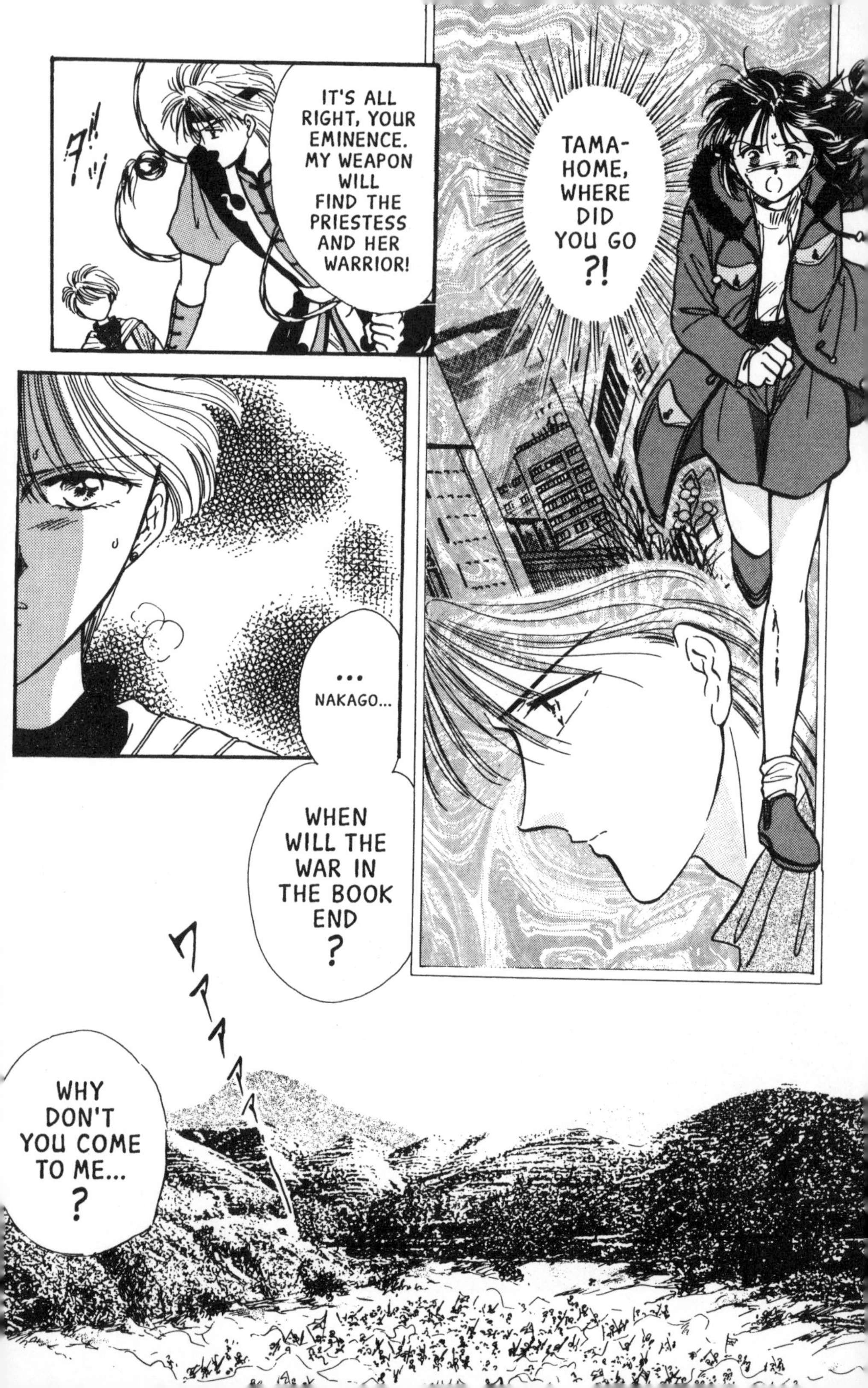
TAMA-HOME, WHERE DID YOU GO?!
IT'S ALL RIGHT, YOUR EMINENCE. MY WEAPON WILL FIND THE PRIESTESS AND HER WARRIOR!
... NAKAGO...
WHEN WILL THE WAR IN THE BOOK END?
WHY DON'T YOU COME TO ME...?

By the way, I came up with the idea of having Tomo use a shell to help with his illusions because in ancient times, it was said the *shinkirō* ("mirage") was created by the *shin*, a giant shell which had dreams in the ocean and exhaled its chi which floated upwards and rose into the air as an illusion. (Of course, I have to wonder how a mirage can still occur in the middle of a desert!)

Ashitare. No comment, really. I think it's all right to have a character who's pretty mindless... But I did enjoy drawing him.

Miboshi. A sorcerer who controlled monsters. The villain who concocted the potion that controlled Tamahome's mind. The temple was based on the famous Pokhara Temple, but the interior resembles an ancient Indian temple. Miboshi isn't holding a rattle, it's a prayer wheel (Tibetans always use them, don't they [?]). His is inscribed with Buddhist sutras to summon demons. (Of course, that's not what they're really for.) If I could afford the pages, I wanted Chichiri to summon a good spirit and have it fight Miboshi's demons! *But this is a shojo manga here...maybe if it were a video game...* He's actually an old man. I don't think we need the background on these two. Sorry! I doubt they have any fans though.

Oh, no! I'm running out of space already... Hm? What about Yui? Hold on, we still have more coming. That's right... the next volume will be the last for *Fushigi Yūgi* (Waaaah! How sad!) After this book is published, the serial will come to an end with issue 5 of *Shojo Comic* which is published on February 5th (1995). But the CD book 3 will come out in February too. The book of illustrations (sorry, it will only contain material from *Fushigi Yūgi*, nothing from *Prepubescence*) will be packed with plenty of material! No definite publication date yet though... See you then in volume 13! *I want to tell the tale of Genbu and Byakko too. Someone give me the chance!*

'94 11/30

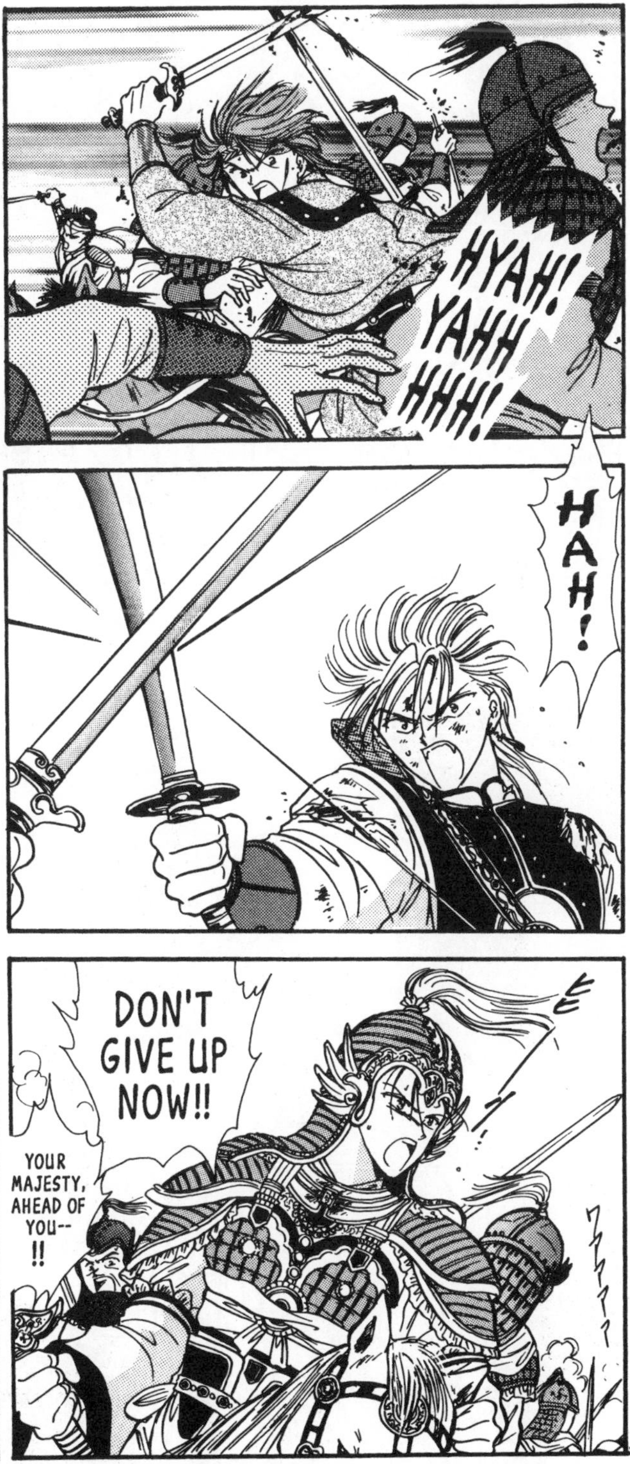
HYAH! YAHH HHH!
HAH!
DON'T GIVE UP NOW!!
YOUR MAJESTY, AHEAD OF YOU-- !!

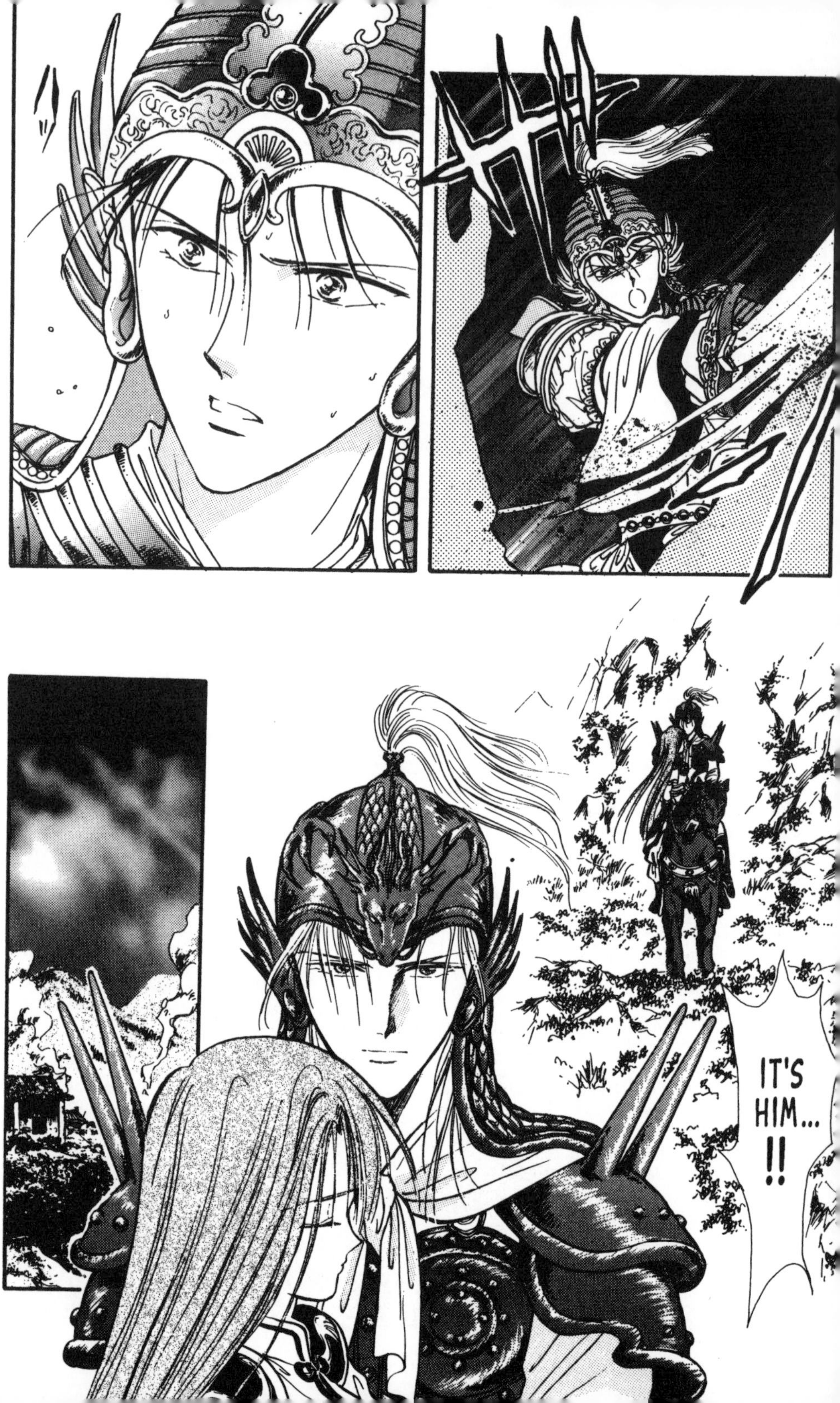
IT'S HIM... !!

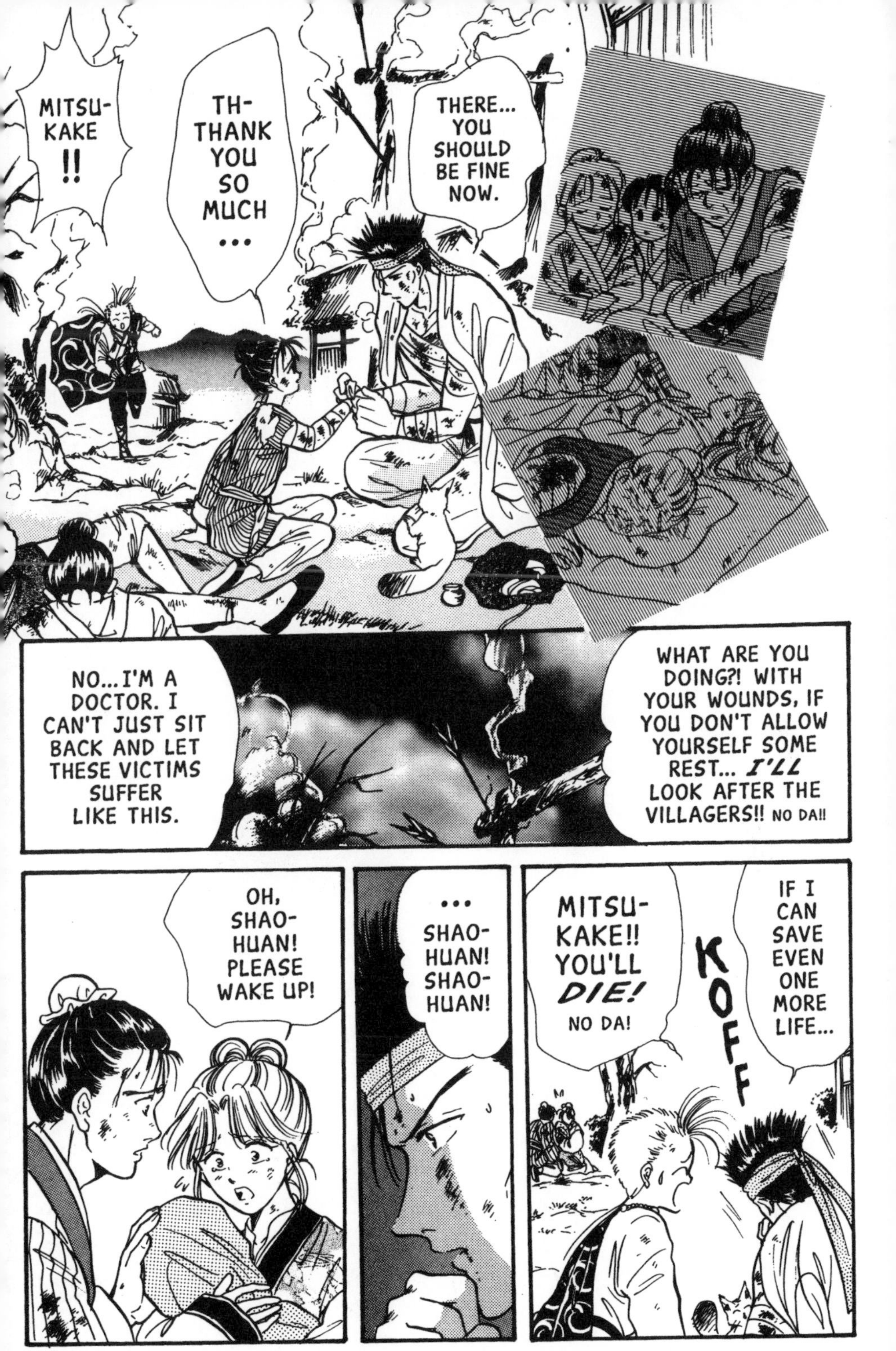

THERE... YOU SHOULD BE FINE NOW.
TH-THANK YOU SO MUCH...
MITSU-KAKE!!
WHAT ARE YOU DOING?! WITH YOUR WOUNDS, IF YOU DON'T ALLOW YOURSELF SOME REST... I'LL LOOK AFTER THE VILLAGERS!! NO DA!!
NO...I'M A DOCTOR. I CAN'T JUST SIT BACK AND LET THESE VICTIMS SUFFER LIKE THIS.
IF I CAN SAVE EVEN ONE MORE LIFE...
KOFF
MITSU-KAKE!! YOU'LL DIE! NO DA!
... SHAO-HUAN! SHAO-HUAN!
OH, SHAO-HUAN! PLEASE WAKE UP!

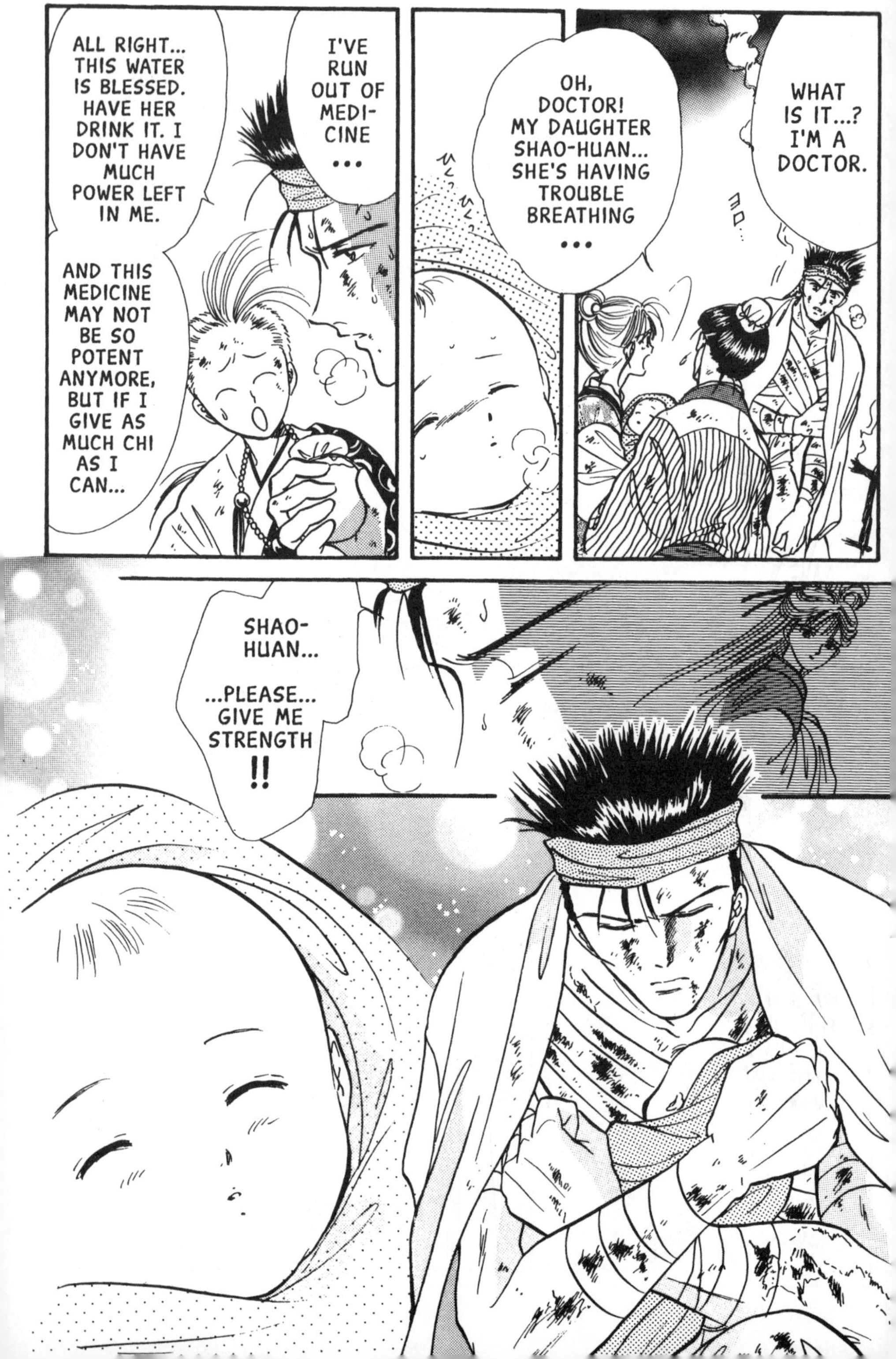
WHAT IS IT...? I'M A DOCTOR.
OH, DOCTOR! MY DAUGHTER SHAO-HUAN... SHE'S HAVING TROUBLE BREATHING ...
I'VE RUN OUT OF MEDI-CINE ...
ALL RIGHT... THIS WATER IS BLESSED. HAVE HER DRINK IT. I DON'T HAVE MUCH POWER LEFT IN ME.
AND THIS MEDICINE MAY NOT BE SO POTENT ANYMORE, BUT IF I GIVE AS MUCH CHI AS I CAN...
SHAO-HUAN... ...PLEASE... GIVE ME STRENGTH !!

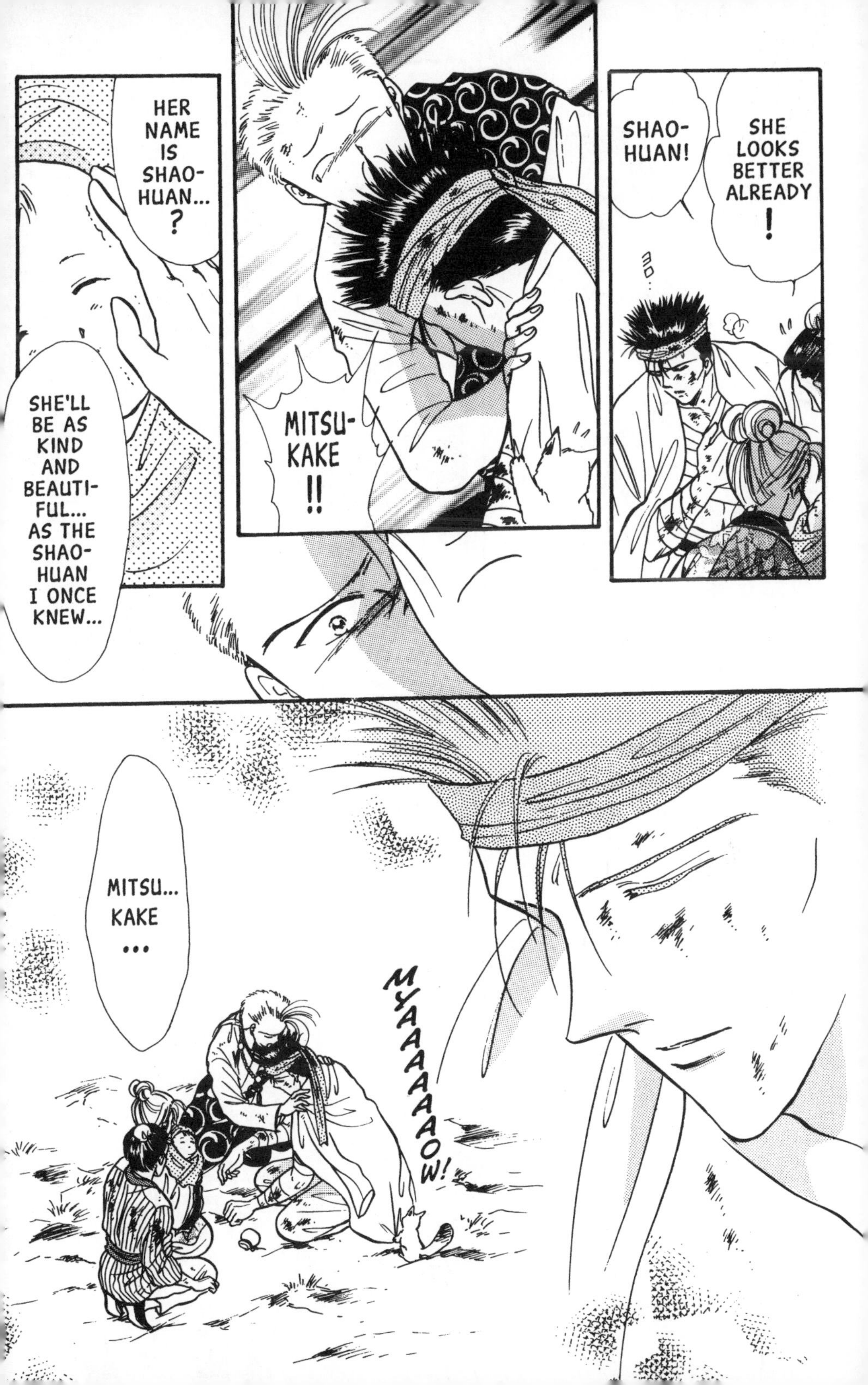
SHE LOOKS BETTER ALREADY!
SHAO-HUAN!
MITSU-KAKE!!
HER NAME IS SHAO-HUAN...?
SHE'LL BE AS KIND AND BEAUTIFUL... AS THE SHAO-HUAN I ONCE KNEW...
MITSU... KAKE...
MYAAAAAAAOW!

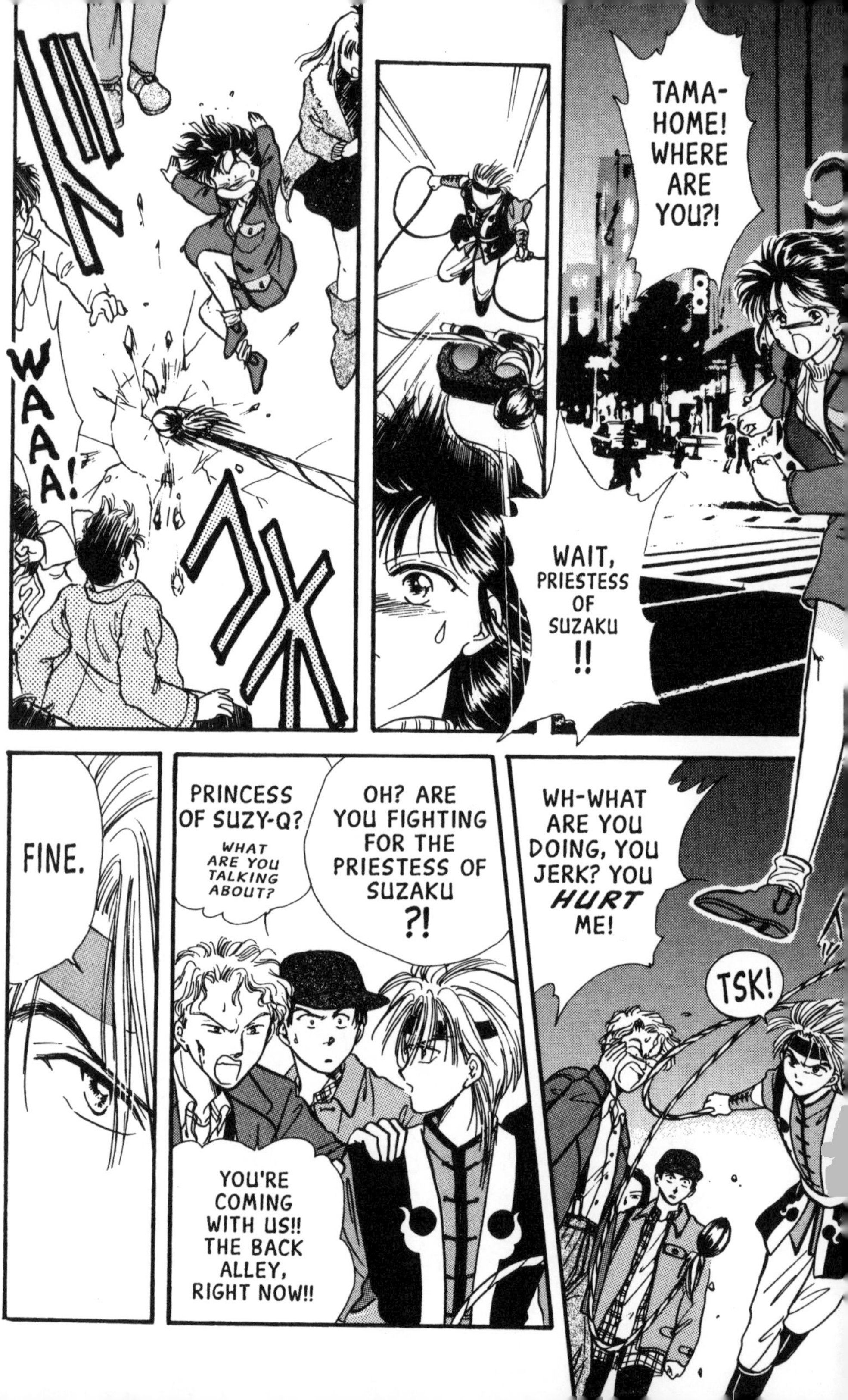
TAMA-HOME! WHERE ARE YOU?!
WAIT, PRIESTESS OF SUZAKU!!
WAAAA!
WH-WHAT ARE YOU DOING, YOU JERK? YOU HURT ME!
TSK!
OH? ARE YOU FIGHTING FOR THE PRIESTESS OF SUZAKU?!
PRINCESS OF SUZY-Q?
WHAT ARE YOU TALKING ABOUT?
YOU'RE COMING WITH US!! THE BACK ALLEY, RIGHT NOW!!
FINE.

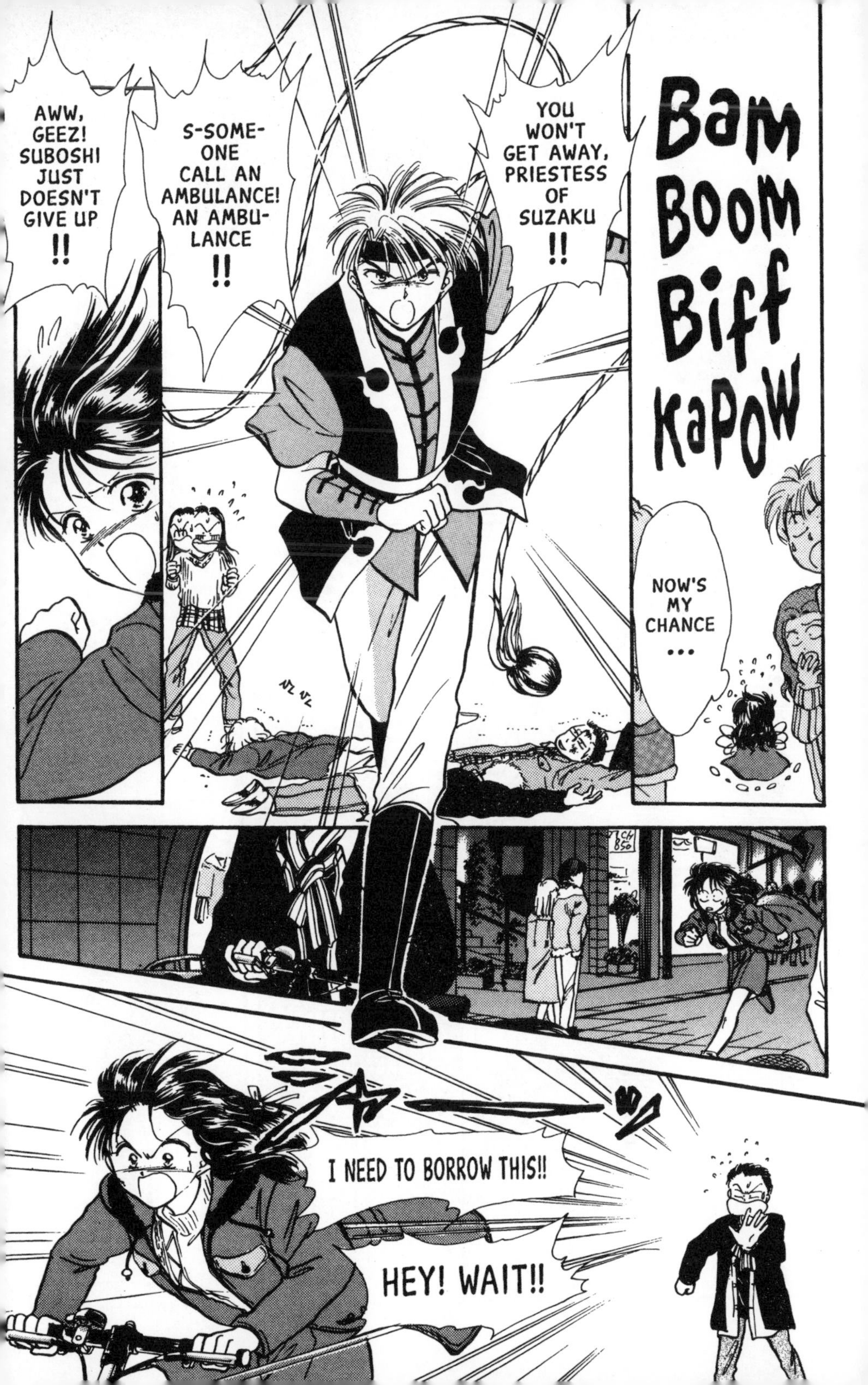
Bam Boom Biff KaPow
NOW'S MY CHANCE...
YOU WON'T GET AWAY, PRIESTESS OF SUZAKU!!
S-SOME-ONE CALL AN AMBULANCE! AN AMBU-LANCE!!
AWW, GEEZ! SUBOSHI JUST DOESN'T GIVE UP!!
I NEED TO BORROW THIS!!
HEY! WAIT!!

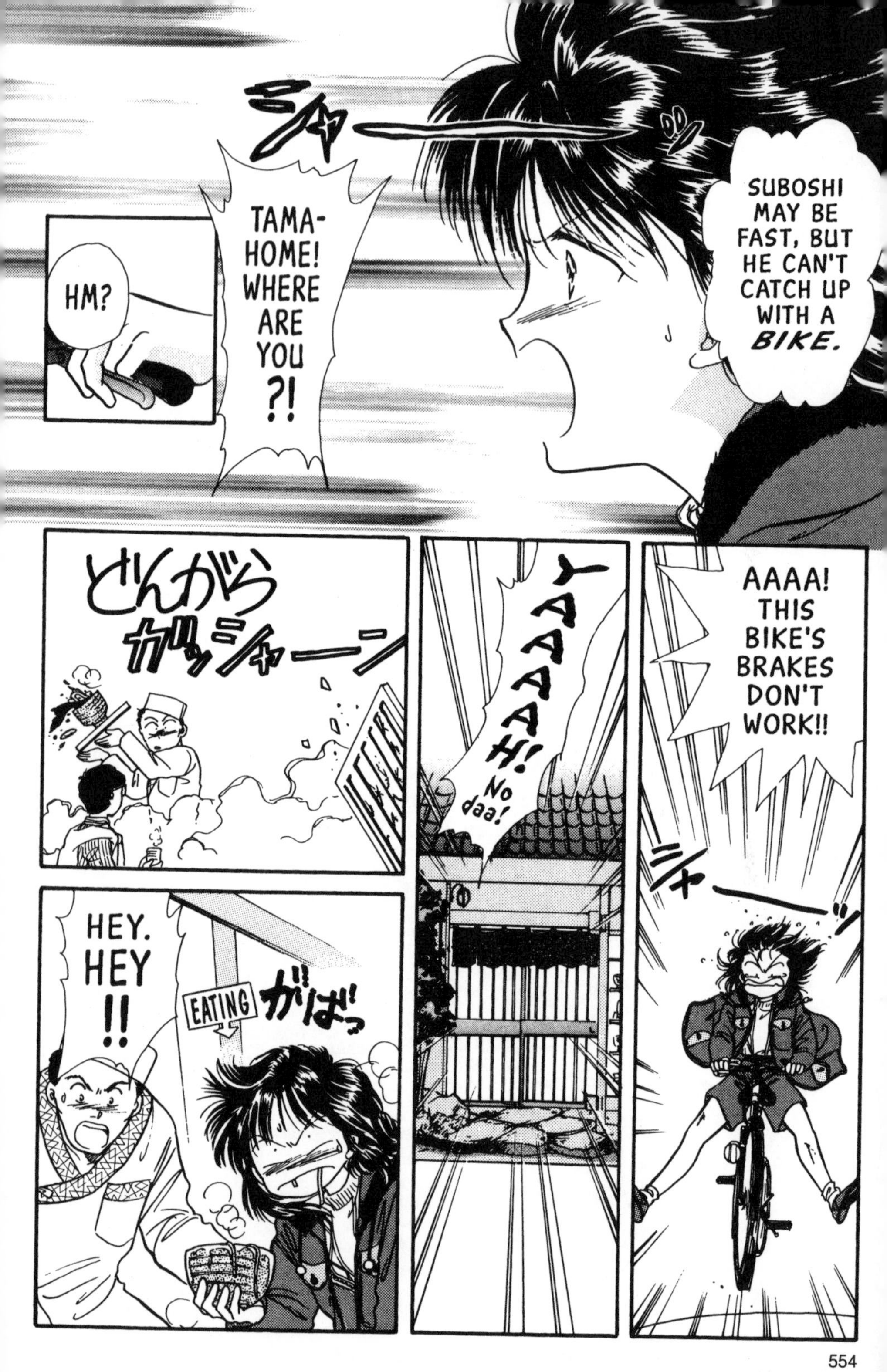
シャー
SUBOSHI MAY BE FAST, BUT HE CAN'T CATCH UP WITH A *BIKE.*
TAMA-HOME! WHERE ARE YOU?!
HM?
AAAA! THIS BIKE'S BRAKES DON'T WORK!!
シャーー"
YAAAAAH! No daa!
どんがらガッシャーン
HEY. HEY!!
EATING
がばっ

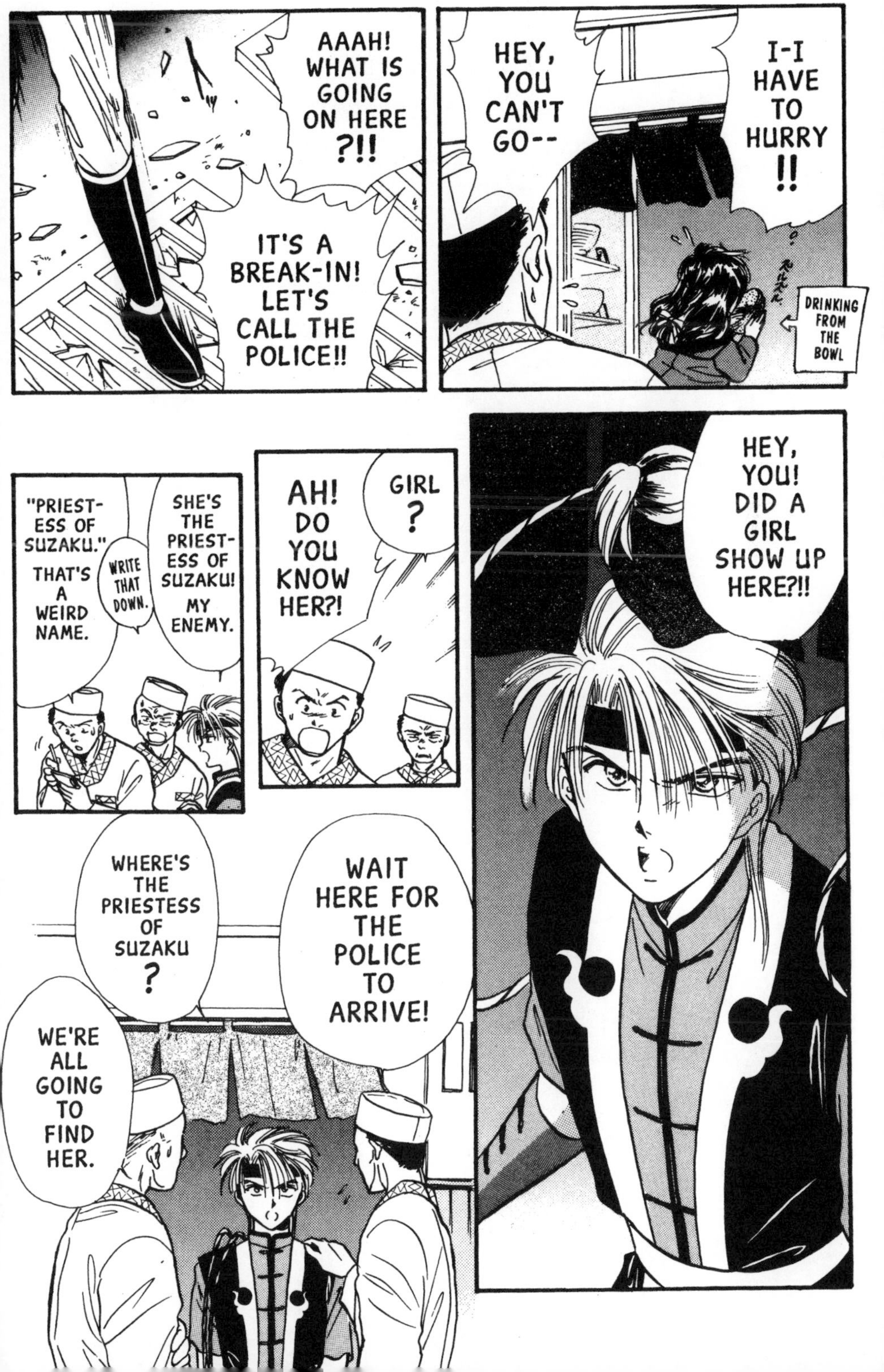
I-I HAVE TO HURRY!!
HEY, YOU CAN'T GO--
DRINKING FROM THE BOWL
AAAH! WHAT IS GOING ON HERE?!!
IT'S A BREAK-IN! LET'S CALL THE POLICE!!
HEY, YOU! DID A GIRL SHOW UP HERE?!!
GIRL?
AH! DO YOU KNOW HER?!
SHE'S THE PRIEST-ESS OF SUZAKU! MY ENEMY.
WRITE THAT DOWN.
"PRIEST-ESS OF SUZAKU." THAT'S A WEIRD NAME.
WAIT HERE FOR THE POLICE TO ARRIVE!
WHERE'S THE PRIESTESS OF SUZAKU?
WE'RE ALL GOING TO FIND HER.

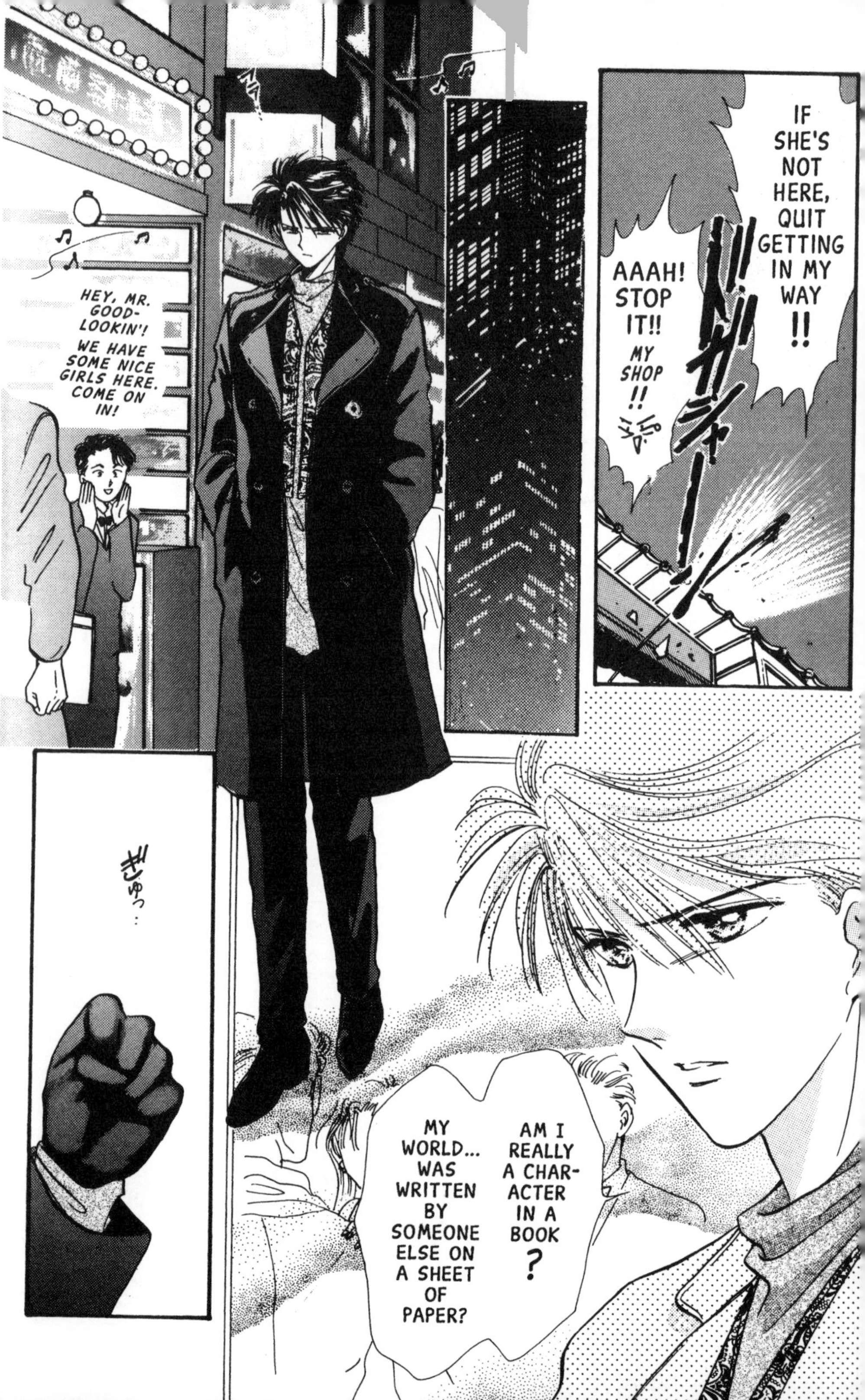
IF SHE'S NOT HERE, QUIT GETTING IN MY WAY!!
AAAH! STOP IT!!
MY SHOP!!
HEY, MR. GOOD-LOOKIN'! WE HAVE SOME NICE GIRLS HERE. COME ON IN!
AM I REALLY A CHARACTER IN A BOOK?
MY WORLD... WAS WRITTEN BY SOMEONE ELSE ON A SHEET OF PAPER?

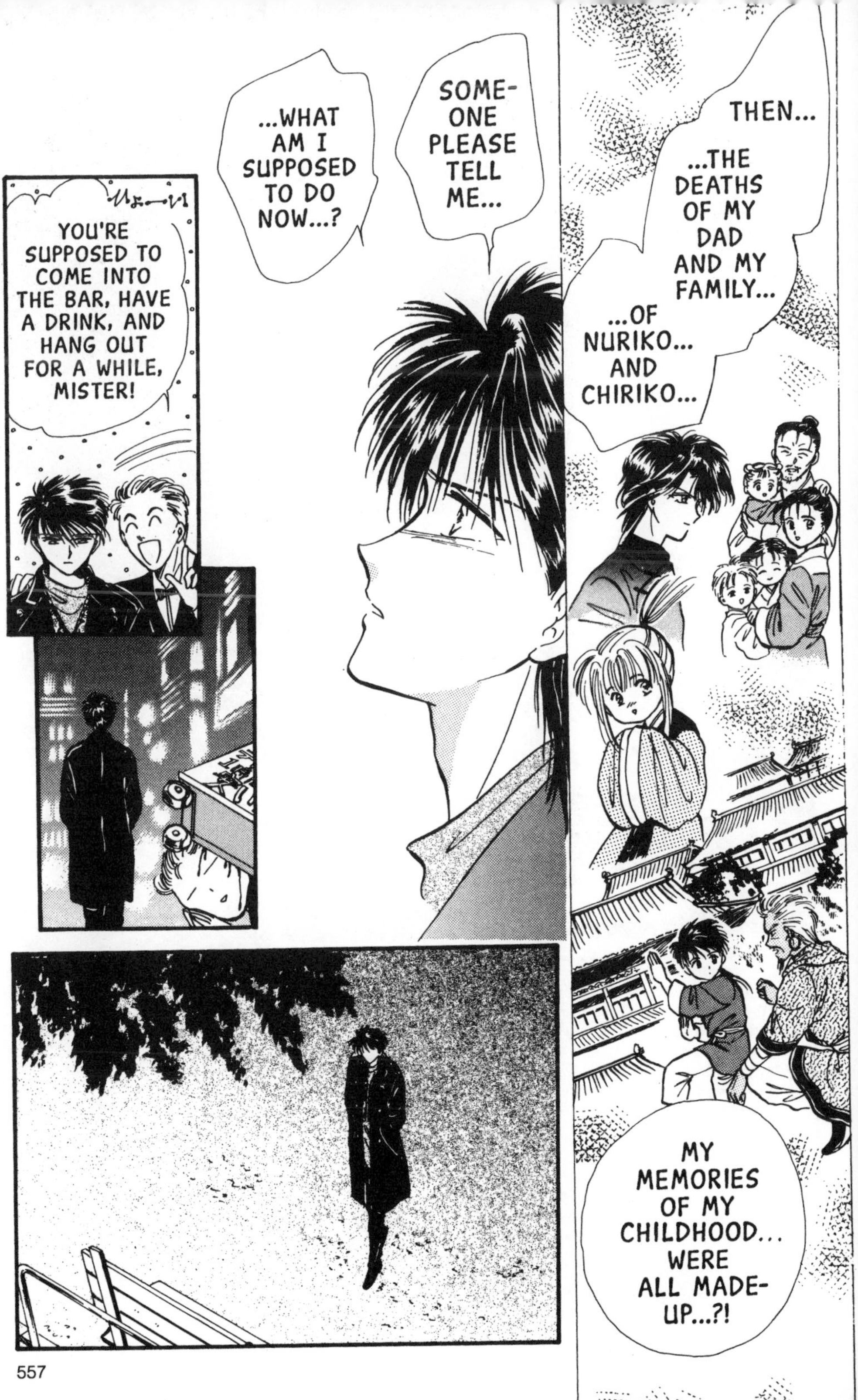
THEN...
...THE DEATHS OF MY DAD AND MY FAMILY...
...OF NURIKO... AND CHIRIKO...
MY MEMORIES OF MY CHILDHOOD... WERE ALL MADE-UP...?!
SOME-ONE PLEASE TELL ME...
...WHAT AM I SUPPOSED TO DO NOW...?
YOU'RE SUPPOSED TO COME INTO THE BAR, HAVE A DRINK, AND HANG OUT FOR A WHILE, MISTER!

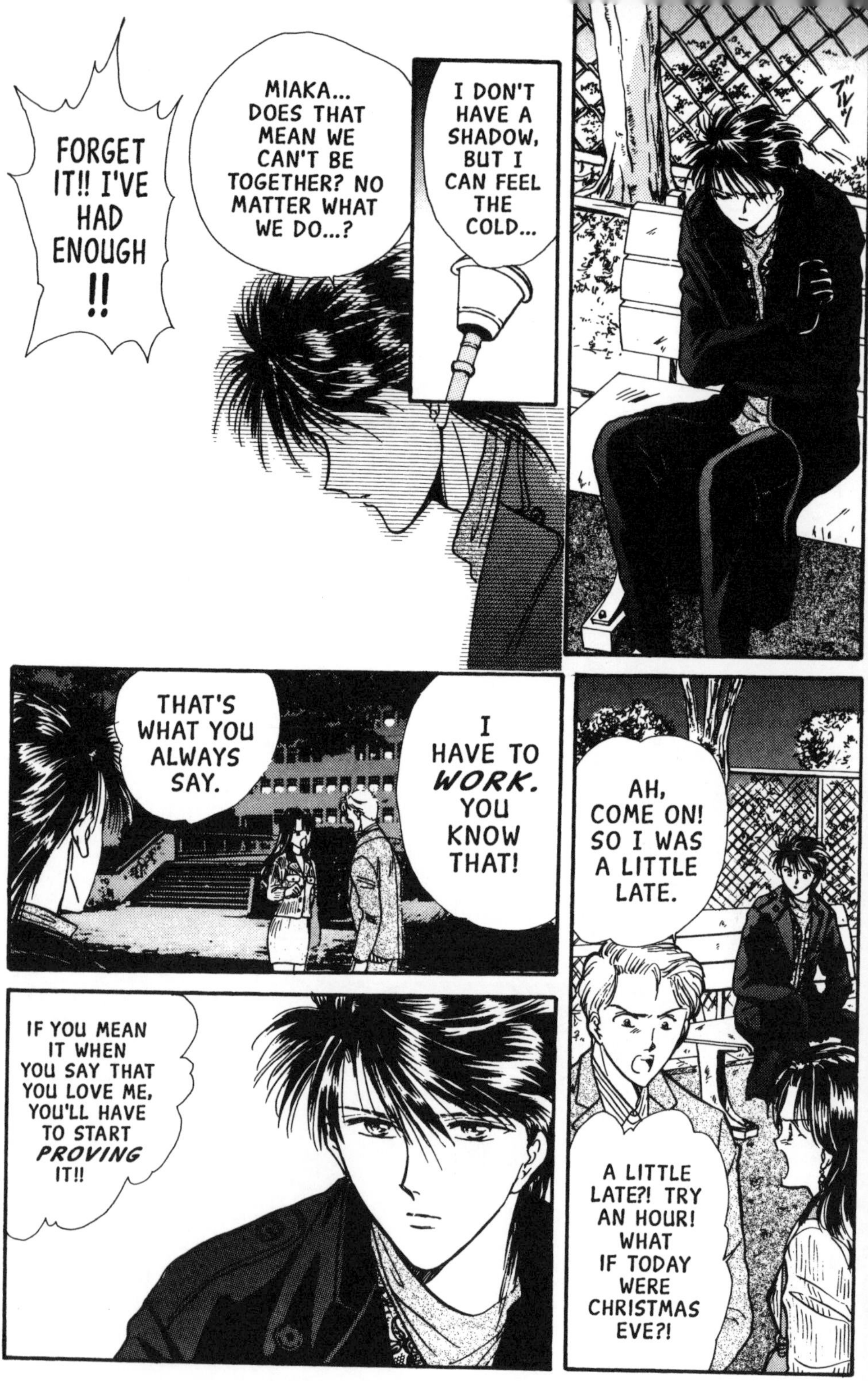
I DON'T HAVE A SHADOW, BUT I CAN FEEL THE COLD...
MIAKA... DOES THAT MEAN WE CAN'T BE TOGETHER? NO MATTER WHAT WE DO...?
FORGET IT!! I'VE HAD ENOUGH!!
AH, COME ON! SO I WAS A LITTLE LATE.
A LITTLE LATE?! TRY AN HOUR! WHAT IF TODAY WERE CHRISTMAS EVE?!
I HAVE TO *WORK.* YOU KNOW THAT!
THAT'S WHAT YOU ALWAYS SAY.
IF YOU MEAN IT WHEN YOU SAY THAT YOU LOVE ME, YOU'LL HAVE TO START *PROVING* IT!!

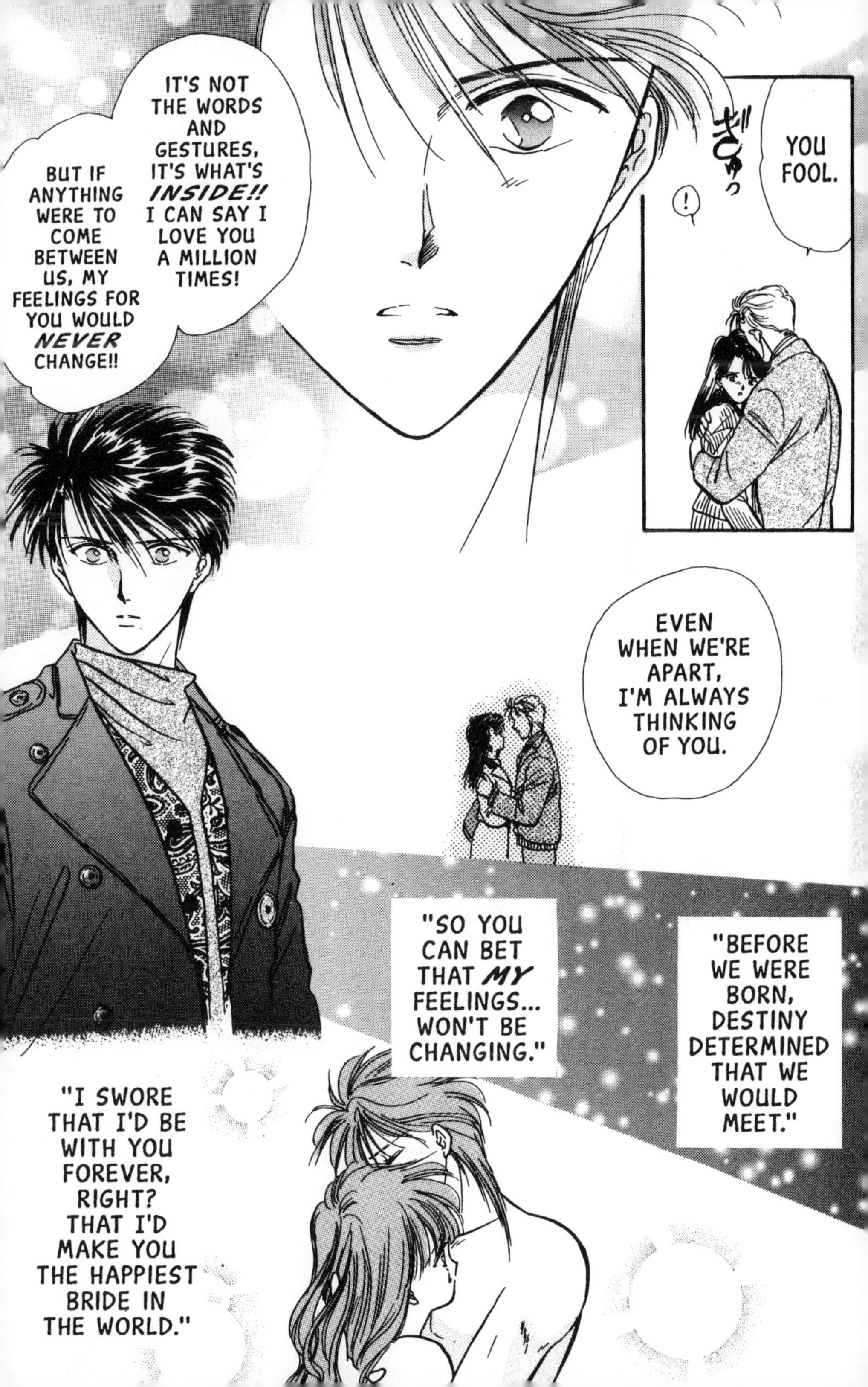
ぎゅっ
!
YOU FOOL.
IT'S NOT THE WORDS AND GESTURES, IT'S WHAT'S *INSIDE!!* I CAN SAY I LOVE YOU A MILLION TIMES!
BUT IF ANYTHING WERE TO COME BETWEEN US, MY FEELINGS FOR YOU WOULD *NEVER* CHANGE!!
EVEN WHEN WE'RE APART, I'M ALWAYS THINKING OF YOU.
"BEFORE WE WERE BORN, DESTINY DETERMINED THAT WE WOULD MEET."
"SO YOU CAN BET THAT *MY* FEELINGS... WON'T BE CHANGING."
"I SWORE THAT I'D BE WITH YOU FOREVER, RIGHT? THAT I'D MAKE YOU THE HAPPIEST BRIDE IN THE WORLD."

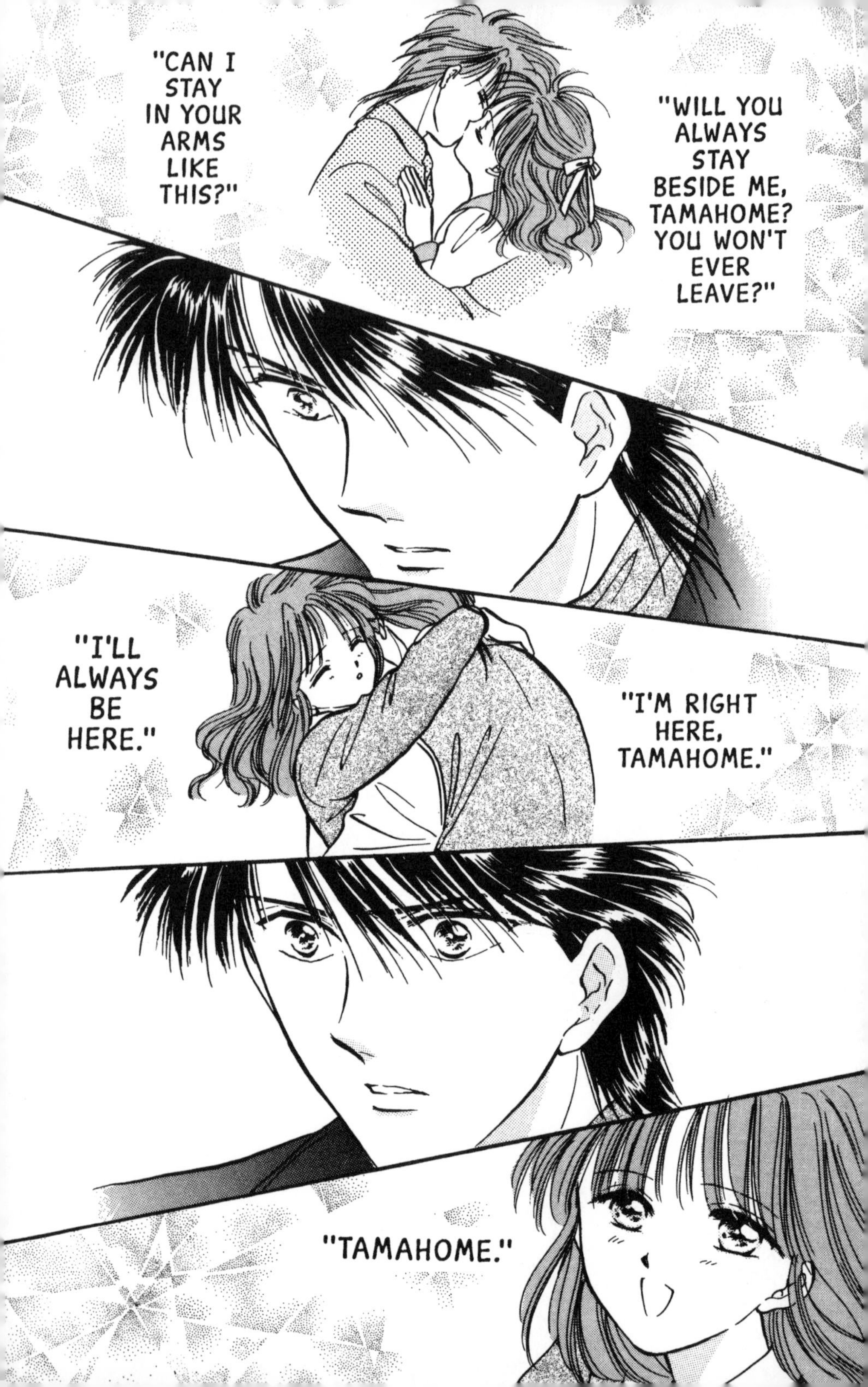
"WILL YOU ALWAYS STAY BESIDE ME, TAMAHOME? YOU WON'T EVER LEAVE?"
"CAN I STAY IN YOUR ARMS LIKE THIS?"
"I'M RIGHT HERE, TAMAHOME."
"I'LL ALWAYS BE HERE."
"TAMAHOME."

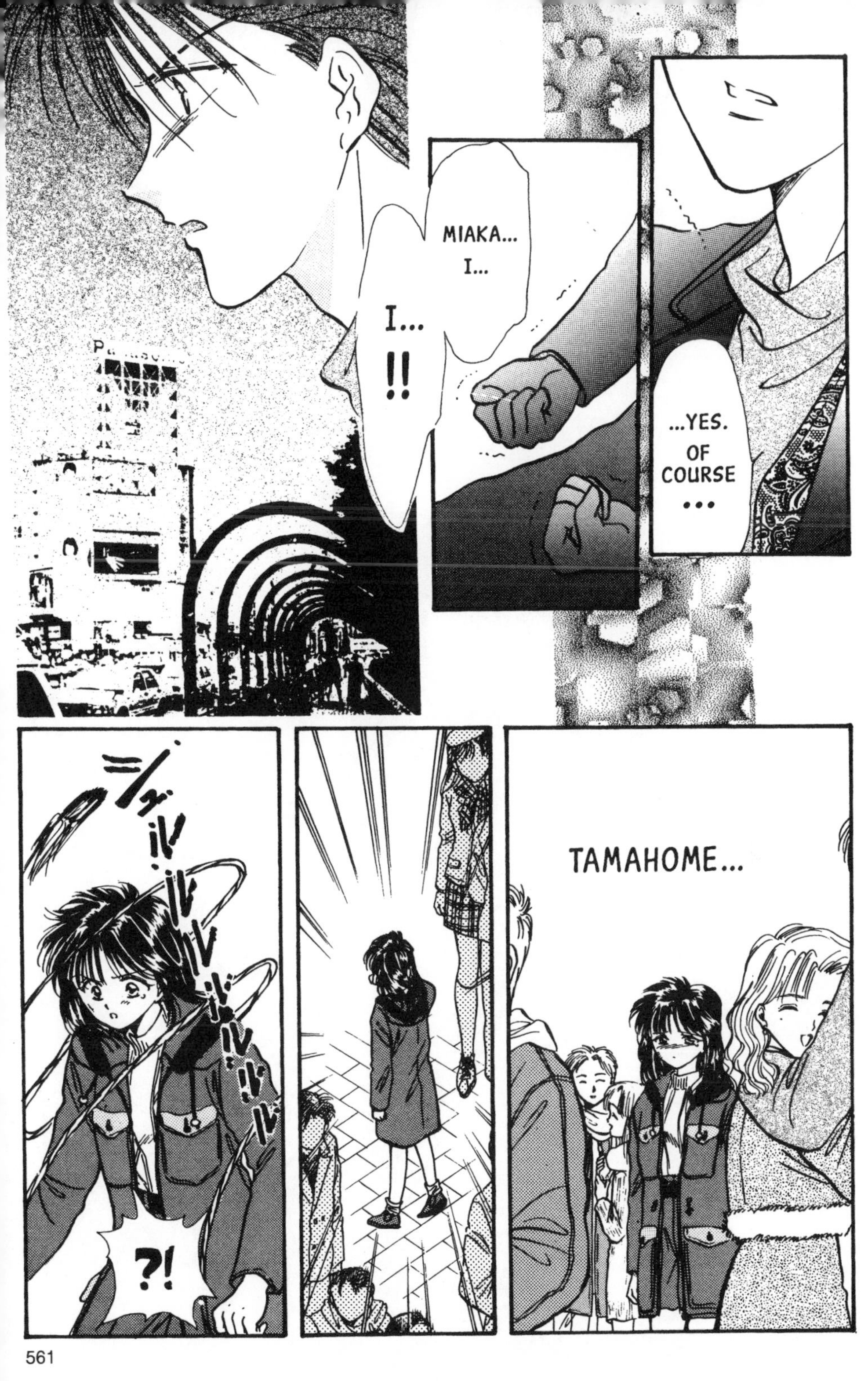
...YES. OF COURSE...
MIAKA... I...
I... !!
TAMAHOME...
?!

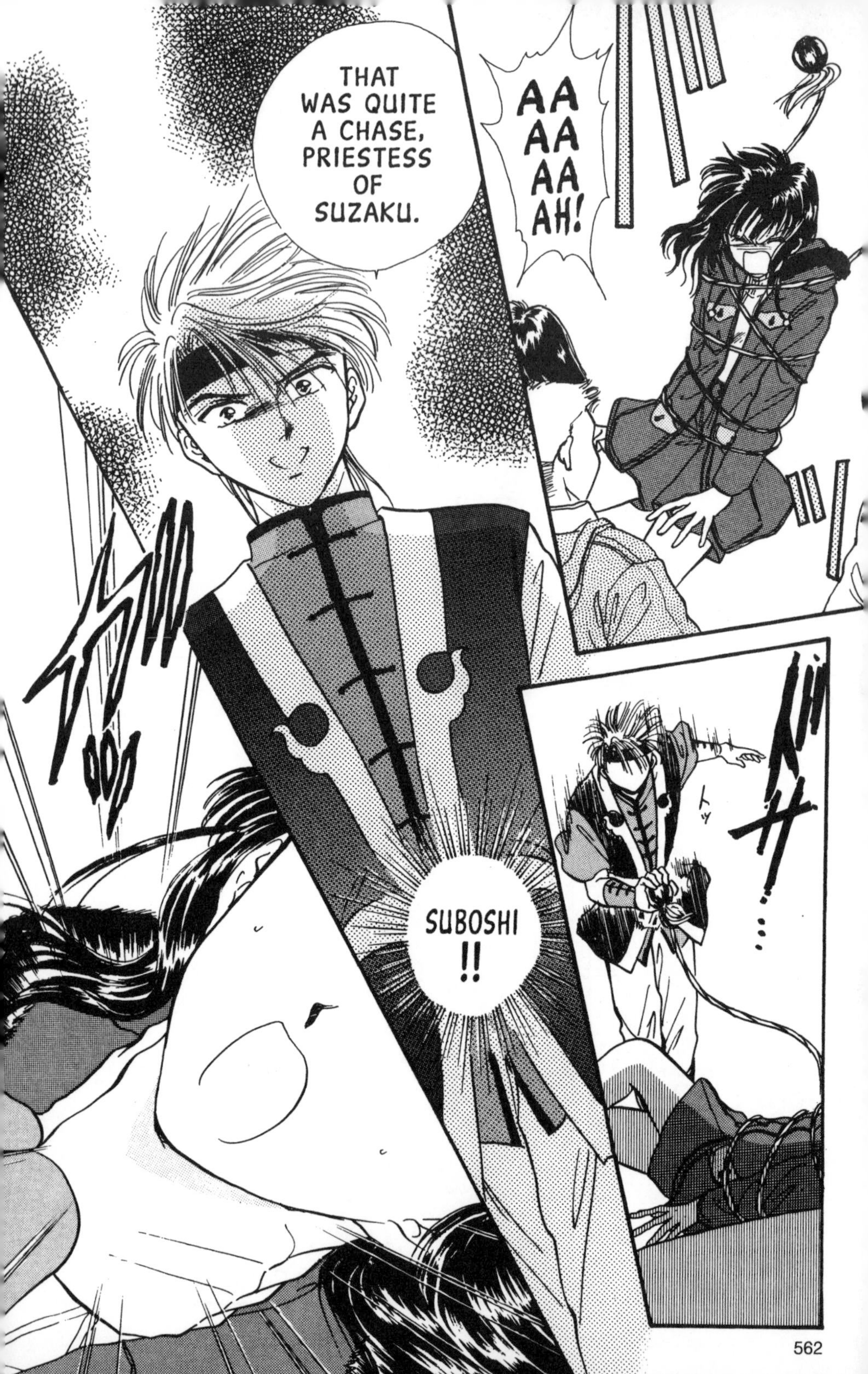
AAAAAAAH!
THAT WAS QUITE A CHASE, PRIESTESS OF SUZAKU.
SUBOSHI !!
...

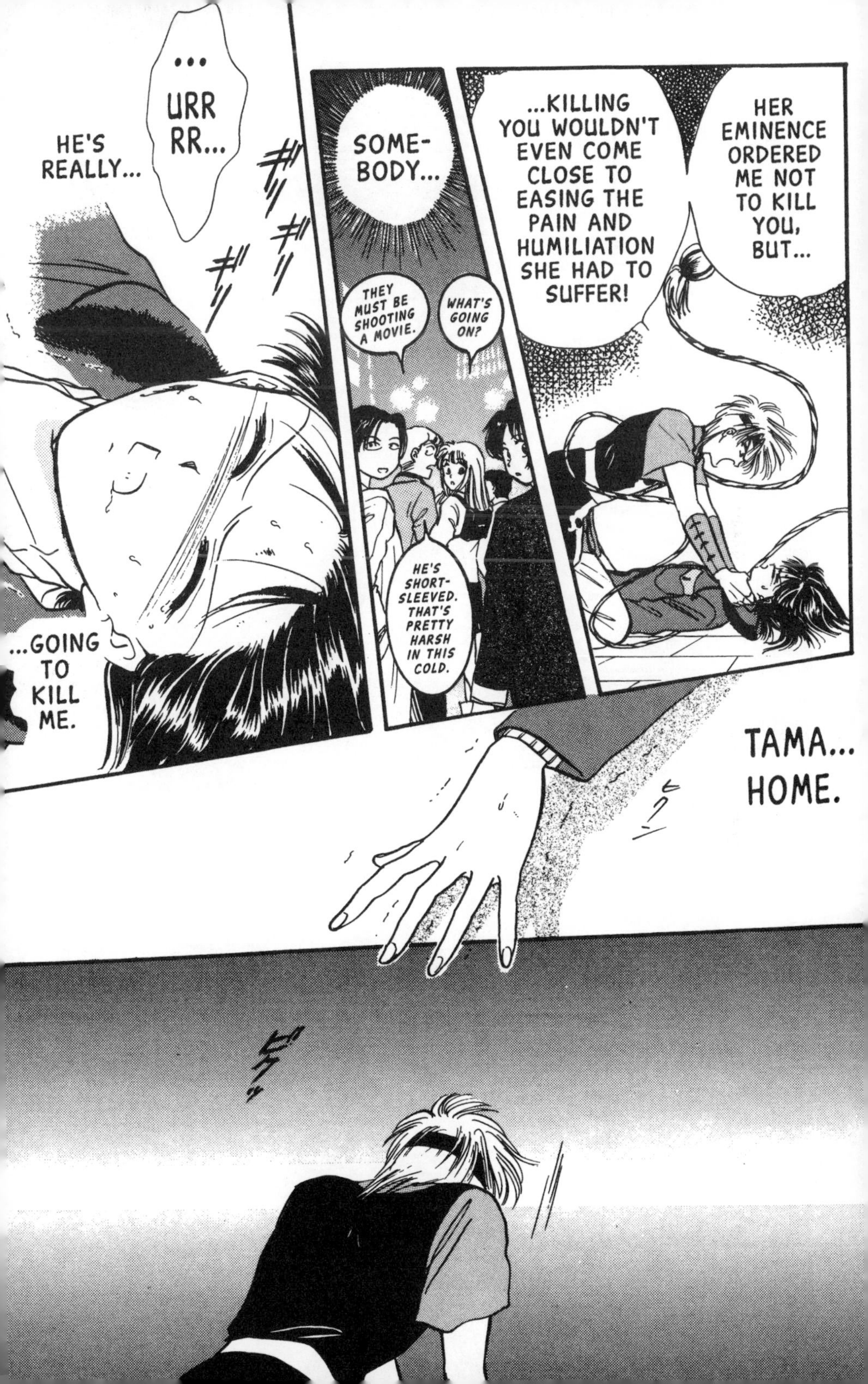
HER EMINENCE ORDERED ME NOT TO KILL YOU, BUT...
...KILLING YOU WOULDN'T EVEN COME CLOSE TO EASING THE PAIN AND HUMILIATION SHE HAD TO SUFFER!
SOME-BODY...
WHAT'S GOING ON?
THEY MUST BE SHOOTING A MOVIE.
HE'S SHORT-SLEEVED. THAT'S PRETTY HARSH IN THIS COLD.
... URRRR...
HE'S REALLY...
...GOING TO KILL ME.
TAMA... HOME.

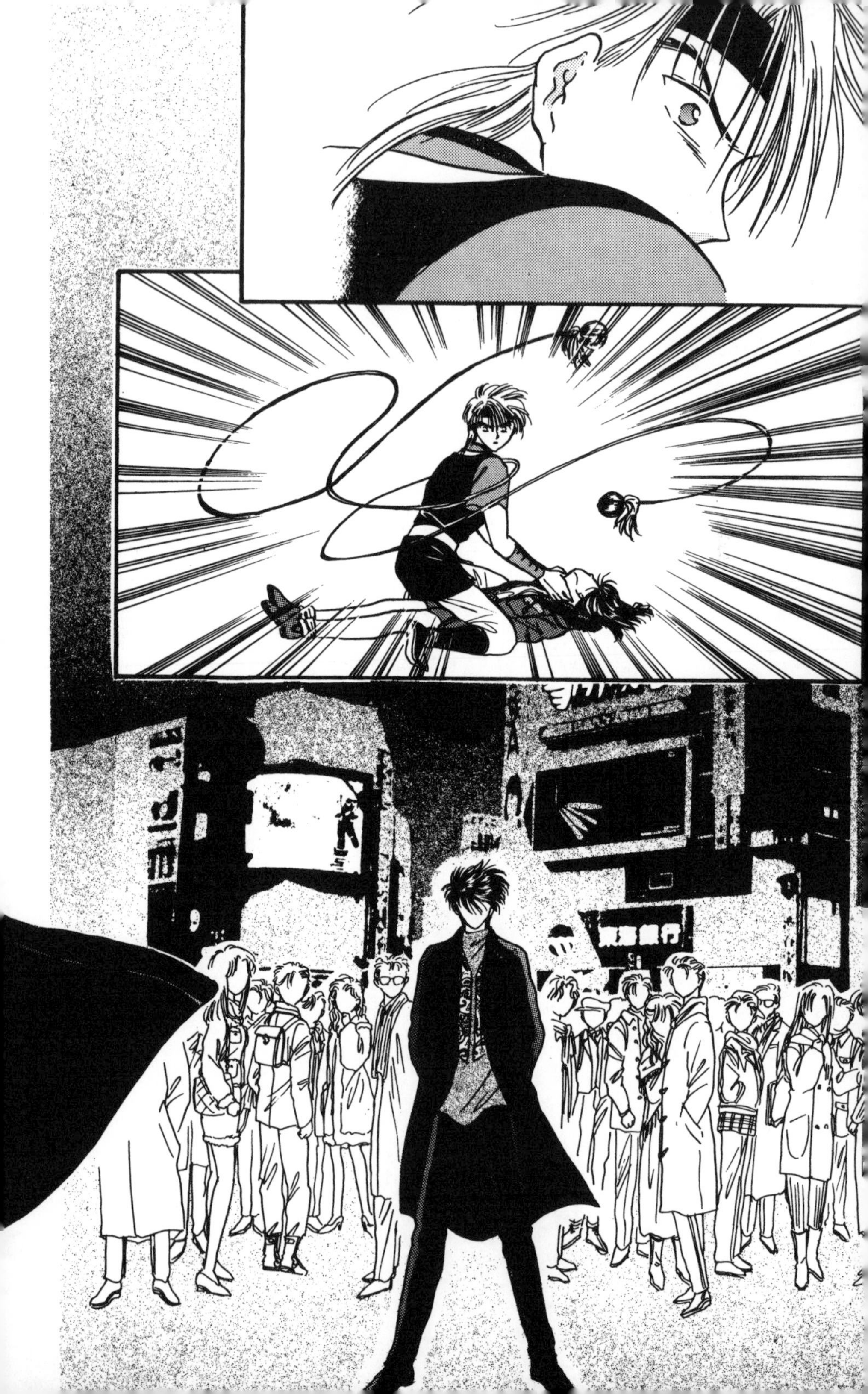

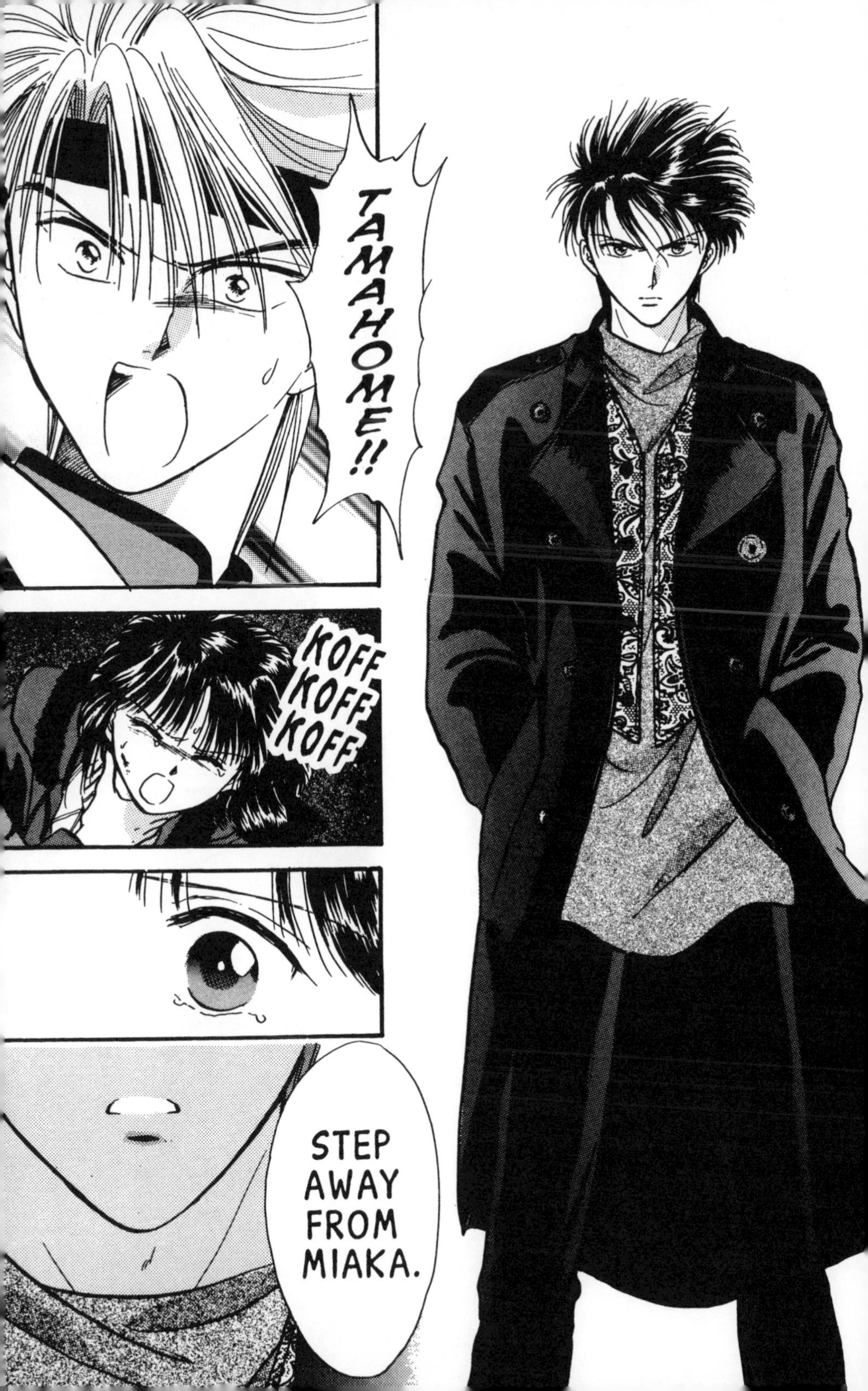
TAMAHOME!!
KOFF KOFF KOFF
STEP AWAY FROM MIAKA.

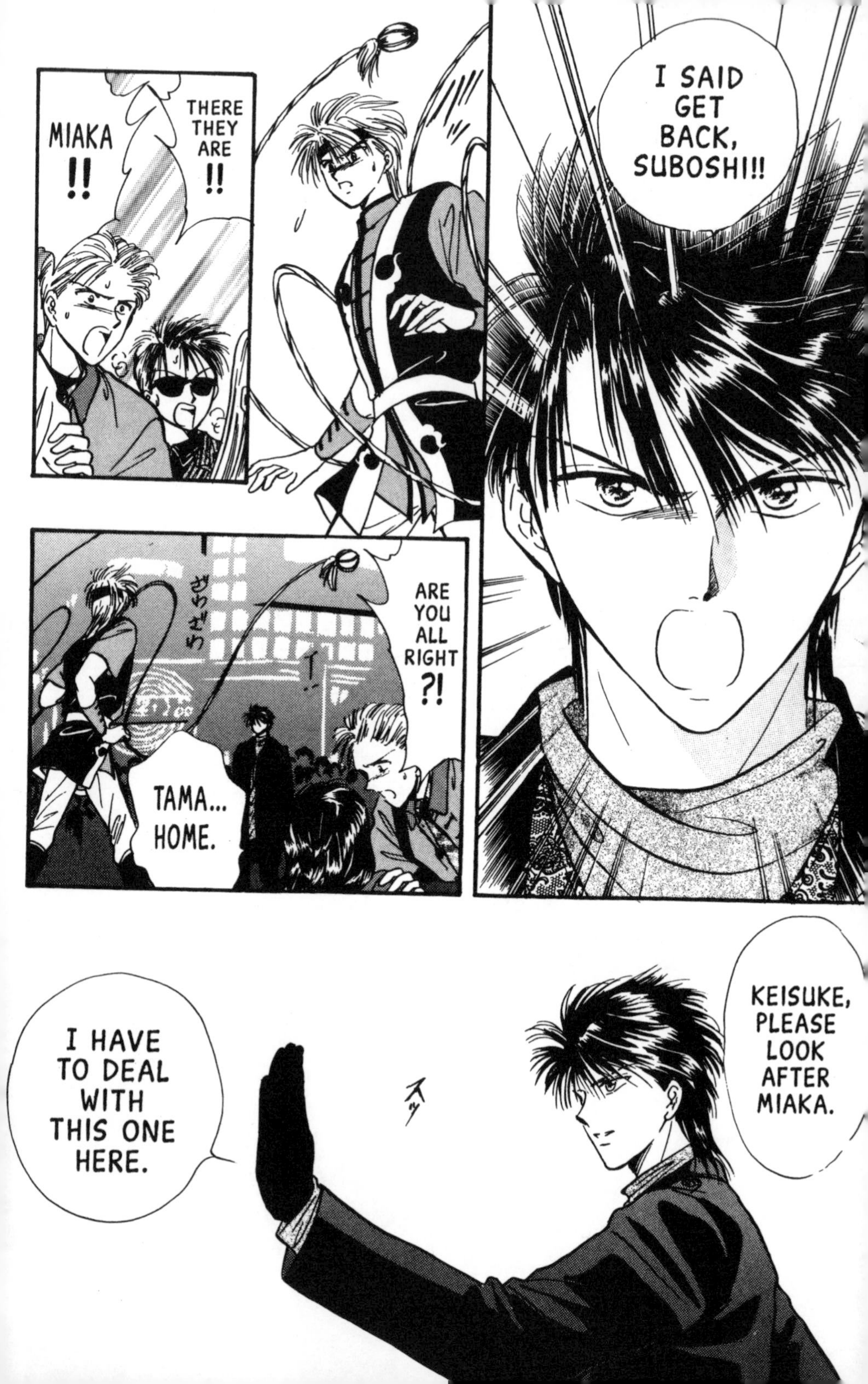
I SAID GET BACK, SUBOSHI!!
THERE THEY ARE!!
MIAKA!!
ARE YOU ALL RIGHT?!
ざわざわ
TAMA... HOME.
KEISUKE, PLEASE LOOK AFTER MIAKA.
スッ
I HAVE TO DEAL WITH THIS ONE HERE.

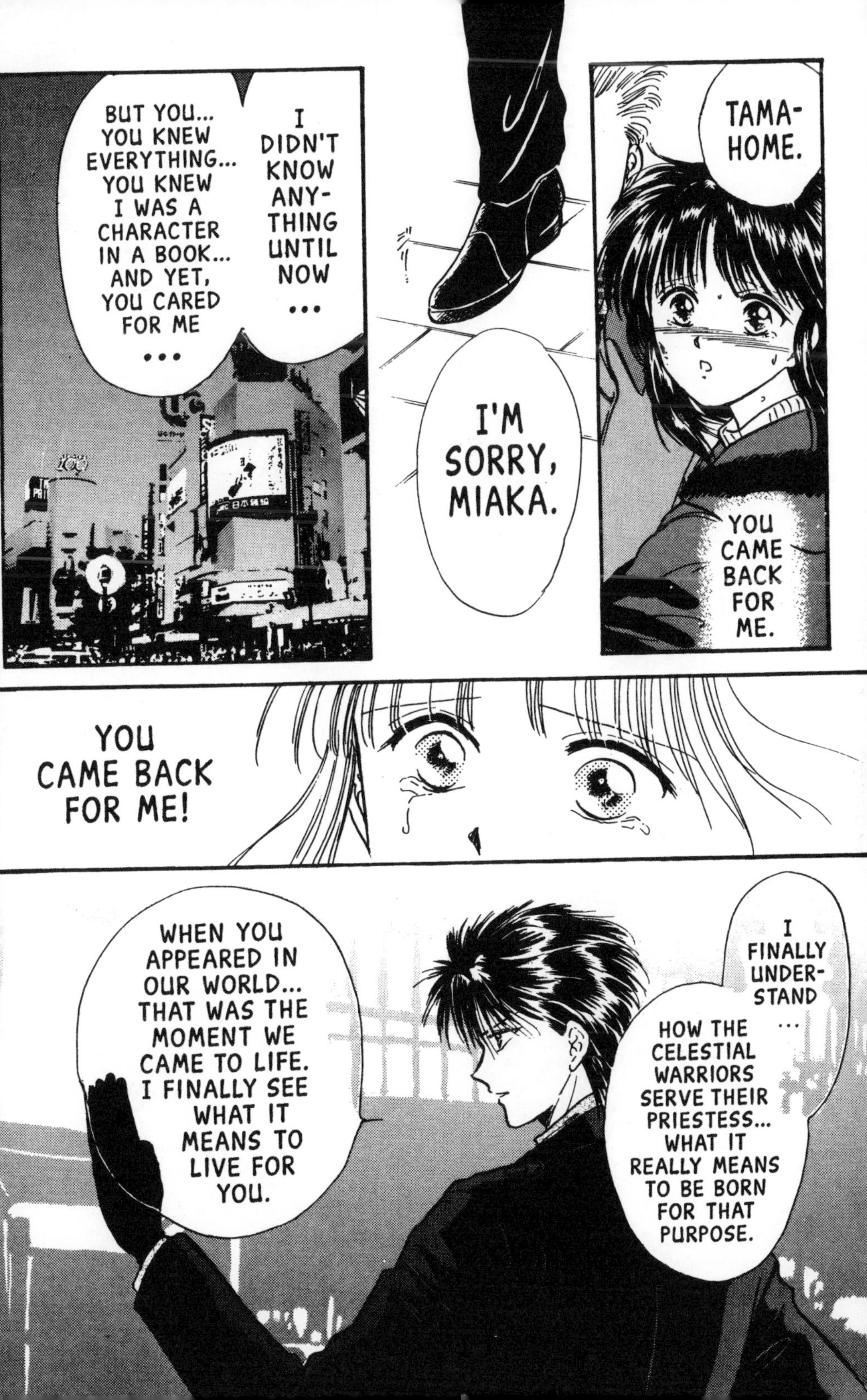
TAMA-HOME.
YOU CAME BACK FOR ME.
I'M SORRY, MIAKA.
I DIDN'T KNOW ANYTHING UNTIL NOW...
BUT YOU... YOU KNEW EVERYTHING... YOU KNEW I WAS A CHARACTER IN A BOOK... AND YET, YOU CARED FOR ME...
YOU CAME BACK FOR ME!
I FINALLY UNDERSTAND...
HOW THE CELESTIAL WARRIORS SERVE THEIR PRIESTESS... WHAT IT REALLY MEANS TO BE BORN FOR THAT PURPOSE.
WHEN YOU APPEARED IN OUR WORLD... THAT WAS THE MOMENT WE CAME TO LIFE. I FINALLY SEE WHAT IT MEANS TO LIVE FOR YOU.

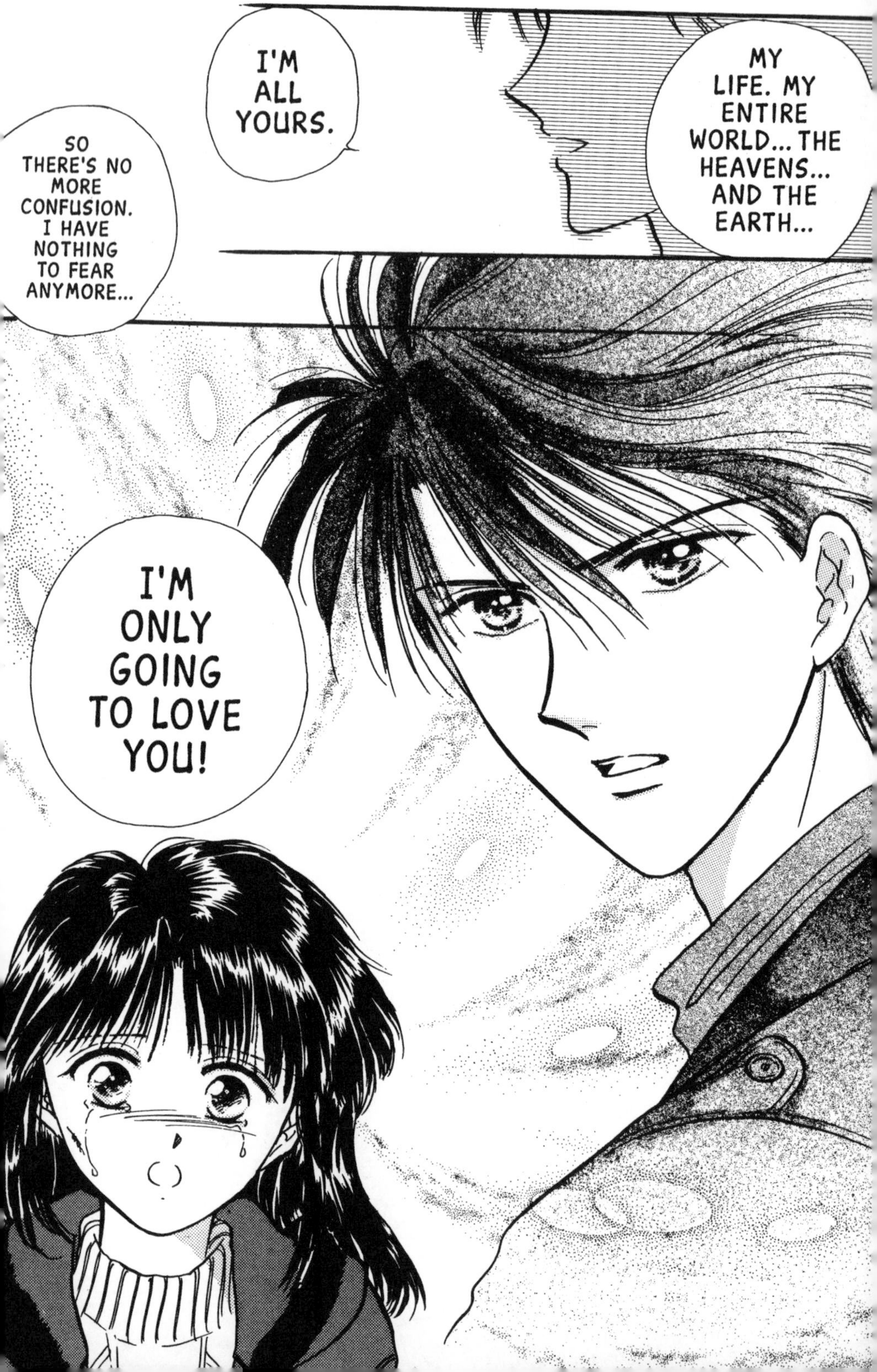
MY LIFE. MY ENTIRE WORLD... THE HEAVENS... AND THE EARTH...
I'M ALL YOURS.
SO THERE'S NO MORE CONFUSION. I HAVE NOTHING TO FEAR ANYMORE...
I'M ONLY GOING TO LOVE YOU!

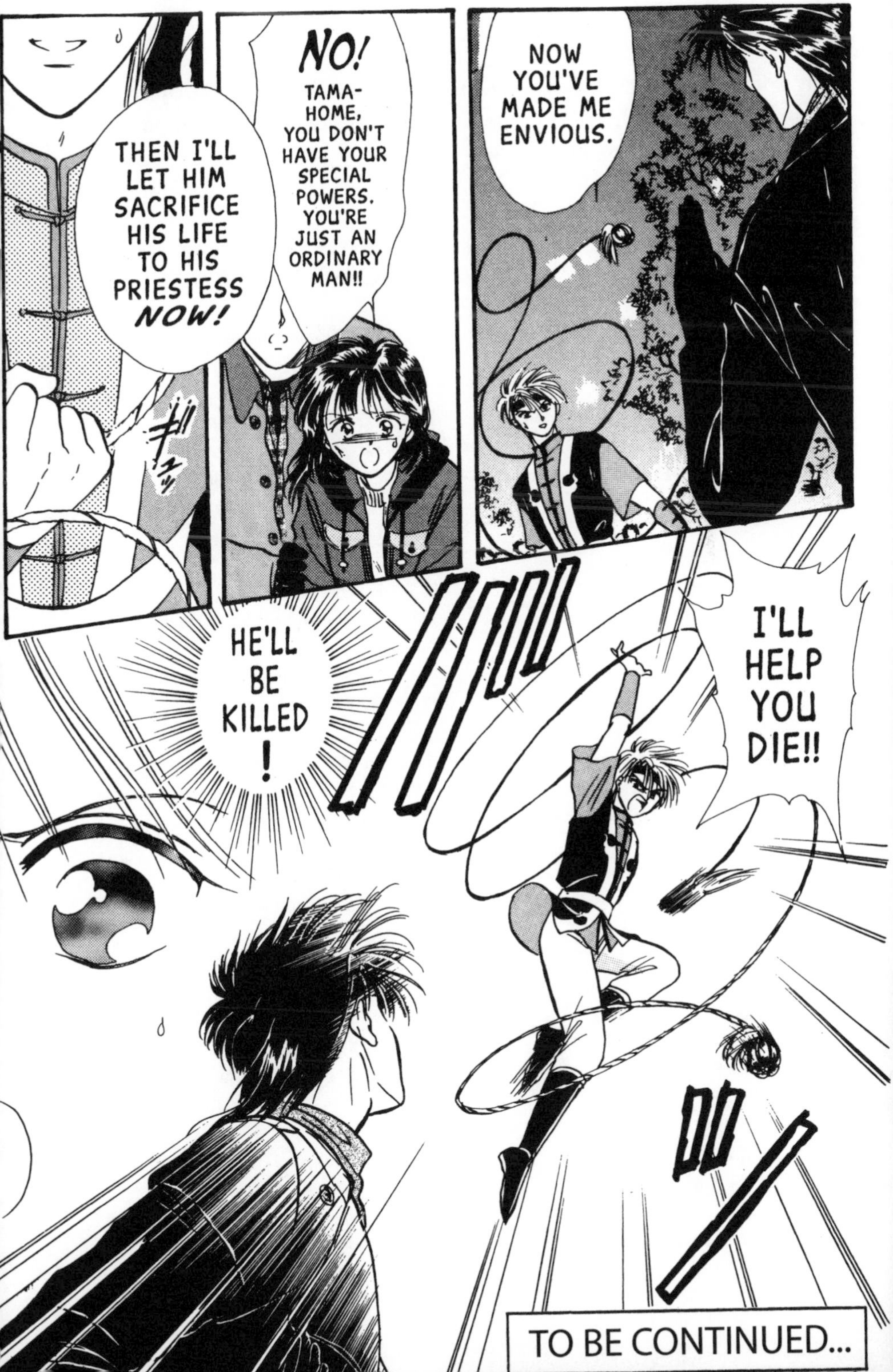
NOW YOU'VE MADE ME ENVIOUS.
NO! TAMA-HOME, YOU DON'T HAVE YOUR SPECIAL POWERS. YOU'RE JUST AN ORDINARY MAN!!
THEN I'LL LET HIM SACRIFICE HIS LIFE TO HIS PRIESTESS NOW!
I'LL HELP YOU DIE!!
HE'LL BE KILLED!
TO BE CONTINUED...

Sound Effects Glossary

Many of the sound effects (FX) in *Fushigi Yûgi* are as Yuu Watase created them, in the original Japanese. This glossary lists the page number followed by the panel number (e.g., "13.3" is page 13, panel 3).

Chapter Fifty-Five
Illusionary Warmth

11.2 FX: DOKUN [heartbeat]
11.3 FX: DOKUN [heartbeat]

15.2 FX: DOKUN [heartbeat]
15.3 FX: GASA... [shifting her weight]
15.4 FX: DOKUN [heartbeat]
15.4 FX: DOKUN [heartbeat]
15.4 FX: SU… [rushing air]

16.3 FX: BYU [flying blade]
16.4 FX: GYAAAAA [a loud scream]

17.1 FX: DOSA [falling to the ground]
17.2 FX: BA [grabbing]

18.1 FX: ZURU… [slipping]
18.3 FX: ZAN [a hard hit]
18.4 FX: SHURURU [whirling]

19.1 FX: GYU [clenching]
19.2 FX: KORO [turning]

20.4 FX: ZAKU ZAKU [steps in sand]

21.1 FX: ZAKU [steps in sand]
21.3 FX: ZURU [going to one knee]
21.5 FX: BAN [striking rock]

24.2 FX: HA [surprise]

26.1 FX: BATA [footsteps]

30.2 FX: GAAA [a mystic sound]
30.3 FX: BASHI [crackling]

31.2 FX: PIKU [surprise]
31.4 FX: SU [moving curtains]

32.1 FX: SHA [moving curtains]
32.5 FX: KYU [tightening]

34.3 FX: ZAZAAAAA [scarfing down food]
34.3 FX: KARAN [dropping chopsticks]
34.4 FX: MOSHA MOSHA [munch munch]
34.6 FX: KATAN [klak]

36.2 FX: POTA [drip]
36.3 FX: HA [gasp]
36.4 FX: PORO PORO PORO [crying]

37.3 FX: GATAN [chair clunking]

38.1 FX: HYOI [lifting]
38.2 FX: MUSHI [ignoring her]
38.3 FX: SUTA SUTA SUTA [quick stomping]
38.4 FX: JITABATA [struggling]

39.3 FX: WAI WAI [crowd noise]
39.4 FX: SUPO [slipping on]

43.2 FX: KURU [a sudden turn]

46.1 FX: PATAN [door closing]

47.7 FX: POKO POKO [pouring]

49.1 FX: GURARI [swaying]
49.3 FX: KARAN… [klak…]
49.3 FX: DOSA… [thud…]

52.2 FX: GYU [squeeze]
52.3 FX: PUCHI PUCHI [unbuttoning]

52.4 FX: BASA BASA [clothes dropping]
52.5 FX: GISHI… [bed noise]

54.1 FX: YORO [wobbling]
54.5 FX: FURA… [falling]

55.3 FX: GYU [hugging]
55.5 FX: HA HA HA!

56.3 FX: BIKUN [a surprised jerk back]
56.4 FX: BIKU [a surprised jerk back]

57.3 FX: SUUU… [a slow appearance]
57.4 FX: HYU [flashing by]
57.4 FX: BIKU [a surprised jerk back]

58.1 FX: FU ["breath" passing]

59.3 FX: TORO [slow movement]
59.4 FX: HA [a small gasp]

60.1 FX: ZURU… [slipping]
60.2 FX: DOKUN DOKUN DOKUN DOKUN [rapid heartbeat]
60.3 FX: DOKUN DOKUN [rapid heartbeat]

CHAPTER FIFTY-SIX
DAWN FOR THE HEART

63.1 FX: DOKI DOKI DOKI [heart thumping]
FX: DOKI DOKI DOKI [heart thumping]

64.4 FX: HA [surprise]
64.4 FX: DOKI DOKI DOKI [heart thumping]
64.5 FX: DOKI DOKI DOKI [heart thumping]

65.2 FX: ZEKUN [tensing up]
65.4 FX: HA… [Oops]
65.5 FX: GISHI [bed movement]

67.4 FX: GURA… [swaying]

68.3 FX: BASA BASA [clothes falling]

69.2 FX: PIKU [sudden surprise]

70.2 FX: HA [gasp]

72.5 FX: PASA [light object falling]

74.2 FX: HA [a gasp]
74.4 FX: SU [quick movement]

78.1 FX: DOKUN DOKUN [heart thumping]
78.2 FX: KIRA [shining]
78.3 FX: BIKU [surprise]

79.3 FX: PAN [crashing]

85.5 FX: BA [sudden movement]

88.4 FX: KYUU [squeeze]

89.3 FX: HA [surprise]
89.4 FX: SU [sudden appearance]

90.3 FX: KYU [tying]

CHAPTER FIFTY-SEVEN
OMINOUS EYES

94.2 FX: KUWAAA [burning]
94.2 FX: KYAAAAA [a scream]

96.3 FX: KA [horse appearing]

97.2 FX: BIKU [surprise]
97.2 FX: KIIIN [piercing noise]
97.3 FX: BA [explosion]

98.2 FX: BIKU [surprise]

100.2 FX: GARA… [pebble falling]

101.3 FX: BOKO BOKO [ground breaking]
101.4 FX: ZAAA [whipping through]

104.1 FX: GIRI GIRI [sliding]
104.4 FX: SHURU [feather movement]
104.5 FX: BIKUN [sudden twitch]

105.2 FX: GIRI [sliding]

108.2 FX: DOKUN DOKUN DOKUN [heart thumping]
108.3 FX: DOKUN DOKUN DOKUN [heart thumping]

110.1 FX: DOKUN DOKUN [heart thumping]
110.1 FX: DOKUN DOKUN [heart thumping]

112.3 FX: BIKU [shock]
112.4 FX: HYU [flash]

113.1 FX: PAN [explosion]
113.2 FX: FU [relief]

115.2 FX: SHU [flash]
115.3 FX: FU [sudden movement]

116.1 FX: DOKA [strike]
116.4 FX: SUTO [landing]
116.4 FX: BASA [falling]

117.2 FX: HA HA HA [rapid breathing]

119.1 FX: HYUUU [wind]

120.3 FX: BA [whipping]
120.5 FX: DO... [piercing]

CHAPTER FIFTY-EIGHT
COUNTERFEIT MEMORY

123.1 FX: ZU [removing]
123.4 FX: GEHO [cough]

124.1 FX: FURA [falling back]
124.2 FX: GARA [rocks falling]

125.4 FX: NYA [smirk]
125.5 FX: KAAA [flash]

126.1 FX: HA [realization]
126.2 FX: ZAAAA... [swirling]

128.3 FX: PITA [freezing]

130.5 FX: DO [burst]

131.5 FX: DOKI... [heartbeat]

132.2 FX: FUWA [floating]
132.3 FX: HYUUUU [wind blowing]

133.3 FX: GIKU [alarm]

134.3 FX: JIIIN [overflowing emotion]

135.1 FX: PISHAN [gleaming]
135.5 FX: DOKA [strike]

136.1 FX: KORO KORO [rolling]
136.2 FX: GAN GAN [throbbing]
136.4 FX: HA [surprise]

137.2 FX: DOKI [heartbeat]
137.5 FX: DOKI DOKI DOKI [heart beating]
137.5 FX: DOKI DOKI DOKI [heart beating]

138.5 FX: DOKI DOKI DOKI DOKI [heart beating]

141.3 FX: ZAKU ZAKU [footsteps]
141.4 FX: HYUU [wind]

144.3 FX: GASA GASA [flipping pages]
144.4 FX: DOSA DOSA [falling objects]
144.4 FX: BASA [opening]

145.1 FX: GIKU [alarm]
145.3 FX: DOKUN DOKUN [heart beating]
145.4 FX: DOKUN DOKUN DOKUN [heart beating]
145.4 FX: DOKUN DOKUN DOKUN [heart beating]

146.1 FX: DOSA [object falling]
146.2 FX: DOKUN DOKUN [heart beating]
146.2 FX: DOKUN DOKUN [heart beating]
146.3 FX: DOKUN [heart beating]

146.4 FX: KARA [door opening]

147.3 FX: PA [light changing]
147.4 FX: KII [door opening]
147.6 FX: ZUZAZAZAA [sliding]

149.1 FX: ZUKIN [pain]
149.2 FX: BUN BUN [shaking off]

150.3 FX: DOKI DOKI DOKI [heart beating]

CHAPTER FIFTY-NINE
COUNTERFEIT LOVE

157.3 FX: DOKA DOKA [hitting]
157.3 FX: GURI GURI [noogies]

158.1 FX: NIKO [smile]
158.2 FX: NIKO [smile]
158.3 FX: NIKO [smile]

159.2 FX: GARA [door opening]
159.3 FX: SAWA SAWA [crowd sounds]

160.2 FX: DOKIN [surprise]

161.4 FX: DOKA [punch]
161.5 FX: DOKI DOKI [heartbeats]

162.2 FX: DOKKUN [heavy heartbeat]
162.2 FX: Koron [clattering]

163.1 FX: NYA [leering smile]

165.4 FX: POKI [crack]
165.5 FX: TON [thump]

166.3 FX: GABA [rising]

168.1 FX: DOKI DOKI DOKI [heart beating]
168.1 FX: DOKI DOKI DOKI [heart beating]
168.4 FX: DOKA DOKA [punching]
168.4 FX: JIRO JIRO [staring]

169.5 FX: KURU [turning]

170.2 FX: TON TON [footsteps]
170.4 FX: KIII [door creaking]
170.5 FX: GACHAN [locking]

171.1 FX: BASA… [clothes falling]

173.1 FX: DOKUN [a heavy heartbeat]
173.1 FX: DOKUN DOKUN DOKUN DOKUN [heartbeats]
173.3 FX: DOKU DOKUN… [heart thumping]
173.6 FX: KASHAN! [shutters closing]

174.1 FX: DOKUN DOKUN DOKUN [heart thumping]
174.1 FX: DOKUN DOKUN DOKUN! [heart thumping]

175.2 FX: FUU FUUU [pencil falling]
175.4 FX: KA [flash]

177.2 FX: PIKU [a twitch]

178.1 FX: PIKU… [alarm]

180.4 FX: BA [shooting out]

181.6 FX: GIRI GIRI [tightening]

182.1 FX: GI GI [tightening]
182.4 FX: GI GI [pulling]
182.5 FX: GU GU [tugging]

183.2 FX: BOKI [cracking]
183.5 FX: GIRI GIRI [tightening]

184.1 FX: PIIIIIII [a musical note]
184.2 FX: HA [realization]

185.1 FX: SHURU… [loosening]
185.4 FX: GUSA [stab]

186.2 FX: PISHI [cracking]
186.3 FX: PISHI PISHI PISHI [crumbling]
186.4 FX: PAN [breaking]

187.2 FX: SUUU [fade in]
187.4 FX: ZA [footstep]

188.1 FX: SA [quick movement]

CHAPTER SIXTY
RAY OF RESURRECTION

194.2 FX: DOOO [explosion]

195.5 FX: BYU [burst]
195.6 FX: BA [flute sound]

196.1 FX: GUA [burst]
196.2 FX: KURURU [spinning]
196.4 FX: BYU BYU BYU [shooting]

197.1 FX: GUSA [stab]
197.3 FX: SUU [appearing]
197.3 FX: DOSA [falling]

198.1 FX: DOSU [stab]
198.2 FX: GOBO [cough]

200.1 FX: DO [slashing]
200.1 FX: DOSU [stabbing]
200.1 FX: DOGO [blow]
200.3 FX: DOSA [falling]

202.6 FX: KORON [tipping over]

203.4 FX: FU [fainting]
203.5 FX: GABA [getting up]

204.2 FX: BA [covering up]

205.1 FX: GUI [tug]
205.3 FX: GOHH [burst]
205.4 FX: DO [explosion]

207.3 FX: GUI [tugging]

209.1 FX: GOHH [roar]
209.2 FX: TA [skip]

210.3 FX: SHAN [clanking]
210.4 FX: ZURURU [sliding]
210.4 FX: BOOO [listlessness]

211.3 FX: SA [picking up]

212.3 FX: PORO PORO [sob sob]

214.3 FX: DOKA [kick]
214.4 FX: DOKOO [kick]

215.1 FX: SUU [quiet snoring]
215.1 FX: GAA [loud snoring]
215.1 FX: PEE [cute snoring]
215.2 FX: PATAN [door shutting]

217.2 FX: ZUDA [falling]
217.5 FX: FUWA [looming over]

218.1 FX: ZAWA [leaves stirring]

219.1 FX: DOKUN DOKUN [ba-dump]
219.1 FX: DOKUN DOKUN [ba-dump]
219.2 FX: DOKUN DOKUN [ba-dump]
219.3 FX: ZURU [sliding]

220.3 FX: ZAAA [swaying branches]

CHAPTER SIXTY-ONE
A SAD FATE

225.2 FX: SHUN [sulking]

226.5 FX: SAWA SAWA [leaves stirring]

227.2 FX: ZUKIN [pang]
227.3 FX: FU [blowing out]

228.1 FX: FU [appearance]

230.1 FX: BATAN [door opening]

232.2 FX: KA [kneeling down]

233.2 FX: DOKUN [ba-dump]

234.2 FX: NIYA [smile]

235.5 FX: FUI [turning around]

236.4 FX: KII [door opening]

240.2 FX: DERORON [ominous appearance]
240.4 FX: DOYA DOYA [chatting]

241.3 FX: TSUN [turning away]
241.4 FX: GATA GATA [furniture moving]

242.1 FX: ZAZAAA [leaves blowing]
242.6 FX: HA [oops]

243.3 FX: GATAN [rising]
243.5 FX: BISHI [pointing]

244.4 FX: GATSU GATSU [eating]
244.5 FX: SAWA SAWA [chatting at a distance]

256.1 FX: ZAZA [bird fluttering]
256.2 FX: DOKI DOKI DOKI [ba-dump ba-dump ba-dump]

257.2 FX: BIKU [alarm]
257.3 FX: DOKUN DOKUN DOKUN [ba-dump ba-dump ba-dump]
257.4 FX: BA [hiding]
257.4 FX: DOKUN DOKUN DOKUN [ba-dump ba-dump ba-dump]
257.4 FX: DOKUN DOKUN [ba-dump ba-dump]
257.6 FX: KA KA [galloping]

CHAPTER SIXTY-TWO
THE UNBREAKABLE WALL

262.3 FX: GYU [tug]
262.4 FX: ZU [moving out]
262.5 FX: ZURU [slip]

263.2 FX: SHAA [pant]

264.1 FX: HA [realization]
264.2 FX: GOOOOH [flame]
264.3 FX: BOOOOH [sizzle]

265.2 FX: CHIIIN [doooong]
265.3 FX: CHIIIN [doooong]
265.3 FX: DOTATATA [running over]

266.1 FX: HETA [exhaustion]

267.4 FX: SU [slight movement]

268.2 FX: PIKU [detecting]

269.1 FX: FU [smile]
269.5 FX: JARA [jangle]

271.4 FX: GAN [thump]
271.4 FX: GON [thump]
271.4 FX: DOTA [fall]
271.5 FX: BATAN [shut]

272.1 FX: HA [noticing]
272.3 FX: KOTSU KOTSU [footsteps]
272.4 FX: GUI [tug]

273.2 FX: PAN [slap]

275.2 FX: DOSU [punch]

276.2 FX: ZURU [slip]

277.1 FX: WAKU WAKU [excited]
277.3 FX: GIKU [alarm]

278.1 FX: PAN [slap]
278.5 FX: DA [dashing out]

279.3 FX: PICHON [drip]
279.4 FX: BURU [shiver]
279.5 FX: HA [waking]

280.2 FX: GASHAAN [rattle]
280.3 FX: HA [detecting]

283.5 FX: BAN BAN [slam slam]

285.3 FX: GA [knock]
285.5 FX: SHIIN [silence]

309.2 FX: GIKU [alarm]
309.6 FX: DOKIN DOKIN DOKIN [ba-dump ba-dump ba-dump]
309.6 FX: DOKIN DOKIN DOKIN [ba-dump ba-dump ba-dump]

311.1 FX: GAKU GAKU GAKU GAKU [shake shake shake shake]

313.1 FX: HAH HAH [huff huff]
313.4 FX: HA [alarm]

316.3 FX: HA HA [laughing]

317.2 FX: GAN [knock]
317.2 FX: HYOHHH [whistling wind]

318.1 FX: BASHA [splash]
318.5 FX: BATAN [shut]

319.1 FX: BAN BAN [thump thump]
319.2 FX: GACHAN [door locking]

CHAPTER SIXTY-FOUR
IMMINENT PARTING

321.2 FX: GYU [squeeze]

323.2 FX: PUCHI [tear]
323.4 FX: SU [hold]
323.5 FX: BA [popping out]
323.6 FX: SHURURURURU [swirl]

329.1 FX: GOOH [burn]
329.3 FX: SU [fade]

325.3 FX: BAN [door opening]

326.3 FX: DOKAA [kick]

328.3 FX: KYU [wipe]

330.1 FX: KA [footstep]

286.3 FX: GU [clench]

288.4 FX: SHIIN [silence]

289.3 FX: HAH [turning around]

CHAPTER SIXTY-THREE
THE TRUTH REVEALED

294.1 FX: GYUUU [choke]
294.2 FX: GEHO GEHO [cough]
294.3 FX: KU [snicker]

295.1 FX: BORO BORO [sob sob]
295.3 FX: GACHAN [click]

296.1 FX: KOKU KOKU [nod nod]

297.1 FX: BA [grab]
297.3 FX: GAKUN [bow]
297.4 FX: GABA [jerking up]

298.2 FX: BA [toss]
298.5 FX: SEH SEH [working hard]

299.4 FX: GEHO GEHO [cough cough]
299.5 FX: HAH HAH [huff huff]

301.2 FX: HA [realizing]

302.4 FX: SU [extracting]

304.2 FX: PAH [opening up]
304.3 FX: SU [appearing]

306.2 FX: DOSA [falling]
306.3 FX: JU [sizzle]

307.4 FX: KURU KURU KURU [spin spin spin]
307.4 FX: KURU KURU KURU KURU [spin spin spin spin]

308.3 FX: FUFU [snicker]
308.4 FX: GOHO [cough]

331.2 FX: KURU KURU KURU [twirl twirl twirl]
331.3 FX: NU [sudden appearance]

332.3 FX: ZORO ZORO [mass movement]

333.2 FX: JITABATA JITABATA [panic]
333.4 FX: GOOOOH [flames]

334.1 FX: Dosa [landing]
334.3 FX: Ba [dramatic turn]

335.3 FX: Kui [gentle tug]
335.5 FX: Pen [slap]

337.1 FX: Doohn [burst]
337.1 FX: Ha [realization]
337.3 FX: Paku paku [mouth movement]
337.6 FX: Doohn [burst]

338.1 FX: Hyun hyun hyun hyun [wrapping around]
338.2 FX: Kuru kuru kuru [spin spin spin]

339.3 FX: Yoro [stagger]
339.5 FX: Ba [grab]

340.4 FX: Bata bata [stomp stomp]
340.6 FX: Giri giri [squeeze squeeze]

341.3 FX: Su [emerge]

342.4 FX: Su [fade]

343.2 FX: Shururururururu [whizzing around]

344.2 FX: Karan [thump]
344.3 FX: Fu [fading]
344.4 FX: Dosa dosa [falls]

345.5 FX: Gan [bump]

348.2 FX: Piku [twitch]
348.5 FX: Niya [smile]

349.1 FX: Kah [flash]
349.2 FX: Don [bump]
349.5 FX: Niya [smile]

CHAPTER SIXTY-FIVE
TRAGIC BATTLE

352.1 FX: Fu [rising]
352.2 FX: Fuwa [float]
352.4 FX: Fu [appearing]
352.5 FX: Pashi [grasp]

353.3 FX: Paku paku [mouth movement]
353.5 FX: Kuru kuru kuru [spin spin spin]

354.1 FX: Ban [burst]
354.2 FX: Su [wave]
354.3 FX: Doohn [burst]

355.2 FX: Su [snag]
355.3 FX: Fuwa [floating]

356.1 FX: Su [twirl]
356.2 FX: Ba [tearing apart]

358.2 FX: Giii [creak]

359.3 FX: Pashi [hit]

360.1 FX: Gakun [arm falling]

361.1 FX: Shaaa [hissing]
361.6 FX: Su [finger motion]

362.1 FX: Ga ga [stab stab]
362.2 FX: Bikun [pain]
362.5 FX: Zuki [pain]
362.6 FX: Shu [flash]

364.1 FX: Zan [slice]
364.4 FX: Fuwa [float]

365.4 FX: Su [flash]

366.2 FX: Gosu [elbow]
366.3 FX: Pita [touch]

367.1 FX: Baku [biting]
367.2 FX: Supon [bounce back]
367.5 FX: Ba [fling]

368.1 FX: Gooohhh [whirlwind]
368.3 FX: Zu zu [rumble rumble]

369.4 FX: Gyu [hug]

370.4 FX: Zukin [pain]

372.1 FX: GOOOHHH [roar]

373.1 FX: KU [grab]
373.4 FX: DOSU [stab]

374.1 FX: SHUUU [fizzing out]
374.1 FX: DOSA [landing]

CHAPTER SIXTY-SIX
EMBRACING EVIL

383.3 FX: KA [flash]
383.4 FX: DOOHN [explosion]

387.1 FX: SUTO [landing]

389.4 FX: HA [realization]
389.5 FX: DOO [wham]

390.1 FX: GUTAA [collapse]

391.6 FX: KAAAH [flash]

393.2 FX: SUU [appearing kanji characters]
393.5 FX: DA [dash forward]

394.1 FX: BASHI [smack]
394.2 FX: GA [grabbing]
394.3 FX: KA [blush]

395.2 FX: DOKA [kick]
395.3 FX: KA [footstep]

397.2 FX: SU [slipping through]
397.3 FX: DA [step]
397.4 FX: BAN [shut]

399.2 FX: KAAAH [flashing]

400.2 FX: DOHHH [burst]

401.1 FX: KA [flash]
401.1 FX: KA [flash]
401.2 FX: GOHH [swirling]
401.3 FX: KA... [footstep]

402-403 FX: OOOOOO [rumbling]

404.2 FX: GO GO GO [tremor]
404.3 FX: GO GO GO [tremor]

405.4 FX: ZAWA [commotion]

407.1 FX: HETA [kneeling down]
407.4 FX: FU [looking down]
407.5 FX: KA [ray]

409.2 FX: BA [sudden movement]
409.4 FX: SUU [removal]

410.1 FX: DON [blow]

411.2 FX: FU [vanishing]
411.5 FX: ZU ZU... [tremor]
411.5 FX: PISHI PISHI [cracking]

412.1 FX: ZU ZU ZU [tremor]
412.5 FX: SHAN [clanking]

413.1 FX: KA [beam]
413.1 FX: SU...[opening]

414.1 FX: SU [vanishing]
414.3 FX: SU [vanishing]
414.3 FX: DOHN [explosion]

452.4 FX: Dokun [heart beating]
452.4 FX: Dokun dokun dokun [heart beating]

453.2 FX: Dokun dokun dokun dokun [heart beating]

459.1 FX: Pa [appearing]
459.2 FX: Pa [appearing]
459.4 FX: Su [open]

463.1 FX: Gyu [squeeze]
463.3 FX: Ba [slam open]
463.5 FX: Sukaa [snoozing]

464.1 FX: Dogashaaan [crashing]
464.2 FX: Doooh [galloping]
464.3 FX: Ohhh [clamor]

465.2 FX: Wahhh [shouting]
465.5 FX: Pori pori [scratching]

466.2 FX: Ka [flash]
466.3 FX: Dooohn [explosion]

467.1 FX: Doka doka doka [galloping]
467.3 FX: Ha [realization]
467.4 FX: Ka [footfall]

468.2 FX: Su [hand movement]
468.3 FX: Ha [sudden realization]
468.4 FX: Dohhh [crashing]

469.1 FX: Dosa [fall]
469.1 FX: Zaku [fall against ground]
469.2 FX: Pishaaan [crackling]
469.2 FX: Heheeen! [neighing]
469.3 FX: Pari pari pari [crackling]

470.4 FX: Ton [step]

471.3 FX: Dosu [stab]
471.5 FX: Yoro [sway]

472.1 FX: Bashi [slap]

416.1 FX: GYU [hug]
416.3 FX: BA [getting up]]

CHAPTER SIXTY-SEVEN
MATRIMONY

420.2 FX: KAAAH [flashing]
420.5 FX: GAKUN [jolt]

423.4 FX: DOSA [fall]

429.1 FX: KI [anger]
429.3 FX: DOKA [kick]

430.2 FX: BAN [slam open]

431.1 FX: GABA [hug]
431.2 FX: Gunya [squish]

434.4 FX: Bata bata bata [running]

437.1 FX: Za [marching]
437.3 FX: Kappo kappo [clopping]

438.5 FX: Gyu [squeeze]

439.3 FX: Bun bun [shaking head]

440.2 FX: Doki doki doki [heart thumping]
440.2 FX: Doki doki doki [heart thumping]

445.4 FX: Gyu [squeeze]

447.2 FX: Shuru [slipping off]
447.5 FX: Pasa [falling lightly]

448.4 FX: Bururu [horse whinny]

CHAPTER SIXTY-EIGHT
THE DIVIDING LIGHT

452.3 FX: Dokun [heart beating]
452.3 FX: Dokun dokun dokun dokun [heart beating]

495.3 FX: GISHI [creak]
495.4 FX: KASHAN [shutter moving]

496.4 FX: KUI [twist]
496.5 FX: KASHAN [shutter opening]

497.3 FX: JUUU [frying]
497.4 FX: BAN [opening door]

498.2 FX: PATAN [door shutting]

500.4 FX: PATAN [door shutting]
500.4 FX: TOSA [sitting down]

501.3 FX: SU [rising]

504.4 FX: PARA [flip]

CHAPTER SEVENTY
SURGE OF THE HEART

511.1 FX: CHI CHI CHI... [chirping]
511.2 FX: CHI CHI CHI... [chirping]
511.2 FX: MOZO... [stir]
511.3 FX: PACHI [opening eyes]
511.5 FX: TA TA TA [scurry]

512.2 FX: CHI CHI [chirping]

514.5 NOTE: Waratte Ii-tomo Zokango (Sure, It's Okay to Laugh Bonus Program) is an ensemble comedy program much like Saturday Night Live.

515.1 FX: KACHA KACHA [dishes]

516.2 FX: KACHA [click]
516.3 FX: FU FU FU FU [laughing]

524.5 FX: KA [step]

525.4 FX: GOTON [train rumbling]
525.5 FX: GOTON [train rumbling]

472.2 FX: Gui [tug]
472.4 FX: Zuru... [slip]

473.4 FX: Para [ribbon undone]

474.3 FX: Kaaaa [flash]

475.3 FX: Kaaaa [flash]

476.1 FX: Suuu [vanishing]
476.2 FX: Suuu [vanishing]

478.3 FX: Gaba [getting up]

CHAPTER SIXTY-NINE
REAL/UNREAL BOY

481.1 FX: Dokun dokun dokun [heart thumping]
481.2 FX: Dokun dokun [heart thumping]
481.2 FX: Dokun dokun [heart thumping]

482.5 FX: Gaba [cowering]
482.6 FX: DOKI DOKI DOKI DOKI DOKI DOKI [heart thumping]

484.3 FX: PORI PORI [crackle crackle]

486.2 FX: SU [held up]

487.1 FX: UOOOO [shout]
487.3 FX: DOOOH [roar]

489.1 FX: HA [alarm]
489.2 FX: BA [impact]
489.4 FX: ZA [footstep]

492.3 FX: BATAN [door shutting]
492.5 FX: SA SA [swift retreat]

493.2 FX: SHIRA [unemotional]
493.2 FX: GATATA [falling]
493.3 FX: PATA PATA [walking away]

494.2 FX: GISHI [creak]
494.4 FX: JUU [frying]

526.1 FX: GYU [squeeze]

532.4 FX: BURU BURU [trembling]

533.1 FX: KACHA [click]
533.3 FX: KYU [rub]

538.1 FX: BAN [slam open]

539.2 FX: YORO [wobbling]
539.5 FX: SU [appearance]

540.5 FX: PAAN [crashing]

CHAPTER SEVENTY-ONE
TO LIVE FOR YOU

543.1 FX: PARIN [cracking]
543.1 FX: SHIRIN [breaking]

544.2 FX: DOKA [smash]

545.2 FX: DA [dash]

546.2 FX: DA [whip]
546.4 FX: WAAAA [battle cry]

547.3 FX: HIHEEN [neighing]
547.3 FX: WAHHH [shouting]

548.1 FX: ZAN [slash]
548.2 FX: HA [alarm]

550.1 FX: YORO [swaying]
550.2 FX: HIKU HIKU [panting]

551.1 FX: YORO [sway]

552.3 FX: DOKOO [smash]
552.4 FX: TO [land]
552.5 NOTE: In Japanese he said, “The beautiful girl of vinegared octopus,” (sudako no miko), which sounds like “Priestess of Suzaku” (Suzaku no Miko).

553.2 FX: HIKU HIKU [twitching]
553.5 FX: SHAAA [coasting]

554.1 FX: SHAAA [riding away]
554.3 FX: SHAAA [coasting]
554.5 FX: DONGARA [crash]
554.5 FX: GASSHAAN [crash]
554.6 FX: GABA [getting up]

555.1 FX: ZURU ZURU [slurping]
555.2 FX: TO [step]

556.1 FX: DOGASHAAN [crash]
556.3 FX: FURA [slump]
556.5 FX: GYU [squeeze]

557.3 FX: HYOOOI [boing]

558.1 FX: BURU [shiver]

559.1 FX: GYU [hug]

561.6 FX: SHURURURURURURURURU [swirling]

562.1 FX: BA [tug]
562.2 FX: DOSA [falling]
562.2 FX: TO [land]
562.4 FX: GA [grab]

563.3 FX: GIRI GIRI GIRI [choking]
563.4 FX: HIKUN [jerk]
563.5 FX: BIKU [alarm]

566.2 FX: BA [retreat]
566.2 FX: ZAWA ZAWA [crowd noise]
566.5 FX: SU [lifting hand]

567.2 FX: JIRI [step]

569.3 FX: GYU [squeeze]
569.4 FX: BA [dramatic move]

CHINESE-TO-JAPANESE GLOSSARY

The Universe of the Four Gods is based on ancient China, but Japanese pronunciation of Chinese names differs slightly from their Chinese equivalents.

Chinese	Japanese	Person, Place, or Object	Meaning
Xong Gui-Siu	Sô Kishuku	Tamahome	Demon Constellation
Hong-Nan	Konan	Southern Kingdom	Crimson South
Gong Wu	Kyûbu	Clue	Palace Strength
Tai Yi-Jun	Tai Itsukun	Oracle	Preeminent Person
Kang-Lin	Kôrin	Lady of Hong-Nan	Peaceful Jewel
Daichi-San	Daikyokuzan	Mountain	Greatest Mountain
Lai Lai	Nyan Nyan	Servant	Nanny
Qu-Dong	Kûto	Eastern Kingdom	Gathered East
Zhong-Rong	Chûei	Second Son	Loyalty, Honor
Chun-Jing	Shunkei	Third Son	Spring, Respect
Yu-Lun	Gyokuran	Eldest Daughter	Jewel, Orchid
Jie-Lian	Yuiren	Youngest Daughter	Connection, Lotus
Shou-Shuang	Jusô	Province	Lasting Frost
Ligé-San	Reikakuzan	Mountain	Strength Tower
Knei-Gong	Kôji	Bandit	Young Victor
Rui-Nei	Eiken	Bandit	Imperial Likeness

Chinese	Japanese	Person, Place, or Object	Meaning
Huan-Lang	Genrô	Bandit Leader	Phantom Wolf
Changhung	Chôkô	Northern Town	Expansive Place
Shao-Huan	Shôka	Mystical Person	Small Flower
Miao Nioh-An	Myo Ju-An	Hermit	Miracle Peaceful Life
Diedu	Kodoku	Potion	Seduction Potion
He-Yan	Waen	Palace Room	Eternal Peace
Bei-Jia	Hokkan	Northern Kingdom	Armored North
Wong Tao-Hui	Ôdokun	Chinese Name	King Bright Path
K'o-Ju	Kakyo	Bureaucracy Exam	Departmental Trial
Hsing-Shin	Shôshi	Second Exam	Ministry Test
Shentso-Pao	Shinzahô	Treasure	God's Seat Jewel
Ming-Ho	Meiga	Canal	Signature Stream
Liu-Chuan	Ryûen	Nuriko's Given Name	Willowy Beauty
Nucheng-Kuo	Nyosei-koku	Island Kingdom	Woman Fort Country
Hua-Wan	Kaen	Woman	Flowery Grace
Dou	To	Tribe	A Measure
Tomolu	Tomoru	Elder	Earth Silent Duty
Teniao-Lan	Touran	City	Unique Crow Orchid
Xi-Lang	Sairô	Western Kingdom	West Tower

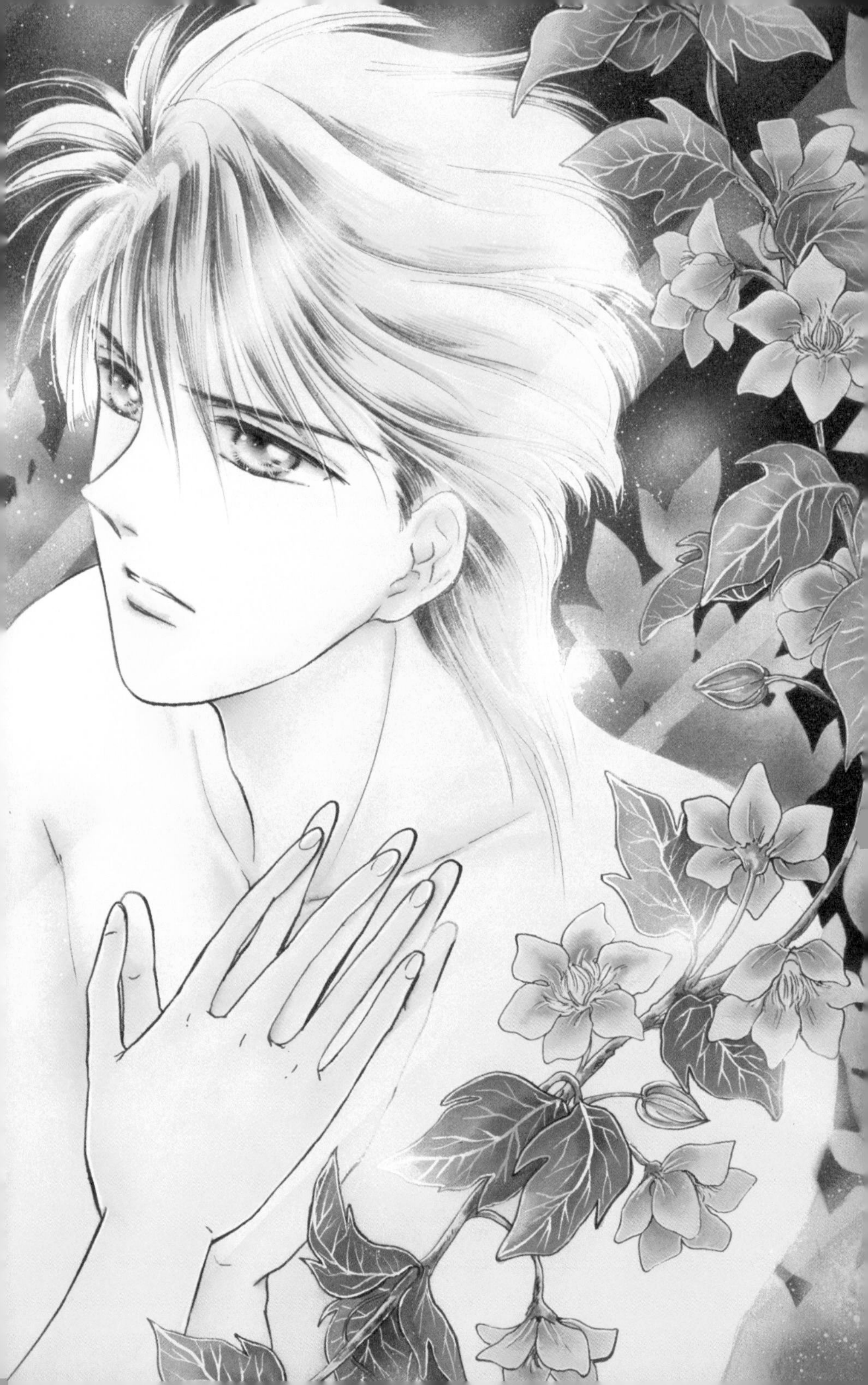

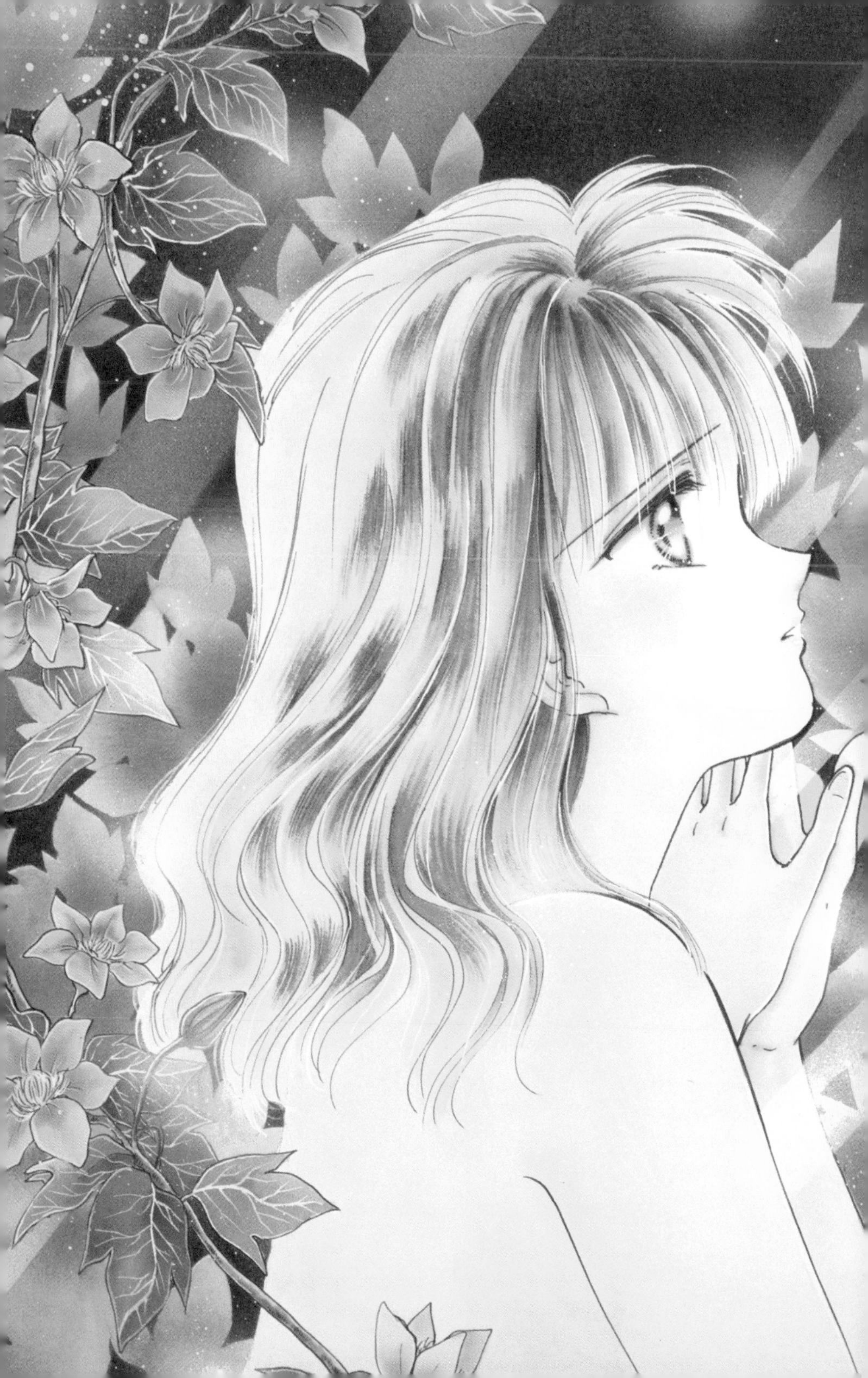

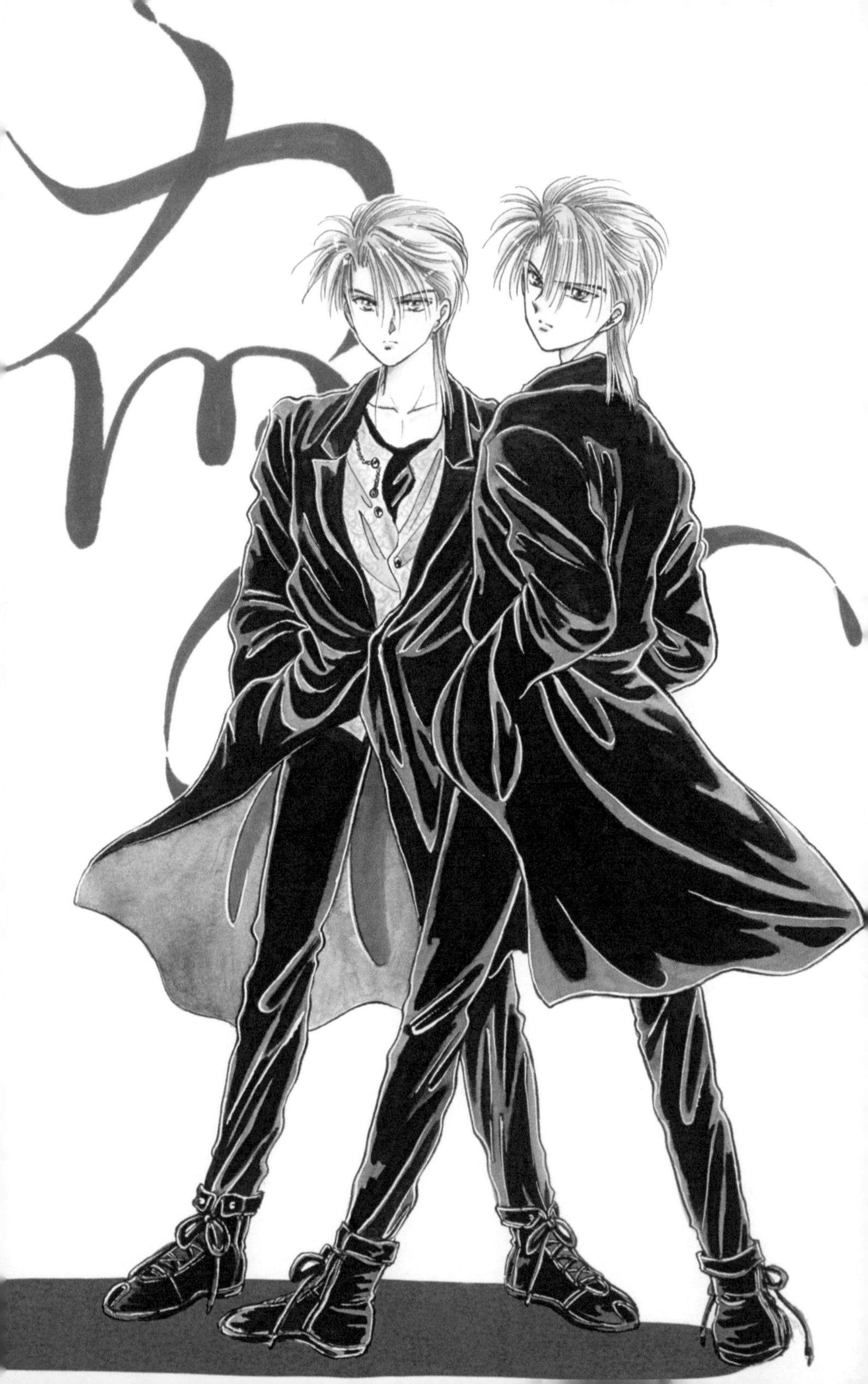

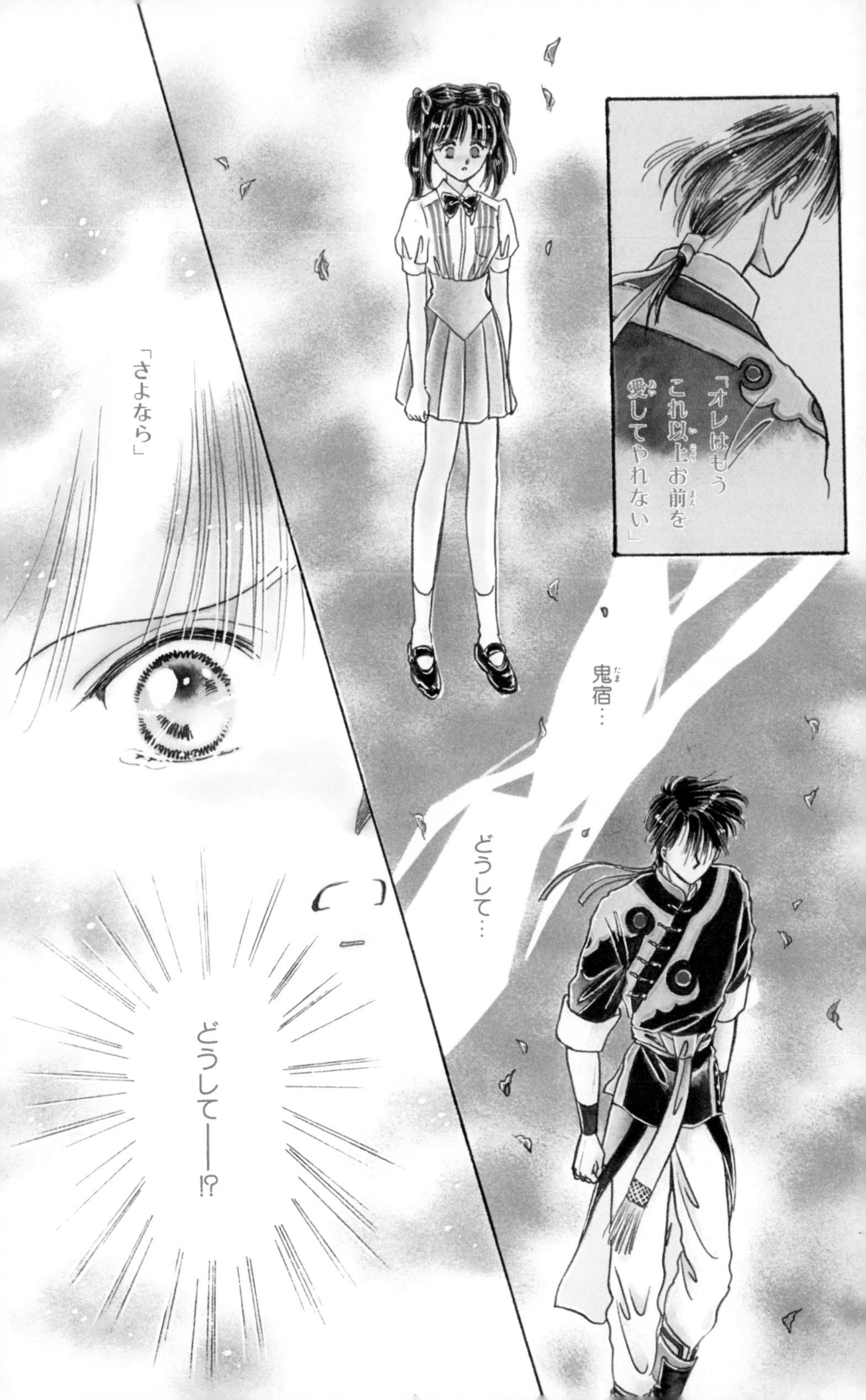
「オレはもう
これ以上お前を
愛してやれない」
鬼宿…
どうして…
「さよなら」
どうして——!?

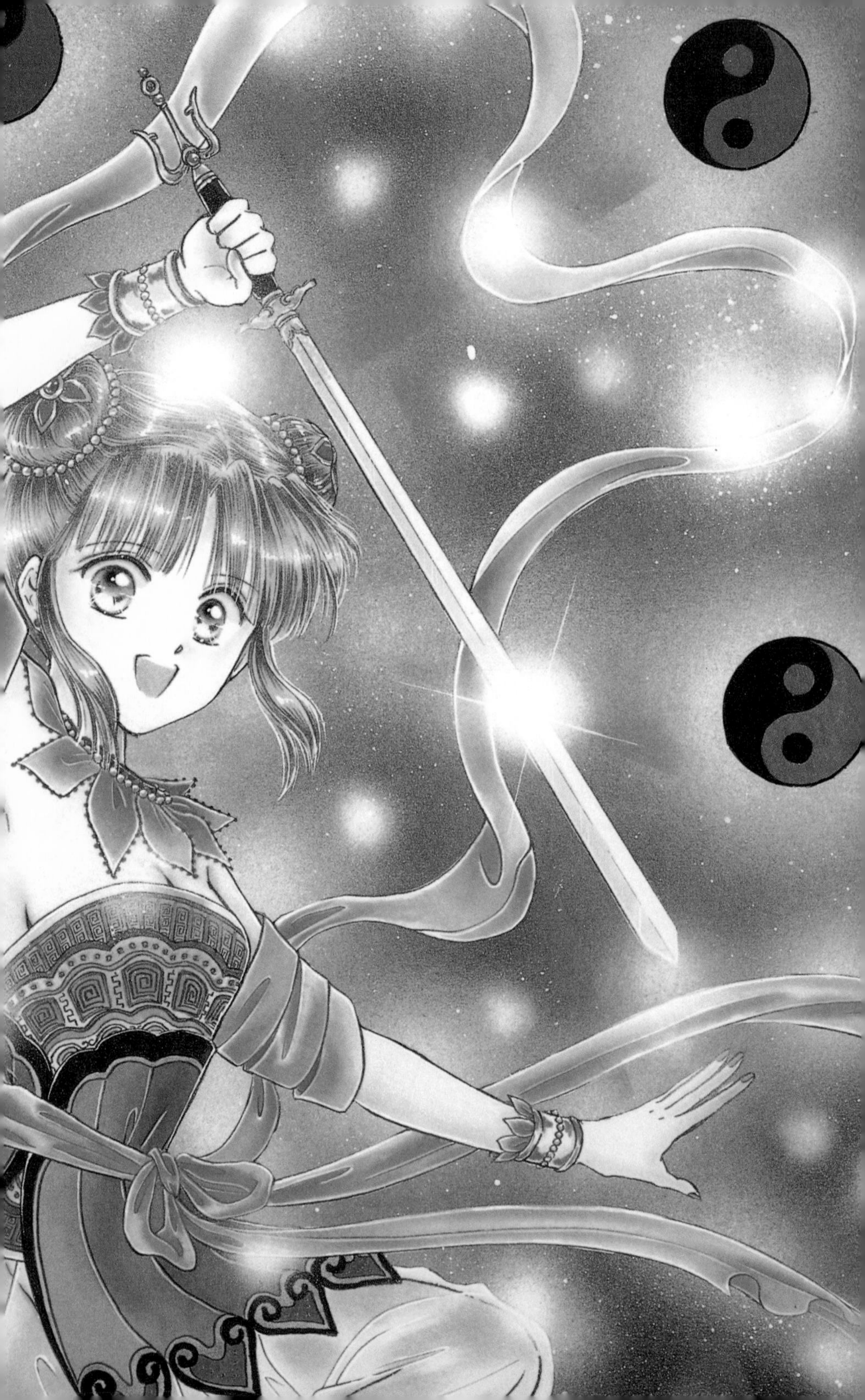

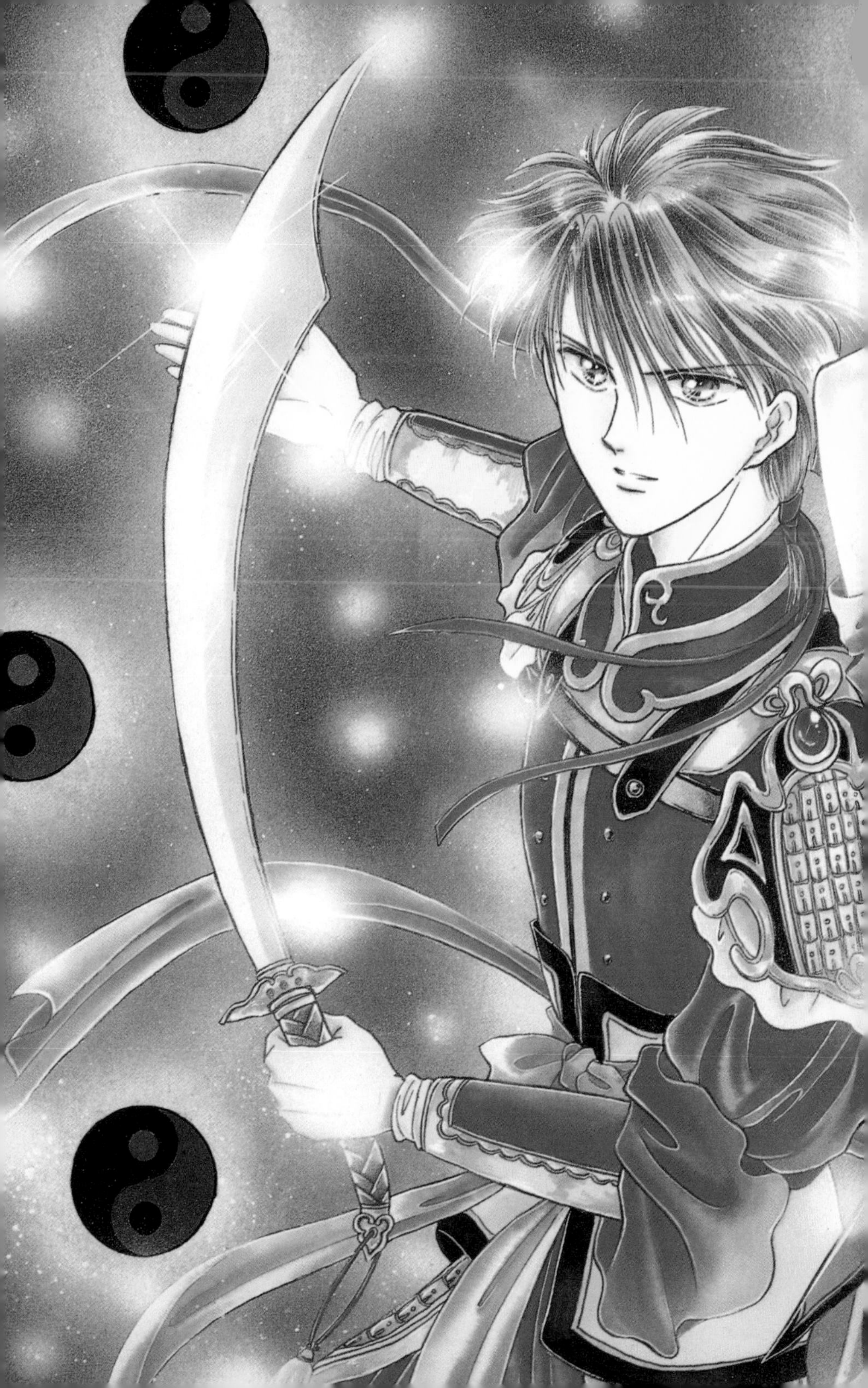

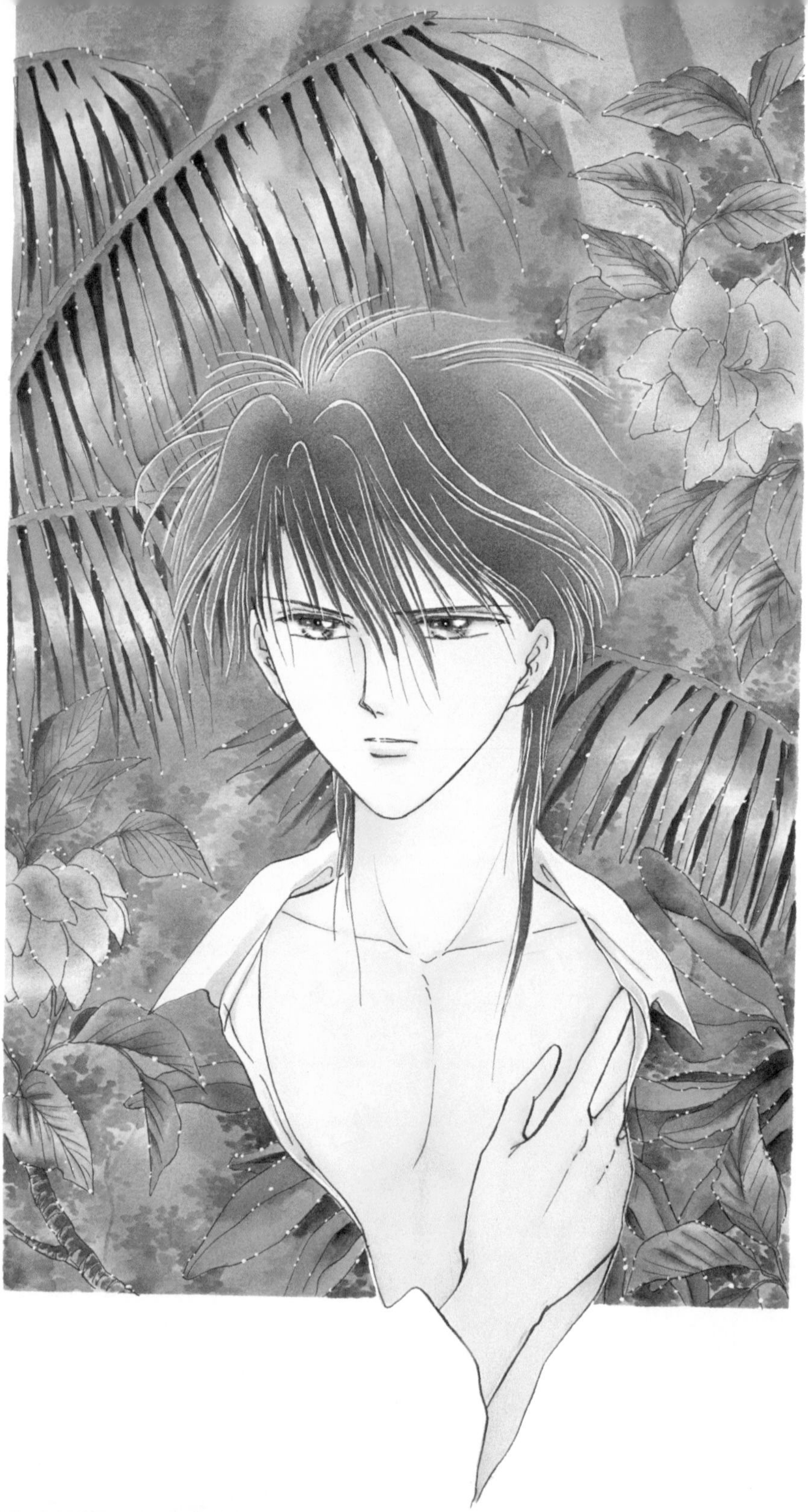

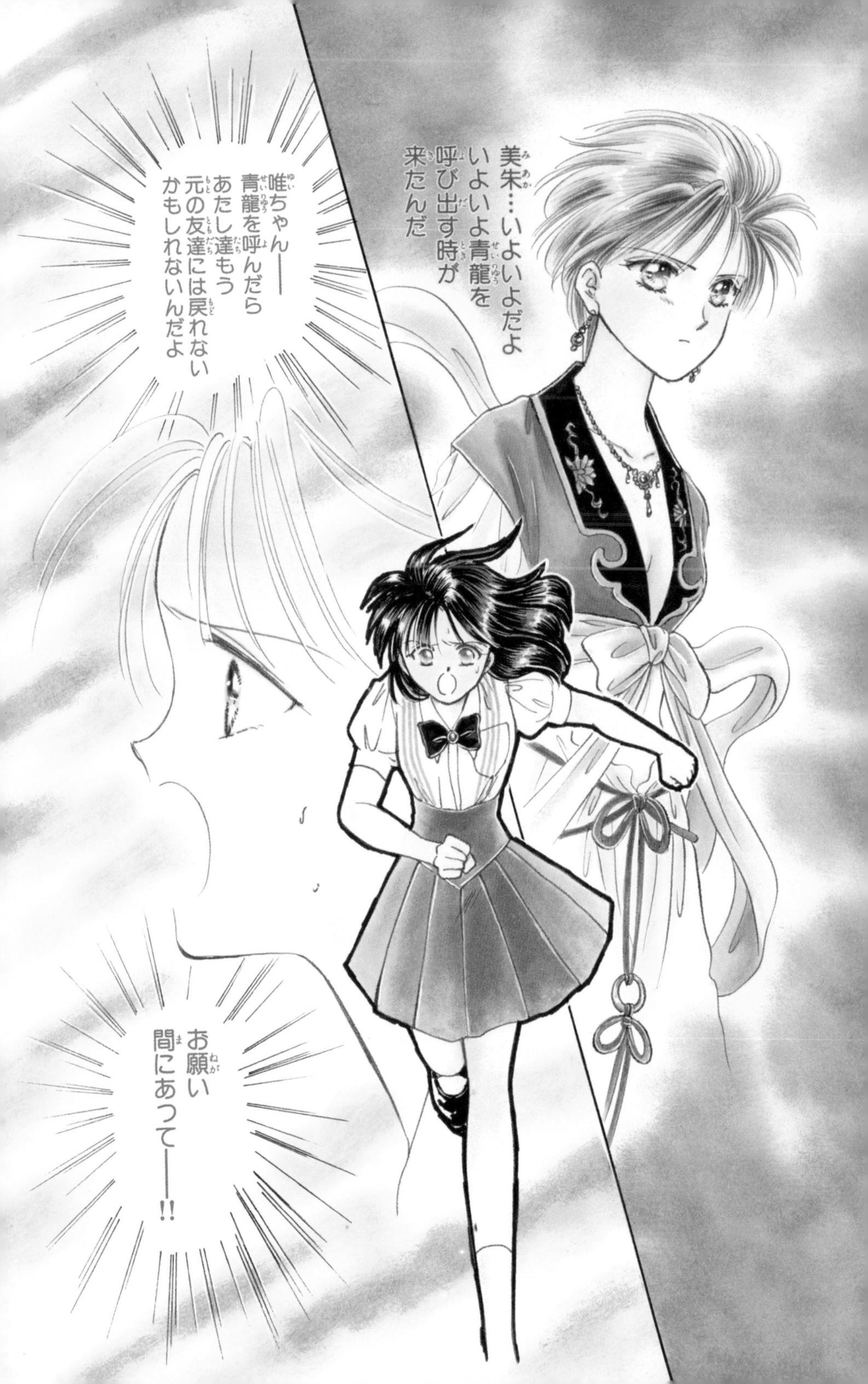
美朱…いよいよだよ
いよいよ青龍を
呼び出す時が
来たんだ
唯ちゃん──
青龍を呼んだら
あたし達もう
元の友達には戻れない
かもしれないんだよ
お願い
間にあって──!!

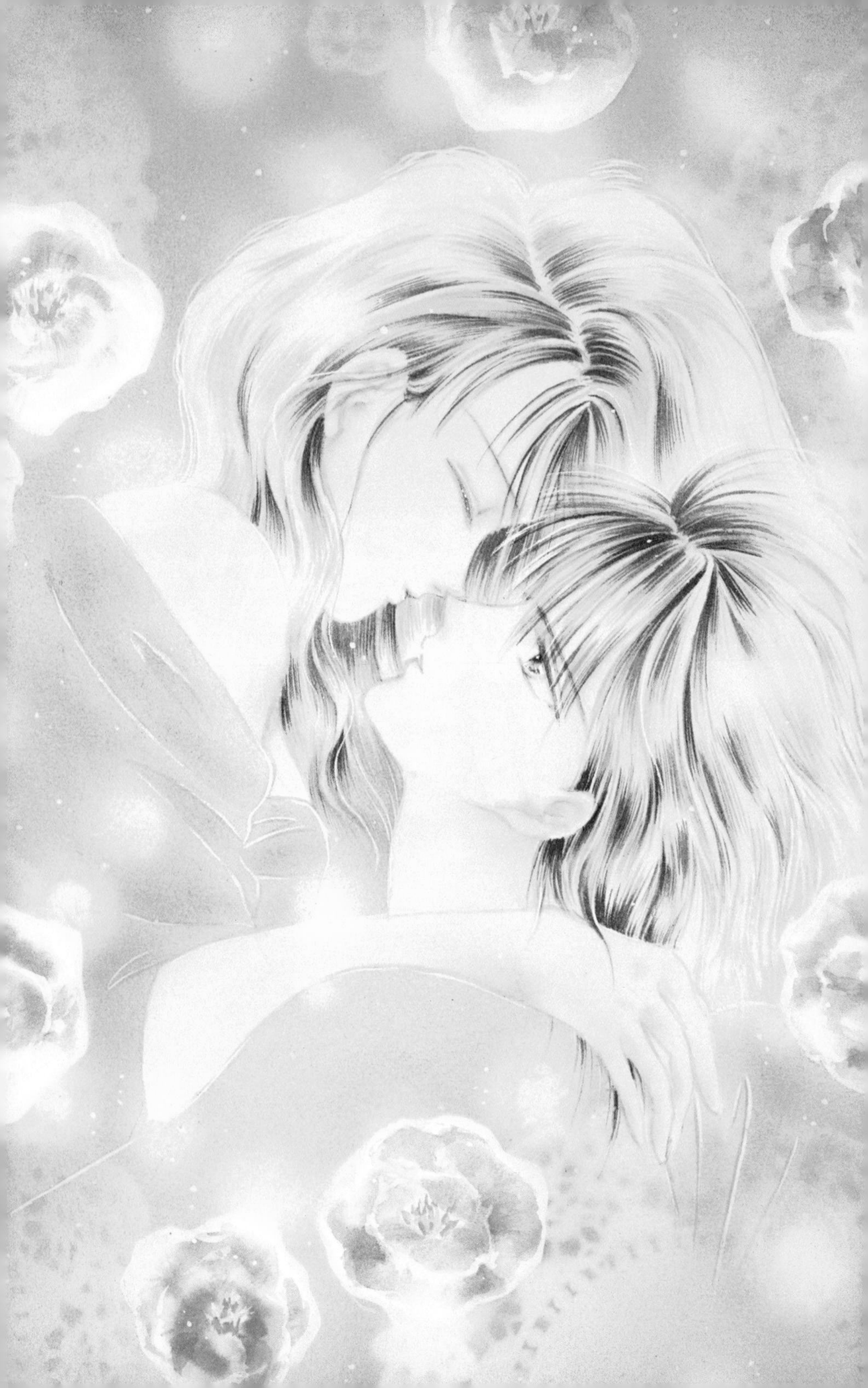

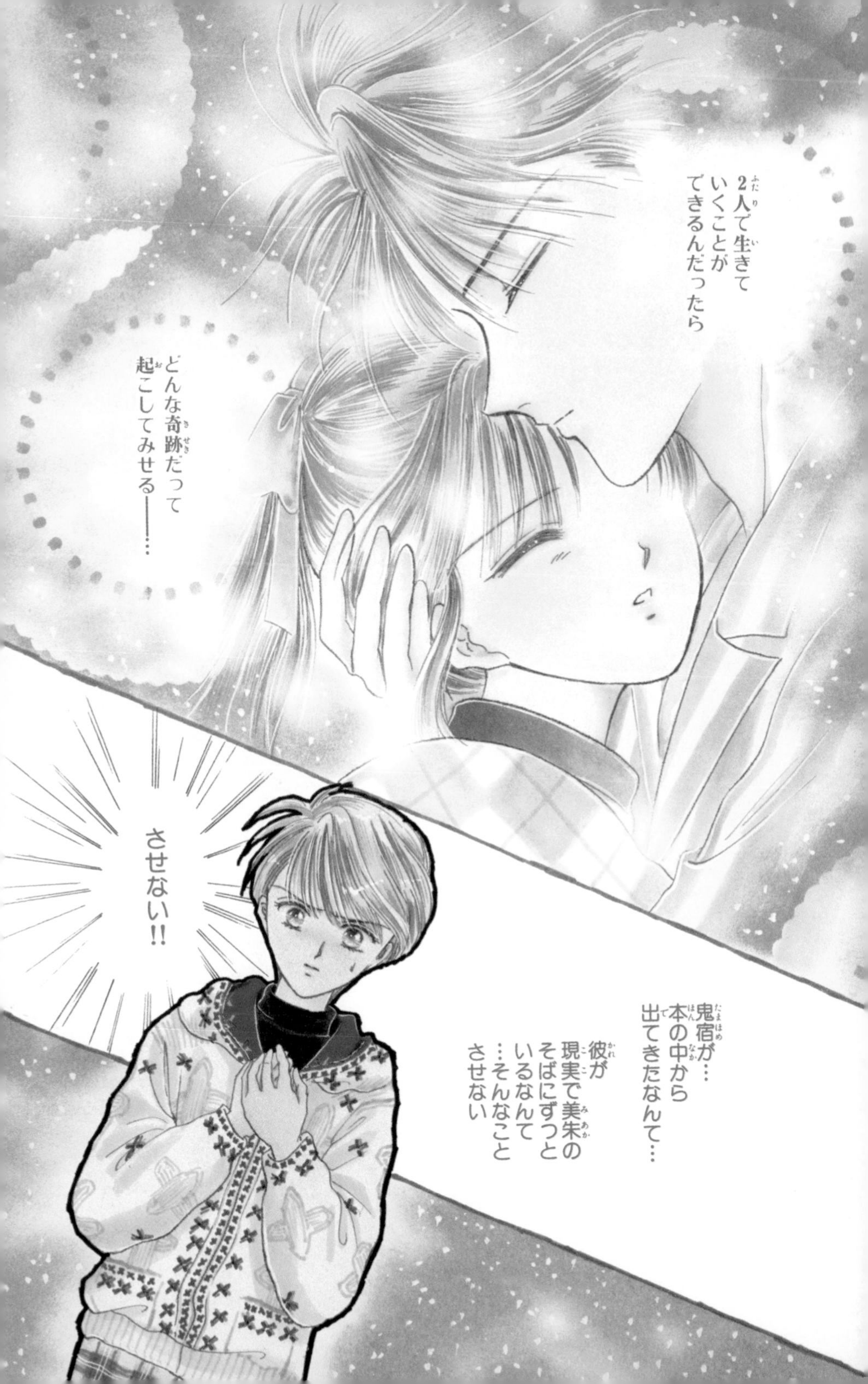
2人で生きていくことができるんだったら
どんな奇跡だって起こしてみせる——…
鬼宿が…本の中から出てきたなんて…
彼が現実で美朱のそばにずっといるなんて…そんなことさせない
させないい!!

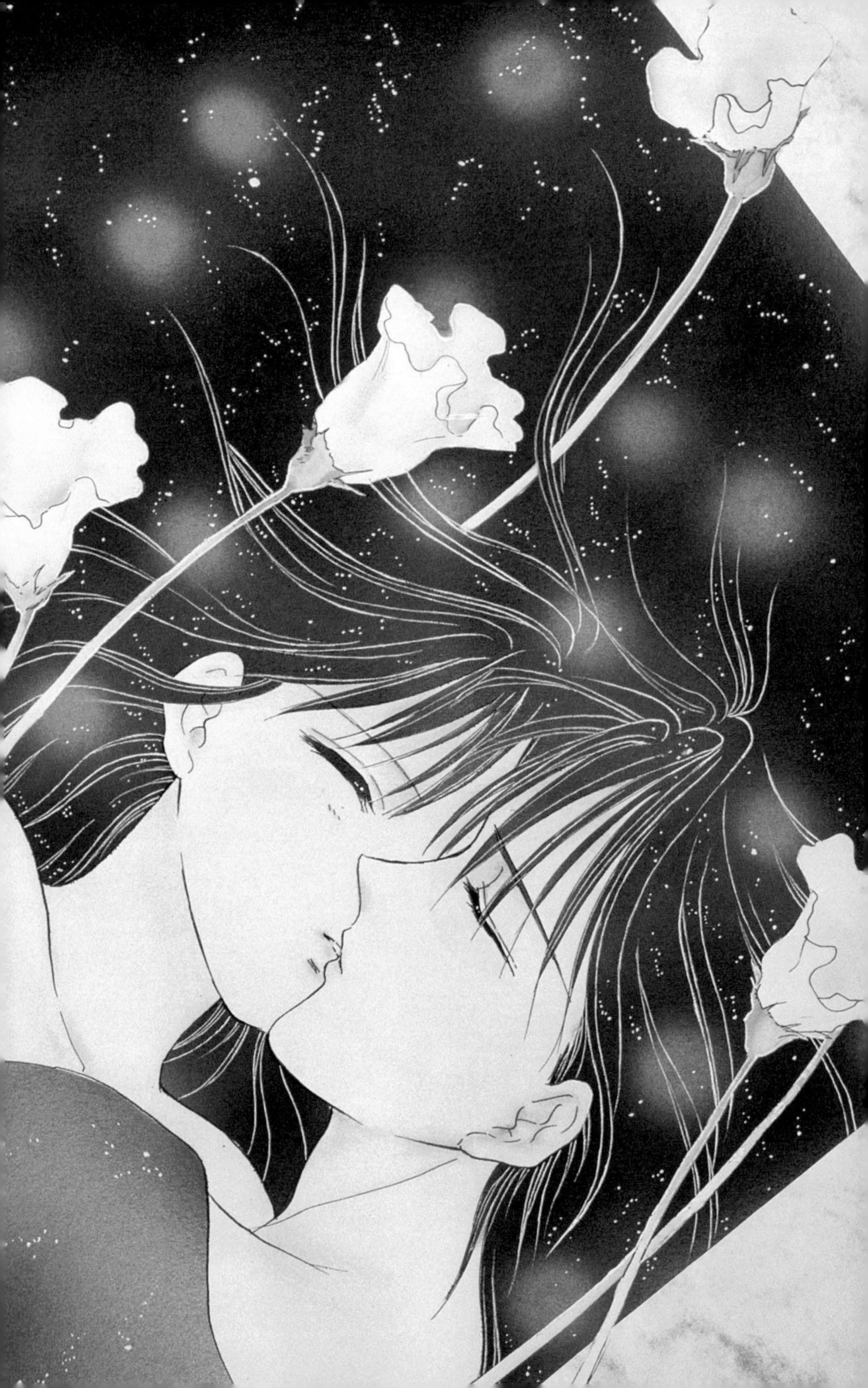

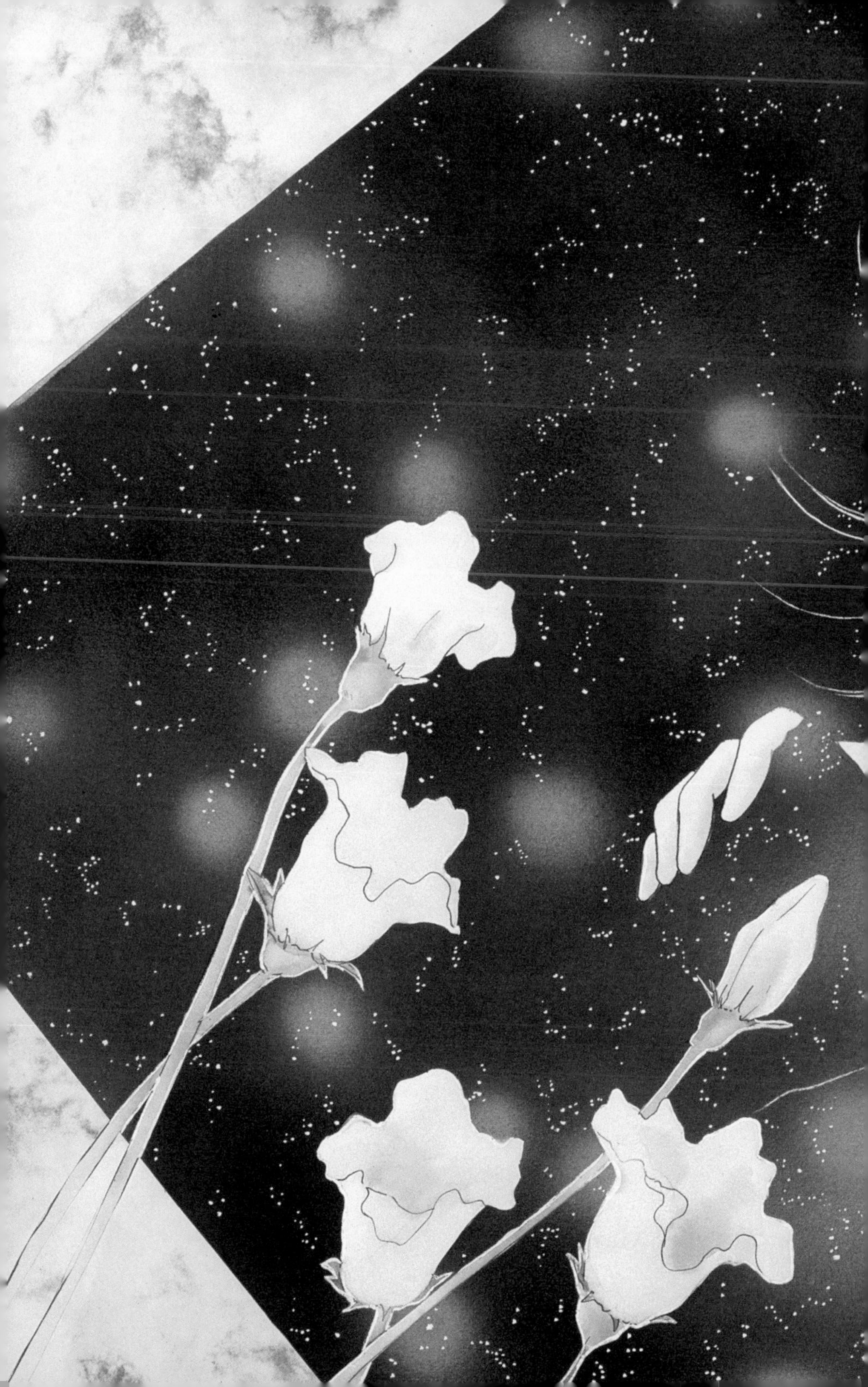

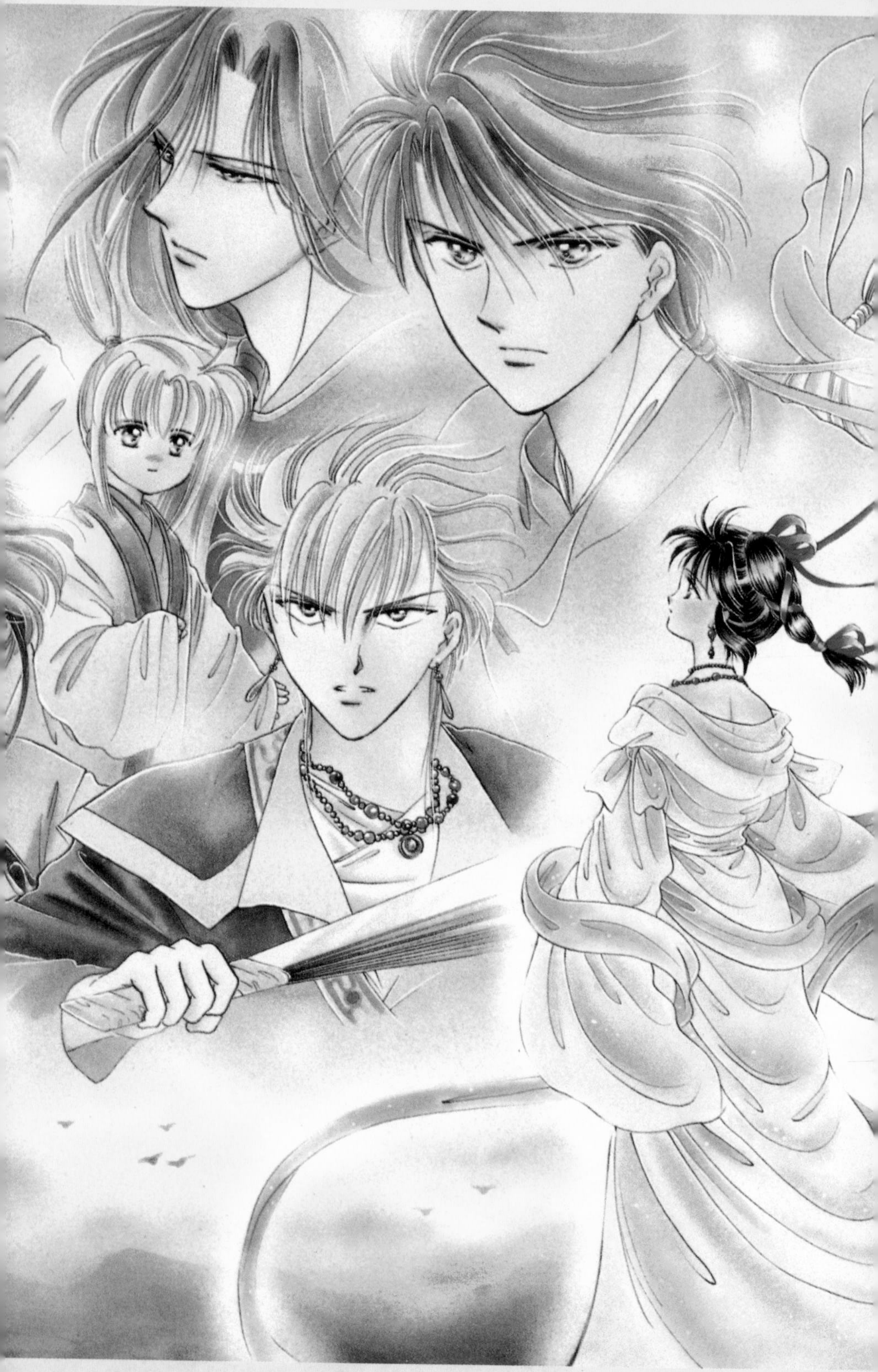

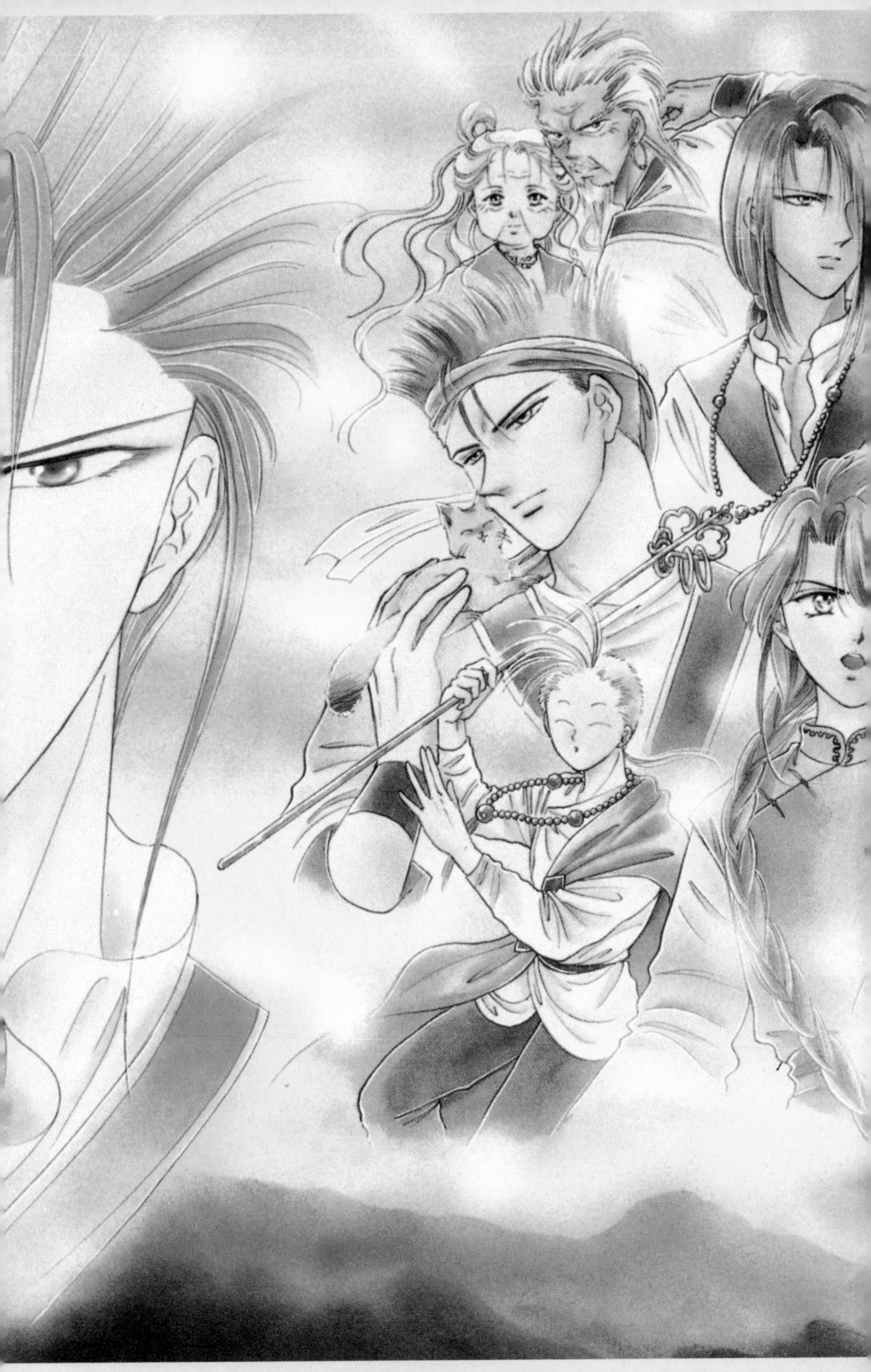

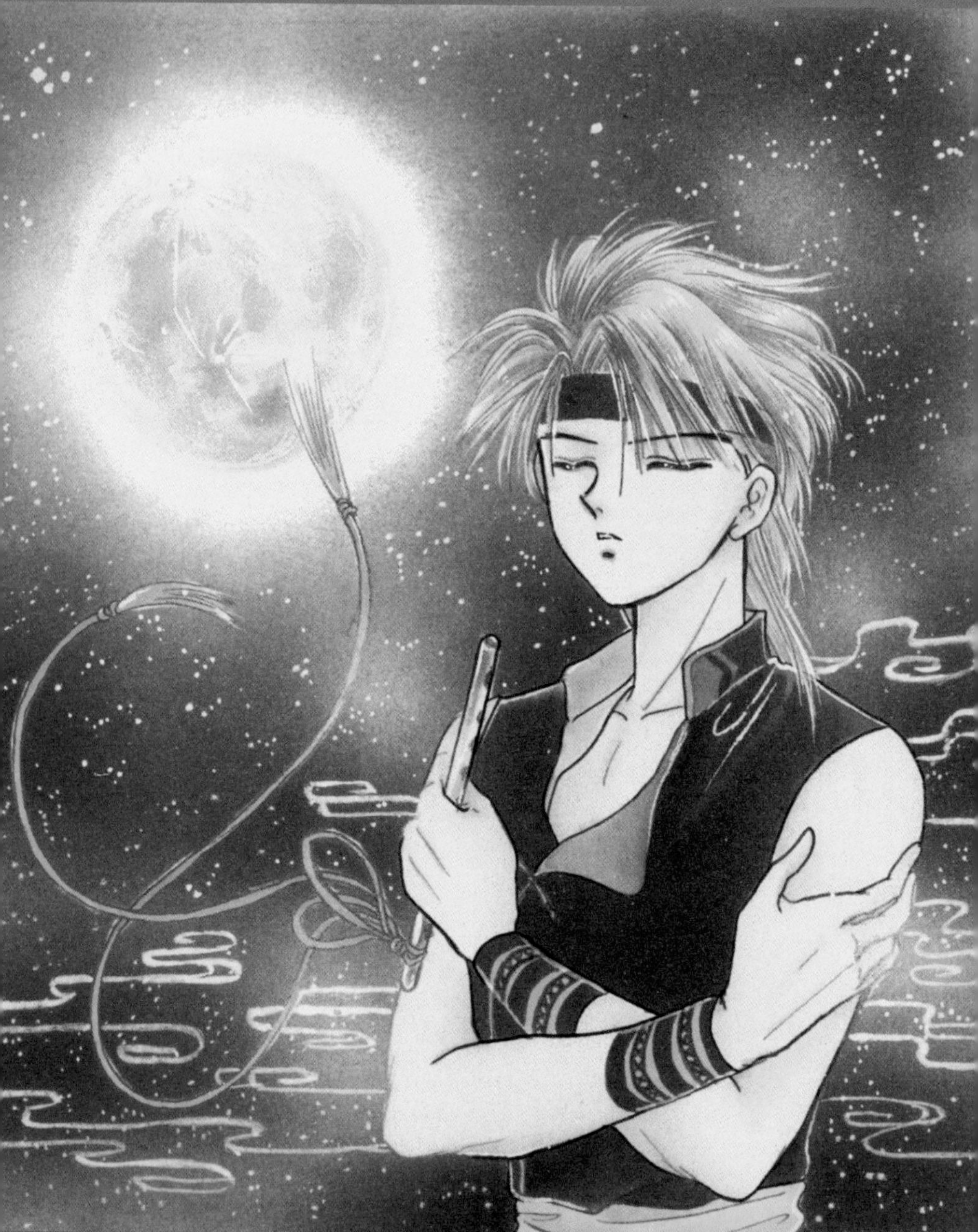

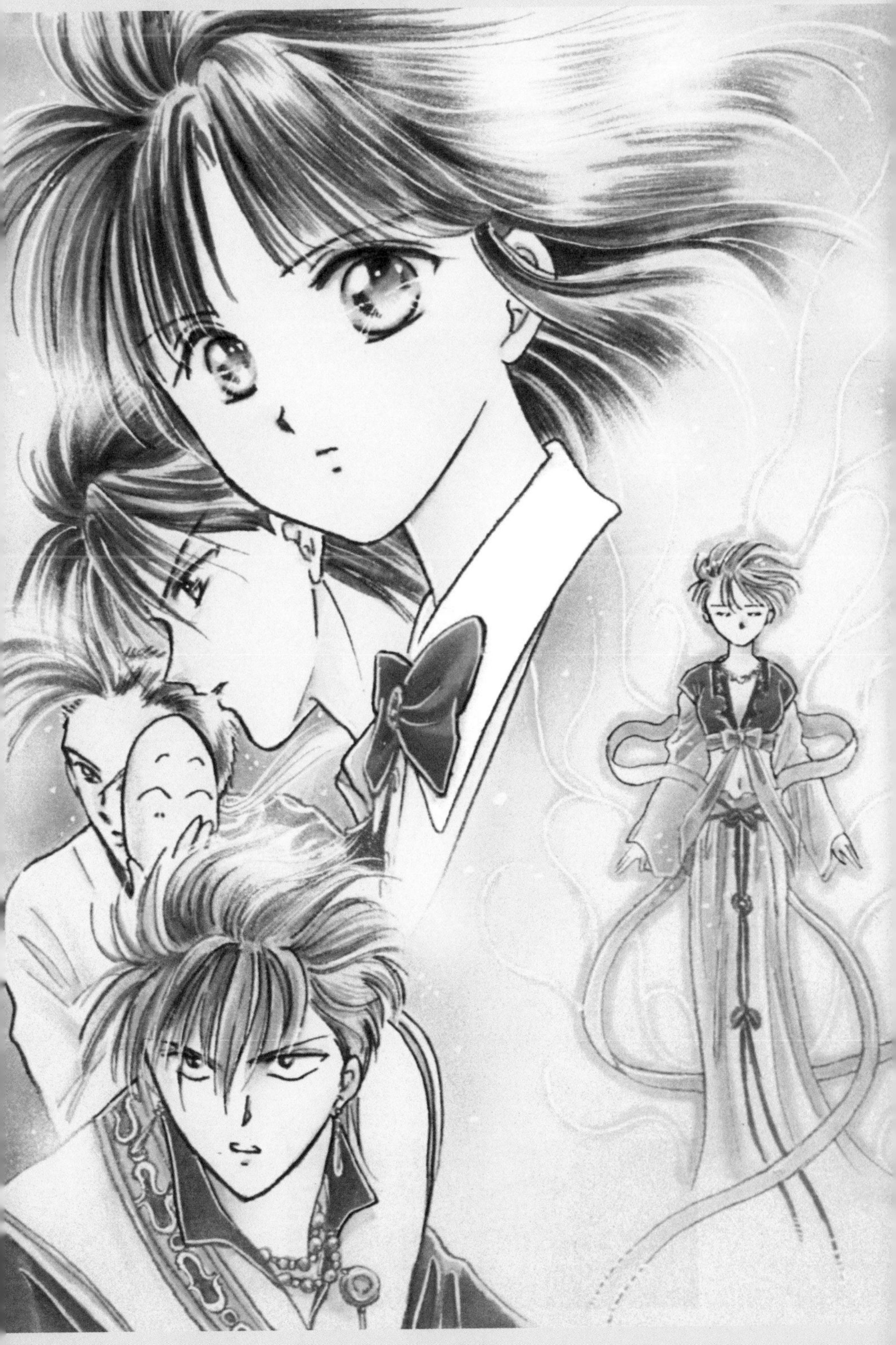

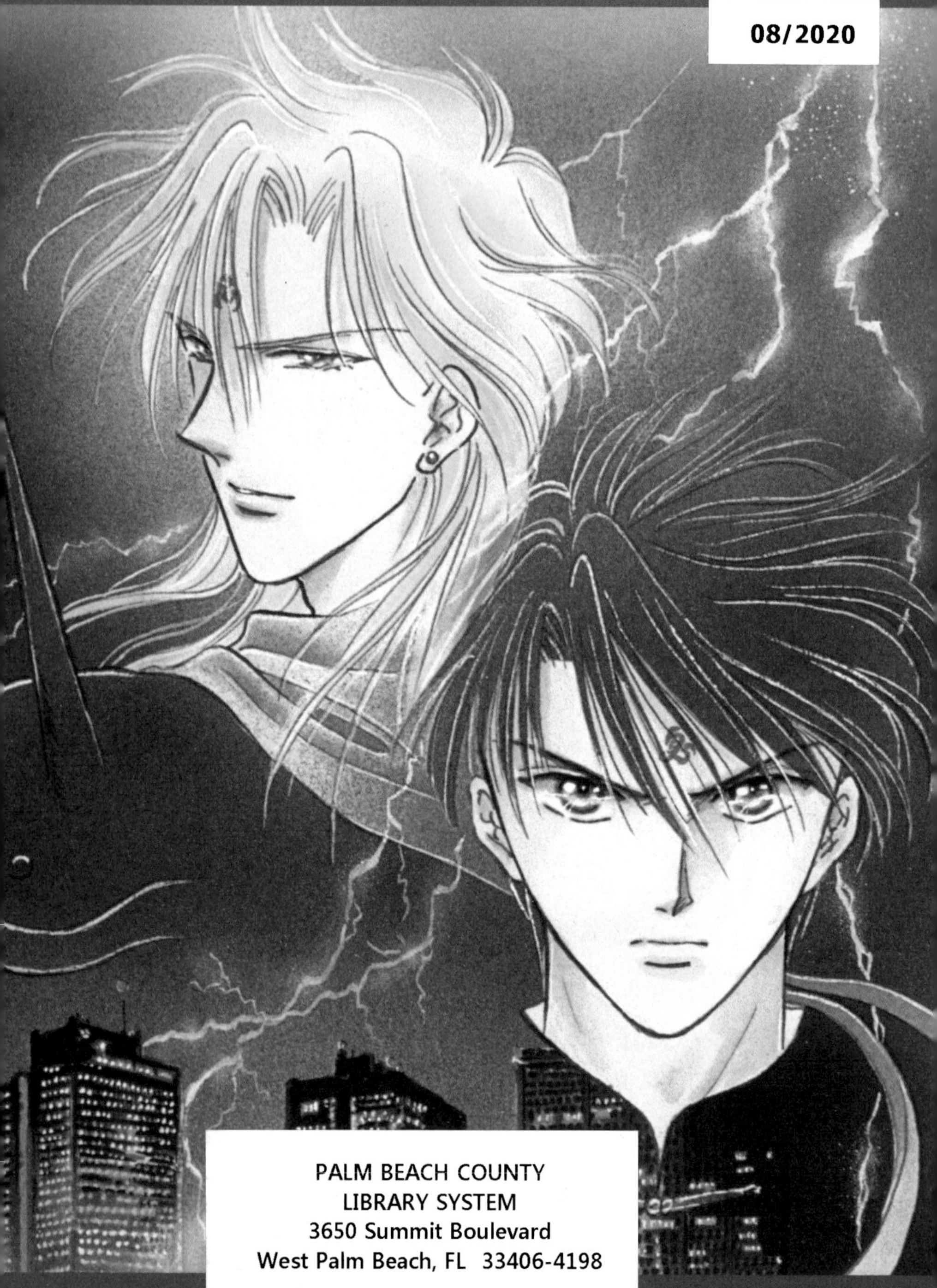